Oct

P

THE ESSENTIALS OF INTERNATIONAL
PUBLIC LAW AND ORGANIZATION

THE MACMILLAN COMPANY
NEW YORK · BOSTON · CHICAGO · DALLAS
ATLANTA · SAN FRANCISCO

MACMILLAN AND CO., Limited
LONDON · BOMBAY · CALCUTTA · MADRAS
MELBOURNE

THE MACMILLAN COMPANY
OF CANADA, Limited
TORONTO

THE ESSENTIALS

OF

INTERNATIONAL PUBLIC LAW
AND ORGANIZATION

BY

AMOS S. HERSHEY, Ph.D.

**PROFESSOR OF POLITICAL SCIENCE AND INTERNATIONAL LAW
IN INDIANA UNIVERSITY**

REVISED EDITION

New York

THE MACMILLAN COMPANY

1939

Set up and electrotyped. Published October, 1912. Reprinted
October, 1914; October, 1915; August, 1916; July, November,
1918; June, 1919; July, October, 1921; January, 1923.
New and revised edition published October, 1927. Reprinted July,
1929; January, May, 1930; June, 1935; April, 1939.

TO

MY STUDENTS

AT

INDIANA UNIVERSITY

PREFACE TO FIRST EDITION

This work—the product of considerable experience in the study and teaching of International Law—aims to furnish the teacher and student with an up-to-date text adapted to the needs of the classroom, and also to present the specialist as well as the general public with a scientific treatise on the subject.

In the execution of this task, the author has tried to be as clear and concise as possible; and, in the body of the text, has carefully confined himself to what he regards as the "Essentials of International Public Law." Minor and controversial details have, for the most part, been relegated to the footnotes. These footnotes are intended to serve a double purpose: to furnish bibliographical and other data for a more extended study or investigation of particular topics; and to provide an additional text for a longer course than is commonly given. It is hoped that the book may thus be readily adapted to a longer or shorter course at the discretion of the instructor.

In the main, the work is based upon modern or contemporary, as distinguished from the older, sources and authorities. A special attempt has been made to review the more important of the many recent contributions to International Law contained in monographs and periodicals—Continental as well as Anglo-American. In the parts dealing with the Law of War and Neutrality, the illustrations are drawn largely from recent wars.

It has been deemed best to incorporate into the body of the text (with notes by way of commentary) those parts of International Law which have been officially codified, viz. the Hague Conventions and the Declaration of the London Naval Conference of 1909.

In the organization of the subject, the writer has adopted the newer and, as he believes, the more convenient as well as scientific system of classification. The Law of Peace is thus mainly divided into "Subjects" and "Objects" of

International Law; the Law of War, into Land, Maritime, and Aërial Warfare. The Adjective Law of Nations is dealt with in Part IV under the heading "Settlement of International Disputes."

It is due to the *American Journal of International Law* to state that the historical chapters, as also the chapters on "The Succession of States" and "Aërial Space" have been previously published in that excellent periodical.

In conclusion, the author wishes to express his gratitude to his friend and colleague Professor Samuel Bannister Harding for valuable advice and assistance in the preparation of this volume.

A. S. H.

BLOOMINGTON, INDIANA,
September 1, 1912.

PREFACE TO REVISED EDITION

A thorough revision of the "Essentials of International Public Law," first published in 1912, has perhaps been expected for some time. Among the reasons for the delay have been the author's temporarily weakened faith in the potency of International Law and the lack of convincing evidence of the stability of the New World Order slowly emerging from the wreck of old Europe.

Not until the dawn of Geneva and Locarno did the writer acquire sufficient resolution to undertake the task of this revision. He is now persuaded not only that the New World Order has secured a fairly firm footing, but that, mainly due to the agency of the League of Nations, International Law is passing through the greatest period in the history of its development. This is especially the case with respect to the pacific settlement of international disputes and the continued progress of international co-operation, legislation (through the treaty-making power), and organization.

In order to emphasize this latter development, the title of this work has been changed from "The Essentials of International Public Law" to "The Essentials of International Public Law and Organization." International Organization is particularly considered in chapter XXII which is wholly new, as also is chapter V on "The Paris Treaties and After." But every chapter (including all notes, references and bibliographies) has undergone a thorough revision.

The main additions to chapters in the previous text have been to the historical chapter IV, chapter XXI on "International Treaties," and chapter XXII on "Amicable Means of Settlement of International .Differences" (see especially pp. 480 ff. on "Judicial Settlement").

Though not, properly speaking, a part of International Law, it has seemed desirable to add pages 101–121 to the historical chapter IV on the main causes and events leading up to the World War. To teachers wishing to confine themselves to International Law and Organization proper, it is suggested that the historical chapters be omitted, either in whole or in part.

In general, the plan and structure of the book outlined in the preface to the first edition has been followed in this revision.

The writer wishes to express his appreciation of the many valuable suggestions and criticisms made by friends and teachers in repsonse to a circular letter sent out a few years ago. To those who suggested the insertion of the bulk of the notes in the body of the text, he would point out that this change, however desirable, would have necessitated at least a two volume work, which would have made its use as a text impracticable.

The author regrets that he is unable to acknowledge by name or specific reference those who have made helpful criticisms. He desires, however, to express his special thanks to Charles S. Hyneman, Rex. M Potterf, Julius R. Bell and Miss Clarice M. Robinson for particular services in the way of verification of references and bibliographies, proof-reading, and the preparation of the index.

A. S. H.

BLOOMINGTON, INDIANA,
October, 1927.

whole or in part.

revision.

A. S. H.

Bloomington, Indiana,
October, 1927.

CONTENTS

INTRODUCTION

PART I

STATES—THE SUBJECTS OF INTERNATIONAL LAW

PART II

THE OBJECTS OF INTERNATIONAL LAW

PART III

INTERCOURSE OF STATES

PART IV

SETTLEMENT AND PREVENTION OF INTERNATIONAL DIFFERENCES

PART V

THE SO–CALLED LAW OF WAR

PART VI

THE SO–CALLED LAW OF NEUTRALITY

LIST OF ABBREVIATIONS

A. J.—American Journal of International Law. New York, 1907–

Am. Histor. Rev.—The American Historical Review. New York, 1895–

Am. Law Rev.—The American Law Review. Boston and St. Louis, 1867–

Am. Pol. Sci. Rev.—The American Political Science Review. Baltimore, 1906–

Anderson and Hershey—Anderson, F. M., and Hershey, A. S.: *Handbook for the Diplomatic History of Europe, Asia and Africa, 1870–1914.* Washington, 1918.

Annals—The Annals of the American Academy of Political and Social Science. Philadelphia, 1890–

Annuaire—Annuaire de l'Institut de Droit International. 1877–

Atherly-Jones—Atherly-Jones, L. A., assisted by Bellot, H. D.: *Commerce in War.* London, 1907.

Atl. Mo.—The Atlantic Monthly. Boston and New York, 1858–

Atlay's Wheaton—*See* Wheaton.

Bluntschli—Bluntschli, J. K.: *Le droit international codifé.* Trad. de l'allemand par C. Lardy. Paris, 1895.

Boeck—Boeck, Ch. de: *De la propriété privée ennemie sous pavillon ennemi.* Paris, 1882.

Boidin—Boidin, Paul: *Les lois de la guerre et les deux conférences de la Haye.* Paris, 1908.

Bonfils (Fauchille)—Bonfils, Henry: *Manuel de droit international public.* ˸ 6è ed. par Paul Fauchille. Paris, 1912. *See* Fauchille.

Borchard—Borchard, E. M.: *The Diplomatic Protection of Citizens Abroad.* New York, 1915.

Bordwell—Bordwell, Percy: *The Law of War between Belligerents.* Chicago, 1908.

Brit. Yr. Bk.—The British Year Book of International Law. London, 1920–

Calvo—Calvo, C.: *Le droit international théorique et pratique,* in 6 v. 5è ed. Paris, 1896.

Cf.—Compare.

Cobbett—Cobbett, Pitt: *Leading Cases on International Law.* 4th ed. by H. H. L. Bellot, Vol. 1, *Peace,* London, 1922 ; Vol. 2, *War and Neutrality,* London, 1924.

Col. Law Rev.—Columbia Law Review. New York, 1901–

Contemp. Rev.—The Contemporary Review. London, 1866–

Crandall—Crandall, S. B.: *Treaties, their Making and Enforcement.* 2d ed. Washington, 1916.

Cur. Hist.—The New York Times Current History, and *Current History, a Monthly Magazine.* New York, 1915–

Cyc. L. P.—Cyclopaedia of Law and Procedure. 40 vols. plus Annotations. New York, 1901–12.

Cyc. Am. Gov.—Cyclopedia of American Government. Ed. by A. C. McLaughlin and A. B. Hart. 3 vols. New York and London, 1914.

xiii

D. L.—Declaration of London.
Dana's Wheaton—*See* Wheaton.
Davis—Davis, G. B.: *The Elements of International Law.* 3d. ed.
New York, 1908.
Despagnet—Despagnet, F.: *Cours de droit international public.* 4è
ed., Paris, 1910.
Edin. Rev.—*The Edinburgh Review or Critical Journal.* Edinburgh,
London and New York, 1804–
Evans, Cases—Evans, L. B.: *Leading Cases on International Law.*
2d ed. Chicago, 1922.
Fauchille—Fauchille, Paul: *Traité de droit international public* (8è ed.
of Bonfils) in 2 v. (vol. 1 is in 3 parts). Paris, 1921–26. See
Bonfils (Fauchille).
Fenwick—Fenwick, Charles G.: *International Law.* New York, 1924.
Fiore—Fiore, P.: *Nouveau droit international public.* 2è ed. Trad.
de l'italien par Ch. Antoine, in 3 v. Paris, 1880.
Fiore, *Int. Law Cod.*—Fiore's *International Law Codified.* Trans. by
E. M. Borchard. N. Y., 1918.
For. Aff.—*Foreign Affairs.* An American Quarterly Review. New
York, 1922–
For. Policy Assoc.—Foreign Policy Association.
Fortn. Rev.—*The Fortnightly Review.* London, 1865–
Funck, Brentano et Sorel—Funck-Brentano. Th., et Sorel, A.: *Précis
du droit des gens.* 2è ed. Paris, 1887.
G. C.—Geneva Conference.
Garner—Garner, J. W.: *International Law and the World War,* in 2 v.
London and New York, 1920.
Grotius—Grotius, Hugo: *De jure belli ac pacis* (1625): accompanied
by an abridged trans. by W. Whewell, in 3 v. Cambridge, 1853.
Grotius Soc.—*Transactions of the Grotius Society.* London, 1915–
H. C.—Hague Convention.
H. R.—Hague Regulations.
Hall—Hall, W. E.: *A Treatise on International Law.* 8th ed. by A.
Pearce Higgins. Oxford, 1924.
Halleck (3d ed.)—Halleck, Gen. H. W.: *International Law,* in 2 v.
3d ed., by Sir Sherston Baker. London, 1893.
Handbuch—Holtzendorff, F. von: *Handbuch des Völkerrechts,* in 4 v.
Berlin, 1885–89. Cited also Holtzendorff.
Harv. Law Rev.—*Harvard Law Review.* Cambridge, 1887–
Heffter—Heffter, A. W.: *Le droit international de l'Europe.* 4è ed.
par F. H. Geffcken. Berlin and Paris, 1883.
Higgins—Higgins, A. P.: *The Hague Peace Conferences.* Cambridge
(Eng.), 1909.
Holland, *Jurisprudence*—Holland, T. E.: *The Elements of Juris-
prudence.* 10th ed. Oxford, 1908.
Holland, *Manual*—Holland, T. E.: *A Manual of Naval Prize Law.*
London, 1888.
Holland, *Studies*—Holland, T. E.: *Studies in International Law.*
Oxford, 1898.
Holland, *War on Land*—Holland, T. E.: *The Laws of War on Land.*
London and New York, 1908.
Holtzendorff—*See Handbuch.*
Hyde—Hyde, C. C.: *International Law chiefly as interpreted and
applied by the United States,* in 2 v. Boston, 1922.

Ill. Law Rev.—Illinois Law Review. Chicago and Evanston, 1907–
Int. J. Ethics—International Journal of Ethics. Philadelphia, Concord
   and Chicago, 1891–
I. L. A.—The International Law Association, Conferences, 1873–
Int. Concil.—International Conciliation: Documents of the American
   Association for International Conciliation. New York, 1909–
J. C. L.—Journal of Comparative Legislation and International Law
   (prior to 1918 entitled *Journal of the Society of Comparative Legis-
   lation*). London, 1896.
J. I. P. (Clunet)—*Journal du droit international privé et de la juris-
   prudence comparée.* Paris, 1874–1915.
J. R. D.—Journal of Race Development. Baltimore, 1911–19.
Kleen—Kleen, Richard: *Lois et usages de la neutralité,* in 2 v. Paris,
   1898–1900.
Klüber—Klüber, J. L.: *Droit des gens moderne de l'Europe.* 2d ed.
   par M. A. Ott. Paris, 1874.
L. Q. R. or *Law Quar. Rev.—The Law Quarterly Review.* London,
   1885–
Lawrence—Lawrence, T. J.: *The Principles of International Law.*
   7th ed. by P. H. Winfield. Boston, 1923.
Liszt—Liszt, F. von.: *Das Völkerrecht systematisch dargestellt.* 12.
   Aufl., Berlin, 1925.
J. de Louter—Louter, J. de: *Le droit international public positif,* in 2
   v. Paris, 1920.
Malloy, *Treaties*—Malloy, W. M., compiler: *Treaties, Conventions,
   International Acts, Protocols and Agreements between the United
   States of American and other Powers.* Vols. I and II, 1776–1909,
   Washington, 1910. Vol. III, 1910–23, compiled by C. F. Red-
   mond. Washington, 1923.
F. de Martens, *Traité*—Martens, F. de: *Traitè de droit international.*
   Trad. du russe, in 3 v., par A. Leo. Paris, 1883–87.
G. F. de Martens—Martens, G. F. de: *Précis du droit des gens de
   l'Europe.* 2 è ed. par Ch. Vergé. Paris, 1864.
Mérignhac—Mérignhac, A.: *Traité de droit public, international,* in
   3 v. Paris, 1905–12.
Mich. Law Rev.—Michigan Law Review. Ann Arbor, 1903–
Minn. Law. Rev.—Minnesota Law Review. Minneapolis, 1907–
Moore, *Arbitrations*—Moore, J. B.: *History and Digest of the Inter-
   national Arbitrations to which the United States has been a Party,*
   in 6 v. Washington, 1898.
Moore, *Digest*—Moore, John Bassett: *A Digest of International Law*
   (with index), in 8 v. Washington, 1906.
Nat. Rev.—The National Review. London.
No. Am. Rev.—The North American Review. Boston and New York,
   1815–
Nys—Nys, E.: *Le droit international,* in 3 v. Vols. 1 and 2, 1st ed.,
   Bruxelles et Paris, 1904–05. Vol. 3, 2d ed., Bruxelles, 1912.
Nys, *Études*—Nys, E.: *Études de droit international public et de droit
   politique,* in 2 v. Bruxelles et Paris, 1896–1901.
Nys, *Les Origines*—Nys, E.: *Les origines de droit international.* Paris,
   1894.
Oppenheim—Oppenheim, L.: *International Law,* in 2 v. 3d ed. by
   R. F. Roxburg. London and New York, 1920–21.

P.-Fodéré, *Cours*—Pradier-Fodéré, P. L. E.: *Cours de droit diplomatique*, in 2 v. 2è ed. Paris, 1881.

P.-Fodéré, or P.-Fodéré, *Traité*—Pradier-Fodéré, P. L. E.: *Traité de droit international public européen et américain*, in 8 v. Paris, 1885–1906.

Pa. Law Rev.—*University of Pennsylvania Law Review and American Law Register*. Successor to *American Law Register*. Philadelphia, 1908–

Perels—Perels, F.: *Manuel de droit maritime international*. Trad. par L. Arendt. Paris, 1884.

Phillimore—Phillimore, Sir R.: *Commentaries upon International Law*, in 3 v. 3d ed. London, 1879–89.

Piédelièvre—Piédelièvre, R.: *Précis de droit international*, in 2 v. Paris, 1894–95.

Pillet—Pillet, Antoine: *Les lois actuelles de la guerre*. 2 è ed. Paris, 1901.

Pol. Sci. Quar.—*Political Science Quarterly*. New York and Lancaster, Pa., 1886–

Pomeroy—Pomeroy, J. N.: *Lectures on International Law in Time of Peace*. Ed. by Th. D. Woolsey. Indianapolis, 1886.

Procs. Am. Soc. I. L.—*Proceedings of the American Society of International Law*. New York, 1908–

Quar. Rev.—*The Quarterly Review*. London and New York, 1809–

R. D. I.—*Revue de droit international et de legislation comparée*. Bruxelles, 1869–

R. D. I. P.—*Revue général de droit international public*. Paris, 1894–

Rev. of Rev.—*The American Review of Reviews*. New York.

Rivier—Rivier, A.: *Principes de droit des gens*. in 2 v. Paris, 1896.

Rolin—Rolin: *Le droit moderne de la guerre*, in 3 v. Bruxelles, 1920.

S. C.—*Stockton's Naval War Code or Laws and Usages at Sea*.

Satow—Satow, Sir Ernest: *A Guide to Diplomatic Practice*, in 2 v. London and New York, 1917.

Scott—Scott, J. B.: *The Hague Peace Conferences of 1899 and 1907*, in 2 v. Baltimore, 1909.

Scott, Cases—Scott, J. B.: *Cases on International Law*. St. Paul, Minn., 1922.

Spaight—Spaight, J. M.: *War Rights on Land*. London, 1911.

Stowell and Munro—Stowell, E. C., and Munro, H. F.: *International Cases*. Vol. 1, *Peace*; vol. 2, *War and Neutrality*. Boston, 1916.

Taylor—Taylor, Hannis: *A Treatise on International Public Law*. Chicago, 1901.

Treaty Series—League of Nations. *Treaty Series*. Publication of Treaties and International Engagements Registered with the Secretariat of the League. London, 1920–

Twiss—Twiss, Sir Travers: *The Law of Nations considered as Independent Political Communities*, in 2 v. new ed. Oxford, 1875–84.

Ullmann—Ullmann, E.: *Völkerrecht*. 2d ed. Tübingen, 1908.

Vattel—Vattel, E. de: *The Law of Nations or the Principles of Natural Law*. v. 3 of *Le droit des gens, ou principes de la loi Naturelle*, in *The classics of International Law*. Trans. by C. G. Fenwick, Washington, 1916.

W. P. F.—World Peace Foundation. *Pamphlet series.* Boston, 1911–16. *A League of Nations.* Boston, 1917–23. *Pamphlets.* Boston, 1924–

Westlake—Westlake, John: *International Law,* in 2 v. Cambridge, Eng. Vol. 1, *Peace,* 2d ed., 1910. Vol. 2, *War,* 1st ed., 1907.

Wharton, *Digest*—Wharton, Francis.: *A Digest of the International Law of the United States,* in 3 v. Washington, 1886.

Wheaton—Wheaton, Henry: *Elements of International Law.* 8th ed., ed. with notes, by R. H. Dana, Jr., Boston, 1866. 4th English ed. by J. B. Atlay, London, 1904.

Wheaton, *History*—Wheaton, Henry: *History of the Law of Nations in Europe and America from the Earliest Times to the Treaty of Washington,* 1842. New York, 1845.

Wilson—Wilson, G. G.: *Handbook of International Law.* St. Paul, Minn., 1910. A new edition has just been published (1927).

Wilson and Tucker—Wilson, G. G., and Tucker, G. E.: *International Law.* 8th ed. by G. G. Wilson. New York, 1922.

Woolsey—Woolsey, Th. D.: *Introduction to the Study of International Law.* 5th ed. New York, 1870.

Yale Law J.— *Yale Law Journal.* New Haven, 1891–

Yale Rev.— *Yale Review.* New York and New Haven, 1892–

Z. I.—*Zeitschrift für Internationales Privat- und Strafrecht.* Erlangen, Munich and Leipzig, 1891–

Z. V.—*Zeitschrift für Völkerrecht.* Breslau, 1907–

TABLE OF CASES

(References are to pages)

xix

ESSENTIALS OF INTERNATIONAL PUBLIC LAW AND ORGANIZATION

INTRODUCTION

CHAPTER I

THE NATURE OF INTERNATIONAL LAW

1. **Definition of International Law.**—*International Law*, or the Common and Conventional Law of Nations, is that body of principles, rules, and customs which are generally recognized as binding upon the members of the International Community of States in their relations with one another or with the nationals of other States.[1]

[1] For various definitions of International Law, see * 1 Calvo, § 1; 1 Hyde, § 1 n.; 1 F. de Martens, *Traité*, § 3; * 1 P.-Fodéré, *Traité*, No. 1; and Ullmann, 9–10 n. Halleck (3d ed., I, 46) simply defines International Law as "the rules of conduct regulating the intercourse of States." This definition is much too inclusive. There are "rules regulating the intercourse of States" which are not, properly speaking, a part of the Law of Nations. International Law is generally and habitually, though not always, observed; but in this respect it does not differ from municipal or State law, the rules of which are also frequently violated. From the standpoints of brevity and general accuracy, Westlake's definition of International Law (I, p. 1) as "the law of the society of states" has much to commend it.

Certain authorities (*e.g.* Liszt, 3d ed., 1904, § 2, p. 13) distinguish between *general* (*allgemeines*) and *particular* International Law. But rules which are not generally or universally recognized as binding can scarcely be said to deserve the name International Law at all. Oppenheim (I, § 1) distinguishes between *universal* in contradistinction to *particular* and *general* International Law. So many divisions seem confusing and unnecessary. However, as long as the League of Nations is not a universal Confederacy, it may sometimes be necessary to refer to the League Law or Law of the League of Nations. According to some authorities (*e.g.* Despagnet, No. 41; and 1 P.-Fodéré, No. 6), the Law of Nations includes a *theoretical* or ideal, and a *real* or actual International Law. They explain that the latter tells us what the law *is*, and the former what it *should* be. This distinction is undoubtedly a sound one, but this volume deals mainly with *positive* or real International Law.

Some writers (*e.g.* Heffter, § 1; and Holtzendorff, in 1 *Handbuch*, §§ 3–4) speak of a European International Law. While it may be readily ad-

1

2. The Term International Law.—The term "International Law"[2] appears to have been coined by Jeremy Bentham in 1780 and is the one generally in use at the present time, although the phrase "Law of Nations" (a translation of *Droit des Gens*—the title of Vattel's famous work published in 1758) is still sometimes employed.

The former term is preferable to the latter inasmuch as *Droit des Gens* is a translation of the Latin *jus gentium*,[3]— a phrase which bore a very different meaning from that of "International Law." Grotius' great work, published in 1625, was entitled *De Jure Belli ac Pacis*, but in 1672 Pufendorf used the title *De Jure Naturae et Gentium*. Early English writers employed the term "Civil Law,"— a phrase still used by Locke toward the close of the seventeenth century.

3. Necessary Distinctions.—International Public Law should be carefully distinguished from International Ethics or Morality, International Comity or the Comity of Nations, Diplomacy or Foreign Policy, International Private Law or Conflict of Laws, and International Administrative Law.

4. International Ethics.—*International Morality* deals with the principles which should govern international relations from the higher standpoints of conscience, justice, or

mitted that the Grotian system is essentially of European origin, the application and development of the Law of Neutrality is largely due to American statesmen and publicists. The distinguished South American publicist Alvarez has even presented us with a valuable work on American International Law—*Le droit int. Americain* (1910). Cf. Alvarez in 3 *A. J.* (1909), 267–359. For a favorable criticism of his thesis, see 1 Fauchille, No. 44.[4-9] But the use of such phrases implying regional limitations, however justifiable from certain points of view, tends to interfere with a broad conception of international rights and duties. The arguments of Alvarez are refuted by Sá Vianna, in *De la non-existence d'un droit int. Américain* (1912).

[2] The term "Interstate Law" or "Law between States" would be somewhat more exact than "International Law," which is a translation of the phrase *juris inter gentes*, used by Zouche as a part of the title of his manual published in 1650 (republished by the Carnegie Institution in 1911 as Vols. I and II of the *Classics of Int. Law*). On the terminology of our subject, see especially "Law between States" Fauchille, No. 3; * Creasy, *First Platform of Int. Law* (1876), pp. 3 ff.; Despagnet, No. 37; Holland, *Jurisprudence* (10th ed., 1908), 380 n.; * Holtzendorff, in 1 *Handbuch*, § 2; Lawrence, § 7; * 1 P.-Fodéré, No. 3; 1 Rivier, 4–6; Ullmann, § 3; 1 Walker, *History of the Law of Nations* (1899), § 1; Atlay's Wheaton, § 12.

[3] See *infra*, No. 38.

humanity. Without certain standards of international morality, International Law could not exist, and many of its principles (as, *e.g.*, respect for treaties) are conditions essential to friendly and stable international intercourse. Though often used as pretexts, ideas and sentiments of humanity sometimes constitute the real motives for certain international rules (even including some relating to warfare, as in the case of the Geneva Conventions). And whatever we may think of their wisdom, it should not be overlooked that in Article 227 of the Treaty of Versailles, the Allied and Associated Powers publicly arraigned William II of Hohenzollern, formerly German Emperor, for a " supreme offence against international morality and the sanctity of treaties." [4] Although the Law of Nations is based largely upon a sense of justice and equity among men, international morality is by no means identical with International Law; [5] for the latter fails to condemn certain practices and principles (as, *e.g.* the right of conquest) which are clearly at variance with ideals of justice and humanity, and it includes many rules which originated in interest and convenience rather than in morality.[6]

5. **The Comity of Nations.**—*International Comity* relates to those rules of courtesy, etiquette, or good will which are or should be observed by governments in their dealings with one another on grounds of convenience, honor, or reciprocity. Such, for example, are the extradition of criminals

---

[4] A special tribunal composed of five judges was to have been created to try the accused. In its decision the tribunal was to be "guided by the highest motives of international policy, with a view of vindicating the solemn obligations of international undertakings and the validity of international morality." Needless perhaps to say, this tribunal was never constituted.

[5] As Pollock (*First Book of Jurisprudence*, 1896, p. 44) justly observes: "Though much ground is common to both, the subject matter of Law and Ethics is not the same. The field of legal rules of conduct does not coincide with that of moral rules, and is not included in it; and the purposes for which they exist are distinct."

[6] Hall (pp. 1 ff.) wisely makes the "existence of rules of positive International Law the sole standard of conduct or law of present authority." He argues: (1) that "it is not agreed in what the absolute standard consists"; and (2) that "even if a theory of absolute right were universally accepted, the measure of the obligations of a State would not be found in its dictates, but in the rules which are received as positive law by the body of States." But he also "unhesitatingly" affirms that essential facts of State existence and moral obligations which are recognized as being the source of legal rules possess a much higher authority than any other part of International Law.

in the absence of express agreement; the observance of certain diplomatic forms and ceremonies; and the faith or credit given in each State to the public acts, records, and judicial proceedings of other States.[7]

6. **Diplomacy or Foreign Policy.**—*Diplomacy* in the wider sense,[8] or *Foreign Policy*, relates to aims of national or international policy and the conduct of foreign affairs or international relations. It is generally based upon considerations of expediency or national interest rather than upon those of courtesy, humanity, or justice. Though its aims and methods should never be illegal or immoral, it must be admitted that its conduct in times past has generally been Machiavellian [9] instead of Grotian.[10] While

[7] Comity is the "recognition which one nation allows within its territory to the legislative, executive, or judicial acts of another nation." Justice Gray, in *Hilton* v. *Guyot* (1894), 159 U. S. Rep. 113, 164. But this definition is too narrow.

For examples of requests for the extradition of criminals on grounds of courtesy, see 4 Moore, *Digest*, § 582.

[8] Diplomacy in the narrower sense may be defined as the "art of conducting the intercourse of nations with one another." Foster, *A Century of American Diplomacy* (1911), p. 2. Twiss (I, p. 163) points out that it is a science as well as an art. He defines diplomacy as "the science which is conversant with Negotiations and Treaties." In the wider sense, "a history of diplomacy properly includes not only an account of the progress of international intercourse, but an exposition of the motives by which it has been inspired and the results which it has accomplished." See preface to the first volume of Hill's monumental *History of Diplomacy in the Development of Europe* (1905–06). For an excellent treatment (with ample references) of the origin, development, organization, and practice of modern diplomacy, see Potter, *Int. Organization* (1922), chs. 7–9 and pp. 612–14.

[9] Machiavellian diplomacy is much older than the publication of Machiavelli's *Prince* in 1513. For examples drawn from the Brâhman Code of Manu, see *infra*, No. 20, and note on p. 34. See also *infra*, No. 34, and notes on the "Diplomacy of Rome."

If one were asked to summarize Machiavellianism as applied to international politics in a single sentence, it might be said that the *end*, which is the creation, maintenance, and increase of political power, is justified by such *means* as force and fraud or intrigue in various forms.

Though the doctrine is usually disclaimed or denounced (as, *e.g.*, by Frederick the Great in his *Anti-Machiavel*), the practice of Machiavellian diplomacy still pervades European international relations to an alarming degree and is not altogether absent from American diplomacy. Its greatest practitioneers in the past include Frederick the Great, Napoleon I, and Bismarck.

Machiavellian diplomacy is not necessarily synonymous with secret diplomacy, though it is true that secrecy furnishes the most favorable conditions under which it thrives and that publicity or open diplomacy (using the word diplomacy in its broader sense of policy) is its best antidote.

there has undoubtedly been some improvement in standards of diplomatic conduct, especially since the close of the Napoleonic wars,[11] the fact has not been sufficiently recognized, at least by publicists, that beyond the well-cultivated field of International Law there still lie vast and but partially explored regions of policy where motives of interest and expediency prevail rather than ideals of law and justice. The aims and methods which govern international relations in these fields of policy or diplomacy may and should be in harmony with established laws and customs, but are often independent of, and sometimes even antagonistic to, recognized rules and principles. At any rate, statesmen exercise a wider discretion and feel less bound by legal checks and moral standards in the realm of Diplomacy or Foreign Policy than within the narrower field bounded by definite rules of positive International Law. The abuse of this freedom frequently leads to intervention and war.[12]

7. **International Private Law or Conflict of Laws.**—*International Private Law* [13] or *Conflict of Laws* is that body of rules or principles which decide between two conflicting systems of law in the decision of cases affecting private rights. It is not a part of International Law proper, and

---

For references on Machiavellian diplomacy, see *infra*, pp. 16–17. See especially Burd, "Machiavelli" in 1 *Cambridge Modern History*, ch. 6; Dunning, *Political Theories, Ancient and Modern* (1902), ch. 11; Figgis, *From Gerson to Grotius* (1907), Lect. 3, pp. 81 ff.; Morley, *Machiavelli* (Romanes Lecture) (1897); and Villari, *The Life and Times of Machiavelli* (1891), *passim*. The views with which the author finds himself most nearly in agreement are those of Figgis, who is of the opinion that Machiavellian methods can only be justified by extreme emergencies.

[10] See *infra*, Nos. 56–57 and note on p. 70.

[11] This appears at least to have been the case down to the Bismarckian régime. Recent publications of documents from the German, Austrian and Russian archives may make it necessary to modify somewhat the statement in the text.

[12] Nys (I, p. 204) quotes von Holtzendorff as saying that "international politics is the use of an international force acting in the interest of the community." He (Holtzendorff) cites the following discriminating words of Bulmerincq: "Law leaves no choice; policy keeps open various means to an end and permits a free choice in respect to these." (See Bulmerincq, in Marquardsen's *Handbuch*, I, § 3.) For a discussion of this subject from the standpoint of an idealist, see Novicow, *La politique int.* (1886).

[13] The term International Private Law seems more exact than Private International Law—the phrase usually employed. *Conflict of Laws* is perhaps preferable to either.

appears to owe its origin to a feeling of comity [14] rather than
to a sense of justice, although it now rests upon a more
positive basis.   " It derives its force from the sovereignty
of the States administering it; it affects only the relations
of individuals as such; and it consists in the rules by which
courts determine within what national jurisdiction a case
equitably falls, or by what national force it is just that it
shall be decided." [15]   It relates especially to such matters as
limits of national jurisdiction; validity of foreign marriages,
wills, and contracts; and questions of residence, domicile,
and nationality.   It is a part of the municipal law in each
State and of the common law in England and the United
States.[16] For the purpose of establishing uniform rules,
large portions of this branch of jurisprudence were codified
through general treaties at the Hague in 1902 and 1905.[17]

   8. International Administrative Law.—International Administrative Law—a branch of international jurisprudence
which is still in its infancy—has been tentatively defined as
" that body of laws and ordinances created by the action of
International Conferences or Commissions which regulate
the relations and activities of national and international
agencies with respect to these material and intellectual
interests which have received an authoritative universal
organization." [18]   It relates to such matters as international
communication by means of postal correspondence and
telegraphy, international transportation, copyright, crime
(*e.g.* the white slave traffic), sanitation, etc.   It is created
by International Congresses or Conferences, and Commissions, and is administered by International Commissions
and Bureaus as well as by national agencies.

   9. Is International Law a Branch of True Law?—The

[14] See *Hilton* v. *Guyot*, 159 U. S. 113, 164–165; and Story, *Conflict of Laws*
(1883), Nos. 28, 33–38.

[15] Hall, § 10, p. 59 of Higgin's 8th ed.

[16] Wharton, *Conflict of Laws* (1905), I, § 1.   Minor (*Conflict of Laws*, 1901,
§ 2) thus distinguishes International Private Law from International Public
Law: (1) as to persons on whom it operates, *i.e.* on private persons; (2) as to
transactions to which it relates, *i.e.* to private interests; (3) as to remedies
applied, *i.e.* these are applied by courts or tribunals.   In the United States, the
States are regarded as sovereign from the standpoint of Conflict of Laws.

[17] See 1 Oppenheim, § 594, who also tells us that several of these Hague
Conventions were set aside by the peace treaties of 1919.

[18] Reinsch, in *Public Int. Unions* (1911), p. 130.   Cf. *infra*, No. 79 and notes.

claim of International Law to be considered a branch of true law or jurisprudence proper has been often denied, more especially by that English school of analytic and positive jurisprudence founded by Bentham and Austin. The Austinian or imperative view of law, which has also found some support on the Continent, seems to-day to be rejected by an overwhelming weight of authority, except possibly in England and the United States.[19]

The objections to considering International Law as a branch of true law fall under three main heads. It is maintained that the Law of Nations lacks: (1) The quality of positive authority or command. It does not conform to Austin's definition of law as " a rule laid down for the guidance of an intelligent being by an intelligent being having power over him." [20] In other words, it is not the general command of a determinate legislator or legislative body with power to enforce its decisions. (2) There is no legal duty or obligation of obedience on the part of those to whom it is addressed, for there are no courts or judicial tribunals to interpret and enforce this so-called law. (3) There is no penalty prescribed for disobedience. Consequently, it lacks sanction or physical power to enforce obedience. The so-called Law of Nations is, it is claimed, a branch of ethics rather than of jurisprudence.[21]

It is now generally agreed that the Austinian view of law is formal, narrow, arbitrary, unhistorical, and unphilological.[22] While it undoubtedly has value for those who practice and administer law in the courts, it does not even furnish a complete definition of municipal law, as many laws are permissive rather than mandatory in their character. It leaves out of account that large and important part

[19] For lists of authorities for and against the Austinian or imperative view of law, see Bibliography at the end of this chapter.

[20] Austin, *Lectures on Jurisprudence* (Campbell's 5th ed., 1911), p.86. Cf. Holland's definition of law as "a general rule of external human action enforced by a sovereign political authority," in *Jurisprudence* (10th ed., 1908), 40.

[21] In this paragraph I have sought rather to summarize the objections generally made to the legal nature of International Law than to state the specific objections of Austin.

[22] This last point has been elaborated by Clark, in his *Practical Jurisprudence* (1883), Pt. I, chs. 2–7. For a summary of the philological argument, see Walker, *Science of International Law* (1893), 21 ff.

of constitutional law which is based upon usage or convention and is not directly administered by judicial tribunals.

The researches inaugurated by Sir Henry Maine and Savigny, the founders of the modern school of historical jurisprudence, have shown that custom is anterior to enacted law, of which indeed it remains the essence even after it has become incorporated into codes and statutes and interpreted by the courts. Even Holland admits that judges do not transform custom into law, for they apply it " retrospectively " as well as " prospectively." They merely place upon it " the stamp of judicial authentication." [23]

Leading authorities even maintain that physical sanction or the threat of physical force is a mere accident and is not an essential characteristic of law. It is but a means to an end—a part of the machinery of society for the enforcement of law. Far more important than the infliction of punishment is the creation of a law-abiding sentiment among the people.[24] Besides, the laws to which the severest penalties are attached are not always those most generally or scrupulously obeyed.[25]

Law in jurisprudence is essentially a body of customs, principles, or rules for the regulation of the external conduct of human beings in their relations with one another as members of a political community.[26] In order fully to

[23] Holland, *op. cit.*, p. 58.

[24] The above is a summary of Walker's argument. See *Science*, 29 ff.

[25] From the point of view of general recognition and habitual obedience, International Law certainly compares favorably with municipal or State law, at least so far as the law of peace is concerned. For example, treaties are, as a rule, faithfully executed, and arbitral decisions are nearly always carried out. The rules of warfare were generally observed during recent wars between civilized States prior to the outbreak of the World War. Even in violating the Law of Nations, modern governments usually render to it the homage of pretended obedience.

[26] Cf. the definitions of Oppenheim, I, § 5, and Clark, p. 134. For numerous definitions of law, see Clark, chs. 4–14; Holland (10th ed.), pp. 41–43; and Pulazky, *Law and Civil Society* (1888), §§ 184–93, pp. 330 ff.

Pollock (*First Book of Jurisprudence*, p. 28) justly observes that "the only essential conditions for the existence of law and legal institutions are existence of a political community and the recognition by its members of settled rules binding upon them in that capacity." But he had previously observed (p. 22) that "the appointed consequences of disobedience, the *sanctions* of law as they

answer the description of law, these rules must be generally recognized as binding and enforceable by external power or appropriate sanction, but they are not necessarily accompanied by the threat or use of physical force in case of their violation. The guarantees or sanctions securing their observance need not be based upon the assertion of force or the danger of speedy and definite punishment. The guarantees for International Law, and still more for the customs and conventions of constitutional law, are mainly of a moral nature; and these rest upon public opinion and law-abiding habits on the part of the people for their observance.[27] Besides, we cannot admit that International Law lacks altogether a determinate lawgiver and sovereign authority.[28] European Congresses, like those of Paris in 1856 and the Hague Conferences, exercised virtual legislative powers and issued commands which have been recognized as binding and were generally obeyed, at least prior to the outbreak of the World War. The thirteen Conventions of the Second Hague Peace Conference of 1907 (compared with the three Conventions of the Conference of 1899) bear witness to the increasing activity and importance of international legislation. True it is that these Conventions bear the form of treaties which each State may refuse to sign and ratify, but they are none the less in essence acts of international legislation.[29] And this is

are commonly called, seem to be not only a normal element of civilized law, but a necessary constituent."

[27] On this point, see especially the profound observations of the eminent German publicist Jellinek, in his *Recht des modernen Staats* (2d ed., 1905), 325 ff., and his *Staatenverträge* (1880), 37 ff.

[28] Creasy (*First Platform*, p. 70) observes on this head: "Although Sovereign States acknowledge no common Superior Lawgiver from which they collectively receive imperative Law, yet they can and do make up a community capable of establishing Laws which shall be binding on each member of the community. In this sense the community at large is a sovereign Lawgiver to each member of the community." So far he seems sound, subject to the reservation that each member of the community can withhold its assent to these laws. But when he makes sanction for this law consist in war or physical force in prospective, we decline to follow him.

[29] This is not merely the author's opinion; it is that of eminent jurists like Jellinek, who says: "Such agreements (*Vereinbarungen*) are not in essence treaties. They create no *jus intra partes*, but a *jus supra partes*, *i.e.*, they give expression to a common juristic conviction; they are not two-sided legal creations, but common irrevocable declarations" (*Öffentlichen Rechte*, 1892, 299). See also Triepel, *Droit int. et droit interne* (1920), 49 ff.

particularly true of the Covenant of the League of Nations which is itself in this sense a law making body.

Nor is International Law wholly without judicial sanction. It is frequently administered and interpreted by judicial tribunals, more particularly by courts of arbitration and national prize courts. The Hague Conference of 1907 even provided for the creation of an International Prize Court which, in the absence of conventions or national legislation, was to apply the rules of International Law.[30] The Permanent Court of International Justice established in 1921 has particular jurisdiction over interpretation of treaties, questions of International Law, and breaches of international obligations. It is to apply international conventions, international customs, principles of recognized law, judicial decisions, and the teachings of the most highly qualified publicists of the various nations (Arts. 36 and 38 of the Statute of the Court).

If physical sanction or the threat or guarantee of physical force is an essential characteristic of law, then it must indeed be admitted that International Law is a law of imperfect obligation. But it has been shown that such is by no means the case. It is impossible to agree with those publicists [31] who hold that war is the real or main sanction of the Law of Nations; for the attempt to characterize war

[30] Title I, Art. 7, of the "Convention for the Establishment of an International Prize Court." It was further provided: "*If generally recognized rules do not exist, the Court shall decide in accordance with the general principles of justice and equity.*" The Court, which never came into existence, was thus expressly authorized to create International Law in such a contingency. Cf. Add. Note at the end of this volume.

[31] For example, Bluntschli, "Introduction," p. 8; Creasy, *First Platform.* §§ 74, 78; Fenwick, 40, 428; Holland, *Jurisprudence,* (10th ed.) 391–93; Salmond, *Jurisprudence,* (3d ed., 1910), 14.

Among those who deny that war is or can be a legal sanction, are: Amos, *Remedies for War* (1880), 137; Bonfils and Fauchille, No. 29; Chrétien, *Principes de droit int. public* (1893), No. 7; Funck-Brentano et Sorel, 7; 1 Hyde, § 4 and notes on p. 10; Nippold, *Die Fortbildung des Verfahrens* (1907), 86; and 1 P.-Fodéré, No. 23. See also Dumas, *Sanctions de l'arbitrage* (1905), *passim*; Moulin, *La doctrine de Drago* (1908), 121–29; Preuss, *Das Völkerrecht im Dienste des Wirtschaftlebens* (1891), 17 ff. and note on p. 58; Lagorgette, *Le rôle de la guerre* (1906), 318 ff.; and Lueder, in 4 Holtzendorff, § 49.

For a number of articles, addresses and editorials on this interesting subject, see under head of "Sanctions," the index volume (1921) of the *A. J.*

It should not be overlooked that war is recognized as a legal sanction by the League of Nations. *Covenant,* Art. 16.

as a guarantee of law or a means of justice in ordinary cases must be considered harmful as well as vain unless concurred in by practically the whole or main body of the International Community. In any case war can only be justified, if ever, as a last resort after every other mode of obtaining justice or redress has failed.

10. **International Law as a Part of Municipal or State Law.**—That International Law, in so far as it is clearly ascertained or recognized as binding, and not contrary to national legislation, is a part of the law of the land is no longer a matter of serious doubt, at least in England and the United States. That the Law of Nations, in its full extent, is a part of the law of England was the view of Blackstone (*Commentaries*, 1765, Bk. IV, ch. 5, p. 67) and of Lords Talbot and Mansfield in the eighteenth century (*Triquet* v. *Bath*, 1764, 3 Burr. 1478, and Scott, *Cases*, 2; and *Heathfield* v. *Chilton*, 1767, 4 Burr. 2015, and Scott, 4n.); as also of Lords Ellenborough and Stowell (*Wolff* v. *Oxholm*, 1817, K. B., 6 M. and S. 92, and Scott, 550; *The Maria*, 1799, 1 C. Rob. 340, and Evans, *Cases*, 535; and the *Recovery*, 1807, 6 Rob. 341) in the early part of the nineteenth century.

This view appears to have prevailed in England [32] until apparently reversed by a bare majority of the Court of Crown Cases Reserved in the famous case of *Queen* v. *Keyn* (L. R., 2 Exchq. Div. 63, and Scott, 243) in 1876. This Court declined, in the absence of an Act of Parliament, to assert British criminal jurisdiction over the captain of the German steamer *Franconia* who had been convicted of manslaughter in the Central Criminal Court for having killed a passenger on board the British steamer *Strathclyde* (as the result of a collision due to negligence) within two and a half miles from the English coast, *i.e.* within the limits of the marine league. In spite of the fact that this decision was promptly nullified by Act of Parliament, and although there was a strong minority opinion supported by six of the thirteen judges, the authority of the older view was considerably shaken.[33] But all reasonable doubt in

[32] See, *e.g.* the leading case of the *Emporor of Austria* v. *Day and Kossuth* (1861), 2 Gifford, 628, 678.

[33] 42 Vict., c. 73. For discussions of the case of *Queen* v. *Keyn*, see 1 Cob-

England as to the legal nature of International Law has now apparently been finally removed by the opinion of Lord Chief Justice Alverstone (formerly Sir Richard Webster) in the case of *West Rand Central Gold Mining Co.* v. *The King* (L. R. 1905, 2 K. B. 391 and Evans, 15 or Scott, 5). Although the petitioners (British mine owners in the Transvaal who sought to recover gold which had been seized by officials acting for the Transvaal Government) were refused redress on the ground that annexation was an act of State which could not be inquired into by the Court, Lord Alverstone assented to the proposition laid down by Lord Robert Cecil that " International Law is a part of the law of England." He said:

" It is quite true that whatever has received the common consent of civilized nations must have received the assent of our country, and that to which we have assented along with other nations in general may properly be called International Law, and as such will be acknowledged and applied by our municipal tribunals when legitimate occasion arises for those tribunals to decide questions to which doctrines of International Law may be relevant." [34]

bett, 132 ff.; Maine, *Int. Law* (1888), 38–45; Picciotto, *Relation of Int. Law to the Law of England and the U. S.* (1915), 86 ff.; 2 Stephens, *Criminal Law* (1883), 29–42; Walker, *Science*, 173 ff.; Westlake, *Collected Papers* (1914), 501 f.; Willoughby, "The Legal Nature of Int. Law," in 2 *A. J.* (1908), 360 ff.

[34] Lord Alverstone, however, added the following warning: "But any doctrine so invoked must be one really accepted as binding between nations, and the International Law sought to be applied must, like anything else, be proved by satisfactory evidence, which must show either that the particular proposition has been recognized and acted upon by our own country, or that it is of such a nature and has been so widely and generally accepted that it can hardly be supposed that any civilized State would repudiate it.   The mere opinions of jurists, however, eminent or learned, that it ought to be so recognized, are not in themselves sufficient.   They must have received the express sanction of international agreement, or gradually have grown to be a part of International Law by their frequent practical recognition in dealings between various nations." On the importance of this case, see Scott, "The Legal Nature of Int. Law," in 1 *A. J.* 855 ff.; Westlake, *Collected Papers*, 498 ff.; and 6 *Columbia Law Review*, 49–50.

During the World War, in 1916, the judicial Committee of the Privy Council in the case of the *Zamora* (2 A. C. 77) gave an authoritative opinion, to the effect that British Orders in Council might not prescribe or alter the law to be administered by a Prize Court, except when the order in question mitigates the Crown's rights in favor of the enemy or a neutral, or unless such reprisals are ordered as are justified by the circumstances of the case and do not entail upon neutrals a degree of unreasonable inconvenience.

This doctrine laid down by Lord Alverstone has in its favor a long, unbroken series of decisions in the United States. As early as 1804 Chief Justice Marshall declared, in the case of *The Charming Betsey* (2 Cranch, 64, 118 and Scott, 11 n.): "An act of Congress should never be construed to violate the Law of Nations if any other possible construction remains." [35]   In the case of the *Nereide* (1815, 9 Cranch, 388, 423) he declared International Law to be " a part of the law of the land." In the *Scotia* (1871, 14 Wall. 170, 187–188, and Evans, 6) Justice Strong said: " No single nation can change the law of the sea. That law is of universal obligation, and no statute of one or two nations can create obligations for the world. Like all the Laws of Nations, it rests upon the common consent of civilized countries. It is of force, not because it is prescribed by any superior power, but because it has been generally accepted

On the other hand, it was distinctly maintained in this decision that while "the law which the Prize Court is to administer is not the national or, as it is sometimes called, the municipal law, but the law of nations"; yet, "it cannot be disputed that a Prize Court, like any other court, is bound by the legislative enactments of its own sovereign state. A British Court would certainly be bound by Acts of the Imperial Legislature . . . The fact, however, that the Prize Courts in this land would be bound by Acts of the Imperial Legislature affords no grounds for arguing that they are bound by the executive orders of the King's Council."

A doctrine similar to that laid down in the *Zamora* case prevails in the United States in reference to Acts of Congress. In *The Amy Warwick* (1862), it was laid down that prize courts are subject to the instructions of their own sovereign. 2 Sprague 123, and case No. 341, 1 Fed. Cas. 799. But it may be doubted whether the British precedent would be followed in respect to executive orders. "In American courts, executive orders are probably of the same effect as statutes, if made under adequate authority. In *Maissoñaire* v. *Keating* Justice Story asserted in dicta that an ordinance would exonerate the captors, and the only recourse open to the injured neutral was through diplomacy or war. There does not seem to have been any doubt expressed as to the binding force of the various blockade orders of the Civil War, or of other executive orders affecting prize in this and other wars." Wright, in 11 *A. J.* (1917), 16.

On the *Zamora* case, which is partially reported in Evans, 343 and Scott, 1052, and fully reported in 10 *A. J.*, 422, see especially Nos. 10 and 11 *A. J.* (1916 and 1917), 564 ff. and 1 ff. respectively; 1 Garner, 173 f.; 2 Hyde § 894, pp. 806, f.; Lawrence (7th ed.), § 188, pp. 461 f.; and 1 & 2 Oppenheim, § 21a, p. 27 and § 434, p. 628 *n*.

[35] But this must not be interpreted to mean that the courts would give effect to a custom of International Law in the face of a statute clearly commanding a violation of its principles. In such a case the State would be responsible to the Community of Nations. It should be added that the jurisdiction of the courts does not extend to questions of a purely political nature.

as a rule of conduct." The most recent and authoritative case in the United States is that of the *Paquete Habana* v. *U. S.* (1899, 175 U. S. 677, and Evans, *Cases*, 602 or Scott, 12) in which our Supreme Court held (p. 686) that even in the absence of treaty, express proclamation, or municipal law, "by an ancient usage among civilized nations, beginning centuries ago, and gradually ripening into a rule of International Law, coast fishing vessels, pursuing their vocation of catching and bringing in fresh fish, have been recognized as exempt, with their cargoes and crews, from capture as prize of war. . . .

"International Law is a part of our law, and must be ascertained and admitted by the courts of justice of appropriate jurisdiction, as often as questions of right depending upon it are duly presented for their determination. For this purpose, where there is no treaty and no controlling executive or legislative act or judicial decision, resort must be had to the custom and usages of civilized nations; and, as evidence of these, to the works of jurists and commentators who, by years of labor, research, and experience, have made themselves peculiarly well acquainted with the subjects of which they treat. Such works are resorted to by judicial tribunals, not for the speculations of their authors concerning what the law ought to be, but for trustworthy evidence of what the law really is." [36]

BIBLIOGRAPHY

Relation between International Law and Municipal or State Law.—Baldwin, in 15 *I. L. A.*, 35; 2 Butler, *Treaty-making Power* (1902), §§ 398–399 and notes; Devlin, *Treaty Power* (1908), § 434 and cases cited in notes; * Evans, *Cases*, 1–20; Fenwick, ch. 575; * Garner, *Recent Developments in Int. Law* (1925), 5–13; Heilborn, *Grundbegriffe*, in 1 *Handbuch*, § 17; * Holland, *Studies*, ch. 10, pp. 176–200; Holtzendorff, in 1 *Handbuch*, 49–53, 117–20; 1 Hyde, § 5 and note on p. 13; Kaufman, *Rechtskraft des int. Rechts* (1899); Maine, *Int. Law*, 36 ff.; * 1 Moore, *Digest*, § 2; 1 Nys, 185–189; * 1 Oppenheim, §§ 20–25; * Picciotto, *The Relation of Int. Law to the Law of England and the U. S.* (1915); * Scott, *Cases*, 1–16, and in 1 *A. J.*, 831 ff.; 2 Stephens, *Criminal Law* (1883), 29 ff.; Triepel, *Völkerrecht und Landesrecht* (1899), 134–55, and in * *Droit int. et droit interne* (1920);

[36] Justice Gray, in the *Paquete Habana, op. cit.*, p. 700. Cf. *Ibid., Hilton* v. *Guyot* (1894), 159 U. S. 113, 163.

Walker, *Science of International Law* (1893), 44 ff.; * Westlake, *Collected Papers* (1914), X, 498–518; (Atlay's) Wheaton, note, § 15a, p. 29; * Willoughby, in 2 *A. J.* (1908), 357–365; Woolsey, § 29; * Wright, "The Enforcement of Int. Law through Municipal Law in the U. S.," *Univ. of Illinois Studies*, Vol. 5, No. 1 (1916), and in 11 *A. J.* (1917), pp. 1–21. See also Index to *A. J.* (1921) under heads of "Municipal Law" and "International Law."

For cases bearing on this subject, the student is particularly referred to Scott, *Cases*, § 1, Introduction, or Evans, *Cases*, ch. 1. See especially *Triquet* v. *Bath* (1764), K. B., 3 Burr. 1478; *The Scotia* (1871), 14 Wall. 170; *The Paquete Habana* (1899), 175 U. S. 677; the *West Rand Central Gold Mining Co.*, v. *The King* (1905), L. R. 2 K. B. 391; and the *Zamora case*, 2 A. C. 77 or 10 *A. J.* 422.

Relation between International Morality and International Law. —Amos, *Jurisprudence* (1872), 393 ff., 504, and in *Remedies for War* (1880), 91–106, 114–16; Atkinson, *Int. Morality* (1851); * 1 Austin, *Lectures on Jurisprudence* (Campbell's 5th ed.), see index; * Bernard, *Lectures on Diplomacy* (1868), 166–71; Bourgeois, in 29 *R. D. I. P.* (1922), 5–22; Burns, *The Morality of Nations* (1915), *passim;* * Creasy, *First Platform of Int. Law* (1876), 11–48; Despagnet (4th ed.), No. 50, pp. 61–62; Dewey, in 1 *For. Aff.* (1922–23), No. 3, pp. 85–95; 1 Fauchille, No. 39; Ferguson, *The International Conference at the Hague* (1899), *passim;* Hibben, in *Int. J. of Ethics*, 156–160; Hobhouse, *Democracy and Reaction* (1904), ch. 8; Holtzendorff, in 1 *Handbuch*, § 17; Jacks, in 3 *For. Aff.* (1924), 266; Lawrence, § 11; Maine, *Int. Law*, 33–34; 1 Nys, 204–06; 1 Rivier, 24–26; Senior, in 77 *Edinburgh Review* (1843), 161 ff.; Sidgwick, *Elements of Politics* (1891), chs. 15, 17; 1 Twiss, § 105; Ullmann, 36–37; Westlake, *Chapters on Int. Law* (1894), 15–16; Woolsey, §§ 3, 15–16, 20b, 21–23. See also 28 *Int. J. of Ethics* (1918), particularly articles by Tufts, etc., pp. 299 ff.

Relation between Law and Morality.—* Ames, *Law and Morals,* in 22 *Harvard Law Rev.* (1908–09), 97–113; * Austin, *Lectures on Jurisprudence* (Campbell's 5th ed.), see index; 1 Ahrens, *Philosophie des Rechts* (1870–71), § 37, pp. 308–12; 1 Bentham, *Works* (Bowring's ed.), *Principles of Morals and Legislation* (1838), especially chs. 1 and 2 on "Utility"; * 1 Clark, *Roman Private Law* (1914–19), § 1, pp. 22–24 and § 3; French, in 2 *Philos. Rev.* (1893), 35–53; * Garner on "Political Science and Ethics," in 17 *Int. J. of Ethics* (1906–07), 194–204; Heron, *Jurisprudence*, chs. 2, 3, and pp. 51–54; 1 Hobhouse, *Morals in Evolution* (1906), chs. 3 and 6; * Holland, *Jurisprudence*, ch. 3; * Jellinek, *Die social-ethische Bedeutung von Recht, Unrecht und Strafe* (1878); 1 Lioy, *Philosophy of Right* (Hastie's trans., 1891), Prolegomena, 131, and Pt. I, ch. 6; Mezes, *Ethics* (1901), Pt. II, ch. 13, pp. 302–324; 1 Oppenheim, §§ 3–10; * Palmer, *The Field of Ethics* (1902), Lect. II; Paulsen, *A System of Ethics* (1899), Book III, ch. 9; * Pollock, *First Book of Jurisprudence* (1896), ch. 2; * Pound, *Law and Morals* (1923); * Pulszky, *Theory of Law and Civil Society*

(1888), chs. 12–13; Rattigan, *Jurisprudence* (1899, 2d ed.), 4–8; Sidgwick, *The Methods of Ethics* (1890), Bk. III, chs. 5 and 6, and *The Elements of Politics* (1891), ch. 13; Taylor, T. W., in 5 *Philos. Rev.* (1896), 36–50; Westlake, *Chapters* (1894), 2–3; * 1 Westermarck, *The Origin and Development of Moral Ideas* (1906–08), chs. 5 and 7; Whewell, *Elements of Morality and Polity* (1845); Willoughby, *The Nature of the State*.(1896), note on pp. 113–14; Wilson, *The State* (1889), §§ 1213–17; 1 Wundt, *Ethics* (1897–1901), Pt. III, ch. 4, pp. 160–87.

International Comity.—Bonfils or 1 Fauchille, No. 38; * Creasy, *First Platform of Int. Law* (1876), 35–37; Dicey, *Conflict of Laws* (2d ed., 1896), 10–15; 1 Fiore, Nos. 198–99; Heffter, § 3, pp. 193–96; Heilborn, in *Handbuch*, § 20; * Holland, *Jurisprudence* (10th ed.), 406–409; * 1 Holtzendorff, *Handbuch*, § 19; 3 Lawrence, *Commentaire* (1868–1880), 54 ff.; Leseur, *Cours de droit int.* (1893), § 30; 1 Lorimer, *Institutes of the Law of Nations* (1883–84), 358–67; 1 Mérignhac, 278 ff.; 1 Nys, 201–03; 1 Oppenheim, § 19; Rivier, 25; Scott, *Cases*, 17; Story, *Conflict of Laws*, §§ 28, 33–38; Ullmann, 38–39; 1 Wharton, *Conflict of Laws* (1905), §§ 1½ and 1a; Wheaton, § 79; Woolsey, §§ 24, 73, 81.   See especially an essay entitled "Völkerrecht und Völkercourtesie," by F. Stoerk, in *Staatsrechtliche Abhandlungen für Laband* (1908), 129–70.

The Nature of Diplomacy or Foreign Policy.—Acton's (Lord) Introduction to Burd's *Il Principe* (1891); Benoist, *Le Machiavélisme*, I, and, *Le Machiavélisme de L'anti-Antimachiavel* (1918); * Bernard, *Lectures on Diplomacy* (1868), Lect. III; Bonfils or 1 Fauchille, No. 66; Bulmerincq, in Marquardsen's *Handbuch*, I, § 3, and in 9 *R. D. I.*, 361 ff.; Calvo, §§ 1310 ff.; Despagnet, No. 50, pp. 63–65; Dunning, *Political Theories, Ancient and Mediaeval* (1902), ch. 11 on "Machiavelli"; Dyer, *Machiavelli and the Modern State* (1904); 1 Flassan, *Histoire de la diplomatie francaise* (1811), "Discours preliminaire"; Foster, *Practice of Diplomacy* (1906), ch. 1; Frederick the Great, *Anti-Machiavel* (French text, ed. 1834); * Figgis, *From Gerson to Grotius* (1907), Lect. 3, pp. 81 ff.; Freemantle, on views of Comte, in 3 *Contemp. Rev.* (1866), 477 ff.; Funck-Brentano, *La politique;* * Funck-Brentano et Sorel, 74, 80; * Harrison on "The Modern Machiavelli," in 42 *Nineteenth Century* (1897), 462–71; Hay in *Addresses* (1906), No. 10, on "American Diplomacy"; * Heffter, §§ 4, 198, 227–40; * 1 Hill, *History of Diplomacy in the Development of Europe* (1905–06), Preface; Hobson, *The Morals of Economic Internationalism* (1920); Holtzendorff, in 1 *Handbuch*, § 18, and *Politik* (1869), Bk. II, chs. 4–7; * 1 Janet, *Histoire de la science politique* (3d ed., 1887), "Introduction sur rapports de la morale et de la politique," and liv. III, chs. 1 and 2, on Machiavelli, 491 ff.; Leseur, *Cours de droit int.* (1893), § 32; Machiavelli, *The Prince* (trans. by Thompson, 1897), particularly chs. 15–19, and *Discourses* (trans. by Thompson, 1883); Morley, Romanes Lecture on Machiavelli in *Miscellanies* (1886–1908), Essay I; von Mohl, *Encyklopädie* (1859),

§§ 86–89, 105–07; * Nippold, *Die Fortbildung des Verfahrens* (1907), 30 ff.; 1 Nys, 205, and *Les origines*, 295 ff.; * Phillips, Article on, in *Ency. Brit.* (11th ed.); 1 P. Fodéré, *Cours*, ch. 1, and *Traité*, No. 37, pp. 100–101; 1 Rivier, 432; Rümelin, *Politics and Morals* (1907); 1 Satow, ch. 1; 1 Sorel, *L'Europe et la Revolution Française* (1893–1904), especially ch. 1 on the diplomacy of the 18th century; 1 Treitschke, *Politik* (1897–98), § 3, and II, § 28; 1 Twiss, § 97; Ullmann, 37–38; * 2 Villari, *Life and Times of Machiavelli* (1891), Bk. II, chs. 2–5; Whewell, *Elements of Morality and Polity* (1845).

Much of the literature on this subject (the theory and practice of diplomacy) centers around the name of Machiavelli. For bibliographies on Machiavelli, see Burd, in 1 *Cambridge Modern History*, 719–726; the Bibliographical Note in the "Introduction" to Burd's *Il Principe* (1891); 1 Janet *Histoire*, 596–601; and the Catalogue of the British Museum.

International Private Law or the Conflict of Laws.—* Amos, *Jurisprudence* (1872), ch. 15; Bonfils or Fauchille, No. 4; * 2 Calvo, liv. VII, 1–23; Despagnet, No. 49; Funck-Brentano et Sorel, ch. 2; Hall, § 10, pp. 58–59; * Holland, *Jurisprudence*, 404 n., 407–12; Holtzendorff, in 1 *Handbuch*, § 16; Lawrence, § 6; 1 Lorimer, *Institutes of the Law of Nations* (1883–84), Bk. III, ch. 9; * 2 F. de Martens, 391–505; Meili, *International Civil and Commercial Law* (1905), Introduction; 1 Mérignhac, 5–9; Neumeyer, *Int. Verwaltungsrecht* (I in 1910, II in 1922); 1 Oppenheim, §§ 1, 594; 4 Phillimore; 1 Piédelièvre, 15–17; 1 Nys, 190–96; * 3 P.-Fodéré, pp. 519–1237; Rattigan, *Jurisprudence* (1899), ch. 11; Ullmann, § 3; 1 Westlake, 249–50; * Wheaton, §§ 77 ff.; Woolsey, §§ 73–74. For a list of the most important works on International Private Law or Conflict of Laws, see the Syllabus to Scott's *Cases on International Law*, § 8, p. xxv (1902 ed.).

The student is especially recommended to read: Beale's *Cases on Conflict of Laws* (1907), Preface, and Summary at the close of the third volume and Minor, *Conflict of Laws* (1901), Introductory chapter to the second edition of 1905.

The most extensive work on this subject is by Weiss, *Traité de droit int. privé* (1907), in 5 vols.

International Administrative Law.—Allen, *Int. Relations* (1920), chs. 3–4, 8–9; * *Annuaire de la vie int.*, since 1905; Bridgman, *The First Book of World Law* (1911); Descamps, *Les offices int.* (1894); Hicks, *New World Order* (1920), chs. 13, 18; Meili, *Die int. Unionen* (1889); Moynier, *Les bureaux int.* (1892); Nippold, *Die Fortbildung des Verfahrens* (1907), 61 ff.; Poinsard, *Études de droit int.* (1894), *Les unions* (1901), and *Le droit int. au XXe siécle* (1907); Overbergh, *L'association int.* (1907); * Potter, *Int. Organization* (1922), Pt. V on "International Administration," chs. 17–19; * Reinsch, "Int. Unions and their Administration," in I *A. J.* (1907), 579–623, "Int. Administrative Law and National Sovereignty," in 3 *A. J.* (1909), 145 ff., and *Public Int. Unions* (1911); Renault, in 3 *R. G. D. I.* (1896),

14 ff.; * Sayre, *Int. Administration* (1918); Toll, *Die int. Bureaux* (1910); Woolf, *Int. Government* (1916), Pt. II, chs. 2–4.

Among the relatively few authorities on International Law who deal with this subject are: Bonfils and 1 (3d Pt.) Fauchille, Nos. 914 ff.; Lizst, §§ 27–28; 2 Mérignhac, 694–718; I Oppenheim, §§ 458–71, 581–96; Ullmann, §§ 68–69; Zorn, *Völkerrechts* (1903), §§ 16–17.

Neumeyer is writing a very comprehensive treatise on what he calls *Internationales Verwaltingsrecht* in three volumes of which the second was published in 1922; but he uses the phrase "international administrative law" in a very different sense from that indicated in our text, and restricts its application to national or internal administration, at least in the two volumes so far published. It appears to belong rather to the subject of International Private Law than to International Administrative Law.

The Austinian or Imperative View of Law.—Among those authorities who may be cited as virtually in favor of the Austinian or imperative view of law or some slight modification thereof, are the following: * Austin, *Lectures on Jurisprudence* (Campbell's 5th ed., 1911), Introductory and Lects. I, V, and VI of the *Province of Jurisprudence Determined*, and Lects. XXII and XXVII on "Sanctions"; Bentham, *Principles*, etc. and *Fragment*, etc. in 1 *Works*, pp. 151 *n.* and 289 *n.*; Fricker, *Das Problem des Völkerrechts*, in 34 *Zeitschrift für Staatswissenschaft*, 368 ff.; * Hobbes, *Leviathan*, chs. 15 *ad fin* and 26; * Holland, *Jurisprudence* (10th ed.), 128–29, 380–83; 1 Ihering, *Zweck im Recht* (1884, 2d ed.), 320 ff.; * Lasson, *Prinzip und Zukunft des Völkerrecht* (1871), 43 ff.; 2 Lorimer, *Institutes of the Law of Nations* (1884), 189; Pollock, *First Book on Jurisprudence* (1896), 13, 96; Pomeroy, §§ 9–30; Pufendorf, *De jure naturale et gentium*, lib. II, cap. 3, § 23; Salmond, *Jurisprudence* (3d ed., 1910), §§ 15–17; * 2 Stephens, *Criminal Law* (1883), 34 ff.; Stephens, J. K., *Int. Law and International Relations* (1884), Pt. I; Wheaton, *History*, etc., 93–95; * Willoughby, *Nature of the State* (1918), 199–204, and * "The Legal Nature of International Law," in 2 *A. J.* (1908), 357–65; Zorn, *Völkerrechts* (1903), § 2.

As against the Austinian or imperative view, the following authorities may be cited: Amos, *Jurisprudence* (1872), 294, 409–413; * Bergbohm, *Staatsverträge und Gesetze als Quellen des Völkerrechts* (1871), 12 ff.; Bernard, *Lectures on Diplomacy* (1868), 171; Bluntschli, 2, 11; * Bonfils or 1 Fauchille, Nos. 26–31; * Bryce, *Studies in History and Jurisprudence* (1901), 499–502; Bulmerincq, in 1 Marquardsen, § 12, and *Praxis und Theorie des Völkerrechts* (1874), 158 ff.; Carter, in *Report of the American Bar Association* (1890), 222 ff.; * Clark, *Practical Jurisprudence* (1883), 5, 181–87, and 1 *Roman Private Law* (1914–15), §§ 1–2; Creasy, *First Platform of Int. Law* (1876), 70–76; Despagnet, Nos. 38–40; 1 Fiore, Nos. 186 ff., and 30 *R. D. I.* (1898), 5–25; Hall, pp. 13–16; * Harrison, Fr., on "The English School of Jurisprudence," in 24 *Fortn. Rev.* (1878), 475–92, 682–703; 1 Halleck (3d ed.), 51, 54; Heffter, § 2, especially note on pp. 3–5; * Higgins,

The Binding Force of Int. Law (1910); Holtzendorff, in 1 *Handbuch*, §§ 6–7; Jenks, *Law in the Middle Ages* (1898), ch. 1; * 1 Jellinek, *Das Recht des modernen Staates* (1905, 2d ed.), 328, 364–68; Kaltenborn, *Kritik des Völkerrechts* (1837), ch. 6; Kebedgy, in 29 *R. D. I.* (1897), 113 ff.; Lawrence, § 9, and *Essays on Int. Law* (1885), 1–36; 1 J. de Louter, § 6; 1 F. de Martens, §§ 1–2; Maine, *Int. Law*, Lect. II, 26–53; and * *Early History of Institutions* (1893), Lects. XII and XIII; 1 Mérignhac, 18–24; Mougins de Roquefort, *La solution juridique des conflits internationaux*, (1889), 36 ff.; 1 Nys, 133–43, and *Les origines*, Introduction; * 1 Oppenheim, §§ 2–10; 1 Phillimore, Introduction, ch. 1; 1 Piédelièvre, 5–11; * Pollock, "Sources of International Law," in 2 *Columbia Law Rev.* (1902), 514 ff.; 1 P.-Fodéré, Nos. 7–12; Rattigan, *Jurisprudence* (1899), 12–20, 355–57; Renault, *Introduction à l'étude de droit int.* (1869), 6 ff.; Rivier, 18–24; * Root, "The Sanctions of Int. Law," in 2 *A. J.* (1908), 451–57; Russell (Lord), in 19 *Reports American Bar Assoc.* (1896), 255 ff.; Salmond, *Jurisprudence* (3d ed., 1910), §§ 21–24; Savigny, *System*, § 11; * Scott, on the "Legal Nature of International Law," in 1 *A. J.* (1907), 831–66; Smith, Munroe, in 12 *Am. Pol. Sci. Rev.* (1918), 1–16; Triepel, *Völkerrecht und Landesrecht* (1899), 103 ff.; 1 Twiss, §§ 104–05; * Ullmann, § 4; * Walker, *History of the Law of Nations* (1899), §§ 2–8, and *Science*, chs. 1 and 2, pp. 1–56; 1 Westlake, 5–9, and *Chapters*, 11–15.

Several of the authorities cited above are difficult to place. Thus Savigny speaks of International Law as at once positive and imperfect. The position of Ihering is also somewhat difficult to determine. Like Savigny he is cited on both sides of the question. He (Ihering) insists upon force as an essential element in law; but he also declares (p. 325) that the legal nature of the Law of Nations is not a subject of doubt.

On p. 13 of his *First Book on Jurisprudence* (1896), Pollock speaks of International Law as consisting of "these customs and observances in an imperfectly organized society which have not fully acquired the character of law, but are on the way to become law;" and on p. 96 he appears to deny that the "duties of independent States to one another" are "legal duties or the subject of legal rules." In an earlier work (*Essays in Jurisprudence and Ethics*, published in 1882, p. 35), he speaks of the "extreme purists of the analytical school, who deny that it (Int. Law) is really law." He asks (on p. 37), "should we not, then, regard public opinion as the final sanction of International Law in every case,—a sanction with physical force behind it, no doubt, in one or another shape, but with a force latent and undefined, and to be called into action only in an extreme case?" I have therefore cited him on both sides of this question.

Salmond (*Jurisprudence*, § 5) defines law as "the rules recognized and acted on in courts of justice." Although he maintains that the imperative theory of law is defective (§ 17) in that it only contains the most important element of the truth, yet he must be classed as essentially Austinian, inasmuch as he holds that "law is based on physical force."

It may be noted that Westlake, who formerly denied the positive character of International Law (see *Treatise on Int. Private Law*, 2d ed., 1880, pp. 3 ff.) is strongly anti-Austinian in his later works.

For references showing a tendency toward a reversion to the Austinian or imperative view of law, due to imperial legislation, in modern Germany, see * Pound on "The Scope and Purpose of Sociological Jurisprudence," in 24 and 25 *Harvard Law Review* (1911 and 1912), 593 and 144–45 respectively.

CHAPTER II

THE BASIS AND SOURCES OF INTERNATIONAL LAW

11. The Basis or Foundation of International Law.—Like the State itself, International Law is ultimately based upon the innate or inherited sociability of human nature directed by specific human needs and interests. Though a fighting animal almost constantly engaged in a desperate struggle for existence with his environment and frequently at war with his fellows, man is also a social and political being who has long since discovered that mutual coöperation and organization are at least as essential to human well-being and progress as are struggle, rivalry, and competition.[1]

Ever since his earliest appearance on this planet, man has apparently lived not in isolation, but in more or less hostile or friendly groups which form ever widening circles (families, hordes, clans, cities, nations, states, confederacies, etc.) within which the practice of mutual aid or coöperation, due to a sense of interdependence, has largely supplanted, or at least greatly modified, the habit of struggle and competition. This habit or practice of mutual aid and coöperation was gradually extended to intergroupal relations, until it now includes all civilized states, races, and nations, and

[1] For illustrations of the operation of this principle even among lower animals and savages, see the first three chapters of Kropotkin's remarkable book, entitled *Mutual Aid, a Factor of Evolution* (1902). Cf. Romanes, *Animal Intelligence* (1883), *passim*; Espinas, *Societés animales* (1877); and Morgan, *Animal Behavior* (1900), ch. 5.

On the general principles, see Giddings, *Principles of Sociology* (1898), *passim*; Durkheim, *De la division du travail social* (1902), liv. 1, ch. 1, 17 ff., chs. 5 and 6; Novicow, *La critique du darwinism social* (1910), ch. 8; Pulszky, *Theory of Law and Civil Society* (1888), ch. 6; Redslob, *Das Problem des Völkerrechts* (1917), Bk. I, chs. 1–4; and Ross, *Social Control* (1901), *passim*. See Tarde, *Laws of Imitation* (1903), chs. 1–3 for the view that conscious and unconscious imitation resulting in fixed habits play an important rôle in the development of the social order. For Professor Giddings' interesting doctrine of Consciousness of Kind and the various forms of Co-operation and Like-mindedness, see his *Inductive Sociology* (1901), Pt. II, chs. 3 and 4.

appears to be entering upon its final phase of world organization.[2]

12. **The Society or Community of States.**—In international relations this solidarity of interests, based on a human need for coöperation and organization, has stimulated the growth of customs and led to the formation of rules and agreements for the maintenance of durable community interests and peaceful intercourse even in time of war. It has given rise in modern times to the conception of a Community, Society, or Family of States,[3] the members of which retain their sovereignty and independence and are regarded as possessed of equal rights and duties in the eyes

[2] For references on International or World Organization, see p. 496n.

Among those authorities who find the basis or foundation of International Law in the principle of human sociability or solidarity of interests in one form or another, may be cited: Bluntschli, 1–2; Bonfils or Fauchille Nos. 5 ff.; Bry, No. 1; Chrétien, *Principes de droit int. public* (1893), No. 1; Despagnet, Nos. 2–3, 38; 1 Fiore, Nos. 151 ff.; Geffcken, *Die Gesamtinteresse als Grundlage des Staates und Völkerrecht* (1898); Grotius (Whewell's trans.), Prolegomena, §§ 7–8, 16–18, 22, 23; Heffter, § 2; Holtzendorff, *Elements de droit int. public* (1891), § 1, and 1 *Handbuch*, 44 ff.; Hautefeuille, ch. I; Kaltenborn, *Kritik des Völkerrechts* (1837), 298; Liszt, § 1; J. de Louter, § 2; 1 F. de Martens, § 1, p. 1 and §§ 3–5, pp. 24–31; 1 Mérignhac, 2, 18; Nippold, *Die Fortbildung des Verfahrens* (1907), § 2, pp. 35 ff.; 1 Nys, 65–66; 1 Ortolan, *Dip. de la mer* (1864), ch. 1, p. 2; 1 Phillimore, ch. 1, § VII; 1 Piédelievre, 1, 13–14; Pillet, in *R. G. D. I.* (1894), 1 ff.; P.-Fodéré, No. 21, p. 72; Preuss, *Das Völkerrecht im Dienste des Wirtschaftslebens* (1891); Suarez, *Tractatus de legibus* (1612), II, ch. 11, No. 9, quoted by Nys, *Les origines*, 11–12; Ullmann, § 1; Westlake, *Chapters* (1894), 26–27; Vattel, Preliminaries, §§ 10–12.

Several of the authorities (*e.g.* 1 Rivier, p. 7 and more recently Jitta, *The Renovation of Int. Law*, 1919, 1 ff.) make the common legal consciousness of the society of nations, based on reason, the primary source of International Law. But in the light of modern psychology, a purely rationalistic basis for International Law may well be doubted. The preamble to the Hague Conventions of 1899 and 1907 for the Pacific Settlement of International Disputes recognizes "the solidarity which unites the members of the society of civilized nations."

[3] Westlake (I, p. 1) defines International Law as "the law of the society of States or nations." Oppenheim (I, § 12) uses the term "family of nations." The majority of the publicists who make use of the conception referred to above seem to prefer the term "international community" or "community of States or nations." On the "Law of the International Community," see especially, 1 F. de Martens, §§ 39, 45–52. In German the term *Staatenverein* is sometimes employed. On the nature, rise, and growth of the "Society of Nations," see especially Lawrence, *International Problems* (1908), chs. 1–3, and *Society of Nations* (1919), Lects. 1–2.

The Spanish theologians of the sixteenth century seem to have been the earliest publicists to give expression to this conception, but it was first given a wide currency by Grotius.

of International Law; but who have also developed a strong sense of interdependence or internationalism. This International Community is by no means a World State or *civitas maxima* based on abstract principles of justice and equity. It is rather a "free society of peoples united by the solidarity of their tendencies and interests." [4]

13. **Utility as the Purpose of International Relations.**— The guiding motive or purpose of international relations should be utility or the satisfaction of collective needs and interests, whether intellectual, moral, or material. These become ever greater, more varied and imperative as the mutual interdependence and solidarity of nations constantly increases. They have, indeed, become so great and complex that it has been found necessary to give certain rules and customs of international intercourse the solemn character of International or World Agreements and thus render them more imperative. There has even been an attempt to create suitable machinery for their better observance and enforcement. In the further development of International Law, motives of utility and a sense of international common interests should be allowed to have at least as much influence as tradition and precedents based upon metaphysical conceptions of natural law or abstract principles of justice. Jurists must learn to look forward as well as backward, and should have regard to the probable or possible social consequences of a given practice rather than to mere conformity with past usages and ideals. Social utility, or adaptability to human needs and social conditions, is thus the ultimate test of international, as of all human law. The better to answer these needs and interests, the Law of Nations tends, like every other branch of jurisprudence, to become more pragmatic and sociological.[5]

[4] Cf. Bonfils or Fauchille, No. 13; and 1 F. de Martens, 268. "To move and live and have its being in the great community of nations is as much the normal condition of a single nation, as to live in a social state is the normal condition of a single man." 1 Phillimore, § VII.

[5] On *Utility* as a test of International Law, see Creasy, ch. 3, especially the citation from Story (*Conflict of Laws*, 1883, § 35) on p. 62. The doctrine is derived from Bentham. See especially Bentham, *Fragment on Government*, ch. 1, sects. 42–47 in 1 *Works* (Bowring's ed., 1838), pp. 271–72.

For a remarkable series of articles on "Sociological Jurisprudence," see Pound, in 24 and 25 *Harvard Law Rev.* (1911 and 1912). For a very sugges-

14. **The Primary Sources of International Law.**—The primary sources of positive International Law are: (1) custom based on tacit consent and imitation; and (2) convention or express agreement by means of treaties.[6]

" Custom as a source of International Law must not be confounded, as Westlake has observed, ' with mere frequency or habit of conduct.' It signifies rather ' that line of conduct which the society has consented to regard as obligatory.' In such a sense international custom is indicative of a general practice which may be fairly accepted as law." [7]

Customary International Law has grown by means of tacit agreement and imitation or consent. It is the Common Law of Nations which has developed gradually from usage or precedents set by particular States as the result of acquiescence or imitation on the part of the other members of the international community. It has as its guarantee or sanction the consensus of opinion and usage of the civilized world, and it forms the oldest and intrinsically the most important portion of International Law; for it is deeply rooted in the habits, sentiments, and interests of mankind.

In dealing with treaties as a source of International Law, it is necessary to distinguish between treaties that are mere bargains or contracts between States, or those which contain no rules for the regulation of international conduct, and treaties that are declaratory or stipulatory of International Law. Especially important are the great International or

tive lecture on "Philosophical Theory and Int. Law," see also Pound, in 1 *Biblitheca Visseriana*, 71–90.

[6] Westlake (I, pp. 14–15) makes "custom and reason" the two sources of International Law. But he thus confuses one of its sources with a means of interpretation. As Oppenheim (I, note on p. 22 of the 1st ed., 1905) justly remarks: "Reason is a means of interpreting law, but it cannot call law into existence." Writers frequently confuse the *sources* of International Law with its *basis* or *foundation* on the one hand, and with the *evidences* or *witnesses* to its existence on the other. Certain Continental publicists (*e.g.* Gareis, *Institutionen des Völkerrechts*, 1887, § 9, and Leseur, *Cours de droit int.*, 1893, pp. 22 ff.) find a source of International Law in the *necessitas* of the Roman jurists. For a criticism of this view, see Ullmann, p. 40.

[7] I Hyde, § 3, p. 6. The reference to Westlake is to I, p. 14. "By custom we mean not merely habit or usage but these developed into a rule which is adhered to in the conviction that an obligation exists," Hicks, *The New World Order* (1920), p. 97.

World Agreements which preserve the form of treaties (reserving to each State the right of sanction or ratification), but which are really great acts of international legislation and create or codify existing international practice. Such are, *e.g.* the Declaration of Paris of 1856, the Geneva Conventions of 1864 and 1906, and the sixteen Conventions of the Hague Conferences of 1899 and 1907.[8]

15. **The Evidences of International Law.**—The evidences or witnesses of International Law are the places where the law as applied or agreed upon is found,[9] or the documents which bear evidence or witness to existing principles and customs. Arranged in the order of their *extrinsic.* importance from the standpoint of formal authoritativeness, they are as follows:

(1) International or World treaties that virtually legislate or codify existing practice. These are the works of International Congresses or Conferences which are composed of delegates vested with full powers to negotiate and conclude treaties of the character indicated above.

(2) The Agreements of International Congresses and Conferences whose work has not received official sanction or ratification. Examples are the Brussels Conferences of 1874 and the Geneva Convention of 1868. The work of such Conferences has sometimes been of great importance, inasmuch as they have codified or influenced existing practice.

(3) Treaties, whether between several or a considerable number of States, which merely purport to be declaratory of existing law or stipulatory of new principles or usages.

---

[8] As pointed out by Jellinek (*Öffentliches Rechte*, 1892, pp. 193 ff. Cf. *Staatenverbindungen*, (1882), 107 ff.), such agreements (*Vereinbarungen*) are the results of the collaboration of many individual wills working for the satisfaction of *common* interests, whereas ordinary treaties (*Verträge*) are the product of several wills working for particular and often opposing interests. See also Binding, *Das Gründung des norddeutschen Bundes* (1889), Nippold, *Das völkerr. Vertrag* (1894), *passim*; 1 Nys, p. 157; and Triepel *Völkerrecht und Landesrecht* (1899), 63 ff.

For a list of lawmaking treaties, see 1 Oppenheim, §§ 556–68; and Introduction to Whittuck, *International Documents* (1908).

[9] This is the sense in which the term "sources" is generally used by historians, but jurists use the term in a different sense. The phrase "evidences of International Law" is borrowed from Walker, *History of the Law of Nations* (1899), ch. 2.

Such are, *e.g.* the Armed Neutralities of 1780 and 1800, the Three Rules of the Treaty of Washington of 1871, and Franklin's famous treaty of 1785 between the United States and Prussia which stipulated for the exemption of private enemy property from capture at sea.

(4) The decisions of judicial tribunals, more especially of Courts of Arbitration, International Commissions of Inquiry, Mixed Tribunals, Prize Courts, the Hague Court of Arbitration, and the Permanent Court of International Justice. The decisions of the Geneva Board of Arbitration which settled the Alabama claims in 1872, the North Sea International Commission of Inquiry of 1906 which investigated the North Sea Incident,[10] and the decisions of the Hague Tribunal created in 1899, will undoubtedly be treated as important precedents in similar cases in the future. The advisory opinions and decisions of the Permanent Court of International Justice established in 1921–22 will probably be regarded as the most authoritative interpretations of International jurisprudence in the future. Indeed, they may aid materially in the creation of new law.

Prize Courts, though hitherto national in character, are supposed to administer International Law;[11] and the decisions of judges of international reputation for learning and impartiality, like Sir William Scott (later Lord Stowell) and Justice Story, have always been treated with great respect, especially in England and the United States. Such decisions have more value for the student of positive International Law than the mere opinions of any publicist, however eminent, partly because they bear a certain stamp of judicial authentication, but still more because the cases have presumably been argued by able counsel and carefully considered from every standpoint, more particularly with a view to their practical bearings.

On the other hand, excessive deference is sometimes paid in England and the United States to judicial opinions which are mere *obiter dicta*, and judicial decisions are often given a

---

[10] See Hershey, *Russo-Japanese War* (1906), ch. 8; and *infra*, No. 308, note 16 on pp. 463–64.

[11] See, *e.g.*, the conception of his office held by Sir Wm. Scott, in the *Maria* (1799), 1 C. Rob. 340 or Evans *Cases*, 282. With some modifications, a similar view is maintained in the case of the *Zamora*. See *supra*, note on p. 13n.

more extended application than they deserve. In dealing
with judicial decisions, the student should always remember
that they are necessarily of limited application, both as to
subject-matter and in respect to nationality, and that International Law is based upon general usage or international
practice. This implies a much wider field of study and
research than is afforded by any supply of judicial decisions,
however copious. This condition of our science is one of
the gravest objections to the teaching of International Law
by the main or exclusive use of the " case system." [12]

(5) Unilateral Acts or Laws, Ordinances, Proclamations,
Decrees, Declarations or Instructions issued by a State to
its naval, military, diplomatic, or consular representatives
for the capture and disposition of prizes, the conduct of its
armies and navies, or the transaction of its business abroad.
Famous examples of this sort are the French Marine Ordinance of 1681; the British Admiralty Manuals and the
American Naval War Code of 1900 (withdrawn in 1904);
the Instructions for the Government of the Armies of the
United States in the Field, issued during our Civil War; the
United States Neutrality Laws of 1794 and 1818 and the
British Foreign Enlistment Acts of 1819 and 1870; and the
various Declarations of Neutrality issued at the outbreak of
important wars.

(6) Opinions of statesmen as expressed in important state
papers and diplomatic correspondence, and opinions of legal
advisors of the various Governments, such as those of the
law officers of the Crown in Great Britian and of the
Attorneys-General of the United States. Such opinions are
important in that they bear a certain official stamp and are
usually well considered and practical; but they are apt to be
biased by advocacy of a particular cause. Moore's monumental *International Law Digest* (in eight volumes, 1906)
illustrates the wealth of material of this sort existing in the
foreign archives of a single modern Government.

[12] "The decisions of the courts of every country, so far as they are founded
upon a law common to every country, will be received, not as authority, but
with respect. The decisions of the courts of every country show how the Law
of Nations, in the given case, is understood in that country, and will be
considered in adopting the rule which is to prevail in this," Chief Justice
Marshall. in *Thirty Hogsheads of Sugar* v. *Boyle* (1815), 9 Cranch 191, 198.

(7) The writings of eminent jurists and authorities on International Law. " In the absence of higher and more authoritative sanctions, the ordinances of foreign States, the opinions of eminent statesmen, and the writings of distinguished jurists are regarded as of great consideration on questions not settled by conventional law. In cases where the principal jurists agree, the presumption will be very great in favor of the solidity of their maxims; and no civilized nation that does not arrogantly set all ordinary law and justice at defiance, will venture to disregard the uniform sense of the established writers on International Law." [13]

" Without wishing to exaggerate the importance of these writers, or to substitute, in any case, their authority for the principles of reason, it may be affirmed that they are generally impartial in their judgment. They are witnesses of the sentiments and usages of civilized nations, and the weight of their testimony increases every time that their authority is invoked by statesmen, and every year that passes without the rules laid down in their works being impugned by the avowal of contrary principles." [14]

The above passages from Kent and Wheaton were approvingly cited by Justice Gray in his opinion in the case of the *Paquete Habana*. He added: " Such works [the works of jurists and commentators] are resorted to by judicial tribunals, not for the speculations of their authors concerning what the law ought to be, but for trustworthy evidence of what the law really is." [15]   Especially valuable

---

[13] 1 Kent, *Commentary on Int. Law* (1877), 19.

[14] Wheaton, § 15.

[15] The *Paquete Habana* (1899), 175 U. S. 677, 700. Cf. *Hilton* v. *Guyot* (1894), 159 U. S. 113, 163–164, 214–215; Lord Coleridge, in *Queen* v. *Keyn* (1876), L. R., 2 Excheq. Div. 63, 154; and Lord Alverstone, in *West Rand Central Gold Mining Co.* v. *The King* (1905), 2 K. B. 391, 401–402, 407.

As in the case of certain great International Treaties, some of the earlier publicists like Grotius, Bynkershoek, and Vattel should perhaps be listed as primary as well as secondary sources or evidences of International Law.   They not only interpreted and systematized existing international custom; but, like the Roman imperial jurists, they virtually exercised legislative functions, and many of their mere opinions were long regarded as authoritative.   In the case of modern writers, a consensus of opinion, or evidence amounting to proof, is necessary before a given rule or custom can be accepted as unquestionable law. It should also be noted that publicists seem to enjoy a greater authority on the

is the work of learned societies like the Institute of International Law.

(8) The histories of International Relations, more particularly of wars, negotiations, and treaties.   Such histories, though they should be used with the greatest caution, contain almost exhaustless stores of information bearing upon the development of the theory and practice of the Law of Nations. Especially important are the histories of diplomacy and International Law, like those of Flassen, Hill, Laurent, Walker, and Wheaton.[16]

BIBLIOGRAPHY

Sources of International Law.—* Bergbohm, *Staatenverträge und Gesetze als Quellen des Völkerrechts* (1877); * Bonfils and 1 Fauchille, Nos. 45–63; Bulmerincq, in Marquardsen, § 11; * 1 Calvo, §§ 27–38; Chrétien, *Principes de droit int. public* (1893), Nos. 10–24; Creasy, *First Platform of Int. Law* (1876), ch. 5; Despagnet, Nos. 54–66; Fenwick, in 16 *Mich. Law Rev.* (1918), 393–401; 1 Fiore, No. 224; Hall, 5–13; 1 Halleck (3d ed.), 55–64; Heffter, § 3; Hautefeuille, *Droit maritime* (1869), ch. 1; * Heilborn, *Grundbegriffe* in 1 *Handbuch*, §§ 6–9; Holtzendorff, *Éléments de droit int.* (1891), § 14, and in 1 *Handbuch*, §§ 21–39; Jellinek, *Die rechtliche Natur des Staatenverträge* (1880); Kaufman, *Rechtskraft des int. Rechts* (1899), *passim;* * Lawrence, Pt. I, ch. 4; 1 Lorimer, *Institutes of the Law of Nations* (1883–84), Bk. I, chs. 1–3; 1 J. de Louter, § 5; Maine, *Int. Law*, Lect. I. 1 F. de Martens, § 43; 1 Mérignhac, 79 ff.; Nippold, *Der völkerrecht-*

Continent than in England and the United States, and their authority seems somewhat greater in the United States than in England.

[16] See Flassen, *Histoire générale de la diplomatie francaise* (1811); Hill, *History of Diplomacy in the Development of Europe* (1905–06); Laurent, *Études sur l'histoire de l'humanite* (1865–80); Walker, *History of the Law of Nations* (1899); Wheaton, *History of the Law of Nations* (1845).

Some authorities lay stress upon the importance of Roman Law as a source of International Law. See, *e.g.* Creasy, *First Platform of Int. Law* (1876), 83–86; 1 Halleck (Baker's 3d ed.), 57 f.; Maine, *Ancient Law* (Pollock's ed.), 92 ff. (Cf. *Int. Law*, 20 ff.) and notes in Appendix, 396 ff.; 1 Phillimore, §§ xxxviii–xl. But whatever value it may have originally possessed as the source from which Grotius and others drew many of their rules, the *Corpus Juris Civilis* cannot, as Calvo (I, § 38) justly observes, "be applied to the international relations of modern peoples without the gravest inconveniences," except in the domain of International Private Law. Halleck (I, ch. 2, § 18 of Baker's 3d ed.), Phillimore (I, § xxiii), and Pomeroy (§ 32) still speak of the Divine Law or principle of justice as a source of International Law; and a few publicists (like Hautefeuille, *Discours preliminaire* to *Droit et des devoirs des neutres*, ch. 1) constantly refer to an imaginary "primitive law" (*droit ou loi primitive*). For an able criticism of Hautefeuille on this point, see Historicus, 75 ff.

liche Vertrag (1894), *passim*, and *Die Fortbildung des Verfahrens*
(1907), 19 ff.; 1 Nys, 144–65; * 1 Oppenheim, §§ 15–19; Perels, § 2;
1 Phillimore, Pt. I, chs. 3–8; 1 Piédelièvre, No. 4; * Pollock, on
"Sources of Int. Law," in 2 *Columbia Law Rev.* (1902), 511–24;
Pomeroy, §§ 31–46; 1 P.-Fodéré, Nos. 24–35; 1 Rivier, § 2; Taylor,
§§ 30–95, 115; * Triepel, *Droit int. et droit interne* (1920), §§ 3–5:
1 Twiss, ch. 6; Ullmann, § 8; * Walker, *History of the Law of Nations*
(1899), ch. 2; 1 Westlake, ch. 2; * Wheaton, § 15 and notes of his
various commentators, notably Atlay and Dana; Wilson, § 4; Woolsey,
§§ 28, 30.

CHAPTER III

THE HISTORY OF INTERNATIONAL RELATIONS DURING ANTIQUITY AND THE MIDDLE AGES

16. **International Law impossible before the Rise of the Modern European State System.**—The history of International Law is essentially a history of the law governing the members of the modern International Community of States in their relations with one another. Inasmuch as the observance of well-established rules and customs of the Law of Nations implies the existence of an International Community of States based upon a general recognition of the fundamental principles of territorial sovereignty and equality of independent States in respect to legal rights and obligations; such a law (in the strict and full sense of this term) could not possibly have been developed prior to the rise of the modern European State System, at the close of the Middle Ages or during the fifteenth and sixteenth centuries of our era. Nevertheless, we are by no means without evidence, even during Antiquity and the Middle Ages, of the observance in intercommunity intercourse of certain rules and customs, mainly with a religious sanction. This was especially the case in Greece, where there were developed rules and customs of *intermunicipal* law which, in many respects, bear a truly remarkable resemblance to our modern system of international jurisprudence.

17. **The International Relations of Antiquity.**—The international relations of the Ancient World have been represented by historians as almost wholly based upon force, and the nations of antiquity are usually described as living in a state either of almost complete isolation or of perpetual warfare with one another. But recent studies and researches, based largely upon archæological discoveries, have demonstrated that such was by no means invariably the case; and that the older conception of the interstate and intertribal life of antiquity, as either non-existent or as

31

characterized by a ceaseless and remorseless struggle, needs considerable modification.   This is even the case with very primitive and backward races.[1]

True it is that the interstate relations of Antiquity, as also of the Middle Ages, were largely controlled by force.   An appeal to arms, the divine right of the stronger, constituted the normal mode of settling disputes and securing concessions or advantages.   War was regarded as the natural condition of mankind; peace, as an artificial state secured by treaty or convention.   Diplomacy, in the sense of statecraft, was by no means unknown; but it was Machiavellian in character, and was usually employed as an aid to war, or a substitute therefor, rather than as a means of preserving peace.   The foreigner, at least technically, was usually regarded as an enemy, *i.e.* as a creature without legal rights or obligations.

18. **The Patriarchal System.**—Under the patriarchal system, which has played such an important rôle in the social and political development of our race,[2] the father and the elders represented the family and the *gentes*, or clans, in their relations with other family or gentile groups.   Political power, at least in its earlier stages, resulted mainly from the application of the principle of confederation; and as the families and *gentes* formed themselves into *phratries* (or *curiae*) and tribes, and finally developed into the city or confederated *gentes* or tribes, this power and responsibility was conferred upon the representative or representatives of

[1] See especially Kropotkin, *Mutual Aid a Factor of Evolution* (1902), ch. 3, on "Savages"; and an interesting study of the relations between Australian groups by Wheeler, in 40 *R. D. I.* (1908), 5–30.   See also Letourneau, *La guerre dans les diverses races humains* (1895), chs. 2–8.

Maine (*Int. Law*, p. 11) justly observes: "Man has never been so ferocious or so stupid as to submit to such an evil as war without some effort to prevent it."   Montesquieu seems to have had some perception of this truth when he said: "All countries have a Law of Nations, not excepting the Iroquois themselves, though they devour their prisoners; for they send and receive ambassadors, and understand the rights of war and peace.   The mischief is, that their law of nations is not founded on true principles." *Esprit des lois*, Bk. I, ch. 3.

[2] This is at least true of the Aryan and some of the Semitic peoples.   It is not implied in the text that the patriarchal system was the primitive form of social and political organization.   It was, relatively speaking, a late and highly developed form of political life.   Nor is it implied that the family preceded the clan historically.

the whole association of associated groups,[3] each group remaining more or less of an independent unit within its own sphere. Each group was bound together by the ties of a real or fictitious kinship,[4] and by common religious observances and beliefs. They naturally regarded all outsiders as foreign or hostile, *i.e.* as having no share in the common worship, and therefore no rights other than those granted by treaty [5] or accorded by religious duties of hospitality.

Such being the general course of early social and political development, we are not surprised to learn that a given tribe, village community, or city possessed little sense of intertribal or community obligations. Although the practice of mutual aid and coöperation had long since greatly modified the struggle for existence and power within the group (which indeed was often socialized to a remarkable extent),[6] the struggle between groups continued—a struggle in which the operation of the law of natural selection, resulting in the so-called survival of the fittest, was only slightly modified by a sense of religious obligation, and by certain rudimentary social interests and feelings.

19. **The Law of the Ancient World.**—" Woe to the conquered " [7]—the right of the stronger to the persons and possessions of the vanquished—was the doom pronounced by the ancient world upon nearly all conquered races and peoples. Any mitigation of the rights of the conqueror was, generally speaking, due to considerations of policy and enlightened self-interest, rather than to a sentiment of pity or a recognition of human rights.

[3] Amongst the Iroquois, "the council of the tribe had power to declare war and make peace, to send and receive embassies, and to make alliances. . . . Intercourse between independent tribes was conducted by delegations of wisemen and chiefs." Morgan, *Ancient Society* (1877), 118.

[4] Fictitious kinship was created by the ceremony of adoption by means of which the newcomer renounced the worship of his former household gods and was initiated into the worship of those by whom he had been adopted. The ancient custom of adoption might be compared with the modern practice of naturalization. See especially Coulanges, *The Ancient City* (1899); and Fowler, *The City State of the Greeks and Romans* (1893), *passim*.

[5] This obligation was also a religious one, being sanctioned by an oath.

[6] This is illustrated by the communism of primitive groups which until recently still survived in the *mirs* or village communities of Russia.

[7] A proverbial saying which Plutarch puts into the mouth of Brennus, the Gallic chieftain. See his *Lives*, "Camillus."

Yet, as intimated above, the history of the international relations of Antiquity is by no means one of unrestrained conquest and slaughter, as too often represented by the older historians. The ancient Egyptians, the Babylonians or Chaldeans, the East Indians, and the Chinese [8] were in the main peaceful, agricultural, and industrial peoples, averse to bloodshed and conquest except when driven thereto by great warriors or conquerors. The Assyrians, the Hebrews, the Phœnicians and Carthaginians, and the Greeks and Romans appear, on the other hand, to have been more cruel and warlike.

20. **India.**—In India the Brâhmans formulated maxims of diplomacy which remind us of Machiavelli's *Prince*; [9] but, unlike the precepts of the great Italian of the Renaissance, they recommend moderation, and even liberality, to the vanquished. The rules of warfare, laid down in the Code of Manu, seem to have been inspired by a genuine regard for the rights of humanity. Humane and even chivalric treatment of combatants as well as of non-combatants is recommended. Although the king is advised to ravage the enemy's territory, " and ever spoil his fodder, food, water, and fuel," to " burst tanks, enclosures, and

[8] On "International Law and Diplomacy in Ancient China," see Martin, *The Lore of Cathay* (1901), chs. 22 and 23; and Mueller, in 3 *Z. V.*, (1908), 192–205.

[9] *E. g.* "He (the king) should also appoint an ambassador learned in all the treatises, who understands gestures, expression, and acts (which are) pure, clever, well-descended. . . . For verily the ambassador alone unites, (and) divides also the united; the ambassador conducts that business by which they are divided or not. In affairs he (the ambassador) should know by (his) obscure signs and acts the emotions, intentions, and efforts of him (the other king), and (should learn) what he intends to do from (his) dependents. . . .

"A king should know the next (king to him to be) an enemy, as also the adherents of (that) enemy; the (one) next to the enemy (to be) a friend; the one beyond both (to be) neutral. All those he should gain by conciliation and the like means, separate or together; also by valor and policy. . . . Whenever (a king) infers a sure increase (of power) of himself in the future, and at the present time (suffers) little annoyance, then let him have recourse to an alliance.

"He (the king) should endeavor to overcome (his) enemy by alliances, bribery, and treachery—all together or separate—never by battle. . . . But in case the three expedients already mentioned do not suit, let (him), prepared, fight, so that he may conquer his enemies. . . ."

See *The Ordinances of Manu*, translated by Burnell and Hopkins (1891), Lect. VII, Nos. 63–68, 155, 158–164, 169, 177, 180, 198, 200–210, etc. The date of this remarkable compilation is uncertain. It is generally set down as about 500 B.C.

trenches," to " assail him and terrify him by night "; [10] yet
" one should not, fighting in battle, slay enemies by concealed weapons, nor with barbed or poisoned (weapons),
nor with firekindled arrows.   Nor should one (mounted)
slay an enemy down on the ground, a eunuch, a suppliant
one with loosened hair, one seated, one who says ' I am thy
(prisoner) '; nor one asleep, one without armor, one naked,
one without weapons, one not fighting, a looker-on, one
engaged with another; nor one who has his arm broken, a
distressed man, one badly hit, one afraid, one who has fled:
remembering virtue (one should not slay them)." [11]

21. **Egypt.**—The most remarkable contribution to our
knowledge of the international relations of the ancient
Orient resulted from the discovery at Tell-el-Amarna, in
1888, of nearly 300 tablets in cuneiform or Babylonian
writing.   These formed a portion of the foreign archives of
the Egyptian Pharaoh Ikhnâton, and contained some of the
diplomatic correspondence of that monarch and his immediate predecessor (Amenhotep III) with Asiatic kings,
togéther with reports of Egyptian governors in Syria.
This correspondence [12] throws a great deal of light, not only
upon the international relations of the early part of the
fourteenth century B.C., but also upon the organization of
the Egyptian Empire by Thutmose III, and the remarkable
Semitic civilization of Syria several centuries prior to the
Exodus of the Hebrews.   It shows that the yoke of Egypt
was much lighter than that of Assyria, Carthage, or even
Rome. [13]   Besides, this correspondence shows that far from

[10] *Ibid.*, Lect. VII, Nos. 195 and 196.

[11] *Ibid.*, Lect. VII, Nos. 90–93.   The Greek writers bear witness to the
humane conduct of the East Indians in warfare.   According to Megasthenes,
they never destroyed the fields of the husbandman nor cut down his trees.
Arrian adds that the peasants fearlessly followed the plow and gathered in their
fruits and harvests in the midst of battle and warfare.   For the passages of the
Greek writers bearing on this subject, see Arrian, *Ind.*, c. II; Diodor. II, 36, 40;
and Strabo, XV, 484, ed. Cassaub.

For an interesting treatment of "International Law in Ancient India,"
see a book with this title recently (1925) published by Viswanatha.

[12] For summaries of the contents of the *Tell-el-Amarna Tablets*, see 2 Petrie,
History of Egypt (1898–1905), 259–311; and Conder, *The Tell-Amarna Tablets*
(1893).   For English translations of many of the tablets, see *Records of the
Past* (new series), *passim*, and Conder.

[13] On the *Organization of the Egyptian Empire*, see Maspero, *Struggle of the
Nations* (1896), pp. 271–80; and Paton, *Early History of Palestine and Syria*

being isolated, as formerly believed, these famous empires of
antiquity were in fairly close and constant commercial and
intellectual intercourse, and that their Governments culti-
vated peaceful and friendly relations with one another.
With the kings of Mitanni, Assyria, and Babylonia, and even
with the Hittites, friendly relations were maintained by
means of a frequent exchange of letters, presents, and
embassies; and even marriage alliances were not unknown.[14]

The oldest treaty of which the text has come down to us is
that between Ramses II (the Sesostris of Greek legend and
the " Pharaoh who knew not Joseph " of Hebrew tradition)
and Khetasar, the King of the Kheta or Hittites (about
1272 B.C.).   It is a very remarkable document, providing
as it does not only for an alliance, with a recognition of
perfect equality and reciprocity between the two sovereigns,
but for the mutual extradition of political refugees and
immigrants, a codicil even providing for humane treatment
of the latter.   It is pleasing to learn that this treaty, which
established a stable balance of power in Syria and was
cemented by a marriage alliance, was loyally observed by
both parties, at least during the reign of Ramses II.[15]

But in spite of the essentially mild and peaceful character
of the ancient Egyptians, the monuments of Egypt bear
witness to their cruelty in warfare and barbarous treatment
of prisoners, whose heads or hands were often cut off and
bodies mutilated [16] in the most frightful fashion, apparently

(1901), 82 ff.   On "Canaan before the Exodus," see especially Sayce, in 88
Contemp. Rev. (1905), 264–77.

[14] With the Mitanni, a treaty of friendship cemented by marriage had been
made at least as early as the reign of Thutmose IV (about 1420–1411 B.C.).
The reigning Pharaoh also obtained several daughters of the king of Babylonia
in marriage, but we learn that a similar request on the part of the latter was
peremptorily refused.   Whereupon the king of Babylonia suggested that any
beautiful Egyptian maiden would do, for who would be able to say, "She is not
a king's daughter."

[15] On this interesting treaty, see especially Breasted, *History of Egypt* (1905),
437–38; Maspero, *Struggle of the Nations* (1896), 401 ff.; 5 Budge, *History of
Egypt* (1902), 48 ff.; and 3 Petrie, *History of Egypt*, 64 ff.   For English translations, see 4 *Records of the Past* (first series), 27–32; 3 Breasted, *Ancient
Records of Egypt* (1906–07), §§ 370–91; and 2 Brugsch, *Egypt under the
Pharaohs* (1881), 71–76.   For a German translation, see, Cybichowski, *Das
antike Völkerrecht* (1907), 10 ff.   The authorities are divided on the question
whether this treaty created a defensive *and* offensive or a merely defensive
alliance.

[16] On the *Mutilation of Prisoners*, see Maspero, *The Struggle of the Nations,*

for the purpose of registration. The Pharaoh himself sometimes presided at these bloody ceremonies, and even conquered princes were subject to the most humiliating treatment. The chariot of the conqueror was ornamented with the heads of the slain; and enslaved captives were chained and set to work, under the whips of hard task-masters, at the public quarries, brickkilns, or dockyards.[17] The lives of women and children were usually, though not always, spared.

22. The Hebrews.—The Hebrews, themselves the victims of Egyptian oppression, appear to have been more cruel and barbarous than their taskmasters. Acting, as they supposed, under the express orders of Jehovah, they waged a relentless war of extermination against the natives of Palestine, with whom they were forbidden to intermarry or make covenants.[18] The adult males were almost invariably slaughtered, and even women and children were frequently massacred. The book of Joshua is filled with accounts of such barbarities. Similar atrocities were also enacted by Saul and David.[19]

But the Mosaic code, so enlightened in many respects, contains the germs of a higher law of warfare than that enjoined and practiced in Palestine. The laws of Deuter-

228 and note (Cf. Maspero, *Life in Ancient Egypt and Assyria*, 1892, p. 189). See especially the Great Karnak Inscription of Merneptah, trans. by Breasted, in 3 *Ancient Records of Egypt*, § 588.

[17] "Therefore, they did set over them taskmasters to afflict them with burdens. . . . And they made their lives bitter with hard bondage, in mortar and in brick and in all manner of service in the field." Exod. I, 11, 14. These captives seem to have been well fed, for the Israelites at times longed for the "flesh pots" of Egypt.

[18] Exod. xxxiv, 10–16, and Deut. vii, 1–3, 22–26.

[19] It is recorded that on one occasion Saul was commanded by the Lord, through Samuel, to "go and smite Amalek, and utterly destroy all that they have and spare them not; but slay both man and woman, infant and suckling, ox and sheep, camel and ass." Saul "utterly destroyed all the people with the edge of the sword," but "spared Agag and the best of the cattle." Whereupon Samuel was angry, and "the Lord repented that he had made Saul king over Israel." 1 Samuel xv. For horrible acts of torture on the part of David, see 2 Samuel viii, 2, and xii, 31. The latter passage states that he put the people of Rabbah "under saws, and under harrows of iron, and under axes of iron, and made them pass through the brickkiln; and thus did he unto all the cities of the children of Ammon."

On Hebrew Warfare, see especially Letourneau, *La guerre dans les diverses races humains* (1895), ch. 13.

onomy provide that, before attacking a city, an offer of peace shall be made. If the offer is accepted, the inhabitants shall be made tributary. But in case of resistance all males shall be put to the sword. The women, children, and cattle may be spared if the cities are very distant; in the case, however, of the " cities of which the Lord thy God doth give thee for an inheritance, thou shalt save alive nothing that breatheth; but thou shalt utterly destroy them." A limit is also set to the right of devastation. Fruit-bearing trees are not to be destroyed, even for use in a siege; for " the tree of the field is man's life." [20]

If the ancient Israelites stand relatively low in the scale of civilization as measured by the standard of humanity in warfare, it should never be forgotten that we owe to Hebrew seers and prophets the highest ideal of peace which the world possesses—the vision of the Millennium or Heavenly Jerusalem. This ideal, which was incorporated into Christianity by its Founder, finds its highest and most poetical expression in the identical language of Micah and Isaiah: " And they shall beat their swords into plowshares, and their spears into pruning hooks; nation shall not lift up sword against nation, neither shall they learn war any more." [21]

23. **The Assyrians and Babylonians.**—The monuments of Assyria and Babylonia, as also the records of the Hebrews, bear witness to the barbarity of the Assyrians and certain of the Babylonian monarchs in warfare. The bodies of the slain were often mutilated, and rebel captives were impaled and subjected to the most horrible tortures.[22] Those who

[20] Deut. xx, 10–20. It was also the custom of the Egyptians to issue a summons to surrender before proceeding to extremities. In case of a favorable response to such a summons, the inhabitants were treated as friends, and a moderate tribute was imposed. 1 Brugsch, *Egypt under the Pharaohs* (1881), 402. From which we may infer that at least some of the provisions of the much lauded Mosaic code were borrowed from the Egyptians.

[21] Isaiah ii, 4, and Micah iv, 3. Cf. Isaiah lxv, 25: "The wolf and the lamb shall feed together, and the lion shall eat straw like the bullock; and dust shall be the serpent's meat. They shall not hurt nor destroy in all my holy mountain, saith the Lord."

[22] For details, see Maspero, *Struggle of the Nations* (1896), 634 ff. See especially the Inscription of Ashurnasirpal, in 2 *Records of the Past* (new series), 134–77.

This cruel and vainglorious monarch makes the following boast: "The

escaped were chained and enslaved. Whole nations were transplanted from one part of the empire to another.[23] The writings of the Hebrew prophets, more especially of Jeremiah, contain a vivid portrayal of the terrible sufferings and devastations which resulted from the invasions of Nebuchadnezzar II, King of Babylon (604–562 B.C.).

24. **The Medes and Persians.**—The barbarous Medes and Persians could hardly be expected to mitigate the horrors and cruelties of oriental warfare. The pages of Herodotus contain many examples of the arrogance and ferocity of their monarchs.[24] Men, women, and children were put to death or enslaved. Whole populations were transported. Mutilation of the dead and torture of the living were freely practiced.[25] Corruption through bribery and the encouragement of habits of luxury appear to have been used as a means of conquest and government.[26]

There are, however, some lighter shades to this picture. The treatment of Themistocles by Artaxerxes was a notable instance of oriental hospitality which the Persians, better than the Jews or the Egyptians, knew how to practice.

nobles, as many as had revolted, I flayed; with their skins I covered the pyramid. Some (of those) I immured in the midst of the pyramid; others I impaled above the pyramid on stakes; others, round about the pyramid, I planted on stakes; many at the exit from my own country I flayed; with their skins I clad the fortress walls," etc.   Col. I, Nos. 90–92, of the Inscription of Ashurnasirpal.   Cf. the translation of another inscription in Goodspeed, *History of the Babylonians and Assyrians* (1902), p. 197. On the "Frightfulness of Ashurnasirpal," see Olmstead, *History of Assyria* (1923), ch. 8.

[23] For example, the Israelites from Samaria to Mesopotamia and Media, and the Jews from Judea to Babylon. This policy of transportation, which appears to have been inaugurated by Tigleth Pileser I (about 1100 B.C.), was carried out on a colossal scale by conquerors like Tigleth Pileser III (745–727) and Nebuchadnezzar II (604–562), There are instances of its application in Roman history. It was also practiced by the Byzantine Emperors and even by Charlemagne.

On the deportation of populations as practiced by the Assyrians, see Maspero, *op. cit.*, 639 f. On "Assyrian Government of Dependencies," and "Oriental Imperialism" see Olmstead, in 12 *Am. Pol. Sci. Rev.* (1918), 63–77, and 23 *Am. Histor. Rev.* (1917–18), 755–62.

[24] Judging from both Greek and Hebrew sources, Cyrus, the founder of the Persian Empire and one of the greatest men of antiquity, appears to have been an exception to this rule.

[25] Cf. *e.g.* the treatment of the corpse of Amasis by Cambyses (Herod. III, 16) with that of Leonidas by Xerxes (Herod. VII, 238).

[26] See *e.g.* the advice of Crœsus of Cyrus—advice which is said to have been followed—to render the Lydians effeminate (Herod. I, 155). Greek statesmen frequently yielded to the temptations of Persian gold.

There was, it seems, at the Persian court a minister specially charged with the care and entertainment of guests.[27] Besides, in dealing with the class of facts cited above, we should remember that the events recorded are scattered throughout an immense period of time, and that the ancient historian, like the mediæval chronicler or present-day journalist, as a rule reported the extraordinary and exceptional rather than the ordinary and normal occurrences of everyday life.   Moreover, as Laurent observes: " The words kingdom, empire, republic, should not mislead us into believing in the existence of political unity where there reigned a great diversity.   India has always formed an assembly of small associations without any consciousness of a common country.   The Persians were only a juxtaposition of peoples and cities." [28]

25. **The Phœnicians and Carthaginians.**—The Phœnicians are the first real commercial people with whom history makes us acquainted.   Ancient commerce, in its beginnings at least, was a species of war, or, worse still, of piracy and brigandage.   The colonies of Phœnicia and Carthage were established by violence.[29]   To the horrible native barbarity of Phœnician warfare,[30] there was added the oppression and suffering wrought by the greed of merchants and systematic commercial exploitation.   Wars partook of the nature of commercial ventures carried on by mercenary soldiers, and the hope of plunder became the guiding motive of foreign

[27] Laurent, who reports this fact, together with many others (see 1 *Études sur l'humanité*, 1865–80, p. 477), adds: "It is a beautiful symbol of the mission which belongs to the department of foreign affairs. The diplomacy of the future, ceasing to be inspired by hate, will have no more important function than that of cultivating relations of friendship between nations."

The Persians were not wholly ignorant of the value of arbitration as a means of preventing war.   Herodotus (VI, 42) relates that Artaphernes, the satrap of Sardis, compelled the cities of Ionia "to make agreements among themselves, so that they might give satisfaction for wrongs and not plunder one another's land."

[28] There were of course some notable exceptions to this rule, as, *e.g.* Egypt, Assyria, and the Hebrew kingdom of David and his successors.   Assyria appears to have been the first of the ancient empires to organize her conquests into provinces and to develop real provincial administration.   Olmstead, *op. cit.*, 606 ff.

[29] Laurent, *op. cit.*, I, 500.

[30] For examples of mutilation and torture, see Judges I, 7; 1 Samuel xi, 2; 2 Kings viii, 12.

policy.   The traders of the Mediterranean were dominated by material considerations, instead of by dreams of military glory and the passions inspired by religious zeal which animated great conquerors like Thutmose III, Tigleth Pileser III, Nebuchadnezzar II, and Cyrus the Great.

The Carthaginian merchants placed restrictions and prohibitions upon trading by foreigners, and the navigation of the seas was forbidden even to colonies, their ports being closed.[31]   Carthage, indeed, resorted to the most violent measures in order to secure commerce in the Mediterranean.[32]   Her treatment of subject races was cruel and selfish in the extreme.[33]

26. The Interstate Relations of the Greeks.—In the Hellenic world the conditions were favorable to the growth of principles and fixed customs of an intermunicipal jurisprudence.   The πόλις or city-state was the center of civic life and the unit or subject of interpolitical relations.   But the passion of the Greek for city autonomy greatly outweighed his sense of nationality.   In spite of a close community of interests and ideas resting on race, religion, and common customs, the Greeks never developed a very definite body of positive intermunicipal law as strictly applicable even amongst themselves.   The relations of the hundreds of Greek cities that dotted the coasts of the Mediterranean, Aegean and Black Seas with each other were governed mainly by considerations of interest, convenience, or sentiment based on a sense of kinship and religion which took such organized forms as religious leagues or amphictyonies,[34] alliances, political leagues or con-

[31] Laurent, *op. cit.*, I, 541.

[32] Montesquieu (*Esprit des lois*, Bk. XXI, ch. 11) observes that "Carthage had a peculiar law of nations.   She caused all strangers who traded in Sardinia and towards the pillars of Hercules to be drowned."   Grote (*History of Greece*, Pt. II, ch. 18) says they drowned " any commercial rivals when they could do so with safety."

[33] Polybius (I, 72, trans. by Schuckburgh 1889) thus describes their treatment of the Libyans: "They had exacted half of all agricultural produce; had doubled the tribute of the towns; and in levying these contributions, had refused to show any indulgence whatever to those who were in embarrassed circumstances."

[34] Of these the most famous and influential was the Delphic Amphictyony, —a body of representatives of twelve tribes,—instituted for the purpose of safeguarding the interests of Apollo at Delphi.   But even the Delphic Amphic-

federacies,[35] the recognition of the military and political leadership of a single State, called the leader or *hegemon* [36] (ἡγεμών) of Greece, and attempts to maintain a balance of power between leading Greek States.[37]

27. Greek Warfare.—The civilization of Greece not only greatly surpassed that of the Ancient Orient, but, in some

tyonic League was essentially a religious body (although sometimes perverted to political uses), and did not extend over the whole Greek world. It did, however, recognize some principles of interstate comity and sought to humanize warfare. This is shown by the oath of its members: "We will not destroy any Amphictyonic town, nor cut if off from running water, in war or peace; if any one shall do this we will march against him, and destroy his city." The Delphic League was in no sense a board of arbitration or Federal Council, as represented by some historians. On the Delphic Amphictyonic Council, see especially Darby, *Int. Tribunals* (1904), 1–10; and 2 Phillipson, *Int. Law and Customs of Ancient Greece and Rome* (1911), 5–11.

[35] The most important of these were the Peloponnesian League, the Delian Confederacy, and the Achæan and Ætolian Leagues. The two latter were genuine Federal Unions. On these Leagues and Confederacies, see especially Freeman's scholarly work entitled *A History of Federal Government* (1893); 2 Phillipson, *op. cit.*, ch. 16; and York, *The League of Nations* (1919), ch. 1. The best brief account of Federal Government in Greece is by Greenidge, *Greek Const. History* (1902), ch. 7. For interesting discussions of Greek Imperialism, particularly that of Athens, see Ferguson, *Greek Imperialism* (1913), Lects. I–II, and in 23 *Am. Histor. Rev.* (1917–18), 763–71.

[36] The first hegemon of Greece (in historical times) was Sparta. Her first hegemony lasted from about 550 to 478 B.C., and included the period of the Persian invasions. Then followed the hegemony of Athens, which lasted until 413, the date of the failure of the Silician Expedition. The second hegemony of Sparta falls within the period of the downfall of Athens (404) and the King's Peace or Peace of Antalcidas (386). During the period which follows we have a brief revival of Athenian power and the short-lived hegemony of Thebes (371–62). The hegemony in Greece is finally (after the battle of Chæronea in 338) seized by Philip of Macedon.

[37] The interstate relations of Greece during the fourth century, B.C., were to a certain extent controlled by attempts to maintain a balance of power between leading Greek States by Persia and leading Greek statesmen like Demosthenes. The idea was suggested to Tissaphernes, the Persian satrap at Sardis in Asia Minor, by that remarkable political adventurer Alcibiades, although there were earlier instances of its actual application.

One object of the Peloponnesian League was to check Athenian hegemony and secure the autonomy of the lesser cities. After the seizure of the Cadmea (the Theban Acropolis) in 397 B.C., Athens entered into an alliance with Thebes in order to check the growing power of Sparta. During the brief period of Theban supremacy that followed, Athens did not hesitate to form an alliance with her old enemy Sparta.

On the balance of power in Greece, see Hume's "Essay on Balance of Power," in 1 *Essays* (ed. by Green and Grose 1889), Pt. II, Essay VII; Wheaton *History*, 16 ff.; and 2 Phillipson, *op. cit.*, ch. 18, pp. 101 ff. On "The Balance of Power" in the ancient Near East during the fifteenth and fourteenth centuries B.C., see Olmstead, *op. cit.*, ch. 2.

respects, compared more than favorably with that of the modern world. Yet Greek warfare was characterized by great cruelty and severity. Except in Homeric times, mutilation [38] and torture were no longer practiced; but quarter was not always given, and Greek freely sold Greek into slavery. If we compare the fierce combats of Homeric times with the relentless struggles of the classical period, especially during the Peloponnesian War, one can hardly pronounce unreservedly in favor of the latter. The treatment of the inhabitants of Melos [39] by the Athenians, and the debates in the Athenian Ecclesia [40] on the fate to be meted out to the revolted Mytilenæans, show to what lengths the democracy of the most civilized State of antiquity was prepared to go in the practice of a sanguinary creed, based not on the brutal instincts of the barbarian but on pure considerations of state policy or political expediency. It should, however, be pointed out that the " Greeks of the fourth century were more humane than those of the fifth." [41]

28. The " Customs of the Hellenes."—In their relations with each other, the Greeks recognized certain laws or " customs of the Hellenes " (τὰ νόμιμα τῶν Ἑλλήνων), such as the inviolability of heralds and envoys, the right of asylum or sanctuary, and truces for the burial of the dead. The Bœotians declared that " it was a principle acknowledged by all, that in an invasion of each other's territory, they should abstain from injuring the temples that were in it " [42]—a principle admitted by the Athenians, provided it

[38] The mutilation of corpses was held by Pausanias to be "more worthy of Barbarians than of Greeks." Herod. IX, 79.

[39] All adult Melians who had surrendered were slain and the women and children sold into slavery. The Dorian people of Melos had committed the offence of trying to remain neutral during the Peloponnesian War. The Athenians frankly repudiated all considerations of justice, and maintained that gods and men alike "always maintain dominion, wherever they are stronger." See Thucyd. V, 105.

[40] For these debates, see Thucyd. III, 37–48. The Ecclesia had decreed that all adult male Mytilenæans should be put to death and the women and children sold into slavery. This decree was afterwards rescinded, and only those guilty of the revolt were tried and executed. But the case was argued in the Ecclesia solely on grounds of public policy or expediency.

[41] 2 Bury, *History of Greece* (1902), 98. On the increasing humanity of the Greeks in the fourth century B.C., see Mahaffy, *Social Life of the Greeks* (1879), 269-71.

[42] Thucyd. IV, 97. The Athenians had garrisoned and fortified the

did not conflict with the law of military necessity.   Truces
or suspension of hostilities for religious purposes, such as
attendance upon the Olympic games,[43] were observed, and
certain territory, like that of Elis, was accounted more or
less sacred and inviolable.[44]

29. **Treatment of Prisoners.**—Prisoners of war, whether
Greek or barbarian, who surrendered unconditionally might
be put to death or sold into slavery;[45] but later customs
brought about a considerable modification of the strict rule.
Captives were sometimes admitted to ransom even in the
Homeric Age, and Thucydides gives several examples of the
exchange of prisoners.[46]   The survivors, including women
and children, were usually sold into slavery.   This was
particularly the case with cities which surrendered unconditionally or which were taken by storm.[47]

It was customary to divide the booty amongst the
victorious soldiery, *i.e.* after devoting one tenth of the spoil
to the gods and a portion to the leaders and warriors who
had particularly distinguished themselves.   Even landed
property was frequently confiscated and thus divided.

30. **Treatment of Foreigners.**—In general, the Greeks

sanctuary of Apollo at Delium in Bœotia.   The Bœotians refused to surrender
the Athenian dead unless Delium were evacuated.   The Athenians entered the
plea of military necessity in reply to the charge of using the sacred water, but
claimed that they had not injured the sanctuary.   Thucyd. IV, 98.   Bury (II,
p. 486) correctly observes: "There seems little doubt that the conduct of the
Bœotians was a greater departure from recognized custom than the conduct of
the Athenians."

[43] Thucyd. V, 49.

[44] Cf. Polyb. IV, 73–74; and Strabo, Bk. VIII, ch. 3, 33.   Yet the "neutrality" of Elis was frequently violated, especially in later times.   Some authorities
have seen in the theoretical exemption of Elis from invasion an ancient instance
of neutralization.   The analogy is evident, but the imperfect "neutralization" of Elis, like that of temples and priests, rested wholly on a religious basis.

[45] The Platæans who surrendered unconditionally to the Spartans in 427 B.C.
claimed that "the law of the Greeks is not to kill such." Thucyd. III, 58.   But
their eloquent plea produced no effect on their hard-hearted judges.   In case
of conditional surrender, the "condition must be observed at the risk of
offending the gods, but only if it had been ratified by an oath."   Greenidge,
op. cit., 47–48.

[46] Thucyd. II, 103, and V, 3.

[47] "It is a perpetual law amongst all men that, when a city is taken from an
enemy, both the persons and property of the inhabitants belong to the captors."
Xenophon, *Cyrop.*, Bk. VII, ch. V, 73.

On the treatment of prisoners by the Greeks and Romans, see especially
2 Phillipson, *op. cit.*, 251 ff.

recognized no obligations to foreigners, *i.e.* citizens of another city or country, unless founded upon the religious duty of hospitality or on treaties (σύμβολα) sanctioned by an oath. The μέτοικοι, or resident aliens, who were extremely numerous in great commercial centers like Athens and Corinth, could as a rule exercise their rights only through a patron (προστάτης).[48] Communities were usually represented in the assemblies and law courts by *Proxeni* (πρόξενοι) who held a position somewhat analogous to that of modern consuls.[49] Treaties of hospitality (ἰσοπολιτεία) sometimes provided for reciprocity or equality of civil rights,[50] and prescribed rules for the settlement of commercial disputes.[51]

31. Arbitration.—But the most remarkable progress made by the Greeks in the development of interstate relations is to be found in their repeated attempts to prevent hostilities or to secure peace through arbitration. It must be admitted that such efforts were often unsuccessful,[52] but

[48] Corinth seems, however, to have been an exception to the general rule. In Corinth the resident alien could probably enforce his private rights in his own name. Greenidge. *op. cit.*, 8. In Athens, the Archon Polemarchus had general jurisdiction over foreigners. See Aristot., *Const. of Athens*, 58. In course of time the Greeks gradually relaxed in their attitude toward foreigners. Actual practice varied greatly at different times and in different places. At the two extremes stood Athens and Sparta—the former being extremely lax or liberal, the latter very strict and exclusive.

[49] But the Greek *Proxenus* was usually a citizen of the State where the aliens whose interests he represented resided. Thus Alcibiades represented the interests of Sparta at Athens. For a very scholarly work on the Greek *Proxeni*, see Monceaux, *Les proxenies grecques* (1886). See also 1 Phillipson, *op. cit.*, 147–56.

[50] Such as intermarriage and property rights. In a few cases they seem to have even provided for an interchange of political rights. Such a close alliance was known as a συμπολιτεία.

[51] They sometimes provided even for the selection of judges who formed a species of international court to which the foreigner might appeal without the intervention of a patron. See Greenidge, *op. cit.*, p. 54. Cf. 2 Laurent, *op. cit.*, 123. On *Rights and Duties of Foreigners in Greece and Rome*, see 1 Phillipson, *op. cit.*, chs. 5–12.

[52] For examples of arbitration, see Plutarch, *Solon*, 10; and *Themis.* 24; Herod. V, 83, 95, and VI, 108; Thucyd. V, 31; No. 2 Phillipson, *op. cit.*, ch. 20; and Egger (*Les traités chez les grecs et les romains* 1866, 67 ff.), who cites a number of cases of arbitration from the inscriptions. For an interesting example of arbitration between Priene and Samos, see 5 *A. J.* (1911), 465–66.

Soon after the publication of the first edition of this text in 1912, the literature on the subject of Greek arbitration was enriched by at least two important contributions: Tod, *International Arbitration amongst the Greeks* (1913); and Raeder, *L'arbitrage international ches les Hellenes* (1912).

they deserve credit for making the attempt. The arbitral clause (an agreement beforehand to submit disputes to arbitral decision) was sometimes inserted in treaties.[53] The arbitrations " related to disputes touching religion, commerce, boundaries, and the possession of contested territories, especially of the numerous islands scattered among the Grecian seas." [54] The arbitrators selected might be noted individuals, friendly cities, or the Oracle of Delphi. It apparently was the opinion of the greatest Greek historian that " it is not right to attack as a transgressor him who offers to submit to judicial decision." [55]

32. Greek Maritime Law.—In the field of maritime law, the Greeks also seem to have made some progress. Although piracy, which was regarded as honorable [56] in the Homeric Age, was still practiced during the classical period, it had been largely supplanted by legitimate and peaceful commerce. The first State which appears to have developed a body of maritime law was Rhodes, the leading commercial State of Greece during the third century B.C. Of this law, which is by some authorities supposed to have been adopted by the Roman Emperors, and some of the principles of which may have survived in the *Consolato de la Mare* of the Middle Ages, but one sentence has survived, at least in its original form. It constitutes the basis of the present doctrine of jettison. " If goods are thrown overboard to lighten the ship, as this is done for the sake of all, the loss shall be made good by a contribution of all." [57]

33. The " Law of All Mankind."—Although even Aristotle regarded barbarians as slaves by nature, to whom the " laws of the Hellenes " did not apply, yet the Greeks recognized a vague and ill-defined " law of all mankind "

[53] As, for example, in the Truce of 423, and the Peace of Nicias between Athens and Sparta in 421 B.C. See especially the treaty between Argos and Sparta, Thucyd. V, 79. Cf. Thucyd. I, 78; IV, 118.

[54] Historical note on Arbitration, in 5 Moore, *Arbitrations*, Appendix III, 4822.

[55] Thucyd. I, 85. For offers of arbitration, see Thucyd. I, 28, V, 39, and VII, 18.

[56] Thucyd. I, 5.

[57] Justinian's *Digest*, XIV, 2. On the so-called Rhodian Law, see an interesting article by Benedict, in 18 *Yale Law J.* (1909); and Ashburner, *The Rhodian Sea-Law* (1909).

(τὰ πάντων ἄνθρωπων νόμιμα).[58] This "law" included at
least the inviolability of heralds and envoys, sanctity of
those treaties which were sanctioned by an oath, and
certain obligations of alliance and hospitality.[59]

34. **The Policy or Diplomacy of Rome.**—The city-state of
Rome first appears in the history of interstate relations as a
member of the Latin League or Confederacy, of which she in
time became the head and master. Through her renewal
of the Latin Alliance in 493 B.C.,[60] and her treaty with the
Hernicans (486),[61] she laid the foundation of Roman power
in Italy, the conquest of which, completed by 272 B.C.,[62] was
at least as much the result of statecraft or diplomacy as of
force.[63] As a result of the Carthaginian and Macedonian

[58] On the "law of all men," see Herod. VII, 136; and Polyb. II, 58, and IV,
6.

[59] Several instances of the violation of this "Law of All Nations" are
recorded by Herodotus (VII, 136) and Thucydides (II, 67).

[60] This treaty, negotiated by Spurius Cassius, the historical founder of
Roman diplomacy, became the model for treaties of equal alliance. "There
shall be peace between Romans and all communities of the Latins, as long as
heaven and earth endure; they shall not wage war with each other, nor call
enemies into the land, nor grant passage to enemies: help shall be rendered by
all in concert to any community assailed, and whatever is won in warfare shall
be equally distributed." Dionys. VI, 95.

[61] Dionys. VIII, 69, 72, 74. The particular object of this alliance was to
sever the Æquians from the Volscians and thus isolate the latter. It seems to
have been the first application of the fundamental principle of Roman
diplomacy—*divide et impera*.

[62] *I.e.* as far north as Cisalpine Gaul and as far south as Sicily. It is not
quite correct to speak of the *conquest* of Italy. It was as the head of a powerful
federation of Latin and Italian allies rather than as the conqueror or absolute
sovereign of subject tribes and cities that Rome first appears as a great World
Power. Though about one fifth of Italy was incorporated directly with the
Roman Republic, it was rather by way of alliance or confederation than of
direct annexation that the Roman mastery over the various races and cities of
the Italian peninsula was obtained. These were placed in a condition of
varied and unequal alliance with and dependence on Rome and isolation from
each other. See especially Beloch, *Der italische Bund* (1880), on the Italian
Confederacy; and Frank, *Roman Imperialism* (1914), particularly chs. 1–3.

[63] Ortolan (*History of Roman Law*, Cutler's ed., 1896, § 181) thus admirably
sums up the foreign policy of the Roman Republic: "To sow discord among
different nations in order to array one against another,—to assist the vanquished in conquering their conqueror,—to husband its own resources, to use
those of its allies to invade the territories of its neighbors,—to interfere in the
disputes of other States, so as to protect the weaker party and finally subju-
gate both,—to wage unnecessary wars, and prove itself stronger in reverses
than in success,—to evade oaths and treaties by subterfuge,—to practice every
kind of injustice under the specious guise of equity—this was the policy that

Wars which followed the conquest of Sicily (241), Rome was drawn into the current of a world-wide imperialism, from which she ultimately emerged (about 146 B.C.) master, indeed, of the nations of the Mediterranean, but with her political liberties destroyed, her economic welfare impaired, and her national character greatly weakened.

35. Roman Attitude toward the Conquered and Idea of a Common Superior.—In the treatment of the conquered and the organization of her conquests, the conduct of Rome was almost wholly controlled by motives of public policy or a more or less enlightened sense of political expediency. Her aims and achievements constitute in themselves a denial of the rights of other communities and nationalities, and it is possible, therefore, to speak of a Roman Law of Nations only in the most restricted sense, unless it be at a very early period in the history of Rome. The world was dominated by a common superior,—first the Roman Senate and later the Roman Emperor,—who, for centuries, either directly or indirectly, ruled the provinces and vassal States and races of the Mediterranean world. This idea of a common superior, mediator, or arbitrator strangely persisted through the Middle Ages. It seems to have been due to the survival of historic traditions and recollections of the benefits conferred upon the world by the " Roman Peace " (*Pax Romana*) and the impartial administration of Roman justice under the Early Empire.

36. The *Jus Belli* of the Romans.—In their attitude toward foreigners and in respect to the laws and customs of warfare (*jus belli*), the Romans greatly resembled the Greeks.[64] As in the case of the Greeks, Roman usages respecting war and treatment of foreigners were based upon a sense of religious obligation, but were modified by considerations of interest and the necessities of intercourse. The treatment of foreigners was more liberal at Rome than

gave Rome the scepter of all Italy, and which was destined to secure for it that of the entire known world."

[64] On the *jus belli* as practiced by the Romans, see the references to Livy and Polybius in Walker, *History of the Law of Nations* (1899), pp. 48–54. The ideas of Cicero were more liberal, but seldom practiced. On Cicero's theory of international morality, see Wheaton, *History*, 20–24. On Greek and Roman treatment of foreigners and rules and customs of warfare, see 1 and 2 Phillipson, *op. cit.*, *passim*; and Redslob, *Histoire du droit des gens* (1923), 87 ff.

in Greece, and the foreign policy of Rome was certainly guided by a wiser statesmanship and a more enlightened sense of self-interest than that which characterized the Greeks. The Romans were both by training and temperament more calculating and judicial than the Greeks, and they had a greater talent for administration and organization.

In view of the general similarity between Greek and Roman conceptions of international rights and duties, we need only notice two branches of Roman law which concern international jurisprudence. One of these is of relatively slight importance, the other of very great influence on the subsequent development of the Law of Nations.

37. The *Jus Fetiale*.—The *jus fetiale* consisted mainly of certain rules and ceremonies or modes of procedure for declarations of war and ratification of treaties of peace, which were of great antiquity and were intended to satisfy the religious scruples and sensitive " legal conscience " of the Romans.[65] They were highly ceremonial and formal in character, and their guardianship was intrusted to a special body of priests known as the College of Fetiales. Only four just (*i.e.* legal) causes of war were recognized,[66] but it cannot be maintained that this had any appreciable influence on Roman practice, at least in historical times. The *fetiales* were mere agents of the Senate, and were practically bound to do its bidding; for in Rome religion was the servant, not the master of the State.

[65] In Greece war was usually declared through a herald; but the Greeks seem to have been less strict in this respect than the Romans, for there are instances of war without declaration.

[66] These were: (1) Invasions or violations of Roman territory; (2) and (3) violation of the rights of ambassadors and of treaties or alliances; and (4) military support given to an enemy or attack upon an ally by a hitherto friendly State. Even in these cases war was only justifiable after satisfaction had been demanded and refused. In case of refusal, war was formally declared by hurling a spear across the Roman frontier into the enemy's territory. For a description of this ceremony, see Livy, I, 32. On the *jus fetiale*, see especially Hill, *History of Diplomacy in the Development of Europe* (1905–06), I, pp. 8–11 and notes; 2 Phillipson. *op. cit.*, ch. 26; and Weiss, *Droit fetiale* (1883).

War might be ended in three ways: (1) By a treaty of friendship or alliance; (2) a *deditio* or unconditional surrender in which case the lives and property of the enemy were generally spared; (3) by *occupatio* or conquest and appropriation of the enemy's territory, or a considerable part thereof. For the formula of *deditio*, see Livy, I, 38.

38. The *Jus Gentium*.—The *jus gentium* belongs to the field of International Private Law rather than to that of the Law of Nations; but owing to its influence upon the thought of the later Middle Ages and the writings of publicists like Gentilis and Grotius, it became a very important factor in the growth of modern International Law.   It consisted in that body of principles and usages common to all nations (including the Italians) among whom justice was administered by Roman magistrates.   Although it included some rules or principles of International Public Law (as, *e.g.* the inviolability of ambassadors), it was wholly different in origin, nature, and subject matter.   It originated in the jurisdiction of the *prætor peregrinus* over foreigners (including Latins and Italians) and in relations between Romans and foreigners in Rome and Italy.   It related to such matters as verbal contracts, partnerships, loans of money, acquisition by delivery and *alluvium*, capture and war, rights over slaves, rights of self-defense, etc.   Some of its rules, as, for example, those relating to the law of *alluvium*, the right of occupation of *res nullius*, and the absolute ownership of land by the Roman *dominus*, were directly appropriated by Grotius and the other founders of International Law, and later applied to international practice.   The *jus gentium* of the Romans may thus be regarded as the source of much of the modern law of occupation and territorial sovereignty or jurisdiction.[67]   In the minds of the later Roman jurists, who were strongly impregnated with the doctrines of Stoic philosophy, its more general principles were practically identified as Laws of Nature.

But the Roman *jus gentium* performed a still more important function in the history of international jurisprudence.   In common with the Canon Law and the Civil Law (into which its more positive rules were incorporated), it greatly influenced the legal conceptions of the Middle Ages, and slowly prepared the way for that " reign of law " and order which is perhaps the most essential condition for a higher civilization, and which is being gradually extended to international relations.

[67] For references on the *jus gentium*, see Bibliography at the end of this chapter.

39. **The " Dark Ages."**—As a result of the decline of the
Roman Empire in the course of the fourth and fifth
centuries B.C., due to internal decay and the irruptions of
the barbarians, the western world relapsed into that
barbarism from which it slowly emerged after the eleventh
century. It has been said that " International Law reached
its nadir in the West " [68] during the so-called " Dark Ages "
between the final disappearance of the Western Empire in
476 and the coronation of Charlemagne as Emperor of the
West by Pope Leo III in 800 A.D. In spite of the pacifist
teachings of Christ and the early Fathers of the Church,
" the history of the wars of Clovis, the hero of the orthodox
clergy, is the tale of savage murder and the most hateful
treachery." [69] Some traditions of a higher civilization (and
also of diplomacy) were, however, preserved at Byzantium, as well as among the Mohammedan Arabs or
Saracens, whose international practice contrasts very
favorably with that of the barbarian Christians of Western
Europe.[70]

40. **The Age of Feudalism.**—The Age of Feudalism,
which characterized the civilization of Western Europe
from the ninth to the fifteenth centuries, was a period of
organized anarchy and private warfare or regulated violence.
Society was divided into feudal groups, of which the basis
was the fief—usually a grant of land by the lord to one of
his vassals. With the social and political relations within
these groups, we need not here concern ourselves. Suffice
it to say that feudalism was essentially a highly complicated
system of land tenure based on military, personal, or
economic service. It was also a form of social and political
organization of which the lord, vassals and other tenants
(villeins, serfs, etc.) constituted the military and political
units, the lord or landowner exercising suzerain or quasi-
sovereign functions based on territorial rights—an idea

[68] Walker, *History of the Law of Nations* (1899), p. 64.

[69] Walker, *op. cit.*, p. 65.

[70] On the international practice of the Saracens, see Bordwell, *Law of War
between Belligerents* (1908), 12–14; Syed H. R. Abdul Majid, in 28 *L. Q. R.*
(1912), 89 ff.; and Walker, *op. cit.*, §§ 45, 66; Cf. 1 Nys, *Études*, 46–74, and
Les origines, 209 f.

which played a highly important part in the development of the science of International Law.[71]

Interfeudal relations were of the loosest kind. In spite of legal forms and customary law, they were controlled by brute force or regulated violence. The wager of battle was a recognized form of judicial trial, and private warfare appears to have been the rule rather than the exception.[72] " War in all its forms may be said to have been the law of the feudal world." It " raged not only between suzerains and vassals of the same fief, but also in the bosom of all the feudal families." [73] The attitude of the feudal lord toward trade and the foreigner is shown by his numerous exactions, such as tolls, the claim of a right to the property of the shipwrecked (*droit de naufrage*), and his claim to inherit the property of the foreigner (*droit d'aubaine*).[74]

41. Influence of the Mediæval Church.—But there were certain unifying, formative, and civilizing influences at work even in Western Europe during the Middle Ages. These were, first and foremost, the Catholic Church as represented by the Roman Papacy. Though mainly intent upon its own aggrandizement and the salvation of the individual soul from torment in another world, the mediæval Church finally awoke to some sense of its humanitarian and international mission, and made efforts to establish peace by means of the

[71] See especially Esmein, *Cours élémentaire d'histoire du droit français* (1901), 175–84 (trans. in Munro and Sellery, *Mediæval Civilization* 1907, 159–67). For a brief but excellent description of feudalism, see Seignobos, *The Feudal Régime* (trans. by Daw, 1902).

[72] Private warfare was regulated in the course of the twelfth, thirteenth, and fourteenth centuries. It was usually preceded by a challenge, and terminated by a truce, peace, or promise to keep the peace by one of the adversaries. As a rule, the right of private warfare was limited to noblemen. As an old adage expressed it, "Only a gentleman may engage in warfare." In any case, ecclesiastics, women, pilgrims, and minors were usually exempt from hostilities. In France, private warfare was prohibited in 1361, but was not suppressed until Louis XI broke the power of feudalism toward the close of the fifteenth century. In Germany, *Faustrecht* (fist-right) continued up to the middle of the sixteenth century. On private warfare in the Middle Ages, see especially Luchaire, *Manuel des institutions françaises* (1882), 228–34; Nys, *Les origines*, ch. 5; and Du Cange, *Des guerres privés* (1838), cited by Bordwell, *op. cit.*, 15.

[73] See the translation from Luchaire, in Munro and Sellery, 171–87. The citations are from pp. 177 and 178.

[74] Of course there were many exceptions to this rule. In England, *e.g.* many statutes were passed for the protection of the foreign merchant. Walker, *History of the Law of Nations* (1899), 120–21.

Truce of God and the Peace of God in the tenth, eleventh and twelfth centuries.[75]

These attempts were, however, only partially successful. More effective were such institutions as the *Quarantaine le Roy* (an enforced lapse of forty days between the outbreak of a quarrel and the opening of hostilities) in France, the King's Peace in England, and the various *Landesfrieden* in Germany. Most effective of all was the gradual substitution of royal for feudal justice.

42. Common Elements in the Civilization of Feudal Europe.—Yet in spite of its reactionary and anarchical tendencies, feudal Europe contained elements which were favorable to the development of a higher civilization based on the idea of a brotherhood of nations. Throughout Christendom, there were common religious beliefs and forms of worship, common customs and standards of living amongst those with the same social status, a language (Latin) common to the educated classes, great Church councils representing various races and nationalities, trade, pilgrimages, and intercourse of various sorts resulting in the interchange of ideas as well as of material goods, and finally the common hatred of the infidel and a general desire to regain possession of the Holy Sepulchre which culminated in the Crusades.

43. The Papacy and Empire.—Although important unifying or organizing and civilizing influences, it cannot be successfully maintained that either the Mediæval Papacy or the Holy Roman (Germanic) Empire exerted strong direct influence upon the amelioration of warfare or the

---

[75] The movement for a "Truce of God," which set aside certain days in the week and seasons of the year for the practice of private warfare, originated in Aquitaine at the close of the tenth century, spread to neighboring French dioceses, and culminated in the Council of Clermont in 1095. But this movement failed to accomplish its purpose.

In the second half of the eleventh century, the Church made a systematic attempt to establish the "Peace of God." Peace Leagues or Associations, with regular statutes, treasury, and magistrates, were established in each diocese under the direction of the bishop, who did not hesitate to use force, if excommunication failed. Violators of the peace were brought before the "judges of the Peace," and if found necessary, punished by an "army of the Peace." Even these efforts were only partially successful. See Luchaire, in Munro and Sellery, *op. cit.*, 183–184.

For texts of Truces of God, see Henderson, *Select Historical Documents of the Middle Ages* (1892), 208–15.

development of International Law.   True it is that the
Papacy and Empire of the later Middle Ages were great
international forces (although often in conflict with each
other), and that the Popes and, to a much less degree, the
Emperors frequently acted as arbitrators and mediators
between kings and princes.   But their power rested mainly
on a theoretical and sentimental or religious basis, and
declined rapidly after the middle of the thirteenth century.[76]

44. Arbitration during the Middle Ages.—Arbitration
was very common in the later Middle Ages, but such was
the almost universal reign of anarchy and violence that it
cannot be said to have very materially mitigated the
prevalence of warfare as the normal condition of that
unhappy time.   Feudalism was in so far favorable to
arbitration as to predispose vassals to accept their lords as
judges, and it accustomed them to the idea of arbitration.
Kings, bishops, eminent jurists, and even cities were also
chosen as arbitrators during the later Middle Ages.   There
are said to have been no less than one hundred instances of
arbitration in Italy alone in the course of the thirteenth
century and we know the practice was common in France
during this period.   Indeed, the arbitral clause was frequently included in treaties as was the case in ancient
Greece (see *supra*, No. 31).   Arbitration declined during the
fourteenth and fifteenth centuries, and almost disappeared
from international usage during the seventeenth and
eighteenth.[77]

[76] On the Struggle of the Empire and Papacy see, especially Bryce, *Holy
Roman Empire* (1880), ch. 10; 1 Hill, *History of Diplomacy*, ch. 5; and Munro,
The Middle Ages (1922), ch. 15.   For further references, see Munro's Bibliography on pp. 415–16, and 1 Hill, *op. cit.*, pp. 248–49.   The pretensions of
both Papacy and Empire at the height of their power went far beyond mere
mediation and arbitration.   Their claims amounted to an assertion of universal
dominion and often resulted in actual intervention.   These claims were usually
admitted in theory, but denied in practice.

A serious obstacle to the efficacy of the Papacy as an arbitrator or mediator
was the doctrine that "no faith need be kept with heretics," and the assertion of
its right to break treaties and annul oaths "contrary to the interests of the
Church."   See an interesting article by White, in 95 *Atlantic Monthly*, 107 ff.

[77] See especially the historical note in 5 Moore, *Arbitrations*, App. III, 4825
ff.; and Nys, *Les origines*, ch. 4.   See also Lange, *Histoire de l'internationalisme*
(1919), I, 125–30.   Lange's pages are based upon the researches of Nova-
covitch (see the latter's *Les compromis et les arbitrages internationaux* 1905).
For a recent review of Arbitration during the Middle Ages, see Fraser, in 11
Cornell Law Quar. (1926), 190–98.

45. **The Influence of Roman Law.**—More important than the direct influence of the Empire, or even than that of the mediæval Church, in the history of the growth of International Law were the indirect influences resulting from the revived study of the Roman Civil Law by the jurists of the twelfth century, the publication of the famous *Decretum* of Gratian in 1144, and the codification of the Canon Law modeled on the *Corpus Juris Civilis* by Gregory IX in 1234. The systematic study and application of the principles of the Roman Law furnished a necessary foundation for the later growth of the royal power and the development of an adequate and enlightened system of international jurisprudence.[78] This study bore fruit later in many a law, custom, decision, pamphlet, monograph, and treatise.

46. **Effect of the Crusades.**—Perhaps the most important single influence of the later Middle Ages upon the development of international relations was that of the Crusades during the twelfth and thirteenth centuries (1096–1291).[79] Though attended with frightful waste and misery, they enlisted the zeal of Christians of various nationalities. They could not therefore fail to stimulate trade and the interchange of ideas, arouse a keener sense of common interests, and awaken a deeper consciousness of the unity of Christendom. They also prepared the way for the destruction of feudalism by weakening the resources of the nobility—a condition from which the free cities and kings were not slow to profit.

47. **Influence of Chivalry.**—The influence of chivalry upon the amelioration of warfare has probably been ex-

[78] On the influence of the Roman Law upon the formation of International Law, see especially Maine, *Ancient Law* (Pollock's ed., 1906), 92 ff. and Pollock's note H in Appendix, and *Int. Law*, 20, 26–29; and Wheaton, *History*, 29 ff. For further references, see Bibliographies on *jus gentium* and *jus naturale infra*, pp. 64–65. For a survey of the doctrines of the theologians and canonists of the Middle Ages, see Vanderpol, *La doctrine scholastique du droit de guerre* (1919), Pt. II.

[79] On the effects of the Crusades, see especially: Adams, *Civilization during the Middle Ages* (1914), ch. 11; Bénont and Monod, *Mediæval Europe* (1902), ch. 22; Emerton, *Mediæval Europe* (1895), 388–97; 1 Hill, *History of Diplomacy in the Development of Europe* (1905–06), 368 ff.; 4 Milman, *Latin Christianity* (1881), Bk. VII, ch. 6; Munro, *The Middle Ages* (1922), 307 ff.; Munro and Sellery, *Mediæval Civilization* (1907), 253–56; Walker, *History of the Law of Nations* (1899), 87 ff.

aggerated. Although it undoubtedly tended somewhat to soften manners and humanize the conduct of the nobles during the later Middle Ages, it is an open question whether its tendency was not rather to increase than to mitigate the barbarities of mediæval warfare which often rivaled, if indeed they did not sometimes exceed, those of the ancient Orient.[80] The obligation of chivalry extended only to equals, and the desire for ransom added the motive of greed to the lust for combat and the exercise of brutal passions.[81]

48. **Influence of Mediæval Commerce.**—Another important influence upon the development of the Law of

[80] On the barbarities of mediæval warfare, see Hosack, *Rise and Growth of the Law of Nations* (1882), chs. 2–4; Nys, *Les origines*, ch. 11; Walker, *History of the Law of Nations* (1899), §§ 63 ff.; and Ward, *Enquiry into the Foundation and History of the Law of Nations* (1795), I, chs. 8–9, and II, ch. 14.

Nys (*Les origines*, p. 188) gives the following summary of the character of mediæval warfare: "In the Middle Ages war bears the stamp of an indescribable cruelty; adversaries injure each other as much as possible; the annihilation of the enemy is the final end of hostilities. Hence, unheard-of acts of barbarity; the use of poisoned weapons; the mutilation of prisoners, devastation, the sack and destruction of towns; recourse to treason and perfidy. We are unable to furnish a complete picture of the atrocities committed."

The Church made some slight efforts to mitigate the horrors of warfare, as, *e.g.* its prohibition of the use of the crossbow and of projectiles hurled from machines, but these efforts were unsuccessful. It also condemned the enslavement of Christian prisoners. Though prisoners were often massacred and some times enslaved, the Church deserves the gratitude of mankind for its crusade against slavery.

Prisoners of note were generally ransomed, sometimes exchanged, and in a few cases released on parole. In the latter case hostages were usually given.

[81] The following passage from a Christian historian descriptive of the capture of Jerusalem, which was taken by storm on July 15, 1099, may serve as an illustration of the unrestrained brutality of the Crusaders when their fierce and unbridled passions were aroused: "No barbarian, no infidel, no Saracen, ever perpetrated such wanton and cold-blooded atrocities of cruelty as the wearers of the cross of Christ on the capture of that city. Murder was mercy, rape tenderness, simple plunder the mere assertion of the conqueror's right. Children were seized by their legs, some of them were plucked from their mother's breasts and dashed against the walls or whirled from the battlements. Others were obliged to leap from the walls; some tortured, roasted by slow fires. They ripped up prisoners to see if they had swallowed gold. Of 70,000 Saracens there were not left enough to bury the dead; poor Christians were hired to perform the office. Every one surprised in the Temple was slaughtered, till the reek from the dead bodies drove away the slayers. The Jews were buried alive in their synagogues. . . ." 4 Milman, *History of Latin Christianity*, p. 37 (American ed., 1881). Cited by Hosack, *op. cit.*, p. 68. Hosack adds that the brutality of the Crusaders has often been contrasted with the remarkable generosity with which Saladin, the renowned Sultan of Egypt, treated the captive Christians when he retook Jerusalem in 1187.

Nations was that of mediæval commerce, which centered in certain Italian cities [82] of the Mediterranean, and was greatly stimulated by the Crusades. It flourished in spite of war, piracy, and the opposition of the Church, and was later extended to the north by way of the Atlantic as well as along overland routes. The desire to protect and extend mediæval commerce led to the formation of leagues of cities. The most important of these confederacies was the Hanseatic League (1250–1450) which, at the time of its greatest extent, " included more than ninety cities of the Baltic and North Sea regions, both seaports and inland towns." [83]

49. **The Discovery of America.**—The necessity for opening up new trade routes to India, which resulted from the Turkish conquests of the fifteenth century, more particularly the capture of Constantinople in 1453, led to the discovery of America and the circumnavigation of Africa and the globe. These, in turn, transferred the center of greatest commercial activity from the Mediterranean to the Atlantic, and greatly extended the circle of international and commercial relations.

50. **The *Consolato del Mare*.**—It is to mediæval commerce that we owe those collections of maritime law which have exercised such a great influence upon the subsequent development of this branch of international jurisprudence. By far the most important of these was the *Consolato del Mare*,[84] a private collection of rules derived from maritime

[82] The most important of these were Amalfi, Venice, Pisa, and Genoa.

[83] Harding, *Essentials in Mediæval and Modern History* (1905), p. 187. See map on pp. 184–185, showing extent of mediæval commerce, trade routes, and the Hansa towns and settlements. The objects of the League were common defense, the acquisition, maintenance, and security of trade; and it provided for the settlement of disputes between members by arbitration.

[84] On the *Consolato del Mare*, see especially Pardessus, *Us et coutumes de la mer* (1847), I, 21–34, 206–209, and II, 1–368 or ch. 12. For English translations of the famous chapter 273 of the *Consolato*, see Wheaton, *History*, 63–65; and Manning, *Law of Nations* (1875), 280–283. Both are copies of Robinson's translation of the Prize Chapters of the *Consolato del Mare*, in *Collectanea Maritima*, No. 5. See also 3 Twiss, *Black Book of the Admiralty* (1871–76), 34, 539 and 611.

Other important mediæval collections or codes of maritime law were: (1) The so-called *Amalfitan Tables*, which appear to date from the eleventh century. (2) The *Laws of Oleron* for Western Europe, which seem to have been completed in the latter part of the twelfth century. (3) The *Laws of Wisby*, dating from about 1288, for the Baltic Nations. (4) The *Maritime Law*

practice in the Mediterranean, which was published in Barcelona, Spain, in 1494.[85]

These rules showed a remarkable liberality toward friends or neutrals.   They made ownership of the ship and goods the test of liability to forfeiture, and laid down the principle that a friend's goods found on board an enemy ship were to be restored to the owner on payment of the freight.   It was even provided that the owner of the cargo might purchase the vessel at a suitable price.   On the other hand, enemy goods found on a neutral vessel were subject to confiscation, although even in this case the vessel, which might be compelled to carry the cargo to a place of safety, was restored to its owner who received the same freight that he would have received if the goods had been carried to their original destination.

51. The Mediæval Origin of the Modern Consulate.— The Crusades and the interests of mediæval commerce led to the establishment of consulates.   At least as early as the twelfth century, naval and merchant consuls chosen by the seamen or merchants themselves, settled disputes among their countrymen and represented the interests of the seamen and merchants of leading Italian, French, and Spanish cities in Mohammedan countries in the Levaut like Egypt and the Ottoman Empire where these rights and privileges were secured and enlarged by treaties known as Capitulations.   Officials known as *consules maritimi* or consul judges were also sent out by the home governments enjoying the same privileges and immunities.   During the thirteenth and fourteenth centuries this institution gradually spread to the West and North; [86] but, owing to the rise

of the Hanseatic League, completed in 1614.   (5) The so-called *Rhodian Sea-Law* of the Roman Empire and the early Middle Ages, which, however, is generally regarded as apocryphal.   It was first published in 1561, though Ashburner (in *The Rhodian Sea-Law*, 1909, p. cxii) presents some strong arguments in favor of his opinion that it was "probably put together by a private hand between A.D. 600 and A.D. 800."

[85] Nys, *Les origines*, p. 232.   But its actual development dates from a much earlier period, probably the fourteenth century.   It was applied by the sea consuls of Barcelona who existed as early as 1279.

[86] In the North, *i.e.* among members of the Hanseatic League, the consular judges were known as aldermen.   Like the consuls of the South, they represented the powerful merchant guilds or corporations rather than the governments.   We should remember in this connection that the Middle Ages were

of permanent embassies and the development of the doctrine of territorial jurisdiction in Europe, the extra-territorial powers of the consuls greatly declined in the course of the sixteenth century, and finally disappeared entirely. Turkey secured the abrogation of the Capitulations by the Treaty of Lausanne in 1923.

52. **The Rise of the Modern European States-system.**— The mediæval consuls were, however, in no proper sense agents or organs of internationalism, though they may in a sense be said to have been " pioneers " in " international organization." [87] Although Christendom was aroused to some sense of its community of interests by the Crusades, mediæval man still lived in a world largely disordered and unorganized, while dreaming of " kingdom come " or the universal rule of Pope or Emperor. The latter dream was dispelled through the mighty forces set in motion by the Renaissance and the Reformation; and the evils of disorder and disorganization were to a degree overcome through the rise of the modern States-system of Europe which was based on the ideas of nationality, the absolute territorial sovereignty of princes, the legal equality of States, and the maintenance of a balance of power or equilibrium of forces between them.

The first distinctly national group to emerge from the relative political chaos of the later Middle Ages was England where the spirit of nationalism, already developed to some extent during the long reign of Henry III, found a fairly complete expression in the Model Parliament of Edward I in 1295 and attained a unity of spirit which may

---

still dominated by the idea of *personality of law,* and that it was entirely natural that colonies or corporations of foreigners residing in a certain quarter of a mediæval city should be permitted to administer their own law, and that they should especially demand these privileges in the Orient.

On the *Mediæval Origin of the Consulate,* see Bonfils and, (3 Pt.) Fauchille, Nos. 734–41; 1 Halleck (3d ed.), 369–70 and note; Hautefeuille, *Histoire de droit maritime int.* (1869), 95 ff.; Holtzendorff, in 1 *Handbuch,* § 77; 2 F. de Martens, *Traité,* § 18; Mérignhac, 314 ff.; 2 Nys, 396–400; 1 Oppenheim, § 419; * Potter, *Int. Organization* (1922), ch. 5; * 4 P.-Fodéré, *Traité,* Nos. 2036–43; Ravndal, in *Am. Consular Bulletin,* III, (1921), Nos. 2, 3, and 4; * Schaube, "La Proxemie au Moyen Age," in 28 *R. D. I.* (1896), 525 ff; I Twiss, § 255.

[87] Potter, *Int. Organization* (1922), 63.

be said to have been cemented on the battlefields of Crecy and Poitiers. [88]

Passing over Scotland where a truly national spirit was developed during this same period in consequence of English attempts at conquest, the next nation-state to emerge was France, who became fully conscious of her nationhood largely as a result of English invasions during the Hundred Years War (1337–1453). The newly awakened national spirit of France " found an inspiring embodiment in that glorious saint of nationality, Joan of Arc." [89]

The next nation-states to emerge were Spain and Portugal inspired by the long crusade against the Moors and pride in foreign conquests. " The national spirit of Portugal was set afire by the great achievements of her navigators; the national unity of Spain, only formally attained by the dynastic union of Castille and Aragon and the conquest of Grenada, was welded by the centralized rule of Charles V and Philip II, and still more by pride in the deeds of the *conquistadores* of the New World, and the prestige won in the wars of Europe by the Spanish infantry." [90]

Then followed a period of rivalries between the new nation-states, particularly the long contest between France and Spain for the leadership of Europe. The Spanish attempt to obtain the mastery of the world during the latter half of the sixteenth century was frustrated, partly by the opposition of England and partly by the revolt of the Spanish Netherlands, more especially by the heroic resistance of the Dutch, who formed a new nation which, however, was not officially recognized by Europe before the

[88] For admirable evaluations of the main but somewhat elusive factors in modern nation-making, such as race, language and literature, religious unity, common subjection to a reigning dynasty or ruling government, common traditions, customs, and sufferings, community of economic interests, and the occupation, real or desired, of a definite geographic area, see particularly, Hays, *Essays on Nationalism* (1926), *passim*; Muir, *Nationalism and Internationalism* (1916), 37–57; and the article entitled "Nation" by Renan in 2 Lalor, *Cyclopaedia of Political Science* (1882–84), 923 ff. For further references on Nationalism, see Krehbiel, *Nationalism, War and Society* (1916), 23. To Krehbiel's list should be added: Gooch, *Nationalism* (1920); and Rose, *Nationality in Modern History* (1916).

[89] Muir, *Nationalism and Internationalism*, (1916), 58. Cf. Rose, *Nationality* (1916), 15–16.

[90] Muir, *op. cit.*, 59.

Peace of Westphalia in 1648. The sixteenth century also saw the birth and independence of a separate but powerful Scandinavian State, Sweden, as a result of the vigorous rule of Gustavus Vasa and the dissolution of the Union of Kalmar (formed in 1397) in 1524.

The main agents in the organization of the European States-system were the leading cities of Italy and the dynasties of France, England, and Spain, more particularly Louis XI, Henry VII, and Ferdinand of Aragon—these " three magicians " as Bacon called them. These kings, whose reigns fall within the latter half of the fifteenth century, all contributed powerfully to the development of that royal power which resulted in the destruction of feudalism as a political force, the unification and nationalization of the State, and the establishment of the modern States-system of Europe. The main organizers of European diplomacy in the narrower sense appear to have been Louis XI, Louis XII, Ferdinand, and the Emperor Maximilian.[91]

The system of permanent or resident embassies was established first in Italy [92] (from the thirteenth to the

[91] 2 Hill, *op. cit.*, 152-58, 208 ff., 308-11.

[92] The researches of Nys (see especially his *Les origines*, ch. 14) and others have rendered almost worthless most earlier accounts of the origin of European diplomacy. The system of *permanent* or *resident* embassies was unknown in antiquity, but the principles and customs of Roman diplomacy seem to have survived in Byzantium where they were practiced, particularly by Justinian and his successors.

Modern diplomacy originated in the leading Italian cities, more particularly in Venice and Rome who were doubtless influenced by their contact with Constantinople, in the course of the thirteenth to the fifteenth centuries. The system of resident embassies existed in Italy by the middle of the fifteenth century. From there the institution was extended to Spain, Germany, France, and England. The States maintained diplomatic relations with one another in the sixteenth century, but the system of permanent embassies or legations cannot be said to have been fully or generally established or perfected in Europe until the age of Richelieu, Mazarin, and Louis XIV in the seventeenth century. However, the terms "diplomatist" and "diplomacy" did not come into general use until the end of the eighteenth century.

On the *Origin of European diplomacy*, see especially, in addition to Nys (cited above): Baschet, *La diplomatie venitienne* (1862), and *Les archives de Venice* (1870); 1 (3 Pt.) Fauchille, No. 656; Flassan, *Histoire de la diplomatie française* (1811), *passim*; * Hill, *History of Diplomacy in the Development of Europe* (1905–06), *passim*, more particularly I, ch. 7, ad. fin., and II, chs. 2, 4, and 7; Holtzendorff in I *Handbuch*, § 83; Krauske, *Die Entwickelung der ständigen Diplomatie* (1885); I Maulde-la Clavière, *La diplomatie au temps de*

fifteenth centuries) and later (during the sixteenth and seventeenth centuries) in Western Europe. The idea of the balance of power and equilibrium of forces also found its first modern application in the intermunicipal relations of the Papacy and leading Italian cities in the fifteenth century,[93] and was later applied in the larger field of general European politics.[94]

53. The Peace of Westphalia.—The actual existence of a secular community of States in Western Europe was first fully revealed to the World by the Treaties of Westphalia— the work of the Congress of Catholic and Protestant States which met at Münster and Osnabrück in 1644–1648.[95]

Machiavel (1892–93); 1 Oppenheim, §§ 358–59; * 3 P.-Fodéré, *Traité*, Nos. 1231–36, and 1 *Cours* 209 ff.; * Potter, *Int. Organization* (1922), ch. 7.
For further references, which are mainly based on French and Italian sources of information, see the "authorities" in Hill, *op. cit.*, and footnotes in Nys, *op. cit.*

[93] *I.e.* Venice, Florence, Milan, and Naples. It was especially applied by Lorenzo de Medici. Italy also seems to furnish us with the first example of the modern administrative State, viz. the centralized administration of Frederick II in Southern Italy and Sicily in the thirteenth century. Burckhardt, *The Civilization of the Renaissance* (Eng. trans. by Middlemore 1892), p. 5. Cited by Nys, *Les origines*, p. 166.

[94] Evidences of the application of this idea may be found in the policies of England and France during the sixteenth century, but the balance of power can hardly be said to have been established as a European system prior to the latter part of the seventeenth century. It was first formally and officially recognized by the Peace of Utrecht in 1713.
On the origin of the system of "European Equilibrium," see Nys, *Les origines*, ch. 8; 2 Hill, *History of Diplomacy*, *passim*, particularly, 158, 238, 294 ff.

[95] In the negotiations at Münster and Osnabrück, which lasted nearly three years and a half, all the leading European powers (except England, Poland, Muscovy, and Turkey) were represented, viz. the Papacy, the German Empire, France, Spain, Sweden, Venice, Denmark, Portugal, and the States General of Holland. The main parties to the negotiations were France and Sweden on the one side and the Roman German Emperor on the other. The various German States, the Grand Duke of Tuscany, and the Dukes of Savoy and Mantua also sent delegates. The Swiss cantons were represented through the good offices of the French and included in the general pacification. The independence of Holland was also recognized. England and Poland were included in the Treaty of Osnabrück as allies both of the Emperor and of Sweden.
These details are taken from Bernard's interesting essay on "The Congress of Westphalia," in his *Lectures on Diplomacy* (1868), Lect. I, and 2 Hill, *History of Diplomacy in the Development of Europe* (1905–06); ch. 7, pp. 592 ff. See also Wheaton, *History*, pp. 69 ff.; Phillimore, *Three Centuries of Treaties of Peace* (1919), ch. 2, pp. 13 ff., and Redslob, *Histoire du droit des gens* (1923), § 38. For further references to the sources and authorities, see Bernard, *op. cit.*, p. 10 and 2 Hill, *op. cit.*, pp. 608 and 611. See also 4 *Cambridge Modern History*, ch. 4 and Bibliography on pp. 866–69.

This Peace, which marks the close of the Thirty Years' War and the establishment of the Modern European States-system on a legal basis, recognized the equality of the Catholic, Lutheran, and Calvinist confessions in Germany; and the independence and legal equality of the States (including the 332 sovereignties of Germany) of Western Christendom, whether Catholic or Protestant, monarchical or republican.[96]

" As a guarantee of faithful execution, the Treaties of Westphalia were accepted as a fundamental law by all contractants, who were empowered and bound to defend their provisions.   Thus, for the first time, Europe received what may be fairly described as an international consti-tution, which gave to all its adherents the right of inter-vention to enforce its arrangements.[97]

BIBLIOGRAPHY

International Law of Antiquity.—I Alcorta, *Cours de droit int. public* (1887), ch. 6, sec. 1; Audinet, in 21 *R. G. D. I* (1914), 29–63; Bender, *Antikes Völkerrecht* (1911); Busolt, in Müller's *Handbuch*, IV, 1, §§ 54–76; * Cybichowski, *Das antike Völkerrecht* (1907); Egger, *Les traités publics chez les grecs et les romains* (1866); * Greenidge, *Handbook of Greek Const. History* (1902), ch. 3, § 2, and *Roman Public Life* (1911), ch. 7; Hermann, *Griechische Antiquitäten* (1882–89), §§ 9–14; * Holtzendorff, in 1 *Handbuch*, §§ 40–64; König, in 11 *Z. V.* (1920), 155 ff.; Korff, in 18 *A. J.* (1924), 246 ff.; * Laurent, *Études sur l'humanité* (1865–80), Vols. I, II, and III; Leseur, *Cours de droit int.* (1893), Nos. 33–38; Müller-Jochmus, *Geschichte des Völkerrechts im Altertum* (1848); * Phillipson, *Int. Law and Customs of Ancient Greece and Rome* (1911), in 2 vols.; Redslob, *Histoire du droit des gens* (1923), §§ 1–13; Scala, *Die Staatsverträge des Altertums* (1898); 2 Schoemann, *Griechische Altertümer* (1902), 1–123; * Tod, *International Arbitration amongst the Greeks* (1913); 2 Vinogradoff, *Historical Jurisprudence* (1920–22), ch. 8; * 1 Walker, *History of the Law of Nations* (1899), 30–64; Wheaton, *History*, Introduction.

International Law of the Middle Ages.—1 Alcorta, *Cours de droit int. public* (1887), ch. 6, sec. 2; Hosack, *The Rise and Growth of the*

---

[96] Of these 332 German States (more or less), "211 were secular states governed by hereditary monarchs (Electors, Dukes, Landgraves, and the like), 56 were free City-states, and 65 were ecclesiastical States governed by Arch-bishops and other Church dignitaries." I Oppenheim, § 44, p. 66.

[97] 2 Hill, *op. cit.*, 602. "All and each of the contracting parties of this treaty shall be held to defend and maintain all and each of the dispositions of this peace, against whomsoever it may be, without distinction of religion." Art. 17 of the Treaty of Osnabrück.

Law of Nations (1882), chs. 2–7; * Holtzendorff, 1 *Handbuch*, §§ 65–84; * Laurent, *Études sur l'humanité* (1865–80), Vols. IV–X, *passim;* Leseur, *Cours de droit int.* (1893), Nos. 38–54; * Nys, *Les origines*, and *Études*, *passim;* Redslob, *Histoire du droit des gens* (1923), §§ 14–38; * 1 Walker, *History of the Law of Nations* (1899), 79–201; Ward, *Enquiry into the Foundation and History of the Law of Nations* (1795), in 2 vols. (still useful).

The historical chapters in treatises of International Law are for the most part either slight or practically worthless in the light of our present knowledge. Among the exceptions are Bonfils, Calvo, Despagnet, Fauchille, J. de Louter, F. de Martens, *Traité*, Nys, Oppenheim, and Wilson and Tucker (the best of the brief sketches).

Jus Gentium.—Austin, *Lectures on Jurisprudence* (Campbell's 5th ed., 1911), see index; * Bryce, *Studies in History and Jurisprudence* (1901), 570–75, 753–54; 1 & 2 Carlyle, *History of Mediæval Pol. Theory* (1903–22, see index); * Clark, *Practical Jurisprudence* (1883), ch. 14; * Dickinson, *Equality of States* (1920, see index); Dunning, *Political Theories, Ancient and Mediæval* (1902), and, *From Luther to Montesquieu* (1905), *passim;* Holland, *Jurisprudence* (10th ed. in 1906), 34–35; Holtzendorff, in 1 *Handbuch*, § 64; 1 Karlowa, *Römische Rechtsgeschichte* (1885–1901), § 59, pp. 451–58; * Maine, *Ancient Law* (Pollock's ed., 1906), 44 ff. and Pollock's note E in Appendix, 396 ff., and *Int. Law*, 27–29; 1 F. de Martens, 84 ff.; 3 Mommsen, *Römisches Staatsrechts*, 603–06 and notes, in Marquardt and Mommsen's *Handbuch;* * Art. on *jus gentium* by Professor Nettleship, in 13 *Journal of Philology*, No. 26; 1 Phillipson, *op. cit.*, ch. 3; 1 Roby, *Roman Private Law* (1902), 5–6, especially note 2 on p. 5; Salkowsky, *Roman Private Law* (Whitefield's trans., 1886), 10, 30–31; 1 Savigny, *System des römischen Rechts* (1840–51), § 23; Sherman, in 12 *A. J.* (1918), 56 ff.; * Sohm, *Institutes* (1904), §§ 13–14; 2 Taylor, *The Mediæval Mind* (1911), ch. 33; * Vinogradoff, in 1 *Bibliotheca Visseriana*, 23–34; 1 Voigt, *Römische Rechtsgeschichte* (1892); § 15, pp. 152–62, and * 1 *Jus naturale und jus gentium der Römer* (1856–76), *passim;* * Walker, *History of the Law of Nations* (1899), §§ 28–29, 85 *et passim* (see index); Westlake, *Chapters* (1894), 18 ff.; Wheaton, *History*, 26 ff.; Wilson, *The State* (1889), Nos. 204 ff.; Willoughby, *Political Theories of the Ancient World* (1903), 252–67.

Jus Naturale.—Ahrens, *Das Naturrecht* (1846), and *Cours de droit naturel* (1868); * Bryce, *Studies in History and Jurisprudence* (1901), Essay XI, 556–606; Burlamaqui, *Principes du droit naturel* (1747), *passim;* 1 and 2 Carlyle, *History of Mediæval Pol. Theory* (1903–22, see index); Clark (A.), on "Natural Rights," in 16 *Annals* (1900), 212–16; * Dickinson, *Equality of States* (1920, see index); * Dunning, *Political Theories, Ancient and Mediæval* (1902), and *From Luther to Montesquieu* (1905), *passim;* Gierke, *Political Theories of the Middle Age* (trans. by Maitland, 1900), *passim;* * Goebel, *Equality of States* (1923), *passim;* Grotius, *De jure belli ac pacis* (Whewell's trans., 1853), see especially "Preliminary," *passim;* Hibben, in 4 *Int. J. of*

Ethics (1893–94), 133–60; Holland, *Jurisprudence* (10th ed.), 6, 30–38; Lorimer, *Institutes of the Law of Nations* (1883–84), and *Institutes of Law* (1880), *passim;* 2 Lowell, *Government of England* (1908), 477–88; * Maine, *Ancient Law* (Pollock's ed., 1906), chs. 3 and 4, and Pollock's notes E–G in Appendix; Mackintosh, *The Law of Nature and Nations* (1828) (see also his *Miscel. Works*, 1878, 27–43); Miller, *Philosophy of Law* (1884), Appendix A, 376–83; * Pound. "The Revival of Natural Law in France," in 25 *Harvard Law Review* (1911–12), 159–62; Pufendorf, *Le droit de la nature et des gens* (trad, par Barbeyrac, 1706), *passim;* Pulszky, *Theory of Law and Civil Society* (1888), ch. 4, 77–83; Reeves, in 3 *A. J.* (1909), 547 ff.; * Ritchie, *Natural Rights* (1895), especially ch. 5; Rutherford, *Institutes of Natural Law* (2d Am. ed., 1832), especially Bk. I, chs. 1, 2, and 5 and ch. 9 of Bk. II; Salmond, in 11 *Law Quarterly* (1895), 121–43; Taylor, T. W. in 1 *Annals* (1891), 558–85; 2 Taylor, H. O. *The Mediæval Mind* (1911), ch. 33; Vattel, *passim;* * 1 Voigt, *Das jus naturale et gentium der Römer* (1856–76), *passim;* Walker, *History of the Law of Nations* (1899), *passim* (see index); * Willoughby, *Political Theories of the Ancient World* (1903), 249 ff. and 281 ff., and *The Nature of the State* (1896), ch. 5, pp. 89–115.

Additional Note on the Forerunners of Grotius.—The most important Precursors of Grotius were: (1) *Alphonso the Wise*, King of Castile (1252–1284), who, with the aid of collaborators, compiled a mediæval code of law called the *Siete Partidas* which contained many rules of land and naval warfare. Nys, I *Études*, 75–86. (2) *Giovanni da Legnano*, Professor of Law at Bologna, who (about 1360) wrote the first substantive treatise on the laws of war. His entire work, which was not published before 1477, was entitled *De bello, de represaliis, et de duello*. (3) *Honoré Bonet*, a Benedictine monk and a Provençal, the author of a remarkable book which bears the peculiar title of *L'arbre des batailles*. It was written about 1384 and contains 132 chapters on the laws of warfare. This work was reëdited by Nys, in 1883. (4) *Christine de Pisan*, perhaps the first advocate of woman's rights, who was born in Venice in 1363 and was educated at the French court. Among the voluminous works of this remarkable woman, there was one entitled *Livre des faits d'armes et de chevalerie*, which is largely copied, with due acknowledgment, from the *L'arbre des battailles* of Honoré Bonet. Both Bonet and Christine were far in advance of their age in humanitarian sentiments, but their works were nevertheless highly successful. On Bonet and Christine, see especially Nys, 1 *Études*, 145–62. (5) *Belli*, an Italian jurist and statesman, who published an important work entitled *De re militari et de bello* about 1563. (6) *Victoria* (1480–1546), a Dominican monk and Professor at Salamanca, whose thirteen *Relectiones theologicæ* were first published in 1557. Two of these, the fifth, entitled *De Indiis* and the sixth, *De jure belli*, deal with the rights of the Indians and the laws of war. Victoria is probably the first modern thinker who conceived the idea of a society or community of nations based upon natural reason and sociability. It was Victoria who first used the phrase *jus inter gentes*. He set up the doctrine of the solidarity and interdependence of States and based the rights of the Spanish in the Indies upon the natural rights of commerce and communication. Barthélemy, in *Les fondateurs du droit int.*, ed. by Pillet, 1904, p. 7. (7) *Ayala* (1548–1584), a military judge in the service of Philip II, who published a treatise in 1582 on the laws of war and military discipline. (8) The great Spanish Jesuit *Suarez*, who published his *Tractibus de legibus* in 1612. In a famous passage which is translated by Westlake (see *Chapters* 1894, pp. 26–27, or *Collected Papers* 1914, 26–27), Suarez for the firsttime clearly states the view that each State is a member of an international community or society of nations which are bound together by the necessity of mutual aid and communion.   He also distinguished clearly between International Law (*jus gentium*) and the Law of Nature (*jus naturale*).   (9) *Gentilis*, a Protestant Italian jurist who was appointed Professor of Civil Law at Oxford in 1587. His chief work, *De jure belli*, which was published in 1598 and reëdited by Professor Holland in 1877, furnished the model and framework for the first and third books of Grotius' *De jure belli ac pacis*.   In 1613 there was published a posthumous work of Gentilis entitled *Advocationis Hispanicæ*.   Gentilis died in 1608.   Gentilis is undoubtedly the most important of the forerunners of Grotius, but lacks the idealism, passion for justice, and broad humanitarianism of the latter.   He is the founder of the historical school of international jurists, and is also in some respects (as *e.g.* in his advocacy of the rights of neutrals) in advance of Grotius.

Among the precursors of the later Grotius of the *Jure belli ac pacis* (*Rights of War and Peace*) there should be listed the earlier Grotius himself.   In 1864 there was discovered at The Hague a MSS. of his entitled *De jure praedae* (*On the Law of Prize or Booty*) written in 1604–05 while the author was 21 years of age.

The *De jure praedae* was an argument or brief written in support of the right of the Dutch East India Company to booty in the defensive war which the Company waged against Portugal on behalf of their trade on the Indian Ocean. This resulted from the Portugese claims to sovereignty over the high seas based upon the Papal Bull of 1493.

This early work of Grotius was essentially a justification of the right under such circumstances to wage war which, in common with the cannonists and scholastics of the later Middle Ages, he erroneously regarded as a means or instrument of international justice.   It is a law of nature, it is maintained, that the one waging a just war is the judge or censor of the one waging an unjust war.   (Grotius seems to have overlooked the fact that from the standpoint of him who wages it, every war is just.)   Consequently, there can be no doubt as to the right to prize or booty (legitimate in itself) captured in a just war.

It remains to add that, with a few alterations, chapter XII of the *Jure praedae* was published as a separate work with the title *De mare liberum* (On the Freedom of the Seas) in 1609, but the main work did not see the light until 1868.

On the *De jure praedae*, see Basdevant, in *Les Fondateurs du droit int.* (ed. by Pillet), *passim*, particularly 131–37, 155–79; Vreeland, *Hugo Grotius* (1917), ch. 3; and Vollenhoven, *Evolution of the Law of Nations* (1919), *passim.*

On the *Precursors of Grotius*, see especially the voluminous researches of Nys, more particularly his *Le droit de la guerre et les precurseurs de Grotius* (1882), *Les origines, Études, passim,* and * *Le droit int.,* (ed. of 1904) I, 213–33.   See *Les fondateurs de droit int.* (1904), ed. by Pillet, for studies of Victoria, Gentilis, and Suarez.   See also Holland's *Studies* and Westlakes *Chapters* (1894), or *Collected Papers* (1914), 25–36 for valuable studies of Ayala, Suarez, Gentilis, etc.   On Suarez, see also Dunning, *From Luther to Montesquieu* (1905), 135–49; and Lange, *Histoire,* etc., 279 ff.   Walker's *History of the Law of Nations, and Science of Int. Law, passim,* Rivier, in Holtzendorff's *Handbuch,* I, § 85, Wheaton's *History*, Introduction, and Kaltenborn, *Die Vorlaüfer des Hugo Grotius* (1848), contain much valuable information. See also Koster, in 4 *Biblitheca Visseriana*, 17–37; Lange, *Histoire*, etc., *passim*; and two recent scholarly works by Meulen, J. Ter, *Die Gedanke der int. Organization* (1917), 269 ff., and Vanderpol, *La doctrine scholastique du droit de guerre* (1919), *passim.*

Among the precursors of Grotius, the following have thus far (1925) been translated and published by the Carnegie Institution in the *Classics of Int. Law*, ed. by J. B. Scott: Ayala, *De jure et oficiis bellicis et disciplina militari*, (1912); Gentilis, *Hispanicae advocationis* (1921); Legnano, *De bello, de represaliis et de duello*, (1917); and Victoria, *De Indiis et de jure belli relectiones*, (1917).

In view of recent movements toward international organization, particular mention should be made of the publication in 1623 (two years before the publication of Grotius' *De jure belli ac pacis*) of a small book entitled *Le Nouveau Cynée* or *The New Cyneas* by Émeric Crucé. This comparatively obscure Parisian monk was a pioneer in the field of international organization rather than a precursor of Grotius. Crucé may even be said to have had the clearer vision; for in the midst of the horrors of the Thirty Years War he had the insight to see that a more drastic solution was needed than a distinction between just and unjust wars, the punishment of state crimes by force, or the humanization of warfare. He had the daring to suggest a Congress or Assembly consisting of ambassadors of the leading sovereigns and great republics of his time which should sit perpetually in some city (preferably Venice) "in order that the differences that might arise should be settled by the judgment of the whole assembly. The ambassadors of those who would be interested would plead there the grievances of their masters and the other deputies would judge them without prejudice. . . . If anyone rebelled against the decrees of so notable a company, he would receive the disgrace of all other Princes, who would find means to bring him to reason. . . ."

"And nevertheless never was a council so august, nor assembly so honorable, as that of which we speak, which would be composed of ambassadors of all the monarchs and sovereign republics, who will be *trustees and hostages of public peace*. And . . . all the said Princes will swear to hold as inviolable law what would be ordained by the *majority of votes* in the said assembly, and to pursue with arms all who would oppose it. This company therefore would judge then the debates which would arise not only about precedence, but about other things, would maintain the ones and the others in good understanding; *would meet discontents half way, and would appease them by gentle means, if it could be done, or in case of necessity, by force.*" (Trans. of *The New Cyneas* by Balch, 1909, 102–04 and 120–22.) It should be added that Crucé based his system of international organization upon freedom of trade and communication and the unity of standards in weights, measures and currency.

For comments on Crucé and his work, see Butler, *Studies in Statecraft* (1920), ch. 5; Lange, I *Histoire de l'internationalisme* (1919), 398–433; Meulen, *Der Gedanke der Int. Organization* (1917), 88–89, 143–52; Nys, 1 *Études*, 308–16; and Redslob, *Das Problem des Völkerrechts* (1917), 182–86.

It should not be overlooked that Grotius himself in a famous passage (lib. II, cap. 23, § 8) declared that "it would be useful, and indeed it is almost necessary, that certain Congresses of Christian Powers should be held, in which the controversies which arise among some of them could be decided by others who are not interested; and in which measures can be taken to compel the parties to accept peace on equitable terms." But to Grotius this idea seems rather incidental and falls considerably short of Crucé's plan of a permanent Assembly which is to include the ambassadors of non-Christian Powers.

In this connection mention should also be made of *Sully's Grand Design* or the so-called *Great Design of Henry IV*, as it has often been misnamed.   It is mainly contained in the last two volumes of Sully's *Memoirs* dictated during the later years of his life (ab. 1635) while that statesman lived in retirement, and was not published (and then not without many alterations) until 1662 or long after his death in 1641.   (The first two volumes were published in 1638.)   The *Memoirs*, which are full of contradictions, attribute to Henry IV (who was assassinated in 1610) the Great Design of grouping, re-grouping, or dividing Christian Europe into six elective monarchies, six hereditary monarchies, and six republics, thus forming a Confederacy which should be controlled by one General and six provincial Councils.   The General Council or Senate, consisting of sixty-six persons chosen proportionally and rechosen every third year, was to deliberate on all matters affecting the joint or several interests of the member-states of the Confederacy, pacify their mutual quarrels, and determine any civil, political, or religious controversies, whether arising within their own territories or those of their neighbors.

It must be admitted that this scheme, while of great interest and importance in the development of ideas of internationalism, was at least partly inspired by political objects, viz., the union of Christian Europe against the Turks (which appears to have been a means rather than an end), the weakening of the Empire of the Hapsburgs, and the possible aggrandizement of France.   It is difficult not to suspect that it was largely a political adaptation of Crucé's plan.

On Sully's "Grand Design," see * Butler, *op. cit.*, ch. 4; Lange, *op. cit.*, 434–76; Meade, *The Great Design of Henry IV* (1909); Meulen, *op. cit.*, 160–70; Redslab, *op. cit.*, 122–36; and York, *Leagues of Nations* (1919), ch. 3.   (The references to Mr. Meade's and Miss York's books are given merely because they contain extracts from Sully's *Memoirs*.   Otherwise, they are not to be relied upon.)

The name of the French advocate *Pierre Dubois*, a precursor of Crucé rather than of Grotius, should not be omitted from this sketch.   Dubois, a contemporary of Dante, wrote a work entitled *De recuperatione Terre Sancta* about 1306 which appears to make him absolutely the pioneer in the history of the development of the idea of modern international organization.   As a means of realizing the recovery of the Holy Land, he substituted for the idea of a world monarchy a Christian Republic or Confederacy headed by a Council of Prelates, Catholic princes and sovereign kings summonéd by the Pope who was also to preside. This Council was to meet on French territory in the vicinity of Toulouse and make such decisions as were necessary to maintain peace.   No Catholic should wage war against another Catholic or shed baptized blood, under penalty of loss of possessions.   For the settlement of controversies between sovereigns there was to be created an International Tribunal which should select six judges—three lay and three ecclesiastical—for the decision of each particular controversy.   It should be added that there is a well-grounded suspicion that Dubois' scheme, advanced as some of its features are, had as its primary aim the aggrandizement of the French monarchy.

On Dubois, see especially, Knight (with bibliography), in 9 *Grotius Soc.* (1924), 1–16; Lange, *op. cit.*, 90–108; Meulen, *op. cit.*, 101–09; and Redslob, *op. cit.*, 105–16.

CHAPTER IV

THE HISTORY OF INTERNATIONAL LAW AND RELATIONS
SINCE THE PEACE OF WESTPHALIA

54. **The Main Factors in the Growth of the Science of International Law.**—As already pointed out, the Peace of Westphalia gave to Europe a sort of international constitution which remained the basis of its public law down to the French Revolution. But it would be a serious error to assume that the International Community of States as revealed to the world in 1648 implied the recognition of the science of International Law as understood and practiced by the Society of Nations at the present time. The science of International Law as it exists to-day is a result of slow historical growth and is the product of two main factors, viz. certain theories or principles on the one hand, and international practice or custom recognized as obligatory on the other. The relative value and influence of the contributions of each of these factors is so difficult to determine that they have never been thoroughly sifted or separated—a task left for the future historians of International Law.

55. **The Importance of Jurists and Publicists.**—It is clear that during its formative period International Law was mainly developed by great thinkers and jurists who were forced to rely upon the weight of general ideas or theoretical considerations rather than upon any satisfactory body of accumulated custom, if they desired to ameliorate conditions or improve international relations. The fundamental principles of the science once firmly established and recognized in international practice, there was less need for theoretical discussion. It then became the main function of the jurist and publicist to apply and interpret the law in conformity with the best and most authoritative precedents or usages.

56. **Grotius the Founder of the Science of International Law.**—The founder of the *Science* of International Law was Hugo Grotius, whose main work, entitled *De jure belli ac*

69

pacis, published in 1625 during the midst of the horrors of the Thirty Years' War, marks an epoch in the history of civilization as well as of International Law. Although there is in it not much that was original and based, as it was, largely upon the labors of his predecessors [1] to whom somewhat scant recognition is given by him, Grotius deserves his title of " Founder of International Law " from the fact that his was the only work in the seventeenth century to obtain wide circulation and general recognition.[2] This was because it answered the needs of the time, and was the fullest, most attractive, systematic, and scholarly exposition of the subject hitherto attempted. Grotius brought to his work great learning, enthusiasm, experience, and a passion for justice which won for him the hearts as well as the heads of his contemporaries and of posterity.

57. His Work based on the *Jus Naturale*.—Like his predecessors and many of his successors, Grotius started from the idea of a universal and immutable Law of Nature (*jus naturale*) based upon right reason and human sociality —a philosophical conception derived from the Stoic philosophers of antiquity that has dominated Ethics and Jurisprudence until recent times. He claimed for the Law of Nations the authority and sanction of this Law of Nature, a doctrine denied by no one in his day,[3] thus giving it an apparently solid, binding, and rational character which few

---

[1] For references and a brief sketch of the "Forerunners of Grotius," see additional note at the end of the preceding chapter.

[2] This is shown by the facts that at least forty-five Latin editions of his book were issued prior to 1748 and that it had been translated into the leading modern languages before the close of the seventeenth century. See Rivier, in 1 Holtzendorff's *Handbuch*, § 88, for list of editions. Grotius' book is said to have made such a great impression upon Gustavus Adolphus that he slept with it under his pillow during his campaigns in Germany.

Grotius was born at Delft, Holland, in 1583. As a child he was a prodigy, writing Latin verses at nine years of age. He entered the University of Leyden when twelve years old, and took his degree of Doctor of Laws at Orleans, France at the age of fifteen. As a result of religious controversy, he was sentenced to imprisonment for life in 1619; but in 1621 he succeeded in escaping from prison and lived for ten years in Paris, where he composed and published his great work in 1623–1625. In 1634 he was appointed Swedish minister to France—a position which he held until the year of his death in 1645. Grotius was poet, philologist, philosopher, historian, and mathematician, as well as diplomatist, lawyer, and jurist.

[3] For references on the *jus naturale*, see Bibliography at the end of the preceding chapter.

cared to dispute. Moreover, he fortified his position by an attractive style and a marvelous display of erudition or citation of authorities from men of all ages and countries (including the Bible, poets, orators, philosophers, and historians, as well as jurists) which went far to enhance his authority in the eyes of his contemporaries. He also borrowed largely from the Roman *jus gentium* the leading principles of which had been practically identified with the *jus naturale*. This " written reason," as the Roman Civil Law has been called, not only commanded the highest respect from its origin, but was sanctioned by general agreement, at least on the part of the educated classes. Grotius thus relied upon positive law (*jus voluntarium*) as determined by general consent, as well as upon the Law of Nature, to give effect to the principles and usages of the Law of Nations.

58. **The Fundamental Principles underlying the Grotian System.**—Many of the principles laid down and usages sanctioned by Grotius are obsolete; others are found only in germ or are incompletely developed; many present-day laws and customs (as *e.g.* those making up the modern Law of Neutrality) were practically overlooked or received scant recognition from him; but the essential principles underlying the Grotian (or perhaps we should say the post-Grotian) system remain the fundamental principles of International Law. Such are the doctrines of the legal equality and the territorial sovereignty or independence of states.[4]

[4] So far as known to the author, the best more or less recent estimates of Grotius' work and various activities are by Basdevant, in *Les fondateurs du droit int.* (ed. by Pillet, 1904); Eysinga, in 6 (3d ser.) *R. D. I.* (1925), 269–79; * Knight, *Life and Works of Hugo Grotius* (Publication No. 4 of the Grotius Society, 1925); Koster, in 4 *Bibliotheca Visseriana*, 38–56; Reeves, in 19 *A. J.* (1925), 12 ff. and 251 ff.; Vollenhoven, *Three Stages in the Evolution of the Law of Nations* (1919), 9–22, 59–77, and in 19 *A. J.* (1925), 1–11; * Vreeland, *Hugo Grotius* (1917), particularly ch. 8, and in 11 *A. J.* (1917), 580 ff.; White, in *Seven Great Statesmen* (1910); and Walker, *Science of Int. Law* (1893), ch. 4. The best brief account of the work of Grotius in English is by Westlake in *Chapters* (1894), 36–51, reprinted in *Collected Papers* (1914) 36–51.

For a very full analysis of the *De jure belli ac pacis*, see Walker, *History of Int. Law*, §§ 143–48. The best modern translation is by Pradier-Fodéré. It is preceded by a valuable biographical and historical essay. For an abridged English translation, see Whewell. A photographic reproduction of the edition of 1646 was published by the Carnegie Institution in 1911. A new translation is in process of publication by this Institution.

These fundamental principles, though not clearly stated by Grotius, underlay his system and were fully developed by his successors, more especially by Wolff, Vattel, and G. F. von Martens. They were the inevitable outcome of the doctrines of natural law and the acceptance of the dogma of the supreme power or sovereignty of states and princes, as defined by Bodin, Grotius, Hobbes, and other political philosophers during the sixteenth and seventeenth centuries.[5]

It only remained to apply this dogma of sovereignty to the international relations of the Community of States recognized by the Peace of Westphalia. It was later seen that if States and princes are sovereign and independent, they must also be regarded as equal before the law, *i.e.*, as entitled under International Law to equal protection in the exercise of their rights and equally bound to fulfil their obligations; and that it was necessary to formulate a doctrine of the fundamental rights and duties of States.

59. **The Successors of Grotius.**—The successors of Grotius, who wrote during the seventeenth and eighteenth centuries, may be divided into three schools—the " Philosophical " or Pure Law of Nature School, the " Positivists " or Historical School, and the " Eclectics " or " Grotians."

60. **The Pure Law of Nature School.**—The Pure Law of Nature School, headed by Pufendorf (1632–1694), denied the existence of any positive International Law based on custom and treaties, and maintained that the Law of Nations is wholly a part of the Law of Nature.[6]   Pufendorf

---

[5] Though differing widely from the latter, both in point of view and details, Grotius (lib. I, c. 3, § 7) practically follows Bodin, who defines sovereignty as "supreme power over citizens and subjects, unrestrained by the laws." Dunning, *Political Theories from Luther to Montesq.* (1905), pp. 96 and 181. Bodin's great work, *De Republica*, was first published in 1576. Grotius has been severely criticized for his defense of the patrimonial State and his repudiation of the doctrine of popular sovereignty, but these views doubtless served to recommend his opinions to the absolute monarchs of his day.

[6] *De jure naturæ et gentium*, II, ch. 3, § 22. On this point Pufendorf followed Hobbes (*De cive*, XIV, 4), who divided Natural Law into "a Natural Law of men and a Natural Law of States," and maintained that the two were composed of identical precepts. In other words, States live in a state of nature in respect to each other. But Hobbes and Pufendorf differed widely in their views as to the sociable nature of man. Pufendorf, however, adpoted Hobbes' imperative view of the nature of law.

occupied the first chair which was founded for the study of the Law of Nature and Nations at a university (at Heidelberg, Germany, in 1661), but his *magnum opus* on *De jure naturæ et gentium* was not published until 1672, when he held the position of Professor of Jurisprudence at the University of Lund, in Sweden. His great service was his insistence upon the supreme importance of natural law at a time when customary law based on good usages was insufficiently developed.[7]

Pufendorf's most famous disciple was Thomasius [8] (1655–1728), a German philosopher who published his *Fundamenta juris naturæ et gentium* in 1705. Thomasius distinguished between perfect and imperfect duties—a distinction afterwards elaborated by Wolff.[9] Other important " Naturalists " of the seventeenth and eighteenth centuries were: Barbeyrac (1674–1744), the famous French translator and commentator of the works of Grotius, Pufendorf, and others; the Genevan Burlamaqui (1694–1748), whose *Principes du droit naturel et politique* was published in 1747; Thomas Rutherford, who published his *Institutes of Natural Law* in 1754; and the French diplomatist De Rayneval (1736–1812), author of the *Institutions de droit de la nature et de gens*.[10]

61. The Positive or Historical School.—The Positive or Historical School of international jurists, while not denying the existence and validity of the Law of Nature, emphasized the importance of custom and treaties as sources of International Law. This school may be said to have originated in England, where it has also attained its fullest development. One of Grotius' predecessors, the Italian Gentilis, who was appointed Professor of Civil Law at Oxford in 1588, and whose chief work, *De jure belli*, was published in 1598,

---

[7] The only part of his work which deals with International Law proper are the last five chapters of the eighth book.

[8] On Thomasius, see especially White, in *Seven Great Statesmen* (1910), 113–161.

[9] Westlake, *Chapters* (1894), p. 72 or *Collected Papers* (1914), 72.

[10] A belated pure "Naturalist" has even appeared during the latter half of the nineteenth century—the Scotch Professor Lorimer. He still defined the Law of Nations as the "law of nature realized in the relations of separate nations" or "political communities." See his *Institutes of the Law of Nations* (1883), I, pp. 1 and 19.

may in a sense be said to have been the founder of this school. At least he enriched his work with examples drawn from contemporary opinion and events—a practice which Grotius condemned—and he preferred historical investigation to abstract reasoning and systematic exposition.

Other representatives of this school in England during the seventeenth century were: the learned Selden [11] who, in a work entitled *Mare clausum* (published in 1635), attacked Grotius' views on the freedom of the sea as expressed in the latter's *Mare liberum* (published in 1609); Zouche (1590–1660), Professor of Civil Law at Oxford and Judge of the Admiralty Court, who published the first *manual* of International Law in 1650; [12] and Sir Leoline Jenkins, Zouche's successor as Admiralty Judge, whose opinions on questions of prize law are of great importance in the history of International Maritime Law. [13]

The three leading positivists of the eighteenth century were the famous Dutch jurist Bynkershoek and the German Professors John Jacob Moser and G. F. von Martens.

Bynkershoek never wrote a treatise on International Law, but he still ranks as one of its leading authorities. [14] Although he recognized reason as an important source of the Law of Nations, he relied mainly upon custom as expressed

[11] In 1640 Selden also recognized the importance of a positive Law of Nations in a work on Law of Nature and Nations among the Hebrews.

[12] The influence of Zouche in England was very great. He was the first publicist to use the term *jus inter gentes* in the title of his work; but he was not the inventor of this phrase, as generally stated. Victoria (see note on p. 65) had employed it in the first half of the sixteenth century, and Grotius had made use of the phrase *jus inter civitates*, though the latter generally employed the ambiguous term *jus gentium*. This work of Zouche was republished and translated under the auspices of the Carnegie Institution as Vols. I and II of the *Classics of Int. Law*, ed. by J. B. Scott (1911).

[13] It should not be forgotten that Germany also produced several representatives of the positive or historical school during the seventeenth century. Of these the most important were Rachel, who published two dissertations on *De jure naturæ et gentium* in 1676; and Textor, *Synopsis juris gentium* in 1680. For reprints and translations of these works, see *Classics of Int. Law* (1916), ed. by J. B. Scott.

[14] The fame of Bynkershoek rests upon three books: *De dominio maris* (1702); *De foro legatorum* (1721); *Questiones juris publici* (1737). Wheaton (*History*, p. 193) says that Bynkershoek was "the first writer who has entered into a critical and systematic exposition of the Law of Nations on the subject of maritime commerce between neutral and belligerent nations."

in treaties and international practice (including unilateral acts) for actual guidance.

John Jacob Moser (1701–1785) was the author of innumerable works bearing mainly on International Law,[15] which are perfect storehouses of historical facts and precedents. Moser was a thoroughgoing positivist, and his attitude toward the law of Nature is one either of indifference or of contempt.

G. F. von Martens (1756–1821) also published numerous works dealing with positive International Law, the most important of which was entitled *Précis du droit des gens moderne de l' Europe*, published in 1788. This work, which appeared in successive editions and has been translated into many languages,[16] has exercised a great influence upon international practice and the subsequent development of International Law. Martens does not wholly repudiate the Law of Nature based on reason and utility, but he admits it only in default of positive rules founded on usage and treaties. As the first systematic manual on positive International Law more or less adapted to modern needs, it became a model and still enjoys considerable reputation. G. F. von Martens is especially clear in his exposition of the fundamental rights and duties of States.[17]

62. **The " Eclectics " or " Grotians."**—A third school of international jurists—the " Eclectics " or " Grotians "— occupy a middle ground between the " Naturalists " and " Positivists." The members of this school followed in the footsteps of Grotius in preserving the distinction between

---

[15] Nys (1 *Droit int.*, p. 257) states that, in 1765, Moser had already composed 200 works and studies. His principal work, entitled *Versuch des neusten Europäischen Völkerrechts in Freidens und Kriegszeiten* in ten volumes, was completed in 1780. It is said by Wheaton (*History*, p. 323) to contain "a rich mine of materials." For a list of his principal works on International Law, see Wheaton, 324–325; and Rivier, in 1 Holtzendorff's *Handbuch*, § 102.

[16] An English translation by Cobbett was published at Philadelphia in 1795. The best and most recent edition, with notes by Pinheiro-Ferreira and Vergé, appeared at Paris in 1864. Martens also began the celebrated collection of treaties which bears his name and which has been continued up to recent times. G. F. von Martens must not be confused with his nephew Charles de Martens, the author of the *Causes célèbres de droit des gens* (1827) and the *Guide diplomatique* (1832), or with the famous Russian jurist and publicist F. de Martens of our own day.

[17] See his *Précis*, liv. IV.

the Law of Nature and the positive or voluntary Law of
Nations, based on custom or consent; but, unlike their
master, they have treated both as about equally important.

The greatest representatives of this school in the eighteenth century were the German philosopher Wolff (1679–
1754) and his Swiss disciple Vattel (1714–67).

Wolff's greatest work in this field was a treatise on the *jus
naturæ* (1740–48) in eight parts. To this was added a
volume on the *jus gentium* in 1749 and an abridgment of the
whole entitled *Institutiones juris naturæ et gentium* in 1763.
But Wolff's highly abstract treatment of these subjects
rendered his works practically unintelligible to those who
might otherwise have profited by them.

The task of introducing Wolff's ideas to men of letters,
statesmen, and diplomatists was undertaken by Vattel, the
famous Swiss publicist, whose influence on the conduct of
international relations is perhaps second only to that of
Grotius. Vattel tells us in the preface of his *Law of
Nations* [18] that he had at first intended only to " clothe "
certain portions of Wolff's system " in a more agreeable
dress," but he soon found it necessary to compose a very
different work. He, therefore, contented himself with
" selecting from the work of M. Wolfius the best parts,
especially the definitions and general principles." His
book, though by no means a wholly original contribution to
the subject, is indeed far from being the mere abridgment or
paraphrase of Wolff's treatise on the *jus gentium* that it is
often represented to have been. He accepts Wolff's
doctrine of perfect and imperfect obligations, and empha-
sizes the fundamental rights and duties of States. He also
adopts his master's complicated and impractical division of
positive International Law into the voluntary, customary,

[18] This famous work, which was published in 1758, bears the additional title:
"Principles of the Law of Nature Applied to the Conduct and Affairs of
Nations and Sovereigns." It has had many editions and translations. The
most recent English translation is by Fenwick. It accompanies the photographic reproduction of the text of 1758 published in *Classics of Int. Law*,
(1916). On Vattel's system and "authority," see especially Fenwick, 7 and 8
Am. Pol. Sci. Rev. (1913 and 1914), 395 ff. and 375 ff. Lapradelle, "Introduction," in 3 Vattel, *Classics of Int. Law* (1916); and Mallarme, in *Les fondateurs du droit int.* ed. by Pillet (1904), 481 ff.

and conventional Law of Nations; [19] but he rejects the Wolffian fiction of a World State or *civitas maxima* as a foundation for the voluntary law of nations. Vattel wrote in an attractive style and enriched his work with illustrations drawn from the history of his own times.[20]

63. The Period between 1648–1713.—The period between 1648 and the Peace of Utrecht (1713) was marked by the aggressive policy of Louis XIV, resulting in a series of wars and conquests and a disturbance of the unstable balance of power in Europe created by the Peace of Westphalia. This in turn led to the formation of the first great European coalition against France headed by England in 1688—a date which also marks the beginning of what Seeley [21] calls the " Second Hundred Years' War " between England and France (1688–1815), which resulted in the conquest of the major portion of the French colonies by England and the establishment of the maritime supremacy of Great Britain. The war of the Spanish Succession (1701–1713) ended in the restoration and first formal acknowledgment of the balance of power as a fundamental principle of European policy, by the Peace of Utrecht.[22]

[19] In addition to these three classes of positive law, we have of course in the Wolffian as in the Grotian system the natural or necessary law which Vattel (Preliminaries, §§ 6–8) says, "consists in the application of the law of nature to nations."

[20] Though not members of any particular school, the following eighteenth century publicists should receive special mention because of their influence upon the development of maritime law, more especially in connection with the Law of Neutrality: the Danish minister Hübner, whose important treatise entitled *De la saisie des bâtiments neutres* (Seizure of Neutral Vessels) was published in 1759; the French jurist Valin, whose excellent Commentary upon the *Marine Ordinance of 1681* and *Traité des prises* (Treatise on Prizes) appeared during 1760–1763; Heineccius, who wrote his treatise *De navibus* in 1721 and *Elementa juris naturalis* which was translated into English in 1763; and the Italians Lampredi and Galiani, who engaged in a famous controversy on the principles of the Armed Neutrality in the latter part of the eighteenth century. On these authors and this controversy, see Wheaton, *History*, especially pp. 200, 219–229, and 309–322.

[21] *Expansion of England* (1883), Lect. II, pp. 24 and 29. There was, however, a long period of peace, and even of alliance, between England and France during 1713–1740.

[22] On the *Peace of Utrecht*, see especially 3 Hill, *History of Diplomacy in the Development of Europe* (1905–06), 323 ff. particularly on pp. 335, 338–39; and 5 *Cambridge Modern History*, ch. 14, pp. 437 ff. For references, see 1 Fauchille, p. 78; 3 Hill, *op. cit.*, 336; and 5 *Cambridge Mod. Hist.*, 854–56.

During this period (1648–1713) lip service was rendered to the leading principles and usages of the Law of Nature and Nations as laid down by Grotius and his successors, but its rules were often practically ignored. The rights and immunities of legations were generally recognized and became fully established; the doctrine of the freedom of the seas made considerable progress; and fixed rules were laid down regulating such matters as the right of visit and search, blockade, and the capture of contraband. In respect to the law of maritime capture a long backward step was taken.

The famous French Marine Ordinance of 1681 [23] admitted the maxim of the *Consolato del Mare* that enemy goods in a friend's vessel are good prize, but it denied the rule that the goods of a friend found on an enemy ship are free. It even declared that neutral vessels carrying enemy goods are liable to confiscation, thus limiting the lawful commerce of a neutral to his own goods carried in his own vessel.[24] With the exception of the latter rule, the principles laid down by the Marine Ordinance of Louis XIV may be said to have entered largely into the theory and international practice (both customary and conventional) of Europe during the seventeenth and eighteenth centuries.

64. The Eighteenth Century.—The most important events in the international relations of the eighteenth century were: the admission of Russia under Peter the

[23] This ordinance was modeled on earlier ones. The law of France varied at different times. On the Marine Ordinance of 1681 and the maritime law of this period, see especially Wheaton, *History*, 107–161.

[24] Wheaton, *op. cit.*, p. 111. "Valin states that this jurisprudence, which prevailed in the French prize courts from 1681 to 1744, was peculiar to them and to the Spanish Courts of Admiralty, the usage of other nations being to confiscate the goods of the enemy only." *Ibid.*, p. 114.

Bynkershoek (*Questiones juris publici*, lib. I, cap. 14) denies that the neutral ship carrying enemy goods might be condemned, but he admits that the goods are subject to confiscation. He also agrees with Grotius (*De jure belli ac pacis*, lib. III, cap. 6) that the rule that "goods found in enemies' ships are to be treated as enemies' goods ought not be accepted as a settled rule of the Law of Nations, but as indicating a certain presumption which may be rebutted by valid proof to the contrary." Grotius adds: "And so it was judged in full senate by our Hollanders in 1338, when war was raging with the Hansa towns; and the judgment has become law." Some eighteenth century publicists like Hübner and F. G. von Martens declared that both neutral goods on enemies' ships and enemy goods on neutral ships were free; but their views were not generally accepted either in theory or practice.

Great to full membership in the circle of European States; the rise of Prussia under Frederick the Great as a first-rate Power; the declaration and achievement of American independence; and the outbreak of the French Revolution.

The colonization of America by the leading nations of Europe, which was begun on a large and effective scale during the seventeenth and continued during the eighteenth century, gave rise to new questions to which the Roman law of *occupatio* and *alluvium* was applied. In Europe the main issues were dynastic, economic, and territorial, and the principle of the balance of power based on an equilibrium of forces was repeatedly affirmed and violated. The *raison d' Etat* (considerations of public interest) became the controlling motive in national policy and the diplomacy of this period was dominated by Machiavellian aims and methods.[25] The end was the glory and aggrandizement of dynasties and States; and to attain these ends all means seemed good. Treaties were violated whenever State interests appeared to demand it, and wars were undertaken on the slightest pretexts. Frederick the Great suddenly invaded Silesia upon the death of Charles VI, in 1740, within a few years after having written his *Anti-Machiavel;* and of all the States which had guaranteed the Pragmatic Sanction of the Emperor, England alone (and she acted from motives of self-interest) kept faith with Austria upon the accession of Maria Theresa after the death of her father. But the greatest crime committed by the Machiavellian statesmen of the eighteenth century was the extinction of one of the most important members of the European family of nations—the threefold division of Poland in 1772, 1793, and 1795.[26]

[25] On the Machiavellian character of the eighteenth-century diplomacy, see especially 1 Sorel, *L'Europe et la révolution française*, (1893–1904), particularly ch. I.

[26] The first division of Poland has been characterized by Wheaton (*History*, p. 269) as the "most flagrant violation of natural justice and International Law which has occurred since Europe first emerged from barbarism." Sorel (*op. cit.*, p. 89) remarks, "Two episodes summarized the custom of Europe on the eve of the French Revolution: the war of the Austrian Succession and the division of Poland." He calls these the "testament of old Europe," and declares that after this had been signed she could only die, leaving as a legacy the pernicious tradition of the abuses from which she perished.

65. **The Armed Neutrality of 1780.**—Early in 1780 the Russian Government laid down the following rules, which were primarily directed against the maritime pretensions of England: (1) all neutral vessels may freely navigate from port to port and on the coasts of nations at war; [27] (2) the goods belonging to the subjects of the Powers at war shall be free in neutral vessels, except contraband articles; [28] (3) such contraband articles shall be restricted to munitions of war; (4) the denomination of blockaded port shall only be given to a port " where there is, by the arrangements of the power which attacks it with vessels, stationed sufficiently near, an evident danger in attempting to enter it." [29] These principles were approved by France, Spain, and the United States, and were incorporated into the conventions of the League of Armed Neutrality of 1780 which was formed by Denmark, Russia and Sweden, and soon joined by Holland, Prussia, Austria, Portugal, and the king of the Two Sicilies.   In 1800 these principles were affirmed anew, with some modifications and additions, [30] by the Second

[27] This is a denial of the famous Rule of 1756 which forbade neutrals to engage in the coasting trade of a belligerent, or in trade between a belligerent and its colonies, when such trade is not permitted during peace.   The rule is now practically obsolete; whether it was ever good law is doubtful.   The principle had been applied to the coasting trade before 1756, and was extended to the colonial trade during the Seven Years' and the Revolutionary wars.   The great champion of the Rule was England.   The leading case is that of *The Immanuel*, 2 C. Rob. 186.   On the *Rule of 1756*, see especially: Hall, § 234; 2 Kleen, § 175; Manning, *Law of Nations* (1875), 260 ff.; 7 Moore, *Digest*, § 1180; 3 Phillimore, Pt. IX, ch. 11; and Wheaton, *History*, 217–19.

[28] This principle of "free ships, free goods" had also been asserted in 1752 by the Prussian commissioners who reported to Frederick the Great on the celebrated Silesian Loan Controversy.   See Ch. de Martens, 2 *Causes célèbres* (1827), cause première.   For a good summary of this controversy between Great Britain and Prussia, see Wheaton, *History*, 206–17.

[29] Wheaton, *History*, 297–298.   Upon the *Armed Neutrality of 1780*, see especially: Bergbohm, *Die bewaffnete Neutralität* (1884); Boeck, *De la propriété privée ennemi* (1882), 55 ff.; Fauchille, *La diplomatie française et la ligue des neutres de 1780* (1893); 1 Kleen, 20 ff.; Manning, 325 ff.; 3 Phillimore, pp. 335 ff.; Scott, *Armed Neutralities of 1780 and 1800* (1918); Wheaton, *History*, 295 ff.   For further citations and authorities, see Scott, *op. cit., passim*.

[30] The main additional article adopted by the Second Armed Neutrality of 1800 affirmed that the "declaration of the officers, commanding the public ships which shall accompany the convoy of one or more merchant vessels, that the ships of his convoy have no contraband articles on board, shall be deemed sufficient to prevent any search on the convoying vessels or those under convoy."   Wheaton, *History*, p. 399.   It will be seen that several of the principles of the Armed Neutrality Leagues are still in advance of International Law

League of Armed Neutrality, consisting of Russia, Prussia, Sweden, and Denmark.

66. The French Revolution.—The outbreak of the French Revolution, and the successful inauguration of the American Union based on principles of democracy, nationality, and federalism, mark a new epoch in the history of international relations, as of civilization in general.

The Abbé de Saint-Pierre had presented the world with his " Project of Treaty for Perpetual Peace " in 1713, aiming at the establishment of a European League or " Christian Republic." Montesquieu taught that the Law of Nations is naturally based upon the principle that the various nations should do each other as much good as possible in times of peace; in war as little harm as possible without injuring their true interests. Rousseau affirmed that war is not a relation between individuals but a relation between States. Mably, the author of an important work entitled *Droit public de l' Europe fondé sur les traités* (The Public Law based on Treaties, 1748), advocated love for justice and humanity, respect for treaties, and the immunity of private property in maritime warfare.

The National Assembly of France solemnly declared on May 22, 1790, that " the French nation renounces wars of conquest and will never use force against the liberty of any people." [31] But on November 19, 1792, the National Convention, abandoning the early principles of the Revolution, issued its famous decree that France " will grant fraternity and aid to all peoples who may wish to recover their liberty," [32] a decree which was, however, abrogated on April 14, 1793, and supplanted by one declaring in favor of non-intervention. The Jacobins incorporated the principle

They were, of course, far in advance of the times in which they were formulated. Though soon violated by some of the very nations which declared them, they do not deserve the cavalier treatment which they receive at the hands of several English publicists. They constitute an important stage in the development of the law of neutrality.

[31] 2 Sorel, *L'Europe et la rév. française* (1893–1904), p. 89; or Nys, 1 *Études*, 365. This decree became part of Tit. VI of the Constitution of 1791. See Anderson, *Constitutions and Documents* (1904), 93; or Helie, *Les constitutions de la France* (1879), 293.

[32] 3 Sorel, *op. cit.*, 170, or Nys, *op. cit.*, 385. This decree was supplemented by that of December 15, 1792, proclaiming liberty and sovereignty to all peoples. See Anderson, *op. cit.*, No. 28, pp. 130–32.

of non-intervention in their still-born Constitution of 1793.[33]
On June 18, 1793, Abbé Gregoire presented a " Project for a
Declaration of the Law of Nations " in twenty-one articles,[34]
as a pendant to the Declaration of the Rights of Man of
1789.   It contained few principles which are unsound.
Some of them form part and parcel of the fundamental
rights of States; others belong to the International Law of
the future; only a few are impracticable.   This Project,
which has been characterized as Utopian, was rejected by
the Convention; but it may nevertheless be regarded as
expressing the altruistic and idealistic spirit of the French
Revolution in its attitude toward foreign nations.   As in
the case of the Declaration of the Rights of Man, its great
defect was that it contained no Declaration of *Duties*.

67. **The Revolutionary and Napoleonic Era.**—Like historical Christianity, the French Revolution proved false to
its principles, and France entered upon a career of aggression and conquest which culminated in the short-lived
Napoleonic Empire (1804–1814), embracing the greater
part of central and southern Europe.   As in the case of the
aggressions of Louis XIV, Great Britain headed a series of
coalitions against Napoleon I which ended in his downfall
and the reduction of France to her former boundaries.
During the period of the gigantic Revolutionary and
Napoleonic struggles (1792–1815), fundamental principles

[33] "The French people declares itself the friend and natural ally of free
peoples; it does not interfere in the governments of other nations; it does not
allow other nations to interfere in its own."   Arts. 118–119 of the Const. of
1793, Anderson, *op. cit.*, No. 39, p. 183.
[34] The more important of these articles are as follows:

ART. 2.   The peoples are independent and sovereign. . . .
ART. 3.   A people should do to others as it would have them do to it.
ART. 4.   The peoples should do each other as much good as possible in times of
           peace; in war, the least harm possible.
ART. 5.   The particular interest of a people is subordinate to the general inter-
           est of the human family.
ART. 6.   Every people has a right to organize and change its governemnt.
ART. 7.   A people has not the right to intevene in the government of others.
ART. 10.   Each people is master of its territory.
ART. 15.   An enterprise against the liberty of one people is a criminal attempt
           against all the others.
ART. 21.   Treaties between the peoples are sacred and inviolable.

For the full text of this remarkable declaration, see Nys, *La révolution française et le droit int.* In *Études*, I, 395–96; or 1 Rivier, 40–41.

and customs of International Law, more especially of maritime law, were set at naught by both France and England, and the rights of neutral commerce were violated in the most outrageous manner. Napoleon, through his Berlin and Milan decrees of 1806 and 1807, not only declared the whole British Isles to be in a state of blockade and interdicted all commerce and correspondence with them, but ordered that all vessels sailing to or from any port in the United Kingdom or its colonies should be confiscated.[35]

The British Orders in Council declared all French ports, together with those of her allies, to be in a state of blockade, and ordered the confiscation of any neutral vessel carrying " certificates of origin "—a device for distinguishing between British and neutral goods. These measures taken together threatened the destruction of all neutral commerce. They called forth the protest and opposition of the United States, who became the main champion of neutral rights and duties at the beginning of Washington's administration in 1793—a position which she has since, on the whole, maintained.[36]

Though a period of conquest, violence, and reaction, it must not be forgotten that the French under Napoleon virtually destroyed old feudalistic and absolute Europe, and sowed the seeds of democracy and nationality which eventu-

[35] The Continental system of Napoleon was only a continuation of a policy begun under the First French Republic. "Already in 1793 England and Russia interdicted all navigation with the ports of France, with the intention to subdue her by famine. The French Convention answered with an order to the French fleet to capture neutral ships carrying provisions to the ports of the enemy or carrying enemy goods." 1 Oppenheim, § 46. For details, see Mahan, *Influence of Sea Power upon the French Revolution and Empire* (1892), II, ch. 17; and Wheaton, *History*, 372 ff.

On Napoleon's *Continental System*, see Manning, *Law of Nations* (1875), Bk. V, ch. 10; and the vast Napoleonic literature, especially Fournier, Rose, Sloane, Lanfrey, etc. Perhaps the best accounts are those by 2 Mahan, *op. cit.*, ch. 18; and Henry Adams, *History of the U. S.* (1889–91), *passim*, particularly Vol. IV, ch. 4. See also Melvin, *Napoleon's Navigation System* (1919).

For documents bearing upon the System, see Anderson, *Constitutions and Documents*, No. 77; and the University of Pa. *Trans. and Reprints*, Vol. II, No. 2, 17–26.

[36] For good accounts of the efforts of the United States to maintain and enforce neutrality during the Revolutionary and Napoleonic period, see Dana's Wheaton, note 215; Moore, *Am. Diplomacy* (1905), chs. 2 and 3; and Henry Adams, *History of the U. S.*, *passim*.

ally bore fruit [37] in a new and in part regenerated and reorganized Europe.

68. The Congress of Vienna.—The balance of power in Europe was once more restored at the reactionary Congress of Vienna in 1814–1815.[38] Though largely basing its work upon the principles of legitimacy [39] and ignoring the powerful forces of democracy and nationality, this Congress nevertheless established a new political order in Europe and proclaimed some important principles of International Law. It defined the relations of ministers, envoys, and ambassadors; declared in favor of the abolition of the African slave trade; and agreed upon general principles intended to secure freedom of navigation on great international rivers, at least by co-riparian States.

Among the political acts of the Congress of Vienna should be particularly noted: the union of Norway and Sweden and of Belgium and Holland; the reorganization and neutralization of Switzerland; the reorganization of the new Germany of thirty-nine States into a loose Confederacy; and, in general, the restoration of the old dynasties in France, Spain, Italy, and Germany.[40]

69. The Period of Reaction (1815–1848).—Under the deadening influence of the Metternich System,[41] the reaction

[37] Especially fruitful were the Secularization and Mediation Acts, which reduced the number of German States to thirty-nine, and prepared the way for Bismarck's work of unification and reorganization in Germany.

[38] On the *Congress of Vienna*, see especially: * 9 and 10 *Cambridge Modern History*, chs. 19, 21, and 1 respectively; Debidour, I *Histoire diplomatique de l'Europe* (1891), ch. 1; 2 Fyffe, *History of Modern Europe* (1881–90), ch. 1; Hazen, in *Three Peace Congresses* (1917), 3–19; Mowat, *European Diplomacy* (1922), ch. 2; Phillimore, *Three Centuries of Treaties of Peace* (1919), ch. 3; * Phillips, *Confederacy of Europe* (1914), 98–120; Rose, *Revolutionary and Napoleonic Era* (1885), ch. 11; Seignobos, *Histoire Politique de l'Europe contemporaine*, (Eng. trans. 1899), ch. 1; Stephens, *Revolutionary Europe* (1907), ch. 11; Wheaton, *History*, 424–506. See Hazen and Seignobos for select bibliographies. For texts of the various treaties, declarations, etc., signed at Vienna, see 1 Hertslet, *Map of Europe* (1875–91) 60 ff., and Oakes and Mowat, *The Great European Treaties of the Nineteenth Century* (1918), 37 ff.

[39] But this principle was not thoroughly and consistently applied, *e.g.* in Sweden and Germany.

[40] The main lines of this resettlement of Europe were laid down by the allies in the treaty of Chaumont signed on March 10, 1814. Sec. 10 *Cambridge Modern History*, 9; and Phillips, *Confederation of Europe* (1914) 77 ff.

[41] On "Europe under the Metternich System," see especially Seignobos, *Pol. History of Europe*, ch. 25.

continued for a generation (1815–1848) after the close of the Congress of Vienna.   Yet there was progress even during this oppressive régime.

70. **The Holy Alliance.**—In 1815 the Emperors of Russia and Austria and the King of Prussia formed what is generally known as the Holy Alliance,[42] pledging themselves to apply the precepts of Christianity, viz. fraternity, justice, charity, and peace, to the conduct of international as well as internal affairs.   But much more important than this paper alliance, based on mere sentiment and vague aspirations possibly cloaking ulterior designs, was the renewal of the Quadruple Alliance the same year between Russia, Austria, Prussia, and England.   In Article 6 it was decided " to renew, at fixed intervals, . . . meetings consecrated to great common objects, and . . . the examination of such measures as . . . shall be judged most salutary for the peace and prosperity of the Nations and for the maintenance of the peace of Europe." [43]

71. **The Concert of Europe.**—This alliance marks the beginning of the European Concert which undertook to suppress revolutions, maintain the treaties of Paris and Vienna, and regulate the affairs of Europe generally.   It marks an attempt to substitute for the old European States-system or community of nations a new society or sort of Confederacy which should be under the control or dictatorship of a committee of the Great Powers.   In 1818 it was joined by France and became known as the Pentarchy, but a rift in the now Quintuple Alliance soon showed itself when England and France failed to sign the Troppau Protocol of 1820.[44]   England withdrew altogether at Verona in 1822.

[42] For the text of the *Holy Alliance*, see the University of Pa. *Trans. and Reprints*, Vol. I, No. 3, or Duggan, *League of Nations*, 318–20.

[43] Phillips, *op. cit.*, 155.   Cf. Webster, *Foreign Policy of Castlereagh* (1925), 55

[44] The Protocol of Troppau was an extension to Europe of the reactionary Carlsbad Decrees which had struck such a severe blow at freedom in Germany. It declared that the "States which have undergone a change of government due to revolution, the results of which threaten other States, *ipso facto*, cease to be members of the European Alliance, and remain excluded from it until their situation gives guaranties for legal order and stability.   If, owing to such alterations, immediate danger threatens other States, the Powers bind themselves, by peaceful means, or if need be by arms, to bring back the guilty State into the arms of the Great Alliance."   Phillips, *op. cit.*, 222.

At Aix-la-Chapelle (1818), the Powers declared for the first time that it was their " unalterable determination never to swerve from the strictest observance of the principles of the Law of Nations, either in their relations with one another or with other States." [45]   In pursuance of their policy of intervention—a principle to which England never assented —they held a series of Congresses (1818–1822) [46] which authorized armed interventions in Naples, Piedmont, and Spain.

72. **The Monroe Doctrine.**—When, however, it was proposed to extend this system to the Spanish colonies in America which had achieved their independence, the President of the United States, acting independently upon a proposal for joint action from the great British statesman Canning, interposed and promulgated the famous Monroe Doctrine, in his annual message to Congress of Dec. 2, 1823. He declared that " we should consider any attempt on their

For the text of the *Carlsbad Decrees* and the *Circular of Troppau*, see Univ. of Pa. *Trans. and Reprints*, Vol. I, No. 3, pp. 16–24.

[45] For the text of this declaration, see Nys on "Le Concert European," in 2 *Études*, p. 27.   On the "Conference of Aix-la-Chapelle" which renewed the Quadruple Alliance and opened the door to France, see Webster, *op. cit.*, ch. 3.

[46] It is to the work of these Congresses and the *System* represented by them that the term "Holy Alliance" has been usually applied.

These Congresses or Conferences were those of Aix-la-Chapelle (1818), Troppau and Laibach (1820), and Verona (1822).   The best recent additions to our knowledge of their work and the policies that prompted them have been made by Cresson, *The Holy Alliance* (1922); and Phillipps, *Confederacy of Europe* (1914).   On the Congresses of Troppau and Laibach, see especially Webster, *op. cit.*, ch. 6.

For the text of what purported to be the secret treaty of Verona, see 24 *Niles Register* (1823), 347.   The text may also be found in Latané, *From Isolation to Leadership* (rev. ed., 1922), 22–24.   This treaty was never officially published, but appeared in the press of Europe and America at the time. Whether authentic or not, it is an interesting document and doubtless exerted some influence upon the course of events.   In this "code of despotism," as Latané calls it, Austria, Russia, Prussia and France are represented as engaging mutually "to use all their efforts to put an end to the system of representative governments, in whatever country it may exist in Europe, and to prevent its being introduced in those countries where it is not yet known" (Art. I).

The High Contracting powers also reciprocally promised to adopt every possible means to suppress the liberty of the press, "not only in their own States, but also in the rest of Europe (Art. II); "and declare it to be their intention to support, each in his own State, the measures which the clergy with a view to their own interests, are enabled to carry into effect for the purpose of maintaining the authority of Princes" . . . (Art. III).

part (*i.e.* of the Allied Powers) to extend their *system* to any portion of this hemisphere as dangerous to our peace and safety." He added:—

" With the existing colonies or dependencies of any European Power we have not interfered and shall not interfere. But with the Governments who have declared their independence and maintained it, and whose independence we have, on great consideration and just principles, acknowledged, we could not view any interposition for the purpose of oppressing them, or controlling in any other manner their destiny, by any European Power in any other light than as the manifestation of an unfriendly disposition toward the United States." [47]

[47] 2 Richardson, *Messages and Papers of the Presidents of the U. S.* (1896), 218. In his famous speech of Dec. 12, 1826, Canning boasted that he had "called the New World into existence to redress the balance of the Old." Of course he referred primarily to his recognition of the Latin American States as part of his policy in resisting French agression in Spain and the Spanish dominions. He had just remarked: "I resolved that if France had Spain, it should not be Spain with the Indies," *i.e.* with the Spanish colonies. See particularly Temperley, *Foreign Policy of Canning* (1925), ch. 6.

In another part of his message (*Ibid.*, p. 209), Monroe also declared that "the American continents, by the free and independent condition which they have assumed and maintain, are henceforth not to be considered as subjects for future colonization by any European Powers." This part of the message was directed primarily against the encroachments of Russia in the Northwest. It did not meet with Canning's approval.

Perhaps the best and most inclusive statement of the entire American policy is contained in a letter from Jefferson to Monroe, dated October 24, 1823; "Our first maxim should be, never to entangle ourselves in the broils of Europe. Our second, never to suffer Europe to intermeddle in cis-Atlantic affairs."

On the *Monroe Doctrine*, see * Alvarez, "Latin American and International Law," in 3 *A. J.* (1909), 269–353, and *The Monroe Doctrine* (1924); * *A. J.* (see index vol., 1921); * *Procs. Am. Soc. I. L.* (1914); *Annals* (July, 1914); *Annals*, "The Centenary of the Monroe Doctrine," Addresses on (Jan., 1924); Beaumarchais, *La Doctrine de Monroe* (1898); Bigelow, *American Policy* (1914); Bingham, *The Monroe Doctrine, An Obsolete Shibboleth* (1913); * Blakeslee [ed.], *Latin America* (Clark University Addresses, 1914), 108–72; * Chadwick, *The Diplomatic Relations of the U. S. with Spain* (1909), ch. 10; Coolidge, *The U. S. as a World Power* (1908), ch. 5; * Dana's note 36 to Weaton's *Int. Law.*, pp. 97 ff.; Edginton, *The Monroe Doctrine* (1904); 1 Fauchille, Nos. 313–31; Fish, *American Diplomacy* (1915), ch. 17 and index; Ford, in 15 *Procs. Mass. Histor. Soc.*, (2d series, 1901–02), and in 7 and 8 *Am. Histor. Rev.* (1902), 676–96 and 28–52; Foster, *Century of American Diplomacy* (1911), ch. 12; Hall, *The Monroe Doctrine and the Great War* (1920); Hart, *The Monroe Doctrine* (1919); * Henderson, in *American Diplomatic Questions* (1901), Pt. IV; Hughes, in 19 *Current History* (1923), 102 ff., in Supp. to *Annals*, (Jan., 1924), and in 17 *A. J.* (1923), 611–28; Hull, *The Monroe Doctrine* (1915); * 1 Hyde, §§ 85–97, pp. 133 ff.; Kimball, "The Monroe Doctrine and the League

The promulgation of the Monroe Doctrine, which was followed by the recognition of the independence of the Latin American States by England, definitely added to the society of nations the leading States of South America and Mexico.[48]

The system and principles of the so-called " Holy Alliance " were finally overthrown by the Revolutions of 1830 and 1848 which, though followed by a period of reaction, eventually substituted the principles of nationality, democracy and constitutional rule for those of legitimacy and absolutism.

73. **The Declaration of Paris** [49] **of 1856.**—The next important step in the development of International Law was taken at the close of the Crimean War in 1856.   Not only

of Nations," in Duggan, *League of Nations* (1919), ch. 16; * Kraus, *Die Monroedoktrin* (1913); * Latané, *The U. S. and Latin America* (1920), ch 2 and index, *From Isolation to Leadership* (1923), *passim*, and *History of American Foreign Policy* (1927), chs. 8 and 20; Mahan, in 40 *Nat. Rev.* (1902–03), 871–89; Moore, in *American Diplomacy* (1905), ch. 6; * 6 Moore, *Digest*, ch. 20; Petin, *Les États unis et la doctrine de Monroe* (1900); Phelps, *Monroe Doctrine* (1916); * Reddaway, *The Monroe Doctrine* (1898); Robertson, *Hispanic Relations* (1923), ch. 4; Shepherd, "New Light on the Monroe Doctrine," in 31 *Pol. Sci. Quar.* (1916), 5–78, and 39 *Pol. Sci. Quar.* (1924), 35–66; * Thomas, *One Hundred Years of the Monroe Doctrine* (1923); Snow, *American Diplomacy* (1893), Pt. II; * Stuart, *Latin America and the United States* (1922), ch. 2 and index; Temperley, *Foreign Policy of Canning* (1925), ch. 5; Tucker, *The Monroe Doctrine* (1885); and Wilson, in 7 *Procs. of Acad. of Pol. Sci.* (1917), 489.

For Bibliographies, see Hart, Kraus, Phelps, Gillman's *James Monroe* (1898), and the Library of Congress, List of References (1919).   See also 1 Fauchille, pp. 592–93.

For further discussion of the Monroe Doctrine in the text, see *infra*, p. 241.

[48] Their recognition by the United States took place in the spring of 1822, by England early in 1825.   See Paxson, *The Independence of the South American Republics* (1903), *passim*.

[49] The Declaration of Paris was signed on April 16, 1856, by all the Powers represented at the Congress, viz. England, France, Austria, Russia, Sardinia, Turkey, and Prussia.   The States not represented at the Congress were invited to sign, and most of them did so before the end of the year.   Japan signed in 1866.   The United States, Spain, Mexico, and a few minor States held out, but the rules of the Declaration were observed in practice, at least until the outbreak of the World War in 1914.   Spain gave notice of her adhesion at the Hague Conference of 1907.   The objection of the United States was based upon the idea that, inasmuch as we did not possess a large navy, the right to fit out privateers must be retained until the capture of private enemy property at sea was abolished.

On the *Declaration of Paris*, see especially Higgins, *The Hague Peace Conferences* (1909), 1–4 with references.

was Turkey expressly admitted to theoretical full standing as a member of the Society of Nations, but the Congress of Paris issued the following epoch-making Declaration of leading principles of Maritime International Law:

(1) Privateering is and remains abolished.
(2) The neutral flag covers enemy's goods, with the exception of contraband of war.
(3) Neutral goods, with the exception of contraband of war, are not liable to capture under an enemy's flag.
(4) Blockades, in order to be binding, must be effective; that is to say, maintained by a force sufficient really to prevent access to the coast of an enemy.

74. **The Period since 1856.**—The half century beginning with the Declaration of Paris in 1856 and ending with the London Conference in 1909 saw greater progress in the direction of internationalism and more successful attempts to improve and codify International Law than any other in history, possibly more than all previous half centuries combined. It was a period of Congresses and Conferences,[50] of International Unions and Associations with definite organs in the shape of Commissions and Bureaus which are rapidly developing a sort of international legislation and an International Administrative Law.

Though the principle of nationality won its greatest triumphs during this period in the achievement of Italian and German Unity (1859–1870), it seemed that the spirit of nationality was being modified or supplemented by that of internationalism, and that the older conceptions of sovereignty and independence were yielding to ideals of solidarity and interdependence.

75. **Codification of the Law of Land Warfare.**—The first important step towards the codification of the laws of land warfare was taken in 1863 when our Government published the " Instructions for the Government of Armies of the United States in the Field," prepared by Dr. Francis Lieber.[51] In 1864 there was concluded, on the initiative of

[50] All real distinction between the words Congress and Conference, if such ever existed, seems to have been lost.

[51] The "Instructions" are printed as an Appendix in Scott, *Texts of the Peace Conferences* (1908), and as Appendix II in Wilson's *International Law.*

Switzerland, the " Geneva Convention for the Amelioration of the Condition of the Wounded in War." [52]   This Convention, which provided for neutralization of persons and things connected with the care of the sick and wounded, was signed by nearly all civilized Powers.   By the Declaration of St. Petersburg of 1868 many States renounced, in case of war among themselves, the use of any " projectile of less weight than 400 grammes (about 14 ounces) which is explosive, or is charged with fulminating or inflammable substances." [53]

76. The London Conference of 1871.—In 1871, the Conference of London [54] solemnly proclaimed " that it is an essential principle of the Law of Nations that no power can liberate itself from the engagements of a treaty, or modify the stipulations thereof, unless with the consent of the contracting Powers by means of an amicable agreement." But it is more than doubtful whether, stated in this absolute form, the above declaration is a principle of International Law.

77. The Brussels Conferences of 1874.—In 1874 the Brussels Conference [55] formulated a Code of Land Warfare

[52] For the text of the *Geneva Convention* (including the *Additional Articles* of 1868) see Higgins, *Hague Peace Conferences*, (1909), 8–17; or Supplement to 1 *A. J.* (1907), 90–95.   But the *Additional Articles* failed of ratification.   The Convention resulted from an agitation aroused by the indefatigable labors of M. Moynier and the publication of a book entitled *Un souvenir de Solférino* by M. Dumant, a Swiss philanthropist who had witnessed the terrible sufferings of the wounded in that battle (1859).

[53] This was based on the principle that the only legitimate object of war "is to weaken the military force of the enemy; that for this purpose it is sufficient to disable the greatest possible number of men; that this object would be exceeded by the employment of arms which uselessly aggravate the sufferings of disabled men, or render their death inevitable."   See preamble of the *Declaration*, in Higgins, *op. cit.*, 5–6; or Whittuck, *International Documents* (1908), 10.

[54] This Conference was attended by representatives of the same Powers which had signed the Treaty of Paris of 1856—an agreement which Russia had violated by reëstablishing her maritime arsenal on the Black Sea upon the outbreak of the Franco-German War of 1870.

[55] For the text of the *Code of the Brussels Conference*, see Higgins, *op. cit.*, 273–80; Supplement to 1 *A. J.* (1907), 96–103; or Scott, *Texts of the Peace Conferences*.

The Brussels Conference was attended by delegates from 15 European States.   Owing to a misunderstanding, the United States was not represented.   The Latin-American States were not invited, and several delegates from South American States were refused admission.   Nys in 2 *Études*, 39–40.   On the

which, though it failed of ratification, obtained great authority and was generally observed. It was largely based on the American " Instructions " and became in its turn the model for the Hague Code of 1899.

78. **The Berlin Congo Conference.**—The next important law-making Conference was the Berlin Congo or West African Conference, which met in Berlin in 1884–1885 to decide certain questions concerning the Congo Free State, whose independence it recognized. This Conference, at which the United States was represented, stipulated for freedom of trade and travel within the Congo basin; agreed to " strive for the suppression of slavery, and especially of the negro slave trade; " [56] engaged to respect the neutrality of the Congo territories; and the Signatory Powers obligated themselves to preserve reasonable order in the territories occupied by them, as also to notify one another of any future occupations or the establishment of future protectorates on the coast of the African continent.

79. **International Unions and Congresses.**—The period since 1850 was also characterized by a remarkable number and variety of International Unions and Conferences,[57] both public and private, dealing with economic, social, and

Brussels Conference, see especially Holland, Studies, 59–78; and F. de Martens, La paix et la guerre (1901), 73–132.

[56] Art. 6 of the "General Act of the Conference of Berlin Concerning the Congo," which is printed in the Supplement to 3 A. J. (1909), No. 1, pp. 7–25. This Act was signed by the leading maritime Powers, the United States, and a number of the minor European States (including Turkey)—14 in all. President Cleveland, however, did not submit the Act to the U. S. Senate for ratification.

It was afterwards supplemented by the Conference of Brussels of 1890, attended by 17 States (including the additional States of Persia, Zanzibar and the Congo), which agreed upon a "General Act for the Repression of the African Slave Trade and the Restriction of the Importation into, and Sale in, a certain defined Zone of the African Continent of Firearms, Ammunition, and Spirituous Liquors." For the text of this Act of 100 Articles, see Supplement, op. cit., 29–59.

On the "Origin of the Congo Free State," see an interesting article by Jesse S. Reeves in 3 A. J. (1909), 99–118. For bibliographies on the Berlin and Brussels Conferences, see Anderson and Hershey, 167 and 196–97.

[57] For a list of 116 such Congresses or Conferences of an official character since 1850, compiled by the Hon. S. E. Baldwin, see 1 A. J. (1907), 808–17. It is followed by a list (pp. 818–29) of nearly 200 International Congresses, Conferences, or Associations, composed of private individuals. These lists must be far from complete, for there are said to have been over 160 International Congresses during the year 1907 alone.

sanitary matters. Beginning with the first International
Sanitary Conference held at Paris in 1851,[58] we have a long
succession of official International Congresses dealing with
all sorts of subjects, such as statistics, sugar duties, weights
and measures, monetary matters, international postal and
telegraphic correspondence, navigation of rivers, the metric
system, submarine cables, private international law, protection of industrial property, railroad transportation, commercial law, international copyright, regulation or suppression of the liquor traffic in certain places, customs duties,
promotion of the interests of the working classes, abolition
of the slave trade, protection of labor in mines and factories,
international arbitration, fisheries, repression of epidemic
diseases, international telephony, suppression of the " white
slave " traffic, international wireless telegraphy, agriculture,
etc.[59]

The most important of these are perhaps the Conference
on Telegraphic Correspondence which met at Paris in 1865
and formed the Universal Telegraph Union; Conferences of
the Universal Postal Union founded in 1874; those of the
European Union of Railway Freight Transportation (1890);
the Union for the Protection of Industrial Property, *i.e.*
patents, trade-marks, etc., created in 1883; the Hague
Union of 1886 for the Protection of Works of Art and

---

[58] At this Conference twelve Powers were represented. There have been
many subsequent International Sanitary Conferences. "In the one field of
sanitation and medicine there are at least twenty separate international organizations."   Reinsch, in N. Y. *Independent* for May 13, 1909.

[59] In addition to the lists referred to above, see the articles on "Int. Conferences" and "Int. Unions" by Judge Baldwin and Professor Reinsch in 1 *A.
J.* (1907), pp. 565–623; and * Reinsch, *Public Int. Unions* (1911). For
general references, see 1 *A. J.* pp. 582 and 602; and Bonfils (Fauchille), note,
pp. 496–97.   Prior to 1912 the main authorities were Descamps, *Les offices
internationaux* (1894); Moynier, *Les bureaux internationaux* (1892); Van
Overbergh, *L'association int.* (1907); Poinsard, *Droit int. conventional* (1894);
Les unions et ententes internationales (2d ed., 1901), and *Le droit int. au XXe
siècle* (1907); Meili, *Die internationalen Unionen* (1885–1889); and B. von Toll,
Die int. Bureaux (1910).   Since 1912 there should be added: Allen, *Int. Rel.*
(1920), chs. 3–4, 8–9; Hicks, *New World Order* (1920), ch. 18; * Potter, *Int.
Organiz.* (1922), ch 17; Sayre, *Int. Administration* (1918), *passim*; and Woolf,
Int. Government (1916), 153–265.

Very few writers on International Law devote much space to this subject.
Exceptions are Bonfils and * 1 (3 pt.), Fauchille, Nos. 914–928; 2 Mérignhac,
688–732; Liszt, §§ 27–28; * 1 Oppenheim, §§ 458–71, 581–96; and Ullmann,
§ 58.

Literature; the four Hague Conferences (between 1893 and 1904) on Private International Law; the five Pan-American Congresses which have been held since 1890; and the Conferences of the International Labor Organization created by the Treaties of Paris in 1919.

Many of the Unions [60] are endowed with permanent organs of legislation and administration.   Their legislative organ may be said to be the Conference or Congress where unanimity is the general rule, but to which there are exceptions.   The administrative organs are Commissions and Bureaus.[61]   One result of the activities of these various organs will doubtless be the development of the science of International Administrative Law—a branch of international jurisprudence which is still more or less in its infancy.

80. **International Arbitration.**—The practice of international arbitration, which had greatly declined at the close of the Middle Ages and which had almost disappeared from international usage during the seventeenth and eighteenth centuries,[62] may be said to have been revived by the Jay treaty of 1794 between England and the United States, which provided for the reference of several questions to arbitration.   But it was not until the smoke had cleared away from the battle fields of the Revolutionary and Napoleonic wars that the practice of arbitration spread or became more or less general.   This movement, which had become a subject of peace agitation, begun in the United States and England, was given a great impetus [63] through

[60] Potter (*op. cit.*, 270–71) gives a list of 45 public international unions with bureaus or commissions exising in 1915.

[61] The Commissions are generally composed of representatives of the members of the Unions, and sometimes exercise a sort of control or supervision over the Bureaus, some of which are located at Berne, Switzerland.

On this subject see especially the excellent article entitled "Administrative Law and National Sovereignty" by Professor Reinsch, in 3 *A. J.* (1909), 1–45, and his *Public Int. Unions* (1911); and * Sayre, *Int. Admin.*   See also references in preceding note 59.

[62] This fact was doubtless largely due to the absolute monarchs of this period who, ruling by divine right, were unwilling to submit their cause to any other than the God of Hosts.

[63] In 1828 the "American Peace Society" was founded by William Ladd of Massachusetts.   In 1840 he published his prize essay on "*A Congress of Nations*," which contained a notable project of a "Court of Nations" as well.

the successful arbitration of the Alabama Claims by the Geneva Arbitration of 1872. Since then arbitrations and arbitration treaties seem to have increased in a sort of arithmetical progression,[64] and they have been particularly numerous since the meeting of the Hague Peace Conferences of 1899 and 1907.

81. **Limitation of Armaments.**—In the latter part of the nineteenth century a kindred movement in favor of a limitation of armaments was making considerable headway. Ever since the Franco-German war of 1870, as a result of a Machiavellian statecraft combined with that policy of " blood and iron " which Bismarck has left as a heritage to modern Germany, and as a consequence of the new colonial imperialism and commercialism [65] which took possession of leading nations (notably of Great Britain, France, and

This suggestive essay was republished by the Carnegie Endowment in 1916. See "Introduction" by J. B. Scott.

The first American Peace Association appears to have been founded by David L. Dodge in New York in 1815. The "London Peace Society" was founded in 1816.

[64] For a very complete account of the arbitrations to which the United States had been a party up to 1898, see Moore's monumental *History and Digest of International Arbitrations*, in 6 vols. Darby (*Int. Tribunals*, 4th ed., 1904, pp. 769 ff.) gives a list of 222 instances of "formal" arbitration between 1794 and 1901. Of these there were 81 cases prior to 1872 and 141 between 1872 and 1901. The United States was a party in 62 cases; Great Britain, 81; France, 28; Prussia or Germany, 17; Russia, 8. Many of these arbitrations were with or between Latin-American States, where this movement has made great progress. Lafontaine (*Pasicrisie Int.*, 1902, VIII–X) says there were 177 instances between 1794 and 1900.

Prior to 1899 the number of arbitration treaties were, comparatively speaking, few in number, but they have greatly increased, especially since 1899. There were 64 such treaties between 1899 and 1907, and the number of arbitration treaties since the meeting of the first Hague Conference had mounted up to about 130 in 1908.

For a list of 67 arbitration treaties between 1900 and 1908, see 2 *A. J.* (1908), pp. 824–26. The United States has been a party to over 20 such treaties. Fried (*Die moderne Friedensbewegung*, 1907, pp. 26–27) gives a list of arbitration treaties between 1899–1907. For a list of 210 arbitration treaties between 1822 and 1903, see Moch, *Histoire sommaire* (1905), 35–40. For Bibliographies on arbitration, see Griffin, *List of References*, published by the Library of Congress (1908); La Fontaine, *Bibliographie de la paix et de l'arbitrage int.* (1904); and Olivart, *Bibliographie du droit int.* (1905–10).

[65] The founder or apostle of this new imperialism appears to have been Lord Beaconsfield. It was not fully adopted by Germany until about 1890. See especially the chapters on "National Imperialism" and "German Imperial Politics" in Reinsch, *World Politics* (1900). For references, see his "Bibliographical Notes."

Germany), Europe was virtually transformed into an "armed camp." This policy, indeed, preserved peace on the European Continent for a generation, but at a fearful economic, social, and moral cost to humanity.

82. The First Hague Peace Conference.—With a view of "seeking, by means of international discussion, the most effectual means of insuring to all peoples the benefits of a real and durable peace, and above all, of putting an end to the progressive development of the present armaments," Czar Nicholas II of Russia [66] called the First International Peace Conference which met at the Hague on May 18, 1899.[67]

The First Hague Peace Conference soon realized that even a limitation of the increase of military and naval expenditure was impracticable at that time, and devoted its chief energies to the secondary purpose for which it had been called, viz. to devise means of securing " the maintenance of general peace."

Owing mainly to the opposition of Germany, the Russian plan of inclusive and limited compulsory arbitration was rejected; but the British and American plan of a so-called " Permanent Court of Arbitration " [68] was adopted in spite of the objections of the German government, and arbitration was recommended " in questions of a judicial character, and especially regarding the interpretation of treaties." [69] A code of arbitral proceeding was also adopted and recommended.[70]

In addition to the " Convention for the Pacific Settlement of International Disputes," the Hague Conference of 1899 also agreed to two other Conventions, three Declarations, and expressed several wishes. Very important seemed the " Convention regulating the Laws and Customs of Land

[66] Russian *Rescript* of August 24, 1898.

[67] Twenty-six States were represented. Of these, twenty were European; five (China, Japan, Persia, Korea, and Siam) were Asiatic; and only two (the United States and Mexico) American.

[68] The so-called Hague Tribunal is not even a Court; it is a panel or list from which judges may be chosen. See *infra*, No. 314.

[69] Art. 16 of the Arbitration Treaty or First Convention for the Settlement of Pacific Disputes.

[70] The great advantage of such a code is that it facilitates arbitration. It was no longer necessary for governments to enter into long and tedious negotiations respecting the mode of procedure on the occasion of each controversy.

Warfare," based on the work of the Brussels Conference of 1874. The Conference also adapted the principles of the Geneva Convention of 1864 to maritime warfare. It " declared " against the launching of projectiles and explosives from balloons for five years; the use of projectiles the only object of which is the diffusion of asphyxiating or deleterious gases; and the use of " dumdum " bullets. The Conference also expressed a series of six wishes in favor of consideration, at a subsequent Conference, of questions relating to the rights and duties of neutrals; the inviolability of private (enemy) property in naval warfare; and the bombardment of ports, towns, and villages by a naval force. It even expressed a wish that the Governments might " examine the possibility of an agreement as to the limitation of armed forces by land and sea, and of war budgets."

83. **The Second Hague Peace Conference.**—On April 3, 1907 the Russian Government proposed a Second Peace Conference which met on June 15th of that year at the Hague.[71] The following were the main items in the Russian program:

1. Improvements in the convention relative to the pacific settlement of international disputes as regards the Court of Arbitration and the International Commissions of Inquiry.

2. Additions to the Convention of 1899 relative to the laws and customs of warfare on land.

3. Framing a convention relative to the laws and customs of maritime warfare.

4. Additions to the Convention of 1899 for adapting to

[71] President Roosevelt had suggested the Conference as early as Sept. 21, 1904; but the summons was deferred owing to the continuance of the Russo-Japanese War, the outbreak of the Russian Revolution of 1905, and the further delay caused by the meeting of the Third Pan-American Conference in 1906. When the time for the meeting of the Second Hague Conference finally arrived, President Roosevelt generously conceded the honor of convoking it to Czar Nicholas II.

Out of the 57 States claiming sovereignty, 44 Governments were represented at this Conference. These included 18 Latin-American States. The other two—Honduras and Costa Rica—were invited, and appointed delegates, but these did not take their seats. Asia was again represented by Japan, China, Persia, and Siam. Korea, having been occupied by Japan, was refused admission. As in 1899, the vote of Montenegro was cast by Russia's representatives, and Bulgaria was again permitted by Turkey to send delegates. The number of delegates had increased from 100 in 1899 to 256 in 1907.

maritime warfare the principles of the Geneva Convention of 1864.

For obvious reasons, " limitations of armaments " was omitted from the Russian program. But Great Britain insisted upon raising this question, and the United States was determined to ask for a consideration of the Drago Doctrine in a modified form, *i.e.* the question of prohibiting the use of armed force for the recovery of contract debts unless arbitration is refused, or in case of failure to submit to an arbitral award.[72]

Owing mainly to the opposition of Germany, Austria, Japan, and Russia, the British Government failed in its attempt to secure a consideration of the question of a limitation of armaments or restriction of military expenditures. Germany even opposed the insertion of the words " more urgent than ever " in the resolution which was adopted confirming the Resolution of 1899 relative to this matter.[73]

Though the Second Hague Peace Conference of 1907 failed in some respects to meet the expectations even of conservative international jurists, it must be admitted that, in appearance, it achieved some success. It had to its credit thirteen Conventions or treaties, one Declaration, three wishes, and several recommendations.

Besides the revisions of the Hague Conventions of 1899 dealing with the Pacific Settlement on International Disputes, the Laws and Customs of Land Warfare, and the Adaptation of the Principles of the Geneva Convention (of 1906) to Maritime Warfare, the Final Act of the Second Hague Conference included Conventions respecting the Employment of Force for the Recovery of Contract Debts (modification of the Drago Doctrine), the Opening of Hostilities, the Duties of Neutral Powers and Persons in case of War on Land, and a Convention respecting the Establishment of an International Prize Court. The Final

[72] For references on the *Drago Doctrine*, see *infra*, p. 255n.

[73] The Conference of 1899 had declared itself of the "opinion that the restriction of military charges, which are at present a heavy burden on the world, is extremely desirable for the increase of the material and moral welfare of mankind"; and it had expressed a wish that the Governments examine the question.

Act also contained various fragments of a code of maritime warfare, *viz.*, Conventions regarding the Status of Enemy Merchant ships at the Outbreak of Hostilities, the Conversion of Merchant Ships into War Ships, the Laying of Submarine Mines, Naval Bombardment, the Rights and Duties of Neutral Powers in Time of War, and Certain Restrictions on the Exercise of the Right of Capture in Maritime Warfare. The latter Convention includes provisions respecting the inviolability of postal correspondence, the exemption from capture of vessels engaged in coast fishing, etc., and regulations regarding the disposition of the crews of enemy merchant ships captured by a belligerent.[74]

The Conference renewed " for a period extending to The Third Peace Conference " the Declaration of 1899 prohibiting " the discharge of projectiles and explosives from balloons or by other new methods of a similar nature." It also declared itself " in principle " in favor of obligatory arbitration,[75] and that certain " differences, notably those relating to the interpretation and application of international conventional stipulations, are susceptible of being

[74] For a table showing which States had signed the various Conventions of the Second Hague Conference by June 20, 1908—the final date set for signatures of the plenipotentiaries—see 2 *A. J.* (1908), 876–77; Higgins, *op. cit.* 530–31; or 2 Scott, 528–31. All but one (Paraguay) had signed the Final Act. The greatest delinquents were China (which had only signed the Declaration, the First Convention, and the Final Act); and Nicaragua (which had only affixed her signatures to the Final Act). Nicaragua has since given her adhesion to nearly all the Hague Conventions. The only Conventions which fared badly were: the Porter Convention *re* the Recovery of Contract Debts which was signed (and even then with many reservations) by only 34 States; the Convention on Submarine Mines, which failed to receive the signatures of seven States (including Russia); the Convention relative to the Establishment of an International Prize Court, which was signed by only 31 States (Great Britain, Japan, Russia, and Brazil being among the non-signatories); and the Declaration prohibiting projectiles from balloons, which failed to secure 17 signatures. The United States did not sign Conventions VI, VII, and XIII. For a table showing ratifications, see 5 *A. J.* (1911), 769–70. It may be noted that the Porter Convention had been ratified (with or without reservations) in 1911 by but 14 states, though there were several adhesions.

[75] The failure of the Conference to agree upon a definite plan of obligatory arbitration was mainly due to the opposition of Germany and Austria. The proposition of the United States in favor of exclusive limited compulsory arbitration had thirty-five votes in its favor and only nine against it, with three abstentions. See Hull, "Obligatory Arbitration and the Hague Conferences," in 2 *A. J.* (1908), 731–42; and 1 Scott, ch. 7.

submitted to obligatory arbitration without any reservation."

A resolution, confirming that of 1899, in favor of the desirability of the limitation of military burdens was adopted; and " in view of the fact that military burdens have considerably increased in nearly all countries since the said year," [76] the Conference declared it " highly desirable for governments to undertake again the serious examination of this question."

The Hague Conference of 1907 made the following notable recommendations and wishes: (1) A recommendation that the Signatory Powers adopt and enforce a Project or Draft of a Convention (of thirty-five articles) for the Organization of a Court of Arbitral Justice [77] as soon as they shall have reached an agreement upon the selection of judges and the constitution of the Court. (4) The wish that " the elaboration of regulations relative to the laws and customs of maritime warfare may figure in the program of the next Conference, and that in any case, the Powers apply, as far as possible, to maritime warfare the principle of the Convention relative to the Laws and Customs of War on Land." (5) A recommendation that the Powers hold a " Third Peace Conference, which might take place within a period similar to that which has elapsed since the preceding Conference, on a date to be set by joint agreement among the Powers."[78]

[76] They went on increasing until they culminated in the catastrophe of August, 1914.

[77] This draft, which was mainly based on a Project presented by the United States, was annexed to the first recommendation of the Conference and is contained in the Final Act. It failed of adoption because of the opposition of many of the smaller States led by M. Ruy Barbosa of Brazil. It provided for a Permanent Court of competent judges (number not specified) "representing the various juridical systems of the world" appointed for a term of twelve years and capable of reappointment. These judges were to meet at the Hague once a year if necessary (in June) to decide pending cases and designate three judges with delegated powers. The Powers were unable to agree upon the constitution of the Court and the apportionment of the judges.

For the text of this very interesting project, see Supplement to 2 A. J. (1908), 29–43; Higgins, The Hague Peace Conferences, 498–509; or Scott, The Texts of the Two Hague Peace Conferences. See especially the excellent article on "The Proposed Court of Arbitral Justice" by J. B. Scott, the real author of the Project in respect to details, in 2 A. J. (1908), 772–810; and ch. 9 of 1 Scott, Hague Peace Conferences.

[78] Wishes 2 and 3 have been omitted from the text. The attention of the

Aside from its inability to agree upon definite plans for securing a limitation of armaments, limited obligatory arbitration, and a real permanent Court of Arbitral Justice, the greatest failures of the Second International Peace Conference at the Hague were: its inadequate Convention relative to Submarine Mines; its failure to provide a Code of Rules for the Regulation of Maritime Warfare; and the unsatisfactory character of the Convention respecting the Rights and Duties of Neutral Powers in Naval War. An International Prize Court was agreed upon; but, owing mainly to the wide divergence between the Anglo-American and Continental systems of maritime jurisprudence, it was found impossible to agree upon a Code of Maritime Law which should govern the decisions of the Court, and the Court never came into being, a bill to establish it having been rejected by the British House of Lords.[79]

Powers was also drawn to the "necessity of preparing the labors of that Third Conference sufficiently in advance to have its deliberations follow their course with the requisite authority and speed." It was added:—

"In order to achieve that object the Conference thinks it would be very desirable that a preliminary committee be charged by the Governments about two years before the probable date of the meeting, with the duty of collecting the various propositions to be brought before the Conference, to seek out the matters susceptible of an early international settlement, and to prepare a program which the Governments should determine upon early enough to permit of its being thoroughly examined in each country. The committee should further be charged with the duty of proposing a mode of organization and procedure for the Conference."

[79] On the *Hague Conferences of 1899 and 1907*, see especially: *Actes et doc. de la deuxieme conférence*; Barclay, *Problems of Int. Practice and Diplomacy* (1907), and *Int. Law and Practice* (1917); Bustamante y Sirven, *La seconde conférence de la paix* (1909); Choate, *The Two Hague Conferences* (1913); Foster, *Arbitration and the Hague Court* (1904); Fried, *Die zweiter Haager Konferenz* (1908); Higgins, *The Hague Peace Conferences* (1909); * Holls, *The Peace Conference at the Hague* (1900); Hull, *The Two Hague Peace Conferences* (1908); De Lapradelle, *La conférence de la paix*, in 6 *R. D. I. P.* (1899), 651 ff.; Lawrence, *Int. Problems and Hague Conferences* (1908); * Lémonon, *La seconde conférence de la paix* (1900); Meurer, *Die Haager Friedenskonferenz* (1905); Myers, in 8 and 10 *A. J.* (1914 and 1916), 769–801, and 270–311; Nippold, *Die Fortbildung des Verfahrens* (1905), and *Die Zweite Haager Friedenskonferenz* (1908); *Proc. Hague Conferences* (with index vol.), in 5 vols.; Renault *L'oeuvre de la Hague* (1908); Schücking, *The Int. Union of the Hague Conferences* (1918); * Scott, *The Two Hague Conferences* (1909), *The Hague Conventions* (1915), *American Addresses at Second Hague Conference* (1910), and *Reports* (1917). For a fairly complete bibliography, see De Lapradelle et Politis in 16 *R. D. I. P.* (1909), 385–87. See also Anderson and Hershey, *Handbook*, 370.

85. **The London Naval Conference of 1909.**—In order to find common meeting ground on some of the most fundamental points of maritime law, a Conference of the leading Maritime Powers was held at London during the winter of 1908-1909. This Conference agreed upon a Declaration consisting of 71 articles embodying a code of rules regulating the rights of neutrals and belligerents with respect to neutral commerce. This code contained important provisions relating to the law of blockade, contraband, continuous voyage, hostile aid or unneutral service, the destruction of neutral prizes, the transfer of the flag, enemy character, the right of convoy, etc.; but, owing to the failure of the Powers to ratify, it never went into force. Nevertheless, it may be regarded as a landmark in the history of International Law, being the first attempt to codify prize law.[80]

86a. **The Bismarckian Regime or Hegemony of Germany, 1871-1890.**—If the development of International Law seemed to be making remarkable headway since the middle of the nineteenth century, this was far from being true in the field of foreign relations where Machiavellian practices of diplomacy continued to prevail just as had been the case in the eighteenth century.[81]

The unification of Italy and Germany by Machiavellian methods and Bismarck's policy of " blood and iron " upset the Balance of Power and led to the hegemony of Germany in Europe. Through his three bold and unscrupulous wars

For texts of the Conferences, see Higgins, *The Hague Peace Conferences*; Scott, *Texts of the Two Hague Conferences*; Supp. to 2 *A. J.* (1908); 2 Scott, *The Hague Peace Conferences*; Whittuck, *International Documents* (1908); or *Int. Law Situations* (1908), 117 ff.

[80] On the *London Conference of 1909*, see especially: * Bentwich, *The Dec. of London* (1911); Bowles, *Sea Law and Sea Power* (1910); Cohen, *The Dec. of London* (1911); *Correspondence*, etc., and *Proceedings* (Cd. 4554 and 4555, 1909); Dupuis, in 18 *R. D. I. P.* (1911), 369 ff.; Harris, in 56 *Nat. Rev.* (1910), 393 ff.; * Lémonon, *La confér. navale de Londrès* (1909); Macdonnell, in 11 *J. C. L.*, 68 ff., and 26 *Rep. I. L. A.* (1911); 89 ff.; Myers, in 4 *A. J.* (1910), 571 ff.; * Naval War College, Int. Law Topics (1910); * Niemeyer, *Das Seekriegsrecht* (1910); Reinsch, in 190 *No. Am. Rev.* (1909). 479 ff.; * Renault, *La confér. navale de Londrès* (1909); * Scott [ed.], *The Declaration of London* (1919); Stockton, in 3 *A. J.* (1909), 596 ff.; Westlake, in 67 *Nineteenth Cent.* (1910), 505 ff.

[81] Cf. *supra*, No. 64, p. 79.

with Denmark, Austria, and France [82] (1864–71), Bismarck placed himself and a Prussianized Germany upon the saddle of Continental Europe—a position which he firmly maintained until his dismissal by Kaiser Wilhelm II in 1890.

After the cession of Alsace-Lorraine in 1871, the Iron Chancellor declared that Germany was " satiated " and he devoted himself to the maintenance of an armed peace with a view of consolidating Germany's new position and possessions. His first and main task was to keep France isolated and prevent her from avenging herself for the loss of Alsace-Lorraine. To this end he formed the so-called League of the Three Emperors (of Germany, Austria and Russia) in 1872.[83]

In 1878 Bismarck undertook to play the rôle of " honest broker " at the Congress of Berlin [84] which was called upon

[82] The Government of Napoleon III seems to have been no less eager for war than were Bismarck and the military clique in Prussia. But Napoleon and his advisors were completely outplayed by Bismarck who from 1866 to 1870 had isolated France and entangled her in the network of his crafty diplomacy. For the texts of the original and "edited" Ems dispatch, see Anderson, *Constitutions and Documents*, 593–94. For a good recent study, see Lord, *Origins of the War of 1870* (1924), ch. 6.

[83] This "League" was a sort of new Holy Alliance based largely on the fear of revolutionary movements like Socialism. The Three Emporers held frequent conferences between 1872 and 1876, but they never formed an actual alliance and did not reduce to writing their verbal agreements relating to the maintenance of the *status quo* in the Orient or elsewhere.   In 1873 the King of Italy visited Berlin and Vienna and a quadruple entente or understanding was formed. See especially 2 Dawson, *The German Empire* (1919), 87–90. For bibliography, see Anderson and Hershey, 55.

[84] On the *Congress of Berlin*, which had no particular significance in International Law but is of great importance in its effect on international relations, see : Anderson and Hershey, 77 ff. ; * Avril, *Négotiations relatives au traité de Berlin* (1887) ; 2 Bismarck, *Reflections and Reminiscences* (1899), ch. 28 ; 2 Dawson, *German Empire* (1919), ch. 16, pp. 132 ff., and in 3 *Cambridge History of British Foreign Policy*, ch. 2, pp. 132 ff. ; 2 Debidour, *Histoire diplomatique de l'Europe* (1891), ch. 12, pp. 519 ff. ; Driault, *La Question d'Orient* (1921), 230 ff. ; Duggan, *The Eastern Question*, ch. 7, in 14 *Columbia Studies* (1902) ; Lord, in *Three Peace Congresses of the Nineteenth Century* (Cambridge, 1917), 47–69 ; Munro, *The Berlin Congress* (1918) ; 2 Morley, *Gladstone* (1911), ch. 5 ; Mowat, *European Diplomacy* (1922), ch. 24 ; Rose, *Development of European Nations* (1922), ch. 9 ; Seton-Watson, *Rise of Nationality in the Balkans* (1917), ch. 10 ; and 4 Walpole, *History of Twenty-Five Years* (1904), ch. 18, pp. 160 ff.

For the text of the Treaty of Berlin and the documents bearing thereon, see 4 Hertslet, *Map of Europe by Treaty* (1875–91), 2697–99. For bibliographies, see Anderson and Hershey, 83–86 ; and Coolidge, *Three Peace Congresses* (Cambridge, 1917), 69.

the insistence of Great Britain and Austria that the Treaty of San Stefano be revised and the designs of Russia on Turkey at the close of the Russo-Turkish War be thwarted. At this Congress Russia suffered a great diplomatic defeat which left its deep imprint upon subsequent international developments.   Not only was her protegé, Bulgaria, divided and greatly reduced territorially, but Austria-Hungary obtained the right " to occupy and administer " the two Turkish provinces of Bosnia and Herzegovina.[85]

In Russia resentment for her failure at the Congress of Berlin was largely directed against the " honest broker " who oftimes loudly proclaimed that to Germany the whole Eastern Question was not worth the " bones of a single Pomeranian grenadier." Consequently, Bismarck, who feared a coalition between France and Russia,[86] turned to Austria-Hungary and concluded with that power the Austro-German Dual Alliance of 1879.   By the terms of this agreement, which was kept secret until 1888, the two Powers mutually bound themselves to make war and conclude peace in common, should either of them be attacked by Russia.   " Should one of the two be attacked by another Power [France], the other will observe at least benevolent neutrality.   Should, however, the attacking party [France] be supported by Russia, either by active coöperation or by military measures which constitute a menace, the other shall aid."[87]

[85] So far as Bulgaria is concerned, the work of the Congress of Berlin was undone in 1885 when the inhabitants of Eastern Rumelia joined their kinsmen north of the Balkans.

[86] During the Franco-German war scare of 1875, the Russian Czar had more than intimated that if France were attacked by Germany, the French would not stand alone.   Germany, he said, would "go to war at her own peril." 2 Dawson, op. cit., 104.   Cf. Robertson, Bismarck (1919), 347 ff.   For further references on the "Franco-German War Scare of 1875," see Anderson and Hershey, 57–58.

[87] Gooch, History of Modern Europe (1923), 46.   For the full text, with accompanying documents, of the Austro-German Alliance, see 1 Pribram, Secret Treaties of Austria-Hungary (1920–21), 19–31.   It will thus be seen that the Dual Alliance of 1879, in form at least, was primarily a defensive alliance against Russia.   Bismarck plead hard for a defensive alliance against France as well as Russia, but Austria persisted in her refusal.

The alliance was concluded for five years.   "It was renewed in 1883, and at subsequent intervals.   Not until 1902 was it agreed that it should be automatically extended at the end of each three-year term."   Gooch, op. cit.

The Austro-German Alliance was soon extended to include Italy who, weary of isolation and angered at the occupation of Tunis by France in 1881,[88] signed a separate or supplementary treaty of alliance with Austria-Hungary and Germany in 1882, the terms of which have been thus summarized by a reliable historian:

" If Italy were attacked by France without provocation, her partners would come to her aid.   Italy, in turn, would help Germany against a French attack.   If one of the Allies (or two) were attacked and engaged in war with two or more Great Powers, the *casus foederis* would arise for all. If a Great Power threatened the security of one of the signatories, and that one was forced to make war, the others would observe benevolent neutrality, reserving the right to take part in the conflict if they should see fit.   If peace was threatened, the Allies would consult with regard to military measures." [89]

The Triple Alliance was joined by several satellites [90] and was frequently renewed [91] until its final extinction in 1915

[88] Tunis, long coveted by Italy, seems to have been promised to France both by Great Britain and Germany at the Congress of Berlin.   Italy had boasted that she had come away from that Congress with clean, *i.e.* empty, hands.

[89] Gooch, *op. cit.*, 67–68.   "The pact was to hold for five years, and to be kept secret.   At Italy's wish, each of the Allies signed an Additional Declaration, affirming that the treaty could in no case be regarded as directed against Great Britain."

For the text of the Triple Alliance of 1882, see 1 Pribram, *op. cit.*, 65 ff. For a detailed account of the negotiations, see 2 Pribram *op. cit.*, ch. 1.   All previous accounts of the terms or successive renewals of the Triple Alliance have been rendered at least partially obsolete by the publication of Pribram's work on *The Secret Treaties of Austria-Hungary* in 1920–21.   For bibliographies or earlier contributions, see Anderson and Hershey, 112 and 115.   For additional references, see Turner, *Europe Since 1870* (1921), 208.   The most available account of *The Origins of the Triple Alliance* is by Coolidge (new ed., 1926).   On various aspects of Italy's relation to the Alliance, see Dillon, *Triple to Quadruple Alliance* (1915), *passim*.   For an excellent recent account of the Triple Alliance, see Dickinson, *Int. Anarchy* (1926), ch. 3.

[90] *I.e.* Serbia and Rumania.   For the Austro-Serb Treaty of 1881 and the secret alliance of 1883 with Rumania, see Gooch, *op. cit.*, 69–71; and 1 Pribram, *op. cit.*, 50 ff., and 79 ff.   See *Ibid.*, *passim* for subsequent renewals.   Rumania's secret obligations to the Triple Alliance continued until 1916.

[91] For the renewals of the Triple Alliance, see 1 and 2 Pribram, *op. cit.*, *passim*.

The Triple Alliance gradually became an offensive alliance, at least so far as the obligations of Austria-Hungary and Germany were concerned.   Italy seems to have pursued what Bismarck once called a "jackal policy."

when Italy denounced her treaties with Austria-Hungary
and entered the World War on the side of France, Russia
and Great Britain.   This network of alliances, which included a new triple entente or League of the Three Emperors
(1881–87) and the Reinsurance Treaty of 1887 with Russia,[92]

[92] In this connection particular mention should be made of Bismarck's "reinsurance" policy in relation to Russia by means of which he sought to keep
open "the wire to St. Petersburg."   No sooner had the Austro-German alliance been formed than he sought reinsurance on the side of Russia by a revival
of the League of Three Emperors.

A tripartite secret treaty good for three years between the three Eastern
Empires was signed in 1881 by which it was agreed that "if one Power should
find itself at war with a fourth Great Power, the others will observe a benevolent neutrality and try to localize the conflict.   This shall apply also to a war
with Turkey," etc., Gooch, *op. cit.*, 53–55.   Cf. Fuller, *Bismarck's Diplomacy*
(1922), 9.   For the text of the treaty, see 1 Pribram, *op. cit.*, 37 ff.

Russia declared it to be her firm intention to respect Austrian interests
resulting from the new position assured her by the Treaty of Berlin.   "The
three Courts will take account of their respective interests in the Balkan
peninsula," etc.   They also "recognize the European and mutually obligatory
character of the principle of the closing of the Straits."

This triple entente of the three Eastern Powers was renewed, with some
modifications, in 1884.   Owing to the unwillingness of Russia to renew it in
1887, the triple entente of the three Eastern Powers lapsed and a secret *Reinsurance Treaty* was signed by Germany and Russia alone without the knowledge
of Austria.   This agreement provided in effect:

Art. 1.   In case either Power should find itself at war with a third Great
Power, the other would maintain a benevolent neutrality, and would try to
localize the conflict.   This provision was not to apply to a war against Austria
or France if resulting from an attack by one of the contracting parties.   This
meant, of course, that Germany would aid Austria if Russia attacked her,
while Russia need not remain neutral if Germany attacked France.

Art. 2.   "Germany recognizes the rights historically acquired by Russia in
the Balkan Peninsula, and particularly the legitimacy of her preponderant and
decisive influence in Bulgaria and Eastern Rumelia . . ."

Art. 3.   The two Courts recognized the European and mutually obligatory
character of the principle of the closing of the Straits and agreed to make common representations to Turkey in case she should infringe this rule.

For the text of the Reinsurance Treaty of 1887 and the *very secret* Additional
Protocol granting German support to Russian policy *re* Bulgaria and the en-
trance to the Black Sea, see 1 Pribram, *op. cit.*, 274 ff.   Cf. Gooch, *op. cit.*,
139–40 and Fuller, *op. cit.*, ch. 9.   For a bibliography, see Anderson and
Hershey, 119.   Note particularly the article by Goriainov on "The End of the
Alliances of the Emperors," in 23 *Am. Histor. Rev.* (1908), 324–49.

On *Bismarck's Policy or Diplomacy* generally, which greatly resembles that
of the reactionary Metternich, see: Barker, *Foundations of Germany* (1916),
chs. 2 and 3 (to be used with caution); Benedetti, *Studies in Diplomacy* (1896),
passim; * 2 Bismarck, *Reflections and Reminiscences* (1899), *passim*; 2 Dawson,
The German Empire (1919), chs. 15–18; * Fuller, *Bismarck's Diplomacy* (1922);
Fullerton, *Problems of Power* (1913), *passim* (see index); * Gooch, *Hist. of
Mod. Eurpoe* (1923, see index); Hayes, *Hist. of Mod. Europe* (1924, see index);

was one of the great contributions of Bismarck to the precarious stability and ultimate downfall of Germany and Europe.

86b. The Restoration of the Balance of Power.   Triple Entente vs. Triple Alliance, World Politics, 1890–1914.— The dismissal of Bismarck [93] in 1890 marks a very important turning point in the history of European international relations.   Emperor Wilhelm II not only insisted upon personal participation in the affairs of government, but he differed greatly from Bismarck in temperament as well as in aims and methods of conducting foreign affairs.   The Reinsurance Treaty of 1887 with Russia was not renewed [94] upon its expiration in 1890.   The result was already visible in 1891 when the French fleet was enthusiastically received in Russian waters at Cronstadt.   An agreement between the two Governments of France and Russia soon followed (August, 1891) to the effect that they would confer and agree upon concerted measures whenever peace was in danger, and especially if one of the two should be menaced by aggression.   But it was not until December 31, 1893, long after considerable quantities of Russian bonds had been subscribed for in Paris, that the *marriage de raison*, as it has been called, between France and Russia was consummated and a military convention signed.

Robertson, *Bismarck* (1919), ch. 6, §§ 3 and 5; Schmitt, *England and Germany* (1916, see index); Seymour, *Diplomatic Background of the World War* (1916, see index); Smith, Munroe, *Militarism and Statecraft* (1918, a very important contribution); Turner, *Europe Since 1870* (1921), chs. 6–8.

For fuller bibliographies, see above cited works of * Fuller, Hayes, Hazen, Robertson, and Turner.

[93] For the main facts and bibliography relating to the dismissal of Bismarck, see Anderson and Hershey, 193–95.   To this list of references should be added *The New Chapters of Bismarck's Autobiography* published in the American edition (1921) with the title *The Kaiser vs. Bismarck.   The Kaiser's Memoirs* by Wilhelm II (1922) do not add much to our knowledge of this or any other subject.

[94] See above, note 92.   There seem to have been several causes for this cutting of the "wire with St. Petersburg," but the main reason probably was that it would have interfered with the new desire manifested in Germany to participate in the game of World Politics, particularly in the Near East, of which the first visit of Wilhelm II to Constantinople in 1889 was a symptom.

Another reason sometimes given is that the new German Empire desired an alliance, or at least more cordial relations, with Great Britain.   The reason given by Count Caprivi was that the treaty was incompatible with Germany's obligations to Austria.

If France is attacked by Germany, or by Italy supported by Germany, Russia shall employ all her available forces to attack Germany. If Russia is attacked by Germany, or by Austria supported by Germany, France shall employ all her available forces to fight Germany.[95]

During the early years of his reign Kaiser Wilhelm II tried to cultivate friendly relations with Great Britain, Russia and even France; but Germany was undergoing a tremendous economic and industrial development which resulted in an increasing demand for participation in the game of World Politics or for a " place in the sun," as she called it. Tempted by the great opportunities opening in Asia and Africa, the leading European Powers were passing through a transition from nationalism to commercial and political imperialism, [96] involving nationalistic aims and rivalries in the exploitation of the world's markets and economic resources, particularly in respect to coal, iron, and latterly oil.

But it was not much before the beginning of the twentieth

[95] The above is the gist of the Franco-Russian Alliance as contained in Art. I of the Military Convention of 1894 which was first published in 1918. The momentous secret was first revealed to the world in January, 1895. The Convention was to have the same duration as the Triple Alliance and neither Power was to conclude peace separately. A Naval Convention was signed on July 16, 1912.

The Franco-Russian Alliance was revised in 1899, adding to the purpose of maintaining the general peace that of "the balance of European power." Instead of lasting as long as the Triple Alliance, the revision of 1899 provided that the Franco-Russian military convention of 1893–94 was to "remain in force as long as the diplomatic agreement for the safeguarding of the common and permanent interests of the two countries." 2 Pribram, *op. cit.*, 219–21.

For the text of these Conventions with exchanges of notes, see 2 Pribram, 207–25. Cf. Gooch, *op. cit.*, 174 and 183.

The most available account of the Franco–Russian *Dual Alliance* is by Tardieu, *France and the Alliances* (1908). The most unbiased account is by Gooch, 172 ff. See also Dickinson, *op. cit.*, 104–12; and Seymour, *op. cit.*, ch. 3, for good brief accounts. For bibliographies, see Anderson and Hershey, 200–01 and 2 Pribram, *op. cit.*, note on p. 204. According to Pribram, "the best single account of the negotiations resulting in this alliance" is Albin's *La paix armée.* See also Turner, *op. cit.*, p. 239. For documents, see Welschinger, *L'Alliance Franco-Russe* (1919).

[96] Lord Beaconsfield may be said to have been the founder of economic imperialism in the twentieth century sense. This is particularly shown by his secret purchase of a controlling interest in the Suez Canal in 1875. Bismarck encouraged the commercial and colonial rivalry between Great Britain and France, especially in Egypt; but was himself forced, albeit reluctantly, to enter upon the German quest for colonies in Africa in 1884.

century that Germany really entered the lists in this
" Struggle of the Nations " for world markets, industrial
exploitation of the world's resources, and national prestige.
Thus far the contest had been waged mainly between Great
Britain and France, and Great Britain and Russia; and
indeed it might be said that by the end of the nineteenth
century the greater parts of Asia and Africa were under the
direct or indirect control of Great Britain, Russia and
France.

Germany, however, had succeeded in establishing at least
a foothold in a few desired localities even outside of Africa,
as, *e.g.* in Samoa, the Caroline Islands, and Kiaochau (1897).
But it was toward Asiatic Turkey that her energies were
mainly directed.   In 1898 the German Emperor made his
second journey to the Near East and declared himself the
" eternal friend of the three hundred million Mohammedans
scattered over the earth." [97]

Meanwhile, the relations between Germany and Great
Britain were becoming somewhat strained.   The unfortunate Kruger telegram [98] of 1896, the growing commercial
and colonial rivalry between the two nations, and the
unfriendly attitude of the German press and people during
the Boer War (1900)—all contributed toward a growing
tensity of relations.   But it was unquestionably the
adoption by the German Government of the naval program

[97] His real purpose seems to have been to obtain economic concessions in
Turkey.   In 1899 came the first concessions for the Bagdad Railway which
soon became the main object of German ambition in the Near East and did so
much to cause concern to the other Powers.

On the *Bagdad Railway*, see Anderson and Hershey, 409–12; Art. on
"Bagdad Railway Negotiations" in 228 *Quar. Rev.* (1917), 487–528; Chéra-
dame, *Le chemin de fer de Bagdad* (1915); * Dickinson, *Int. Anarchy* (1926),
ch. 9; * Earle, *Turkey, The Great Powers and the Bagdad Railway* (1923); 2
Ewart, *Roots and Causes of the Wars, 1914–18* (1925), 729–44; Jastrow, *The
War and the Bagdad Railway* (1917); Lémonon, in 17 and 19 *R. D. I. P.*
(1910 and 1912), 201 ff. and 318 ff.; * Lewin, *The German Road to the East*
(1916); Lynch, in 89 *Fortn. Rev.*, n.s. (1911), 375 ff. and 771 ff.; and Rohrbach,
Die Bagdadbahn (1911).

[98] This was a telegram of congratulations to President Kruger of the Boer
Republic on the occasion of the failure of the indefensible Jameson raid in 1896.
The incident gave great offense to the British public who were never permitted
to forget it by the British press.   On the *Kruger Telegram*, see Anderson and
Hershey, pp. 229–31; Gooch, *op. cit.*, 218 ff.; and Schmitt, *England and
Germany* (1916), 143–246.

embodied in the Navy Laws of 1898 and 1900 [99] that led to the abandonment by Great Britain of her so-called " policy of splendid isolation " [100] and the formation of the Triple Entente (1904–1907) preceded by the Anglo-Japanese Alliance of 1902.[101]

In 1904 there was taken the first step in that diplomatic revolution which eventually resulted in the overthrow of the balance of power in Europe which had been at least partly restored by the formation of the Franco-Russian Alliance during 1891–93. Indeed, it may be said that when the British Empire shifted its support from the Triple to the Dual Alliance, the see-saw or scales of the balance were tipped against the Triplice even more than they had been formerly tipped in its favor. Germany began to fear she was being " encircled," and Europe marched rapidly toward the world catastrophe of 1914.

[99] The preamble of the German Naval Bill of 1900 declared: "Germany must have a fleet of such strength that a war against the mightiest sea-power would involve risks threatening the supremacy of that power." From an article by the author entitled "Germany—The Main Obstacle to the World's Peace," published in 66 *N. Y. Independent* (1909), 1071 ff. On the *Naval Rivalry between Great Britain and Germany*, see especially ch. 8 entitled "The Admiralty of the Atlantic," in Schmitt, *op. cit.* On the German "Navy Bills," see 1 Churchill, *The World Crisis* (1923), ch. 5; and 1 Von Tirpitz, *Memoirs* (1919), ch. 11.

[100] Great Britain had always favored the Triple Alliance, at least she leaned strongly to that side. Indeed, it might be said that at times she was almost a silent supporter, if not a partner. For example, in 1887 Great Britain joined a triple entente with Italy and Austria directed against Russia to preserve the *status quo* in the Mediterranean. See Fuller, *Bismarck's Diplomacy* (1922), ch. 12. For some interesting correspondence between Bismarck and Lord Salisbury, see *Ibid.*, App., 329 ff.

In 1889 Bismarck directly proposed a defensive alliance against France, but Lord Salisbury declined on the ground that he could not face Parliament on this issue. Gooch, *op. cit.*, 192. "Perhaps in 1875, probably in 1879, and certainly in 1876 and again in 1889, Bismarck made definite overtures to Great Britain for an alliance." Schmitt, in 39 *Am. Histor. Rev.* (1924), 454 *n.*

During 1898–1901 Chamberlain, then Colonial Secretary, suggested an Anglo-German Alliance, but the proposal was rejected by the Kaiser and his Chancellor Count von Bülow. See Gooch, *op. cit.*, 300 ff. for a very interesting letter of the Kaiser's on this subject. See especially the interesting revelations of Baron von Eckardstein, *Ten Years at the Court of St. James* (1922), ch. 8. For various proposals of an Anglo-German Alliance, see Dickinson, *op. cit.*, 56 ff. In 1901 there were negotiations in London looking toward an Anglo-German-Japanese alliance, but again the proposals were thwarted by the Kaiser and his advisors in Berlin. Gooch, *op. cit.*, 326 ff. See also Eckardstein, *op. cit.*, chs. 11–12; and Dawson, in 126 *Contemp. Rev.* (1924), 575–85.

[101] For references on the Anglo-Japanese Alliance, see *infra*, 147n.

The Franco-British Entente Cordiale, begun in 1904, took the form not of a written alliance, but of a series of understandings and agreements, partly public and partly secret. Outstanding Anglo-French controversies relating to the Newfoundland fisheries, Siam, Madagascar, the New Hebrides, and the Niger region were settled, but the principal part of these agreements consisted in a British recognition of the paramount interests of the French in Morocco [102] in return for the abandonment by France of her " policy of pin-pricks " directed against the British occupation of Egypt.   Thus was begun the so-called " encirclement " of Germany through a complete reversal of Anglo-French relations.[103]

[102] The public "Declaration" regarding Morocco affirmed that the French Government had no intention of changing the political status of Morocco, but that the British Government would not obstruct any action taken by France to preserve order and carry out necessary reforms.   Both Governments agreed to "afford to one another their diplomatic support in order to obtain the execution" of the agreement.

To this "Declaration" there were added several secret articles (first published in 1911) making provision for compensation to Spain or a virtual partition of Morocco in the "event of either Government finding themselves constrained by force of circumstances to revise their policy in regard to Egypt or Morocco," though in the published Declaration the French Government declared that it had "no intention of altering the political status of Morocco." For texts in English of the Anglo-French Agreements *re* Egypt and Morocco, see Mowat, *Select Treaties and Documents* (1918), 1 ff.; or Morel, *Morocco in Diplomacy* (1912), 230 ff.

These Anglo-French agreements were supplemented by a public Declaration and an accompanying secret Convention between France and Spain.   While the Declaration declared the attachment of the French and Spanish Governments to the "integrity of the Moorish Empire under the sovereignty of the Sultan," the secret convention contained elaborate provisions for the conditions under which a possible future partition of that Empire should take effect.

On the *Franco-Spanish Arrangement of 1904*, see especially Morel, *Morocco in Diplomacy* (1912), ch. 11; * Stuart, *French Foreign Policy* (1921), ch. 6, pp. 145 ff.; and Tardieu, *France and the Alliances* (1908), 95 ff.   For the texts, see Morel, *op. cit.*, 236 ff.

[103] As late as 1898 France and England found themselves on the verge of war in consequence of the *Fashoda Incident*.   A French exploring expedition had planted the French flag at the mud village of Fashoda in the valley of the upper Nile, thus blocking the Cape-to-Cairo project of Cecil Rhodes and other British imperialists.   In consideration of the recognition by Great Britain of French claims to extensive regions around Lake Chad, France abandoned her pretentions.   For a good account of the *Fashoda Incident*, see Gooch, *op. cit.*, ch. 8. For further references, see Anderson and Hershey, 224–27.

For a bibliography on the *Anglo-French Entente Cordiale*, see *Ibid.*, 286–88. Note especially the following references on this subject: Barclay, *Thirty Years*, (1914), *passim*; 2 Crispi, *Memoirs* (1912), *passim*, particularly ch. 10; * 2 Daw-

In consequence of the dramatic appearance of Kaiser Wilhelm II at Tangier on March 31, 1905, and his recognition of the Sultan of Morocco as an absolutely independent sovereign,[104] the Congress of Algeciras [105] met in

son, *The German Empire* (1919), ch. 22; 1 Debidour, *Histoire diplomatique de l'Europe* (1917), ch. 11; Dickinson, *op. cit.*, ch. 4; * Gooch, *History of Modern Europe* (1923), ch. 10, and in 3 *Cambridge History of British Foreign Policy*, ch. 5, pp. 305 ff.; Kennedy, *Old Diplomacy and New* (1922), Pt. II, ch. 2; Lémonon, *L'Europe et la politique britannique* (1910), ch. 9; Loreburn, *How the War Came* (1920), ch. 4 (criticism of Grey's policy); * Morel, *Morocco in Diplomacy* (1912), *passim* (a severe attack on British and French policy *re* Morocco); Mowat, *European Diplomacy* (1922), ch. 27; Murray, *The Foreign Policy of Sir Edward Grey, 1906-15* (1915, defence of Grey's policy); Perris, *Our Foreign Policy and Grey's Failure* (1912, opposed to the Entente); Russell, Bertrand, *Justice in War Time* (1916), 138-70 (a severe attack on Grey's policy); Schmitt, *England and Germany* (1916), ch. 9; Seymour, ch. 7 on "The Diplomatic Revolution," in his *Diplomatic Background of the War* (1916); * Stuart, *French Foreign Policy* (1921), ch. 5; Tardieu, *France and the Alliances* (1908), ch. 5.

The path to the *entente* with England had been prepared by a French *rapprochement* with Italy during 1896-1902. According to the Franco-Italian Convention of 1902, Italy agreed to give France a free hand in Morocco in return for a recognition by France of Italy's designs on Tripoli. "From this date Italy, though still a member of the Triple Alliance, stood in many respects closer to France than to her associates in the Triple Alliance." Anderson and Hershey, 222. On the *Franco-Italian Convention of 1902*, see Anderson and Hershey, 221-22 and 338-39; * 2 Pribram, *op. cit.*, 226 ff.; * Stuart, *op. cit.*, ch. 4, pp. 77-89; and Tardieu, *op. cit.*, 86-95.

[104] This constituted the *First Moroccan Crisis*. Its real purpose seems to have been to test the Entente Cordiale and challenge the right of Great Britain and France to dispose of Morroco without the consent of Germany. It should be remembered that the Russian army had just been defeated at Mukden (in February, 1905). The Kaiser's speech at Tangier was delivered in pursuance of the advice of the German Chancellor von Bülow (see latter's *Imperial Germany*, Am. ed., 1914, p. 98).

On the *Moroccan Crisis of 1905*, see in addition to the references on the *Entente Cordiale* (*supra*, note 103), Anderson and Hershey, 333-34; * Dickinson, *op. cit.*, 124 ff.; 2 Ewart, *op. cit.*, 773 ff.; and 1 Grey, *Twenty-Five Years* (1925), ch., 5, 6-7.

Another daring effort to break the *Entente Cordiale* was made this same year (1905) by the German Emporer. By means of an alliance with the Czar, he sought to detach France from the *entente* with Great Britain and force her (France) into a new Triple Alliance between Germany, France and Russia. He prevailed upon the still weaker and more vacillating Czar to sign the secret Russo-German draft of the Treaty of Björko, countersigned by a Russian admiral who had no knowledge of its contents. The agreement remained a dead letter, but affords evidence of the folly of the two leading monarchs of Europe prior to the World War. For the "Secret Negotiation between the Kaiser and the Czar and the text of the Treaty of Björko," see Anderson and Hershey, 288-92; Dillon, *Eclipse of Russia* (1918), chs. 16-18; Gooch, *op. cit.*, 385-88; Isvolksky, *Recollections* (1921), ch. 2; Welschinger, *L'alliance Franco-Russe* (1919), ch. 5; and Witte, *Memoirs* (1921), ch. 11.

1906 to attempt an international settlement of Moroccan affairs—an attempt which must be pronounced a failure.[106]

For the extraordinary *Willy-Nicky Correspondence*, see Bernstein, *The Willy-Nicky Correspondence* (1918, exchange of telegrams); and Levine, *Letters from the Kaiser to the Czar* (1920).

[105] This Conference was called by the Sultan of Morocco at Germany's behest. It consisted of the delegates from the thirteen States that had signed the Treaty of Madrid of 1880 (except Norway), including the United States, and, in addition, Russia. For the important political, though secret, rôle which President Roosevelt played in persuading France to agree to the Conference, in influencing the course of negotiations at Algeciras, and in securing the consent of Germany to some of its most important provisions, see 1 Bishop, *Theodore Roosevelt* (1920), chs. 26–27.

The United States signed and ratified the Act of Algeciras, with an additional protocol declining responsibility for its enforcement.

The Act of Algeciras, consisting of 123 articles, laid down the "threefold principle of the sovereignty and independence of His Majesty the Sultan, the integrity of his dominions, and economic liberty without any inequality. . . ." Its main provisions concerned the organization of a police force and a State bank. The organization of the police was entrusted to French and Spanish officers. While France and Spain were to act as the mandatories of the powers in the matters of banking and the police force, they were really given a privileged position. The only supporter of Germany at this Conference was Austria-Hungary. Anderson and Hershey, 332–33.

For references on the *Congress of Algeciras*, see *Ibid.*, 333–34. Note particularly Tardieu, *La Conférence d'Algeciras* (1908). The best accounts in English seem to be by * Dickinson, *op. cit.*, ch. 5; 2 Ewart, *Roots and Causes of the Wars* (1925), 786 ff.; and Stuart, *op. cit.*, ch. 8. · For further references, see Index to *A. J.* (1920). For the Act of Algeciras, see Morel, *op. cit.*, App. XII, 252 ff. or Supp. to 1 *A. J.*, 47 ff.

[106] Further economic and diplomatic conflicts between France and Germany and conditions in Morocco culminating in rebellion and the French expedition to Fez led to the *Second Morocco Crisis of 1911.* This crisis arose from the dispatch of the German gunboat Panther to Adagir on July 1 which was intended as a notice that France would not be allowed to establish a protectorate over Morocco without the consent of Germany (Bethmann-Holweg, *Reflections on the World War*, 1920, 32). The British Government, which suspected Germany of the design of procuring a naval harbor on the west coast of Morocco threatened war with Germany if British interests were ignored. Germany gave the necessary assurances, but it was not until November 4, 1911 that the Franco-German Convention was signed by which Germany received compensation in the French Congo in return for the concession to France of a free hand in Morocco politically.

On the whole, the settlement was a great triumph for France, especially as a demonstration of Anglo-French solidarity. But it did not improve the German temper or Anglo-German or Franco-German relations.

For a bibliography on *The Morocco Crisis of 1911*, see Anderson and Hershey, 406–07. See also Churchill, *The World Crisis* (1923), ch. 3; * Dickenson, *op. cit.*, ch. 7; 2 Ewart, *op. cit.*, 814–55; 1 Grey, *op. cit.*, ch. 13; * Gooch, *op. cit.*, ch. 14, and in 3 *Cambridge History of British Foreign Policy*, 438 ff.; Kennedy, *Old Diplomacy and New* (1922), Pt. II, ch. 5; Montgelas, *Case for the Central Powers* (1925), 41–47; Schmitt, *op. cit.*, ch. 11; and * Stuart, *op. cit.*,

The so-called " Encirclement of Germany " was completed by the enlargement of the Anglo-French Entente Cordiale into the Anglo-Franco-Russian Triple Entente in 1907 which tipped the scales of the balance of power still more heavily against Germany and Austria-Hungary.[107] As in the case of the Anglo-French Entente, the Anglo-Russian Entente was made possible by a settlement of outstanding differences through the Convention signed by Britain and Russia on August 31, 1907.

This Convention related to Persia, Afghanistan and Thibet. Persia was divided into two spheres of influence—Russian and British—and a neutral zone; Russia agreed that Afghanistan was outside her sphere of influence and recognized the preponderant diplomatic position of Great Britain there; [108] and in Thibet the suzerainty of China, as also its territorial integrity, was recognized by both Governments.[109] Thus the diplomatic revolution of 1904–07 was completed and Europe was divided into two groups of Powers, the Triple Alliance and the Triple Entente, which " faced one another in an atmosphere full of distrust and tension." [110]

ch. 11. For the documents, see Appendices to Morel, *op. cit.*, 219 ff. and Supp. to 6 *A. J.*, 31 ff.

On the *Casablanca Incident* of 1908, the case of six deserters (three of them German) from the French Foreign Legion in Morocco who were given protection by the German consul, see: Anderson and Hershey, 398–401; Gidel, in 17 *R. D. I. P.* (1910), 326–407; Gooch, *op. cit.*, 459–60; Scott, *Hague Court Rep.* (1916), 110 (for the award); Schoen, *Memoirs of an Ambassador* (1922), 90 ff.; 1 Stowell and Munro, 377–85; Stuart, *op. cit.*, 257–61; Wilson, *Hague Arbitration Cases* (1915), 82–101 (documentary). For editorial comment and the award, see also 3 *A. J.* (1909), 176 ff., 698 ff., 755 ff., 946 ff.

[107] Italy need hardly be taken into account in this connection as she played a double rôle, being in a sense a member of both combinations. For the Franco-Italian Agreement of 1902, see *supra*, note 103.

In October, 1909 Italy also entered into a very secret Agreement with Russia. For the text of the Agreement, see 1 *Un livre noir* (ed. by Marchand, Paris, 1922–23), 357–58. "The Germans were rightly suspicious of Italy's 'extra dances' with France and Russia." Schmitt, in 29 *Am. Histor. Rev.* (1924), 463. On the Racconigi Agreement between Italy and Russia, see Dickinson, *op. cit.*, 221–22, 304–06.

[108] Under reserve, however, of the maintenance of the political *status quo* and commercial freedom.

[109] For the text of the Anglo-Russian Agreement of 1907, see Mowat, *Select Treaties and Documents* (1918), 9–15.

[110] Schoen, *op. cit.*, 159. As in the case of France and England a few years prior to the formation of the Entente Cordiale (see above, *Fashoda Incident,*

The Triple Entente was greatly strengthened and consolidated [111] by the Bosnian Crises of 1908–09 which resulted from the annexation of Bosnia-Herzegovina by Austria-Hungary early in October, 1908,[112] several months after the outbreak of the revolution of the Young Turks on July 24 of that year.

During this crisis Great Britain, France and Italy strongly supported the Russian demands for a Congress of

note 103), Great Britain and Russia had been on the verge of war in consequence of the North Sea Incident in 1905 (see *infra*, p. 463 n.).   In fact, Anglo-Russian hostility dated from the Crimean War (1854–56) and had been particularly virulent during the Russo-Turkish War (1877–78).

It should not be overlooked that the Anglo-Japanese Alliance had been renewed in 1905 and that in June and July of 1907 there were also signed Conventions between France and Japan and Russia and Japan respectively. "It must be admitted that the situation was not pleasant for Germany. . . . By 1907, in addition to the Franco-Russian Alliance, Germany was confronted by a network of agreements involving Great Britain, Spain, Italy, and Japan, of which Powers two were closely connected with the Dual Alliance.   The Triple Alliance was now opposed by a Triple Entente, which was in a position to restrain the policy of Germany and Austria in the very regions they regarded as the theatres of their political and economic expansion.   Indubitably the strength of the new combination lay in the support which British sea power could give to the military pressure exerted by France and Russia."   Schmitt, *England and Germany* (1916), 242.

But Germany had largely brought all this upon herself by her challenge to British naval power and her unwise and blundering diplomacy since the accession of Emperor Wilhelm II.

On the *Triple Entente*, with particular reference to the Anglo-Russian Entente, see (in addition to some of the references on the *Anglo-French Entente Cordiale, supra,* note 103), the bibliography in Anderson and Hershey, 361–62. See also references in Turner, *Europe Since 1870* (1921), 419 and particularly the references in an admirable article by Schmitt on "The Triple Alliance and Triple Entente," in 29 *Am. Histor. Rev.* (1924), 449 ff.   For brief accounts, with special reference to the *Anglo-Russian Entente*, see Andrassy, *Diplomacy and the War* (1921), Pt. I, ch. 3; Asquith, *Genesis of the War* (1923), chs. 9–10; * 1 Dawson, *German Empire* (1919), ch. 23; * Gooch, *History of Modern Europe* (1923), ch. 11, and in 3 *Cambridge History of British Foreign Policy,* 356 ff.; Lémonon, *L'Europe et la politique britannique* (1910), ch. 10; Russell, *Justice in War Time* (1916), 171 ff. (an attack upon British Policy); Schmitt, *England and Germany* (1916), ch. 9 and * Article, in 29 *Am. Histor. Rev.* (1924); Tardieu, *France and the Alliances* (1908), ch. 6, pp. 237 ff.

[111] "The crisis due to the annexation had brought us far nearer to England and had consolidated the entente once for all." Nekludoff, *Diplomatic Reminiscences* (1920), 20.   "Altogether, the crisis of August, 1908 to March, 1909 marked the end of a policy of compromise between Russia and Austria and accentuated the division of Europe into two directly opposed camps." *Ibid.,* 22.

[112] It should be recalled that the Treaty of Berlin had sanctioned the "occupation and administration" by Austria-Hungary of these former Turkish provinces.

the Powers to consider the matter, but Germany threw her
" sword into the scales " on the side of her ally and notified
Russia (in March, 1909) that if she (Russia) intervened to
aid Serbia, she (Germany) would support Austria. Russia
backed down at once and, though greatly humiliated and
apparently determined on a future reckoning,[113] recognized
the annexation.

The Triple Alliance and Entente successfully weathered
the various Balkan crises of 1912–13,[114] but the settlement

[113] On March 31, Serbia withdrew her opposition to annexation and promised
to live on good neighborly terms with Austria.

Recent documentary evidence seems to show that the initial move toward
the annexation of Bosnia-Herzegovina really came from Russia. On July 2,
1908, the Russian Foreign Minister Isvolsky proposed to permit such annexation in return for the opening of the Straits of Constantinople to Russian warships. Conversations between Count Aehrenthal, the Austrian statesman,
and Isvolsky occurred at Buchlau in Bohemia on September 15. The Russian
proposal for the opening of the Straits at that moment did not find favor in the
eyes of the British Government, as did the demand for a European Congress.
Consequently, Count Aehrenthal decided to act. Isvolsky loudly complained
that he had been tricked by the wily Austrian. See Gooch, *History of Modern
Europe* (1923) 411 ff.

On the *Bosnian Crisis* see especially: Anderson and Hershey, 374 ff. and
382 ff.; * Dickinson, *op. cit.*, ch. 6; 2 Ewart, *Roots and Causes of the Wars*
(1925), 926–48; * Gooch, *op. cit.*, 410 ff., and in 3 *Cambride History of British
Foreign Policy*, 402–12; 1 Grey, *op. cit.*, ch. 11; Loreburn, *How the War Came*
(1920), 38 ff.; Montgelas, *Case for the Central Powers* (1925), 30–38; * Schmitt,
England and Germany (1916), ch. 10 (see also index); Seymour, *Diplomatic
Background of the War* (1916), 179 ff., 213 ff.; * Siebert, *Entente Diplomacy*
(1921, documentary), 213–72.

For references, see the bibliographies in Anderson and Hershey, 376–78 and
385; and the references in Gooch, 410 n.

[114] There were several of these crises. The first arose in November, 1912,
when Serbia sent troops to occupy Durazzo on the Adriatic coast. Austria,
supported by Germany and Italy, demanded their withdrawal; and, lacking
the support of England and France, the Russian Minister Sazonoff declared
"we are not going to war with the Triple Alliance on account of a Serbian port
on the Adriatic." Siebert, *op. cit.*, 396. Though Poincaré appears to have
used his influence in favor of peace, he repeatedly declared that "Russia could
absolutely rely on armed assistance from France, if the Austro-Serbian conflct
should lead to a general war." Siebert, 407. Cf. *Ibid.*, 403, where Isvolsky
represents Poincaré as saying, "If Russia makes war, France also will make
war." See also 1 *Un livre noire* (Paris, 1922–23), 346–48, 362 ff. Germany
maintained a similar attitude toward Austria.

During the period of the meetings of the *London Conference* from December
16, 1912 to May 30, 1913, the situation remained very dangerous. On the
work of this Conference, see particularly 1 Grey, *Twenty-five Years* (1925), ch.
14, pp. 248 ff. A general European War was averted mainly through the untiring efforts of Sir Edward Grey and the moderation of Germany, France and
Russia. London and Berlin worked in cordial harmony at this time. The

of Bucharest [115] (August 10, 1913) was regarded by Austria and Germany as most humiliating to their prestige and menacing to their interests.

main political result of this Conference was the creation on paper of the ephemeral principality of Albania in deference to the wishes of Austria and Italy.

The situation was particularly acute in April, 1913, when King Nicholas of Montenegro was forced by the Powers to evacuate Scutari which had been assigned to Albania.   So imminent did a conflict appear that even Germany prepared for mobilization.   Gooch, *op. cit.*, 508.   It seems that Austria and Russia had already partly mobilized.

According to the revelations of the Italian ex-Premier Giolitti, Austria-Hungary again planned to attack Serbia in the late summer of 1913.   This appears to have been due to the refusal of Serbia to evacuate Albanian territory which she had occupied.   On August 9, 1913, the day before the signing of the Treaty of Bucharest, the Italian statesman received a telegram from the Italian Ambassador at Vienna stating that Austria had communicated to Italy and Germany her "intention of taking action against Serbia," and defining such action as defensive, "hoping to apply the *casus fœderis* of the Triple Alliance." To this Giolitti replied that such contemplated action not being defensive, "it is evident that there can be no question of the *casus fœderis.*"   Giolitti, *Memoirs* (1923), 372–73.   Serbia finally yielded to a threat of force by Austria on Oct. 20, 1913 "in accordance with advice from the Triple Entente." Pribram, *Austrian Foreign Policy* (1923), 49.   On the crises during the Balkan Wars of 1912–13, see especially Dickinson, *op. cit.*, ch. 12.

[115] Austria was now confronted by an enlarged and aspiring Serbia bereft of access to the sea, but a protegé of Russia and on good terms with Rumania now veering from the Triple Alliance to the Triple Entente.   The road to Saloniki on the Aegean Sea was practically closed to Austria, and Germany's protegé Turkey had been defeated and weakened, thus doubly threatening her route to the Near East (*Drang nach Osten*).   In any case, Germany felt that a weakened and thwarted Austria was a menace to her prestige and interests. Austria had also incurred the increased hostility of Russia and jealousy of Italy. Russia, ever bent upon her "historic mission," was awaiting an opportune moment to secure the opening of the Straits and, if possible, the possession of Constantinople.   Bulgaria was sullenly discontented.   Most pregnant of all, the national feelings of the South Slavs of Bosnia and Croatia had been awakened and they had discovered their kinship with the Serbs to whom they looked for leadership in their nationalistic aspirations.

On the *Treaty of Bucharest*, see Duggan, in 28 *Pol. Sci. Quar.* (1913), 627 ff.; Gibbons, *New Map of Europe* (1916), ch. 17; Marriot, *The Eastern Question* (1917); and Seymour, *Diplomatic Background of the War* (1916), 236 ff.   For a good statement of the attitude of the German Government, see Bethmann-Holweg, *Reflections on the World War*, (1920), 76–78 who remarks that "the scale had been heavily weighted against the Central Powers."   For the attitude of Russia, see 1 Buchanan, *Mission to Russia* (1923), chs. 10–11.

On the *South Slav Question*, see especially, Seton-Watson, *The Southern Slav Question* (1911), particularly chs. 9–12 on the Agram and Friedjung Trials and the Vasic Forgeries.   They illustrate the Machiavellian depths of pre-war Austrian diplomacy and administration.   See also Durham, *Twenty Years of Balkan Tangle* (1920), *passim*; Taylor, *The Future of the South Slavs* (1917), and a more recent book by Seton-Watson entitled *Sarajevo* (1926).

For bibliographical references on the Balkan Wars and Slavic Europe

Meanwhile, the Triple Entente was being further strengthened by a general increase in armaments, especially in Russia and France, and by naval arrangements between France and Russia [116] and France and Great Britain. On November 22, 1912, through an exchange of letters between Sir Edward Grey and M. Paul Cambon, the French ambassador at London, it was agreed that " if either Government had some grave reason to expect an unprovoked attack by a third Power, or something that threatened the general peace, it should immediately discuss with the other whether both Governments should act together to prevent aggression and to preserve peace, and, if so, what measures they would be prepared to take in common." [117]

This Anglo-French Agreement, closely bordering on an alliance, was followed by the concentration of the French fleet on the Mediterranean, leaving the northern coast of France undefended except by the British fleet. Thus there was created at least a strong moral obligation on the part of Great Britain to defend France against a German attack at sea.

In the spring of 1914 " conversations " relating to naval coöperation were begun between Russia and Great Britain. Though they failed to secure an alliance, the Russian diplomats expressed the " greatest satisfaction " at the complaisance exhibited by the British.[118]

generally, see Anderson and Hershey, 425 ff.; and Kerner, *Slavic Europe* (1918, a bibliography.)

[116] On the Franco-Russian negotiations, see Beard, *Cross Currents in Europe To-day* (1922), 22–27. For the text of the naval convention of 1912, see 2 Pribram, *Secret Treaties of Austria-Hungary* (1920–21), 223–25.

[117] Schmitt, "Triple Alliance and Triple Entente" in 29 *Am. Histor. Rev.* (1924), 459. Schmitt also gives the text of the political clauses of the Franco-Russian Alliance and remarks: "We can hardly make any distinction between the engagements contracted." Yet if the texts printed on p. 459 of Schmitt's article be closely studied, certain distinctions may be observed. For the text of the Grey-Cambon letters, see also Gooch, in 3 *Cambridge History of British Foreign Policy*, 467–68.

On the Anglo-French naval and military understandings, particularly of 1912, see Anderson and Hershey, 444–45; Beard, *op. cit.*, 29–34; Gooch, *History of Modern Europe* (1923), 497–99; Schmitt, *op. cit.*, and *England and Germany* (1916), 364; and Siebert, *Entente Diplomacy* (1921), 723–24 (for the Grey-Cambon letters).

[118] See Schmitt (in article, cited above, p. 461) who adds: "The episode is of the greatest importance, for it appeared to the French and Russians as the first step in the consolidation of the Triple Entente; just as the military arrange-

The relations between the leading members of the Triple Alliance and the Triple Entente were thus strained more than ever [119] during the fateful days of July, 1914 when the next Balkan Crisis arose. This resulted from Austria's " formidable " ultimatum to Serbia occasioned by the murder [120] at Sarajevo in Bosnia on June 28 of the Archduke Ferdinand, heir to the Austrian throne.

After Serbia's qualified acceptance of the Austrian ultimatum, Austria-Hungary, eager for vengeance and de-

ments of a month before marked the rejuvenation of the Triple Alliance. Thus, at last, the two diplomatic groups stood face to face, on the very eve of Sarajevo."

The Anglo-Russian conversations were apparently still going on when the World War broke out. Gooch tells us that on May 23 the Grey-Cambon letters were given to the Russian Ambassadors with the information that there was no objection to a similar agreement with Russia.

On the Anglo-Russian negotiations of 1914 for naval coöperation, see Beard, *op. cit.*, 34 ff.; Dickinson, *op. cit.*, 399 ff.; 1 Ewart, *op. cit.*, 531–41; Gooch, *History of Modern Europe*, 529 ff., and, in 3 *Cambridge History of British Foreign Policy*, 483–86; Schmitt, *op. cit.*, and Siebert, *op. cit.*, 713 ff.

[119] True it is that the relations between Great Britain and Germany had shown promise of material improvement in consequence of a new secret agreement relating to the commercial development and ultimate political disposition of the Portuguese African colonies, the friendly coöperation between the British and German Governments during the Balkan crises of 1912–13, a settlement of the Bagdad Railway problem on the eve of the World War, and the friendly character of the negotiations for a limitation of naval armaments initiated by the Haldane Mission early in 1912. This Mission, though a failure at the time, was followed by a somewhat better understanding and a certain relief in the tension produced by naval rivalry. Yet there is evidence that the German Government was greatly disturbed over the revelations of Anglo-Russian negotiations for naval coöperation in the spring of 1914.

On the *Haldane Mission* of 1912, see Anderson and Hershey, 412–16; Begbie, *Vindication of Great Britain* (1916), ch. 3, pp. 127 ff.; Bethmann-Holweg *op. cit.*, 49 ff.; * Dickinson, *op. cit.*, 387–99; Gooch, in 3 *Cambridge History of British Foreign Policy*, 456 ff.; Haldane, *Before the War* (1920), 72 ff.; Schmitt, *England and Germany* (1916), 346 ff.; Siebert, *op. cit.*, 613–39.

On the *Bagdad Railway Settlement*, see Anderson and Hershey, 449–51; Gooch, *op. cit.*, 478–81; Lichnowsky, *Mission to London* (1918), 20; Schmitt, *op. cit.*, 369–71. See also references in note 97, *supra.*

[120] It is now known that the murder was instigated by one Colonel Dimitrjevitch, Chief of the Intelligence Bureau of the Serbian General Staff, though the Austrian Government appears to have had no knowledge of the fact at the time. See Barnes, in *Current History* for May, 1924, p. 178; and Schmitt, in 29 *Am. Histor. Rev.* (1923–24), 470–71 and the references cited in these articles. See also Barnes, *Genesis of the War* (1926), ch. 5; Durham, *The Sarajevo Crime* (1925); Fay, "Serbia's Responsibility for the World War," in *Cur. Hist.*, Oct. and Nov., 1925 and references therein cited; and Seton-Watson, *Sarajevo* (1926) and in 3 *For. Aff.* (1924–25), 489 ff.

termined to crush [121] the leader of the Greater Serbian or South Slavic movement at any cost, promptly declared war on Serbia and invaded Serbian territory. The German Government, which had given a free hand to its ally in the early days of July, tried in vain to localize the Austro-Serbian struggle and refused Sir Edward Grey's proposals for mediation through a Conference of the Four Powers—Great Britain, Germany, France and Italy. The Kaiser and his Chancellor did not attempt to mediate or apply the brakes to Austria until it was too late, for on July 29 Russia mobilized fifty-five divisions in reply to Austria's twenty-two. The Russian Government, bent upon its " historic mission " [122]—the leadership of the Pan-Slavic movement and control of the Straits of Constantinople—and apparently believing that the time for fulfillment had arrived, had mobilized her entire forces by July 31. Austria seems to have mobilized simultaneously. Thus these two Powers may be said to have precipitated the World War, for Germany felt bound to meet the Russian mobilization by a declaration of war.

During the crisis of the twelve days preceding the World War, the French Government refused to exert a moderating influence at St. Petersburg [123] and seems to have confined

[121] The various reports and dispatches printed in the *Austrian Red Book* (in 3 vols., ed. by Goos) make this abundantly clear. The contention that Austria was a tool of Germany's was baseless in 1914 as in 1908. The Austrian Government appears to have been unwilling to compromise at any point. Yet, Austria's attitude toward Serbia is more understandable if we imagine what our attitude toward Mexico would be if one of our leading statesmen were assassinated in Texas as a consequence of agitation or conspiracy in that country.

[122] The dispatches of Isvolsky from Paris make frequent reference to this "historic mission." See Siebert, *op. cit.*, and *un livre noir, passim.* Nekludoff (*Diplomatic Reminiscences*, 1920, 4–5), reports that in an interview with the Czar in 1911, the latter had said to him it would be out of the question for Russia to face a war before 1917, or 1915 at the earliest. But the military authorities evidently considered the army ready on July 13, 1914, when an extremely provocative article entitled "Russia is ready. France must be ready too" appeared in the St. Petersburg *Bourse Gazette.* This article aroused much anger in Berlin. Gooch, *History of Modern Europe*, 524.

The Russian Crown Council had met on February 21, 1914, to consider "the necessity of a comprehensive program of action, in order to assure for us a satisfactory solution of the Straits in the event of being compelled at no distant period to defend our interests in the Bosphorus and Dardanelles." Gooch, *op. cit.*, 520.

[123] See, *e.g.*, 2 *Un livre noir*, 280 and 283–84. Cf. *Falsifications of the Russian Orange Book* (ed. by Romberg, 1923), 30.

itself mainly to efforts to secure the support of Great Britain; and Italy appears to have been concerned throughout merely with her prospects and hopes of compensation. The British Government,[124] while apparently believing it had kept its hands free, had allowed them to become entangled in the network of the secret Machiavellian diplomacy of France and Russia to such an extent that certain moral obligations, at least to France, had been created which could not be honorably evaded when the World War finally came.   Besides, there was the great fear (and perhaps jealousy too) of Germany and the menace of a European War to British interests in various parts of the world.   Particularly were vital British interests threatened in the countries bordering on the English Channel, notably in Belgium and northern France.   Under the circumstances. it is hardly surprising that Great Britain, taking advantage of the excellent pretext afforded by the German violation of Belgian neutrality,[125] entered the struggle.

If we look for the deeper and more fundamental causes of the World War, we shall find them mainly in the fears, hatreds and suspicions engendered by imperialistic, economic and nationalistic rivalries between the Great Powers,

[124] Of all the Powers, Great Britain was least responsible for the World War. Her attitude throughout, both before and since, appears to have been the most upright and enlightened.   And of all modern European diplomats, Sir (now Viscount) Edward Grey exhibits the cleanest and most straight-forward record. See particularly the first volume of his *Twenty-five Years*—an honest and straight-forward account of his work in the British Foreign Office prior to the World War.   As during the Balkan Crisis of 1912–13, Sir Edward Grey seems to have done everything humanly possible under the circumstances to avert an armed conflict, though even he cannot be acquitted of a Machiavellian evasion of the truth (in fact, he admits as much himself) in replies to questions in the British Parliament.   Under the old or secret diplomacy, truth-telling on all occasions was, indeed, quite impossible.

Of course the British policy, first inaugurated in 1904 by King Edward VII and Lord Landsdowne, of secret entanglements with France has been severely criticised.   But the alternative would seem to have been one of practical isolation in Europe which might have ended in disaster.

For good appreciations of the diplomacy of Viscount Grey, see Murray, *The Foreign Policy of Sir Edward Grey* (1915); and Stowell, *Diplomacy of the War* (1915), 268–70.   For severe criticism, see Barnes, *Genesis of the War* (1926), ch. 8 and references; Loreburn, *How the War Came* (1920), *passim*; Perris, *Our Foreign Policy and Sir Edward Grey's Failure* (1912); and Russell, *Justice in War Time* (1916), *passim*.   See the Appendix in Loreburn for the text of Grey's great speech of August 3, 1914.

[125] For references on German violation of Belgian neutrality, see *infra*, p. 196 n.

more particularly between the two great groups of Powers known as the Triple Alliance and the Triple Entente.[126] Diplomatically speaking, it may be said that it was largely the struggle for the Balance of Power between these two groups by Machiavellian methods that caused the World War. The historical causes of the conflict as between Germany and France are rooted in the Alsace-Lorraine Problem; as between England and Germany, in their naval, colonial and commercial rivalry; and as between Austria and Germany on the one hand and Russia on the other, in the Pan-Slavic and nationalistic movements in the Balkans and the natural desire of Russia to obtain control of the Straits and, if possible, of Constantinople. From the viewpoint of the international jurist the World War must be considered as primarily the result of that armed international anarchy [127] still prevailing in the world and the want of an adequate system of international organization. It indicates the partial collapse and inadequacy of the Grotian system of International Law based largely on a theoretical distinction between just and unjust wars, the assumed right of sovereigns to appeal to force in the interest of law and justice, the impracticable belief in the possible humanization of warfare, and extreme conceptions of the rights of sovereignty and independence.[128]

[126] "It was the schism of Europe in Triple Alliance and Triple Entente which fused the various quarrels and forces into one gigantic struggle for the balance of power; and the war came in 1914 because then, for the first time, the lines were sharply drawn between the two rival groups, and neither could yield on the Serbian issue without seeing the balance pass definitely to the other side." Schmitt, in 29 *Am. Histor. Rev.* (1923-24), 450.

[127] See, *e.g.*, Dickinson, *The European Anarchy* (1916), and * *The International Anarchy* (1926), *passim.* "The outbreak of the Great War is the condemnation not only of the clumsy performers who strutted for a brief hour across the stage, but of the international anarchy which they inherited and which they did nothing to abate." Gooch, *History of Modern Europe*, 559.

[128] In the above paragraph it is intended to suggest rather than to exhaust the fundamental causes of the World War. On the Fundamental Causes of War, see *infra*, pp. 546 ff.

For more or less impartial treatments in English of the *Causes of the World War*, see especially Beard, *Cross Currents in Europe To-day* (1922), chs. 1-3; Boghitschnevitsch, *Causes of the War* (English edition in 1925); * Dickinson, *International Anarchy* (1926); 1 and 2 Ewart, *Roots and Causes of the Wars, 1914-18*, (1925), *passim;* * Fay, "New Lights on the Origins of the War," in 25 and 26 *Am. Histor. Rev.* (1919-21), 616 ff., 37 ff., 224 ff.; Hays, "The Causes of the Great Wars," in 1 *These Eventful Years*, ch. 5, pp. 194 ff.; * Gooch,

BIBLIOGRAPHY

History of Int. Law and Relations since the Peace of Westphalia.
—1 Alcorta, *Cours de droit int. public* (1887), ch. 6, secs. 3–4; Alvarez,
Le droit int. américain (1910); Bex, *Essai sur l'évolution de droit des
gens* (1910); Boeck, *De la propriété privée ennemie sous pavillon
ennemi* (1882), 1–153; Debidour, *Histoire diplomatique* (in 2 vols.,
1891); Dupuis, *Le principe d'equilibre* (1909); * 3 Hill, *History of
Diplomacy in the Development of Europe* (1905–06), *passim;* Hosack,
Rise and Growth of the Law of Nations (1882), chs. 8–10; 1 Kleen,
"Introduction historique," 1–70; Laurent, *Études sur l'humanité*
(1865–80), Vols. X–XVIII; Leseur, *Cours de droit int.* (1893),
§§ 49–59; 1 Mohl, *Geschichte und Literatur der Staatswissenschaften*
(1885), 337–475; * Muir, *Nationalism and Internationalism* (1916);

History of Modern Europe (1923); Loreburn, *How the War Came* (1920), *passim*;
Montgelas, *Case of the Central Powers* (1925); Owen, Senator, in 65 Cong.
Record, Pt. I, 68th Congress, 1st Session, Dec. 18, 1923, 355–99; and * Schmitt,
"Triple Alliance and Triple Entente," in 29 *Am. Histor. Rev.* (1923–24).   For
Bibliography, see Gooch, *Recent Developments of European Diplomacy* (1927).
   The book by Barnes entitled "Genesis of the World War," (1926) is neither
impartial nor reliable.
   For references to the best recent sources of information, see Gooch, *op. cit.*,
note on p. 552; the references given by Barnes, Dickinson, Fay and Schmitt, in
the articles and books cited above; and the excellent bibliography in 2 Hayes,
Modern Europe, (ed. of 1924), 719–22.
   The student should be warned that most of the books and official documents
produced during and immediately after the war are often worse than useless,
being either one-sided or misrepresentative.   We owe out great knowledge of
the causes of the World War—a knowledge possibly greater than in the case
of any other war in history—to the opening of the archives by the Russian,
German and Austrian revolutionists.
   It should be noted that during the past few years (1921–25) there have been
a considerable number of remarkable works produced by French publicists
tending to expose the share of France in the responsibility for the war under
the Poincaré régime.   The animus is of course partly political.   The following
seem to be the most important of these works: Demartial, *La guerre de 1914*
(1922); Fabre-Luce, *La victoire* (1924); Gouttenoire de Toury, *Poincaré
a-t-il voulu la guerre* (1920), and *La politique russe de Poincaré*, and
Javres (1923); Mornhardt, *Les preures*; Pevet, *Les responsables de la guerre*
(1921); and Renouvin, *Les origines immédiates de la guerre* (1925).
   Particularly noteworthy are the Isvolsky dispatches contained in *Un livre
noir* (2 vols., 1922–23), edited by Marchand; and Stieve, *Der Diplomatische
Schrifturchsel Iswolskis, 1911–1914* (1924), in 5 vols.   See Siebert, *Entente
Diplomacy* (1921), for many of these dispatches translated into English.
They yield much damaging evidence against the Poincaré régime, particularly
in respect to Russian subventions to leading organs of the French press (with
the connivance of the French Government) and the aggressive designs of the
Russian Government during the period extending from 1910 to 1914.   But
the most important source of information is the collection of German documents in 30 odd vols. known as *Die Grosse Politik der Europäische Kabinette,
1871–1914*.

* Nys, *Études*, especially I, 318–406 on "La révolution française *et* le droit int.";Ompteda, *Literatur des Völkerrechts im XIX Jahrhundert* (trans. from Italian into German by Scholz, 1785); Redslob, *Histoire du droit des gens* (1923), §§ 39 ff.; Vollenhoven, *The Three Stages in the Evolution of the Law of Nations* (1919); Walker, *History of the Law of Nations* (1899); * Wheaton, *History, passim*, and *Histoire des progrès du droit des gens en Europe* (4th French ed., 1865).

Among the treatises which deal with the subject in a more or less satisfactory manner are: Bonfils, Calvo, Chrétien, *Principes de droit Int. public* (1893), Despagnet, * Fauchille, Fenwick, Fiore, Halleck (3d. ed.), J. de Louter, * F. de Martens, *Traité*, * Mérignhac, * Nys, * Oppenheim, and Taylor.

History of the Science of Int. Law.—I Alcorta, *Cours de droit int. public* (1887), ch. 7; 1 Mohl, *Geschichte und Literatur der Staatswissenschaften* (1855), 337–475; * Nys, 213–328; * Ompteda, *Literatur des Völkerrechts* (1785), *passim*; Nys, *Notes sur l'histoire dogmatique et literaire de droit int. en Angleterre* (1888), *Les théories politiques et le droit int. en France jusqu'au XVIII siècle* (1899), and *Études, passim; Les fondateurs du droit int.*, ed. par Pillet (1904); Rivier, in 1 Holtzendorff's *Handbuch*, §§ 85–123; Walker, *Science of Int. Law* (1893), *passim*; Wheaton, *History, passim*. Among the treatises, see Bonfils, Calvo, * Fauchille, Fenwick, Fiore, Halleck, J. de Louter, Manning, *Law of Nations* (1875), F. de Martens, * Nys, * Oppenheim, and Taylor.

For *Bibliographies*, see * Bonfils, * Fauchille, von Mohl, *op. cit.*,* Nys, Ompteda, *op. cit.*, * Oppenheim, Rivier in 1 Holtzendorff, and * Olivart, *Bibliographie du droit int.* (1905–10).

For current bibliographies, see numbers of the *American Journal of Int. Law* and the * *American Political Science Review.*

For *Treaties*, see the Collections and Summaries contained in the compilations of * De Clercq, Dumont, Flassan, Gardner, * Hertslet, Koch, * Malloy (for treaties to which the U. S. has been a party), * Martens, Strupp, * *Archives Diplomatiques* and the *League of Nations Treaty* Series. See also the Supplements to *A. J.*, the volumes on the Foreign Relations of the United States, published as *House Documents*, the British and Foreign *State Papers*, the *Parliamentary Blue Books*, and the documents published in the *American Journal of Int. Law*, the *Revue générale de droit int. public*, the *Zeitschrift für Völkerrecht*, etc.

The leading available periodicals on International Law are as follows: *American Journal of International Law* (since 1907); *Jahrbuch für Völkerrecht* (since 1913); *Revue générale de droit international public* (since 1894); *Revue de droit international et de legislation comparée* (since 1869); *Zeitschrift für internationales Recht* (since 1891); *Zeitschrift für Völkerrecht und Bundesstaatsrecht* (since 1907); and the *Annuaire de l'Institut de Droit Int.* (since 1887). See also *British Year Books* (since 1920–21).

Valuable articles and notes on Int. Law also frequently appear in the *American Law Review*, the *Green Bag*, the *Harvard Law Review*, the *Law Quarterly Review*, the *Minnesota Law Review*, the *Yale Law Review*, the *Juridical Review*, the *Journal of Comparative Legislation and Int. Law*, the *American Political Science Review*, the *Archiv. für öffentliches Recht*, the *Annelen des deutschen Reichs*, *Revue de droit public et de la science politique*, and the *Journal du droit international privé*.

CHAPTER V

THE PARIS TREATIES AND AFTER, 1919-1925

86c. The Wilsonian Principles.—In an address to Congress on January 8, 1918, President Wilson announced " the program of the world's peace," including the famous Fourteen Points [1] which, together with four subsequent addresses of President Wilson's and eight diplomatic notes exchanged between the President and the German Government during October and November, 1918, were formally accepted by the Allies as well as by Germany as the legal basis of the Armistice and the Peace Settlement.

With slight abridgements, the Fourteen Points which were to constitute the main basis of the peace, and which may also be considered as fundamental principles of a proposed New World Order, were thus stated by President Wilson:

" 1. Open convenants of peace, openly arrived at, . . . [2]

[1] In respect to the Fourteen Points there was one reservation made by the Allies—that relating to the "freedom of the seas" (see below, note 3)—and a modification or interpretation of the meaning of "restoration" (see below, note 8) as used by President Wilson.

The subsequent addresses were: the Address to Congress on Feb. 11, 1918 (containing the Four Principles); the Speech at Baltimore on April 6, 1918; the Speech at Mount Vernon on July 4, 1918 (stating the Four Ends or Objects); and the Speech at New York on Sept. 27, 1918 (with the Five Particulars).

For the text of these speeches, see 1 Temperley, *Hist. of the Peace Conference of Paris* (1920–24), 431–48. With the exception of the two latter, they are also printed in Scott, *Pres. Wilson's Foreign Policy* (1918). For the text of the Fourteen Points, see Scott, *op. cit.*, 359–62 or 1 Temperley, *op. cit.*, 433–35. They may also be found in Latané, *Isolation to Leadership* (2d ed., 1923), 205 ff. These should be read in the light of Premier Lloyd George's statement of British War Aims on January 5, 1918. See 1 Temperley, *op. cit.*, 189–92.

For the text of the diplomatic notes referred to in the text, see 1 Temperley, *op. cit.*, 448–58.

[2] It is added: "after which there shall be no private international understandings of any kind, but diplomacy shall proceed always frankly and in the public view."

Obviously, under the conditions which existed there, this point could be observed very imperfectly at Paris in 1919; but it nevertheless constitutes an ideal or a fundamental principle of the New Diplomacy which can be increasingly realized under a New World Order.

" 2. Absolute freedom of navigation upon the seas outside territorial waters, alike in peace and in war, except as the seas may be closed in whole or in part by international action for the enforcement of international covenants.[3]

" 3. The removal, so far as possible, of all economic barriers, and the establishment of an equality of trade conditions among all nations consenting to the peace and associating themselves for its maintenance.[4]

In a letter to the Sec'y of State, dated June 12, 1918, President Wilson thus explained this point: "When I pronounced for open diplomacy, I meant, not that there should be no private discussions of delicate matters, but that no secret agreements should be entered into, and that all international relations, when fixed, should be open, above board and explicit." Cited by 1 Baker, *Wilson and World Settlement* (1922–23), 46. In this sense, it may be claimed that Art. 18 of the Covenant, requiring the registration and publication of treaties, is at least a partial fulfillment of the First Point.

[3] On this second point, the Allied Governments reserved to themselves "complete freedom." In their memorandum accepting the terms of peace laid down by President Wilson (see 1 Temperley, *op. cit.*, 457), they pointed out that "clause 2, relating to what is usually described as freedom of the seas, is open to various interpretations, some of which they could not accept." The phrase "was generally taken to mean complete freedom of passage to all neutral shipping in time of war," though some of the more extreme advocates also "asked for immunity of passage to all enemy private property at sea." 2 Temperley, *op. cit.*, 145.

So far as known to the writer, President Wilson never explained what he meant by "freedom of the seas." It appears he believed that this freedom would be realized, so far as desirable, under the League of Nations, "in which there would be no neutrals." 1 and 2 Baker, *op. cit.*, 383 and 319.

On the *Freedom of the Seas*, cf. *supra*, Nos. 202–206 (see Bibliography on p. 336) and *infra*, No. 433 and note on pp. 651–53.

[4] The ideal expressed in the Third Point is twofold: the removal of economic barriers, so far as possible, *i.e.*, freer trade; and an equality of trade conditions, viz. the removal or absence of *discriminations* in trade. It has found expression in such phrases as the "open door" and "most-favored-nation treatment." It includes the idea of "freedom of transit" in ports, rivers, and railways. Under certain conditions, it might possibly be held to include the right of access to raw material also.

In a letter to Senator Hitchcock, dated Oct. 22, 1918, President Wilson rather heatedly repudiated the idea that his words implied a restriction upon the right of every nation to determine its own economic policy (see 2 Baker, *op. cit.*, 413), though they might well bear that interpretation. He emphasized the prohibition of "hostile discrimination."

Though the Third Point presents economic ideals of "removal of economic barriers" and "equality of trade conditions" which are far from realization, it cannot be denied that progress in these directions has been made. Art. 23 (*e*) of the Covenant contains a promise that the members of the League "will make provision to secure and maintain freedom of communications and of transit and equitable treatment for the commerce of all Members of the League." The "Régime of Ports, Waterways and Railways," contained in

" 4. Adequate guaranties given and taken that national armaments will be reduced to the lowest point consistent with domestic safety.[5]

" 5. A free, open-minded and absolutely impartial adjustment of all colonial claims, based upon a strict observance of the principle that in determining all such questions of sovereignty the interests of the populations concerned must have equal weight with the equitable claims of the Government whose title is to be determined.[6]

" 6. The evacuation of all Russian territory and such a settlement of all questions affecting Russia as will secure the best and freest coöperation of the other nations of the world in obtaining for her an unhampered and unembarrassed opportunity for the independent determination of her own political development and national policy and assure her of a sincere welcome into the society of free nations under institutions of her own choosing; . . . The treatment accorded Russia by her sister nations will be the acid test of their good will, . . . " [7]

Pt. XII (Arts. 321 ff.) of the Treaty of Versailles, include provisions which, though partly devised as penalties and not immediately granting reciprocal rights to Germany, probably mark an epoch in the development of freedom of traffic in transit (Cf. *infra*, note 52 on p. 525). The Conventions on Transit and Waterways of "international concern" adopted by the Barcelona Conference in 1921 also mark an important step in this direction. See an article on this subject by Toulmin, in *Brit. Yr. Bk.* (1922–23), 167–78. For the texts of the Barcelona Conventions and Statutes, see Supp. to 18 *A. J.* (1924), 118–27, 151–67.

[5] This principle was incorporated into Art. 8 of the Covenant with the substitution of the word "national" for "domestic." It was applied to Germany, Austria, Hungary and Bulgaria in the Treaties (see *e.g.* Arts. 159 ff. of the Treaty of Versailles), and it should not be overlooked that in the preamble to the Military, Naval and Air Clauses of that Treaty, the Signatories declared that the purpose of German disarmament is to "render possible the initiation of a general limitation of the armaments of all nations."

On the struggle for a limitation of armaments at the Paris Peace Conference, see especially: * 1 Baker, *op. cit.*, chs. 19–24; and 2 Temperley, *op. cit.*, (see index).

On the efforts of the League of Nations and the Washington Conference to solve this difficult problem, see *infra*, pp. 507 ff. and 145 ff.

[6] On the *Mandatory System*, which may be said to go farther than the requirements of this Fifth Point in some respects, see *infra*, pp. 160 ff.

[7] The "sister nations," have not stood this "acid test." In spite of her recognition by many States, Russia remains more or less of an outlaw nation and as such (not because of the character of her people or the nature of her institutions) a menace to the Western World.

" 7. Belgium . . . must be evacuated and restored. . . .
" 8. All French territory should be freed and the invaded
portions restored,[8] and the wrong done to France by Prussia

On the *Foreign Policy of Soviet Russia*, see * Dennis, *The Foreign Policies
of Soviet Russia* (1924); Kelly, in 3 *For. Aff.* (1924–25), 91 ff.; Miliukov,
Russia Today and Tomorrow (1922), ch. 5; and *Russian-American Relations,
1917–20* (documents publ. by For. Policy Assoc., New York, 1920).

[8] Respecting the meaning of the word "restored" as used in the Seventh,
Eighth and Eleventh points, the Allied Powers insisted upon the following
interpretation—an interpretation which President Wilson accepted:

"By it they understand that compensation will be made by Germany for all
damages done to the civilian population of the Allies and their property by the
aggression of Germany by land, by sea, and from the air."   1 Temperley, *op.
cit.*, 457–58.

The absence of any clear rule or principle respecting *reparations* or indemnities was perhaps the weakest point in the Wilsonian peace program.   The
substitute or interpretative principle offered by the Allies might perhaps have
been fair and well within Germany's capacity to pay if it had been restricted
to illegal acts or violations of International Law, more especially the rules of
warfare.   The inclusion of pensions and separation allowances in damages to
civilian populations has been generally condemned.   (It should perhaps be
explained that, strictly speaking, the use of the word "reparation" implies
actual damages, whereas "indemnity" might possibly include indirect or
punitive compensation; but as applied to the situation at Paris, these words
appear to have about the same meaning).

There seems to be no rule in International Law or practice restricting the
right of a victor or conqueror to exact such indemnity or reparation as he can
after a successful war.   In agreement with the Russian formula of 1917,
"peace without annexations or indemnities on the basis of self-determination
of peoples," President Wilson had declared on Feb. 11, 1918: "There shall be no
annexations, no contributions, no punitive damages,"

Great Britain at first demanded that Germany pay the entire costs of the war.
This demand was opposed by the United States, and it was abandoned.   After
interminable controversies, a compromise between the Allies was finally
attained by which Germany was made to accept responsibility "for all the loss
and damage to which the Allied and Associated Governments and their nationals have been subjected as a consequence of the war imposed upon them
by the aggression of Germany and her allies" Art. 231 of the Treaty of Versailles.   But the allies recognized that the resources of Germany were inadequate for complete reparation and she was only required to make compensation for damages done to civilian populations.   This was unfortunately
made to include pensions and separation allowances, thus about doubling the
amount of reparations.   In Annex I attached to the Reparation Clauses ten
categories of such damages were listed.

The Allies were unable to agree upon a lump sum as advocated by the
American delegation.   They did, however, accept our suggestion of a Reparation Commission which was given extensive powers, but the prestige and reputation for moderation and impartiality of this Commission was seriously impaired by our subsequent withdrawal from European affairs.

According to Art. 233 of the Treaty, Germany was to be notified of the extent of her obligations by the Reparations Commission on or before May 11,
1921, by which date she was to have paid the equivalent of 20,000,000,000 gold

in 1871 in the matter of Alsace-Lorraine . . . should be righted. . . .

" 9. A readjustment of the frontiers of Italy should be effected along clearly recognizable lines of nationality.[9]

marks (Art. 235) or nearly $5,000,000,000. By that date Germany claimed that she had paid more than the equivalent of this amount. The Allies claimed that about $3,000,000,000 was still due. By Sept. 30, 1922, Germany appears to have paid in cash, state property, or deliveries over 25,000,000,000 gold marks or more than $6,000,000,000. See Moulton and McGuire, *Germany's Capacity to Pay* (1923), 74–75.

On May 5, 1921 the Allies presented to Germany an ultimatum requiring the payment of a total of 132,000,000,000 gold marks by the delivery of a, b, and c bonds of which the latter, the c bonds, amounting to 82,000,000,000 marks, were to be without coupons and issued by the Reparation Commission at its discretion. Until the redemption of the bonds Germany was to pay annually 2,000,000,000 gold marks and 26 per cent of the value of her exports. See Hershey, in 15 *A. J.* (1921), 411–18; and * Toynbee, *Survey of Int. Affairs, 1920–23* (1925), 140 ff.

The question of German reparations remained one of the main causes of European chaos and unrest until the adoption of the so-called Dawes plan at the London Conference of 1924 effected at least a temporary solution of the problem. Alpha, in 2 *For. Aff.* (1923–24), 55–83.

On *Reparations*, see especially: * 2 Baker, *Wilson and World Settlement* (1922–23), chs. 42–43; * Baruch, *Reparations* (1920); Bass and Moulton, *America and the Balance Sheet of Europe* (1921), Pt. II; * Dulles, in Baruch, *op. cit.*, 289–97, 323–37, and in *These Eventful Years*, I, ch. 19; Finch, in 16–19 *A. J.* (1922–24), see index; Gooch, *Mod. Germany* (1925), ch. 12; * Keynes, *Econ. Conseq. of the Peace* (1920), ch. 5, and *A Revision of the Treaties* (1922), *passim*; Lamont, in *What really Happened in Paris* (ed. by House and Seymour, 1921), ch. 11, pp. 259 ff.; * Moulton and McGuire, *Germany's Capacity to Pay* (1923); Moulton and Pasvolsky, *World War Debt Settlements* (1926); Nitti, *Peaceless Europe* (Eng. ed., 1922) or *The Wreck of Europe* (Am. ed., 1922), and *The Decadence of Europe* (1923), *passim*; Nogaro, *Reparations* (1922); *Round Table* (1919–25), *passim*; * Tardieu, *The Truth about the Treaty* (1921), chs. 9–10; 2 Temperley, *Hist. of the Peace Conference of Paris* (1920–24), *passim*, (see index); W. P. F. 5 *League of Nations* (1922), Pts. I–III, Nos. 1–3, pp. 5–209; Vanderlip, *What Next in Europe?* (1922), ch. 6; and Young, in 1 *For. Aff.* (1922–23), No. 3, pp. 35–47. A good brief account may be found in Buell, *Int. Relations* (1925), ch. 22.

On the *Dawes Plan*, see: Anon., in 240 *Edin. Rev.* (1924), 261–83; Boyden, in 2 *For. Aff.* (1923–24), 583–97; * Dawes, *The Dawes Plan* (1925); Finch, in 18 *A. J.* (1924), 419 ff. and 707 ff.; Greer, in 219 *No. Am. Rev.* (1924), 769–82; Kuczynski, in 4 *For. Aff.* (1926), 254–63; * Moulton, *The Reparation Plan* (1924); Parmentier, in 3 *For. Aff.* (1924–25), 244–52; 14 *Round Table* (1923–24), 683–95; Toynbee, *Survey, 1924* (1926), 323–99; and W. P. F., 6 and 8 *Pamphlets* (1923 and 1925), Pts. V and VI, Nos. 5, 5–6.

For a good brief account, see Buell, *op. cit.*, ch. 22, op. 513–22. For the text of the *Report*, see Moulton, *op. cit.*, App. A., pp. 149 ff. or Supp. to 19 *A. J.* (1925), 23 ff.

[9] This was in accordance with President Wilson's well-known doctrine of self-determination and the rights of nationalities repeatedly declared in his speeches.

" 10. The peoples of Austria-Hungary . . . should be accorded the freest opportunity of autonomous development.[10]

" 11. Rumania, Serbia, and Montenegro should be evacuated; occupied territories restored; Serbia accorded free and secure access to the sea; and the relations of the several Balkan States to one another determined by friendly counsel along historically established lines of allegiance and nationality; and international guaranties of the political and economic independence and territorial integrity of the several Balkan States should be entered into.[11]

In the case of Italy, both in the Trentino and on the Adriatic, this doctrine collided with economic and political (partly strategic and partly imperialistic) aspirations and the secret Treaty of London (see below, note 19) by which Great Britain and France felt themselves bound, and it was not possible to make a strict application of the principle.   Besides, Italy had made a reservation regarding her rights under the Ninth Point and President Wilson said he "fully realized that Italy was not bound by the Fourteen Points in making peace with Austria" 2 Baker, *op. cit.*, 133.   Nevertheless, he put up a strong open fight against the excessive Italian demands which threatened to disrupt the Paris Conference.

On *Fiume and the Adriatic Question*, see especially; * 2 Baker, *op. cit.*, chs. 31–33; Ferrero, in 120 *Atl. Mo.* (1917), 61–68; Gayda, in 105 (n.s.) *Fortn. Rev.* (1919), 478–91; Haskins and Lord, *Some Problems of the Peace Conference* (1920), 244–61; Johnson, in *What Really Happened at Paris*, (ed. by House and Seymour, 1921), ch. 6, pp. 112–39; Marriott, *The Europ. Commonwealth* (1918), ch. 14; Savic, *So. East. Europe*, (1918), ch. 7; Seton-Watson, *The Balkans, Italy and the Adriatic* (1915); Woodhouse, *Italy and the Jugoslavs* (1920), especially chs. 10–11; and * Toynbee, *Survey, 1924* (1926), 408 ff.

For documents, see 3 Baker, *op. cit.*, 259–307; and 5 Temperley, *op. cit.*, 384–432.

[10] In his Note of Oct. 18, 1918, Austro-Hungary was informed that, because of "certain events of the utmost importance" (referring to our recognition of the belligerency of Czecho-Slovakia and the nationalistic movement of the Jugo-Slavs), President Wilson "is no longer at liberty to accept a mere 'autonomy' of these peoples as a basis of peace, but is obliged to insist that they, and not he, shall be the judges of what action on the part of the Austro-Hungarian Government will satisfy their aspirations and their conception of their rights and destiny as members of the family of nations." 1 Temperley, *op. cit.*, 452–53.

Thus modified, it may be said that, broadly speaking, the Tenth Point was applied on the bases of nationality and self-determination.

[11] Though subject to adverse criticism in detail (particularly in the case of Rumania), it may also be said that, broadly speaking, the Wilsonian principles of nationality and self-determination were applied in the cases of Rumania, Serbia and Montenegro.

Rumania acquired Transylvania and part of the Banat from Hungary, most of Bukovina from Austria, and Bessarabia from Russia (the latter a doubtful disposition to which Russia has never assented).   Serbia was merged in the larger Jugo-Slavia to which Montenegro (at her own request) was joined.

" 12. The Turkish portions of the present Ottoman Empire should be assured a secure sovereignity, but the other nationalities which are now under Turkish rule should be assured an undoubted security of life and an absolutely unmolested opportunity of autonomous development, and the Dardanelles should be permanently opened as free passage to the ships and commerce of all nations under international guarantees.[12]

" 13. An independent Polish State should be erected which should include the territories inhabited by indisputably Polish populations, which should be assured a free and secure access to the sea, and whose political and economic independence and territorial integrity should be guaranteed by international covenant. [13]

" 14. A general association of nations must be formed under specific covenants for the purpose of affording mutual guarantees of political independence and territorial integrity to great and small States alike." [14]

It might be suggested that the international guaranties provided by the Covenant of the League of Nations are perhaps inadequate. They should be supplemented by a Balkan Pact similar to the Locarno Pact of 1925 between France and Germany (see *infra*, pp. 151–54).

[12] The intrigues of some of the Powers at Paris and the procrastination of the Peace Conference in respect to the settlement of the Turkish question constitute a blot upon its record. Consequently, the Turks were able to recuperate their strength and reject the long delayed Treaty of Sèvres (Aug. 20, 1920). However, it could hardly be said that the settlement at Lausanne (in 1923) constituted a rejection of the Wilsonian principles. Cf. *infra*, pp. 140–41.

[13] The Polish settlement has been much criticized, especially the arrangements respecting Danzig and the Polish corridor (see *infra*, p. 138 and note 27), but this was a case where not only was it difficult to determine the proper limits of Polish nationality, but where two Wilsonian principles—those of nationality and "free access to the sea"—were in conflict. The result was a compromise which must be characterized as an honest attempt to apply apparently irreconcilable principles.

On the *Polish Question*, see especially: Askenazy, *Danzig and Poland* (1921); Butler, *The New Eastern Europe* (1919), chs. 4–6; Dennis, *The Foreign Policies of Soviet Russia* (1924), ch. 6; * Lord, in *What Really Happened at Paris* (ed. by House and Seymour, 1921), ch. 4, and in *Some Problems of the Peace Conference* (Haskins and Lord, 1920), ch. 5; Marriott, *The Europ. Commonwealth* (1918), chs. 9–10; Namier, in 81 *Nineteenth Cent.* (1917), 300–06; *Poland's Case for Independence* (London, 1916); Skryzyniski, *Poland and Peace* (1923), chs. 2 and 9–10; * Temperley, *Hist. of the Peace Conference of Paris* (1920–24), 233–83; and * Toynbee, *Survey of Int. Affairs, 1920–23* (1925), 248–73. Cf. *infra*, pp. 172–73 n. and note 43 on p. 142.

[14] On the *League of Nations*, which was the fulfillment of this last Point, see *infra*, ch. 23.

In his Speech of February 11, 1918, President Wilson proclaimed the following Four Principles:

" 1. Each part of the final settlement must be based upon the essential justice of that particular case and upon such adjustments as are most likely to bring a peace that will be permanent.

" 2. Peoples and provinces are not to be bartered about from sovereignty to sovereignty as if they were mere chattels and pawns in a game, even the great game, now forever discredited, of the Balance of Power.

" 3. Every territorial settlement involved in this war must be made in the interest and for the benefit of the populations concerned and not as a part of any mere adjustment or compromise of claims among rival States.

" 4. All well defined natural aspirations shall be accorded the utmost satisfaction that can be accorded them without introducing or perpetuating old elements of discord and antagonism that would be likely in time to break up the peace of Europe, and consequently of the world." [15]

[15] With the exception of the first, these *principles* may be regarded as restatements of the principles of nationalistic and self-determination which are applied to particular countries in the Fourteen Points. It may be noted that the fourth principle considerably limits the applications of the doctrine of self-determination.

The principle of self-determination or consent of the governed had been reiterated over and over again. For example, in his Address to the Senate on Jan. 22, 1917, the President had said: "No peace can last, or ought to last which does not recognize and accept the principle that governments derive all their just powers from the consent of the governed, and that no right anywhere exists to hand peoples about from sovereignty to sovereignty as if they were property." See Scott, *Pres. Wilson's Foreign Policy*, 250. Cf. *Ibid.*, 271 and 368.

On July 4, 1918, President Wilson thus described the Four *Ends* for which the "associated peoples of the world are fighting and which must be conceded them before there can be peace":

"1. The destruction of every arbitrary power anywhere that can separately, secretly, and of its single choice disturb the peace of the world, or, if it cannot be presently destroyed, at the least its reduction to virtual impotence.

"2. The settlement of every question . . . upon the basis of the free acceptance of that settlement by the people immediately concerned. . . .

"3. The consent of all nations to be governed in their conduct towards each other by the same principles of honor and of respect for the common law of civilized society that govern the individual citizens of all modern States, and in their relations with one another to the end that all promises and covenants may be sacredly observed, no private plots or conspiracies hatched, no selfish injuries wrought with impunity, and a mutual trust established upon the handsome foundation of a mutual respect for right.

Aside from reparations,[16] the treatment of Russia, the readjustment of the Italian frontier, the disposition of Shantung,[17] and some other decisions like the refusal of the

"4. The establishment of an organization for peace which shall make it certain that the combined power of free nations will check every invasion of right and serve to make peace and justice the more secure by affording a definite tribunal of opinion to which all must submit and by which every international readjustment that cannot be amicably agreed upon by the peoples directly concerned shall be sanctioned."

These great ends or objects, he declared, can be put into a single sentence: "*What we seek is the reign of law, based upon the consent of the governed and sustained by the organized opinion of mankind.*" 1 Temperley, *op. cit.*, 444.

Finally, on Sept. 27, 1918, our President stated Five *Particulars* which, he said, constituted an authoritative interpretation of this Government's duty with regard to peace:

"1. The impartial justice meted out must involve no discrimination between those to whom we wish to be just and those to whom we do not wish to be just. It must be a justice that plays no favorites and knows no standards but the equal rights of the several peoples concerned.

"2. No special or separate interests of any single nation or any group of nations can be made the basis of any part of the settlement which is not consistent with the common interest of all.

"3. There can be no leagues or alliances or special covenants and understandings within the general and common family of the League of Nations.

"4. And, more specifically, there can be no special selfish economic combinations within the League and no employment of any form of economic boycott or exclusion, except as the power of economic penalty, by exclusion from the markets of the world, may be vested in the League of Nations itself as a means of discipline and control.

"5. All international agreements and treaties of every kind must be made known in their entirety to the rest of the world." . . . 1 Temperley, *op. cit.*, 447.

[16] See above, note 8.

[17] By Art. 156 of the Treaty of Versailles Germany renounced in favor of Japan all "rights, title and privileges—particularly those concerning the territory of Kiao-Chow, railways, mines and submarine cables—which she acquired in virtue of the Treaty concluded by her with China on March 6, 1898, and of all other arrangements relative to the province of Shantung."

Under the conditions existing at the Paris Conference at the time (the Italian crisis, etc.), in view of the secret treaties with Japan, and the fact that China (under duress, to be sure) had signed away her rights, it is difficult to see how President Wilson could have avoided consenting to the transfer of German rights in Shantung to Japan. As a result of the Washington Conference (see *infra*, p. 148), these rights, etc., were substantially restored to China by Japan a few years later.

Among the voluminous literature on the *Shantung Question*, see especially; 2 Baker, *Wilson and World Settlement* (1922–23), chs. 35–36; Bau, *The Foreign Relations of China* (1921), ch. 27; Buell, *The Washington Conference* (1922), ch. 8, pp. 255–63; Elliot, in 13 *A. J.* (1919), 651–737; * Godshall, *The Int. Aspects of the Shantung Question* (1923); Kawakami, *Japan's Pacific Policy* (1922), chs. 28–32; Lansing, *Peace Negotiations* (1921), ch. 18; Reinsch, *An American Diplomat in China* (1922, see index); 6 Temperley, *Hist. of the Peace*

Allies to permit the union of Austria and Germany,[18] it may be justly claimed that the Wilsonian principles were fairly well carried out or at any rate were given a certain recognition and application which compares more than favorably with results achieved at any former World Congress.   And no former World Conference has to its credit any such an achievement as the League of Nations.   Some of the principles were extremely difficult, if not impossible, to apply under given conditions, and at certain points they came into collision with the secret treaties [19] or under-

Conference of Paris (1920–24), 368–90; Toynbee, *Survey of Int. Affairs, 1920– 23* (1925), 456–63; * Willoughby, *China at the Conference* (1922), ch. 23, and *Foreign Rights and Interests in China* (1920), chs. 12–13; and Wood, *The Chino-Japanese Treaties of 1915* (1921), and * *China, Japan and the Shantung Question* (1921).

For documents and treaties, see 3 Baker, *op. cit.*, 311–16; *The Sino-Jap. Negotiations of 1915*; and *Shantung* pamphlets published by the Carnegie Endowment.

[18] This was inspired by fear of a Greater Germany.   In some cases there was a conflict between the principles of self-determination and the demand for military security, as in the case of France on the Rhine and of Italy in the Tyrol.   In other cases the conflict was with secret treaties.   In the case of Danzig and the Polish Corridor, it was a conflict between nationality and the principle of "access to the sea."

[19] The first of these secret arrangements was that of March 20, 1915 between Great Britain and Russia by which Great Britain consented to the annexation of Constantinople and the Straits by Russia in return for a similar benevolent attitude on Russia's part toward British aims elsewhere, *e.g.*, in Persia and Turkey.   But the renunciation by the Russian Revolutionary Government of the desire to make this annexation and the subsequent withdrawal of Russia from the World War freed Great Britain from her obligation in this matter.

The next and most important secret agreement was the Treaty of London (April 26, 1915) by which, as the price for her entry into the War, Italy was promised the Trentino, Southern Tyrol, Trieste, and considerable Slavic territory (including many islands) on the Adriatic coast, as also twelve Greek islands off the coast of Asia Minor, a prospective share in the partition of Asiatic Turkey, etc.   It may be noted that Fiume was not included in these allotments.

There was also an agreement (Aug. 8, 1916) with Rumania by which this country was to receive Transylvania up to the River Theiss, the Bukovina up to the River Pruth, and the Banat.

The most remarkable secret agreement was that of Mar. 11, 1917 between France and Russia, the purpose of which was "to allow France and England complete freedom in drawing up the western frontiers" of Germany in return for "equal freedom in drawing up our (Russian) frontiers with Germany and Austria." "In other words, France was to decide what should be done with all of Germany west of the Rhine, and Russia was to have a free hand with Poland." 1 Baker, *op. cit.*, 56.

On Feb. 16, 1917 Great Britain agreed to the Japanese demands that German rights, etc., in Shantung be transferred to Japan, together with the

standings that had been negotiated during the World War
and which the Allies felt bound to observe.

86d. **The Paris Peace Conference.**—The Paris Peace
Conference first met in plenary session on January 18, 1919.
It met under the worst possible political, economic and
psychological conditions, with a large portion of Europe in a
state of unrest and chaos bordering on anarchy.   Russia
was in the throes of social revolution and the terrible
economic distress in Germany and many parts of Central
and Southeastern Europe furnished fertile fields for the
seeds of Bolshevist and other revolutionary propaganda.
Problems almost infinite in number and often of the greatest
complexity called for a speedy solution.   From the very
outset, the Conference was dominated by the personalities
and energies of three men—Premiers Clemenceau and Lloyd
George, and President Wilson, the representatives of
France, Great Britain and the United States—who, together
with Premier Orlando of Italy, became known as the " Big
Four " and who after two months of mere discussion
assumed a virtual dictatorship.[20]   Finally, after more than
five months of the most strenuous labor, there was signed on
June 28, 1919 the Treaty with Germany in the Hall of
Mirrors at Versailles on the very spot where Bismarck had
proclaimed the German Empire in 1871.[21]

German islands in the Pacific north of the equator, while the German islands
south of the equator were to go to the British.

There were not less than six secret agreements providing for the political or
economic partition of Turkey.   1 Baker, *op. cit.*, 66.

On the *Secret Treaties*, see: * 1 Baker, *op. cit.*, chs. 2–4; Bass, *The Peace
Tangle* (1920), ch. 2; * Cocks, *The Secret Treaties* (1918); Laloy, *Les documents
secrets publiés par les Bolcheviks* (1919); Reinsch, *Secret Diplomacy* (1922),
ch. 8; Seymour, in 1 *These Eventful Years*, ch. 6; and 1 and 6 Temperley, *op.
cit.*, (see index to Vol. 6).   For texts and documents, see Cocks, Laloy, and
Temperley.

[20] For interesting characterizations of the "Big Three" of the Conference,
see Keynes, *Economic Consequences of the Peace* (1920), ch. 3; and Gooch,
Modern Europe (1923), 662–66.

The major decisions were made by the Big Four (really the Big Three), but
the real work of the Conference was done by many technical commissions and
numerous experts.   On the Organization of the Paris Conference, see *infra*,
note on pp. 429–30.

For a Bibliography on the Peace Conference, see end of this chapter.

[21] The treaty was not a negotiated one, so far as Germany was concerned.
Oral discussions were denied her, though Germany was permitted to make
Counter Observations in writing.   She only obtained one really important
concession—the plebiscite in Upper Silesia.

86e. **The Treaty of Versailles.**—By far the most important of the Paris Treaties was the Treaty of Versailles. The most difficult problem confronting the Paris Peace Conference was perhaps that of satisfying the desire of France for security against Germany on her eastern frontier. The militarists headed by Marshall Foch insisted upon the control of the left bank and the bridgeheads of the Rhine. It was only after fierce and prolonged controversy and the ordering of the *S. S. George Washington* to France that these matters were finally adjusted during the latter part of April, 1919.[22]

Alsace-Lorraine was restored to France with the frontiers prior to 1871.[23]

Germany was " forbidden to maintain or construct any fortification either on the left bank of the Rhine or on the right bank to the west of a line drawn fifty kilometers to the East of the Rhine." Within this area the maintenance and assembly of armed forces, military manoeuvres of any kind, as well as the upkeep of all permanent works for mobilization, were also forbidden. In case of any violation of these articles, Germany was to be " regarded as committing a hostile act against the Powers signatory of the present Treaty and as calculated to disturb the peace of the world."[24]

[22] The almost equally difficult question of reparations (see above, note 8) was also settled (so far as it can be said to have been settled) at about the same time.

[23] Arts. 51–79 and Annex of the Treaty of Versailles.

[24] Arts. 42–44 of the Treaty of Versailles. These articles have been incorporated into the Locarno Pact of 1925 between France and Germany. See *infra*, p. 151 and note 70. Cf. Art. 180.

"As a guarantee for the execution of the present Treaty by Germany, the German territory situated to the west of the Rhine, together with the bridgeheads, will be occupied by the Allied and Associated troops for a period of fifteen years from the coming into force of the present Treaty." Art. 428.

Art. 429 makes provision for three successive evacuations at the expiration of three five-year periods. "If at that date [the end of fifteen years] the guarantees against improvoked aggression by Germany are not considered sufficient by the Allied and Associated Governments, the evacuation of the occupying troops may be delayed to the extent regarded as necessary for the purpose of obtaining the required guarantees."

The reference here seems to be to the Treaties of Guarantee or Assistance to France between Great Britain and France and the United States and France, signed on June 28, 1919. For the texts of these Treaties, see 2 Temperley, *op. cit.*, 337–40. They never came into force because the undertaking by Great Britain was contingent upon consent to ratification by the United States

As compensation for the destruction of the coal mines in the north of France and as part payment of reparations, Germany was required to cede to France the coal mines situated in the Saar Basin. The government of this territory was to be entrusted to the League of Nations, acting in the capacity of trustee. " At the end of fifteen years from the coming into force of the present Treaty the inhabitants of the said territory shall be called upon to indicate the sovereignty under which they desire to be placed." [25]

and our Senate failed to give its consent.   Tardieu (*The Truth about the Treaty*, 1921, ch. 6, pp. 210–12) argues that, failing the ratifications of these treaties, the occupation may be prolonged until their coming into force, or equivalent agreements.   "In a word," he says, "no Treaties of Guarantee, no evacuation in 1935."   But it should be noted that the Allied and Associated Governments are the judges as to whether the guarantees against unprovoked aggression by Germany are to be considered sufficient.

Art. 30 declares that "in case either during the occupation or after the expiration of the fifteen years referred to above the Reparation Commission finds that Germany refuses to observe the whole or part of her obligations under the present Treaty with regard to reparation, the whole or part of the areas specified in Article 429 will be re-occupied immediately by the Allied and Associated forces."

On the *Rhine Frontier* and the *Saar Basin*, see especially: * 2 Baker, *Wilson and World Settlement* (1922–23), chs. 25–28; Bisschop, *The Saar Controversy*, in *Grotius Soc. Publication* (1924), No. 2; * Haskins, in *Some Problems of the Peace Conference* (Haskins and Lord, 1920), ch. 4, pp. 117–50, and *What Really Happened at Paris* (ed. by House and Seymour, 1921), ch. 3, pp. 49–66, and in 1 and 3 *For. Aff.*, 46–58, and 199–210; Osborne, *The Saar Question* (1923); * Tardieu, *The Truth about the Treaty* (1921), chs. 5–6, 8; 2 Temperley, *op. cit.*, 176–84; and Toynbee, *Survey of Int. Affairs* (1920–23), 76–85.

For documents, see 3 Baker, *op. cit.*, 227–56; Bisschop, *op. cit.*, Annexes; and * Osborne, *op. cit.*, Appendices.

[25] Arts. 45–49.   In an elaborate Annex to these articles provision is made for the cession and exploitation of the mining property (which is to become the absolute property of the French State), the Government of the territory, and the plebiscite at the end of fifteen years, *i.e.*, in 1935.

The government is to be entrusted to a Commission of five members chosen by the Council of the League of Nations.   The decisions of the Commission are by majority vote.   The inhabitants retain their existing nationality, local assemblies, etc., and are free from military service, but are not permitted to vote for the President of Germany or members of the German Reichstag.   The territory is submitted to the French customs régime.   It should be added that the President of the Governing Commission, who exercises very extensive administrative powers, must be a Frenchman, according to the recommendations adopted by the Council of the League of Nations.

At the coming plebiscite in 1935, the present population will vote by communes or districts on the three following alternatives: (*a*) maintenance of the existing régime; (*b*) union with France; (*c*) union with Germany.   Only those resident in the territory at the date of the signature of the present Treaty

Germany also lost considerable territory, population and mineral resources [26] to Poland (including the greater part of Posen, the Polish Corridor [27] in West Prussia, and nearly one-third of Upper Silesia) and smaller bits of territory to Belgium, Denmark, etc.[28]

Germany was also required to renounce " in favor of the Principal Allied and Associated Powers all her rights and titles over her oversea possessions." [29]

" In order to render possible the initiation of a general limitation of the armaments of all nations," [30] the German army was to be reduced to 100,000 men with 4,000 officers, the Great General Staff was to be dissolved, and it was declared that " universal military service shall be abolished

will have the right to vote.   In case of union with Germany, provision is made for the repurchase of the ownership of the mines by Germany at a price payable in gold.

[26] It is not merely or mainly the loss of population and territory that should be considered.   In Lorraine Germany lost about three-fourths of her iron ore; and her supply of coal was considerably curtailed (nearly one-third) by the at least temporary cession to France of the coal mines of the Saar Basin and the much criticised decision of the Council of the League of Nations in 1921 which awarded to Poland about three-fourths of the coal production of Upper Silesia. On *Upper Silesia*, see Finch, in 16 *A. J.* (1922), 75–80; 1 Kellor, *Security Against War* (1924), ch. 7; and Osborne, *The Upper Silesian Question* (1920). On Germany's losses of coal and iron ore, see Keynes, *Economic Consequences of the Peace* (1920), 81–101.

[27] German East Prussia is thus cut off from the main body of Germany. This is undoubtedly an undesirable arrangement, but it is difficult to see how it could have been avoided.   See Lord, in Haskins and Lord, *Some Problems of the Peace Conference* (1920), 179–80.   For references on the Polish Settlement, see above, note 13.

[28] The Treaties provided for a number of plebiscites.   See Temperley, *op. cit.*, (index in vol. 6).   Cf. *infra*, note 15 on p. 281.

[29] Art. 118.   Not only was "all movable and immovable property in such territories belonging to the German Empire or to any German State" confiscated (Art. 119), but "the Allied and Associated Powers reserve the right to retain and liquidate all property, rights and interests belonging . . .to German nationals, or companies controlled by them, within their territories, colonies, possessions and protectorates, including territories ceded to them by the present Treaty" (Arts. 121 and 297 b).   These provisions also apply to Alsace-Lorraine (Arts. 53 and 74) and in fact to private German property generally outside the German frontiers and within Allied jurisdiction or in particular countries like Russia, China, Turkey, Austria, etc. (Art. 260).

The provisions authorizing the general expropriation without compensation of private enemy property are, from the standpoint of the international jurist, the least defensible sections of the Treaty of Versailles.   See *e.g.*, the comments of Keynes, *op. cit.*, 67–81.

[30] Preamble to Pt. V of the Treaty of Versailles.

in Germany." [31]   The German naval forces were limited to a relatively few vessels,[32] and the armed forces of Germany must not include any military or naval air forces.[33]

Excepting Pt. I containing the Covenant of the League of Nations and the provisions regarding reparations,[34] these are perhaps the main provisions of the Treaty of Versailles. The Treaty was ratified by all the Signatory Powers with the main exceptions of China [35] and the United States.[36]

86f. The Other Treaties of Paris.—On October 17, 1919 the Austrian National Assembly ratified the Treaty of St.

[31] Art. 173.   Germany is also severely restricted in the manufacture, importation and exportation of munitions and war material.   For the Military, Naval and Air Clauses of the Treaty, see Arts. 159–202.

[32] Six battleships, six light cruisers, twelve destroyers, and twelve torpedo boats.   Art. 181.   "The construction or acquisition of any submarine, even for commercial purposes, shall be forbidden in Germany."   Art. 191.   It should be noted that Germany also ceded to the Allies all German merchant ships of 1600 tons gross and upwards, one-half the vessels between 1000 and 1600 tons, and one-quarter of her steam trawlers and other fishing boats.   Furthermore, Germany agreed to build for the Allies such ships as they may specify up to 200,000 tons annually for five years, the value of such vessels being credited to the Reparation Fund.   Thus the German mercantile marine was virtually swept from the seas for many years.   This may have been justified on the theory that the methods by which she conducted her submarine warfare were illegal.   See Annex III (1, 3, and 5) to Pt. VIII on Reparations.

[33] Art. 198.   For the execution of the Military, Naval and Air Clauses of the Treaty, Inter-Allied Commissions of Control were instituted.   Arts. 203–10.

[34] For the provisions regarding reparations which have been only partially carried out and have been seriously modified by the Dawes plan, see Arts. 231 ff.   Cf. above, note 8.

[35] The other exceptions were Ecuador and the Hedjaz.   China refused to ratify because of the transfer of German rights and interests in Shantung to Japan, but her subsequent ratification of the Treaty with Austria admitted her into the League of Nations.

[36] Owing to partisan differences and in part to genuine objections to the Treaty (particularly to the Shantung Settlement and certain obligations incurred by membership in the League of Nations), our Senate on March 19, 1920, refused to consent to ratification by a vote of 49 for and 35 against the treaty, including the Lodge reservations.   The necessary two-thirds were lacking by 7 votes.   For good commentaries, see Finch, in 14 *A. J.* (1920), 155–206; 6 Temperley, *op. cit.*, 391–425; and Thomas, *Monroe Doctrine* (1923), ch. 20.   See also Lodge, *The Senate and the League of Nations* (1925), ch. 10. For the text of the Lodge reservations, see Lodge, *op. cit.*, 199–202.   On "Amendments and Reservations" to the Treaty, see Wright, in 4 *Minn. Law Rev.* (1919–20), 14 ff., and in 20 *Col. Law Rev.*, 121 ff.

In 1921 the United States concluded separate treaties of peace with Germany, Austria and Hungary.   For the text of the Treaty with Germany, which practically granted to us all rights, etc., we would have enjoyed under the Treaty of Versailles, see Supp. to 16 *A. J.* (1922), 10–13.

Germain by which Austria recognized the complete independence of the succession States of Hungary, Czecho-Slovakia, Poland and Jugoslavia, and ceded so much territory and population that she was reduced to a small German state with entirely inadequate resources.[37]

By the Treaty signed at Neuilly on November 27, 1919, Bulgaria lost most of the territory gained in the Balkan Wars of 1912–13 and the World War.[38] She was, however, promised economic outlets in the Aegean,[39] and was left in a somewhat sullen but apparently acquiescent mood.

The Treaty of the Trianon with Hungary was finally signed on June 4, 1920.   She was stripped of the bulk of her non-Magyar subjects and reduced to a small Magyar state.[40]

86g. **The Treaty of Lausanne.**—The above treaties are in large part repetitions of the Treaty of Versailles.[41]   The Treaty of Sevres with Turkey signed on August 10, 1920,

[37] The new republic of Austria was left with an area of about 32,000 square miles and a population of over 6,500,000. She was deprived of seaports; her army was reduced to 30,000; and she was required to pay such indemnities as might be determined by the Reparations Commission. For a summary of the Treaty of St. Germain, see Bowman, *The New World* (1921), ch. 11, pp. 214–15.

Her main grievances were that she lost the southern Tyrol with a considerable German population to Italy, about 3,000,000 Bohemian Germans to Czecho-Slovakia, and that she was not permitted to unite with Germany unless with the unanimous consent of the Council of the League of Nations. This is undoubtedly a serious impairment of sovereignty and a denial of the principle of self-determination. However, such union would have been unpalatable not merely to France, but to Italy, Poland, Rumania, Jugo-Slavia and particularly to Czecho-Slovakia as well.

No attempt was made to collect reparations from Austria. On the contrary her finances were rehabilitated through the aid of the League of Nations.

[38] The Dobrudja was ceded to Rumania; the greater part of Macedonia to Jugo-Slavia; and Western Thrace was assigned to Greece. Bulgaria also promised to pay an indemnity of nearly half a billion dollars and to reduce her army to 20,000 men.

[39] Art. 48 of the Treaty of Neuilly. On "Bulgaria under the Treaty of Neuilly," see Bowman, *The New World* (1921), ch. 16.

[40] The new so-called republic of Hungary was left with an area of 35,800 square miles, a population of nearly 8,000,000 and an army of 35,000 men. Of all the Succession States, Hungary seems to have been the most resentful over her treatment by the Allies. It was mainly against Hungary that the Little Entente was formed. See *infra*, No. 86 i.

[41] Whole sections were copied almost verbatim. They all begin with the Covenant of the League of Nations. For the texts of these treaties, see *Treaties of Peace, 1919–23* (New York, 1924), in 2 vols.; Supp. to 13 and 14 *A. J.* (1919 and 1920), and to 15 *A. J.* (1921), 1 ff.; or 3 and 5 Temperley, *op. cit.*

which would have reduced her outlying possessions in Europe practically to Constantinople, remained unratified. The Treaty of Lausanne, signed on July 24, and ratified by the Turkish National Assembly on August 23, 1923, provided for the retention of Eastern Thrace by Turkey; the recognition of the French and British mandates in Syria, Mesopotamia and Palestine; and the abrogation, with certain exceptions, of the old régime of the Capitulations under which foreigners in the Ottoman Empire had been free from the jurisdiction of the Turkish courts for centuries.[42]

86h. The Supplementary Treaties of Paris.—There were also concluded at Paris a number of supplementary treaties. The most important of these were the Polish and other Minorities Treaties which imposed certain obligations for the protection of the racial, linguistic, or religious minorities

[42] As a result of the World War, the old Ottoman Empire was destroyed and the new Turkey was practically restricted to Eastern Thrace, Constantinople, and the old homeland of Anatolia in Asia Minor. Turkey was relieved of a great number of old servitudes resting upon her, and her former mere *de jure* sovereignty might be said to have been transformed into a *de facto* sovereignty.

A separate Turko-Greek Agreement, concluded at Lausanne on July 24, 1923, provided for the compulsory transfer to Greece of Turkish nationals of the Greek orthodox religion in exchange for the transfer to Turkey of Moslem inhabitants in Greek territory. This was accomplished on a scale unprecedented in modern history.

It should be noted that the Treaty of Lausanne was preceded by the dethronement of the Sultan (Nov., 1922) and followed by the abolition of the Caliphate (March, 1924). On the "Abolition of the Sultanate" and the "Caliphate," see Toynbee and Kirkwood, *Turkey* (1926), chs. 10–11.

On the *Conference and Treaty of Lausanne*, see: Brown, in 17 and 18 *A. J.* (1923–24), 290–96, 113–16; 17 and 19 *Cur. Hist.* (1922–24), 531–35, 743–48, 929–30, and 87–101 respectively; * Hughes, in 18 *A. J.* (1924), 237–43; 13 *Round Table* (1922–23), 342 ff.; Thomas, *Monroe Doctrine* (1923), ch. 22; Toynbee and Kirkwood, *Turkey* (1926) ch. 7; Toynbee, in 2 *For. Aff.* (1923-24), No. 1, pp. 84-99; Turlington, in 18 *A. J.* (1924), 698–706.

On the "New Status" of Turkey, see Toynbee, in 123 *Contemp. Rev.* (1923), 281 ff. On the "Capitulations," see especially Brown, in 1 *For. Aff.* (1922–23), No. 4, pp. 71–81; Thayer, in 17 *A. J.* (1923), 207 ff.; and Toynbee and Kirkwood, *op. cit.*, ch. 9.

For the text of the Treaty of Lausanne, see Supp. to 18 *A. J.* (1924), 1 ff. or 2 *Treaties of Peace, 1919–23*, 959 ff. For the provisions of the Treaty relating to the Straits of Constantinople, see *infra*, note 19, p. 305.

On August 6, 1923 the United States signed two Treaties—one of amity and commerce and another of extradition—with Turkey based on the principles of reciprocity and the most-favored-nation treatment. For a good account of the American Treaties, see article on "The Lausanne Treaty," in 134 *Atl. Mo.* (1924), 693 ff. See also Hughes, in 18 *A. J.* (1924), 239–42. The U. S. Senate has failed to consent to the ratification of these treaties.

upon Poland, Czecho-Slovakia, Jugo-Slavia and Rumania.[43] There was also a convention, signed at St. Germain on September 10, 1919, revising and practically abrogating the

[43] Similar obligations were imposed upon Austria, Hungary, and Bulgaria. It should be added that the principles of the Minorities Treaties were extended to Albania, the Baltic States (particularly to Finland in respect to the Aland Islands), to Upper Silesia, Danzig, Greece, and Turkey (see Arts. 37–45 of the Treaty of Lausanne).

In the Treaty with Poland, which may be regarded as the model or proto-type of the Minorities Treaties, it is declared that "Polish nationals who belong to racial, religious or linguistic minorities shall enjoy the same treatment and security in law and in fact as the other Polish nationals. In particular they shall have an equal right to establish, manage and control at their own expense charitable, religious and social institutions, schools and other educational estab-lishments, with the right to use their own language and to exercise their religion freely therein" (Art. 8).

In towns and districts in which there reside a "considerable portion of Polish nationals of other than Polish speech," the positive duty is enjoined of providing "adequate facilities for ensuring that in the primary schools in-struction shall be given to the children of such Polish nationals through the medium of their own language"; and "minorities shall be assured an equitable share in the enjoyment of the sums which may be provided out of public funds under the State, municipal or other budget, for educational, religious or charitable purposes" (Art. 9).

There are also in the Polish Treaty two special provisions in favor of the Jews. One of them confers on the Jewish communities the right, subject to the general control of the State, to appoint educational committees for the dis-tribution of the proportional share of public funds allocated to Jewish schools; and the other provides against legislative or administrative action which would force the Jews to violate their Sabbath (Arts. 10 and 11).

The observance of these Articles, "so far as they affect persons belonging to racial, religious or linguistic minorities," are placed under the guarantee of the League of Nations. "They shall not be modified without the assent of the majority of the Council of the League."

"Poland agrees that any member of the Council of the League of Nations shall have the right to bring to the attention of the Council any infraction, or any danger of infraction, of any of these obligations, and that the Council may thereupon take such action and give such direction as it may deem proper and effective in the circumstances."

Poland also agrees that any differences of opinion as to questions of law or fact arising out of these Articles shall, if the other party demands, be referred to the Permanent Court of International Justice. "The decision of the Permanent Court shall be final and shall have the same force and effect as an award under Art. 13 of the Covenant" (Art. 12).

For the texts of the Polish and other Minorities Treaties, see Supp. to 13 and 14 A. J. (1919 and 1920), 426 ff. and 311 ff., or 5 Temperley, op. cit., 439 ff. For the important covering letter of Clemenceau, see 13 A. J. (1919), 416 ff. or 5 Temperley, op. cit., 432–37. For an interesting speech by President Wilson on this subject, see 5 Temperley, op. cit., 130–32.

On the *Protection of Minorities*, see: * Buell, *Int. Relations* (1925), ch. 8; Duparc, *La protection des minorités* (1922); * Evans, in *Brit. Yr. Bk.* (1923–24), 95–123; 1 Fauchille, Nos. 258, 409 [9–14]; Fauchille et Sibert, in 32 *R. D. I. P.*

General Berlin Act of 1885 relating to the Congo and the General Act of the Brussels Anti-Slavery Conference of 1890; [44] a convention providing for prohibition in the greater part of Africa of " trade spirits " and distilled beverages containing ingredients injurious to health; [45] a convention for the Regulation of Aerial Navigation; [46] and the St. Germain Convention of 1919 for the Control of the Trade in Arms and Ammunitions over large areas.[47]

86i. **The Little Entente.**—One of the most important political developments of the post-war period was the formation of the Little Entente by Czecho-Slovakia. This is a defensive alliance consisting of a series of treaties with and between Jugo-Slavia and Rumania in 1921. It was originally formed against Hungary and aims at the maintenance of peace and the *status quo* in Central Europe.[48]

(1925), 5–31; Heyking, in 7 and 10 *Grotius Soc.* (1921 and 1924), 119 ff., and 143 ff.; Hofmannsthal, in 31 *I. L. A.* (1922), 155–70; Hudson, in 1 House and Seymour, *What Really Happened at Paris* (1921), ch. 9; Krstitch, *Les minorités, l'etat et la communauté international* (1924); Information Section, League of Nations, *League of Nations and Minorities* (1923); Lucien-Brun, *Le problème des minorités* (1923); Rappard, *Int. Relations Viewed from Geneva* (1925), 40 ff.; * Rosting, in 17 *A. J.* (1923), 641–60; Ruyssen, *Les minorités nationales* (1923), *passim*; * 5 Temperley, *Hist. of the Peace Conference of Paris* (1920–24), ch. 2; Tenekides, in 31 *R. D. I. P.* (1924), 72 ff.; * Toynbee, *Survey of Int. Affairs, 1920–23* (1925), 213–26; Visscher, *The Stabilization of Europe* (1924), ch. 2; and 8 and 9 W. P. F., *Pamphlets* (1925 and 1926), 568–74 and 316 ff.

[44] Cf. *supra*, No. 78 and note 56, and *infra*, No. 216. The St. Germain Convention renews the provisions of the Berlin Act for commercial equality within the Congo basin and for freedom of navigation for merchant vessels on the Congo and the Niger. It also provides for an attempt to secure the complete suppression of slavery and of the slave trade by land and sea. The Convention is to be revised at the end of ten years. For the text of this Convention, see Supp. to 15 *A. J.* (1921), 314–21. For a summary, see 1 Oppenheim, § 564.

[45] For the text of this convention, see Supp. to 15 *A. J.* (1921), 322–28. For a summary, see 1 Oppenheim, § 566.

[46] For its main provisions, see *infra*, No. 221a.

[47] The execution of this treaty has been much hampered by the failure of the United States to consent to ratification and the refusal of our Government to coöperate in the work. See especially Toynbee, *Survey of Int. Affairs, 1920–23* (1925), 390–93. For reasons for the refusal of our Government to become a party to the Treaty of St. Germain, see Hughes, in 18 *A. J.* (1924), 236. For the text of this Convention, see Supp. to 15 *A. J.* (1921), 297 ff. For a summary, see 1 Oppenheim, § 588c. It seems to have been replaced by a new Convention, in 1925.

[48] The Little Entente has also formed close commercial and political relations with Poland, Italy and Austria. Broadly speaking, it may be regarded

86j. **The Continuation Conferences.**—As in the case of the period following the Vienna Congress,[49] a characteristic feature of the period (1920–22) immediately following the Paris Peace Conference was a series of what may be called Continuation Conferences.[50] These Conferences, most of them of an Inter-Allied character,[51] were devoted mainly to vain attempts to solve the problems of reparations [52] and the effective disarmament of Germany, though other matters were also discussed and considered.[53]

as an antidote against what has been termed "The Balkanization of Central and Southeastern Europe." See, *e.g.*, Mowrer, *Balkanized Europe* (1921). On the *Little Entente*, see especially: * Benes, in 1 *For. Aff.* (1922–23), No. 1, pp. 66–72; Huddleson, in 118 *Contemp. Rev.* (1920), 620 ff.; Machray, in 119 N. S. *Fortn. Rev.* (1926), 764–74; Mc Bain and Rogers, *The New Consts. of Europe* (1922), 60–61; Mousset, *La petite entente* (1923, see annexes for the texts of the treaties); Seton-Watson, in 17 *New Europe* (Oct. 14, 1920); 4 Temperley, *op. cit.*, 493, and 519 (for texts in English); Toynbee, *Survey of Int. Affairs, 1920–23* (1925); Pt. III, and Toynbee, *Survey*, etc., *1924* (1926), 440–56; and 6 W. P. F., *Pamphlets* (1923), No. 2, pp. 112 ff.

[49] Cf. *supra*, No. 71 and note 46, p. 86.

[50] For a list of 24 such International Conferences, see Toynbee, *op. cit.*, 7–8. For a summary of the work of each of these Conferences, see * *Ibid.*, 9–34. On *Continuation Conferences*, see also Bardoux, *De Paris à Spa* (1921); *Cur. History* (1920–23), *passim*; Gibbons, *World Politics* (1922), ch. 48; Harris, in 119 *Contemp. Rev.* (1921), 433–41; Kennedy, *Old Diplomacy and New* (1922), Pt. III, ch. 4; and *Round Table* (1920–23), *passim*.

There was also established at Paris in July, 1919, a permanent Conference or Commission of Ambassadors to act as the official representatives of the Principal Allied Powers for the interpretation and execution of the Paris Treaties. This body, which came to consist of the Allied Ambassadors to France, held numerous meetings and displayed great activity in the decision of minor problems. On the Conference of Ambassadors of whose work little is known, see 1 Kellor, *Security Against War* (1924), ch. 4; and Toynbee, *op. cit.*, 1–5.

[51] The Germans were first admitted at Spa in July, 1920 and they also attended several other Conferences. Usually only Great Britain, France (in some cases, merely these two), Italy, Japan and Belgium were represented as a rule by their Premiers.

The most ambitious of these Conferences was that of Genoa (April–May, 1922) which was inspired by Lloyd George and aimed at nothing less than the economic reconstruction of Europe, and particularly at better relations with Russia. There were represented 29 European States and 5 British Dominions. Owing mainly to the attitude of France and Belgium, it proved an almost absolute failure.

On the *Genoa Conference*, see especially: 16 *Cur. Hist.* (1922), 316–27, 479–96; Dillon, in 117 (n.s. 111) *Fortn. Rev.* (1922), 353 ff. and 881 ff.; Harris, in 121 *Contemp. Rev.* (1922), 681–90; Mills, *The Genoa Conference* (1922); 12 *Round Table* (1921–22), 469–92; Simonds, in 65 *Rev. of Rev.* (1922), 371–75, 597–606; * Toynbee, *Survey of Int. Affairs, 1920–23* (1925), 25–34.

[52] On *Reparations*, see above, note 8.

[53] Thus, the Adriatic question was the main problem considered at Paris in

86k. The Washington Conference.—Aside from the work of the League of Nations,[54] the most important of the International Conferences held during the period immediately following the World War was the Conference which was called by the United States,[55] and which met at Washington during November, 1921 to February, 1922 to consider the closely interrelated series of problems connected with " limitation of armament " and " Pacific and Far Eastern questions."

The most tangible result of the Washington Conference, perhaps its greatest concrete achievement, was the Five-Power Naval Treaty which established a naval holiday and a national ratio [56] in shipbuilding, as also a limitation in strength of such capital ships [57] as might thereafter be built

Jan., 1920, as also were war criminals and trade with Russia; the Near East at London and San Remo in Feb. and April of the same year; the Russo-Polish War at Spa and Hythe in July and August, 1920; Upper Silesia at Paris in Aug., 1921; an Anglo-French Pact at Cannes in Jan., 1922; and relations with Russia at Genoa and the Hague in April–May and August, 1922.

[54] On the work of the League, see *infra*, ch. 23.

[55] The Powers originally invited were Great Britain, France, Italy, Japan and China. Invitations were later extended to Belgium, The Netherlands and Portugal. For the invitations, see *Conference on the Limitation of Armaments* (Washington, 1922), 4 ff. For the agenda, personnel and proceedings, see *Ibid.*, 10 ff. Cf. 16 *A. J.* (1922), 159 ff.

[56] The ratio was based on "existing naval strength." It was 5–5–3 between the British Empire, the United States and Japan. It involved the scrapping of 30 ships by the United States, 25 by Great Britain, and 25 by Japan. For tables, see Buell, *The Washington Conference* (1922) 143–44, 153–54, and 161–63.

The United States and Great Britain were allowed 525,000 tons each and Japan, 315,000. In the case of these three Powers, this involved the scrapping of about 40 per cent of their existing strength in capital ships. France and Italy were permitted a tonnage of 175,000 each which was considerably above their ratio on the basis of existing strength.

[57] A capital ship is defined in the Naval Treaty (ch. II, pt. 4) as a "vessel of war, not an aircraft carrier, whose displacement exceeds 10,000 tons . . . or which carries a gun with a calibre exceeding 8 inches."

To be sure, it might be urged that recent developments in aerial and submarine warfare had rendered these great cumbersome battleships practically obsolete, and that in scrapping them the Great Naval Powers were only discarding relatively useless and unnecessarily expensive weapons of warfare. But the saving was a real one, though much more important was the removal of a fundamental cause of war by the cessation of rivalry in the building of great battleships.

Unhappily there was no limitation placed on the number or general tonnage of cruisers or auxiliary vessels, though the particular tonnage of such ships was limited to 10,000 tons and their calibre of guns to eight inches. Owing to the opposition of France, no restriction could be placed on the building of sub-

to 35,000 tons, for nearly fifteen years, i.e. until December 31, 1936. Thus there was removed the immediate possibility of war between the United States and Japan and the remote danger of a struggle between Great Britain and the United States for naval supremacy.[58]

In order to quiet the fears and suspicions of Japan, the United States, the British Empire and Japan also agreed that, with certain exceptions,[59] the *status quo* " with regard to fortifications and naval bases shall be maintained in their

marines; but, due to the insistance of the United States, there was signed a separate Five-Power Treaty dealing with submarines and poison gas, and the rules of International Maritime Law prescribing visit and search in case of capture were reaffirmed and specifically applied to submarine warfare. Cf. *infra*, p. 649 n.

The British delegation proposed the total prohibition of the maintenance, construction, or employment of submarines; but this drastic resolution was opposed not only by France, Italy, and Japan, but by the United States as well.

[58] It may be said that this was a fateful hour in the destiny of nations. In 1916 the United States had embarked on a naval building program which would have given her the supremacy of the seas by 1925. The avowed object of the American program had been the creation of a "navy equal to the most powerful maintained by any other nation in the world." By 1924 our navy would have been equal to that of Great Britain in ships and superior in guns and tonnage. See Table in Buell, *op. cit.*, 143.

It has been well said that in one speech on Nov. 12, 1921, Sec'y Hughes "sunk more ships than all the admirals in history." Perhaps the most significant result of the Conference was the partial renunciation by Great Britain of a naval supremacy which she had held for two centuries and the admission of the United States to equal partnership in great battleships.

[59] The following are the exceptions and more specific provisions:

(1) The United States is not obliged to maintain the *status quo* in the Hawaiian Islands or in any of our insular possessions "adjacent to the United States, Alaska and the Panama Canal Zone." However, the *status quo* applies to the Aleutian Islands as well as to Guam and the Phillipines.

(2) Great Britain agreed to maintain the *status quo* in "Hongkong and the insular possessions which the British Empire now holds or may hereafter acquire in the Pacific Ocean, east of the meridian of 110 degrees east longitude, except (a) those adjacent to the coast of Canada, (b) the Commonwealth of Australia and its territories, and (c) New Zealand." It should be noted that Great Britain is not precluded from enlarging her great naval base at Singapore.

(3) Japan specifically agreed to maintain the *status quo* in the Kurile Islands, the Bonin Islands, Amani-Oshima, the Loochow Islands, Formosa, and the Pescadores, and any insular territories or possessions in the Pacific Ocean which she may hereafter acquire. See Art. 19 of the Five-Power Naval Treaty.

So far as the effect of this important Article upon the future relations of the United States and Japan is concerned, it means that by the withdrawal of our naval frontier from Guam and the Manila Bay to the Hawaiian Islands we cease to appear to be a menace to Japan; but in depriving ourselves of a means of offense, we have lost our power to defend the Philippines, except under the Four-Power Treaty.

respective territories and possessions " in the Pacific Ocean. This provision may be said to have prevented or put an end for the time being to any possible rivalry between Japan and the United States in constructing and maintaining fortifications and naval bases.

In order further to placate Japan, more particularly to obtain her assent to the abrogation of the Anglo-Japanese Alliance,[60] there was negotiated the Four-Power Treaty or Pacific Pact which may be described as a regional agreement by which the British Empire, the United States, Japan and France sought to protect their respective insular possessions in the Pacific Ocean.[61]

[60] This alliance had become very unpopular in the United States and Canada.

On the *Anglo-Japanese Alliance*, see especially: Buell, *The Washington Conference* (1922), ch. 4; Dennis, *The Anglo-Japanese Alliance* (1923); Dickinson, *Int. Anarchy* (1926), 291–96; * Hayashi, *Secret Memoirs* (1915), chs. 1–5; and Wood, *China, the U. S., and the Anglo-Japanese Alliance* (1921).

[61] This agreement, which is to remain in force indefinitely subject to termination at the will of any of the contracting parties upon one year's notice at the end of ten years, carries with it an obligation on the part of the Four Powers not merely to "respect their right in relation to their insular possessions and insular dominions in the region of the Pacific Ocean," but to call a joint Conference to consider and adjust any "controversy arising out of any Pacific question and involving their said rights which is not satisfactorily settled by diplomacy and is likely to affect the harmonious accord now happily subsisting between them" (Art. 1). "If said rights are threatened by the aggressive action of any other Power, the High Contracting Parties shall communicate with one another fully and frankly in order to arrive at an understanding as to the most efficient measures to be taken, jointly or separately, to meet the exigencies of the particular situation" (Art. 2).

It may be noted that the phrases "region of the Pacific" and "any Pacific question" used in the Treaty are somewhat vague. A supplementary treaty excluded the main islands of Japan from the purview of the Four-Power Treaty.

It may likewise be noted that a leaf was taken from Art. 10 of the Covenant of the League of Nations. But the legal obligation created is merely to discuss, whether in conference or by an exchange of notes, the measures to be taken in case of serious controversies or threatened acts of aggression. But it can hardly be claimed that this regional entente (it seems to involve an entente rather than an alliance) is wholly free from "entangling possibilities."

Accompanying the Four-Power Treaty was a Declaration to the effect: (1) that the Treaty shall apply to the Mandated Islands in the Pacific Ocean, with certain reservations on the part of the United States; and (2) that the controversies referred to in Art. 1 "shall not be taken to embrace questions which according to principles of International Law lie exclusively within the domestic jurisdiction of the respective Powers," such as tariffs and immigration. For the text of the Declaration, see Buell, *op. cit.*, 403. See *Ibid.*, ch. 6 for a severe criticism of the Four-Power Treaty. But this author, who has furnished us with the best work on the Washington Conference, displays a strong anti-Japanese bias and is therefore probably unjust to Japan.

Next perhaps in the order of their importance, among the concrete results of the Washington Conference were: the restoration of Shantung, more particularly the lease of Kiaochow and the Shantung Railway to China by a separate treaty between China and Japan; [62] the Nine-Power Treaty relative to the Open Door in China; [63] and a series of Resolutions designed to afford some relief to China.[64]

The U. S. Senate consented to the ratification of the Treaty with the following reservation: "The United States understands that . . . there is no committment to armed force, no alliance, no obligation to join in any defence."

[62] For references on the Shantung Question, see above, note 17.

[63] This treaty defined more clearly and concretely the scope and application of the open door or equal opportunity for trade principle than had been done before, e.g. by Secretary Hay in his famous Circular Note of Sept. 6, 1899, who mainly attempted to prevent preferential charges in respect to customs duties, harbor dues, and railway rates. It may even be claimed that the scope of the Hay doctrine was somewhat extended and to a certain extent made to include what has been called the Hughes-Root doctrine which aims at the abolition of spheres of influence and the prevention of special rights or privileges that would abridge the rights of nationals of other States. A supplementary Resolution even provided for a Board of Reference, but its functions were merely to investigate and report. A Resolution was also adopted providing for the publicity of existing and future commitments of China and with respect to China.

Coördinate with the principle of equal opportunity for trade in China is that of the territorial integrity of China which has usually been included in what has been called the Open Door Policy.

On the *Open Door Policy*, see: * Bau, *The Open Door Doctrine* (1923); * Dennett, *Americans in Eastern Asia* (1922, see index), and in Bau, *op. cit.*, "Introduction"; Hershey, *Russo-Japanese War* (1906), 329 ff. or *Modern Japan* (1919), 364 ff.; * Kawakami, *Japan's Pacific Policy* (1922), chs. 23–26; Latané, *From Isolation to Leadership* (1923), ch. 5; Millard, *Democracy and the Eastern Question* (1919), ch. 11; * Willoughby, *Foreign Rights in China* (1920), ch. 9, and *China at the Conference* (1922), ch. 16; and Yen, *Open Door Policy* (1923). Dennet shows that the Open Door Policy was an old policy based on the most-favored-nation treatment.

On "Treaties and Agreements with and concerning China, 1894–1919," see the monumental collection by MacMurray, in 2 vols. published under the auspices of the Carnegie Endowment in 1921.

[64] Thus, in addition to those named in the above note, there were Resolutions providing for the establishment of a Commission to investigate the Chinese judicial system with a view to the future abolition of extraterritorial rights of foreigners; the future control by China of the foreign post offices and radio stations on her own territory; the unification of Chinese railways, etc. There was also a treaty relating to revision of the Chinese customs tariff for the purpose of raising it to an effective five per cent *ad valorum*.

It can not be said that these resolutions and agrements relating to China (with the possible excepting of the abolition of foreign post offices) constituted solid achievements. Besides, owing to the delay of the French Government in ratifying the agreements relating to China, they do not seem to have become

861. The Struggle for Security through Disarmament and Arbitration culminating in the Locarno Pact (1925).— Largely because of the withdrawal of the United States from European political affairs, the failure of the United States to ratify the Treaty of Versailles and the Guarantee Treaty of 1919 with France,[65] the increasing divergence between French and British policies, and the failure to secure adequate German reparations, etc., France exhibited decided militaristic and imperialistic tendencies for several years after the World War. Among other things, she sought to surround Russia with a *cordon sanitaire* as a barrier against revolutionary ideas, entered into military alliances with Belgium, Poland and Czecho-Slovakia, and finally (in 1923) occupied the rich and highly industrialized region of the Ruhr [66] in German Westphalia to obtain

operative until 1925. Certainly, while the Washington Conference was a notable success in securing the cessation of rivalry in capital shipbuilding between the Great Naval Powers, in securing the abrogation of the Anglo-Japanese Alliance, and in furthering good relations between the Great Pacific Powers (perhaps even to the extent of preventing another world catastrophe), it can hardly be said to have more than scratched the surface in solving the Chinese problems.

On the *Washington Conference*, see: Archimbaud, *La Conférence de Washington* (1923); *Cur. Hist.* (1921–22), 374 ff., 521 ff., 699 ff., and 986 ff.; Buell, *The Washington Conference* (1922); Hershey, in *Indiana University Alumni Quarterly* (1922), 138–45; Kawakami, *Japan's Pacific Policy* (1922), *passim;* Mérignhac, in 29 *R. D. I. P.* (1923), 127–51; Root, in *Men and Policies* (1925), 452–68; 12 *Round Table* (1921–22), 1 ff. and 294 ff.; Simonds, in 64 *Rev. of Rev.* (1921), 599–605; Sullivan, *The Great Adventure at Washington* (1922, journalistic); Taft, *Japan and the Far Eastern Conference* (1922); * Toynbee, *Survey of Int. Affairs* (1920–23), 452 ff.; * Willoughby, *China at the Conference* (1922).

For brief accounts, see Adams, *Foreign Policy of the U. S.* (1924), 418–26; Latané, *From Isolation to Leadership* (1923), ch. 12; and Thomas, *Monroe Doctrine* (1923), ch. 21.

For the texts of the Treaties and Resolutions see Buell, *op. cit.*, 371 ff.; or Supp. to 16 *A. J* (1922), 41 ff. For the *Report* of the American Delegation, see 16 *A. J.* (1922) 159 ff. For the full proceedings of the Conference in both French and English, see *Conference on the Limitation of Armaments* (Washington 1922).

[65] On this Treaty, see above, note 24.

[66] "The Ruhr Basin ... furnished nearly eighty per cent of Germany's coal and coke. In it are located 65 per cent of her ingot steel and rolling mills. The whole region is covered with a network of railroads, and is highly industrialized. . . . It is the heart of Germany's industrial system." Roosevelt, in 4 *For. Aff.* (1925), 113.

Partly as a condition for and partly as a result of the adoption of the Dawes plan (see above, note 8), the French occupation of the Ruhr came to an end in July, 1925.

" productive guarantees " for the payment of German reparations.

In the meantime [67] the League of Nations was engaged in the study and discussion of disarmament.   It was soon seen that the problem of disarmament was inseparably bound up with that of security.   But the first proposal of a Treaty of Mutual Assistance [68] (1923) was rejected by the MacDonald (Labor) Government of Great Britain which emphasized the importance of arbitration as a means of security.   In the summer of 1924 there was elaborated at Geneva the remarkable Protocol [69] for the Pacific Settlement of Inter-

The legality of the occupation has excited considerable controversy.   In favor of the legality of the occupation, see Finch, in 17 *A. J.* (1923), 724–33; and Smith, in 219 *No. Am. Rev.* (1924), 160–77.   As opposed to the legality of the occupation, see: Dreher, in 35 *New Republic* (1923), 9–11; Grimm, in 17 *Cur. Hist.* (1922–23), 916–23; Keynes, in 36 *New Republic* (1923), 9–10; McNair, in *Brit. Yr. Bk.* (1924), 17–37; and Miller, in New York *Evening Post*, Aug. 21, 1923, and in 34 *Yale Law J.* (1924), 46–59; and Schuster, in 18 *A. J.* (1924), 407–18.

On the *French Invasion and Occupation of the Ruhr*, see especially: 17–19 *Cur. Hist.* (1922–24), 711 ff., 901 ff., 12–20 (Art. by Painlevé, 33 ff., 197 ff., 257–61 (Tardieu), 261–65 (Lord Curzon), 1037 ff. (British notes), 61 ff.   (Poincaré's reply); Lichtenberger, *The Ruhr Conflict* (pamphlet publ. by the Carnegie Endowment, 1923, No. 19); * Roosevelt, in 4 *For. Aff.* (1925), 112–22; 13 *Round Table* (1922–23), 237 ff., 494 ff., 712 ff.; Simonds in 67 *Rev. of Rev.* (1923), 151 ff., 258 ff., 371 ff.; and * Toynbee, *Survey*, etc., *1924* (1926), 268 ff.

[67] During the same period (1920–22), the French and British Governments were unable to agree upon a guarantee pact which would secure France and Belgium against another much feared German invasion.

[68] The main objection to this treaty was that it recognized regional treaties and alliances as the principle means of rendering assistance in case of attack. For the text of this treaty, see 7 W. P. F., *Pamphlets* (1924), No. 8, pp. 480 ff.

[69] Cf. *infra*, 471 n.

The main principles of the Protocol were the prohibition or outlawry of aggressive war which was declared an international crime, and the submission of every international dispute that might give rise to armed hostilities to compulsory arbitration (using the term "arbitration" in a very broad sense) or a pacific mode of settlement.

The aggressor was defined as "every State which resorts to war in violation of the undertakings in the Covenant or in the present Protocol," (Art. 10), *i.e.*, as any State that refuses artibration or a pacific settlement of the dispute.

On the *Geneva Protocol*, see: * Baker, *The Geneva Protocol* (1925); Buell, *Int. Relations* (1925), ch. 26; Chamberlain, in 38 (8th ser.) *Liv. Age* (1925), 225–31; Clark, Hudson, Lowell, and Root, in 7 W. P. F., *Pamphlets* (1924), Nos. 7 and 9, pp. 391–400 and 509–27; 21 *Cur. Hist.* (1924–25), 313 ff. and 506 ff.; Dennis, in 221 *No. Am. Rev.* (1925), 665–79; Erich and Wehberg, in 51 (3d ser. 5) *R. D. I.* (1924), 509 ff. and 548 ff.; * Garner, in 19 *A. J.* (1925), 123–32; Hudson, in 3 *For. Aff.* (1924–25), 226–35; Mainsty, in 10 *Grotius Soc.* (1925), 159 ff.; * Miller, *The Geneva Protocol* (1925); Parmoor, in 127 *Contemp. Rev.*

national Disputes.   It was supported by France, now under the control of the Radicals and Socialists, and unanimously adopted by the Assembly of the League, but was rejected by the Conservative Government of Great Britain which had succeeded the Labor Government late in 1924.

Acting upon a German proposal that the Great Powers guarantee the *status quo* on the Rhine,[70] representatives of Great Britain, France, Germany, Italy, Belgium, Czecho-Slovakia and Poland met at Locarno during October, 1925 and negotiated the remarkable complex of treaties forming the Peace of Locarno.

The most important of these treaties—that of the Rhine Security Pact between Germany, Great Britain, France, Italy and Belgium—is thus summarized by one of the leading statesmen of Europe who was a prominent participant in their negotiation:

" 1. Germany, France, Belgium bind themselves to respect, and England and Italy guarantee, the inviolability of the Franco-Belgian-German frontiers.[71]

" 2. Germany, France and Belgium bind themselves mutually not to undertake any invasion and not to have recourse to any warlike step.

" 3. The obligation not to wage war does not apply to cases of necessary defence, the violation of a demilitarized frontier, the fulfilling of the duty of a Member of the League of Nations, and the carrying into effect of Articles 15 and 16

(1925), 1–8 and 145–47; Phillips, in 241 *Edin. Rev.* (1925), 19-37; *Round Table* (Dec., 1924), 52–64; Shotwell, in 53 *Survey* (1924–25), 145–47; Sibert, in 32 *R. D. I. P.* (1925), 207 ff.; Taisne, 32 *R. D. I. P.* (1925), 238 ff.; * Toynbee, *Survey of Int. Affairs, 1924* (1926), 36–64; Williams, *The League, the Protocol, and the Empire* (1925), *passim;* and Wright, Wood, and Garner, in *Prize Essays* (publ. by the Chicago Council on For. Rel., 1925).

For the text of the Protocol and other documents, see Baker, *op. cit.*, or Miller, *op. cit.*, and 7 W. P. F., *Pamphlets* (1924), Nos. 7 to 9.

[70] See Arts. 42 and 43 of the Treaty of Versailles relating to the demilitarization of the right and left banks of the Rhine, which were incorporated into the Locarno Pact.   Cf. *supra*, p. 136.

[71] In express terms all the High Contracting Parties "collectively and severally guarantee" the territorial status and inviolability of this frontier (Art. 1), but the real guarantee is that of the outside Powers—Great Britain and Italy.

"The present treaty shall impose no obligation upon any of the British Dominions, or upon India, unless the Government of such Dominion or of India signifies its acceptance thereof."   Art. 9.

of the League of Nations Covenant (which includes, for France, the case of assistance to Czecho-Slovakia and Poland).[72]

" 4. Germany, France and Belgium, having made a decision not to wage war against one another, bind themselves at the same time by special arbitration treaties to settle all their disputes by peaceful means, or by accepting the verdict of a court of arbitration.

" 5. England and Italy guarantee the observance of these obligations on the part of the participating States.

" 6. All the rights and duties of the participating States arising from the League of Nations Covenant remain unaffected, *i.e.*, all these negotiations are conducted within the compass of the Covenant and are really the carrying out of certain of its principles and articles. These obligations will enter into effect with the entry of Germany into the League of Nations." [73]

Perhaps equal in importance to the Rhine Security Pact were the integral arbitration treaties negotiated at Locarno between Germany and France, Belgium, Poland and Czecho-Slovakia. These treaties are based essentially on the distinction (indicated in Art. 13 of the Covenant) between legal and political differences.[74]

So-called legal disputes, or those in which " the parties are in conflict as to their respective rights," that cannot be settled by the normal methods of diplomacy, shall be-

[72] " In this case military intervention is not bound down to any previous decision of the Council of the League, if it is a question of necessary defence, a flagrant violation of a demilitarized frontier, a flagrant attack, or violence."

[73] Benes, in 4 *For. Aff.* (1926), pp. 205–06. Questions incapable of settlement by diplomacy or unsuitable for judicial decision shall be submitted to a conciliation commission. " If the proposals of the commission are not accepted by the two parties, the question shall be brought before the Council of the League of Nations, which will deal with it in accordance with Art. 15 of the Covenant of the League." Art. 3. The detailed arrangements for effecting a peaceable settlement are made the subject of special arbitration treaties. See below.

In a separate collective note regarding the interpretation of Art. 16 of the Covenant, Germany was assured that this article "must be understood to mean that each State Member of the League is bound to coöperate loyally and effectively in support of the Covenant and in resistance to any act of aggression to an extent which is compatible with its military situation and takes its geographical situation into account."

[74] Cf. *infra*, No. 304, and pp. 512–13.

submitted for decision either to an arbitral tribunal or to the Permanent Court of International Justice. But *before* any resort is made to arbitral or judicial procedure, such dispute *may be submitted* to a Permanent Conciliation Commission.[75] The task of this Commission shall be to elucidate questions in dispute, collect all necessary information, and endeavor to bring the parties to an agreement. At the close of its labors [76] it shall draw up a report.

" In the event of no amicable agreement being reached before the Permanent Conciliation Commission, the dispute shall be submitted by means of a special agreement either to the Permanent Court of International Justice . . . or to an arbitral tribunal. . . ." [77] All questions, meaning primarily so-called political controversies or conflicts of interest, which cannot be settled by diplomacy, arbitral methods, or judicial decision *shall be submitted* to the Permanent Conciliation Commission, " whose duty it shall be to propose to the parties an acceptable solution and in any case to present a report." If no agreement has been reached within a month after the labors of this Commission, " the question shall, at the request of either party, be brought before the Council of the League of Nations, which shall deal with it in accordance with Art. 15 of the Covenant of the League." [78]

[75] This Commission shall consist of five members appointed as follows: "The High Contracting Parties shall each nominate a commissioner chosen from among their respective nationals and shall appoint, by common agreement, the three other commissioners from among the nationals of third Powers; these three commissioners must be of different nationalities and the High Contracting Parties shall appoint the President of the Commission from among them. The commissioners are appointed for three years and their mandate is renewable." Art. 4 of the Arbitration Treaty between Germany and Poland.

[76] These labors are not public except with the consent of the parties. *Ibid.*, Art. 11. The parties shall be represented before the Commission by agents, "whose duty it shall be to act as intermediary between them (the parties) and the Commission." Counsel and experts may also be appointed. Art. 12.

"Unless otherwise provided in the present treaty, the decisions of the Permanent Conciliation Commission shall be taken by a majority." Art. 13.

[77] Art. 16 of the Treaty cited above which adds: "If the parties cannot agree on the terms of the special agreement after a month's notice, one or other of them may bring the dispute before the Permanent Court of International Justice by an application."

[78] *Ibid.*, Arts. 17 and 18. Except for names and with the omission of Art. 21 in the conventions between Germany and France and Germany and

There were, in addition, negotiated at Locarno two security or mutual guarantee pacts between France on the one hand and Czecho-Slovakia and Poland on the other [79] which were so formulated as to constitute a complement to the Rhine Pact and the arbitration treaties.

These Locarno Treaties, which have been well called the Peace of Locarno, were signed at London on December 1, 1925. But their going into effect was conditioned upon the entry of Germany into the League of Nations. Owing to the intrigues of certain Powers for seats on the Council, this was delayed until early in September, 1926 when Germany finally entered. Consequently, the Locarno Treaties did not actually come into force until their ratification on September 14 of that year. This date is important because it seems to mark the real end of the World War and, together with the strengthening of the League of Nations by the admission of Germany, points toward the beginning of a new pacific era in the history of Europe and of international relations. [80]

Belgium, all the Locarno Arbitration Treaties are practically identical. Art. 21 provides that the present treaty "shall not in any way affect the rights of and obligations of the High Contracting Parties as Members of the League of Nations and shall not be interpreted as restricting the duty of the League to take whatever action may be deemed wise and effectual to safeguard the peace of the world."

[79] "In the event of Poland (or Czecho-Slovakia) or France suffering from a failure to observe the undertakings . . . between them and Germany . . . , France and reciprocally Poland (or Czecho-Slovakia), acting in application of Art. 16 of the Covenant of the League of Nations, undertake to lend each other immediately aid and assistance, if such a failure is accompanied by an unprovoked recourse to arms.

"In the event of the Council of the League of Nations, when dealing with a question brought before it in accordance with the said undertakings, being unable to succeed in making its report accepted by all its Members other than the representatives of the parties to the dispute, and in the event of Poland (or Czecho-Slovakia) or France being attacked without provocation, France, or reciprocally Poland (or Czecho-Slovakia), acting in application of Art. 15, parag. 7, of the Covenant of the League of Nations, will immediately lend aid and assistance." Art. 1 of the French Treaties of Security with Poland and Czecho-Slovakia.

[80] On the *Peace of Locarno*, see particularly: * Benes, in 4 *For. Aff.* (1926), 195–210; Bisschop, in 11 *Grotius Soc.* (1926), 79–115; 23 *Cur. Hist.* (Dec. 1925), 316 ff.; Glasgow, *From Dawes to Locarno* (1925); Hyde and Fenwick, in 20 *A. J.* (1926), 103–11; * MacDonald, in *For. Policy Assoc.*, *Pamphlet* No. 35 (1925–26), summary on pp. 10 ff.; *Round Table* (Dec., 1925), No. 61; Seymour, in 15 *Yale Rev.* (1926), 209–25; Simonds, in 72 *Rev. of Rev.* (1925), 517 ff.; Strupp, *Das Werk von Locarno* (1926); and * 9 W. P. F., *Pamphlets* (1926), No. 1, pp. 1–75.

BIBLIOGRAPHY

Paris Peace Conference.—* Baker, *Woodrow Wilson and World Settlement,* in 3 vols. (1922–23), and *What Wilson Did at Paris* (1920); Dillon, *Inside Story of the Peace Conference* (1920); * Gooch, *History of Modern Europe* (1923), ch. 19 (best brief account); Harris, *The Peace in the Making* (1920); Haskins and Lord, *Some Problems of the Peace Conference* (1920); House and Seymour, *What Really Happened at Paris* (1921); Huddleston, *Peace-Making at Paris* (1920); Lansing, *The Peace Negotiations* (1921), and *The Big Four and Others at the Peace Conference* (1921); * Tardieu, *The Truth About the Treaty* (1921), ch. 3; Temperley, *A History of the Peace Conference of Paris,* in 6 vols. (1920–24, see index to 6th vol.); Thompson, *The Peace Conference Day by Day* (1920).

Treaties of Paris, particularly of **Versailles.**—Bainville, *Les conséquences politiques de la paix* (1920); Barthou, *Le traité de paix* (1919); Bougeois, *Le traité de paix de Versailles* (1919); Finch, "The Treaty of Peace with Germany in the U. S. Senate," in 14 *A. J.* (1920), 155–206; Hanotaux, *Le traité de Versailles* (1919); Lodge, *The Senate and the League of Nations* (1925, for the Lodge Reservations); Pillet, *Le traité de paix de Versailles* (1920); Scelle, *La morale des traités de paix* (1920); Scott, *Introduction to the Peace Treaties* (1920); Stegemann, *Das Triegbild von Versailles* (1926); * Tardieu, *The Truth About the Treaty* (1921); * Temperley, *History of the Peace Conference,* in 6 vols. (1920–24, see index to 6th vol.); *Treaty of Peace with Germany; Hearings* before the U. S. Senate Committee on For. Rel., 66th Cong., 1st sess., 1919; *Treaties of Peace,* in 2 vols. (New York, 1924, texts).

Period After the World War, 1919–25.—* Baruch, *Reparations* (1920); Bass, *The Peace Tangle* (1920); Bass and Moulton, *America and the Balance Sheet of Europe* (1921); Bowman, *The New World* (1921); * Buell, *International Relations* (1925); *Cur. Hist.,* 1919–1926, *passim;* Dawes, *The Dawes Plan* (1925); Dennis, *The Foreign Policies of Soviet Russia* (1924); Fabre-Luce, *La crisis des alliances* (1922); Fisk, *The Inter-Ally Debts* (1924); Gibbons, *Europe since 1918* (1923); * Keynes, *Economic Consequences of the Peace* (1920), and *A Revision of the Treaty* (1922); McBain and Rogers, *The New Consts. of Europe* (1920); Moulton and McGuire, *Germany's Capacity to Pay* (1923), and *The Reparation Plan* (1924); Mowat, *A Diplomatic History of Europe, 1914–25* (1927); Nitti, *Peaceless Europe* (Eng. ed., 1922), or *The Wreck of Europe* (Am. ed., 1922), *The Decadence of Europe* (1923), and *They Make a Desert* (1924); Quigly, *From Versailles to Locarno* (1927); *Round Table,* 1919–1926, *passim;* Simonds, *How Europe Made Peace* (1927); Toynbee, *The World After the Peace Conference* (1925), and * *Survey of Int. Affairs* (1920–23), and (1924); and Visscher, *The Stabilization of Europe* (1924).

Toynbee's admirable *Surveys* are to be published annually.

For texts of the treaties, see 23 *Cur. Hist.* (1925), 323–27; and Supp. to 20 *A. J.* (1926), 21 ff.; or 9 W. P. F., *op. cit.,* 54 ff.

PART I

STATES—THE SUBJECTS OF INTERNATIONAL LAW

CHAPTER VI

STATES AS INTERNATIONAL PERSONS AND MEMBERS OF THE INTERNATIONAL COMMUNITY

87. States the Main Subjects of International Law.—The International Persons or Subjects of International Law are mainly States [1]—the only entities which can become real members of the international community. Strictly speaking, in international relations States alone have legal rights and duties. Though the Law of Nations, in certain cases, regulates relations between States and individuals as well as between the States themselves and thus appears to deal directly with individuals (as in the case of pirates and blockade runners), the laws themselves are rules between States, and it is only as members of a recognized political community that individuals can really be said to possess international rights and obligations. [2]

[1] The main exception to this rule is the League of Nations which is an International Person *sui "generis."* I Oppenheim (3d ed.), p. 125. The other exceptions are insurgent communities whose belligerency has been recognized. These enjoy a certain legal status as International Persons for purposes of warfare. They may be regarded as inchoate or embryonic States. See *infra*, No. 115. The Papacy is an apparent rather than a real exception. See *infra*, No. 89.

[2] Some publicists (as *e.g.* Heffter, §§ 14, 58; Kaufman, *Die Rechtskraft des international Rechts*, 1899, §§ 1–4; Westlake, *Chapters*, 1894, p. 2; and Wheaton, § 19) claim that individuals also are subjects of International Law; but this view is obviously based upon a confusion of terms. Persons and things are *objects*, not *subjects* of the Law of Nations. Westlake (*Chapters*, p. 2) asserts that "it would be pedantic to deny that the pirate and the blockade runner are subjects of International Law," but he admits that "it is only by virtue of rules prevailing between States that they are so." Rehm (*Untertanen als Subjekte völkerrechtliche Pflichten*, in I Z. V. 53–55) thinks that individuals partake of the nature of subjects of the international community as far as international duties are concerned. He raises the very interesting question

157

88. The Essential Characteristics of a State.[3]—A State is a permanent association of people politically organized upon a definite territory and habitually obeying the same autonomous government.   Its essential and distinguishing characteristics are: (1) A people permanently organized for

whether such International Commissions as that of the Danube do not create international rights and obligations for individuals? We might also ask whether International Unions do not partake of the nature of International Persons and create international legislation directly binding upon individuals as well as upon States?   This is particularly the case with such International Public Unions as the former International Sugar Commission and the European Danube River Commission which virtually legislate as well as administer by majority vote.   Sayre, *Int. Administration* (1918), 121 ff. and 38 ff.   However, at the present imperfect stage in the development of the organization and functions of these bodies, it is probably safer to deny them the character of international personality and to maintain that they only create law binding upon States.

Several of the authorities (Bluntschli, Arts. 23, 360–63, 370; Bonfils or 1 Fauchille, Nos. 154, 157, 397 ff.; 1 Fiore, Nos. 680 ff.; Heffter, § 58; and 1 F. de Martens, §§ 85–87) maintain that man is a subject of International Law by reason of his existence as a human being; and that as such he possesses certain primordial, inherent, fundamental rights which are guaranteed by the Law of Nations.   Such are, *e.g.* the rights of existence, liberty, protection of life and property, emigration and expatriation, freedom of worship, etc.   These so-called rights of mankind are undoubtedly supported by a powerful public opinion; but, with the exception of the rights of protection against the depredations of pirates and slave traders, they cannot be said to be guaranteed by the positive Law of Nations.   Still less do they confer international personality upon individuals who must ordinarily look to the respective governments to which they owe allegiance for the effective protection of their international rights and interests.

For the correct view, see especially: Fenwick, 85; Heilborn, *System des Völkerrechts* (1896), 58–138; Holland, *Jurisprudence* (10th ed.), 126, 355, 384 ff.; Jellinek, *Oeffentlichen Rechte* (1892), 310–14; Liszt, § 7; 2 Lorimer, (*Institutes of Law* 1880), 131; * 1 Oppenheim, §§ 13, 288–93, 344; 1 Rivier, 48; Stoerk, in 2 Holtzendorff, §§ 113–14; Triepel, *Völkerrechts und Landesrecht* (1899), 13–21; Ulmann, §§ 19, 107; and Zorn, *Völkerrechts* (1903), §6.

Arts. 3–5 of the Convention relative to the Establishment of an International Prize Court adopted by the Second Hague Peace Conference (1907) provided for appeal in certain cases by individuals as well as States. Such right of appeal to an International Court might doubtless be considered an exception to the rule that States are the sole subjects of international law.   On the other hand, it may be argued that even in these cases individuals enjoy this right of appeal only as nationals of some particular State.

[3] For various definitions of the State, see * 1 Fauchille, Nos. 160–63; 1 Calvo, § 39; * Evans, *Cases*, 33–59; * Garner, *Introd. to Political Science* (1910), 39 ff.; Heffter, § 15; Holland, *Jurisprudence* (10th ed.), 45 ff.; 1 Hyde, § 7; Jellinek, *Das Recht des modernen Staates* (2d ed., 1905), 173; Liszt, § 7 II; * 1 Moore, *Digest*, § 3; 1 Oppenheim, § 64; Pomeroy, §§ 49 ff.; * 1 P.-Fodéré, Nos. 69–81; Lawrence, 48; 1 Rivier, 45–48; * Scott, *Cases*, 19–57, particularly on pp. 35 and 39 *n.*

political purposes, *i.e.* the maintenance of law, liberty, and a relative equality of opportunity as conditions necessary for individual and social wellbeing.   (2) A definite territory containing inhabitants sufficiently civilized and numerous [4] and resources sufficient to insure a certain degree of permanence, stability and independence.   (3) A certain degree of sovereignty or autonomy and independence (*i.e.* relative freedom from a higher or an external control), and a government which is habitually obeyed.

89. **Associations or Institutions which do not enjoy International Personality.**—Among associations or institutions which do not enjoy international personality may be mentioned:

(1) Member-States of a Federal Union like that of the United States.

(2) Savages, nomads, pirates, and certain barbarous tribes and societies or States which have not as yet attained a sufficient degree of civilization or form of political organization adapted to the needs of international intercourse.

(3) Mere racial, social, political, and religious groups or institutions, such as nationalities,[5] social classes, political parties, and churches.[6]   These may and often do exercise an

---

[4] No rule can be laid down as to the number of inhabitants or amount of territory necessary to the existence or recognition of a State.   Sovereignty and international personality are enjoyed by States as small as Monaco with a territory of 8 square miles and 22,956 inhabitants, and as vast as the British Empire.   It has been reported that Liechtenstein was refused admission to the League of Nations because of its small size.   This tiny principality has an area of 65 square miles and had a population of 10,716 in 1912.

[5] The main champions of the theory that nationalities are real, or at least desirable, subjects of International Law are Italian publicists.   This theory is based upon the view that nations are the natural units of international relations, and have an inherent right to form themselves into States.   Even admitting this to be the case, the legal status of such units would depend upon their recognition as members of the International Community.

Upon the principle of nationality, see especially De Roquette-Buisson, *Du principe des nationalitiés* (1895).   For good criticisms of this theory, see 1 Fauchille, No. 22; 1 Nys, 337–48; 1 P.-Fodéré, Nos. 48–68; and 1 Mérignhac, 330 ff.

For references, see the notes in 1 Fauchille, p. 13; 1 Fiore, 244; 1 Rivier, 49; and the Bibliography in De Roquette-Buisson, *op. cit.*

[6] Fiore (*Int. Law Cod.*, 1918, Arts. 12, 70–71, 705 and n.), places the Roman Catholic Church in the category of international persons.   The only adherents to this view we have found are Chrétien, *Principes de droit int. public* (1893), No. 77; and Pillet, note in Sirey, *Rec. pér* (1895), II, 57 (cited from 1 Fauchille, No. 155).

important influence upon international relations, but they do not have even *de facto* international personality.

(4) Commercial corporations and Chartered Companies [7] like the old British East India or present-day African Companies. These companies sometimes exercise enormous political powers, even to the extent of making treaties and waging war; but their powers, however great, are merely delegated ones. In the case of Great Britain at least, the charters are mere grants of the British Crown which may be revoked at any time for sufficient cause. Besides, they are at the mercy of the sovereign Imperial Parliament which did not hesitate to abolish the old East India Company altogether in 1858. Yet it cannot be denied that some of these Companies do enjoy a sort of *de facto* international personality, though they have no legal status in international law.

(5) The same may in general be said of colonies or provinces. In the case, however, of four self-governing Dominions of the British Empire, viz., Canada, Australia, South Africa, and New Zealand, it must be said that they enjoy a considerable degree of *de jure* as well as *de facto* international personality.[8] This is also true of the Irish Free State [9] and India.[10]

---

[7] In his earlier editions, Lawrence (*Principles*, 3d ed., § 54) claims that such privileged corporations are subjects of International Law in a double sense: (*a*) as are individuals and ordinary corporations; (*b*) as occupying a special international position. Lawrence does not appear to have succeeded in making converts to this opinion, and has somewhat modified his views in his later editions, §§ 34, 42.

[8] For some years prior to 1919 when they signed the Treaties of Paris separately and became members of the League of Nations, the Dominions may be said to have enjoyed a varying degree of *de facto* international personality. Thus, generally speaking, they framed their own tariffs, negotiated their own commercial treaties (*e.g.* the famous Reciprocity Agreement of 1911 between Canada and the United States), and were consulted on political matters or questions of general policy in which they were supposed to be specially interested. The Imperial Government retained control over foreign relations of a purely political nature; but, in the case of commercial agreements, the Dominions had acquired a practical autonomy. They were also given separate representatives in certain International Administrative Unions like the Universal Postal Union.

In general, prior to the World War, there may be discerned in the British Commonwealth of Nations "a steady development in two directions: (*a*) towards increased coöperation and interdependence; (*b*) towards greater independence, that is, the acquisition by the Dominions of a status of complete

At the Paris Peace Conference of 1919, as a result of their activities and sacrifices during the World War,[11] four of the Dominions and India were accorded representatives as members of the British Empire delegation in the Council of twenty-five composed of five delegates from each of the five Great Powers,[12] as also in the Plenary Conferences both as

equality with the United Kingdom." Hall, *The British Commonwealth of Nations* (1920), 140–41. The status of Canada in the Empire was thus expressed by Kipling in "Our Lady of the Snows":

> "Daughter am I in my mother's house;
> But mistress in my own."

[9] In the Articles of Agreement for a Treaty between Great Britain and Ireland ratified January 8, 1922, it was declared:

"Ireland shall have the same constitutional status in the Community of Nations known as the British Empire as the Dominion of Canada, the Commonwealth of Australia, the Dominion of New Zealand, and the Union of South Africa, . . . (Art. 1).

"Subject to the provisions hereinafter set out, the position of the Irish Free State in relation to the Imperial Parliament and Government and otherwise shall be that of the Dominion of Canada, . . . (Art. 2).

"The oath to be taken by members of the Parliament of the Irish Free State shall be in the following terms:

I . . . do solemnly swear true faith and allegiance to the Constitution of the Irish Free State as by law established and that I will be faithful to His Majesty King George V, his heirs and successors, in virtue of the common citizenship of Ireland with Great Britain and her adherence to and membership of the group of nations forming the British Commonwealth of Nations" (Art. 4). Borden, in 12 *Yale Review* (1922–23), 784.

Art. 1 of the Constitution declared: "The Irish Free State is a co-equal member of the Community of Nations forming the British Commonwealth of Nations." She is a member of the League of Nations and maintains a Minister at Washington.

For the texts of the Constitution and the Articles of Agreement with Great Britain, see Figgis, *The Irish Constitution* (1922), 64 ff., and 96 ff. On "The Significance of the Irish Free State" see Kennedy, 218 *No. Am. Rev.* (1923), 316 ff.

[10] India, while not enjoying dominion status, has also been accorded a degree of *de jure* international personality. This "important portion" of the British Empire is a member of the League of Nations and was permitted to sign the Treaties of Paris separately.

[11] In its famous Constitutional Resolution, the Imperial War Conference of 1917 declared itself in favor of "a full recognition of the Dominions as autonomous nations of an Imperial Commonwealth, and of India as an important portion of the same," as also of recognizing "the right of the Dominions and India to an adequate voice in the foreign policy and in foreign relations, . . . Hall, *op. cit.*, 177. Hall describes the ideal as that of "an intimate society of equal and autonomous states, conducting their common affairs by continuous consultation followed by concerted action."

[12] This Council never actually met and it was of course impossible to secure direct or separate Dominion representation on the Council of Ten or among the

small nations and as forming part of the British Empire Delegation.   The Treaty of Versailles with Germany was signed separately June 28, 1919 by the representatives for India and of four of the British Dominions [13] as well as by plenipotentiaries representing the British Empire as a whole. " They were all equally plenipotentiaries of His Majesty the King, who was the ' High Contracting Party ' for the whole Empire." [14]   The four Dominions and India were also admitted as original members of the League of Nations. They are directly represented in the Assembly of the League, and " there is no legal obstacle to one or more of the Dominions being elected to the Council of the League as the representatives of the Assembly." [15]   The Dominions are also members of the International Labor Organization and various other International Public or Administrative Unions.

In the Report of the Inter-Imperial Relations Committee of the Imperial Conference, dated November 20, 1926, the Dominions and Great Britain are defined as " autonomous communities within the British Empire, *equal in status*, in no way subordinate one to another in any aspect of their domestic or external affairs, though united by common allegiance to the Crown and freely associated as members of the British Commonwealth of Nations." [16]

Big Four or the Big Three who ultimately became the dictators at Paris. However, several of the Dominion representatives, like General Smuts of South Africa, Premier Hughes of Australia, and Premier Borden of Canada, played exceedingly important rôles, more particularly in connection with the disposition of the German colonies and the establishment of the mandatory system.

[13] Viz., Canada, Australia, South Africa, and New Zealand.   Newfoundland is apparently a self-governing Dominion without international status or personality.

[14] Lord Milner, quoted by Hall, *op. cit.*, 193.   Lord Milner adds: "The United Kingdom and the Dominions are partner nations; not yet indeed of equal power, but for good and all of equal status. . . ."   He apparently forgets to mention India.

A similar procedure was followed in ratification, *e.g.*, the Treaty was approved by a resolution passed by the Canadian Parliament, and an Order in Council was at once cabled to the Colonial Secretary advising the Crown to ratify in behalf of Canada.

[15] Lewis, in *Brit. Yr. Bk.* (1922–23), 33.   Three of the Dominions were appointed Mandatory States over certain former German colonies.   See *infra*, p. 188 n.   "It is significant that these mandates were received by the Dominions direct from the Secretariat of the League of Nations, and correspondence thereon is not being conducted through the imperial Government."   *Ibid.*

[16] The phrase "United Kingdom" was omitted from the title of the King.

Provision was made for the independent negotiation of treaties by each of the Dominions through plenipotentiaries selected by them, but with full powers granted by the king.[17] Each Dominion appears to be bound only by treaties to which it has definitely assented, either expressly or tacitly; [18]

For the text of this very important constitutional and international document, see *N. Y. Times*, Nov. 21, 1926, sect. I, p. 28; *Cur. Hist.*, Jan., 1927, pp. 564–69; or *N. Y. Nation*, Dec. 8 and 15, 1926, pp. 590 ff. and 648 ff. For the text of the resolution respecting the treaty-making power adopted by the Imperial Conference of 1923, see *Round Table* for March, 1924, pp. 227–28.

[17] It appears that in one instance at least, a treaty with the United States—the one designed to protect the halibut fishery of the North Pacific Ocean—was signed (on May 2, 1923) by Canada alone without submitting it to the approval of any British authority. It was a moot point whether the Canadian minister who signed the treaty acted as the representative of the Canadian Government or as a plenipotentiary of the British King who appears to have cabled full powers at the last moment. Marriot, in 113 (n.s.) *Fortn. Rev.* (1923), 788 ff.

[18] Though the Imperial Conference declared its approval of the methods by which Great Britain had become a party to the Treaty of Locarno, it did not favor ratification by the Dominions. The projected Anglo-French Treaty of 1919 provided that it "shall impose no obligation on any of the Dominions of the British Empire unless and until it is approved by the parliaments of the Dominion concerned."

At the Washington Conference of 1922 for the limitation of armaments. the Dominions were not included in the invitations sent out by the United States Government; but their representative was included in the British Empire delegation as at Paris in 1919.

In May, 1920, it was agreed between the British and Canadian Governments that the British Crown might appoint, on the advice of the Canadian Cabinet, a Canadian Minister Plenipotentiary at Washington to have charge of Canadian affairs. But the appointment of a Canadian Minister was delayed until November, 1926.

The propriety of Dominion diplomatic representation in foreign capitals was recognized by the Imperial Conference of 1926.

On *Dominion Status*, see: Allin, in 17 *Am. Pol. Sci. Rev.* (1923), 612–22; Borden, *Canad. Const. Studies* (1922), 72 ff., 114 ff., and * in 12 *Yale Rev.* (1922–23), 774–89; Buell, *Int. Relations* (1925), ch. 9, pp. 194–205; Curtis, *The Problem of the Commonwealth* (1916), *passim*; Dennis, in 16 *Am. Pol. Sci. Rev.* (1922), 584 ff.; Ewart, in 7 *A. J.* (1913), 268 ff., and in * 216 *No. Am. Rev.* (1922), 773 (reply to Kennedy); * Hall, *The British Commonwealth* (1920), particularly chs. 9 and 11; Keith, *Imperial Unity*, (1916), 510 ff., *War Gov't. in the Dominions* (1921), *passim*, particularly ch. 7; and * *Dominion Home Rule* (1921), ch. 4 (good brief account); * Kennedy, *The Canadian Constitution* (1922), chs. 21 and 25, "Canada's National Status," in 216 *No. Am. Rev.* (1922), 299–311, "The British Dominions," in 6 Temperley, *Hist. of the Peace Conference* (1920–24), 335 ff., and in 123 *Contemp. Rev.* (1923), 737 ff.; * Lewis, in *Brit. Yr. Bk.* (1922–23), 21–41, and *Ibid.*, (1925), 31 ff.; Lowell, "Treaty Making Power in Canada," in 2 *For. Aff.* (1923), 12–23; MacKenzie, "Treaty Making Power in Canada," 19 *A. J.* (1925), 489 ff.; Marriot, in 113 (n. s.), *Fort. Rev.* (1923), 788 ff.; Nathan, in 8 *Grot. Soc.* (1923), 117 ff.; Pollard, in 6

but it is recognized that the major share of responsibility for the general conduct of foreign affairs still rests upon Great Britain.

Though it might seem to an onlooker that the British Confederacy was in process of dissolution, the formal unity of the British Empire is, however, recognized by common allegiance to one Sovereign and devotion to one flag, as its essential unity is preserved by a sense of common interests and a spirit of coöperation that makes it a sort of model for the international community as a whole. Indeed, the British Empire has been officially described as a " free association of free and equal nations."

(6) The Papacy or the Pope,[19] who ceased to be a real

Temperley, *Hist. of the Peace Conference* (1920–24), 84–98; Rolin, in 50 (3d ser. 4), *R. D. I.* (1923), *Round Table*, since 1915, *passim.* particularly Sept., 1916, Dec., 1920 and March and Sept. 1924; Stevanson, in 3 *For. Aff.* (1924), 135 ff.

For detailed accounts covering the period prior to 1914, see Hall, *op. cit.*, chs. 5–6; 3 Keith, *Responsible Gov't. in the Dominions* (1912), 1101–51; and Porrit, *Fiscal and Diplomatic Freedom of the British Overseas Dominion* (1922), 161–212.

[19] The international status of the Pope is regulated by the Italian Law of Guarantees of 1871. For the English text of this law, see 1 Halleck (3d ed.), 142–45. It guarantees his inviolability and secures him in the enjoyment of certain rights and privileges ordinarily enjoyed only by sovereigns.

On the *International Status of the Pope*, see Bluntschli, *De la responsibilité du pape* (1877); Bompard, *La pape et le droit des gens* (1888), and, in 7 *R. D. I. P.* (1900), 369 ff.; Chrétien, in 6 *R. D. I. P.* (1899), 281 ff.; Cougny, *La papauté en droite int.* (1906); * Despagnet, Nos. 147–64; Dubois, in 37 *J. I. P.* (Clunet, 1910), 374 ff.; * 1 Fauchille, Nos. 156, 370–96; 1 Fiore, Nos. 520–21, and *Int. Law Cod.* (1918), Nos. 356–57, 706–32; Flaischin, in 36 *R. D. I.* (1904), 85 ff.; * Geffcken, in 2 Holtzendorff, §§ 40–42; * Gidel, in 18 *R. D. I. P* (1911), 589 ff.; Heffter, §§ 40–41; Heilborn, *System des Völkerrechts* (1896), 194–211; Higgins, in 9 (n.s.) *J. C. L.* (1909), 252 ff.; Imbart-Latour, *La papauté en droit int.* (1893); 2 Mérignhac, 119–53; 1 Moore, *Digest*, § 18; Müller, *Die Völkerrechtliche Stellung des Papstes* (1916); * 2 Nys, 297–323 (mainly historical); De Olivart, *La pape les états de l'eglise et l'Italie* (1897); * 1 Oppenheim, §§ 104–07; Pillet, in Sirey, *Rec. pér.* (1895), II, 57; 1 Rivier, 120–23; 2 Phillimore, Nos. 278–440 (historical); Rostworowski, in *Annales de l'ecole libre des sciences politiques* (1892), 102 ff.; Ullmann, § 28; Vergnes, *La condition int. de la papauté* (1905); 1 Westlake, 37–39.

The above selections from the extensive literature on this subject represent a great variety and diversity of opinion, but it is believed that the view presented in the text is the most dominant and authoritative.

See also Scott, *Cases*, 49 ff. for the French cases of *Gustave Gaultier et al.* (1911) and *Appeal of Chesnelong*, Court of Cessation (1913), in which it was held that the Pope, having lost his sovereignty in 1870, the Pontifical flag was not a foreign flag and could not be displayed in the Department of the Sarthe according to a prefectural ordinance which had the force of law. See especially

member of the international community upon the annexation of Rome by Italy and his consequent loss of all temporal power in 1870. But the Pope is in an anomalous position. He still retains an *apparent* or *quasi*[20] international personality. He continues to send and receive diplomatic envoys and to make ecclesiastical treaties named Concordats. These agreements are not, however, treaties in the international sense of that term; and, although his representatives enjoy the privileges and immunities of diplomatic agents as a matter of traditional usage and courtesy, they are ecclesiastical rather than international officials. The Pope as such has no international rights or duties, inasmuch as he is without temporal subjects or territory. He is an *object* rather than a *subject* of International Law. As an evidence of his exclusion from the society of nations, we may point to the fact that he was not invited to either of the Hague Peace Conferences of 1899 or 1907 or to Paris in 1919.

90. Extent of the Application of International Law to Barbarians and Savages.—Leading authorities [21] on International Law accept Lorimer's division of humanity into three concentric circles or spheres—civilized, barbarous, and savage.[22] Only States with a certain degree of civilization somewhat resembling that of Western Europe and America are held to be entitled to full recognition as members of the international community. This is because a certain amount of mutual understanding and reciprocity of interests is essential to advantageous and continued international intercourse, and the existence of States with the will and capacity

the comments of Gidel in article cited above. For the decision that the Roman Catholic Church in Porto Rico is a legal personality with capacity to sue, etc., and the dictum that the Holy See still occupies a recognized position in International Law, see C. J. Fuller in *Ponce v. Rom. Cath. Church in Porto Rico* (1907), 210 U. S., 296, 318.

For a fuller bibliography, see 1 Fauchille, pp. 726–28.

[20] Gidel, *op. cit.*, note 17, makes out a very interesting case for attributing to the Pope an *artificial* international personality which Oppenheim (I, pp. 126 and 185 *n*.) characterizes as not admissable.

[21] *E.g.* 1 Fauchille, No. 44; 1 Nys, 123 f.; and Pillet, in 1 *R. D. P. I.* (1894), 1 ff.

[22] Lorimer, *The Institutes of the Law of Nations* (1883), I, Bk. II, chs. 2 and 17, and Bk. III, ch. 2.

to fulfill their international obligations is a necessary qualification for membership in the modern family of States.

Although our system of International Law has undoubtedly had a Christian origin in the sense that it was
developed by the so-called Christian nations of Western
Europe and bears some traces of Christian influence, it
should not be described as essentially Christian or European
in character, as has been done by some publicists.[23] It is as
applicable to non-Christian and non-European States as to
States of Christian and European origin. From the standpoint of the Law of Nations, the *main test of civilization* [24] *is
to be found in the quality of the existing Government.* As far
as race and religion are concerned, China, Japan, and
Turkey are as well qualified for membership in the international community as are Russia, Spain, and the United
States.

On the other hand there are publicists [25] who maintain
that the scope of International Law is as wide as humanity
itself and that its range extends over the whole earth. This
view is in conflict with the actual practice of nations, more
particularly with the practice of those States exhibiting
colonizing or imperialistic tendencies.

The Law of Nations can be only partially applied to
barbarians or half-civilized peoples,[26] and still less to
savages; but it should be applied to the greatest extent
practicable. Treaties with such peoples are morally
binding, but it cannot be maintained that they are, strictly
speaking, a legal obligation; for savages at least are almost
wholly without that sense of understanding and capacity for
government which would make them the proper subjects of
legal rights and duties. They could not be held to a
sufficient degree of accountability. But this makes the
moral responsibility of those who deal with them all the
greater.

[23] For example, by Heffter, § 7.
[24] Westlake, *Chapters* (1894), p. 141 or *Collected Papers* (1914), 143.
[25] For example, Bluntschli, Arts. 7–8; and Bonfils or 1 Fauchille, No. 40.
[26] For judicial opinions on the status of half-civilized peoples like the Moroc-
cans and Algerine pirates, see Sir William Scott in the cases of *The Helena*
(1801), 4 C. Rob., 3; *The Madonna del Burso* (1802), 4 C. Rob., 169; and *The
Hurtige Hane* (1801), 3 C. Rob., 324. See Scott, *Cases* (ed. of 1902), 2–3 *n.*
and 45.

With the exception of the Russian Union of Soviet Republics, and the United States,[27] the most active members of the international community, as evidenced by membership in the League of Nations, are as follows:

Abyssinia [28]   Argentina [30]
Albania [29]   Austria

[27] The following are the most important States still remaining outside the League of Nations:

Afghanistan	Nejd, Sultanate of
Ecuador	Russian Union of
Egypt	Soviet Republics
Iceland	Turkey
Mexico	United States

On Nov. 22, 1921, a treaty was signed with Afghanistan whereby Great Britain recognized the complete independence of this country. See *Annual Register* for 1921, p. 267; and Toynbee, *Survey of Int. Affairs, 1920–23* (1925), 383–84. Afghanistan appears to be one of the few remaining sovereign States not an active member of the international community. Prior to 1921, Afghanistan had been for some years a British protectorate. Willoughby and Fenwick, *Types of Restricted Sovereignty* (1919), 14–15.

Among the signatories of the Treaty of Versailles were two plenipotentiaries of the King of the Hedjaz, a "free and independent State" of Arabia, important by reason of the fact that its capital is Mecca. The Sultanate of Nejd is now dominant in the Arabian peninsula, where it controls the Hedjaz and other political groups.

Since Dec. 1, 1918, Iceland is an independent State under a Danish protectorate. 1 Oppenheim, § 93, note 3, p. 167.

In consequence of their dissatisfaction with the refusal of the League to give them permanent seats in the Council upon the occasion of the admission of Germany in Sept., 1926, Brazil and Spain give notice of withdrawal from the League after the expiration of the two years' interval stipulated in Art. 1 of the Covenant. Costa Rica withdrew in Jan., 1927, after two years' notice.

[28] *Abyssinia* (or Ethiopia) was admitted to the League of Nations on Sept. 28, 1923. Its independence had been recognized by Italy in 1896 after the defeated Italians had vainly sought to make good their claims to a Protectorate. On the former international status of Abyssinia, see Willoughby and Fenwick, *op. cit.*, 13 f. On the admission of Abyssinia, see Toynbee, *op. cit.*, 393–96.

[29] The independence of *Albania* was proclaimed in 1912 and was recognized by the Great Powers as well as the Balkan States in 1913. In 1920 its complete independence was recognized by Italy which had established a military government there during the latter part of the World War, and on Dec. 17, 1920 Albania was admitted to membership in the League of Nations. On the recent history and status of Albania, see especially 30 *Ency. Brit.* (new vols., 1922); International Year Book (since 1912); Fenwick, *Wardship in Int. Law* (1919), 21; and 4 Temperley, *Hist. of the Peace Conference* (1920–24), ch. 5, Pt. II, pp. 338–46.

[30] The *Argentine Republic* withdrew her delegates from the League of Nations Assembly in 1920 in consequence of dissatisfaction over the failure of several proposed amendments. Her delegates seem to have absented themselves from its meetings ever since, but Argentine has not withdrawn from the League and, to a certain extent, participates in League activities.

Belgium	India
Bolivia	Irish Free State
Brazil	Bulgaria
British Empire [31]	Chile
Australia	China [32]
Canada	Colombia
South Africa (Union of)	Cuba [33]
New Zealand	

[31] As stated above (p. 164), the *British Empire* has been officially described as a "free association of free and equal nations." See also the description by the Imperial Conference of 1926, on p. 162. This description applies to only that portion of the Empire which may more accurately be called the British Commonwealth. In the list given above, its members are arranged in the order of their signatures attached to the Treaties of Paris or their subsequent admission to the League of Nations, as in the case of the Irish Free State. On the status of India and the Irish Free State, see *supra*, p. 161, note 9.

[32] In view of the many practical limitations placed upon their sovereignty, the status of countries like *China* as sovereign states might be considered doubtful were it not for the generally accepted legal fiction that contractual agreements or treaties, whether in fact voluntary or involuntary, which do not strike at the heart of their freedom or independence, do not constitute infringements upon sovereignty. Such states might, indeed, be said to enjoy a *de jure* rather than a *de facto* sovereignty.

[33] *Cuba* is on the whole free to conduct her own external and internal affairs, but nevertheless her relations with the United States seem those of a Protectorate; for several of the restrictions imposed by the Platt Amendment appear to be legal limitations upon sovereignty. According to the Platt amendment of 1901 (which was incorporated into an ordinance appended to the Cuban constitution and embodied in the treaty of 1903–1904 between Cuba and the United States), "the Government of Cuba shall never enter into any treaty or other compact with any foreign power or powers which will impair or tend to impair the independence of Cuba," nor "assume or contract any public debt" for the payment of which the ordinary revenues of the island shall be inadequate. Cuba also agreed that "the United States may exercise the right to intervene for the preservation of Cuban independence, the maintenance of a Government adequate for the protection of life, property, and individual liberty and for discharging the obligations with respect to Cuba imposed by the treaty of Paris on the United States, now to be assumed and undertaken by the Government of Cuba." 6 Moore, *Digest*, § 910; and 1 Malloy, *Treaties*, 362. On the Platt Amendment which was really the work of Secretary Root, see especially editorials in 8 *A. J.* (1914), 585 ff. and 886 ff. The substance of the Amendment was inserted in the Treaty of 1916 with Haiti, but omitted in the Treaty of the same year with Nicaragua. See editorials in 10 *A. J.* (1916), 859 ff. and 344 ff. Cf. notes below.

For select references on recent relations with Cuba, see Jones, *Caribbean Interests of the U. S.* (1916), 356–58; and Stuart, *Latin America and the U. S.* (1922), 158 and 181.

Upon several occasions, the United States has intervened in Cuba in pursuance of the rights thus granted. Stuart, *op. cit.*, 173 ff. For the erroneous view that Cuba remains a fully sovereign State, see Benton, *Int. Law and Diplomacy of the Spanish-American War* (1908), 290–91; Fenwick, (see index), and *Wardship*, 19–20; and Stuart, *op. cit.*, 179–80. See Whitcomb, *La situa-*

Czecho-Slovakia [34]

Denmark

Dominican Republic [35]

  (Santo Domingo)

Esthonia [36]

Finland

France

Germany

Greece

Guatemala

tion int. de Cuba (1905), ch. 5, for the view that Cuba is a part-sovereign State. Fauchille (No. 181, p. 271) uses the term "quasi-protectorate."

Lawrence (p. 59) prefers to call Cuba a client State which is his name for a Protectorate. But the writer sees no reason why the term Protectorate should not be frankly used to describe the relations between the United States and such States as Cuba and Haiti. The fact is that they have signed away several of the essential rights of sovereignty. Their membership in the League of Nations and exercise of considerable diplomatic activity does not make them fully sovereign States.

[34] *Czecho-Slovakia* is one of the Succession States formed mainly out of the Slavic regions of the old Austro-Hungarian Empire in 1918 when the Czechs (formerly known as Bohemians) regained the independence they had lost nearly 300 years earlier. Czecho-Slovakia is the heart or nucleus of the Little Entente—a defensive alliance (consisting of a series of treaties with Jugo-Slavia and Rumania and between the two latter States) originally formed against Hungary and which aims at the maintenance of peace and the *status quo* in Central Europe.

See especially Hobza, in 29 *R. D. I. P.* (1922), 385 ff.; and an article on Czecho-Slovakia by T. J. Masaryk, the President of the Republic, in the new volumes added to the Ency. Brit. in 1922. On the *Little Entente*, see *supra*, No. 86 i and note 48, pp. 143–44.

[35] Since 1905, when President Roosevelt, without the consent of the U. S. Senate, put into force an executive agreement with the Dominican Government and proceeded to administer the financial affairs of San Domingo, the *Dominican Republic* has been operating under a sort of receivership or financial Protectorate instituted and administered by the United States. The Senate finally agreed to a treaty signed on Feb. 8, 1907 which provided that our Government should administer the customs of San Domingo for fifty years. See Hollander in 1 *A. J.* (1907), 287 ff. For the text of the Convention of 1907, see Supp. to 1 *A. J.*, 231 ff.

This arrangement proved highly successful from a fiscal point of view; but, owing to political disorders, the United States Government felt obliged to intervene and proclaimed a military administration in San Domingo on Nov. 29, 1916. This military rule continued until Oct. 21, 1922 when a provisional Dominican Government was installed, a plan for the withdrawal of the American occupying force having been agreed upon. This withdrawal appears to have been virtually effected and, though the United States still exercises the functions of a receivership, from a legal standpoint at least, the Dominican Republic has resumed her former status as a sovereign State. In November, 1924 she was admitted into the League of Nations.

Unlike the Haitians (see note below), the Dominicans never signed away their rights of sovereignty. Though not an International Protectorate, San Domingo may be described as an independent State under the protection of the United States.

[36] *Esthonia*, and *Latvia* are Baltic States which severed their connection with Russia in 1917–18 after the Bolshevik Revolution of November, 1917 and later (1920–21) were admitted to membership in the League of Nations. In March,

Haiti [37]	Italy
Honduras	Japan
Hungary	Latvia

1922 a treaty was signed between Esthonia, Finland, Latvia and Poland on the basis of the "community of their mutual political and economic interests."

The Contracting Parties declare that "if one of them shall be attacked without provocation, they will preserve a benevolent neutrality toward the attacked State and will immediately consult together as to the measures to be undertaken." (Art. 7). McBain and Rogers, *The New Constitutions of Europe* (1922), 61. For the text of the Treaty, see 16 *Cur. Hist.* (1922), 471.

On the "Recognition of the Baltic States," see 6 Temperley, *Hist. of the Peace Conference* (1920–24), 284–310. On the "Int. Rel. of the new Baltic States," see Toynbee, *Survey of Int. Affairs, 1920–23* (1925), 238–45.

[37] In consequence of frequent revolutions and pressure by foreign powers, the United States Government felt itself obliged to intervene in the internal affairs of *Haiti* late in July, 1915. On Feb. 28, 1916 the U. S. Senate ratified a treaty with Haiti which placed that republic under the political as well as financial control of the United States.

This Treaty provides that, on nomination by the President of the United States, the President of Haiti shall appoint a general receiver of customs, a financial adviser, American officers to organize a Haitian constabulary, etc. Haiti agreed not to increase her public debt without the previous consent of the United States whose Government undertook to intervene when necessary for the preservation of Haitian independence and the maintenance of a government adequate for the protection of life, property, and liberty. It should be particularly noted that this treaty was concluded only for a period of ten years with privilege of renewal at the option of either party for another period of ten years. For the text of the Treaty, see 39 *U. S. Statutes*, Pt. II, 1654. See also summary in 1 Hyde, § 22.

If the matter were tested in an international court, there might be grave doubts as to the legal validity of this treaty. Serious personal pressure appears to have been brought to bear upon the President, the Cabinet, and other officials of Haiti to secure its ratification. They were threatened by Secretary Daniels with loss of back payment of salaries and were told that in case the treaty failed of ratification, the United States Government would remain in control of Haiti until the desired end should be accomplished. See a pamphlet on the *Seizure of Haiti* issued by the Foreign Policy Association (1922), signed by Bausman *et. al.*; *Hearings on Haiti and Santo Domingo* (1922); and Stuart, *Latin America and the U. S.* (1922), 233.

It is suggested that the student make an application of the third condition for the validity of treaties (see *infra*, No. 297, p. 443) to the case of Haiti.

However, if this treaty is to be considered valid, Haiti must be considered a Protectorate of the United States.

On the intervention of the United States in Haiti and San Domingo, see especially: *Hearings on Haiti and Santo Domingo* (1922); Hughes, Sec'y, in 17 *A. J.* (1923), 621–24; Jones, *Caribbean Interests of U. S.* (1916), chs. 8–9; Kelsey, in 100 *Annals*, No. 189 (March, 1922); Schoenrich, in *Mexico and the Caribbean* (ed. by Blakeslee, 1920), 206–23; * Stuart, *Latin America and the U. S.* (1922), ch. 11.

For select references on our relations with Haiti and San Domingo, see Jones, *op. cit.*, 358–59 and 360; and Stuart, *op. cit.*, 218 and 238.

Liberia [38]   Netherlands
Lithuania   Nicaragua [39]
Luxemburg   Norway

[38] Founded by the American Colonization Society in 1820–28 for negro freedmen, *Liberia* should be of particular interest to Americans. Though never *de jure* a colony, Liberia is an offshoot of the United States, and may, indeed, be said to be the only *de facto* colony ever established by us overseas. For many years the settlements were generally considered as more or less under the protection of the United States, but in 1847 they set up as an independent republic, adopting a constitution closely modelled on that of the United States.

Since 1912 when an international loan of $1,700,000 to Liberia was arranged and an American receiver-general appointed who also acts as financial adviser to the Liberian Government, the negro republic may again be said to be under the protection of the United States. Following our example, Liberia declared war against Germany in 1917 and $5,000,000 were placed to her credit by the United States Government for war purposes. An application to have this credit, which remained almost wholly unexpended, transformed into a loan has hitherto (1925) been resisted by the United States Senate. The opposition is in part motivated by fear that the conditions under which the loan is to be granted will transform Liberia into a Protectorate.

Having ratified the Treaties of Paris of which she was a Signatory, Liberia is an original member of the League of Nations.

On "Relations between the United States and Liberia," see Faulkner, in 4 *A. J.* (1910), 529–45 and Finch, in 3 *A. J.* (1909), 958–63. For official documents see *Supplement* to 4 *A. J.* (1910), 188 ff.

[39] In consideration of the sum of $3,000,000 *Nicaragua*, by the ratified Bryan-Chamorro Treaty of 1916, agreed (1) to grant in perpetuity to the United States the exclusive proprietary rights necessary for the construction of a canal by way of the San Juan River and the Great Lake or any other route; and (2) to lease to the United States for 99 years the Great and Little Corn Islands and to grant the right to establish a naval base on such Nicaraguan territory bordering on the Gulf of Fonseca as the United States shall select. 3 Malloy, *Treaties* 2740. For summaries, see 1 Hyde, § 23 and Stuart, *op. cit.*, 274 f.

Costa Rica, Salvador, and Honduras protested against the ratification of this treaty on the ground that it impaired their existing rights. The Central American Court of Justice, to which the cases of *Costa Rica* and *San Salvador*, v. *Nicaragua* were appealed, held that Nicaragua had violated the rights of these States by consenting to the treaty; but that, inasmuch as the United States was not subject to the jurisdiction of the Court, it declined to declare the Convention null and void. Nicaragua also denied the jurisdiction of the Court. The United States thus found itself in an embarrassing position, more especially since the controversy ultimately led to the dissolution of an International Court which was essentially our own creation. For editorial comment on the decision in the case of *Costa Rica* v. *Nicaragua*, see 11 *A. J.* (1917), 156 ff. See also González on "The Neutrality of Honduras, etc.," in 10 *A. J.* (1916), 508–42. For the decisions themselves, see 11 *A. J.* (1917), 181 ff. and 674 ff.

Since 1909 the United States Government has repeatedly intervened in the affairs of Nicaragua. It has in general found a force of 100 marines sufficient to secure order and maintain the government it desired in power. However, it must be said that neither these interventions nor the Treaty of 1916 constitute an infringement of the legal sovereignty of Nicaragua. It should be noted that

Panama [40]   Peru
Paraguay   Poland [41]
Persia   Portugal

the substance of the provisions of the Platt Amendment which had been incorporated in the proposed Treaty of 1913 were carefully omitted from the
ratified Treaty of 1916.   Finch, in 10 *A. J.* (1916), 344 ff.   Consequently,
like the other Central American States, Nicaragua remains *de jure* a fully
sovereign state; but like Panama and San Domingo, it may be said to
be under the special protection of the United States.

On the *Relations between the United States and Nicaragua* since 1909, see
especially: Brown, in 4 *J. R. D.* (1914), 409–26, and, in *Latin America*, (ed.
Blakeslee, 1914), 245 ff.; Jones, *Caribbean Interests of U. S.* (1916), ch. 10, pp.
172 ff.; Latané, *U. S. and Latin America* (1920), 280–88; Lopez, in *Mexico
and the Caribbean* (ed. Blakeslee, 1920), 305 ff.; Munro, *Five Republics of
Central America* (1918), ch. 11; * Stuart, *Latin America and the U. S.* (1922),
ch. 13, pp. 269 ff.   For references on the recent intervention in Nicaraugan
affairs by the U. S., see 24 and 26 *Cur. Hist.* (1926–27), 345 ff and 104 ff.

For select references on our relations with Nicaragua and Central America
generally, see Jones, *op. cit.*, 361–62; and Stuart, *op. cit.*, 261 and 288–89.

[40] By the Hay-Varilla Treaty concluded Nov. 18, 1903 the United States
agreed to guarantee and "maintain the independence of the Republic of
Panama" which granted to the United States "in perpetuity the use, occupation and control of a zone of land and land under water for the construction,
maintenance, operation, sanitation and protection" of a Canal ten miles in
width, as also rights akin to sovereignty over the zone and auxillary land and
waters (Arts. 1–4).   It was also agreed (Art. 23) that "if it should become
necessary at any time to employ armed forces for the safety or protection of
the canal, . . . the United States should have the right . . . to use its police
and its land and naval forces or to establish fortifications for these purposes."
The United States was also granted certain property rights and rights of maintaining public order and sanitation in the cities of Panama and Colon and
within the harbors and territory adjacent thereto (Art. 7).

It is evident that the above grants and concessions are serious limitations
upon the actual or *de facto* independence of Panama in respect to a considerable
portion of its territory, property, and freedom of action; but, except possibly
for the right of intervention for the protection of the Canal and the maintenance
of public order in the cities of Colon and Panama, they appear to be in the
nature of leases or servitudes and are not in derogation of *de jure* sovereignty.
Consequently, *Panama*, though a dependent state politically, is not, strictly
speaking, a Protectorate.

As bearing upon Panama's relation to the League of Nations of which it is
an original member, Art. 24 of the Hay-Varilla Treaty may be of interest:
"If the Republic of Panama shall hereafter enter as a constituent into any
other Government or into any union or confederation of states, so as to merge
her sovereignty or independence in such Government, union or confederation,
the rights of the United States under this convention shall not be in any respect
lessened or impaired."   Of course this provision had original reference to the
possibilities of Panama's entering the Central American Union or Confederation.

For the text of the Treaty, see 2 Malloy, *Treaties*, 1349.   For a summary,
see 1 Hyde, § 20.

[41] After nearly a century and a half one of the "greatest crimes of the eight-

Rumania

Salvador

Serb-Croat-Slovene State [42]

  (Jugo-Slavia)

Siam

Spain

Sweden

Switzerland

Uruguay

Venezuela

eenth century"—the threefold partition of *Poland* in 1772, 1793, and 1795—was atoned for through the creation at Paris in 1919 of a new Poland.

In Art. 87 of the Treaty of Versailles, Germany recognized the "complete independence" of Poland and her rights and duties in respect to the new State (including provisions as to boundaries and plebiscites) were laid down in subsequent articles.

As in the cases of Czecho-Slovakia, Jugo-Slavia, Rumania, etc., the relations between Poland and the leading Allies, more particularly in respect to the protection of minorities, were dealt with in separate treaties. See *supra*, note 43 on p. 142. For the texts of these treaties which were signed but not ratified by the United States, see 5 Temperley *Hist. of the Peace Conference* (1920–24); App. IV, 432–68.

But the provisions in these and other treaties, restricting the freedom of these states in their treatment of minorities are not considered limitations on sovereignty *de jure*, being rather in the nature of personal servitudes. Cf. *infra*, p. 274 n.

The status of *Danzig*, Poland's sole outlet to the sea, is interesting as illustrating the difference between the status of a Protectorate and that of mere "protection." Art. 102 of the Treaty of Versailles describes it as "a Free City" and declares that "it will be placed under the protection of the League of Nations." A High Commissioner, appointed by the League but resident at Danzig, is "entrusted with the duty of dealing in the first instance with all differences arising between Poland and the Free City of Danzig in regard to this Treaty or any arrangements or agreements made thereunder" (Art. 103). In accordance with another provision of this article, a constitution was drawn up by elected representatives of the City in agreement with the High Commissioner, proclaimed in Nov., 1920, and placed under the guarantee of the League. For the text of the Constitution, see McBain and Rogers, *New Constitutions of Europe* (1922), 429

In accordance with Art. 104 of the Treaty of Versailles, a Treaty between Poland and Danzig negotiated by the Allied Powers came into force Nov. 15, 1920, which not only included this City within the Polish Customs frontiers, but provided that Poland should conduct the foreign affairs of Danzig as also afford diplomatic protection to citizens of that City when abroad. Consequently, Danzig seems to be a Polish Protectorate under the protection of the League of Nations.

On the *Int. Status of Danzig*, see Corbett, in *Brit. Yr. Bk.* (1924), 138–41; Lannoy, in 3 (ser. 2) *R. D. I.* (1921), 436 ff.; Le Vesque, *La Situation int. de Dantzig* (1924); *Lewis, in *Brit. Yr. Bk.* (1924), 89–102; Piccioni, in 28 *R. D. I. P.* (1921), 84 ff.; and Toynbee, *Survey of Int. Affairs, 1920–23* (1925), 261–66. See also Loenig, in 12 *Z. V.* (1923), 489 ff.; and Makowski, in 30 *R. D. I. P* (1923), 169 ff.

[42] From a strictly legal standpoint the *Serb-Croat-Slovene State*, commonly known as Jugo-Slavia, appears to be an enlargement of Serbia rather than a new State. It came into being on Dec. 1, 1918 when the Prince-Regent Alexander of Serbia accepted the invitation of the Jugo-Slav National Council to assume the regency over the Jugo-Slavic provinces (Seton-Watson in 32 *Ency. Brit.*, new vols., 1922).

BIBLIOGRAPHY

States as International Persons and Members of the International Community.—Bluntschli, Arts. 17–27; 1 Calvo, §§ 39–41; 1 Cobbett, 42 ff.; Despagnet, Nos. 69–74; * Evans, *Cases*, ch. 2, pp. 33 ff.; * 1 Fauchille, Nos. 154–64; Fenwick, ch. 6, pp. 83 ff.; 1 Fiore, Nos. 275–309, and *Int. Law Cod.*, Nos. 56 ff.; Hall, § 1, pp. 17 ff.; Heffter, § 15; Holtzendorff, in 2 *Handbuch*, 5–11; Lawrence, §§ 34–37, 42–44; Liszt, § 71; 1 J. de Louter, §§ 11–12, pp. 160 ff.; 1 F. de Martens, §§ 53–54, 63, 84–85; 1 and 2 Mérignhac, 114–232 and 154–221; 1 Nys, 63–68; * 1 Oppenheim, §§ 63–70; 1 Piédelièvre, Nos. 71–76; 1 Phillimore, §§ 61–68; 1 P.-Fodéré, Nos. 43–81; * 1 Rivier, § 1, pp. 7–18 and § 3, pp. 45–51; * Scott, *Cases*, Pt. I, ch. 1, pp. 19–57; Ullmann, §§ 19, 38; 1 Vattel, §§ 1–12; 1 Westlake, 1–5; Wheaton, § 16 ff.; Willoughby and Fenwick, *Types of Restricted Sovereignty* (1919).

For an additional Bibliography, see 1 Fauchille, p. 223.

CHAPTER VII

CLASSIFICATION OF STATES

92. **Double Classification of States.**—From the standpoint of International Law, States may be doubly classified into Sovereign and Part-Sovereign; and into Simple, Composite and Dependent.

93. **Sovereign States and Sovereignty Defined.**—Sovereign States are those which are fully autonomous and independent, *i.e.* relatively free from higher or outside control—a freedom not fully enjoyed by Part-Sovereign States. Sovereignty [1] is one and the same power, will, or capacity

---

[1] It is not necessary for our purpose to enter into any discussion of the many and complicated theories respecting the nature of sovereignty which have been held since the term was introduced into political science by Bodin in 1576. His definition of sovereignty as "supreme power over citizens and subjects, unrestrained by the laws," is still perhaps the best, as it is certainly the simplest that has ever been formulated. Bodin, *De republica*, lib. 1, cap. 8. But, as pointed out by Borchard in *History of Political Theories* (ed. Merriam and Barnes, 1924), p. 125, Bodin, "while an absolutist in the internal aspect of sovereignty, viewed external sovereignty as subject to the Law of Nations." Cf. Garner, in 19 *Am. Pol. Sci. Rev.* (1925), 4. (On Bodin, see especially Coker, *Readings in Pol. Philosophy*, 1914, pp. 225 ff.; Dunning, *From Luther to Montesquieu*, 1905, ch. 3; and the select references given in Coker and Dunning, pp. 236–37 and 123 respectively). Grotius (lib. I, cap. III, § 7) defined sovereignty as "the power whose acts are not subject to the control of another, so that they may be made void by the act of any other human will." For other definitions, see Garner, *Introd. to Pol. Science* (1910), 239.

A few recent publicists like Duguit, Laski and Follett deny the sovereignty as well as the personality of the State. Duguit, the leading representative of this pluralistic school, substitutes the ideas of solidarity and public services which he declares to be the fundamental facts of human society. 1 Duguit, *Etudes de droit public* (1901), Introduction and ch. 1, and *Law in the Modern State* (1919), Introduction and chs. 1–2. Cf. Follett, *The New State* (1918), *passim*; Gettell, *Hist. of Pol. Thought* (1924), ch. 29; Laski, *Problem of Sovereignty* (1917) *passim*, and *Foundations of Sovereignty* (1921), Essay I. See also Barker, "The Discredited State," in 5 *Political Quarterly* (Feb., 1915); Ellis, "The Pluralistic State," in 14 *Am. Pol. Sci. Rev.* (1920), 393 ff.; "Guild Socialism and Pluralism," in 17 *Am. Pol. Sci. Rev.* (1923), 585 ff.; and Sabine, "Pluralism," in the same volume, 34–40. For an excellent review of "Pluralistic Theories," see Coker, in Merriam and Barnes, *Hist. of Political Theories* (1924), ch. 3. For a vehement attack upon the doctrine of sovereignty as applied in International Law, see Edmunds, *The Lawless Law of Nations* (1925),

inherent in the State;[2] but it has a double aspect—an external as well as an internal face.[3]

94. Internal Sovereignty.—On its internal side, sovereignty implies such supreme control over everything found on a State's territory and such power to regulate the conduct of its subjects as may be necessary tõ realize the purpose for which the State exists.   To this end it sets its own limits to the extent and scope of its power or jurisdiction.   The Germans call this the *Competenz-Competenz*.

95. Limitations on External Sovereignty.—On its external side, sovereignty may be limited in various ways:

(1) By the rules, principles, and customs of International Law.   For a violation of these rules, which are binding upon all members of the international community, a State is internationally responsible.

(2) The conventional Law of Nations or treaties, subject to the clause *rebus sic stantibus* (see *infra*, p. 43 n.) which is generally implied.   For a serious breach of its express agreements, a State is responsible to those members of the family of nations whose rights have been violated.

(3) Certain delegations of sovereignty and State servitudes[4] not deemed in derogation of sovereignty, such as the exercise of financial, judicial, or administrative functions by representatives of a foreign Power, and the temporary occupation of territory by foreign troops, etc.

(4) Treaties of alliance, guarantee,[5] and protection by which a State obligates itself to give aid to another under certain conditions or to assist in maintaining a certain state of affairs agreed upon.

passim, particularly the introductory chapter.   For sane and well-considered views in respect to the "Limitations on National Sovereignty in International Relations," see * Garner, in 19 *Am. Pol. Sci. Rev.* (1925), 1–24.   See note on p. 2 of his article for a list of publicists who criticise adversely the prevailing conception of sovereignty as applied to international relations.

[2] The authorities are divided on the question whether sovereignty is an essential characteristic of the State.

[3] On the distinction between external and internal sovereignty see Bluntschli, Arts. 64 ff.; Despagnet, No. 74; Fauchille, No. 164; Holland, *Jurisprudence* (10th ed.), 48–49, 359–361, 384; * Jellinek, *Das Recht des mod. States* (2d ed., 1905), 461–470; * Le Fur, in 1 *Z. V.* (1907), 232 ff.; and *L'État fédéral et confédération d'états* (1896), 443 ff.; * 1 Mérighnac, 117 ff., 162 ff.; 1 P.-Fodéré, Nos. 132–36; Ullmann, § 19, p. 89; Wheaton, § 20.

[4] On International Servitudes, see *infra*, Nos. 166–68.

[5] On Treaties of Guarantee, see *infra*, No. 301.

(5) Certain relations of suzerainty and vassalage or protection and dependence only in partial derogation of sovereignty. Such were the feudal relations between the Holy Roman Empire and the States of Germany between 1648 and 1806, the position of Napoleon I in his relations with the members of the Confederacy of the Rhine and other European States like Spain and Naples, the former relations between the Ottoman Empire and such states as Bulgaria, Rumania, etc., and the numerous cases of dependence and protection or the various restricted types of sovereignty that exist today.

(6) Membership in a Confederacy, such as the League of Nations, in which all members enjoy equal rights and are equally and reciprocally bound.

It is generally held that the above limitations or restraints are not legal restrictions on sovereignty on the grounds that they are mere delegations of power, or that they do not really bind the will or power of the sovereign who has thus freely chosen to bind himself [6] through *auto-limitation* or *auto-determination*.

But there are many instances where the relations between States are of such a nature that it cannot be maintained that all the States involved in the relationship are sovereign. To these cases the terms " part-sovereign," " semi-sovereign," " non-sovereign," and " dependent " have been variously applied. They include members of Federal and Real Unions, Confederacies, and the majority of those States which are said to be under the protection of another State.

The above analysis shows that external sovereignty or independence must not be understood in any absolute or unrestricted sense. Whatever may be the case in theory, in practice it is very much limited [7] and wholly relative.

---

[6] By means of a legal fiction, the sovereign defeated in warfare is supposed to have freely consented to such humiliating terms (*e.g.* the cession of territory, the limitation of his land or naval forces, and the demolition of fortresses) as may have been imposed upon him by a treaty of peace.

But "if a State . . . parts with its rights of negotiation and treaty, and loses its essential attributes of independence, it can no longer be regarded as a sovereign State, or as a member of the great family of nations." 1 Halleck (3d ed.), p. 69. Cf. 1 Phillimore, §§ 75–76.

The mere payment of tribute is not regarded as in derogation of sovereignty.

[7] That sovereignty does not imply unlimited power is clearly shown by

Although it is well to insist that States must enjoy a certain degree of autonomy and independence in order to possess an international status, the Law of Nations must also take cognizance of the other great facts of dependence and interdependence or the international solidarity of modern States and peoples.

96. **Classification of States.**—Besides the division into sovereign and part-sovereign, States may also be classified into simple or unitary, composite, and dependent or semi-sovereign.

97. **(I) Simple States.**—*Simple or Unitary States* are those with a single supreme central government representing the will and power of the State, " whether it be the will of a sovereign ruler, or the collective will of a popular body or a representative assembly." [8]

They include such complex incorporate unions with colonies and dependencies as the British Empire prior to 1919 as well as simple unitary States like Holland, Italy and France. The majority of Simple States are fully sovereign and independent, and enjoy complete international personality.

" The Simple State may be either single, *i.e.* wholly separate and distinct from any other State, or it may be connected with another State by what is called a Personal Union." [9]

98. **Personal Unions.**—A *Personal Union* consists of several States accidentally or temporarily united under the same ruler or sovereign. It is not, properly speaking, a composite State, nor does it enjoy any degree of international personality. Each State retains its own sovereignty, and remains a distinct and separate International Person or Subject of International Law. [10]

With the annexation of the Congo Free State by Belgium

Jellinek, *Das Recht des mod. Staates* (2d ed., 1905), 461–170. Cf. Jellinek, *Die Lehre von den Staatenverbindungen* (1882), 35 ff.; and *Gesetz und Verordnung* (1887), 196 ff.   See also Le Fur, *État fédéral* (1896), 438 ff.; and 1 Mérignhac, 219 ff.

[8] 1 Moore, *Digest*, § 5, p. 21.

[9] *Ibid.*

[10] The question has often been raised whether one member of a Personal Union may wage war against another. Theoretically, this would be possible; practically, it is improbable in the highest degree.

in 1908, the last existing example of a Personal Union disappeared. The other historical illustrations of this form of so-called union most frequently cited are: the dynastic Union between Great Britain and Hanover extending from 1714 to 1837; that between the Netherlands and Luxemburg between 1815 and 1890; the Union between Spain and the Holy Roman Empire during the reign of the Emperor Charles V in the sixteenth century; and that from 1885 to 1908 between Belgium and the former Congo Free State.[11]

99. **(II) Composite States.**— *Composite States* are permanent Unions or associations of two or more States with certain common functions and organs of government. From the standpoint of International Law, they may be classified into Real Unions, Confederacies, and Federal Unions.

100. (1) **Real Unions.**—A *Real Union* exists where several States, otherwise sovereign and independent, are perpetually united by an express agreement under the same dynasty, so that they together form a single International Person.[12] Each member of the Union retains its internal sovereignty and its own constitution; but there are at least common ministers or joint councils who advise the monarch on questions affecting the interests of the Union [13] as a whole, more especially in matters pertaining to war and

[11] On Personal Unions, see especially 1 Fauchille, No. 166, [1-12] pp. 228 ff. and the literature there cited.

[12] Nevertheless the separate members may also enjoy a certain degree of international personality. Thus Norway and Sweden had separate commercial flags and extradition treaties.

[13] Norway-Sweden did not have even a common Minister of Foreign Affairs, the king acting through the Swedish Foreign Minister; in questions touching the interests of both kingdoms, the monarch was bound to take the advice of joint Councils of State. Matters of interest common to both countries were regulated by concurrent identical laws or resolutions. There was no common legislature.

Austria-Hungary had three common Ministers for Foreign Affairs, War, and Finances. There was even a sort of rudimentary common legislature consisting of two Delegations or Committees of sixty members, each representing the Austrian and Hungarian Parliaments. But the bulk of the legislation common to both countries (including the tariff) was in the form of practically identical statutes passed for a term of years. In substance these statutes were treaties resulting from negotiations.

On the "Dual Monarchies," see especially Lowell, *Governments and Parties in Continental Europe* (1896), II, ch. 10; Wilson, *The State* (1889), Pt. IX, and the authorities there cited.

peace, the common finances, the control of the army and navy, and the conduct of foreign affairs.

Since the separation of Norway and Sweden [14] in 1905, and the breakup of the Austro-Hungarian Empire in 1918, there is no surviving example of a Real Union.[15]

101. (2) **Confederacies.**—A *Confederacy (Staatenbund* or league of States) is a permanent association or union of States joined together by treaty or compact for purposes of common defense and general welfare. The Union has organs and functions of its own, especially for the conduct of foreign affairs; but each State remains otherwise sovereign and independent, and also enjoys international personality.[16]   The main organ of the Union is a Diet or Congress exercising delegated powers and consisting of delegates from each of the member States whose votes are usually cast as a unit.   The central power does not, as a rule, attempt to deal directly with individuals as such; it operates upon and through the member-States themselves.

With the important exception of the League of Nations and the possible exception of the British Commonwealth of Nations, which seems to be a Confederation in spirit if not in form (see *supra*, p. 162), there are no existing examples of a Confederacy, but this form of International Union has been a very important factor in State making. The most important historical instances are: The United Netherlands from 1580 to 1795; the United States of America under the Articles of Confederation from 1781 to 1789; the Swiss

[14] The authorities differ in their opinions on the nature of the former Union between Norway and Sweden, but the majority rightly consider it to have been a Real Union.

Higgins (Hall, 8th ed., p. 26 *n*.) regards the relations existing between Denmark and Iceland since 1918 as those of a Real Union, but I am inclined to agree with Oppenheim (I, p. 167) that Iceland is a Danish Protectorate.

[15] There is a difference of opinion as to whether the Pragmatic Sanction of 1723 created a Real or a mere Personal Union between Austria and Hungary. The main authorities on the Real Union are Jellinek, *Staatenverbindungen* (1882), 197–248; Juraschek, *Personal and Real Union* (1878); and Blütigen, in 1 *Z. V.* (1907), 237 ff.   See especially 1 Fauchille, No. 167, [1–7], pp. 233 ff. and the literature there cited.

[16] Most of the authorities deny international personality to the Union on the ground that it is not a State, but this view contradicts the facts for the sake of a theory.   On *Confederacies*, see especially 1 Fauchille, Nos. 169–71, pp. 241 ff. and the references there given.

Confederacy before 1798 and from 1815 to 1848; and the Germanic Confederation from 1815 to 1866.

102. (3) **Federal Union.**—A *Federal State (Bundesstaat* or Union of States) is a perpetual Union of non-sovereign States with a constitution, central organs, and government of its own. The member-States possess certain inherent, original, or non-delegated powers of their own; but although both central and State governments are supreme within their own respective spheres, the central government deals directly with individuals and practically (if not legally) fixes the limits to its own competence, *i.e.*, the extent and scope of its power and jurisdiction. Consequently, the Federal Union is fully sovereign and independent. The Federal State alone is a complete International Person, but the member States may enjoy some degree of international personality.[17]

Existing examples of a Federal Union enjoying *de jure* international personality [18] are: The United States since 1789, Switzerland since 1848, Mexico since 1857, the Argentine Republic since 1860, Germany since 1871, Brazil since 1891, Venezuela since 1893, and Canada since 1919.[19]

103. (III) **Dependent or Semi-Sovereign States.**—*Dependent* or *Semi-Sovereign States* [20] are States which, without

[17] This is denied by most publicists, but their opinion on this subject is not in strict accord with the facts. It is certainly true that the member states of the United States are wholly without international personality; but this is not altogether true of the Swiss Cantons and the German States prior to the World War. The member States of the former German Federal Union retained the rights of legation and treaty-making within certain limits. The Swiss Cantons also preserve a very limited treaty-making power.

Under the German Constitution of 1919, Germany remains a Federal State in principle, though with stronger unitary tendencies than ever; but the member-States have lost the active and passive rights of legation and they cannot enter into treaty relations with foreign States except through the intermediary of the *Reich*. (Arts. 45 and 78 of the German Constitution.) Brunet, *The New German Const.* (1922), 63, 307–08, 315.

[18] Canada, Australia, and South Africa are examples of Federal Unions with Dominion status and international personality. See *supra*, pp. 160 ff.

[19] For bibliographies on the Federal Union, see 1 Fauchille, pp. 245 ff.; Hart, *Introduction to Fed. Gov't.* (1891), 178–192; and Le Fur, *État fédéral et confédération d'états* (1896), x–xvii.

[20] The best definition is perhaps that given by Klüber (§ 24): "When one State is dependent on another in the exercise of one or more of the essential rights of sovereignty, but is otherwise free, it is called dependent, or *mi-souverain.*"

being members of a composite State, retain a certain degree of sovereignty and international personality in spite of the fact that in the conduct of foreign relations they are at least partially subject to the control of another State. This control usually extends to internal affairs as well.

The relation is one which is almost necessarily anomalous, more or less vague, and difficult to maintain. It usually ends in either annexation or complete independence. There are no general or hard and fast rules governing the relationship; for the degree of dependence varies in each particular case, and ranges from almost complete dependence to virtual independence

In general, it may be said that the foreign relations of the subordinate State are commonly subject to the control or direction of its superior which usually exercises the most important powers of external sovereignty, such as the right of legation and the treaty-making power. But the inferior State may share in the exercise of these functions to a greater or less degree; and it is not necessarily treated as a belligerent in a war to which the superior is a party.[21]

It is customary to subdivide Dependent or Semi-Sovereign States into two classes:

104. (1) **States under Suzerainty.**— *Vassal States or States under Suzerainty.* These terms are derived from feudalism and were originally used to describe the feudal relation of service and protection between the vassal and his lord who became known as the former's suzerain in the course of the fifteenth century. They have often been used to characterize the relations between the German princes and the Holy Roman Germanic Empire, at least during the period from 1648 to 1805. After becoming almost extinct, the term " suzerainty " was revived in the nineteenth century and applied to the relations between the Ottoman

---

[21] This was recognized in 1855 by the British Court of Admiralty, which decided that the Ionian Islands (then in the relation of a Protectorate to Great Britain) remained neutral during the Crimean War. *The Ionian Ships*, 2 Spinks, 212; Scott, *Cases*, 21.

There is no reason why the same principle should not be applied to a State under suzerainty which apparently enjoys a greater *de facto* independence. Turkey did not interfere in the war betweeh Bulgaria and Servia in 1885. Egypt issued a separate Declaration of Neutrality during the Russo-Japanese War.

Empire and such tributary States as Rumania, Servia, and Bulgaria,[22] even after these had become practically independent. This terminology is no longer applicable to modern conditions, but it still survives in treatises and diplomatic documents.

Theoretically, Vassal States are supposed to possess only those rights and privileges which have been expressly granted to them, but actually they would seem to be well-nigh independent of their suzerain.

This class of States has almost disappeared from international relations,[23] and there only remains the class

[22] All of these States now enjoy a *de jure* as well as a *de facto* independence. The last to declare its complete independence was Bulgaria in 1908. Up to that time Bulgaria was still theoretically a vassal and tributary State, but went to war with Servia without consulting Turkey or the Powers in 1885. The conditional independence of Rumania and Servia, was recognized by the Great Powers at the Congress of Berlin in 1878.

[23] The status of the *Transvaal or South African Republic* prior to the outbreak of the Boer War in 1899 has been a subject of much controversy. In the Convention of 1881 it was declared to be under the suzerainty of Great Britain The word "suzerainty" was omitted in the Convention of 1884, but the Republic remained under such restrictions in respect to the exercise of the treaty-making power (Great Britain reserving the right of veto) that it must be considered to have been a British Protectorate. For references on the former international status of the *Transvaal*, see 1 Fauchille, p. 281.

Prior to 1914 when she was formally declared to be a British Protectorate, *Egypt* was the main surviving example of a Vassal State. After the British occupation of 1882, Egypt remained (until 1914) a Vassal State at least nominally subject to the suzerainty of Turkey.

The British Protectorate was formally terminated on Feb. 28, 1922 when Egypt was recognized as "sovereign and independent" by Great Britain; but this recognition was accompanied by four reservations respecting the Sudan, the Suez Canal, the defense of Egypt, and the protection of foreign interests and of minorities in Egypt. These matters were to be made the subjects of agreements with the Egyptian Government. "Until such agreements, satisfactory to ourselves and the Egyptian Government, are concluded, the *status quo*, will remain intact." Lloyd George, in the House of Commons on Feb. 28, 1922. See *Round Table* for Sept., 1924, p. 669. Cf. 6 Temperley, *Hist. of the Peace Conference* (1920–24) 203.

From what has been said, it will be seen that the present status of Egypt is difficult to determine. As pointed out by the *Manchester Guardian* (Nov. 28, 1924, weekly ed.), strictly speaking, "Egypt is not and never has been a part of the British Empire. . . . "Egypt's international status is unlike that of any other country. She is independent and yet without certain sovereign powers which were reserved in 1922 for future settlement between her and Great Britain."

Whatever else may be said regarding the present doubtful status of Egypt, it is certainly true that Great Britain occupies a privileged political position there and that it certainly remains under British protection.

generally known as International Protectorates to be classified under the head of Dependent States.

105. (2) **International Protectorates.**—An *International Protectorate* is the status or relation which exists where a weak or dependent State has through treaty or otherwise [24] been placed under the legal protection of a more powerful one (at least as far as the control of its foreign affairs are concerned) for the sake of greater safety, or because it was virtually forced into this position.   Although the practice of keeping client or vassal States in a condition of dependence or partial subjection was freely practiced by the Romans as a means of conquest, the modern Protectorate is ostensibly instituted for the benefit of the protected State.   But it is frequently employed as a means of exploitation and disguised conquest even in modern times.

The position of the protecting State is supposed to be like that of a trustee, and its obligations resemble somewhat those of a guardian toward its ward.   But it must be admitted that the conditions on which the trust is held are

The *Sudan*, for many years under Egyptian rule, revolted in 1882 and was reconquered by an Anglo-Egyptian force in 1898.   In 1899 there was established an Anglo-Egyptian *condominium* or joint control over this region which continued until early in December, 1924 when, following the assassination of Sir Lee Stack Pasha, Sirdar of the Egyptian army and Governor-General of the Sudan, the Egyptian Government submitted to a number of very severe demands made by the British Government.   These demands included not merely the apologies and assurances usual in such cases and an indemnity of £500,000, but also the withdrawal of Egyptian officers and military units from the Sudan within twenty-four hours.

For accounts of these demands, see *Round Table* for Jan., 1925; and Simonds in 71 *Rev. of Rev.* (1925), 45–46.

The status of the Sudan prior to these British demands was thus described by a competent authority: "The Sudan is an Anglo-Egyptian Protectorate controlled by Great Britain."   6 Temperley, *op. cit.*, 205.

On the status of *Egypt* and *The Sudan*, see particularly: Chirol, in 243 *Quar. Rev.* (1924), 145–60; 21 *Current Hist.*, (1925), 721–27; Crabitès, in 3 *For. Aff.* (1924), 320–30; Lybyer, in 21 *Current Hist.* (1925), 594–99; *Round Table*, Dec., 1920, No. 41, pp. 32 ff., and Sept., 1924, No. 56, pp. 667–82; Ruzé, in 49 and 50 (3d ser. 3–4) *R. D. I* (1922), 385 ff., 66 ff.; 6 Temperley, *op. cit.*, ch. 1, Pt. IV, pp. 193 ff. and 204 f., Visscher, in 51 (3d ser. 5) *R. D. I* (1924), 564 ff.

For bibliography on *Egypt*, see 1 Fauchille, pp. 288–90.

[24] "Protection may be tacit: thus the relationship of Russia to Bulgaria, between 1878 and 1885, can hardly be described as anything but Russian protection of Bulgaria, subject to Bulgarian subservience to Russia."   The question here is whether this was more than mere political subservience.   Baty, in *Brit. Yr. Bk.* (1921–22), note 2 on p. 109.

often violated.   The main duty is that of protection, and the protector incurs a certain measure of international responsibility for the conduct of his ward which gives him the right of intervention in the internal as well as the external affairs of the protected State.   The dependent State is bound to submit to such control and allow such intervention as it has agreed to permit; and it usually retains only a slight degree of international personality.

In contradistinction to States under Suzerainty, treaties made by the protector do not apply to States under a Protectorate unless it is expressly so stipulated; the dependent State is not necessarily a party in a war waged by its superior; and protected States retain all rights and privileges which have not been expressly yielded.[25]   But, as a matter of fact, International Protectorates are usually much more dependent than vassal States have been. Neither in principle nor in practice is there any clear or fundamental difference between the two classes.   The Protectorate is in fact the modern form of clientage or vassalage.

Existing Protectorates [26] are those of Great Britain [27] in

[25] It should be added that the establishment of a Protectorate does not necessarily invalidate treaties made between the protected and other States; the State protected does not become a part of the territory of its protector; nor does the new relation in itself effect any change in the nationality of the nationals of the two States.

As bearing upon the latter point, in a dispute between France and Great Britain respecting the applicability to British subjects of certain nationality decrees issued in Tunis and Morocco, the Permanent Court of International Justice gave an advisory opinion on Feb. 7, 1923 to the effect that this controversy was not solely a matter of domestic jurisdiction, as claimed by France. The Court was of the opinion that the French decrees in question related to persons born upon the territory of the French Protectorates of Tunis and the French zone of Morocco, and not upon the territory of France itself.

"The powers of the protecting over the protected State, depend, first, on the treaties between them establishing the Protectorate; and, secondly, upon the conditions under which the Protectorate has been recognized by third Powers 'against whom there is an intention to rely on these treaties.' Protectorates, under International Law, have common features but also individual characteristics resulting from the special conditions under which they were created and the stage of their development."   The quotation is from Gregory, in 17 *A. J.* (1923), 302.   See *Collection of Advisory Opinions*, Series B, No. 4 (Leyden, 1923).   See also Hudson, *Court of Int. Justice* (1925), 48–54.

[26] The main historical Protectorates of the 19th century were those of Great Britain over the Ionian Islands (1815–63) and the Transvaal (1881–1902); and of Austria, Prussia, and Russia over the "free and independent" city of Cracow (1815–46).

[27] For the doubtful case of Egypt, see above, note 23.

the Malay States, Borneo, certain islands in the Western Pacific, and numerous so-called Protectorates in various parts of Africa like Bechuananland, Somaliland, Uganda, Nyasaland and particularly Zanzibar; of France [28] over

Many former British Protectorates, like Gambia, the Gold Coast, Nigeria, and Kenya, have been annexed as Crown Colonies. In fact it may be said that, outside India, British Protectorates approximate more and more to annexed territory. Indeed, most of them are Colonial Protectorates or disguised occupations (see *infra*, No. 185). This is perhaps partly the cause and partly the result of the transfer, since 1880, of the administration of such present or former Protectorates as British East Africa, Nigeria, Nyasaland, Somaliland, Uganda, and Zanzibar, from the Foreign to the Colonial Office.

There are still a few cases, like that of the Protectorate in North Borneo, of administration by a Chartered Company. There is at least one case—that of a petty sovereignty in Borneo—of direct government by a British subject, the Rajah of Sarawak.

In the best organized British Protectorates, a British official called a Resident acts as advisor to the native Government; less well organized countries or regions, where tribal government prevails, are administered by British Commissioners or Consul-Generals.

There are two cases of a *condominium*, *i.e.* joint administration or Protectorate—the Anglo-Egyptian in the Sudan and the Anglo-French in the New Hebrides.

A British Protectorate is defined by Jenkyns (*British Rule and Jurisdiction beyond the Seas*, 1902, p. 165) as a "country which is not within the British dominions, but as regards its foreign relations is under the exclusive control of the King . . ." In *Rex* v. *Crewe* (1910), 79 *L. J.*, 874, the Court of Appeals held that the Bechuanan Protectorate was not a part of the dominion of the Crown, but foreign territory.

It does not follow that there is no exercise of British jurisdiction or interference in internal affairs. Indeed, there seems to be a tendency not restricted to the British Empire for the protecting State to assert jurisdiction over foreigners as well as its own citizens within the territory of the protected State, but this seems to be largely limited to what are regarded as uncivilized regions. See Hall, *Foreign Powers and Jurisdictions of the British Crown* (1895), Pt. III, ch. 3, pp. 204 ff.; * Jenkyns, *op. cit.*, ch. 9; and Westlake, *Collected Papers* (1914), 181 ff.

On *British Protectorates*, in addition to the above references, see Colonial Office List (1920); * Lucas, in 6 *Oxford Survey of the British Empire* (Oxford, 1914), 34 ff., 66 ff.; Macdonell, Art. on "Protectorates," in 22 *Ency. Brit.*, 11th ed.; *Statesman's Year Book* (1924); and 1 Westlake, 125–29.

[28] Like the British, the French Protectorates are mostly disguised annexations or occupations. Madagascar, formerly a French Protectorate, was annexed in 1896. The international personality of Tunis is very slight. After almost provoking a general European War (see *supra*, p. 112), France finally succeeded in definitely establishing and organizing her Protectorate over Morocco in 1912.

On the *French Protectorates* over Tunis, Annam, etc., and Morocco, see 1 Fauchille, No. 187 and the references on pp. 273 ff. and 279–80. For an account of the historical development of "The New Moroccan Protectorate," see Harris, in 7 *A. J.* (1913), 245–67.

Tunis, Annam, Cambodia, and Morocco; and of the United States over Cuba.[29] With the exception of the latter whose international activities are considerable and whose external sovereignty is only subject to the control of the United States in a few essential matters, the great majority of the Protectorates above named are either colonial in character or the international personality remains very slight.[30]

105a. **Mandatory System.**[31]—What appears to be a new or

[29] On the Cuban and Haitian protectorates, see *supra*, notes 33 and 37 on pp. 168 and 170.

[30] Aside from the British Protectorates or Native States in India (see *infra*, No. 108), there appear to be three main types or classes of present-day Protectorates or client States: (1) Protectorates like Cuba and Egypt (from 1914 to 1922) which are almost sovereign and practically independent; (2) British and French Protectorates like Zanzibar, the Sultanate of Johore near Singapore, Brunei in Borneo, Tunis, Annam, and Cambodia, which are more or less highly organized and where native States or rulers still exist; and (3) pure Colonial Protectorates which are disguised occupations (see *infra*, No. 185).

On *Protectorates and Vassal States*, see Baty, *Int. Law in South Africa* (1900), ch. 2; * Boghitchévitch, *Halbsouveränität* (1903); * Despagnet, *Essai sur les protectorats* (1896); Englehardt, *Les protectorats* (1896); * 1 Fauchille, Nos. 176–92; Fenwick, *Wardship in Int. Law* (1919); Hall, § 4, pp. 28–29 and § 38a, pp. 150–53; Heilborn, *Das völkerrechtliche Protektorat* (1891), and in 8 *Z. V.* (1914), 217 ff.; Gairal, *Le protectorat international* (1896); Jenkyns, *British Rule and Jurisdiction beyond the Seas* (1902), ch. 9; Lindley, *Acquisition and Government of Backward Territory in Int. Law* (1926), ch. 23; Macdonell, in 22 *Ency. Brit.* (11th ed.); * 1 Oppenheim, §§ 90–95; Pic, in 3 *R. D. I. P.* (1896), 613–47; Pillet, in 2 *R. D. I. P.* (1895), 583 ff.; De Pouvourville, in 4 *R. D. I. P.* (1897), 176 ff.; Rouard de Card, *Les traités de protectorat conclus par la France en Afrique, 1870–95* (1897); Sirmagieff, *Des états mi-souverains* (1889); Stubbs, *Suzerainty* (1880); * 1 Westlake, 22–27, 121–29; Wilhelm, in 17 *J. C. I. P.* (Clunet, 1890), 204 ff., and in 22 *J. C. I. P.* (Clunet, 1895), 760 ff.

For more complete bibliographies, see 1 Fauchille, pp. 259–60, 268 ff., and 285 ff.

[31] The main architect of the mandatory system was undoubtedly General Smuts who served on the League of Nations Commission and whose pamphlet entitled "The League of Nations: A Practical Suggestion," prepared in collaboration with the "Round Table" group, was published in 1918 and circulated at the Paris Peace Conference. This is within the author's personal knowledge.

But the real source of the plan and of the ideas of General Smuts and his collaborators was their knowledge and observation (derived partly from experience) of the principles of British administration of colonies and dependencies. As an application of his own principles of self-determination and the rights and interests of the governed, President Wilson derived these ideas from General Smuts and incorporated them into the Covenant of the League of Nations.

The theory and practice of the mandatory system seems also to have been influenced by the conception of a *mandatarius* in Roman Private Law as an agent to whom a commission is entrusted and who may not exceed the limita-

modified form of the Protectorate is prescribed in Article 22 of the Covenant of the League of Nations which was adopted as at least a partial antidote or substitute for the economic and political imperialism that was one of the fundamental causes of the World War.

Article 22 of the Covenant of the League of Nations runs as follows:

" To those colonies and territories which as a consequence of the late war have ceased to be under the sovereignty of the States [32] which formerly governed them and which are inhabited by peoples *not yet able to stand by themselves* under the strenuous conditions of the modern world, there should be applied the principle that the *well being and development of such peoples form a sacred trust of civilization* and that securities for the performance of this trust should be embodied in this Covenant.

" The best method of giving practical effect to this principle is that the *tutelage of such peoples should be intrusted to advanced nations* [33] who, by reason of their resources, their

tions of the mandate. The ideals of trusteeship as applied to colonies or dependent tribes may also be said to have a strong background in American history, as, *e.g.* in relation to the North American Indians and the Philippine Islands.

The only previous analogies in international relations to the mandatory system may be found in the Berlin-Congo Act of 1885 and the Act of Algeciras in 1906 (see *supra*, p. 91 and *infra*, p. 112).

On the *Origin of the Mandatory System*, see: * 1 Baker, *Wilson and World Settlement* (1922–23) 226–27, 261–75; Bileski, in 13 *Z. V.* (1924), 77 ff.; Potter, in 16 *Am. Pol. Sci. Rev.* (1922), 363 ff.; * Smuts, *League of Nations* (1918), 11–23; 2 and 6 Temperley, *op. cit.*, 231 f. and 502 f. respectively; and Wright, in 23 *Mich. Law Rev.* (1925), No. 7.

[32] *I.e.*, of Germany and the Turkish Empire. The mandates were to apply only to former enemy territory.

[33] The "advanced nations" or Allied and Associated Powers arrogated to themselves the right of distributing the mandates. On May 7, 1919, even before the signature of the Treaty of Versailles, the Supreme War Council allocated the bulk of Togoland and the Cameroons to France; German East-Africa, etc., to Great Britain; German South-West Africa (Tanganyika) to the Union of South Africa; the four ex-German Islands in the Pacific north of the equator to Japan; the former Pacific possessions south of the equator (excepting Nauru and German Samoa) to Australia. Nauru was allocated to the British Empire, German Samoa to New Zealand. To Belgium there was awarded (a little later) a portion of German East-Africa. It was not until May 5, 1920 at San Remo that France was definitely selected as the mandatory for Syria and Great Britain for Palestine and Mesopotamia. Owing mainly to the demands of the United States that she be consulted, more particularly in regard to the oil of Mesopotamia, the terms of the A and B man-

experience or their geographical position, can best undertake this responsibility, and who are willing to accept it, and that this tutelage should be *exercised by them as Mandatories on behalf of the League.*

" The character of the mandate must differ according to the stage of the development of the people, the geographical situation of the territory, its economic conditions and other similar circumstances.

The mandates were divided into three classes or types:

A. " Certain communities formerly belonging to the Turkish Empire [34] have reached a stage of development where their existence as independent nations can be provisionally recognized subject to the rendering of administrative advice and assistance by a Mandatory until such time as they are able to stand alone. The wishes of these communities must be a principal consideration in the selection of the Mandatory.

B. " Other peoples, especially those of Central Africa, are at such a stage that the Mandatory must be responsible for the administration of the territory under conditions which will guarantee freedom of conscience and religion, subject only to the maintenance of public order and morals, the

dates were considerably delayed. For selections from the correspondence between the United States and Great Britain, see 6 Temperley, *op. cit.*, 507–10. See also Wright, in 23 *Mich. Law Rev.* (1925), No. 7.

[34] The A mandates are those of the British Empire for Iraq (or Mesopotamia) and Palestine (with a separate mandate for Trans-Jordania since 1924), and that of France in Syria and Lebanon. The avowed purpose is to prepare these peoples for independence. The ultimate recognition of Iraq's complete independence is, indeed, embodied in a bilateral treaty of alliance signed Oct. 10, 1922, between that country and Great Britain. This form of the mandate approaches most nearly the most liberal type of the Protectorate (see *supra*, p. 168) like Cuba.

It is apparently contemplated that Iraq, which is now a separate kingdom, shall become in the course of time a member of the League of Nations. For texts of the British mandate for Palestine and the French mandate for Syria and Lebanon, see 3 Levermore, *League of Nations* (1923), 402 ff.; or Supp. to 17 *A. J.* (1923), 164 ff. and 177 ff. The terms of the mandate for Iraq (Mesopotamia) did not formally go into effect until Sept. 27, 1924, though in its relations with that kingdom the British Government has acted in the spirit of a mandatory since 1920.

An Anglo-Iraq Treaty, signed on Jan. 13, 1926, provides for the continuance for 25 years of the relations between Iraq and Great Britain as defined by the Treaty of Alliance of 1922, unless Iraq should be admitted as a Member of the League of Nations before the expiration of that period. For the text of this Treaty, see *Manchester Guardian* (weekly ed., Feb. 12, 1926), 128.

prohibition of abuses such as the slave trade, the arms traffic and the liquor traffic, and the prevention of the establishment of fortifications of military and naval bases and of military training of the natives for other than police purposes and the defense of territory, and will also secure equal opportunities for the trade and commerce of other Members of the League.[35]

C. " There are territories, such as Southwest Africa and certain of the South Pacific islands which, owing to the sparseness of their population or their small size, or their remoteness from the centers of civilization, or their geographical contiguity to the territory of the Mandatory, and other circumstances, can be best administered under the laws of the Mandatory as integral portions of its territory, subject to the safeguards above mentioned in the interests of the indigenous population.[36]

[35] It should be noted that the B mandates provide particularly for the open door for members of the League. They contemplate a system of direct administration by the mandatories who, however, pledge themselves to prohibit certain abuses such as the slave trade, and traffic in arms and liquor. The mandatory also agrees to prevent the establishment of fortifications, etc., and the military training of natives except for police purposes and the *defense of territory*.

The omission of the article *the* before "territory" appears to leave the above italicized phrase ambiguous. France has insisted on the right to train natives in Togoland and the Camaroons in order to "repulse an attack, or for the defense of the territory outside that over which the mandatory is administered." This is certainly contrary to the spirit and intent of the mandatory system.

[36] The C mandates approximate most closely to Colonial Protectorates (see *infra*, No. 185), and are by some considered as being virtual colonies or disguised annexations. The mandate territories are recognized as integral portions of the territory of the mandatories.

On the other hand it might be urged that even in the case of the C mandates, the Council of the League has insisted that the nationality of the peoples be distinct from that of the governing or mandatory power. 4 Levermore, *League of Nations* (1924), 138–39.

The principles of the open door are not prescribed for the C mandates, but there are very strict provisions regarding the slave trade, forced labor, traffic in arms and liquor, etc.

A perusal of the texts of some of the draft A, B, and C mandates will show that they are conceived in the most liberal spirit and apparently inspired by a genuine desire to give effect to the provisions of Article 22 of the Covenant, in some cases actually going beyond its requirements. In all cases full powers of legislation and administration, subject to the provisions of the mandates, are given to the mandatories. These mandates are virtually constitutions for the peoples or areas to which they apply.

For the texts of the C mandates, see *Supp.* to 17 *A. J.* (1923), 138–93 or 1 Levermore, *op. cit.*, 59–69.

" In every case of mandate, the Mandatory shall render to the Council an annual report in reference to the territory committed to its charge.

" The degree of authority, control or administration to be exercised by the Mandatory shall, if not previously agreed upon by the Members of the League, be explicitly defined in each case by the Council.

" A permanent Commission shall be constituted to receive and examine the annual reports of the Mandatories, and to advise the Council on all matters relating to the observance of the mandates." [37]

[37] The Mandatory Commission which meets annually at Geneva and is appointed by the Council of the League, consists of nine members, five of whom must be nationals of non-mandatory States. It examines the annual reports of the various mandatories and frequently interprets the obligations of the mandatory powers. It appears to be an efficient, authoritative, impartial body to which the League has delegated its supervisory powers. It does not hesitate to inquire into the entire spirit of the administration of the mandatories and call their attention to complaints and abuses. It even occupies itself with such matters as land tenure, labor conditions, education, and public health. See, *e.g.* the questionnaire for the B and C mandates in 2 Levermore, *op. cit.*, 205–08. The Mandate Commission has passed a resolution to the effect that the Mandatory Powers do not possess "any right over any part of the territory under mandate other than that resulting from their being entrusted with the administration of the territory." Buell, *Int. Relations* (1925), 342. But the Commission seems to need larger powers and should have observers on the spot. On the "Working of the Machinery" of the mandate system, see especially *League of Nations and Mandates* (League of Nations Secretariat, Geneva, 1924), 29 ff.

On *International Mandates*, see articles in 96 *Annals* (July, 1921), 70–97; 1 * Baker, *Wilson and World Settlement* (1922–23), 226–27, 261–75; Baty, in *Brit. Yr. Bk.* (1921–22), 115 f.; Bentwich, in *Brit. Yr. Bk.* (1921–22), 48–56; Bileski, in 13 *Z. V.* (1924), 77 ff.; * Buell, *Int. Relations* (1925), ch. 15, pp. 339 ff.; Burckhard, *Le mandat français en Syrie* (1925); and in 20 *Cur. Hist.* (1924), 386 ff.; Buxton and Evans, *Oppressed Peoples and the League of Nations* (1922), ch. 3; Corbett, in *Brit. Yr. Bk.* (1924), 128–36; Coriceanu, *Les mandats int.* (1921); Dienna, *Les mandats int.* (1926); Fanshawe, *Reconstruction* (1925), 70–84; Furukaki, *Les mandats int.* (1923); Gore, in *The League of Nations Starts* (1920), ch. 7; Harris, in 122 *Contemp. Rev.* (1922), 604–11; *Int. Concil.*, No. 166; Keith, in 4 *J. C. L.* (1922), 71 ff.; Lansing, *Peace Negotiations* (1921), ch. 13; League of Nations, Information Section, *League of Nations and Mandates* (Geneva, 1924); Levermore, *League of Nations* (annual Yearbooks since 1921), see index; Lewis, in 39 *Law Quar. Rev.* (1923), 458–75; * Lindley, *Acquisition and Govt. of Backward Territory* (1926), ch. 26; Lugard, in 238 *Edin. Rev.* (1923), 398–408; Mills, in 17 *A. J.* (1923), 50–62; Millot, *Les mandats int.* (1924); * Moon, *Imperialism and World Politics* (1926), ch. 18; * Pic, in 5 (2 ser.) *R. D. I. P.* (1923), 322 ff.; Potter, in 16 *Am. Pol. Sci. Rev.* (1922), 563 ff.; Rappard, *Int. Relations Viewed from Geneva* (1925), ch. 2, pp. 27–40; Rolin, in 47 *R. D. I.* (1920), 329–63; Schücking and Wehberg, *Die*

106. Distinctions between an International Protectorate, a merely Protected State, and a Colonial Protectorate.—

International Protectorates should be distinguished from merely politically *protected States* like Panama and San Domingo [38] on the one hand, and from *Colonial Protectorates* on the other. The latter, in which the inhabitants and territory protected do not form States within the modern meaning of this term, will be discussed under the head of " Modes of Acquiring Territory." [39]

Some of the authorities place the North American Indian tribes and the vassal or protected Princes and States of India under the head of International Protectorates. They are undoubtedly, in a sense, Protectorates, but certainly not International Protectorates. Neither do they fit into the category of Colonial Protectorates. They seem to constitute a class by themselves. [40]

107. The North American Indians.—Prior to 1871, the North American Indian tribes were regarded by the United

Satzung des Völkerbundes (2d ed., 1924), 684–711; * Smuts, *League of Nations* (1918); Stoyanowsky, *La théorie des mandats int.* (1925); 2 Strupp, *Wörterbuch des Völkerrechts* (1924–25), 12 ff.; * 6 Temperely, *Hist. of the Peace Conference* (1920–24 see index), particularly 500–23, and *Second Year of the League* (1922), 81–91; * White, *Mandates* (1925); W. P. F., *League of Nations and Pamphlets* (1918 ff.) see index and particularly 8 *Pamphlets, Yearbook of the League of Nations*, 1925, pp. 485–93; Woolf, *Mandates and Empire* (1920), and 29 *I. L. A.* (1920), 128 ff.; * Wright, in 17 *A. J.* (1923), 691 ff., 18 *A. J.* (1924), 306–15, and 23 *Mich. Law Rev.* (1925), No. 7.

For Bibliographies, see Library of Congress, *List of References on Mandates* (1924); and (for French references), Pic, in 5 (2d ser.) *R. D. I. P.* (1923), 322–23.

[38] For Panama and San Domingo, see, *supra*, notes 40 and 35 on pp. 172 and 169.

A good historical example of the merely protected State is the Confederacy of the Rhine (1806–1813), which recognized Napoleon I as its "Protector." Its members were, however, virtually client or vassal states.

The small Republic of San Marino is under the "exclusive protective friendship" of Italy, but is not a Protectorate.

In a very broad general sense, the Latin-American States might be said to be under the political protection of the United States.

[39] See *infra*, No. 185, pp. 289 ff.

[40] An Act of Congress, dated March 3, 1871, declared: "No Indian nation or tribe within the territory of the United States shall be acknowledged or recognized as an independent nation, tribe, or power with whom the United States may contract by treaty; but no obligation of any treaty lawfully made and ratified with any such Indian nation or tribe prior to March 3, 1871, shall be hereby invalidated or impaired." But agreements with Indian tribes, subject to the approval of Congress, have been made since the passage of this act, 1 Moore, *Digest*, § 17, p. 37.

States as " domestic dependent nations " in a " state of pupilage resembling that of a ward to his guardian." [41] They were held to possess certain rights of occupancy to the soil, but the real title to their lands, which was originally based on discovery and conquest,[42] had become vested in the National Government by virtue of the rights of succession. As long as they remained connected with their tribal organizations, they were regarded as " domestic subjects "; but it was held that " an Indian treaty, when duly solemnized, is as much a law of the land as is a treaty with a foreign power." [43]

108. **The Princes and States of India.**—Closely analogous to the status of the North American Indian tribes before 1871, and yet differing from it on some points, is that of the Princes and States of India in their relations with Great Britain. Like the Indian tribes in the United States, the six hundred protected Princes and States of India have no international relations with foreign Powers or with each other. The preamble of an Act of Parliament [44] of 1876 described them as in " alliance with Her Majesty," and they are held to be entitled to British protection on the high seas or in foreign parts. They cannot even send representatives to Calcutta, but must communicate with the British Government through the British representatives at their courts. In 1891 the official Gazette published [45] by the Government of India declared:

" The principles of International Law have no bearing

---

[41] See especially Chief Justice Marshall, in *Cherokee Nation* v. *Georgia* (1831), 5 Peters, 1, and *Worcester* v. *Georgia* (1832), 6 Peters, 515; Justice Gray, in *Elk* v. *Wilkins* (1884), 112 U. S. 94; and Justice *Miller* in *U. S.* v. *Kagama* (1886), 118 U. S. 375. For a review of these and other decisions, see Snow, *Question of the Aborigines* (1921), ch. 3.

[42] Chief Justice Marshall, in *Johnson* v. *McIntosh* (1823), 8 Wheaton 543, and Evans, *Cases*, 281 or Scott, 175.

[43] 1 Moore, *Digest*, p. 37. On the *Status of the American Indian*, see: * 2 Butler, *Treaty-making Power* (1902), ch. 14; 1 Calvo, § 71; Devlin, *Treaty Power* (1908), ch. 12; 1 Halleck (3d ed.), 75–78; Lawrence, 1 *Commentaire* (1868–80), 264 f.; * 1 Moore, *Digest* §§ 15–17; * Scott, *Cases* (ed. of 1902), 398–412, or Snow, *Cases on Int. Law* (1893), 230–41; 2 Wharton, *Digest*, ch. 8, §§ 208–11; Wheaton, § 38 (Atlay's ed., § 38 *a* and Dana's ed., note 24); and 1 Willoughby, *The Const. Law of the U. S.* (1910), ch. 20.

[44] 39 and 40 Vict., c. 46. See Westlake, *Chapters* (1894), p. 212 or *Collected Papers* (1914), 217.

[45] Westlake, *op. cit.*, 215–16 or 220–21.

upon the relations between the Government of India as representing the Queen Empress on the one hand, and the native States under the suzerainty of Her Majesty on the other. The paramount supremacy of the former presupposes and implies the subordination of the latter." [46]

109. (**IV**) **Neutralized States.**—There is another class of States which does not fit well into our scheme of classification. This is the permanently neutralized State. Neutralized States are those whose neutrality, independence,[47] or territorial integrity are recognized and permanently guaranteed by an international agreement of the Great Powers on condition that they agree never to go to war except in case of attack, and never to assume international obligations (as *e.g.* enter into a treaty of alliance or guarantee) which might lead them into hostilities. The purpose of such permanent neutralization has generally been the maintenance of the balance of power in Europe by removing a temptation to aggression and creating a Buffer-State between rival Powers. A violation of the neutrality of a permanent neutralized State imposes upon the guaranteeing Powers the duty of intervention [48] in behalf of the injured State.

[46] Cited also by Westlake, I, p. 42. Westlake, our main authority on this subject, quotes freely from Lee-Warner, *The Protected Princes of India* (1894); and Tupper, *Our Indian Protectorate* (1893).

On the *Indian States* or *Princes*, see also Hall (8th ed.), 28 n.; *Round Table* (Dec., 1916), pp. 91–113; 2 Nys, 80–86; Wheaton (Atlay's ed.), § 38 *c*. They really seem to be a form of the Colonial Protectorate (see *infra*, No. 185).

[47] Independence is not expressly guaranteed in the case of Switzerland. Unlike Switzerland, the integrity and inviolability of the territory of Belgium was not expressly guaranteed. Luxemburg was merely given a guarantee of neutrality. But guarantees of independence as well as of territorial integrity and inviolability must be implied; for, as Westlake (*Int. Law*, 1st ed., I, p. 28) justly remarks: "The territory of a State cannot be violated without infringing its neutrality, and it may be added that a similar infringement would result from an attack by force on its independence."

[48] There is a difference of opinion among the authorities as to whether in such a case as the "collective" guarantee of the neutrality of Luxemburg, the guarantors are bound to act singly or separately, should any of them decline to join in common or collective action. For the contrary views of Bluntschli and Lord Derby, see Hall § 113, pp. 401–02. For a refutation of Lord Stanley's (Derby's) view that the collective guarantors are not bound to act separately, see Piccioni, *Essai sur la neutralité* (2d ed., 1902), 20 ff. See also Sanger and Norton, *England's Guarantee to Belgium and Luxenburg* (1915), ch. 4. Such a doctrine would deprive the guarantee of efficacy. There can be no question as to legal obligation in case of several, separate or individual guarantees, as in the case of Belgium.

The permanent neutralization [49] of States should be distinguished from the status of mere temporary neutrality during war on the one hand, and from the possible neutralization of parts of a State,[50] or of rivers, straits, canals, lakes, gulfs, and seas on the other.[51] By analogy the term has also been applied to certain persons and things like surgeons, hospitals, and hospital ships in time of warfare.[52]

The authorities seem to be about equally divided on the question whether permanently neutralized States remain fully sovereign. On the one hand it is argued that neutralization " does not carry with it the renunciation of any faculty of state life. It is merely an undertaking not to do certain things, and no more impairs sovereignty than does an undertaking not to interfere in a particular war. . . . Besides, it is necessary that for every part of the civilized world the full powers of sovereignty should exist." [53] On the other hand, it is justly urged that to permanently deprive a State of the right to declare war or contract alliances at will, is manifestly a serious restriction on external sovereignty or freedom of action such as fully sovereign States have hitherto exercised. This is a fact which no amount of plausible argument can extinguish.[54]

[49] We might also distinguish between permanent and temporary neutralization, as in the case of China during the Russo-Japanese War. See Hershey, *Russo-Japanese War* (1906), 248.

[50] The most conspicuous example of the neutralization of a part of a State has been that of a portion of Savoy which was included in the neutralization of Switzerland in 1815. In 1860, Savoy, until then belonging to Sardinia, was ceded to France, which thus succeeded to the rights and duties pertaining to the neutrality of these provinces. These duties were recognized in 1883, when the French Government discontinued the construction of fortifications near Geneva in deference to the complaints of the Federal Council of Switzerland. There is no agreement as to how far these rights and duties extend in the case of a neutralized province. The neutralized zone in Savoy ceased in 1919. See Treaty of Versailles, Art. 435 and Annexes thereto. On the neutralization of Savoy, see particularly Lawrence, § 226. For bibliography, see 1 Fauchille, pp. 717–18.

Another historical case of neutralization of a part of a State was that of the two Ionian islands of Corfu and Paxo, together with their dependencies, which were declared permanently neutral by England, France, and Russia when the group to which they belong were annexed by Greece in 1864. The king of Greece on his part agreed to "maintain such neutrality."

[51] See *infra*, Nos. 195 ff.

[52] See *infra*, Nos. 369 ff.

[53] This is the argument of Westlake, I, pp. 28–29.

[54] It is not merely that a neutralized State is not fully sovereign; it is less

The sole surviving example of a permanently neutralized
State is Switzerland,[55] the neutralization of Belgium [56] and
free in its choice of means than are other States. Oppenheim (I, p. 174) points
out that a State does not lose any part of its sovereignty by concluding a treaty
of arbitration. This is true, but suppose it were generally bound to arbitrate
all or any class of international disputes, while other States retained the right
to go to war. Would such a State be fully sovereign? If we had a general
treaty of obligatory arbitration, the contracting States would remain sovereign
because all would be equally and reciprocally bound.

Mérignhac (II, p. 43) urges that treaties of guarantee do not destroy
sovereignty. Such treaties do not necessarily imply a limitation of sovereignty
—not unless the State whose rights are guaranteed binds itself permanently not
to exercise important or essential sovereign powers such as other States enjoy.

[55] The neutrality of Switzerland was formally recognized and guaranteed by
the Powers at the Congresses of Vienna and Paris in 1815. It had been largely
maintained from the Peace of Westphalia down to the French Revolution, but
had not withstood the test of the struggles of the Revolutionary and Napoleonic
period. No case of violation has occurred since 1815. The neutralization of
Switzerland was reaffirmed by Art. 435 of the Treaty of Versailles. Indeed,
it may be said to form a part of the public law of Europe.

Upon her entry into the League of Nations in 1920, Switzerland was
permitted to make certain reservations bearing upon her obligations under
Arts. 10 and 16 of the Covenant. The Council of the League recognized her
"unique situation," and declared that she "shall not be forced to participate in
a military action or to permit the passage of foreign troops or the preparation of
military enterprises upon her territory." Mowat, in *Brit. Yr. Bk.* (1923–24),
92. See also Borel, in 27 *R. D. I. P.* (1920), 153 ff.; Borgeaud, *La neutralité
Suisse* (1921), ch. 4; Huber, in 2 *Les origines et l'oeuvre de la Societé des Nations*,
(ed. by Munch, 1923), 68–136; and Rappard, in 1 *Ibid.*, 360 ff.

On the *Neutralization of Switzerland*, see especially: Borgeaud, *La neutralité
Suisse* (1921); Hilty, *Die Neutralität der Schweiz* (1889); Schweizer, *Geschichte
der schweizerischen Neutralität* (1893–95); and Sherman, in 12 *A. J.* (1918), 241
ff., 462 ff., and 780 ff.

For further references, see 1 Fauchille, p. 705.

[56] The independence and permanent neutrality of Belgium was guaranteed
by the Great Powers (including Prussia) in the two treaties of London of 1831
and 1839; the neutrality of Luxemburg by the same Powers at the London
Conference of 1867.

On the German violation of Belgian neutrality in Aug., 1914, see particularly
* Visscher, *Belgium's Case* (1916), especially ch. 2. See also 2 Garner, chs.
28–29; Stowell, *Diplomacy of the War* (1915), ch. 9; and Warrin, *The Neutrality
of Belgium* (1918). For bibliographies on Belgian Neutrality, see Visscher, *op.
cit.*, 161–64 and 1 Fauchille, pp. 709, 712. On the causes and effects of the
abrogation of Belgian neutrality, see Roussel Le Ray, *L'abrogation de la
neutralité de la Belgique* (1923).

The most important historical instances of permanent neutralization usually
cited are the "free and independent city" of Cracow (1815–46) and the
Congo Free State (1885–1908). The neutrality of Cracow was guaranteed by
Austria, Prussia, and Russia. It was annexed by Austria in 1846.

The Congo Free State was not a case of perfect neutralization. At the West
African Congress of 1884–85, Mr. Kasson, the American plenipotentiary,
proposed that the territories comprised within the conventional Congo basin be

Luxemburg having been abolished in 1919 in consequence of the German violation of the guaranteed neutrality of these countries at the outbreak of the Great War.

permanently neutralized. After much discussion, the Powers merely agreed (see Arts. 10–11 of the Final Act of the Conference, in Supplement to 3 *A. J.*, 1909, 14) "to respect the neutrality" of the region on certain conditions and to "use their good offices" to this end. In 1885 the Congo State declared itself perpetually neutral. It will be interesting to observe the effect of the recent (1908) annexation of the Congo Free State by Belgium upon the status of this territory. It is the first example of "a neutralized State holding a colony within neutralized territory." See Reeves on "The Origin of the Congo Free State," in 3 *A. J.* (1909), 99 ff. For references on the neutrality of the Congo, see 1 Fauchille, pp. 363 and 715.

The first historical instance of attempted permanent neutralization was that of the island of Malta, which was declared neutral by the treaty of Amiens (Art. 10) between France and England in 1801–1802. But this treaty was never executed. See Morand, in 1 *R. D. I. P.* (1894), 522 ff.

The most recent case of the neutralization of a portion of a State known to the author is that of the Aaland Islands which was effected through the instrumentality of the Council of the League of Nations. On Oct. 20, 1921, Germany, France, Great Britain, Italy, and the Baltic States signed at Geneva a treaty providing for the non-fortification and neutralization of these islands which form a small group in the Gulf of Finland between the coasts of Sweden and Finland. The Islands themselves were awarded to Finland by the League of Nations, though the inhabitants, being Swedish in origin, language and culture, greatly desired to be annexed to Sweden. Cf. *infra*, p. 511 n.

On "The Neutralization of the Aaland Islands," see Gregory, in 17 *A. J.* (1923), 63–76. For the text of the treaty, see Supp. to 17 *A. J.*, 1 ff.

The present-day form of neutralization seems to be that of the *demilitarized zone*. At least it is somewhat analagous. On the demilitarization of the right and left banks of the Rhine, see Treaty of Versailles, Arts. 42–44. These have been incorporated into the Locarno Pact. On the demilitarized zones and islands on the shores of the Straits of Constantinople, see Convention Relating to the Régime of the Straits concluded at Lausanne on July 24, 1923, Arts. 4–9. For the text of this treaty, see 2 *Treaties of Peace, 1919–23* (1924), 1025 ff.

On *Neutralized States* generally, see Bluntschli, Arts. 745–47; Descamps, *La neutralité de la Belgique* (1902), and *L'État neutre à titre permanent* (1912); Despagnet, Nos. 137–46; Erich, in 7 *Z. V.* (1913) 452–76; Eyschen, "La position du Luxembourg," in 31 *R. D. I.* (1899), 5 ff.; * 1 Fauchille, Nos. 348–69; Geffcken, in 4 *Handbuch*, § 137; Hagerup, in 12 *R. D. I. P.* (1905), 577 ff.; * 1 Kleen, §§ 12–22, pp. 85 ff.; Liszt, §§ 11 and 580 II; Littell, *Neutralization of States* (1920); Morand, in 1 *R. D. I. P.* (1894), 522–37; 1 Nys, 379–96, in 2 *Etudes*, 47–163, and in 32 and 33 R. D. I. (1900 and 1901), 461 ff., 583 ff., and 15 ff. respectively; * 1 Oppenheim, §§ 95–101; Piccioni, *Essai sur neutralité perpetuelle* (1902), 2 P.-Fodéré, Nos. 1001–15; Regnault, *Des effets de la neutralité perpétuelle* (1898); Richter, *Die Neutralization von Staaten* (1913); * 1 Rivier, § 7, pp. 108–20; Tswettcoff, *De la situation juridique des états neutralisés* (1895); Ullmann, § 27; * 1 Westlake, 27–31 and in 33 *R. D. I.* (1901), 389–97; Wicker, *Neutralization* (1911) and in 5 *A. J.* (1911), 639–52; Wilson, in 4 *Yale Rev.* (1914–15), 474–86.

BIBLIOGRAPHY

Classification of States.—Bluntschli, Arts. 70–80; Brie, *Theorie der Staatenverbindungen* (1886); 1 Calvo, §§ 44 ff.; Despagnet, Nos. 75–78, 109–46; Ebers, *Die Lehre von dem Staatenbunde* (1910); * 1 Fauchille, Nos. 165–94; 1 Fiore, Nos. 332 ff., and *Int. Law Cod.* (1918), Arts. 102–23; * Garner, *Introduction to Political Science* (1910), ch. 5, pp. 136 ff.; Hall, § 4; 1 Halleck (3d ed.), 68 ff.; Heffter, §§ 18–21, and Geffcken's notes on pp. 53–54; Holtzendorff, in 2 *Handbuch*, 98–141; * 1 Hyde, §§ 12–29; * Jellinek, *Recht des mod. Staates* (3d ed.), ch. 21, pp. 719–67, and *Die Lehre von den Staatenverbindingen* (1882); Klüber, §§ 29–35; Lawrence, §§ 37–43; Lawrence, 1 *Commentaire*, 225–345; Le Fur, *État federal et confederation d'états* (1896); Liszt, §§ 9–11; 1 J. de Louter, §§ 12–13; 1 F. de Martens, §§ 55–62; 1 G. F. de Martens, *Précis du droit des gens* (1864), §§ 16–21; 2 Mérignhac, 6–226; * 1 Moore, *Digest*, §§ 5–15; * 1 Nys, 349–98; * 1 Oppenheim, §§ 85–111; 1 Phillimore, §§ 69–123; 1 Piédelièvre, Nos. 76–114; Pomeroy, §§ 58–66; 1 P. Fodéré, Nos. 90–123; * 1 Rivier, 75–120; Taylor, §§ 120–44; 1 Twiss, §§ 23–81; Ullmann, §§ 20–27; Westerkamp, *Staatenbund und Bundestaat* (1892); * 1 Westlake, ch. 3; Wheaton, §§ 34–59.

CHAPTER VIII

THE ORIGIN, RECOGNITION, AND CONTINUITY OF STATES

110. **The Origin and Existence of the State.**—It is not within the province of the Law of Nations to deal with the causes of the origin or of the existence and growth of States —a subject which belongs to the province of general political science rather than to that of international jurisprudence. It is impossible to lay down juridical rules which shall determine the legality of the existence of an independent political community. The State is an historical and political fact,[1] the creator rather than a creature of law; but it is possible to determine, in a general way, the rules which should govern their recognition by, or admission to, the international community. The most important of these is that they must bear the essential marks or distinguishing characteristics of a State as set forth in a previous chapter.[2]

The State exists independently of its recognition,[3] but some form of recognition is necessary in order to secure its admission into the family of nations. There is, strictly speaking, no *right* to admission,[4] though there are many cases in which recognition cannot long be withheld without danger of serious or embarrassing consequences.

---

[1] Jellinek, *Das Recht des mod. Staates* (2d ed. 1905), 265 ff. Cf. *Die Lehre von den Staatenverbindungen* (1882). See also 1 Fauchille, No. 195; Liszt, § 7 III; 1 Nys, 70 ff.; 1 Rivier, 55 ff.; and Ullmann, § 29, p. 123.

[2] See *supra*, No. 88.

[3] "It has never been admitted by the United States that they acquired anything by way of cession from Great Britain by the treaty of Peace, 1783. It has been viewed only as a recognition of preëxisting rights." . . . *Harcourt* v. *Gaillard* (1827), 12 Wheat, 523, 527. Cf. *McIlvaine* v. *Coxe's Lessee* (1808), 4 Cranch, 209, 212.

[4] Consequently, there is no legal *duty* of recognition. This is the opinion of 1 Fauchille, No. 203 f.; Liszt, § 7 IV; 1 F. de Martens, § 64; 1 Oppenheim, § 71; and Le Normand, *La reconnaissance internationale* (2d ed., 1899).

But the contrary view is maintained by equally good authorities. See *e.g.* Bluntschli, Art. 35; Hall, pp. 20, 103; 1 Piédelièvre, No. 122; Pomeroy, § 215; 1 Rivier, 57; and Ullmann, § 30, p. 125.

The right and duty of recognition seems to be of a moral nature. Several of the authorities (see *e.g.* 1 P.-Fodéré, No. 144) speak of a theoretical right of recognition which may be ignored in practice.

III. **Modes of Recognition.**—The members of the international community are such by virtue of original membership in the European family of nations, or their subsequent admission.   Recognition of such admission may be tacit or express.

A new State may be tacitly or impliedly recognized by an older State through the conclusion of a treaty, the sending or reception of diplomatic agents, or the establishment of such official relations as indicate an intention to treat it as an International Person.[5]   Instances of tacit admission are Russia, the United States, Japan, and China. It is impossible, in some cases, to fix a definite date of admission.

Express or formal recognition may also assume various forms.   It may be formal and collective, as in the case of Turkey which was formally admitted to full membership [6] to the society of nations by the Great Powers at the Congress of Paris in 1856.   It may also be conditional, as in the case of the Balkan States which were admitted at the Congress of Berlin in 1878 on condition [7] that they impose no religious disabilities on their subjects.

Though tacit or express recognition binds only the recognizing State, it usually amounts to a certificate of admission to the international community.

II2. **The Conditions under which New International**

---

[5] For example, the flag of the Congo Free State was recognized by the United States in 1884.

It is a disputed question whether the appointment of consuls implies recognition. See *e.g.* Hall (109 *n.*) in the negative and 1 Oppenheim (§ 428) in the affirmative.   It would seem from a study of historical instances that the mere appointment of consuls does not imply recognition, but that the granting of an *exequatur* or document authorizing them to act does involve such recognition.   The British Government appointed consuls to various South American States at least eighteen months before their recognition by Great Britain, and a number of South American States were recognized by the United States through the issuance of *exequaturs*. See 1 Moore, *Digest*, pp. 79, 90–91, 206.   The British consuls continued to perform their functions during our Civil War.

[6] This membership was, however, somewhat qualified in practice.   It can scarcely be maintained that, prior to the World War, Turkey was actually treated in all respects as a fully sovereign and independent member of the family of nations.

[7] It appears to be agreed that the violation of such conditions does not render the recognition invalid, for recognition cannot be withdrawn if once given.   It might possibly justify intervention in certain cases.   It certainly would justify protest, suspension of diplomatic relations, and perhaps reprisals.

Persons may Arise.—New International Persons may arise in consequence of the following events:

(1) The division of an existing State or International Person into several separate international entities, as in the case of the separation of Norway and Sweden,[8] or the successful secession of members of a Federal Union.

(2) The Union of a number of States into a Confederacy or Federal State, as in the case of the United States, the Swiss Cantons, and the former German Empire.

(3) The entrance of hitherto barbarous, half-civilized or Oriental States into the international community, as in case of Russia under Peter the Great in the early part of the eighteenth, and of Japan and China [9] in the latter part of the nineteenth century.

(4) The erection of a new State in a region previously uncivilized, as in the case of the Transvaal or South African Republic (1852–1902), the Congo Free State (1884–1908), and Liberia (recognized since 1847).

(5) The formal recognition of new members by international agreement of the Powers, as in the case of the Balkan States in 1878, the Congo Free State in 1885, and of Belgium in 1831.

(6) The recognition of insurgent political communities which have revolted from the parent country.

The recognition of the latter class of communities has given rise to more definite rules and a more regular and consistent practice than in most of the other cases. Consequently, these merit a somewhat extended discussion.

The recognition of insurgent communities may be considered in three successive stages. These will be discussed in turn.

113. (I) **Recognition of Insurgency.**—*A Status of Insurgency* may be recognized when an insurrection with a political purpose has assumed the proportions of a war " in a material sense," and when it seriously interferes with the exercise of sovereignty or with normal foreign intercourse.

---

[8] As indicated above (p. 179 n.), Norway and Sweden were not wholly devoid of separate international personality prior to their separation, but each State is now a complete International Person.

[9] As in the case of Turkey, it may be questioned whether the membership of China is not somewhat qualified in international practice.

Though it is held that such a contest (one in which belligerency proper is not recognized) does not amount to civil war " in a legal sense," [10] it has passed beyond the stage of a mere mob outbreak or riot into that of an organized insurrection with responsible leaders, etc.

The recognition of a status of insurgency affects the relations between all parties concerned. Such recognition by the parent State implies the admission of certain rights and duties relating to the conduct of hostilities, as e.g. the treatment of combatants as prisoners of war instead of as traitors and pirates.[11] It also probably frees the parent State from a certain measure of responsibility for the acts of the insurgents, and imposes certain obligations upon the latter.

114. **Effects of a Recognition of Insurgency.**—Recognition of insurgency by third Powers implies certain obligations on the part of the latter, such as the enforcement of neutrality laws,[12] as also certain rights, such as the protection, wherever possible of the lives and property of neutrals,[13] and freedom from search and capture by in-

[10] The distinction between "recognition of belligerency and recognition of a condition of political revolt, between recognition of the existence of war in a material sense and war in a legal sense" was made by Chief Justice Fuller in the case of *The Three Friends* (1897), 166 U. S. 1, Evans, *Cases*, 66 or Scott, 830. The status of insurgency was also recognized by President Cleveland in his Proclamation of 1895 enjoining a strict observance of our Neutrality Laws during the second Cuban insurrection which broke out in that year. A similar British Proclamation had been issued in the Bahamas during the first Cuban insurrection in 1869. See 1 Moore, *Digest*, p. 242, and the case of *The Salvador* (1870), 3 Privy Council 218, and Scott, *Cases* (ed. of 1902), 743. In 1899 the German Consul-general at Cape Town issued a proclamation impliedly recognizing the insurgency of the Boers. See Campbell, *Neutral Rights and Obligations in the Anglo-Boer War*, in John Hopkin's *Studies* for 1908, p. 47.

[11] On the question "Can insurgents be treated as Pirates?" see *infra*, No. 214.

[12] See cases of *The Salvador* and *The Three Friends*, cited above. In 1900 the Institute of Int. Law declared that "in case of insurrection or civil war, International Law imposes upon third powers certain obligations toward established and recognized governments which are struggling with an insurrection." The supply of arms, munitions of war, and subsidies to the insurgents is prohibited; and it is especially forbidden to permit the "organization within its territory of military expeditions hostile to established or recognized governments." See Scott, *Resolutions of the Institute* (1916), 157.

The rights and duties implied in a recognition of insurgency have never been fully determined or officially declared.

[13] See Secretary Hay to Mr. Bridgman, Minister to Bolivia, March 14, 1899, *For. Rel.* (1899), 105. Cited by 1 Moore, *Digest*, p. 243.

surgent vessels. This involves a certain measure of responsibility for both the insurgents and the parent State.

On the other hand, certain rights and privileges are recognized as belonging to the insurgents, as *e.g.* freedom from treatment as pirates, the right to prevent " access of supplies to their domestic enemy ";[14] and it is maintained that " a status of insurgency may entitle the insurgents to freedom of action in lines of hostile conflict which would not otherwise be accorded, as was seen in Brazil in 1893–1894, and in Chile in 1891. It is a status of potential belligerency which a State, for the purpose of domestic order, is obliged to recognize. The admission of insurgency does not place the foreign State under new international obligations as would the recognition of belligerency, though it may make the execution of its domestic laws more burdensome."[15]

Unless recognized as belligerents, insurgents are not supposed to exercise the rights of visit and search, capture of contraband, or to institute blockades.

115. **(II) Recognition of Belligerency.**—A *Status of Belligerency* may be recognized when the insurrection has assumed the proportions of a public civil war in a legal sense, *i.e.* a war waged by insurgents politically organized under a responsible government exercising sovereign powers over a definite territory and having the will and capacity to fulfill its neutral obligations. It goes without saying that it must be able to protect the lives and property of neutrals so far as these are consistent with the ends and methods of civilized warfare, the rules of which it is bound to observe.

[14] Sec'y Hay to the Sec'y of the Navy, Nov. 15, 1902. Cited by Wilson in article entitled "Insurgency and Int. Maritime Law," in 1 *A. J.* (1907), 56. But Mr. Hay adds: "The existence of the power is restricted to the precise end to be accomplished. No right of confiscation or destruction of foreign property in such circumstances could well be recognized, and any act of injury so committed against foreigners would necessarily be at the risk of the insurgents." In another connection, he justly observes: "To deny to an insurgent the right to prevent the enemy from receiving material aid cannot well be justified without denying the right of revolution."

[15] Wilson, in the article cited above, pp. 59–60. Professor Wilson is entitled to the credit of having first called the attention of students of International Law to this important subject and of formulating the law of insurgency; but it has nevertheless been ignored, even by some recent publicists.

For the events in Brazil and Chile referred to in the text, see 1, 2 and 7, Moore, *Digest*, §§ 70, 333–34, 1172.

For References on the Recognition of Insurgency, see Bibliography at the end of this chapter.

116. Effects of Recognition of Belligerency.—The effect of a recognition of belligerency, which, like the recognition of independence, may be either tacit or express,[16] is to admit the insurgents to all the rights and privileges, and to impose upon them all the duties of a State so far as the conduct of the war is concerned. It confers an international status, though merely for purposes of warfare; but diplomatic relations between neutrals and insurgents should be un-official or informal in character,[17] and should be strictly confined to matters affecting the private and business interests of the nationals of both parties. Consuls may be sent or may continue to perform their duties among the insurgents when belligerency has been recognized, but no *exequatur* should be granted to a consul sent by an insurgent belligerent community.[18]   It goes without saying that there must be no treaties or exchange of diplomatic agents.

Special attention should be called to the fact that recognition of belligerency by third Powers is by no means necessarily or solely to the advantage of the insurgents. To be sure, it may give them moral comfort and support, enable them to float their bonds, etc.; and it permits them to exercise the rights of visit and search, capture contraband and institute blockades. But the insurgents may not be in as good a position to take advantage of these opportunities as the parent State, which also acquires these same rights and privileges.[19]   It should also be remarked that recognition by the parent State does not carry with it the same consequences or indicate the same attitude as recognition by third Powers.   The parent State binds itself to treat those

[16] It is now usually express, *i.e.* it occurs through a formal Declaration or Proclamation of Neutrality, such as was issued by Great Britain soon after the outbreak of our Civil War. But authorities are in error when they assert or imply that this has always been the case. The recognition of the belligerency of the South American States was tacitly recognized by the admission of their vessels to the ports of the United States on equal terms with those of Spain. See 1 Moore, *Digest*, § 61. Of course there is no doubt as to which method is preferable. Recognition by the parent States is always tacit or implied.

[17] On this subject, see especially "Acts Falling Short of Recognition," in 1 Moore, *Digest*, § 72.

[18] See *supra*, note on p. 200.

[19] This was notably the case with Spain and Cuba. See Hershey, "The Recognition of Cuban Belligerency," in 7 *Annals* (1896), 450 ff.; Moore, in 21 *Forum* (1896), p. 297 f.; Woolsey, *America's Foreign Policy* (1898), 25 ff.

recognized as enemies instead of as rebels and pirates, at least until the war is over, and it declines full responsibility for acts of the insurgents.   But it does not recognize their neutrality or international status.

117. History of Status of Belligerency.—The status of belligerency is a very modern addition to International Law. It was invented during the first quarter of the nineteenth century by the United States and Great Britain, and applied by them to the revolts in Spanish America and Greece; but it is only within a comparatively recent period that the doctrine has been clearly defined, more particularly in connection with the American Civil War and the Cuban Insurrections of 1868–1878 and 1895–1898.

118. The Tests of Belligerency.—It is now pretty generally agreed that a justifiable recognition of belligerency rests upon a double basis of law and policy.   " The question of belligerency is one of fact not to be decided by sympathies for or prejudices against either party.   The relations between the parent State and the insurgents must amount, in fact, to war in the sense of International Law." [20]

" Among the tests are the existence of a *de facto* political organization of the insurgents, sufficient in character, population, and resources to constitute it, if left to itself, a State among nations capable of discharging the duties of a State; the actual employment of military forces on each side, acting in accordance with the rules and customs of war . . . ; and, at sea, employment by the insurgents of commissioned cruisers, and the exercise by the parent government of the rights of blockade of insurgent ports against neutral commerce, and of stopping and searching neutral vessels at sea.   If all these elements exist, the condition of things is undoubtedly war; and it may be war before they are all ripened into activity." [21]

[20] President Grant, in Special Message of June 13, 1870. See 1 Moore, *Digest*, p. 194.

[21] See Dana's valuable note 15 to Wheaton, pp. 34–39. A portion of this note, which is perhaps the clearest exposition of the law of belligerency ever published, may be found in 1 Moore, *Digest*, § 59, and Snow, *Cases on Int. Law* (1893), 24–27. Cf. the first part of President Grant's message of 1870 cited above, which is couched in almost identical language. Dana's edition of Wheaton was published in 1866.

It should be noted that Dana does not assert that all of the tests must be

The true ground of recognition as a matter of policy is thus stated by another leading authority: " The right of a State to recognize the belligerent character of insurgent subjects of another State must, then, for the purposes of International Law, be based solely upon a possibility that its interests may be so affected . . . as to make a recognition a reasonable measure of self-protection.[22]   According to Dana, the only justification for recognition is that the neutral's " own rights and interests are so affected as to require a definition of its own relations to the parties."   If not justified by such necessity, " it is a gratuitous demonstration of moral support to the rebellion, and of censure upon the parent government "; and premature recognition may be regarded in the light of an unfriendly act,[23] though it should not be looked upon as an intervention.

119. **Historical Examples of Recognition of Belligerency.** —Among the historical instances of recognition of belligerency are those of the various States of Spanish America [24] by the United States and Great Britain during the first quarter of the nineteenth century; the recognition of the belligerency of Greece by Great Britain in 1825; that of

applied in every case.   To insist upon a navy as a *sine qua non* would be equivalent to a claim that war in a legal sense cannot be carried on solely on land.   Where it can be applied in conjunction with the others, this test is almost conclusive, although it is not likely that a mere fleet will be recognized, as was shown in the cases of Brazil and Chile in 1893 and 1891.   See Lawrence, § 142; and 1, 2 and 7, Moore, *Digest*, §§ 70, 333–34, 1172.

On the proper tests for belligerency, see also the rules adopted by the Institute of International Law, in 1900.   Scott, *Resolutions of the Institute* (1916), 158–59.   See also Féraud-Giraud, in 3 *R. D. I. P.* (1896), 277 ff.; Olivart, in 28 *R. D. I.* (1896), 101–03; Rougier, *Les guerres civiles* (1903), Pt. III, chs. 3 and 4; and Wiesse, *Le droit int. appliqué aux guerres civiles* (1898), § 4.

Some of the publicists are satisfied with much less than are the authorities indicated above.   See *e.g.* Bluntschli, Art. 512; Pomeroy, § 224 ff.; 2 Rivier, 213 f.; and Vattel, Bk. III, §§ 293–94.   See also Justice Grier, in *The Prize Cases* (1862), 2 Black, 635.

[22] Hall, p. 39.   Hall distinguishes three classes of cases in this connection: (1) The case of insurgents isolated in the midst of loyal provinces.   In this case the question could hardly arise.   (2) The case of a State contiguous with a revolted State.   Here the presumption of propriety is rather against recognition, but the contiguous State decides whether its "interests will be better secured by conceding or withholding recognition."   (3) In the case of maritime warfare, the presumption is in favor of recognition.

[23] See Dana, in note cited above.

[24] See Latané, *The Diplomatic Relations of the United States and Spanish-America* (1900), 56; and Paxson, *The Independence of South American Republics* (1903), 253–64.

Texas by the United States in 1836 [25]; and that of the Southern Confederacy [26] by Great Britain, France, etc. in 1861. The United States was on the verge of recognizing the belligerency of Cuba [27] in 1869, and again in 1896; but the Executive Department of our Government in each instance refrained from doing so on the ground mainly that a responsible government had not been established.

120. **(III) The Recognition of Independence.**—*The Status of Independence* should not be recognized until the contest between the parent State and belligerent insurgents is virtually decided, and the independence of the latter has been practically established as a matter of fact. As in the case of the recognition of belligerency, there is a double question of law and policy involved. The real questions to be asked and answered are: (1) Is there a *bona fide* contest still going on or has it practically ceased? (2) If the fact of virtual independence has been fully established, is it to the interest of the third Power to recognize the revolted or seceding community as a member of the international com-

[25] 1 Moore, *Digest*, § 62.

[26] On the famous controversy regarding the so-called premature recognition of the Southern Confederacy by Great Britain, see especially 1 Moore, *Digest*, § 66, and the authorities cited on p. 189. To these should be added Bernard, *Neutrality of Great Britain* (1870), etc., chs. 6 and 7; Bluntschli, in 2 *R. D. I.* (1870), 452 ff.; and Harris, *The Trent Affair* (1896).

It is now generally admitted even by publicists in the United States that the recognition of the Southern Confederacy by Great Britain on May 13, 1861, was not premature, though perhaps a trifle hasty. It was fully justified, if not necessitated, by President Lincoln's Proclamation of April 19, 1861, instituting a blockade of Southern ports.

[27] It is known that President Grant was only prevented from taking this step by the opposition of his Secretary of State, Hamilton Fish. That the country was prepared for such recognition may be seen by consulting the Congressional debates of the period. See *Cong. Globe*, 2d sess. of 41st Cong. (1869–1870), Pts. 5 and 6.

In the spring of 1896 the two Houses of our National Legislature passed a concurrent resolution in favor of the recognition of the belligerency of Cuba. Later, the Senate voted a joint resolution of like import. For the voluminous debates on this subject, see *Cong. Record*, 54th Cong., 1st and 2d sess.

On the agitation for the *Recognition of Cuban Belligerency*, see Benton, *Int. Law and Diplomacy of the Spanish-American War* (1908), 36–41; Hershey, in 7 *Annals* (1896), 450 ff.; Moore, in 2 *Forum* (1896), 288–300; and in 1 *Digest*, and 1900 § 67; Olivart, in 5 and 7 *R. D. I. P.* (1898 and 1900), 518 ff., and 575 ff.; Woolsey, *America's Foreign Policy* (1898), 25 ff.

For further references on *Recognition of Belligerency*, see Bibliography at end of this chapter.

munity? [28] It is not necessary to await recognition by the parent State.[29]

121. **Effects of Premature Recognition of Independence.** —The justice of a cause or sympathy with an oppressed people are wholly insufficient grounds of recognition either of belligerency or independence. Premature or unjustified recognition of independence is a gross affront to the parent State and practically amounts to an intervention in the internal affairs of another nation that may result in war. Such was the recognition of the independence of the United States by France in 1778, which was followed by a declaration of war on the part of Great Britain. Other examples of intervention in the guise of recognition were the recognition of the independence of Greece and Belgium by the Powers in 1827–1830, Cuba [30] in 1898, and Panama [31] in 1903.

122. **Examples of Recognition of Independence.**—Sound precedents bearing on the law of recognition of independ-

[28] See 1 Moore, *Digest*, §§ 30 ff., pp. 87–110, for good statements of the law of the recognition of independence by American statesmen. See *Letters of Historicus* (1863), III, by Sir W. Harcourt for citations from the speeches of British statesmen on this subject.

There is perhaps no rule of International Law respecting which there is greater agreement than that governing the recognition of the independence of insurgent communities.

[29] Thus, the Spanish-American States were not recognized by Spain until many years after their recognition by the United States and Great Britain. Holland was not recognized by Spain until 1648, *i.e.* nearly seventy years after Holland's declaration of independence.

[30] The United States, not wishing to recognize the so-called government of the Cuban insurgents, declared the *people* of Cuba free and independent. On the *Recognition of Cuban Independence*, see Benton, *Int. Law and Diplomacy of the Spanish-American War* (1908), ch. 4; Cameron's *Report* No. 1160, in Senate Doc. of 5th Cong., 2d sess. (38827); Chadwick, *Relations of the U. S. and Spain* (1909), ch. 29; Hershey, in 11 *Annals* (1898), 353 ff.; 1 and 6 Moore, *Digest*, §§ 40, 909–10.

[31] The independence of Panama was formally recognized by President Roosevelt on Nov. 13, 1903, *i.e.* within ten days after the so-called revolutionists had declared their independence. It was virtually recognized within three days after the birth of this Republic. It was really a case of political intervention, only to be justified, if at all justifiable, on grounds of national policy and the "collective interests of civilization."

On the *Recognition of Panama*, see 3 Moore, *Digest*, § 344 for the main documents bearing upon the case. See also Hershey, in 16 *Green Bag* (1904), 265–66; Scott (G. W.), in 75 *Outlook* (1903), 947–50; Woolsey, in 16 *Green Bag* (1904), 6–12; Rougier and Viallate, in 11 *R. D. I. P.* (1904), 481 ff. and 567 ff.: and * Chamberlain, in 195 *No. Am. Rev.* (1912), 145 ff.

ence, or cases in which the legal rule was observed, may be
found in the numerous recognitions of Spanish American
States by the United States and Great Britain in the first
half of the nineteenth century; and in the recognition of
Texas by the United States in 1837, one year after Mexico
had ceased all attempts to recover her lost territory.[32]

123. **There is no Legal Right or Duty of Recognition.**—
Strictly speaking, there is no legal right or duty of recognition, although the new State which has fully established
its independence undoubtedly has a strong moral claim to
diplomatic intercourse and admission to membership in the
family of nations. It should be added that recognition,
whether of insurgency, belligerency, or independence, is
usually regarded as an executive act, and falls within the
prerogative of the Executive Department of the United
States Government.[33]

123a. **Recognition of New Governments.**—Generally
speaking, the same rules and principles should be held to
apply to the recognition of changes in the form of government. The recognition is primarily a question of policy
which should be based upon considerations of the facts in
the particular case, viz. whether the new government shows
evidences of sufficient stability and capacity to carry out its
international obligations.[34]

[32] On the *Recognition of the Independence of the Spanish-American Republics
and Texas*, see 1 Moore, *Digest*, §§ 28–37; Latané, *The Diplomatic Relations of
the United States and Spanish America* (1900), ch. 2; Paxson, *The Independence
of the South American Republics* (1903), and *Letters of Historicus* (Sir W.
Harcourt, 1863), 3–35.

[33] For a citation and discussion of the American cases, see Penfield, in 32
Am. Law Rev. (1898), 390–408. For a fuller citation of cases, see *Jones* v.
United States (1890), 137 U. S. 202. See Scott, (ed., 1902), 38–44, for an
abridged report of this leading case. See also Berdahl, "Power of Recognition," in 14 *A. J.* (1920), 519–39; and Field, "Doctrine of Political Questions
in Fed. Courts," in 8 *Minn. Law Rev.* (1924), 500 ff.

For references on Recognition of Independence, see Bibliography at the
end of this chapter.

[34] Except for a somewhat different course followed by Secretary Seward and
several of his successors, *de facto* recognition has been the policy of the United
States, at least until recent years. It was based upon Jefferson's view expressed in 1792 that "it accords with our principles to acknowledge any
government to be rightful which is formed by the *will of the nation substantially
declared.*" This principle was reiterated again and again by leading American
statesmen during subsequent years, *e.g.* by Secretary Buchanan who declared
in 1848: "In its intercourse with foreign nations, the Government of the

123b. **Distinction between *de facto* and *de jure* Recognition.**—Within recent years there has developed a distinction between the *de facto* and the *de jure* recognition of new States and Governments. *De jure* recognition is complete recognition, involving full or normal diplomatic intercourse, whereas mere *de facto* recognition is recognition for purposes of trade or to satisfy practical needs. Thus, the United States recognized the Government of President Carranza in Mexico, first as *de facto* in 1915, and later as *de jure* in 1917; and Great Britain accorded to the Government of Soviet Russia a *de facto* recognition by the con-

United States has, from its origin, always recognized *de facto* governments: We recognize the right of all nations to create and re-form their political institutions according to their own will and pleasure.   We do not go beyond the existing government to involve ourselves in the question of legitimacy.   It is sufficient for us to know that a government exists, capable of maintaining itself, and then its recognition inevitably follows. . . . "

It was only toward the close of the 19th century that the capacity of a new government to fulfill its foreign obligations began to be stressed, *e.g.* by Secretary Hay in 1899.   The lack of both the will and capacity to meet its foreign obligations was given as one of the main reasons for refusal on the part of the United States to recognize the Bolshevik régime in Soviet Russia.

In 1913–14, President Wilson refused to recognize General Huerta as President of Mexico on the ground that he was a usurper and had set up a mere military despotism.   Indeed, Wilson may be said to have announced a new principle of recognition when he asserted almost at the outset of his administration that "coöperation is possible only when supported at every turn by the orderly processes of government based upon law, not upon arbitrary or irregular force."

Under Secretary Hughes the United States Government withheld recognition of the Obregon Government from Jan. 1, 1920 to Aug. 31, 1923, pending reassurances as to the protection of American interests in Mexico.

But the most extreme instance of reluctance on the part of our government to recognize an apparently stable *de facto* government has been its attitude toward the Bolshevik régime in Soviet Russia.   In justification of this policy, Secretary Hughes said on Mar. 21, 1923: "The fundamental question in the recognition of a government is whether it shows ability and a disposition to discharge international obligations.   Stability, of course, is important; stability is essential.   Some speak as though stability was all that was necessary. What, however, would avail mere stability if it were stability in the prosecution of a policy of repudiation and confiscation?   In the case of Russia we have a very easy test in a matter of fundamental importance, and that is of good faith in the discharge of international obligations.   I say that good faith is a matter of essential importance because words are easily spoken.   Of what avail is it to speak of assurances, if valid obligations and rights are repudiated and property confiscated?"   17 *A. J.* (1923), 296 f.   Cf. Secretary Colby, in 1 Hyde, § 45.

On the "Recognition Policy of the United States," see especially: Goebel, in 66 Columbia University *Studies* (1915), No. 1, *passim;* 1 Hyde, §§ 44–45; and 1 Moore, *Digest,* §§ 43–58.

clusion of a trade agreement in 1921 several years prior to *de jure* recognition early in 1924.[35]

124. The Continuity of States.—It is a cardinal principle of the Law of Nations that changes in the internal government or constitution of a State, as from a monarchy to a republic or a change of dynasty, do not affect its identity or continuity as an International Person.[36] But in case such a change is effected by revolution or violence, other States should be allowed a reasonable time within which to recognize the new government. In the meantime, however, necessary business may be transacted with the *de facto* or local government, but such business should be of a distinctly non-political character; or, if political, it should not pass beyond the stage of negotiation.[37]

Generally speaking, treaties remain obligatory except in the case of personal or purely dynastic treaties;[38] the financial obligations incurred by the previous government must be paid; property rights, whether public or private, remain unaffected unless alienated or confiscated; and the new government is responsible for wrongs and injuries done to the government or citizens of another State.[39]

[35] In 1919 the British foreign office recognized the Esthonian National Council as a *de facto* independent body which was held to be such a government as could set up a prize court and send informal diplomatic representatives. Hershey, in 14 *A. J.* (1920), 511.

As to legal effects of the recognition or non-recognition of a *de facto* Government (with citation of cases), see Borchard, §§ 84–85; * Dickinson, in 22 *Mich. Law Rev.* (1923), No. 1 and 2, and in 19 *A. J.* (1925), 263–72; Hershey, *op. cit.*, 512–14; Mc Nair, in *Brit. Yr. Bk.* (1919–21), 57 ff.; and Wright, in 17 *A. J.* (1923), 742–46.

For references on the Recognition of New or *de facto* Governments, see Bibliography at the end of this chapter.

[36] Of course this principle does not apply in cases of a total or partial loss of independence, or in changes which involve the union of several States into one or the division of one State into several. For judicial assertions of this fundamental principle which is now universally accepted, see *Texas* v. *White* (1868), 7 Wall. 700 and *Keith* v. *Clark* (1878), 97 U. S. 454. For an abridged report of these cases, see Scott (ed., 1902), 25–36.

[37] For the practice of the United States, see 1 Moore, *Digest*, §§ 43–58, particularly pp. 120 and 139.

[38] An example of such a treaty is the Family Compact of 1761 between the king of France and other members of the House of Bourbon. A change in the form of government might also affect political treaties or alliances.

[39] Under the convention of 1831, France finally paid the United States a money indemnity in settlement of claims of American citizens growing out of illegal acts committed by Napoleon I. 1 Moore, *Digest*, pp. 249 and 252. For

The same principles apply where there has been a mere loss of territory.   Thus the obligations of Prussia remained the same after she had been deprived of almost one third of her territory by the Peace of Tilsit in 1807.[40]   Such loss of territory might, however, be conceivably so great as to make it practically impossible for a State to fulfill its legal obligations.   "On the same principle, when a State is extinguished, and its territory incorporated with another State, the continuity of the annexing State and the obligations of its treaties are unaffected, and the treaties of the extinguished State fall to the ground." [41]   Thus, upon the "incorporation of the kingdom of Hanover in the Prussian monarchy, in 1860, the Hanoverian treaties of amity, commerce, navigation, extradition, and copyright ceased to exist.   They were replaced by the Prussian treaties on the same subjects." [42]

BIBLIOGRAPHY

Recognition of States as International Persons.—Bluntschli, Arts. 28–38; 1 Calvo, §§ 87–98; Chrétien, *Principes de droit int. public* (1893), Nos. 149–59; Creasy, *First Platform of Int. Law* (1876), 677–81; Despagnet, Nos. 79–85; * 1 Fauchille, Nos. 195–213; Fenwick, 103–08; 1 Fiore, Nos. 309–21, and *Int. Law Cod.*, Arts. 165–82; Goebel, *Recognition Policy of the U. S.*, in 66 Columbia University *Studies* (1915), No. 1; * Hall, § 2, p. 20, and § 26; 1 Halleck (3d ed.), 79–86; Heffter, § 23; Holtzendorff, in 2 *Handbuch*, 23–33; * 1 Hyde,

the full history of the French indemnities paid to citizens of the United States, see 5 Moore, *Arbitrations*, 4399–4485.   For the history of the indemnity paid by the king of the Two Sicilies, see *Ibid.*, 4575 ff. and especially 4576–4581 as to the principle of liability involved.

[40] The same principles would apply where a State had increased its territory. "Even Sardinia, while enlarging its area to nearly four times its original size by the absorption of the rest of the Italian States, and after changing its name to that of the kingdom of Italy, did not consider its indentity to be destroyed, and held its existing treaties to be applicable as of course to the new provinces." Hall, 21–22 n.

[41] 1 Westlake, pp. 59–60.   As we shall see in the next chapter (p. 218), the latter part of this statement is too absolute.   Not all treaties of the extinguished State are abrogated.

[42] 1 Rivier, 73.   Cited by 1 Westlake, 60.   Other instances mentioned by Westlake are the extinction of the commercial treaties of England and France with Texas after the incorporation of the State into our Federal Union in 1845, and the abrogation of the Tariff Conventions of England and the United States with Madagascar upon the annexation of this island by France in 1896.   For a discussion of the latter case, see Lawrence (3d ed.), App. I, 647–51.

§§ 36–42; Lawrence, §§ 44–47; Lawrence, 1 *Commentaire* (1868–80), 195 ff.; 1 and 2 Lorimer, *Institutes of the Law of Nations* (1883–84, see index); 1 J. de Louter, § 14; 1 F. de Martens, §§ 63–64; 1 Mérignhac, 320–30; * 1 Moore, *Digest*, ch. 3, §§ 27–42; * Le Normand, *La reconaissance internationale* (1899); 1 Nys, 68–115; * 1 Oppenheim, §§ 71–75; 2 Phillimore, Pt. V, ch. 4; 1 Piédelièvre, Nos. 119–24; * Pomeroy, Ch. 7, §§ 215–49; 1 P.-Fodéré, Nos. 136–45; * 1 Rivier, 54–61; Snow, *Int. Law* (1898), § 8; Taylor, §§ 153–59; Ullmann, § 30; Walker, *Manual*, § 1, and *Science*, 116–18; 1 Westlake, 57–58; Wheaton (Atlay's ed.), §§ 26–27, and (Dana's ed.), Dana's note 16; Wilson and Tucker, § 21.   For further references, see Griffen, *List of References on Recognition* published by Library of Congress (1904).

Recognition and Effects of Belligerency.—* Bernard, *Neutrality of Great Britain during the Civil War* (1870), *passim*, especially 114–17, 122–50, 151–66; Bluntschli, Art. 512, and in 2 *R. D. I. P.* (1870), 452 ff.; Borchard, § 94; 1 Calvo, §§ 84–86; * 1 or 2 Fauchille, Nos. 202–03, 1045–46; Fenwick, 108–10; Hall, § 5; 1 Halleck (3d ed.), 79–84; * (Harcourt) *Letters of Historicus* (1863), 1–37; 1 Hyde, §§ 47–50; * Lawrence, §§ 41, 141; 1 Kleen, § 34; Féraud-Giraud, in 3 *R. D. I. P.* (1896), 277 ff.; * 1 Moore, *Digest*, §§ 59–71; Le Normand, *La reconnaissance internationale* (1899); Olivart, *Del reconocimiento de belligerancia* (1895), and in 28 *R. D. I. P.* (1896), 100–03, 3 *R. D. I. P.* (1896), 503 f., 5 *R. D. I. P.* (1898), 499 ff., 7 *R. D. I. P.* (1900), 575 ff.; Pomeroy, §§ 224–235; 6 P.-Fodéré, No. 2658; 2 Rivier, 213–14; * Rougier, *Les guerres civiles* (1903), especially §§ 45–50, 89–102; Snow, *Int. Law* (1898), § 10; Taylor, §§ 145–47; Walker, *Manual* (1895), § 1, and *Science* (1893), 115–16; 1 Westlake, 50–57; Wiesse, *Le droit int. appliqué aux guerres civiles* (1898), §§ 3–12; 1 Wharton, *Digest*, § 69; Wheaton, Dana's note 15; Wilson and Tucker, § 29; Woolsey, §§ 41, 180.   For a fuller bibliography on belligerency, see Rougier, *op. cit.*, xi–xvi.

Recognition and Effects of Insurgency.—Benton, *Int. Law and Diplomacy of the Spanish American War* (1908), 34–38; 1 Fauchille, No. 199; Fenwick, 110 f.; Hall, § 5a; 1 Hyde, § 50; Lawrence, § 142; * 1 Moore, *Digest*, § 74; Stockton, 77–81; Wilson and Tucker, § 27; * Wilson, § 18, *Lectures on Insurgency* (1900), Naval War College, Newport, R. I., in 1 *A. J.* (1907), 46–60, and in 40 *Cyc.*, *L. P.* 313 ff.   The subject is one which is almost wholly ignored even by some recent authorities.

Recognition of New or de facto Governments.—* Anderson, in 9 and 10 *Inter-America* (1924 and 1925), 503–34 and 21–42; Baty, in 31 *Yale Law J.* (1921–22), 469 ff.; Borchard, §§ 84–85; Despagnet, No. 82; * Dickinson, in 22 *Mich. Law Rev.* (1923), Nos. 1 and 2, and in 19 *A. J.* (1925), 263–72 (for cases); * 1 Fauchille, No. 205; Fenwick, 112–15; Goebel, "Recognition Policy of the United States," in 66 Columbia University *Studies* (1915), No. 1, *passim;* * Hershey, in 14 *A. J.* (1920), 499–518; * 1 Hyde, §§ 43–46; Larnaude, in 3 (2d ser.)

R. D. I. P. (1921), 457 ff.; McNair, in *Brit. Yr. Bk.* (1921–22), 59 ff.;
Podesta Costa in 31 *I. L. A.* (1922), 94 ff., and in 29 (4 second series)
R. D. I. P. (1922), 47 ff.; * Rougier, *Les guerres civiles* (1903), 478–560;
Scelle, in 21 *R. D. I. P.* (1914), 117 ff.; Stinson, in 9 *Minn. Law Rev.*
(1924), 1–20; Wiesse, *Le droit int. appliqué aux guerres civiles* (1898),
237 ff.   See also *Procs. Am. Soc. I. L.* (1924).

Continuity or Identity of States.—Bluntschli, Arts. 39–45; 1 Calvo,
§§ 99, 104; Creasy, *First Platform of Int. Law* (1876), 99–110; Despagnet, Nos. 87–88; Fenwick, 111–16; 1 Fiore, Nos. 321–31, and
Int. Law Cod. (1918), Arts. 124–46; Field, *Outlines of an Int. Code*
(1876), Art. 19; Hall, § 2, pp. 20–22; 1 Halleck (3d ed.), 90; Lawrence,
§ 48; 1 F. de Martens, § 65; * 1 Moore, *Digest*, §§ 78–79; * 1 Phillimore, Pt. II, ch. 7; * 1 Piédelièvre, Nos. 135–42; Pomeroy, §§ 68–75;
1 Oppenheim, §§ 76–77; 1 P.-Fodéré, Nos. 149–55; 1 Twiss, §§ 18,
21; 1 Rivier, 52–63; Ullmann, § 35; * 1 Westlake, 58–59; Wheaton,
§§ 28–32; Woolsey, §§ 38–40.

CHAPTER IX

THE EXTINCTION AND SUCCESSION OF STATES

1. THE EXTINCTION OF STATES

125. Total Extinction.—A State ceases to exist when it has lost the essential marks or distinguishing characteristics of a State.[1] It may become extinct through voluntary action or as a result of conquest. Theoretically, extinction might result from natural causes, such as depopulation, extermination, total emigration, or a permanent condition of anarchy. But practically, States are extinguished through voluntary incorporation, forcible annexation, division into several States, or union with other States.[2]

Like the recognition of a new State or government, the recognition of a conquest, merger, division, or cession is the recognition of an accomplished fact, and should not be refused after resistance has virtually ceased, or when the old government has practically ceased to function. But a reasonable time should be permitted to elapse in order to enable the recognizing State to judge of the permanence and stability of the new condition of affairs, or to determine the capacity of the new State or States to carry out their international obligations. Such recognition is generally tacit.

States fully extinguished lose all international personality, and acquire the rights and obligations of the annexing or incorporating State. The observance of any agreements or promises made by the latter to such annexed or incorporated State is a matter of conscience, or of moral rather than of legal obligation.

[1] See *supra*, No. 88.

[2] Examples of voluntary incorporation are the Union of England with Scotland and Ireland, and the admission of Texas into the Federal Union of the United States.

History abounds in examples of forcible annexations or cessions and conquests. Modern instances are the annexation of the South African (Transvaal) Republic and the Orange River Free State by Great Britain; and of the division of Poland in the 18th century.

126. **Partial Extinction.**—There is a partial loss of international personality when a State loses a part of its external sovereignty or independence, either by placing itself under the Protectorate of a stronger Power or by joining a Confederacy. Such partial loss of independence may materially affect its international obligations.

2. THE SUCCESSION OF STATES

127. **Universal Succession.**—When one State takes the place of another and undertakes a permanent exercise of its sovereign territorial rights or powers, there is said to be a succession of States.[3]   This succession may be called universal in case of total absorption, whether through voluntary agreement, forcible annexation or subjugation, the division of a State into several International Persons, or the union of several States into a single International Person.   Universal succession may also be said to exist where a State is broken up and divided among several previously existing States, as in the case of the division of Poland between Russia, Prussia, and Austria.

128. **Partial Succession.**—Partial succession occurs in the following cases:

(1) When a State acquires a portion of the territory of another through cession or conquest.

(2) When a new State is formed in consequence of a successful revolt or declaration of independence.

(3) When a fully sovereign State loses a portion of its external sovereignty or independence through incorporation into a Confederacy or Federal Union, or places itself under the Protectorate of a stronger Power.

(4) When the latter process is reversed, and the State under Suzerainty or a Protectorate, or the member of a Federal Union, becomes a fully Sovereign state.

Instances of division or separation are Belgium and Holland in 1831, and Norway and Sweden in 1905.

Examples of union are the Federal Unions of the United States, Germany, and Switzerland.

[3] There may of course be a succession of several States, as in the case of the division of Poland.

On the meaning and propriety of the phrase "succession of States," see note at the end of this chapter.

I. Universal Succession

129. **Effects of Total Absorption.**—In case of total extinction and absorption or incorporation, the authorities are generally agreed that the annexing or absorbing State succeeds in the main to the rights and obligations of the extinguished State.   " The conqueror who reduces a nation to his subjection receives it subject to all its engagements and duties toward others, the fulfillment of which then becomes his own duty." [4]

There is no reasonable doubt that the successor assumes responsibility for the financial obligations, more particularly the public debt, of the extinguished State.   The former falls heir to the latter's assets, credits, revenues, and resources subject to the charges or burdens resting upon them.[5] " *Res transit cum suo onere.*"   Thus, the United States [6]

[4] Mr. Adams, Sec. of State, to Mr. Everett on Aug. 10, 1818.   1 Moore, *Digest*, p. 334.

[5] This principle extends to the case of an extinguished government.   "It was applied by the English courts to the cotton in England belonging to the Government of the Confederate States, which was held to pass by their overthrow to the United States, subject to such right of account against the latter as the holders of it would have had against the former."   1 Westlake, p. 75.   See the *United States* v. *Prioleau* (1866), 2 H. and M. 563, and Evans, *Cases*, 84; *United States of America* v. *McRae* (1869), L. R. 8 Eq. 69, or Evans, 87; and the *King of the Two Sicilies* v. *Wilcox* (1851), 1 Sim. N. S. 301, 327–36.

An exception to the application of this principle exists where a loan has been contracted for the purpose of the war which results in extinction or absorption. 1 Westlake, 78.

[6] The famous case of the *Texan bonds* is only an apparent exception to this rule.   When Texas was admitted to the American Union in 1845, the power to lay and collect customs duties passed to the United States.   It was agreed that the vacant and unappropriated lands within its limits were to be retained by the State and "applied to the payment of the debts and liabilities of the Republic of Texas; and the residue of the lands, after discharging the debts and liabilities, were to be disposed of as the State might direct, but in no event were said debts and liabilities to become a charge upon the Government of the United States."   5 *U. S. Statutes at Large*, 798.   Cited by 1 Moore, *Digest*, p. 343.   Subsequently, in 1850, the United States took over a portion of these lands, and in return for this and other considerations, the United States agreed to pay to Texas $10,000,000, but stipulated that five millions thereof should remain unpaid until the creditors holding Texan bonds for which duties on imports had been specially pledged, should file releases of all claims against the United States.

In 1854, before a final settlement was made, a British holder of a Texan bond brought a claim against the United States for the payment thereof before a mixed commission which had been instituted for the adjustment of claims between the United States and Great Britain.   The British and the United

assumed the public obligations of the former colonies in 1789, the enlarged Sardinia or the new Italy took over the public debts of the lately annexed Italian States in 1861, as did Prussia those of the incorporated German States in 1866.

In case there are several successors, the debt should be rateably divided, preferably in proportion to the revenues and taxable resources [7] of that portion of the divided territory which each receives.

In principle, the absorbing or incorporating State also succeeds to the contractual obligations of the extinguished State, at least as far as the rights of third parties are involved; and, *vice versa*, the contractual rights and obligations of the annexing State extend to the inhabitants and territory of the people absorbed.

There are, however, important exceptions to this rule. It is clear that political (including personal and dynastic) treaties and alliances of the extinguished State fall to the ground. It is equally clear that transitory or dispositive treaties remain in force. Of such a character are stipulations respecting boundary lines, servitudes, or easements resting on the land relating to the use and repair of roads (including railways) or the navigation of rivers, etc. In

States commissioners gave diametrically opposed opinions. The umpire, Mr. Joshua Bates, an American citizen, decided that the commission could not entertain the claim, apparently for lack of jurisdiction.

Whatever the merit of this decision, there can be no reasonable doubt that the United States was bound in equity to pay these bonds. As Dana (note 18 to Wheaton) has well said: "It certainly would not be satisfactory to say that the United States discharges its obligation to the creditors of Texas, to whom her customs were pledged, by paying only the amount of the customs received."

In 1855 Congress passed an act providing that, in lieu of the $5,000,000 payable to Texas in 5% stock under the act of 1850, the Secretary of the Treasury should pay to those creditors of Texas who held bonds for which the revenues of the Republic were pledged, the sum of $7,500,000, to be apportioned among the holders *pro rata*. See 1 Moore, *Digest*, p. 347.

On the *Texan Bond Controversy*, see especially: 1 Calvo, § 101; * Dana's Wheaton, note 18 p. 49; 1 Hyde, § 128; Lawrence, 1 *Commentaire* (1868–80), 211 ff.; Magoon, *Law of Civil Government under Military Occupation* (1902), 190–91; * 1 Moore, *Digest*, § 97, pp. 343–47; * 4 Moore, *Arbitrations*, 3591–94; Scott, *Cases*, (ed., 1902), 94–96 n.; Snow, *Cases on Int. Law* (1893), 18–20; 1 Westlake, 77–78; Ullmann, 132 n.

[7] The extent of territory and number of the population have also been suggested. These have in a few cases furnished the basis of the division, but they furnish very crude and unsatisfactory criteria.

these cases the rights of third parties, which it would be illegal to ignore or destroy, are involved.

There is a serious difference of opinion in respect to treaties of commerce, navigation, extradition, etc. According to some authorities,[8] such treaties are extinguished like those of a political alliance or friendship. According to another, but more infrequent, view, " treaties of commerce and other international conventions which bind the annexed State " [9] remain in force. There is a third opinion which considers " a general answer to these questions based on principle, to be impossible and leaves them to the nature and scope of the treaties and concrete circumstances for decision." [10] The better opinion (and the one most consonant with international practice) would seem to be that such treaties may be annulled at the option of the absorbing State. True it is that the rights and interests of third parties are affected; but the interests involved are for the most part economic or quasi-political in their nature, and cannot as a rule resist the pressure of changed social and political conditions.

As in the case of partial succession,[11] the universal successor acquires complete rights of sovereignty over the territory which has been absorbed; and can, therefore, make any change in the laws or political institutions of the extinguished State which it deems necessary or desirable. But civil and criminal law as opposed to constitutional and purely administrative law, and the private rights of the inhabitants of the extinguished State, remain unaltered unless changed by express enactment. Contracts, franchises, and concessions to private companies and individuals should also, as a rule, be maintained. The universal suc-

---

[8] *E.g.* Despagnet, No. 91; I Piédelièvre, No. 148; I Rivier, 72; I Westlake, p. 67 n.

[9] I F. de Martens, p. 369.

[10] Ullmann, p. 132. Cited by I Westlake, p. 67 n. Ullmann cites Bluntschli and I Calvo, § 100, in favor of this opinion—a view which he himself seems to share in spite of his criticism of it as being "much too elastic." He claims that the annexing State succeeds to the legal order (*Rechtsordnung*) of the incorporated State, but admits that, in deciding on the question whether such treaties shall be maintained, it (the absorbing State) takes its own interests into account.

[11] See *infra*, p. 224.

cessor also succeeds to the public and private domain of the extinguished State.

II. Partial Succession

130. **Effects of Partial Succession.**—The general rules and principles governing partial succession are practically the same as in the case of universal succession or total extinction and absorption. But these rules may be greatly modified in international practice by considerations of public policy based on the interests of the ceding as well as on those of the annexing States. There is even a greater modification of these principles in the case of a colony or province which has achieved its independence.

The main difference between the two categories of universal and partial succession is that in case of partial succession, whether by cession or conquest, there is a continuity of State life or personality on the part of the State which has lost a portion of its territory. This materially affects international rights, interests, and obligations.

In such cases it may be necessary to distinguish between the general rights and obligations of the ceding or dismembered State and the *special or local rights and obligations of the inhabitants of the ceded territory*. This distinction also applies to the case of a colony or province which has achieved its independence. There may be certain charges or burdens in the nature of servitudes resting upon the land, or the assets, revenues, or resources of the new State or ceded province may have been mortgaged or hypothecated as security for the payment of a portion of the public debt of the ceding or dismembered State.

It is generally agreed that the purely local or personal rights and obligations of the ceded or conquered territory, as also those of the new State which has achieved its independence, remain with the new State or ceded territory. This is particularly true of the public domain, public property such as government railways, and of purely local and personal debts or of any portion of the public debt which may have been contracted in the interest of the new State or ceded province, more particularly for internal improvements.

Many of the authorities [12] maintain that the partial successor must also take over a proportional part of the general public debt of the ceding or dismembered State; but,

[12] It is often claimed that this is also the case with debts which are secured by the assets, revenues, or resources of the ceded province or of an insurgent or belligerent community which has won its independence.   But the rule would certainly not apply to a loan thus secured which had been contracted for general purposes, or for the special purpose of waging the war or crushing the rebellion resulting in cession or independence.

The United States in 1898 refused to assume in behalf of Cuba any portion of the so-called Cuban debt, for the payment of which the Cuban revenues were pledged, on the ground that it consisted of a "mass of Spanish obligations and charges," and was "in no sense created by Cuba as a province or department of Spain or by the people of the island."   This debt had been mainly contracted "for the purpose of supporting a Spanish army in Cuba," and the creditors "took the chances of the investment" with a full knowledge of the risks involved.   "From no point of view can the debts above described be considered as local debts of Cuba or as debts incurred for the benefit of Cuba."   1 Moore, *Digest*, § 97, pp. 351–85.   The citations given above may be found on pp. 352, 357, 358, 367, and 368.

There can be no question that the United States acted wisely in refusing to assume for her protégé the major portion of this debt, but Cuba would seem to have been liable in equity for such a portion of the loan as had been spent on internal improvements, such as railways, harbors, etc.   See an interesting article contributed by Von Bar to the German periodical *Die Nation* for April 22, 1899.   Cited by 1 Westlake, 79 n.

On the *Cuban and Philippine Debts*, see Magoon, *Law of Civil Government under Military Occupation* (1902) p. 187, for a citation from an article by Hon. Whitelaw Reid contributed to the *Anglo-Saxon Review* for June, 1899.   Mr. Reid says: "Warned by the results of their inquiry as to the origin of the 'Cuban Debt,'" and having "learned that over one-fourth of the Philippine Debt had actually been transferred to Cuba to carry on the war against the Cuban insurgents," the American commissioners at Paris abandoned all idea of assuming the so-called "Philippine Debt."   But the United States paid to Spain the sum of $20,000,000 for the cession of the Philippine Islands—an amount which was at least equal to the face value of that debt.

The views of Le Fur on this subject (see 6 *R. D. I. P.*, 1899, 615 ff.) are so obviously prejudiced that they are unworthy of serious refutation.

The Spanish Commissioners made much of the fact that the Spanish-American colonies had assumed their local debts (see 1 Moore, *Digest*, pp. 342–43, 355); but the circumstances were very different, and "historically we know that the assumption of said obligations was a price paid by said colonies for independence and recognition of sovereignty."   Magoon, *op. cit.*, p. 188.

There are numerous historical examples of the assumption of purely local debts (see 1 Moore, *Digest*, pp. 339–51, 361), and it undoubtedly amounts to an obligation in International Law.

The following authorities hold that the partial successor should assume a proportional part of the public debt: Despagnet, No. 97; 1 Fauchille, No. 225; 1 Fiore, No. 360; Huber, *Die Staatensuccession* (1898), Nos. 125–35 and 205; 1 Piédelièvre, Nos. 154 ff.; 1 Rivier, 214; Taylor, § 165; Ullmann, § 33. To the contrary may be cited: Bluntschli, Arts. 47–48; Hall (8th ed.), pp. 116 n, 120, 21 n; 1 Halleck (3d ed.), 91; 1 Oppenheim, § 84; 1 P.-Fodéré, No. 157.

however equitable and just such an arrangement may be, it cannot be maintained that this is a positive rule of the Law of Nations. There have, indeed, been a considerable number of historical instances of such division,[13] but the

The Ayes thus seem to have it, but it should be noted that a number of them qualify their statement of the law by the use of such phrases as *should*, it is *just and rational*, *theoretically*, etc. This indicates a subjective rather than a positive or objective attitude toward the subject. They evidently endeavor to state the law as they think it *should* be, rather than *as it is*—a frequent fault with Continental publicists.

[13] The main instances of a division of the general public debt prescribed in modern treaties are as follows:

(1) The assumption by Sweden of a part of the Danish debt upon the cession of Norway by Denmark in 1814. (2) The agreement by France to take over a small portion of the national debt of Sardinia upon the latter's cession of Savoy and Nice in 1860. (3) The apportionment of the Danish debt between Denmark and the ceded duchies upon the annexation of Schleswig, Holstein, and Lauenburg by Austria and Prussia in 1864 and 1866. (4) The assumption by Italy of a part of the Papal debt in 1864. (5) The assumption by Sardinia of three-fifths of the Monte-Lombardo-Veneto debt, and of a part of the Austrian national loan of 1854, by the treaty of Zürich in 1859. (6) The division by the Powers of the public debt of the Netherlands between Belgium and Holland in 1839. (7) The obligations imposed by the Powers upon Bulgaria, Servia, Montenegro, and Greece to discharge portions of the debt of the Ottoman Empire in accordance with the treaty of Berlin of 1878. But no part of the Ottoman debt was assumed by Russia on account of her acquisitions in Asia. It may be noted that the two latter instances are examples of a division secured through European intervention rather than by conquest or a treaty of cession. For a few more relatively unimportant examples, see Huber, *Die Staatensuccession* (1898) No. 127. In the Treaty of Lausanne of 1912, it was stipulated that Italy, to whom Tripoli was ceded, should take over a part of the Turkish debt.

Among the important historical instances where there was no assumption of any portion of the general debt are those of the cession of Alsace-Lorraine by France to Germany in 1871, and of Cuba and the Philippine Islands by Spain in 1898. The United States did not take over any portion of the British debt upon the acknowledgment of her independence by Great Britain in 1783, nor have any of her various acquisitions of territory been charged with such obligations excepting Texas. The Spanish-American colonies appear to have assumed only their local debts.

The Treaty of Versailles (Art. 254) provides that the Powers to which German territory is ceded shall undertake to pay a portion of the pre-war debt of the German Empire, as also of the pre-war debt of the German State to which the ceded territory belonged. The portions and methods of discharging the obligations were to be determined by the Reparation Commission. Since, however, Germany had refused to assume any part of the French debt in 1871, France was exempted from any payment in respect of Alsace-Lorraine (Art. 255).

"In the case of Poland that portion of the debt which, in the opinion of the Reparation Commission, is attributable to the measures taken by the German and Prussian Governments for the German colonization of Poland shall be excluded from the apportionment" (Art. 255).

international practice is by no means uniform. If the debt is divided, it should be in proportion to the taxable assets or resources of the new State or ceded province as compared with those of the remaining portion of the dismembered State.

Contrary to the general principle governing in the case of universal succession,[14] all treaties, excepting transitory and dispositive conventions, affecting the incorporated or ceded province fall to the ground in cases of partial succession. This also holds when an insurgent or seceding colony, province, or State has achieved its independence.[15]

" On the cession [16] of territory by one nation to another,

In the case of Austria, Art. 203 of the Treaty of St. Germain provided that "each of the States to which territory of the former Austro-Hungarian Monarchy is transferred, and each of the States arising from the dismemberment of that Monarchy, including Austria, shall assume responsibility" for a portion of the unsecured as well as the secured bonded debt of the former Austro-Hungarian Government, as it existed on July 28, 1914. The Reparation Commission was to determine the amount of liability thus assumed. None of the Succession States, other than Austria, are to be held liable for the *bonded war debt* of the former Austro-Hungarian Government; but they are to have no recourse against Austria in respect of war debt bonds of which they or their nationals are the owners (Art. 205).

"The public debt of Bosnia and Herzegovina shall be regarded as the debt of a local area and not as part of the public debt of the former Austro-Hungarian Monarchy" (Art. 204).

For the agreement to apportion the Ottoman public debt between Turkey and its detached parts, see Arts. 46–57 of the Treaty of Lausanne (1923). For text of this Treaty, see 2 *Treaties of Peace, 1919–23* (1924), 959 ff., particularly 974–80.

[14] See *supra*, p. 218.

[15] Thus the United States did not share in either the rights or obligations of British treaties after she had achieved her independence. A long and bitter controversy arose in connection with the fishing rights granted by Great Britain in 1783. The United States claimed that the right to fish on the coast of Newfoundland and on the other coasts of the British dominion in North America was merely a recognition of preëxisting and imprescriptible rights which were not abrogated by the War of 1812. On the other hand, the British justly held that these rights were created by treaty and were extinguished by the war. By the treaty of 1818 the citizens of the United States were merely granted the *liberty* to fish, etc. This constituted a virtual abandonment of the untenable contention that these rights existed independent of treaty stipulation.

On the *Northeastern Fisheries*, see especially: J. Q. Adams, *The Fisheries and the Mississippi* (1828); * Elliot, *The United States and the Northeastern Fisheries* (1887); Isham, *The Fishery Question* (1887); Hall, § 27, pp. 117–18 (8th ed.); Lawrence (3d ed.), § 111; * 1 Moore, *Digest*, §§ 163 ff.; Dana's Wheaton, 341–50 and note 142; 3 Wharton, *Digest*, §§ 301 ff.; and the *U. S.* v. *Great Britain* (case of Atlantic Coast Fisheries), in 4 *A. J.* (1910), 948 ff.

[16] The same rule applies, of course, to cases of conquest.

those internal laws and regulations of the former designated as municipal continue in force and operation until the new sovereign imposes different laws and regulations." But those " laws which are political in their nature, and pertain to the prerogatives of the former government, immediately cease upon the transfer of sovereignty." [17] The Constitution and laws of the annexing or conquering State do not necessarily extend *ex proprio vigore* to the annexed or ceded territory,[18] which is nevertheless completely subject to the will of its new sovereign.

Private property rights, particularly in land, are unaffected by a change of sovereignty. " It is very unusual, even in cases of conquest, for the conqueror to do more than displace the sovereign and assume dominion over the country. The modern usage of nations, which has become law, would be violated; that sense of justice and of right which is acknowledged and felt by the whole civilized world would be outraged if private property should be generally confiscated. The people change their allegiance; their relation to their ancient sovereign is dissolved; but their

[17] Griggs, Att'y-Gen., in 1 Moore, *Digest*, § 93, p. 310. See also the opinions of Chief Justice Marshall, etc., on pp. 332–33.

[18] See especially the series of decisions known as the "Insular Cases" decided by our Supreme Court in 1901. In the leading case of *De Lima* v. *Bidwell* (1901), 182 U. S. 1, it was held that Porto Rico was not a foreign country within the meaning of the tariff laws after its cession, but a territory of the United States. Consequently, the Dingley Tariff Act of 1897, which was exclusively applicable to foreign countries, did not apply to Porto Rico. See also *Fourteen Diamond Rings* v. *United States* (1901), 183 U. S. 176, which applied the same doctrine to the Philippine Islands. In *Downes* v. *Bidwell* (1901), 182 U. S. 244, it was held that Porto Rico "is a territory appurtenant and belonging to the United States within the revenue clauses of the Constitution; that the Foraker Act (of 1900) is constitutional, so far as it imposes duties upon imports from such islands." In *Dooley* v. *United States* (1901), 182 U. S. 222, it was held that duties upon imports from the United States to Porto Rico prior to the ratification of the treaty of peace were lawfully collected under the war power. It is a remarkable fact that the decision in each case represented a bare (but not always the same) majority of one, the vote of the judges standing five to four.

On the *Insular Cases*, see especially: Littlefield, in 15 *Harv. Law Rev.* (1901–02), 169 ff., and 281 ff.; * 1 Moore, *Digest*, § 94, pp. 313 ff.; 1 Willoughby, *The Const. Law of the U. S.* (1910), §§ 170–71 and ch. 30; Scott, *Cases*, (ed., 1902), 667–74, including note on p. 674. For further references to cases, see 1 Moore, *Digest*, p. 331.

For other cases showing the effect of a change of sovereignty on laws, see Beale, *Cases on the Conflict of Laws* (1900), 65–84. See also Scott, *Cases*, 109 ff.

relations to each other, and their rights of property remain undisturbed. If this be the modern rule even in cases of conquest, who can doubt its application to the case of an amicable cession of territory? " [19]

In Cuba and the Philippines the rights of property entitled to protection under the phrase " property of all kinds " (see Arts. I and VII of the treaty of peace with Spain) were believed to include trade-marks and the property rights of municipalities,[20] but they were held not to include rights to public office, whether purchased or inherited.[21]

The annexing State, as also the colony or province which has achieved its independence, succeeds to the public domain of that portion of the ceding or dismembered State which is located in the ceded territory or the new State; but it appears to be somewhat doubtful as to whether it succeeds to the whole of its private domain or property as well. The better opinion would seem to be that it only succeeds to that portion of the private property of the ceding or dismembered State which is destined for local use. Thus, State-owned railways, telegraph and telephone plants, etc., pass to the annexing or new State; [22] but State loans to corporations or

[19] Marshall, in the leading case of *United States* v. *Percheman* (1833), 7 Peters, 51, 86; and (in abridged form) Evans, *Cases*, 320 or Scott, *Cases*, 99. Our great Chief Justice also stated that even had the treaty by which Florida was ceded to the United States contained no stipulation safeguarding the property of individuals, their property rights would have been unaffected by the change. In *United States* v. *Soulard* (1830), 4 Pet. 511, he had remarked *apropos* of the cession of Louisiana that "the United States, as a just nation, regards this stipulation (viz. that the inhabitants of the ceded territory should be protected in the free enjoyment of their property rights) as the avowal of a principle which would have been held equally sacred, though it had not been inserted in the contract." For the citation of numerous other cases and expressions of official opinion on this subject, see 1 Moore, *Digest*, § 99; 1 Hyde, § 132, p. 236 *n*.; and Sayre, in 12 *A. J.* (1918), 481 *n*.

[20] Magoon, *The Law of Civil Government and Military Occupation* (1898), 305–15, 463–71, 515–45, etc. The rights of property secured by copyrights and patents acquired by Spaniards was specifically protected by Art. XIII of said treaty. 1 Moore, *Digest*, p. 427.

[21] Magoon, *op. cit.*, 194–209 and 454 ff. See also 1 Moore, *Digest*, § 99, pp. 428–29; and the cases of *Sanches* v. *United States* (1907) and the *Countess of Buena Vista* v. *United States* (1908), in 2 *A. J.* (1908), 678–88. For criticism of these decisions, see Bordwell, in 3 *A. J.* (1909), 119–36.

[22] See *e.g.* Despagnet, No. 99; 1 Piédelièvre, No. 161; and 1 P.-Fodéré, No. 161.

individuals should not, as a rule, be confiscated.   In the case of privately owned railroads, the principle of succession only applies to the public rights of regulation or control. In view of the increasing tendency toward State socialism, this subject deserves more attention than it has yet received.

There is a difference of opinion respecting the obligations of the new or annexing State to execute the contracts, concessions, or franchises, etc., granted by the ceding or dismembered State within the ceded territory or territorial borders of the colony or province which has achieved its independence.   It would certainly seem that such contracts and concessions should, as a rule, be respected, and this has been the general practice of nations for at least a century; [23]

[23] Such provisions were contained in the treaties of Campo Formio (1797), Paris (1814), Zürich (1859), Paris (1860), London (1864), Vienna (1864), Frankfort (1871), and Berlin (1878).   The various treaties by which the United States acquired Louisiana, Florida, and Texas contained similar stipulations.   But these provisions seem to have been ignored in several recent cases of cession or conquest, viz. by France in Madagascar (1896), by the United States in the treaty of Paris (1898) with Spain, and by Great Britain in South Africa (1900).   1 Moore, *Digest*, § 98, pp. 385–90, and Gidel, *Des effets de l'annexion sur les concessions* (1904), ch. 11.

The United States of course acknowledged the validity of Spanish contracts and concessions in Cuba, Porto Rico, and the Philippines, which were of a purely local nature or in the exclusive interests of the inhabitants of these islands (1 Moore, *Digest*, p. 406); but it refused to admit a legal obligation to continue payments to the Manila Railway Co., which was a concession with a guarantee of 8 per cent granted by Spain partly in the imperial and partly in the local interest. See 1 Moore, § 98, pp. 395 ff., and Magoon, *op. cit.*, pp. 177 ff. See also Magoon, pp. 529–31, for the opinion of this law officer that the United States was not legally bound to continue the payment of the Spanish subsidy to an English telegraph company in the Philippine Islands.

The Transvaal Concessions Commission of 1901, which was appointed by the British Government to inquire into concessions presenting examples of mixed public and private rights granted by the South African Republic, declared: "It is clear that a State which has annexed another is not legally bound to any contracts made by the State which has ceased to exist, and that no court of law has jurisdiction to enforce such contracts if the annexing State refuse to recognize them."   In commenting upon these dicta, Westlake (I, pp. 81–82) observes: "The latter dictum is true, since courts of law are bound by the will of the sovereign power of the country, whether that will be just or unjust.   The former dictum . . . is to be explained by the narrow meaning which the commissioners evidently attached to the term 'legal' . . ."   The Commissioners add: "But the modern usage of nations has tended in the direction of the acknowledgment of such contracts."   And, with certain reservations, England appears to have acted on this principle.

In the cases which were brought up for judicial determination, the British Courts declined to assert jurisdiction on the ground that annexation was an act of State, and they held that municipal tribunals lacked authority to enforce

but international practice is by no means uniform, and the rule is not without important exceptions.

The general principle which should govern this important but much neglected subject has been correctly stated by a leading Italian authority: " The annexing Government succeeds to the rights and obligations resulting from contracts regularly stipulated by the ceding government in the relative public interest of the territory ceded." [24]

To this rule there seem, however, to be several exceptions. The grant or concession must have been not merely *regularly* obtained or duly acquired, *i.e.* from the proper authority and with a proper observance of legal forms, but it must have been made in good faith.[25]   It must not be in violation of a treaty with the annexing or dismembered State nor contracted for the purpose of the war which results in annexation.   The concession may also be canceled if the grantee has without lawful excuse failed to fulfill the essential conditions of the grant.   The new government is, moreover, justified in canceling or modifying the concession in case it is injurious to the public interest or in conflict with the public order or the fundamental principles governing the legislation or policy of the annexing State.   In the various classes of cases covered by the last sentence compensation or indemnity should, however, be made.[26]

contractual obligations alleged to have been incurred by an adversary.   The leading cases are those of *Cook* v. *Spring* (1899), A. C. 572; and the *West Rand Central Gold Mining Co.* v. *The King* (1905), 2 K. B. 498, 1 *A. J.* (1907), 217, or (in abridged form) Scott, *Cases*, 74.   See especially Keith, "Colonial Cases Relating to the Succession of States," in 3 *Z. V.* (1909), 618–20, and Westlake, in 17 *Law Quar. Rev.* (1901), 392 ff.

It appears to be authoritatively established that "the conquest and annexation of the territory of a State does not render the annexing State liable for the torts of the State which it has displaced."   Hurst on "State Succession in Matters of Tort," in *Brit. Yr. Bk.* (1924), 163, ff.   The citation is on p. 178 *ad fin.*

[24] 1 Fiore, No. 356, p. 313.

[25] See on this point the instructions of Secretary Root, in 1 Moore, *Digest*, pp. 392 ff., and Magoon, *op. cit.*, 595 ff.

[26] For the exceptions, see *Report* of the Transvaal Concessions Commission in 1 Moore, *Digest*, § 98, pp. 411–414; Gidel, *Des effets de l'annexion sur les concessions* (1904), chs. 7–10; and Sayre, in 12 *A. J.* (1918), 723 ff.

Add. note on "Succession of States."—The authorities are very much divided as to the meaning and propriety of the phrase "succession of States." Several (*e.g.* Gareis, *Institutionen des Völkerrechts*, 1887, § 16, pp. 59 ff.; Keith, *Theory of State Succession*, 1907, *passim;* and Zorn, *Völkerrechts*, 1903,

The same principles of course apply to a colony or province which has achieved its independence.

32, 77) even deny that it ever takes place, and one (Liszt, § 34) only admits it in a few cases.   Others maintain that it is a pure fiction or metaphor, whether useful or otherwise.   But the majority accept the doctrine of succession either in pure or modified form.

The Roman idea of succession upon death as the continuation of the person of the deceased by the heir was introduced into the Law of Nations by Grotius who said: "It is undoubted law that the person of the heir, in respect to the continuation of public as well as private ownership, is to be conceived as the same with the person deceased" (lib. II, cap. 9, § 12).   This view was adopted by Pufendorf and Vattel, but denied by the commentator Cocéji, who claimed that the Grotian doctrine of succession was a fiction based upon a principle of Roman private law which is inapplicable, in all its content, to International Public Law.   On the views of Cocéji, see Gidel, *Des effets de l'annexion sur les concessions* (1904), pp. 35 and 57 ff.

Among the publicists who hold more or less strictly to the Grotian doctrine of succession are: Despagnet, Nos. 90 ff.; Hall, 99; 2 Halleck, (3d ed.), 495; 1 F. de Martens, § 67, pp. 368 f.; and 1 Rivier, 70 ff.

The following authorities are among those who hold to the doctrine of succession in modified form: Bluntschli, Arts. 50, 54, and 55; 1 Calvo, §§ 99 ff.; 1 Fiore, No. 355; Heffter, § 25; 1 Oppenheim, §§ 80 ff.; 1 P.-Fodéré, Nos. 158 and 160; and Ullmann, § 32.

Among the publicists who evidently consider the phrase "succession of States" a mere fiction or metaphor are Appleton, Gabba, and Gidel, who have produced valuable monographs on this important subject.   But Huber, the most important of them all, does not hesitate to use the phrase "Staaten-succession" as the title of his remarkable work.   It must be admitted that these monographs are, for the most part, highly abstract and theoretical, and that their conclusions are often at variance with international practice. Thus Appleton (*Des effets des annexion de territoires*, 1895, p. 51) holds that the annexed or extinguished State still continues to exist in spite of its loss of sovereignty; and Gidel, *op. cit.* (chs. 3 and 4) bases his theory of "continuity" upon the right of the occupant.   He claims that cession is a recognition rather than a source of rights.   The views of Max Huber, although highly abstract, are more reasonable and are largely based upon a study of international practice.   He declares (p. 18):

"The notion of succession is a general one in law, and belongs exclusively neither to private nor to public law.   Succession is a substitution *plus* continuation.   The successor steps into the place of the predecessor and continues his rights and obligations; so far the succession of private and public law agree.   But we now have to distinguish between those kinds of succession. A civil successor who steps into the place of his predecessor steps into his rights and obligations as though he were himself the predecessor.   That is the universal succession of private law in the human sense, at least according to the prevailing doctrine.   But the successor of international law steps into the rights and obligations of his predecessor as though they were his own. . . ."   Cited and translated by Westlake, I, p. 69.

For an excellent review and criticism of the authorities, see Gidel, *Des effets de l'annexion sur les concessions* (1904), chs. 2–3.

BIBLIOGRAPHY

Succession and Extinction of States.—Appleton, *Des effets de l'annexation sur les dettes de l'état demembré ou annexé* (1895); Bentwich, *Leading Cases*, ch. 4; Bluntschli, Arts. 46–61; Borchard, § 83; Bry, *Précis élémentaire de droit int. public* (1906), Nos. 56–72; Cabouat, *Des annexions de territoires et de leurs principales consequences* (1881); 1 Calvo, §§ 99–104; Cavaglieri, *Die dottrina della successione di stato a state* (1910); 1 Cobbett, 70–77; Descamps, in 15 *R. D. I. P.* (1908), 385 ff.; Despagnet, Nos. 86–102; * Evans, *Cases*, 84–107; * 1 Fauchille, Nos. 214–34; Fenwick, 116–22; Field, *Outlines of an Int. Code* (1876), Arts. 22–26; * 1 Fiore, Nos. 348–66; Gabba, *Questioni di diritto civile* (1880); Gareis, *Institutionen des Völkerrechts* (1887), 16, 59 ff.; * Gidel, *Des effets de l'annexion sur les concessions* (1904); Grotius, liv. II, cc. 9 and 10; * Hall, §§ 27–29; 1 and 2 Halleck (3d ed.), 90–92, 495; Hartmann, *Institutionen des praktischen Völkerrechts in Friedezeiten* (1878), §§ 12–13; Heffter, §§ 24–25; Holtzendorff, in 2 *Handbuch*, 33–43; * Huber, *Die Staatensuccession* (1898); Hurst, in *Brit. Yr. Bk.* (1924), 163 ff.; * 1 Hyde, §§ 120–33; * Keith, *Theory of State Succession* (1907), and in 3 *Z. V.* (1909), 618 ff.; Larrivière, *Des consèquences des transformations territoriales des états sur les traités anterieurs* (1892); Lawrence, § 49; Liszt, § 34; 1 J. de Louter, § 15; * Magoon, *Law of Civil Government under Military Occupation* (1902), *passim;* 1 F. de Martens, §§ 66–69; * 1 Moore, *Digest*, ch. 4, §§ 92–99; * 1 Oppenheim, §§ 79–84; * 1 Piédelièvre, Nos. 134–200; 1 Phillimore, §§ 126–37; Phillipson, *Termination of War* (1916), chs. 4, 11–13; 1 P.-Fodéré, Nos. 156–63; * 1 Rivier, 65–75, 213 ff.; * Sayre, in 12 *A. J.* (1918), 475 ff. and 705 ff.; Schönborn, *Staatensukzessionen* (1913); * Scott, *Cases*, 74–115; Selosse, *Traité de l'annexion au territoire français et de son démembrement* (1880); Taylor, §§ 163–68; Ullmann, §§ 31–34; * 1 Westlake, 59–83; Westlake, *Collected Papers* (1914), 475–97; 1 Wharton, *Digest*, § 5; Wheaton, §§ 28–32.   For a fuller bibliography, see 1 Fauchille, pp. 337–38.

CHAPTER X

THE ESSENTIAL RIGHTS AND DUTIES OF STATES

131. **Their Nature.**—Until recently, authorities were generally agreed that there exist certain essential or fundamental rights and duties of States which underly the positive rules and customs of International Law. These rights (to which are attached corresponding duties) are usually described as primary, inherent, absolute, fundamental, essential, permanent, etc. They were formerly identified with natural rights and formed part of the so-called law of nature. Some publicists now regard them as moral rather than legal principles, and a few even deny them altogether.[1] But these rights have, in fact, a broader

---

[1] For example, Brown, in 26 *Yale Law Rev.* (1916), 85–93, and in 9 *A. J.* (1915), 305–35; Cavaglieri, in 18 *R. D. I. P.* (1911), 261; * Heilborn, *System des Völkerrechts* (1896), 279–306; Jellinek, *System der subjectiven öffentlichen, Rechte* (1892), 302 ff.; 1 Oppenheim, § 112; and 1 Westlake, 306 ff.

Jellinek considers the fundamental rights of States tautological, and Heilborn's main argument appears to be that they lack sanction or are included under other categories. But the lack of sanction is not greater than in the case of many of the more positive rules of International Law. The fact that authorities are not fully agreed on the content and meaning of the fundamental rights and duties of States is no proof of their non-existence. Oppenheim says he agrees with the publicists cited above, but he admits these rights and duties under a different name.

The most suggestive treatment of this question is by Pillet, in 5 and 6 *R. D. I. P.* (1898 and 1899), 66 ff., 236 ff., and 503 ff.; but many of his suggestions are too tentative for acceptance in a textbook.

Some of the older publicists adopted the Thomasian classification of perfect and imperfect rights and duties. This division is now generally abandoned. See 1 Westlake (153, 285, 288) for modern instances of adherence to the doctrine of imperfect rights.

At its first session, held in 1916, the American Institute of International Law adopted the following "Declaration of the Rights and Duties of Nations":

"I. Every nation has the right to exist, and to protect and conserve its existence; but this right neither implies the right nor justifies the act of the state to protect itself or to conserve its existence by the commission of unlawful acts against innocent and unoffending states.

"II. Every nation has the right to independence in the sense that it has a right to the pursuit of happiness and is free to develop itself without interference or control from other states, provided that in so doing it does not interfere with or violate the rights of other states.

and deeper significance than the ordinary positive rules of the Law of Nations of which they are in large measure the ultimate basis or source, and have even greater obligatory force. Though far from absolute and not inherently unchangeable, they are in the nature of controlling or fundamental principles based upon conditions essential to State existence and international life in our time.

I. THE RIGHT OF SELF PRESERVATION

132. The Right of Self-preservation.—The most important of these fundamental rights of States is that of existence, which involves the rights of self-preservation and defense. To this right there is attached the corresponding duty of respecting the existence of other States. The right of self-preservation takes precedence, in a sense, over all other rights and duties, and is much more than a right in the ordinary use of this term. It is a principle which underlies all positive rules and customs, and is based upon an instinct which in the last resort controls all living organisms.

A State has unquestionably the right, under modern conditions, to make such preparations and to take such measures as it may deem necessary for its own safety and defense, but it has no right to make a disposition of its forces or assume an attitude threatening to the existence or safety of another State. It should also have the right to take such

"III. Every nation is in law and before law the equal of every other nation belonging to the society of nations, and all nations have the right to claim and, according to the Declaration of Independence of the United States, 'to assume, among the powers of the earth, the separate and equal station to which the laws of nature and of nature's God entitle them.'

"IV. Every nation has the right to territory within defined boundaries and to exercise exclusive jurisdiction over its territory, and all persons whether native or foreign found therein.

"V. Every nation entitled to a right by the law of nations is entitled to have that right respected and protected by all other nations, for right and duty are correlative, and the right of one is the duty of all to observe.

"VI. International law is at one and the same time both national and international: national in the sense that it is the law of the land and applicable as such to the decision of all questions involving its principles; international in the sense that it is the law of the society of nations and applicable as such to all questions between and among the members of the society of nations involving its principles." 10 *A. J.* (1916), 125 f. See *Ibid.*, 211–21 for comments by Root. See also Dupuis, in 24 *R. D. I. P.* (1917), 300 ff. For text and comments, see Scott, *Am. Inst. of I. L.*, 87–101.

measures as are necessary to prevent organized propaganda or espionage on its own soil directed against its institutions or morale by other States, and it has the corresponding duty to refrain from such propaganda or espoinage in foreign territory. It is also bound to use due diligence or the means at its disposal to prevent organized conspiracies or military preparations against a friendly State on its own soil, as also to forbid the direct use of its territory and resources for hostile purposes. In short, it is under obligations to preserve a strict and impartial neutrality between warring Powers unless it itself decides to go to war or has assumed obligations contrary to neutrality as a Member of the League of Nations.

The right of self-preservation [2] includes the right to preserve the integrity and inviolability of its territory with the corresponding duty of respecting that of other States. In order to protect and preserve this right, it may in extreme cases of necessity [3] commit what would ordinarily be an infraction of the Law of Nations and violate the territorial sovereignty or international right of another State, as was done, e.g. by England through the seizure of the Danish fleet in 1807,[4] by Canada in the case of the *Caroline*,[5] by

[2] Some publicists (e.g. Bonfils and 1 Fauchille, No. 243; Chrétien, *Principes de droit int. public*, 1893, Nos. 187 ff. 1 P.-Fodéré, Nos. 219 and 261; and 1 Rivier, 265–268) also include the right of progress or perfectibility, *i.e.* the development of power, resources, etc., but these are certainly not legal or positive rights.

[3] The excuse of necessity is denied by Bonfils and 1 Fauchille, No. 247[3]; 1 Mérignhac, 246 f.; 1 Piédelièvre, No. 207; and 1 Westlake, 309 ff.

It is admitted by Grotius, lib., c. II; §§ 6–10; Hall, Pt. II, ch. 7; Heffter, § 30; 1 Phillimore, Pt. III, ch. 10; 1 P.-Fodéré, Nos. 220–34; 1 Rivier, 277–79; 1 Twiss, § 102; and Vattel, liv. II, c. 9, § 119.

The excuse of necessity may, as some publicists assert, be theoretically unsound and practically dangerous (being liable to abuse); but, as P.-Fodéré (I, p. 367) observes: "This theory, however, admirable for saints and heroes, is not made for common humanity;" or, as Westlake (I, 320) remarks in another connection: "Laws are made for men and not for creatures of the imagination."

[4] The seizure of the Danish fleet by England in 1807 to prevent its falling into the hands of Napoleon has been almost unanimously condemned by Continental writers. Naturally it has been upheld by British publicists like Hall (p. 326 f., 8th ed.) and Westlake (I, 315 f.). Surely an American is capable of rendering an impartial verdict. See the comments of Captain Mahan (*Influence of Sea Power upon the French Revolution*, 1894, II, 277), who justifies the seizure. This so-called act. of "piracy" or "brigandage"

Spain in the case of the *Virginius*,[6] and by Japan in the invasion of Korea and Manchuria, the very objects of the conflict, at the outbreak of the Russo-Japanese War.   The

appears to have been wholly justifiable.   See also Rose, *Life of Napoleon* (1901–02), II, 129 ff., and *Napoleonic Studies* (1906), 133–52.

[5] During the Canadian insurrection in the winter of 1837–38, the American steamboat *Caroline*, was being used by Canadian insurgents and their American sympathizers to transport recruits and military supplies from Schlosser, N. Y., on the American side of Niagara River, to Navy Island, the headquarters of the insurgents.   This island, through which ran the boundary line between Canada and the United States, was located in the midst of the Niagara River.   It was believed that the *Caroline* would also be used to transport the expedition from Navy Island to the Canadian shore. On the night of Dec. 29, 1837, she was seized by Canadian forces at Schlosser, N. Y., and set adrift over the Niagara Falls.   It appears that only two persons were killed.

In the course of the correspondence between the American and British Governments which followed the arrest and imprisonment in 1841 of McLeod, one of the supposed British participants in the seizure of the *Caroline*, on a charge of murder, Daniel Webster, then Secretary of State, laid down the rule which Lord Ashburton admitted was applicable to the case.

Webster contended that to justify the conduct of the Canadian authorities, England must show a "necessity of self-defense, instant, overwhelming, and leaving no choice of means and no moment for deliberation . . ." as also that the "local authorities of Canada did nothing unreasonable or excessive, since the act justified by the necessity of self-defense must be limited by that necessity and kept clearly within it."   Professor Westlake (I, p. 313) justly remarks: "This was good law, except as to the emergency's leaving no moment for deliberation."

It should be added that reparation by way of apology or idemnity should always be promptly made for such violations of territorial sovereignty or international rights.   Lord Ashburton expressed regret that an explanation and apology for this "violation of territory" had not been made immediately.

On the case of the *Caroline*, see especially 2 and 7 Moore, *Digest*, §§ 217 and 300.   See also 3 Moore, *Int. Arbitrations*, 2419 ff.; Gen. Scott, *Autobiography*, I, 305–17; Hall, § 84; 1 Hyde, § 66; Lawrence (3d ed.), § 249; 1 Stowell and Munro, 121–23; and 1 Westlake, 313 f.

[6] The case of the *Virginius* is more doubtful.   The *Virginius* was the property of Cuban insurgents and was employed in aid of the Cuban rebellion against Spain during the Ten Years' Insurrection (1868–78).   Registered as an American vessel and carrying the flag of the United States, she was captured by the Spanish man-of-war *Tornado* about ten or fifteen miles from the coast of Jamaica on October 31, 1873.   The pursuit had begun and ended on the high seas.

The *Virginius* was taken to Santiago de Cuba, where, after a summary trial by court-martial, fifty-three of her officers, crew, and other persons on board (including Americans, Englishmen, and Cubans) were condemned to death and executed as pirates.   The remainder were held as prisoners and afterwards surrendered to the United States.   Mr. Williams, the Attorney-General of the United States, gave it as his opinion that the *Virginius* "was as much exempt from interference on the high seas by another power, on that ground, as though she had been lawfully registered."

excuse of necessity might also be alleged in case the United States were forced to invade a Latin-American State in defence of the Monroe Doctrine.

II. THE RIGHT OF INDEPENDENCE

133. The Right of Independence.—The second essential right of States is that of sovereignty, or autonomy and independence. This right involves the corresponding duty or respecting the autonomy or internal sovereignty and the independence or external sovereignty of other States, and it results from that liberty or freedom from restraint which is a necessary condition for the exercise of State activity. As indicated in a previous chapter, this independence or external sovereignty is far from absolute or unlimited; [7] it is a question of degree, and should be measured by the amount of liberty which it is needful or desirable that a State should

As agreed upon, the vessel was afterwards delivered to the navy of the United States with the American flag flying; but owing to proof by Spain of her fraudulent registry, the salute to the flag was dispensed with. Spain also paid to the United States an indemnity of $80,000.

The British Government also demanded and obtained compensation for the families of the executed, but did not complain of the seizure of the vessel, which is evidently regarded as justifiable on the grounds of necessity or self-defense. This seems to have been the correct view. It is also the view of Taylor (§§ 404 ff.), Woolsey (§ 214), and Westlake (I, 171 ff.). Hall (§§ 82, 86) is doubtful.

Of course the plea of necessity or self-defense can in no wise be extended to the execution of the prisoners. That was a gross and unwarranted outrage. The charge of piracy was absurd. One is surprised to see this charge justified to a degree in Scott's *Cases* (ed., 1902), 322 n.

On the case of the *Virginius*, in addition to the authorities cited above, see especially 2 Moore, *Digest*, pp. 895 ff., 967 ff., 980 ff.; Chadwick, *The Relations of the United States and Spain* (1909), chs. 16 and 17, pp. 314 ff.; 1 Hyde, § 68; and 1 Stowell and Monroe, 368–71.

The plea of necessity entered by Germany in defense of the invasion of Belgium in August, 1914 cannot be justified on any of the grounds indicated above. On the part of Germany, this was either a case of self-defense against acts of aggression committed or intended to be committed by France (for which no proof has ever been presented); or a case of so-called political or military necessity based on political motives (*raison d'etat*) or strategical considerations (*Kriegsraison*). The acceptance of this monstrous doctrine would result in international anarchy and is the very negation of law in international relations. Cf. *infra*, note 56 on p. 196.

See especially * Visscher, *Belgium's Case* (1916), ch. 3. See also 2 Garner, chs. 28–29; and Stowell, *Diplomacy of the War* (1915), ch. 9.

[7] For the main restrictions on independence or external sovereignty, see *supra*, ch. 6, No. 95.

have in order properly to perform its functions—international as well as national.

134. **Rights flowing from Sovereignty and Independence.**
—The following are the most important of the rights of
a State flowing from of sovereignty, or autonomy and
independence:

(1) To establish, maintain, and change its own constitution or form of government and select its own rulers.
This implies the right of social and political revolution, even
if effected by violent means.[8] Unless such revolutions
become chronic and fail to afford reasonable protection to
the lives and property of foreigners, other States have no
right to intervene for the restoration of order or the institution of a stable and responsible government.

(2) To negotiate and conclude treaties and alliances that
are not in violation of International Law, and to maintain
diplomatic intercourse with other members of the international community.

(3) To make and change its own laws, subject to the
qualification that these should be in conformity with the
rules and principles of the Law of Nations. A sovereign
State has especially the right to make rules and regulations
regarding religion, restrict or prohibit immigration, etc.—
rights which are sometimes denied.

(4) To administer its own laws and create its own
administrative machinery.

(5) With some exceptions, to be noted hereafter,[9] to
exercise exclusive jurisdiction over all persons and things
within its territory.

(6) Without violating the rights of others or prohibiting
international intercourse, to frame its own policies, more
especially those of a commercial nature.

135. **Intervention.**—Unless on grounds of self-preservation or on the basis of treaty rights or International Law,
the right of sovereignty or autonomy and independence
implies in general the duty of non-intervention in the

[8] It is impossible for any one who believes in progress to agree with those
authorities who maintain that it is permissible to crush revolutions which
threaten the security of other States by reason of their ideas or principles.

[9] See *infra*, Nos. 166, 200, 209, 211, 270 ff., 287 ff.

internal and external affairs of other nations by forcible means.

The subject of forcible intervention,[10] which may be defined as dictatorial (*i.e.* as implying the use or threat of force) interference in the affairs of another nation, is one of great difficulty and complexity. This arises from the fact that nowhere else within the wide range of international relations does there exist such an apparent conflict between political theory or fundamental principles on the one hand and actual international practice on the other.

136. **The Practice of Intervention.**—The whole modern or post-Grotian system of International Law rests upon the doctrine of the legal equality and independence of sovereign States. This doctrine presupposes full liberty of action on the part of each sovereign within his own sphere or jurisdiction, and non-interference in the internal or external affairs of other sovereigns. Non-intervention is, therefore, in principle a necessary corollary of the doctrine of the equality and independence of sovereign States and must be considered a fundamental principle of International Law.

[10] Armed or forcible intervention should be distinguished from mere diplomatic intervention which is unaccompanied by a threat or the use of force. Such interposition usually takes the form of notes addressed to a foreign government in which grievances are stated, claims urged for injuries or non-payment of obligations, or protests made against alleged wrongs, bad treatment, or unjustifiable conduct.

Intervention should also be carefully distinguished from the following acts: (1) Mediation or the use of good offices between States on the verge of or during hostilities. (2) Purely defensive measures by way of preparation for war. (3) Measures of retorsion and reprisal which are essentially retaliatory in their nature. (4) Mere intercession or friendly advice. (5) Aid or assistance rendered to another State upon request. (6) Diplomatic protests against the conduct of other governments. (7) Diplomatic interposition to collect claims or otherwise protect the rights of a State or its nationals. (8) Alliances showing an intention to assist or coöperate in case of war. (9) War itself— a status to which intervention often leads, but which it may be intended to avoid.

The intervening State may, however, use the various coercive means which are applicable in war, such as the occupation of a port, or the seizure of a strategic position, etc. Or it may prefer measures of self-help which fall short of war, as an embargo, pacific blockade, etc. Often a mere veiled threat has the desired effect.

Recognition of the independence of a revolted community, if premature, may be a disguised intervention. Recognition of belligerency, even if premature, does not amount to an intervention.

But International Law is supposed to rest upon international practice as well as upon fundamental principles; and when we examine the actual practice of nations, more especially that of the Great Powers during the nineteenth century,[11] we find numerous examples of armed intervention on all sorts of grounds and pretexts.

137. **Classification of Interventions.**—Broadly speaking, interventions may be thus classified:

(1) Interventions on grounds of morality or humanity, *i.e.* to put an end to great evils and acts of injustice, such as gross forms of cruelty and oppression, religious persecution, needless effusion of blood, danger of race extermination, etc.

(2) Interventions on grounds of policy or interest, *e.g.* to maintain the Balance of Power or the Monroe Doctrine, to prevent the spread of political heresy, to crush dangerous

[11] During antiquity intervention was perhaps the rule rather than the exception. The history of the Roman Republic is that of a long series of interventions. Under the Roman Empire, intervention lost its significance as an act of interference in the affairs of foreign nations, and acquired the character of a legal and legitimate exercise of the generally recognized sovereignty of Rome.

In the absence of anything like the city-states or the great Empires of the ancient world on the one hand or of the nations and states-system of the modern world on the other, we can scarcely speak of intervention in the proper sense of this term in connection with the history of the Middle Ages. But it should be noted that Popes, Emperors, Kings, feudal lords, etc., were continually interfering in one another's affairs. The wars of religion of the sixteenth and seventeenth centuries afforded new pretexts for intervention.

The publication of Machiavelli's *Prince* in 1513 undoubtedly contributed to the frequency of the practice of intervention during the centuries that followed. He recommended intervention in war on the ground of self-interest alone, and characteristically advised his Prince never to remain neutral in any war in which his neighbors might become involved, inasmuch as "it is always more advantageous to take part in the struggle."

On the contrary, Grotius set up the principle that the mere possibility of being attacked does not justify intervention, though he admitted that the aggrandizement of another State may operate as a *casus belli* in a war which is otherwise just. He urged the neutral State to "do nothing which may strengthen the side which has the worse cause, or which may impede the motions of him who is carrying on a just war"—a position which obviously falls far short of the modern view of the obligations of neutrality. Grotius, however, set up the principle of justice and equity as opposed to the Machiavellian doctrine of self-interest as the guiding star through the troubled sea of international relations. See *The Prince*, ch. 21; and *De jure belli ac pacis*, lib. III, cap. 17, § 3.

These two principles may be said to have striven for mastery ever since the days of Machiavelli and Grotius. For further facts bearing on the history of intervention, see *supra*, ch. 4, *passim*.

revolutions, to advance the general welfare or the collective interests of civilization, etc.

(3) Interventions on so-called legal grounds, for the sake of self-preservation, to prevent or terminate an illegal or unjustifiable intervention by another State, in pursuance of a right to intervene granted by treaty or to enforce treaties of guarantee, for the protection of the lives and property of nationals of the intervening State, and to secure the enforcement of rights granted by treaty or based on fundamental rules or principles of International Law.

138. **Intervention on Legal Grounds.**—Authorities have always differed widely on what constitute legal or justifiable grounds for intervention, or, indeed, as to whether any such right exists. The only approach to unanimity is in respect to intervention for the sake of self-preservation, which, be it observed, is not, properly speaking, a right or law in the ordinary sense of these terms as applied to positive rules and regulations, but a fundamental right or principle which underlies and takes precedence of all systems of positive law and custom. To justify intervention on this ground, the danger must, of course, be direct and immediate, and not merely contingent or remote.[12]

Aside from the need of self-preservation, the only cases in which intervention may be said to be in a sense legally justifiable are the following:

(1) In pursuance of a right to intervene granted by treaty, as in the case of Cuba (see *supra*, p.168), or to enforce treaties of guarantee provided these do not stipulate for the maintenance of a particular dynasty or a particular form of government in the State to which the guarantee is applied.[13]

(2) To prevent or terminate an illegal intervention on the

[12] The seizure by England of the Danish fleet in 1807 (cited in note 4) is a good example of intervention on the ground of self-preservation or imminent danger.

The numerous interventions for the preservation of the Balance of Power in Europe are often used to illustrate this same principle. But many of them were mere pretexts, and it is generally difficult, if not impossible, to determine in a given case whether and to what extent the principle of self-preservation was involved. Certainly in most cases the danger was remote rather than immediate. These should be classed as political interventions.

[13] Such stipulations in a treaty of guarantee are probably null and void, inasmuch as they constitute a denial of one of the essential rights of independence. See especially Milanovitch, *Des traités de guarantie* (1888), 37 ff.

part of another State, as in the case of the United States against the French in Mexico in 1865. It cannot be maintained that this is a duty as well as a right, for States cannot afford to spend their strength and resources in redressing wrongs unless their interests are seriously involved.

(3) To protect the lives and property of the nationals of the intervening State, and to secure the enforcement of important rights granted by treaty or recognized by the Law of Nations. Intervention in these cases should, however, always be diplomatic in character, and forcible means should never be employed unless as a last resort.[14] Mere danger of injury to the lives or property of foreigners affords no ground for intervention, inasmuch as aliens, unless in case of discrimination against them, can claim no special exemption from the ordinary risks run by nationals during times of riot, insurrection, or civil war (see *infra*, No. 155).

139. **Intervention on Moral and Humanitarian Grounds.** —International practice also admits other exceptions to the rule of non-intervention, on moral or political grounds. Forcible interference in the internal affairs of another State has been justified on grounds of humanity in extreme cases like those of Greece, Bulgaria, and Cuba, where great evils existed, great crimes were being perpetrated, or where there was danger of race extermination. The humanity of our time, combined with an increasing desire for justice and a growing consciousness of interdependence and international solidarity, will doubtless make such interventions more frequent in the future than they have been in the past.[15]

[14] Art. I of the Second Hague Convention (1907) respecting the Limitation of the Employment of Force for the Recovery of Contract Debts declared:

"The Contracting Powers agree not to have recourse to armed force for the recovery of contract debts claimed from the Government of one country by the Government of another country as being due to its nationals.

"This undertaking is, however, not applicable when the debtor State refuses or neglects to reply to an offer of arbitration, or, after accepting the offer, prevents any agreement (*compromis*) from being agreed on, or, after the arbitration, fails to submit to the award."

This same principle might well be applied to all claims of a pecuniary nature.

[15] For example, with our present knowledge of the causes of disease, it can hardly be supposed that States would hesitate to intervene, if necessary, in order to prevent the spread of a disease like cholera.

The time may be not far distant when nations will not hesitate to use

But to prevent their being used as mere pretexts, interventions on grounds of morality and humanity should be collective in character, *i.e.* there should be at least several participants, or if one nation intervenes, it should act as the agent or mandatory of the others.

140. Interventions on Political Grounds.   The Balance

their power of intervention to prevent or terminate an unnecessary or unjustifiable war by insisting on arbitration or some other peaceful method of adjusting their disputes.   They would be justified in doing so because of the injurious effects of modern war on commerce as well as on grounds of humanity.

The Government of the United States insisted, almost to the point of ultimatums, upon arbitration as a mode of settling the two Venezuelan disputes of 1895 and 1902 with Great Britain and Germany.   The significance of these interventions on the part of the United States seems to have escaped the attention of the authorities on International Law or on the Monroe Doctrine.   On the "Two Venezuelan Episodes," see Latané, *United States and Latin America* (1920), ch. 6.   See also Thomas, *Monroe Doctrine* (1923), 53 ff. and 207 ff.   For documents, see 6 and 7 Moore, *Digest*, §§ 966–67, 1094.

Art. 11 of the Covenant of the League of Nations declares that "any war or threat of war, whether immediately affecting any of the Members of the League or not, is hereby declared a matter of concern to the whole League, and the League shall take any action that may be deemed wise and effectual to safeguard the peace of nations."

It is also declared to be the "friendly right of each Member of the League to bring to the attention of the Assembly or of the Council any circumstance whatever affecting international relations which threatens to disturb international peace or the good understanding between nations upon which peace depends."

This article seems to authorize intervention by the League in case of "any war or threat of war" or of any threatened disturbance of international peace.

Art. 10 (see Covenant) might also be said to constitute an agreement of guarantee which includes the right of intervention for the purpose of respecting and preserving "*as against external aggression* the territorial integrity and existing political independence of all Members of the League," though the means and methods of fulfilling this obligation are left to the separate members.

Art. 19 also grants to the Assembly of the League the right to "advise the reconsideration by Members of the League of treaties which have become inapplicable, and the consideration of international conditions whose continuance might endanger the peace of the world."   But this scarcely amounts to the grant of the right of intervention, as Fauchille (I, No. 331, p. 663) seems to imply.

It should be noted that disputes "arising out of a matter which by International Law is solely within the domestic jurisdiction" of one of the parties are removed from the jurisdiction of the Council of the League (Art. 15, paragraph 8 of the Covenant), as also "regional understandings like the Monroe Doctrine" the purpose of which is to secure peace (Art. 21).

Broadly speaking, it might almost be said that the Covenant of the League provides a system of collective interventions for the maintenance of international peace, in case of the failure of amicable modes of settling international disputes such as mediation, arbitration, and judicial settlement.   Cf. *infra*, pp. 461 and 510 ff.

of Power and the Monroe Doctrine.—There remains for consideration intervention on political grounds. The leading Powers of Europe have always maintained a " set of primary interests," for the maintenance of which they have not scrupled to intervene whenever occasion demanded. In the seventeenth and eighteenth centuries they frequently combined to preserve the Balance of Power—a system based upon the idea of an equilibrium of forces. Endangered by Louis XIV, this system was revived by the Peace of Utrecht in 1713. Temporarily destroyed by Napoleon I, it was restored at the Congress of Vienna in 1815. In the name of the so-called " Holy Alliance," the Quadruple Alliance, renewed Nov. 20, 1815, undertook to prevent and to crush revolution in Italy and Spain, and even threatened to extend its activities to the Western Hemisphere. It was mainly against the extension of this system of intervention to Latin America that the Monroe Doctrine was proclaimed in 1823 [16]—a doctrine which also included a declaration that the American Continent was not open to further colonization. The Monroe Doctrine has since been more fully developed, and, in its existing form, may perhaps be defined as the prohibition of any further acquisition, colonization, or permanent occupation of American territory, or the control in any manner of the destiny of Latin-American States, by any European Power.

141. The European Concert of Powers.—In the course of the nineteenth century, the European idea of a Balance of Power gradually developed into that of the European Concert—a sort of loose Confederacy of five or six of the leading Powers whose members usually interfered jointly or collectively in matters which were deemed of paramount

[16] For discussions of and references on the Monroe Doctrine, see *supra*, No. 72.

On the *European Concert* and *Balance of Power in Europe*, see especially: Bernard, *Lectures on Diplomacy* (1868), 97–100; Brougham, 8 *Works* (1857), 1–50; * Dickinson, *Equality of States* (1920), 292–310; Donnadieu, *Essai sur la théorie de l'equilibre* (1900), *passim*, and *Les rapports des grandes puissances* (1921); * 1 Fauchille, Nos. 23, 108, 153[57], 248; Fenelon, in Wheaton, *History*, 82–84; Holland, *European Concert in the East*. *Quest.* (1885); 2 Nys, *Études*, 1–46; Wheaton, *History, of the Law of Nations* (1845), *passim*.

For bibliographies, see 1 Fauchille, p. 15, and *List of References on Europe and Int. Politics* published by the Library of Congress (1914), 49–57.

importance.   They have thus intervened in the affairs of Holland and Belgium, Greece, etc., but their principal field of activity has been the Ottoman Empire, where their interventions have been so constant and frequent as to create, in the opinion of some publicists, a body of jurisprudence which is part of the public law of Europe.

Toward the close of the nineteenth century they attempted to extend their system to the Far East, but encountered the diplomatic opposition of the United States and the armed resistance of Japan.

It should especially be noted that the whole fabric of European supremacy in Asia and Africa rests upon this system of political intervention—a policy which the Powers are now beginning to apply jointly or collectively instead of severally, as was formerly the case.

142. **The Primacy of the United States in America.**—A political Primacy, similar in kind, though of a less positive character, is wielded by the United States on the American Continent.   It is a Primacy essentially political in its nature which has no legal basis whatsoever, but which rests upon certain maxims enunciated by the fathers of the Republic and applied by American statesmen.   Based originally upon the principle of non-intervention in the affairs of Europe, the Monroe Doctrine is essentially a system or policy of intervention derived from our conception of primary or permanent American interests.

With one exception [17] prior to the World War, the United States has confined its interventions to American affairs. The most notable instances have been the intervention against the unjustifiable interference of Napoleon III in the affairs in Mexico in 1865; the intervention on grounds of humanity and American interests in behalf of Cuba against Spain in 1898; and the premature recognition of the independence of Panama (really a disguised intervention) by President Roosevelt in the " interests of collective civilization " and of the United States in 1903.

[17] The participation of the United States in the intervention of the Powers against China during the great Boxer Uprising of 1900.   The protests of Secretary Hay and President Roosevelt against the treatment of the Jews in Rumania and Russia in 1902 and 1903 were not interventions in the proper sense of this term.   One is surprised to see Mérignhac (I, p. 299 and n.) so characterize them.

143. **Collective Intervention.**—Theoretically, intervention on political grounds should likewise be collective. It is actually becoming so in Europe, where the Great Powers have usually acted more or less in concert in the solution of European problems and where the League of Nations may find a promising field for collective intervention. But the Monroe Doctrine forbids European intervention in American affairs, and no Concert of Powers has thus far been developed on the American Continent.

144. **The Doctrine of Non-intervention.**—The present tendency among publicists [18] is toward the acceptance of the

[18] The principle of non-intervention appears to have been first put forth by Kant in his Essay on Perpetual Peace published in 1795. "No State should interfere in the constitution or government of another State." Art. 5. In 1798 Washington wrote to Lafayette to the effect that no government should interfere in the internal affairs of another government, unless it acted in the interest of its own security. See 2 Nys, 187. For the attitude assumed by France during the Revolution, see *supra*, No. 66. But owing to the reaction which followed, little headway was made in securing support for the principle of non-intervention before the Revolutions of 1830 and 1848, except in the United States and England. In 1820–23 Lord Castlereagh and Mr. Canning laid down the English doctrine that intervention is only to be justified on grounds of danger to immediate security or permanent essential interests. Cf. Webster, *Foreign Policy of Castlereagh* (1925), 237 ff.; Temperley, *Foreign Policy of Canning* (1925), 13 ff., 458, 470 ff.; and 2 *Cambridge History of British Foreign Policy* (1923), 53–54, 622 ff. The fiasco of Napoleon III in Mexico (1861–66) seems to have aided in discrediting the doctrine of the right of intervention still prevailing on the Continent at that time. On the "Policy of the U. S. as Regards Intervention," see Martin, in 93 Columbia University *Studies* (1921), No. 2; and 6 Moore, *Digest*, ch. 19.

Among modern publicists who either deny a right of intervention or accept the principle of non-intervention (with or without exceptions), the following may be cited: Bluntschli, Arts. 68, 474–80; Brocher de la Flechére, in 26 *R. D. I.* (1894), 415–31; Bourgeois, in 4 *R. D. I. P.* (1897), 745 ff.; Bry, *Précis élémentaire de droit int. public* (1906), Nos. 96 ff.; Carnazza-Amari, in 5 *R. D. I.* (1873), 352–89 and 531–61; Despagnet, Nos. 193 ff.; Bonfils and * 1 Fauchille, Nos. 300–33; 1 Halleck (3d ed.), 95 ff. and 512 ff.; Heffter, §§ 44–46; 1 Fiore Nos. 561 ff., and *Int. Law Cod.* (1918), Arts. 556–62; Geffcken, in 4 *Handbuch*,131–68; De Floeckher, *De l'intervention* (1896), ch. 2, § 3; Funck-Brentano et Sorel, 212–16; * Kebedgy, *De l'intervention* (1890), ch. 2, pp. 39 ff.; Liszt, § 55, III; 1 F. de Martens, § 76; 1 Mérignhac, 284 ff.; Neumann, *Elements du droit des gens* (1886), § 14; 2 Nys, 182–93; 1 Piédelièvre, Nos. 289 ff.; * 1 P.-Fodéré, Nos. 287 ff., especially 355; * 1 Rivier, 389 ff.; * Rougier, *Les guerres civiles* (1903), Pt. III, chs. 1 and 2, pp. 315–70; Vattel, liv. II, §§ 54–62; Walker, *Manual of Public Int. Law* (1895), §§ 5–7 and *Science of Int. Law* (1893), 112, 151; Wheaton, §§ 63–71; Wilson, § 23; Wilson and Tucker, § 41; Woolsey, § 43.

Several of the authorities cited above (De Floeckher, Funck-Brentano et Sorel, Piédelièvre, and P.-Fodéré) deny the legal character or validity of the principle of non-intervention as the correct and normal rule of international practice. But most of them admit intervention as a legitimate exercise of sovereign power in extreme and exceptional cases on high moral or political rather than on purely legal grounds, as, *e.g.* in case of the commission of great crimes against humanity (Greece, Bulgaria, Armenia, and Cuba), or where essential and permanent national or international interests of far-reaching importance are at stake (Ottoman Empire in 1865, or Panama).

It seems necessary to admit another class of exceptions to the rule of non-intervention. The application of this important principle in its fullest extent is necessarily limited to fully sovereign States and to nations which possess governments capable of maintaining a fair degree of order and of affording reasonable protection to the lives and property of foreigners. Whether such States as those of Central America, with all their boasted sovereignty, are capable of affording such a degree of order and protection is, to say the least, very doubtful.

145. The Nature of Intervention.—Like war, intervention is not, commonly or strictly speaking, a law or a right in the ordinary legal sense of these terms, although, like war, it may become a source of legal rights and duties. Like war, it is really an exercise of sovereign or high political power— a right inherent in sovereignty itself. The government

principle of non-intervention, as well as that of intervention. Fauchille (I, p. 562) considers intervention less a right than a sanction of the rights of States. The majority hold that the correct rule of International Law is non-intervention, but that intervention is either legally or morally permissible in extreme cases. Even those authorities who appear to admit a legal right of intervention (*e.g.* Arntz, in 8 *R. D. I.* 1876, 675 ff.; Amos, *Remedies for War* 1880, 75–81, 139–62; Creasy, *First Platform of Int. Law* 1876, 278–96; * Hall, Pt. II, ch. 8; * Lawrence, Pt. II, ch. 1; Kebedgy, *op. cit.;* * 1 Oppenheim, §§ 134 ff.; 1 Phillimore, Pt. IV, ch. 1; 1 Westlake, 317–21) restrict its application as much as possible.

On the right of collective intervention, see especially Hall, § 95; Dumas, *Les sanctions de l'arbitrage* (1905), 166 f.; Horning, in 18 *R. D. I.* (1886), 188 ff. and 281 ff.; Rolin Jecquemyns, in 8 *R. D. I.* (1876), 295, 673.

For discussion of and references on intervention on grounds of humanity, see Stowell, *Intervention in Int. Law* (1921), § 8, pp. 51–62, particularly notes on pp. 55–56 and 58–65.

For divers views and instances of intervention, the student is especially referred to 1 Calvo, §§ 110–207; 6 Moore, *Digest*, ch. 19; 3 Moore, *Arbitrations*, 2313–47; 1 P.-Fodéré, Nos. 287 ff.; and 1 Wharton, *Digest*, §§ 45–72.

which intervenes performs a political act. " It is a high and summary procedure which may sometimes snatch a remedy beyond the reach of law; " [19] but which is usually either a justifiable exception to the ordinary, everyday rule of non-intervention or an act based upon the mere possession of physical force. Inasmuch as a sovereign who chooses to exercise this supreme political power cannot be restrained except by the counter use of force, it may become necessary for another or other interested sovereigns to assert a similar political power and intervene against such unjust or injurious act of intervention.[20]

146. **The Right of Legal Equality.**—The third essential right of sovereign States is that of equality before the law. All fully independent or sovereign States, however weak or powerful, are entitled to equal protection in the enjoyment of their rights under treaties and International Law.[21] To this right there is attached the corresponding duty of respecting the legal equality of other States. This principle, which is almost universally admitted,[22] is a necessary consequence of the fundamental right of sovereignty and independence. As Vattel [23] said: " A small republic is no less a sovereign State than the most powerful Republic." Or, as Chief Justice Marshall expressed it: " Russia and Geneva have equal rights. It results from this equality

---

[19] *Letters of Historicus* (1863), p. 41.

[20] Considerable portions of the text on intervention are drawn from the following articles to which the student is referred for a fuller exposition of the author's previously expressed, if somewhat immature, views on this subject: "Intervention and Recognition of Cuban Independence," in 11 *Annals* (1898), 353 ff.; "Justification for Intervention," in 31 *Rev. of Rev.* (1905), 199 ff.; and "The Calvo and Drago Doctrines," in 1 *A. J.* (1907), 26–45.

[21] From the rules of equality and independence must be excepted half-civilized and part-sovereign States together with those under Suzerainty and Protectorates.

[22] This principle is denied or doubted by a few leading authorities: Lawrence (3d ed.), § 134 (Cf. 7th ed., §§ 112 ff.); 1 Lorimer, *Institutes of the Law of Nations* (1883–84), 170–71; Pillet, in 5 *R. D. I. P.* (1896), 70 ff.; 1 Westlake, 321–24, and *Collected Papers* (1914), 92 ff. See especially * Dickinson, *Equality of States* (1920), *passim*, for a very keen and comprehensive criticism of the historical and still prevailing conception of the nature of the principle of the legal equality between States. He shows, for example, that it does not imply an equal status or capacity for rights. See also Baker, in *Brit. Yr. Bk.* (1923–24), 1–20; and Goebel, *The Equality of States* (1923).

[23] Preliminaries, § 18.

that no one can rightfully impose a rule on another. Each legislates for itself, but its legislation can operate on itself alone." [24]

Each sovereign State has also the right of selecting such arms and flags, etc., and of conferring upon its rulers such rank and titles as it chooses, though it cannot always insist upon their recognition by other States. Although their influence varies greatly, all members of the international community have as a rule one vote and one vote only at International Congresses and Conferences where [25] the vote of the weakest State counts equally with that of the strongest.

There still exist, however, certain differences of rank between States which have not wholly disappeared from international practice. Monarchies and great Republics enjoy what are called *royal honors*, which entitle these States to the exclusive and reciprocal privilege of sending diplomatic agents of the first rank (ambassadors) with rights of precedence and a certain priority of rank.[26]

Because States differ greatly in political power and influence, it does not follow that they are not entitled to equal protection under the Law of Nations. Just as there is a natural and artificial inequality between individuals whose evil effects are visible even in the administration of justice, so there are between States natural and artificial inequalities which sometimes result in a violation of the rights of the weak by the powerful.

Moreover, as pointed out previously,[27] the Concert of the six Great Powers in Europe and the United States in America assert and maintain a sort of Primacy or He-

---

[24] The *Antelope* (1825), 10 Wheaton, 66, 122, or Scott, *Cases*, 9. Cf. Sir Wm. Scott, in *Le Louis* (1817), 2 Dod. 210, 243, or Scott, *Cases*, 338.

[25] To avoid questions of rank and precedence, the principle of the *alternat* has often been used. *E.g.* in signing documents, certain Powers alternate, in such a manner that each Power occupies the first place in the list of signatures, in the copy which it receives. The alphabetical device was employed at the Hague Conferences, *i.e.* the Powers signed as they were seated —in alphabetical order.

It is of interest to note that, though the French language is usually employed at these Conferences, each State has the privilege of using its own language.

[26] The monarchical chiefs of these States also address each other as brothers.

[27] *Supra*, Nos. 141–42.

gemony.   These are facts of vast importance and significance, but their leadership is political in character and has no legal basis whatever.   Neither the United States nor the Great Powers have any definite rules of conduct, they have no permanent organization or machinery, their action in any given case is by no means certain.   They deal with each particular situation as it arises from political motives and by political methods.

It may have seemed to a few publicists some years ago that " Europe is working round again to the old notion of a common superior; " [28] but such important social and political events as the rise of modern Japan, the Turkish and Chinese Revolutions, the Hague Peace Conferences, and the increase in the number of members of the international community since the World War together with the formation of the League of Nations, have tended to discredit such prophecy.

IV. THE RIGHT TO RESPECT

147. **The Right to Respect.**—From the rights of sovereignty and equality flows a fourth fundamental right of States—the so-called right to respect.[29] A failure to observe the forms of respect due a sovereign State is usually regarded as an affront to its dignity, and may entail serious consequences.   The right to respect involves the duty of a reciprocal observance of certain rights and ceremonial forms. These include diplomatic privileges,—a topic which will be considered in a subsequent chapter,[30]—the observance of a certain etiquette in diplomatic intercourse, and the use of

[28] *E.g.* Lawrence (3d ed.), § 134.   For an interesting attack on the principle of the legal equality of States, see Hicks, in 2 *A. J.* (1908), 530–61.   But legal equality, or equality under the protection of the law, does not necessarily imply equality of voting power, as Mr. Hicks appears to think, though it may be admitted that there is great confusion of thought on this subject.

Perhaps the best defense of the traditional doctrine is by Max Huber, *Die Gleichheit der Staaten* (1909).   For references on the so-called "Equality of States," see Dickinson, *op. cit.*, particularly on pp. 123 and 124; and 1 Fauchille, 460–61.   For a review of leading authorities, see Armstrong, in 14 *A. J.* (1920), 540 ff.

[29] Some publicists speak of a right of reputation in this connection.   This is obviously absurd.

[30] See *infra*, ch. 18.

the customary military and maritime ceremonials between armies or between vessels, and between vessels and forts belonging to different States.[31]

The right to respect is especially held to include: (1) Respect for a State's moral and political personality as represented by its sovereigns, warships, and diplomatic agents. This is shown by paying the customary honors and marks of respect. Besides, a State may not appropriate the flag, arms, etc., nor copy the emblems or inscriptions found on the coins of another State. (2) Respect for its civil or legal personality. Unless there is well-grounded suspicion of a denial or gross perversion of justice, full faith and credit should be given in each State to the judicial proceedings of other States.[32]

V. THE RIGHT TO COMMERCE OR INTERCOURSE

148. **The Right to Commerce or Intercourse.**—The fifth essential right and duty of States is that of mutual commerce or intercourse. These result from the interdependence and solidarity of the intellectual, social, and economic interests of modern peoples; and include various forms of

[31] These ceremonials have no longer the importance they had in the days when they implied pretentions to supremacy over portions of the high seas. As far as the open sea is concerned, they are mere matters of courtesy. But States may require the observance of certain maritime ceremonials within territorial waters.

For details regarding the rules of *Military and Maritime Ceremonial*, the student may consult: * 1 Calvo, §§ 231–59; De Cussy, *Phases et causes célèbres du droit maritime* (1856), liv. I, tit. II, §§ 61–63; Davis (3d ed.), 128–31; Despagnet, No. 171; * 1 Halleck, ch. 5, §§ 16–28; Heffter, § 197; Klüber, §§ 117–22; G. F. de Martens, §§ 158–59; * 1 Ortolan, *Diplomatie de la mer* (1864), liv. II, ch. 15; * 2 Phillimore, Pt. V, ch. 5; 1 Pomeroy, ch. 8, §§ 255–57; * 2 P.-Fodéré, Nos. 549–94; the U. S. Army Regulations of 1895, the U. S. Navy Regulations of 1896, and the Queen's Regulations and Admiralty Instructions of 1879.

[32] The question has been much debated, *apropos* of the *Zappa Affair*, which led to a breach of diplomatic relations between Greece and Rumania in 1892, whether one State may inherit real property in another State which prohibits the acquisition of such property by foreigners. For a brief account of the *Zappa Incident*, see 1 Westlake, 251. For bibliography of the *Zappa Affair*, see 1 Fauchille, p. 477.

On the so-called "Right to Respect," see especially: 3 Calvo, §§ 1300–02; Despagnet, Nos. 184–86; * 1 Fauchille, Nos. 279–84; 1 Fiore, Nos. 439–51; Heffter, §§ 32, 102–03; Holtzendorff, in 2 *Handbuch*, § 17; 1 Oppenheim, §§ 120–22; 2 Phillimore, §§ 27–43; 2 P.-Fodéré, Nos. 451–83; and Vattel, liv. II, ch. 3, §§ 35–48.

modern intercourse, more especially diplomatic and commercial relations.[33] It is perhaps rather a necessary condition for modern progress and development than a right in the legal sense of this term,[34] but it is at least an open question whether the violation of the most rudimentary of these rights is not a serious violation of the Law of Nations. For example, a breach of diplomatic intercourse is apt to be followed by war, and a total prohibition of the imports of a particular nation would certainly be regarded as an unfriendly act. To be sure, a State might conceivably refuse all diplomatic and commercial intercourse with the outside world, but by such action it would cease to be a member of the family of nations. A member of the international community may use its taxing power to levy custom dues which are practically prohibitory; it may favor one State and discriminate against another by means of treaties of commerce and navigation; it may refuse to all foreigners or those of a particular nationality the rights of trade and settlement; it may close certain of its ports to foreign commerce, prohibit foreign trade in certain articles, or reserve its coasting trade for the use of its own nationals. But it may not refuse all trade with foreign nations or with a particular people; it may not refuse the protection of its courts to foreigners whom it admits within its territory; it accords a certain measure of protection to its own nationals on foreign soil; and it must permit the passage of foreign merchantmen through its maritime belt and international passageways, as also the innocent use of its territorial waters, at least by coriparian States.

It will thus be seen that the right of mutual commerce or intercourse is far from absolute. It is limited by other essential and fundamental rights which take precedence or restrict its application.[35]

---

[33] It would also seem to include the innocent use of postal and telegraphic facilities, and a right to the innocent use of rivers, etc., for purposes of trade and travel.

[34] In one respect the right of intercourse is certainly a legal right, *i.e.* as against third Powers. Except in time of war, no State has the right to interfere in the commerce between two States.

[35] On the so-called "Right of Commerce" or "Intercourse," see especially. 3 Calvo, §§ 1303–05; * 1 Fauchille, Nos. 285–89; Grotius, liv. II, ch. 2, §§ 13–17; Hall, § 13; Heffter, § 33; Holtzendorff, in 2 *Handbuch*, § 16; F. de Martens,

149. **The Right of Jurisdiction.**—One of the essential or fundamental rights of a State flowing from territorial sovereignty is that of jurisdiction over practically all things and persons on its territory.[36] By virtue of its personal supremacy or sovereignty, it may, in addition, exercise a limited jurisdiction over its nationals travelling or residing in foreign lands, who are thus subject to a double or concurrent jurisdiction,[37] at least in principle.   Some States even wrongly claim the right to punish aliens for certain crimes committed abroad.[38]   A State also has jurisdiction over all its vessels (including all persons and things thereon) on the high seas, and any State may punish piracy.   Finally, in time of war, belligerent States or communities may exercise the rights of visit and search, capture and confiscate contraband goods, and institute and enforce blockades, etc. These matters will be considered more in detail in subsequent chapters.

§ 79; 1 Mérignhac, 256–58; 1 Oppenheim, § 141; 4 P.-Fodéré, Nos. 1899 ff.; 1 Rivier, 262–64; and Vattel, liv. II, ch. 2, §§ 21–26.

In conformity with President Wilson's third point which called for the "removal, so far as possible, of all economic barriers and the establishment of an equality of trade conditions," Art. 23 of the Covenant of the League of Nations declares that the Members of the League "will make provision to secure and maintain freedom of communication and of transit and equitable treatment for the commerce of all Members of the League."   Cf. *supra*, p. 126 and note 4, and *infra*, p. 525 n.

[36] For exceptions to this rule, see *infra*, Nos. 166, 209, 211, 270 ff., and 287 ff.

[37] For an interesting case of possible concurrent triple jurisdiction, see *Regina* v. *Anderson* (1868), 11 Cox, C. C., 198, or Evans, *Cases*, 172.

[38] The claim of many States to jurisdiction over aliens for certain crimes committed in foreign countries cannot be too strongly condemned, for it is a dangerous abuse of power and has no sound theoretical basis.   It is contrary to the principle of territorial sovereignty as well as that of personal supremacy.   In the famous *Cutting Case* in 1886, the United States refused to admit the validity of the Mexican law under which an American citizen was convicted for a libel on a Mexican published in Texas.

On this case and subject, see Gamboa, in 22 *R. D. I.* (1890), 234–50; * Beckett, in *Brit. Yr. Bk.* (1925), 44 ff.; 1 Hyde, § 243; Lawrence, § 104; * 2 Moore, *Digest*, §§ 200–02 (including Moore's admirable *Report* on the Cutting Case); 1 Oppenheim, § 147; Rolin, in 20 *R. D. I.* (1888), 559–77; Scott, *Cases*, 387 ff.; Snow, *Cases*, 172–74; Taylor, §§ 191–94; Wheaton, § 113; 1 Westlake, 261–63.

On the *Right of Jurisdiction*, see especially: Bluntschli, Arts. 381–93; 1 Fauchille, Nos. 263–66; 1 Fiore, Nos. 475–558; Hall, §§ 62, 75–80; 1 Halleck, 198–254; Heffter, §§ 34–39; 1 Hyde, § 218; 2 Moore, *Digest*, §§ 175–249; 1 Oppenheim, §§ 143–47; Praag, *Jurisdiction et droit int. public* (1915), Nos. 25–48; 1 Rivier, 326 ff.; 1 Westlake, 246–52; and Wheaton, §§ 77 ff.

149a. **Fundamental Duties of States.**—In the preceding sections, attention is repeatedly called to the fact that each essential or fundamental right of States involves the duty of respecting the corresponding right of other members of the international community. It should be noted, however, that there has been a tendency to assert the rights rather than the duties of States, and special emphasis should be placed upon the legal as well as the moral duty of governments to observe their treaty obligations [39] and obey the rules and principles of International Law, more particularly in their relations with foreign States and aliens. This involves a consideration of the subject of the responsibility of States.

BIBLIOGRAPHY

The Fundamental Rights and Duties of States.—Bluntschli, Arts. 64–94, 375–93; Brown, in 9 *A. J.* (1915), 305–35; Bry, *Précis élémentaire de droit int. public* (1906), Nos. 73–94; Bulmerincq, in 1 Marquardsen's *Handbuch*, §§ 21–26; 1 and 3 Calvo, §§ 107–09, 208–59, 1261–62, 1300–09; 1 Chrétien, *Principes de droit int. public* (1893), Nos. 160–302; Despagnet, Nos. 165–86; * Dickinson, *Equality of States* (1920), *passim;* * 1 Fauchille, Nos. 235–97; Fenwick, chs. 8–11; 1 Fiore, Nos. 367–658, and *Int. Law Cod.* (1918), Arts. 185–351, 393–426, 545–95; Fontenay, *Des droit et des devoirs des états entre eux* (1888); Gareis, *Institutionen des Völkerrechts* (1887), §§ 24–28; Hall, §§ 7–13, 62, 75 ff.; * 1 Halleck (3d ed.), 93 ff., 116–42, 186 ff.; Heffter, §§ 26–39; Heilborn, *System des Völkerrechts* (1896), 279–306 (for criticism); * Holtzendorff, in 2 *Handbuch*, pp. 47–69; * Klüber, §§ 36–122; Lawrence, §§ 112 ff., and *Essays on Int. Law* (1885), 208–33; Liszt, § 55 III; 1 J. de Louter, § 16; 1 F. de Martens, §§ 72–79; 1 Mérignhac, 233–84, 310–20; Neumann, *Eléments du droit des gens* (1886), § 8; 2 Nys, 176–228; * 1 Oppenheim, §§ 112–47; 1 and 2 Phillimore, Pt. III, chs. 2–3, 10, 18, and Pt. V, chs. 1–3, 5; 1 Piédelièvre, Nos. 201–372; * Pillet, in 5 *R. D. I. P.* (1898), 66 ff., 236 ff., and in 6 *Ibid.* (1899), 503 ff.; Pomeroy, §§ 76–124, 204–14; 1 and 2 P.-Fodéré, Nos. 164–95, 211–332, 442–594; 1 Rivier, §§ 9, 19–30; Ullmann, §§ 36–38; Vattel, Introduction, §§ 13–23, liv. I, §§ 13–25, and liv. II, §§ 1–137; 1 Westlake, 246 ff., 306–17, and *Collected Papers* (1914), chs. 7 and 8; Wheaton, §§ 60–62, 77, 152–60; Wilson, ch. 2.

---

[39] On the *Duties of States*, see particularly: Bernard, "The Obligation of Treaties," in *Lectures on Diplomacy* (1868), Lect. IV, 163 ff.; 3 Calvo, §§ 1261–62, 1299–1309; * 1 Fauchille, Nos. 290–95; 1 Fiore, Nos. 559–658, and *Int. Law Cod.* (1918), Arts. 545–618; Hall, §§ 11, 13; 1 Halleck (3d ed.), ch. 13; and Redslob, *Histoire de droit des gens* (1923), 17–24, 47–57, 122–28, 224–26, 337–39, 355–59, 397–403, 433–40.

For references on *Intervention*, see *supra*, note on pp. 243 f.   To this list should be added: Hodges, *The Doctrine of Intervention* (1915); * 1 Hyde, §§ 69–84, and in 6 *Ill. Law Rev.* (1911), No. 1; Linglebach, in 16 *Annals* (1900), 1–32; Martin, "The Policy of the United States as regards Intervention," in 93 Columbia University *Studies* (1921), No. 2; Stowell, *Intervention in Int. Law* (1921); and Winfield, in *Brit. Yr. Bk.* (1922–23 and 1924), 130 ff. and 149 ff.   Stowell's book is the best and most extensive work on this subject, but is somewhat discursive and too broad in some of its ideas and applications.

CHAPTER XI

RESPONSIBILITY OF STATES

150. **International Delinquencies.**—For a failure to observe its international obligations, as also for a positive violation of the rights of other members of the international community, a State is internationally responsible.[1] Such act of commission or omission is called an International Delinquency.[2]

A State is *directly* responsible for its own actions or for acts of its officials [3] and agents performed at its command or acting under its authority.[4]   State acts which violate Inter-

[1] Some publicists of the positive or historical school still teach the false and dangerous doctrine that a State is the sole judge of its international responsibilities.   But the fact that a State is theoretically sovereign or that there is no International Court of Justice with general obligatory jurisdiction over infractions of the Law of Nations does not free a State from international responsibility or make it the sole judge of its international actions.

[2] "International Delinquencies" should be distinguished from "Crimes against the Law of Nations" and "International Crimes."   "Crimes against the Law of Nations" are such acts against foreign States as are pronounced criminal by Municipal Law.   The phrase "International Crimes" refers to such outrages against mankind as piracy and slave trading, which every State has the right to punish.   See 1 Oppenheim, § 151.

International delinquencies should also be distinguished from unfriendly or merely discourteous acts.   For examples of international delinquencies, see 1 Oppenheim, §§ 155, 162–63.

[3] This responsibility is to States rather than to individuals.   In International Law the individual as such has as a rule neither rights nor obligations other than those belonging to him as a citizen or subject of a member of the Family of Nations.

[4] This principle applies particularly to diplomatic and administrative officials and military and naval commanders.   It does not fully apply to judicial functionaries, for these are more or less independent of the executive in all well-regulated modern States.   "All therefore that can be expected of a government in the case of wrongs inflicted by the courts is that compensation shall be made, and if the wrong has been caused by an imperfection in the law of such kind as to prevent a foreigner from getting equal justice with a native of the country, that a recurrence of the wrong shall be prevented by legislation."   Hall, § 65, p. 269.

On "State Responsibility for Acts of State Organs," see especially * Borchard, §§ 75–81; 1 Hyde, §§ 286–88; 6 Moore, *Digest*, §§ 998–1018; and 1 Oppenheim, §§ 157–63.

It should be noted that the international responsibility of a State "does

national Law or inflict injuries upon other nations constitute serious international delinquencies, if committed wilfully or as a consequence of culpable negligence. Such acts should be promptly disavowed, an apology tendered, their authors punished, and, in case of material damage, pecuniary reparation made.

151. **Direct *versus* Indirect Responsibility.**—In ordinary times a State is also *indirectly* responsible for the orderly and law abiding conduct of all those residing or domiciled (including foreigners) within its jurisdiction and subject to its laws. It is bound to use due (*i.e.* reasonable) diligence or at least the means at its disposal to prevent injurious acts against other States on the part of its own nationals or of foreigners residing on its territory. For an international delinquency of this sort, due satisfaction and reparation should also be made. But the punishment of the offenders or payment of an indemnity to those injured is usually deemed a sufficient satisfaction in these cases.

In case of inability to agree upon proper terms of settlement, the dispute should be referred to arbitration or the Permanent Court of International Justice. If arbitration be refused or satisfaction denied, recourse may be had to one of the means of self-help described in a subsequent chapter.[5]

152. **General Principle of Responsibility for Injuries to Foreigners.**—The general principle governing the responsibility of States for acts injurious to foreigners within its own jurisdiction is that a State is bound to furnish the same degree and kind of protection to foreigners and provide the same means of redress or measure of justice that it grants to its own nationals; but that ordinarily (*i.e.* in the absence of special privileges conferred by treaty or municipal law) foreigners are not entitled to a greater degree of protection or better guarantees of justice than are afforded to a State's own citizens or subjects.[6]

not as a general rule extend to the tortious acts of minor officials." Borchard, § 79, p. 189.

A State is not responsible for the utterances of members of Parliament or legislative and representative bodies. But "a statute is no defense against a breach of international obligations." Borchard, § 75, p. 181.

[5] See *infra*, ch. 24.

[6] This principle, though it is not without exceptions, is generally admitted to be an undoubted rule of International Law. Upon it is based the famous

153. The Rules governing the Responsibility of States in Respect to Foreigners.—In attempting to secure redress or justice, foreigners should, in the first instance, generally speaking, have recourse to the local or territorial tribunals of the district in which they are domiciled, or, as Vattel put it,[7] to the "judge of the place." In cases of indirect responsibility, judicial remedies should, as a rule, be exhausted before resorting to diplomatic interposition as a means of obtaining redress.[8] But this rule does not apply in cases of gross perversion or evident denial of justice, where local remedies have been superseded, where judicial action is waived or wanting, where the acts complained of are in themselves violations of treaty or of International Law, or where there is undue discrimination against foreigners on the part of the authorities.[9] It "does not

Calvo Doctrine, which condemns intervention (diplomatic as well as armed) as a legitimate method of enforcing any or all private claims of a pecuniary nature, at least such as are based upon contract or are the result of civil war, insurrection, or mob violence. "To admit in such cases the responsibility of governments, *i.e.* the principle of indemnity, would be to create an exhorbitant and fatal privilege essentially favorable to powerful States and injurious to weaker nations, and to establish an unjustifiable inequality between nationals and foreigners." 3 Calvo, § 1280. Cf. 1 and 3, and 6 Calvo, §§ 205, 1271–97, and 6 *Ibid.*, § 256.

This doctrine is undoubtedly sound in principle, but subject to certain exceptions. It has been incorporated, though in too absolute a form, into some of the laws and constitutions and into many treaties by Latin American States. See Arias, in 7 *A. J.* (1913), 755–60; and Borchard, § 97.

The broader *Calvo Doctrine* should be distinguished from the narrower *Drago Doctrine* which merely forbids the forcible collection of public debts— a doctrine equally sound in principle and wise as policy, but which its author, the distinguished Argentine statesman, Señor Drago, supported by the erroneous and in part obsolete contention that "it is an inherent qualification of all sovereignty that no proceedings for the execution of a judgment may be instituted or carried out against it."

On the *Calvo and Drago Doctrines*, see especially: Barclay, *Problems of Int. Practice and Diplomacy* (1907), 115–22; Borchard, §§ 119–23, 371–78, 390–93; 1, 3, and 6 Calvo, §§ 110, 185–206, 1271–97, 256; * Drago, "State Loans," in 1 *A. J.* (1907), 692–726, and *Cobro coercitivo de duedas publicas* (1906); * Hershey, "The Calvo and Drago Doctrines," in 1 *A. J.* (1907), 26–45; * Moulin, *La doctrine de Drago* (1908, with comprehensive bibliography), and in 14 *R. D. I. P.* (1907), 417 ff.; Scott (G. W.), in 183 *No. Am. Rev.* (1906), 602–10; Triana, *La doctrina Drago* (1908, documentary); and Vivot, *La doctrina Drago* (1911); Williams, in 2 *Bibliotheca Visseriana*, 1–66. Cf. references on *The Porter Convention, infra*, p. 263 n.

[7] Liv. II, ch. 8, § 103. Cf. ch. 6, §§ 72 and 73.

[8] 6 Moore, *Digest*, § 987. Cf. 2 Wharton, § 241.

[9] For examples of such exceptions, see 1 Hyde, §§ 283–85; 6 Moore, *Digest*, §§ 913–14, 986–93, 102.; and 2 Wharton, *Digest*, §§ 230 and 242.

apply to countries of imperfect civilization, or to cases in which prior proceedings show gross perversions of justice." [10]

The question of the liability of a State for injuries to the persons and property of foreigners resulting from mob violence is one in which the people of the United States should be deeply interested. Whether due to the intensity of feeling engendered by race and labor problems or (as is more likely) to a lax enforcement of law resulting from cumbrous and antiquated legal methods of trial and procedure, the American custom of lynching, though it shows some signs of abatement, is not likely to disappear until the causes which lead to it are removed.

154. **The Practice of the United States.**—The rule which has generally been verbally maintained by American statesmen appears to have been first laid down by Daniel Webster upon the occasion of the riots at New Orleans and Key West in 1851, which resulted from the summary execution of a number of American filibusters in Cuba. While admitting that the Spanish consul (whose office had been attacked and furniture destroyed) [11] was entitled to indemnity, he maintained that those Spanish subjects who had been injured in person or property were not entitled to compensation, on the ground that many American citizens suffered equal losses from the same cause and foreigners are merely " entitled to such protection [12] as is afforded our own citizens." As a mark of courtesy and out of respect to the magnanimity of the Queen of Spain (in liberating American prisoners), Congress nevertheless granted compensation to Spanish subjects as well as to the Spanish consul for losses sustained during these riots.

History has repeated itself in respect to a number of claims made by foreigners for injuries resulting from mob violence in the United States from that day to this. In the majority of these cases, our Government has refused to admit liability in principle, but has usually granted compensation as a matter of grace or favor, or from a sense of

[10] 2 Wharton, *Digest*, p. 695.

[11] The archives of the consulate had been thrown into the street, the portrait of the Queen of Spain defaced, and the Spanish flag torn to pieces.

[12] 2 Wharton's *Digest*, § 226, p. 601. Cf. Moore, *Digest*, § 1023, pp. 812–13. See also Snow, *Cases on Int. Law* (1893), 181–83.

sympathy, benevolence, or policy.[13] Many of our statesmen, however, admit liability in case of a failure on the part
of the local authorities to use due (*i.e.* reasonable) diligence
in preventing or punishing such crimes, and this is unquestionably the rule of International Law.[14]

On the other hand the United States has shown com-
mendable zeal in protecting its citizens from such attacks
abroad. It has repeatedly interposed diplomatically in
behalf of its citizens in China, Turkey, Mexico, Panama,
Chile, Brazil, and other Central and South American
States.[15]

In view of this double inconsistency—that of theory and
practice on the one hand, and our attitude at home and
abroad on the other—it is highly desirable that our State
Department should in the future frankly admit liability in

[13] This was notably so in the cases of the 43 Chinese killed and wounded
at Rock Springs, Wyoming, in 1885; and of the Italians lynched at New Orleans
in 1891. For these and numerous cases, see 6 Moore, *Digest*, §§ 1025 ff. See
also the notes and references as well as the text in Borchard, §§ 86–92; and
1 Hyde, §§ 290–91. A number of cases are also cited by Goebel, in 8 *A. J.*
(1914), 802–52; and Ralston, *Int. Arbitral Law* (2nd ed., 1926), *passim*.

[14] This rule is usually stated in language ascribed to Secretary Evarts:
"A government is liable internationally for damages done to alien residents
by a mob which by due diligence it could have repressed." See 2 Wharton,
Digest, p. 602. But the absence of quotation marks in Wharton and a refer-
ence to Evart's dispatch as given in 6 Moore, *Digest* (pp. 817–18) shows
that Mr. Evarts did not use the language which has been ascribed to him.
It is, however, a good statement of an undoubted principle of the Law of
Nations if we add the words—"and which it fails to punish."

The fact that our Federal Government has sometimes been unable to
secure justice for foreigners by reason of constitutional or statutory limitations
does not free it from international responsibility in such cases.

On "Responsibility of the Federal Government for Violations of the
Rights of Aliens," see Gammans, in 8 *A. J.* (1914), 73–80; Ex-Sec'y Root,
in 4 *A. J.* (1910), 523–26; and Watson on "Need of Federal Legislation,"
in 25 *Yale Law J.* (1915–16), 561 ff.

On Mar. 13, 1924, the Council of the League of Nations unanimously
adopted the following opinion given by a committee of ten jurists: "The
responsibility of a State is only involved in the commission in its territory of
a political crime against the persons of foreigners if the State has neglected
to take all reasonable measures for the prevention of the crime and the pursuit,
arrest, and bringing to justice of the criminal. The recognized public character of a foreigner, and the circumstances in which he is present in its territory,
entail upon a State a corresponding duty of special vigilance on his behalf."
4 *Monthly Summary of League of Nations* (1924), 53.

[15] 1 Hyde, § 293 and 6 Moore, *Digest*, §§ 1019–30, *passim*. For our diplomatic interposition in China, see Moore's digest of the extremely able communication of the Chinese minister Cheng Tsao Ju to Secretary Bayard on
pp. 822–26.

all cases of attack by mobs upon foreigners as such or upon those of a particular nationality whenever the local authorities show themselves unwilling or unable to use reasonable diligence to prevent, and whenever the courts are unable or unwilling to punish, such crimes. For foreigners have an undoubted right to demand better protection against this species of violence than is afforded by our courts and local authorities in some parts of this country.

But it may be urged that the admission of such a principle might, in some cases, give to foreigners a protection superior to that enjoyed by our own citizens. This may be true in countries like our own where life and property are insecure from mob violence and where criminal procedure is notoriously defective; but civilized States are supposed to grant at least a fair or average degree of such protection in ordinary times, and it is no adequate reply to a charge of denial of justice to,[16] or an undue discrimination against, foreigners to urge that our own citizens frequently suffer similar or even greater injustice. There would, of course, be no responsibility in the case of an ordinary miscarriage of justice, where the spirit as well as the forms of the law had been complied with, or in the case of one accidentally killed or injured in the course of a riot or insurrection.[17]

In view of the protest by Japan in 1906 against the segregation of Japanese school children in San Francisco,[18]

[16] On what constitutes a denial of justice, see especially Anzilotti, in 13 R. D. I. P. (1906), 21–24; * Borchard, §§ 81, 127–29, 381 ff.; 1 Hyde, §§ 281–82; 6 Moore, Digest, §§ 913, 986; Procs. Soc. D. L. (1927); 2 Wharton, Digest, § 230; and Vattel, liv. II, ch. 18, § 350.

[17] See, e.g. the case of Bain, in 6 Moore, Digest, § 1027.

[18] On the Japanese School Question, see especially Barthélemy, in 14 R. D. I. P. (1907), Chronique, 636 ff.; Baldwin, in 7 Col. Law Rev. (1907), 85 ff.; Hershey, in 1 Am. Pol. Sci. Rev. (1907), 393 ff.; and Ex-Sec'y Root, in 1 A. J. (1907), 273 ff. For a very brief account of this controversy, see Hershey, Modern Japan (1919), 321–24.

This dispute was primarily a question of treaty construction and constitutional law (the extent of the treaty-making power in the United States); but it was contended that the right of education was included under the right of residence granted by the treaty of 1894 on reciprocal terms, and this may be considered a question of International Law as well as treaty construction. There seems to have been no warrant for this contention.

In the paper cited above, Sec'y Root maintained that under the treaty, the State of California might decline to furnish all aliens with school privileges but could not discriminate against those of a particular nationality in the

it should be noted that a State is under no obligation to extend to foreigners the enjoyment of civil and private rights or to place them upon an equal footing with its own nationals in these respects. Whatever rights or privileges of this kind (whether of an educational, economic, or religious nature) foreigners may enjoy are based upon convention or the principle of reciprocity, or are granted as a matter of grace and favor.[19] All that an alien who is permitted to set foot on foreign territory (and this permission is purely optional) can demand as a matter of strict right in the absence of privileges granted by treaty, is protection of life and property together with access to the administrative authorities and local courts for this purpose.

155. **Responsibility for Injuries to Foreigners during Civil War and Insurrection.**—The same principles may, in general, be said to apply to cases of injuries or losses sustained by foreigners during civil war and insurrection; but the law of necessity or the physical inability (*force majeure*) to furnish adequate protection under such circumstances usually absolves governments from responsibility in these cases. The general rule is that " a sovereign is not ordinarily responsible to alien residents for injuries they receive on his territory from belligerent action, or from

use of her public school system. There appears to be no other authority for this view, whether regarded as a principle of treaty construction or a rule of the Law of Nations. The theory of "undue discrimination" has been applied to the responsibility of a State for the *protection* of foreigners, but I am not aware that it has been extended beyond this duty. There is much, however, that might be said in its favor.

A similar controversy involving the question of national or race discrimination arose in 1913 in consequence of the passage by the California legislature of the Heney-Webb land act which provided in effect that aliens ineligible to citizenship should not be permitted, except by a short term lease, to hold or acquire land in California. The Japanese Government repeatedly protested against this act as unfair and discriminatory as well as inconsistent with treaty provisions, but our Government maintained that the enactment was the result of particular economic conditions in California rather than the outcome of race prejudice.

For the diplomatic correspondence on this subject, see *For. Rel. of U. S.* (1913 and 1914), 625 ff. and 426 ff. or *Japan Year Book* (1914), 572 ff. For summaries, see Hershey, *Modern Japan* (1919), 327–32; and an editorial in 8 *A. J.* (1914), 571–78. For the text of the California Alien Land Tenure Law, see Supp. to 8 *A. J.* (1914), 177–79. For discussion of some of the legal aspects of this law, see Buell, in 17 *A. J.* (1923), 35–47.

[19] On this head see especially Anzilotti, 13 *R. D. I. P.* (1906), 18–20.

insurgents whom he could not control, or whom the claimant government had recognized as belligerents." They are " not entitled to greater privileges or immunities than the other inhabitants of the insurrectionary district. . . . By voluntarily remaining in a country in a state of civil war they must be held to have been willing to accept the risks as well as the advantages of that domicile." [20]

These principles have been repeatedly enunciated by our leading statesmen,[21] as also by those of Europe,[22] and they have the almost unanimous sanction of leading authorities on International Law. Almost invariably they have been applied by European States in their relations with each other, though frequently ignored in their dealings with weaker States, more particularly in the cases of China, Turkey, and the Republics of Latin America.

156. **Exceptions to General Principles.**—There are, however, several exceptions which must be made to the general principles laid down in this chapter. Indemnity would seem to be due to foreigners by way of exception in the following cases: (1) Where there has been shown a lack of due diligence on the part of the authorities either to prevent or to punish injuries. (2) Where the act complained of is directed against them because they are foreigners, or as belonging to some particular nationality. (3) Where the injury results from an act contrary to the laws or treaties of the country in which the act is committed, and for which no redress can otherwise be obtained. (4) When there has been a serious violation of International Law, more especially of the rules of civilized warfare. (5) In cases of a gross violation or an evident denial of justice, or of undue

[20] 2 Wharton, *Digest*, § 223, pp. 576–78. Cf. 6 Moore, *Digest*, § 1032, p. 885.

On "Claims based on War," see especially: * Borchard, §§ 93 ff.; 1 Hyde, §§ 294–302; * 6 Moore, *Digest*, §§ 1032 ff.; Ralston, *Int. Arbitral Law* (1926), ch. 12; and 2 Wharton, *Digest*, §§ 223–25. Moore's monumental *History and Digest of International Arbitrations* (in 6 vols.) contains a mine of material on this subject.

[21] For numerous opinions of American statesmen, see 6 Moore, *Digest*, §§ 1032–49. Cf. 2 Wharton, *Digest*, §§ 223–25.

[22] See especially the notes of Prince Schwartzenburg (Austrian) and Count Nesselrode (Russian) in reply to certain claims of the British Government which were based upon injuries to British subjects during the revolutions in Tuscany and Naples, in 1848. Cited by 6 Moore, *Digest*, pp. 886–87; and 1 P.-Fodéré, § 205, pp. 343–45.

discrimination against foreigners on the part of the authorities.[23]

157. **Claims based on Contract.**—There is another class of claims, viz. those based upon contract, which have given rise to much controversy. These consist mainly of public loans (bond issues), government contracts or concessions, and private investments which have been guaranteed by a defaulting government. The question is here not so much one of responsibility (for the responsibility of a State is conceded in these cases) as of the means by which such claims may be enforced. Though the authorities who discuss this question are divided in their opinions, the majority of them appear to be opposed to their forcible collection,[24] except possibly as a last resort or in exceptional cases.

It is argued, on the one hand, that the public faith—the so-called " honor of the prince "—is particularly engaged in case of contracts of this nature, inasmuch as a government cannot be sued without its own consent; that creditors may have no other means of redress than that of appealing to the State to which they owe allegiance; that stock in the public debt even if held by an enemy is exempt from seizure and its interest payable even in time of war; and that States, being in legal theory free and independent and owning no common superior, each State may enforce its rights at its own discretion by any means whatsoever.

On the other hand, it is urged that hazardous loans and investments should be discouraged; that those making

[23] See especially: Borchard, §§ 86–97; 1 Hyde, §§ 281–97, 300–01; 6 Moore, *Digest*, §§ 912 ff., 986 ff., 1010 ff., 1019 ff., 1022 ff., 1032 ff., 1040 ff., and 1044 ff.; and the rules adopted by the Institute of International Law (1900). See Scott, *Resolutions* (1916), 159–61.

[24] The right of a State to use coercive measures in the collection of public debts is asserted, *e.g.* by Hall (8th ed.), 333–34; 1 Halleck (3d ed.), 105 ff.; 2 Phillimore, Pt. V, ch. 3; 1 Rivier, 272–73.

The right is denied with or without reservations by 1 Calvo, § 205; Kebedgy, in 1 *R. D. I. P.* (1894), 261; F. de Martens, in 19 *R. D. I.*, 386; Moulin, *La doctrine de Drago* (1908), 99–129; 2 Nys, 225; Politis, *Les emprunts d'État* (1894), 217 ff.; 1 P.-Fodéré, No. 405; Rolin-Jaequemyns, in 1 *R. D. I.* (1869), 145 ff.; and 1 Westlake, 331–34.

For the opinions of ten leading publicists on this question, see 35 *R. D. I.* (1903), 597–623. They are nearly all strongly in sympathy (with or without reservations) with the principles of the Drago note.

them usually do so with a full knowledge of the risks incurred and in the expectation of exceptionally large returns; that the natural penalty of a failure on the part of a State to fulfill its obligations is a loss of credit; that foreigners cannot hope to be preferred to native creditors; that coercive measures for the collection of bad debts are never or seldom employed except against weak States and are likely to be employed as a pretext for aggression or conquest; and that " it is an inherent qualification of all sovereignty that no proceedings for the execution of a judgment may be instituted or carried out against it.[25]

In 1907, at the Second Hague Peace Conference, a considerable number of States signed the so-called Porter Convention, *i.e.* the Convention respecting the Limitation of the Employment of Force for the Recovery of Contract Debts," which declares:

" The Contracting Powers agree not to have recourse to armed force for the recovery of contract debts claimed from the Government of one country by the Government of another country as being due to its nationals. This undertaking is, however, not applicable when the debtor State

[25] Senor Drago in the note referred to above, p. 255 n. But this argument is based upon an erroneous and partly obsolete view of the nature of sovereignty. For the text of the Drago Note, see Supp. to 1 *A. J.* (1907), 1–6.

The views of British and American statesmen are not in complete harmony upon this subject, although the general policy of Great Britain and the United States had been substantially the same, except for the British interventions in Mexico, Egypt, and Venezuela, and those of the United States in San Domingo and Central America.

The English view, as stated by Lord Palmerston in 1848 and reaffirmed by Lord Salisbury in 1882 and by Premier Balfour in 1902, is that financial intervention, though legally permissible, is inexpedient. It is a question of policy rather than of law. For the text of Lord Palmerston's circular, see Hall (8th ed.), 334–35 n.; and 2 Phillimore, Pt. V, ch. 3.

In usually refraining from diplomatic as well as forcible intervention to secure the payment of public and contract debts, the United States appears to have been influenced by respect for what it believes to be a principle of the Law of Nations as well as by policy or expediency. For the views of American statesmen, see 6 Moore, *Digest*, §§ 916, 995–97. Cf. 2 Wharton, *Digest*, §§ 231–32.

In his Message of Dec. 4, 1906, President Roosevelt admitted that "the non-payment of public debts may be accompanied by such circumstances of fraud and wrongdoing or violation of treaties as to justify the use of force." See Hershey, "The Calvo and Drago Doctrines," in 1 *A. J.* (1908), p. 40. See pp. 43–44 of this article for data showing how excessive in amount many claims (particularly Civil War Claims) have been.

refuses or neglects to reply to an offer of arbitration, or, after accepting the offer, renders a *compromis* impossible, or, after the arbitration, fails to submit to the award." [26]

In view of the fact that the Porter Convention was ratified by only a limited number of States, it can hardly be maintained that it forms a part of the conventional Law of Nations. Indeed, it must be admitted that International Law speaks with a very uncertain voice on the subject of the right of a State to resort either to diplomatic interposition or forcible methods for the collection of contract claims except in the case of a clear denial of justice or where the conduct of a government has been otherwise tortious.[27] There will probably be little dissent from the

[26] H. C. (1907), Art. I. See Higgins, *Hague Peace Conferences* (1909), 180.

By referring to the Table of Signatures appended to the Hague Conventions of 1907 (see Higgins, *op. cit.*, 530–31, or 2 Scott, 529), it may be noted that thirty-four States had signed this Convention by June 30, 1908—the final date set for signatures of their plenipotentiaries. Among the ten who did not sign were Brazil, China, and Venezuela. Many of the Contracting Powers signed under such reservations (see Higgins, *op. cit.*, 191–93, 534–36, and 2 Scott, 533–35) as somewhat to weaken its force.

By referring to the Table of Ratifications in 5 *A. J.* (1911), 769–70, it will be seen that only fourteen States had ratified this Convention by 1911, but these included most of the leading Powers.

It may be noted that the so-called Porter Convention is at once broader and narrower than the famous Drago Doctrine—broader in that it includes public loans as well as ordinary contract debts, and narrower in that it does not absolutely forbid the use of force in the collection of public debts. It is narrower than the Calvo Doctrine, which forbids even diplomatic intervention as a means of collecting all pecuniary debts, except as a final resort. It should be observed that the Convention does not authorize or sanction the use of force in any case.

On the *Porter Convention*, see especially: Borchard, §§ 122–23; * Higgins, *The Hague Peace Conferences* (1909), 180–97; Lémonon, *La seconde conférence* (1908), 97–120; * Moulin, *La doctrine de Drago* (1908), 213 ff.; Scott, G. W., in 2 *A. J.* (1908), 78–94; and * 1 Scott, J. B., *The Hague Peace Conferences* (1909), ch. 8. Cf. references on the *Calvo and Drago Doctrines, supra*, p. 255 n.

[27] As, for example, "when the contracting State, contrary to the terms of its agreement, forfeits a concession without judicial procedure, or when it arbitrarily, and without regard for the decisions of its own courts grants away to others rights lawfully vested by contract in the concessionaire, thereby impairing or destroying the value of the concession." 1 Hyde, § 304.

The United States Government has resorted to diplomatic interposition in exceptional instances, as where diplomacy furnished the only means of redress, or in cases of the non-performance of a government contract, the arbitrary confiscation of property rights, or the annulment of charters or concessions. For examples, see Borchard, § 114; 6 Moore, *Digest*, §§ 918, 996–97; and 2 Wharton, *Digest*, § 232.

view that, in general, pecuniary claims, whether based on torts or contracts, should be submitted to arbitration or judicial decision.

BIBLIOGRAPHY

Responsibility of States.—* Anzilotti, in 13 *R. D. I. P.* (1906), 5–29 and 285–309; Arias, in 7 *A. J.* (1913), 724–65; * Bar, in 31 *R. D. I.* (1899), 464 ff.; Baty, *Int. Law in So. Africa* (1900), chs. 4–5 (for examples of claims by Great Biitain); Bluntschli, Arts. 375–93; * Borchard, Pt. I, chs. 4–8, and Pt. IV, chs. 4–5, and in 34 *Yale Law J.* (1924), 1 ff.; Brewer and Butler, in 22 *Cyc. of Law and Procedure* (1906), 1734 ff. (Art. on Int. Law); Brusa, in 17 *Annuaire de l'Institut* (1898), 96 ff.; * 3 and 6 Calvo, §§ 1263–98, and 256 respectively; Clunet, *Offenses et actes hostiles commis par particuliers contre un état entranger* (1887); 11 *Corpus Juris*, 816–25; Devlin, *Treaty Power* (1908), ch. 15; * 1 Fauchille, ch. 7, Nos. 398 [1–18]; Fenwick, 156–60, 386–96; 1 Fiore, Nos. 659–79, and *Int. Law Codified* (1918), Arts. 596–615; Funck-Brentano et Sorel, ch. 12; Goebel, in 8 *A. J.* (1914), 802–52; Hall, §§ 11, 65; Heffter, §§ 101–04; * Hershey, in 1 *A. J.* (1907), 26–45; Holtzendorff, in 2 *Handbuch*, 70–74; Huffcut, in 2 *Annals* (1891–92), 69 ff.; * 1 Hyde, §§ 270–309, and 8 *Ill. Law Rev.* (1914), No. 6; Liszt, § 35; * Moulin, *La doctrine Drago* (1908); * 6 Moore, *Digest*, ch. 21 (for claims by the United States); * 1 Oppenheim, §§ 148–67; 1 Piédelièvre, 317–22; * 1 and 3 P.-Fodéré, Nos. 196–210, 402 ff., 1363 ff.; Ralston, *Int. Arbitral Law* (1910), *passim*, 204 ff., 274 ff.; * *Report* by Committee of Experts on " Responsibility of States for Damages Done to the Property of Foreigners," in Supp. to 20 *A. J.* (1926), 116–203; * 1 and 2 Rivier, 271–73 and 40–44, respectively; Ex-

"International commissions have frequently allowed claims based on the infraction of rights derived from contracts where the denial of justice was properly established." 6 Moore, *Digest*, p. 718.

Borchard (§ 110) properly distinguishes between "three important classes of contract claims: first, those arising out of contracts concluded between individuals who are citizens of different countries; second, those arising out of contracts between the citizen and a foreign government; and third claims arising out of the unpaid bonds of a government held by the citizens of another." He rightly points out that the distinction between the second and third classes is particularly important, "inasmuch as there is far less reason for governmental intervention to secure the payment of defaulted bonds of a foreign government than there is in the case of breaches of concession and similar contracts." In the first class of cases, contracts between individuals, there would seem to be no occasion for interposition at all unless the local courts denied or unduly delayed justice.

On *Claims based on Contracts*, see especially: * Borchard, Pt. I, ch. 7, §§ 109–26; 1 Hyde, §§ 303–09; * 6 Moore, *Digest*, §§ 916–19, 995–97; 1 Westlake, 331–34; 2 Wharton, *Digest*, §§ 231–32.

For numerous references, especially to the foreign literature on this subject, see Borchard, *op. cit.*, notes to ch. 7.

Sec'y Root, in 4 *A. J.* (1910), 517–28; * Rougier, *Les guerres civiles* (1903), 448–78; Schoen, *Die völkerr. Haftung der Staaten* (1907); * Strupp, *Das völkerr. Delikt* (1920), in Stier-Somlo's *Handbuch*, III, 1a, and in 31 *I. L. A.* (1923, Vol. I), 127 ff.; Tchernoff, *Le droit de protection*, especially liv. III, ch. 4; Thorpe, *Int. Claims* (1924); * Triepel, *Völkerrecht u. Landesrecht* (1899), 324–81, or *Droit int. et droit interne* (1920), 321–78; Ullmann, § 39; Vattel, liv. II, §§ 63–78; Visscher, in 2 *Bibliotheca Visseriana*, 89–119; Wiesse, *Le droit int. appliqué aux guerres civiles* (1898), § 14, pp. 43–55; * 1 Westlake, ch. 14; Wheaton, § 32; 2 Wharton, *Digest*, ch. 9, §§ 223 ff.

For copious references to the sources and authorities, see Borchard, *op. cit., passim.*

PART II

THE OBJECTS OF INTERNATIONAL LAW

158. **Introductory.**—The objects of the Law of Nations are: (1) material goods or things; and (2) individuals or persons (including corporations).

The main *things* to which the rules of International Law apply are land territory, territorial waters, the open sea, aerial space, public vessels (mainly warships), private vessels (mainly merchantmen), and other public and private property of various sorts.

In the following chapters we shall first consider the various forms of a State's territory, and the modes of acquisition. This will be followed by chapters on aerial space and the open sea (including the non-territorial or property rights of States, more especially the jurisdiction over warships and merchant vessels in times of peace). Finally, we shall consider the rights and duties of individuals as objects of International Law during peace.

CHAPTER XII

A STATE'S TERRITORY, BOUNDARIES, AND STATE SERVITUDES

159. **The Nature of Territorial Sovereignty.**—A State's territory is that definite portion of the earth's surface which is subject to its sovereignty or *imperium*. According to the old maxim, *Quidquid est in territorio, est etiam de territorio.*[1] This territorial supremacy should be distinguished from the non-territorial or property rights which a State enjoys over its public and private domain.[2] Nor should it be confused with the right of eminent domain by virtue of which a State may expropriate private property for public purposes, though it should be noted that this right of eminent domain[3] is essentially an exercise of territorial sovereignty, and may be exercised for international as well as national purposes. It cannot, however, be said that an international right of eminent domain has as yet been developed.

The jurisdiction of a State extends, with certain exceptions to be noted hereafter,[4] over all persons and things found on its territory, and may also be employed for international as well as national purposes. Territorial sovereignty is of the nature of *imperium* rather than *dominium*,[5] *i.e.* it is an imperial rather than a property right. With certain exceptions,[6] this *imperium* or territorial supremacy is exclusive in character, and cannot be exercised by more than one sovereign State over a given territory.

[1] Or in respect to persons, *qui in territorio meo est, etiam meus subditus est.*

[2] See *supra*, Nos. 129–30.

[3] On the right of *Eminent Domain*, see especially: Beach, *Public Corporations in the United States* (1893), §§ 653–688; Cooley, *Constitutional Limitations* (7th ed., 1903), 752; 20 *Corpus Juris*, 501–1237; * Elliot, *Municipal Corporations* (1910, 2d ed.), ch. 10, §§ 83–98; Lewis, *The Law of Eminent Domain* (3d ed., 1909).

[4] See *infra*, Nos. 209, 211, 270 ff., 289–91.

[5] The saying of the great French jurist Portalis is frequently cited in this connection: "Property belongs to the citizen, empire to the sovereign."

Some publicists still speak of territorial sovereignty as a property right. This is doubtless a mediæval survival of the terminology introduced into public law by the feudal confusion of rights based upon the exercise of sovereignty and those derived from the ownership of land.

[6] See I Oppenheim, § 171, for these exceptions.

160. **Extent of a State's Territory.**—The territory of a State consists of land, water, and air. It may be thus classified: (1) The Land Domain. (2) The Maritime and Fluvial Domain or Territorial Waters, using the latter phrase in a general sense. (3) Aerial Space.

161. **The Land Domain.**—The Land Domain consists of all the land (including colonies and dependencies) [7] to which the State has a valid title. Especially important are such means of communication as the public highways, telegraph lines, etc., which are subject to public control.

The Land Domain of a State also includes all islands formed within its territorial waters,[8] and the territorial subsoil beneath its land and water surface. This jurisdiction over the subsoil, which extends to an indefinite depth, arises from the necessity—a need increasingly felt—of conserving for future generations the rich treasures found beneath the earth's surface. In certain cases, international regulation may be deemed desirable.[9]

162. **Boundaries or Frontiers of a State.**—The frontiers or boundaries of a State are usually classed as natural or physical, and artificial or conventional. To avoid international conflicts and controversies, it is very important that they be accurately drawn and definitely ascertained.

163. **Natural Boundaries.**—Natural boundaries [10] have been formed, for the most part, by mountains, forests,

---

[7] It does not, strictly speaking, include a Vassal State under Suzerainty or a Protectorate. But inasmuch as the Suzerain or Protector frequently exercises jurisdiction within the Vassal or Protected State, no general rule can be laid down in respect to such territory. It certainly does not include the Back Country (*Hinterland*), spheres of interest, and the like. It probably includes leased territory.

[8] In the case of the *Anna* (1805), 5 C. Rob. 373, Sir Wm. Scott held that a chain of uninhabited mud islands situated at a distance of a mile and a half from the western shore of the principal entrance of the Mississippi River formed natural appendages to the coast, and that the extent of territory or marine league should be measured from these islands. For the case of the *Anna* in abridged form, see Evans, *Cases*, 148; 1 Moore, *Digest*, § 82, pp. 269–70; and Scott, *Cases*, 195. For comments, see Lawrence, § 72, p. 143; 1 Oppenheim, § 234, and 1 Westlake, 120.

[9] On the importance of the subsoil and the different systems of mine exploitation, see 1 Nys, 411–12.

[10] Natural boundaries have played a very important rôle in the history of international relations (witness, *e.g.* the repeated attempts of the French to establish the Rhine, Rhone, and the Pyrenees as the natural boundaries of

deserts, valleys, steppes or plateaus, marshes, the open sea, rivers, and other territorial waters. They rest upon prescription or immemorial custom, or are more definitely defined by conventions.

164. **Artificial Boundaries.**—Artificial boundaries are necessarily fixed by treaties and usually follow imaginary astronomical or mathematical lines based on latitude or longitude. They are often marked by various signs or landmarks, such as stones, posts, walls, trenches, roads, canals, buoys, etc.

165. **Rules for Fixing Natural Boundaries.**—In the absence of treaties, the following rules regulating natural boundaries are laid down by the customary Law of Nations:

(1) In case of a navigable river, the boundary line follows the middle of the so-called *thalweg* (down way or valley way),[11] *i.e.* the strongest current of the midchannel or navigable portion of the stream.[12] If the river be not navigable, the line runs down the middle of the stream.[13]

France); but, owing to ever increasing facilities for interstate communication by artificial means, the subject is one of decreasing importance. A consideration of the value of natural frontiers would be beyond the scope of a work on International Law, which merely prescribes the rules to be followed in the absence of boundary treaties or conventions. For references on *Boundaries*, see Bibliography at the end of this chapter.

[11] For the etymological meaning of this word, see 1 Westlake, 144 n.

[12] As the result of convention or prescription, it sometimes happens that the whole bed of the stream belongs to one of the co-riparian States. This is the case with the Ohio River, no part of which was included in the cession of Virginia to the United States (in 1781) of "the territory northwest of the river Ohio." In *Handly's Lessee* v. *Anthony* (1820), 5 Wheaton 374, and Scott, *Cases*, 200, it was held that the State of Kentucky extended to low-water mark on the western and northwestern side of the Ohio, and that an island or peninsula (whether island or peninsula depending on the height of the river) formed by the Ohio and a channel or bayou on the north side of the river belongs to the State of Indiana. See also *Indiana* v. *Kentucky* (1889), 136 U. S. 479.

In *Buttenuth* v. *St. Louis Bridge Co.* (1888), 123 Illinois 535, and *Iowa* v. *Illinois* (1893), 147 U. S. 1, the phrase "middle of the Mississippi River" was construed as meaning the "middle of the main channel" or "thread of the stream."

The former of the cases cited above may be found in Scott, *Cases*, 206. For a long citation from *Iowa* v. *Illinois*, see 1 Moore, *Digest*, § 128, pp. 618–19. See Evans, *Cases*, 140 and 143 for the cases of *Louisiana* v. *Mississippi* (1906), 202 U. S. 1; and *Arkansas* v. *Tennessee* (1918), 246 U. S. 158.

[13] This is the earlier rule, but it has the disadvantage of being a shifting line. Yet the modern rule of the *thalweg* is not without similar inconveniences.

(2) " Where a boundary follows mountains or hills, the water divide constitutes the frontier." [14] This is readily determined where there is a range or ridge of mountains with a sharply defined crest. But where the mountain barriers consist of " a tumbled mass of peaks and gorges," [15] the problem becomes very difficult. [16]

(3) When States are separated by lakes or landlocked seas, the boundary line follows the middle of such seas or lakes. But these are sometimes divided between the bordering States by convention. [17]

(4) " In a narrow strait separating the lands of two different States, the boundary line runs either through the middle or through the midchannel, unless special treaties make different arrangements." [18]

Though it is held in the United States that questions of boundary between independent nations are political in their nature, [19] boundary disputes are eminently proper subjects

It also is subject to change, though to a lesser degree. "The law, as stated by law writers and in the adjudged cases, seems to be well settled that where a river is declared to be the boundary between States, although it may change imperceptibly from natural causes, the river as it runs continues to be the boundary. But if the river should suddenly change its course or desert the original channel, the rule of law is, the boundary remains in the middle of the deserted river bed." This is the identical language of Justices Scott and Smith in *Buttenuth* v. *St. Louis Bridge Co.* (1888), 123 Illinois 535, and *Cooley* v. *Golden* (1893), 52 Missouri Appeals, 229. See Scott, *Cases*, 209 and 216.

See also *St. Louis* v. *Rutz* (1891), 138 U. S. 226; *Nebraska* v. *Iowa* (1892), 143 U. S. 359, 368; and the opinion of Cushing (1856), 8 Opp. Atty. Gen., 175–76. For a summary of *Nebraska* v. *Iowa* and citation of cases, see 1 Moore, *Digest*, § 82, pp. 271–73. For other cases, see *Ibid*, § 128.

[14] Hall, § 38, p. 147. Cited by Moore, *Digest*, I, § 127, who adds: "This rule, while simple enough in principle, is often exceedingly difficult of application." For examples, see his references to Moore, *Arbitrations* on p. 616 of the *Digest*.

[15] Curzon, *Frontiers* (1907), p. 19. In this very remarkable Romanes lecture, Lord Curzon calls attention to the "well-known geographical fact that in the greatest mountain systems of the world, for instance, the Himalayas and the Andes, the water divide is not identical with the highest crest."

[16] It is, of course, possible that a mountain range may belong wholly to one or the other of the coterminous States.

[17] For examples, see 1 Oppenheim, § 179. The use of the water is, however, common to the bordering States.

[18] 1 Oppenheim, § 199, p. 362. He cites 1 Twiss, §§ 183–84.

[19] See especially *Foster and Elam* v. *Neilson* (1829), 2 Peters 253 and Scott, *Cases*, 429; *U. S.* v. *Texas* (1891), 143 U. S. 621, and the cases therein cited.

But the United States courts do not hesitate to assume jurisdiction over

for judicial determination; and, in case of serious controversies, should always be referred to courts of Arbitration,
the Permanent Court of International Justice, or mixed
commissions for settlement.[20]

166. **State Servitudes.**—State servitudes are exceptional
and perpetual restrictions not involving a loss of sovereignty
in itself on the territorial or personal sovereignty of one
State in favor of another State or of other States.[21]   They
are based either on express convention or upon a tacit
agreement resulting from immemorial usage, and are in the
nature of real and permanent rights rather than of ordinary
rights and obligations.   Since they are in a sense limitations
upon sovereignty, they should be construed strictly.[22]   On

boundary disputes between States or between a Territory and a State of the
Union.   There is no sound reason why the Permanent Court of International
Justice should not be given obligatory jurisdiction for the decision of boundary
and other disputes of a judicial nature between members of the Society of
Nations.

[20] "The usual practice adopted by the Peace Conference in 1919 with
regard to boundaries was to specify them in words, so far as was practicable,
and leave the actual delimitation to Boundary Commissions, which were to
fix the frontier line on the spot in conformity with the provisions of the
treaties."   1 Oppenheim, § 198, pp. 360–61 *n*.

[21] Though State Servitudes have usually been restrictions on territorial
sovereignty, *i.e.* servitudes *in rem*, the author knows of no good reason why
the use of the term should be confined to this class of limitations on sovereignty,
as most publicists would have it.   There may be servitudes *in personam* as
well as servitudes *in rem*, as far as the Law of Nations is concerned; and
servitudes may be restrictions upon personal as well as territorial sovereignty.
The term is often misapplied, *e.g.* by Hall (p. 203 of 8th ed.) when he
includes "the right of innocent use of territorial seas" in his list of servitudes.
This is a general restriction on territorial sovereignty imposed upon all States
by International Law.   The characteristic mark of an International Servitude
is that it is an easement or limitation on the exercise of sovereignty in favor
of some particular State or States.   But such restrictions are not sufficiently
important to involve any actual loss of sovereignty, as they do, *e.g.* in the
case of a Protectorate.
The prevalent conception and theory of International Servitudes is denied
by the following publicists: Bulmerincq, in 1 Marquardsen, *Handbuch*, § 49;
Gareis, *Institutionen des Völkerrechts* (1887), § 71; Jellinek, *Das Recht des
Modernen Staates* (1905), 391–93; Liszt, § 14, pp. 131–34; and 2 Nys, 271–79,
who uses the chapter-heading "Pretended International Servitudes."
In the case of the *North Atlantic Fisheries* (1910), the Hague Tribunal
denied that fishery rights granted by Great Britain to the United States
constituted an International Servitude.   For a convincing refutation of the
grounds upon which this denial was based, see 1 Oppenheim, § 203.   See
Ibid., p. 365 *n*. for references.

[22] For citation of the authorities on this point, see 9 *North Atlantic Fisheries
Arbitration* (1910), 306 ff.

the other hand, they are as a rule not extinguished by war or conquest and usually continue to be obligatory upon the succeeding or annexing State.[23] But they may be extinguished by common agreement, by express or tacit renunciation on the part of the State or States for whose benefit they were created, and possibly, in extreme cases, by denunciation or revocation.

State servitudes have commonly been divided into two classes—positive and negative.

167. **Positive Servitudes.**—Positive servitudes are those which grant to a State the right to perform certain acts on the territory of another State, such as fishery rights in territorial waters, the construction and operation of a railway, the collection of customs dues, the passage of an army or the garrisoning of a fortress, and the exercise of certain judicial, military, and police functions on foreign territory. Examples of positive servitudes are: the Russian and Japanese railways in Manchuria, the collection of customs dues by the United States in San Domingo, the exercise of consular rights of jurisdiction in the Orient, and the former French fishery rights on the coasts of Newfoundland.

168. **Negative Servitudes.**—Negative servitudes are those which obligate a State to abstain from exercising its territorial or personal sovereignty in certain ways, such as a convention not to exercise certain judicial, military, or police functions on its own territory; an agreement not to fortify certain places; an obligation not to permit certain classes of foreigners to reside on national territory or to abstain from acts of jurisdiction over nationals of another State; and the conditions sometimes imposed by treaties of peace requiring a limitation of naval or land armaments, etc. Examples of negative servitudes are: the agreement of Russia and Japan (see Art. 9 of Treaty of Portsmouth in 1905) " not to construct in their respective possessions on the island of Sakhalin or the adjacent islands any fortifications or other similar military works; " the promise of

---

[23] There is a difference of opinion as to whether the clause *rebus sic stantibus* (vital change of circumstances), supposed to be implied in every treaty, is applicable to state servitudes.

France to England made several times in the eighteenth century not to fortify Dunkirk (these clauses were abrogated in 1783); and the obligation imposed by the Powers upon Russia at the Congress of Paris in 1856 to demolish all fortresses upon the Black Sea and not to maintain a fleet of warships in these waters,—an intolerable servitude which Russia did not hesitate to declare no longer binding upon the outbreak of the Franco-German War in 1870.[24]

BIBLIOGRAPHY

Nature of Territorial Sovereignty.—Bluntschli, Arts. 276–77; Bonfils, Nos. 483–89: 1 Calvo, §§ 260 ff.; Despagnet, Nos. 385–86: 1 (2 Pt) Fauchille, Nos. 484–85; 1 and 2 Fiore, Nos. 522 ff., 798; Fricker, *Von Staatsgebiet* (1867); 1 Halleck (3d ed.), 150 ff.; * Heilborn, *System des Völkerrechts* (1896), 5–36; Heimburger, *Der Ewerb der Gebietshoheit* (1888); Henrich, in 13 *Z. V.* (1924), 28 ff.; Holtzendorff, in 2 *Handbuch*, 225–28; * Jellinek, *Das Recht des modernen Staates* (2d ed., 1905), 381–93; 1 F. de Martens, § 87; 2 Mérignhac, 352 ff.; 2 Moore, *Digest*, § 175; 1 Nys, 402–12; * 1 Oppenheim, §§ 168–75; 2 P.-Fodéré, Nos. 595–612; 1 Phillimore, §§ 150–54; * 1 Rivier, 135–42; 1 Twiss, §§ 140–44; Ullmann, § 86; Vattel, liv. I, § 205

[24] The Treaties of Peace with Germany, Austria, etc. at the close of the World War imposed numerous servitudes upon these former belligerents. Thus, not only were they limited as to the size, etc. of their aerial, naval and military forces, but Germany and Austria were obliged to grant freedom of transit through their territories, either by rail, navigable waterway, or canal, to persons, goods, vessels, carriages and mails coming from or going to the territory of any of the Allied and Associated Powers (see *e.g.* Arts. 321–26 of the Treaty of Versailles). Czecho-Slovakia was given the right to lease for 99 years areas in the ports of Hamburg and Stettin, as also the right to run its trains over certain sections of the Austrian railways (Art. 363 of the Treaty of Versailles and Art. 322 of the Treaty of St. Germain).

Very interesting and important are the obligations for the protection of the racial, linguistic, and religious minorities imposed upon Poland and a number of other States by the Minority Treaties. See *supra*, note 43, p. 142.

Unless the view of the majority of the authorities prevails to the effect that servitudes must needs be territorial, there would seem to be no good reason for rejecting the author's view that the rights and obligations created by the Minorities Treaties are in the nature of personal servitudes. The only objection that occurs to the writer is that it might be urged that they are not specifically in favor of particular States, but rather in the interest of the international community as a whole. However, it may be replied that they were exacted by particular States and presumably in the several as well as the collective interest. Unlike the rights of innocent passage, they are not, strictly speaking, international in character, and they constitute particular obligations resting upon the servient State.

and liv. II, §§ 79–83; * Walker, *Science of Int. Law* (1893), 41–43, 56, 69, 90–91; * 1 Westlake, 86–90, and *Collected Papers* (1914), ch. 9, pp. 131 ff.; Wheaton, §§ 161–63; Woolsey, § 56.

Frontiers and Boundaries.—Bluntschli, Arts. 296–303; Bonfils and * 1 (2 Pt.) Fauchille, Nos. 486–89; 1 Calvo, §§ 342, 353; * 1 Cobbett, 99 ff.; Creasy, *First Platform of Int. Law* (1876), Nos. 230–31; Curzon, *Frontiers* (Romanes Lecture for 1907); Despagnet, No. 387; Evans, *Cases*, 140–48; Fawcett, *Frontiers* (1918); Fenwick, ch. 15; Field, *Outlines of an Int. Code* (1876), Arts. 28–36; 2 Fiore, Nos. 799–806, and *Int. Law Codified* (1918), Arts. 1045–54; Funck-Brentano et Sorel, 17–20; Grotius, lib. II, c. 3, § 18; Hall, § 38; 1 Halleck (3d ed.), 171 ff.; * Hart, "Boundaries of the U. S.," in 1 *Cyc. Am. Gov.*, 150 ff.; Heffter, § 66; Holdich, *Political Frontiers* (1916) and *Boundaries in Europe* (1918), *passim;* Holtzendorff, in 2 *Handbuch*, 232–39; * 1 Hyde, §§ 135–40; Kluber, § 133; Liszt, § 9; 1 F. de Martens, § 88; * 1 Moore, *Digest*, §§ 126–28, 154–62; * 1 Nys, 412–22; * 1 Oppenheim, §§ 198–202; 2 P.-Fodéré, Nos. 759–77; * 1 Rivier, 165–71; * Scott, *Cases*, 200 ff.; Taylor, § 251; 1 Twiss, §§ 147–48, 153; Ullmann, § 91; Vattel, liv. I, §§ 266 ff.; 1 Westlake, 144–45; Wheaton, §§ 192, 194–96, 202.

State Servitudes.—Basdevant, in 19 *R. D. I. P.* (1912), 512 ff.; Baty, *Int. Law in South Africa* (1900), 48–49, 74 ff.; Bluntschli, Arts. 353–59; Bulmerincq, in 1 Marquardsen's *Handbuch*, § 49; * Clauss, *Die Lehre von den Staatsdienstbarkeiten* (1894); 3 Calvo, § 1583; Creasy, *First Platform of Int. Law* (1876), Nos. 257–61; Despagnet, Nos. 190–92; Fabre, *Des servitudes* (1901); 1 Fauchille, Nos. 339–43; Fenwick, ch. 16, pp. 261–63 and 279–85; 2 Fiore, Nos. 829–30, and *Int. Law Cod.* (1918), Arts. 1100–02; Gareis, *Institutionen des Völkerrechts* (1887), § 71; * Hague Tribunal (1910) in *North Atlantic Coast Fisheries Arbitration* (Washington, 1912–13), particularly vols. 8 and 9, pp. 17 ff. and 570 ff. (for English translations of the authorities), and 4 and 5 *A. J.* (1910 and 1911) 957–59 (for the decision, and 11–14 for commentary by Lansing); Hall, § 42, pp. 203–05; Heffter, § 43; * Holland, *Jurisprudence*, 214–21; Hollatz, *Begriff und Wessen der Staats-Servituden* (1908); Holtzendorff, in 2 *Handbuch*, 246–52; 1 Hyde, §§ 152–53; Klüber, §§ 137–39; Labrousse, *Des servitudes* (1912); Liszt, § 14, pp. 131–34 of 12th ed.; * 1 F. de Martens, §§ 93–95; McNair, in *Brit. Yr. Bk.* (1925), 111–27; 2 Mérignhac, 366–68; 1 and 2 Moore, *Digest*, §§ 163–68, 177; * 2 Nys, 271–79, and in 37 *R. D. I.* (1905), 118 ff.; * 1 Oppenheim, §§ 203–08; 1 Phillimore, §§ 280–83; 1 Piédelièvre, Nos. 448–52; Potter, in 9 *A. J.* (1915), 627–41; * 2 P.-Fodéré, Nos. 834–45, 1038; * 1 Rivier, 73, 258, 296–303; Stall-Holstein, in 49 (3d ser.) *R. D. I.* (1922), 424 ff.; Taylor, § 252; 1 Twiss, § 245; * Ullmann, §§ 99 ff.; 1 Westlake, 61; Wilson and Tucker, §§ 55, 68; Wilson, § 52. For further references, see 8 *North Atlantic Coast Fisheries Arbitration* (Washington, 1912), 19, 22, 29 ff.

CHAPTER XIII

MODES OF THE ACQUISITION AND LOSS OF TERRITORY

169. There are five modes by which a State may acquire a legal title to territory.

Accretion.—(I) By *Accretion*, which is, comparatively speaking, of slight importance. It consists in the increase or enlargement of the land territory of a State mainly [1] through the action of its rivers or the ocean. These formations are usually caused by gradual alluvial deposits at the mouths of rivers (deltas) and on the seacoast. New islands formed in rivers, lakes, or within the maritime belt belong to the neighboring State or States. In the latter case, the marine league is measured from the shores of such islands.[2]

170. **Prescription.**—(II) By *Prescription*, which has been well defined as " the acquisition of sovereignty over a territory through continuous and undisturbed exercise of sovereignty over it during such a period as is necessary to create under the influence of historical development the general conviction that the present condition of things is in conformity with international order." [3]

It has been denied [4] that *usucapion* or acquisitive prescription can furnish a good title to territory, but the majority of publicists admit that long-continuous and

[1] Such formations may also be artificial, as in the case of embankments, dikes, etc., built along a river or on the seacoast. Holland has wrested considerable portions of her territory from the ocean.

The rules governing accretion are derived from Roman Law. See Justinian, 2 *Institutes*, I, 20–24; 42 *Digest*, I, 7, 29, 65; and Grotius, II, c. 8, §§ 8–16.

[2] See *supra*, No. 161, 8 n., for the decision of Lord Stowell in the case of *The Anna* (1805), 5 C. Rob. 373, and Scott, *Cases*, 195. For the rules relating to river boundaries, see *supra*, No. 165.

[3] 1 Oppenheim, § 242, p. 401.

[4] By Heffter, § 12; Klüber, § 6; 2 Mérignhac, 415–18; * Pomeroy, §§ 107–14; 1 G. F. de Martens, §§ 70–71; 1 F. de Martens, § 89; and Ullmann, § 92, p. 308. Some of the authorities follow Grotius (11, c. 4, §§ 1, 7, 9) who rejects the *usucapion* or acquisitive prescription of the Roman law, *i.e.* when property is taken from the original owner, but accepts a title based upon immemorial possession; others wholly reject international prescription.

uninterrupted possession purges a title which may originally have been tainted with fraud or violence.   This latter view, which is in accord with international practice,[5] is based upon the need of international order and stability.   There is, however, no definite time limit in International Law which acts as a bar to claims against the possessor.

171. **Conquest or Subjugation.**—(III) By *Conquest* or *Subjugation*.[6]   A completed conquest is the incorporation of foreign territory, *i.e.* its complete and permanent subjection to the territorial jurisdiction of the conquering or occupying State, after its subjugation by armed forces.   This incorporation must be shown by some act showing intention (such as a decree of annexation) and ability to maintain permanent possession.

Several leading authorities [7] refuse to recognize conquest as a legal mode of acquiring territory, but this view is in

---

[5] Considerable portions of the territory of modern Europe (*e.g.* Poland) may be said to be held by a title originally based on prescription and conquest, and later recognized by treaties, etc.

The treaty of Washington (1897) for the settlement of the boundary dispute between Great Britain and Venezuela laid down the following rule (among others) for the conduct of the arbitrators: "Adverse holding or prescription during a period of fifty years shall make a good title.   The arbitrators may deem exclusive political control of a district, as well as actual settlement thereof, sufficient to constitute adverse holding or to make title by prescription."   1 Moore, *Digest*, § 88, p. 297.

For other instances of international practice, see Ralston, in 4 *A. J.* (1910), 133–44, and *Int. Arbitral Law* (1926), ch. 12.   For references on *Prescription*, see especially Audinet, in 3 *R. D. I. P.* (1896), 314; and 1 Oppenheim (3d ed.), p. 400.

[6] Oppenheim (I, § 236 and II, § 264) distinguishes between conquest and subjugation.   This is correct from his point of view, for he uses the term "conquest" in the sense of effective military occupation.   While this undoubtedly corresponds with the usual or popular use of the term, it does not represent the technical meaning of the words as employed by most of the authorities on the Law of Nations.   The substitution of "subjugation" for "conquest" as a source of title to territory would scarcely remove all danger of misunderstanding, for it would also be necessary to distinguish between its popular and technical meaning.

On *Military or Belligerent Occupation*, which should be clearly distinguished from conquest, see *infra*, ch. 28.

[7] Bonfils, No. 535; Despagnet, Nos. 396–98; 2 and 3 Fiore, Nos. 863 and 1693, and *Int. Law Cod.* (1918), Arts. 1083–86.   Audinet (3 *R. D. I. P.*, 1896, 320) appears to think that titles usually cited as based upon conquest are really based upon prescription; but this view, while applicable in some cases, is clearly untenable in other instances.   On conquest as a mode of acquiring territory, see particularly 1 (2 Pt.) Fauchille, Nos. 557[10–12], pp. 763–70 and the references there given.

contradiction with the facts of historical development and international practice. Whatever may be said as to the desirability of abolishing the so-called right of conquest, and however desirable that the validity of titles based upon fraud and violence be denied,[8] we cannot substitute our wishes for realities or create rules of International Law by ignoring the practice of nations.[9]

Titles based upon conquest should be clearly distinguished from those derived from prescription on the one hand, and cession on the other. Most titles popularly supposed to be based upon conquest are, technically speaking, based upon cession.[10]

172. **Distinction between Conquest, Cession, and Prescription.**—" Title by conquest differs from title by cession

[8] The author is among those who ardently desire that some future International Conference may abolish this so-called right of conquest, or at least declare titles based upon future conquests invalid. He is of the opinion that this would be an important step in the direction of international peace.

Respecting this so-called right of conquest, it would seem that modern International Law neither denies nor affirms, but it unquestionably recognizes the validity of titles based upon conquest.

[9] "Conquest gives a title which the courts of the conqueror cannot deny, whatever the private and speculative opinions of individuals may be respecting the original justice of the claim which has been succesfully asserted." Chief Justice Marshall, in *Johnson* v. *McIntosh* (1823), 8 Wheat. 543, 588.

It should, however, be noted that while Article 10 of the Covenant of the League of Nations does not formally abolish title to territory based on future conquest, its observance would make aggression and conquest practically impossible. It should also be mentioned that the Pan-American Congress held at Washington in 1890 passed a resolution that "conquest shall never hereafter be recognized as admissible under American public law." 1 Moore, *Digest*, § 87, p. 292.

[10] Thus, our title to the Philippine Islands is technically based upon cession. It would be based upon conquest if they had been formally annexed without express cession by Spain, and if we had continued to hold and govern them after the substantial cessation of hostilities. It would be based upon prescription if we had simply continued to hold and govern them for an indefinite length of time without notification or an act of formal annexation. Of course, these suppositions ignore constitutional obstacles.

Modern instances of conquest have been those of Hanover, etc., by Prussia in 1866, and the Orange Free State and South African Republic by Great Britain in 1900–1901.

Napoleon the Great's conquests were generally recognized, having, indeed, usually been secured by cessions. There were, however, several cases in which the legality of his acts was disputed. The most famous of these was the *Case of the Elector of Hesse Cassel*. For the main facts bearing on this case, see Hall, § 204; 2 Halleck (3d ed.), 496–99; 3 Phillimore, §§ 568–74; Snow, *Cases on Int. Law* (1893), 381–83.

in that the transfer of the territory is not effected by treaty, and from title by prescription in that there is a definite act or series of acts out of which the title arises. These acts are successful military operations; but if a province conquered in a war is afterwards made over to the victorious power by treaty, it is acquired by cession. Title by conquest arises only when no formal international document transfers the territory to its new possessor." [11]

173. **Effects of Conquest.**—The main effects of conquest, like those of cession, on the native inhabitants of the conquered or ceded territory have been considered in the chapter on " The Succession of States." The most important general principle governing this subject is that the conquering or annexing sovereign does not, by the mere fact of cession or conquest, acquire any special rights over the lives and private property of his new subjects. They fall, of course, under his personal and territorial jurisdiction; but in the absence of express legislation, their private and property rights remain unaffected.

174. **Cession.**—(IV) By *Cession*, which consists in the formal transfer by convention of territory from one State to another. The treaty of cession usually contains stipulations respecting the rights and duties of allegiance or nationality, the proportionate share of the public debt to be assumed by the annexing or ceding State, etc.; but no general rules can be laid down governing these matters.

From the standpoint of International Ethics, cessions might be classified as voluntary or forcible, *i.e.* as due to the voluntary action of the ceding State during a time of peace or as resulting from armed coercion at the close of a war. But such a division would be valueless from the point of view of International Law, inasmuch as there is a legal fiction that all cessions are voluntary, whether brought about by conquest or by more peaceable means.

175. **Classification of Cessions.**—From a legal standpoint, cessions may be said to be with or without consideration.

(1) They may be sold or exchanged. *Sales* of territory are less frequent than formerly, but they are familiar to the student of American History who will readily recall the

[11] Lawrence, § 77.

purchase of Louisiana, Florida, and Alaska. *Exchange* is also less frequent than formerly, though there are several instances in recent European History. By the Treaty of Berlin in 1878, Rumania ceded to Russia a portion of Bessarabia in exchange for the Dobrudja, and the island of Heligoland in the North Sea was ceded by England to Germany in exchange for territory adjoining East Africa in 1890.

(2) The great majority of modern cessions are in the form of *gifts*. Free or voluntary gifts of territory are, indeed, rare, and cessions of territory without consideration are usually found in treaties of peace, *i.e.* they are really forced gifts made under duress. Recent instances are the cession of the southern portion of the island of Sakhalin by Russia to Japan in 1905, and the cession of Porto Rica by Spain to the United States in 1898.[12]

176. The Plebiscite.—Several publicists [13] maintain that an affirmative popular vote is desirable or necessary on the part of the inhabitants of the ceded district in order to give validity to a cession of their territory. The theory of the plebiscite was first systematically applied to territorial cessions during the first few years of the French Revolution, and was especially advocated by Napoleon III by whom it was applied to the annexation of Nice and Savoy by France in 1860, and to the cession of Venice to Italy in 1866.[14]

[12] Cessions by marriage settlement and testament have practically ceased since the disappearance of the patrimonial conception of the State. That the latter form of cession is not wholly obsolete under an absolutistic régime is shown by the will of Leopold II, King of the Belgians, bequeathing the Congo Free State to Belgium. For the text of this "curious will," see 1 Oppenheim, § 216, p. 271 n.

[13] Among the relatively few advocates of the plebiscite in the case of cession are: Funck-Brentano et Sorel, 157 f. and 335 ff.; Rouard de Card, *Études de droit int.* (1890), 37–74; and Rotteck, Art. "Abtretung" in *Staatswoerterbuch* (begun in 1834 and cited by 1 Rivier, 210). This theory has hitherto found very little favor among authorities on International Law except in Italy and, to some extent, in France.

[14] The plebiscite was also applied on a large scale by Sardinia (1860 to 1870) in the creation of the modern kingdom of Italy, and by France to the island of St. Barthelemy which was ceded to France by Sweden in 1877. It should be especially noted that the plebiscite has never found favor in the practice of either Great Britain or the United States, though the principle of "consent of the governed" was proclaimed by the Declaration of Independence.

In his speech to the Senate on January 22, 1917, President Wilson declared that " no peace can last or ought to last, which does not recognize and accept the principle that governments derive all their just powers from the consent of the governed, and that no right anywhere exists to hand peoples about from sovereignty to sovereignty as if they were property." This same principle of self-determination, which had in the meantime become one of the cardinal principles of the Russian Revolution, was made the basis of several of the " fourteen points " and reiterated by Wilson in several speeches a year later as one of the necessary bases of the coming peace settlement. It was applied to a considerable extent in the Treaties of Paris (1919), where the use of the plebiscite was prescribed in a number of cases.[15]

The use of the plebiscite, while highly desirable in itself, is liable to certain abuses in practice, and can be said to have only a limited sanction, either in theory or in practice. In any case, it is certain that the legal validity of a title based on cession does not require such action on the part of the inhabitants of the ceded territory.

177. **The Option.**—It has, on the other hand, been customary to insert in treaties of cession a clause granting

[15] Thus, the inhabitants of Eupen and Malmédy were "entitled to record in writing" on registers opened by the Belgian authorities a desire to remain under German sovereignty, and the League of Nations was to decide whether these districts should be retained by Belgium after this vote had been taken (Art. 34 of the Treaty of Versailles).

The Saar Basin was placed under the temporary trusteeship of the League of Nations, and at the end of fifteen years "the inhabitants of the said territory shall be called upon to indicate the sovereignty under which they desire to be placed" (Art. 49). See Annex, Ch. III, Arts. 34–40 for details as to how the plebiscite is to be taken and executed.

The frontier between Germany and Denmark was to be "fixed in conformity with the wishes of the population." Arts. 109–11. The boundary between Poland and Germany in a portion of Upper Silesia was to be determined by a plebiscite, as also certain boundaries of East Prussia. Arts. 88, 94–97. For references on "The Upper Silesian Question," see *supra*, note 26 on p. 138.

"The net result of the several peace treaties, therefore, may be said to be a recognition by the Powers that were parties to them of the general principle that transfers of territory should be conditioned upon the wishes of the inhabitants of the territory wherever the circumstances make it possible to consult local opinion." Fenwick, 238. On the Plebiscites of the Treaties of Paris, see Temperley, *Hist. of the Peace Conference* (1920–24), index to vols. 1–6.

to the inhabitants of the ceded territory the *option* of retaining their old allegiance or citizenship by means of an express declaration to this effect. But it appears to be the law that, in the absence of an express stipulation to the contrary, the annexing State may, for the sake of safety, expel those of the inhabitants who choose to retain their old allegiance. Many treaties stipulate for the option to emigrate within a certain period. Some permit option without requiring emigration.[16]

178. **Disguised Cessions.**—There are several forms of cessions which have been aptly described as disguised, veiled, or indirect cessions.

[16] The Treaty of 1898 between the United States and Spain appears to have granted the right of option to the Spanish-born residents of the Phillipine Islands, but refused it to the native Filipinos. See Randolph, *The Law and Policy of Annexation* (1901), 60. On the cession of Alsace-Lorraine, see Cogordan, *La nationalité* (2d ed., 1890), 358 ff. For the law and practice of the United States, see 3 Moore, *Digest*, §§ 379–80.

"The nationality of the inhabitants of territory acquired by conquest or cession becomes that of the government under whose dominion they pass, subject to the right of election on their part to retain their former nationality by removal or otherwise, as may be provided." Chief Justice Fuller, in *Boyd* v. *Thayer* (1892), 143 U. S. 135. See 3 Moore, *Digest*, p. 311, for citation of additional cases.

The provisions in the Paris Peace Treaties of 1919 relating to this matter are fairly liberal. The Treaty of Versailles grants to German nationals over 18 years of age habitually resident in the territories transferred to Belgium, Czecho-Slovakia, and Poland the right to choose German nationality within two years, in which case they must, however, transfer their residence to Germany, though they may retain their immovable property in the ceded territory. Arts. 37, 85, 91. See Art. 106 for a similar provision regarding the German residents of Danzig. The rules regulating the status of the inhabitants of Alsace-Lorraine are more elaborate. See Arts. 53–54 and Annex. The provisions relating to nationality contained in the treaties for the protection of minorities (see *supra*, note on p. 142) also deserve study in this connection.

On the *Plebiscite and Option*, see especially: Bonfils and 1 Fauchille, 427–31, 567–71; Buell, *Int. Relations* (1925), ch. 2, pp. 37–50; Cabouat, *Droit int. des annexions* (1881), 192–218; * Cogordan, *La nationalité* (1890), ch. 7; Despagnet, Nos. 334–39, 400; * 1 Fauchille, Nos. 427–31, 561–78; * Fenwick, 234–40; Funck-Brentano et Sorel (2d ed., 1887), 157 f., 335 ff., 503 f.; Heatley, in 3 *J. C. L.* (1921), 258 ff.; 1 Hyde, §§ 108–09; Lieber, in 3 *R. D. I.*, 139 ff.; Liszt, § 17; 1 F. de Martens, § 90; * 3 Moore, *Digest*, §§ 379–80; 2 Nys, 16–26; * 1 Oppenheim, § 219; Randolph, *The Law and Policy of Annexation* (1901), 59 ff.; 1 and 2 Rivier, 204–12, 438–39; * Selosse, *Traité de l'annexion* (1880), 218–351; Ullmann, § 98; * Wambaugh, *Plebiscites* (1920); and 1 Westlake, 70–74.

Particular attention should be called to the admirable monograph on Plebiscites by Miss Wambaugh published by the Carnegie Endowment for Int. Peace in 1920.

(1) The various *leases* of territory for a term of years (usually 99 years) which have been quite frequent, particularly in China, within recent years. Examples are the lease of the ports of Kiao-chau to Germany, of Port Arthur and Talien-wan (Dalny) to Russia, Wei-hai-wei to Great Britain in 1898, and of the Panama Canal Zone to the United States in 1903.[17]

(2) Administrative occupation, *i.e.* the indefinite occupation of certain districts, islands, or provinces, as those of Cyprus and of Egypt by England in 1878 and 1882, and of Bosnia and Herzegovina by Austria in 1878. The latter provinces were formally annexed by Austria-Hungary in 1909, Cyprus by Great Britain in 1914, and Egypt is an " independent " State under British protection.[18]

179. Occupation.—(V) By *Occupation* which has been defined as " the act of appropriation by a State through which it intentionally acquires sovereignty over such territory as is at the time not under the sovereignty of another State." [19]

[17] On the lease of the Panama Canal Zone to the United States, see *supra*, note 40, p. 172.

It should be noted that the 25 year Russian lease of Port Arthur and Dalny was transferred to Japan in 1905 and later extended by China to 99 years. The lease of Kiao-chau was renounced by Germany in favor of Japan in 1919, who agreed to restore it to China on certain conditions a few years later (1922).

A lease would seem to be a disguised cession in which the exercise of the rights of sovereignty is practically taken over by the lessor, leaving nothing but the shell of a bare *de jure* sovereignty in the hands of the lessee.

On *Leases*, see: * Bau, *Foreign Relations of China* (1921), ch. 20; Buell, *Int. Relations* (1925), ch. 20, pp. 443–47; Despagnet (3d ed.), No. 394 *bis;* 1 (2 Pt.) Fauchille, No. 557[15]; Fenwick, 243–44; Lawrence, § 82; Lindley, *Acquisition and Gov't. of Backward Territory in Int. Law* (1926), ch. 25; 2 Nys, 104–08; Stowell and Munro, 203–08; * 1 Westlake, 135–36; and * Willoughby, *Foreign Rights and Interests in China* (1920), ch. 8, and *China at the Conference* (1922), ch. 14. For the texts of the Chinese leases, see Mac-Murray, *Treaties with China, 1894–1911* (1921).

[18] See *supra*, note 23 on p. 183. On *Disguised Cessions* generally, see Gérard, *Des cessions déguisés* (1904); De Pouvourville, in 6 *R. D. I. P.* (1899), 113 ff.; Perrinjaquet, in 16 *R. D. I. P.* (1909), 316 ff.; and 1 Westlake, 135–41.

[19] 1 Oppenheim, § 220, p. 383. Oppenheim thus distinguishes occupation from conquest and cession: "Occupation as a mode of acquisition differs from subjugation chiefly in so far as the conquered and afterwards annexed territory has hitherto belonged to another State. Again, occupation differs from cession in so far as through cession the acquiring State receives sovereignty over the respective territory from the former owner State."

180. **Conditions of Occupation.**—Under the modern law of occupation which is derived from the Roman law of *occupatio*, at least two conditions are essential for complete title to territory thus acquired.

(1) The occupied territory must be *res* or *territorium nullius*, *i.e.* at the time of occupation it must be either uninhabited or, if peopled by uncivilized tribes which are not politically organized under any government possessing the marks of sovereignty,[20] it must have remained unappropriated by any civilized State.

(2) Occupation must be real or effective. This includes: (a) The *animus domini* or expression of intention as shown by a formal act of annexation [21] or of notification to the other Powers. It must be a State act, *i.e.* made by properly authorized agents of the government, or subsequently ratified in case of settlement by unauthorized colonists. (b) Actual settlement or real and effective occupation. This involves at least the establishment of a responsible administration capable of maintaining a degree of order sufficient for the protection of existing rights.[22]

[20] Such territory may once have been occupied and abandoned, but as a rule it has never been occupied.

At the West African Conference of Berlin held in 1885, Mr. Kasson, the plenipotentiary of the United States, declared that his Government "would gladly adhere to a more extended rule, to be based on a principle which should aim at the voluntary consent of the natives whose country is taken possession of, in all cases where they had not provoked the aggression." But the Conference "hesitated to express an opinion" upon such "delicate questions."

It is generally admitted, at least by Anglo-American authorities, that so-called treaties of cession by uncivilized chiefs or tribes have, strictly speaking, no legal validity. These lack the necessary "capacity" to make valid contracts or treaties. In International Law, the possession of a government having the marks of sovereignty is the test of civilization. See especially, Westlake, *Collected Papers* (1914), 139–57; and Chief Justice Marshall, in *Johnson* v. *McIntosh* (1823), 8 Wheat. 543 and Scott, *Cases*, 175 or Evans, *Cases*, 281. Cf. *supra*, No. 90.

[21] "The formalities accompanying annexation are not prescribed by International Law. In modern times it is usual to hoist the national flag and read a proclamation setting forth the intention of the government to take the territory in question as its own; but any ceremony of clear import done on the spot in a public manner is sufficient." Lawrence, § 74, p. 149.

[22] Art. 35 of the General Act of the Berlin Conference (1884–1885) declares: "The signatory Powers of the present Act recognize the obligation to assure, in the territories occupied by them, upon the coasts of the African Continent, the existence of an authority sufficient to cause acquired rights to be respected, and as the case may be, the liberty of commerce and of transit

181. **Discovery as a Title.**—It will thus be seen that mere discovery,[23] or even annexation, does not confer a valid title to territory. At the most it constitutes an inchoate title [24] which in practice operates as a bar to occupation by another State within a reasonable time. For a State failing to respect the clearly expressed intention of another State to

in the conditions agreed upon." For an English translation of the text of the General Act, see Supp. to 3 *A. J.* (1909), 7 ff. For Arts. 34 and 35, see p. 24. For comment, see 1 Westlake, 106 ff.

Art. 34 declares: "Any Power which shall henceforth take possession of territory upon the coasts of the African continent outside of its present possessions, or which being hitherto without such possessions shall require them, as also any Power which shall assume a protectorate there, shall accompany the respective act with a notification addressed to the other signatory Powers of the present Act, in order to enable them, if need be to make good any claims of their own."

It can hardly be successfully maintained that *notification* is at present essential to the validity of a title to territory acquired by occupation. It should be noted that the requirement of notification is omitted from the Convention of St. Germain of 1919 which revised on broader lines and practically abrogated the Berlin Act of 1885. See *Treaty Series*, No. 18 (1919, Cmd.) 477.

The Institute of International Law adopted a Project of ten articles Relative to the Occupation of Territory in 1888. It made notification a condition of effective occupation. For the text of this Project, see Scott, *Resolutions of the Institute of Int. Law* (1916), 86–88.

[23] Vast claims to territory were formerly based on mere discovery, especially if accompanied or followed by an assertion of possession. Thus England granted a wide stretch of territory in America extending "from sea to sea" to the Plymouth Company in 1620, and Spain and Portugal claimed vast territory based on discovery and Papal grants.

The history of occupation has been divided into three periods: (1) Up to the sixteenth century, acquisitions of new territory were mainly based upon Papal grants. (2) In the sixteenth and seventeenth centuries the English, French, and Dutch, having refused to recognize the validity of the Papal grants to Spain and Portugal, based their claims on a priority of discovery or possession, or both. (3) During the eighteenth century, the publicists declared in favor of effective possession—a doctrine which was put into practice in the partition of Africa in the latter half of the nineteenth century.

On the history of occupation, see especially Jèze, *Étude sur l'occupation* (1896), 1–40; and Salomon, *L'occupation des territoires sans maître* (1889), 31–101. For brief accounts, see * Bonfils and 1 (2 Pt.) Fauchille, Nos. 537–41; and Despagnet, No. 403.

Mere discoveries in the Artic and Antarctic Polar regions afford no basis for the assertion of title by Great Britain or the United States. See Scott and Balch, in 3 and 4 *A. J.* (1909 and 1910), 928 ff. and 265 ff. See also Lindley, *Acquisition of Territory*, etc. (1926), ch. 2; Miller, in 4 *For. Aff.* (1925), 47 ff.; Waultrin, in 15 *R. D. I. P.* (1908), 78 ff., 185 ff., and 16 *R. D. I. P.* (1909), 649 ff.

[24] On "Inchoate Title by Discovery or Occupation," see particularly Westlake, *Collected Papers* (1914), 163 ff.

appropriate a newly discovered or recently annexed *territorium nullius* would be guilty of an unfriendly act.

182. **Extent of the Area of Occupation.**—So far we are on solid ground, for the authorities appear to be unanimous. But there is a wide difference of opinion when it comes to the difficult question of determining the extent of the area within which an effective occupation operates.

The older Anglo-American view is thus expressed by Twiss: "When a nation has discovered a country and notified its discovery, it is presumed to intend to take possession of the whole country within those natural boundaries which are essential to the independence and security of its settlement." [25] Generally speaking, this view is repudiated, especially by recent Continental authorities, who demand actual or effective occupation of the whole area claimed. "No State can appropriate more territory through an act of occupation than it can regularly govern in time of peace with its effective means on the spot." [26]

---

[25] 1 Twiss, § 124. Cf. Twiss, *The Oregon Question* (1846), p. 174. Cited by Westlake, *Collected Papers* (1914), 175, who adds: "But the principle of security can hardly be relied on as governing the distribution of territory except for very small areas contiguous to real settlements."

The principle of security is thus stated by Hall (p. 129, 8th ed.), as to which he erroneously claims that "there is no difference of opinion": "A settlement is entitled, not only to the lands actually inhabited or brought under its immediate control, but to all those which may be needed for its security, and to the territory which may fairly be considered to be attendant upon them."

This view is apparently shared by most of the Anglo-American publicists with the exception of Walker and Westlake. See *e.g.* Lawrence, § 74; 1 Phillimore, § 237; Pomeroy, §§ 98 ff.; and Taylor, § 99.

[26] Holtzendorff, in 2 *Handbuch*, 263. Cited with approval by Westlake, *op. cit.*, 170.

"The limits of occupation are determined by the material possibility of making the authority of the government respected within the extent of the territory occupied. There is no occupation where the power of the State is not felt." 1 F. de Martens, § 89, p. 464. See also to the same effect, Jèze, *Étude sur l'occupation* (1896), 285 ff.; 2 Mérignhac, 458; 1 Rivier, 196; Salomon, *L'occupation des territoires* (1889), 319 ff.; Art. 35 of the General Act of the Conference of Berlin, cited above; and Art. 1 of the "Project Relative to the Occupation of Territory" adopted by the Institute of International Law in 1888, in Scott, *Resolutions of the Institute of Int. Law* (1916), 86.

But Bonfils (6th ed., No. 553) justly remarks: "It is reasonable that one should recognize in the occupying State a certain right of preference in respect

In view of the conditions laid down with such apparent unanimity as essential to effective occupation, it is difficult to avoid the conclusions of the more recent continental writers on this subject. The area of effective occupation can extend no farther than real possession or the actual exercise of sovereign rights over the region claimed. So much is necessary in order to confer a complete or legally valid title. But, as in the case of territory claimed on the basis of mere discovery or annexation, the occupier has a presumptive or inchoate title to such portions of the contiguous [27] or neighboring country (if it be *territorium nullius*) as may be deemed necessary for defense or future settlement within a reasonable time, or which form a part of the geographical unity of the region actually settled. Such presumptive or inchoate title operates as a bar to settlement or colonization by another State.

183. **Islands.**—It is almost unanimously [28] admitted that the occupation of a portion of an island of moderate size amounts to occupation of the whole; and that, in the case of a group of small islands, the actual occupation of one furnishes at least a presumptive title to all the rest. It is generally agreed that islands lying or forming within the marine league belong to the territory on the coast.

184. **Large Islands and Continents.**—There is considerable authority in theory and practice for the view that in case of occupation of a certain seacoast, " possession is understood as extending into the interior country to the sources of the rivers emptying within that coast to all their

to the future and definite acquisition of a free zone contiguous to its actual possessions." As to the extent of this zone, Bonfils favors the "reasonable principle, acceptable in theory, but more than difficult to apply in practice" —that the zone should include all the country "forming a geographical unity with the point occupied."

[27] The doctrines of *continuity* and *contiguity*, as set forth by Secretaries Calhoun and Webster (see 1 Moore, *Digest*, § 81, pp. 264–65), have been generally denied. For references, see Jèze, *Étude sur l'occupation* (1896), 288 *n.* They can only be said to confer inchoate or presumptive titles, and then only for comparatively small or moderate areas.

This theory of contiguity has been revived in our day in connection with the partition of Africa under the German name of *Hinterland* (Back Country), *Sphere of Influence*, etc. See *infra*, Nos. 186–87.

[28] Salomon (*op. cit.*, 323) dissents from this view, but it is generally admitted both in theory and practice.

branches and the country they cover." [29]   This theory of the watershed should only be applied to rivers of moderate length, such as those emptying into the Atlantic Ocean on the eastern coast of the United States.   It could have no reasonable application to such rivers as the Mississippi or the Columbia.

In cases where there is intermediate vacant land contiguous to the settlements of two nations, " each nation has an equal title to extend its settlement over the intermediate vacant land, and thus it happens that the middle distance satisfies the juridical title, whilst it is the nearest approximation to a natural boundary, and the most convenient to determine." [30]

The above statements may be regarded as fairly descriptive of the correct theory and practice, provided it be understood that the " title " or " possession " thus claimed are merely inchoate or presumptive.   In no case can a fort or settlement at the mouth of a river give title to the whole basin, as claimed by the United States in the Oregon controversy. [31]   And the occupation of one bank of a

[29] Messrs. C. Pinckney and Monroe, U. S. ministers, to Mr. Cevallos, Spanish Minister, respecting the boundaries of the Louisiana territory (April 20, 1805), in 2 *Am. State Papers* (*For. Rel.*), 664.   Cited by 1 Moore, *Digest*, § 81, p. 263.

This is the first principle laid down by the United States.   The second lays down the principle of the middle distance in language differing from that cited in the text.   "A third rule is, that, whenever any European nation has thus acquired a right to any portion of territory on that [the American] continent, that right can never be diminished or affected by any other Power, by virtue of purchases made, by grants or conquests, of the natives within the limits thereof."

These rules are expressly cited and adopted by 1 Phillimore, § 238; and 1 Twiss, § 125.   The principle of the watershed is criticised by 1 Westlake, 115 f.

[30] 1 Twiss, § 132, p. 216.   The boundary line between the United States and Mexico (case of Texas) was finally drawn in accordance with this principle. See Hall, § 33, pp. 132–34.   "But there can be no doubt that natural boundaries would be preferred to an imaginary line in cases where these exist." Lawrence, (3d ed.), § 94, p. 152.

[31] Mr. Gallatin to Mr. Addington, Dec. 19, 1826, in 6 *Am. St. Papers* (*For. Rel.*), 667.   Cited by 1 Moore, *Digest*, § 81, p. 263.

The claim of the United States to the so-called Oregon Territory (between the Rocky Mountains and the Pacific Ocean, and between the 42d degree and 54th degree and 40 minutes of north latitude) was based upon the following grounds: (1) Prior discovery and exploration, and the establishment of the first posts and settlements.   (2) The virtual recognition of the title of the

river does not confer a title to territory upon the opposite bank.

There are several forms of disguised or qualified occupation which remain to be considered.

185. Forms of Disguised or Qualified Occupation. The Colonial Protectorate.

—The most important of these is the Colonial Protectorate [32] which may, indeed, amount to a virtual annexation. It has been defined as " a region in which there is no State of International Law to be protected, but which the Power that has assumed it does not yet claim to be internationally its territory, although that Power claims to exclude all other States from any action within it." [33] Yet " the powers exercised in a [colonial] protectorate are in fact territorial." [34] Jurisdiction is

United States by the British Government as shown by the restitution of Astoria in accordance with the Treaty of Ghent in 1814. (3) The acquisition by the Treaty of 1819 of the titles of Spain derived from discovery. (4) The ground of continuity and contiguity.

The exclusive claim of the United States was opposed by Great Britain on the following grounds: (1) Prior discovery and contemporary exploration and establishment of posts. (2) The express reservation of the British claims upon the restoration of Astoria in 1818. (3) A denial of the Spanish claims. (4) A denial of the doctrine of continuity and contiguity.

The controversy ended, as such controversies usually result, in a compromise. The Treaty of Washington (1846) established the 49th degree of north latitude as the permanent boundary between the United States and the British possessions.

On the *Oregon Controversy*, see especially: Foster, *A Century of American Diplomacy* (1911), 302–13; Hall, § 33; * Moore, 1 and 5 *Digest*, §§ 80–81, 104, 835, and 1 *Arbitrations*, chs. 7 and 8; Pomeroy, § 103; * Twiss, *The Oregon Question* (1846); * Wheaton, §§ 172–76. For the text of the Treaty of Washington, see 1 Malloy, *Treaties*, 656.

In the equally famous boundary dispute between Great Britain and Venezuela, the claims of Venezuela were based mainly upon Spanish discoveries and settlements; those of Great Britain on prescription, conquest, and occupation, due to subsequent Dutch and British settlements. Through the intervention of the United States in 1895, the questions at issue were finally arbitrated in 1899. Great Britain secured through this award the greater part of the territory in dispute between Venezuela and British Guiana, but Venezuela retained the entire mouth of the Orinoco River.

On the *Venezuelan Boundary Dispute*, see Cleveland, *Venez. Boundary Controversy* (1913); Moore, 1 and 6 *Digest*, §§ 88, 966. For a brief summary, see Hall, § 33, pp. 136–37; and Latané, *U. S. and Latin America* (1920), ch. 6, pp. 238–49.

[32] See *supra*, No. 106, for comparison with International Protectorates. It is sometimes difficult to draw the line of demarkation.

[33] 1 Westlake, 125 f.

[34] Hall, *A Treatise on the Foreign Powers and Jurisdiction of the British Crown* (1895), § 98, p. 224.

claimed and asserted over foreigners as well as over nationals of the protecting State, which incurs a certain measure of *de facto* international responsibility for the maintenance of order and the conduct of the natives over whom it exercises a certain amount of authority or control. The powers exercised within such a region usually have the sanction of treaties with the native chiefs or tribes, although the source of the legal validity of such authority and control as is exercised must be sought for in the laws, decrees, or charters of the protecting State rather than in these treaties with the natives.

The main advantages of a colonial protectorate for the protecting State are that it affords a means of excluding other Powers and preparing the way for annexation without incurring the burden of complete sovereignty and international responsibility involved in real and effective occupation; for the natives, it affords a means of gradual initiation into the mysteries of so-called civilized life. It appears also to be less objectionable to neighboring Powers than complete occupation.

Article 34 of the General Act of the Berlin Conference laid down the same condition of notification for protectorates as for occupation on the African coast; but it is only to *occupations* that Article 35 attached the obligation of insuring the establishment of authority [35] " sufficient to

[35] The original proposal to extend this obligation to protectorates met with the opposition of England and Germany. But Arts. 1 and 2 of the "Draft regarding Occupation of Territories" adopted by the Institute of International Law in 1888 insists upon "the establishment of a responsible local power, provided with sufficient means to maintain order and to assure the regular exercise of its authority within the limits of the occupied territory" in the case of protectorates as well as of ordinary occupations. Scott, *Resolutions of the Institute of Int. Law* (1916), 87. This also appears to be the opinion of most of the authorities. Westlake (I, 126), for example, says: "There can be no doubt that the principle of that obligation applies equally to all colonial protectorates."

On *Colonial Protectorates*, see especially: Bonfils and 1 (2 Pt.) Fauchille, No. 558; Bry, *Précis élémentaire de droit int. public* (1906), No. 169; 1 Cobbett, 115–16; * Despagnet, *Essai sur protectorats* (1896), ch. 3; Fiore, *Int. Law Cod.* (1918), Arts. 1087–92, and in 14 *R. D. I. P.* (1907), 148 ff.; Gairal, *Le protectorat int.* (1896), 267–300; Hall, § 38a, and * *Foreign Powers and Jurisdiction* (1895), 204–38; * Jenkyns, *British Rule and Jurisdiction* (1902), ch. 9; Lawrence, §§ 43, 80; Lindley, *Acquisition and Gov't. of Backward Territory in Int. Law* (1926), ch. 23, pp. 182–88; Meyer, *Die staatsrechtliche Stellung der deut-*

protect acquired rights," etc.   The authorities hold, however, that the exercise of a certain amount of authority (at
least sufficient for the maintenance of a degree of order) is
obligatory in a colonial protectorate as in a territory under
real occupation.   The difference is merely one of degree.
The latter assumes the exercise of complete, the former of
partial, sovereignty.

186. **2. The Hinterland.**—The American theory of continuity and contiguity has been revived in recent times in
connection with the partition of Africa in the form of claims
to the *Hinterland* (Back Country).   Extensive regions in
China and Africa extending far beyond any territory which
could properly be denominated *Hinterland* have also been
divided up between the Powers into what are called *Spheres
of Influence or Interest.*[36]

187. **3. Spheres of Influence or Interest.**—Such divisions
are based upon conventions which appear to be mainly of
two kinds:

(1) Agreements for reciprocal abstention from territorial
acquisition within a given line or area.   An example is the
Agreement of 1886 between England and Germany:
" Germany [or Great Britain] engages not to make
acquisitions of territory, accept protectorates, or interfere
with extension of British [or German] influence, and to give
up any acquisitions of territory or protectorates already
established in that part of the Western Pacific lying to the

schen Schutsgebiete (1888); * 2 Nys, 80–98; Perrinjaquet, in 16 *R. D. I. P.*
(1909), 320 ff.; 1 Rivier, 89–91; Snow, *Question of the Aborigines* (1921), *passim;* * 1 Westlake, ch. 6, pp. 120–29, and *Collected Papers* (1914), 181–91.

[36] There seems to be no clear distinction between these terms.   Both are
vague.   Spheres of Influence appear to have more of a political, Spheres of
Interest rather an economic significance.

On the *Hinterland* and *Spheres of Influence* (which, however, should be
kept mentally distinct), see * Bau, *Foreign Relations of China* (1921), ch. 21;
Bonfils, Nos. 559–60; Bry, *op. cit.*, No. 170; Buell, *Int. Relations* (1925),
ch. 20, pp. 447–50; 1 Cobbett, 116–18; * Despagnet, in 1 *R. D. I. P.* (1894),
103 ff.; 1 (2 Pt.) Fauchille, No. 552[8]; Fiore, *Int. Law Cod.* (1918), Arts. 1093–
97, and in 14 *R. D. I. P.* (1907), 155 ff.; Hall, § 38b, and * *Foreign Powers
and Jurisdiction* (1895), § 101; Holdich, *Political Frontiers*, ch. 6; Kawakami,
Japan's Pacific Policy (1922), ch. 22; Lawrence, § 81; * Lindley, *op. cit.*,
ch. 24; 2 Nys, 98–102; De Pouvourville, in 6 *R. D. I. P.* (1899), 120–22;
1 Rivier, 177–79; Rutherford, in 20 *A. J.* (1926), 300–25; * 1 Westlake,
130–35, and *Collected Papers* (1914), 191–93; and * Willoughby, *Foreign
Rights and Interests in China* (1920), ch. 10.

east, southeast, or south [or west, northwest, or north] of the said conventional line." [37]

(2) Agreements not to alienate territory. An example is the Agreement of 1898 between Great Britain and China that the latter " will never alienate any territory in the provinces adjoining the Yangtsze to any other Power, whether under lease, mortgage, or any other designation." [38]

It is hard to see how such agreements can have any legal validity except for the contracting parties. At the most they confer a feeble inchoate or reversionary title which may act as a bar to trespass by third Powers.

188. **Loss of Territory.**—As there are five modes of acquiring title to territory, so there are five corresponding modes of losing it, viz. physical loss, prescription, conquest, cession, and dereliction. There is also a sixth, viz. a successful revolt [39] or rebellion, to which there is no corresponding mode of acquisition. There are only two modes of loss of territory which require any special discussion.

189. **Physical Loss of Territory.**—As territory may be increased through accretion, it may be diminished through physical means, such as earthquakes, volcanic action, the washing of the waves, the gradual subsidence of the earth's surface, etc. In case of the disappearance of an island near the coast through volcanic action, the marine league would thereafter be measured from the mainland instead of from the site of the former island.[40]

190. **Dereliction.**—Dereliction corresponds to occupation. It is " effected through the owner-State completely abandoning territory with the intention of withdrawing from it forever, thus relinquishing sovereignty over it. Just as occupation requires, first, the actual taking into possession (*corpus*) of territory and, secondly, the intention (*animus*) to acquire sovereignty over it, so dereliction requires, first, actual abandonment of a territory, and, secondly, the intention to give up sovereignty over it. Actual abandon-

[37] Cited by 1 Westlake, 130.

[38] *Ibid.*, 134.

[39] The case of successful revolt has been considered under the head of "Recognition of Independence," *supra*, No. 122.

[40] For the rules governing changes in river boundaries, see *supra*, No. 165.

ment alone does not involve dereliction as long as it must be presumed that the owner has the will and ability to retake possession of the territory.   Thus, for instance, if the rising of natives forces a State to withdraw from a territory, such territory is not derelict as long as the former possessor is able and makes efforts to retake possession.   It is only when a territory is really derelict that any State may acquire it through occupation." [41]

BIBLIOGRAPHY

Modes of Acquiring and Losing Territory.—Bluntschli, Arts. 276–95; Bonfils and * 1 (2 Pt.) Fauchille, Nos. 532–71; Bry, *Précis élémentaire de droit int. public* (1906), Nos. 162–75; Bulmerincq, in 1 Marquardsen, *Handbuch*, §§ 47, 50; Cabouat, *Droit int. des annexions* (1881), 100 ff.; 1 and 5 Calvo, §§ 263–300, 3117–18; Chrétien, *Principes de droit int. public* (1893), Nos. 121–46; 1 Cobbett, 110–19; Creasy, *First Platform of Int. Law* (1876), Nos. 212–27, 249–55; Despagnet Nos. 388–409; Engelhardt, in 18 *R. D. I.* (1886), 433 ff., 573 ff.; * Evans, *Cases*, 281–305; Fenwick, ch. 14, pp. 221–44; Field, *Outlines of an Int. Code* (1876), Pt. I, ch. 7; 2 Fiore, Nos. 840–65, and *Int. Law Cod.* (1918), Arts. 1055–97; Gérard, *Des cessions déguisées* (1904); Grotius, II, cc. 3, 4, 8, §§ 8–16; * Hall, §§ 31–37, 204–05; 1 and 2 Halleck (3d ed.), p. 154, and ch. 34, pp. 467–99; Heffter, §§ 69–70, 72, 178, and Geffcken's note on p. 431; Heimburger, *Der Erwerb der Gebietshoheit* (1888), 103 ff.; Holtzendorff, in 2 *Handbuch*, 252–76, and *Eroberungen und Eroberungsrecht;* * 1 Hyde, §§ 99–119; Jèze, *Étude sur l'occupation;* * Lawrence, §§ 74–83; * Lindley, *Acquisition and Gov't. of Backward Territory in Int. Law* (1926); Liszt, §§ 17–18; 1 J. de Louter, § 20; 1 F. de Martens, §§ 89–91; 1 G. F. de Martens, §§ 35–45 and notes by Vergé; 2 Mérignhac, 410–98; * 1 Moore, *Digest*, §§ 80–89; * 2 Nys, 1–108; * 1 and 2 Oppenheim, §§ 209–47 and 264–65; 1 and 3 Phillimore, §§ 222–95, 568–74; Phillipson, *Termination of War* (1916), 9 ff. and 277 ff.; 1 Piédelièvre, Nos. 419–43; Pomeroy, §§ 91–123; 2 P.-Fodéré, Nos. 781–833, 850–66; 1 and 2 Rivier, 172–220 and 436–42; * Salomon, *L'occupation des territoires sans maître* (1889); Scaife, in 4 *Papers of Am. Histor. Assoc.* (1890), No. 3, pp. 269–93; * Scott, *Cases*, 173–200, 694–732; Selosse, *Traité de l'annexion* (1880), 61–98, 281 ff.; Taylor, §§ 217–27; * 1

[41] 1 Oppenheim, § 247.   For the cases of Santa Lucia and Delagoa Bay, see Hall, § 34; and Oppenheim, *op. cit.*   On the disputed claims of Brazil and England to the island of Trinidad, see 1 Moore, *Digest*, § 89.

"The United States maintained that Navassa Island in 1857, when a citizen of the United States took possession of it under the Guano Islands Act, was 'derelict and abandoned.'"   1 Moore, *Digest*, p. 299.   See *Jones v. U. S.* (1890), 137 U. S. 202, and Scott, *Cases* (ed., 1902), 38.

Twiss, ch. 8, §§ 113–39, and *The Oregon Question* (1846); Ullmann, §§ 92–100; * Vattell, liv. I, §§ 81, 203–10, and liv. II, §§ 79–98, 140–51; Walker, *Manuel of Int. Law* (1895), §§ 9–13; 1 Wharton, *Digest*, §§2–3; Wheaton, §§ 161–76; * 1 Westlake, 90–143, and *Chapters* (1894), 134–89 or *Collected Papers* (1914), 136–93; Wilson, § 28.

For further references, see 1 (2 Pt.) Fauchille, pp. 664–65 and 1 Oppenheim (3d ed.), pp. 372, 376, 383, 390, 394, 400, 403.

CHAPTER XIV

TERRITORIAL WATERS

191. (I) **The Marginal Sea.**—The territory of a State bordering on the open sea also includes the Territorial or Marginal Sea, which is usually held to be a marine league measured from the low-water mark.[1]

192. **History of the Marine League.**—The three-mile limit, or marine league, was originally based upon the principle first clearly enunciated by Bynkershoek [2] in the early part of the eighteenth century that the territorial sovereignty or jurisdiction of the State is limited by its power to defend its seacoast by force of arms—*imperium terræ finiri ubi finitur armorum vis*, i.e. *quousque tormenta exploduntur.* The range of the cannon of that day seems to have been about a marine league or three nautical miles, and this distance became the generally recognized limit of the marginal sea in the course of the eighteenth century. During the nineteenth century the rule of the marine league

---

[1] That the jurisdiction of a State over its littoral or marginal sea is based upon territorial sovereignty is denied by some good authorities on what appear to be insufficient grounds. For a criticism of their views, see especially Heilborn, *System des Völkerrechts* (1896), 37–58; 1 Oppenheim, § 185; Schücking, *Das Küstenmeer* (1897), 14–20; and 1 Westlake, 195–96. For a review of the various theories, see 1 (2 Pt.) Fauchille, Nos. 492[1–10].

For the argument against the doctrine of territorial sovereignty as applied to territorial waters, see De Lapradelle, in 5 *R. D. I. P.* (1898), 264 ff. For the views of leading authorities on this point, see De Lapradelle, *op. cit.*, 271–72. For an English translation of this brilliant but not convincing article, see Crocker, *Extent of the Marginal Sea* (1919), 183–236.

Jurisdiction over territorial waters may, of course, include property rights, but it is not essentially based upon property, as many of the older authorities supposed.

The low-water mark is usually taken as the starting point for the measurement of the marine league, but there is a considerable variety of opinion on this point. See, *e.g.* Latour, *La mer territoriale* (1889), 20 ff.; 1 Nys, 502–05; and 1 Oppenheim, § 186. The low-water mark has the sanction of many treaties, the British Territorial Waters Jurisdiction Act of 1876, and of the Institute of International Law.

[2] *De dominio maris* (1702), c. 2. Cf. the vaguer statements of Grotius (lib. II, cap. 3, §§ 13 and 14), and Vattel (liv. I, ch. 23, § 289).

appears to have completely supplanted the principle upon which it was originally based; and, instead of being extended to meet the demands of new modern guns of ever increasing range, it has always remained the same until it is now apparently as fixed and unalterable as were the laws of the Medes and the Persians. And this in spite of the protests of publicists and the efforts of statesmen.[3]

There can be no doubt that an extension of the three-mile limit for all territorial purposes, particularly for the exercise of exclusive fishing rights, would be highly desirable. Besides, the marine league no longer satisfies the needs of modern requirements for defense. An extension to meet these requirements is certainly favored by an ever increasing number of publicists, and was strongly recommended by the Institute of International Law in 1894.[4]

[3] The great majority of modern publicists favor an extension of the three-mile limit, but some of them do not distinguish clearly between the present three-mile rule and the principle upon which it was originally based. For references, see the Bibliography at the end of this chapter.

In 1806 the Government of the United States attempted to obtain a recognition of a six-mile limit from England, but refused to admit a claim of six miles made by Spain to the Cuban coast in 1863 and 1864. Secretary Seward, in 1 Moore, *Digest*, § 146. In 1864 Secretary Seward proposed a zone of five miles to the British Legation at Washington. 1 Moore, § 152. The British Government has, however, always insisted upon the three-mile limit. Until 1918 Norway claimed four miles. See Aubert, in 1 *R. D. I. P.* (1894), 429 ff.; and Böye, in 33 *I. L. A.* (1924), 294–98. Spain "has always claimed a six-mile limit," and Russia "claims a fishing limit of twelve miles." Bower, in 3d series 7 (Pt. IV) *J. C. L.* (1925), 137.

The three-mile limit has the sanction of a considerable number of State Acts and Treaties, *e.g.* the Russian Prize Rules of 1869, the British Territorial Waters Acts of 1876, French legislation in 1866 and 1888, the North Sea Fisheries Convention of 1882, the Convention of Constantinople relating to the Suez Canal of 1888, and the Convention of 1893 concerning the Behring Sea. For additional treaties, see 1 Calvo, § 356; 1 Nys, 509; and Crocker, *op. cit.*, 485 ff.

[4] The Institute of International Law, after an exhaustive discussion of this question, voted by a decisive majority (there was no division of opinion as to the desirability of extending the three-mile limit) in favor of a zone of six marine miles for all territorial purposes. It even permitted the extension of this zone for purposes of neutrality beyond six miles in time of war, provided the range of cannon shot were not exceeded. Scott, *Resolutions of the Institute of Int. Law* (1916), 113–15. Preamble and Arts. 1–2, 4.

The maritime Powers were urged to hold an International Congress for the adoption of these or similar rules, but no such Congress has even been held. It is highly desirable that this recommendation by the Institute be acted upon.

193. Right of Innocent Passage.—Though the marginal sea is undoubtedly territorial, " all ships without distinction have the right of innocent passage through the territorial sea, saving to belligerents the right of regulating such passage and of forbidding it to any ship for the purpose of defense, and saving to neutrals the right of regulating the passage of ships of war of all nationalities through the said sea." [5]   But such vessels, if merchantmen, are probably liable in principle to the jurisdiction of the riparian State.[6]

The United States was largely instrumental in definitely fixing the three-mile limit during Washington's administration.   The judicial decisions which introduced the rule of the marine league into Anglo-Saxon jurisprudence were those of Sir William Scott at the beginning of the 19th century, notably in the cases of the *Twee Gebroeders* (1800), 3 C. Rob. 162 or Evans, *Cases*, 771.

For the history of the "General Adoption of the Three-mile Limit," see particularly Fulton, *Sovereignty of the Sea* (1911), Sec. II, ch. 2.   For a strong reaffirmation of the three-mile limit by the Imperial Supreme Prize Court in Berlin, see *The Elida* (1915), 10 *A. J.* (1916), 916 or Evans, *Cases*, 184.

"It now is settled in the United States and recognized elsewhere that the territory subject to its jurisdiction includes the land areas under its dominion and control, the ports, harbors, bays and other inclosed arms of the sea along its coast, and a marginal belt extending from the coast line outward a marine league, or three geographical miles." *Cunard S. S. Co.* v. *Mellon* (1922), 262 U. S. 100, 122.   For an interesting comment on this important decision, see Conboy, in 2 *Canad. Bar Rev.* (1924), 8–23.

[5] Art. 5 of the Rules adopted by Institute.   Scott, *op. cit.*, 114.

This is unquestionably a rule of International Law based on the universal practice of nations.   It, of course, does not include sabotage or the right to engage in the coasting trade, which is usually reserved by the coastal State.

Art. 7 declares that "ships which pass through territorial waters shall conform to the special regulations decreed by the littoral State in the interest and for the safety of navigation or as a matter of maritime police."   As Westlake (I, p. 190) points out: "The right of the littoral State to publish regulations in the interest of navigation does not include a right to exact payment of dues, by ships not entering its harbors, under pretext of providing the navigation with necessary lights and buoys."   See also 1 Oppenheim, § 188.

There is a difference of opinion as to whether warships with inoffensive purpose enjoy the right of innocent passage through the territorial waters. They certainly have the customary right of passage through such portions of the marginal sea as constitute international highways.   See 1 Oppenheim, §§ 188 and 449.   Hall (p. 198 of 8th ed.) denies that the right of innocent passage extends to warships.   For a refutation of his view, see Westlake (I, 196) who points out that the "ship of war as well as a merchantman may have a lawful errand beyond the littoral sea in question," which "in the course of its lawful voyage it may be difficult for it to avoid."

Oppenheim (I, § 449) is of the opinion that "a State is in strict law always competent to exclude men-of-war from all or certain of its ports and from those territorial waters which do not serve as highways for international traffic."

194. **Exercise of Authority beyond the Marine League.**—
There is considerable authority and practice in favor of the
view that for purposes of defense and in order to execute its
revenue and sanitary laws, a State may exercise a limited
authority beyond the three-mile limit.   Such limited authority or jurisdiction has been asserted and exercised, at
least by Great Britain,[7] the United States,[8] and France;[9]

This is undoubtedly the law in respect to ports and international highways.
But Oppenheim (I, § 188) elsewhere admits that "as a rule, however, in
practice no State actually opposes in time of peace the passage of foreign
men-of-war and other public vessels through its maritime belt," and that
"a usage has grown up by which such passage, if in every way inoffensive
and without danger, shall not be denied in time of peace."

[6] The authorities are divided on this point.   Art. 6 of the Rules adopted
by the Institute (see *supra*) declares: "Crimes and offences committed on
board foreign ships passing through the territorial sea by persons on board
of them against persons or things on board the same ships, are as such outside
the jurisdiction of the littoral State, unless they involve a violation of the
rights or interests of the littoral State or of its subjects not forming part of
the crew or passengers."

This is a good practical rule and it represents the prevailing custom, but
it may be doubted whether it is a principle of International Law.   As in
the analagous case of jurisdiction over foreign merchantmen in port (see
infra, No. 211), it would seem that there is no good reason for denying local
jurisdiction over passing vessels *in principle*.   The British Territorial Waters
Act of 1878 claims such jurisdiction.   See especially Hall, § 59; 1 Oppenheim,
§ 189; and 1 Westlake, 264.

On the *Immunity of Public Vessels from Local Jurisdiction*, see *infra*,
No. 209.

[7] The British Hovering Acts of 1736 and 1784 asserted a jurisdiction, for
revenue purposes and for the prevention of "hovering" on the coast in a
menacing and annoying manner, to a distance of four leagues from the shore.
They have been long since repealed.   Atlay (note 179a to Wheaton) tells us
that "the present customs legislation [of Great Britain] makes a distinction
as regards the extent of jurisdiction claimed for revenue purposes between
ships belonging to British subjects and ships belonging to foreigners."   While
asserting a jurisdiction extending *three leagues* from the shore in case of British
subjects, it only claims *one league* if the owners are not British.   See Customs
Act of 1876, 39 and 40 Vict., c. 36.   "British Acts of Parliament require
vessels liable to quarantine or having infectious diseases on board to observe
certain regulations when within two leagues of the coast of the United Kingdom, but they authorize no enforcement of those regulations except by the
recovery of a penalty from the captain when the vessel arrives within the
territory."   1 Westlake, 176.

For a very full discussion and defense of the British Hovering and Quarantine or Public Health Acts, see 2 Piggott, *Nationality* (1907), 40–60.

[8] The revenue laws of the United States, embodied in the Act of 1797
(§ 27) and incorporated into the Revised Statutes (sec. 2760), direct the officers
of the revenue cutters to "go on board all vessels which arrive within the
United States or within four leagues thereof, if bound for the United States,

and, whether on the basis of comity [10] or of law, appears to

and search and examine the same, and every part thereof, and [they] shall demand, receive, and certify the manifests required to be on board certain vessels, . . . and [they] shall remain on board such vessels until they arrive at the port or place of their destination." 1 Moore, *Digest*, § 151, pp. 725–726.

It should be especially noted that the law does not authorize the *seizure* of a foreign vessel beyond the three-mile limit, as has sometimes been asserted. It merely prescribes visit and search. "The statute (of 1797) may well be construed to mean only that a foreign vessel, coming to an American port, and there seized for a violation of revenue regulations committed out of the jurisdiction of the United States, may be confiscated; but that, to complete the forfeiture, it is essential that the vessel shall be bound to and shall come within the territory of the United States, after the prohibited act. The act done beyond the jurisdiction is assumed to be part of an attempt to violate the revenue laws within the jurisdiction." Dana's note 108 to Wheaton, § 179, p. 258. See also 1 Moore, *Digest*, § 151, p. 726.

The Tariff Act of Sept. 21, 1922 (§ 586), provides that a master who, without a permit, allows goods to be unloaded from his vessel within four leagues of the coast, subjects himself to liability for a fine and the vessels and cargoes to forfeiture. There is also an older act of 1884 forbidding the trans-shipment of cargoes by night.

Among the vessels seized outside the three-mile limit in consequence of efforts to enforce prohibition were the British schooners *Grace* and *Ruby* which were found guilty of attempting to smuggle intoxicating liquor into United States territory in violation of Rev. St., §§ 2872, 2874 (Comp. St. §§ 5563, 5565) and the National Prohibition Act (41 Stat. 305). Consequently, the vessels were held subject to forfeiture. *Grace and Ruby* (1922), 283 Fed. 475.

On Jan. 23, 1924, a treaty was signed and later ratified between the United States and Great Britain which provides that, while upholding the principle of the marine league, the United States may search and seize British vessels attempting to violate its liquor laws within the distance from the coast "that can be traversed in one hour by the vessel suspected of endeavoring to commit the offense." In exchange for this concession the United States agreed to allow British vessels with liquor aboard listed as sea stores or as cargo destined for a port foreign to the United States to enter American jurisdiction, provided the liquors are kept under seal continuously while the vessel remains in territorial waters, and that no part of such liquors be unladen within the United States.

"The treaty is an experiment; it is limited to one year, with power on behalf of either party to propose amendments three months before its expiration, and the treaty itself is to expire within the year unless the amendments proposed have been agreed upon." Editorial, in 18 *A. J.* (1924), 305.

For the text of this treaty, see Supp. to 18 *A. J.* (1924), 127. Similar treaties have been negotiated with other Powers, *e.g.*, with Italy, Sweden and Germany. For texts, see Supp. to 19 *A. J.* (1925), 6 ff.

[9] It appears that France authorizes visit and search for the enforcement of revenue laws to a distance of two myriameters or about four leagues. The French Government insisted that the battle between the *Alabama* and *Kearsarge* should not take place within the range of cannon shot from the coast. 1 Moore, *Digest*, § 150.

[10] Twiss (I, 190) remarks on this head: "Such laws and regulations, how-

encounter no opposition on the part of other States.   But such exercise of limited authority to enforce revenue or quarantine regulations does not justify the seizure [11] of foreign vessels outside the territorial waters, except possibly in cases of extreme necessity on grounds of self-defense, or

ever, have no foundation of *strict right* against other nations. . . . It is only under the *Comity of Nations* in matters of trade and health that a State can venture to enforce any portion of her Civil Law against foreign vessels, which have not as yet come within the limits of her maritime jurisdiction." He calls it a "permissive" jurisdiction and cites the case of *The Appollon* (1824), 9 Wheaton 362.

The main point of this decision is thus stated in the syllabus at the head of the case: "It seems that the right of visitation and search, for enforcing the revenue laws of a nation, may be exercised beyond territorial jurisdiction, upon the high seas, and on vessels belonging to such nation, or bound to its ports."

Oppenheim (I, § 190) disagrees with the view of Twiss and Phillimore. He says: "I believe that, since Municipal Laws of the above kind have been in existence for more than a hundred years and have not been opposed by other States, a customary rule of the Law of Nations may be said to exist which allows riparian States in the interest of their revenue and sanitary laws to impose certain duties on such foreign vessels bound to their ports, as are approaching, although not yet within, their territorial maritime belt."

[11] In *Rose* v. *Himeley* (1808), 4 Cranch 241, Chief Justice Marshall and a majority of our Supreme Court held that "a seizure beyond the limits of the territorial jurisdiction for breach of municipal regulations, is not warranted by the Law of Nations."   Cf. to the same effect *Le Louis* (1817), 2 Dodson 210 and Scott, *Cases*, 338.

It has been claimed (Taylor, § 248) that *Rose* v. *Himeley* was overruled by *Hudson* v. *Guestier* (1810), 6 Cranch 281 and Scott, *Cases*, 365.   This was the opinion of Chief Justice Marshall himself, but the report of the latter case leaves this point doubtful.   See Dana's note 108 to Wheaton, § 179, pp. 259–60; and 1 Moore, *Digest*, § 151, p. 729.

Rose v. *Himeley* is certainly in conflict with certain views previously expressed by Chief Justice Marshall in *Church* v. *Hubbart* (1804), 2 Cranch 187; Evans, *Cases*, 157 or Scott, *Cases*, 361; and 1 Moore, *Digest*, 727–28. But the real purport of this decision was that "the court did not undertake to pronounce judicially, in a suit on a private contract (a policy of insurance) that a seizure of an American vessel made at four leagues, by a foreign power was void," holding that a State's "power to secure itself from injury may certainly be exercised beyond its territory."   Dana, note 108 to Wheaton, p. 259; and 1 Moore, *Digest*, p. 729.   For a review of these cases, see Dickinson, in 11 *Harv. Law Rev.* (1926), 4–12.

A novel question was raised in Alaska in 1904.   Driven from the region of Cape Nome, the gamblers of that section established a gambling house on the ice beyond the three-mile limit.   Did the United States Government have jurisdiction?   For various answers, see Rolland, in *Chronique*, 11 *R. D. I. P.* (1904), 340–45; 2 Mérignhac, 384; and Brown, in *Procs. Am. Soc. I. L.* (1923), 21.

when a hot pursuit begun in marginal waters is continued on the open sea.[12]

195. **(II) Bays and Gulfs.**—The territorial waters naturally include ports, harbors, roadsteads, and river mouths. Indeed, these waters may be said to be national. They also include such bays and gulfs as are almost wholly inclosed by the territory of a single State and whose entrance from the ocean is narrow enough to be commanded by forts or shore batteries erected on one or both sides of the entrance, even if the entrance be wider than six miles or two marine leagues.[13] The entrance is formed by a straight line from headland to headland, at which the three-mile limit begins. Some States claim jurisdiction over certain bays whose entrance is too wide to be effectively commanded by coast

[12] Art. 8 of the rules adopted in 1894 by the Institute of International Law declares: "The littoral State has the right to continue on the high seas a pursuit commenced in the territorial sea, and to seize and judge the ship which has broken its laws within its waters. In case, however, of capture on the high sea, the fact shall be notified without delay to the State whose flag the ship flies. The pursuit must be interrupted as soon as the ship enters the territorial sea of its own country or of a third Power. The right to pursue is at an end as soon as the ship has entered a part of its own country or of a third Power." Scott, *Resolutions, op. cit.*, 115. This Resolution was voted unanimously.

For a review of the doctrine of "hot pursuit" with ample citations from the authorities, see Hershey, in 13 *A. J.* (1919), 562 ff.

In 1891 the *Itata*, a transport in the service of Chilean insurgents, was accused of violating the neutrality laws of the United States. She was pursued by American naval forces from San Diego, California to Iquique, Chile where she was said to have surrendered to Admiral McCann under duress, but without resistance. The United States and Chilean Claims Commission decided that "the United States committed an act for which they are liable to damages and for which they should be held to answer." 3 Moore, *Arbitrations*, 3070. See also *U. S.* v. *Trumbull* (1891), 48 Fed. 94 and Scott, *Cases*, 318; and 2 Moore, *Digest*, § 316.

It appears, however, that this decision was made on the basis of a demurrer on the part of the United States; the real facts seem to have been that the *Itata* was never pursued into Chilean waters and that her surrender on the part of Chilean authorities was voluntary. See *U. S. and Chilean Claims Commission* (1901), Decision No. 21, pp. 200 ff.

[13] The statement of this rule is that of Oppenheim (I, § 191) somewhat modified.

Some publicists claim that gulfs or bays with an entrance wider than ten miles cannot be claimed as wholly territorial. But the Institute of International Law voted in favor of twelve miles, unless a long continued usage had established a more extensive jurisdiction. Art. 3 of Scott, *Resolutions, op. cit.*, 114.

defenses,[14] and such claims would seem to have the sanction of the Law of Nations, provided they are based upon immemorial custom.[15]

[14] The United States claims the whole of the Delaware and Chesapeake Bays as territorial. See 1 Moore, *Digest*, § 153, pp. 735–39, for the opinion of Att.-Gen. Randolph (1793) in the case of the *Grange;* and 4 and 5 Moore, *Int. Arbitrations*, 4333, 4675, and Scott, *Cases*, 232, for the *Alleganean* (1885).

Great Britain holds Conception Bay in Newfoundland (which has an average width of about fifteen miles, an entrance of twenty miles, and a depth of about forty miles), to be territorial. See 1 Moore, *Digest*, § 153, p. 740, and Snow, *Cases on Int. Law* (1893), 45–47 for *The United States Cable Co.* v. *The Anglo-American Telegraph Co.* (1877). Great Britain has also asserted jurisdiction over foreign as well as native fishermen in the Moray Firth. *Mortensen* v. *Peters* (1906), 14 Scots Law Times Rep. 227, Pts. 13 and 14. See also 1 *A. J.* (1907), 5–26 for a full report, and Evans, *Cases*, 29, 151 for abridged reports of this interesting case.

It appears that Russia also claims jurisdiction over the White Sea. See "L'affair de l'Onward Ho" (1910), in 18 *R. D. I. P.* (1911), 94–99. For Canadian claims to the Hudson Bay, see Balch, in 6 *A. J.* (1912), 409 ff.

[15] "For bays, the territorial sea follows the sinuosities of the coast, except that it is measured from a straight line drawn across the bay at the place nearest the opening toward the sea, where the distance between the two sides of the bay is twelve miles in width, at least unless a continuous and secular usage has sanctioned a greater width." Art. 3 of the rules of the Institute, cited above.

"In case of bays the three marine miles are to be measured from a straight line across the body of water at the place where it ceases to have the configuration and characteristics of a bay. At all other places the three marine miles are to be measured following the sinuosities of the coast." The Hague Tribunal in *United States* v. *Great Britain* (case of North Atlantic Coast Fisheries), in 4 *A. J.* (1910), 948, 983. For comment on this arbitral decision, see Borchard, in 11 *Col. Law Rev.* (1911), 1 ff.; and Lansing, in 5 *A. J.* (1911), 1–31, particularly pp. 19–25.

There is considerable usage in favor of permitting exclusive fishery rights within a bay whose entrance does not exceed ten miles in width. Such stipulations are found in the Anglo-French Fishery Treaty of 1839, the Hague Convention of 1882 for the Regulation of Fisheries on the North Sea, and the project of the Anglo-American Treaty of 1888. See particularly Fulton, *Sovereignty of the Sea* (1911), Sec. II, ch. 3.

The claims of Great Britain to the "Narrow Seas" and the "Kings Chambers" have probably been abandoned. See 1 Oppenheim, §§ 191 and 194 with notes on pp. 344 and 348. In any case they are no longer valid.

The vague and shadowy claims to jurisdiction for domestic purposes over large portions of the Atlantic Ocean and Gulf of Mexico sometimes made by American publicists in behalf of the United States have been taken too seriously by Continental authorities. For the source of these misrepresentations, see 1 Kent, *Commentaries* (1884), 30.

On *Bays and Gulfs*, see particularly: Balch, in 6 *A. J.* (1912), 409 ff.; * Charteris, in 23 and 27 *I. L. A.* (1908 and 1912), 103 ff. and 107 ff. respectively, and 16 *Yale Law J.* (1906–07), 471 ff.; 1 (2 Pt.) Fauchille, § 516; Gregory, in 1 *Am. Pol. Sci. Rev.* (1906–07), 410 ff., in 16 *Harv. Law Rev.*

With the exception of the marginal sea or marine league, gulfs and bays, whose entrance is too wide to be commanded by forts and shore batteries, usually belong to the open sea. This is also the case with such gulfs and bays as are surrounded by the land territory of more than one riparian State. In general, it may be said that the right of innocent passage and use applies to gulfs and bays as well as to the marginal sea, as far as private vessels or merchantmen are concerned, but that States need not admit foreign warships to these waters which may in a sense be regarded as national.

196. (III) **Straits.**—A strait dividing the land territory of a single State which is not too wide to be commanded by shore batteries [16] is territorial. But if such a narrow strait divides the land of two different States, it belongs to the territory of both, the boundary line running through the mid-channel. [17] Foreign merchantmen have the right of

(1902–03), 150 ff., and in 21 *Harv. Law Rev.* (1887), 65 ff.; * Hurst, in *Brit. Yr. Bk.* (1922–23), 42–54; and Oppenheim in 1 and 5 *Z. V.* (1906 and 1911), 579–87, and 74–95.

See also Bibliography at the end of this chapter.

[16] Examples are the British Strait of Solent, which divides the Isle of Wight from England; the Dardanelles and the Bosphorus, which are Turkish waters; and the Russian Strait of Kertch, connecting the Sea of Azov with the Arctic Ocean.

By a treaty in 1846 and through subsequent acts, the United States and Great Britain claimed jurisdiction over the Strait of Juan de Fuca between Vancouver Island and the State of Washington, a channel which seems to have an average width of about fifteen miles. See 1 Moore, *Digest*, § 133; and Hall, 195. See also 1 Moore, *Arbitrations*, ch. 7. This appears to be the only exception to the rule stated in the text.

In 1894 the Institute of Int. Law (see Scott, *Resolutions, op. cit.*, 115, Art. 10) declared that the rules relating to the territorial sea (marginal sea and bays, cf. *supra*, Nos. 191–95) apply also to straits whose width does not exceed twelve miles, with the following distinctions and modifications:

"1. Straits whose shores belong to different States form part of the territorial sea of the littoral States, which will exercise their sovereignty to the middle line.

"2. Straits whose shores belong to the same State and which are indispensable to maritime communication between two or more States other than the littoral State always form part of the territorial sea of such State, whatever the distance between the coasts.

"3. Straits which serve as a passage from one free sea to another can never be closed."

Straits actually subject to conventions or special usages are reserved from the operation of these rules.

[17] Slightly adapted from Oppenheim (I, § 194), who cites the Lymoon

innocent use and passage in territorial straits as well as in territorial bays, gulfs, and the marginal sea; but foreign warships do not have this right unless the strait forms an international highway.

If the strait forms an international highway, the right of innocent passage [18] for foreign warships and merchantmen exists even in the case of straits which are less than six miles in width.[19] For such innocent use no tolls may be collected,

Pass which separates the British island of Hong Kong from the Asiatic mainland as an historical example. It was "half British and half Chinese as long as the land opposite Hong Kong was Chinese territory."

[18] "In time of war, the territorial Power, if belligerent, may of course deal with the ships of the enemy as it pleases. The enemy will similarly exercise his belligerent right within the straits as elsewhere." Holland, *Studies in Int. Law* (1898), 278.

[19] In 1879 the United States declared that it would not tolerate exclusive claims to the Straits of Magellan. Art. 5 of the Treaty of 1881 between Chile and the Argentine Republic provides: "Magellan's Straits are neutralized forever, and free navigation is guaranteed to the flags of all nations." 1 Moore, *Digest*, § 134, p. 664. See also Abribat, *Le détroit de Magellan* (1902). It should be noted that the term "neutralized" as applied in this connection is somewhat of a misnomer.

The Dardanelles and the Bosphorus, which form the entrance to the Black Sea, should be regarded as an exception to this rule. Their status is based on convention. According to a series of great international treaties, warships (with a few exceptions) were not allowed to pass through these Turkish Straits, but merchantmen were expressly permitted to do so. The modern rule dates from the latter part of the eighteenth century. The Treaty of 1809 between Great Britain and Turkey expressly sanctioned the ancient rule of the Ottoman Empire forbidding all foreign warships from entering these waters. (As long as the Black Sea was wholly Turkish water, the Sultan had a right to prohibit merchantmen as well as war vessels from entering the Straits.) These stipulations were reaffirmed by the London Treaty of 1841, the Treaty of Paris of 1856, the London Conference of 1871, and the Berlin Treaty of 1878.

This rule was evaded or violated by Russia during the Russo-Japanese War when she sent several cruisers belonging to her Volunteer Fleet in the Black Sea through the Straits flying the commercial flag in the guise of merchantmen for the purpose of exercising the rights of search and capture in the Red Sea. Hershey, *Russo-Japanese War* (1906), 128 ff. and 148 ff. Prior to her entrance into the World War, Turkey allowed two German cruisers, the *Goeben* and the *Breslau*, to pass through the Straits.

On the *Straits of Constantinople*, see especially: 1 (2 Pt.) Fauchille, Nos. 499–503; Gorianow, *Le Bosphore et les Dardanelles* (1910); Holland, *European Concert in the Question* (1885), 225–27; Lawrence, § 89; Mischef, *La mer noire et les détroits de Constantinople* (1899); 1 Moore, *Digest*, § 134, pp. 664–67; 1 Nys, 459–70; 1 Oppenheim, §§ 181 and 197; * Phillipson and Buxton, *The Question of the Bosphorus and the Dardanelles* (1917); Schuyler, *American Diplomacy* (1886), 317–18; and Wheaton, §§ 182, 191, with Dana's note 111 on p. 264. For further references, see 1 (2 Pt.) Fauchille, p. 216.

even on the ground of immemorial usage sanctioned by
treaties;[20] although it is perhaps permissible to make
necessary charges for the maintenance of buoys, lighthouses,
pilots, etc.

197. (IV) **Inland Lakes and Landlocked Seas.**—It is
universally agreed that lakes and landlocked seas which are

On July 24, 1923, there was signed at Lausanne a separate Straits Convention with Turkey which proclaims the "principle of freedom of transit and
of navigation by sea and by air" in the Straits, but which abandons the
old practice of excluding warships in favor of that of admitting all ships
provided they observe certain prescribed restrictions. Merchantmen are
granted "complete freedom of navigation and passage" in time of war as
well as in peace on condition that, in case of a war in which Turkey is a belligerent, the vessels shall give no aid to the enemy (Annex to Art. 2, I c).
Warships are also to have "complete freedom of passage" under certain
restrictions as to numbers, etc. (Annex I, 2–5).

The Convention further creates "demilitarized zones" on both shores of
the Straits within which there shall exist "no fortifications, no permanent
artillery organization, no submarine engines of war other than submarine
vessels, no military aerial organization, and no naval base" (Art. 6). At
Constantinople there may be maintained an arsenal and a naval base as well
as a garrison of 12,000 men (Art. 8).

For the execution of the Convention an International Straits Commission
is to be constituted at Constantinople which shall exercise its functions under
the auspices of the League of Nations to which it will make an annual report.
This Commission shall be composed of a representative of Turkey (who
shall be President) and representatives of France, Great Britain, Italy, Japan,
Bulgaria, Greece, Rumania, Russia, and the Serb-Croat-Slovene State, in so
far as these Powers are signatories of the Convention and have ratified the
same. In the event of the United States acceding to the Convention, it will
be entitled to a representative on the Commission (Arts. 10–16).

"Should the freedom of navigation of the Straits or the security of the
demilitarized zones be imperiled by a violation of the provisions relating to
freedom of passage, or by a surprise attack or some act of war or threat of
war, the High Contracting Parties, and in any case France, Great Britain,
Italy, and Japan, acting in conjunction, will meet such violation, attack,
or other act of war or threat of war, by all the means that the Council of the
League of Nations may decide for this purpose" (Art. 18).

For the text of the Straits Convention, see 18 *A. J.* (1924), 53 or 2 *Treaties
of Peace, 1919–23* (New York, 1924), 1023.

On the *Straits Convention of Lausanne,* see Visscher, in 50 and 51 (4 and
5 third ser.) *R. D. I.* (1923 and 1924), 537 ff. and 13 ff.

[20] Through the persistence of the United States, the *Sound Dues* levied
from time immemorial on vessels and cargoes passing through the Sound
and the two Belts which form a passage between the North Sea and the
Baltic, were abolished in 1857. They were redeemed by pecuniary indemnities. This topic, which is discussed at considerable length in many works
on International Law, is now one of mere historical interest.

On the *Danish Sound Dues,* see especially: 1 Moore, *Digest,* § 134; 1 Oppenheim, § 196; Schuyler, *American Diplomacy* (1886), 306–16; Snow, *Americans
Diplomacy* (1893), 124–27; and Wheaton, §§ 183–84, including Dana's note 112.

wholly surrounded by the land territory of a single State are territorial. And most publicists [21] also agree that in the absence of special treaties,[22] such lakes and seas as are wholly inclosed by the territory of more than one State belong to the territories of the various riparian States in proportional parts, the boundary line running through the middle of these bodies of water. But the use of such territorial waters is common to all the bordering States.

198. (V) **International Lakes and Seas.**—International lakes and seas, *i.e.* such as are surrounded by several States and are at the same time connected with the open sea by a narrow navigable strait or channel, are also territorial; but they should be considered free and open to all the world,[23] at least as far as merchantmen and international trade are concerned.[24]

Thus, " so long as the shores of the Black Sea were exclusively possessed by Turkey, that sea might, with propriety, be considered a *mare clausum*; . . . but since the territorial acquisitions made by Russia, and the commercial establishments formed by her on the shores of the Euxine, both that Empire and the other maritime Powers have become entitled to participate in the commerce of the Black Sea, and consequently to the free navigation of the Dardanelles and the Bosphorus." [25]

[21] So far as known to the author, the following publicists are the only ones who claim that such lakes and seas as are wholly inclosed by the territory of several States are free: Calvo, 1, § 301; Caratheodory, in 2 Holtzendorff, 378; and Despagnet, No. 416.

[22] For examples of treaties which make a division of these seas and lakes between the riparian States, see 1 Oppenheim, § 179.

"The Caspian Sea is surrounded by Russia and Persia, but, by virtue of the treaties of Gulistan (1813) and Tourkmantschai (1828), it is subject practically to Russian control."   1 Moore, *Digest*, § 135.

[23] Though the authorities are not all agreed upon this point, such is the actual practice.

Among the authorities who claim that international lakes and seas are necessarily free to all the world are the following: 1 Calvo, § 301; Caratheodory, in 2 Holtzendorff, 378; Liszt, § 36, p. 293; 2 Mérignhac, 587; 1 Nys, 448 ff.; and 1 Rivier, 153, 230.

Oppenheim (I, § 180) and Ullmann (§ 88, p. 293) admit that this is the actual practice, but deny that it has been established as a rule of International Law.

[24] This does not, of course, apply to the coasting trade.

[25] Wheaton, § 182. Cf. *supra*, note 19, p. 304. This principle is not admitted in respect to the *Great Lakes* of Ontario, Erie, Huron, and Superior

199. (VI) **National Rivers.**—It is generally [26] agreed that all streams lying wholly within the territory of a single State are national in character and are subject to the exclusive jurisdiction of the State within whose boundaries they flow. When navigable, such rivers are usually open to the merchantmen of all nations so far as *international* trade is concerned, but such freedom of navigation is a privilege rather than a right unless secured by treaty.

(Lake Michigan is wholly within the territory of the U. S.) which are connected with the Gulf of the St. Lawrence by the St. Lawrence River. But the St. Lawrence River is not an international highway to the extent that are the Dardanelles and the Bosphorus. Besides, there are several important canals which render the connection between the Great Lakes and the Gulf of St. Lawrence partly artificial.

"At the time when the United States achieved independence the Great Lakes belonged exclusively to Great Britain. No other nation had any rights in or over them. By the treaty of peace of 1783 the lakes were divided between the contracting parties and the boundary fixed as running through the middle of the lakes and of the waterways connecting them. The United States and Great Britain thus shared thenceforth, to the exclusion of any claim whatsoever of a third nation, the territorial sovereignty over the lake waters, which had therefore been wholly British. . . ." Mr. Uhl, Acting Sec. of State, May 23, 1894. See the same effect, Mr. Gresham, Sec. of State, Jan. 2, 1895, who said: "The Department concurs in the view expressed by the Canadian Judge (McDougall in the case of the American vessel *Grace*) that the lake waters on either side of the international boundary line are under the exclusive municipal jurisdiction of the respective countries." 1 Moore, *Digest*, § 137, pp. 673 and 675.

For the international boundary in the Great Lakes, see 1 Moore, *Arbitrations*, chs. 5 and 6, and Vol. 6 for maps.

On the meaning of the term "high seas" as applied to the Great Lakes, see 1 Moore, *Digest*, § 136, p. 670. See especially *United States* v. *Rodgers* (1893), 150 U. S. 249, and Scott, *Cases*, 222. See also Hunt, in 4 *A. J.* (1901), 285–313.

"In respect of the right of navigation, the lakes that separate the two countries, *i.e.* Lakes Ontario, Erie, Huron, and Superior, and their water communications, are treated as international waters, being dedicated in perpetuity to the common navigation of all the inhabitants." But this common right of navigation does not include the coasting trade. Lake Michigan is open to British subjects by treaty. 1 Moore, *Digest*, § 138, pp. 675–76.

The Baltic Sea is an open sea, in spite of the fact that the entrances to it from the North Sea are controlled by Denmark and Sweden. Various more or less successful attempts to close it to foreign warships during war have been made by the riparian States, but this pretention has never been admitted by the other Powers. See, *e.g.* Bonfils and 1 (2 Pt.) Fauchille, No. 504, and Wheaton, § 185.

[26] A few publicists seem to be of the opinion that the principle of the freedom of navigation applies to navigable rivers generally. See, *e.g.* Despagnet, No. 428; and Fiore, *Int. Law Cod.* (1918), Art. 983. Bluntschli (Art. 314)

200. **(VII) International Rivers.**—Navigable rivers which flow through or between several States into the open sea are called International Rivers.   They are undoubtedly territorial in the sense that such portions of these rivers as lie within the territory of a single State are subject to the jurisdiction of that State.[27]

Boundary rivers belong to the States whose territory they divide, the boundary line running, as a rule, either through the middle of the river or through the middle of the *thalweg* or navigable portion of the stream.[28]   The use of boundary rivers is certainly common to all the co-riparian States. " Where a river forms the boundary between two countries, and the only access to the adjacent territories is through such river, the waters of the whole river must be considered as common to both nations, for all purposes of navigation, as a common highway." [29]   It should also be open to the merchantmen of other nations for purposes of international trade.[30]

In respect to rivers flowing successively through or between several States to the open sea, the majority of the more modern authorities [31] are of the opinion that the State

erroneously asserts that "streams and navigable rivers which are in communication with a free sea are open to the vessels of all nations in time of peace."

[27] The State does not ordinarily assert jurisdiction over the foreign vessel or its crew as long as their conduct does not affect the peace and comfort of the native inhabitants.   It may not levy tolls for profit, but may collect charges for lights, buoys, dredging, and other incidental expenses.   Cf. *infra*, No. 210 and notes on pp. 328–29.

[28] Cf. *infra*, No. 165.

[29] 1 Moore, *Digest*, § 131, p. 627.

[30] In the case of *The Appollon* (1824), 9 Wheaton 362, it was held that "the mere transit of a French vessel through the waters of a river which forms the boundary between the United States and the territory of a foreign State, for the purpose of proceeding to such territory, cannot be taken to subject the vessel to penalties imposed by the United States upon French vessels for entering their territory."   1 Moore, *op. cit.*

[31] Allowing for a few corrections, the authorities are thus tabulated by 1 Westlake, 161–62.

Those asserting the right of innocent passage: Bluntschli, § 314; Caratheodory, in 2 Holtzendorff's *Handbuch*, § 60; Despagnet, § 428; Engelhardt, in 2 *R. D. I.*, 372; 2 Fiore, No. 774; Geffcken, in Heffter, § 77; Grotius, lib. II, cap. 2, § 13; Institute of Int. Law, *Annuaire* for 1887–88, 182 (see also Scott, *Resolutions of the Institute of Int. Law*, 1916, p. 78); Pufendorf, lib. III, cap. 3, n. 5–8; 1 Rivier, 226; Ullmann, § 105; Vattel, liv. II, § 130; Wheaton, § 193.   To this list should be added: 1 Halleck (3d ed.), 173–74; 2 Mérignhac, 160 ff.; and 1 Westlake 153–59.

or States located on the upper waters of such rivers, have a right to the innocent use of their navigable portions, and this view is in accordance with modern practice based on treaties.[32] The right of innocent passage undoubtedly

Those denying the right of innocent passage as a matter of strict law: 1 Calvo, §§ 219, 293; Hall, § 39; Heffter, § 57; Klüber, §§ 76, 135; 1 F. de Martens, § 101; G. de Martens, § 84; 1 Phillimore, § 160; 1 Twiss, § 145. To this list should be added: Creasey, *First Platform of Int. Law* (1876), No. 233; Lawrence (3d ed.), § 112, somewhat modified in 7th ed., § 92; 1 Oppenheim, § 178; Pomeroy, § 132; 2 P.-Fodéré, Nos. 728, 749; and Woolsey, § 62.

Bonfils, No. 524, simply says that "the general tendency of the modern doctrine is favorable to freedom of navigation, subordinated to measures of precaution and safeguard for the security of riparian States and in respect to their rights of jurisdiction, police, customs regulations," etc.

[32] The freedom of river navigation as a principle of public law is a modern doctrine. True it is that the "Roman law declared all navigable rivers to be so far public property that a free passage over them was open to everybody, and the use of their banks (*jus littoris*) for anchoring vessels, lading and unlading cargo, and acts of the like kind, to be incapable of restriction by any right of private domain." 1 Phillimore, § 155. But this was not a principle of International Law.

In the Middle Ages the idea of the public character of river navigation almost wholly disappeared. It was revived as a principle of the Law of Nations by Grotius (lib. II, c. 2, § 13), who proclaimed the doctrine of the freedom of navigation on rivers as well as on the open sea. The doctrine of the right of innocent passage on rivers was more fully elaborated by Vattel (liv. II, §§ 117, 123, 127–29, 134). But it was practically disregarded in international practice until the outbreak of the French Revolution.

In November, 1792, the provisional Executive Council of France declared *apropos* of the Scheldt, which had been closed by the Treaty of Münster in 1648, that "the stream of a river is the common, inalienable property of all the countries which it bounds or traverses; that no nation can, without injustice, claim the exclusive right to occupy the channel of a river and prevent the neighboring peoples who inhabit its upper waters from enjoying the same advantages." Engelhardt (*Du régime conventionnel des fleuves int.*, 1879, p. 24), perhaps the leading authority on this subject, considers this proclamation "the first charter of contemporary fluvial liberties." A limited application of this principle was made by a number of treaties to which France was a party during the Revolutionary and Napoleonic period.

The Grotian principle was also adopted by the allied Powers in Art. 5 of the Treaty of Paris of 1814 which proclaimed the freedom of navigation upon the Scheldt, and upon the Rhine "from the point at which it becomes navigable *to the sea*" so that "it can be prohibited to no one." In 1815 the Powers represented at the Congress of Vienna declared that "those States which are separated or traversed by the same navigable river engage to regulate by common consent all matters relating to the navigation of this river." To this end they agreed to name a commission. Art. 108 of the Final Act of the Congress of Vienna. Art. 109 declared that "navigation on the rivers referred to in the preceding article, from the point where each of them becomes navigable to *its mouth*, shall be entirely free, and cannot, in respect to commerce, be prohibited to any one; it is understood, however, that respect will

carries with it the incidental right to use the banks of such rivers for mooring, loading, and unloading cargoes, etc., provided such use is innocent and necessary.   No charges

be paid to police regulations.   These regulations shall be uniform for all and as favorable as possible to the commerce of all nations."

"In order to assure the application of this principle, articles were inserted expressly regulating in certain respects the free navigation of the Rhine; and it was provided that 'the same freedom of navigation' should be 'extended to the Necker, the Main, the Moselle, the Meuse, and the Scheldt, from the point where each of them becomes navigable to their mouths.'   And in order to 'establish a perfect control' over the regulation of the navigation, and to 'constitute an authority which may serve as a means of communication between the States of the Rhine upon all subjects relating to navigation,' it was stipulated that a central commission should be appointed, consisting of delegates named by the various bordering States. . . ."   1 Moore, *Digest*, p. 628.   These articles form part of Annexe XVI to the Final Act of the Congress of Vienna.   Some of the provisions of the Vienna agreements appear to have been rendered illusory on certain European rivers.

On the free navigation of the Rhine, see especially: Barel, in *Brit. Yr. Bk.* (1921-22), 75 ff.; * Chamberlain, in 105 Columbia University *Studies* (1923), 47 ff.; Engelhardt, in 11 *R. D. I.* (1879), 363 ff.; 1 (2 pt.) Fauchille, No. 526; 1 Hyde, § 169; * Kaeckenbeeck, *Int. Rivers* (1918), 31 ff.; 1 Moore, *Digest*, p. 628; Schuyler, *American Diplomacy* (1886), 345 ff.; 1 Westlake 149 f.; and Wheaton, *History*, 498-506.

The next important step was taken by the Congress of Paris in 1856. Arts. 15-17 of the Treaty of Paris stipulated that the principles established by the Congress of Vienna should apply to the Danube and its mouths, and provided for the creation of two commissions composed of delegates from each of the interested Powers—a temporary "European" Commission to clear the mouths of the river and the adjacent seas from obstructions, and a permanent "Danube River" Commission to prepare regulations for navigation and river police, etc.   The jurisdiction of this "temporary" European Commission was extended in 1878 and 1883 and it endures to this day.   In 1883 a new "mixed Commission of the Danube" was created for the purpose of supervising the execution of the regulations made for the navigation of the river.   The most noteworthy features of the European Commission are that a majority of votes are sufficient for a decision, and that the Commission appears to form a distinct International Person, having the power of prescribing and enforcing penalties for the violation of its regulations.

It should be noted that the Treaties of Paris (see, *e.g.* Art. 331 of the Treaty of Versailles) declared the Danube from Ulm eastwards to be international.   In order to provide fresh regulations and authority, an International Commission, consisting of representative of the riparian states and of Belgium, France, Greece, Italy and Great Britain, met in Paris during 1920 and 1921. It drafted a Statute for the Danube which was ratified by the signatory Powers June 22, 1922.

The Danube Statute of 1921 confirmed the powers of the European Commission which was to consist of representatives of Great Britain, France, Italy, and Rumania, with power to add to their number in certain circumstances.   It also made permanent the "International Commission of the Danube," provisionally set up by the Paris Treaties, which consists of two representatives from Germany, and one of each of the other riparian States

are permissable beyond such as are necessary for the maintenance or improvement of navigation or for the use of special appliances.

and of such non-riparian States as are represented on the European Commission.

The Statute also lays down the duties of this Commission (which are mainly administrative) and of the riparian States in order to secure freedom of navigation. "Provision is also made for the settlement of disputes between the Commission and separate riparian States, ultimate recourse to the Permanent Court of International Justice being provided in certain cases." Toulmin, in *Brit. Yr. Bk.* (1922–23), 167–69. See also Sherman, in 17 *A. J.* (1923), 451 ff.; and Toynbee, *Survey of Int. Affairs, 1920–23* (1925), 328–32.

On the free navigation of the Danube, see especially: * 1 (2 Pt.) Fauchille, No. 528; * Chamberlain, in 105 Columbia University *Studies*, 47 ff.; Engelhardt, in 16 *R. D. I.* (1884), 360 ff.; Kaeckenbeeck, *Int. Rivers* (1918), 83 ff.; * 1 Moore, *Digest*, 630–31; Sayre, *Int. Administration* (1918), 38–47; Schuyler, *American Diplomacy* (1886), 352 ff.; Sherman, in 17 *A. J.* (1923), 438 ff.; Ullmann, § 105, pp. 335–38; 1 Westlake, 151–53.

In 1884–85 the Conference of Berlin agreed upon the free navigation of the Congo and the Niger, together with their tributaries, and created the International Congo Commission as a special international organ similar to the Mixed Commission of the Danube for the regulation of the navigation of the Congo which was also neutralized, the regulations respecting the Niger being left to the enforcement of the co-riparian States. On the *Congo* and the *Niger*, see particularly Kaeckenbeeck, *op. cit.*, 137 ff. For references, see 1 (2 Pt.) Fauchille, pp. 571–72.

It should be added that the General Act of the Berlin Conference of 1884–85 was practically abrogated by a Convention signed at St. Germain on Sept. 10, 1919. Art. 1, which prescribed the area within which freedom of trade was to be enjoyed by all nations, was re-enacted; and new rules providing for the freedom of navigation on the Congo, the Niger, and their tributaries were laid down. See Supp. to 15 *A. J.* (1921), 314. For a summary of the three Conventions of St. Germain, see Hall (Higgins 8th ed.), § 38c.

After Spain obtained control of both banks of the Mississippi River at its mouth, she claimed the exclusive right of navigation below the point reached by the southern boundary of the United States—a claim strongly resisted by the latter Power on treaty grounds and as forbidden by the Law of Nature and Nations. The dispute was terminated by the Treaty of 1795, which declared that the navigation of the Mississippi should be free to the United States as well as to subjects of the King of Spain. Through the subsequent acquisition of Louisiana and Florida by the United States, "the Mississippi ceased to be an international stream, and the right to control its navigation passed exclusively to the United States" (1 Moore, *Digest*, p. 625), although Great Britain put in a claim, which was based upon Article VIII of the Treaty of Peace (1782–83), to the right of the free navigation of the river. This article declared that "the navigation of the river Mississippi, from its source to the ocean, shall forever remain free and open to the subjects of Great Britain and the United States." This right was granted, however, under the erroneous idea (as shown by Art. II of the same treaty) that the source of the Mississippi was in British or Canadian territory. The claim of Great Britain was afterwards abandoned.

There was also a controversy in 1823 and 1826 between Great Britain and

201. **(VIII) Interoceanic Canals.**—The same rules applicable to international rivers and straits should be applied to international canals, which are artificial waterways forming

the United States respecting the right of the free navigation of the St. Lawrence. As in the case of the dispute with Spain, the United States based its claim mainly on the "general principles of the law of nature"—an argument whose validity was denied by Great Britain. It may be noted that Westlake (I, 157) admits that "the American argument appears to have been well founded." The United States also urged that the St. Lawrence was analogous to a *strait* connecting navigable seas.

"By Article IV of the Reciprocity Treaty of June 5, 1854, it was agreed that the inhabitants of the United States should have 'the right to navigate the river St. Lawrence, and the canals in Canada, used as a means of communicating between the Great Lakes and the Atlantic Ocean,' as fully and freely as British subjects, subject only to the same tolls and assessments as the latter." The treaty of 1854 was terminated in 1866 in pursuance of a notice given by Congress.

"By Article XXVI of the Treaty of Washington of May 8, 1871, it was declared that the navigation of the river St. Lawrence, ascending and descending from the 45th parallel of north latitude, where it ceases to form the boundary between the two countries, 'from, to, and into the sea, shall forever remain free and open for the purposes of commerce to the citizens of the United States, subject to any laws and regulations of Great Britain, or of the Dominion of Canada, not inconsistent with such privilege of free navigation.'" On the other hand, it was reciprocally provided that the navigation of the rivers Yukon, Porcupine, and Stikine in Alaska should be free and open for purposes of commerce to the subjects of Great Britain as well as to citizens of the United States.

"By Article XXVII of the same treaty the British Government engaged to urge upon that of Canada to secure to the citizens of the United States the use of the Welland, St. Lawrence, and other canals in the Dominion on terms of equality with its inhabitants; and the United States engaged to grant to British subjects the use of the St. Clair Flats Canal on terms of equality with the inhabitants of the United States," etc. See 1 Moore, *Digest*, § 131, pp. 634–35, for the citations and facts given above.

On the navigation of the Mississippi and the St. Lawrence, see especially: * 1 *Am. State Papers*, 253–57, and 6 *Ibid.*, No. 464, pp. 757–77; 1 Cobbett, 119–23; Hall, § 39; Kaeckenbeeck, *Int. Rivers* (1918), 205 ff.; * 1 Moore, *Digest*, §§ 130–31; 1 Phillimore, §§ 160, 169–70; Pomeroy, §§ 133–34; * Schuyler, *American Diplomacy* (1886), 265–91; Snow, *Cases on Int. Law* (1893), 33–40; 1 Westlake, 154–58; Wheaton, §§ 200–05, and Dana's note 118 on pp. 287–88.

The Argentine Confederation declared the navigation of the rivers Paraná and Uruguay open to merchantmen of all nations in 1852. In 1867, after a prolonged resistance, Brazil finally opened the Amazon and its tributaries to the merchant ships of all friendly States. By decree of July 1, 1867, Venezuela opened the Orinoco and its branches to foreign merchant vessels.

On South American Rivers, see especially 1 Calvo, §§ 323–32; 1 (2 Pt.) Fauchille, No. 529$^{1-3}$; 1 Hyde, §§ 166–67; Kaeckenbeeck, *op. cit.*, 213 ff.; * 1 Moore, *Digest*, § 131, pp. 640–53; and * Schuyler, *op. cit.*, 319–44.

The Paris Treaties of 1919 probably mark an epoch in the development not merely of the freedom of river navigation, but of freedom of traffic in

an international passageway. The only permissible variation from these rules would seem to be that reasonable tolls may be collected to pay for the construction as well as the maintenance of the canal.

From the standpoint of the Law of Nations, purely internal canals are wholly national,[33] but international

transit as a whole, whether by rail or waterways. Though partly devised as penalties and not immediately granting reciprocal rights to Germany, the "Régime of Ports, Waterways and Railways" contained in Pt. XII (Arts. 321 ff.) of the Treaty of Versailles in particular includes provisions that may serve as future precedents for international agreements.

For example, Germany agreed to "grant freedom of transit through her territories, on the routes most convenient for international transit, either by rail, navigable waterway, or canal, to persons, goods, vessels, carriages, wagons and mails coming from or going to the territories of the Allied and Associated Powers (whether contiguous or not)." Such persons, goods, etc., it was declared, "shall not be subject to any transit duty or to any undue delays or restrictions, and shall be entitled in Germany to national treatment as regards charges, facilities, and all other matters" (Art. 321).

Regarding freedom of navigation it was agreed that the "nationals of any of the Allied and Associated Powers as well as their vessels and property shall enjoy in all German ports and on the inland navigation routes of Germany the same treatment in all respects as German nationals, vessels and property." In particular vessels are to be treated on a footing of equality with national vessels in German territory (Art. 327).

Among the rivers declared international are the Elbe, the Oder, the Nieman, the Danube from Ulm, and all navigable parts of these river systems, together with lateral canals and channels. On these waterways "the nationals, property and flags of all Powers shall be treated on a footing of perfect equality" (Arts. 331–32).

A temporary régime for the administration of these waterways was provided which was to be superseded by a General Convention relating to international waterways. Germany undertook in advance to adhere to said General Convention which was to be approved by the League of Nations (Art. 338). Presumably the Waterways Convention adopted by the Barcelona Conference in 1921 (see *infra*, note 53 on p. 525) which was attended by German delegates is intended to fulfill this promise.

Separate International Commissions were established for the administration of the Elbe, the Oder, and the Nieman (in the latter case if requested by the League of Nations) and special arrangements were made for the Danube, the Rhine and the Moselle (Arts. 340–62).

For a summary of Arts. 321–63 of the Treaty of Versailles, see 1 Hyde, §§ 173–80. For an able analysis of Pt. XII of the Treaty of Versailles, see Miller, in 13 *A. J.* (1919), 669–86. Mr. Miller calls special attention to Art. 378 which "provides not only that the provisions mentioned shall be subject to revision by the League of Nations at any time after five years after the coming into force of the present treaty, but also that after the five years' period no Allied or Associated Power can claim the benefit of any of the stipulations of these Articles, 'in which reciprocity is not accorded in respect of such stipulations.'"

[33] An example of such a canal would be the Erie Canal in New York State.

canals, or those forming a passageway for international traffic, while territorial and therefore under the control and jurisdiction of the State in which they lie, should be open to the warships as well as merchantmen of all nations for purposes of innocent use.

These principles should govern in the absence of treaties, but they have as a matter of fact been applied by convention in the cases of the two great interoceanic Canals of the Suez and the Panama.[34] Both of these Canals are declared " free and open " on terms of equality to warships and merchantmen of all nations.[35] Neither are to be blockaded —a purely conventional stipulation which does not apply to

[34] The Emperor William or Kiel Canal which connects the Baltic with the North Sea was open to the vessels of all nations even prior to the World War, but it was regarded by Germany as purely territorial, having been built for strategic rather than commercial purposes.

By the Treaty of Versailles the Kiel Canal and its approaches were declared "free and open to the vessels of commerce and of war of all nations at peace with Germany on terms of entire equality." Only such charges may be levied as are intended to cover the cost of maintaining or improving the Canal or its approaches; and in respect to charges, etc., the nationals, property, and vessels of all Powers shall be treated on a footing of perfect equality with those of Germany. "In the event of violation of any of the conditions of Arts. 380 to 386, or of disputes as to the interpretation of these Articles, any interested Power can appeal to the jurisdiction instituted for the purpose by the League of Nations."

In the case of the *Wimbledom*, a British steamer laden with munitions for Poland, the Permanent Court of International Justice decided on Aug. 17, 1923, that the action of the German Government in excluding this vessel from the Kiel Canal was a violation of the obligations assumed by Germany in the Treaty of Versailles. The Court held that the Canal had ceased to be an inland waterway and damages were awarded. See *Collection of Judgments* (Ser. A), No. 1; and Hudson, *Court of Int. Justice* (1925), 59–64 and index.

The Corinth Canal is of secondary importance. It connects the Gulf of Corinth with the Aegean Sea, and, though open to the use of all nations, is regarded as entirely under Greek control as lying wholly within Greek territory. Yet it is difficult to see why the principles governing international straits should not be applicable to this Canal as well.

[35] Cf. Art. 1 of the Convention of Constantinople (1888) and Art. 3 § 1 of the Hay-Pauncefote Treaty of 1901. The latter significantly omits the phrase, "in time of war as in time of peace" contained in the former. It would seem from this that the United States reserves to itself the right to close the Panama Canal during a war, if necessary. Of course such a power will never be exercised except for purposes of self-protection. It is not likely that foreign warships, except those of an enemy, will ever be excluded from the innocent use of the Canal. Sect. 3 of Art. 3 contemplates the transit of the Canal by warships of a belligerent.

natural straits—nor shall any act of war or hostility be committed within either.[36]

" Vessels of war of a belligerent shall not revictual nor take on stores in the Canal except so far as may be strictly necessary; and the transit of such vessels through the Canal shall be effected with the least possible delay in accordance with the regulations in force, and with only such intermission as may result from the necessities of the service. Prizes shall be in all respects subject to the same rules as vessels of war of belligerents.

" No belligerent shall embark or disembark troops, munition of war, or warlike material in the Canal except in case of accidental hindrance of the transit, and in such case the transit shall be resumed with all possible dispatch.

" The provisions of this article shall apply to waters

[36] This, of course, includes the marine league. The Treaty of Constantinople (Art. 11) also forbids the "erection of permanent fortifications." "The United States, however, shall be at liberty to maintain such military police along the Canal as may be necessary to protect it against lawlessness and disorder." Art. 3, § 2, of the Hay-Pauncefote Treaty. For the texts of these treaties, see Supp. to 3 A. J. (1909), 123 ff. and 127 ff.

The first draft of the Hay-Pauncefote Treaty (which was rejected by the Senate), as also the treaty as amended by the Senate (which was rejected by Great Britain), contained a clause declaring that "no fortifications shall be erected commanding the Canal or the waters adjacent." This clause, which had also formed part of the Clayton-Bulwer Treaty of 1850 (now superseded), was omitted in the second Hay-Pauncefote Treaty at the suggestion of Great Britain, on the ground that it was not in harmony with the clause cited above, and might give rise to grave misunderstanding.

This omission appears to leave the question open, but there can be little doubt that the United States possesses the right to fortify the entrances to the Panama Canal. Surely this would be the case if it were a natural strait. Any limitation of this right must rest upon convention. That clause of the Clayton-Bulwer Treaty prohibiting fortification is certainly not in force. Art. 2 of the Hay-Pauncefote Treaty distinctly states that the Government of the United States "shall have and enjoy all the rights incident to such construction [of the Canal], as well as the exclusive right of providing for the regulation and management of the Canal." Art. 23 of the Treaty of 1903 with Panama expressly grants the right of fortification to the United States.

For an able argument against the fortification of the Panama Canal, see Hains, in 3 A. J. (1909), 354–94. For a reply, see General Davis, in Ibid., 885–908. See also Knapp, in 4 A. J. (1910) 314–58; Olney, Wambaugh, and Kennedy in 5 A. J. (1911), 298 ff., 615 ff., and 620 ff.; and Jones, Caribbean Interests of the U. S. (1916), ch. 12. For the treaties and documents bearing on this interesting subject, see Supp. to 3 A. J. (1909), 106 ff., especially 123–39.

adjacent to the Canal, within three marine miles of either end. . . .

"The plant, establishments, buildings, and all work necessary to the construction, maintenance, and operation of the Canal, shall be deemed to be part thereof, for the purpose of this treaty, and in time of war, as in time of peace, shall enjoy complete immunity from attack or injury by belligerents, and from acts calculated to impair their usefulness as part of the Canal." [37]

It may be observed that these provisions are intended to secure the neutrality and open use of these great inter-oceanic canals. This neutrality is not effectively guaranteed; and they cannot be said to be fully *neutralized*,[38] inasmuch as the transit of friendly belligerent warships is permitted. The so-called neutralization of the Suez Canal is strengthened by an agreement of the leading Powers of Europe; [39] that of Panama by a treaty between the United

[37] Art. 3, §§ 3–6 of the Hay-Pauncefote Treaty. Except for a part of the last paragraph, these sections are substantially identical with Arts. 2–6 of the Treaty of Constantinople.

[38] To use a happy term of Lord Cromer's, they are *internationalized* rather than completely *neutralized*. Lord Cromer (2 *Modern Egypt*, 1908, 384) cites Lord Pauncefote as saying that the word "neutralization" as applied to the Suez Canal "had reference only to the neutrality which attaches by International Law to the territorial waters of a neutral State, in which a right of innocent passage for belligerent vessels exists, but no right to commit an act of hostility." Perhaps it would be best to say that these Canals are internationalized and partly neutralized.

[39] Art. 10 of the Treaty of Constantinople recognizes the right of the Sultan of Turkey and the Khedive of Egypt to take such measures as they "might find it necessary to take for securing by their own forces the defense of Egypt and the maintenance of public order." Such measures had indeed been taken by England in 1882 when she crushed the revolt under Arabi Pasha— an insurrection which resulted in her "temporary" occupation of Egypt. At a Paris Conference in 1885 the British delegates formulated a general reservation as to the application of the provisions proposed in so far as they "might fetter the liberty of their Government during the occupation of Egypt by the forces of Her Brittanic Majesty." In 1887 this reservation was renewed by Lord Salisbury. In 1898 Lord Curzon declared in the British House of Lords that, owing to these reserves, the Convention of Constantinople had not been brought into practical operation." By Art. 6 of the Anglo-French Declaration of April 8, 1904, respecting Egypt and Morocco, Her Majesty's Government declared that they "adhere to the stipulations of the Treaty of the 29th October 1888, and that they agree to their being put in force." 1 Westlake, 345–46. Westlake adds, however; "But whether with or without an express reservation, it must be considered that, in future as in 1882, rules having the freedom of the Suez Canal for their object cannot

States and Great Britain. But the main provisions of these conventions may also be said to constitute rules or principles of the Law of Nations which would operate even in the absence of such agreements. It can at least be said that canals which constitute international highways are free and open to the warships as well as the merchant vessels of all nations in time of peace on terms of entire equality. There should be no discrimination in conditions or charges of traffic and these must be just and equitable.[40] The same rights or privileges probably extend to warships for purposes of innocent (*i.e.* inoffensive) passage even in time of war.

BIBLIOGRAPHY

Marginal Sea, Bays or Gulfs, Lakes or Seas, and Straits.—* Barclay, in 27 *I. L. A* (1912), 81 ff., and in 12 and 13 *Annuaire*, 104 ff. and 125 ff.; Bluntschli, Arts. 302–10; Bonfils, Nos. 491–511, 516–19; Bower, in 7 (3d ser.) *J. C. L.* (1925), 137 ff.; Bry, *Précis élémentaire de droit int. public* (1906), Nos. 130–37, 139–41; Brown, in 17 *A. J.* (1923), 89–95, and in *Proc. Am. Soc. I. L.* (1923), 15–31; * Bynkershoek, *De Dominio Maris* (1702), cap. 2, and *Questiones juris publici* (1737), I, 1, c. 8; 1 Calvo, §§ 353–75; Caratheodory, in 2 Holtzendorff's *Handbuch*, 378–85; * Charteris, in 23 and 27 *I. L. A.* (1908 and 1912),

be interpreted as hindering the protection of that freedom by the Power best able to give it, in good faith and with no avoidable disturbance of commerce."

The control of the Suez Canal by Great Britain rests partly upon her occupation of Egypt and partly upon her ownership of nearly half of the shares in the Suez Canal Co.; that of the United States over the Panama Canal upon the construction and ownership of the Canal, and upon the "grant in perpetuity" by the Republic of Panama of "the use, occupation, and control of a zone of land, and land under water" of the width of ten miles in the Isthmus of Panama. Art. 2 of Treaty of 1903. See Supp. to 3 *A. J.* (1909), 130.

[40] Cf. Arts. 1 and 3 (1) of the Treaty of Constantinople and of the Hay-Pauncefote Treaty.

In 1912 Congress passed an Act exempting our coastwise trade from tolls on the Panama Canal. Great Britain protested on the ground that this exemption was a violation of the Hay-Pauncefote Treaty. After considerable controversy, President Wilson (in 1914) finally secured the repeal of the Panama Canal Act.

The main question involved was whether the words "all nations" (who were assured the free and open use of the Canal on terms of entire equality) were susceptible of being interpreted "all nations except the United States."

For legal arguments on both sides of this question, see especially *Proc. Am. Soc. I. L.* (1913), *passim*. The arguments are briefly summarized by Jones, *Caribbean Interests of U. S.* (1916), ch. 11. For references, see *Ibid.*, 362–66.

103 ff. and 107 ff. respectively: 1 Cobbett, 136–54; Colombos, in 9 *Grot. Soc.* (1924), 89 ff.; Conboy, in 2 *Canad. Bar Rev.* (1924), 8–23; Creasy, *First Platform of Int. Law* (1876), Nos. 240–46; * Crocker, *The Marginal Sea* (extracts from leading authorities, conventions, etc., 1919); Despagnet, Nos. 412–27; Dickinson, in 11 *Harv. Law Rev.* (1926), 1–29; * Evans, *Cases*, 148–57; * 1 (2 Pt.), Fauchille Nos. 490–511, 516–19; Fenwick, 250–60, 268–73; 2 Fiore, Nos. 146–54, 801–15, and *Int. Law Cod.* (1918), Arts. 993–1005; * Fulton, *Sovereignty of the Sea* (1911), sec. II, pp. 537 ff.; Godey, *La mer côtierè* (1896); Grotius, lib. II, cap. 3, § 13; Guerra on "Straits," in 31 *R. D. I. P.* (1924), 232–54; Hall, §§ 41–42; 1 Halleck (3d ed.), 157–70; 1 Hautefeuille, *Droits et devoirs des neutres* (1868), 51–68; Heffter, §§ 75–77; Heilborn, *System des Völkerrechts* (1896), 37–58; * 1 Hyde, §§ 141–50; Latour, *La mer territororiale* (1889), 20–65; Lawrence, §§ 72, 87–89; Liszt, § 16; J. de Louter, § 21; 1 F. de Martens, §§ 98–100; 2 Mérignhac, 370–98, 587–97; * 1 Moore, *Digest*, §§ 133–53; Nielson, in *Procs. Am. Soc. I. L.* (1923), 32–39; * 1 Nys, 437–74, 497–522; * 1 Oppenheim, §§ 179–81, 185–97; 1 Ortolan, *Diplomatie de la mer* (1864), 139–62; Paulus in 5 (3d ser.) *R. D. I.* (1924), 397–424; Perels, § 5; 1 Phillimore, §§ 180–206; 1 Piédelièvre, Nos. 386–418; Pomeroy, §§ 139–57; 2 P.-Fodéré, Nos. 617–57, 661–81; Raested, "La mer territoriale," in 19 *R. D. I. P.* (1912), 598 ff., and in 21 *R. D. I. P.* (1914), 401 ff.; * 1 Rivier, 143–59, 230; "Report of Neutrality Committee," in 33 *I. L. A.* (1924), 259–335; Salmond, in 34 *Law Quar. Rev.* (1918), 235–52; * Scott, *Cases*, 217–51; Schücking, *Das Küstenmer* (1897); Snow, *Cases on Int. Law* (1893), 41–71; * Stoerk, in 2 Holtzendorff's *Handbuch*, 409–53; Taylor, §§ 229–31, 247–50; 1 Twiss, §§ 181–84, 187–92; Ullmann, §§ 87–88, pp. 290 ff.; Vattel, liv. I, chs. 22–23, §§ 274–78, 287–95; Du Vigneaux, *Le droit de l'état sur la mer territoriale;* Walker, *Manual of Public Int. Law* (1895), §§ 17–18, and *Science of Int. Law* (1893), 171 ff.; * 1 Westlake, 175–78, 187–201; 1 Wharton, *Digest*, §§ 27–29, 32; Wheaton, §§ 177–91 and Dana's notes 105, 108, 112 (see also Atlay's notes); Wilson, §§ 35–38, 40, and in *Int. Law. Topics* (1913), 11 ff.; and Woolsey, §§ 56–61.

For additional references, see 1 (2 pt.) Fauchille, pp. 126 ff., *passim*; Crocker, *Marginal Sea* (1919); and 8 *North Atlantic Coast Fisheries Arbitration* (Washington, 1912–13), 202 ff.

Free Navigation of Rivers.—Bluntschli, Nos. 311–15; Bonfils, Nos. 520–31; Bousek, in 7 *Z. V.* (1913), 39 ff.; Bry, *Précis élémentaire de droit int.* (1906), Nos. 143–57; 1 Calvo, §§ 302–40; * Caratheodory, in 2 Holtzendorff's *Handbuch*, 279–377; * Chamberlain, *The Régime of Int. Rivers: Danube and Rhine* in 105 Columbia University *Studies* (1923); 1 Cobbett, 119–27; Despagnet, Nos. 428–30; * Engelhardt, in 16 *R. D. I.* (1884), 360 ff., *Du Régime conventionnel des fleuves int.* (1879), and *Histoire du droit fluvial conventionnel* (1889); Van Eysinga, in 2 *Bibliotheca Visseriana*, 123–57; * 1 (2 Pt.) Fauchille, Nos. 520–31; Fenwick, 263–68; 2 Fiore, Nos. 755–97, and *Int. Law Cod.* (1918), Arts. 288–90, 961–87; Grotius, lib. II, cap. 2, §§ 11–

15; Hall, § 39; 1 Halleck (3d ed.), 171–79; Heffter, § 77; Huber in 1 Z. V. (1907), 29 ff. and 159 ff.; * 1 Hyde, §§ 159–84; * Kaecken-beeck, *Int. Rivers* (1918); Lawrence, § 92; Liszt, § 38; J. de Louter, § 23; 1 and 2 F. de Martens, §§ 101, 157; 2 Mérignhac, 605–32; * 1 Moore, *Digest*, §§ 130–31; 1 and 2 Nys, 423–37 and 109–31; 1 Oppenheim, §§ 176–78; Oglive, *Int. Waterways* (1920); Orban, *Droit fluvial int.* (1896); * 1 Phillimore, §§ 155–71; Pomeroy, §§ 129–38; 2 P.-Fodéré, Nos. 682–757; 1 Piédelièvre, Nos. 376–84; * 1 Rivier, 142, 221–29; Schulthess, *Das int. Wasserrecht* (1915); * Schuyler, *Am. Diplomacy* (1886), 265–366; Scott, *Resolutions of the Institute of Int. Law* (1916), 78–83 and 168–70 (for rules adopted by the Institute of International Law in 1887 and 1911); Snow, *Cases* (1893), 32–41; Taylor, §§ 233–41; 1 Twiss, § 145; * Ullmann, § 105; Vallotton, in 45 (2d series 15) *R. D. I.* (1913), 271 ff.; Vattel, liv. II, §§ 123–34; Walker, *Manual of Public Int. Law* (1895), § 16; * 1 Westlake, ch. 7, pp. 145 ff.; 1 Wharton, *Digest*, § 30; * Wheaton, §§ 192–205, and *History*, 498–517; Wilson, § 39; Woolsey, § 62.

For further references or bibliographies, see Chamberlain, Fauchille, Kaechenbeeck, and Orban, *op. cit.*

Interoceanic Canals.—* Arias, *The Panama Canal* (1911); Asser, in 20 *R. D. I.* (1888), 529 ff.; 1 Bishop, *Roosevelt* (1920), chs. 24–25; Bonfils, Nos. 511–15; Bustamante, 27 in *R. D. I.* (1895) , 112 ff.; 1 Calvo, §§ 376–80, and 6 *Ibid.*, §§ 14 ff.; * Caratheodory, in 2 Holtzendorff's *Handbuch*, 386–406; Cromer, 2 *Modern Egypt* (1908), ch. 47, pp. 382–87; Davis, in 3 *A. J.* (1909), 885–908; Van Eysinga, in 2 *Bibliotheca Visseriana*, 123–57; Fauchille, *Blocus maritime* (1882), 184 ff.; *1 (2 Pt.) Fauchille, Nos. 511–15; Fenwick, 273–78; Fiore, *Int. Law Cod.* (1918), Arts. 988–92; Freycinet, *La question d'Egypt* (1905), ch. 2, 99–204; Haines, in 3 *A. J.* (1909), 354–94; Hall, § 39a; * Henderson, in *Am. Diplomatic Questions* (1901), 65–201; Holland, *Studies in Int. Law* (1898), 27–29; * 1 Hyde, §§ 197–98; Johnson, *Four Centuries of the Panama Canal* (1906); Keasbey, *The Nicaragua Canal and the Monroe Doctrine* (1896), *passim;* Latané, *The Diplomatic Relations of the United States and Spanish America* (1900), ch. 4, and *United States and Latin America* (1920), ch. 4; Latour, *Le mer territoriale* (1889); 66–118; Laun, *Die Internationalisierung der Meerengen and Kanäle* (1918); Lawrence, §§ 90, 227, and *Essays on Int. Law* (1885), 41–162; Liszt, § 37; 2 F. de Martens, § 59; 2 Mérignhac, 597–605; * 2 and 3 Moore, §§ 178, 336–71; Munroe, in 17 *Annals* (1901), 13–34; * 1 Nys, sec. III, ch. 6; * 1 Oppenheim, §§ 182–84, and *Panama Canal Conflict* (1913); Pensa, *La republique et le canal de Panama* (1906); 1 Phillimore, §§ 99a and 207 ff.; 2 P.-Fodéré, Nos. 658–60; 1 Rivier, 231–33; Root, *Addresses* (1916), 207 ff.; Roosevelt, in *Pacific Ocean in History* (ed. Stephens and Bolton, 1917), 137–50, and *Autobiography* (1916), 526–43; Twiss, in 7 *R. D. I.* (1875), 682 ff., in 14 *R. D. I.* (1882), 572 ff., and in 17 *R. D. I.* (1885), 615 ff.; Ullmann, § 106; * Viallate, in 10 *R. D. I. P.* (1903), 5 ff., in 11 *R. D. I. P.* (1904), 481 ff., and *Essais d'histoire diplomatique* *américaine* (1905), 57–206; * 1 Westlake, ch. 15; 2 and 3 Wharton, *Digest*, §§ 150 f. and 287 ff.; White, *Expansion of Egypt* (1899), 315 ff.; Wilson, § 40; Woolsey, in 1 *Report Am. Histor. Assoc.* (1902), 307–11.

For further references, see 1 (2 Pt.) Fauchille, pp. 294 ff., 340 f. For Bibliography of 160 pages on "Interoceanic Canals and Railway Routes," see *List of Books and of Articles* by the Library of Congress (1909), 95–121. See also bibliographies in Arias, *op. cit.*, and (for the Suez Canal) Anderson and Hershey, 107–08.

On the Panama Canal, consult the Index volume to *A. J.* (1920). See particularly the *Proc. Am. Soc. I. L.* (1913) for numerous addresses on various stages of the Panama Canal controversy.

CHAPTER XV

THE OPEN SEA

I. THE FREEDOM OF THE OPEN SEA

202. History of the Freedom of the Open Sea.—During Antiquity and the early Middle Ages, the open sea was theoretically free and common to the use of all mankind,[1] though by no means free from depredation by pirates even under the rule of the Roman Empire. But owing to the universal prevalence of piracy and the revival of commerce during the Later Middle Ages, the leading maritime States of Europe claimed territorial jurisdiction over adjacent seas. Thus Venice and Genoa respectively laid claim to the Adriatic and the Ligurian Seas, Portugal regarded herself as sovereign over the whole of the Indian and the southern portion of the Atlantic Ocean, and Spain preferred the modest claim of sovereignty over the Pacific Ocean and the Gulf of Mexico. Sweden and Denmark were apparently satisfied with the Baltic and the Arctic regions, but England claimed the Narrow Seas, the North Sea, and the Atlantic from Cape Finisterre in Spain to Stadland in Norway.

These enormous pretentions led to a great controversy [2]

---

[1] This was at least the view of the Roman jurists, who are supposed to have derived the doctrine from the Rhodian Laws of the Sea. For a learned article on "Justinian and the Freedom of the Sea," see Henn, in 19 *A. J.* (1925), 716–27.

[2] Thus Gentilis defended the Spanish and English claims in a work entitled *Hispanicae Advocationis* (1613). In the same year William Welwood defended the English claims in a work entitled *De dominio maris*. In 1633 Sir John Burroughs wrote his *Sovereignty of the British Seas*. In 1676 Sarpi published a book in defense of the claims of Venice to the Adriatic. The work of Grotius written in behalf of Holland was directed against the exorbitant claims of Portugal. Selden's work (published in 1635), was an official defense of the claims of England to the British Seas. 1 Oppenheim, § 250. See Fulton, *Sovereignty of the Sea* (1911), ch. 9; Nys, *Les origines*, 379–87, and 2 *Études*, 260–72; and Potter, *Freedom of the Seas* (1924), ch. 4, for additional information regarding this great controversy.

Very interesting is the reply of Queen Elizabeth to the Spanish envoy Mendoza who complained (in 1580) of the intrusion of English vessels in East Indian waters. The great queen refused to admit any right of Spain

on the freedom of the sea to which the most notable contributions were the *Mare liberum* by Hugo Grotius, in 1609, and the *Mare clausum* by John Selden, written in 1618 but not published before 1635. The main contention of Grotius was that the sea is by nature incapable of appropriation or occupation. This was denied by Selden, who claimed that portions of the sea had actually been appropriated, especially by England.

The final victory for the freedom of the open sea may be said to have been won [3] by 1824, when Great Britain [4] joined with the United States in protesting against the claim of Russia to the exclusive use of the waters of the Bering Sea within 100 Italian miles of the Alaskan and Siberian coasts, or islands belonging to Russia.[5]

to debar her subjects from trade, or from "freely navigating that vast ocean, seeing the use of the sea and air is common to all; neither can a title to the ocean belong to any people or private persons, forasmuch as neither nature nor public use and custom permitteth any possession thereof." Cited by Hall (Higgins, 8th ed.), 181.

[3] Special mention should be made of the important book by Bynkershoek, *De dominio maris*, published in 1702.

[4] In the early part of the nineteenth century, Great Britain had silently dropped her claim that foreign vessels should "strike their topsail and take in their flag, in acknowledgment of His Majesty's sovereignty within His Majesty's seas" (which were supposed to extend to Cape Finisterre). Cited by Hall, p. 185; and 1 Oppenheim, § 249.

[5] This claim, abandoned by Russia in 1824, was afterward (1886–1893) partly revived by the United States in respect to the seal fisheries; but it is a mistake to assert, as has frequently been done, that the United States Government based its claim mainly on the right of *mare clausum*.

True, this was the view taken by Judge Dawson of the District Court of Alaska (the *Onward*), and Chief Justice Fuller assumed (in the *Sayward* case) that the seizures were made on the ground of *mare clausum;* but Mr. Phelps (our minister at London) admitted that this so-called right was not applicable to the case, and Secretary Blaine, referring to the *mare clausum*, declared: "The Government has never claimed it and never desired it. It expressly disavows it." 1 Moore, *Digest*, p. 903. His main argument was that the Canadian vessels which had been seized and confiscated were engaged in a pursuit that was in itself *contra bonos mores*, though in one of his notes to Lord Salisbury, he also asserted for the United States a claim to jurisdiction derived from Russia north of the 60th parallel of north latitude.

The main argument of the United States was, however, that of property in the seals and consequent right of protection on the high seas. This claim was based on the well-known fact that the seals habitually resort, for breeding purposes, to the Pribyloff Islands belonging to the United States, from whence they go out on the high seas in search of food, and to which they regularly return during successive years.

The Court of Arbitration, to which all questions relating to the controversy

203. The Freedom of the Open Sea.—It may, therefore, now be regarded as a universally accepted rule of International Law that the open sea [6] is free for the common use of all nations, at least in times of peace. Being practically insusceptible of effective occupation, it cannot be appropriated by any sovereignty or subjected to any jurisdiction; being indispensable for free intercourse, more particularly as an international highway, it is free and common to all. It is not so much *res nullius* as *res communis omnium*.

The freedom of the open sea has three main practical consequences:

were referred, decided (in 1893) in favor of Great Britain on all points; but for the better safeguarding of the seals, it drew up a series of rules which unfortunately remained largely ineffective, owing mainly to the failure of Japan to agree to these regulations.

However, in July, 1911, the four Powers directly concerned finally "agreed on the suspension of pelagic sealing for fifteen years. Here we have the beginning of an 'International Game Law,' which is undoubtedly the solution of the difficulty." Lawrence, § 86, p. 181 of 7th ed. For editorial comment, see 5 *A. J.* (1911), 1025 ff. For the text of the convention, see Supp. to 5 *A. J.* (1911), 267 ff.

On the *Bering Sea Controversy*, see Barclay, in 25 *R. D. I.*, 417 ff.; 1 Cobbett, 127–35; * 1 (2 Pt.) Fauchille, No. 505 (see pp. 245–46 for references); Geffcken, in 22 *R. D. I.*, 230 ff., and 53 *Fortn. Rev.* (1890), 741 ff.; Engelhardt, in 26 *R. D. I.*, 388, and in 5 *R. D. I. P.* (1899), 193 and 347 ff.; * Henderson, in *Am. Diplomatic Questions* (1901), 3–62; 1 Hyde, note on pp. 260–61; Knott, in 27 *Am. Law Rev.* (1893), 684 ff.; Lawrence, § 86; * 1 Moore, *Digest*, § 172; F. de Martens and Renault, in 1 *R. D. I. P.* (1894), 32 ff. and 44 ff.; Scott, *Cases*, 248–51 (for the Award of the Tribunal of Arbitration); * Snow, *Cases on Int. Law* (1893), 521–28, and *Am. Diplomacy* (1893), 471–509; Walker, *Science of Int. Law* (1893), 175–204. For a complete account of the Bering Sea Controversy, see the *Proceedings of the Fur Seal Tribunal Arbitration* at Paris (1895) in 15 vols.

For good brief accounts of the *History of the Freedom of the Open Sea* in international theory and practice, see Bonfils, Nos. 573–76; 1 (2 Pt.) Fauchille, No. 483[8]; * Hall, § 40; 2 Nys, 135–39; and 1 Oppenheim, §§ 248–51. For fuller accounts, consult Brown, *Freedom of the Seas* (1919); Fulton, *Sovereignty of the Sea* (1911); and Potter, *Freedom of Seas* (1924), *passim*.

For some very extreme but interesting views as to what is involved in the modern "German Conception of the Freedom of the Sea," see an article by the writer, in 13 *A. J.* (1919), 207 ff.

[6] The open sea (or "high seas") has been well defined as "the ocean, and all connecting arms and bays or other extensions thereof, not within the territorial limits of any nation whatever." Field, *Outlines of an Int. Code* (1876), Art. 53. It includes such bodies of partially land-locked water as the Black Sea and the Sea of Marmora, which are connected with the open sea by navigable straits open to international navigation; but it does not include the Sea of Azov which, though connected with the Black Sea by a navigable strait, is considered Russian territory. 1 Oppenheim, § 252.

204. (1) **The Right of Free Navigation. Collisions.**—
The right of free navigation has certain necessary restrictions. For example, to prevent collisions, certain regulations respecting signs, signals, etc., are prescribed and observed.[7] But these derive their origin and sanction from municipal rather than International Law.

205. (2) **Free Fishing on the High Seas.**—Freedom of fishing on the high seas—a right which can only be limited through an international servitude [8] or by treaty. Thus, the fisheries on the North Sea are regulated by the Hague Convention of 1882,[9] and the Tribunal which arbitrated the Bering Sea Controversy adopted a series of regulations

[7] Such regulations are found in the laws of most countries, *e.g.* the British Merchant Shipping Act of 1873 and 1894, the French Regulations of 1897, and the Regulations decreed by the Belgian King in 1880 which have been adopted by various maritime States. For the French text of these rules, see Perels, 373–80.

The Institute of International Law adopted a "Project for a Uniform Law of Maritime Collisions" in 1888. Scott, *Resolutions of the Institute of Int. Law* (1916), 83–86. The first rule is that if a collision has been caused by a fault, damages fall upon the ship on board of which the fault has been committed. In 1889 a Conference of leading maritime States met at Washington to consider this subject. Its discussions and regulations have had a great influence upon subsequent legislation.

At the Brussels Conference of 1909–10, which was attended by most of the maritime States of Europe and America (including the United States), two conventions were signed on Sept. 23, 1910—one for the "unification of certain rules of law with respect to collisions between vessels," and the other "respecting assistance and salvage at sea." An International Conference also met at London in 1913 to draw up a convention for safety of life at sea. 1 Oppenheim, § 265. But the outbreak of the World War appears to have interfered with the enactment of the legislation necessary to secure all the desired results. For the text of the Convention respecting Collisions, see Supp. to 4 *A. J.* (1910), 121–25. For editorial comment, see 4, 5 and 6 *A. J.* (1910–1912), 412 ff., 192 f. and 488 ff. respectively.

On *Collisions*, see especially: Bonfils, Nos. 578–80; Bry, *Précis élémentaire de droit int.* (1906), No. 180; 1 (2 Pt.) Fauchille, No. 483[17]; 2 Fiore, Nos. 740–42, and *Int. Law Cod.* (1918), Arts. 1031–32; Marsden, *Collisions at Sea* (1923), *passim;* 2 Mérignhac, 523 ff. and 552; 2 Nys (1st ed.), 171–74; * 1 Oppenheim, § 265; Perels, §§ 19–20 and pp. 373 ff.; 5 P.-Fodéré, Nos. 2362–75; and Smith, *Rule of the Road at Sea* (1910), *passim.*

It has been claimed that there is an international legal obligation of assistance in case of collision, shipwreck, etc. There is undoubtedly a strong moral obligation, and some countries, *e.g.* the United States, France, and England, have made it a legal obligation in municipal law.

[8] Thus, until 1904, the French claimed to have an international servitude in the fisheries upon the banks of Newfoundland.

[9] See Bonfils, No. 582; 1 Oppenheim, § 282; and 5 P.-Fodéré, Nos. 2457–58.

which were intended to prevent the extermination of the seals in that region.[10]

206. (3) **Submarine Cables.**—The right of laying and protecting submarine cables. In accordance with a wish expressed by the Institute of International Law in 1879 [11] that the destruction or injuring of submarine cables on the high seas be declared an international delinquency, a Conference at which 26 States (including the United States) were represented met at Paris in 1884 and signed a Convention which placed submarine cables under the collective protection of the Powers. According to the terms of this Convention, the rupture or injury of a submarine cable, whether due to voluntary action or to culpable negligence, is punishable by the laws and courts of the State to which the offending party belongs.[12]

[10] See *supra*, note on p. 323. For the text of these regulations, which unfortunately were not adopted by the other Powers, excepting Italy, see 1 Moore, *Digest*, § 172, pp. 914–16.

On *Fishery Rights on the Open Sea and in Territorial Waters* (with special reference to the North Atlantic Fisheries), see: * 1 Cobbett, 158 ff.; Elliot, *The U. S. and the N. E. Fisheries* (1887); Isham, *The Fishery Question* (1887); * Lawrence (3d ed.), § 111; * 1 Moore, *Digest*, §§ 163 ff. and *Am. Diplomacy* (1905), ch. 4; *U. S.* v. *Great Britain* (1910)—case of *Atlantic Coast Fisheries*, in 4 *A. J.* (1910), 948 ff.

A very curious exception to the rule laid down in the text is the British pearl fishery off Ceylon which extends to a distance of twenty miles from land. This is a "claim to the products of certain submerged portions of land which have been treated from time immemorial by the successive rulers of the island as subjects of property and jurisdiction." Hall, *Foreign Jurisdictions of the British Crown* (1895), 243 n. Westlake (I, 190–91) regards it as "an occupation of the bed of the sea." On the question whether the bed of the sea can be occupied (with special reference to the proposed Anglo-French Channel Tunnel), see Hurst, in *Brit. Yr. Book* (1923–24), 34–43; 1 Oppenheim, § 287c, and 2 Z. V. (1908), 1–16; 1 Piggott, *Nationality* (1907), 25–28; and Robin, in 15 *R. D. I. P.* (1908), 50 ff.

[11] Scott, *Resolutions of the Institute of Int. Law* (1916), 24–25.

[12] Arts. 2, 8, and 12 of the Convention of 1884. Art. 15 is brief, but its importance has been overestimated. It reads: "It is understood that the stipulations of this convention shall in no wise affect the liberty of action of belligerents." This has been interpreted as giving unlimited freedom of action to belligerents in time of war, but it cannot free them from their general neutral obligations. See *infra*, note 13, pp. 621–22.

For the text of this treaty, see 2 Malloy, *Treaties*, 1949. For good summaries, see Bonfils, No. 583; and 1 Oppenheim, § 287.

On *Submarine Cables in Time of Peace*, see: Bonfils, No. 583; Bry, *op. cit.*, No. 184; * 1 (2 Pt.) Fauchille, No. 483[29–34]; 2 Fiore, No. 822; 1 Hyde, § 211; Jouhannaud, *Les câbles sous-marines* (1904); 2 Mérignhac, 532–35; 2 Nys, 170 f.; * 1 Oppenheim, §§ 286–87; Perels, 75 ff.; Poinsard, *Études de*

II. Jurisdiction Over Vessels

207. Nationality of Ships.—The main objects of International Law on the high seas are ships, which are under the jurisdiction and protection of the State whose flag they fly and under the laws of which they are registered. Each State with a maritime flag stipulates the conditions under which vessels may obtain a certificate of registry or other document, such as a passport, sea letter, etc., entitling them to the protection of her flag.[13]

208. Theory of Exterritoriality as applied to Vessels.—All vessels having a right to sail under the maritime or military flag of a State may be said to partake of its nationality and are under its protection and jurisdiction on the high seas. It has often been asserted that ships are floating portions of the State's territory, but this is a pure fiction which, though comparatively harmless, is wholly unnecessary. It might be said that vessels are treated *as though* they were floating parts of the territory of the State under whose flag they rightfully sail, but the jurisdiction to

droit int. conventionnel (1894), 55–60; 5 P.-Fodéré, No. 2548; * Renault, in 12 and 15 *R. D. I.*, 251 ff. and 619 ff.; 1 Rivier, 386–87; Roper, *Die Unterseekabel* (1910); Stoerk, in 2 Holtzendorff, 507 f.; * Wilson, *Submarine Telegraphic Cables* (1901). For additional references, see 1 (2 Pt.) Fauchille, p. 55; and 1 Oppenheim, p. 446.

On *Submarine Cables in Time of War*, see *infra*, p. 622 n.

In 1912 an International Conference on Wireless Telegraphy attended by the representatives of 30 States (including the United States) met at London. They signed the International Radiotelegraphic Convention which superseded two previous Berlin Conventions of 1906. For the text of this Convention, see 3 Malloy, *Treaties*, 3048, or Supp. to 7 *A. J.* (1913), 229 ff. For brief summaries of the Berlin and London Conventions, see 1 Oppenheim, §§ 287 "a" and "b." For references on "Wireless Telegraphy on the Open Sea," see *Ibid.*, p. 448.

[13] Without such flag as evidenced by her papers, a merchant vessel is entitled to no protection whatever. Nor is she entitled to protection if she sails under the flags and registry of more than one State. The other papers or documents usually required are the muster roll, the log book, the manifest of the cargo, bills of lading, and the charter party or contract between the owner and the one chartering the vessel.

In case of a warship, the word of the commander is usually held to be sufficient to establish the nationality of the vessel. In any case, the production of his commission would be conclusive evidence.

For details respecting conditions of nationality, ships, papers, etc., see Hall (3d ed.), Appendices 1 and 2; Holland, *Manual*, Nos. 178–94; * 2 Moore, §§ 321–28; 1 Oppenheim, §§ 261–62; 5 P.-Fodéré, Nos. 2270–94; and Snow, *Int. Law. A Manual* (1898), App. I.

which they are subject may be readily justified on other and better grounds.[14]

209. Jurisdiction over Public Vessels on the Open Sea and in Foreign Ports and Waters.—The jurisdiction of a State over its warships on the open sea is absolute even in time of war, *i.e.* the right of search does not extend to them. This jurisdiction also extends to them in foreign ports and foreign territorial waters, where it is known as immunity from local jurisdiction.[15] Though public vessels have no *right* of entry into foreign ports and waters,[16] freedom of permission to enter is assumed in the absence of an express prohibition. Such privilege of entry constitutes an " implied license," which should be " construed as containing an exemption from the jurisdiction of the sovereign within whose territory she (the vessel) claims the rites of hospitality." [17]

210. Jurisdiction over Private Vessels on the Open Sea. —The jurisdiction of a State over its private vessels on the high seas is less absolute and complete. Such vessels, in

---

[14] Thus, a warship is an organ or direct representative of a State, and a merchantman partakes of the State's nationality. The sovereignty of a State over its vessels is therefore personal rather than territorial.

The great majority of the more modern authorities reject the fiction of exterritoriality, at least as applied to merchantmen. For good criticisms of this theory, see Hall, § 76; (Harcourt), *Letters of Historicus*, 201–12; and Pietri, *Étude sur la fiction d'exterritorialité* (1895), ch. 2, and conclusion.

[15] This immunity also extends to organized land forces or armed troops where these have been given permission to use the territory of a State. These are under the jurisdiction and control of their own commanders. See *infra*, Nos. 451–52.

[16] Except probably where such waters constitute an international passageway. See *supra*, No. 196.

[17] Chief Justice Marshall, in *Exchange* v. *McFaddon* (1812), 7. Cranch, 116, and Evans, *Cases*, 232, 240 or Scott, *Cases*, 300, 308. See also the opinions of Sir Robert Phillimore, in *The Constitution* (1879), L. R. 4 Pro. Div. 39; and of L. J. Brett, in *The Parlement Belge* (1878), Law Rep., 5 Pro. Div., 197. These cases should be studied by every student. They may also be found in Evans, *Cases*, 232–50; Scott, *Cases*, 300–10; and Snow, *Cases*, 103–20. For the *Status of Mail Ships*, see 2 Piggott, *Nationality*, 15 f.

This immunity is not, however, quite absolute. They must "demean themselves in a friendly manner" and observe harbor, port, sanitary, and neutrality regulations. But the remedy against an abuse of hospitality is diplomatic rather than judicial. In no case can judicial process be served on board such a vessel. It should be added that the crew, etc., of a public vessel are subject to local jurisdiction for offenses committed on shore. See 2 Moore, *Digest*, § 256.

time of war, are subject to the rights of visit and search by belligerent warships; but in times of peace they are free from the exercise of these rights, except in case of a strong or well-grounded suspicion of piracy.[18] Other exceptions to complete freedom from interference on the high seas are based upon the right of self-defense as in the case of the *Virginius*,[19] and the probable right of hot pursuit on the high seas for violation of municipal law where the pursuit has begun in territorial waters.[20]

This jurisdiction extends to all goods and persons on board the vessel, whether native or foreign-born. A limited authority for the time being is vested in the captain. No foreign State has a right to interfere with his management or discipline, and he, in turn, is limited to the care and governance of his own vessel. Children born during the voyage, at least according to the law of some countries, partake of the ship's nationality, and crimes committed on board are punishable by the courts of the State to which the vessel belongs.[21]

[18] A limited right of visit and search is granted by treaty in a few cases. The most important of these is for the regulation of the slave trade. See *infra*, No. 216. On the "Prohibition of Visit and Search in Time of Peace," see 2 Moore, *Digest*, § 309.

Even leading English authorities now admit that there was no warrant for the exercise of these rights by Great Britain to secure the impressment of native-born seamen, found on board American vessels in the early part of the 19th century. On the *Impressment of Seamen*, see especially: Adams, *History of the U. S. under Jefferson and Madison* (see index); Foster, *Am. Diplomacy*, 235–38; * 2 Moore, *Digest*, §§ 317–20; 3 Wharton, *Digest*, § 331; Walker, *Science*, 124 ff.; Dana's Wheaton, §§ 108–09 and note 67 on pp. 175 ff.

Several authorities (*e.g.* 3 Phillimore, §§ 323–26, and 5 P.-Fodéré, No. 2543) speak of a right of visit or of approach for verification of flag or inspection of papers; but such a right can hardly be said to exist, except in the possible case of a strong suspicion of piracy. See on this point, *The Marianna Flora*, 11 Wheat. 1, and Evans, *Cases*, 160 or 1109. For the masterly reply of Secretary Webster to the British contention that there is a distinction between the rights of visit and search, see 2 Moore, *Digest*, pp. 935–39.

[19] See *supra*, No. 132, note on pp. 233–34.

[20] See *supra*, No. 194, note on p. 301.

[21] "It is clear that an English ship on the high sea, out of any foreign country, is subject to the laws of England; and persons, whether foreign or English, on board such ship are as much amenable to English law as they would be on English soil." *Regina* v. *Lesley* (1860), Bell's Crown Cases, 220, and Scott, *Cases*, 349. For other leading cases, see Evans, *Cases*, 172 ff.; and Scott, 351 ff.

211. **Jurisdiction over Private Vessels in Foreign Ports and Waters.**—It has also been claimed that immunity from local jurisdiction extends to private vessels in foreign ports and waters. There is, it is true, customary immunity for all offenses which merely affect the crew or internal discipline of the ship or which are of such a character as not to disturb the peace of the port; but this appears to be a usage based on comity or convention [22] rather than a strict rule of International Law. This so-called " French rule " is, however, a very convenient and desirable practice from the standpoint of commercial interests, and deserves the heartiest commendation and support. [23]

212. **Jurisdiction over Cases Arising from Salvage or Collision.**—As a rule admiralty courts will decline to assume

Another interesting and important case is that of *John Anderson*, reported in 1 Moore, *Digest*, pp. 932–35, and 1 Wharton, *Digest*, 123–25.

[22] See especially 2 Piggott, *Nationality*, 17–32, for the English law and discussion of doubtful or controverted points. Exclusive jurisdiction over matters that concern only the internal order or discipline of merchantmen (including disputes as to wages) are frequently conferred upon consuls by consular conventions. For the law and practice of the United States, see 2 Moore, *Digest*, § 206. In *Ellis* v. *Mitchell* (1874) the Supreme Court of Hongkong held that the American consul could not settle a dispute as to seamen's wages in the absence of express authority under treaty. See Scott, *Cases* (ed. of 1902), 234 or Snow, 133.

[23] This rule appears to be of French origin. See *The Newton and the Sally* and the *Jally* or the *Tempest*, Snow, *Cases*, 121–23; 1 Ortolan, 446 ff.; and Wheaton, § 103.

The leading American case is that of *Wildenhus* (1886) (120 U. S. Rep. 1, and Evans, *Cases*, 176) in which the French cases cited above are reviewed. In this case murder between decks of the Belgian steamer *Noordland* moored to a dock in Jersey City was held to be a crime which affected the peace and tranquillity of the port. (There was a convention of the character above described between Belgium and the United States.) Cf. the *L'anemone* (1875, Snow, 124–25) in which the Supreme Court of Mexico held that the murder of a Frenchman by another on board a French merchant vessel in a Mexican port was not necessarily a disturbance of the peace of the port. In *The Tempest* (cited above) murder was held to be such a crime by the Court of Cassation in France.

A most interesting case in which three States had concurrent jurisdiction is that of *Regina* v. *Anderson* (1868), 11 Cox, C. C., 198 and Evans, *Cases*, 172 or Scott, 351. It is that of murder by an American citizen on a British merchant vessel in French waters.

In 1898 the Institute of International Law adopted a "Project of Regulations for Legal Régime of Ships and their Equipages in Foreign Ports." The Institute adopted the French Rule (Art. 29) as an exception to the principle of territorial jurisdiction, which was strictly upheld (Art. 28). See Scott, *Resolutions*, 151.

jurisdiction over disputes concerning mariners' wages in a foreign vessel, but they may decide cases of salvage or collision between foreigners where the questions at issue are *communis juris*.[24]

III. PIRACY

213. **Definition of Piracy.**—Piracy consists of an act or acts of violence adequate in degree and committed with piratical intent on the open sea by a private vessel,[25] without authority from any State or belligerent community.[26]

214. **Marks of Piracy.**—The following marks or characteristics of a piratical act should be emphasized: (1) It must be an overt act of violence adequate in degree.[27] It is usually, though not necessarily, an act of depredation committed with intent to plunder (*animus furandi* or *lucri causa*) and the pirate is nearly always a sea robber. (2) It must be committed on the open sea or at least outside the territorial jurisdiction of any State. Opinions differ [28] as to

---

[24] In the case of the British ship *Reliance* (1848), 1 Abbott's Adm. Rep. 317, the United States Circuit Court for the Southern District of New York declared: "The admiralty courts of the United States will decline jurisdiction of controversies arising between foreign masters and owners unless the voyage has been broken up or the seamen unlawfully discharged." The *Reliance*, having rescued goods from the wreck of another British vessel, had instituted proceedings for salvage. See Scott, *Cases* (ed. of 1902), 230; Snow, *Cases*, 129; or 2 Moore, *Digest*, 294.

In the case of the *Belgenland* (1884), 114 U. S. 355 (see also Evans, 166 or Snow, 189), which grew out of a collision, the Supreme Court of the United States assumed jurisdiction. For references to other cases of this character, see note in Snow, 132, or Scott (ed. of 1902), 233. See especially 2 Moore, *Digest*, § 205. For an International Convention concerning "Assistance at Sea and Salvage," signed at Brussels in 1910, see Supp. to 4 *A. J.* (1910) 126 ff. For editorial comment, see 4–6 *A. J.* (1910–12), 412 ff., 192 f., and 488 ff., respectively.

[25] Or by the mutinous crew or passengers against their own vessel for the purpose of converting it to their own use.

[26] See note to *U. S.* v. *Smith* (1820), 5 Wheaton 153, 160–83, for various definitions of piracy, collected by Judge Story The other leading American cases are *U. S.* v. *Palmer* (1818), 3 Wheaton 610; *U. S.* v. *Klintock* (1820), 5 Wheaton 144; and *U. S.* v. *Pirates* (1820), 5 Wheaton 184. The earlier definitions of piracy are inadequate rather than incorrect.

[27] For instance, robbery, murder, destruction by fire, etc. It would not include such acts as petty larceny or a mere threat.

[28] Hall (§ 81, p. 313), and Lawrence (§ 102, p. 215), agree that piracy may include descent from the sea and depredations upon traders on an unappropriated island; and Hall even maintains that though piracy "cannot take place independently of the sea," "a pirate does not so lose his piratical

whether piracy includes descents from the sea upon the coast for purposes of kidnapping or plunder, but it certainly must be directly connected with the sea.   (3) It must be piratical and non-political in motive and unauthorized by any State or insurgent community.[29]   Consequently, insurgent vessels should not be regarded as pirates unless they commit depredations against neutral commerce.[30]

character by landing within State territory that piratical acts done on shore cease to be piratical." Lawrence, in dissenting from this latter view, justly observes: "Surely the fact that the crime was committed within territorial jurisdiction would make the perpetrators amenable to the law of the State, not to the provisions of an international code." Westlake (I, 182) agrees with Lawrence, whose view on this point is undoubtedly the correct one. Oppenheim (I, § 277) denies that acts of violence committed by descent from the open sea can ever be considered piracy.

[29] The acceptance of commissions from both belligerents is deemed equivalent to a total lack of authority, but acts done in excess of authority are not piracy. However, if an insurgent vessel knowingly continues hostilities after the government she serves has ceased to exist, her acts may be regarded as piratical. For the case of the *Shenandoah*, see Lawrence, 216–17.

[30] The main case cited in contravention of this view is that of the *U. S.* v. *The Ambrose Light* (1885), 25 Fed. 408 or Scott, *Cases*, 544, in which a Federal District Court held that a vessel found on the high seas in the hands of insurgents who had not been recognized as belligerents by any independent nation, is technically piratical. But the judgment in the case of the *Ambrose Light* has called forth much adverse criticism; and on the whole the weight of opinion would seem to be against the position that insurgent vessels not molesting the ships of other nations may be treated as pirates. See a criticism of this case by Mr. Francis Wharton in 3 Wharton, *Digest*, p. 469. See also Snow's note in *Cases on Int. Law* (1893), on p. 204.

Westlake (I, 184) calls attention to the fact that the court made the following statement as to the grounds of its decision: "When a seizure has been made by the navy department under the regulations, and the case is prosecuted before the court by the government itself, claiming *summum jus* —its extreme rights—the court is bound to apply to the case the strict technical rules of International Law." The court also stated that "where insurgents conduct an armed strife for political ends, and avoid any infringement or menace of the rights of foreign nations on the high seas, the modern practice is, in the absence of treaty stipulations or other special ties, to take no notice of the contest."

It should be added that the ship was released on the ground that the Secretary of State had impliedly recognized a state of war by his note of April 24, 1885, to the Columbian Minister—an inference which Secretary Bayard denied. See 2 Moore, *Digest*, p. 1099. On the case of the *Ambrose Light*, see especially 2 Moore, *Digest*, § 332, and 3 Wharton, *Digest*, § 381. See also 1 Hyde, § 233.

The other cases sometimes cited in contravention of the view upheld in the text are those of *The Magellan Pirates* (1853), 1 Spinks Eccl. and Adm. Rep. 81, and Scott, *Cases*, 345; and *The Huascar* (1877), 2 Moore, *Digest*, p. 1086.

215. **Jurisdiction over Pirates.**—" Pirates being the common enemies of all mankind, and all nations having an equal interest in their apprehension and punishment, they may be lawfully captured on the high seas by the armed [?] vessels of any particular State, and brought within its territorial jurisdiction, for trial in its tribunals." [31] It was

In *The Magellan Pirates*, Dr. Lushington held that certain Chilean insurgents, who had seized a British and an American vessel and appropriated treasure found on board one of these vessels, were pirates, but it was not on the ground that they were insurgents. The learned judge said: "It does not follow that rebels and insurgents may not commit piratical acts against subjects of other States, especially if such acts were in no degree connected with the insurrection or rebellion. See 1 Phillimore, § 360, for a fuller report of this case.

The Huascar was a Peruvian monitor whose crew had revolted in 1877 and declared for the insurgent Government. It stopped several British vessels and had taken coal from one of them, and several officers from the other. After an unsuccessful attempt to capture her on the part of a British cruiser, she subsequently surrendered to Peru, who claimed an indemnity from Great Britain. In the controversy which followed, the British Government maintained that the *Huascar* was technically a pirate. On this interesting case, see 1 Calvo, § 504; 1 Cobbett, 299 f.; Hall, § 81, p. 319; 1 Halleck (3d ed.), 447–49 n.; Lawrence, § 102; 2 Moore, *Digest*, p. 1086; 5 P.-Fodéré, No. 2512; Walker, *Manual of Public Int. Law* (1895), 56–59.

In the case of the *Montezuma* (1877), a vessel in the service of the Cuban insurgents which attacked Spanish merchantmen in the Rio de la Plata, the Brazilian Government refused to regard as a pirate a ship which confined its hostile acts to Spanish vessels. See 1 Calvo, § 502, and Snow, *Cases*, 206 ff. See also in support of this view, *The Republic of Bolivia*, 1 K. B. 785, reported in 3 *Z. V.* (1909), 165 ff., 341 ff.

England, France, and Germany took a similar view of their rights and duties when the Spanish Government declared the Spanish squadron at Carthagena, which had fallen into the hands of insurgents, to be piratical. 1 Calvo, §§ 497–500. This was also the view of Secretary Bayard in his correspondence with the Columbian Government. See 2 Moore, *Digest*, p. 1089.

The parent State may, of course, treat rebels or insurgents as pirates by municipal law, but they are not pirates *jure gentium*. The piratical intent is wholly lacking. It is a perversion of the original and essential meaning of piracy to regard them as such. Recognized belligerents should not be treated as pirates even by the parent State, for they have acquired an international status which should be respected.

[31] Wheaton, § 124. This is an admirable statement of the law of piracy. The only modification it appears to need is the omission of the word *armed* before *vessels*. A few German writers (see 1 Oppenheim, p. 439 *n.*, for references) claim that only warships may seize pirates, but this view is probably incorrect. Of course only armed vessels would be apt to venture to attack them.

The text should not be interpreted to mean that pirates can only be tried and punished in the jurisdiction of the State whose vessel has captured them. For, as Wheaton remarks in the next paragraph: "Piracy, under the law of

formerly customary to exercise a summary jurisdiction on the spot, but it would seem that this cannot now be done, unless it is impossible to bring them into the nearest home port for trial. They may be tried by any competent court, and piracy is usually regarded as a capital crime.[32]

It is pretty generally conceded that the warships of all nations [33] have the right of approach for the purpose of verifying the flag in case of suspicious conduct on the part of a vessel on the high seas, and that they may exercise the right of visit and search if there is grave reason for suspicion. But the exercise of this right on insufficient grounds may furnish a good cause for complaint, and even be made the basis of a claim for damages. "With regard to property captured by pirates, it is a rule of the Law of Nations, derived from Roman Law, that it must be presumed never to have been divested from its original owners. On recapture no *postliminum* is necessary, and the property re-vests in the former owner, although salvage may be payable." [34]

IV. THE SLAVE TRADE

216. **The Slave Trade.**—It is a serious reflection upon our civilization that the slave trade was permitted to flourish almost unchecked until the close of the Napoleonic wars. The main credit for having undertaken a crusade against this fearful traffic belongs to England,[35] which secured a

nations, may be tried and punished in the courts of justice of any nation, by whomsoever and wheresoever committed; but piracy created by municipal statute can only be tried by that State within whose territorial jurisdiction, and on board of whose vessels, the offence thus created was committed.''

[32] However, this is not necessarily the case. It should also be said that a State is not obliged to punish piracy. "According to the German Criminal Code, piracy committed by foreigners against foreign vessels cannot be punished by German courts." 1 Oppenheim, p. 439 *n*.

[33] Judge Story, in the *Marianna Flora* (1826), 11 Wheat. 1; Evans, *Cases*, 160; or Scott, *Cases*, 1009.

[34] Cobbett (2d ed), 130. Cf. 1 Oppenheim, § 279.

[35] The English Prize Courts had already refused restitution in two cases of American vessels engaged in the slave trade on the ground that it is a "trade which, being unprotected by the domestic regulations of their legislature and Government, subjects the vessel engaged in it to a sentence of condemnation." The *Amédie* (1810), 1 Aeton 240, and *The Fortuna* (1811), 1 Dodson 81. See Dana's Wheaton, §§ 128–29 and note 86; and 2 Moore, *Digest*, § 310, pp. 914–15.

The British Parliament had abolished the slave trade in 1807.

declaration in favor of the abolition of this " scourge which has so long desolated Africa, degraded Europe, and afflicted humanity " at the Congress of Vienna in 1815, and again at Verona in 1822. The United States joined the crusade in 1820 through an Act of Congress which declared the slave-trade piracy—a doctrine which found its way into a number of laws and treaties, but which had been repudiated by the highest authorities [36] and found no warrant in the Law of Nations.

The great obstacle encountered by England in her efforts to suppress the slave trade was opposition to the exercise of the right of visit and search in time of peace, more particularly on the part of France and the United States. It was not before 1841 that she succeeded in negotiating the so-called Quintuple Treaty with France,[37] Prussia, Austria, and Russia granting a reciprocal right of search of vessels suspected of slave trading and punishing it as piracy. But the French Chamber of Deputies refused to ratify the treaty, and would only consent (in the treaty of 1845) to a right of visit for a verification of the flag and papers. By 1850 England had concluded nearly 50 treaties for the suppression of slave trading.[38] But the United States remained obstinate, and it was only in 1862, after Great Britain had officially renounced all claim to the rights of visit and search,[39] that the United States agreed to a treaty

[36] The leading case is that of *Le Louis* (1817, 2 Dodson 210, and Scott, *Cases,* 338) one of Sir William Scott's (or Lord Stowell's) most famous decisions. *Le Louis* was a French vessel which was captured for slave trading in 1816 after the close of the Napoleonic wars. Lord Stowell denied the right of visit and search in time of peace except for piracy or in pursuance of a treaty (or possibly for purposes of self-defense); and maintained that the slave trade, though unjust and condemned by the law of England, was not legal piracy, nor was it legally a crime by the universal Law of Nations. See especially Wheaton, § 131, and Dana's note 86. This line of reasoning was followed by Chief Justice Marshall, in the case of the *The Antelope* (1825), 10 Wheaton 66 or Scott, 9. See also Wheaton, § 133, and Dana's note 88; and 2 Moore, *Digest,* 917–18.

[37] A very limited right of search had been mutually granted by the treaties of 1831 and 1833 between France and England.

[38] See the lists in 1 Phillimore, § 308, and 1 Halleck (3d ed.), 254–55.

[39] This was in 1858. The renunciation was made by Lord Malmesbury who acted on the advice of the law officers of the Crown. 2 Moore, *Digest,* pp. 943–45. But the United States had (in 1842) agreed to maintain a fleet on the African coast to assist in the suppression of the African slave trade.

granting the mutual rights of detention, search, and seizure of merchantmen suspected of slave trading within 200 miles of the African coast and 30 leagues of the coast of Cuba.[40]

The abolition of slavery in the various States of America and in Cuba finally put an end to the West African slave trade; but there still remained the trade on the East African coast and the overland traffic. The fourteen States (including the United States), which signed the General Act of the Conference of Berlin concerning the Congo (1884–85), obligated themselves " to strive for the suppression of slavery and especially of the negro slave trade " (Art. 6); and Article 9 declared:

" Conformably to the principles of the Law of Nations, as they are recognized by the Signatory Powers, the slave trade being interdicted, and as the operations which by land and sea, furnish slaves to the trade ought to be equally considered as interdicted, the Powers who exercise or shall exercise rights of sovereignty or an influence in the territories forming the conventional basin of the Congo declare that these territories shall not serve either for a market or way of transit for the slaves of any race whatever. Each of these Powers engages itself to employ all the means in its power to put an end to this commerce and to punish those who are occupied in it." [41]

But these provisions were not effective, and the same Powers [42] which had participated in the Conference of Berlin, signed (in 1890) the General Act of the Conference of Brussels called for the purpose of " putting an end to the crimes and devastations engendered by the traffic in African slaves, of efficiently protecting the aboriginal population of Africa, and of securing for that vast continent the benefits of peace and civilization." [43] This convention

[40] "By an additional article of Feb. 17, 1863, this reciprocal right was extended to waters within 30 leagues of the islands of Madagascar, Porto Rico, and Santo Domingo." 2 Moore, *Digest*, p. 947.

[41] Supp. to 3 *A. J.* (1909), 13–14.

[42] With the addition of the King of Belgium in his capacity of "Sovereign of the Independent State of the Congo," the Shah of Persia, and the Sultan of Zanzibar.

[43] See preamble to the General Act of the Brussels Conference as translated in Supp. to 3 *A. J.* (1909), 29 ff. The Act consists of 100 Articles and includes regulations for the suppression of the traffic on land as well as by sea.

conceded a limited right of visit and search [44] of vessels whose tonnage is less than 500 tons within certain maritime zones in the Indian Ocean.

In view of the work of the Brussels Conference and of the numerous treaties providing means for the prevention and punishment of this traffic, Lord Stowell's dictum that the slave trade is not a crime in the eyes of the Law of Nations can hardly be said to be longer tenable. True it is that it is not piracy, and slavery itself is a domestic institution which International Law does not, strictly speaking, condemn as illegal; [45] but slave trading undoubtedly stands condemned at least by the conventional Law of Nations. Indeed, like piracy, it may be said to be an International Crime.

BIBLIOGRAPHY

Freedom of the Open Sea in Time of Peace.—Angell, *The World's Highway* (1915), *passim;* Bluntschli, Arts. 304–08; * Bonfils, Nos. 572–83; Brown, *Freedom of the Seas* (1919), *passim;* Bry, *Précis élémentaire de droit int.* (1906), Nos. 176–84; * Bynkershoek, *De dominio maris* (1702)—Carnegie trans. by Magoffin (1923); 1 Calvo, §§ 343–52; Castel, *Du principe de la liberté des mers* (1900); 2 Cauchy *Le droit maritime int.* (1862), 92–124; Cole, in 4 *Grotius Soc.* (1919), 15–25; Creasy, *First Platform of Int. Law* (1876), Nos. 236–39; Despagnet, No. 410; * 1 (2 Pt.) Fauchille, Nos. 4831–48; Fenwick, ch. 18; 2 Fiore, Nos. 718–44; Fulton, *Sovereignty of the Sea* (1901); * Grotius, *De mare liberum* (1609)—Carnegie trans. by Magoffin (1916), and, *De jure belli ac pacis,* liv. II, cap. 2, § 3; * Hall, § 40; Hautefeuille, *Histoire de droit maritime int.* (1869), 13–25; Hays, in 12 *A. J.* (1918), 283 ff.; Heffter, §§ 73–74; Hershey, on "German Conception of the Freedom of the Seas," in 13 *A. J.* (1919), 207 ff.; Lawrence, §§ 85–86; Liszt, § 36; 1 F. de Martens, §§ 96–98; 2 Mérignhac, 498–505; * Meurer, *The Freedom of the Sea* (1919); * 2 Moore, *Digest,* § 309, and *Am. Diplomacy* (1905), ch. 3; 2 Nys, 132–39, *Les Origines,* 379–87, and 2 *Études,* 260–72; * 1 Oppenheim, §§ 248–59; 1 Ortolan, *Diplomatie de la mer* (1864), 113–38; Perels, § 4; 1 Phillimore, §§ 172–96; Pomeroy, §§ 155–58; * Potter, *Freedom of the Seas* (1924), *passim;* 2 P.-Fodéré, Nos. 871–85; Reeves, in 22 *Am. Histor. Rev.* (1916–17), 535 ff.; * 1 Rivier, 234–39; * Selden,

---

[44] See Arts. 42 to 49 for the rules regulating the right of visit and search.

[45] There are a few Continental authorities like Fauchille (I, No. 398), who maintain that the Law of Nations condemns domestic slavery.

A new Slavery Convention signed by twenty States was approved by the Assembly of the League of Nations at its seventh session at Geneva in Sept., 1926. See *Seventh Year Book L. of N.* (1927), p. 198.

Mare clausum (1635); Stier-Somlo, *Die Freiheit der Meere* (1917); Stoerk, in 2 Holtzendorff, 483 ff.; Taylor, §§ 242–46; 1 Twiss, § 172 ff.; Ullmann, §§ 101–02; * Vattel, liv. I, §§ 279–86; Walker, *Science of Int. Law* (1893), 163–71; 1 Westlake, 164–67; Wheaton, §§ 186–87, and Dana's note 113; Woolsey, § 59.

For references to and citations from German views and publicists, see Hershey, in 13 *A. J.* (1919), 207 ff. For an extensive bibliography, see Potter, *op. cit.*, 253–74. See also 1 (2 Pt.) Fauchille, pp. 11–12.

Nationality of Ships and Jurisdiction over Vessels on the High Seas and in Foreign Ports and Waters.—Bluntschli, Arts. 317–52; * Bonfils, Nos. 584–629; Bry, *op. cit.*, Nos. 193–204; 1 and 3 Calvo, §§ 385–484, 155–1568; * Charteris, in *Brit. Yr. Bk.* (1920–21), 45–96; 1 Cobbett, 261–95; Davis, 70–83; Despagnet, Nos. 431–39; * Evans, *Cases*, 172–86, 231–61; * 1 (2 Pt.) Fauchille, Nos. 596–629; Fedozzi, in 4 *R. D. I. P.* (1897), 202 ff.; Fenwick, ch. 12; 1 and 2 Fiore, Nos. 535–55, 730–42, and *Int. Law Cod.* (1918), Arts. 1006–33, 1198–1205; Gregory, in 2 *Mich. Law Rev.* (1904), No. 5; * Hall, §§ 44–45, 54–59, 76–79, and *Foreign Jurisdictions of the British Crown* (1895), §§ 106–09; 1 Halleck (3d ed.), 215–32, 438; Heffter, §§ 78–90; Heilborn, *System des Völkerrechts* (1896), 211–78; Heyking, *L'exterritorialité* (1889), §§ 44–47; * 1 Hyde, §§ 221–29; Jordan, in 40 (2 ser. 10) *R. D. I.* (1908), 341 ff. and 481 ff.; Latour, *La mer territoriale* (1889), 280–317; * Lawrence, §§ 99–100, 107; 2 Mérignhac, 536–86; * 1 and 2 Moore, *Digest*, §§ 174, 204–08, 321–28; Nielson, in 13 *A. J.* (1919), 1–21; 2 Nys, 140 ff.; * 1 Oppenheim, §§ 260–71; * 1 Ortolan, *Diplomatie de la mer* (1864), 163–206, 228–92; * Perels, §§ 7–15; 1 Piédelièvre, Nos. 622–35; 1 Phillimore, §§ 344–55; 2 Piggott, *Nationality* (1907), *passim;* Pomeroy, §§ 178–87; * 5 P.-Fodéré, Nos. 2275–2470; Pietri, *La fiction d'exterritorialité* (1895), 355–72; 1 Rivier, 150–51, 156, 239–48, 333–35; * Scott, *Cases*, 300–10, 349–60; Snow, *Int. Law. A Manual* (1898), §§ 16–17, 23–26; Stoerk, in 2 Holtzendorff, 428–53, 518–50; Stowell and Munro, §§ 26, 28; Taylor, §§ 253–71; Walker, *Manual of Public Int. Law* (1895), §§ 20, 27; * 1 Westlake, 167–80, 264–72; 1 and 3 Wharton, *Digest*, §§ 33–38, 41, 325–27, 331, 408–10; * Wheaton, §§ 100–09 and * Dana's notes, Nos. 63, 66, 67.

Piracy.—Bernard, *Neutrality of Great Britain* (1870), 118–21; Bluntschli, Arts. 343–40; Bonfils, Nos. 592–94; Bry, *op. cit.*, Nos. 185–88; * 1 Calvo, §§ 485–512; 1 Cobbett, 295 ff.; Despagnet, Nos. 440–42; * Dickinson, in 38 *Harv. Law Rev.* (1925), 334–60; 1 (2 Pt.) Fauchille, Nos. 483[49–58]; 1 Fiore, Nos. 494–95, and *Int. Law Cod.* (1918), Arts. Nos. 300–05; Gareis, in 2 *Holtzendorff*, 571–81; * Hall, §§ 81–82; 1 Halleck, (3d ed.), 444–50; Heffter, § 104; * 1 Hyde, §§ 231–33; * Lawrence, § 102; 2 Mérignhac, 506–11; * 2 Moore, *Digest*, §§ 311–14; * 1 Oppenheim, §§ 272–80; 1 Ortolan, *Diplomatie de la mer* (1864), 207–27; Perels, §§ 16–18; Piédelièvre, Nos. 637–44; 1 Phillimore, Pt. III, ch. 20, §§ 356–61; Pomeroy, §§ 188–92; * 5 P.-Fodéré, Nos. 2490–2512; * 1 Rivier, 248–51; Schuyler, on

"The Piratical Barbary Powers," in *Am. Diplomacy* (1886), 193–232;
* Scott, *Cases*, 337–38, 544–48, 1009; Snow, *Cases on Int. Law* (1893),
195–212, and, *Int. Law. A Manual*, § 27; Stiel, *Der Tatbestand der
Piraterie* (1905); Taylor, §§ 188–89; Ullmann, § 104; * Walker,
Manual of Int. Public Law (1895), § 21; * 1 Westlake, 181–86; 3
Wharton, *Digest*, §§ 380–81; Wheaton (Dana's ed.), §§ 122–24,
and * Dana's notes, 83–84; Woolsey, §§ 144–45.

Slave Trade and the Brussels Conference.—Barclay, in 22 *R. D. I.*
(1890), 316 ff., 454 ff.; Bry, *Précis élémentaire de droit int.* (1906), Nos.
189–92; 5 Calvo, §§ 2997–3003; 1 Cobbett, 302–05; Creasy, *First
Platform of Int. Law* (1876), 262–78; Engelhardt, in 22 *R. D. I.*
(1890), 603 ff.; * 1 Fauchille, Nos. 398–408 (see pp. 761–62 for references); Fenwick, 206–09; Gareis, in 2 *Holtzendorff*, 553–91, and
Die Sklavenhandel und das Völkerrecht (1885); 2 Halleck (3d ed.),
247–56; 1 Hyde, § 230; Lawrence, § 103; Lindley, *Acquisition and
Gov't. of Backward Territory* (1926), ch. 27; Liszt, § 49; 1 F. de Martens,
§ 85; 2 Mérignhac, 512–23; De Montardy, *La Traité et le droit int.*
(1899); 2 Nys, 147–56, and in 22 *R. D. I.* (1890), 57 ff. and 138 ff.;
* 2 Moore, *Digest*, § 310; Moynier, *Les Bureaux int.* (1892), 111–21;
* 1 Phillimore, Pt. III, ch. 17, §§ 296–313; Poinsard, *Études de droit
int.* (1894), 38–47; Pomeroy, § 193; * 5 P.-Fodéré, Nos. 2513–41;
* Queneuil, *La Conférence de Bruxelles et ses resultats* (1907); 1 Rivier,
374–79; Rolin-Jaequemyns, in 23 and 24 *R. D. I.* (1891 and 1892),
560 ff., 206 ff.; * Schuyler, *Am. Diplomacy* (1886), 233 ff.; Scherling,
Die Bekämfung von Sklavenraub (1897); * Scott, *Cases* (*Le Louis*),
338 ff.; Snow, *Question of the Aborigines* (1921), ch. 7; Taylor, § 190;
Ullmann, § 133; * Walker, *Manual of Int. Public Law* (1895), § 21,
pp. 60–65; * Wheaton, §§ 125–33, and * Dana's notes 85–89; Woolsey,
§ 146.

CHAPTER XVI

THE LAW OF THE AËRIAL SPACE IN TIME OF PEACE [1]

217. Criticism of the Principles Formulated by the Institute of International Law.—The inventions of wireless or radiotelegraphy and radiotelephony, but more especially improvements in the aeroplane and dirigible airships, have greatly extended the possibilities of international aërial communication and navigation, and have thus rendered necessary a discussion of the law of the so-called aërial domain in works on International Law.

During its session at Ghent in 1906, the Institute of International Law adopted the following principles: " The air is free. States have over it, in time of peace and in time of war, only the rights necessary for their self-preservation." [2]

These principles, which were based upon the views of Fauchille [3] and accepted by a vote of 14 against 9, have

[1] For the *Law of Aërial Warfare*, see *infra*, ch. 30.

[2] Article I of the Regulations adopted by the Institute for Aërostats and Wireless Telegraphy. Scott, *Resolutions of the Institute of Int. Law* (1916), 164. Cf. Art. 3 of the Rules adopted at Madrid in 1911 which states that "international aërial circulation is free," saving the rights of the subjacent States to take certain measures to insure security. The Madrid Rules also declared that every aircraft must have but one nationality—that of the country in which it has been registered. Otherwise they have little importance. Scott, *op. cit.*, 171.

The following is the text of the remaining articles adopted at Ghent in so far as they relate to the Law of Peace:

Art. 2.—In default of special arrangements, the rules applicable to ordinary telegraphic correspondence are applicable to communication by wireless telegraphy.

Art. 3.—Each State has the power (*faculté*) to the degree necessary for its security, to oppose, above its territory and its territorial waters, and to as great a height as it may find useful, the passage of Hertzian waves, whether these be emitted by apparatus belonging to the State or by private apparatus placed upon the earth, on board a vessel, or in a balloon.

Art. 4.—In case of prohibition of correspondence by wireless telegraphy, the government must at once notify the other governments of the prohibition which it decrees.

[3] For the extremely interesting and suggestive views of M. Fauchille, the late brilliant and versatile editor of the *Revue générale de droit int. public*,

been justly criticised. They are not in agreement with subsequent theory or practice,[4] and do not answer the practical needs either of aërial navigation or of wireless telegraphy, especially in time of war.

218. **The Correct Principles.**—The correct principles were undoubtedly those formulated by Professor Westlake, who proposed the following alternative article at the above-named session of the Institute: " The State has a right of sovereignty over the aërial space above its soil, saving a right of inoffensive passage for balloons or other aërial machines and for communication by wireless telegraphy." [5]

219. **Territorial Sovereignty over the Aërial Space.**— From the standpoint of State or municipal law there can be little, if any, doubt that the aërial space is subject to the territorial sovereignty of the State underneath, at least as far as it can be utilized or controlled. " Justinian tells us that the air, like the high seas, is by natural right common to all. In the sense that all can breathe it in as they have opportunity this is certainly true; but it can hardly be accepted as a proposition of jurisprudence with respect to its use for the support of a vehicle of transportation." [6]

There existed, however, another principle of the Civil Law which declared that the lord of the soil was also lord of the heavens (*dominus soli; dominus cæli*),[7] which, with

see 1 (2 Pt.) Fauchille, No. 531[2-21]; Draft Convention in Supp. to 7 *A. J.* (1913), 148 ff.; *Le domain aërien*, in 8 *R. D. I. P.* (1901), 414–85; *Rapports a l'Institut de droit int.*, in 19 and 21 *Annuaire*, 19–86 and 76–87; *Rapports*, in 23 and 24 *Annuaire*, 297 ff., 23–122, and 303–46; and 17 *R. D. I. P.* (1910), 55 ff.

[4] See especially Art. 1 of the Paris Convention of 1919 Relating to International Air Navigation (for text, see Supp. to 17 *A. J.* 1923), 198; Hazeltine, *The Law of the Air* (1911), Sect. I; Spaight, *Aircraft in Peace* (1919), ch. 1; and Woodhouse, *Textbook of Aërial Laws* (1920), *passim*.

[5] See 21 *Annuaire* (1906), 299. Westlake's article received but three votes at the time of its proposal (1906) to the Institute, but it has since won wide support. There is a difference of opinion among jurists respecting this so-called right of innocent or inoffensive passage.

[6] Baldwin, in 4 *A. J.* (1910), 95. He cites *Inst.* I, 1, de rerum divisione, § 1; and *Digest*, I, 8, de rerum divisione, § 2, 1.

[7] Julliot, *De la Propriété du domaine aërien* (1909), 7. The Roman tradition of ownership in the aërial space was revived in the later Middle Ages and came down to Blackstone through Coke upon Littleton. Blackstone says: "Land hath also, in its legal signification, an indefinite extent upwards as well as downwards. *Cujus est solum ejus est usque ad cælum* is the maxim

certain limitations and modifications, appears to have been incorporated into our common law.[8]

220. Why Control is Necessary.—Control of the aërial space by the territorial power underneath is necessary for various purposes in time of peace as well as in time of war. As far as the use of wireless telegraphy is concerned, it is necessary in order to oppose the passage of Herzian waves to the degree that the security or interests of the State may demand.[9] In respect to aërial navigation, it may be desirable or necessary in order to prevent espionage, to enforce the collection of customs duties, maintain sanitary and quarantine regulations, prevent various crimes, particularly smuggling, and, in general, for purposes of security or defence.

221. The Nature of this Control.—From the standpoint of International Law, it would seem that the State underneath has a right of territorial sovereignty or jurisdiction over the aërial space above, at least as far as it can be utilized or controlled.[10] The aërial space above the ocean

of the law. . . . So that the word 'land' includes not only the face of the earth, but everything under it, or over it," Cooley's *Blackstone* (4th ed.), Bk. II, p. 18. Cf. Coke upon Littleton (Thomas ed., 1836), Bk. II, ch. 1.

According to De Montmorency, this Roman tradition is a mediaeval gloss which first appeared in England in the latter part of the 13th century. See *Brit. Yr. Bk.* (1921–22), 168 and 3 *Grotius Soc.* (1918), 62–66. See also Spaight, *op. cit.*, 54.

[8] It is expressly incorporated into the codes of Germany, France, and Switzerland. For citation and discussion of cases bearing on the rights of the owner of the soil in the United States, see Baldwin and Kuhn, in 4 *A. J.* (1910), 102 ff., and 123 ff. As far as the State is concerned, the theory of ownership has, of course, been abandoned for that of *imperium* or territorial sovereignty. Grünwald appears to stand alone in clinging to the theory of *dominium* or ownership.

For citations from the German, French, and Swiss codes, see 4 *A. J.* (1910), 98 f., 127 f.; Julliot, *op. cit.*, 7 f.; and Meurer, *Luftschiffahtsrecht* (1909), 13 ff. See also Lycklama à Nijeholt, *Air Sovereignty* (1910), 34 ff.

[9] Art. 3 of the Rules of the Institute. See note 2, *supra*.

[10] Some publicists have favored the division of the aërial space, for purposes of jurisdiction, into an upper and a lower zone. Rolland (13 *R. D. I. P.*, 1906, 65) held the atmosphere to be territorial to a distance of 330 meters. Fauchille advocated exclusive control for purposes of self-defense to a distance of 500 meters (17 *R. D. I. P.*, 1910, 60). The zone proposals have been, I think, generally abandoned as impracticable.

A number of the older authorities favored the rule or principle of the cannon shot; but, since modern aëronautic cannon are said to have a vertical range of 5500, 7400, and even 11,500 meters, this would render freedom in

or unoccupied territory is of course free; but this can hardly be claimed in respect to that portion of the atmosphere above the territorial waters (including the marginal seas) or above that part of the land surface of the earth which is inhabited by peoples organized into political communities.

The nature of this control appears to be analogous to that exercised over a State's territorial waters, more particularly the marginal seas, straits, and international rivers. Foreign airships should be granted a right of innocent or inoffensive passage; and, in general, the same rules should be applicable to them in the territorial atmosphere as are applied to foreign vessels in territorial waters. Their nationality will doubtless be determined by their flag or registry; and, though in principle subject to the jurisdiction of the State above whose territory they pass, they will be practically exempt from its criminal jurisdiction except in respect to crimes which affect the interests or disturb the peace of its inhabitants.[11]

221a. **The International Air Convention.**—A "Convention for Regulation of Aërial Navigation" was drawn up by the Peace Conference of 1919 and signed on October 13, 1919 by fifteen Powers.[12] It forms the main legal basis for

the upper zone wholly illusory. Besides, the analogy between the marine league or range of cannon shot as applied to the ocean and aërial space soon breaks down. In the case of the ocean the reasons for control decrease in proportion to the distance from the shore; in the case of aërial space, the danger (as, *e.g.* from the weight of falling bodies) may increase in proportion to the distance from the earth's surface.

[11] This would at least be the case with private airships. Public airships will probably enjoy the rights and privileges of so-called exterritoriality, as in the case of public vessels or warships.

[12] The Signatories included the British Empire, the United States, France, Italy, Japan and a number of minor Powers. The following States deposited their ratifications on June 1, 1922: the British Empire, France, Italy, Japan, Belgium, Bolivia, Greece, Portugal, Jugo-Slavia, and Siam. 3 Malloy, *Treaties*, 3768. The United States signed the Convention with certain reservations, but apparently has not ratified it.

It should be noted that the *American Journal* prints the final and correct text, but omits (with one exception) the interesting Annexes. These may be found in Spaight, *op. cit.*, who, however, does not give the correct text. The Annexes are printed in Malloy, *Treaties*.

For the text of this interesting and important Convention, see Supp. to 17 *A. J.* (1923), 198 ff.; Spaight, *Aircraft in Peace* (1919), App. I, pp. 137 ff.; or 3 Malloy, *Treaties*, 3768.

such conventional rules relating to international aërial navigation as exist in time of peace.

The contracting States recognize that every State has "complete and exclusive sovereignity in the air space above its territory and territorial waters" (Art. 1), but agree "in time of peace to accord freedom of innocent passage" above their territory and territorial waters to the aircraft of the other contracting States who observe the conditions prescribed in the convention (Art. 2).[13] Any State has, however, the right "for military reasons or in the interest of public safety," to map out "prohibited areas," provided such areas are published and notified to the other contracting States (Art. 3).

The nationality of aircraft is determined by rules similar to those existing for seagoing vessels. "An aircraft possesses the nationality of the State on the register of which it is entered" (Art. 6), and "cannot be validly registered in more than one State" (Art. 8).[14]

Aircraft engaged in international navigation shall carry certificates of registration, airworthiness, and of competency; licenses for pilots, navigators, and engineers; a list of passengers, if any; bills of lading and manifests for cargo; log books, etc.[15]

"Every aircraft of a contracting State has the right to cross another State without landing. In this case it shall

[13] It will be observed that the principles proposed by Professor Westlake in 1906 (see *supra*, No. 218) were the ones virtually adopted. The authorities are divided on the question as to whether this "freedom of innocent passage" is a right in International Law or is merely based on convention or comity. In other words, does it exist apart from favor or agreement?

[14] The owner must be a national; or, in the case of a corporation, the president and two-thirds of the board of directors must be nationals (Art. 7).

"No contracting State shall, except by a special and temporary authorization, permit the flight above its territory of an aircraft which does not possess the nationality of a contracting State" (Art. 5). This is an extraordinary provision. As pointed out by Kuhn (14 *A. J.*, 1920, p. 373), it would seem to exclude the aircraft of the United States from the territory of all the contracting States, including Canada. However, Art. 5 appears to have been amended by a subsequent Protocol drawn up at London on October 25, 1922. Spaight, in *Brit. Yr. Bk.* (1924), 184.

[15] Arts. 11–13, 19 and Annexes A–E. The annexes furnish details relating to the marks and numbers an aircraft shall carry, conditions governing the issue of certificates of airworthiness, regulations as to the keeping of log books, rules as to lights and signals, rules of the air, etc. The Annexes may be found in Spaight, *Aircraft in Peace* (1919), 149 ff.

follow the route fixed by the State over which the flight takes place. However, for reasons of general security it will be obliged to land if ordered to do so by means of signals provided in Annex D " (Art. 15).[16]

" The carriage by aircraft of explosives and of arms and munitions of war is forbidden in international navigation."[17]

[16] Art. 15 also provides that "every aircraft which passes from one State into another shall, if the regulations of the latter State require it, land in one of the aerodomes fixed by the latter." Notification of these aerodomes shall be given.

"The establishment of international airways shall be subject to the consent of the States flown over" (Art. 15).

The right of *cabotage* is reserved for the aircraft of the territorial State by Art. 16 which declares that "each contracting State shall have the right to reserve to its national aircraft the carriage of persons and goods for hire between two points on its own territory."

"Upon the departure or landing of an aircraft, the authorities of the country shall have, in all cases, the right to visit the aircraft and to verify all the documents with which it must be provided" (Art. 21).

"Aircraft of the contracting States shall be entitled to the same measure of assistance for landing, particularly in case of distress, as national aircraft" (Art. 22).

"With regard to the salvage of aircraft wrecked at sea the principle of maritime law will apply, in the absence of any agreement to the contrary" (Art. 23).

There are also provisions for equality of charges for the use of aerodomes as between national and foreign aircraft (Art. 24).

Art. 23 of the original draft which was omitted in the final convention contained the following interesting provisions relating to jurisdiction:

"All persons on board an aircraft shall conform to the laws and regulations of the State visited. . . .

"Legal relations between persons on board an aircraft in flight are governed by the law of the nationality of the aircraft.

"In case of crime or misdemeanor committed by one person against another on board an aircraft in flight, the jurisdiction of the State flown over applies only in case the crime or misdemeanor is committed against a national of such State and is followed by a landing during the same journey upon its territory.

"The State flown over has jurisdiction:—(1) With regard to any breach of its laws for the public safety and its military and fiscal laws; (2) In case of a breach of its regulations concerning air navigation."

[17] Art. 26 which adds: "No foreign aircraft shall be permitted to carry such articles between any two points in the same contracting State." Each State may also prohibit or regulate the carriage or use of photographic apparatus (Art. 27).

For provisions relating to *State Aircraft*, see Arts. 30–31.

State Aircraft is divided into two classes: (a) military, *i.e.* those "commanded by a person in military service" and (b) "aircraft exclusively employed in state service such as posts, customs, police."

"All state aircraft other than military, customs, and police aircraft shall

The Convention established an International Commission for Air Navigation as a permanent body placed under the direction of the League of Nations.[18]   Its main duties are to make and receive proposals for amending the convention, to amend the technical annexes, to collect and communicate information of interest to air navigation, to give opinions on questions submitted to it, and to carry out certain specific duties imposed upon it by the convention.[19]

BIBLIOGRAPHY

Law of Aërial Space in Time of Peace.—2 Baker, *Wilson and World Settlement* (1922–23), ch. 46; * Baldwin, in 4 *A. J.* (1910), 49 ff.; Bielenberg, *Die Freiheit des Luftraums* (1911); Blachère, *L'air et le droit* (1911); Catellani, *Le droit aérieu* (1912); * 1 (2 Pt.) Fauchille, Nos. 531[2–17], * in 8 *R. D. I. P.* (1901), 414 ff, in 17 *R. D. I. P.* (1910), 55 ff., in 19 *Annuaire* (1902), 19–86, in 21 *Annuaire* (1906), 76 ff., in 23 *Annuaire* (1910), 297 ff., in 24 *Annuaire* (1911), 23 ff., 303 ff., and in Supp. to 7 *A. J.* (1913), 148 ff.; Fenwick, ch. 17: Fleischmann, *Grundgedanken eines Luftrechts* (1910); Garner, *Recent Developments in Int. Law* (1925), 141 ff.; Grahame, White and Harper, *Air Power* (1917), 197 ff.; Grünwald, *Das Luftschiff* (1908); Hall,

be treated as private aircraft and as such shall be subject to all the provisions of the present convention."

"No military aircraft of a contracting State shall fly over the territory of another contracting State nor land thereon without special authorization. In case of such authorization the military aircraft shall enjoy, in principle, in the absence of special stipulation the privileges which are customarily accorded to foreign ships of war."   But a military aircraft which is forced, requested, or summoned to land shall have no right to these privileges.   Special arrangements between the States concerned will determine in what cases police and customs aircraft may be authorized to cross the frontier.   In no case shall these be entitled to the privileges referred to above.

[18] This Commission was to have consisted of two representatives of the United States, France, Italy and Japan; one of Great Britain and one of each of the British Dominions and of India; and one of each of the other contracting States (Art. 34).   But the United States and Japan have not joined this body.

[19] Art. 34.   See also Arts. 9, 14–17, 28–29.   Any disagreement relating to the interpretation of the convention shall be determined by the Permanent Court of International Justice.   But disagreements relating to technical matters shall be settled by a majority vote of the International Commission (Art. 37).

"In case of war, the provisions of the present Convention shall not affect the freedom of action of the contracting States either as belligerents or as neutrals" (Art. 38).

For summaries of or comments on this important Convention, see Hazeltine, in 29 *I. L. A.* (1920), 387 ff.; 1 Hyde, §§ 190–91; Kuhn, in 14 *A. J.* (1920), 369–81; Lee, in 33 *Harv. Law Rev.* (1919), 23–38; and 1 Oppenheim, §§ 197 a–c.

§ 42a; * Hazeltine, *The Law of the Air* (1911); Hilty, in 19 *Archiv des Öffent. Rechts* (1905), 87 ff.; D'Hooghe, *Droit aérien* (1912); 1 Hyde, §§ 182–93; Julliot, *De la proprieté du domain aérien* (1909); Kausen, *Die Radiotelegraphie im Völkerrecht* (1910); Kenny, in 4 *Z. V.* (1910), 472 ff.; Kohler, in 4 *Z. V.* (1910), 588 ff.; * Kuhn, in 4 *A. J.* (1910), 109 ff.; Latey, in 7 *Grotius Soc.* (1922), 73 ff., and 7 *J. C. L.* (Pt. I, 1925), 96–100; Lawrence, § 73; Lee, in 7 *A. J.* (1913), 470 ff., and in 33 *Harv. Law Rev.* (1920), 23–38; Loubeye, *Les principes du droit aérien* (1911); * Lycklama a Nijeholt, *Air Sovereignty* (1910); Meili, *Die drahtlose Telegraphie* (1908), and *Das Luftschiff* (1908); 2 Mérignhac, 398 ff., and 21 *R. D. I. P.* (1914), 205 ff.; Meurer, *Luftschiffahrtsrecht* (1909), and in 16 *R. D. I. P.* (1909), 76 ff.; Meyer, *Die Erschliessung des Luftraumes* (1909); De Montmorency, in *Brit. Yr. Bk.* (1921–22), 167–73, and in 3 *Grotius Soc.* (1918), 61–69; 1 Nys, Sect. III, ch. 8, in 34 *R. D. I. P.* (1902), 501 ff., and in 19 *Annuaire*, 86–114; * 1 Oppenheim, §§ 197 a–c: Richards, *Sovereignty over the Air* (1912); Rolland, in 13 *R. D. I P.* (1906), 58 ff.; Schneeli, *Radiotelegraphie und Völkerrecht* (1908), §§ 7–13; Schroeder, *Der Luftflug* (1911); * Spaight, *Aircraft in Peace* (1919), *passim;* Sperl, *Die Luftschiffahrt* (1911), and in 18 *R. D. I. P.* (1911), 473 ff.; Ullmann, § 86, p. 289, and § 147, pp. 426–27; Warner, in 4 *For. Aff.* (1925), 278–93; * Westlake, in 21 *Annuaire* (1906), 227–29; Wilson, §§ 30, 43, and in 5 *Am. Pol. Sci. Rev.* (1911), 171 ff.; * Woodhouse, *Textbook of Aërial Laws* (1920).

For fuller Bibliographies, see 1 (2 Pt.) Fauchille, pp. 581–84; Lycklama a Nijeholt, *op. cit.*, Appendices; and Spaight, *op. cit.*, 217–27. For reviews of the earlier authorities, see Hazeltine, *op. cit.*, Lect. I; and Lee, in 7 *A. J.* (1913), 470 ff.

For some additional references on and discussion of *Wireless Telegraphy* (with special reference to the International Radiotelegraphic Convention of 1912), see 1 Oppenheim, §§ 287 a–b. For the text of that Convention, see 3 Malloy, *Treaties*, 3048 or Supp. to 7 *A. J.* (1913), 229 ff.   Cf. note 12 in previous chapter.

CHAPTER XVII

INDIVIDUALS AS OBJECTS OF INTERNATIONAL LAW

222. Individuals as Objects of the Law of Nations.—As stated in an earlier chapter,[1] individuals are objects rather than subjects of International Law. Inasmuch as their international rights and obligations are mainly secured and determined by the States or political communities to which they belong, their nationality or political allegiance is a matter of the first importance.

223. What is Nationality?—Nationality is usually defined[2] as the status or tie which unites an individual to a particular State. It involves reciprocal relations of allegiance and protection, and generally, though not always, implies that the individual clothed with a national character is a citizen[3] or subject of the State to which he owes allegiance. This national character is determined by municipal or State Law, and it frequently happens that several States lay claim to the allegiance of the same individual (this is a case of so-called double nationality) or that an individual is left without any nationality whatever (the Germans call it *Staatslos* or *Heimatlos*).[4] In the former case conflicts between States are likely to arise which call for the exercise of the greatest tact and forbearance. In the latter case injustice may be done to those individuals who

[1] See *supra*, note 2 in ch. 6. See, in addition, Borchard, §§ 7–10; Diena, in 16 *R. D. I. P.* (1909), 57 ff. See especially 1 Oppenheim, §§ 288–92, for a good discussion and references on this point.

[2] Nationality as here defined is a legal term and should be distinguished from the vague political or ethnological sense in which it is often used. Thus we speak of an individual as possessing German, Italian, Polish, or even Jewish nationality, without any necessary reference to a particular State.

[3] The terms *citizen* and *subject* have the same meaning in International Law. *Citizen* is usually applied to members of a State having a republican form of government; *subject* to those with monarchical institutions. Thus we speak of British subjects and American citizens. Since individuals who are not citizens in the strict or narrow sense are sometimes clothed with a national character, the term *national* is now preferred by many statesmen and publicists.

[4] For discussion of, and references on, "Double and Absent Nationality," see * 1 Oppenheim, §§ 308–13, p. 481.

347

are in a sense outlaws from the standpoint of International Law.

I. Native-born Citizens or Subjects

224. **Native-born Citizens.**—The most numerous and important class of individuals over whom a State claims jurisdiction are native-born citizens or subjects. But when it comes to the application of this term, there is a wide divergence in theory and practice.

All modern legislation supports the principle that children born within the territory of a State to parents who are themselves citizens are clothed with the nationality of their parents. But there is not the same unanimity in respect to those born outside the State's territory to parents who are citizens, nor in respect to those born within the State's territory to alien parents.

225. **The *jus soli*.**—According to the feudal principle of the *jus soli*,[5] nationality is primarily determined by the place or locality of birth. Consequently, children born to alien parents within the State's territory are clothed with its nationality. If carried out to its logical conclusion, this system would also require that those born outside the State's territory to parents who are citizens should not inherit the nationality of their parents. But this conclusion is not drawn nowadays.[6] Modern States are practically unanimous in claiming for children born abroad to its citizens the nationality of their parents.[7]

The *jus soli* prevails predominantly in Great Britain, the United States, and most of the States of Latin America.

226. **The *jus sanguinis*.**—According to the Roman and early Germanic principle of the *jus sanguinis*, nationality is

---

[5] The *jus soli* is of feudal origin and was originally based upon the territorial relation of a fief to its lord. During the Middle Ages it gradually supplanted the more ancient *jus sanguinis*, which was again given wide currency in Europe through the adoption of the Napoleonic Code.

[6] However, this seems to have been the doctrine of the French publicists of the old régime. See the citation from Bacquet, in Weiss, *Manuel de droit int. privé* (1909), p. 7, and 1 *Traité de droit int. privé* (1898), 43.

[7] But many American States (including the United States) only actually claim those who show an intention to reside in the country of their origin. Others grant them the right of option after they have attained their majority.

based primarily upon descent or parentage.[8] Thus, according to this system, children born outside a State's territory to parents who are citizens, are clothed with the nationality of their parents, whereas those born within a State's territory to alien parents are regarded as foreigners.

This system prevails predominantly in Germany,[9] Austria, Hungary, Norway, and Switzerland.

[8] The *jus sanguinis* was not merely a Roman and early Germanic conception, but this principle of inheritance or descent may be said to have been that of antiquity itself. As stated above, it was incorporated into the Napoleonic Code, and thus given a wide currency in Europe.

The Civil Code of Napoleon (1804) does not declare in express terms that children inherit the nationality of their parents. Art. 9 gave to a child born to alien parents on French soil, and who is not domiciled in France at the time of his majority (those having French domicile being considered French unless they have made a contrary choice), the right to choose French nationality within a year after attaining his majority, provided he acquires a French domicile within a year after his declaration. For the text, see Cogordan, *La nationalité* (2d ed., 1890), 431.

Art. 10, § 1 simply declares that "every child born of a Frenchman in a foreign country is French." The new Art. 8, § 1° of the Civil Code (law of 1889) is thus conceived: "Any individual born of a Frenchman in France or abroad" is French. For the text of the law of 1889, see Andreani, *La condition des étrangers en France* (1907), ch. 3, pp. 111 ff., or 2 Sieber, *Das Staatsburgerrecht* (1907), 84 ff.

"Every individual born in France to foreign parents (one of whom is himself born there) is French, saving the privilege (if it is the mother who is born in France) of declining French nationality within the year following his majority." Art. 1, § 3° of the law of 1893. See Andreani, *op. cit.*, p. 123. For an English translation of the laws of 1889 and 1893, see *Report on Citizenship*, 72 House Doc., No. 326, 59th Cong., 2d sess. (1906–1907), 317 ff.

[9] The German Nationality Law of 1913 contained some novel provisions. § 13 makes it possible for a German non-resident or one descended from a former German or one who has been adopted as a child of such to be naturalized. According to the German commentator Delius (*Reichs und Staatsangehörikeitsgesetz*, 1913) this section "aims to facilitate as far as possible the reinstatement of lost members of our population as citizens again. . . . Reference is here made especially to representatives of commerce, to members of the German communities in Palestine, to missionaries, and in general to persons who by being especially active in the fostering of German-dom abroad, for example in German societies, and particularly by maintaining German schools and churches, do a worthy service." Flournoy, in 8 *A. J.* (1914), 478–79.

§ 25 is in some respects still more extraordinary. It contains the provision that "citizenship is not lost by one who before acquiring foreign citizenship has secured on application the written consent of the competent authorities of his home State to retain his citizenship. Before this consent is given the German consul is to be heard." This seems to be a direct encouragement of dual nationality. Apparently the performance of services to the State rather than residence or even descent is to be made the basis of German nationality abroad.

On the "German Law of Nationality," see Flournoy, *op. cit.*, 477–86. For

227. Mixed Systems.—A mixed system prevails in France, Belgium, Holland, Greece, Turkey, Russia, Spain, Italy, etc. In France, *e.g.* (which may be regarded as a type of this class of States) every child of a Frenchman is held to be of French nationality, whether born in France or abroad; whereas an individual born in France to alien parents, and not domiciled in France at the age of majority, is regarded as a foreigner. But until the completion of his twenty-second year, such an individual has the option of making an act of submission by declaring his intention to acquire a French domicile; and if he acquires such a domicile within a year after his act of submission, he may claim French nationality by means of a declaration which will be registered with the Ministry of Justice.[10] Every individual born in France to a foreigner and who is domiciled there at the time of his majority is regarded as French unless, within the year following his majority, he has declined French nationality and proved that he has preserved the nationality of his parents by means of an attestation drawn up in due form by his government.[11]

Some special comments on the practice of Great Britain and the United States may be found useful.

228. Native-born British Subjects.—England formerly stood almost exclusively upon the ground of the *jus soli*, and claimed the allegiance of all children born to aliens on British soil or within British jurisdiction,[12] as well as of the

editorial comment, see 9 and 12 *A. J.* (1915 and 1918), 939 ff. and 356 ff. respectively. For the text of the law, see Supp. to 8 *A. J.* (1914), 217 ff.

[10] Cogordan, *op. cit.*, 81. For commentaries on Art. 9 of the Civil Code and Art. 8, § 4° of the law of 1889, see Cogordan, *op. cit.*, § 5., and Andreani, 125 ff. This article is slightly modified by the law of 1893. For a good treatment of "French Nationality Laws," in English, see McGovney, in 5 *A. J.* (1911), 324–54.

[11] Cogordan, *op. cit.*, 84. He must also produce a certificate showing that he has complied with the military law of his country.

Some minor points in the laws on nationality may here be noted: The nationality of foundlings is governed by the *jus soli*. Illegitimate children usually inherit the nationality of their mother, though they may acquire the nationality of the father through subsequent legitimation. The nationality of the wife is generally merged in that of her husband. Thus, when a woman marries a foreigner, she usually loses her former nationality.

[12] There were, however, several exceptions: (1) Children of foreign ambassadors. (2) Children born to an enemy father at a place within the British dominions, but in military occupation of an enemy State. (3) Children

children born to British subjects abroad. But since 1870 the right of legitimate children born to alien parents within British jurisdiction to acquire the nationality of their parents by means of a declaration of alienage at the age of majority, is recognized.

According to the Naturalization Act of 1870, the following were regarded as native-born British subjects:

" (1) Persons born within the British dominions or on board British ships on the high seas or in foreign territorial waters, whether born of British or alien parents, and whether legitimate or illegitimate, provided that, if legitimate children born of alien parents, and if of the age of twenty-one years or more, they have not made a declaration of alienage, in accordance with the provisions of the Naturalization Act of 1870.[13]

" (2) Legitimate children and grandchildren by male descent, of British subjects, born out of the dominions of the crown.[14]

" (3) Persons whose father, being a British subject, or whose mother being a British subject and a widow, has become naturalized during the infancy of such persons in a country under the laws of which infant children do not become naturalized by the naturalization of their parents; and like persons, notwithstanding that they have become naturalized by the naturalization of their parents, if they

of persons attainted of high treason, or in the actual service of any foreign prince or State at enmity with Great Britain at the time of the birth of such children. See Hall, *Foreign Powers and Jurisdiction of the British Crown* (1894), pp. 18–19 n.

Children born abroad to any whose fathers are in the military service of the Crown have also been considered British subjects, at least since the statute of Edward III, as also those born on board a British ship on the high seas. Piggott, *Nationality* (1907), I, 42–46.

[13] Thus, "a child born of foreign parents even during an accidental stay is fully, and until the age of twenty-one years, irretrievably a British subject." Hall, *op. cit.*, 20.

[14] "4 Geo. II, c. 21, and 13 Geo. III, c. 21. The meaning of these Acts was decided in *De Geer* v. *Stone*, 22 Ch. D. 243, to be that 'the grandchild born abroad, whose father was also born abroad, being respectively grandchild and child of a man who was by the common law a natural born British subject, would be himself a natural born British subject, but that his children born abroad would be aliens.'" Hall, *op. cit.*, 19 n. But Great Britain does not pretend to afford protection to such subjects if claimed by the country in which they are born. *Ibid.*, 66. The paternal grandfather disappears in subsection (b) of the British Act of 1914. See below, note 16.

have not during infancy been *resident*,[15] within the meaning of section 10 of the Act of 1870, in the country where the father or mother is naturalized." [16]

229. **Native-born Citizens of the United States.**—In the United States, the principle of *jus soli* of the common law was followed, and it was held that " children born in the United States of alien parents, who have never been naturalized, are native citizens of the United States." [17]

The Civil Rights Act of 1866 (the first law containing a provision on this subject) declared: " All persons born in the United States *and not subject to any foreign Power*, excluding Indians not taxed, are declared to be citizens of

[15] On the probable meaning of the term *resident* in this connection, see Hall, *op. cit.*, § 17.

[16] *Ibid.*, pp. 18–19. Subject to certain exceptions, such as foreign naturalization or a declaration of alienage, the following are the main classes of natural born British subjects: (*a*) Children born within the dominions. (*b*) Children born abroad of a father who falls within category *a*. (*c*) Children born abroad of a person who falls within category *b*. For this classification, see 1 Piggott, *Nationality* (1907), 53.

The British Nationality and Status of Aliens Act of 1914 (4 and 5 Geo. V, ch. 17) declares:

"1. (1) The following persons shall be deemed to be natural-born British subjects, namely:

(*a*) Any person born within His Majesty's dominions and allegiance; and

(*b*) Any person born out of His Majesty's dominions, whose father was a British subject at the time of that person's birth and either was born within His Majesty's allegiance or was a person to whom a certificate of naturalization had been granted; and

(*c*) Any person born on board a British ship whether in foreign territorial waters or not:

"Provided that the child of a British subject . . . shall be deemed to have been born with His Majesty's allegiance if born in a place where by treaty, capitulation, grant, usage, sufferance, or other lawful means, His Majesty exercises jurisdiction over British subjects."

To subsection (*b*) the British Law of 1918 adds: "or had become a British subject by reason of any annexation of territory, or was at the time of that person's birth in the service of the Crown." McNair, in 35 *Law Quar. Rev.* (1918), 215.

"In the main, the above provision was practically declaratory of existing British law. There are two notable changes, however. The first is the provision that children born abroad of naturalized as well as native British subjects are themselves born British subjects. The second is that citizenship is not transmitted beyond the first generation," with the exception noted above in the paragraph beginning "Provided." Flournoy, in 9 *A. J.* (1915), 880. See also McNair, *op. cit.*, 213–32.

[17] 3 Moore, *Digest*, p. 277.

the United States." [18] But the modifying phrase set in italics appears to have been rendered null and void by the adoption of the Fourteenth Amendment to the Constitution of the United States: " All persons born or naturalized in the United States, and *subject to the jurisdiction thereof*, are citizens of the United States and of the State wherein they reside." [19]

The Act of Congress of 1855 declared: " All children heretofore or hereafter born out of the limits and jurisdiction

[18] *Revised Statutes*, § 1992. See Moore, *op. cit.* The *italicized* phrase appears to have meant that if it be shown that one born in the United States owes allegiance to another State, he is not a citizen of the United States. Art. "Nationality," in 2 Lalor's *Cyclopedia* (Chicago, 1882–84). A different view is held by Van Dyne, *Citizenship of the U. S.* (1904), No. 2.

For a review of the juridical *dicta* to the effect that the phrase "subject to the jurisdiction thereof" in the Fourteenth Amendment also included children who bore a foreign allegiance *jure sanguinis*, see Moore's *Am. Notes* in the first edition of Dicey's *Conflict of Laws* (1896), 201. These valuable notes have unfortunately been omitted in the second edition (1908) of this excellent work.

[19] The phrase set in *italics* does not appear to exclude children subject to a foreign Power by reason of a *jure sanguinis* allegiance, but merely excludes children born in the United States of diplomatic agents and Indians still living in tribal relations. It is also believed to exclude children of alien enemies in hostile occupation of the United States.

In the leading case of *United States* v. *Wong Kim Ark* (1898), 169 U. S. 649, or Scott, *Cases*, 138, our Supreme Court held that "a child born in the United States, whose parents, though of Chinese descent and subjects of the Emperor of China, are domiciled in the United States, is a citizen of the United States by birth, within the meaning of the Fourteenth Amendment." 3 Moore, *Digest*, p. 280. See also *In re Look Tin Sing* (1884), 21 Fed. 905; * *Ex parte Chin King* (1888), 35 Fed. 354, and Scott *Cases*, (ed. of 1902), 379; and the other cases cited in 3 Moore, *Digest*, 280, and 1 Willoughby, *Constitutional Law of the U. S.* (1910), § 125.

The decisions of the Department of State do not appear always to have agreed with those of the courts. For example, in *Hausding's Case* (1885), Secretary Frelinghuysen supported Mr. Kasson, U. S. minister to Germany, in the opinion that one Ludwig Hausding, who was born in the United States of a Saxon subject, but who had resided in Saxony since his infancy, was not entitled to a passport as a citizen of the United States. And this in spite of the fact that his father had, subsequently to his birth, become a naturalized citizen of the United States. "The fact of birth under circumstances implying alien subjection, establishes of itself no right of citizenship." This case may possibly be harmonized with the Chinese cases, cited above, on the theory that Hausding had never shown any fixed or definite intention to return, such as was manifested in the case of the subjects of the Emperor of China. But the fact remains that the State Department gave the Fourteenth Amendment a different construction from that given by the Federal Courts. This former construction of the State Department has, however, since been abandoned.

On *Hausding's Case*, see 3 Moore, *Digest*, 278–79, and Snow, *Cases*, 222–23. For two other somewhat similar cases, see 3 Moore, 279–80.

of the United States, whose fathers were or may be at the time of their birth citizens thereof, are declared to be citizens of the United States; *but the rights of citizenship shall not descend to children whose fathers never resided in the United States.*" [20]

The Act of 1907 declares: " All children born outside the limits of the United States who are citizens thereof in accordance with the provisions of section 1993 of the Revised Statutes of the United States and who continue to reside outside the United States shall, in order to receive the protection of this Government, be required upon reaching the age of eighteen years to record at an American consulate their intention to become residents and remain citizens of the United States and shall be further required to take the oath of allegiance to the United States upon attaining their majority." [21]

II. NATURALIZED CITIZENS OR SUBJECTS

230. Naturalized Citizens.—Another important class of citizens, especially in the United States, are naturalized citizens or subjects. These are persons between whom and the State the tie of allegiance has been artificially created by a process termed naturalization. " Naturalization in the narrower sense of the term, in contradistinction to naturalization through marriage, legitimation, option, domicile, and appointment as government official, may be defined as the reception of a foreigner into the citizenship of a State through a formal act on application of the individual." [22] It is in this narrower sense that we shall use the term.

[20] § 1993 of the Revised Statutes of the United States, incorporating the provisions of the act of Feb. 10, 1855. See 3 Moore, *Digest*, p. 282. Hence an illegitimate child born abroad of an American woman is not a citizen of the United States.

[21] § 6 of The Act of 1907 in "Reference to the Expatriation of Citizens and their Protection abroad." See Supp. to 1 *A. J.* (1907), 259; or Van Dyne, *Law of Naturalization of the U. S.* (1907), App., 440.

§ 5 of this Act declares: "That a child born without the United States of alien parents shall be deemed a citizen of the United States by virtue of the naturalization of or resumption of American citizenship by the parent: *Provided* That such naturalization of or resumption takes place during the minority of such child; *And provided further*, That the citizenship of such minor child shall begin at the time such minor child begins to reside permanently in the United States."

[22] Slightly adapted from 1 Oppenheim, § 303. Cf. *Ibid.*, § 299. In the

Naturalization is regulated by municipal or State law, but it is of special importance to students and statesmen, since the conflict of legislation on the subject may give rise to serious international conflicts.

230a. The So-Called Right of Expatriation.—Some authorities and legislators have maintained that the individual has a natural right of expatriation, *i.e.* to transfer his allegiance and claim to protection from one sovereign to another at will, and that this right is guaranteed by the Law of Nations. The United States has especially championed this view since 1868,[23] even at times undertaking to

wider sense, naturalization may take place without special formalities, as where a foreign wife acquires the nationality of her husband or minor children that of their father.

There is also a process of collective naturalization, as when a country or province is annexed or incorporated by another. See especially 1 Hyde, § 352; 3 Moore, *Digest*, §§ 379–80; and Van Dyne, *op. cit.*, ch. 4. Several of the Latin-American States, as, *e.g.* Brazil, Mexico, Peru, consider such acts as the purchase of real estate, or residence for a term of years, as *ipso facto* evidence of naturalization.

[23] Roused to a fever heat of excitement by the refusal of England to grant the right of trial by mixed juries to naturalized American citizens accused of Irish (Fenian) outrages, Congress passed the famous Act of 1868 declaring expatriation to be "a natural and inherent right of all people," and denouncing as inconsistent with the fundamental principles of the republic "any declaration, instruction, opinion, order, or decision of any officers of this Government, which denies, restricts, impairs, or questions the right of expatriation." It was also enacted that "all naturalized citizens of the United States, while in foreign States, are entitled to, and shall receive from this Government the same protection of persons and property that is accorded to native-born citizens in like situations and circumstances." 3 Moore, *Digest*, § 439.

Prior to 1868 the courts and legal authorities in the United States accepted the common-law doctrine that a subject or citizen cannot renounce his allegiance without the consent of his Government. See especially the *Case of MacDonald* (1747), and *William's Case* (1799), Scott, *Cases*, 134 and 158; and the judicial opinions on *Ballard's* and *Talbot's* citizenship (*Talbot* v. *Jansen*, 1795, 3 Dallas 133) in 3 Moore, *Digest*, § 432. For references to the older authorities, see *Ibid.*, § 431, p. 552.

Not until 1845–48, when Buchanan was Secretary of State, did our State Department claim that naturalized American citizens were entitled to the same degree of protection as native-born citizens in the country of their origin. After 1848 Secretary Webster reverted to the earlier rule laid down in 1840 by Mr. Wheaton, minister to Prussia, in the case of Mr. *Knoche*, a naturalized American citizen who had been forced to enter the Prussian army after his return to Prussia. "Had you remained in the United States or visited any other foreign country except Prussia on your lawful business, you would have been protected by the American authorities at home and abroad, in the enjoyment of all your rights and privileges as a naturalized citizen of the United States. But, having returned to the country of your birth, *your native domicile*

protect its naturalized citizens without respecting the rights of the country of their origin; but, within recent years, our Government appears to have abandoned its extreme and

and national character revert (so as long you remain in the Prussian dominions), and you are bound in all respects to obey the laws exactly as if you had never emigrated." 3 Moore, *Digest*, p. 564.

Replying to an inquiry whether M. *Depierre* (a native of France, but a naturalized citizen of the United States) could "expect the protection of this Government in that country, when proceeding thither with a passport" from the Department of State, Secretary Webster said in 1852: "If, as is understood to be the fact, the Government of France does not acknowledge the right of natives of that country to renounce their allegiance, it may lawfully claim their services when found within French jurisdiction." 3 Moore, *Digest*, p. 567. Similar ground was taken by Secretary Everett in 1853, Secretary Marcy in 1855, and Attorney-General Cushing in 1856.

During Buchanan's Presidency, the State Department again changed its tone. In 1859, Secreatry Cass instructed Mr. Wright, American Minister to Prussia, to demand the immediate discharge of *Christian Ernst*, a naturalized American citizen, from compulsory military srevice in Hanover on the ground that the offense charged—evasion of military service—had not been committed before the emigration of Ernst to the United States at the age of nineteen. In these instructions, which were issued in circular form to other Governments, President Buchanan (the views expressed were really his) took the broad ground that "the moment a foreigner becomes naturalized his allegiance to his native country is severed forever. He experiences a new political birth. A broad and impassable line separates him from his native country. . . . Should he return to his native country, he returns as an American citizen and in no other character. In order to entitle his original government to punish him for an offense, this must have been committed while he was subject and owed allegiance to that government. . . . It must have been of such a character that he might have been tried and punished for it at the moment of his departure." 3 Moore, *Digest*, pp. 574–75.

During the Civil War Secretary Seward permitted the controversy to rest. It was soon afterward revived in connection with the Fenian outrages in Ireland and led to the Act of 1868, cited above. In the same year the historian Bancroft, then United States Minister to Prussia, negotiated a Treaty of Naturalization with Prince Bismarck in behalf of the North German Confederation which had been formed in 1866 and which four years later (1870) developed into the German Empire. It was followed by the conclusion of similar treaties with other States.

The Bancroft treaties provide for the reciprocal recognition of naturalization combined with five years' uninterrupted residence. But if the naturalized emigrant returns to the country of his origin, he is liable to punishment for offences (such as evasion of military service) committed before his emigration unless the liability has ceased through prescription. If the returning emigrant renews, without intent to return, his residence in the old country, he shall be deemed to have renounced his naturalization in the new; and a presumption of an intention not to return and of consequent loss of the newly acquired nationality arises after a residence of more than two years in the old country. On the Bancroft treaties, see especially: 1 Hyde, § 361; and 3 Moore, *Digest*, §§ 390 ff.

For various Naturalization Conventions to which the United States is a party, see Van Dyne. *Law of Naturalization of the U. S.* (1907), App., 441 ff.

indefensible attitude in this matter. Though nearly all States now permit the expatriation of their citizens, they do so at their own discretion. Consequently, the so-called right of expatriation is not a principle of International Law.

231. **Naturalization in Great Britain.**—Until 1870, England held to the equally indefensible doctrine of perpetual allegiance—*nemo potest exuere patriam*—and refused to recognize any right of expatriation on the part of her subjects. But she abandoned this illiberal attitude in 1870, when she not only recognized the right of expatriation of her own subjects, but provided improved facilities for the naturalization of foreigners.[24]

" By the seventh section of the Naturalization Act of 1870, any alien who has resided in the United Kingdom for not less than five years, or who has been in the service of the Crown for a like period, and who *intends either to reside* [25] in

The Treaty of Naturalization between the United States and Great Britain (1870) merely provides for a reciprocal recognition of the naturalization of British subjects or American citizens, and the resumption of British or American nationality. For commentary, see 1 Piggott, *Nationality* (1907), ch. 17.

The United States has also concluded Treaties of Naturalization with Belgium (1868), Sweden and Norway (1869), Austria-Hungary (1870), Ecuador (1872), Denmark (1872), Haiti (1902), San Salvador (1908), Portugal (1908), Honduras (1908), Uruguay (1908), and Peru (1907). These treaties are mainly drawn on the line of the Bancroft treaties, referred to above. The treaties with San Salvador, Portugal, Uruguay, and Peru, which are of special interest as illustrating the later views of our Government, are printed in 2, 3, and 4 Supp. to *A. J.* (1908–1910), 342–43, 159–60, 284–85, 134–35 respectively. For additional data, see 1 Hyde, § 361, p. 360 notes.

Owing to their stringent enforcement of military conscription, our main conflicts have been with Germany, Austria-Hungary, and Russia. These countries have frequently resorted to expulsion of naturalized Americans even in apparent violation of treaty rights. But our Government appears to have receded from the extreme and untenable positions which it has sometimes assumed, except in the case of the Russian Jews (1911).

For the subject-matter of this note, see especially 3 Moore, *Digest*, particularly §§ 390–407, 431–40, 453; Moore, *American Diplomacy* (1905), ch. 7; and Art. on "Nationality," in 2 Lalor, *Cyclopedia* (Chicago, 1882–84).

For several cases of dual nationality involving controversy with the French and Italian Governments during the World War, see Fenwick, 167–68.

[24] Prior to 1844 an alien could only be naturalized by special Act of Parliament or by letters of denization. The Act of 1844 permitted naturalization at the discretion of a Secretary of State.

[25] It is doubtful whether the phrase *intends to reside* has any particular meaning or importance. In the case of *M. Bourgoise* (1889), L. R. 41 Ch. D. 310 (or 1 Cobbett, 186), who spent the remainder of his life in France after having been naturalized in England, it was not even mentioned. See 1 Piggott, *Nationality* (1907), 101 f. and 122 ff.

the United Kingdom or to serve under the Crown may, at the discretion of a Secretary of State, be granted a certificate of naturalization which carries with it all the rights and obligations of a British subject within the United Kingdom." [26]

" A person to whom a certificate of naturalization is granted by a Secretary of State shall . . . be entitled to all political and other rights, powers, and privileges, and be subject to all obligations, duties and liabilities to which a natural-born British subject is entitled or subject, and, as from the date of his naturalization, have to all intents and purposes the status of a natural-born British subject." [27]

Children born to naturalized parents in the United Kingdom are of course natural-born British subjects according to the *jus soli*, and those who become resident in the United Kingdom with their naturalized father, or with their mother if she is a widow at the time of her naturalization, are naturalized British subjects. But children born to naturalized parents abroad and continuing to reside there are presumably aliens. [28] Married women are deemed subjects of the State to which their husbands belong;

[26] Hall, *Foreign Powers and Jurisdiction* (1894), § 18. The British Nationality and Status of Aliens Act of 1914 adds that the applicant must satisfy the Secretary of State that he is of "good character and has an adequate knowledge of the English language." Sect. 2, (b).

In Sect. 8 (1) of this Act the Government of any British possession is given the same power as the Secretary of State to grant or revoke certificates of imperial naturalization; but, except in the case of the Dominions and India, any certificate of imperial naturalization must first be submitted to the Secretary of State for approval.

The main purpose of the Act of 1914 seems to have been to put aliens naturalized in the Dominions in the same position as natural-born British subjects. Thus, prior to Jan. 1, 1915 (the date when the Act went into effect) citizens of the United States naturalized in Canada were not regarded as British subjects, and this in spite of the fact that they were obliged to take the oath of allegiance to the British king.

It is interesting to note that the law was not to become effective in the separate Dominions until approved by their legislatures. See particularly Flournoy, in 9 *A. J.* (1915), 870 ff.; and McNair in 35 *Law Quar. Rev.* (1919), 213 ff.

[27] Sect. 3 (1) of the Act of 1914. Cf. Art. 7, § 3 of the Naturalization Act of 1870 as printed in Hall, *op. cit.*, p. 243. The qualifying phrase of the older law is omitted in the new Act.

[28] This is the opinion of Hall, *op. cit.*, § 19, and Dicey in 5 *Law Quar. Rev.* (1889), 438. It is not shared by Westlake (I, 235 n.). Piggott (*Nationality*, 1907, I, 126) leaves one in doubt.

consequently, they acquire the nationality of their naturalized husbands, at least in the United Kingdom.

232. Loss of British Nationality.—Since 1870, " the status
of a British subject may be lost—

" (1) By natural-born British subjects of British origin:

" (*a*) Through [voluntary] naturalization in a foreign
State;

" (*b*) By declaration of alienage, . . .

" (*c*) Through marriage, in the case of a woman, with an
alien.

" (2) By natural-born British subjects of foreign origin,
and by naturalized persons:

" (*a*) By declaration of alienage;

" (*b*) Through marriage, in the case of a woman, with an
alien." [29]

233. Naturalization in the United States.—Beginning
with the Act of 1790, Congress has passed various statutes
for the naturalization of aliens. The present law, which
was enacted on June 29, 1906, provides:

(1) That an alien desiring to be naturalized " shall
declare on oath before the clerk of any court authorized by
this Act to naturalize aliens, [30] or his authorized deputy, in
the district in which such alien resides, two years at least
prior to his admission, and after he has reached the age of
eighteen years, that it is *bona fide* his intention to become a
citizen of the United States, and to renounce forever all
allegiance and fidelity to any foreign prince, potentate,
state, or sovereignty, and particularly, by name, to the

[29] Hall, *op. cit.*, § 25. Cf. §§ 13–16 of the British Nationality and Status of
Aliens Act of 1914. For the text of this Act, see Supp. to 9 *A. J.* (1915),
413–23. The Act of 1870 requires as conditions for recognition of the validity
of the expatriation of British subjects that the act be voluntary on the part of
the individual, that he be not under any disability, and that he reside in the
foreign State at the time of his naturalization; but it does not prescribe any
formalities or rules, such as length of residence, etc. On the Conditions of
Naturalization, cf. Hall, *op. cit.*, §§ 25–26, and 1 Piggott, *op. cit.*, 136 ff.

An especially valuable commentary on the Naturalization Act of 1870 is the
Report of the Interdepartmental Committee of 1901, (*Par. Paper, op. cit.*, 1901,
Cd. 723). It is printed in the *Report on Citizenship*, etc., 72 House Doc., No.
236, 59th Cong. 2d sess. (1906–1907), 343–61.

[30] Naturalization in the United States is a judicial act. For a list of courts
having jurisdiction, see Van Dyne, *op. cit.*, App., 493 ff.

prince, potentate, state, or sovereignty, of which the alien may at the time be citizen or subject. . . ." [31]

(2) Not less than two years nor more than seven years after he has made such declaration of intention,[32] he shall file a petition verified by the affidavits of at least two credible witnesses—citizens of the United States—setting forth that " he is not a disbeliever in or opposed to organized government, or a member of or affiliated with any organization or body of persons teaching disbelief in or opposed to organized government, a polygamist or believer in the practice of polygamy, and that it is his intention to renounce, etc., . . . and that it is his intention to reside permanently in the United States. . . ."

(3) He shall, furthermore, " declare in open court that he will support the Constitution of the United States "; prove that " he has resided continuously within the United States five years at least, and within the State or Territory where such court is at the time held one year at least, and that during that time he has behaved as a man of good moral character, attached to the principles of the Constitution of the United States . . ."; and, finally, that he expressly renounces any hereditary title or order of nobility which he may have borne in the State of his origin.[33]

[31] Sec. 4 of the Act of 1906 (34 Stat. at L. 596) printed in Supp. to 1 *A. J.* (1907), 31 ff.; Van Dyne, *op. cit.*, 417 ff.; or *Naturalization Laws and Regulations*, Nov. 11, 1911, issued by the Department of Commerce and Labor.

[32] According to the law of 1906, the declaration of intention may be made immediately after the alien's arrival in the United States, but it must be made at least two years before his admission to citizenship. The life of the declaration is limited to seven years. In any case five years' residence in the United States and one year within the State or Territory where the application is made is necessary before a certificate of citizenship can be obtained.

There are several exceptions to these rules. No declaration is required and one year's residence is sufficient in the case of aliens who have performed honorable service in the army or navy of the United States. Widows and minor children of deceased aliens who have declared their intention may be naturalized without making such declaration. Residence in Hawaii, the Philippine Islands, or Porto Rico is accepted as fulfilling the five-year residence requirement. An exception is also made in favor of an alien seaman who has declared his intention and served three years on board a United States merchanman. He may at once be admitted to citizenship. Van Dyne, *op. cit.*, 61 ff., 74 ff.

[33] Sec. 4 of the Act of 1906, *op. cit.* Sec. 8 also provides that "no alien shall hereafter be naturalized or admitted as a citizen of the United States who cannot speak the English language, "unless he is physically unable to speak."

234. **Persons Capable of Naturalization in the United States.**—Those capable of naturalization in the United States are " white persons " and " persons of African descent." [34]

It has been judicially held that neither Chinese, Japanese, Burmese, Hawaiians, American Indians, nor Hindus can be naturalized under the statutes.[35] Alien women, whether married or unmarried, may be naturalized in the same manner and under the same conditions as alien men, and prior to the Act of 1922, the naturalization of the husband and father conferred this status upon his wife [36] as well

Sec. 15 provides that "if any alien who shall have secured a certificate of citizenship under the provisions of this Act shall, within five years after the issuance of such certificate, return to the country of his nativity, or go to any other foreign country and take permanent residence therein, it shall be considered *prima facie* evidence of a lack of intention on the part of such alien to become a permanent citizen of the United States at the time of filing his application for citizenship, and, in the absence of countervailing evidence, it shall be sufficient in the proper proceeding to authorize the cancellation of his certificate of citizenship as fraudulent. . . ."

[34] "By the Acts of 1802 and 1824, only "free white persons" were capable of naturalization. By the Act of 1870, the benefits of the law were extended to "aliens of African nativity and to persons of African descent." The law, as consolidated in the Revised Statutes, thus stands, embracing only "white persons," and " persons of African descent." 3 Moore, *Digest*, p. 329.

[35] See especially 3 Moore, *Digest* § 383; and Van Dyne, *op. cit.*, 40 ff. But "Indians are capable of naturalization by special law or treaty, and have often been so naturalized." Alien enemies are also excluded.

It was not until November, 1922 that a decision of our Supreme Court was finally had upon the question whether a Japanese subject can be naturalized. In the case of *U. S.* v. *Ozawa*, 260 U. S. 178, our highest judicial tribunal indicated its agreement with the almost unbroken line of decisions (citing the decisions) of our federal and State courts which have held that the words "white persons" were "meant to indicate only a person of what is popularly known as the Caucasian race" from which the Japanese are clearly excluded.

In *U. S.* v. *Bhagat Singh Thind*, 43 Sup. Ct. 338, decided on Feb. 19, 1923, the Supreme Court answered in the negative the following question certified to it by a Circuit Court of Appeals: "Is a high caste Hindu of full Indian blood. born at Amritsar, Punjab, India, a white person?" The Court said: "What we now hold is that the words 'free white persons' are words of common speech, to be interpreted in accordance with the understanding of the common man, synonymous with the word 'Caucasian' only as that word is popularly understood."

For the texts of these interesting and important decisions, see 17 *A. J.* (1923), 151 ff. and 572 ff. For editorial comment, see *Ibid.*, 328–30. See also Parker, in 19 *A. J.* (1925), 26–27.

[36] Provided she was a person who may be lawfully naturalized under our laws, *i.e.* a white person or of African descent.

By an Act of Congress, approved on Sept. 22, 1922 (the result of an agita-

as upon his minor children "dwelling in the United States." [37]

235. Modes of Expatriation.

—In spite of our championship of the doctrine of expatriation as a natural, inherent right, it was not until 1907 that the United States defined the conditions under which an American citizen should be deemed to have expatriated himself. [38]

The Law of 1907 provides:

(1) " That any American citizen shall be deemed to have expatriated himself when he has been naturalized in any foreign state in conformity with its laws, or when he has taken an oath of allegiance to any foreign State.

tion in favor of equal rights or independent citizenship for women), the United States departed from its former policy and the general practice of States in respect to the status of American women married to foreigners or foreign women married to citizens of the United States. The Act provides: (a) that any woman who marries a citizen of the United States or whose husband is naturalized after the passage of the Act shall not acquire citizenship of the United States by reason of such marriage or naturalization, though if eligible to citizenship she may be naturalized. In the latter case, the usual requirements are relaxed in her favor by waiving the necessity of a declaration of intention and by requiring but one year's residence instead of five. (b) No woman citizen shall lose her American citizenship by reason of her marriage to an alien, unless she makes a formal renunciation of citizenship or unless the husband is ineligible to citizenship. In this case she ceases to be an American citizen, and cannot be naturalized as long as she is married to such alien.

It already appears that the enforcement of this law will result in severe hardships to married women who have lost citizenship in their own country and who are denied American citizenship by reason of their marriage to foreigners. Not only will it increase the number of those stateless persons with no or with an absent nationality, but it will greatly increase the number of those with dual or double nationality, e.g. in the case of many American women married to alien husbands residing abroad. Controversies regarding the nationality of children born of marriages between Americans and foreigners are also likely to arise.

On the "New Married Women's Citizenship Law," see Flournoy, in 33 Yale Law J. (1923), 159 ff.; Garner, in Brit. Yr. Bk. (1923–24), 169–72; Hill, in 18 A. J. (1924), 720 ff.; and Reeves, in 17 A. J. (1923), 97–100. For the text of the act, see Supp. to 17 A. J. (1923), 52–53.

[37] This includes those minor children born abroad who come to the United States after the father's naturalization, as well as those born abroad who reside in the United States at the time of naturalization. 3 Moore, Digest, § 413, p. 464; and Van Dyne, Law of Naturalization of the U. S. (1907), ch. 2, pp. 197 ff.

[38] It had, however, frequently been held by the State Department (see especially 3 Moore, Digest, § 430) that children born abroad of an American father might, at the age of majority, surrender the nationality of their parents and accept that of the country of their birth and residence. This election need not be formal, but may be inferred from acts showing an intention to reside (animo manendi) permanently abroad.

(2) " When any naturalized citizen shall have resided for two years in the foreign State from which he came, or for five years in any other foreign State, it shall be presumed that he has ceased to be an American citizen, and the place of his general abode shall be deemed his place of residence during said years.[39] *Provided, however*, That such presumption may be overcome on the presentation of satisfactory evidence to a diplomatic or consular officer of the United States, under such rules and regulations as the Department of the State may prescribe: And *provided also*, That no American citizen shall be allowed to expatriate himself when his country is at war." [40]

[39] These provisions have been incorporated into many of the Naturalization Conventions to which the United States has been a party.

[40] Sec. 2 of the Act of 1907 in "Reference to the Expatriation of Citizens and their Protection Abroad." See Supp. to 1 *A. J.* (1907), 258–59; or Van Dyne, *op. cit.*, 438–40. For the Instructions to Diplomatic Officers and Consular Regulations referred to above, see Van Dyne. 475 ff.

"It will be observed that the Act declares that expatriation may be effected in four different ways, viz., By naturalization in a foreign State, by taking the oath of allegiance to a foreign State, by marriage of an American woman to a foreigner [now changed], and by residence of a naturalized citizen of the United States in a foreign country." Van Dyne, 337.

"While residence of a naturalized citizen of the United States in a foreign country is not sufficient evidence of expatriation, long-continued residence abroad raises a presumption of abandonment of citizenship. The presumption of law, with respect to residence in a foreign country, especially if it be protracted, is that the party is there '*animo manendi*,' and it lies upon him to explain it." *Ibid.*, 345.

A person "may reside abroad for purposes of health, of education, of amusement, of business, for an indefinite period; he may acquire a commercial or a civil domicile there; but, if he does so sincerely and *bona fide animo revertendi*, and does nothing inconsistent with his preëxisting allegiance, he will not thereby have taken any step toward self-expatriation." Secretary Fish to the President (in 1873). Cited, *Ibid.*, 345.

"Voluntary expatriation by a naturalized citizen which forfeits a right to diplomatic intervention may be inferred from a long residence abroad in the place of his birth, by the non-payment of taxes and non-possession of property in this country, and by failure to express an intention to return." 2 Wharton, *Digest*, § 176, pp. 368–69.

Another way (than the four modes above-mentioned) in which expatriation may be effected is by desertion from the army or navy. Contrary to the practice in some countries, foreign military or naval service or the acceptance of a public office in a foreign country do not in themselves effect expatriation in the view of the United States.

"The doctrine of implied renunciation of citizenship by continuous residence in a foreign country does not completely apply to countries where citizens of the United States enjoy exterritoriality. In such countries they live under the protection, more or less, of their own Government, and are answer-

236. Effect of Declaration of Intention.—Though mere declaration of intention in no wise confers citizenship or absolves the party making it from allegiance to the Government of the country from which he comes,[41] yet our Secretary of State is authorized by Act of Congress to issue passports, at his discretion, to persons who are not fully naturalized in certain cases.[42]

III. Aliens, Particularly Domiciled Aliens

237. Domiciled Aliens.—There is a third class of persons who, under certain circumstances, may be said to be clothed with the national character of the country in which they

able to its laws. Consequently, they are generally held to retain their American domicile." 3 Moore, *Digest*, p. 776. The presumption in favor of retention of nationality by missionaries in foreign lands is particularly strong.

On *Modes of Expatriation* or *Loss of American Nationality*, see especially 3 Moore, *Digest*, §§ 466–80; Van Dyne, *Citizenship of the U. S.* (1904), Pt. IV, ch. 1, *Law of Naturalization of the U. S.* (1907), ch. 5; and 2 Wharton, *Digest*, §§ 176–79.

[41] See especially *Minneapolis* v. *Reum* (1893), 56 Fed. 576, and Scott, *Cases* (ed. of 1902), 390; 3 Moore, *Digest*, § 387; Van Dyne, *Citizenship*, Nos. 24, 26–38, 43, and *Naturalization*, pp. 64–76, 224, 262–63.

[42] "Where any person has made a declaration of intention to become such a citizen as provided by law, and has resided in the United States for three years, a passport may be issued to him entitling him to the protection of the Government in any foreign country: *Provided*, that such passport shall not be valid for more than six months and shall not be renewed, and that such passport shall not entitle the holder to the protection of this Government in the country of which he was a citizen prior to making such declaration of intention." Sec. 1 of Act of March 2, 1907, cited above.

In the famous *Koszta Case* (see below, note 48), Secretary Marcy did not, as frequently misrepresented, base his argument upon the fact that Koszta had declared his intention to be an American citizen, but he merely used this fact as evidence of domicile. The State Department has, in a few instances, held that such declaration gives a "quasi right to protection as against the claim of a third Power to allegiance." Secretary Frelinghuysen to Mr. Wallace, Minister to Turkey, 1884. See 3 Moore *Digest*, p. 340. It is more than doubtful whether this can be maintained as a principle of International Law.

In the case of *Boyd* v. *Thayer* (1891), 143, U. S. 135, 178, the United States Supreme Court declared that minors acquire an inchoate status by declaration of intention on the part of their parents which entitles such minors, in case the naturalization of their parents remains incomplete, to retain American nationality at the age of majority or accept the allegiance of some foreign Power. See Van Dyne, *Citizenship of the U. S.* (1904), Nos. 28 and 43.

In some States of the American Union, an alien who has declared his intention may vote at elections for Federal as well as State officers, but this does not make him a citizen of the United States.

reside, but they are in no wise to be regarded as subjects or citizens. They are domiciled aliens.[43]

238. **What is Domicile?**—" By a person's domicile is meant, generally speaking, his permanent home [or residence].   It is the criterion, in English and American law, of civil as distinguished from political status.   The case is the same in the law of other countries, though not of all.   In Italy, for example, civil status follows the political; and so it does to a great extent in France, and in the countries which, like Belgium, have followed the French Civil Code. It is not, however, conversely true that in countries where civil status is derived from domicile that political status follows the civil.   In such countries, the two conceptions are distinct, neither being dependent upon the other." [44]

239. **Questions to which the Law of Domicile Applies.**— Thus, the question of domicile is quite distinct from that of allegiance or nationality proper.   In most countries, the law of a man's domicile (*lex domicilii*) regulates such matters as legitimacy, minority, capacity to contract, marry,[45] or hold property, the validity of a will relating to personality, and the succession to personal property in cases of intestacy.

[43] The laws of England still recognize a sort of inferior naturalization called denization.   Denization is by letters patent issued under the Great Seal and denizens appear to occupy an intermediate position between aliens and subjects.   Under the old law, they could not inherit real property or transmit it to their children born before denization, but this distinction seems to have disappeared.   The main advantage of this form of naturalization appears to be that it affords a means of avoiding the requirement of five years' residence in the United Kingdom required for ordinary naturalization.   On *Denization*, see Hall, *Foreign Powers and Jurisdiction* (1894), § 22; and 1 Piggott, *Nationality* (1907), ch. 6.

[44] 3 Moore, *Digest*, § 487, p. 811.   Moore adds: "In primitive times it was not so.   In days when the people were generally attached to the soil, . . . domicile was the general criterion of status, political as well as civil, if, indeed, it can be said that such a distinction then existed.   But, with the passing away of the feudal system and the rise of the modern national State, together with the coincident development of commerce and industry, political allegiance— allegiance to the nation—became, as a distinct conception, the test of national character, while domicile, whether national or quasi-national, or merely municipal, remained the test of rights in civil relations."

[45] This refers merely to capacity to contract a marriage, as the age of consent, etc.   The effects of marriage itself appear, generally speaking, to be governed by the law of the place (*lex loci rei sitæ*) where the marriage has been celebrated.

240. The Principle of Nationality.—Some countries, however, like France [46] and Italy, where the rules of the Civil Code are in force, apply the principle of nationality to many or all of these questions. Such matters really fall within the field of International Private Law or Conflict of Laws whose particular function it is to furnish the jurist with precedents, rules, and principles for the decision of cases arising under these heads. He has to determine, in any given case, whether to apply the law of domicile, the law of allegiance, or the simple rule of the *lex loci rei sitæ.*[47]

Although the law of domicile as a part of International Law is mainly confined to matters of prize or to cases arising from belligerent capture,[48] it may be of interest to

[46] France applies the principle of nationality to marriages by Frenchmen abroad. Thus, a marriage contracted by a Frenchman in which the forms required by French law have not been observed, will not be regarded as valid by French tribunals. The marriage of Jerome Bonaparte in 1803 to Miss Patterson of Baltimore was invalidated on this ground. Dana, note 55 to Wheaton, § 93, p. 151.

[47] The *lex loci* is especially applied to cases involving the conveyance of real property.

[48] Cf. *infra*, No. 434. In the famous *Koszta Case* (1853), Secretary Marcy made the astonishing claim that "it is a maxim of International Law that domicile confers a national character," and that persons domiciled in the United States had a right to the protection of our Government while abroad.

Martin Koszta, a Hungarian refugee involved in the revolution of 1848, came to the United States, where he declared his intention of American citizenship on July 31, 1852. After a residence of nearly two years in the United States, he went to Turkey and placed himself under the protection of the American consul at Smyrna. Here he was seized and confined on board an Austrian brig of war, but was rescued by the prompt intervention of Captain Ingrahm, in command of the United States sloop of war *St. Louis*, who threatened to use force in case Koszta was not released. Fortunately, an arrangement was made by which the prisoner was delivered into the custody of the French Consul-General until the United States and Austria should agree as to the manner of disposing of him. Subsequently, he was sent back to the United States.

In the controversy which followed, Secretary Marcy supported the action of the United States mainly on two grounds: (1) That Koszta, having acquired a domicile in this country, was entitled to national protection. This argument was clearly untenable, as mere domicile only confers national (enemy) character under certain circumstances in time of war (see *infra*, No. 434). (2) "By the laws of Turkey and other eastern nations, the consulates therein may receive under their protection strangers and sojourners whose religion and social manners do not assimilate with the religion and manners of those countries. The persons thus received become thereby invested with the nationality of the protecting consulate. These consulates and other European establishments in the East are in the constant habit of opening their doors for the reception of

indicate some of the more general rules of the *lex domicilii* in this connection because of their importance in international relations.

241. **Kinds of Domicile.**—According to most authorities, domicile is of two kinds—*Domicile of Origin* and *Domicile of Choice*.[49]   *Domicile of Origin* is that derived from the place of birth.   Legitimate children acquire the domicile of the father and illegitimate children that of the mother at the time of birth.   Foundlings have the domicile of the country in which they are born.   *Domicile of Choice* is that deliberately adopted by a person of full age.   It consists of a combination of actual residence (*factum*) and intention of permanent or indefinite residence (*animus manendi*).   The domicile of origin is retained until a domicile of choice is actually acquired; a domicile of choice until it is abandoned, when the domicile of origin reverts or a new domicile of choice is acquired.

242. **Special Rules of Domicile.**—The wife usually takes the domicile of her husband and retains it after his death. But if she should marry again, she acquires the domicile of her second husband.   A legitimate minor has the domicile of his father or of his mother during widowhood, or, perhaps, in some cases, of his legally appointed guardian.   In no case can the minor change his domicile of his own accord.

243. **Time and Intention the Controlling Principles De-**

such inmates, who are received irrespective of the country of their birth or allegiance.   It is not uncommon for them to have a large number of such *protégés*.   International Law recognizes and sanctions the rights acquired by this connection."   This position was clearly tenable, and furnishes ample justification for the action of our Government.

On the *Koszta Case*, see 3 Moore, *Digest*, §§ 490–91; and Borchard, §§ 250–51.   The accounts of this case usually found in the treatises and textbooks are either inadequate or practically worthless, owing to the fact that they are, for the most part, based upon misconceptions or misrepresentations.   For abridged citations from the documents, see 2 Wharton, *Digest*, §§ 175, 198.

In a subsequent case (that of *Simon Tousig*), an Austrian who had acquired a domicile in the United States and was later arrested and imprisoned in Austria, Secretary Marcy properly refused to intervene on the ground that Tousig had "voluntarily returned to Austria and placed himself within the reach of her municipal laws."   3 Moore, *Digest*, p. 838.

[49] Some authorities speak of a third kind—Domicile by Operation of Law, as where a minor or dependent person passes under the control of a legal superior or a person acquires a domicile by virtue of employment by the State.   But it would seem that persons falling under this category may be readily classified under one or the other of the heads indicated in the text.

termining Domicile.—The two controlling principles in determining domicile are *intention* and *time*. But mere intention, without some overt act, is not sufficient.[50]   The most material circumstance showing intention is actual residence, but it may also be deduced from the nature of the occupation, correspondence, or business relations of the one claiming a domicile.   Thus, the pursuit of a regular trade or business would clearly indicate domicile or permanent residence.   The presumptions, in these cases, would be strongly in favor of intention (*animo manendi*); but this presumption may be overcome by proof that the original intention was only to remain for a short and definite time, and that the original domicile has not been lost or a new domicile acquired.

Domicile of origin easily reverts in cases of acquired domicile.   To effect this it is sufficient that the person with a domicile of choice should actually begin his return journey to his native country with the intention of resuming his residence there.[51]

[50] Sir Wm. Scott, in *The President* (1804), 5 C. Rob. 277, and Scott, *Cases*, 664 n.   But a few days' residence was held sufficient in the case of *Mr. Whitehill* who was shown to have intended to take up his permanent residence in the island of St. Eustatius shortly before the British took it from the Dutch in 1781.   Lawrence, p. 356; and Wheaton, § 321.

The importance of time or long-continued residence was carefully considered by Sir Wm.   Scott in the case of *The Harmony* (1800), 2 C. Rob. 322 and Evans, *Cases*, 411.   Lord Stowell held that "a special purpose may lead a man to a country which shall detain him the whole of his life . . . against such a long residence, the plea of an original purpose could not be avowed.   It cannot happen, with but few exceptions, that mere length of time shall not constitute a domicile."

The presumption against an acquired domicile would be strong in the case of a mere student, a prisoner, or a missionary.

[51] Thus, in the case of *The Indian Chief* (1801), 3 C. Rob. 12, (Evans, *Cases*, 414, or Scott, 659), Lord Stowell ordered the restoration of the property of Mr. Johnson, an American domiciled in England, on proof that, at the time of capture, he had actually left England for the United States with the intention of remaining there.   Lord Stowell said: "The character that is gained by residence ceases by non-residence.   It is an adventitious character, and no longer adheres to him from the moment that he puts himself in motion *bona fide* to quit the country *sine animo revertendi*."

The leading American case is that of *The Venus* (1814), 8 Cranch, 253, and Scott, *Cases*, 672.   It adopts the principles of the British decisions, cited above, and in connection with these, should be carefully considered by the student. for commentaries, see Hall, § 168;   2 Hyde, § 789;   Lawrence, § 154;   and Wheaton, §§ 322 ff.

244. The Right of Admitting and Excluding Aliens.—
" Every State is free to admit foreigners upon its territory
or to exclude them, in case of necessity, from motives of
public order; with stronger reason it is free to admit them
on certain conditions, under certain restrictions. At the
same time the usage generally followed by governments
permits to foreigners, in times of peace, entrance upon their
territory, freedom to trade, passage, temporary sojourn, and
settlement; but it is well understood that every individual
presenting himself upon foreign territory, by this fact alone
tacitly agrees to submit to the laws of the country that
receives him, to pay the imposts due from any commercial
operations in which he may engage or any business which he
may establish, and to observe the local police regulations." [52]

245. The Practice of the United States.—The United
States has exercised the power of total exclusion in the case
of the Chinese [53] (and this in violation of treaty), and with

---

[52] 2 Calvo, § 700.   Those authorities like Bonfils, Fauchille, Fiore, Heffter,
etc., who claim that the Law of Nations guarantees certain natural rights to
the individual, speak of a *right* of emigration as "flowing logically from the
principle of individual liberty."   But these same publicists admit that some
States discourage emigration and that "the freedom of emigration does not
imply the absolute right of *immigration*."   Bonfils and 1 Fauchille, Nos.
410–14.

It is true that nearly all modern States freely permit emigration, but this
is not legally obligatory upon the State.

Some publicists maintain that, as a result of the fundamental right of commerce or intercourse between States, a member of the family of nations is
under obligation to open its territory to the nationals of all civilized States.
True it is that a modern State which excluded all foreigners would practically
place itself outside the pale of the international community, and that the exclusion of those of a particular nationality would probably justify measures of
retorsion (a form of reprisal—see *infra*, No. 321); but there can be no legal
obligation in the premises.   "The reception of aliens is a matter of discretion,
and every State is by reason of its territorial supremacy competent to exclude
aliens from the whole, or any part, of its territory."   1 Oppenheim, § 314.

Rivier (I, p. 307) states the correct doctrine when he says: "The State is
master in its own house.   It may refuse to foreigners access to its territory,
interdict all immigration, or the immigration of certain individuals or of certain
categories of individuals, for example, nationals of certain countries."   Rivier
adds, however, that this principle, which flows logically from the rights of
independence and self-preservation, is to-day greatly tempered by the rights of
mutual commerce and inoffensive passage.

For resolutions on the admission and expulsion of aliens adopted in 1892 by
the Institute of International Law, see Scott, *Resolutions of the Institute of
Int. Law* (1916), 103–10.   See especially Art. 6.   For 10 Articles and 14
wishes on the subject of emigration, see *Ibid.*, 137–41.

[53] For the legislation and treaties relating to the Chinese, see 4 Moore,

certain exceptions, since 1924 of all aliens ineligible to citizenship. Congressional legislation to this effect has been upheld by our Supreme Court.

" It is an accepted maxim of International Law, that every sovereign nation has the power, as inherent in sovereignty, and essential to self-preservation, to forbid the entrance of foreigners within its dominions, or to admit them only in such cases and upon such conditions as it may see fit to prescribe. In the United States, this power is vested in the national Government, to which the Congress has committed the entire control of international relations, in peace as well as in war. It belongs to the political power of the Government, and may be exercised either through treaties made by the President and Senate, or through statutes enacted by Congress." [54]

246. **The Immigration Laws of the United States.**—Since 1875 the Congress of the United States has shown ever increasing severity in its general restrictions upon foreign immigration. The Act of February, 1917,[55] which appears

Digest, §§ 567–78. For 28 rules regulating the admission of the Chinese in 1909, see *Treaty Laws, and Regulations Governing the Admission of the Chinese*, published by the Bureau of Immigration and Naturalization of the Department of Commerce and Labor (1917), 3 ff. For a selected bibliography on the Chinese Question, see Coolidge, *Chinese Immigration* (1909), 505 ff. For more complete bibliographies, see Cowan and Dunlap, *Bibliography of the Chinese Question in the United States* (1909); Griffin, *Select List of References on Chinese Immigration* (1904); and *A List of Books on Immigration* (1907).

As a result of agitation for an anti-Japanese exclusion law, a *modus vivendi* between the Japanese and the United States Governments was effected in 1907–08 whereby Japanese laborers were practically excluded by the Japanese Government itself. This so-called "Gentlemen's Agreement," which proved highly effective and was attached to the Commercial Treaty of 1911 between Japan and the United States in the form of a declaration by the Japanese Government, was annulled by the U. S. Immigration Law of 1924 which excluded all aliens ineligible to citizenship. For the text of the Japanese protest and the reply of Sec'y Hughes, see 20 *Cur. Hist.* (1924), 649 f. and 881 f.

[54] Justice Gray, in *Nishimura Ekiu* v. *United States* (1891), 142 U. S. 651, 659. Cf. Justice Field in *Chae Chan Ping* v. *U. S.* (1889), 130 U. S. 581, 609; and Justice Gray in the *Chinese Cases* (1892), 149 U. S. 698, and Scott, *Cases* (ed. of 1902), 382.

[55] For previous legislation, see 4 Moore, *Digest*, § 562; *Immigration Laws*, Dept. of Labor (1921); and Bouvé, *Exclusion and Expulsion of Aliens* (1912), 51 ff.

The Act of 1875 merely prohibited the importation of women for purposes of prostitution and the immigration of aliens "who are undergoing conviction in their own country for felonious crimes, other than political. . . ." The

to be still in force except where supplanted by subsequent laws, levied, for purposes of an " immigrant fund," a head tax of eight dollars for every alien entering the country. It broadened the scope of excluded classes, and required all aliens over 16 years of age to have a reading knowledge of some language.

Among excluded classes (according to Sec. 3 of the Act of 1917), are the following: Idiots, imbeciles, feeble-minded persons, epileptics, insane persons, and persons of constitutional psychopathic inferiority; persons with chronic alcoholism, paupers, professional beggars, vagrants, persons afflicted with tuberculosis or with a loathsome or dangerous disease, or persons found otherwise mentally or physically defective (such physical defect being of a nature affecting the ability of such alien to earn a living); persons convicted

Act of 1882 levied a head tax of fifty cents "for every passenger not a citizen of the United States," and forbade the landing of convicts, lunatics, idiots, or of "any person unable to take care of himself or herself without becoming a public charge." The Act of 1885 forbade the immigration of aliens under contract to labor. The Acts of 1891 and 1903 made a number of further additions to the excluded classes (such as anarchists, polygamists, and epileptics), the latter Act raising the head tax to two dollars; but it was not before 1907 that this tax was raised to four dollars, and imbeciles, the feeble-minded persons afflicted with tuberculosis, those physically defective, etc., were excluded. The Act of 1907 increased the head tax to four dollars and greatly broadened the scope of exclusion.

In 1905 the British Parliament passed an Aliens Act largely modeled on the Act of Congress of 1882. It merely excluded undesirable aliens who belong to one or more of the following classes:

"(a) If he cannot show that he has in his possession or is in a position to obtain the means of decently supporting himself and his dependents (if any).

"(b) If he is a lunatic or an idiot, or owing to any disease or infirmity appears likely to become a charge upon the rates or otherwise a detriment to the public.

"(c) If he has been sentenced in a foreign country with which there is an extradition treaty for a crime, not being an offense of a political character, which is, as respects that country, an extradition crime within the meaning of the extradition Act, 1870.

"(d) If an expulsion order under this Act has been made in his case."

But, unlike the legislation of the United States, the Act provides for exemption in case of an immigrant who proves that he is seeking admission solely to avoid religious persecution. The Act also provides specific directions for the expulsion of undesirable aliens.

For an analysis of the Aliens Act of 1905, see Sibley and Elias, *The Aliens Act and Right of Asylum* (1906), 43 ff. For the text, see *Ibid.*, App. I, 83 ff. See also Henriques, *Law of Aliens and Naturalization* (1906).

Immigration laws exist in a number of countries, but the power of *expuslion* is much more general than that of prohibitions against admission. Sibley and Elias, 19.

of having committed a felony or other crime or misdemeanor involving moral turpitude; polygamists, or persons who practice polygamy or believe in or advocate the practice of polygamy; anarchists, or persons who believe in or advocate the overthrow by force or violence of the Government of the United States, or of all forms of law, or who disbelieve in or are opposed to organized government, or who advocate the assassination of public officials or who advocate or teach the unlawful destruction of property; persons who are members of or affiliated with any organization entertaining and teaching disbelief in or opposition to organized government, or who advocate or teach the duty, necessity, or propriety of the unlawful assaulting, or killing of any officer or officers, either of specific individuals or of officers generally, of the Government of the United States, or of any other organized government, because of his or their official character, or who advocate or teach the unlawful destruction of property; prostitutes, or persons coming into the United States for the purpose of prostitution or for any other immoral purpose, or who directly or indirectly procure or attempt to procure or import prostitutes, or who are supported by or receive in whole or in part the proceeds of prostitution; contract laborers; [56] persons who have come in consequence of advertisements for laborers printed, published, or distributed in a foreign country; person likely to become a public charge; persons who have been deported under any of the provisions of this act; stowaways; all children under sixteen years of age, unaccompanied by or not coming to one of their parents (except that as in the case of stowaways they may be admitted in the discretion of the Secretary of Labor); unless otherwise provided for by existing treaties, natives of a portion of the continent of Asia and of islands within a given area adjacent to the continent of Asia defined by latitudinal and logitudinal lines not possessed by the United States; [57] all aliens over sixteen years of age, physically

56 For judicial interpretations of the term "contract laborers," see 4 Moore, *Digest*, § 564.

57 This provision shall, however, not apply to persons of the following status or occupations: Government officers, ministers or religious teachers, missionaries, lawyers, physicians, chemists, civil engineers, teachers, students, authors,

capable of reading, who can not read the English language, or some other language or dialect, including Hebrew or Yiddish.[58]

The Immigration Act of 1924 presents several novel features. In the first place, it marks a real attempt to control immigration at its source through a system of consular certificates or visas; and in the next place, it makes ineligibility to become naturalized a reason for exclusion.[59] It also greatly improves the quota system [60] introduced for

artists, merchants, and travelers for curiosity or pleasure, nor to their legal wives or their children under sixteen years of age who shall accompany them or who subsequently may apply for admission to the United States. This will give a good idea of the classes generally excepted from the provisions of our immigration laws.

[58] Immigration Act of Feb. 5, 1917, sec. 3, somewhat abridged. For the text of this Act, see *Immigration Laws and Rules*, U. S. Dept. of Labor (1917).

Sec. 3 also provides that any admissible alien or any citizen of the United States may bring in or send for his father or grandfather over 55 years of age, his wife, his mother, his grandmother, or his unmarried or widowed daughter, if otherwise admissible, whether such relative can read or not. It also exempts from the illiteracy test all aliens who shall prove that they are seeking admission to the United States to avoid religious persecution.

"Nothing in this act shall exclude, if otherwise admissible, persons convicted, or who admit the commission, or who teach or advocate the commission, of an offense purely political."

The provisions of the law applicable to contract labor shall not exclude professional actors, artists, lecturers, singers, nurses, ministers of any religious denomination, professors for colleges or seminaries, persons belonging to any recognized learned profession, or persons employed as domestic servants.

Very severe penalties (far more severe than in the case of previous immigration laws) are prescribed for certain violations of the act.

[59] On non-eligibility to become naturalized, see *supra*, No. 234 and note 35.

[60] The main objects of the quota system are to reduce the number of annual immigrants and to make the reduction fall most heavily on the countries of southern and eastern Europe (the countries of recent immigration) and most lightly on those of northern and western Europe from which our earlier immigration was principally derived.

Under the law of 1921 the "quota base" was the census of 1910 and the number of immigrants alotted to any nationality annually was three per cent of the number of foreign born of that nationality in the United States as shown by that census.

The law of 1924 makes the census of 1890 the "quota base" and the percentage two instead of three. The quota so calculated is to remain in force until July 1, 1927 when the "national origins" plan shall come into effect. According to this scientific plan, "the annual quota of any nationality" will be "a number which bears the same ratio to 150,000 as the number of inhabitants in continental United States in 1920 having that national origin . . . bears to the number of inhabitants in continental United States in 1920." Sec. 11, sub. (b).

The term "immigrant" is defined as "any alien departing from any place

the first time in the Quota Act of 1921 which expired by
limitation on June 30, 1924 and was superseded by the new
Quota Act of that year.

247. **Expulsion of Aliens.**—The right of expelling foreigners is also generally held to be an attribute or incident of
sovereignty,[61] and is probably practiced, to a greater or less
extent, by all political communities.   It is usually justified
on grounds of self-protection or public interest.   Expulsion
is necessarily an administrative act, but it is not a punitive
measure and should not be performed in an arbitrary or
needlessly injurious manner or for insufficient cause.   It is

outside the United States destined for the United States, except (1) a government official, his family, attendants, servants, and employees, (2) an alien
visiting the United States temporarily as a tourist or temporarily for business
or pleasure, (3) an alien in continuous transit through the United States, (4)
an alien lawfully admitted to the United States who later goes in transit from
one part of the United States to another through foreign contiguous territory,
(5) a bona fide alien seaman serving as such on a vessel arriving at a port of the
United States and seeking to enter temporarily the United States solely in the
pursuit of his calling as a seaman, and (6) an alien entitled to enter the United
States solely to carry on a trade under and in pursuance of the provisions of a
present existing treaty of commerce and navigation." Sec. 3.

For two very important articles on "The Quota" and "Ineligible to Citizenship" provisions of the Immigration Act of 1924, see 18 and 19 *A. J.* (1924 and
1925), 737 ff. and 23 ff. respectively.   For the text of the Act, see Supp. to
18 *A. J.*, 208 ff.

There are two classes of immigrants—quota and non-quota immigrants.
Among the latter are: (*a*) an unmarried child under 18 years of age, or the wife
of a citizen of the United States residing therein; (*b*) an immigrant previously
lawfully admitted to the United States who is returning from a temporary visit
abroad; (*c*) an immigrant born in the Dominion of Canada, Newfoundland,
Mexico, Cuba, Haiti, the Dominican Republic, the Canal Zone or an independent country of Central or South America, and his wife, and his unmarried
children under 18 years of age, if accompanying or following to join him; (*d*)
ministers of religion, or college professors, and their wives and minor children;
and (*e*) bona fide students at least fifteen years of age.

Very drastic penalties are prescribed for violation of the law, and the burden
of proof is placed upon the alien to establish that he is not subject to exclusion
or liable to deportation (sec. 23).

[61] A few publicists like Fiore (*Traité de droit penal int.*, 1880, 100 ff.), Pinheiro-Ferreira (*Notes sur Vattel*, liv. II, c. 8, § 100), and Tchernoff (*Droit de
Protection*, 1898, 461), are of the opinion that the practice of expulsion is an
invasion of natural rights; but the majority of the authorities justify it on
grounds of public interest.

In *Turner* v. *Williams* (1904), 194 U. S. 279, the Supreme Court of the
United States declared the right to expel aliens inherent in sovereignty.   For
the resolutions on expulsion of foreigners adopted by the Institute of International Law, see Scott, *Resolutions of the Institute of Int. Law* (1916), 88–90
and 103 ff.   For some foreign laws relating to expulsion and exclusion of aliens,
see Bouvé, *op. cit.*, App. A, 685 ff.

maintained that the expelled person has a right to know the reason for his expulsion, and that this reason should be communicated to the Government of the State to which he belongs. Unless there is imperative reason for urgency, he should be given a reasonable time to adjust his affairs, more especially in the case of a domiciled alien with business or property interests.[62] There should be no discrimination because of race or religion.[63]

If these rules are violated, an indemnity[64] may be demanded by the Government of the injured alien. If this be refused, the case should be arbitrated. As a last resort, recourse may be had to reprisal in the form of retorsion.

248. **Rights of Aliens.**—Nearly all modern nations place the foreigner upon substantially the same footing as the native in respect to the enjoyment of civil as distinguished from political rights. In a few States they are still under certain disabilities as far as trade, the practice of certain occupations and professions, religious worship, and the ownership, transfer, and inheritance of real property are concerned.[65]

[62] For cases of expulsion, see 3 and 4 Moore, *Digest*, §§ 393, 399, 463, 550–59. See especially the case of *Hollander*, in 4 Moore, pp. 102–08.

[63] Such discrimination was formerly practiced by Russia in the case of the Jews. See 4 Moore, *Digest*, § 554.

[64] The British exacted an indemnity from Nicaraugua for the arbitrary seizure and expulsion of twelve British subjects in 1894. See the *Bluefields* case, in 4 Moore, *Digest*, § 551, pp. 99–101.

For claims on account of expulsion, decided by mixed commissions, see 4 Moore, *Arbitrations*, ch. 60.

[65] Trade restrictions are still very great in China. It is generally known that foreigners are only legally permitted to trade in certain ports or places opened by treaty.

In Japan property in land is still forbidden to foreigners as individuals. It also appears that the personality of foreign corporations is not recognized in Japan.

In several States of the American Union, aliens are still prohibited from purchasing, holding, or inheriting real estate; but these disqualifications have, in the case of those belonging to certain nationalities, been overridden by treaties which our courts hold to be the law of the land, State laws or constitutions to the contrary notwithstanding. See 4 Moore, *Digest*, §§ 544–45.

The British Act of Naturalization of 1870 removed the disabilities until then resting upon aliens in the United Kingdom in respect to the acquisition and disposition of real property. In Great Britain "an alien has full proprietary capacity (except that he may not be the owner of a British ship), full contractual testamentary, and procedural capacity, but no parliamentary, municipal, or other franchise, and no qualification for a public office." McNair

All that aliens can claim, however, from the strictly legal standpoint, is protection of life and property, and access to the courts for the sake of securing this protection.[66]   But most modern States permit to alien friends the free use of their courts on the same terms as natives or citizens.   The United States even recognizes the right of non-resident aliens to sue in the Federal courts.[67]

249. **Duties of Aliens.**—In return for this protection, mere passing travelers or visitors, as well as resident aliens, owe a local and temporary allegiance and obedience to the laws or the sovereign in whose country they live or through whose territory they pass.   They are subject to the local administration and may be punished for any crimes or misdemeanors committed within the jurisdiction of such sovereign.[68]   They must obey all reasonable regulations instituted for their welfare or for the convenience of the local authorities, such as requirements in respect to the *visé* of passports,[69] registration, etc.

The power to impose taxes being an attribute of sover-

---

in 35 *Law Quar. Rev.* (1919), 225.   The registry laws of the United States, as in some other countries, place certain restrictions upon aliens in respect to the registration of vessels.   2 Moore, *Digest*, § 322.

For references on the special rights of exterritoriality still enjoyed by foreigners in some Mohammedan countries in Africa and the Orient, see *infra*, pp. 425–26.

[66] For a fuller discussion of this subject, see *supra*, ch. 11.

[67] France refuses the use of her tribunals where the plaintiff and defendant are both foreigners.   This system is justly condemned by Bonfils, (5th ed.), No. 447.   It should be noted, however, that the many exceptions to this rule have greatly limited its application.

[68] Aliens traveling or residing in foreign lands are none the less subject to the laws of their own country.   They are thus theoretically subject to a double or concurrent jurisdiction.   But it is not customary for the home State to assert jurisdiction over crimes committed by its citizens abroad except for particular offences (such as treason, counterfeiting, etc.) or in particular places (in barbarous countries or communities).

Aliens traveling or residing abroad are subject to recall for military service. Their government owes them a certain measure of protection against arbitrary or oppressive acts on the part of foreign governments, but this protection is exercised at the discretion of the home government.   See *supra*, ch. 11 and Bibliography on pp. 264–65.

Some countries even wrongfully assert jurisdiction over foreigners for acts committed on foreign territory.   See *supra* No. 149 and p. 250 for references on the *Cutting Case.*

[69] On *American Passports*, see especially 3 Moore, *Digest*, §§ 493–533; and Gaillard Hunt, *The American Passport* (1898).

eignty, aliens must pay all just and ordinary taxes, but they are not bound to submit to the exaction of forced loans [70] or to taxes which are discriminatory and confiscatory. Resident aliens, who have not declared their intention to become naturalized citizens or who have not exercised the right of suffrage, are not liable to military service, though it is generally held that they may be called upon to perform police or militia service in case of necessity.[71]

IV. EXTRADITION OF FUGITIVE CRIMINALS AND POLITICAL OFFENDERS

A fourth category of individuals who may, from a certain point of view, be regarded as objects of the Law of Nations, are Fugitive Criminals and Political Offenders.

250. **Fugitive Criminals.**—Fugitive criminals or persons accused of crime committed in one country and fleeing into another may be extradited or delivered by the government of the latter into the hands of the authorities of the former, upon the demand of the government of the nation in whose territory the crime has been committed.

In the absence of a treaty, extradition is not, strictly speaking, a legal obligation in International Law; [72] for

[70] 2, 4, and 6 Moore, *Digest*, §§ 183–84, 540, and 1036. For the consideration of the subject of forced loans by international commissions, see 4 Moore, *Arbitrations*, ch. 62, pp. 3409 ff.

[71] On the *Exemption of Aliens from Ordinary Military Service*, see especially Bluntschli, Art. 391; Bonfils, No. 445; Despagnet, No. 354; * Hall § 61; * Halleck (3 d ed.), 419–20 n., 558–59 n.; Lawrence, (3d ed.), § 117: * 4 Moore, *Digest*, § 458; 1 Westlake, 218–19; 2 Wharton, *Digest*, § 202.

[72] Clarke (*Extradition*, ch. 1, 4th ed., 1903) vainly attempts to show that the assertion that "the majority of jurists deny the existence of any right to demand extradition" is incorrect. He quotes from Grotius, Pufendorf, Kent, Story, etc.; but he is not fully borne out even by these authorities, for the majority of them evidently consider extradition a natural right or moral duty rather than a legal right or obligation. He himself finally concludes (p. 14) that the refusal to surrender fugitive criminals is "a serious violation of the moral obligations which exist between civilized communities."

The great majority of the more modern authorities clearly regard extradition, in the absence of a treaty, as a mere matter of comity, discretion, interest, or moral obligation. This is also the view of the great majority of jurists and statesmen, and it is borne out by international practice. See especially 4 Moore, *Digest*, §§ 580 ff., and 1 *Extradition* (1891), §§ 9–15; and Spear, *The Law of Extradition* (1885, 2d ed.), ch. 1, for views of American jurists and statesmen.

Some modern authorities are, however, not quite clear upon this point

there is no generally recognized rule of the Law of Nations which requires that the worst criminal be given up by one sovereign upon the request of another. But it is to the interest of civilization and the international community that all persons guilty of serious crimes be extradited for trial to the place where the crime has been committed. And since the third decade of the nineteenth century [73] a number of laws have been enacted and numerous treaties of extradition concluded which prescribe the mode and conditions of delivery and enumerate crimes for which extradition shall take place.

251. The Nature of Extradition.—Except in Great

Fiore (I, Nos. 626–27) considers extradition a duty of mutual aid or assistance. Despagnet (No. 291) speaks of it as a "theoretical obligation founded upon the principles of International Law," but denies that it is a "positive obligation," in the absence of convention. Westlake (I, p. 254) classes it as an "imperfect right." Rivier (I, p. 348) appears to be practically alone in holding, apparently without reserve, that "independently of all conventional arrangement, there is an obligation of extradition existing between States of equal civilization, members of the international community." But even he adds: "This principle is to-day more or less generally recognized, at least in theory." Fauchille (I, No. 457) tries to harmonize these more or less opposing stand-points between the advocates of the rights of sovereignty and the duties of coöperation and interdependence.

[73] Treaties of extradition were comparatively infrequent prior to the French Revolution. Contrary to the modern usage, they were usually directed against political offenders rather than ordinary criminals. Art. 20 of the Treaty of Amiens (1802) provided for the reciprocal extradition of fugitives accused of certain heinous crimes between England, France, Spain, and the Batavian Republic. But it was not until after 1840 that Treaties of Extradition may be said to have become frequent. This was doubtless owing to increased facilities of interstate communication.

The first municipal law on the subject appears to have been the Belgian law of 1833, but it was not until 1870 that the British Parliament passed an Extradition Act. The Congress of the United States passed General Extradition Laws in 1848 and 1869—Acts which are now replaced by secs. 5270–77 of the Revised Statutes, supplemented by the Act of 1882 (22 U. S. Stat. at Large, 215).

With the exception of Art. 27 of Jay's Treaty of 1794 with Great Britain (which expired by limitation in 1807), the first treaties of the United States were with Great Britain in 1842 and France in 1843.

For the Extradition Treaties and Laws of the United States, see Hawley, *Int. Extradition* (1893); Moore, *Extradition* (1891), in 2 vols., App. I; Spear, *The Law of Extradition* (1885), Appendices; Supplements to *A. J.* (see index vol.).

For the Laws and Treaties of Great Britain, see Biron and Chalmers, *Extradition* (1903); Clark, *Extradition* (1903); and Piggott, *Extradition* (1910), App. For the laws of various countries, see 2 Martitz, *Int. Rechtshilfe* (1897), 771 ff.

Britian and the United States, States as a rule refuse to extradite their own citizens or subjects.[74] Just as a government, unless bound by treaty, may refuse extradition for any crime whatsoever, so it may grant extradition at its discretion, unless restrained by municipal law.[75] For

[74] England and the United States are exceptions to this rule. This arises from the fact that the United States does not, except for such international crimes as piracy and the slave trade, punish her citizens for crimes committed out of the country; and England only punishes her subjects for such crimes as treason, murder, bigamy, etc., when these are committed abroad.

In the absence of a clause expressly exempting nationals from extradition, the State Department at Washington has held that they should be surrendered upon demand. Italy, however, has refused to deliver up her subjects to the United States in spite of the fact that the Extradition Treaty between the two countries contains no such exemption. See 4 Moore, *Digest*, § 594, pp. 290 ff. In 1890 the Swiss Federal Tribunal decided in favor of the position taken by the United States. *Ibid.*, pp. 298 ff.

In the case of *Charlton* v. *Kelly* (1913), 229 U. S. 447, Scott, *Cases*, 415, or Evans, *Cases*, 340, the Supreme Court of the United States affirmed the judgment of a district court which had refused a writ of habeas corpus to prevent the extradition of a citizen of the United States who had murdered his wife in Italy and escaped to the United States.

The main objection urged against Charlton's extradition was that the treaty with Italy had been abrogated, since it lacked mutuality; for Italy had refused to deliver up its own citizens, the Italian code, indeed, forbidding such extradition.

The Court held that this lack of reciprocity rendered the treaty voidable but not void, and did not deprive the executive department of its right to deliver up American citizens. The court declared, that "there is no principle of International Law by which citizens are excepted out of an agreement to surrender 'persons' where no such exception is made in the treaty itself."

For editorial comment on the *Charlton Case*, see 5 and 7 *A. J.* (1911 and 1913), 182 ff. and 580 ff. For a full report of this interesting case, see 7 *A. J.* 637 ff.

In *Trimble's Case* (1884) the United States declined to order the surrender of one of its citizens to the Mexican Government "on the ground that, as the treaty negatived any obligation to do so, the President was not invested with legal authority to act." 1 Moore, *Extradition* (1891), § 135.

Art. 6 of the Treaty of 1861 with Mexico declared that neither of the contracting parties shall be "bound to deliver up its own citizens." Sec'y Frelinghuysen construed this provision (which, as he said, was identical with clauses in numerous other Extradition Treaties of the United States) as conferring upon the President no discretionary power whatever—a view which was judicially upheld in *Ex parte McCabe* (1891), 46 Fed. 363. Art. 4 of the Treaty of 1899 between the United States and Mexico expressly granted such discretionary power to the President. 4 Moore, *Digest*, pp. 301 and 303. "In July, 1895, the Mexican Government declined to surrender to the United States, Chester W. Rowe, a fugitive from justice, on the ground that he had, by the purchase of real estate in Mexico, assumed Mexican nationality." *Ibid.*, p. 302.

[75] This at least appears to be the prevailing doctrine in France and on the

extradition is essentially a political or executive act, though the judiciary usually decides the legal or technical points involved, at least in England and the United States. Extradition is generally granted on the bases of reciprocity, and is applied to a considerable number and variety of crimes.[76]

252. Rules of Extradition.—There are several customary rules governing extradition which are so generally observed that they may be claimed as virtual rules of International Law. One of these is that the names of the crimes enumerated in Extradition Treaties should be construed in accordance with the law prevailing in the State which asks for the surrender of the fugitive criminal. In other words, the

Continent. But it is not the view in England or the United States. In the United States it has been almost uniformly held that, in the absence of a treaty, the President is not authorized to order an extradition. An exception was the unauthorized surrender by Secretary Seward of *Arguelles* to Spain in 1864. But this violation of constitutional law and custom has been generally condemned. On the *Arguelles Case*, see Clark, *op. cit.*, 72–74; * 1 Moore, *Extradition*, § 27, and 4 *Digest*, § 581, pp. 249 f.; Spear, *Extradition* (1885), 1–3, 6, 43; Dana's Wheaton, § 115, note 73; Woolsey, § 78.

In England it is held that the common law gives the Government no right to surrender an alien. The Crown may negotiate extradition treaties, but they are given effect by Orders in Council under the authority of an Act of Parliament.

[76] The Extradition Act of Great Britain (1870) specified the following crimes as extraditable: murder, and attempt and conspiracy to murder; manslaughter; counterfeiting and altering money and uttering counterfeit or altered money; forgery, counterfeiting, and altering, and uttering what is forged or counterfeited or altered; embezzlement and larceny; obtaining goods or money by false pretenses; crimes by bankrupts against bankruptcy law; fraud by a bailee, banker, agent, factor, trustee, or director, or member, or public officer of any company made criminal by any Act for the time being in force; rape; abduction; child stealing; burglary and housebreaking; arson; robbery with violence; threats by letter or otherwise with intent to extort; piracy by law of nations; sinking or destroying a vessel at sea, or attempting or conspiring to do so; assaults on board a ship on the high seas with intent to destroy life or to do grievous bodily harm; revolt or conspiracy to revolt by two or more persons on board a ship on the high seas against the authority of the master.

To this list the Extradition and Slave Trade Acts of 1873 added the following; kidnapping and false imprisonment; perjury, and subornation of perjury; and slave trading. See Biron and Chalmers, *op. cit.*, 78–79, 88; and 1 Oppenheim, § 331. For commentary on the Extradition Act of 1870, see Piggott, *Extradition* (1910), ch. 3.

Art. 27 of the Jay Treaty of 1794 with Great Britain merely provided for extradition in case of murder or forgery; the Treaty of 1842 enumerated seven extraditable crimes; the Convention of 1890 with Great Britain adds twenty more.

name of the crime is to be determined rather by the law that has been violated than by the law of the county in which the fugitive is found. Thus, our Supreme Court held that the Spanish word *falsificacion* used as a corresponding word for *forgery* in the Mexican text of the Treaty of 1861 was equivalent to a charge of forgery, even though the crime committed (that of forgery of theatre tickets) might not be forgery at common law—a point which was left undetermined.[77]

Another rule now fully established is that a criminal cannot be tried for any other crime than that named in the warrant of extradition.[78]

[77] *Benson* v. *McMahon* (1888), 127 U. S. 457, 466. Cf. *In re Farez*, 7 Blatch. 345. On these two cases, see Hawley, *Int. Extradition* (1893), 5–7; and 4 Moore, *Digest*, pp. 276–78.

[78] See especially *United States* v. *Rauscher* (1886), 199 U. S., 407, Evans, *Cases*, 346, or Scott, *Cases*, 405. Prior to this important decision, judicial opinion in the United States had been divided. On the *Rauscher Case*, and the earlier judicial decisions in the United States, see 4 Moore, *Digest*, § 597, and 1 *Extradition*, § 187.

During the famous *Winslow* controversy between the United States and Great Britain (1876), Secretary Fish contended that a person could be indicted and tried for an offense other than that for which he had been extradited. Lord Derby, on the other hand, claimed that it was "an essential principle of extradition" that a person surrendered for one offense should not be tried for another.

Before the requisition for Winslow's extradition had been presented at London, the British Minister at Washington suggested that it would probably be refused unless the United States entered into a stipulation that Winslow would not be tried for any other offense than that for which he was to be surrendered. As a consequence of this difference, the execution of the treaty of 1842 was suspended until the British Government temporarily receded from its position.

On the *Winslow Case*, see especially: Hawley, *Int. Extradition* (1893), 8–13; * 1 Moore, *Extradition* (1891), 196–219, and 4 *Digest*, § 596; 2 Wharton, *Digest*, § 270. For further references on this case and an excellent summary of the judicial history of this subject in the United States, see 4 Moore, *Digest*, pp. 308–11.

The rule is different in "Inter-State Rendition" or the Law of Extradition between States of the American Union. In the States persons can be tried for crimes other than those for which they have been extradited. It has even been held that persons kidnapped in one State and carried forcibly into another may be tried. The State Courts merely assert jurisdiction; they will not inquire into irregularities of this kind. For citation of numerous cases, see *State* v. *Patterson* (1893), 116 Missouri 505, and Scott, *Cases*, 413. On "Interstate Extradition," see especially 1 Willoughby, *The Const. Law of the U. S.* (1910), ch. 14; 2 Moore, *Extradition* (1891); and Scott, *Interstate Rendition* (1917).

For the interesting but not very important *Savarkar Case* (1911) which involved irregularities in the surrender of a Hindu prisoner who escaped from a

It is also customary, at least in England and the United States, before a warrant of extradition is issued, to require such evidence of guilt as, according to the laws of the country where the fugitive is found, would justify his (or her) commitment for trial if the crime had been there committed. But this can hardly be considered a principle of International Law, for a State has discretionary power in this matter. In England and the United States aliens have the privilege of habeas corpus.

253. **Political Offenders.**—There is one class of offenses which are not extraditable, according to modern usage. It is now universally held that political offenders are exempt from extradition process.[79] But there is unfortunately no agreement as to the nature or content of a political offense, and no satisfactory definition of a political crime has as yet been evolved.

254. **Difficulties of Definition and Application.**—The difficulties of definition [80] and its application arise from two

British ship in the French port of Marseilles, see Scott, *Hague Ct. Reports* (1917) 275; and 1 Stowell and Munro, 416–22.

[79] This exemption holds, whether expressed in treaties or not.

The recognition of the non-extradition of political offenders as a general principle of conduct dates from the European Revolutions of 1830 and 1848, though it may be said to owe its origin to the French Revolution of 1789. It was particularly England, Switzerland, France, Belgium, and the United States who championed the cause of political freedom. In 1830 even Austria and Prussia refused Russia's demand for the extradition of Polish refugees. But a reaction set in (1833) when Austria, Prussia, and Russia concluded agreements stipulating that persons who had committed high treason and *lèse majesté*, or who were guilty of conspiracy or revolt against a throne or legitimate government should be surrendered. The same year (1833) Belgium passed her famous Extradition Law (see *supra*, p. 378 n.) which expressly forbade the extradition of political offenders—a provision which finds its first incorporation in a modern treaty in the Convention of 1834 between Belgium and France. Since 1866 even Russia has felt herself obliged to agree to the non-extradition of political offenders. Grivaz, *Nature et effects de l'asile politique* (1895), ch. 2, particularly pp. 89 ff.; and 2 Martitz, *Int. Rechtshilfe* (1897), 134–84. For a good summary, see 1 Oppenheim, § 333.

[80] For various definitions of a political offense, see 2 Calvo, § 1034; and 3 P.-Fodéré, No. 1872. One of the best characterizations is that by Lord Denman in the *Castioni* case (1891), 1 Q. B. 149; Evans, *Cases*, 352; or Scott, *Cases*, 420.

"The question really is whether, upon the facts, it is clear that the man was acting as one of a number of persons engaged in acts of violence of a political character with a political object, and as part of the political movement and rising in which he was taking part." Cf. *In re Meunier* (1894), 2 Q. B. 415 or Scott, *Cases*, 427.

sets of facts. In the first place, a crime may be purely political or it may have a double motive or end—it may be partly political and partly personal or private. Such crimes have been named *délits connexes* (mixed) by French publicists. In the next place, a crime may be political in appearance, but really private or *vice versa*.

In the latter case, no serious difficulty presents itself, provided the facts are clearly established. For the determination of these facts, a judicial inquiry would seem to be desirable. A more serious difficulty arises in the case of mixed crimes. Here it may be extremely difficult or well-nigh impossible to determine the dominant or controlling motive or purpose, as where theft, arson, or homicide, have been committed. In these cases, too, a judicial decision based on a thorough investigation would seem to be the best solution.

The following solution adopted by the Swiss Extradition Law of 1892 is championed by Oppenheim (I, § 337): "Art. 10 recognizes the non-extradition of political criminals, but lays down the rule at the same time that political criminals shall nevertheless be surrendered in case the chief feature of the offense wears more the aspect of an ordinary than of a political crime, and that the decision concerning the extraditability of such criminals rests with the *Bundesgericht*, the highest Swiss Court of Justice."

Arts. 13, 14, and 15 of the Oxford Rules of 1880 adopted by the Institute of International Law as modified at Geneva in 1892 declare:

"Art. 13.   Extradition is inadmissible for purely political crimes or offenses.

"Nor can it be admitted for unlawful acts of a mixed character or connected with political crimes or offenses, also called relative political offenses, unless in the case of crimes of great gravity from the point of view of morality and of the common law, such as murder, manslaughter, poisoning, mutilation, grave wounds inflicted wilfully with premeditation, attempts at crimes of that kind, outrages to property by arson, explosion of flooding, and grave robbery, especially when committed with arms and violence.

"So far as concerns acts committed in the course of an insurrection or of a civil war by one of the parties engaged in the struggle and in the interest of its cause, they cannot give occasion to extradition unless they are acts of odious barbarism or vandalism forbidden by the laws of war, and then only when the civil war is at an end.

"Art. 14.   Criminal acts directed against the bases of all social organization, and not only against a certain State or a certain preceding form of government, are not considered political offenses in the application of the foregoing rules.

"Art. 15.   In any case, extradition for crimes having the characters both of political and common law crime ought not to be granted unless the requesting State gives the assurance that the person surrendered shall not be tried by extraordinary courts." Scott, *Resolutions of the Institute of Int. Law* (1916), 44 and 103. Cf. 1 Westlake, 256–67.

These rules have been criticised, but they seem to embody the best opinion on this subject.

Then, too, a political crime may be of such a gross and outrageous character, as in the case of the assassination of a constitutional sovereign or chief of State, that it is not to the interest of other States to refuse extradition. Such cases should be exempted from the operation of the rule that political offenders are not extraditable.[81]

[81] See Arts. 13 and 14 cited above. There is still considerable difference of opinion respecting anarchistic and nihilistic attempts and attacks upon the life of a reigning sovereign or Chief of State. Many States have accepted the so-called *attentat* clause enacted by Belgium in 1856. This clause stipulated that the murder of the head of a foreign government or of a member of his family should not be considered a political crime. 1 Oppenheim, § 335. The United States has even included it in a few of its Extradition Treaties. For clauses dealing with political offenses in Extradition Treaties between the United States and other countries, see Supplement to 3 *A. J.* (1909), 144 ff.

As Oppenheim (I, § 339) justly observes: "The Belgian clause goes too far, since exceptional cases of murder of heads of States from political motives or for political purposes might occur which do not deserve extradition." There have been attempts of this nature which were either legitimate as part of a political insurrection or which, because of the tyranny and oppression exercised, are not condemned by the moral sense of mankind.

On the other hand, mere anarchistic attempts should receive no quarter. Communists and socialists, however, stand upon an entirely different footing, for their efforts are not "directed against the bases of all social organization"; they aim at the reorganization of society on a juster and sounder foundation.

It should be added that press offenses are usually regarded as political, but not necessarily so.

On *Political Offenses*, see especially: Bluntschli, Art. 396; Bry, *Précis élémentaire de droit int.* (1906), No. 329; 2 Calvo §§ 1034–45; 1 Cobbett, 247–48, 250; Despagnet, No. 304 B.; Diena, in 2 *R. D. I. P* (1895), 306 ff.; * 1 Fauchille, Nos. 464–72; Grivaz, *Nature et effets du principe de l'asile politique* (1895); * 1 Hyde, §§ 315–18; Laire, *Extradition et les délits politiques* (1911); Lammasch, *Das Recht der Auslieferung* (1884), and in 3 Holtzendorff, 485 ff.; Lawrence, § 111; Mérignhac, *Traité*, 754–78; * 4 Moore, *Digest*, § 604; and * 1 *Extradition* (1891), ch. 8; 3 F. de Martens, § 96; * 2 Martitz, *Int. Rechtshilfe*, (1897); * 1 Oppenheim, §§ 333–40; 3 P.-Fodéré, Nos. 1871–1873; Renault, in 7 *J. I. P.* (Clunet), 65 ff.; 1 Rivier, 351–57; Rolin, in 12 *Annuaire*, 156 ff., and in 24 and 26 *R. D. I.*, 285–93 and 125–52; * Scott, *Cases*, 420–28; Soldan, *Extradition des criminels politiques* (1882); Taylor, § 212; Ulmann, § 129, IV; 1 Westlake, 256–58. See also the papers by Clark, Coudert, and Mack in *Procs. Am. Soc. I. L.* (1909), 95–166.

The student should especially study the case of *In re Castioni* (1890), L. R. Q. B., Div. 149, and Evans, *Cases*, 352 or Scott, *Cases*, 420. See also the cases of *Cazo*, 1 Moore, *Extradition*, § 217; *The St. Alban's Raid, Ibid.*, § 215; the *Salvadorean Refugees* and *San Ignacio Raid*, in 4 Moore, *Digest*, § 604, pp. 334 ff.; and the case of *Rudowitz*, Maxey, in 21 *Green Bag* (1909), 147 ff.; Coudert, in *Procs. Am Soc. I. L.* (1909), 140 f.; and Hyde, in 8 *A. J.* (1914), notes on pp. 491–95.

On Jan. 15, 1920 Holland rightly refused the demand of the Supreme Council, representing the Allied and Associated Powers, "to deliver into their hands William of Hohenzollern, former Emporer of Germany, in order that he

V. The So-called Right of Asylum

255. The So-called Right of Asylum.—This so-called right applies especially to criminals, political refugees, and slaves, and has been claimed on warships, in legations, and consulates, and even on merchantmen in the case of political refugees who, having escaped to another country, take passage on a foreign merchant vessel for a third country, said vessel being bound on a voyage which includes calls at ports of their own country.[82]

There is no right of asylum appertaining to individuals. So far as this so-called right exists, it belongs to the State; but to this right there is attached no corresponding duty.

In the absence of treaty obligation, every State has of course the right to give or withhold asylum to foreigners, including criminals, political offenders, and fugitive slaves. But it has no right to harbor criminals either on its warships or in legations.[83]   It is also agreed that, except in Spanish-

may be put to trial." The demand for this extradition was based upon Art. 227 of the Treaty of Versailles which arraigned him for "a supreme offense against international morality and the sanctity of treaties." For a summary of the facts and arguments, see Scott on "The Trial of the Kaiser," in House and Seymour, *What Really Happened at Paris*, 231–58. Cf. *supra*, ch. i., p. 3 and note 4.

For the "Extradition of the Assassins of the Spanish Premier Dato by the German Reich (Fort Extradition Case)," see 16 *A. J.* (1922), 542 ff.

[82] In the *Barrundia Case* (1890), Mr. Mizner, U. S. Minister to Central America, was unjustly censured and recalled by President Harrison for having advised the surrender of General Barrundia, a Guatemalan political refugee who had taken passage on the Pacific Mail Steamer, then anchored in transit in the port of San José de Guatemala. General Barrundia resisted capture and was killed. 2 Moore, *Digest*, § 307, pp. 871–77. Secretary Blaine's labored defense of our Government's position in this case fails to carry conviction. A more correct statement of the law is that of Secretary Bayard in the case of *Gámez* (2 Moore, *Digest*, pp. 867–68, and Snow, *Cases on Int. Law*, 1893, 149) or of Sec'y. Gresham in 1893 (see 1 Hyde, § 225, p. 403). See also the case of *Sotelo*, 2 Moore, *Digest*, 856, Snow, *op. cit.*, 147, and Scott, *Cases*, 336–37 n. In 1893 Honduras promptly disavowed all responsibility for the firing upon the American steamer *Costa Rica* because her captain refused to surrender Dr. Bonilla, a political refugee. 2 Moore, *Digest*, pp. 879 ff.

[83] See *infra*, Nos. 209, 278. In no case may a process be served on board a public vessel, nor can one charged with crime be even forcibly removed. Ordinary criminals should be given up upon proper demand. But the demand should be made diplomatically and, in extreme cases, the vessel might be refused the hospitality of the port.

The immunities of legations are not as great as those of warships. It is now generally admitted that an ambassador or other foreign minister cannot afford shelter to ordinary criminals, even to servants of the embassy, if the offense

American States (where a special usage seems to have obtained recognition) and perhaps in the Orient, legations and consulates no longer have the right of granting asylum to political refugees.[84]

A different practice appears to obtain in the case of warships. It would seem that according to general usage, commanders of warships may, under circumstances of serious danger and at their discretion, grant asylum to political refugees from motives of humanity upon condition of observing a strict neutrality between both parties. But asylum should never be offered nor should the refugees be permitted to maintain communication with the shore. The same principles probably extend to fugitive slaves.[85]

charged is committed outside the minister's residence. But the arrest should, if possible, be arranged diplomatically, and the convenience or wishes of the minister should be carefully consulted. See *infra*, p. 409 n. as to the time and mode of arrest.

[84] The right of asylum of legations has almost disappeared in European practice. The classic case is that of the *Duke of Ripperda* (1726). See Ch. de Martens, *Causes célèbres*, 174; 1 Satow, § 338; Snow, *Cases*, 139; and 2 Moore, *Digest*, 765–66. But owing to the frequency of political revolutions, it still persists in Spanish-America and perhaps in Spain where it was revived during the Carlist Wars in the middle of the nineteenth century. There was a case in Spain as late as 1873. There have also been a few sporadic cases in southeastern Europe, one in Greece (1862), and one in Constantinople (1895). The practice also obtains in some parts of the Orient.

The United States discourages the practice in Spanish-American States, but does not prohibit it entirely. For the opinion of Secretary Fish and the Instructions to diplomatic agents issued by our State Department on this point see Snow, *Cases*, 142, and *Int. Law. A Manual* (1898), 28. See also 2 Moore, *Digest*, §§ 295–304, particularly § 300, for the views of Secretary Fish.

[85] For the instructions of the British Admiralty and the Regulations of the United States Navy on these points, see 2 Moore, *Digest*, § 305, and Snow, *Int. Law. A Manual*, 29.

Art. 28 of the General Act of the Brussels Conference of 1890 provided that "any slave who may have taken refuge on board a ship of war flying the flag of one of the Signatory Powers shall be immediately and definitely freed; such freedom, however, shall not withdraw him from the competent jurisdiction if he has committed a crime or offense at common law." On *Fugitive Slaves*, see especially Charteris, in *Brit. Yr. Bk.* (1920–21), 85 ff.; and Perels, 126–31.

For the rules respecting the reception of refugees on board warships and merchantmen in foreign ports adopted by the Institute of Int. Law, see Scott, *Resolutions of the Institute of Int. Law* (1916), 148–49, 152, 154, Arts. 19–21, 34, 42. For an interesting controversy between Brazil and Portugal, in 1894, see 2 Moore, *Digest*, § 305, pp. 853 ff.

BIBLIOGRAPHY

Nationality, Naturalization, Expatriation, and Citizenship.—Andreani, *La condition des étrangers en France* (1907); Arts. "Aliens," "Citizens," etc., in *Am. Digest, Corpus Juris*, and *Ruling Case Law;* Bluntschli, Arts. 364–74; * Borchard, §§ 4–5, 198–282, and in 7 *A. J.* (1913), 497 ff.; 2 Calvo, §§ 539–654, and 6 *Ibid.*, §§ 92–117; *Citizenship, Expatriation*, etc., in 72 House Doc., No. 326, 59th Cong., 2d sess. (1906–07); 1 Cobbett, 176–203; Cockburn, *Nationality* (1869); * Cogordan, *La nationalité* (2d ed., 1890); Davis, ch. 4, pp. 135–51; Delécaille, *De la naturalization* (1893); Despagnet, Nos. 329–44, and *Droit int. privé* (5th ed., 1909), liv. I; * Dicey and Keith, *Conflict of Laws* (1922), Bk. I, ch. 3; * 1 Fauchille, Nos. 417–32; Fenwick, ch. 11, pp. 165–75; 1 Fiore, Nos. 644–58, 684–712, and *Int. Law Cod.* (1918), Nos. 530–44, 643–47; Flournoy, in 9 *A. J.* (1915), 870 ff., and in 30, 31, and 33 *Yale Law J.* (1921–24), 545 ff., 702 ff., and 159 respectively; De Folleville, *Traité de la naturalization* (1888); Foote, *Private Int. Jurisprudence* (3d ed., 1904), Pt. I, ch. 1; Franklin, *The Legislative History of Naturalization in the United States* (1906); Hall, Pt. II, ch. 5, and, *Foreign Powers and Jurisdiction* (1894), Pt. II, ch. 1; 1 Halleck (3d ed.), ch. 12; Gargas, in 5 *Z. V.* (1911), 278 ff. and 478 ff.; * Garner, *Introduction to Pol. Sci.* (1910), ch. 11; Howard, *The German Empire* (1906), ch. 8; * 1 Hyde, §§ 342–98; Arts. on "Nationality" and "Naturalization" in 2 Lalor, *Cyclopedia of Political Science* (Chicago, 1882–84); De Lapradelle, *De la nationalité* (1893); Lawrence, §§ 94–96; Lehr, *La nationalité* (1909); G. de Leval, *La protection diplomatique des nationaux a l'étranger* (1907); Liszt, § 19; 1 J. de Louter, § 18; 1 and 2 F. de Martens, §§ 85–86 and 44–48 respectively; Martitz, *Das Recht der Staatsangehörigkeit* (1875); Meili, *Int. Civil and Commercial Law* (1905), 119–28: McGovney, in 5 *A. J.* (1911), 325 ff. and 11 *Col. Law Rev.* (1911), 231 ff. and 326 ff.; * Moore, *American Diplomacy* (1905), ch. 7, * 3 *Digest*, ch. 10, and 3 *Arbitrations*, ch. 54; Nielson, in 20 *Col. Law Rev.* (1920), 840–61; * 1 Oppenheim, §§ 293–313; * Piggott, *Nationality*, in 2 vols. (1907); 3 P.-Fodéré, Nos. 1645–91; 1 Rivier, 303–07; Salmond, in 17 and 18 *Law Quar. Rev.*, 270–82 and 49–63; Snow, *Cases on Int. Law* (1893), 213–30, and *Int. Law. A Manual* (1898), §§ 29–31; * Scott, *Cases*, Pt. I, ch. 2, pp. 134–72; * Sieber, *Das Staatsburgerrecht*, in 2 vols. (1907); Stoerk, in 2 Holtzendorff, 583 ff., and in 2 *R. D. I. P.* (1895), 273 ff.; Taylor, §§ 172–83; Ullmann, §§ 108–12; Van Dyne, *Citizenship of the U. S.* (1904), and *Law of Naturalization of the U. S.* (1907); Vattel, liv. I, §§ 212–23; Walker, *Manual of Public Int. Law* (1895), § 19, and, *Science of Int. Law* (1893), 204–18; Webster, *Law of Naturalization* (1895); 1 Weiss, *Traité de droit int. privé* (1907), and, *Manuel de droit int. privé* (1909), liv. I; * 1 Westlake, ch. 10, and, *Private Int. Law* (4th ed., 1905), ch. 15; 1 Wharton, *Conflict of Laws* (3d ed., 1905), §§ 5–14, 2 *Ibid.*, ch. 14, and 2 *Digest*, §§ 171–98;

Wheaton (Atlay's ed.), §§ 85, 151 A, 151 H, 151 T, and (Dana's ed.), § 85 and note 49; 1 Willoughby, *The Const. Law of the U. S.* (1910), chs. 17–19, and in 1 *A. J.* (1907), 914 ff.; Wilson, §§ 44–47; Zeballos, *La nationalité*, in 2 vols. (1914).

For a fuller bibliography on Nationality, etc., see 1 Fauchille, pp. 841–43. See also Index (1920) to *A. J.* For articles in legal periodicals, see Jones and Chipman, *Index*, in 4 vols. (1882–1922).

Domicile.—Art. on " Domicile " in *Am. Digest, Corpus Juris*, and *Ruling Case Law;* Bouvé, *Exclusion of Aliens* (1912), 427 ff.; Borchard, §§ 243–46, 250–51; 2 Calvo, §§ 655–97; 1 Cobbett, 214–20; Davis, 156 ff; * Dicey, *Conflict of Laws* (1908), Bk. I, ch. 2; * Evans, *Cases*, 136–37, 411–33; Foote, *Private Int. Jurisprudence* (1904), Pt. I, ch. 2; Hall, §§ 72, 168; 1 Halleck (3d ed.), 415 ff.; 2 Hyde, §§ 789–90; Jacob, in 10 *Grotius Soc.* (1925), 89 ff.; Jacobs, *Law of Domicile* (1887); Lawrence, § 154; 2 F. de Martens, §§ 69, 76–80; Lewis, in *Brit. Yr. Bk.* (1923–24), 60–77; * 3 Moore, *Digest*, ch. 11, and 3 *Arbitrations*, ch. 55; * 4 Phillimore, chs. 4–14; * Scott, *Cases*, Pt. III, ch. 8, pp. 659–93: Story, *Conflict of Laws* (8th ed., 1883), ch. 3; Taylor, §§ 170–72, 179, 202 f., 517; 1 Twiss, §§ 168–71; Walker, *Manual of Public Int. Law* (1895), § 40, and, *Science of Int. Law* (1893), 251 ff.; 1 Westlake, 210–13, and *Private Int. Law* (4th ed., 1905), chs. 2 and 14; * Wharton, *Conflict of Laws* (3d ed., 1905), ch. 2, §§ 20–80; Wheaton (Atlay's ed.), §§ 81–94, and Pt. II, ch. 2 A, §§ 151a–151t, pp. 238–51, and Dana's ed., note 55; 1 Willoughby, *Constitutional Law of the U. S.* (1910), § 122; Woolsey, §§ 71–72, 74, 183, and App. II, pp. 502 ff.

Rights of Emigration, Immigration, Exclusion, and Jurisdiction over Aliens.—Berc, *De l'expulsion des étrangers* (1888); Bléteau, *De l'asile et du droit d'expulsion* (1886), 305 ff.; Bluntschli, Arts. 375–93; * Borchard, §§ 6–8, 14–32, 34–46, 133–36, and in 7 *A. J.* (1913), 497–520; * Bouvé, *Exclusion and Expulsion of Aliens in U. S.* (1912), *passim;* 2 and 6 Calvo, §§ 700–06 and 119–25; Darut, *De l'expulsion des étrangers* (1902); Despagnet, Nos. 340–55; Davis, 151–56; * 1 Fauchille, Nos. 410–16, 433–54; Fenwick, 175–80; Féraud-Giraud, *Droit d'expulsion;* Fiore, Nos. 48–93, 699, 709–12, and *Int. Law Cod.* (1918), pp. 42–43 and Nos. 257–64; Hall, §§ 10, 61–64, 87; 1 Halleck (Baker's 3d ed.), 418–20n, 460, 558 n.; Heffter, §§ 60–62; Henriques, *The Law of Aliens* (1906); * 1 Hyde, §§ 59–64, 266–69; *Immigration Laws*, U. S. Dept. of Labor (1917); Jeancourt-Galignani, *L'immigration en droit. int.* (1908); Langhard, *Das Recht der politischen Fremdausweisung* (1891); Lawrence, §§ 98, 101; G. de Leval, *La protection diplomatique* (1907), §§ 72 ff.; 1 J. de Louter, § 18, pp. 274–99; 1 G. F. de Martens, §§ 83–100; 1 and 2 F. de Martens, §§ 79, 86, and 44, 69–70, 81; * Martini, *L'expulsion des étrangers* (1909); Médecin, *Étude sur l'admission des étrangers en France* (1909); * 4 Moore, *Digest*, ch. 13; 2 Nys, 229–43; * 1 Oppenheim, §§ 314–26; Overbeck, *Niederlassungsfreiheit und Ausweissungsfreiheit* (1907); Parker, in 18 and 19 *A. J.* (1924 and 1925), 737 ff. and 23 ff.; 1 Phillimore, §§ 317–

35; 3 P.-Fodéré, Nos. 1857–59; 1 Rivier, 137, 307–14, 337–47; Rolin-Jacquemyns, in 20 *R. D. I.* (1888), 499 and 615; Root, in 4 *A. J.* (1910), 517–28; Sibley and Elias, *The Aliens Act* (1906); Stoerk, in 2 Holtzendorff, 630–55; Taylor, §§ 173, 186–87, 201–03, 467; Tchernoff, *Le droit de protection* (1898); Thomas, in 4 *R. D. I. P.* (1897), 620 ff.; Ullmann, §§ 113–16; Vattel, liv. I, § 213, and liv. II, §§ 100–15; Walker, *Manual of Public Int. Law* (1895), § 19; Weiss, *Manuel de droit int. privé* (1909), liv. II, 211–337, and 2 *Traité de droit int. privé* (1907); 1 Westlake, 215–19, 327–30; 2 Wharton, *Digest*, §§ 201–06; Wheaton, §§ 82, 113, 140 ff.; Wheeler, in 3 *A. J.* (1909), 869–84; * 1 Willoughby, *Constitutional Law of the U. S.* (1910), ch. 16; Wilson, § 48; Woolsey, §§ 65–67.

For numerous addresses, see 5 *Procs. Am. Soc. I. L.* (1911), *passim.* For fuller bibliographies, see 1 Fauchille, pp. 820–21, 880, 888–90, 922–24, 947, 960, 963.

Extradition.—Barrett, in 25 *I. L. A.* (1908), 101 ff.; Beauchet, *Traité de l'extradition* (1899); Bentwick, *Leading Cases* (1913), ch. 8; * Bernard, *Traité de l'extradition*, in 2 vols. (2d ed., 1890); Biron and Chalmers, *The Law and Practice of Extradition* (1903): Bluntschli, Arts. 394–401; Bry, *Précis élémentaire de droit int.* (1906), Nos. 320–31; 1 and 2 Butler, *Treaty Making Power* (1902, see index); 2 Calvo, §§ 949–1071; * Clarke, *Extradition* (4th ed., 1903); Delius, *Das Auslieferungsrecht* (1898); Devlin, *Treaty Power* (1908), ch. 11; Despagnet, Nos. 289–315; * Evans, *Cases*, 341–44, 346–58; * 1 Fauchille, Nos. 455–81; Fenwick, ch. 13; Féraud-Giraud, *De l'extradition* (1890); Fiore, *Traité de droit penal int. et de l'extradition*, in 2 vols. (trans. by Antoine, 1880); Hall, §§ 13 and 63; 1 Halleck (3d ed.), 235–39, 257–68; Hawley, *The Law of Int. Extradition* (1893); Heffter, § 63; * 1 Hyde, §§ 310–41, and in 8 *A. J.* (1914), 486–514; Lamasch, *Auslieferungspflicht und Asylrecht* (1887), and in 3 Holtzendorff, 454 ff.; Lawrence, §§ 110–11; Lawrence, W. B., 4 *Commentaire*, 362–540; Liszt, § 44; 1 J. de Louter, § 18, pp. 303–15; 3 F. de Martens, §§ 84–98; * Martitz, *Int. Rechtshilfe in Strafsachen*, 2 vols. (1888, 1897); * 4 Moore, *Digest*, ch. 14, and * 1 *Extradition* (1891); 2 Nys, 244–56; 1 Phillimore, §§ 363–89 d; * Piggott, *Extradition* (1910); Pomeroy, §§ 198–201; 3 P.-Fodéré, Nos. 1860–93; 1 Rivier, 348–57; Saint-Aufin, *L'extradition*, in 2 vols. (1913); * Scott, *Cases*, 404–28: Spear, *The Law of Extradition* (1884); De Stieglitz, *Étude sur l'extradition* (1883); 1 Stowell and Munro, 403–22; Taylor, §§ 205–12; Travers, *Droit penal int.* (1921), Nos. 1932 ff. *ad fin.;* 1 Twiss, 405–17; Ullmann, §§ 127–31; Walker, *Science of Int. Law* (1893), 232–38; * 1 Westlake, 217, 252–61; Wheaton, §§ 115–21 and notes; Wilson, § 49; Wilson and Tucker, § 67; Woolsey, §§ 77–78; 2 Wharton, *Digest*, §§ 268–82.

For bibliographies on *Extradition*, see especially Beauchet, *op. cit.*, Bernard, *op. cit.*, and 1 Fauchille, pp. 987–90, 1014. For selected references on *Political Offenses*, see *supra*, note 81 on p. 384.

Right of Asylum.—Bléteau, *De l'asile et du droit d'expulsion* (1886);

Bonfils, Nos. 622, 696–98; Bry, *op. cit.*, Nos. 198, 200, 250; 1 and 2 Calvo, §§ 469–71, 1521 ff.; Despagnet, No. 349; 1 (1 and 2 Pt.) Fauchille, Nos. 441^{23}, 619$^{6-21}$, 624$^{25-34}$; * Gilbert, in 15 *Harv. Law Rev.* (1901), 118–39, and in 3 *A. J.* (1910), 562–95; * Hall, §§ 52, 55, 63; Heffter, §§ 63, 212; * 1 Hyde, §§ 224–25, 254, 443; Lawrence, § 108; Lehr, *Manuel des agents diplomatiques* (1888), Nos. 1059–70; 2 F. de Martens, §§ 12, 56; * 2 Moore, *Digest*, §§ 291–307, and in 7 *Pol. Sci. Quar.* (1892), 1 ff., 197 ff., and 397 ff.; 1 Oppenheim, §§ 316, 390, 450; 2 Perels, 125–31; * 3 P.-Fodéré, Nos. 1416–25, and in 2 *Cours*, 88 ff.; 1 Rivier, 314, 499–502; Robin, in 15 *R. D. I. P.* (1908), 461 ff.; * 1 Satow, §§ 330–45, and ch. 20; * Scott, *Cases*, 323–36; Snow, *Cases on Int. Law* (1893), 139–50, and *Int. Law. A Manual* (1898), § 18; Sibley and Elias, *The Aliens Act and Right of Asylum* (1906); Stoerk, in 3 Holtzendorff, 465 ff., 485 ff.; 1 Stowell and Munro, 16–17, 242–46; Taylor, §§ 186, 256–60, 271, 311–12; Tobar y Borgoño, *L'asile interne;* 1 Wharton, *Digest*, § 104; 1 Westlake, 267–69, 281–84; Wilson and Tucker, 127, 145–46, 185–86; Wilson, 118, 172, 188.

PART III

INTERCOURSE OF STATES

CHAPTER XVIII

RIGHTS AND DUTIES OF DIPLOMATIC AGENTS AND SOVEREIGNS

I. DIPLOMATIC AGENTS

256. The Head or Chief of State.—The supreme organ and representative of a State in its diplomatic relations is the Head or Chief of the State. He may be either a monarch or a President [1] and represents the State in its international relations with all other sovereigns; and, if traveling or resident in other States, is entitled to certain honors and marks of respect.[2] His person, residence and suite are inviolable, and he is exempt from local jurisdiction in criminal and civil, as also in certain fiscal matters. It will be more convenient to consider these immunities after we have studied those of diplomatic agents.[3]

257. Minister of Foreign Affairs.—The actual control or management of international relations is usually in the hands of the Secretary or Department of State for Foreign Affairs.[4] He supervises the work of public ministers and

---

[1] The monarch or President may be the nominal rather than the real Head of the State, as in the case of the King of England and the President of France. In Switzerland, which has a plural executive, the President of the Federal Council represents the State in its international relations.

[2] Unless he chooses to remain *incognito*. On *Heads of States and Titles and Precedence among Sovereigns and States*, see especially: * 1 Oppenheim, §§ 341–56; 1 P.-Fodéré, *Cours*, chs. 2–4; and 1 Satow, Bk. I, chs. 4–5.

[3] See *infra*, No. 281.

[4] On the *Organization of our Departments of State and the Conduct of Foreign Relations Generally*, see: Corwin, *The President's Control of Foreign Relations* (1917); Foster, *Century of Am. Diplomacy* (1911), ch. 4; Hughes, in 16 *A. J.* (1922), 355 ff.; * Lay, *Foreign Service of the U. S.* (1925), especially chs. 2–3; Mathews, *The Conduct of American Foreign Relations* (1922), *passim*, particularly ch. 3; 1 P.-Fodéré, *Cours*, ch. 6; 1 Satow, particularly ch. 3; Schuyler, *Am. Diplomacy* (1886), 1–40; Van Dyne, *Our Foreign Service* (1909), ch. 1; Wright, *Control of American Foreign Relations* (1922), *passim*. For a *History*

other diplomatic agents sent abroad, and he conducts the business of the State in its relations with the various members of the *diplomatic corps*.[5]

258. The Right of Legation.—The main instruments of diplomatic intercourse are public ministers or other diplomatic agents. Every recognized sovereign State, and also the League of Nations, enjoys the active and passive rights of legation or representation, *i.e.* the rights of sending and receiving diplomatic agents.[6] But there is no corresponding obligation to send and receive foreign ministers, though a State which refused all diplomatic intercourse would practically lose its membership in the international community.

259. The Right to refuse a Particular Individual.—Each State is free in the choice of its agents, though the Government to which they are accredited is not, strictly speaking, bound to receive them. It may refuse to enter into or to continue diplomatic relations with a particular State, but under certain circumstances such refusal might be construed as unfriendly, or even hostile.[7]   It may, of course, refuse to

of the Department of State of the United States, see a series of articles by Gaillard Hunt, in 1 to 6 *A. J.* (1907–1912), published in book form in 1914.

On the *Organization and Work of the British Foreign Office*, see especially: Cecil in 3 *Cambridge History of British Foreign Policy*, ch. 8; and 2 Grey, *Twenty-five Years* (1925), ch. 30.

[5] The *diplomatic corps* consists of all the ministers or diplomatic agents accredited to a particular government. It possesses a certain sense of solidarity or collectivity and sometimes speaks with a certain authority, more particularly in the Orient, on questions of ceremony or diplomatic etiquette; but it is in no sense a legal or even a political personality. Its members are completely independent of one another. The dean or presiding officer of the diplomatic corps is usually its oldest ranking member or the Papal Nuncio. The term is also sometimes applied to all the diplomatic agents sent abroad by a particular State.

On the *diplomatic corps*, see especially 2 Fiore, No. 1111; 1 P.-Fodéré, *Cours*, 253–56; 1 Rivier, 452–53; and 1 Satow, ch. 23, §§ 368 ff.

[6] But the exercise of this right is discretionary. Several authorities (Heilborn, *System des Völkerrechts*, 1886, 182, and Wheaton, § 207) claim that this is a mere competence or an imperfect right rather than a right in the strict sense. It would seem to be both. It is in fact a fundamental right of States. See *supra*, No. 148. On the *Right of Legation*, see especially: 1 Oppenheim, §§ 360–69; and 1 Satow, ch. 12. For references, see 1 Oppenheim (3 ed.). p. P542.

Part-sovereign States may enjoy a more or less limited right of legation. See *supra*, Nos. 101–05. The Pope enjoys the right by courtesy based on traditional usage, but his agents are not real international functionaries See *supra*, No. 89, pp. 164–65.

[7] See *infra*, Nos. 267–69.

enter into negotiations which have a particular purpose.   A State may decline to receive a particular agent who is *persona non grata*, one of its own citizens or subjects, or one whose duties or powers are deemed incompatible with the institutions of the receiving State.[8]

But the grounds for rejection should not be frivolous and should be clearly stated, if possible.[9]   In order to avoid unpleasant incidents of this nature, it is customary (though not obligatory) to make confidential inquiries beforehand as to whether the appointment of a certain person would be agreeable to the Government of the country to which he is to be accredited.   This custom is usually referred to as *l'agreation* (consent).[10]

260. **Duties of Diplomatic Agents.**—The main duties or functions of permanent diplomatic agents are those of observation, protection, and negotiation.   It is the duty of the resident minister to observe and report upon all matters of interest to his Government, to protect by means of his mediation or good offices [11] nationals of his own State against acts of illegality and injustice in the country to which he is sent, and to enter into negotiations for the purpose of settling any outstanding difficulties between his own Government and that to which he is accredited.   But he may perform other miscellaneous functions, such as the registration of births, marriages, and deaths of his fellow nationals, the authentication of certain documents, the issuance of passports, etc.   In no case should he intervene

[8] Thus, Protestant States do not, as a general rule, receive Papal envoys. Most countries, including the United States, will not receive their own nationals.   A *persona non grata* is one who is unacceptable on personal or political grounds.   On "*Persona Grata*," see 1 Satow, ch. 14.

[9] England insists upon a statement of the grounds of rejection in all cases. But her practice appears to be exceptional.   It is not legally obligatory.

[10] On *l'agreation*, see especially: 1 P.-Fodéré, *Cours*, 395 ff.; and 1 Satow, § 230.   The United States has had several disagreeable experiences as a result of its failure to observe this custom.   On the famous *Keiley* case, see 4 Moore, *Digest*, pp. 480–83;   and 1 Satow, § 232.   For this and other cases, see also Foster, *Practice of Diplomacy* (1906), ch. 3;   Hall, § 98;   Lay, *op. cit.*, 108 ff.; 4 Moore, § 638;   1 Oppenheim, § 375;   Satow, ch. 14, §§ 231–33;   and Taylor, §§ 289–90.

Since the United States began to appoint ambassadors in 1893, it has observed the practice of *agreation* for envoys of that grade.

[11] But he should not act as an agent for the collection of private claims.   4 Moore, *Digest*, § 647.

in the internal affairs of the country by which he has been received.[12]

261. **Classification of Public Ministers.**—In accordance with the seven rules adopted at the Congress of Vienna (1815), supplemented by the eighth rule of Aix-la-Chapelle (1818), public ministers are divided into four classes:

(1) Ambassadors and Papal Legates or Nuncios.[13]

(2) Envoys, Ministers, or other persons accredited to Sovereigns.[14]

(3) Ministers Resident accredited to sovereigns.

(4) Chargé d'Affaires accredited to Ministers for Foreign Affairs.

262. **Necessary Documents.**—Before setting out on his mission, a public minister is in general furnished by his home Government with the following documents:

(1) A *Letter of Credence*, stating the name, rank, etc., of the agent, together with the general object of his mission, and bespeaking for him full faith and credit in the conduct of the business with which he is charged. This Letter of Credence is usually addressed by his sovereign to the sovereign or Chief of State to whom he is accredited.[15]

[12] See 4 Moore, *Digest*, § 649, for the case of *Gouveneur Morris*. On the *Bulwer Incident*, see *infra*, note 26 on p. 402.

On the *Duties of Diplomatic Agents*, see especially Bonfils, Nos. 681–83; Despagnet, Nos. 229–30; * 1 (3 Pt.), Fauchille, Nos. 681–83; Foster, *Practice of Diplomacy*, chs. 5 and 6; 1 Hyde, §§ 444–50; * 4 Moore, *Digest*, §§ 647 ff.; 1 Oppenheim, §§ 378–83; 1 P.-Fodéré, *Cours*, ch. 10, and *Traité*, Nos. 1346 ff.; * 1 Rivier, § 37, pp. 467 ff.

[13] It may be recalled that Papal Legates or Nuncios are no longer to be regarded as real public ministers since the abolition of the temporal power of the Pope in 1870. Ambassadors are supposed to represent the person and dignity of their sovereign in a personal sense and are entitled to precedence and special honors, such as the right of personal audience with the sovereign and royal honors generally.

[14] This class may be said now to include Permanent Envoys, Ministers Plenipotentiary, and Envoys Extraordinary. There is no substantial difference between the first three classes.

For curious information and amusing incidents growing out of the struggles for precedence which formerly prevailed between public ministers, see Bernard, *Lectures on Diplomacy* (1868), Lect. I; 4 Macaulay, *History of England* (ed. 1855); and Wicquefort, *L'ambassadeur et ses fonctions* (1676). See also 1 Satow, chs. 4–5.

[15] Except in the case of a Chargé d'Affaires, when it is written by one Foreign Minister to the other. For details on *Letters of Credence, Full Powers, Instructions*, etc. see especially 1 Hyde, § 420; 1 P.-Fodéré, *Cours*, ch. 9, pp. 403 ff.; * 1 Satow, chs. 8 and 15; 1 Twiss, §§ 212–14; and Wheaton, §§ 217–20.

263. **Full Powers.**—(2) *Full Powers*, or authority to negotiate.   These Powers may be contained in the Letter of Credence [16] or conferred by letters patent.   Their purpose is to define the limits within which the agent may negotiate and to what extent his acts may be considered binding on his Government.   Full Powers are no longer interpreted or understood as legally binding upon the sovereign, the right to ratify being in all cases either expressly or tacitly reserved. [17]

264. **Instructions.**—(3) *Instructions* are directions furnished to the agent by his home Government, either at the beginning or in the course of his mission, to serve as a guide in his relation with the Government to which he is accredited or in the conduct of negotiations.   They usually state the object of the mission, lay down rules for the transaction of his business, and inform him as to the extent of his powers or the real intentions of his Government. These instructions may be general or special, oral or written (they are usually written), secret or public.   They may be changed or modified in the course of the negotiation. [18]

265. **Other Documents.**—(4) *Special Passports* and, in some cases, a *Safe-conduct*.   These contain a description of the agent's person and office and authorization to travel to the seat of the Government to which he is sent.   (5) The *Cipher* or secret key for communication with the home Government.

266. **The Commencement of the Diplomatic Mission.**— " When a diplomatic minister reaches the capital of the

---

[16] In case of a permanent minister, the Full Powers are usually inserted in the Letter of Credence or, rather, the Letter of Credence ordinarily serves as authority to negotiate.   But when the minister resident is charged with a special task, as, for example, the negotiation of a commercial treaty, he is furnished with special letters patent for this purpose.   Envoys or ministers sent to a Congress or Conference are not generally furnished with Letters of Credence, but with General Full Powers, copies of which are exchanged.   Cf. Hall, pp. 356–57; P.-Fodéré, *Cours*, 422; and 1 Satow, ch. 8.

[17] On this much-controverted point, see *infra*, No. 298.

[18] They are generally secret, and should not be communicated without the consent or direction of the home Government.   It has happened that negotiators have been furnished with a double set of instructions—one secret, the other to be communicated.   Rivier (I, 464) justly observes on this point: "The respect and loyalty which States owe one another requires that these (instructions) be not contradictory."   According to Satow (I, § 241) written instructions are not always provided.

country to which he is accredited, he notifies his arrival to the Minister for Foreign Affairs and demands an audience of the sovereign for the purpose of delivering his Letters of Credence. Ambassadors are entitled to a public audience, whereas ministers of the second and third classes have only a right to a private audience, and Chargés d'Affaires are obliged to be content with an audience of the Foreign Minister." [19] Though it is only after this public reception that a public minister enters upon the actual exercise of his functions and is fully entitled to diplomatic privileges and immunities as a matter of strict law,[20] it is customary to

[19] Lawrence, p. 283.

[20] This appears to be the view of most of the authorities, but they are not all agreed upon this point. While international practice seems to support the opposite view from that set forth in the text, it is difficult to find in this custom a sound basis for a principle of public law. As the diplomatic relation is a mutual one, it can scarcely be maintained that full or legal immunity can be conferred by the sending State alone.

However, it would appear that a limited application of the principles of inviolability and immunity from arrest or detention apply during the voyage, even through third countries. The minister and his suite are protected by their passports or public character, provided the third State is not at war with the sending or receiving State. The case of *Soulé* is an interesting one. In 1854 Mr. Soulé, United States Minister at Madrid, was provisionally stopped at Calais, France, under an order of the French Minister of the Interior that he should be not allowed to "penetrate into France" without the knowledge of the French Government. Upon the protest of the United States Minister at Paris, the French Minister of Foreign Affairs replied that the Government of the Emperor had "not wished . . . to prevent an envoy of the United States crossing French territory to go to his post in order to acquit himself of the commission with which he was charged by his Government; " that "if Mr. Soulé was going immediately and directly to Madrid, the route of France was open to him;" that if, on the contrary, he "intended to go to Paris with a view of tarrying there, that privilege was not accorded him." It was explained that he had been stopped with a view of consulting him as to his intentions. 4 Moore, *Digest*, pp. 557–58.

It should be explained that Mr. Soulé was a native of France and a naturalized American citizen. He had fought a duel with the French ambassador at Madrid and was reported to have criticised the Government of Louis Napoleon.

On the *Right of Transit or Innocent Passage of Public Ministers*, particularly as illustrated by the case of *Soulé*, see especially 3 Calvo, §§ 1534–36; Foster, *op. cit.*, 53 f.; * Hall, § 99; * 4 Moore, *Digest*, §§ 643–44; 1 Oppenheim, § 398; Pomeroy, §§ 340 f.; 3 P.-Fodéré, *Traité*, Nos. 1257, 1394; 1 Rivier, § 39, pp. 508–12; 1 Satow, ch. 22, particularly § 352; Taylor, §§ 293–94; 1 Twiss, § 222; 1 Westlake, 274–75; Wheaton, §§ 244–47.

The right for public ministers of innocent passage through third States and immunity from civil suit has judicial sanction, at least in the United States. See *Wilson* v. *Blanco* (1889), 56 N. Y. Superior Court, 582, and Scott, *Cases*, 293. This right probably exists to a certain extent even on belligerent or

accord them these rights and immunities during their voyage to the seat of the Government to which they are accredited and while awaiting their formal reception.

267. The Termination of Diplomatic Missions.—Diplomatic missions terminate by the death or recall of the minister; the expiration of the term fixed for the duration of the mission; the success or failure of the object of the mission if it be of a special nature; the death, abdication, or dethronement of the sovereign or Chief of State to whom or by whom the minister has been accredited; [21] dismissal or withdrawal as a consequence of some serious offense on one side or the other; a change in the rank or class of the agent or embassy; a declaration or outbreak of war; or a radical change in the form of government of either country. In every case the diplomatic agent retains his privileges and immunities until his return to his own country.

268. Recall of Ministers.—The normal and most frequent mode of termination is by *Recall*. Before his departure, a public minister usually has another audience with the sovereign or foreign minister, and presents his Letter of Recall. He receives in return a letter or papers of commendation (*lettre de récréance*), his passport and, at some courts, presents or decorations.[22]

occupied territory. It is, or course, subject to the law of military necessity. During the siege of Paris, in 1870, the diplomatic corps protested against the refusal of Count Bismarck to permit them to correspond with their Governments, except by means of "open letters." The United States especially remonstrated against this refusal as an "uncourteous proceeding," and maintained that the rights of legation "must be regarded as paramount to any belligerent right" under the circumstances. 4 Moore, *Digest*, § 675, pp. 696–701.

It is clear, at least since the discussions growing out of the *Trent Affair* (see *infra*, p. 726 n.), that the diplomatic agent of an enemy State cannot be taken from a neutral vessel or on neutral territory. Neutral States have a right to the use of the high seas for diplomatic communication with either belligerent as well as with one another.

[21] In case of death, the Letter of Credence is usually renewed; in case of abdication or dethronement, the minister is provided with a new Letter. These rules do not necessarily apply to Chargés d'Affaires who are merely accredited by one Foreign Minister to another. A radical change in the form of government also requires new Letters of Credence. The election of a new President in a Republic does not terminate the mission.

For references on *Termination of Diplomatic Missions*, see 1 Oppenheim, (3d ed.), p. 581. To his list should be added Foster, *Practice of Diplomacy* (1906), ch. 9; and particularly 1 Satow, ch. 24.

[22] It was formerly a general custom to send presents to all departing minis-

Just as a State may, on reasonable grounds, decline to receive any particular person as a public minister, so it may, at any time, demand the recall of a resident minister or other diplomatic agent,[23] for good and sufficient reasons; if, for example, the minister has rendered further intercourse difficult or impossible or if he has made himself personally obnoxious to the sovereign or foreign minister of the Government to which he is accredited.   Such a request, if made in good faith and for sufficient reason, should be at once complied with, but there can be no legal obligation in the matter.[24]   The Government by whom the minister has

ters whose mission was not terminated abruptly.   Fortunately, this custom has almost disappeared from international practice, but some courts still confer orders and decorations suitable to the rank of the minister.   The United States set a good example in refusing to give or permit the acceptance of such presents or decorations.   See especially Foster, *op. cit.*, 141 ff.; 4 Moore, *Digest*, § 651; and 3 P.-Fodéré, *Traité*, No. 1521.

[23] The sending State may of course recall any of its ministers or agents at its own discretion.

[24] For the contrary but erroneous view, see 3 Calvo, § 1365; and 1 Halleck (3d ed.), 366.   For the correct view, see Hall, (8th ed.), pp. 359–60; Lawrence, (7th ed.), § 126, p. 279; and Taylor, § 321.

Generally speaking, the Continental authorities present a very inadequate or superficial discussion of this question.   This may possibly be due to the fact that the United States appears to have furnished most of the instances of requests for recall, as of dismissal of public ministers.

The circumstances which led to the request for the recall of the French minister *Genet* in 1793 are so well known to nearly every schoolboy in the land that it is unnecessary to recapitulate them here.   Suffice it to say that his conduct was such that our Government would have been amply justified in sending him out of the country.

The request of the French Government for the recall of *Gouverneur Morris* made at the same time was also fully justified.   Morris had been engaged in intrigues in favor of the monarchical or Court party.

The United States seems also to have been justified in its request for the recall (in 1871) of the Russian Minister *Catacazy*, who had rendered himself personally obnoxious by conversation and publications abusive of President Grant.

An interesting incident was that of the Spanish Minister *De Lôme*.   On Feb. 8, 1898, the New York *Journal* published a private letter abstracted from the mails at Havana by a Cuban sympathizer, in which the Spanish Minister had described President McKinley as "weak and a bidder for the admiration of the crowd, besides being a would-be (or rather second-rate) politician (*politicastro*)"; and he intimated that it would be advantageous for Spain to take up, "even if only for effect," the question of commercial relations.   The United States promptly asked for his recall; but De Lôme, recognizing that his usefulness was at an end, had offered his resignation before the matter could be laid before the Spanish Government.   It was promptly accepted.

For these and other cases, see 4 Moore, *Digest*, § 639.

been accredited has the right to pass upon the facts and decide for itself whether the conduct of its agent has been such or whether its interests in the premises are of such a nature as to make it desirable to comply with the wishes of the Government which has requested the recall.

269. Dismissal of Ministers.—A minister should only be positively dismissed [25] under the most extreme circumstances, as when hostilities are on the point of breaking out, an impossible ultimatum has been delivered, if his Government has positively refused reparation for a serious wrong, when his personal conduct has been such as to make it practically impossible to continue further relations with

Though it is not strictly obligatory to accede to a request for recall, "the instances must be rare indeed in which such a request ought not to be granted." Mr. Buchanan, Secretary of State, to Mr. Jewet, 1847, 4 Moore, *Digest*, p. 494.

Reasons for the request should always be given if possible. In 1852 Secretary Everett refused to give reasons for a request for the recall of the Minister from Nicaragua, but these reasons were afterwards given. Moore, *op. cit.*, p. 498.

That a government must be its own judge as to the validity of alleged reasons is shown by the circumstances which led to the request for the recall of the United States Minister Wise by the Brazilian Government in 1847. The conduct of Mr. Wise in attempting to secure the release of Lieut. Davis and the American sailors who had been imprisoned by the Brazilian authorities, was highly approved by the United States Government, and his subsequent failure to appear at several Court fêtes (the acts nominally alleged as reasons for his recall) was due to a sense of "recent insult and indignity." No government could afford to recall a minister under circumstances which involved an implied censure for acts of which it heartily approved. 4 Moore, *Digest*, 495–97. For a fuller account, see Stuart, *Latin America and the U. S.* (1922), 365–71.

The most recent case of a request to recall known to the writer is that of the Austrian ambassador Dumba whose recall was demanded by the United States on Sept. 9, 1915 by reason of his pernicious activities prior to our entrance into the World War. He admitted that he had proposed to his Government plans to instigate strikes in American manufacturing plants engaged in the production of munitions of war, and committed "a flagrant violation of diplomatic propriety in employing an American citizen protected by an American passport as a secret bearer of official dispatches through the lines of the enemy of Austro-Hungary." Special Supp. to 10 *A. J.* (1916), 361. For editorial comment, see 9 *A. J.* (1915), 935 ff.

On Dec. 4, 1915, our State Department informed the German Government that because of their "connection with the illegal and questionable acts of certain persons within the United States," the "continued presence" of Capt. Boy-Ed, naval attaché, and Capt. von Papen, military attaché, "would be unacceptable to this Government." For the main documents, see Special Supp. to 10 *A. J.* (1916), 363–66; or Hershey, *Diplomatic Agents and Immunities* (1919), 53–56.

[25] This is done by sending him his passports and, if necessary, escorting him to the frontier.

him, or in case of interference in internal or domestic affairs.[26]

[26] Hall (8th ed., p. 361), who exhibits an anti-American bias upon several occasions in his otherwise admirable work, sneeringly remarks: "The United States has had the misfortune to supply almost all the modern instances in which a Government has felt itself unable to continue relations with a minister accredited to it." Upon a superficial view this reproach appears to be deserved, but an impartial examination of the cases themselves will show that, except in one instance, the dismissals were wholly justifiable. Indeed, it must be admitted that, in some of these cases, our Government showed a forbearance bordering upon pusillanimity.

The first of these unfortunate cases was that of the Spanish Minister *Yrujo* in 1804-1806. After denouncing an Act of Congress as "an atrocious libel," Yrujo attempted (in 1804) to corrupt the editor of a newspaper by offering a pecuniary consideration for opposing certain measures and views of the Government of the United States and advocating those of Spain. Though the Spanish Government had granted him "permission" to return to Spain in response to a request for his recall, Yrujo failed to take his departure, and returned to Washington early in 1806, where he was officially informed that his presence was "dissatisfactory" to the President. Thereupon he notified the United States Government that he intended to remain in Washington as long as it might suit the "interests of the king" and his own "personal convenience," and that he remained in possession of all his rights and privileges. He not only communicated his correspondence with our Government to his colleagues of the diplomatic corps, but he also caused it to be published in the newspapers. His conduct appears, however, to have been approved by the Spanish Government. Though virtually dismissed early in 1806, he remained in the country until late in 1807. Together with Merry, the British Minister, Yrujo was also implicated in the Burr conspiracy.

On the *Yrujo Incident*, see especially 2 Adams, *History of the U. S.* (1889-91), 258-68, 362-73, and 3 *Ibid.*, 184-89, 194, 209, 236-64; Foster, *Century of Am. Diplomacy* (1911), 217-20, 225; * 4 Moore, *Digest*, § 640, pp. 508-11; 1 Wharton, *Digest*, §§ 84 and 106, pp. 605 and 698.

The second case is that of the British Minister *Jackson* in 1809-1810, who twice intimated that our Government had been guilty of falsehood and duplicity in its negotiations with the British Government. He was consequently informed that no further communications from him would be received, and Mr. Pinkney, then United States Minister in London, was instructed to ask for his recall (Nov. 23, 1809). Diplomatic relations having been suspended pending his recall, Mr. Jackson was finally (March 14, 1810) directed to return to England, though Lord Wellesley stated that his conduct was not disapproved by the British Government.

In the meantime Mr. Jackson had withdrawn from Washington to New York and Boston, where he gave a toast "so flagitiously insolent to the Government of the United States that Mr. Madison was compelled to direct that his recall should be immediately demanded." Any one who will read the long amusing note published by Wharton in his *Digest* (I, § 107, pp. 713 ff., reprinted in 4 Moore, *Digest*, § 640, pp. 515 ff.), cannot fail to be convinced that if the administration of Mr. Madison is subject to criticism in this matter, it is that it was insufficiently vigorous.

On *Jackson's Case*, see 5 Adams, *op. cit.*, 96-132, 154-57, 212-19; Foster, *op. cit.*, 220-23; * 4 Moore, *Digest*, 511-25; Wharton, *Digest*, 606-09. 713-23.

270. The Fiction of Exterritoriality.—For the sake of preserving harmonious relations, and in order to ensure independence or freedom in the exercise of their functions,

In 1849 Secretary Clayton refused to hold any further correspondence with the French Minister *Poussin* on the ground that he had used language disrespectful to our Government. 4 Moore, *Digest*, pp. 531–33.

In 1856 Secretary Marcy announced to the British Minister Mr. *Crampton* the determination of the President to "discontinue further intercourse" with him on the ground that he had continued to violate the Neutrality Laws of the United States by participation in the recruiting of troops for the Crimean War after he had been admonished not to do so. His recall had been refused by the British Government which placed a different construction upon our Neutrality Laws than maintained by the United States. 4 Moore, *Digest*, pp. 533–35.

A later case was that of *Lord Sackville-West*, a curious "breach of diplomatic privilege and invasion of purely domestic affairs." During the Presidential campaign of 1888, the British Minister was made the victim of a common electioneering trick. He received a letter marked "private," purporting to come from a naturalized Anglo-American residing in California, asking his advice as to the Presidential candidate most likely to favor British interests. In his reply to this decoy letter, Lord Sackville intimated that the Democratic party was secretly, though not openly, friendly to Great Britain, and he inclosed an extract from a newspaper in which electors were advised to vote for President Cleveland.

The letter was published a few weeks before the election, and used as a campaign document against the candidate whom it was intended to favor. The situation was rendered more difficult by reason of Lord Sackville's unsuccessful attempts to explain matters to American newspaper reporters, in the course of which he accused the administration of acting for political effect. Secretary Bayard promptly cabled Mr. Phelps, the United States Minister in London, to request his lordship's recall as speedily as possible.

Lord Salisbury properly declined to act until he had received Lord Sackville's explanation, but suggested that dismissal was preferable to immediate recall, as dismissal need not end his diplomatic career. Inasmuch as election day was drawing nigh, Lord Sackville promptly received his passports.

The British Minister was undoubtedly guilty of an indiscretion, but it cannot be seriously maintained that his offense was of such a character as to justify a dismissal or even a demand for recall. Indeed, the London *Times* (cited by Foster, *Practice of Diplomacy*, 1906, 189) scarcely put the case too strongly when it said: "A more ridiculous spectacle has rarely been witnessed in any civilized country than the flurried and unmannerly haste with which the Government of President Cleveland has endeavored to put a slight on this country, obviously for electioneering purposes, before her Majesty's ministers could deal, one way or the other, with the alleged indiscretion of the British representative at Washington."

However, the case has its extenuating circumstances. Perhaps the very absurdity or humor of the situation prevented too great resentment on the part of the English. They knew that the Irish vote was not to be trifled with.

On the *Sackville Incident*, see 5 Calvo, § 258; * Foster, *op. cit.*, 187–89; Hall, note on pp. 362–63; 1 Halleck (3d ed.), 367 f.; Lawrence, § 126, pp. 280–81; * 4 Moore, *Digest*, § 640, pp. 536–48; 1 Satow, § 428; Wheaton (Atlay's ed.), § 225 d.

There is one other case of dismissal deserving of special mention to which

diplomatic agents enjoy certain privileges and immunities in the countries to which they are accredited. These rights have been frequently grouped under the head of exterritoriality. But there is a growing disposition on the part of the more recent authorities to frown upon the use of this term as a useless, misleading, if not dangerous fiction or metaphor.[27]

the United States was *not* a party. It is that of Mr. *Bulwer*, British Minister at Madrid in 1848. Acting upon the instructions of Lord Palmerston, he warned the Spanish Government of the danger of the course it was taking in not pursuing a sufficiently liberal policy, and recommended the adoption of a legal and constitutional course of government. To this interference in its domestic affairs, Spain replied by sending Mr. Bulwer his passports with an intimation that he must leave Madrid within forty-eight hours.

This case is particularly important because Lord Palmerston, though clearly wrong in applying them in this case, laid down the correct principles governing the conditions under which a demand for the recall of a public minister should be complied with. They are thus summarized by Lord Salisbury:

"It is, of course, open to any government, on its own responsibility, suddenly to terminate its diplomatic relations with any other State, or with any particular minister of any other State. But it has no claim to demand that the other State shall make itself the instrument of that proceeding, or concur in it, unless that State is satisfied by reasons, duly produced, of the justice of the grounds on which the demand is made." 4 Moore, *Digest*, p. 538. The reply of Secretary Bayard to this argument (pp. 539 ff.) is unconvincing. He is misled on this point by the "high authority" of Calvo (see p. 547).

On the *Bulwer Incident*, see Hall, 362; * 4 Moore, *Digest*, § 640, pp. 538–39, 545–46; and 1 Satow, § 423.

[27] Among those opposed to the idea of exterritoriality as a principle of Int. Law, may be cited: Barthélemy, in 13 *R. D. I. P.* (1906), 125 f.; * Bonfils, No. 693; Bry, *Précis élémentaire de droit int.* (1906), Nos. 214, 245, 249; Crouzet, *De l'inviolabilite et de l'exemption de jurisdiction* (1875), 71 ff.; * Dana, note 129 to Wheaton, pp. 303 ff.; Despagnet, Nos. 233, 238, 251; 2 Fiore, Nos. 1147, 1154, 1161; * Hall, §§ 48, 57, 76; 1 Halleck (3d ed.), 332 ff.; 1 Hyde, § 245; * Kebedgy, *Die diplomatischen Privilegien* (1901), 8 ff.; Lawrence, § 100; 2 Mérignhac, 249–57; 4 Moore, *Digest*, 630 f.; 2 Nys, 366 ff.; Odier, *Des privileges des agents diplomatique* (1890), 307 ff.; Piétri, *La fiction d'exterritorialité* (1895), Pt. I, ch. 2; 2 P.-Fodéré, *Cours*, 47–50; and 3, *Traité*, Nos. 1396–97; Pinheiro-Ferreira, notes *sur le Précis de* G. F. de Martens, (1831) II, § 172, 215; 1 Satow, § 278; 1 Westlake, 273 f.; Ullmann, § 50, pp. 182–83.

Among those in favor of exterritoriality, either as a right or a useful legal fiction are the following: Bluntschli, Arts. 135–53; Bynkershoek, *De foro legatorum* (1721), *passim*, particularly cap. 8, § 1; 3 Calvo, §§ 1451 ff., 1499 ff.; and 1 *Dictionnaire de droit int.* (1885), 315–20; Droin, *L'exterritorialité* (1895), 57 ff.; Funck-Brentano et Sorel, 63–64; Geffcken, in 3 Holtzendorff, 654; * Grotius, lib. II, cap. 18, §§ 4–11; Heffter, §§ 205, 215; * Heyking, *L'exterritorialité* (1889), particularly §§ 14–16; Klüber, §§ 49, 204; Lehr, *Manuel des agents diplomatiques* (1888), Nos. 1071 ff.; Lisboa, *Les fonctions diplomatiques* (1908), 3; 2 G. F. de Martens, §§ 172 and 215; 1 and 2 F. de Martens, § 82,

1. *Inviolability*

271. The Principle of Inviolability. Its Application.—
The main special right or privilege of diplomatic agents is
that of inviolability or exemption from restraint, injury, or
interference. This principle, based originally upon the
supposed sacred character of the herald or envoy and
sanctioned by religion, was one of the oldest and most
fundamental " laws of all mankind " [28] known to the
ancients. It extends to the family and suite as well as to
the person of the agent, and applies to all things or persons
necessary for the accomplishment of his mission, such as his
residence,[29] furniture, carriages, archives, couriers, and correspondence. It begins as soon as the envoy enters the
country to which he is accredited, and only ends when he
leaves it, even in case of a rupture or suspension of diplomatic relations.

272. In Third Countries.—The authorities are divided on
the question whether the diplomatic agent is inviolable in
third countries which he is obliged to traverse in order to
reach his destination; but the better opinion would seem to
be that he enjoys a limited inviolability conditioned on his
good behavior, and the right of innocent passage, provided
the third State is not at war with the sending or receiving
State.[30] He is also probably immune from arrest and

12–14 respectively; 1 Lorimer, 248; * 1 Oppenheim, § 389; 1 Piédelièvre,
Nos. 488 ff.; 2 Phillimore, §§ 104, 108, 140, 176 ff.; 1 Rivier, 330–35, 417 ff.,
481–99; Stoerk, in 2 Holtzendorff, 656 ff.; Vattel, liv. IV, §§ 80–119; Vercamer, *Des franchises diplomatiques* (1891), 142 ff.; 1 Twiss, §§ 165 and 217;
Wheaton, § 224. For reviews of the older authorities, see Droin, *op. cit.*, Pt. I,
chs. 1–2; and Heyking, *op. cit.*, §§ 6–13.

These authorities differ greatly from each other as to the nature, basis, and
extent of exterritoriality. Some consider it a mere fiction, others a legal right
or principle; some make it include inviolability, others restrict it to immunity
from criminal and civil jurisdiction; some extend it to the person and suite of
the agent, others limit to the hotel, etc., etc.

The main objections to this term are well summed up by Kebedgy (*Diplom.
Privilegien*, 1901, p. 8): It is insufficient, since jurisdiction is not exclusively
territorial; incorrect, inasmuch as the hotel or residence of the embassy is not,
under all circumstances, exempt from local jurisdiction; unnecessary, because
the immunities are explicable on other grounds. It is also dangerous, as apt
to give rise to extravagant pretensions.

[28] See *supra*, No. 33.
[29] See *infra*, No. 278.
[30] Cf. *supra*, note 20 on pp. 396–97.
As in favor of the view that diplomatic agents are inviolable in third States,

detention [31] except in serious cases, but it is doubtful whether he is legally entitled to any other immunities in third States.

273. **Limits of Inviolability.**—Except in cases of necessity or self-defense,[32] the right to inviolability in the country which receives them, is nearly absolute.   In most countries public ministers are protected by special laws.[33]   In any

Bonfils and Fauchille (No. 689) mention Vattel, Merlin, Holtzendorff, Klüber, de Martens, Wheaton, Twiss, Lorimer, and Satow; as opposed, Grotius, Bynkershoek, Gentilis, Zouch, Wicquefort, Heffter, Calvo, and Carnazza-Amari. Bonfils and Fauchille themselves share the affirmative opinion. To this affirmative list may be added: Halleck, Taylor, Ullmann, Phillimore, Rivier; to the negative list, Hall, Oppenheim, Mérignhac, Pomeroy, P.-Fodéré, and Westlake. For good discussions of this subject, see 1 Oppenheim, §§ 397–400 (with references on p. 573); and 1 Satow, ch. 22.

It should be added that the Institute of Int. Law suppressed Art. 19 of the Rules on Diplomatic Immunity adopted in 1895. This article had recognized the inviolability and immunities of public ministers in third countries. See 14 *Annuaire*, 239.

[31] *Wilson* v. *Blanco* (1889), 56 N. Y. Superior Court, 582, and Scott, *Cases*, 293. For a criticism of this decision, see 1 Westlake, 275–76 n.

[32] When the safety of the State is threatened, as in cases of conspiracy; voluntary exposure to danger, as in case of a riot, an assault, acceptance of a duel, etc.; or when the diplomatic agent is traveling incognito.

The classic cases of conspiracy are *Count Gyllenborg*, Swedish Ambassador to England (1717), and the *Prince of Cellarmare*, Spanish Ambassador to Paris (1718). Both were placed under arrest and held as prisoners. These cases are cited in nearly all the treatises. For full reports, see 1 Ch. de Martens, *Causes célèbres*, 75–138 and 139–73. For brief reports, see 1 Satow, §§ 281–82; and Snow, *Cases on Int. Law* (1893) 87–88.

"A foreign minister, by committing the first assault, so far loses his privilege, that he cannot complain of an infraction of the Law of Nations; if, in his turn, he should be assaulted by the party aggrieved." *U. S.* v. *Ortega* (1825), 4 Wash. Circ. Ct. 531, citing and affirming *U. S.* v. *Liddle* (1808), 2 Wash. Circ. Ct. 205. See Scott, *Cases*, 296 n.

[33] The Revised Statutes of the United States, §§ 4063–4064, declare any judicial process null and void whereby "the person of any public minister of any foreign prince or State authorized and received as such by the President, or any domestic or domestic servant of any such minister, is arrested or imprisoned, or his goods or chattels are distrained, seized, or attacked"; and every person suing out or executing such process is declared to be "a violator of the Law of Nations, and a disturber of the public repose," and shall be imprisoned for not more than three years and fined at the discretion of the Court, 4 Moore, *Digest*, § 660, p. 631.

For foreign legislation on this subject, see Heyking, *L'exterritorialité* (1889), § 21; Odier, *Des privileges des agents diplomatiques* (1890), 53–78; and Vercamer, *Des franchises diplomatiques* (1891), Pt.I, ch. 2. France has special press laws providing for the punishment of the defamation of ambassadors, etc. See Odier, *op. cit.*, 103 ff.; 3 P.-Fodéré, *Traité*, 1385, and 2 *Cours*, 16–19. For the text of the English law (7 Anne, c. 12), see Blackstone, *Com.*, Bk. I, c. 7, § 255, or Halleck (3d ed.), 337–38 n. The ordinary alien is also in a sense in-

case there is an obligation to punish violations of this principle of the Law of Nations on the part of individuals. If an infraction is committed by the Government itself or by one of its officials, suitable reparation by way of explanation, apology, indemnity, etc., must be made.

2. *Immunity from Criminal Jurisdiction*

274. Immunity from Criminal Jurisdiction.—Diplomatic agents also enjoy immunity from criminal and civil jurisdiction.[34] Immunity from criminal jurisdiction is absolute. It consists in freedom from arrest and punishment for alleged crimes or violations of law by the local authorities,[35] but this does not mean that public ministers are exempt from the moral obligation of obedience to local or municipal law.[36] In case the minister commits a serious crime or offense, he may be punished in his own country, where he is supposed to have retained his domicile, and he is responsible to his own Government, to which the proper representations should be made. A request for his recall may be made or, if his conduct be extremely reprehensible, he may be dismissed, or even, should necessity require it, be temporarily imprisoned or conducted to the frontier.

A public minister cannot be compelled to give evidence or to act as a witness in a lawsuit or criminal trial, though he may, with the consent of his Government, waive this privilege.[37] He cannot, in general, waive his privilege of

violable, *i.e.* as entitled to the protection of the ordinary law and the courts; but the diplomatic agent is inviolable in a special sense.

[34] These immunities are closely connected, and partly identical with inviolability, of which they seem to be a consequence and from which they cannot be completely separated.

[35] This is well shown by Beling, *Die strafrechtliche Bedeutung der Exterritorialität* (1896), §§ 4–6.

[36] This includes freedom from police jurisdiction as well, but public ministers are expected to observe local police or municipal regulations relating to sanitation, fire protection, license taxes for hunting, etc. In case of failure to comply with such regulations, complaint may be made to their own Government. On Police Regulations, see especially 4 Moore, *Digest*, § 669; and 2 P.-Fodéré, *Cours*, 112–16, and 3, *Traité*, Nos. 1427 ff.

[37] This privilege was waived by *Señor Comancho*, Minister from Venezuela, who was present at the assassination of President Garfield in 1880. Acting upon instructions from his Government, he gave evidence as a chief witness at the trial of the assassin Guiteau.

In 1856 the *Dutch Minister* refused to appear as a witness at the trial in a

immunity from criminal jurisdiction without the consent of his sovereign.

3. Immunity from Civil Jurisdiction

275. Immunity from Civil Jurisdiction. Exceptions.— Diplomatic agents also enjoy a limited immunity from jurisdiction in civil matters. They are exempt [38] in principle, but there are important exceptions like the following:

(1) Real actions, relating to immovables which the minister possesses in the country to which he is sent. With the exception of his residence, these are subject to territorial jurisdiction.

(2) When the agent or minister engages in a trade, profession, or in commerce, he is subject to local jurisdiction in his business or professional dealings. [39]

(3) If he acts in a fiduciary character, such as guardian or trustee, he is liable for the obligations contracted in this capacity. [40]

(4) When the minister, whether with or without the authorization of his government, [41] voluntarily submits to judicial process without pleading his immunity, or if he himself sets the machinery of justice in motion. In such cases he must bear the judicial consequences of his action,

case of homicide which had occurred in his presence. He was supported by his own Government and his colleagues of the diplomatic corps. His recall was afterwards requested by the United States Government which regarded his refusal to testify as discourteous and disrespectful under the circumstances. See especially 3 Calvo, § 1520 n.; 1 Halleck (3d ed.), 353; * 4 Moore, *Digest*, § 662; 1 Oppenheim, § 392; Snow, *Cases*, 98.

In countries which permit of such a practice, the deposition of a public minister is usually taken and produced at the trial.

[38] There are a few dissentients (*e.g.* Fiore) from this opinion, but it is the view of the great majority of publicists and has the sanction of international practice. See, *e.g.* 1 Oppenheim, § 391; and 1 * Satow, §§ 288–300.

[39] This is the consensus of opinion among the authorities. But the contrary view was taken by English judges in *Taylor* v. *Best* (1854), 14 Common Bench 487, and Snow, *Cases*, 90; and in *Magdelena Steam Navigation Co.* v. *Martin* (1859), 2 Ellis and Ellis 94, and Evans, *Cases*, 212.

In *Musurus Bey* v. *Godham*, L. R. (1894), 1 Q. B. 533, it was held that the Statute of Limitations does not begin to run against his creditors while a foreign ambassador is in England and accredited to the sovereign.

[40] This would also be the case with property which he received by will or inheritance.

[41] It is a disputed point whether the prior consent of his Government is necessary or not. See especially on this point Piétri, *Étude critique sur la fiction d'exterritorialité* (1895), No. 56.

though the means of execution would probably be limited to any real property he may possess.

But as a general rule, diplomatic agents are not subject to suit for debt or in any civil action,[42] and their movable property [43] cannot be seized, attached, or confiscated. Injured parties should address themselves to the Minister of Foreign Affairs,[44] who may, at his discretion, bring the matter to the attention, first of the accused public minister, and later, if deemed advisable, to the Government he represents.

4. *Other Immunities and Privileges*

276. Fiscal Immunities.—" The person of a diplomatic agent, his personal effects, and the property belonging to him as representative of his sovereign, are not subject to taxation.[45] Otherwise, he enjoys no exemption from taxes

[42] For the amusing case of the *Ambassador of Peter the Great* (1708), see Blackstone, *Com.*, Bk. I, ch. 7, § 255, or Snow, *Cases on Int. Law* (1893), 89.

In 1772 the passports of the *Baron de Wrech*, Minister Plenipotentiary of the Landgrave of Hesse-Cassel at the Court of Paris, were withheld for non-payment of debts. The diplomatic corps remonstrated against this act as a violation of International Law. So far as we are aware, it has never been repeated. Snow, 97, and 2 Ch. de Martens, *Causes célèbres*, 110–21.

[43] See *Wheaton's case* (4 Moore, *Digest*, § 663; Snow, *Cases*, 94–97; and Wheaton, §§ 228–41) for an apparent exception to this rule.

The Prussian Government supported the claim of Wheaton's landlord to detain his furniture for alleged damages on the ground that "the lessor is entitled, as a security for the rent and other demands arising under the contract, to the rights of a *Pfandgläubinger* (a creditor whose rights are secured by hypothecation), upon the goods brought by the tenant upon the premises and there remaining at the expiration of the lease." Prussian Civil Code.

In other words, "the Prussian Government decided that the general exemption of the personal property of a foreign minister from the local jurisdiction did not extend to the case in question, where, it was contended, the right of detention was created by the contract itself and by the effect given to it by the local law." The United States Minister maintained that this position was in violation of diplomatic immunities. Those authorities who discuss the case appear to agree with Wheaton.

[44] In Austria there is a special court for this purpose, but submission to its jurisdiction is voluntary. Neumann, *Éléments du droit des gens* (1886), § 42, p. 260. For Minister Jay's experiences before this court (1875), see 4 Moore, *Digest*, § 661.

[45] This exemption includes direct personal taxes, such as the capitation or poll tax; special taxes like those on income and capital (unless the minister is engaged in commerce); sumptuary taxes like those on doors and windows; those for military purposes, quartering troops, etc.

It does not necessarily include such indirect taxes as the excise, rates or assessments for local purposes from which he derives a benefit, inheritance

or duties as of right. By courtesy, however, most, if not all, nations permit the entry free of duty of goods intended for his private use." [46]

277. **Other Privileges.**—Other privileges of public ministers are the right of private worship (which is no longer of great importance in this age of toleration); the right, according to their rank, to certain ceremonial honors and marks of respect; [47] a very limited and purely voluntary disciplinary jurisdiction over members of their suites or official families; [48] and, if permitted by their home Governments, the right of performing certain civil functions, such as the issuance of passports to fellow nationals, the authentication of certain documents like wills, contracts, etc., and the performance of the marriage ceremony. [49]

taxes, customs dues, stamp and registry duties, tolls, etc. Nor does the immunity include taxes on realty. Even the residence of the minister is not necessarily exempt from the land tax. In respect to indirect taxes and the tax on his residence, the principles of reciprocity or courtesy are usually applied. On "Exemption from Taxation," see particularly 1 Satow, ch. 19.

For the practice of the United States, see 4 Moore, *Digest*, §§ 667–68.   Art. 11 of the "Rules on Diplomatic Immunities" adopted by the Institute of Int. Law in 1895 declares: "A public minister abroad, the functionaries officially connected with his mission, and the members of their families living with them, shall be exempt from paying: (1) direct personal imposts and sumptuary taxes; (2) general imposts on wealth, whether upon capital or upon income; (3) war taxes; (4) customs duties on articles for personal use.   Each Government may indicate the evidence required in order to secure these exemptions from taxation."   Scott, *Resolutions of the Institute of Int. Law* (1916), 122.

[46] Hall, § 53, p. 235.

[47] See especially 2 P.-Fodéré, *Cours*, pp. 273 ff., and 3 *Traité*, Nos. 1287 ff., 1496–1501.

[48] See Bonfils and 1 (3 pt.), Fauchille, Nos. 726–29; 3 Calvo, §§ 1540–49; Heffter, § 216; 2 P.-Fodéré, *Cours*, 254 ff., and 3, *Traité*, Nos. 1472–90; 1 Rivier, 504 f.; and 1 Satow, §§ 301 ff.

But the old idea of the right of criminal and civil jurisdiction over members of the suite, formerly claimed and sometimes exercised, has disappeared from the doctrine as well as the practice of the Law of Nations, excepting in some parts of the Orient. See *infra*, No. 291.

[49] On *Diplomatic and Consular Marriages*, see Hall, § 53 p. 236 and note on pp. 236–37; 1 Hyde, § 453; 3 Lawrence, *Commentaire sur Wheaton* (1868–80), 357 ff.; * 2 Moore, *Digest*, §§ 238–39; Odier, *Des privilèges des agents diplomatiques* (1890), 328–86; and Westlake, *Private Int. Law* (4th ed. 1905), §§ 27–30.

The marriage of two fellow nationals of the diplomatic agent celebrated at the embassy is generally valid, if performed in conformity with the law of their State; but no State is under any international obligation to recognize such marriages.   And the State in which the ceremony is solemnized may refuse to recognize their validity, unless performed in accordance with its laws.   There

278. The Freedom of the Hotel or Immunity of Domicile.
—It is generally agreed that the hotel or residence [50] of the foreign minister is protected from forcible entry or invasion by his diplomatic inviolability and immunities. But this freedom is not absolute. The embassy must not harbor criminals or refugees from justice,[51] and no violation of territorial sovereignty should be permitted. The minister should surrender those accused of crime and, if necessary, even permit the premises to be searched. In case of persistent refusal, the legation may be surrounded with guards, and if extremely urgent, forcible entry may be made.[52]

appears to be no general rule on this interesting subject, and the whole matter remains in great confusion.

In its instructions to consular and diplomatic agents, the United States Government has always emphasized the importance of observing the law of the country in which the marriage ceremony takes place. 2 Moore, *Digest*, § 237. But this rule does "not apply to non-Christian or semi-civilized countries where consular courts are established." *Ibid.*, § 238.

It would seem that mixed marriages or the marriage of a national with a foreigner in the embassy would not, as a rule, be upheld. Thus, mixed marriages solemnized at foreign embassies in Paris have been repeatedly declared void by the French Tribunals; and the marriage between an Austrian and an English woman celebrated at the British embassy in Vienna was annulled by the Supreme Court of Austria in 1880. For the latter case, see Von Bar, *Int. Law, Private and Criminal* (Gillespie's trans., 1883), 493 n. For the French case of *Meffray and Mudge*, see Odier, *op. cit.*, 332 ff.

[50] This includes his stable, carriages, etc.

[51] The old "freedom of the quarter" has disappeared, except in some parts of the Orient. On the so-called *Right of Asylum*, see *supra*, No. 225.

But the protection of the embassy may well be extended from motives of humanity to refugees from mob violence or a criminal conspiracy.

[52] In the case of *Gallatin's coachman* (1827), who had committed an assault outside the embassy, the English Government claimed the right of arresting him within the stable of the minister. It admitted, however, that as a matter of courtesy, the convenience of the minister should have been consulted as to the time and manner of making the arrest. 4 Moore, *Digest*, pp. 656 f. On this case, see also * 1 Satow, § 329; and 1 Stowell and Munro, 7–8.

This case is mentioned by nearly all the authorities, who generally cite it as an example of the "English practice." which they consider exceptional. It certainly does not seem to have been a case of extreme urgency.

In 1865 a Russian subject, *Mickilchenkorff*, having wounded one of the attaches of the Russian embassy at Paris, was removed by police officials who had been called upon for aid. Upon his being imprisoned and indicted, the Russian ambassador requested his extradition on the ground that the hotel of the embassy was extraterritorial; but the French Government refused this request and proceeded with the trial. 3 Calvo, § 1505.

The Chinese refugee, *Sun Yat Sen*, was induced to enter the house of the Chinese Legation in London (in 1896), and kept under arrest there with the

279. **The Family and Suite of the Envoy.**—To a greater or less degree, these immunities are shared by the family and suite of the envoy.[53]   His retinue or suite include:

(1) The members of his family, as wife, children, and other near relatives living under his roof.

(2) His official suite and their families, such as Councillors, Naval and Military Attachés, Secretaries of Legation,[54] the Chancellor of the Legation, various assistants, clerks, interpreters, the chaplain, doctor, official legal adviser, and the like.

(3) Couriers or bearers of dispatches.

(4) Domestics like private secretaries, tutors, and servants [55] such as cooks, coachmen, etc.

280. **Extent of these Immunities.**—It is generally agreed that the various members of the family and of the official suite of the envoy, together with their families, enjoy the same inviolability and the same immunities that he himself does.   Children born to them during their mission are regarded as having been born on the territory of the home State.   These privileges cannot be waived [56] without the

purpose of sending him back to China for trial.   But the English Government properly insisted upon his release.   1 Oppenheim, § 390, p. 567.

On "Immunities of Residence," see especially 1 Satow, ch. 20.

[53] It is customary to furnish to the local authorities a list of the members of the family and domestics, but, according to Taylor (p. 346 n.), this custom is more honored in the breach than the observance.   The best evidence of diplomatic character is a certificate of the Secretary of State.   *In re Baiz* (1908), 135 U. S. 403, and Scott, *Cases*, 314; and *U. S.* v, *Liddle* (1808), 2 Wash. C. C. 205.

[54] "The wife of a secretary of a foreign legation in this country is, while with him in his official capacity, subject, in respect to her personal estate, to the laws of the country he represents."   Secretary Frelinghuysen to Mr. Lawrence (1883).   Cited in 4 Moore, *Digest*, § 664, p. 652.

[55] These do not include workmen occasionally employed on the premises. To entitle one to immunity, the service must be real, and not colorable.   *Triquet* v. *Bath* (1764), 3 Burr. 1478, and Scott, *Cases*, 2; *Heathfield* v. *Chilton* (1767), 4 Burr. 2015, and Scott, *Cases*, 288; and *Sarmiento's Case*, in 4 Moore, *Digest*, p. 654.

The immunity does not extend to matters unconnected with the service.   In *Novello* v. *Toogood*, 1 B. and C. 554, a chorister of the Portuguese ambassador was held liable for poor rates on a house in which he lived and let lodgings. This appears to have been on the ground that he was carrying on the business of lodging house keeper; for, in a later case, it was held that an attaché of the Portuguese embassy was not liable for parochial rates on a house which had been sublet to him.   *Parkinson* v. *Potter* (1885), L. R. 16 Q. B. Div. 152, and Evans, *Cases*, 216.

[56] This is at least true in respect to those immunities belonging to any member of his *official* family or suite.

consent of the home Government.   They are also shared by couriers or dispatch bearers of the legation (who also share in the right of innocent passage through third States) during the performance of their duties.   The dispatches they bear are also exempt from search and seizure.

It is also customary to grant exemption from civil and criminal jurisdiction to all persons in the private service of the envoy or of members of his legation, provided such persons are not nationals of the receiving State.   But these privileges may be waived at discretion, and mere servants or domestics cannot claim exemption from taxes, immunity of domicile, or freedom from arrest for crime committed outside the residence of their employers.   In case of arrest, they should, however, be released if the envoy refuses to waive their immunity from criminal jurisdiction.[57]

Mere visitors and hangers-on of the embassy do not enjoy diplomatic privileges and immunities.[58]   They do not

[57] In this case they should be sent home for trial.   Nationals of the receiving State should be handed over to the local authorities.

There is a considerable diversity both in the doctrine and practice respecting immunities of domestics or non-official members of the diplomatic suite.   The Italian school of publicists deny immunity from all criminal as well as civil jurisdiction.   Others make a distinction between these two kinds of jurisdiction.   Some authorities distinguish between offenses committed outside and inside the embassy; others between nationals and foreigners.

Anglo-American law and practice, which grant immunity from suit to domestics of public ministers, seem more liberal than necessary; for the modern tendency should be to restrict the diplomatic privileges and immunities of mere servants or non-official members of the legation.   These extensive immunities are no longer necessary (if, indeed, they ever were) to the freedom of the diplomatic agent.   At any rate, there appears to be no good reason why domestics should enjoy immunity from civil jurisdiction.

[58] The case of *Don Pantaleon Sa* (1653) is the one usually cited in this connection.   But it is not clear whether this brother of the Portuguese ambassador, who was executed by Cromwell for murder committed under circumstances of peculiar atrocity, was a mere visitor or an actual member of the Portuguese embassy.   It appears that he had received a promise from his sovereign that he would be appointed to succeed his brother (whose recall was momentarily expected) as ambassador to England.

As Lawrence (7th ed., p. 288) says: "If he is to be regarded as a member of his brother's suite, all we can say is that International Law has developed since this time and would not now permit a trial and execution under similar circumstances by the authorities of the State where the crime was committed. But if he was simply a visitor at the embassy, he would not be protected by diplomatic immunity to-day any more than he was two hundred and forty years ago."

For the case of *Don Pantaleon Sa*, see 1 Satow, § 286; Snow, *Cases on Int. Law* (1893), 86; and 2 Ward, *Hist. of the Laws of Nations* (1795), 535–46.

necessarily extend to consuls as such, public or secret political agents, military or naval officers, or mere commissioners not clothed with a diplomatic character. But they do extend to the judges of the Hague Tribunal or Court of Arbitration and of the Permanent Court of International Justice, members of the Assembly and Council of the League of Nations, public officials of the League at Geneva, members of official International Congresses and Conferences, and, in general, to all agents clothed with a diplomatic or representative character, such as commissioners if they are properly accredited and do not have a mere technical or administrative character.[59]   It should be added that if a State consents to receive one of its own nationals in a diplomatic capacity, it should extend to him all privileges and immunities belonging to his mission, unless it has made their abandonment a condition of his reception.[60]

II. Sovereigns and Heads of State

281. **Immunities of Sovereigns.**—Sovereigns and Heads of State traveling or residing abroad enjoy, in time of peace, inviolability and absolute immunity from criminal and police jurisdiction.[61]   They are also exempt from civil process except in the following cases:

[59] According to an editorial in the *Christian Science Monitor* for Aug. 11, 1925, "with a unanimity that suggests concerted action, the European nations, in quick succession are replying negatively to the requests of the United States Government for an extension of the diplomatic immunity privileges so as to include agents of the American Treasury Department, sent abroad to investigate production costs under the Fordney-McCumber Tariff Act."

[60] English judges hold that even a British subject may enjoy the immunities of a diplomatic agent.   *Macartney* v. *Garbutt* (1890), L. R. 24 Q. B. Div. 368, and 1 Cobbett, 309.   See to the contrary, Art. 15 of the Rules adopted by the Institute of Int. Law.   Scott, *Resolutions of the Institute of Int. Law* (1916), 123.

[61] Unless they travel *incognito*.   But this is no real exception, inasmuch as they may, at any time, reveal their identity and thus claim the privileges and immunities of sovereigns.

Another apparent exception is where a sovereign enters the military service of another sovereign.   In this case, his immunities are partly suspended. Where a person is subject in one country and sovereign in another, he is subject to the laws of the former in his private capacity.

If the safety of the State requires it, as in case of conspiracy, they may be sent out of the country.   This is rather an application of the supreme law of necessity than an exception to complete immunity.

Presidents of Republics, when traveling in a representative capacity, have a right to the same privileges and immunities as Monarchical Sovereigns.

(1) In respect to any real property which they may possess as private individuals in the foreign State.   (2) Respecting civil actions based upon the capacity of the State or sovereign as heir or legatee in an open succession upon foreign territory.   (3) In case the State or foreign sovereign voluntarily accepts the local territorial jurisdiction.[62]   (4) For damages resulting from a delinquency committed by a sovereign upon foreign territory, unless such injuries are due to acts of sovereignty.[63]

Foreign sovereigns or Heads of State also enjoy certain fiscal immunities, such as freedom from direct personal taxes, customs dues, etc.; but they are not necessarily exempt from indirect taxes other than customs dues, or from taxes on realty.

These immunities extend to his residence, family, and suite; but, contrary to the older practice, the sovereign [64] has no criminal jurisdiction over members of his suite on foreign territory.   Nor may he afford asylum to criminals or refugees from justice.   Sovereigns who have abdicated or been deposed do not have a right to the privileges and immunities of reigning sovereigns, though they may enjoy them as a matter of courtesy.

282. A State not Liable to Suit or Judicial Process.— That a State cannot be sued without its own consent has long been a fundamental principle of the Law of Nations, as it is of the Constitutional Law of the United States.[65]

See *De Haber* v. *Queen of Portugal* (1851), 17 Q. B. 196, and Scott, *Cases,* 278; and *Mighill* v. *Sultan of Johore* (1894), L. R. 1 Q. B. Div. 149, Evans, *Cases,* 205, and Scott, *Cases,* 280.   See also 3 Calvo, §§ 1462–73; 2 Phillimore, § 109; and 2 Moore, *Digest,* § 250.

[62] For important English and American cases on exemptions of sovereigns from jurisdiction, see Evans, *Cases,* 205–12; Scott, *Cases,* 278–85; Snow, *Cases,* 72–82; and 2 Phillimore, § 113 A.

[63] For these exceptions see the Rules adopted by the Institute of Int. Law in 1891.   *Resolutions of the Institute of Int. Law* (1916), 91.

The fourth exception is very doubtful.   It appears to be a principle of French jurisprudence, but it would certainly be rejected in England, where it has been held that a foreign sovereign was not liable in damages for a breach of promise of marriage which he had made while living in England under an assumed name.   See *Sultan of Johore,* cited above in note 61.

[64] The older practice is illustrated by the famous case of *Queen Christina of Sweden* (1657).   Walker, *Manual,* 70 f.   In 1873 the Shah of Persia condemned a member of the suite to death in London, but the British Government refused to permit the execution.

[65] See Amend. XI of the Constitution of the United States.   This rule is

BIBLIOGRAPHY

Rights and Duties of Diplomatic Agents.—14 *Annuaire* (1895–96), 201–44; Baty, in 8 *Grotius Soc.* (1923), 21–36; Bluntschli, Arts. 159–243; Bonfils or * 1 (3 Pt.) Fauchille, Nos. 652–732; Bry, *Précis élémentaire de droit int.* (1906), Nos. 215–58; Bulmerincq, in 1 Marquardsen, *Handbuch*, §§ 71, 73, 76, 80; Bynkershoek, *De foro legatorum* (1721); * 3 Calvo, §§ 1310–67, 1480–1549, 6 *Ibid.*, §§ 258-- 262, 285, 304–23, and Art. on "Exterritorialité" in 1 *Dictionnaire de droit int.* (1885), 315–20; Chrétien, *Principes de droit int. public* (1893), Nos. 442–542; 1 Cobbett, 305–21; Corwin, *The President's Control of Foreign Relations* (1917); Crouzet, *De l'inviolabilité* (1875); Dana, note 129, Dana's ed. of Wheaton, 303–07; Davis, ch. 7; Despagnet, Nos. 218–52; De Clercq et de Vallat, *Formulaire des Chancelleries diplomatiques et consulaires* (1908); Droin, *L'exterritorialité des agents diplomatiques* (1895); Eagleton, in 19 *A. J.* (1925), 293–314; Egerton, in 19 *A. J.* (1925), 293 ff.; * Evans, *Cases*, 212–31: Fenwick, ch. 21; Féraud-Giraud, *États, souverains, personnel diplomatique et consulaire, etc., devant les tribunals étrangers* (1895); 2 Fiore, Nos. 1103–75, and *Int. Law Cod.* (1918), Arts. 427–94; "Foreign and Diplomatic Service," in *Brit. Yr. Bk.* (1920–21), 97 ff.; Foster, *Practice of Diplomacy* (1906), *passim*; Field, *Outlines of an Int. Code* (1876), Arts. 91–158: Funck Brentano et Sorel, liv. I, ch. 5; * Garcia de la Vega, *Guide pratique* (4th ed., 1905); Geffcken, in 3 Holtzendorff, 605–84; Gentilis, *De legationibus* (1612), lib. III; * Grotius, (1629), lib. II, cap. 18; * Hall, §§ 50–54, 98–101; 1 Halleck (3d ed.), 269–73, 325–68; * Heffter, §§ 198–240; Hershey, *Diplom. Agents and Immunities* (1919); * Heyking, *L'exterritorialité* (1889); Hubler, *Die Magistraturen* (1895); Hughes, in 16 *A. J.* (1922), 355 ff.; Hunt, *Department of State of U. S.* (1914); * 1 Hyde, §§ 408–59; *Instructions to Diplomatic Officers of the U. S.* (1897); * Kebedgy, *Die diplomatischen Privilegieu* (1901); Klüber, §§ 166–230; Lawrence, §§ 106, 121–30; * Lay, *Foreign Service of the U. S.* (1925); particularly ch. 3; * Lehr, *Manuel des agents diplomatique* (1888); Lisboa, *Les fonctions diplomatiques* (1908); Liszt, § 23; J. de Louter, §§ 32–33; Ch de Martens, *Le guide diplomatique* (5th ed., 1866), and *Causes célèbres* (1827); * 2 G. F. de Martens, §§ 175–250; 2 F. de Martens, §§ 6–17; * Mathews, *The Conduct of Am. Foreign Policy* (1922), *passim;* McIlwrath, "The

not universal, so far as constitutional law is concerned. In many countries States may be sued as ordinary litigants, but International Law does not admit the submission of one State to the jurisdiction of another. See, especially Bisschop, on "Immunities of States Marinitime Law," in *Brit. Yr. Bk.* (1922–23), 159 ff.

To the principle laid down in the text, there seems to be an exception, viz. where the State owns or inherits real property or conducts a business enterprise in the territory of another State. On the much-discussed *Zappa Affair*, see especially 6 Calvo, §§ 286–99; Despagnet, No. 186; and 1 Westlake, 251–52. For references on the *Zappa Affair*, see 1 Fauchille, p. 477.

Diplomatic Service," in 86 *19th Cent.* (1919), 731 ff.; 2 Mérignhac, 229–94; * 4 Moore, *Digest*, ch. 15, §§ 623 ff.; Myers, in 11 *Am. Pol. Sci. Rev.* (1917), 24–58; Neumann, *Éléments du droit des gens* (1886), §§ 53–67; 2 Nys, 335–93, and *Les origines;* * Odier, *Des privilèges des agents diplomatique* (1890); * 1 Oppenheim, §§ 358–417; Ozanam, *L'immunité civil* (1912); 2 Phillimore, §§ 114–242; * Piétri, *Étude sur la fiction d'exterritorialité* (1895); * 1 Piédelièvre, Nos. 453–516; Pomeroy, ch. 11; * Praag, *Jurisdiction et droit int.* (1915), Nos. 49–68, 163, 203–36: * P.-Fodéré, 1 and 2 *Cours, passim,* and 3 *Traité,* Tit. I, ch. 1; * 1 Rivier, 429–518; Roederer, *De l'application des immunités* (1904); * 1 Satow; Schuyler, *Am. Diplomacy* (1886); 105–90; * Scott, *Cases,* 286–300; * Snow, *Cases on Int. Law* (1893), 83–99; 1 Stowell and Munro, ch. 1, 1–18; Taylor, §§ 273–324; 1 Twiss, ch. 12; Ullmann, §§ 44–53; Van Dyne, *Our Foreign Service* (1909), ch. 2 (very elementary); Vattel, liv. LV, §§ 55 ff.; Vercamer, *Des franchises diplomatiques* (1891); Walker, *Manual de droit int. public* (1895), § 26; Walpole, *Foreign Relations* (1882), ch. 4; 1 Westlake, 273–87; * 1 Wharton, *Digest,* ch. 4; Wheaton (Atlay's ed.), Pt. III, ch. 1, §§ 206–51; Wicquefort, *L'ambassadeur et ses fonctions* (1780); Wilson, ch. 5; Wilson and Tucker, ch. 13; Woolsey, §§ 86–98.

For further references, see the Bibliographies in Bonfils, Droin, *op. cit.,* Fauchille, Heyking, *op. cit.,* Oppenheim, and Olivart, *du droit int. Bibliographie.*

Rights and Duties of Sovereigns.—Angell, in 35 *Yale Law J.* (1925), 150–68; (1905–10), 11 *Annuaire* (1881), 436 ff., or Scott, *Resolutions of the Institute of Int. Law* (1916), 91–92 (for draft of regulations of the Institute of Int. Law); Audinet, in 2 *R. D. I. P.* (1895), 385 ff.; Bar, in 12 *J. I. P.,* 645 ff.; Bluntschli, Arts. 115–58; * Bonfils or 1 (3 Pt.) Fauchille, Nos. 632–47; Borchard, § 72 and note on p. 176; Bry, *Précis élémentaire de droit int.* (1906), Nos. 206–14; Bulmerincq, in 1 Marquardsen, *Handbuch,* § 66; * 3 Calvo, §§ 1454–79, and 6 *Ibid.,* §§ 282–303; Clunet, in 14 *J. I. P.,* 5 ff.; 1 Cobbett, 92–99; * Despagnet, Nos. 253–58; * Evans, *Cases,* 205–12; Fenwick, 183–86, 351; Féraud-Giraud, *États, souverains* (1895); 1 and 2 Fiore, Nos. 501 ff., 1097–1102; * Foote, *Private Int. Jurisprudence* (3d ed., 1904), 148–66; Gabba, in 15, 16, and 17 *J. I. P.* (Clunet), 180 ff., 538 ff., and 25 ff.; Hall, § 49; Heffter, §§ 48–57; 1 Hyde, §§ 408–10; Liszt, § 22; 2 J. de Louter, § 31; 1 F. de Martens, §§ 80–83; * 2 Mérignhac, 294–314; Neumann, *Éléments du droit des gens* (1886), §§ 15–16; * 1 Oppenheim, §§ 341–56; 2 Phillimore, Pt. VI, ch. 1; 1 Piédelièvre, Nos. 517–28; Piétri, *La fiction d'exterritorialité* (1895), Pt. II, ch. 2; 3 P.-Fodéré, *Traité,* Nos. 1537 ff.; * 1 Rivier, 413–25; * Scott, *Cases,* 278–86; Snow, *Cases on Int. Law* (1916), 72–82; Stoerk, in 2 Holtzendorf, 658 ff.; Taylor, § 184; Ullmann, § 41; Vattel, liv. I, §§ 38–45, and liv. IV, § 108; Visscher, in 49 (3d ser.), *R. D. I.* (1922), 149 ff., 300 ff.; 1 Westlake, 250–52, and *Private Int. Law* (4th ed., 1905), §§ 190–94; Weston, in 32 *Harv. Law Rev.* (1918–19), 266 ff.; Wheaton, §§ 95–98; Woolfman, in 4 *A. J.* (1910), 373–83.

CHAPTER XIX

RIGHTS AND DUTIES OF CONSULS

283. **Definition.**—Consuls are official agents sent by a State to foreign ports and cities, mainly for the purpose of watching over and promoting the commercial and industrial interests of the appointing State and its citizens or subjects, and of protecting its nationals traveling or residing in these places.[1]

284. **Classification.**—With reference to their character, modern consuls are usually said to be of two kinds: (1) *Consuls missi*, or professional consuls (*consuls de carriére*), who are not permitted to engage in any other business or profession. They are real public officials or functionaries of the sending State and enjoy full consular privileges and immunities. (2) *Consuls electi*,[2] or commercial consuls, who are chosen by the appointing government, either from its own citizens engaged in business in the city or country in which they are permitted to exercise their functions, or from among the nationals of a foreign State (usually of the country in which they serve). They are of distinctly inferior competence and status, and do not enjoy full consular privileges and immunities.[3]

[1] On the *Mediæval Origin of the Consulate*, see *supra*, No. 51, and note on pp. 58–59, for references.

[2] This term is now a misnomer, since this class of consuls is also appointed by the sending State. They were formerly elected by foreign merchants themselves.

[3] Some States (*e.g.* France, Great Britain, and the United States) do not, as a rule, appoint merchant or business consuls.

The United States has always preferred to appoint native American citizens, if properly qualified candidates for the position could be found. "No person who is not an American citizen shall be appointed hereafter in any consulate-general or consulate to any clerical position the salary of which is one thousand dollars a year or more." Act of April 5, 1906, sec. 5. See 5 Moore, *Digest*, § 697, p. 12. This Act also abolished the grade of commercial agent.

All consular officers whose respective salaries exceed $1,000 a year are prohibited from transacting business, practicing or being interested in the practice of the law. They are even forbidden to invest money in business enterprises or real estate (except for their own use) in the country from the Government of

With respect to rank, consuls are usually divided into four classes: (1) Consuls-general who exercise supervision or control over several consular districts or one large consular district. (2) Consuls for smaller districts or certain towns or ports. (3) Vice-consuls with consular character. (4) Consular agents with consular character.[4]

which they have received their exequaturs. *Consular Regulations* (1924), No. 37 and note.

Through the enactment of the Rogers Bill by Congress on May 24, 1924 (for the text of this important Act, see Lay, *Foreign Service of the U. S.*, 1925, App. E, 407 ff.), our foreign service was reorganized and (presumably) greatly improved.

This Act provides for the amalgamation of the Diplomatic and Consular Services under the name of "Foreign Service of the United States." Officers of this service, known as "Foreign Service Officers" are to be graded and classified on the basis of a new and common salary scale, ranging from $9,000 in class one downward to $3000 in class nine, with unclassified grades from $3000 downward to $1500. Appointments to a particular class and promotions from class to class are to be made by the President (by and with the advice and consent of the Senate).

Appointments as Foreign Service Officers shall be made after examination and a suitable period of probation in an unclassified grade "or after five years of continuous service therein, by transfer from the Department of State." Promotions are to be based on merit as shown by a system of inspection and efficiency records. Transfers may be made from one service to the other which, in respect to function, are kept quite distinct. The President is authorized to grant representation allowances to diplomatic missions as well as to consular offices under certain conditions, and fairly liberal retirement allowances are provided.

By subsequent Executive Order (June 7, 1924, see Lay, *op. cit.*, App. F., 417 ff.), the Board of Examiners were instructed to include the following subjects among those in which candidates shall be examined: "at least one modern language other than English (French, Spanish, or German by preference), elements of International Law, geography, the natural, industrial, and commercial resources and the commerce of the United States; American history, government and institutions; the history since 1850 of Europe, Latin America and the Far East; elements of political economy, commercial and maritime law." (Art. 14).

A Foreign Service School for the instruction of new applicants has been established in the Department of State at Washington. See Arts. 25–30, Exec. Order, June 7, 1924, and Dpt. order, No. 296, printed in Lay, *op. cit.*, 422, 425–26. Cf. *Ibid.*, pp. 335–38.

On our "Reorganized Foreign Service," see * Lay, *Foreign Service of the U. S.* (1925), ch. 9, and in 18 *Am. Pol. Sci. Rev.* (1924), 697–711; Dennis, in 219 *No. Am. Rev.* (1924), 178–86; Lansing, in 17 *A. J.* (1923), 285–87; and Sullivan, in 51 *World's Work* (Nov., 1925), No. 1, pp. 45–52.

[4] 1 Oppenheim, § 422. Prior to 1919 at least, the British Consular Service had six ranks. *Ibid.*, p. 593.

In the United States "the order of official precedence in the service is as follows: (1) Consuls-general: (2) consuls; (3) vice-consuls de carrière, and interpreters; (4) consular assistants and student interpreters when commis-

Consuls are, as a rule, placed under the direction of the Minister of Foreign Affairs or Secretary of State, with whom they correspond and to whom they send their reports; but they are also under the general supervision of the diplomatic agent or public minister accredited to the Government of the country in which they are located.

285. **The Appointment of Consuls.**—Every State is free to appoint such consuls, whether of its own or of a foreign nationality, as it deems qualified; but no State is legally bound either to admit them generally [5] or to permit the exercise of consular functions in a particular place or locality.

The consul receives from his home Government letters patent (*lettres de provision*) or a commission which is transmitted through diplomatic channels to the Minister of Foreign Affairs of the country in which he is to serve. If he prove acceptable, he is furnished with an *exequatur*,[6] or authorization to exercise consular functions by the foreign Government. The exequatur may be refused [7] or it may be

sioned as vice-consuls; (5) vice-consuls not of career; (6) consular assistants and student interpreters when not commissioned as vice-consuls; (7) consular agents." *Consular Regulations* (1924), No. 440.

"By the Act of April 5, 1906, for the reorganization of the United States consular service, Consuls-general are divided into seven classes, according to the salary, and consuls into nine classes. . . ." 5 Moore, *Digest*, p. 8. For this Act and regulations governing consular appointments and promotions in the United States, see Supp. to 1 *A. J.* (1907), 308–16. See also Lay, *Foreign Service in the United States*, 21 ff. and 389 ff. This Act and these regulations aimed to substitute the merit for the spoils system in the consular service. In 1909, by Executive Order, the merit system was also extended to all grades in the diplomatic service below that of minister.

[5] By refusing to appoint or receive consuls, a State would, of course, practically lose many of the advantages of membership in the international community.

[6] "An *exequatur* usually consists in a letter patent signed by the sovereign, and countersigned by the Minister of Foreign Affairs; but it is not necessarily conferred in so formal a manner; in Russia and Denmark the consul merely receives notice that he is recognized, and in Austria his commission is indorsed with the word 'exequatur' and impressed with the imperial seal." Hall, 373.

On the *exequatur*, see especially 1 Hyde, §§ 462–63; 5 Moore, *Digest*, §§ 698–700; and *Consular Regulations* (1924), Nos. 48–50.

[7] A State may refuse to receive a consul on personal or political grounds. No reasons for refusal need be given.

The case usually cited in this connection is that of *Major Haggerty*, a naturalized Irish-American who was known to have been connected with Fenian plots. England properly refused to grant him an exequatur in 1869.

withdrawn [8] without assigning any reason. In serious cases the receiving Government may ask for a consul's recall, though such a request need not be entertained by the appointing Government, unless it is satisfied that it is well grounded. In extreme cases a consul may be summarily dismissed.

286. **Duties or Functions of Consuls.**—One of the leading authorities [9] on this subject has classified or summarized the duties or functions of consuls under the following heads:

(1) As commercial agents of their Government and as protectors of the commerce and navigation of their nationals. [10]

(2) As agents for their Government for securing political information and as overseers of the execution of treaties. [11]

(3) As agents for the administration of the marine of the state, and as agents charged with the police of the merchant marine. [12]

[8] Mérignhac (II, 327) justly observes: "This measure should only be taken after ripe reflection, for it is more serious than the refusal to grant an exequatur."

For cases of *Refusal, Revocation, Dismissal* and *Recall,* see 1 Calvo, §§ 1381, 1383–84, 1391; Hall, § 105; pp. 373–75 and note (8th ed.); * 5 Moore, *Digest,* §§ 700–01; and 4 P.-Fodéré, Nos. 2036–64.

[9] P.-Fodéré, in 4 *Traité,* Nos. 2019–96. On the *Duties or Functions of Consuls,* see also Bonfils, Nos. 762–71; Carr, 55 *Pan Am. Union Bulletin* (1922), 366–80; * Foster, *Practice of Diplomacy* (1906), 223–37; Hall, *Foreign Powers and Jurisdiction* (1894), etc., 73–101; Lay, *Foreign Service of the U. S.* (1925), 131 ff.; * 5 Moore, *Digest,* §§ 717–31; 1 Oppenheim, §§ 429–33; 2 Phillimore, §§ 257–60; * Stowell, *Le consul* (1909), 15–136, 225–97, and *Consular Cases and Opinions* (1909, see index); *Consular Regulations of the United States* (1924); Ullmann § 61.

[10] They furnish all sorts of information relating to municipal laws, tariffs, trade conditions, industries, navigation, agriculture, finances, institutions, etc., to their Government or fellow nationals. Much of this information, which is often extremely valuable, is embodied in consular reports.

They are also expected to lend their good offices in securing for their fellow citizens fair treatment and protection from injustice; and in maintaining for them all the privileges and advantages to which they are entitled through municipal law, international usage, or treaties, more particularly the most-favored-nation clause.

[11] Their rôle as political agents is entirely secondary and passive, if not exceptional. The function of overseeing the execution of treaties of commerce and navigation is, however, of prime importance.

[12] They control and legalize "ship's papers," inspect vessels and certify invoices of their cargoes, settle disputes between master and crew or passengers, assist sailors in distress, secure their arrest or extradition for desertion, mutiny, or other crimes.

(4) As agents of administration in general.[13]

(5) As officers of the home State for the performance of civil functions.[14]

(6) As officials acting in a ministerial capacity.[15]

(7) As protectors and, under certain circumstances, guardians of the interests of their fellow nationals.[16]

(8) As arbitrators or judges exercising a very limited and purely voluntary jurisdiction over fellow nationals.[17]

(9) As sanitary police agents and administrators.[18]

The rights and duties of consuls are determined, in any

[13] This includes a wide range of functions, such as the issuance and visé of passports to fellow nationals, the authentication and legalization of documents, the granting of certificates of various sorts, the registry of births, deaths, and marriages, etc.

[14] For example, the consular right to celebrate marriages, as to which the practice varies greatly. It is, in general, limited to marital unions between fellow nationals. Great Britain permits it where one of the parties is a British subject. The United States does not authorize its consuls to solemnize marriages, but they may act as witnesses.

On *Consular Marriages*, see especially: Hall, *Foreign Powers and Jurisdiction*, 85–101; 1 Halleck (3d ed.), 381 f. and notes; 2 Moore, *Digest*, § 240; 4 P.-Fodéré, No. 2079; Stowell, *Le consul* (1909), 34–51, and *Consular Cases* (see compendium and index); Westlake, *Private Int. Law* (4th ed., 1905), § 27.

[15] Such are notarial acts of various sorts, like the attestation of contracts, the attestation and reception of wills, the reception of moneys and goods deposited by fellow nationals, the examination of witnesses and administration of oaths, etc.

[16] Most consular conventions give them the right of appealing to the local authorities to secure this protection, which may even be extended to nationals of other States who are under their protection (protégés). Generally speaking, it is the duty of consuls to render such aid to their fellow nationals as is necessary to enable them to earn their living or return to their own country; but this obligation is a moral rather than a legal one, and great care and caution must be used in its exercise.

It is also customary for consuls to intervene in the administration of successions and see that justice is done in case of the death of fellow nationals, and they may have to act as guardians in behalf of minors, idiots, etc., and administer estates.

[17] Except in the case of crews they have no contentious or compulsory jurisdiction in so-called Christian countries.

It is a custom based on treaties and usage for consuls to exercise a disciplinary jurisdiction (though not to the exclusion of local jurisdiction) over such offenses committed by the crews of vessels of their own nationality as do not disturb the peace or dignity of the port.

[18] Their rôle in this capacity is mainly that of furnishing their Government with information relating to epidemics, the state of public health in the cities or ports where they are located, the measures taken to prevent or check the spread of disease, etc. They also inspect vessels bound for a port of their own country for this purpose.

particular case, by treaties, by custom or international usage, by such conditions as may be laid down in the exequatur, and by the consular laws and regulations of the appointing State. But consuls may not discharge functions at variance with the law of the receiving State.[19] The duties of American consuls are rendered particularly onerous by reason of our tariff and immigration laws, which impose upon them many functions in connection with their execution.

287. **Consular Privileges and Immunities.**—Though consuls do not, as a rule, exercise diplomatic functions, they nevertheless enjoy certain privileges and immunities; but these are, for the most part, derived from treaties (particularly the most-favored-nation clause), local usage, or general custom based upon considerations of respect or reciprocity.

288. **Those forming Part of International Law.**—There are, however, a few rules which may be said to form a part of International Law itself. It is generally agreed that professional consuls are under the special protection of International Law, and that they are entitled to a certain degree of respect and protection [20] or personal immunity, though they are not inviolable.[21] It is also agreed that the official archives [22] and correspondence of the consulate are

[19] Opinion of Att.-Gen. Cushing in 8 *Opinions of Attorney's-General*, 100 and 470, or Stowell, *Consular Cases and Opinions*, 570 and 582.

[20] States are prone to resent any affront offered to their consuls or consulates, such as an attack by a mob or insult to the consular flag. In the *New Orleans Affair* (see *supra*, No. 154), Webster admitted liability for the attack on the Spanish consulate.

For numerous cases illustrative of the protection due to consular officers and archives, see 5 Moore, *Digest*, §§ 704–05. For the famous *Pritchard Affair* between France and England, which almost resulted in war, see 3 Calvo, § 1392 or 2 Phillimore, § 247. On the *Imbrie Incident* (the killing of an American vice-consul by a mob at Teheran in Persia), see Stowell, in 18 *A. J.* (1924), 768–74.

[21] But the personal inviolability of consuls is usually secured by treaty. To the same effect is Art. 7 of the "Regulations relating to Immunities of Consuls," adopted by the *Institute of International Law* in 1896. Scott, *Resolutions of the Institute of Int. Law* (1916), 125. "In no case may consuls be arrested or detained, except for grave infractions of the law."

[22] This immunity naturally carries with it the inviolability of the consulate or of that portion of the consul's residence in which the archives are contained, but it does not extend to the private papers or personal effects of the consul.

The consulate should not be used as an asylum for refugees or criminals, These should be surrendered upon request by the local authorities.

inviolable; and that consuls are permitted to place above the outside entrance of the consulate the arms of their country, and to display the flag [23] of their country on public occasions unless they reside in a city where their Government is represented by a diplomatic mission.

The measure of consular privileges and immunities in International Law would seem to be the amount or degree necessary for the proper performance of consular duties. Thus, a consul, not a citizen of a foreign State, may claim exemption from service on juries and in the militia, and no troops should be quartered upon the consulate or consular residence.

Such are the consular privileges and immunities which may be said to constitute a part of International Law.   In addition, they enjoy considerable privileges which are based on treaties, the most-favored-nation clause, local usage and reciprocity. [24]

289. **Privileges and Immunities Based on Treaties and Usage.**—One of the most common consular immunities based on treaty or reciprocity is that of exemption from direct personal contributions, such as the poll tax, and from taxes on income, furniture, doors and windows, [25] etc.; but

[23] Art. 14 of the "Regulations" adopted by the *Institute* (1896). Scott, *op. cit.*, 127. But the Consular Regulations of the United States (1924) state that "permission to display the national flag is not a matter of right, though it is usually accorded, and it is often provided for by treaty." No. 73.

[24] "Generally, a consul may claim for himself and his office not only such rights and privileges as have been conceded by treaty, but also such as have the sanction of custom and local laws, and have been enjoyed by his predecessors or by consuls of other nations, unless a formal notice has been given that they will not be extended to him." *Consular Regulations of the United States* (1924), No. 72.

On *Consular Treaty Rights*, see particularly a scholarly work with this title by Ludwig (1913). See especially his comments on the effect of the most-favored-nation clause, pp. 119 ff.

[25] In some countries exemption from customs dues is granted as a matter of courtesy. "Article 476 of the Customs Regulations of the United States provides for free entry in the United States 'of articles sent by a foreign government, for its use, to an agent in this country, on application through the Department of State.'" 5 Moore, *Digest*, § 716.

Art. 13 of the "Regulations on Immunities of Consuls" adopted by the Institute of International Law (1896) declares: "Consuls are exempt from paying: (1) direct personal taxes, and sumptuary taxes; (2) general taxes upon wealth, whether on capital or income; (3) war taxes.

they are never exempt from taxes on realty, or on business in which they are themselves engaged.[26]

Another common consular immunity found in treaties is that of freedom from the obligation of serving as witness or giving testimony in court except through deposition.[27]

Nearly all authorities agree that consuls, whether engaged in trade or not, are amenable to the local courts in civil as well as criminal matters; [28] but it is also generally held they should not be " arrested or detained except for grave infractions of the law." [29]

[26] "With reference to a complaint that the consul of the Elector of Hesse at New York had been enrolled in a military company, and had been fined by a court-martial for non-attendance upon the company's parades, the Department of State said that the case was one that belonged primarily to the courts of law, which had, when resorted to in such cases, always decided, according to the principles laid down by the Law of Nations, and embodied in treaties, that 'all persons recognized in the consular character by the President's exequatur, *who are not citizens of the United States*, are exempted from all public service, and from all taxes, imposts, and contributions except such as they may have to pay on their property, or in consequence of their engaging in commercial pursuits, they remaining in all cases amenable to the laws of the country.' " Secretary Forsyth to Mr. Faber (1840), in 5 Moore, *Digest*, § 715.

This passage throws light upon the practice of the United States; but it cannot be successfully maintained that the exemption from taxes is a principle of the Law of Nations, for it is not universally recognized, nor is it essential to freedom in the performance of consular duties.

[27] Secretary Marcy contended (in 1854) that the provision in the Federal Constitution granting to an accused person the right of compulsory process to procure the presence of witnesses in his favor, prevailed over a treaty with France which exempted consuls from the obligation of appearing in court and giving testimony. This contention "was not acquiesced in by the French Government, which required their flag, when raised to the mastheads of certain of their men-of-war at San Francisco, to be saluted as a reparation for the alleged indignity to their consul." 5 Moore, § 714, p. 81. See also Snow, *Cases on Int. Law* (1893), 99; 1 Wharton, *Digest*, 665; and *In re Dillon* (1854), 7 Sawy., 561, or Stowell, *Consular Cases*, 139.

All reasonable doubt on this subject has been removed (if any ever existed) by the decisions in *Baiz* v. *Malo* (1899), 58 N. Y. Supp. 806; and *U. S.* v. *Trumbull* (1891), 48 Fed. 94. For summaries, see Stowell, *op. cit.*, 51 and 418.

[28] The principle that consuls are not entitled to the immunities of public ministers from civil and criminal jurisdiction appears to have been first laid down judicially in *Barbuit's Case* (1737), Forrester's Cases Temp. Lord Talbot 281, Stowell, *Consular Cases*, 52, or Scott, *Cases*, 311. It has been repeatedly affirmed. For numerous other cases, see 5 Moore, *Digest*, §§ 711–12; and Stowell (see compendium, *op. cit.*, pp. 758–60, and index, 799). A particularly interesting case is that of *Com.* v. *Kosloff* (1816), 5 S. and R. 545; 5 Moore, *Digest*, § 712; and Stowell, *op. cit.*, 112.

[29] Art. 7 of the Regulations of the Institute, cited above. In the United States the Federal Courts have exclusive jurisdiction over consuls. 5 Moore, *Digest*, § 713.

290. **Termination of Consular Functions.**—The consular office terminates through death, recall or dismissal, revocation of the exequatur, or war.[30]   It is a principle universally recognized that a change in the headship of the appointing or receiving State does not terminate the functions of a consul. Neither a new commission nor exequatur are necessary.[31]

291. **Consular Jurisdiction in non-Christian Countries.**— In China and a few non-Christian countries in Asia and Africa,[32] the consuls have not only retained their earlier jurisdiction [33] over their own countrymen, but they also enjoy most of the diplomatic privileges and immunities. These include inviolability, certain marks of honor and respect, immunity from civil and criminal jurisdiction, and other miscellaneous rights and privileges.[34]

BIBLIOGRAPHY

Consuls.—11, 12, 13, and 15 *Annuaire* (1896), 348 ff., 277 ff., 179 ff., and 275 ff., respectively; Bluntschli, Arts. 244–75; Bodin, *Les immunités consulaires* (1899); Bonfils or *1 (3 Pt.) Fauchille, Nos. 733–75; Bulmerincq, in 3 Holtzendorff, 687–720, 738–53, and in 1 Marquardsen, *Handbuch*, §§ 70, 72, 74, 77, 81; 3 Calvo, §§ 1368–1430, 1445–50, and 1 *Dictionnaire de droit int.* (1885), Art. Consul;

[30] It is doubtful whether the functions of a consul terminate when his district is annexed, ceded to, or conquered by another State. Oppenheim (I, § 437) thinks the answer should be in the affirmative.

On the status of American consuls in Belgium after the occupation by German troops, see documents in Spec. Supp. to 10 *A. J.* (1916), 445–59. Cf. comments in 2 Hyde, § 701, p. 386; and 1 Oppenheim (3d ed.), p. 603.

For Instructions to Diplomatic and Consular Officers of the United States entrusted with the interests of foreign governments at war with the governments to which such officers are accredited, see Supp. to 9 *A. J.* (1915), 118–20.

[31] 1 Oppenheim, § 438.

[32] The extraterritorial privileges and immunities of consuls were abolished in Japan in 1899. They were practically abolished in Turkey by the Treaty of Lausannes in 1923, and seem now in process of abolition in China.

[33] This extraterritorial jurisdiction seems to be based upon the right of protection—a right which extends even to natives who are taken under the protection (protégés) of the foreign diplomatic or consular legations. It is derived from treaties or capitulations (see Brown, *Foreigners in Turkey* (1914), ch. 2; and 1 Twiss, ch. 14), and reenforced by custom or prescription.

[34] Since this highly complicated and technical subject forms no part of general International Law and seems destined soon to disappear altogether, it has not been deemed necessary to enter upon a detailed discussion of it, either in the text or in notes. For Bibliography, see pp. 425–26.

* Carr, in 1 *A. J.* (1907), 891 ff., and in 55 *Pan American Union*, Bulletin (1922), 366–80; De Clercq et de Vallet, *Guide pratique des consulats* in 2 vols. (1908); 1 Cobbett, 321–26; Devlin, *Treaty Power* (1908, see index); Despagnet, Nos. 363–78; Engelhardt, in 20, 21, 22, and 25 *R. D. I.*, 505 ff., 588 ff., 336 ff., and 132 ff., respectively; Field, *Outlines of an Int. Code* (1876), Arts. 159–85; 2 Fiore, Nos. 1176–87, and *Int. Law Cod.* (1908), Arts. 495–529; "Foreign and Diplomatic Service," in *Brit. Yr. Bk.* (1920–21), 97–108; "Foreign Service," Report on, publ. by National Civil Service Reform League (1919); * Foster, *Practice of Diplomacy* (1906), ch. 11; Funck-Brentano et Sorel, ch. 6; * Hall, *Foreign Powers and Jurisdiction* (1894), 73–101, and *Int. Law*, § 105; 1 Halleck (3d ed.), ch. 11; Heffter, §§ 244–48 and Geffcken's notes; Hübler, *Die Magistraturen* (1895), §§ 12–18; * 1 Hyde, §§ 460–88; Jones, *Consular Service of the United States* (1906); Jordan, in 38 (2 ser.) *R. D. I.* (1906), 479 ff., and 717 ff.; Koenig, *Handbuch des deutschen Konsularwesens* (6th ed., 1902); Lawrence, § 131; 4 Lawrence, *Commentaire* (1868–80), 1–304; * Lay, *Foreign Service of the United States* (1925), particularly chs. 5 and 9, and in 18 *Am. Pol. Sci. Rev.* (1924), 697–711; Lehr, *Manuel des agents diplomatiques et consulaires* (1888); Lisboa, *Les functions diplomatiques* (1908), ch. 5; Liszt, § 24; 2 J. de Louter, §§ 34–35; * Ludwig, *Consular Treaty Rights* (1913); 1 Ch. de Martens, *Guide diplomatique* (5th ed., 1866), §§ 68–78; 2 F. de Martens, §§ 18–23; McAneny in 35 *Cent. Mag.*, n. s. (1898–99), 604 ff.; 2 Mérignhac, 314–38; Monnet, *Manuel diplomatique et consulaire* (1905); * 5 Moore, *Digest*, ch. 16; 2 Nys' 394–403; * 1 Oppenheim, §§ 418–38; * 2 Phillimore, §§ 243–71; 1 Piédelièvre, Nos. 567–616; Pillaut, *Manuel de droit consulaire* (1910); Pomeroy, §§ 370–85; * 4 P.-Fodéré, Nos. 2034–2146; * 1 Rivier, 519–42; Salles, *L'institution des consulats* (1898), 311–22; Schuyler, "Our Consular System," in *American Diplomacy* (1886); * Scott, *Cases*, 311–22; Stewart, in 20 *A. J.* (1926), 81 ff.; Stockton, *Outlines of Int. Law* (1914), ch. 11; * Stowell, *Le consul* (1909), and, * *Consular Cases and Opinions* (1909); Taylor, §§ 325–30; 1 Twiss, § 223; * Ullmann, §§ 54–62; Van Dyne, *Our Foreign Service* (1909), ch. 3; Walpole, *Foreign Relations* (1882), ch. 5; 1 Westlake, 279, 287–89; 1 Wharton, *Digest*, ch. 5; Wheaton (Atlay's ed.), §§ 110, 216, 249; *Ibid.* (Dana's ed.), notes 68 and 135, on pp. 178, 324–25; Wilson, ch. 6; Wilson and Tucker, No. 82; Woolsey, §§ 99–100; and Zorn, *Das Konsulargesetzgebung des deutschen Reiches* (1901).

See also * *Consular Regulations of the United States* (1924); and *General Instructions* to Her Majesty's Consular Officers (1893).

For further references see the bibliographies in Bonfils, Fauchille, Lay, *op. cit.*, and Stowell, *Le Consul*.

Consular Jurisdiction in Mohammedan Countries and the Orient. —Arminjon, *Étrangers et protégés dans l'Empire Ottoman* (1903); Bau, *Foreign Relations of China* (1921), ch. 18; * Bulmerincq, in 3 Holtzendorff, 720–38, 753 ff., and in 1 Marquardsen, *Handbuch*, §§ 75, 78–79; Bonfils or * 1 (3 Pt.) Fauchille, Nos. 776–91; Brown

Foreigners in Turkey (1914) and in 1 *For. Aff.* (1922–23), No. 4, pp. 71–81; Bruillat, *Étude sur la jurisdiction consulaire* (1898); 3 Calvo, §§ 1431–44; Denby, "Exterritoriality in China," in 18 *A. J.* (1924), 667 ff.; Despagnet, Nos. 356–62; *Hall, *Foreign Powers and Jurisdiction of the British Crown* (1894), 132–203; 1 Halleck (3d ed.), 386–400; * Hinckley, *American Consular Jurisdiction in the Orient* (1906); Hübler, *Die Magistraturen* (1895), §§ 19–21; 1 Hyde, §§ 259–65; Jenkyns, *British Rule beyond the Seas* (1902), ch. 8; Jones, *op. cit.*, ch. 3; Kebedgy, in 27 *R. D. I.*, 313 ff.; Lippmann, *Die Konsular-jurisdiktion im Orient;* Liszt, § 25; Liu, *Exterritoriality*, in 118 Columbia University *Studies* (1925); 2 J. de Louter, § 36; * Mandelstam, "La justice ottomane,"etc., in 14 and 15 *R. D. I. P.* (1907 and 1908), 5 ff., 534 ff. and 329 ff., respectively; 2 F. de Martens, §§ 24–26, and *Das Consularwesen* (1874); 2 Mérignhac, 69–118, 338–56; 5 Moore, *Digest*, § 703; 2 Nys, 403–18, and in 7 *R. D. I.* (2d series), 237 ff.; 1 Oppenheim, 439–42; Pélissié du Ransas, *Le régime des capitulations dans l'Empire ottomane* (2 vols., 1902 and 1905); 2 Phillimore, §§ 273–77; * Piétri, *La fiction d'exterritorialité* (1895), 282–354; Piggott, *Extraterritoriality* (1907); 4 P.-Fodéré, Nos. 2122–2138; Quigley, "Exterritoriality in China," in 20 *A. J.* (1926), 46–68; * Rey, *La protection diplomatique et consulaire dans les Echelles du Levant* (1899); 1 Rivier, 543–58; Tarring, *British Consular Jurisdiction in the East* (1887); Taylor, §§ 331–33 ; * 1 Twiss, ch. 14, and in 25 *R. D. I.*, 213 ff.; Tyau, "Exterritoriality in China," in *Brit. Yr. Bk.* (1921–22), 133–49; Ullmann, §§ 63–65; 1 Wharton, *Digest*, § 125; * Willoughby, *Foreign Rights and Interests in China* (1920), ch. 2; Woolsey, §§ 99–100.

For further references, see 1 (3 Pt.) Fauchille, pp. 141–43 and pp. 168–69 for references on the Mixed Tribunals of Egypt—a subject of special interest.

CHAPTER XX

ORGANIZATION AND PROCEDURE OF INTERNATIONAL CONGRESSES AND CONFERENCES

292. Purpose and Character of International Congresses and Conferences.—The enormous increase in the number, variety, and importance of International Congresses and Conferences [1] since the middle of the nineteenth century has been pointed out in Chapter IV.[2] The organization and work of the Council and Assembly League of Nations will be discussed in Chapter XXIII. In this connection it will be merely necessary to point out a few of the rules governing the organization and procedure of these bodies.

They usually consist [3] of delegates or representatives of a number of Sovereign States clothed with diplomatic privileges and immunities, and bearing full powers and instructions, who meet for the purpose of discussing matters of common interest, or for that of negotiating agreements on certain subjects. The most important are those which meet to make peace and settle great political questions, like the Congress of Vienna in 1815 or that of Berlin in 1878, and the Paris Peace Conference of 1919; to discuss and decide matters of common interest, like the various Pan-American Conferences; or to negotiate great Lawmaking Treaties or World Agreements like the Hague Peace Conferences of 1899 and 1907.[4]

---

[1] These terms appear to be used interchangeably at the present time. Only official Congresses and Conferences are dealt with in this chapter.

[2] See, *supra*, No. 79.

[3] Heads of States now seldom attend these Conferences in person. The States represented are usually, though not necessarily, fully sovereign.

[4] The number and importance of Lawmaking and Peace Conferences increased during the 19th century. The first important Lawmaking Congress was that of Vienna in 1815, but its work as an International Legislature was entirely secondary. The same is true of the Congress of Paris in 1856. But after 1870 we had a series of lawmaking Conferences and Congresses, beginning with the Brussels Conference of 1874 (including the Hague Peace Conferences), which did not have their origin in the need of a political settlement after a great war or series of wars, but which were called in times of peace for the purpose of preventing or regulating war.

The Great Powers have, in times past, undertaken to speak for the whole of Europe or the world, more particularly in the solution of political questions; but the modern tendency appears to be toward a more general inclusion of the smaller or weaker Powers, even of Asia and Latin America.[5]

293. **Rules of Organization and Procedure.**—There are no fixed rules for the organization and procedure of these bodies. It would seem that any State or Government may call such a Congress or Conference and invite such Powers as it pleases,[6] though it may be said to be a reasonable rule that all Powers interested in the purpose of the Conference should be invited. The invited Powers may accept with or without conditions, or may decline the invitation altogether.[7] Each State which has been invited may send as many delegates or representatives as it chooses, but these together have but one vote, usually cast by the head of the delegation.

After the selection of the President [8] and other officers, and the exchange and verification of their powers, special commissions or committees [9] are chosen for the discussion

[5] See *supra*, pp. 241 and 247. This tendency is also illustrated by the organization of the League of Nations.

[6] The inviting Power also usually formulates the program, as did Russia for the two Hague Peace Conferences.

[7] "No State can be a party which has not been invited, or admitted at its own request." 1 Oppenheim, § 484, p. 647. But it is customary to invite all States interested in the particular objects of the Conference. No sovereign State should be excluded from a Congress or Conference dealing with questions which interest the international community as a whole.

[8] It has been customary to select as President the First Plenipotentiary or Minister of Foreign Affairs of the State in whose territory the Congress or Conference is held, but this custom was not followed at the two Hague Peace Conferences. The First Plenipotentiary of Russia was selected as a compliment to the Czar who had called these Conferences. At Paris (1919) the French Premier Clemenceau presided at the plenary sessions.

[9] The Hague Peace Conference of 1907 was divided into four general commissions which were divided (with one exception) into two subcommissions. These subcommissions were too large, for they ranged from 75 to 103 members (inasmuch as any plenipotentiary could attend one or all of them). In some cases, Committees of Examination were appointed to report to the subcommittees. In addition, there was a small Commission on Petitions and a larger Commission on Editing for the Conference as a whole. There is great need for a better organization of future Conferences.

For further information on the organization and procedure of the Second Hague Peace Conferences, see Hull, *Two Hague Conferences* (1908), 31–34; and Scott, 112–24.

and determination of particular subjects. These are again discussed and voted upon in full session by the Congress or Conference as a whole. To give full legal validity to a vote

At the Paris Peace Conference of 1919, twenty-seven different States (all States that had either declared war or broken off diplomatic relations with Germany) were represented, besides four British dominions and India (which were doubly represented—both on their own account and as members of the British Empire Delegation). There were seventy authorized delegates or plenipotentiaries. Each of the Great Powers had five of these, while the smaller powers had from one to three each. In most cases the Head of the State (Premier or President), acted as chief Plenipotentiary.

The neutral States were permitted to participate in discussions which affected their own special interests. There were also claimants like the Zionist Jews, the Armenians, the Esthonians, etc., who were allowed to lay their claims before the Council of the Conference. Russia was conspicuous by her absence.

The British Delegation alone numbered nearly two hundred, with as many clerks and typists. (Castlereagh is said to have had a staff of fourteen at Vienna). The American Commission to Negotiate Peace was nearly as numerous. One of the special features at Paris was the great number of technical delegates or so-called experts, many of them experts in name only. The author can testify that comparatively little use was made of the experts in International Law as such.

The Treaties of Paris were really imposed, not negotiated. The Great Powers were in actual control of the Conference—a control which was exercised at first through the Council of Ten (consisting of the chief plenipotentiaries of the four Great Powers and their Foreign Ministers), and later (after the middle of March, 1919) through the Council of Four (Clemenceau, Lloyd George, Wilson and Orlando). The Great Powers had control of the various Commissions or Committees on which the smaller powers were represented to a certain extent. These latter could also sit and vote in the six plenary sessions of the Conference, but these meetings were almost wholly formal and cut-and-dried performances.

At the outset only a few committees were set up. These included the important League of Nations Commission and the Commissions on Responsibility for the War, on Reparation, and on the International Régime for Ports, Waterways, and Railways. On these Commissions the Great Powers were allowed two-thirds of the representation. The smaller powers were asked to draw up all their claims in writing, and were also called upon to state them orally before the Council of Ten.

This led to the appointment of further Commissions not merely on territorial, but on economic and financial questions as well. Particular mention should be made of the Commission on International Labor Legislation. Subcommittees were organized for the consideration of details and special committees for the study or decision of particular questions like that of Teschen.

There appear to have been ultimately fifty-eight of these committee groups which held 1,646 meetings. The Council of Ten held 72 sessions and the Council of Four 145 sessions. There was also a Council of Five, consisting of Ministers of Foreign Affairs attending to minor matters, which held 39 sessions. After the disappearance of the Council of Four in the summer of 1919, the Council of Five continued to sit as a sort of superior Commission of the Conference.

The recommendations of these various Commissions were sometimes ac-

or resolution, practical unanimity [10] is necessary, though the majority may consider the motion binding upon its members. The results achieved at each session are collected into a *procés-verbal* (minutes) or Protocol. The body of articles or resolutions adopted are finally collected into a whole—the Final or General Act, which is signed by the plenipotentiaries of the several States, with or without reservations.

294. **Language.**—The official or customary language used at these Conferences was formerly French—the language of diplomacy *par excellence*; but any delegate has a right to the use of his own mother tongue, and English is now regarded as equally valid or official as French. [11]

BIBLIOGRAPHY

Congresses and Conferences.—* Baldwin, in 1 *A. J.* (1907), 565–78; Bluntschli, Arts. 12, 108–14; Bonfils or * 1 (3 Pt.) Fauchille, Nos. 796–815; * Buell, *Int. Relations* (1925), ch. 27; 3 Calvo, §§ 1674–81; Despagnet, Nos. 484–88; 2 Fiore, Nos. 1216–24, and *Int. Law Cod.* (1918), Arts. 1211–50; Geffcken, in 3 Holtzendorff,

cepted, particularly if they were unanimous. Often they were altered or modified and sometimes were altogether rejected or ignored by the Council of Four which usually passed upon them. In case of acceptance, they were incorporated into the treaties by the Drafting Committee. In any case the smaller powers were almost wholly excluded from participation in the decisions. It should also be mentioned that many of the major problems of the settlement, such as the French, Italian, and Japanese claims, were not referred to commissions, but discussed in secret council.

On the *Organization of the Paris Peace Conference*, see: * 1 Baker, *Wilson and World Settlement* (1922–23), chs. 10–11; House and Seymour, *What Really Happened at Paris* (1921), ch. 2; Tardieu, *The Truth About the Treaty* (1921), ch. 3; and * 1 Temperley, *Hist. of the Peace Conference* (1920–21), ch. 7 and pp. 497 ff.

[10] By practical or quasi-unanimity is meant the agreement of nearly all the States, including all the more important ones. The continued and persistent opposition of a Great Power is nearly always fatal to a proposal, though it may not oppose its insertion in the Final Act; the opposition of several smaller or relatively unimportant States is, on the other hand, frequently ignored. Their legal rights remain unimpaired, for they are not bound to sign the Final or General Act, or they may withdraw from the deliberations of the Conference.

[11] Thus the English and French texts of the Treaty of Versailles (1919) are both regarded as official—a condition which has its disadvantages, inasmuch as there are instances of ambiguity or discrepancy.

In case of discrepancy between the meaning of two different texts, "each party is only bound by the text in its own language. Moreover, a party cannot claim the benefit of the text in the language of the other party." 1 Oppenehim, § 554, p. 704.

679–84; 1 Halleck (3d ed.), 468–69; * Hankey, "Diplomacy by Conference," in *Round Table* (1921), No. 42; Heffter, No. 240 and Geffcken's note; Kamarowsky, *Le tribunal int.* (1887), 91–102; 1 Ch. de Martens, *Guide diplomatique* (1866), § 58; 1 F. de Martens, § 52; Myers, in 8 *A. J.* (1914), 81–108; Nippold, *Die Fortbildung des Verfahrens* (1907), § 20, pp. 481 ff.; * 1 Oppenheim, §§ 483–85; Phillipson, *Termination of War and Treaties of Peace* (1916), Pt. II, ch. 4, pp. 111 ff.; * Potter, *Int. Organization* (1922), Pt. VI, chs. 20–22; * P.-Fodéré, 2 *Cours*, pp. 339–454, and 6 *Traité*, Nos. 2593–99; 2 Rivier, 8–18; * 2 Satow, chs. 25–26, and *Int. Congresses and Conferences* (1920); * 1 Scott, chs. 1–3; Taylor, §§ 34–36; Ullmann, §§ 72–73; Woolf, *Int. Gov't.*, ch. 5; Zaleski, *Die Völker-Bedeutung der Kongresse* (1874).

For a list of 116 *Official Congresses*, or *Conferences*, see Baldwin, in 1 *A. J.* (1907), 808 ff. For an annual review of official Conferences, see Fried's *Annuaire de la vie internationale.*

CHAPTER XXI

INTERNATIONAL TREATIES

295. Definition and Scope of Treaties.—International Treaties or Conventions [1] are agreements or contracts between two or more States, usually negotiated for the purpose of creating, modifying or extinguishing mutual rights and reciprocal obligations.

[1] For various definitions of treaties, see Devlin, *Treaty Power* (1908), § 2; and Myers, in 11 *A. J.* (1917), 538.

The terms "treaty" and "convention" are practically synonymous, though the latter term is perhaps applied more frequently to treaties of lesser importance. There are various other kinds of agreements between States, such as *protocols, cartels* (see *infra*, note on p. 606), *capitulations* (see *infra*, pp. 606–07), the *compromis* (in arbitration, see *infra*, No. 310), *declarations, modi vivendi* (provisional working arrangements), exchange of *notes or letters*, and *sponsiones*, (agreements made between representatives who are not properly commissioned or who act in excess of authority).

Concordats are agreements between Catholic States and the Pope concerning the affairs of the Roman Church in Catholic countries.

The term *protocol* is used in a variety of senses. "Used to denote the form taken by an international compact, the word may be regarded as describing a somewhat informal record of an agreement between the High Contracting Parties.

"During a Congress or a Conference, . . . the minutes of the meetings of the plenipotentaries are styled either *protocol* or *procès-verbal*, indifferently. . . . Obviously protocol in this sense does not mean an agreement." 2 Satow, § 559.

Protocols are sometimes explanatory of the text of a treaty or are signed by way of fulfilment of a previous compact. Again the form may be used to record ratification or non-ratification of a treaty or to record compacts more or less independent of other international agreements, as, *e.g.* the Protocol of Agreement between the United States and Spain (1898) embodying the terms on which negotiations for peace were to be undertaken. For discussion and examples of these various senses in which the term "Protocol" is used, see 2 Satow, ch. 29.

For the three senses in which the term "Declaration" is applied, see *Ibid.*, ch. 28. In the treaty sense Satow (II, § 535) follows Oppenheim (I, § 487) in describing it as "the title of a body of stipulations of a treaty according to which the parties engage themselves to pursue in future a certain line of conduct. The Declaration of Paris, 1856, the Declaration of St. Petersburg, 1868, and the Declaration of London, 1909, are instances of this. Declarations of this kind, differ in no [essential] respect from treaties."

On *Exchange of Notes* and *modi vivendi*, see 2 Satow, §§ 584 ff. and 599 ff. See also 2 Hyde, §§ 508–09 and notes.

The practice of treaty-making is very ancient,[2] and treaties constitute an important source and evidence of International Law.[3] The noun " treaty " seems to have been formed on the basis of the verb " to treat," [4] and the negotiation of treaties has come to be one of the most important functions of modern diplomacy. Indeed, the scope of treaty-making has broadened to such an extent that it may be said that the treaty nexus of the present day includes within its extensive and complicated network, almost every conceivable variety of subject matter,[5] and the great law-making treaties of the past century, particularly since the Declaration of Paris (1856) inclusive, constitute in substance, though not in form, a species of international legislation.[6]

295a. **The Treaty-Making Power.**—" The treaty-making power of States is, as a rule, exercised by their heads, either personally, or through representatives appointed by these heads." [7]   In principle, all treaties are signed *ad referendum*, *i.e.* they are not complete or fully valid until they are ratified.[8]

[2] On the oldest treaty of which the text has come down to us, see *supra*, No. 21, p. 36.   For treaties in Ancient Greece and Rome, see 1 and 2 Phillipson, chs. 15–17; and Egger, *Études historiques sur les traités* (1866).

[3] Cf. *supra*, Nos. 14–15.

[4] Potter, *Int. Organization* (1922), 142.

[5] "It has been estimated that the number of treaties in force between the several States at the outbreak of the World War exceeded eight thousand." 1 Oppenheim, § 491.   According to Potter (*op. cit.*, p. 160), "it appears that modern States have concluded somewhat over ten thousand treaties with one another since the dawn of international relations."   Myers (11 *Am. Pol. Sci. Rev.*, 1917, note on p. 31) concludes that there are in existence some 25,000 treaties, of which about two fifths are in force.   Wright (13 *A. J.*, 1919, p. 242) says: "With a total of 595 treaties from its foundation to August, 1914, the United States has averaged more than four a year, and for the twentieth century fifteen a year or a treaty ratified every three weeks."

[6] Cf. *supra*, No. 14.   On *Law-Making Treaties*, see especially: 1 Oppenheim, §§ 18, 492, 555 ff.; and Potter, *op. cit.*, 168–71, 177–79, 190.

[7] 1 Oppenheim, § 495, p. 657.   He adds: "Yet, as a rule, heads of States do not act in person, but authorize representatives to act for them."   These receive full powers and instructions, together with other documents.   See *infra*, Nos. 263–65.

[8] The following steps or stages in treaty-making should be carefully distinguished: (1) the negotiation (negotiation in the narrow sense) by the plenipotentiaries; (2) the signing of the treaty by those fully empowered to sign it; (3) the ratification of the treaty by the Head or Chief of State—a solemn act by which he gives it his final approval (see 2 Satow, § 606, and

" The organization and powers of the agencies through
which States enter into treaties are defined by their fundamental laws, or constitutions.   This delegation of power by
the State, in first instance, is final, and an obligation
constitutionally contracted is binding on the entire State.
. . . It is a principle of International Law that a sovereign
State is restrained only by self-limitations or by such as
result from a recognition of like powers in others." [9]

In modern States, the treaty-making power lies mainly in
the hands of the Executive, though parliamentary and
democratic tendencies point toward an increasing participation of representative bodies in treaty-making.   In
England treaty-making seems still to be regarded as essentially a prerogative of the Crown, [10] but on the European

Foster, *Practice of Diplomacy*, 1906, 286); (4) the exchange or deposit of
ratifications (usually provided for in the treaty) by representatives of the
respective governments;   and (5) the publication or proclamation of the
treaty where this is required, as in the United States, to make it a part of the
law of the land.

This latter step is not necessary to making the treaty fully valid or binding
upon the respective Governments.   "It will be noted that the range of
binding effect of the treaty increases at each stage, from signature through
ratification and exchange to promulgation.   Signature binds the government,
ratification and exchange of ratifications binds the State, promulgation binds
the people of the State individually."   Potter, *op. cit.*, 150.

States may also become participants in treaty rights and obligations
through *adhesion* or *accession*.   The terms are used loosely or interchangeably,
and there seems to be no practical difference between them.   On *adhesion* or
accession, see Foster, *op. cit.*, 281–82; 1 Oppenheim, § 533; and 2 Satow,
§§ 613–18.

It should be noted in this connection that according to Art. 18 of the Covenant of the League of Nations, "every treaty or international engagement
entered into hereafter by any Member of the League shall forthwith be registered with the Secretariat and shall as soon as possible be published by it.
No such treaty or international engagement shall be binding until so registered."
For memorandum on the registration and publication of treaties approved by
the Council of the League of Nations, see Supp. to 14 *A. J.* (1920), 366–70.

[9] Crandall, §§ 1–2.   The author of this—perhaps the best—work on
treaties continues: "Accordingly, the full power to enter into treaties is an
attribute of every such State, as likewise a limitation on its exercise is a first
mark of dependence.   It does not follow that the power resides unrestricted
in the regularly constituted treaty-making organ."

[10] Of course this power is exercised through a responsible Cabinet and
Secretary of State, and is indirectly subject to the control of Parliament.
2 Anson, *Law and Custom of the Const.* (4th ed., 1907–09), Pt. II, 97.   Cf.
Ridges, *Const. Law of Eng.* (2d ed., 1915), 534.   For a severe criticism of the
British system and proposed reforms, see Ponsonby, *Democracy and Diplomacy*
(1915), *passim*.   However, "treaties involving a charge on the people, or a

Continent parliaments have attained to a considerable direct share in the exercise of this power.[11]

change in the law of the land can be carried into effect only by an Act of Parliament." Crandall, p. 280. This is particularly the case with treaties abridging the private rights of British subjects (*Ibid.*, § 123), and "those modifying the established laws of trade and navigation" (Phillipson, *Termination of War*, 1916, 157).

It has not been customary to submit treaties to Parliament before ratification, though it seems that the Treaties of Paris (1919–20) were so submitted in the form of a bill for carrying them into effect. On April 1, 1924, Mr. Ponsonby, the Parliamentary Under-Secretary of State for Foreign Affairs, declared in the House of Commons:

"It is the intention of His Majesty's Government to lay on the table of both Houses of Parliament every Treaty, when signed, for a period of 21 days, after which the Treaty will be ratified and published and circulated in the Treaty Series. In the case of important Treaties, the Government will, of course, take an opportunity of submitting them to the House for discussion within this period . . ." *Brit. Yr. Bk.* (1924), 191, citing 171 Hansard, 2007.

It should be noted that this announcement does not appear to contemplate any change in the British procedure respecting the negotiation or ratification of treaties, but it does aim to secure publicity of the terms of all treaties and to keep Parliament informed of agreements, excepting those of a minor or technical character, with foreign Powers.

It appears that the practice referred to above, inaugurated by the McDonald or Labor Government, was abandoned by the succeeding Conservative Government.

For an interesting address on the "Treaty-Making Power of the Crown," see Atherley-Jones, in 4 *Grotius Soc.* (1919), 95–109.

[11] The example and influence of France on the Continent of Europe has been most important in this respect. Art. 8 of the Constitutional Law of July 16, 1875 provides that the President of France shall negotiate and ratify treaties. The French law classifies under five general heads the treaties that shall receive legislative approval—treaties of peace, of commerce, treaties that involve the finances of the State, those relating to the persons of French citizens in foreign countries, and the cession, exchange or annexation of territory. The approval of the legislature in these cases is given in the form of a law authorizing the President to ratify the treaty and cause it to be executed.

The French Chamber of Deputies has a Commission on Foreign and Colonial Affairs which "exercises a more constant and effective supervision over the executive than is exercised by the parliamentary body in any other country." McBain and Rogers, *New Consts. of Europe* (1922), 150, citing Barthélemy, *Democratie et diplomatie* (1917), 130 ff. and 322 ff.

The Fundamental Statute of Italy (1848) declares (Art. 5): "To the King alone belongs the executive power. He is the supreme head of the State; . . . declares war; makes treaties of peace, alliances, commerce, and other treaties, communicating them to the Houses as soon as the interest and security of the State permit, . . . ; treaties involving financial obligations or alterations of the territory of the State shall not take effect until after they have received the approval of the Houses."

It should be added that "in practice, however, treaties of commerce, as well as treaties touching upon matters, the regulation of which belongs to Parliament, are, it appears, regularly submitted to that body prior to their ratifica-

295*b*. The Treaty-Making Power in the United States.—

The constitution of the United States declares that the
President " shall have power, by and with the advice and

tion. The legislative approval is given in the form of a law authorizing that
the treaty be carried into effect." Crandall, § 140, p. 321.

There exists in the Italian Parliament no Committee of Foreign Affairs and
the Italian Government enjoys a wide independence in dealing with international questions.

Art. 11 of the former German Constitution of 1871 provided that "it shall
be the duty of the Emperor . . . to declare war and conclude peace . . . to
enter into alliances and other treaties with foreign countries. . . .

"So far as treaties with foreign countries relate to matters which, according
to Art. 4, are to be regulated by imperial legislation, the consent of the Bundes-
rat shall be required for their conclusion, and the approval of the Reichstag
shall be necessary to render them valid." Art. 4 lists no less than sixteen
matters which shall be subject to imperial legislation.

The new German Constitution (1919) declares (Art. 45): "The National
President represents the Commonwealth (*Reich*) in matters of International
Law. He concludes in the name of the Commonwealth, alliances and other
treaties with foreign powers . . . War is declared and peace concluded by
national law. Alliances and treaties with foreign States relating to subjects
within the jurisdiction of the Commonwealth, require the consent of the
National Assembly."

The National Assembly (Reichstag) is to appoint a Standing Committee on
Foreign Affairs (Art. 35). "Its purpose is to submit the foreign policies of the
Cabinet to a constant surveillance by the popular representation." Brunet,
The New German Const., (1922), 150 f.

In general, "the new European constitutions follow the model of France.
Certain classes of treaties are enumerated that require legislative ratification;
inferentially other treaties may be concluded by the executive. War and
peace may be declared only by the legislature. In most of these constitutions
no provision is made for a Commission of Foreign Affairs similar to the French,
although presumably such commissions may be established under the standing
orders of the Parliaments without express constitutional authorization."
McBain and Rogers, *op. cit.*, 150–51. See, *e.g.* Art. 64 of the Constitution of
Czechoslovakia, Arts. 51, and 79 of that of Jugoslavia, and Art. 49 of the
Polish Constitution.

The latter, which is more or less typical, declares: "Commercial and customs treaties, as well as treaties which impose a permanent financial burden on
the State, or contain legal rules binding on the citizens, or change the frontiers
of the State, also alliances, require the consent of the *Sejm*."

" It is interesting to note that even though the new constitutions contain
liberal provisions for the initiative and referendum, they make no attempt to
bring foreign affairs within the scope of direct government." McBain and
Rogers, *op. cit.*, p. 151. The only modern State which admits the people to a
direct share in the treaty-making power is Switzerland. In January, 1921,
the Swiss electorate adopted by an overwhelming majority the following
amendment to Art. 89 of the Federal Constitution: "Treaties with foreign
powers which are concluded without limit of time or for a period of more than
fifteen years shall also be submitted to the people for acceptance or rejection
upon demand of 30,000 Swiss citizens qualified to vote, or of eight cantons."
It may be recalled that in May, 1920 the Swiss people voted in favor of entering

consent of the Senate, to make treaties, provided two-thirds of the Senators present concur "; and that " this Constitution, and the *laws* of the United States which shall be made *in pursuance thereof*, and all *treaties* made, or which shall be made *under the authority of the United States*, shall be the supreme law of the land; and the judges in every State shall be bound thereby, anything in the constitution or laws of any State to the contrary notwithstanding." [12]

Thus in the United States the Senate is an important part of the treaty-making power,[13] and treaties [14] are not mere

the League of Nations. Brooks, in 14 and 15 *Am. Pol. Sci. Rev.* (1920 and 1921), 477–80 and 423–25 respectively. Cf. McBain and Rogers, *op. cit.*, 152 f.

For additional data bearing on Parliamentary Participation in the Treaty-Making Power, see * Crandall, chs. 18–20; Dodd, *Modern Consts.* (1909); Harley, in 13 *A. J.* (1919), 393 ff.; * McBain and Rogers, *op. cit.*, Pt. I, ch. 7 and Pt. II, *passim;* Phillipson, *Termination of War* (1916), 156–59; Ponsonby, *Democracy and Diplomacy* (1915), App. II, 128 ff.; and "Ratification of Treaties," in 14 *Sen. Doc.*, No. 26, 66 Cong., 1st session (1919).

[12] Art. II, sec. 2, par. 2 and Art. VI, par. 2. The italics used above are intended to call attention to a difference in respect to phraseology between laws and treaties. It is also provided that "no State shall enter into any treaty, alliance, or confederation"; and that "no State shall, without the consent of Congress . . . enter into any agreement or compact with another State, or with a foreign power." Art. I, sec. 10, paragraphs 1 and 3.

[13] The Senate may be said to participate in the negotiation of treaties in the broader but not in the narrower sense. The earlier custom inaugurated by Washington of seeking the advice of that body prior to the negotiations of treaties has been followed only in rare or exceptional instances; though individual members, particularly those on the Committee of Foreign Relations, are not infrequently consulted on the conduct of important negotiations.

The President is the sole organ of communication with foreign powers, but the Senate has frequently exercised its right of participating in the negotiation of treaties in the broader sense by advising amendments or reservations or by making these a condition for its consent to ratification by the President.

The President may withhold from the Senate a treaty already negotiated, or may submit a treaty to that body with recommendations for amendments. He may even refuse to ratify treaties approved by the Senate or withdraw treaties from its consideration.

The custom seems to be growing, on the part of our Senate, of making *reservations* to treaties. These may be *distinghished from amendments* as not involving formal or textual changes as do the latter. They may be merely interpretative, in which case the meaning of the treaty remains unchanged. As in the case of amendments, reservations or interpretations may be attached to the treaty draft or proposal by a mere majority of the Senators present. For this and other reasons (one is that it tends to make the conduct of foreign affairs more complicated and difficult), this tendency toward an increasing participation of the Senate in the negotiation of treaties in the broader sense is to be deplored.

The President is not bound to accept either amendments or reservations at the hands of the Senate any more than the Senate is bound to accept them from

international contracts, but a part of the law of the land.[15]
They are paramount over State laws and State Consti-.

him. The other Signatories to a signed treaty must give their consent to
reservations as well as to amendments, but this consent may be tacit or express.
It is believed that reservations as well as amendments to a treaty on the part
of other Signatories must be submitted to the Senate.

On *Reservations*, see Anderson and Kellogg, in 13 *A. J.* (1919), 526–30,
767–73; 2 Hyde, § 519; * Mathews, *Conduct of Am. Foreign Relations* (1922),
154–61; Miller, *Reservations to Treaties* (1919); Washburn, in 5 *Cornell Law
Quar.* (1920), 257 ff.; and * Wright, in 4 *Minn. Law Rev.* (1919), 17–39.

For a "Compilation of Treaty Reservations," see 15 *Sen. Doc.* (1919),
66th Cong., 1st sess. No. 135.

On the various reservations proposed to the Versailles Treaty, see Finch, in
14 *A. J.* (1920), 175 ff.

[14] The word "treaty" is here used in its constitutional rather than in its
international law sense, *i.e.* it means an international contract for the ratification of which the concurrence of two-thirds of the Senators present is necessary.
There are many international agreements—so-called *executive agreements*—
which are not submitted to that body.

Executive agreements are of two main kinds:

(a) Simple executive agreements, such as arbitrations or conventions for
the adjustment of private claims against foreign governments, agreements
involving the military power of the President, agreements serving as the basis
of future negotiations or of foreign policy like the Lansing-Ishii Exchange of
Notes in 1917 with Japan, *modi vivendi* or provisional and working arrangements of various sorts, and agreements in execution of treaty stipulations.
Perhaps the most important simple executive agreements have been the armistice or Peace Protocol with Spain of 1898 and the Final Protocol signed with
China in 1901 at the close of the Boxer uprising. The Senate has insisted on
substituting the word "treaty" for special agreement (*compromis*) in certain
arbitration treaties, but "there have been numerous instances in which the
Senate has approved treaties providing for the submission of specific matters
to arbitration, leaving it to the President to determine exactly the form and
scope of the matter to be arbitrated and to appoint the arbitrators." 1
Willoughby, *Constitutional Law of the U. S.* (1910), 475.

(b) Agreements under Acts of Congress. These have related to trade and
navigation, including reciprocity arrangements, international copyright,
trade-marks, international postal and money order conventions, agreements
with Indian tribes, and the acquisition of territory.

On *Executive Agreements*, see: Barnett, in 15 *Yale Law J.* (1905), 18 ff.
and 63 ff. (reprinted with additions, in pamphlet form); Corwin, *The President's
Control of Foreign Relations* (1917), 116–25; * Crandall, chs. 8–9; Foster,
The Practice of Diplomacy (1906), ch. 16, and in 11 *Yale Law J.* (1901), 69 ff.;
2 Hyde, §§ 505–09 and notes; * Mathews, *op. cit.*, ch. 10; 5 Moore, *Digest*,
§§ 752–56, and in 20 *Pol. Sci. Quar.* (1906), 385–420; 1 Willoughby, *op. cit.*,
ch. 33; and Wright, *Control of Am. Foreign Relations* (1922), see index.

[15] The assertion that treaties are "the supreme law of the land" must be
taken with considerable allowance. In the first place, it only applies to treaties
in the constitutional sense as explained above. In the second place, it is only
true of treaties or stipulations in treaties that have been proclaimed and may
be said to be self-executing, *i.e.*, such as "require no legislation to make them
operative." J. Field, in *Whitney* v. *Robertson* (1888), 124 U. S., 190, 194, and

tutions which are null and void if in conflict with them.[16]
An Act of Congress, however, "supersedes a prior inconsistent treaty as a law binding the courts. Conversely, it
has frequently been declared that so far as a treaty operates
of its own force as municipal law, it supersedes inconsistent
Acts of Congress." [17]

There is no certain agreement as to the extent of the
treaty-making power in the United States. The classic
statement of the prevailing doctrine is that of Justice Field
in a dictum contained in *Geofroy* v. *Riggs*; [18] " The treaty-

Scott, *Cases*, 458, 461. Cf. Marshall, in *Foster* v. *Neilson* (1829), 2 Pet. 253
and Scott, *Cases*, 429, 432.

The House of Representatives has from time to time asserted a right to
refuse to enact legislation, more particularly to pass the appropriations,
necessary to carry a treaty into effect. It is of course true that there is no
legal means of compelling Congress to pass legislation essential for the enforcement of treaty agreements, and that payments of money can be made only on
the authority of an Act of Congress; but the assent of the House is not necessary to the validity of a treaty, though it may be essential to its execution.
However, "while the House still holds to the existence of its discretionary
power in the enforcement of treaties, as a matter of fact it has seldom, if ever,
refused to take the necessary action to provide the means of enforcement."
Mathews, *op. cit.*, 203.

On this subject, see Burr, *Treaty-Making Power in the U. S.* (1912), ch. 5,
pp. 376 ff.; 1 and 2 Butler, *Treaty-Making Power of the U. S.* (1908), chs. 10
and 12, §§ 363–75; * Crandall, chs. 12–13; Corwin, *National Supremacy*
(1913), ch. 10, and *The President's Control of Foreign Relations* (1917), 92–109;
* Mathews, *op. cit.*, ch. 11, pp. 201–12; 5 Moore, *Digest*, §§ 758–61; Tucker,
Limitations on the Treaty-Making Power (1915), ch. 8; and 1 Willoughby, *op.
cit.*, § 206.

[16] This principle was first judicially asserted by our Supreme Court in very
sweeping fashion in the case of *Ware* v. *Hylton* (1796), 3 Dall. 199, 236, and has
been reasserted in many subsequent cases. For reviews of the leading cases,
see especially: 2 Butler, *Treaty-Making Power* (1902), ch. 91, particularly
§ 359 for conclusion); Corwin, *National Supremacy* (1913), *passim*, particularly
chs. 4, 8, 11; Crandall, ch. 16; Devlin, *Treaty Power*, ch. 9; and 1 Willoughby,
Const. Law of the U. S., ch. 35, §§ 212–15.

[17] Crandall, § 72, p. 161. See *Ibid.*, note 12 for citation of leading cases.
For reviews of cases, see also 2 Butler, *op. cit.*, ch. 12; Devlin, *op. cit.*, ch. 8;
and 1 Willoughby, *op. cit.*, §§ 207–09.

"There would seem to be certainly one exception to the rule that the later
treaty abrogates the prior inconsistent statute, and this is in reference to acts
for raising revenue." 1 Willoughby, *op. cit.*, § 209, p. 488. Cf. Crandall, § 89.

"When the two relate to the same subject, the courts will always endeavor
to construe them so as to give effect to both, if that can be done without violating the language of either; but if the two are inconsistent, the one last in date
will control the other, provided always the stipulation of the treaty on the
subject is self-executing." J. Field in *Whitney* v. *Robertson* (1888), 124 U. S.,
190, 194, and Scott, 458, 461.

[18] (1890), 133 U. S. 258, 267. Justice Field continues: "The treaty-power,

making power in the United States extends to all proper subjects of negotiation between our Government and the Governments of other nations." But it is generally admitted that "a treaty cannot change the Constitution or be held valid if it be in violation of that instrument." [19]

as expressed in the Constitution, is in terms unlimited except by those restraints which are found in that instrument against the action of the government or of its departments, and those arising from the nature of the Government itself and of that of the States. It would not be contended that it extends so far as to authorize what the Constitution forbids, or a change in the character of the Government or in that of one of the States, or a *cession of any portion of the territory of the latter without its consent*. But with these exceptions, it is not perceived that there is any limit to the questions which can be adjusted touching any matter which is properly the subject of negotiations with a foreign country."

It should be pointed out that the limitation expressed in the phrase set in italics is questionable.

Perhaps the most noteworthy expression of the prevailing nationalistic view is that by Ex-Secretary Root: "In international affairs there are no States; there is but one nation, acting in direct relation to and representation of every citizen in every State . . . So far as the real power goes, there can be no question of State rights, because the Constitution itself, in the most explicit terms, has precluded the existence of any such question." Root, in 1 *A. J.* (1907), 273, 278–79.

[19] J. Swayne, in *The Cherokee Tobacco Case*, 11 Wall. (1870), 616, 620. There are, says Sec'y Root in the article cited above, no express limitations, but "there are certain implied limitations arising from the nature of our government, and from other provisions of the Constitution." But he does not attempt to state what these are beyond quoting the dicta from J. Field in *Geofroy v. Riggs* given in note 18.

On this difficult and complicated subject of the limitations on the treaty-power in the United States, consult especially the works of Butler, Corwin and Crandall, cited above. See particularly Willoughby's view on the reserved rights of the States in their relation to the treaty-power, as expressed in Vol. I, § 215, pp. 502–03 of his *Const. Law of the U. S.*

On the *Treaty-Making Power in the U. S.*, see: Anderson, in 1 *A. J.* (1907), 636–70, and in 14 *A. J.* (1920), 400–02; Bacon, in 180 *No. Am. Rev.*, 502 ff.; Burr, *Treaty-Making Power in the U. S.* (1912), *passim*, and in 51 *Procs. of the Am. Philos. Soc.*, No. 206; * 1 and 2 Butler, *Treaty-Making Power in the U. S.* (1902), *passim*; Clancey, in 7 *Mich. Law. Rev.* (1908–09), 19 ff.; * Corwin, *National Supremacy* (1913), and *The President's Control of Foreign Policy* (1917), *passim*; * Crandall, *passim*; Devlin, *Treaty Power* (1908), *passim*; Foster, in 11 *Yale Law J.* (1901), 69 ff., and *Practice in Diplomacy* (1911), chs. 12–16; Hayden, *The Senate and Treaties, 1789–1817* (1920); Hall and Hyde, in 7 *Procs. Acad. Pol. Sci.* (1917), No. 3, Pt. II, 548 ff.; Kuhn, in 7 *Col. Law Rev.* (1907), 172 ff.; Lewis, in 34 *Annals* (1909), 313–43; Lodge, in 31 *Scribners* (1902), 33–43; * Mathews, *The Conduct of Am. Foreign Relations* (1922), chs. 8–13; Mikell, in 57 *Univ. of Pa. Law Rev.* (1908–09), 435 ff. and 528 ff.; Miller, in 41 *Am. Law Rev.* (1907), 527 ff.; 5 Moore, *Digest*, §§ 734–38; Pomeroy, *Const. Law of the U. S.* (1888), §§ 669–81; * Root, in 1 *A. J.* (1907), 273–86; Sutherland, *Const. Power and World Affairs* (1919), chs. 6–7; Tansill, in 18

However, no case has even arisen in which a treaty has been held unconstitutional by our Supreme Court.

296. Classification of Treaties.—Treaties are of many kinds and variety of content. Since all attempts at a scientific classification of treaties have failed,[20] it is perhaps

A. J. (1924), 459–82; Tucker, *Limitations on the Treaty-Making Power* (1915, for criticism of prevailing doctrine); Wheeler, in 17 *Yale Law J.* (1907–08), 151 ff.; 1 Willoughby, *Const. Law of the U. S.* (1910), chs. 32–35; Wright, *The Control of Am. Foreign Relations* (1922), *passim*, particularly ch. 8, in 13 *A. J.* (1919), 247–64, and in 12 *A. J.* (1918), 64–95.

See also Gregory, Ion, Lewis, Kuhn, and Willoughby in *Procs. Am. Soc. I. L.* (1907), 150 ff.; and Meyer, *List of References on the Treaty-Making Power* (Washington, 1920).

[20] 1 Oppenheim, § 492, and note on p. 654 (3d ed.). The old division of treaties into real and *personal* has no longer any practical value. More useful is F. de Marten's (I, § 112) classification of treaties into *political* and *social*, but it is suggestive rather than exhaustive. Some authorities substitute the term "economic" for "social." Pradier Fodéré (II, Nos. 920 ff.) divides treaties, considered as to their object, into *general* and *special*. This division seems somewhat arbitrary, but it affords a convenient means of summary. Under General Treaties, he includes treaties of peace, of political union, alliance guarantee and protection, neutrality, cession, commerce, and customs unions. Under the head of Special Treaties, he deals with concordats, boundary treaties, those establishing servitudes, treaties of navigation, consular conventions and capitulations, conventions relating to literary and artistic property, industrial property, extradition treaties, postal, and telegraphic conventions, and conventions relating to railroads.

Perhaps the most scientific classification of treaties is that which divides them into executed, transitory, or dispositive treaties on the one hand; and executory, continuing, or permanent treaties on the other. "An executory contract is one in which a party binds himself to do, or not to do, a particular thing. . . . A contract executed is one in which the object of the contract is performed; and this, says Blackstone, differs in nothing from a grant." Chief Justice Marshall, in *Fletcher* v. *Peck*, (1810), 6 Cranch 87, 136. Cited by Taylor, § 343, p. 367.

Westlake (I, 60 f.) defines what he prefers to call dispositive treaties as those "which dispose of or about things by transferring or creating rights in or over them, as a deed conveying a field or granting a right of way over it, disposes of or about the field by transferring the property in it to the purchaser, or creating the right of way over it in the grantee." Cf. *Ibid.*, 294–95.

Examples of executed or transitory treaties are boundary treaties, treaties of cession, or those clauses in a treaty which create servitudes. Examples of executory treaties are treaties of alliance, commerce, extradition, guarantee, etc.

This classification has the additional advantage, at least in the case of transitory treaties, of furnishing us with a category of obligations which usually persist in spite of changes brought about by war or the Succession of States. See *supra*, No. 129; and *infra*, No. 344. For a recent article on "La classification des traités int.", see Rapisardi-Mirabelli in 50 (3d ser. 4) *R. D. I.* (1923), 653–67. This seems to be the only monographic contribution to the subject.

From the standpoint of International Law and Organization, the most

most convenient to refer to them in terms of their nature, purpose, or subject matter; as, for example, treaties of alliance, protection, guarantee, peace, neutrality, commerce, extradition, arbitration, copyright, monetary treaties, consular conventions, etc. We may also speak of treaties as simple or conditional, unilateral or bilateral (as to whether the contracting parties are reciprocally bound or not), preliminary or definitive, accessory, additional, subsidiary, or principal (as to whether they depend on a previous treaty or not) etc.

Especially important [21] is the distinction between ordinary treaties which are mere bargains or contracts and the great Lawmaking or International Law Treaties, such as those negotiated by the Hague Peace Conferences, which will probably mark an epoch in the development of internationalism.

297. Conditions for the Validity of Treaties.—The following are the essential conditions for the validity of a treaty:

(1) The parties to it must be capable of contracting. Fully sovereign States have complete contracting power, and part- or semi-sovereign States such measure of contracting power as has been retained by or conferred upon them.[22] All treaties in excess of this power are null and void.

(2) The persons or agents who negotiate the treaty must have full powers from their government.[23] If they exceed these powers, their government is not bound. But where certain material advantages have been derived from such action, it is the duty of the State receiving such benefits either to make compensation or to restore things to their

useful classification would probably be that between treaties dealing with legal and governmental matters, *i.e.* Lawmaking Treaties and those dealing with concrete or particular subjects, such as cession of territory, boundary treaties, etc. See Potter, *Int. Organization* (1922), 168.

[21] See *supra*, p. 25.

[22] As in the case of a member State of a Confederacy, or a State under Suzerainty. The capacity of a State to contract may be also limited in certain respects by its constitution. See *supra*, Nos. 295 a and b.

[23] "There are also persons who in virtue of being intrusted with the exercise of certain special functions have a limited power of binding it by contracts relative to matters within the sphere of their authority. Thus officers in command of naval or military forces may conclude agreements for certain purposes in time of war." Hall, § 108, p. 380.

former condition so far as practicable, " unless the contract made was evidently in excess of the usual powers of a person in the position of the negotiator, in which case the sovereign State, having prejudiced itself by its own rashness, may be left to bear the consequences of its own indiscretion." [24]

(3) Freedom of consent. But in interpreting this phrase we must remember that " in International Law force and intimidation are permitted means of obtaining redress for wrongs, and it is impossible to look upon permitted means as vitiating the agreement, made in consequence of their use, by which redress is provided for." Consequently, International Law " regards all compacts as valid, notwithstanding the use of force and intimidation, which do not destroy the independence of the State which has been obliged to enter into them." [25]

" Violation or intimidation used against the person of a sovereign, of a commander, or of any negotiator invested with power to bind his State, stand upon a different footing." " The only kind of duress which justifies a breach of treaty is the coercion of a sovereign or plenipotentiary to such an extent as to induce him to enter into arrangements which he never would have made but for fear on account of his personal safety. Such was the renunciation of the Spanish crown extorted by Napoleon at Bayonne, in 1807, from Charles IV and his son Ferdinand. The people of Spain broke no faith when they refused to be bound by it and rose in insurrection against Joseph Bonaparte, who had been placed upon the throne." [26] Gross error or fraud, as the use of a forged map, also vitiates a treaty. [27]

(4) The treaty must not be in conflict with the undoubted rules and principles of International Law. Thus a treaty would not be binding which had as its object the subjugation or partition of a country, an assertion of a proprietary right

[24] *Ibid*, 381.
[25] *Ibid*.
[26] *Ibid*., 382 and Lawrence § 134, p. 303.
[27] "But the rule that a contract is vitiated by fraud applied, subject to the observation that some latitude must be allowed in negotiating treaties of peace to the right of misleading an adversary which is incident to war." 1 Westlake, 290.

over a portion of the open sea, or the establishment of the slave trade.

298. Form and Ratification of Treaties.—Although no prescribed form [28] is necessary, treaties are usually written and signed with some degree of formality.[29] After being signed by the plenipotentiaries or negotiators, they are usually ratified or confirmed by the head of the treaty-making power itself [30] and ratifications are exchanged by authorized agents.

Mutual consent may be inferred; and the treaty is, therefore, actually concluded from the moment it is signed by negotiators acting with full powers. Partial or conditional ratification is not permissible, and the date of signature marks the beginning of the binding force of the treaty, though its operation is practically suspended until it has been ratified.[31] The effects of ratification are retroactive so far as public rights or the contracting governments are concerned, but " a different rule prevails when the treaty operates on individual rights. The principle of relation does not apply to rights of this character, which were vested before the treaty was ratified; it is not considered as conclusive until there is an exchange of ratification." [32]

[28] Agreements may even be made by the display of symbols, as when a white flag is raised in token of surrender. Less formal agreements are sometimes made by exchange of notes.

[29] At present treaties are usually signed in the alphabetical order of the names of the States in the French language. Sometimes the order is determined by lot. "In the draft of the treaty for his own state, the representative of that State may, following the principle of the alternat, sign first." Wilson, p. 197.

[30] In absolute monarchies, this is generally the monarch; in republics, the President or some representative body. In the United States it is the President. Ratification is customary even where the treaty does not prescribe ratification. If no time is specified, a reasonable period is presumed. Ratification is usually evidenced by an exchange of documents, but it may be tacitly shown by execution.

[31] Some publicists (*e.g.* Jellinek, *Die rectliche Natur der Staatenverträge*, 1880, 55; Nippold, *Der völkerrechtliche Vertrag*, 1894, 123; and Ullmann, § 78) maintain that mutual consent and the conclusion of the treaty are indicated by ratification; but this view is not in agreement with the facts of international practice. Wegemann appears to be the only modern writer on this subject who holds that "ratification is somewhat superfluous (*etwas ueberflüssiges*) and inconsequential (*nicht sagendes*). *Ratification von Staatsvertraegen*, p. 4, note 9. Cited from Harley, "The Obligation to Ratify Treaties," in 13 *A. J.* (1919), 390.

[32] 5 Moore, *Digest*, § 762, p. 245, citing Davis, *Notes*, etc. The leading

The question as to whether a State may legally refuse to ratify a treaty concluded by its properly accredited agents acting within their powers was long controverted,[33] but it may be now regarded as definitely resolved in the affirmative. In practice, ratification is given or withheld at discretion.[34] There are still publicists who maintain that a State is morally bound to ratify, but none (so far as known to the writer) [35] claim that a State is thus legally bound. Ordinarily, ratification will follow signature as a matter of course, and a State refusing to ratify on insufficient grounds or from mere caprice would soon lose credit with the rest of the international community.

299. **Rules for the Interpretation of Treaties.**—The rules for the interpretation of treaties are derived from general jurisprudence. Strictly speaking, they form no part of International Law proper, and the contracting States are free to apply any rules they may agree upon; but it may nevertheless be found useful to indicate a few of the rules of interpretation which have found most general acceptance.

" The important point is to get at the real intention [36] of

decision on this point is *Haver* v. *Yaker* (1869), 9 Wall. 32, and Scott, *Cases*, 443. See also 2 Butler, *Treaty-making Power of the U. S.* (1902), § 383; and * Crandall, ch. 21. Treaties providing for the cession of territory have been held to be binding from the date of signature, but they do not go into effect until actual transfer or delivery. Crandall, § 157. "As in the case of other treaties, a treaty of peace is not, however, definitely binding until the exchange of ratification; and a state of war in the technical sense continues until the date of the exchange." *Ibid.*, § 159. See Phillipson, *Termination of War* (1916), 188 ff. for sound arguments in favor of the view that the date of signature should mark the end of the war and that the exchange of ratifications should have a retroactive effect so far as hostilities are concerned.

[33] The older authorities like Grotius, Bynkershoek, Vattel, G. F. de Martens, etc. generally held that ratification was obligatory, at least by natural law. It should be remembered that they wrote before the modern period of parliamentary participation in the treaty-making power. This view has been generally abandoned.

[34] "The ratification may be refused by any party, and although this would be offensive if done without grave reason, it is impossible to limit the right of doing it." 1 Westlake, 291.

Of course there has never been any question of the right to refuse ratification in the case of States in which, like the United States, a representative body has an important share in the treaty-making power. Foreign governments are presumed to have knowledge of such facts.

[35] With the exception of Wegemann, cited above in note 33.

[36] In his very suggestive treatment on the "Interpretation of Jural Acts" (see 5 *Evidence*, 1923, §§ 2248 ff.), Wigmore calls attention to the vital dis-

the parties, and that enquiry is not to be shackled by any rule of interpretation which may exist in a particular national jurisprudence, but is not generally accepted in the civilized world." [37]

With this word of caution from a leading authority, we may venture to lay down the following rules:

(1) The language of a treaty should be interpreted according to its plain or reasonable sense. Ordinary words should be taken in their ordinary or everyday sense, and technical words in their technical sense. The interpretation should be neither too literal nor too technical, and should follow the spirit rather than the letter of the document. [38]

(2) Words having more than one meaning should be interpreted in the general rather than the technical sense, unless clearly used in the technical sense. "When terms used in a treaty have a different legal sense within the two contracting States, they are to be understood in the sense

tinction between *intention* and *meaning*. He observes: "The person's actual will or intent to utter a given word can seldom be used for juristic purposes."

[37] 1 Westlake, 293. Westlake does not consider specific rules of "much practical use," but he favors a "large and liberal spirit of interpretation." On the *Interpretation of Treaties*, see especially: Adler, in 26 *Law Mag. Rev.* (5th ser.), 62 ff. and 164 ff.; Appert, in 26 *J. I. P* (Clunet, 1899), 433 ff.; Bonfils, Nos. 835–37; * Crandall, chs. 22–23; 1 Cobbett, 341–47; Devlin, *Treaty Power* (1908), §§ 94, 115–32; 1 (3 Pt.) Fauchille, Nos. 840–44; 2 Fiore, Nos. 1032–46, and *Int. Law Cod.* (1918), Arts. 797–821; Foster, *Practice of Diplomacy* (1911), ch. 14; * Hall, §§ 111–12; * 2 Hyde, §§ 530–37, and in 3 *A. J.* (1910), 46 ff.; * Mathews, *op. cit.*, ch. 12; 5 Moore, *Digest*, §§ 763–64; * 1 Oppenheim, §§ 553–54; 2 Phillimore, Pt. V., ch. 8, §§ 64–95; Phillipson, *Termination of War* (1916), 180–84; 2 P.-Fodéré, Nos. 1171–88; Pic, in 17 *R. G. I. P.* (1910), 5–35; Ralston, *Int. Arbitral Law* (1926), ch. 2; Taylor, §§ 377–93; Vattel, Bk. II, ch. 17, §§ 262–322; 2 Wharton, *Digest*, § 133; Wilson, ch. 7, § 75; Woolsey, § 113.

[38] Thus, Art. 9 of the Treaty of Utrecht (1713) stipulated that the port and fortifications of Dunkirk be destroyed and never rebuilt. France complied with this stipulation, but proceeded to violate its spirit by building a larger port at Mardyck, within a league of Dunkirk. France ultimately recognized the reasonableness of the British protest and discontinued the building of the new port.

The phrase *jusqu'à la mer* (to the sea) in articles annexed to the Treaty of Vienna of 1815 was interpreted to include the several continuations of the Rhine which by a subsequent convention (1831) were declared open to the sea. It has also been held by our Supreme Court (in *Geofroy* v. *Riggs*, 1890, 133 U. S., 258, 271, and Scott, *Cases*, 446) that the District of Columbia, as a political community, was included in the expression "States of the Union," as used in Art. 8 of the consular convention of 1853 with France. For these and other examples, see Crandall, § 165.

which is proper to them within the State to which the provision containing them applies; if the provision applies to both States the terms of double meaning are to understand in the sense proper within them respectively." [39]

(3) " If the meaning of a stipulation is ambiguous, the reasonable meaning is to be preferred to the less reasonable, the adequate meaning to the meaning not adequate for the purpose of the treaty, the consistent meaning to the meaning inconsistent with general recognized principles of International Law and with previous treaty obligations toward third States." Furthermore, in case of ambiguity, that " meaning is to be preferred which is less onerous for the obliged party, or which interferes less with the parties' territorial and personal supremacy, or which contains less general restrictions upon the parties." [40]

(4) " There is no rule of construction better settled either in relation to covenants between individuals or treaties between nations than that the whole instrument containing the stipulations is to be taken together, and that all articles *in pari materia* should be considered as parts of the same stipulations." [41]

(5) A treaty should, if possible, be so construed as to give effect to the fundamental rights of a State, such as independence, etc., and in conformity with the accepted rules, customs and principles of International Law. In case of doubt the language of the treaty should be construed as favorable to the party assuming the obligation.

(6) In case of conflict between different treaties with the same State, or different provisions of the same treaty, (*a*)

---

[39] Hall, § 111, p. 392. Hall gives the following illustration: "Thus by the treaty of 1866 it was stipulated between Austria and Italy, that the inhabitants of the provinces ceded by the former power should enjoy the right of withdrawing with their property into Austrian territory during a year from the date of the exchange of ratifications. In Austria the word inhabitant signifies such persons only as are domiciled according to Austrian law; in Italy it is applied to every one living in a commune and registered as resident. . . . As the provision referred to territory which was Austrian at the moment of the signature of the treaty, the term inhabitant was construed in conformity with Austrian law."

[40] 1 Oppenheim, § 554, p. 703.

[41] Secretary Livingstone to Baron Lederer, cited in 5 Moore, *Digest*, p. 249. It should be noted that this is a rule of construction rather than of interpretation proper.

the later treaty is binding, and (b) that which is specifically stated or permitted prevails over the more general provision. (c) An imperative or specific prohibition usually takes precedence of a general permission.

(7) " It is a general principle of construction with respect to treaties that they shall be liberally construed, so as to carry out the apparent intention of the parties to secure equality and reciprocity between them." [42]

(8) " Prior negotiations are merged in the written instrument, and cannot be resorted to for the purpose of contradicting or explaining its plain provisions." [43]

(9) A practical and common construction of the terms of a treaty by the parties through proper representatives shortly after its conclusion is quite conclusive as to their meaning." [44]

300. **Most-favored-nation Clause.**—Especially important is the interpretation of the most-favored-nation clause in commercial treaties. This is a clause which provides that the citizens or subjects of the contracting States may enjoy

[42] J. Field, in *Geofroy* v. *Riggs* (1890), 133 U. S., 258; and Scott, *Cases*, 446. Cf. the same Justice, *In re Ross*. (1890), 140 U. S., 453, 475. "Treaties are to be construed in a broad and liberal spirit, and when two constructions are possible, one restrictive of rights that may be claimed under it and the other favorable to them, the latter is to be preferred." *Asakura* v. *Seattle*, U. S. Sup. Ct. Adv. Op. (1923–24), 577, 578. (Cited from 19 *A. J.*, 1925, 44).

[43] Crandall, § 166, p. 377. "However," continues this excellent authority, "in case of ambiguity or doubt in the application of the terms of a treaty, reference is frequently made to the contemporaneous declarations of the negotiators who framed the treaty, and to prior negotiations, not to make a treaty where the parties have failed to do so, nor to change the terms of the treaty actually made, but to determine the general object of the negotiations, the particular sense in which the terms, otherwise uncertain of application, were used at the time, or the conditions as they existed at the time of the conclusion of the treaty."

[44] Crandall, p. 383. See *Ibid.*, § 167 for examples. For cases of discrepancies between texts, see § 169.

In the United States, treaties are subject to interpretation by the judicial as well as by the executive and (to some extent even) by the legislative departments of the government. But it should be particularly noted that "on public rights, the courts follow the political departments of the government, both as to the interpretation of a treaty and as to whether an alleged treaty is actually in force. . . . When, on the other hand, treaties confer private rights on citizens or subjects of the contracting powers—rights such as are enforceable in a court of justice—the courts accept such treaties as rules of decision and place upon them their own interpretation, in so far as the treaties are self-executing." Mathews, *op. cit.*, 219. On "Political Questions," see especially Crandall, § 163; and Field, in 8 *Minn. Law Rev.* (1924), 485 ff.

the privileges accorded by either party to the most-favored-nation.[45] Until recently the United States has usually denied that this clause, whether in its general gratuitous or simple reciprocal form, applies to reciprocity treaties or

[45] "It may be a gratuitous conferring of privileges, it may be conditional, or it may depend upon like concessions on the part of the other nation." Wilson, 204.

Hornbeck (*The Most-Favored-Nation Clause in Commercial Treaties*, 1910, ch. 2, pp. 18–20) distinguishes five forms: (1) The form of simple transfer which grants a privilege without reciprocity or condition. (2) The specialized reciprocal form which applies only to favors mentioned in the treaty. (3) The simple reciprocal form. (4) The imperative and unconditioned form. (5) The qualified, or conditional reciprocal form. Cf. the classification by Herod, *Favored Nation Treatment* (1901), 5–6.

"The majority of the commercial treaties of the United States do not contain the most-favored-nation clause in its general form, but in what is called its conditional, qualified, or reciprocal form. In this form it stipulates that all favors granted to third States shall accrue to the other party unconditionally, in case the favors have been allowed unconditionally to the grantee, but only under the same compensation, in case they have been granted conditionally. The United States, however, has upheld the opinion that, even if the commercial treaty contains the clause in its general, and not in its qualified form, it must always be interpreted as though it were worded in its qualified form, and the Supreme Court of the United States has confirmed this interpretation." I Oppenheim, § 580, p. 750. See *Bartram* v. *Robertson* (1887), 122 U. S. 116, and *Whitney* v. *Robertson* (1888), 124 U. S. 190, and Scott, *Cases*, 458.

Oppenheim regards the American interpretation as unjustifiable, as do indeed, most British and European writers on the subject. Exceptions are F. de Martens (II, 322), and Westlake (I, 294).

On the *Most-favored-nation Clause*, see especially: Barclay, in 17 *Yale Law J.*, (1907–08), 26 ff., and *Problems of Int. Practice and Diplomacy* (1907), 137–42; Calwer, *Die Meistbegünstigung in den Vereinigten Staaten* (1902); Cavaretta, *La Clarisola della nazione più favorita* (1906); * Crandall, ch. 24, and in 7 *A. J.* (1913), 708–23; * Culbertson, *Int. Economic Policies* (1925), ch. 3; Farra, *Les effets de la clause de la nation la plus favorisée* (1912); * Geir, *Die Meistbegünstigungs-Klausel* (1906); Harris and Crandall, in *Procs. Am. Soc. I. L.*, (1911), 288 ff.; Hepp, *Theorie générale de la clause de la nation la plus favorisée* (1914); Herod, *Favored Nation Treatment* (1901); * Hornbeck, *The Most-favored-nation Clause* (1910), or in 3 *A. J.* (1909), 395 ff., 619 ff., 797 ff.; 2 Hyde, §§ 536–37, and in 3 *A. J.* (1909), 57 ff.; Kasson, *Reciprocity* (1901); Lederle and Springer, in 27 *Z. I.* (1918), 154–76; * Ludwig, *Consular Treaty Rights and Most-favored-nation Clause* (1913), 119 ff.; * 5 Moore, *Digest*, §§ 765–69; I Oppenheim, § 580, and in 24 *Law Quar. Rev.* (1908), 328–34; Osborne, in 181 *No. Am. Rev.* (1905), 731 ff.; 4 P.-Fodéré, Nos. 2020 ff.; * Visser, in 4 (2d ser.) *R. D. I.* (1902), 66–87, 159–77, and 270–80; 2 Wharton, *Digest*, § 134; *Whitney* v. *Robertson*, (1888), 124 U. S. 190, and Scott, *Cases*, 458 (citing *Bartram* v. *Robertson* 1887, 122 U. S. 116); Wilson, § 76.

For a fuller Bibliography, see Hornbeck, *op. cit.*, 113 ff.

On the "Most-favored-nation Clause in China's Treaties," see Bau, *Foreign Relations of China* (1921), Pt. IV. ch. 22; and Phen, in 8 and 9 *Chinese Soc. and Pol. Sci. Rev.* (1924–25), 157 ff., 56 ff., 252 ff.

concessions based upon reciprocal advantages;[46] Great Britain, on the other hand, has maintained that the most-favored-nation clause should be unconditional in all cases, and that a favor or advantage granted to one State should extend to all other nations enjoying most-favored-nation privileges with that State.[47]

301. **Treaties of Guarantee.**—Treaties of guarantee merit particular attention by reason of their special character. They are " agreements through which one or more Powers engage to maintain given conditions or rights "[48] or to secure certain guaranteed objects, as, for example, the permanent neutralization of Belgium or Switzerland, the independence and integrity of the Ottoman Empire, or the undertaking by the Members of the League of Nations to " respect and preserve as against external agression the territorial integrity and existing political independence of all Members of the League."[49]

Guarantee treaties may be mutual or unilateral, several or collective (or both). " The effect of guarantee treaties

---

[46] See especially the discussions between the United States and France, England and Germany, in 5 Moore, *Digest*, § 765.

[47] "The United States, both as regards form and interpretation, has been a regular adherent of the conditional usage, with a few exceptions. Great Britain has regularly adhered to the unconditional, with, likewise a few exceptions. The countries of Europe followed first the unconditional, then the conditional, and then again the unconditional." Hornbeck, *op. cit.*, 56.

In its Commercial Treaty of Dec. 8, 1923 with Germany, the United States has inserted the unconditional form of the most-favored-nation clause. See McClure, in 19 *A. J.* (1925), 688, 699. See also treaties with Brazil, Czechoslovakia, etc., in 19 *A. J.*, 119 ff. They seem to indicate the adoption of a new policy by the United States. See Culbertson, *Int. Economic Policies* (1925), 92 ff.

[48] Wilson, p. 205. On *Treaties of Guarantee*, see especially: Bluntschli, Arts. 430–40; Bonfils or 1 (3 Pt.) Fauchille, Nos. 882–93; Despagnet, Nos. 144 and 461; Erich, *Ueber Allianzen* (1911), and in 7 *Z. V.* (1913), 452–76; * 1 Evarts, *Roots and Causes of the Wars* (1914–18), 418–43; * Hall, § 113; Heffter, § 97; Idman, *Le traité de guarantee* (1913); * Milanovitch, *Des traités de guarantie* (1888); * 1 Oppenheim, 574–76a; 2 Phillimore, §§ 56–63; 2 P.-Fodéré. Nos. 969–1020; Quabbe, *Die völkerr. Guarantie* (1911); * 2 Rivier, 97–105; Sanger and Norton, *England's Guarantee to Belgium and Luxemburg* (1915), especially chs. 2, 4, and 6; Taylor, §§ 350–53; Vattel, II, §§ 235–39; Wheaton, § 277; Wilson, § 77; and Woolsey, § 109.

[49] Art. 10 of the Covenant. Cf. *supra*, note 48, p. 194, and *infra*, pp. 508–09. The United States has guaranteed the independence of Cuba and Panama. See *supra*, notes on pp. 168 and 172. The integrity of Norway was guaranteed by Great Britain, France, Germany and Russia by the Treaty of Christiania in 1907. See Supp. to 2 *A. J.* (1908), 267.

is the imposition of the duty upon the guarantors to do what is in their power to secure the guaranteed objects." [50] The kind and quantity of coercion to be applied to carry out this purpose depends upon various circumstances, such as ability to render assistance at the particular time, the request of the party whose rights are guaranteed, his behavior, vital changes in political conditions, etc.

There is a difference of opinion respecting the duty of a State in case of a *collective* guarantee. In 1867 Lord Derby maintained that in the event of the violation of the neutrality of Luxemberg, the guarantors were not bound unless they acted in concert. But if this view were to prevail, it would be difficult to see the worth of a collective guarantee. [51]

302. **Effect of Treaties upon Third States.**—Treaties are directly binding upon the contracting parties alone, [52] but they may also affect the relations of third States by creating conditions which these are bound to respect, or from which they may derive advantage. [53] They may affect previous treaty rights of third States, as in the case of the most-favored-nation clause in commercial treaties (see *supra*, No. 300); and while a third State cannot incur legal obligations under a treaty to which it was not a party and cannot acquire rights under a treaty which benefits it merely incidentally, there are good grounds for holding that treaties (even when they do not provide for " adhesion " or " accession "), may become a basis for the growth of customary law and thus the source of general international rights and duties. This is particularly the case with Law-making Treaties and International Settlements. [54]

[50] 1 Oppenheim, § 575, p. 739.

[51] Cf. *supra*, note 48 on p. 194.

[52] Treaties are not, as a rule, directly binding upon the nationals or subjects of a State; they bind the States and governments themselves, in so far as they are self-executing. See *supra*, note 15. But the Constitution of the United States makes them a part of our municipal law.

[53] An example would be a treaty providing that a State's navigable waters shall be open to the merchantmen of all nations. Third States would ordinarily feel bound to respect boundary treaties.

In case of adherence or accession (see *supra*, note 8), third States undoubtedly acquire legal rights and duties under the treaty.

[54] See the excellent and highly suggestive monograph by Roxburgh, *Int. Conventions and Third States* (1917), especially §§ 23–40, 46–62, and 71 (for conclusions). See also 1 Oppenheim, § 522.

302*a*. **Sanctions of Treaties.**—Of the various means formerly employed to secure the performance of treaties—oaths, hostages, pledges, occupation of territory,[55] and treaties of guarantee—the latter is the only one still generally in use.

303. **Termination of Treaties.**—Treaties may become extinct through the expiration of their time limit,[56] by the performance of the specific object of the contract, or by a later agreement superseding the earlier one, in whole or in part. They may be dissolved by mutual consent, an express renunciation of advantages, a voluntary release by one of the contracting parties, or by denunciation or withdrawal by notice in accordance with the terms of the agreement.

They may become void upon the cessation of conditions essential to the continuance of the treaty or upon the extinction either of the subject [57] (*i.e.* contracting party), or object of the treaty (*i.e.* purpose or subject-matter); if found legally, physically, or morally impossible of execution; or, in certain cases, upon the outbreak of war.

They may become voidable (*i.e.* subject to annulment or cancellation), through war, a subsequent change of status of international personality on the part of one of the contracting parties, if their terms are inconsistent with subsequent International Law (as, *e.g.* in the case of the abolition

As to violations of rights of third States, Roxburgh says (p. 32): "If . . . the treaty infringes the legal rights of a third State, the State is immediately entitled to intervene. In practice, there seem to be three classes of cases in which such rights are liable to be violated: (*a*) When the treaty violates any universally accepted rule of International Law, (*b*) when it is inconsistent with the safety of the third State, and (*c*) when it violates rights previously acquired by the third State."

[55] Temporary occupation of territory is still employed to secure the payment of a debt or the exaction of a war indemnity. The last case of a treaty secured through hostages was that of Aix-la-Chapelle in 1748. For discussion and references, see 1 Oppenheim, §§ 523-28. See also Phillipson, *Termination of War* (1916), 207 ff.

See Arts. 429-32 of the Treaty of Versailles for the conditions under which the German territory west of the Rhine, together with the bridge-heads, are to be evacuated by allied troops at the end of fifteen years.

[56] The right to give notice after a specified lapse of time for the cessation of the treaty is frequently provided for in the text. 2 Hyde, § 539. This would seem to be a case of dissolution rather than of expiration.

[57] For the effect upon treaties of the "Succession of States," see *supra*, Nos. 129-130; for the effects of war, see *infra*, No. 344.

of privateering), or if any of the implied conditions [58] under which the treaty has been made are violated. Such implied conditions are that the treaty shall be observed in its essentials [59] by both parties, that it shall remain consistent with the fundamental rights of independence and self-preservation, and that there shall be no *vital* change in the circumstances or conditions under which the treaty was made. The clause *rebus sic stantibus* is an implied condition in all treaties.[60]

[58] This principle is thus stated Hall (§ 113, p. 407): "Neither party to a contract can make its binding effect dependent at will upon conditions other than those contemplated at the moment when the contract was entered into, and on the other hand a contract ceases to be binding so soon as anything which formed an implied conditions of its obligatory force at the time of its conclusion is essentially altered."

[59] This is the view of Hall (*op. cit.*, 408) and a minority of publicists. For the opinion of the majority that there is no distinction in this respect between the essential and non-essential parts of a treaty, and that the breach of any portion of the agreement renders the whole compact voidable, see 1 Oppenheim, § 547.

[60] This is the view of the great majority of publicists, and it is in accord with international practice. For examples drawn from the practice of the United States, see Crandall, § 180, p. 441; Foster, *Practice of Diplomacy* (1911), ch. 15; 2 Hyde, § 541, note 4; and 5 Moore, *Digest*, § 772.

The Conference held in London in 1871 to settle the Black Sea Question declared: "It is an essential principle of the Law of Nations that no power can liberate itself from the engagements of a treaty, nor modify the stipulations thereof, unless with the consent of the contracting powers by means of an amicable arrangement."

As Lawrence (7th ed., p. 304), observes: "This doctrine sounds well; but a little consideration will show that it is as untenable as the lax view which would allow any party to a treaty to violate it on the slightest pretext. . . ."

The clause *rebus sic stantibus* should only be resorted to in very exceptional circumstances. All are agreed that a change of government or even in the form of government does not, in general, affect the obligation of treaties. As there is great danger in the abuse of this principle, it should be emphasized that the principle *rebus sic stantibus* " implies a complete change in the state of things which was the basis of the treaty and one of its tacit conditions. The change of circumstances must be such as either to render the execution of the treaty difficult or impossible or to entail the performance of obligations which were not foreseen by the contracting parties and which, had they been foreseen, would never have been assumed." 2 Garner, § 449, p. 218.

"When the existence, or the vital development, of a State stands in unavoidable conflict with its treaty obligations, the latter must give way, for self-preservation and development, in accordance with the growth and the vital requirements of the nation, are the primary duties of every State. . . . Every treaty implies a condition that, if by an unforeseen change of circumstances an obligation stipulated in the treaty should imperil the existing or vital development of one of the parties, it should have a right to demand to be released from the obligation concerned." 1 Oppenheim, § 539, pp. 689–90. For a summary of the views of various authorities, see Fenwick, 345–47.

303a. Treaties of Peace.—Treaties of peace are of such particular importance that they demand a special consideration, though not generally so dealt with in the texts or treatises.   While they usually purport to be of a permanent character or aim to set up a permanent state of things (amounting to an international settlement in the case of the great treaties like those of Vienna, Berlin and Paris), it must be admitted that they are often most unsatisfactory and sadly in need of revision.[61]   By reason of the psychological conditions under which they were made at the close of a war, they are apt to contain unjust provisions which the defeated party resents and seeks to evade at the earliest opportunity.   Besides, being made under strong pressure or duress,[62] they fail to evoke the sense of moral obligation which is ordinarily aroused by treaties made under happier auspices.

After the establishment of peace, all hostile operations must discontinue.   " Any acts whatever of a hostile character committed by forces ignorant of the restoration of peace must be made good, and the *status quo* existing on the day of the termination of the war must as far as possible be reinstated. . . .

On *rebus sic stantibus*, see Bonuca, in 4 *Z. V.* (1910), 449–71; *Crandall, *Treaties*, § 180; Foster, *op. cit.*, 299–305; * 2 Garner, § 449; 2 Hyde, § 541; Kaufmann, *Das Wesen des Völkerrechts und die Clausela rebus sic stantibus* (1911); Lammasch, *Das Völkerrecht nach dem Kriege* (1918), 142–58; * 5 Moore, *Digest*, § 772; * 1 Oppenheim, § 539; Phillimore, *Three Centuries of Treaties of Peace* (1919), 135–40; Schmidt, *Über die völkerr. clausula rebus sic stantibus* (1907); Taylor, in *Procs. Am. Soc. I. L.* (1913), 223 ff.; and 2 Westlake, 295–96.

On the *Termination of Treaties* generally, see especially: 2 Butler, *op. cit.*, §§ 384–89; 1 Cobbett, 334–41; * Crandall, ch. 25; Devlin, *op. cit.*, ch. 5, §§ 95–99, and ch. 8; Foster, *op. cit.*, ch. 15; 2 Hyde, §§ 538–51; * Mathews, *op. cit.*, ch. 13; * 5 Moore, *Digest*, §§ 770–80; * 1 Oppenheim, §§ 534–49; Phillimore, *op. cit.*, ch. 8; 1 Willoughby, *op. cit.*, §§ 207, 220–21, 223–24.

[61] Art. 19 of the Covenant of the League of Nations provides that the Assembly may "advise the reconsideration by Members of the League of treaties which have become inapplicable"; but, as Higgins remarks (8th ed. of Hall, 407), "the method of revision appears to be too cumbersome to be effective."   See also the criticisms of Oppenheim, I, § 167° (2) and 167⁸ (4); and Pollock, *League of Nations*, (2d ed., 1922), 172.

[62] Phillipson (*Termination of War*, 1916, 162) distinguishes between duress and pressure which, he says, "cannot properly be described as duress."   However, the popular mind will probably be unable to grasp this distinction.   On the effect of fraud, violence, or intimidation on the validity of treaties, see *supra*, No. 297 (3).

"If any such acts are committed the injured party is entitled to compensation, the responsibility resting either on those who did the acts or on their own governments." [63]

"Unless otherwise stipulated, conditions remain conformably to the principle of *uti possidetis*," *i.e.* the state of possession existing at the end of the war. But "where the principle of *uti possidetis* is not stipulated or implied, that of the *status quo ante bellum* applies," *i.e.* the state of possession as it was before the war.[64]

BIBLIOGRAPHY

Treaties.—Amos, *Remedies for War* (1880), 173–88; 12 *Annuaire* (1892), 226–57; Bergbohm, *Staatsverträge als Quellen des Völkerrechts* (1876); * Bernard, "Obligation of Treaties," in *Lectures on Diplomacy* (1868), Lect. IV; Bigelow, *Breaches of Anglo-American Treaties* (1917); Bluntschli, Arts. 402–61; Bonfils or * 1 (3 Pt.) Fauchille (see pp. 289–91 for references), Nos. 816–929; Bulmerincq, in 1 Marquardsen, *Handbuch*, §§ 53–64; Bry, Nos. 283–340; 3 Calvo, §§ 1567–1669; 1 Cobbett, 327–47; * Crandall, *Treaties;* Davis, ch. 8; Despagnet, Nos. 443–74; Fenwick, ch. 20; 2 Fiore, Nos. 976–1095, and *Int. Law Cod.* (1918), Nos. 744–927; * Foster, *Practice of Diplomacy* (1911), chs. 12–16; Funck-Brentano et Sorel, chs. 7–9; Geffcken and Gessner, in 3 Holtzendorff, 5–139; Grotius, lib. II, cc. 15–16; * Hall, Pt. II, ch. 10; 1 Halleck (3d ed.), 275–324; Heffter, §§ 81–99; * 2 Hyde, §§ 489–551; Jellinek, *Staatenverträge* (1880), *Staatenverbindungen* (1882), 100–13, and 1 *Das Recht des modernen Staats* (2d ed., 1905), see index; Klüber (Ott's 2d ed., 1874), §§ 141–65; Lawrence, §§ 132–34, and *Essays on Int. Law* (1885), 89–162; Liszt, §§ 31–32; 2 J. de Louter, §§ 24–30; 1 F. de Martens, §§ 102–

---

[63] Phillipson, *op. cit.*, 216. "For example, territory occupied in such circumstances must be immediately evacuated . . . , contributions collected must at once be repaid, persons taken as prisoners must be set free again, ships captured must be released, and so on."

In support of these sound views, Phillipson cites the interesting cases of *The Mentor* (1799), 1 C. Rob. 179, 182–83; and *The John* (1818), 2 Dodson 336.

[64] *Ibid.*, 221 and 222. "The *uti possidetis* clause is nowadays unusual in peace treaties, if not obsolete. In its stead, the practice is adopted of stipulating the cession of certain territory demanded by one State or the other as a result of successful invasion or successful prosecution of the war in general, all other invaded territory being restored.

On *Treaties of Peace*, see: * Baker and McKernan, *Laws of Warfare* (1919), 679–767 (for citations from the authorities); Bower, in 3 *Grotius Soc.* (1918), 1–21; 1 Halleck, ch. 9; * 2 Oppenheim, §§ 266–78; Phillimore, *Three Centuries of Treaties of Peace* (1919); and * Phillipson, *Termination of War and Treaties of Peace* (1916), *passim*. For further references, see 2 Oppenheim, pp. 361, 366, and 371 of 3d ed.

16; Mathews, *Conduct of Am. Foreign Relations* (1922), chs. 8–13;
2 Mérignhac, 633–790; Mill, "Treaty Obligations" in 8 *Fortn. Rev.*
(1870), 715–20; * 5 Moore, *Digest*, ch. 17; Myers, "Treaty Violation,"
in 11 and 12 *A. J.* (1917 and 1918), 538 ff., 794 ff., and 96 ff.; Nippold,
Der völkerrechtliche Verträge (1894); * 1 Oppenheim, §§ 491–580;
2 Phillimore, Pt. V, chs. 6–9; 1 Piédelièvre, Nos. 314–64; * Potter,
Int. Organization (1922), chs. 10–12; P.-Fodéré, 2 *Cours*, 461–98,
and 2 *Traité*, ch. 6, Nos. 886–1224; * 2 Rivier, 33–146; Roxburgh,
Int. Conventions and Third States (1917); * 2 Satow, ch. 27–31; Schuyler, "Commercial Treaties," and "Fisheries," in *Am. Diplomacy*
(1886), 404–57; * Scott, *Cases*, 429–73; Stockton, chs. 13–14; Stowell
and Munro, Pt. I, ch. 3 (see also index); Taylor, §§ 334–400; Triepel,
Völkerrecht und Landesrecht (1889), 27–90, or *Droit international et
droit interne* (1920), see index; 1 Twiss, ch. 13; Ullmann, §§ 74–85;
* Vattel, liv. II, cc. 12–17, 152–322; Walker, *Manual of Public Int.
Law* (1895), §§ 30–31; * 1 Westlake, 290–98; Wegeman, *Die Ratification von Staatsverträgen* (1892); 2 Wharton, *Digest*, ch. 6; * Wheaton,
Pt. III, ch. 2, and Dana's notes 139, 142, etc.; * Wilson, ch. 7; Wilson
and Tucker, ch. 14; Woolsey, ch. 5, §§ 101–13 and Appendix II,
423 ff. (for list of the most important treaties since the Reformation,
with a brief statement of their provisions); and Wright, *Control of
Am. Foreign Relations*, see index; and in 10 *A. J.* (1916), 706–36.

See also special bibliographies on *Treaty-Making Power in the U. S.,
Parliamentary Participation in the Treaty-Making Power, Interpretation
of Treaties, Most-Favored-Nation Clause, Treaties of Guarantee, Clause
rebus sic stantibus, Termination of Treaties, and Treaties of Peace,*
in this chapter.

For Treaty Collections, see Myers, *Manual of Collection of Treaties*
(Cambridge, 1922). The most extensive and celebrated collection is
that of G. F. de Martens with its various supplements and continuations (1761—to our own time). See *Catalogue of Treaties* (Washington, 1919) which lists over 3000 international agreements concluded between 1814 and 1918.

PART IV

SETTLEMENT AND PREVENTION OF INTERNATIONAL DIFFERENCES

304. Introductory.—International differences may arise on various grounds which have been broadly distinguished as legal or political in their nature.[1] Legal differences or conflicts of rights are those arising from disputes or controversies to which recognized legal principles or more or less clearly established rules and customs of International Law may be more or less readily applied. Political differences or conflicts of interest are those which result from a conflict of political, social, or economic interests and to which it is difficult or impossible to apply such rules or principles. Modes of settling international differences may be broadly classified as peaceful or amicable, and forcible or non-amicable. It is manifestly easier to apply amicable modes of settlement to legal than to political differences. All States are morally bound to exhaust all peaceful or amicable modes of settling their differences before resorting to forcible or non-amicable means.

It is now also becoming increasingly recognized that prevention of international disputes is even more important than their pacific settlement after they have arisen, and that the best and surest means of prevention lie in international coöperation and organization. Consequently, a chapter altogether new on this subject (chapter XXIII) has been added to Pt. IV.

[1] It is not always possible to separate legal and political differences in practice, for they are usually of a mixed character, and legal claims have often been made a pretext for disguised political aggression.

On this distinction between legal and political differences, see especially: * Buell, *Int. Relations* (1925), ch. 25, pp. 589–604; Bulmerincq, in 4 Holtzendorff, 5 ff.; Castberg, in 6 (3d ser.) *R. D. I.* (1925), 156 ff.; 2 Hyde, § 560; Jelf, in 7 *Grotius Soc.* (1922), 59 ff.; Loder, *La difference entre l'arbitrage int. et la justice int.*; 2 J. de Louter, § 37; Nippold, *Die Fortbildung des Verfahrens* (1907), 127 ff.; * 2 Oppenheim, §§ 1–3; Potter, *Int. Organization* (1922), 212–14; Reeves and Scott, in *Procs. Am. Soc. I. L.* (1915), 78–94; * Reinsch, in 5 *A. J.* (1911), 604–14; 2 Rivier, 149 f.; Ullmann, § 148; * 1 Westlake, 357 ff.; Wilson, § 81; * Woolf, *Int. Government* (1916), ch. 6, and *Frame Work of a Lasting Peace* (1917), sects. 2 and 3. See also Fenwick, *et. al.*, in *Procs. of Am. Soc. I. L.* (1924), 44 ff.

CHAPTER XXII

AMICABLE MEANS OF SETTLEMENT OF INTERNATIONAL DIFFERENCES

There are at least six recognized amicable modes of settling international differences.

305. (I) **Negotiation.**—The more usual or customary mode is by means of *negotiation*.[1] Diplomacy is constantly at work avoiding friction, smoothing over difficulties, effecting compromises, and settling claims.[2] In case of a serious difference, States are bound to try this mode of settlement before resorting to forcible means of coercion or redress—a rule which appears to have been violated by Italy in 1911 in sending an ultimatum to Turkey without suitable prior negotiations. Negotiations may be carried on orally, by an exchange of notes, by written communications, or at a Congress or Conference.[3]

[1] On *Negotiation*, see especially: Bonfils or 1 (3 Pt.) Fauchille Nos. 931–32; Bulmerincq, in 4 Holtzendorff, 13–17; 3 Calvo, §§ 1670 ff.; Despagnet, No. 470; Fenwick, 399–400; Foster, *Practice of Diplomacy* (1911), ch. 12; Hoijer, *La solution pacific des litiges int.* (1925), 2–25; 2 Hyde, § 552; Kamarowsky, *Le tribunal int.* (1887), 73–79; * 1 and 2 Oppenheim, §§ 477–82 and § 4 respectively; * 1 and 2 P.-Fodéré. *Cours*, 514 ff. and 298 ff., and 6 *Traité*, Nos. 2585–86.

See also the references on the nature of diplomacy, in Bibliography at the end of ch. I, *supra*, pp. 16–17. Among more recent works dealing with various phases of diplomacy are the following: Barthelémy, *Démoctratie et politique étrangère* (1917); Brown, *Int. Realities* (1917), 174–200; Kennedy, *Old Diplomacy and New* (1922); Lippmann, *The Stakes of Diplomacy* (1915); Mowrer *Our Foreign Affairs* (1924); Ponsonby, *Democracy and Diplomacy* (1915); Poole, *The Conduct of Foreign Relations* (1924); Potter, *Int. Organization*, (1922), chs. 7–9; Reinsch, *Secret Diplomacy*; and Young, *Diplomacy Old and New* (1921).

[2] On *Claims*, see especially: * Borchard, (see index); Brewer and Butler, Article on "International Law," in *Cyc., of L. and P.* IX (1906); 6 Moore, *Digest*, ch. 21; Moore, *Arbitrations, passim* (see index); Thorpe, *Int. Claims* (1924); and 2 Wharton, *Digest*, ch. 9.

[3] See *supra*, ch. 20. On "Diplomacy by Conference," which had been introduced into European practice for a short period by Lord Castlereagh after the Congress of Vienna (Webster, *Foreign Policy of Castlereagh*, 1925, pp. 56–58), see a very remarkable paper by * Hankey, in *Round Table* for March, 1921, pp. 287 ff. This reference is not to diplomacy through great International

306. (II) **Good Offices.**[4]—*Good offices* consist in suggestions or advice on the part of third Powers, offered for the purpose of inducing States at variance with each other to come together and attempt by negotiation, or otherwise, an amicable settlement of their differences.

307. (III) **Mediation**—*Mediation* partakes more of the character of an actual diplomatic intervention on the part of third Powers. The mediator assumes the rôle of a middleman and plays a leading and regular part in the conduct of negotiations; but he acts as a conciliator or mutual friend rather than as a judge, and he is usually more anxious to effect a compromise than to secure a settlement of the dispute on a judicial basis. This mode of procedure is especially adapted to the settlement of *political* differences. Mediation may be single or collective in character, and it may be designed to terminate as well as to prevent a war or other serious international conflict.

The Hague Peace Conferences of 1899 and 1907 laid down the following rules in respect to the use of Good Offices and Mediation:[5]

Conferences, but rather to a recent tendency developed during and after the World War of personal conferences between the responsible Ministers themselves. In a sense the League of Nations may be said to be the best illustration of the possibilities of personal diplomacy by conference. Viscount Grey (*Twenty-five Years*, 1925, I, 340) thought the World War might have been averted by such a Conference as he proposed to Germany.

[4] The terms "good offices" and "mediation" are often confused, especially in diplomatic documents. This is very natural, as the former may lead to the latter, of which it is frequently the first step. There is no warrant for the use of the phrase *armed* mediation, which would amount to a forcible intervention. Likewise is mediation accompanied by threats an intervention rather than a mediation.

The term "good offices" is also used in another sense than that indicated in the text. It may mean the "unofficial advocacy of interests which the [diplomatic] agent may properly represent, but which it may not be convenient to present and discuss on a full diplomatic footing." Communication from Sec'y. Hay to Mr. McNally, No. 235, March 16, 1900. Cited from 2 Hyde, § 553.

[5] Through treaties, States occasionally agree to submit to a sort of obligatory mediation in advance. For examples, see Bonfils or 1 (3. pt.) Fauchille, Nos. 934, 936–41; 2 Piédelièvre, Nos. 670–78; and 2 Rivier, 164.

For historical examples of mediation (which are very numerous) see: Bonfils or 1 (3 Pt.) Fauchille, Nos. 937–42; 3 and 6 Calvo, §§ 1684–1704, 349–51 respectively; and 6 Moore, *Digest*, §§ 1065–67 (for instances of the tender of good offices and mediation on the part of the United States). For references on Good Offices and Mediation, see Bibliography at the end of this chapter.

" In case of serious disagreement or dispute, before an appeal to arms, the Contracting Powers agree to have recourse, as far as circumstances allow, to the good offices or mediation of one or more friendly Powers (Art. 2).[6]

" Independently of this recourse, the Contracting Powers deem it expedient *and desirable*[7] that one or more Powers, strangers to the dispute, should, on their own initiative and as far as circumstances may allow, offer their good offices or mediation to the States at variance.

" Powers, strangers to the dispute, have the right to offer good offices or mediation, even during the course of hostilities.

" The exercise of this right can never be regarded by either of the parties at variance as an unfriendly act (Art. 3).

" The part of the mediator consists in reconciling the opposing claims and appeasing the feelings of resentment which may have arisen between the States at variance (Art. 4).

" The duties of the mediator are at an end when once it is declared, either by one of the contending parties, or by the mediator himself, that the means of reconciliation proposed by him are not accepted (Art. 5).

" Good offices and mediation, undertaken at the request of the contending parties or on the initiative of Powers

An interesting example of the use of good offices and mediation by the United States is that by ex-President Roosevelt during the Russo-Japanese War which resulted in the Treaty of Portsmouth in 1905. Mr. Roosevelt's activities during the negotiations show that good offices developed into mediation. See Hershey, *Int. Law and Diplomacy of the Russo-Japanese War* (1906), 347 ff., and 353 ff. (including notes). For more recent light on this subject, see 1 Bishop, *Theodore Roosevelt* (1920), chs. 31–32; and Dennett, *Roosevelt and the Russo-Japan. War* (1925), chs. 8–10.

[6] 1 H. C. (1899 and 1907), Arts. 2 to 7 (inclusive). It should be noted that the tender of good offices or mediation on the part of third Powers prior to or during hostilities is a legal right, but not an obligation. However, the Powers at variance are bound to have recourse to this mode of settling disputes, *as far as circumstances allow.* But this qualification renders the obligation largely illusory.

The conventions of the two Hague Conferences may be most conveniently consulted in Higgins, *The Two Hague Conferences* (1910), where they are printed on parallel pages. See also 2 Scott, *The Hague Peace Conferences* (1909), and *Texts of the Peace Conferences* (1908).

[7] The phrase in *italics* is the sole contribution to this subject by the Conference of 1907.

strangers to the dispute, have exclusively the character of advice, and never have binding force (Art. 6).

" The acceptance of mediation cannot, in default of agreement to the contrary, have the effect of interrupting, delaying, or hindering mobilization or other measures of preparation for war.

" If mediation takes place after the commencement of hostilities, the military operations in progress are not interrupted, in default of agreement to the contrary (Art. 7)." [8]

Article 11 of the Covenant of the League of Nations declares any war or threat of war anywhere " a matter of concern to the whole League " and instructs it (the League) to " take any action that may be deemed wise and effectual to safeguard the peace of nations."   It is also declared to be the " friendly right of each Member of the League to bring to the attention of the Assembly or of the Council any circumstance whatever affecting international relations which threatens to disturb international peace."

Thus there is incorporated into the constitution of the League a provision which is undoubtedly intended to make the Council of the League the mediator in international disputes.[9]

308. (IV) **Conciliation and Commissions of Inquiry.**—

[8] Article 8 recommended the following form of special mediation, when circumstances allow:

"In case of a serious difference endangering peace, the contending States choose respectively a Power, to which they intrust the mission of entering into direct communication with the Power chosen on the other side, with the object of preventing the rupture of pacific relations.

"For the period of this mandate, the term of which, in default of agreement to the contrary, cannot exceed thirty days, the States at variance cease from all direct communication on the subject of the dispute, which is regarded as referred exclusively to the mediating Powers.   These Powers shall use their best efforts to settle the dispute.

"In case of a definite rupture of pacific relations, these Powers remain jointly charged with the task of taking advantage of any opportunity to restore peace."

This form of special mediation, which is based upon the use of seconds in duelling, was fathered by Mr. Holls, one of the American delegates.   It has never been employed.   On *Special Mediation*, see Holls, *Peace Conference at the Hague* (1900), 187–203.   For references on Good Offices and Mediation, see, Bibliography at the end of this chapter.

[9] The Council has exercised its mediatorial functions in several international disputes, *e.g.* in the *Aaland Islands* and *Corfu* cases.

The Hague Conference of 1899 created a new mode of [10] settling a certain class of international disputes. It recommended that " in differences of an international nature, involving neither honor nor vital interests, and arising from a difference of opinion on points of fact, . . . the parties who have not been able to come to an agreement by means of diplomacy should, as far as circumstances allow, institute an International Commission of Inquiry, to facilitate a solution of these differences by elucidating the facts by means of an impartial and conscientious investigation." [11]

In subsequent articles [12] the Convention of 1899 provided that International Commissions of Inquiry should be constituted by special agreement between the parties in dispute and, unless otherwise stipulated, in the manner fixed by Art. 32 of the Convention for the Pacific Settlement of International Disputes.[13] This convention, or special agreement, defines the facts to be examined, determines the extent of the powers of the commissioners, and settles the procedure.[14]   " The report of the Commission is limited to a

[10] This institution appears to owe its origin mainly to the great Russian publicist, F. de Martens. He maintained that International Commissions of Inquiry are not an innovation, and pointed to the various Mixed Commissions selected to trace boundary lines, settle claims, etc., as historical precedents. While there is a certain amount of justification for this view, I rather agree with those who hold that Mixed Commissions constitute a special form of arbitration, and that the International Commission of Inquiry, as instituted by the Hague Conventions, furnishes us with a new form of International Tribunal. See, *e.g.* Beaucourt, *Les commissions int. l'enquête* (1909), 15–47; Kamarowsky, *Le tribunal int.* (1887), 165–84; Nippold, *op. cit.*, § 19.

[11] 1 H. C. (1899 and 1907), Art. 9. Owing to the opposition of the smaller States, both Conferences refused to make recourse to International Commissions of Inquiry obligatory.

[12] 1 H. C. (1899), Arts. 10 to 14.

[13] Art. 12 of the Convention of 1907 provides that they shall be formed in accordance with Arts. 45 and 57—the substitutes of Arts. 24 and 32 of the Convention of 1899. These prescribe the mode in which the Arbitration Tribunal is to be formed and organized in case the parties at variance fail to come to a direct agreement as to its composition.

It should be noted that the revised Convention of 1907 provides that only one of the two commissioners chosen by each contracting party may be taken from its own "nationals," whereas the original convention of 1899 permitted the choice of two of its own citizens or subjects.

[14] 1 H. C. (1899), Art. 10. Art. 10 of the Convention of 1907 adds: "It determines the mode and time in which the Commission is to be formed. . . . It also determines, if there is need, where the Commission is to sit, and whether it may remove to another place, the language the Commission shall use and the languages the use of which shall be authorized before it, as well as the date

statement of facts, and has in no way the character of an award.   It leaves to the parties at variance entire freedom as to the effect to be given to this statement." [15]

In consequence of the successful settlement of the North Sea or Dogger Bank Incident [16] of 1904 by means of a

on which each party must deposit its statement of facts ,and, generally speaking, all the conditions upon which the parties have agreed."

"If the Convention of Inquiry has not determined where the Commission is to sit, it will sit at the Hague."   1 H. C. (1907), Art. 11.

"The parties are entitled to appoint special agents to attend the Commission of Inquiry, whose duty it is to represent them and to act as intermediaries between them and the Commission.   They are further authorized to engage counsel or advocates, appointed by themselves, to state their case and uphold their interest before the Commission."   1 H. C. (1907), Art. 14.

"The International Bureau of the Permanent Court of Arbitration acts as registry for the Commissions which sit at the Hague," and is given charge of the archives.   Arts. 15 and 16.

[15] 1. H. C. (1899 and 1907), Arts. 14 or 35.

[16] This was a very strange and sensational incident.   On the night of October 21–22, 1904, a fleet of British fishermen trawling for cod off the Dogger Bank in the North Sea were suddenly attacked by warships belonging to the Russian Baltic Squadron, then on its ill-fated voyage to the Far East.   Considerable damage was done and two lives were lost.

British feeling was stirred to its highest pitch of excitement by this event (which was regarded as the culmination of a series of Russian "outrages"), and the two countries seemed on the brink of war, when France tendered her good offices and it was finally agreed (on Nov. 25, 1904) that an International Commission of Inquiry should be appointed, consisting of five members of high naval rank, three of whom were in the service of neutral Powers.

It was further agreed that "the Commission shall inquire into and report on all circumstances relative to the North Sea incident, *and particularly on the question as to where the responsibilities and the degree of blame* attaching to the subjects of the two High Contracting Parties or of other countries in case their responsibility should be established by the inquiry."   Art. 2 of the *Declaration of St. Petersburg.*   For the English text of this Declaration, and the Report of the Commission, see 2 *A. J.* (1908), 929–36.

It should be noted that the powers granted to the North Sea Commission were much broader than those contemplated by the Hague Convention.

The North Sea Commission met in Paris on January 9, 1905, and rendered its verdict on February 25th.   The majority held in effect that the Russian Admiral Rojestvensky was responsible for the action and results of the firing upon the fishing fleet, but that he was not personally to blame, *i.e.* though responsible for the firing and not justified in fact, there was an apparent justification for what he did and he was not subject to trial and punishment.

There can be little doubt that the firing was due to a state of panic among the Russian officers of the fleet, induced by a fear or belief that they were in great danger of attack by Japanese torpedo boats.   The Russian Government recognized its responsibility by the payment of £65,000 as indemnity due the Hull fishermen.

"The institution of the North Sea Commission and its successful working under such trying circumstances must be pronounced a great victory both for the principle of international inquiry and of international arbitration.   Al-

Commission of Inquiry modeled somewhat on that contemplated by the Hague Convention of 1899, the Hague Conference of 1907 revised the rules of 1899 and adopted a code of procedure for this new form of International Tribunal, based largely upon experience gained through the establishment and working of the North Sea Commission of 1905.[17]

though nominally called an International Commission of Inquiry analogous to those provided for by Arts. 9–14 of the first Hague Convention, it really combined the functions of an International Court of Tribunal of Justice with those of a Commission of Inquiry and, in accordance with the purposes for which it was organized, it passed upon the questions of *responsibility* and *degree of blame* as well as inquired into and reported upon the facts or circumstances of the case. It was in fact an arbitration *sui generis*, of a kind new and unprecedented in the history of international relations; for it was not only applied, at a time of great excitement, to a question affecting the so-called national honor and vital interests (?) of both parties to the dispute, but it introduced into our administration of international justice a new method of procedure in cases of alleged violation of the Law of Nations.   It has set a precedent for the establishment of tribunals combining the functions of an International Court of Arbitration with those of a Court of Inquiry for the investigation and trial before the bar of the public opinion of the world, of those charged with international crimes and misdemeanors, or serious violations of International Law.   It is true that the accused in this case, if found guilty, were to have been punished by a national penal sanction; but the power of imposing an international censure was vested in the North Sea Commission by the Declaration of St. Petersburg, and, although the organization and procedure of the Commission may be open to criticism in matters of detail, there is no valid reason why the principles involved in this case should not be given even a more extended application."
Hershey, *Int. Law and Diplomacy of the Russo-Japanese War* (1906), 240–41.

Though this mode of settling international disputes appears to be without precedent, there have been many serious controversies to which it might have been applied with good hope of success.   Had the blowing up of the *Maine* not been complicated with other and even more serious matters, our war with Spain might possibly have thus been averted by recourse to this means.   A number of international incidents, exhibiting more or less analogy to the North Sea incident, are cited by Smith and Sibley, *op. cit.*, 295–319.

On the *North Sea Incident*, see Beaucourt, *Les commissions internationales d'enquête* (1909), ch. 3; Hershey, *Int. Law and Diplomacy of the Russo-Japanese War* (1906), ch. 8; Higgins, 167–70; Mandelstam, in 12 *R. D. I. P.* (1905), 161 ff. and 351 ff.; I Mérignhac, 442–47; De la Penha, *La commission internationale d'enquête sur l'incident Anglo-Russe de la Mer de Nord* (1905); Smith and Sibley, *International Law during the Russo-Japanese War* (1905), 283 ff., 446–458, 468–71.

For references on Conciliation and Commissions of Inquiry, see Bibliography at the end of this chapter.

[17] For these rules of procedure, which are purely optional, see 1 H. C. (1907), Arts. 18–34. For a summary, see Hershey, in 2 *A. J.* (1908), 38.

The Russian De Martens also proposed in effect to render recourse to International Commissions of Inquiry obligatory in a certain very limited

Though there is no specific mention of Commissions of Inquiry in the Covenant of the League of Nations, the Members of the League have agreed that " if there should arise between them any dispute likely to lead to a rupture, they will submit the matter either to arbitration or judicial settlement *or to inquiry by the Council*; " and, in the latter case, they have agreed in no case to resort to war until three months after the report by the Council which " shall be made within six months after the submission of the dispute." [18]

In case such a dispute is submitted to inquiry by the Council, it shall try to effect a settlement; and, " if such efforts are successful, a statement shall be made public giving such facts and explanations regarding the dispute and the terms of settlement thereof as the Council may deem appropriate." If the dispute is not thus settled, the Council shall nevertheless " make and publish a report containing a statement of the facts of the dispute and the recommendations which are deemed just and proper in regard thereto." [19]

If the report is unanimous (other than the representatives of one or more of the parties to the dispute), the " Members of the League agree that they will not go to war with any party to the dispute which complies with the recommendations of the report." If the report is not unanimous, the " Members of the League reserve to themselves the right to take such action as they shall consider necessary for the maintenance of right and justice." [20]

sense and include the fixing of responsibility among their duties, but the Conference of 1907 rejected his wise proposals.

[18] Art. 12 of the Covenant.   Cf. *infra*, p. 512 and note 37.

[19] Art. 15.   Cf. *infra*, pp. 514-16 and notes.

[20] The thirty *Bryan Peace Treaties* of 1913-14, though never applied, mark an interesting and important step in the evolution of the idea of the International Commission of Inquiry from its inception at the first Hague Conference of 1899 up to its present incorporation in the Constitution of the League of Nations.

In general each treaty set up a permanent Commission of five members (with three neutrals) and provided that "the High Contracting Parties agree that all disputes between them, of every nature whatsoever, other than disputes the settlement of which is provided for and in fact achieved under existing agreements between the High Contracting Parties [*i.e.*, through arbitration] shall, when diplomatic methods of adjustment have failed, be referred for investigation and report to a permanent International Commission . . . ;

309. (V) **International Arbitration. Definition.**—*International Arbitration* is a quasi-judicial mode of settlement of international disputes in which by agreement of the parties concerned, one or more arbiters are selected for the decision of the controversy. It " has for its object the settlement of differences between States by judges of their own choice, and on the basis of respect for law." [21]

and they agree not to declare war or begin hostilities during such investigation and before the report is submitted" (Art. 1 of the Treaty between the United States and Great Britain).

"In case the High Contracting Parties shall have failed to adjust a dispute by diplomatic methods, they shall at once refer it to the International Commission for investigaiton and report. The International Commission may, however, spontaneously by unanimous agreement offer its services to that effect, and in such case it shall notify both governments and request their co-operation in the investigation" (Art. 3 of the same treaty). (Only some of the treaties grant to the Commission the right of initiative which appears in various forms).

All the High Contracting Parties agree that the report of the Commission shall be completed within one year after the date on which it shall declare its investigation to have begun, unless they shall limit or extend the time by express agreement; and they all "reserve the right to act independently on the subject matter of the dispute after the report of the Commission shall have been submitted" (Art. 3).

A common provision is to the effect that the treaty shall remain in force for five years and thereafter until twelve months after notice on the part of one of the contracting parties of an intention to terminate it. Presumably many of these treaties are still in force.

The main advantages claimed for the treaties are that they give time for calm consideration or a "cooling-off process," afford an opportunity to mobilize public opinion in favor of a peaceful settlement, and may be applicable to questions involving national honor as well as to justiceable disputes. But the evolution of methods and machinery for the pacific settlement of international controversies seems to have advanced beyond them.

On the *Bryan Peace Treaties*, see especially: Buell, *Int. Relations* (1925), 590–93; 1 (3 Pt.) Fauchille, No. 970 [15–16]; Finch and Scott, Editorials in 7–10 *A. J.* (see Index of *A. J.* under head of "Peace," 219); 2 Hyde, § 558; Myers, in 3 W. P. F. (1913), No. 11, Pt. 1, pp. 18 ff.; and Scott, "Introduction," in *Treaties for the Advancement of Peace* (Carnegie Endowment, 1920). For the texts of the treaties, see the above volume and Supp. to 10 *A. J.* (1916), 263 ff.

At the fifth Pan-American Congress held at Santiago in 1923, a treaty was signed extending the principle of the Bryan Treaties to the American Republics generally. See Buell, *op. cit.*, 591–92.

[21] 1 H. C. (1899 and 1907), Arts. 15 and 37. "As Dr. Lammasch says in his work upon international arbitration (*Die Rechtscraft internationales Schiedssprüche*, 1913, p. 37), the significance of the words 'on the basis of respect for law' have no other meaning than that 'the arbiter shall decide in accordance with equity, *ex aequo et bono*, when positive rules of law are lacking.'" Decision of the Hague Court of Arbitration in the case of *Norway* vs. *The United States*, 17 *A. J.* (1923), 362, 384.

310. **The Compromis.**—It is customary for the parties at variance to frame a special agreement called the *compromis*,[22] defining the nature and limits of the controversy and the powers of the arbiters, naming the arbiters or designating the mode of their selection,[23] formulating or indicating the rules of procedure to be followed, the rules or principles (whether of equity or International Law) which should determine the decision,[24] the language, place of meeting, etc. " Recourse to arbitration implies an engagement to submit in good faith to the award." [25]

311. **The Arbitral Clause.**—Arbitration was originally [26] purely voluntary or facultative in character, but it became

Owing to the nature of the interests involved, the mode of selection of arbiters, and the lack of definite rules or a clearly defined jurisdiction, arbitration has a semi- or quasi-judicial rather than a purely judicial character. The arbitrators are often not sufficiently judicial and independent, and sometimes they seem bent upon effecting a satisfactory compromise rather than administering judicial rules.

[22] See 1 H. C. (1907), Arts. 52–54, 58. The progress of arbitration in the United States has been considerably hampered by the insistance at times of our Senate to be consulted on each separate *compromis*. See, *e.g.* Moore, *Int. Law and Current Illusions* (1924), 85 ff., and Scott, in 2 *A. J.* (1908), 387 ff. and 624 ff.

"The Permanent Court (*i.e.* the Hague Tribunal or Court of Arbitration) is competent to settle the *compromis*, if the parties are agreed to have recourse to it for the purpose." It is similarly competent, even if the request is only made by one of the parties, in certain cases. Art. 53.

[23] The arbitrator or arbitrators most frequently selected in modern times have been sovereigns or Heads of States, simple individuals (statesmen, magistrates, jurists, etc.), or a corporate body of individuals.

On the composition and selection of the Hague Court of Arbitration, see *infra*, No. 314.

The United States has made frequent use of Mixed Commissions, consisting of both partisan and neutral elements, particularly for the settlement of claims, the tracing of boundary lines, etc. Mixed Commissions may have an administrative, diplomatic, or arbitral character.

On *Mixed Commissions*, see especially Beaucourt, *Les commissions international d'enquête* (1909), 15–47; Kamarowsky, *Le tribunal int.* (1887), 165–84; Moore, *Arbitrations* (in 6 vols.,—see index); 6 P.-Fodéré, No. 2601; 1 Scott, 216–23.

[24] Perhaps the most famous rules thus laid down were the "Three Rules of the Treaty of Washington" for the determination of the *Alabama Controversy* in 1871.

[25] 1 H. C. (1899 and 1907), Arts. 18 and 37.

[26] On the *History of Arbitration*, see *supra*, Nos. 31, 44, and 80.

The student should particularly read the note in 5 Moore, *Arbitrations*, 4821 ff. See Darby, *International Tribunals* (1904), 769 ff., for a useful digest of cases.

in a sense obligatory when States began to insert the arbitral clause (*clause compromissoire*), an *a priori* agreement to arbitrate, into treaties.[27] This was the second stage in the history of arbitration.[28]

312. **Special Treaties of Permanent Arbitration.**—Arbitration entered upon its third stage when the arbitral clause expanded into special treaties [29] of permanent arbitration in the latter part of the nineteenth century. This movement, which appears to have begun in Latin America, was given a tremendous impetus by the Hague Conferences of 1899 and 1907, and it has reached such proportions that almost all civilized States are now connected by a network of such treaties.

313. **Projects for General Treaty of Obligatory Arbitration.**—During the next and present stage in the history of arbitration we have witnessed various projects for a general treaty of obligatory arbitration. In 1890 the First Pan-American Conference adopted a project for a general

[27] The arbitral clause was not wholly unknown to the Greeks. See *supra*, No. 31.

The first modern instance of the insertion of this clause seems to have been that contained in the treaty of 1796 between the United States and Tripoli. It was vaguely included in the Treaty of Guadalupe Hidalgo (1848) between the United States and Mexico, and in a number of treaties between Latin-American States, but does not appear to have become general until the last quarter of the nineteenth century. Mérignhac, *Traité de l'arbitrage int.* (1895), 199–214. On the *Arbitral Clause*, see also 6 P.-Fodéré, Nos. 2606 ff.; and 2 Rivier, 170 ff. For lists of arbitral clauses, see La Fontaine, *Pasicrisie, Int.* (1902), X–XIV.

[28] The arbitral clause appeared: (*a*) in a special or particular form, *i.e.* limited to the treaty itself, or to certain subjects which were specifically enumerated; or (*b*) in a more general form.

[29] See Mérignhac, *op. cit.*, p. 206 n., for a list of such treaties between 1876 and 1883. A treaty of permanent arbitration was negotiated between England and the United States in 1897, but it failed to obtain the sanction of that grave-yard of good projects, the United States Senate. However, in 1908 this body approved no less than twelve arbitration treaties between the United States and France, Switzerland, Mexico, Italy, Great Britain, Norway, Portugal, Spain, Netherlands, Sweden, Japan, and Denmark. For the texts of these treaties which contained reservations respecting vital interests, independence, or honor, see Supp. to 2 *A. J.* 296–336. For a list of 77 arbitration treaties between 1900 and 1908, see 2 *A. J.* (1908), 824–26. Cf. Fried, *Die moderne Friedensbewegung* (1906), 26–27. For a very complete list of arbitration treaties between 1822 and 1905, see Moch, *Histoire sommaire de l'arbitrage* (1905), 35–40. See end of this useful volume for a series of graphic representations.

treaty of obligatory arbitration, but it failed of ratification.[30]
Various projects for limited obligatory arbitration [31] were

[30] The Conference adopted obligatory arbitration as a "principle of American International Law," and declared that the "principle of conquest is eliminated from American Public Law." All of the States represented (including the United States), except Chile, voted in favor of these declarations. Alverez, "Latin America and International Law," in 3 *A. J.* (1909), 329; and Quesada, *Arbitration in Latin America* (1907), 15–43. See Supp. to 1 *A. J.* (1907), 299, for a Treaty of Obligatory Arbitration between nine Latin-American States; and *Ibid.*, 303, for Treaty of Arbitration of Pecuniary Claims between the United States and sixteen Latin-American States.

[31] At the Hague Peace Conference of 1899, Russia proposed *inclusive* obligatory arbitration for pecuniary claims and disputes relating to the interpretation or application of about twelve different kinds of treaties. 1 Scott, 321 ff., 803 ff. A majority of States voted in favor of these proposals, which were dropped on account of the opposition of Germany. Nevertheless, the Powers reserved to themselves the right of concluding new treaties of obligatory arbitration. 1 H. C. (1899), Art. 19. There followed a perfect avalanche of arbitration treaties.

In 1907 a similar but larger list of about thirty specified subjects, based on the proposals of Portugal, was discussed. "Of the twenty-four classes voted on by the committee, only eight received a majority vote. . . . The vote in the commission resulted in thirty-three ayes and eleven noes for *some* list of classes, and thirty-one ayes and thirteen noes for the proposed list." Hull, in 2 *A. J.* (1908), 736 and n.

The Anglo-American project of *exclusive* obligatory arbitration was based on the prevailing type of treaty as concluded between France, Great Britain, the United States and other leading Powers. It provided that "differences of a legal nature and, primarily, those relating to the interpretation of treaties existing between two or more of the Contracting Nations, which may arise between them in the future and which cannot be settled by diplomatic means, shall be submitted to arbitration, on condition, however, that they do not involve the vital interests, independence, or honor of either of the said nations, and that they do not affect the interests of other nations not concerned in the dispute." (Each nation is its own judge as to whether the dispute falls within any of these of excepted categories.)

To this project there were added the eight classes of *inclusive* arbitration agreed to in committee. The whole project was adopted in commission by a vote of thirty-two against nine, with three abstentions. But since the opposition included Germany and Austria, it was dropped, much to the disgust of Mr. Choate, the head of the American delegation, who said: "The minority has been so feeble that one could almost count its number upon the fingers of a single hand."

On *Obligatory Arbitration at the Hague Conferences*, see André, *De l'arbitrage obligatoire* (1903); Higgins, 82–84; Holls, *Peace Conference at the Hague* (1900), 227–31; Hull, *The Two Hague Conferences* (1908), 297–348, and in 2 *A. J.* (1908), 731–42; Fried, *Die zweite Haager Konferenz* (1907), 39–119; * Lammasch, in 4 *A. J.* (1910), 83–94; Lémonon, *La seconde conférence de la paix* (1908), 121–87; 1 Nippold, *Die zweite Haager Friedens-Konferenz* (1908), §§ 5–8; *Parl. Papers*, Misc. No. 4 (1908), 351–423; "Report of Baron Guillaume," in 1 *Actes et doc. de la deux. confer.*, 455–552; * 1 Scott, ch. 7, and, *American Addresses at the Hague* (1910), 34–68; Stoika, *L'arbitrage obligatoire* (1909), chs. 2–3.

proposed at the Hague Conferences of 1899 and 1907; but they were defeated, owing mainly to the opposition of Germany. In its Final Act, the Conference of 1907 declared that it was " unanimous: (1) In admitting the principle of compulsory arbitration. (2) In declaring that certain disputes, in particular those relating to the interpretation of treaties and application of the provisions of international agreements, may be submitted to compulsory arbitration without any restriction." [32]

But the Conference of 1907 went one step beyond this platonic declaration. It practically prescribed obligatory arbitration in one class of cases, viz., the collection of contract debts, though under such reservations and with such failures of ratification as to make it a very doubtful rule of International Law.[33]

313a. The League of Nations and Arbitration.—As stated above (No. 308, p. 465), the Members of the League have agreed that they will submit any dispute likely to lead to a rupture either to arbitration or judicial settlement, or to inquiry by the Council, and in case of arbitration or judicial decision not to resort to war until three months after the award by the arbitrators which " shall be made within a reasonable time."

They further agreed to submit the whole subject-matter of any dispute " which they recognize as suitable for submission to arbitration or judicial settlement," and declared the following classes of disputes among those that are generally suitable to arbitration:

" Disputes as to the interpretation of a treaty, as to any question of International Law, as to the existence of any fact which if established would constitute a breach of international obligation, or as to the extent and nature of the reparation to be made for any such breach."

They also agreed that " they will carry out in full good faith any award or decision that may be rendered, and that they will not resort to war against a Member of the League which complies therewith. In the event of any failure to

---

[32] F. A. (Final Act, 1907), Higgins, 67; or 2 Scott, 287.

[33] 2 H. C. (1907), Art. 1. See *supra*, No. 157.

For references on the *Porter Resolution*, see *supra*, p. 263 n.; on the *Calvo and Drago Doctrines*, see *supra*, p. 255 n.

carry out such award or decision, the Council shall prepose what steps should be taken to give effect thereto." [34]

314. The So-called Permanent Court of Arbitration at The Hague.—The idea of a permanent International Court or Tribunal had long been a favorite theme with publicists.[35] It was at last partially realized in 1899, and some further improvements in its organization and procedure were effected in 1907.

The Convention for the Pacific Settlement of International Disputes of 1907 declares:

" With the object of facilitating an immediate recourse to arbitration for international differences, which it has not been possible to settle by diplomacy, the *Contracting*

[34] Arts. 12 and 13 of the *Covenant*. The Geneva Protocol of Arbitration, Security, and Disarmament for the Pacific Settlement of International Disputes (1924) was based on the idea of securing a reduction of armaments and preventing wars of aggression by substituting compulsory arbitration and judicial settlement for war as a last resort after the failure of other means, such as diplomacy, mediation or conciliation, and voluntary arbitration.

In respect to arbitration, the Protocol provided (see Art. 4 which is too extensive and complicated for reproduction here) that, failing settlement by the Council of the League in accordance with Art. 15 of the Covenant (see *infra*, pp. 514–16), it (the Council) (1) shall endeavor to persuade the parties to the dispute to submit the dispute to judicial settlement or voluntary arbitration; (2) failing such agreement, there shall, at the request of at least one of the parties, be constituted a Committee of Arbitrators; (3) in case there is no request for arbitration and the Council is unable to agree upon a unanimous report, it (the Council) shall itself determine the composition, powers and procedure of the Committee of Arbitrators.

It should be noted that the above scheme applies particularly to non-justiceable disputes, provision having been made (in Art. 3 of the Protocol) for the submission of legal disputes to the Permanent Court of International Justice.

The Protocol was recommended by forty-seven States represented in the Fifth Assembly of the League of Nations which met at Geneva in Sept., 1924 and signed by eighteen of them, including France. It failed, however, of ratification, owing mainly to the opposition of the Tory Government of England and several of the British Dominions, particularly Canada. Fear of the opposition of the United States appears to have been one of the reasons for rejection.

On the *Geneva Protocol*, cf. *supra*, pp. 150–51. For references, see *supra*, p. 150 n.

For compulsory arbitration as provided by the Locarno Pact, see *supra*,

[35] For a history and development of this idea, see especially the remarkable works of Kamarowsky, *Le tribunal int.* (1887); Mérignhac, *L'arbitrage int.* (1895); and Descamps, in 28 *R. D. I.* (1896), 5–75. The latter's "Essai sur l'organization de l'arbitrage international" appears to have made a particularly favorable impression on the Conference of 1899 among the documents of which it lies incorporated.

Powers undertake to *maintain the Permanent Court of Arbitration, as established by the First Peace Conference*, accessible at all times, and acting, unless otherwise stipulated by the parties, in accordance with the rules of procedure inserted in the present Convention. The Permanent Court is competent for all arbitration cases, unless the parties agree to institute a special Tribunal." [36]

The following is the mode prescribed for the selection of arbitrators:

" Each Contracting Power selects four persons at the most, of known competency in questions of International Law, of highest moral reputation, and disposed to accept the duties of arbitrator. The persons thus selected are inscribed, as members of the Court, in a list which shall be notified to all the Contracting Powers by the Bureau.[37] . . . The members of the Court are appointed for a term of six years. Their appointments are renewable." [38]

When the Contracting Powers desire to have recourse to the so-called Permanent Court for the settlement of a particular difference, they must choose arbitrators from this list.[39]

" Failing the agreement of the parties on the composition of the Arbitration Tribunal, the following course shall be pursued:

" Each party appoints two arbitrators, *of whom one only can be its national or chosen from among the persons who have been selected by it as members of the Permanent Court.* These arbitrators together choose an umpire. If the votes are equally divided, the choice of the umpire is intrusted to a

[36] 1 H. C. (1907), Arts. 41 and 42. Cf. 1 H. C. (1899), Arts. 20 and 21. The phrase set in *italics* was added in 1907.

[37] An *International Bureau* was created to serve as registry or record office for the Court. "It is the channel for communications relative to the meetings of the Court; it has charge of the archives and conducts all the administrative business. . . ." 1 H. C. (1907), Art. 43. See also Arts. 46–50, and 63.

"The *Permanent Administrative Council*, composed of the diplomatic representatives of the Contracting Powers accredited to the Hague and of the Netherland Minister for Foreign Affairs, who acts as President, is charged with the direction and control of the International Bureau." *Ibid.*, Art. 49.

[38] 1 H. C. (1899), Art. 44. Cf. 1 H. C. (1899), Art. 23.

"The members of the tribunal, in the exercise of their duties and out of their own country, enjoy diplomatic privileges and immunities." 1 H. C. (1899 and 1907), Arts. 26 and 46.

[39] For a list of members of the Court in 1910, see Supp. to 4 *A. J.*, 264–78.

third Power, selected by agreement between the parties. If an agreement is not arrived at on this subject, each party selects a different Power, and the choice of the umpire is made in concert by the Powers thus selected.

" *If, within two months' time, these two Powers cannot come to an agreement, each of them presents two candidates taken from the list of members of the Permanent Court, exclusive of the members' selected by the parties and not being nationals of either of them. Which of the candidates thus presented shall be umpire is determined by lot.*[40]

315. **The Hague Code of Procedure.**—The Hague Conference of 1899 also formulated quite an elaborate code of procedure, modeled largely on that adopted by the Institute of International Law in 1875,[41] consisting of twenty-eight articles. It was revised and considerably enlarged in 1907,[42] and a short code for arbitration by a more summary pro-

[40] 1 H. C. (1907), Art. 45. The *italicized* portions of this article were added in 1907. Cf. 1 H. C. (1899), Art. 24.

[41] See Scott, *Resolutions of the Institute of Int. Law* (1916), 1–7.

[42] 1 H. C. (1907), Arts. 51–85. Cf. 1 H. C. (1899), Arts. 30–57.

"Unless the *compromis* has specified the languages to be used, the question shall be decided by the Tribunal." Art. 61.

"Art. 37 of the Convention of 1899 left it to the absolute discretion of the parties to employ such agents and counsel as they wished. This freedom seems to have been abused by some of the parties in employing as counsel members of the Hague Tribunal itself, thus inviting severe criticism in some quarters. In view of this danger, the German amendment to Article 62 was adopted: ' The members of the Permanent Court may not act as agents, counsel, or advocates except on behalf of the Power which appointed them members of the Court.'" Hershey, in 2 *A. J.* (1908), 45.

This article is still objectionable as it stands. Members of the Court should have been excluded altogether from service as counsel, as the United States proposed. 1 Scott, 294.

Discussions are to be "public, if it be so decided by the Tribunal, with the assent of the parties." Art. 66.

"The deliberations of the Tribunal take place in private and the *proceedings remain secret*. All questions are decided by a majority of the members of the Tribunal. The award must state the reasons on which it is based." Arts. 78 and 79. "Each party pays its own expenses and an equal share of those of the Tribunal." Art. 85.

On the *Convention for the Pacific Settlement of International Disputes*, see 1 *Actes et doc. de la deux. confér.*, 399–454; Barclay, *Problems of Int. Practice and Diplomacy* (1907), 9–45, 191; Descamps, in 32 *R. D. I.* (1900), 117, 270, 353, 498; Hershey, in 2 *A. J.* (1908), 29–49; * Higgins, 95–179; Holls, *The Peace Conference* (1900), ch. 5; Hull, *The Two Hague Conferences* (1908), 267 ff.; Lémonon, *La seconde conference* (1908) 69 ff.; 1 *Die Haager Friedenskonferenz* (1905); Nys, in 8 *R. D. I.* (2d series, 1906), 5 ff.; 2 Oppenheim, §§ 19–25; *Parl. Papers*, Misc. No. 4 (1908), 302–51; * 1 Scott, ch. 6.

cedure added.[43] Thus, the nations are freed from the necessity of framing rules of procedure for each and every controversy.

316. Defects of the Hague Tribunal or Court of Arbitration.

—Though this so-called Permanent Court of Arbitration was a step in advance, its constitution and organization are obviously very defective. In the first place it is not even a Court, but rather a panel or list of judges. The so-called Court is wanting in cohesion, continuity, and independence. Litigation is slow and expensive. During the period between the meeting of the two Hague Conferences of 1899 and 1907, the Hague Tribunal or Court of Arbitration was only called into existence upon four occasions.[44] The formation of a system of international jurisprudence by such means is manifestly impossible.

[43] 1 H. C. (1907), Arts. 86–90. "Each of the parties at variance appoints an arbitrator. The two arbitrators thus selected choose an umpire. . . . " Art. 87. This procedure is designed to aid in the solution of disputes of a special or technical character. It is more simple, rapid and inexpensive.

[44] 1. The first case was that of the *Pious Fund of the Californias* (1902). It supports the important principle of *res judicata* in public law. For the protocol and text of the award, see 2 *A. J.* (1908), 893–902. See also 1 Cobbett, 24–28.

2. The *Claims* v. *Venezuela* (1904) for preferential treatment on the part of Great Britain, Germany, and Italy, who had blockaded Venezuelan ports and thus obtained a recognition of their claims. The Tribunal decided in favor of these claimants over against those who had not used force, thus establishing an unfortunate precedent in favor of the use of force in such cases. The decision is bad both in law and morals. For the protocols and text of this award, see 2 *A. J.* (1908), 902–11. See also Mallarmé, in 13 *R. D. I. P.* (1906), 423 ff.

3. The *Japanese House Tax*. It was held that these leases exempt the lands and all buildings constructed on them from "all imposts, taxes, charges, contributions, or conditions whatsoever other than those expressly stipulated in the leases in question." 2 *A. J.* (1908), 911–21.

4. The *Muscat Dhows Case* (1905), which is relatively unimportant. See 2 *A. J.* (1908), 923 ff.

Among the most important of the ten cases decided by the Hague Tribunal between 1907 and 1915 were the * *North Atlantic Coast Fisheries Case*; that of the *Orinoco Steamship Co*; the *Russian Indemnity*; and the *Carthage Case between France and Italy*. For reports of the cases decided by the Hague Tribunal, see Scott, *Hague Ct. Rep.* (1916); and Wilson, *The Hague Arbitration Cases* (1915).

One of the most recent cases (the 17th) decided by the old Hague Court of Arbitration is that of the *Norway* vs. *United States Arbitration* (1922) of claims to compensation of Norwegian citizens for the seizure of ships under construction in the United States during the World War. The decision went against the United States which paid the Norwegian Government the sum of $12,239,852.47 on Feb. 16, 1923. For the decision of the Hague Court and

317. **The Proposed Court of Arbitral Justice.**—To remedy these defects and provide the nations with a real Permanent Court for the settlement of judicial disputes, the second Hague Conference, mainly through the efforts of the American delegation, attempted to create a so-called " Court of Arbitral Justice." But their labors were only partially successful. A Draft Convention providing for the organization, jurisdiction, and procedure of such a Court was elaborated and readily adopted in plenary session,[45] but the Conference was unable to agree upon a mode of selection for the appointment of judges.[46]

This Project was annexed to the following wish expressed by the Conference:

" The Conference calls the attention of the Signatory Powers to the advisability of adopting the annexed draft

editorial comment (including a letter from Sec'y Hughes criticising the award), see 17 *A. J.* (1923), 362 ff. and 287 ff. See also Garner, note in *Brit. Yr. Bk.* (1923–24), 159–62; and Smith, in 16 *A. J.* (1922), 81–84.

[45] Upon the final vote, there were thirty-six yeas and six abstentions. A number of States made reservations to the effect that the principle of the legal equality of States be recognized in the composition of the Court. Higgins, 517.

[46] There were three methods of selection proposed: (1) A system of rotation practically identical with that adopted for the International Prize Court (see *infra*, p. 740 n.). This plan was proposed and ably defended by Messrs. Choate and Scott of the American delegations. According to the revised American project, the judges (seventeen in number) were to represent the leading nations, main languages, and the various judicial systems of the world. The eight leading nations or World Powers (Great Britain, the United States, Germany, Russia, Japan, France, Austria-Hungary, and Italy) were to be represented by judges sitting during their full term of appointment for twelve years, the judges from the lesser States sitting in rotation for periods varying from one to ten years. See Table, in 1 Scott, 823–25. This plan encountered the unyielding opposition of the smaller States, headed by their vigorous champion, M. Barbosa, head of the Brazilian delegation.

(2) A system based upon the idea of the absolute equality of States proposed by Brazil. According to this project (which was not seriously considered), there were to be as many judges as there are States, *i.e.* forty-six judges divided into three groups, each group to sit by rotation during a period of three years.

(3) A system of election proposed by the United States. According to this plan, each State was to select a candidate whose name should be sent in to the International Bureau at the Hague. This Bureau should then transmit a list of the forty-six persons thus designated to the Minister of Foreign Affairs of each country, with the request that he check the names of fifteen of the candidates. Those receiving the highest number of votes were to form the Court during a period of twelve years. This system, which would appear to meet the tests both of equality and sovereignty, was, however, objectionable to the smaller as well as to the larger States.

For a discussion of these various systems, see especially 2 Scott, 457–59.

Convention for the creation of a Judicial Arbitration Court, and of bringing it into force as soon as an agreement has been reached respecting the selection of the judges and the constitution of the Court." [47]

The Proposed Judicial Arbitration Court was to be "composed of judges representing the various judicial systems of the world, and capable of insuring continuity in arbitral jurisprudence." The judges and deputy judges were to be "chosen from persons of the highest moral reputation, and all fulfilling conditions qualifying them, in their respective countries, to occupy high legal posts, or be jurists of recognized competence in matters of International Law." They were to be appointed for a term of twelve years.[48]

"The Court annually nominates three judges to form a special Delegation and three more to replace them if the former are unable to act." This election was to be by ballot and plurality vote.[49]

The Delegation was declared competent: (1) To decide all cases of arbitration submitted to it. (2) To perform the functions of a Commission of Inquiry. (3) To settle the *compromis* if the parties so agree (or even at the request of one of the parties in certain cases).[50]

[47] F. A. (Final Act) of H. C. (1907), in Higgins, 67–69 or 2 Scott, 289. On Oct. 18, 1900, Secretary Knox suggested to the Powers that the International Prize court be invested with the functions of a Court of Arbitral Justice.

[48] D. C. (Draft Convention) of H. C. (1907), Arts. 1–3. See Higgins, 498 ff.; 2 Scott, 291 ff.; or Whittuck, *op. cit.*, 220 ff.

It should be especially noted that the proposed Court was to be "without derogation" to the so-called Permanent Court of Arbitration. It appears to have been the idea of its promoters that the new Court, "though competent to deal with all cases submitted to it" (Art. 17), would be particularly adapted to the trial of purely *judicial* disputes, and that the older Hague Tribunal might serve for the settlement of political differences capable of such settlement.

[49] D. C. Art. 6. This idea of a Delegation was proposed in Russia.

[50] D. C., Arts. 17–19. Cf. 1 H. C. (1907), Arts. 52–54. "Each of the parties concerned has the right to nominate a judge of the Court to take part, with power to vote, in the examination of the case submitted to the Delegation. If the Delegation acts as a Commission of Inquiry, this task may be intrusted to persons other than the judges of the Court." Art. 20.

For rules of procedure, see Arts. 22–30. In general, the rules of 1 H. C. were to be followed. See *supra*, No. 315.

On the proposed *Court of Arbitral Justice*, see 1 and 2 *Actes et doc. de la deux.*

318. The Finality of the Award in Arbitration.—It is generally agreed that an arbitral award, properly made and duly pronounced, is final and binding, unless otherwise stipulated in the agreement (*compromis*).[51] But there are certain conditions under which an arbitral verdict is not binding, *e.g.* if the arbitrators have been bribed or coerced, if they have exceeded their instructions, or in case of fraud.[52]

319. The Scope of Arbitration.—There has been much controversy as to the possible scope of arbitration. Theoretically this method is applicable to any international difference, but practically it is much easier of application in the settlement of disputes of a legal nature.[53]

confér. (Hague, 1908), 332–35, 347–98, 144–61, 309–25, 331–51, 596–630, 1031–1070; Bustamente, *The World Court* (1925), ch. 4; Fried, *Die zweite Haager Konferenz* (1907), 98–119; Higgins, 498–517; Hull, *The Two Hague Conferences* (1908), 410–26; Lémonon, *La seconde conférence* (1908), 220–79; Myers, in 10 *A. J.* (1916), 270–311; Nippold, *Die zweite Haager Friedens Konferenz* 1; Teil, *Das Prozessrecht* (1908), § 9; * Scott, ch. 9, in 2 *A. J.* (1908), 772–810, and in *American Addresses at Second Hague Conference* (1910), 77–111.

[51] "The award, duly pronounced and notified to the agents of the parties, settles the dispute definitely and without appeal. Any dispute arising between the parties as to the interpretation and execution of the award shall, in default of agreement to the contrary, be submitted to the decision of the Tribunal which pronounced it. The parties may in the *compromis* reserve the right to demand the revision of the award." 1 H. C. (1907), Arts. 81–83. See Art. 83 for the conditions under which the demand for a revision of the award may be made.

"An arbitral decision may be disregarded in the following cases: viz. when the tribunal has clearly exceeded the powers given it by the instrument of submission, when it is guilty of an open denial of justice, when its award is proved to have been obtained by fraud or corruption, and when the terms of the award are equivocal." Hall, § 119, p. 420.

In the case of *La Ninfa* (1896), 75 Fed. 513, and Scott, *Cases*, (ed. of 1902), 443, 447, it was held that an arbitral award "is to be construed as a treaty which has become final. A treaty when accepted and agreed to, becomes the supreme law of the land. It binds courts as much as an Act of Congress."

[52] There have been comparatively few cases in which arbitral awards have been set aside or even seriously questioned. For some instances of improper awards, see Clarke, in 1 *A. J.* (1907), 361 ff. See also 7 Moore, *Digest*, §§ 1081–83. On "Sanctions of Int. Arbitration," see Dumas, in 5 *A. J.* (1911), 934–57.

[53] This view obtained official recognition at The Hague Conferences. "In questions of a legal nature, and especially in the interpretation or application of International Conventions, arbitration is recognized by the Contracting Powers as the most effective, and, at the same time, the most equitable means of settling disputes which diplomacy has failed to settle. *Consequently, it would be desirable that, in disputes regarding the above-mentioned questions, the Contracting Powers should, if the case arise, have recourse to arbitration, in so far*

It has been customary, in treaties of arbitration, to exlude questions involving national honor,[54] vital interests,[55] or independence,[56] as also questions affecting the interests of third Powers.[57] The States themselves are of course the

as circumstances permit." 1 H. C. (1907), Art. 38. The *italicized* part of this article was added in 1907.

[54] There is a growing sentiment in favor of admitting so-called questions of "honor" to arbitration. Indeed, there is no sound reason for excluding them. Many of them are of a nature particularly susceptible of arbitration when diplomacy or mediation fails. On national honor, see an interesting little volume by Perla, entitled *What is National Honor?* (1918). See particularly ch. 3 containing a list of 135 citations illustrating different views of national honor. But Perla fails to distinguish clearly "national honor" which involves prestige, from "vital interests" which are essentially political and economic in their nature. On "national honor" and "vital interests" see especially Barclay, *New Methods of Adjusting Int. Disputes* (1917), ch. 6; Dickinson, *Int. Anarchy* (1926), 32–37; and Veblen, *The Nature of Peace* (1917), 27–30.

[55] The phrase "vital interests" is nowhere adequately explained. But the fact that it is vague does not prove that the difficulty is not a real one. It of course refers to questions of a far-reaching political, economic, or social character. Illustrations may be found in the various applications of the Monroe Doctrine, or in a study of such wars as those between Russia and Japan, and Spain and the United States. Fundamental racial differences may also be involved.

[56] Mérignhac (*De l'arbitrage int.*, 1895, Nos. 188–93) points out that the exclusion of questions relating to integrity and independence is not in the interest of the smaller States. He only admits exceptions to the practicability of arbitration in two cases: in case of differences between a civilized and a barbarous nation, and between an established government and insurgents.

[57] A typical treaty is that between France and the United States (1908). "Differences which may arise of a legal nature, or relating to the interpretation of treaties existing between the two Contracting Parties, and which it may not have been possible to settle by diplomacy, shall be referred to the Permanent Court of Arbitration at The Hague by the Convention of July 29, 1899, *provided*, nevertheless, they do not affect the vital interests, the independence, or the honor of the two Contracting States, and do not concern the interests of third parties." Art. 1. For text, see 2 Supp. to 2 *A. J.* (1908), 299. For nine such treaties, see *Ibid.*, 296–336. During the latter part of 1923, the United States renewed such belated arbitration treaties with Great Britain, France, Japan, Portugal and Norway.

It appears that "Great Britain is a party to some 200 arbitration treaties, but all have the reservation that they shall not apply to issues affecting the 'vital interest' or the 'national honor' of the country. This reservation was recently abandoned by France in a treaty with Switzerland." *Manchester Guardian* (weekly), for Oct. 2, 1925, pp. 261 and 269.

On "Restrictive Clauses in Int. Arbitration Treaties," see Wehberg and Cavalcanti, in 7 and 8 *A. J.* (1913 and 1914), 300–14 and 723–37 respectively.

A very interesting attempt to solve the difficulties encountered by the "honor" and "vital interests" problems was that of the *Taft-Knox Treaty*, negotiated in 1911 between Great Britain and the United States, but mutilated by our Senate in 1912. A similar treaty was negotiated with France.

judges as to whether the dispute falls within any of these categories. A few of the smaller States have agreed to arbitrate *all* their differences.[58]

"All differences hereafter arising between the High Contracting Parties, which it has not been possible to adjust by diplomacy, relating to international matters in which the High Contracting Parties are concerned by virtue of a *claim of right* made by one against the other, under treaty or otherwise, and which are *justiceable* in their nature by reason of being susceptible of decision by the *application of the principles of law and equity*, shall be submitted to the Permanent Court of Arbitration established at The Hague by the Convention of October 18, 1907, or to some other arbitral tribunal, as may be decided in each case by special agreement, which special agreement shall provide for the organization of such tribunal if necessary, define the scope of the powers of the arbitrators, the question or questions at issue, and settle the terms of reference and the procedure thereunder (Art. I, par. 1). . . .

"The High Contracting Parties further agree to institute, as occasion arises, and as hereinafter provided, a *Joint High Commission of Inquiry*, to which, upon the request of either party, shall be referred, for impartial and conscientious investigation, any controversy between the parties within the scope of Article I, before such controversy has been submitted to arbitration, and also any other controversy hereafter arising between them, even if they are not agreed that it falls within the scope of Article I; *provided, however, that such reference may be postponed until the expiration of one year after the date of the formal request therefor*, in order to afford an opportunity for diplomatic discussion and adjustment of the question in controversy, if either party desires such postponement.

"Whenever a question or matter of difference is referred to the Joint High Commission of Inquiry, as herein provided, each of the High Contracting Parties shall designate three of its nationals to act as members of the Commission of Inquiry for the purpose of such reference; or the Commission may be otherwise constituted in any particular case by the terms of reference, the membership of the Commission and the terms of reference to be determined in each case by an exchange of notes (Art. II, par. 1). . . .

"The Joint High Commission of Inquiry, instituted in each case as provided for in Article II, is authorized to examine into and report upon the particular questions or matters referred to it, for the purpose of facilitating the solution of disputes by elucidating the facts, and to define the issues presented by such questions, and also to include in its report such recommendations and conclusions as may be appropriate.

"The reports of the Commission shall not be regarded as decisions of the questions or matters so submitted either of the facts or on the law, and shall in no way have the character of an arbitral award.

"It is further agreed, however, that in cases in which the parties disagree as to whether or not a difference is subject to arbitration under Article I of this treaty, that question shall be submitted to the Joint High Commission of Inquiry; and if all or all but one of the Commission agree and report that such difference is within the scope of Article I; it shall be referred to arbitration in accordance with the provisions of the treaty (Art. III)."

For the full text of this attempt to minimize the danger of war, see Supp. to 5 *A. J.* (1911), 253 ff. For editorial comment, see 6 *A. J.* (1912), 167 ff. See also Dennis, in 6 *A. J.* (1912), 614 ff.

[58] *E.g.* Denmark and Holland. Brazil and the Argentine Republic have

320. **Is a State under an Obligation to Arbitrate?**—Aside from treaty stipulations, there is, in general, no legal obligation resting upon States to arbitrate their differences.[59] But they are morally bound to employ every possible amicable mode of redress of grievances before resorting to the use of force, and they are probably legally bound to have recourse to negotiation.[60]

320a. (VI) **Judicial Settlement and The Permanent Court of International Justice.**—The main difference between arbitration and judicial settlement seems to be that whereas " international arbitration has for its object the settlement of differences between States by judges of their choice," [61] in judicial settlement the parties in controversy

agreed to submit to arbitration all controversies in so far as they "do not turn upon questions involving constitutional rules of the one or the other of the two countries." Supp. to 3 *A. J.* (1910), 1–4, Art. I.

Norway and Sweden have agreed to submit to The Hague Court questions as to whether the disputes involve vital interests. In 1902 the Argentine Republic and Chile bound themselves to submit all controversies except those affecting the Constitution of either country. 1 *Ibid.*, 290.

[59] There would seem to be an exception in case of a claim for the collection of contract debts. But only the creditor State is bound to offer arbitration by the terms of the Porter Convention on this subject. The debtor State has the alternative of acceptance or refusal. In the latter case, the creditor nation may employ force. 2 H. C. (1907), Art. 1. Cf. *supra*, pp. 262–63 and notes.

[60] So, at least, thinks Oppenheim, II, § 3. And this view appears to be borne out by international practice. The so-called *duty* article of the Convention of 1899 declared: "The Signatory Powers consider it their duty, if a serious dispute threatens to break out between two or more of them to remind these latter that the Permanent Court is open to them. . . ." The Conference of 1907 added: "In case of a dispute between two Powers, one of them may always address to the International Bureau a note containing a declaration that it would be ready to submit the dispute to arbitration. The Bureau must at once inform the other Power of the declaration." 1 H. C. (1899 and 1907), Arts. 27 and 48.

It has been well said that this article provides for a sort of appeal to the Hague Tribunal, but it does not make arbitration in any sense obligatory. For discussion and a very interesting comment by Baron d'Estournelles de Constant, see Hershey, in 2 *A. J.* (1908), 42–43.

In this connection, it might be well to take into account the obligatory character of the arbitration provided for in the *Locarno Pact* of 1925. See *supra*, pp. 151–54. It should also be noted that, aside from those negotiated by the United States and some by Great Britain, the important exceptions of "honor" and "vital interests" have been omitted in most recent arbitration treaties. This in itself represents an enormous advance. For recent progress in arbitration see a pamphlet published by the W. P. F. entitled "Arbitration and the United States."

[61] 1 H. C. (1899 and 1907), Arts. 15 and 37.

submit their dispute to a permanent court or to judges who are not selected by them.

Since 1899 there has been a growing dissatisfaction with the old Hague Court of Arbitration and in 1907 an attempt had been made to create a real permanent Court—the so-called Court of Arbitral Justice—which failed owing to the inability of the States represented to agree upon a method of selecting the judges.[62]

The Covenant of the League of Nations provided (in Article 14) that " the Council shall formulate and submit to the Members of the League for adoption plans for the establishment of a Permanent Court of International Justice. The Court shall be competent to hear and determine any dispute of an international character which the parties thereto submit to it. The Court may also give an advisory opinion [63] upon any dispute or question referred to it by the Council or by the Assembly."

The Jurisdiction of the Court Voluntary.—In order to give effect to this mandate, the Council of the League appointed a Committee of Jurists which sat at The Hague during June and July, 1920 and formulated a plan by which the Court, without any special agreement (or *compromis*), was to have jurisdiction of cases of a legal nature falling

---

[62] See *supra*, No. 317.

[63] The majority of the judgments (using the word "judgment" in a broad or non-technical sense) of the Court of International Justice have thus far been in the form of advisory opinions which are looked upon askance in some quarters. But in giving these "opinions" to the Council, the Court seems to be performing a very useful and even necessary function. In one case—that of the dispute between Russia and Finland over the autonomy of Eastern Carelia—the Court refused to give an advisory opinion on the ground that Russia, a non-member of the League of Nations, had expressly repudiated any attempted interference in this matter by the League. It held that this would be a violation of the independence of State which is a fundamental principle of International Law.

The advisory opinions of the Court appear to have a judicial character and, with due deference to the contrary view of Judge Moore, in giving them the Court seems to be performing a judicial function.

On *Advisory Opinions*, see especially: Bustamente, *The World Court* (1925), ch. 14; Hudson, *The Permanent Court of Int. Justice* (1925), 80–86, 136–59; Kellor and Hatvany, *U. S. Senate and Int. Court* (1925), chs. 10–11; and Moore's *Memorandum on Advisory Opinions*, in *Publications of the Court*, Series D, No. 2. See also *Rules of the Court*, Arts. 71–74 relating to advisory opinions. Judge Moore seems to have modified his views somewhat in *Int. Law and Current Illusions* (1924), 114–15.

within the four categories enumerated in Article 13 of the Covenant.[64]   Owing to objections made in the Council by Great Britain, France and Italy, the Statute for the establishment of the Permanent Court which was finally approved by the Assembly of the League of Nations on December 13, 1920 merely provides (Article 36) that " the jurisdiction of the Court comprises all cases which the parties refer to it and all matters specially provided for in Treaties and Conventions in force." [65]   Thus for compulsory jurisdiction in these cases there was substituted a purely voluntary jurisdiction.[66]

The Election of the Judges.—As indicated above (No. 317), the Draft Convention for the Court of Arbitral Justice proposed by the Second Hague Conference of 1907 failed of adoption because the Conference was unable to agree upon a mode of selection of the judges.   An ingenius suggestion

[64] Cf. *supra*, p. 470.   These are: (1) the interpretation of a treaty; (2) any question of International Law; (3) the existence of any fact which, if established, would constitute a breach of an international obligation; and (4) the nature or extent of the reparation to be made for the breach of an international obligation.   Art. 13, parag. 2 of the Covenant.

[65] But Art. 36 of the Statute further provides for what is known as the "Optional Clause" attached to a separate Protocol or treaty.   "Any Power may declare that it recognizes as compulsory, *ipso facto* and without any special agreement, as regards any other Power accepting the same obligation, the jurisdiction of the Court in all or any of the categories above enumerated."

Art. 36 also contained the important provision that "in the event of a dispute as to whether the Court has jurisdiction, the matter shall be settled by the decision of the Court."

The Optional Clause had, on Dec. 1, 1924, been signed by 23 States, including France, China and Brazil which were the most important signatories in respect to size.   The ratifications numbered 15.   But the adherence of France was contingent on the entrance into force of the Geneva Protocol (see *supra*, p. 471 n.) which was rejected by Great Britain.

On the *Optional Clause*, see particularly Hudson, *op. cit.*, (see index.)   For the text of the Optional Clause and a list of the States that have signed it, see *Ibid.*, 335–39.

[66] The Court may in a sense be said to have compulsory jurisdiction conferred upon it by treaty, not merely for those States that have signed and ratified the Optional Clause, but for the Signatories of the Paris Peace Treaties which confer on the new Court jurisdiction respecting ports, waterways and railways, etc.   The special treaties with Poland, etc., for the protection of minorities (cf. *supra*, p. 142 n.) also give the Court a certain obligatory jurisdiction.   For these and other instances, see Bustamente, *op. cit.*, 208–18; Fachiri, *Permanent Court of Int. Justice* (1925), 71–84; Hudson, *op. cit.*, 20–21, 40–43, 119–23, 204, 221–22, 235–36; and Kellor and Hatvany, *op. cit.*, ch. 8.   See also a publication by the Court (series D, No. 4) containing "Extracts from International Agreements affecting the Jurisdiction of the Court" (1924).

by Ex-Secretary Root enabled the Committee of Jurists of which he was a distinguished member to hit upon a plan for the election of judges which proved highly satisfactory. He suggested that inasmuch as there was a preponderance of the Great Powers in the Council [67] and of smaller Powers in the Assembly of the League,[68] a solution of the baffling problem might possibly be found in the election of judges by the concurrent vote of the Assembly and the Council.

Accordingly, a scheme was devised that is too complicated for textual reproduction here, but which has thus far worked admirably.[69]

Composition of the Court.—The Permanent Court of International Justice [70] consists of fifteen members—eleven judges and four deputy-judges.[71] The members of the Court are elected for nine years and may be re-elected. " The ordinary Members of the Court may not exercise any

[67] This is no longer the case, as far as actual representation is concerned, since the decision of the Council of the League of Nations in Sept., 1922 to increase the non-permanent members from four to six—an action approved by the third Assembly. In 1926 the number of non-permanent members of the council was increased to nine. See *infra*, p. 501 and notes.

[68] For the argument of Ex-Sec'y. Root on this point, see 15 *A. J.* (1921), 2–6.

[69] The judges are elected by the concurrent vote of the Council and the Assembly, acting separately, from a list of candidates nominated by the various national groups of members of the older Hague Court of Arbitration. For the exact process, see *Statute* of the Court, Arts. 4–12. The text of the Statute may be found, *e.g.* in Bustamente, *op. cit.*, 353 ff.; Hudson, *op. cit.*, 340 ff.; Moore, *op. cit.*, 148 ff.; or Supp. to 17 *A. J.* (1923), 57 ff.

The results of the first election showed that the judges elected fully met the qualifications set by the Statute (Art. 2) that the Court "shall be composed of a body of independent judges, *elected regardless of their nationality* from amongst persons of high moral character, who possess the qualifications required in the respective countries for appointment to the highest judicial offices, or are jurisconsults of recognized competence in International Law."

It is also declared that "the whole body should represent the main forms of civilization and the principal legal systems of the world" (Art. 9).

For lists of the judges elected, with some description of their qualifications, see Hudson, *op. cit.*, 366–68; and Moore, *op. cit.*, 105–08.

[70] It should be explained that this Court is in addition to the Court of Arbitration organized under the Hague Conventions of 1899 and 1907 and to the special Tribunals of Arbitration to which States are always at liberty to submit their dispute for settlement" (Art. 1 of the *Statute*).

[71] "The number of judges and deputy-judges may hereafter be increased by the Assembly, upon the proposal of the Council of the League of Nations, to a total of fifteen judges and six deputy-judges" (Art. 3). The deputy-judges are substitutes for absent judges.

political or administrative function." [72]   " No member of
the Court can act as agent, consul or advocate in any case of
an international nature." [73]   " Judges of the nationality of
each contesting party shall retain their right to sit in the
case before the Court." [74]

The Court shall sit at The Hague at least once a year, but
the President of the Court may summon an extraordinary
session whenever necessary. Nine judges constitute a
quorum sufficient to constitute the Court.[75] " The expenses of the Court shall be borne by the League of
Nations." [76]

Competence of the Court.—" Only States [77] or Members

[72] Art. 16. "This provision does not apply to the deputy-judges except
when performing their duties on the Court."

[73] "This provision only applies to the deputy-judges as regards cases in
which they are called upon to exercise their functions in the Court."

"In interpreting the provision of the Statute forbidding the judges to act as
counsel 'in any case of an international nature, or to exercise any political or
administrative function,' the Court held that the political function exercised
by Viscount Finley as a member of the House of Lords, and by Mr. Altamira
as a senator, did not fall within this inhibition."   Moore, *op. cit.*, 116.

"No member may participate in any case in which he has previously taken
an active part, as agent, counsel or advocate for one of the contesting parties as
a Member of a national or international Court, or of a commission of enquiry
or in any other capacity" (Art. 17).

"A member of the Court cannot be dismissed unless, in the unanimous
opinion of the other members, he has ceased to fulfill the required conditions,"
(Art. 18).

[74] But if the Court includes upon the bench a judge of one of the parties only
or if the Court includes no judge of the nationality of the contesting parties,
provision is made for selection of national judges.   Art. 31 of the *Statute* and
Art. 4 of the *Rules of Court*.   For these *Rules*, see Bustamente, *op. cit.*, 365 ff.;
Hudson, *op. cit.*, 351 ff.; Moore, *op. cit.*, 161 ff.; or Supp. to 16 *A. J.* (1922),
173 ff.

[75] Arts. 22, 23 and 25.

[76] Art. 33.   For information regarding the compensation of judges, see
Moore, *op. cit.*, 110.

Arts. 26–29 provide for three classes of cases for the decision of which a full
Court is not necessary: (1) The Court will appoint every three years a special
chamber of five judges for the consideration of labor cases.   (2) The Court
will also appoint every three years a special chamber for cases relating to transit
and communications.   (3) "With a view to the speedy dispatch of business,
the Court shall form annually a chamber composed of three judges who, at the
request of the contesting parties, may hear and determine cases by summary
procedure" (Art. 29).

[77] The projected *International Prize Court* (see *infra*, pp. 740–41 n.) had
provided for appeals by enemy as well as neutral individuals in certain cases.

The *Central American Court of Justice*, which was inaugurated in 1908 and
lasted until virtually destroyed by its creator, the United States, in 1918, had

of the League of Nations can be parties in cases before the Court " which " shall be open " not merely to the Members of the League, but " also to States mentioned in the Annex to the Covenant." [78]

" The conditions under which the Court shall be open to other States shall, subject to the special provisions contained in treaties in force, be laid down by the Council, but in no case shall such provisions place the parties in a position of inequality before the Court." [79]

jurisdiction over cases arising between any of the Contracting Governments and individuals as well as between the Governments themselves. The five Central American States had also bound themselves to submit to this Court "all controversies or questions which may arise among them, of *whatsoever nature*, and no matter what their origin may be, in case the respective Departments of Foreign Affairs shall not have been able to reach an understanding." Arts. 1–3 of the Convention of 1907, in Supp. to 2 *A. J.* (1908), 231 ff. For comment see Scott in 2 *A. J.* 140–43, and in 12 *A. J.* (1918), 380–82. See Supp. to 8 *A. J.* (1914), 179–213 for "Regulations" and "Procedure" of the Court. For a brief survey of the inauguration and work of the Court, see 7 W. P. F. (1917), No. 1, pp. 131–44. Cf. *supra*, ch. 6, note 39. See also Bustamente, *op. cit.*, ch. 5.

[78] This provision appears to have been primarily intended to make it possible for the United States to participate in the working of the Court without joining the League of Nations.

[79] Art. 35 which adds: "When a State which is not a Member of the League of Nations is a party to a dispute, the Court will fix the amount which that party is to contribute towards the expenses of the Court."

On May 17, 1922, the Council adopted a resolution laying down the conditions under which the Court shall be opened to States not members of the League or mentioned in the Annex to the Covenant. This resolution merely requires the previous deposit with the Registrar of a declaration accepting the jurisdiction of the Court, in accordance with the Covenant, Statute and Rules, and undertaking to carry out in good faith its decisions and not to resort to war against a State complying therewith. Such declaration may be either particular, as respecting a particular dispute; or general, as embracing all or a particular class of disputes. For the text of the Resolution, see Hudson, *op. cit.*, 364–65.

On Feb. 17, 1923 Sec'y Hughes recommended that the Senate be asked for its consent to the adhesion of the United States to the Protocol of Dec. 16, 1920 on four conditions. These were: (1) that such adhesion shall not be taken as involving any legal relation to the League of Nations or obligations under the Covenant; (2) that the United States be permitted to participate in the election of judges; (3) that the United States pay a fair share of the expenses of the Court; and (4) that the Statute for the Court be not amended without the consent of the United States. To these reservations President Coolidge added another to the effect that the United States should not be bound by advisory opinions which it had not joined in requesting.

On Jan. 27, 1926, by a vote of 76 to 17, our Senate finally approved the resolution in favor of the adherence of the United States to the Protocol of Signature of the Statute of the Permanent Court of International Justice with

Law to be Applied by the Court.—Article 38 of the Statute declares: " The Court shall apply:

1. International conventions, whether general or particular, establishing rules expressly recognized by the contesting States;

2. International custom, as evidence of a general practice accepted as law;

3. The general principles of law recognized by civilized nations;

4. Subject to the provisions of Article 59,[80] judicial decisions and the teachings of the most highly qualified publicists of the various nations, as subsidiary means for the determination of rules of law."

It is added that " this provision shall not prejudice the

the Hughes reservations including an express assertion of the right of withdrawal. Instead of the harmless Coolidge reservation, there was added a fifth—the only one of real significance—which provides that the Court shall not "without the consent of the United States entertain any request for an advisory opinion touching any dispute or question in which the United States *has or claims an interest.*"

This reservation, which amounted to an American right of veto on advisory opinions, caused great concern at Geneva. See an interesting article by Baker, in the London *Nation*, Sept. 4, 1926. The Juridical Committee, which considered the matter, proposed that the United States should exercise all the rights enjoyed by members of the League Council on the basis of equality, their exercise being made the subject of an understanding between the Government of the United States and the Council of the League. There the matter rests and will probably continue to rest for a long time. An institution like the United States Senate is evidently ill-fitted for international coöperation. For the text of the Reply of the Nations to the U. S. World Court Reservations, see *Cur. Hist.* for Nov. 1926, pp. 244–46.

The objections to the Court in the United States have been based mainly on the idea that it is a League Court, *i.e.* the creation or instrument of the League of Nations which, having been an object of misrepresentation for political purposes is still anathema to many Americans. But the fact is, as Sec'y Hughes has well pointed out, that "the Court is an independent judicial body with appropriate judicial functions and abundant safeguards for their proper discharge. It is not a servant of the League; and its decisions are not supervised or controlled by the League." *Procs. Am. Soc. I. L.* (1923), 86.

On "America's Relation to the Court" and the views of Harding, Hughes, Root, etc., see 17 *A. J.* (1923), 331–43; Hudson, *op. cit.*, 95–96, 173 ff.; *Int. Concil.* (May, 1923), No. 186; W. P. F., 5 *League of Nations* (1922), No. 5; and 85 *Advocate of Peace* (1923), 169–87.

[80] Art. 59 declares that the "decision of the Court has no binding force except between the parties and in respect of that particular case." This seems to mean that the Court is not bound to follow its previous decisions, but of course they are certain to have great moral weight as precedents.

power of the Court to decide a case *ex aequo et bono*, if the parties agree thereto."

Procedure of the Court.—French and English are the official languages of the Court.[81]   Cases are brought before the Court either by the notification of the special agreement or by a written application addressed to the Registrar. The parties shall be represented by agents who may be assisted by counsel or advocates.   Proceedings are both oral and written.   The hearings are to be public, unless the Court shall decide otherwise or unless the parties demand that the public be not admitted.   Minutes, which shall be the only authentic record, must be made at each hearing.

The deliberations of the Court shall take place in private and remain secret.   All questions are to be decided by a majority of the judges present at the hearings and, in the event of an equality of votes, the President or his deputy shall have the casting vote.   The judgment shall state the reasons on which it is based with the names of the judges who have taken part in it.   Dissenting judges are entitled to deliver separate opinions.   The judgment shall be read in open Court, and is to be regarded as final and without appeal.[82]   Unless otherwise decided by the Court, each party shall bear its own costs.

[81] However, at the request of the parties, the Court may authorize another language to be used.

[82] But in the "event of dispute as to the meaning or scope of the judgment, the Court shall construe it upon the request of any party" (Art. 60).

"An application for revision of a judgment can be made only when it is based upon the discovery of some fact of such a nature as to be a decisive factor which fact was, when the judgment was given, unknown to the court and also to the party claiming revision, always provided that such ignorance was not due to negligence" (Art. 61).

"Should a State consider that it has an interest of a legal nature which may be affected by the decision in the case, it may submit a request to the Court to be permitted to intervene as a third party.   It will be for the Court to decide upon this request.

"Whenever the construction of a convention to which States other than those concerned in the case are parties is in question, the Registrar shall notify all such States forthwith.

"Every State so notified has the right to intervene in the proceedings; but if it uses this right, the construction given by the judgment will be equally binding upon it" (Arts. 62 and 63).

For the procedure of the Court, see Arts. 39–64 of the *Statute* and Arts. 32–75 of the *Rules of Court*.   Both are printed in Hudson, *op. cit.*, 340–65; and Moore, *op. cit.*, 147–78.

The Permanent Court of International Justice began its first session on January 20, 1922 and has already given a considerable number of advisory opinions and decisions of more or less interest.   It promises to become an important organ in the pacific settlement of international controversies and the development of International Law.[83]

BIBLIOGRAPHY

Good Offices and Mediation.—Barclay, *Problems of Int. Practice and Diplomacy* (1907), 191–97, and *New Methods of Adjusting Int. Disputes* (1917), 23–31; Bluntschli, Arts. 483–87; Bonfils or * 1 (3 Pt.) Fauchille, Nos. 932–43; Bulmerincq, in 4 Holtzendorff, 17–30, and in 1 Marquardsen, *Handbuch*, § 87; * 3 and 6 Calvo, §§ 1682–1705, 349–51, respectively; Despagnet, 473–76; Fenwick, 400–03; 2 Fiore, Nos. 1199–1201, and *Int. Law Cod.* (1918), Nos. 1259–67; Fourchault, *De la médiation* (1900); * Garner, *Recent Developments of Int. Law*, 563 ff.; Heffter, §§ 88, 107; 1 Halleck (3d ed.), 465–66; Higgins, 167; Hoijer, *Litiges int.* (1925), 25–79; * Holls, *Peace Conference at The Hague* (1900), 176–203; Hull, *The Two Hague Conferences* (1908), 267–76; * 2 Hyde, §§ 553–56; * Kamarowsky, *Le tribunal int.* (1887), 80–102; Lémonon, *La seconde confér.* (1908), 69–73; Liszt, § 52; 2 J. de Louter, § 39, pp. 129–35; 3 F. de Martens, § 103; Mélik, *La médiation et bons offices* (1900); * Mérignhac, *L'arbitrage int.* (1895), 158–71, and 1 *Traité*, 429–40; 1 Meurer, *Die Haager Friedenskonferenz* (1905–07), 104 ff.; * 7 Moore, *Digest*, §§ 1065–68; Nippold, *Die Fortbildung des Verfahrens* (1907), § 18, pp. 411 ff.; * 2 Oppenheim, §§ 7–11; 2 Piédelièvre, Nos. 665–78; Phillipson, *Termination of War* (1916), ch. 3, pp. 76–91; Politis, in 17 *R. D. I. P.*

[83] On Dec. 1, 1924 the States that had signed the Protocol of Signature numbered 48.   The number of ratifications was 37.   For a list of signatories, see Hudson, *op. cit.*, 334; or W. P. F., *Yearbook of L. of N.* (1925), 581–92.

The most important advisory opinions have perhaps been those with regard to the Nationality Decrees issued in Tunis and Morocco, involving the meaning of "domestic" jurisdiction; the status of Eastern Carelia, denying the jurisdiction of the Court over Russia, a non-member of the League; certain intricate questions arising from the application of the Polish Minorities Treaty to German settlers in Poland; and an opinion in (Sept., 1925) to the effect that, under the Treaty of Lausaanne, the Council of the League had a right to fix the boundaries between Iraq and Turkey in respect to Mosul.

The most important judgment or decision has been that of the *S. S. Wimbledon*, respecting the freedom of the Kiel Canal.

For lists of judgments and advisory opinions given prior to 1925, see Hudson, *op. cit.*, 369; and W. P. F., *op. cit.*, 583–84.   For discussions of cases, see Bustamente, *op. cit.*, ch. 15; Fachiri, *op. cit.*, ch. 5; Hudson, *passim*; 2 Kellor, *Security against War* (1924), chs. 27–32; and * Moore, *op. cit.*, 119–40.   For the text of the opinions and decisions, see Publications of the Court, *Series A and B*.

(1910), 136 ff.; * Potter, *Int. Organization* (1922), ch. 13, pp. 194–205; 2 and 6 P.-Fodéré, *Traité*, Nos. 1132–43, 2588–93, and 2 *Cours*, etc., 501 ff.; * 2 Rivier, 161–65; * 2 Satow, chs. 22–23; 1 Scott (see index); Taylor, §§ 359–60; Ullmann, § 152; * Vattel, liv. II, c. 17, § 328; Wheaton (Atlay's ed.), § 288 a; Wilson, § 83; and Zamfiresco, *De la médiation* (1911). For cases of mediation to which the United States has been a party, see 5 Moore, *Arbitrations*, 5042–56, and 7 *Digest*, §§ 1065–68.

Conciliation and Commissions of Inquiry.—Barclay, *Problems of Int. Practice and Diplomacy* (1907), 13–14, 35–42, 217, and *New Methods of Adjusting Int. Disputes* (1917), ch. 8; * Beaucourt, *Les commissions int. d'enquête* (1909); Bokanowski, *Les commissions int. d'enquête* (1908); Brown, *La conciliation int.* (1925); Despagnet, No. 477; 1 (3 pt.) Fauchille, No. 970$^{6-17}$; Fenwick, 414–17; Finch, in 10 *A. J.* (1916), 882–90; Fiore, *Int. Law Cod.* (1918), Nos. 1268–98; * Garner, *op. cit.*, 526 ff.; * Hershey, *Int. Law and Diplomacy of the Russo-Japanese War* (1906), ch. 8; Higgins, 167–69; Hoijer, *op. cit.*, 79–100; * Holls, *Peace Conference at The Hague* (1900), 203–20; Hull, *Two Hague Conferences* (1908), 277–97; 2 Hyde, §§ 557–58; Lapradelle, in 6 *R. D. I. P.* (1899), 767 ff.; Lémonon, *La seconde confer.* (1908), 73–94; 2 J. de Louter, § 39, pp. 135–41; * Mandelstam, in 12 *R. D. I. P.* (1905), 161 ff., 351 ff.; 1 Mérignhac, *Traité*, 440–47, and *La conférence int. de la paix* (1900), 279 ff.; Meurer, *Die Haager Friedenskonferenz* (1905–07), 129 ff.; Nippold, *Die Fortbildung des Verfahrens* (1907), § 19, and *Die zweite Haager Friedenskonferenz* (1908), § 3; 2 Oppenheim, § 5, and * §§ 11a–d (4th ed.); Politis, in 19 *R. D. I. P.* (1912), 149 ff.; Potter, *Int. Organization* (1922), 205–09; 1 Scott, 265–73; Smith and Sibley, *Int. Law during the Russo-Japanese War* (1905), 275–317, 446–58, 468–71; Ullmann, § 158; Wilson, § 84.

Arbitration.—*American Conference on Int. Arbitration* (1896); Amos, *Political and Legal Remedies for War* (1880), 164–72; Balch, in 15 *Col. Law Rev.* (1915), 590 ff. and 662 ff.; Barclay, *Problems of Int. Practice and Diplomacy* (1907), index, and *New Methods of Adjusting Int. Disputes* (1917), chs. 5–7; Baty, *Int. Law* (1909), ch. 1; Bluntschli, Arts. 488–98; Bonfils, or 1 (3 Pt.) Fauchille, Nos. 944–70; Bry, *Précis élémentaire de droit int.* (1906), Nos. 361–68; Bulmerincq, in 4 Holtzendorff, 30–58, and in 1 Marquardsen, *Handbuch*, § 87; * 3 and 6 Calvo, §§ 1706–1806, 352–90, respectively; Castberg, in 6 (3d ser.) *R. D. I.*, 155 ff. and 310 ff.; Clarke, in 1 *A. J.* (1907), 342–408; 1 Cobbett (3d ed.), 36–41; Coudert, *Addresses* (1905), 3 ff.; * Darby, *Int. Tribunals* (4th ed., 1904), 767–917 (for instances of arbitration); Dennis, in 11 *Col. Law Rev.* (1911), 493–513; * Descamps, *Essai l'organization de l'arbitrage int.* (1896), and in 28 *R. D. I.* (1896), 5–76; Despagnet, *Cours de droit int.* (1910), Nos. 697–713; Dreyfus, *L'arbitrage int.* (1892); * Dumas, *Les sanctions de l'arbitrage int.* (1905), and in 5 *A. J.* (1911), 934–57; Dungern, in 7 *Z. V.* (1913), 257–71; Duplessix, *L'organization int.* (1909);

Fenwick, 403–09; 2 Fiore, Nos. 1202–15, *Int. Law Cod.* (1918), Nos. 1299–1385, and in 30 *R. D. I.* (1898), 5 ff.; Foster, *Arbitration and The Hague Court* (1904); Fraser, "History of Arbitration," in 11 *Cornell Law Quar.* (1926), 179–208; * Fried, *Die moderne Schiedsgerichts-bewegung* (1904), *Die moderne Friedensbewegung* (1907), and *Die zweite Haager Konferenz* (1907); * Garner, *Recent Developments in Int. Law* (1925), Sect. 10; Grotius, II, c. 23, § 8; Hall, § 119; 1 Halleck (3d ed.), 102–03, 467–68, 485–87; Heffter, § 109; * Hicks, *The New World Order* (1920), ch. 11; * Higgins (see index); Hoijer, *op. cit.*, 101–290; * Holls, *Peace Conference at The Hague* (1900), (see index); Hull, *Two Hague Conferences* (1908), 297–427, 470–77, 490–95; * 2 Hyde, §§ 559–85; Interparliamentary Union, *Reports of,* since 1892; * Kamarowsky, *Le tribunal int.* (1887); Lafontaine, *Pasicrise Int.* (1902), and in 34 *R. D. I.* (1902), 349 ff., 558 ff., 623 ff.; Lake Mohonk Conference, *Reports on International Arbitration,* since 1895; * Lammasch, *Die Rechtskraft Internationaler Schiedsspruche* (1913), in 2 *Publications de l'Institute Nobel Norwegien* (1912), and *Die Lehre von den Schiedgerichtsbarkeit* (1913); Lapradelle et Politis, *Recueil des arbitrages int.* I (1798–1855), in 1900, and II (1856–72), in 1924; Lapradelle, "La Conférence de la Paix," in 6 *R. D. I. P.* (1899), 651–846 (see p. 651 for bibliography), and in 16 *R. D. I. P.* (1909), 385 ff. (see pp. 385–87 for bibliography); Laveleye, *Des causes actuelles de la guerre et de l'arbitrage* (1873); Lawrence, *Essays on Int. Law* (1885), 234–77, *Principles* (7th ed.), § 221, and *International Problems and Hague Conferences* (1908), 62–82; Le Fur, in 16 *R. D. I. P.* (1909), 437 ff.; Lémonon, *La seconde confér.* (1908), 95–279; Liszt, § 53; 2 J. de Louter, § 40; Maine, *Int. Law* (1888), 211–28; Manning, *Arbitration Treaties among the American Nations* (1924, texts of treaties); 3 F. de Martens, § 104, and *La conférence de la paix* (1900); * Mérignhac, *De l'arbitrage int.* (1895), 1 *Traité,* 448–574, and *La conférence int. de la paix* (1900); 1 Meurer, *Die Haager Friedenskonferenz* (1905); * Moch, *Histoire sommaire de l'arbitrage* (1905); * Moore, *History and Digest of International Arbitrations to which the United States has been a Party,* in 6 vols. (see especially note on pp. 4821 ff. for a translation from Mérignhac on "The History of Arbitration"); * 7 Moore, *Digest,* §§ 1069-89; Moore, in 22 *Annals* (1903), 35–44, in *American Diplomacy* (1905), 200–20, in 6 *Papers of American Historical Assoc.* (1891), 63–85, and in *Int. Law and Current Illusions* (1924), ch. 3, pp. 81–96; Morris, *Int. Arbitration and Procedure* (1911) Mougins de Roquefort, *De la situation juridique des conflits int.* (1889); Myers, in 5 W. P. F. (1915), No. 5, pt. III (for list of arbitration engagements), and in 23 *Cur. Hist.* (1925), pp. 656–62; National Peace Congresses, *Proceedings of,* since 1908; * Nippold, *Die Fortbildung des Verfahrens* (1907), and *Die Zwiete Haager Friedenskonferenz* (1908); Nys, in 38 *R. D. I.* (1906), 5 ff.; * 2 Oppenheim, §§ 12--25; 2 Piédelièvre, Nos. 679–758; 3 Phillimore, §§ 3–5; Phillipson, *Two Studies in Int. Law* (1908), 1–49, 118–27; * 6 P.-Fodéré, Nos. 2602–30; * Ralston, *Int. Arbitral*

Law and Procedure (1910); Reinsch, in 5 *A. J.* (1911), 604–14; Revon, *L'arbitrage int.* (1892); 2 Rivier, 166–88; Rouard de Card, *L'arbitrage int.* (1877), and *Les destinées de l'arbitrage* (1892); Rolin-Jacquemnys, *De l'arbitrage* (1883); Schücking, *The Int. Union of the Hague Conferences* (1918, see index); Scott, *Cases* (ed. of 1902), 443–49 (for the case of the *Ninfa*), and 1 *The Hague Peace Conferences*, especially chs. 5–9, and *Treaties for the Advancement of Peace* (1920), "Introduction"; Taylor, §§ 33, 356–58; Ullmann, §§ 154–57; * Vattel, liv. II, § 329; * 1 Westlake, 350–68; 3 Wharton, *Digest*, § 316; Wilson, §§ 85–86; and * Woolf, *Int. Government* (1916), ch. 6.

For articles on arbitration, see especially the files of the *Advocate of Peace; Annuaire de la vie int.* (since 1905); the New York *Independent;* and Jones and Chipman, *Index to Legal Periodicals* (since 1887).

For fuller bibliographies, see Bonfils, Fauchille, Lafontaine, *op. cit.*, Olivart, *Bibliographie du droit int.* (1905–10), and *List of References on Int. Arbitration* published by Library of Congress (1908).

Judicial Settlement and Permanent Court of Int. Justice.—Baker, in *Brit. Yr. Bk.* (1925), 68–102; Blociszeksoski, in 3 (3d ser.) *R. D. I. P.* (1922), 23 ff.; Borchard, in 218 *No. Am. Rev.* (1923), 1–16, and in 4 *Ill. Law Quar.* (1922), 67–73; Borel, in 17 *A. J.* (1923), 429–37; Bourgeois, in *The League of Nations Starts* (London, 1920); Bourquin, in 2 (3d ser.) *R. D. I.* (1921), 17 ff.; Buell, *Int. Relations* (1925), 582–88; * Bustamente, *The World Court* (1925); Castberg, in 6 (3d ser.) *R. D. I.* (1925), 156 ff. and 310 ff.; Finch, in 17 *A. J.* (1923), 521–26; Fanshawe, *Reconstruction* (1925), 32–55; * Facchira, *The Permanent Court of Int. Justice* (1925); Fry, *Key-Book of the L. of N.*, ch. 6; Hammerskjoeld, in 3 (3d ser.) *R. D. I.* (1922), 125 ff., and in 36 *Harv. Law Rev.* (1922–23), 704–25; Garnet, *op. cit.*, Lect. 13; * Harding, Hughes, etc., in 17 *A. J.* (1923), 331–43, in *Int. Concil.* (1923), No. 186, in 85 *Advocate of Peace* (1923), 169–87, or W. P. F., 5 and 6 *League of Nations* (1922 and 1923), Nos. 5 and 1; Hoover, in *Int. Concil.* (1923), No. 186; * Hudson, *The Permanent Court of Int. Justice* (1925), *passim*, and in 20 *A. J.* (1926), 1–32; * Hughes, in *Procs. Am. Soc. I. L.* (1923), 75–89, and in 10 *Procs. Acad. Pol. Sci.* (1923), 140–59 (see also Addresses in *Pathway to Peace*, 1925); 2 Hyde, §§ 573–76; 2 Kellor, *Security against War* (1924), chs. 24–33, *The U. S. Senate and the Int. Court* (1925); Keen, *Towards Int. Justice* (1923), 197–225; Magyary, *Die Int. Shiedsgerichtsbarkeit* (1922); * Moore, *Int. Law and Current Illusions* (1924), 96–148, or in 22 *Col. Law Rev.* (1922), 497–511, and in *Int. Concil.* (1924), No. 197; Morellet, *L'organization de la Cour* (1921); Mougins de Roquefort, *De la solution juridque des conflits int.* (1889), *passim;* Nyholm, in 2 *Les origines et l'oeuvre de la societé des nations* (ed. Munch, 1924), 241–63; * 2 Oppenheim (4th ed.), §§ 25ab–ag; Phillimore, in 1 *Brit. Inst. Int. Affairs* (1922), 113–23, and in 6 *Grot. Soc.* (1921), 89 ff.; Politis, *La justice int.* (1924), and in 4 *For. Aff.* (1926), 443–53; *Proceedings*, Society Settlement Judicial Dispute for 1910–16; Potter, *Int.*

Organization (1922), ch. 16; Richards and Loder, in *Brit. Yr. Bk.* (1921–22), 1–26; * Root, in 15 *A. J.* (1921), 1–12, and in *Procs. Am. Soc. I. L.* (1923), 1–15 (see also Addresses in *Men and Policies*, 1925, 324–426); Schücking and Wehberg, *Die Satzung des Völkerbundes* (1924), 313–50; * Scott, *The Project of a Permanent Court* (1920), and in 15 *A. J.* (1921), 52–56, 260–66, 556–58; Wehberg, *The Problem of an Int. Ct. of Justice* (1918), and in 4 (3d ser.) *R. D. I.* (1923), 179 ff.; and * Woolf, *Int. Government* (1916), ch. 6.

For bibliographies, see Bustamente, *op. cit.*, 323 ff.; Hudson, *op. cit.*, 373 ff.; and 85 *Advocate of Peace* (1923), 198–99 and 438–40.

The publications of the Court are in the form of Series A.—Collection of Judgments; Series B.—Collection of Advisory Opinions; Series C.—Acts and Doc. Relating to Judgments and Advisory Opinions; and Series D.—Acts and Doc. Concerning the Organization of the Court.

CHAPTER XXIII

PREVENTION AND SOLUTION OF DIFFERENCES THROUGH INTERNATIONAL ORGANIZATION AND COÖPERATION

320a. Historical Sketch of Plans for International Organization.—The real pioneer in the history of disinterested plans for international organization was the Parisian monk Emeric Crucé whose remarkable book entitled *Le Nouveau Cynée* or *The New Cyneas* was published in 1623.[1] Crucé suggested a permanent Congress or Assembly of ambassadors of the leading sovereigns and great republics of his time which should settle international differences by majority vote, and whose decisions the princes and sovereigns were sworn to enforce.[2] Since Crucé's day many similar plans have been formulated.[3]

[1] It will be recalled that this was two years prior to the publication of Grotius' *De jure belli ac pacis*.

The really remarkable feature of Crucé's work is perhaps his insistence upon freedom of trade and communication as a basis for international organization. Crucé was not absolutely the pioneer in this field. He had been preceded by several others, notably by the French advocate Pierre Dubois in the early part of the 14th century. But there are good reasons for suspecting that Dubois was not a genuine internationalist and that, like Sully's Grand Design, his scheme had as its real aim the aggrandizement of the French monarchy.

[2] The *New Cyneas* (trans. by Balch, 1909), 102–04 and 120–22. For a slight discussion of and references on Crucé, Sully's *Grand Design*, and Dubois, see *supra*, pp. 67–68.

[3] Prominent among these plans were the following: the Grand Design of Sully or Henry IV (ab. 1635); the Diet proposed by William Penn in his *Essay* (published in 1693); Abbé Saint-Pierre's "Project of a Treaty for Perpetual Peace" (1712–17); Bentham's *Essay* entitled "A Plan for an Universal and Perpetual Peace" (not published until 1843, but apparently written from 1786–89); Kant's *Essay* on "Perpetual Peace" based on the principles of representative government and federation (1795); and Ladd's *Essay* on "Congress of Nations" (1840).

For accounts of many and various *Plans of International Organization*, see: Butler, *Studies in Statecraft* (1920); Lange, *Histoire de l'internationalism* (1919); J. ter Meulen, *Der Gedanke der Int. Organization* (1917); Redslob, (1917); *Das Problem des Völkerrechts*; Schücking, *Die Organization der Welt* (1908); and York, *Leagues of Nations* (1919). For good brief accounts, see Hicks, *The New World Order* (1920), ch. 5; and Morrow, *The Society of Free States* (1919), ch. 2.

320b. **Beginnings of International Organization.**—But it can hardly be said that actual attempts at real world organization were made prior to the Congress of Vienna in 1815. The attempt to substitute for the old European state-system a sort of new European Confederacy or Concert [4] under the control of the Great Powers failed largely because of autocratic tendencies and because the Alliance intervened in internal as well as in external affairs. Later interventions of the European Concert of Powers [5] had at times a certain limited success, particularly in the cases of Holland and Belgium, Greece and Turkey, but they usually failed to achieve much that was desired because of the rivalry of the Great Powers. The rapid and extensive growth of Congresses or Conferences and of International Administrative Unions during the latter half of the nineteenth century culminating in the Hague Conferences of 1899 and 1907 has been noted,[6] as has also the more recent development of Diplomacy by personal Conference.[7]

320c. **Genesis of the League of Nations.**—Perhaps the earliest expression by a modern statesman in favor of a " League of Peace " was by Sir Henry Campbell Bannerman in 1905.[8] In his Nobel Prize Address delivered at Christiania, Norway on May 5, 1910, Ex-President Roosevelt made what appears hitherto to have been the most definite suggestion for a " League of Peace." [9] But it was not until after the World War was in progress that the various

[4] Cf. *supra*, Nos. 70–71.

[5] See *supra*, No. 141.

[6] See *supra*, Nos. 74–79, 82–83.

[7] See *supra*, note 3 on pp. 458–59.

[8] Baker, in 2 *Les origines et l'oeuvre de la societé des nations* (ed. by Munch, 1924), 16. "He did not explain the detail of his plan, . . . but he had sown a seed which grew in the mind of the British public."

[9] He said: "Finally, it would be a master stroke if these great powers honestly bent on peace would form a League of Peace, not only to keep the peace among themselves, but to prevent, by force if necessary, its being broken by others . . . Such power to command peace throughout the world could best be assured by some combination between those great nations which sincerely desire peace and have no thought themselves of committing aggressions." For a report of this speech, see, *e.g.* 95 *Outlook* (May 7, 1910), 19–21.

Particularly noteworthy are the "Proposals for a League of Peace" by Williams in 106 *Contemp. Rev.* (1914), 628–36. The support of the movement for such a League during the earlier years of the World War by the British Premier Asquith and Sir Edw. Grey should also be noted.

movements and organizations [10] favoring a more or less radical solution of the problems of international reorganization made much headway.

By far the most important of these organizations, at least in the United States, was the League to Enforce Peace, formed in 1915.[11] Its platform called not merely for a judicial tribunal and periodical Conferences to formulate and codify rules of International Law, but for a Council of Conciliation for hearing, consideration and recommendation in the case of all non-justiciable questions not settled by negotiation.[12]

[10] At least outside of socialistic and labor circles. Even the professional pacifists and internationalists did not for the most part see much beyond the need of disarmament, arbitration and judicial settlement, or confined themselves to vague aspirations and humanitarian devices.

The most stimulating and influential of the pre-war publicists was Norman Angell whose main work—*The Great Illusion* (of which the first American edition was published in 1910)—demonstrated in brilliant fashion the economic and political futility of war.

[11] On the *League to Enforce Peace*, see especially: *League to Enforce Peace* (Procs. of Conference of 1915); *Ibid.* (Procs. of Conference of 1918); * Marburg, *League of Nations* (1917), and *Draft Convention for L. of N.* (1918); Short, *Program and Policies of the League* (1916); Taft, *Papers on League of Nations* (1920).

Ex-President Taft was President of the League. The practical work of Mr. Hamilton Holt, former Editor of The New York *Independent*, in the cause of peace generally, and particularly in connection with this League, should receive due recognition.

[12] The platform also declares: "The Signatory Powers shall jointly use forthwith both their economic and military forces against anyone of their number that goes to war, or commits acts of hostility against another of the Signatories before any question arising shall be submitted." For the text of the platform, see *League to Enforce Peace* (1915), 4, or Short, *op. cit.*, VII.

The same year (1915) there was founded in London a "League of Nations Society" with a similar program. It secured perhaps a greater following than the American branch in the United States.

There were a considerable number of other similar projects for world organization elaborated either by individuals, organizations or groups in Great Britain as also on the Continent of Europe. Among these, as especially noteworthy, should be mentioned: the Minimum Program of the Central Organization for a Durable Peace; the Proposals for the Prevention of Future Wars, by Lord Bryce's group (Dickinson and others); the Draft of a General Treaty for the Pacific Settlement of International Disputes, by a Dutch Committee; and the Draft Treaty of the Fabian Society.

The latter of these is the most detailed and comprehensive. For text and comment by Woolf, see Woolf, *Framework of a Lasting Peace* (1925), 91–123, and 5 *The New Statesman* (Spec. Supp. for July 10 and July 17, 1915), 336 ff., 360 ff. For the texts of the other projects above mentioned, see Woolf, *op. cit.*, 61 ff. For a list of fifty-one plans or projects, see Schücking and Wehberg, *Die Satzung des Völkerbundes* (1924), 6–10.

The most influential recruit for the League to Enforce Peace was enlisted in May, 1916 when President Wilson declared that the United States was " willing to become a partner in any feasible association " formed in order to realize certain "fundamental things." [13]   Later he made

Speaking generally, most of the plans or drafts examined appear to have in common a realization of the need of machinery (Council of Conciliation or Inquiry) for the settlement of non-legal or *political* disputes (conflicts of interests as against conflicts of right).   This the older advocates of arbitration and judicial settlement had not understood.

Most detailed and comprehensive are two German schemes—one drawn up by Erzberger, the famous leader of the Centre Party, in 1918, and the other formulated under the auspices of the German Revolutionary Government in April, 1919.   The main reliance of the Erzberger draft was on obligatory arbitration.   The German official plan was very radical and democratic.   It provided for an indirectly elected World Parliament, having the right of initiative as well as for a Congress of States; and compulsory mediation for the settlement of conflicts of interest.   Both schemes aimed at freedom of the seas and of communication.

For Erzberger's draft, see Erzberger, *League of Nations* (1919), ch. 15. On the German official plan, see Pollock, *League of Nations* (2d ed., 1922), App. III, 239 ff.; and Schücking, in 1 *Les origines et l'oeuvre de la societé des nations* (1924), 138–60.   On "Das deutsche Volk und der Völkerbund," see Wehberg, in *Ibid.*, 440 ff.   See latter article for references to German works on the League of Nations.   On the various plans for international organization elaborated during the World War, see particularly: Lange, in 1 *Ibid.*, 1–61; and Woolf, *op. cit.*,

Among the more or less important books in advocacy of a League of Nations or International Organization that were published during or soon after the war period are the following: * Brailsford, *A League of Nations* (1917); Goldsmith, *A League to Enforce Peace* (1917); Hobson, *Towards Int. Government* (1915); Kallen, *The World in Alliance* (1915), and *Hammering Out the Details* (1917); Keen, *League of Nations* (1918); * La Fontaine, *The Great Solution, Magnissima Charta* (1916); Lammasch, *Das Völkerrecht nach dem Kriege*, in 3 *Public. de l'Institut Nobel*, (1917), and *Völkermord oder Völkerbund* (1920); Minor, *A Republic of Nations* (1918); Otley, *Les problèms int. et la Guerre* (1916); Paish, *The Nations and the League* (1920), and *A Permanent League of Nations* (1918); Pollard, Pollock, Barker, etc., in *League of Nations Series* (1918); Wells, *Idea of a League of Nations* (1919); and * Woolf, *Int. Government* (1916), and *The Framework of a Lasting Peace* (1925).

One of the most able and energetic writers against the League in its present form in the United States, has been D. J. Hill.   See *Present Problems in Foreign Policy* (1919), and *American World Policies* (1920).   His earlier views are embodied in a work on *World Organization* (1911).

[13] These he declared to be: "First, that every people has a right to choose the sovereignty under which they shall live. . . . Second, that the small States have a right to enjoy the same respect for their sovereignty and for their territorial integrity that great and powerful nations expect and insist upon.   And, third, that the world has a right to be free from every disturbance of its peace that has its origin in aggression and disregard of the rights of peoples and nations."   Shaw, *President Wilson's State Papers and Addresses* (1917), 274 or Scott, *President Wilson's Foreign Policy* (1918), 193.

the principle of a general association of nations the last of his famous fourteen points [14] and succeeded in incorporating the Covenant of the League of Nations [15] into the Paris Treaties.

320d. Purpose and Methods of the League as Indicated in the Preamble of the Covenant.—The League is created:

" In order to promote international coöperation and to achieve international peace and security,[16]

" by the acceptance of obligations not to resort to war,

" by the prescription of open, just and honorable relations between nations,

" by the firm establishment of the understandings of International Law [17] as the actual rule of conduct among Governments, and

" by the maintenance of justice and a scrupulous respect for all treaty obligations in the dealings of organized peoples with one another."

320e. Membership in and Withdrawal from the League.

---

[14] See *supra*, pp. 125 ff.

[15] Space does not permit a consideration of the making of the Covenant at the Paris Peace Conference or of the struggle for its incorporation into the Paris Treaties.   Those interested in these matters should consult: * 1 Baker, *Wilson and World Settlement* (1922–23), Pt. III, chs. 13–18; * Baker, P., on "The Making of the Covenant," in 2 *Les origines et l'oeuvre de la societé des nations* (1924), 16–67; Miller, "The Making of the League," in *What Really Happened at Paris* (ed. by House and Seymour, 1921), ch. 17, pp. 398–424; Scelle, "La Élaboration du pacte," in 1 *Ibid.*, 62–137; and 2 and 6 Temperley, *Hist. of the Peace Conference* (1920–24), pp. 21–31 and 426–61 respectively.

Suffice it to say here that hardly a single idea contained in the Covenant was original with President Wilson.   "His relation to it was mainly that of editor or compiler, selecting or rejecting, recasting or combining the projects that came to him from other sources."   1 Baker, *op. cit.*, 214.

The Covenant is really the product of the League of Nations Commission of 19 members of which Wilson was Chairman and which included many of the leading statesmen of the world, such as the British Lord Cecil and Gen. Smuts, the French M. Bourgeois, the Japanese Baron Makino and Viscount Chinda, the Chinese Wellington Koo, the Greek Venizelos, the Italian Orlando, etc.

The Commission held 15 long sessions in Col. House's office at the Hotel Crillon.   Its first meeting was on Feb. 3, and the last on April 11, 1919.   The first completed draft was presented and read by President Wilson to a plenary session of the Conference on Feb. 14, and (after the incorporation of certain amendments relating to the Monroe Doctrine, the right of withdrawal, etc. demanded in the United States) adopted at the plenary session of April 28, 1919.

[16] This double purpose of the League should be particularly noted.

[17] On "Understandings of International Law," cf. Brown, in 13 *A. J.* (1919), 738–41 and Wright, in 14 *A. J.* (1920), 565–80.

—" The original Members of the League of Nations shall be those of the Signatories which are named in the Annex to this Covenant, and also such of those other States named in the Annex as shall accede without reservation to this Covenant. Such accessions shall be effected by a declaration deposited with the Secretariat within two months of the coming into force of the Covenant   Notice thereof shall be sent to all other Members of the League.

" Any fully self-governing State, Dominion or Colony not named in the Annex may become a Member of the League if its admission is agreed to by two-thirds of the Assembly, provided that it shall give effective guaranties of its sincere intention to observe its international obligations, and shall accept such regulations as may be prescribed by the League in regard to its military, naval and air forces and armaments.

" Any Member of the League, may, after two years' notice of its intention so to do, withdraw from the League, provided that all its international obligations and all its obligations under this Covenant shall have been fulfilled at the time of its withdrawal " (Art. 1 of the *Covenant*).[18]

[18] The last paragraph of Art. 1 relating to withdrawal from the League should be read in connection with that portion of Art. 26 which declares that no amendment "shall bind any Member of the League which signifies its dissent therefrom, but in that case it shall cease to be a Member of the League." See also Art. 16, parag. 4, which provides: "Any member of the League which has violated any covenant of the League may be declared to be no longer a Member of the League by a vote of the Council concurred in by the representatives of all the other Members of the League represented therein."

So far (July 1, 1927) there have been no actual withdrawals from the League, except in the case of Costa Rica. In 1920 the Argentine Republic withdrew from the Assembly, but not from the League. In Sept., 1926, owing to failure to secure permanent seats in the Council, Spain and Brazil gave notice of withdrawal.

According to Art. 1, there are two classes of members:

(I) Original Members, consisting (1) of the 32 States and Dominions or Allied and Associated Powers that were at war with Germany (excepting Russia) and signed the Paris Treaties; and (2) of the 13 neutral States invited to accede to the Covenant, making 45 States and Dominions. All these are named in the Annex to the Covenant. From this list must be subtracted the United States, Ecuador and the Hedjaz which signed but did not ratify the Treaties. China became a Member by signing the Treaty of St. Germain with Austria.

(II) Admitted members, now 14 in number, which have been admitted by a two-thirds vote of the Assembly. The conditions laid down for subsequent admission are: (1) they must be "fully self-governing;" (2) they shall give effective guaranties of sincere intention to observe their international obliga-

320f. **The Organs of the League.**—" The action of the League under this Covenant shall be effected through the instrumentality of an Assembly and of a Council, with a permanent Secretariat " (Art. 2).[19]

a. **The Assembly.**—" The Assembly shall consist of representatives of the Members of the League.

" The Assembly shall meet at stated intervals and from time to time, as occasion may require, at the Seat of the League, or at such other place as may be decided upon.

" The Assembly may deal at its meetings with any matter within the sphere of action of the League or affecting the peace of the world.

" At meetings of the Assembly each Member of the League shall have one vote, and may not have more than three Representatives " (Art. 3).[20]

tions; and (3) they shall accept such regulations as may be prescribed by the League in regard to their military, naval and aërial forces and armaments.

When the Covenant of the League came into force on Jan. 10, 1920, there were 23 Members. Now (1926) there are 56. The latest recruit is Germany which was admitted in Sept., 1926. For a list of Members and non-Members, see 10 W. P. F. *Pamphlets* (1927), 155. Cf. *supra*, pp. 167–73. "There is no difference between original and non-original members, except in the fact of the history of their admission and except as conditions may be set at the time of admission. Once admitted, all members are on a basis of complete equality in their enjoyment of the privileges of membership." Hudson, in 18 *A. J.* (1924), 436.

The Assembly seems to have been fairly lenient in applying the conditions for admission. It appears to have insisted upon: (a) *de jure* or at least *de facto* recognition; (b) a stable government which could be described as "fully self-governing" with more or less settled frontiers; and (c) satisfactory assurances respecting intention to observe international obligations and the prescriptions of the League respecting armaments. Hudson, *op. cit.*, 453. The application of Liechtenstein appears to have been rejected because of its small size. Before being admitted to membership, Abyssinia was required to sign a declaration adhering to the Convention of St. Germain (1919) respecting slavery. Guaranties as to the protection of minorities were required from a number of States before admission to the League.

On "Admission" or "Membership in the League of Nations," see Coucke, in 48 (3d ser. 2) *R. D. I.* (1921), 520 ff.; Hoijer, *Le pacte de la Societé des Nations* (1926), 34 ff.; * Hudson, in 18 *A. J.* (1924), 436–58; and Scello, in 28 *R. D. I. P.* (1921), 122 ff.

[19] To these main constitutional organs of the League should be added "The Permanent Court of International Justice" which is, however, a practically independent body. See *supra*, pp. 480 ff. Certain Commissions like the permanent Mandates Commission (cf. *supra*, p. 191 n.) might also be considered as virtually independent organs of the League. The functions of these organs are primarily executive in their nature.

[20] The First Assembly met at Geneva in November, 1920, with representa-

b. **The Council.**—The Council shall consist of representatives of the Principal Allied and Associated Powers

tives from 42 Members of the League present.   Since then it has met on the first Monday of each September, its sessions lasting about a month.   It now forms a body of about 150 members, or rather of nearly 300, counting the substitutes, technical delegates and secretaries.   Its meetings are public unless it decides otherwise.   Hitherto, the right of secret sessions has never been exercised.   There may be extraordinary meetings for emergencies.   There was one such in March, 1926 relative to the admission of Germany.   A special session of the Assembly may be summoned at the request of a Member, provided a majority of the Members concur.

Already in the First Assembly the question arose whether the Members necessarily represented their Governments in the discussions as well as in their decisions.   It was agreed that this was certainly the case when they voted; but, though there was a difference of opinion on this point, it appears to have been generally conceded that in the debates a certain latitude might be allowed in the expression of personal views.   It should be particularly noted that the veto is by States.

Among the special duties of the Assembly are: the admission of new Members of the League (Art. 1); the election of the nine non-permanent Member-States represented on the Council (Art. 4); the approval of the additional Member-States represented on the Council (Art. 4); the approval of the appointment by the Council of the Secretary-General; the election (with the Council) of the judges of the Court of International Justice; participation in the amendment of the Covenant (Art. 26); consideration of disputes referred to it by the Council, or at the request of either party to a dispute (Art. 15); the adoption of the Annual Budget of the League and its allocation among the Member-States (Art. 6); the reconsideration of inapplicable treaties and the consideration of dangerous international conditions (Art. 19); and the consideration of the Annual Report on the work of the Council.

The Assembly functions in (*a*) plenary sessions and (*b*) committees.

Aside from the General Committee which assists the President of the Assembly in the general direction of its work, there are six committees among whom the work of the Assembly is apportioned.   These six Committees deal respectively with: (1) Legal and Constitutional Questions; (2) Technical Organizations; (3) Armaments; (4) The Budget and Financial Questions; (5) Social and General or Humanitarian Questions; and (6) Political Questions (including Mandates).

Except the report on the work of the Council and Secretariat, all matters are first dealt with in these Committees and are then referred to the Assembly in plenary session.   But since all Member-States are entitled to representation on all these committees, sub-committees are often created.   In order to present the results of its labors to the Assembly, each Committee (or sub-committee) elects a Reporter who acts as Secretary and makes a report to the Assembly.   Each Assembly has also a number of special committees.

The *agenda* of the Assembly is drawn up by the Secretary-General.   It includes: (1) A report on the work of the Council and of the Secretariat, as also on the measures taken to execute the decisions of the preceding Assembly; (2) items ordered by the Assembly at a previous session, items proposed by the Council and items proposed by any Member of the League; and (3) the Budget.   There are arrangements for placing additional items on the agenda by the Assembly itself.

[United States of America,[21] the British Empire, France, Italy and Japan], together with Representatives of four [now nine] [22] other Members of the League. These four [now nine] Members of the League shall be selected by the Assembly from time to time in its discretion. Until the appointment of the Representatives of the four Members of the League first selected by the Assembly, Representatives of Belgium, Brazil, Spain and Greece shall be Members of the Council.

" With the approval of the majority of the Assembly, the Council may name additional Members of the League, whose Representatives shall always be Members of the Council; the Council with like approval may increase the number of Members of the League to be selected by the Assembly for representation on the Council.[23]

The official languages are English and French, and the proceedings are published in both languages. If a speaker chooses, he may use a third language but in this case he is responsible for translation into English or French.

On the *Assembly and Council* and the relation between them, see especially: Brett, *The First Assembly* (1921); Fanshawe, *Reconstruction* (1925) 14–30; Fosdick, in *The League of Nation Starts* (London, 1920), ch. 1; * Fry, *Key-Book of the League of Nations*, 22–34; Harris, *What the League of Nations Is* (1925), ch. 3, and *Geneva, 1923*; Hoijer, *op. cit.*, 49–94; Hymans, "L'oeuvre du conseil," in 1 *Les origines et l'oeuvre de la societé des nations* (1924), 501–53; *Lange, "L'assemblée des délégues," in 2, *Les Origines*, etc., 358–415; Laski, *A Grammer of Politics* (1926), 626–38; Pollock, *The League of Nations* (2d ed., V, 1920), 98–112; Rougier, in 28 *R. D. I. P.* (1921), 197–412; Schücking and Wehberg, *Die Satzung des Völkerbundes* (1924), 260–333; Sweetser, *The League of Nations at Work* (1920), 29–48; Temperley, *The Second Year of the League* (1922), chs. 1–2; Williams, *The League of Nations Today* (1923), ch. 3; and * 8 W. P. F., *Pamphlets* (1925), 392–400.

[21] Of course the United States should be omitted from this list, but it continues to form part of the text of the Covenant.

[22] At the request of the Council, the Assembly, on Sept. 25, 1922, approved "the decision of the Council to increase the number of Members of the League chosen by the Assembly for representation on the Council from four to six." This decision went into effect at once.

[23] In 1921 the Assembly voted in favor of the following amendment, forming a second paragraph in Art. 4:

"The Assembly shall fix by a two-thirds majority the rules dealing with the election of the non-permanent Members of the Council, and particularly such regulations as relate to their term of office and the conditions of re-eligibility."

This amendment came into force in August, 1926.

In Sept., 1926, the Assembly elected nine of its members to non-permanent seats on the Council. Poland, Rumania and Chile were elected for three years; Holland, Columbia and China for two years; and Belgium, Czechoslovakia and Salvador for one year. By more than the necessary two-thirds majority, Poland was declared eligible for re-election at the end of her three

" The Council shall meet from time to time as occasion may require, and at least once a year, at the Seat of the League, or at such other place as may be decided upon.

" The Council may deal at its meetings with any matter within the sphere of action of the League or affecting the peace of the world.

" Any Member of the League not represented on the Council shall be invited to send a Representative to sit as a Member at any meeting of the Council during the consideration of matters specially affecting the interests of that Member of the League.

" At meetings of the Council, each Member of the League represented on the Council shall have one vote, and may have not more than one Representative " (Art. 4).[24]

years' service. This was evidently for the purpose of placating Poland who had demanded a permanent seat on the Council. Spain and Brazil were not to be so placated, and gave notice of withdrawal at the end of the two years prescribed in Art. 1 of the Covenant.

[24] The Council meets at least four times a year and as much oftener as is deemed necessary. Art. 11 also provides for an immediate meeting on the request of any Member of the League in case of emergency arising from war or threat of war. The sittings are usually held at Geneva, but there have been a number of meetings at London and Paris and a few at Rome and Brussels. From Jan. 16, 1920 to June 8, 1925 there were 33 meetings or an average of about six a year. During this period the Council acted upon 1483 agenda items. See 8 W. P. F., *Pamphlets* (1925), 399–400.

The Council is confronted by an ever-increasing volume of work. Most of its business is now conducted in public (it seems to be increasingly public), though it has the right to hold private sessions. In any case all the minutes of Council proceedings are published.

At each session the Council decides the items to be placed on the agenda of the next session. Should a Member-State request a subject to be considered at the next session, the Secretary-General will place it on the agenda. By a majority vote, new items may be placed on the agenda in the course of a session.

Among the special duties of the Council are: the appointment (with the approval of the Assembly) of the Secretary-General and the approval of the appointment by him of his staff (Art. 6); the election (with the Assembly) of the judges of the Court of International Justice; to name (with the approval of the Assembly) the "additional Members of the League whose representatives shall always be members of the Council (Art. 4); to increase (with the approval of the Assembly) "the number of Members of the League to be selected by the Assembly for representation on the Council" (Art. 4); to formulate plans for the reduction of armaments (Art. 8); to take such action as it may deem proper regarding any violation of the Covenant relating to the protection of minorities; to consider any action that may be deemed necessary when it is summoned in case of war or threat of war (Art. 11); to deal with disputes between Member-States submitted to the Council for inquiry and report (Arts. 12 and 15); to propose measures necessary to give effect to arbitral awards or the judicial

c. **Relation Between the Assembly and Council.**—The Assembly has been officially described as the " supreme organ " of the League, but the Council is a far more active and effective working body. Both Assembly and Council may deal at their meetings " with any matter within the sphere of action of the League or affecting the peace of the world." [25]

Aside from their special duties and activities, we thus have the unique spectacle of two political bodies endowed with practically equal and coördinate powers. Their relation appears to have been left purposely vague and ill-defined. It is neither the relation between a Senate and House of Representatives nor that between an executive and a legislature, either under the Presidential or under the Parliamentary systems of government. [26]

Since the Council is a much smaller body than the Assembly and meets much more frequently, it has naturally attracted to itself the greater part of the work of the League. It also performs many of its most important special duties

settlement of disputes between Member-States (Art. 13); to consider disputes not submitted to arbitration or judicial settlement, to report on them and, if necessary, refer such disputes to the Assembly (Art. 15); to decide whether a breach has been committed by any Member-State in resorting to war in contravention of the Covenant and to recommend to the several Governments what effective military, naval or aërial forces they shall severally contribute for the protection of the Covenants of the League (Art. 16); and to take whatever steps may be necessary for the settlement of disputes, or the prevention of hostilities, between a Member and a non-Member of the League or between non-Members (Art. 17).

[25] See above, Arts. 3 and 5 of the Covenant.

[26] "It is impossible to consider the Assembly as a chamber of deputies and the Council as an upper chamber. . . . It is equally impossible to consider the Council as invested with the executive and the Assembly with the legislative power. . . ." *Records of the First Assembly*, Plenary Meetings, 318. Cited by 8 W. P. F., *op. cit.*, 393.

Respecting the relations between the Assembly and Council, the following principles have been adopted for practical guidance:

" (*a*) The Council and the Assembly are each invested with particular powers and duties. Neither body has jurisdiction to render decision in a matter which has been expressly committed to the other organ of the League, but either body may discuss and investigate any matter which is within the general competence of the League.

" (*b*) Under the Covenant, representatives on the Council and the Assembly render their decisions as the representatives of their respective States, and in rendering such decisions they have no standing except as representatives.

" (*c*) The Council presents each year to the Assembly a Report on the Work performed by it." Fry, *Key-Book of L. of N.*, 33–34

or functions.   In practice it may be described as the main working or executive organ of the League.

Yet the Assembly is by no means a mere " debating society."   It also performs some very important special duties,[27] and freely criticises the work of the Council.   In practice it might almost be said to have become the general directing force of the League's activities.   Perhaps its most important rôle in the future will be that of furnishing an international forum where grievances may be ventilated and the pressure of public opinion throughout the world brought to bear upon the pacific solution of international disputes.[28]

d. **The Rule of Unanimity and Procedure.**—" Except where otherwise expressly provided in this Covenant, or by the terms of the present Treaty, decisions at any meeting of the Assembly or of the Council shall require the agreement of all the Members of the League represented at the meeting."[29]

[27] On the special duties of the Assembly and Council, see above, notes 20 and 24.

[28] Thus, during the Italo-Greek crisis of September, 1923 which had arisen from the occupation of Corfu, by Italy, the mere silent presence of the Assembly at Geneva (which showed admirable self-restraint in remaining silent until the crisis was over) undoubtedly contributed toward the withdrawal of Italy.

On the *Corfu Incident*, (more interesting than important from a legal point of view), see: Fosdick, in 68 *Rev. of Rev.* (1923), 481–86; Hill, in 18 *A. J.* (1924), 98–104; * 1 Kellor, *Security Against War* (1924), ch. 9; * Lowell and Hudson, in 6 W. P. F., *League of Nations* (1923), No. 3, pp. 169–210; Nicoglori, *L'affaire de Corfu* (1925); Strupp, in 31 *R. D. I. P.* (1924), 255 ff.; Visscher, in 51 (3 ser. 5) *R. D. I.* (1924), 213 ff., 377 ff.; Wright, in 18 *A. J.* (1924), 536–44.

[29] Apart from admission of new Member-States, approval of amendments by the Assembly, etc., the main exception to the rule of unanimity is that the consent of the representatives of the parties to a dispute is not required for a report on it by the Council to be considered unanimous (Art. 15).

The requirement of unanimity has been much criticised.   But as long as modern notions of sovereignty prevail, it is not likely to be changed.   As the Swiss Commentary (W. P. F., 3 *League of Nations*, 114–15) says: "In point of form, it constitutes a great obstacle to decisions; but in reality it is frequently easier to obtain unanimity than to secure a qualified majority, for the reason that a State will not assume without serious reasons the direct responsibility of defeating by its veto a resolution seriously desired by all the other Powers.   Moreover, to admit that a great Power could be controlled by a majority would raise the risk of provoking dangerous tensions.   The efficacy of the League of Nations might thus be put to a severe ordeal. . . ."

In practice States are very loathe to exercise their right of veto.   They often prefer to indicate their disapproval by absence or abstention from voting.   A compromise will usually be made to which all can agree.   It should be added that a resolution carried by a majority, and not unanimously be-

" All matters of procedure [30] at meetings of the Assembly or of the Council, including the appointment of Committees to investigate particular matters, shall be regulated by the Assembly or by the Council and may be decided by a majority of the Members of the League represented at the meeting " (Art. 5).

e. **The Secretariat and Expenses.**—" The permanent Secretariat shall be established at the Seat of the League. The Secretariat shall comprise a Secretary-General and such secretaries and staff as may be required.

" The first Secretary-General shall be the person named in the Annex; [31] thereafter the Secretary-General shall be appointed by the Council with the approval of the majority of the Assembly.

" The secretaries and the staff of the Secretariat shall be appointed by the Secretary-General with the approval of the Council.

" The Secretary-General shall act in that capacity at all meetings of the Assembly and of the Council. [32]

comes a recommendation upon which Member-States are severally entitled to act.

The rule of unanimity does not apply to wishes (*voeus*). As to these a bare majority suffices. See an important article by Williams, on "The League and Unanimity," in 19 *A. J.* (1925), 475–88, particularly 479–82, 485–88.

[30] All matters of procedure may be decided by a majority vote of the Member-States present and voting. These include appointment of committees and, in general, all decisions taken under the Rules of Procedure. For the Rules of Procedure adopted by the First Assembly, see W. P. F., 4 *League of Nations* (1921), 31–39.

[31] The Secretary-General named in the Annex is The Hon. Sir James Eric Drummond. He still (1927) holds this important position. It is doubtless due to his ability as an organizer that the League owes much of its success.

[32] "The members of the Secretariat act, during the period of office, in an international capacity, and are not in any way representatives of their own country." Memorandum of the Sec'y.-Gen. to Fifth Session of the Council, May 19, 1920. They constitute a sort of international civil service, consisting in 1925 of about 465 persons of 34 different nationalities, including both men and women. Only 75 of these are, however, classed as public officials.

Certain special duties are assigned to the Secretary-General by the Covenant. Thus, according to Art. 11, he shall, on the request of any Member of the League, forthwith summon a meeting of the Council in case of an emergency of war or threat of war; according to Art. 15, he will make all necessary arrangements for a full investigation and consideration of a dispute between Members of the League likely to lead to a rupture of which he has been duly notified by any party to the dispute; and Art. 18 prescribes that treaties between Members of the League shall be registered with the Secretariat. However,

" The expenses of the League shall be borne by the Members of the League in the proportion decided by the Assembly " (Art. 6).[33]

f. **Seat, Diplomatic Immunities, etc.**—" The Seat of the League is established at Geneva.

" The Council may at any time decide that the Seat of the League shall be established elsewhere.

" All positions under or in connection with the League, including the Secretariat, shall be open equally to men and women.

" Representatives of the Members of the League and officials of the League when engaged on the business of the League shall enjoy diplomatic privileges and immunities.

" The buildings and other property occupied by the

the Secretariat performs many other duties that are not indicated in the Covenant.

The Secretariat is essentially an administrative organ common to all and forming a link between the other organs of the League. Its function is mainly twofold: "(1) it provides machinery, administrative or other, for the operations of the various organs of the League; and (2) it is responsible for its own internal administration." It "carries out the work of the League (*a*) through its own Special Sections, and (*b*) in coöperation with a number of Auxiliary Organizations set up and convened by the Assembly and Council." Fry, *op. cit.*, 34.

There are 11 Special Sections, viz.,—Administrative and Minorities, Mandates, Political, Armaments, Economic and Financial, Transit and Communications, Humanitarian and Social, Health, Information, Legal, and Supervision of International Bureaux. Among the Auxiliary Organizations of the League with which the Secretariat coöperates are various Technical Organizations like those of Health, Transit and Communications, etc., the Permanent Mandates Commission, two Commissions on Armaments, the Intellectual Coöperation Committee, etc. For a list and description of these, see Fry, *op. cit.*, ch. 4, pp. 35–53. On the "Technical Organizations" of the League, see Cummings, in 2 *Les origines et l'oeuvre de la societé des nations* (1924), 282–89; * Fanshawe, *Reconstruction* (1925), ch. 6, pp. 122 ff.; Fry, *op. cit.*, and W. P. F. 4 *League of Nations* (1921), 64–103.

The higher officials hold office for seven years. Both higher and lower officials are appointed for twenty-one years subject to review of their appointments at the end of each period of seven years. The subordinate staff holds office for twenty-eight years, also subject to review at the end of each seven years.

On the *Secretariat*, see especially: Fanshawe, *op. cit.*, 30–32; * Fry, *op. cit.*, 34–53; Hoijer, *op. cit.*, 95 ff.; * Krabbe, in 2 *Les origines, op. cit.*, 264–82; * Laski, *A Grammer of Politics* (1926), 638–45; Schücking and Wehberg, *op. cit.*, 340–78; Williams, *The League of Nations Today* (1923), ch. 4; and W. P. F. 4 *League of Nations* (1921), 115 ff.

[33] The latter paragraph is an amendment which came into force on Aug. 13, 1924. The budget for 1925 totalled $4,371,963.49.

League or its officials or by Representatives attending its meetings shall be inviolable " (Art. 7).

320g. **Prevention of War.** *a.* **Reduction of Armaments.** —" The Members of the League recognize that the maintenance of peace requires the reduction of national armaments to the lowest point consistent with national safety and the enforcement by common action of international obligations.

" The Council, taking account of the geographical situation and circumstances of each State, shall formulate plans for such reduction for the consideration and action of the several Governments.

" Such plans shall be subject to reconsideration and revision at least every 10 years.

" After these plans shall have been adopted by the several Governments, the limits of armaments therein fixed shall not be exceeded without the concurrence of the Council.

" The Members of the League agree that the manufacture by private enterprise of munitions and implements of war is open to grave objections. The Council shall advise how the evil effects attendant upon such manufacture can be prevented, due regard being had to the necessities of those Members of the League which are not able to manufacture the munitions and implements of war necessary for their safety.

" The Members of the League undertake to interchange full and frank information as to the scale of their armaments, their military, naval and air programs, and the condition of such of their industries as are adaptable to warlike purposes (Art. 8).

" A permanent Commission shall be constituted to advise the Council on the execution of the provisions of Articles 1 and 8 and on military, naval and air questions generally " (Art. 9).[34]

---

[34] Though rivalry in armaments was recognized as a fundamental cause of modern war, little was accomplished in the direction of securing even a partial limitation of armaments prior to the World War. The only successful attempt was the Rush-Bagot Agreement of 1817 between the United States and Great Britain limiting the number of warships on the Great Lakes to three vessels for each Power. On the *Rush-Bagot Agreement*, see Callahan, *The Neutrality of the American Lakes* (1898), ch. 4; and Foster, *Report* on "Limitation of

b. Guaranties against Aggression.—" The Members of the League undertake to respect and preserve as against

Armament on the Great Lakes," reprinted by the Carnegie Endowment, pamph. No. 2, in 1914.

The Hague Conferences failed even to secure a limitation of the "progressive increase of armaments." Cf. *supra*, Nos. 82–83. On the history of efforts to secure a limitation of armaments prior to the World War, see Buell, *Int. Relations* (1925), ch. 23, pp. 528–31; Picard, *La question de la limitation des armaments* (1911); * Wehberg, *Limitation of Armaments* (1921), and *Die Int. Beschränkung der Rüstungen* (1919).

The reduction of national armaments to the "lowest point consistent with *domestic* safety" was the fourth of Wilson's Fourteen Points. At the Paris Conference the word *domestic* was changed to *national*. Cf. *supra*, p. 127. On the "Struggle for Limitation of Armaments" at Paris, see especially: 2 Baker, *Woodrow Wilson and World Settlement* (1922–23), Pt. IV, chs. 19–24. For documents, see 3 *Ibid.*, 197–224. On the disarmament of Germany through the Versailles Treaty, see *supra*, pp. 138–39 and notes. On the work of the *Washington Conference re* naval armaments, see *supra*, pp. 145 ff.

The League of Nations has devoted more of its time and attention to this difficult and intricate problem than perhaps to any other, but thus far with few positive results, though it is hoped that the forthcoming International Conference on Armaments may accomplish something substantial.

Under Art. 8 the Council of the League is charged with these duties: (1) to formulate plans for the reduction of armaments for the consideration and action of the several Governments; and (2) to advise as to how the evil effects attendant upon the manufacture by private enterprise of munitions and implements of war can be prevented. The Members of the League agree to interchange full and frank information regarding their armaments, etc. Art. 9 provides that a permanent Commission shall be constituted to advise the Council on these matters.

Such a Permanent Advisory Commission known as the P. A. C. was appointed some months before the meeting of the First Assembly in November, 1920, but it consisted exclusively of naval, military and air representatives of each of the States represented on the Council and was subject to criticism. Yielding to pressure by the First Assembly, there was created an additional Commission, known as the T. M. C. or Temporary Mixed Commission which included statesmen like Lord Cecil, representatives of the International Labor Bureau, as well as military, economic and financial experts.

The T. M. C. began its work in March, 1921 with the consideration of the illicit traffic in as well as the private manufacture of arms and ammunition. The consideration of the trade in war materials was rendered necessary by the failure of the Great Powers, mainly due to the opposition of the United States, to ratify the Treaty signed at St. Germain in 1919 (cf. *supra*, p. 143).

It was not until 1924 that the American Government would condescend to explain its objections to the St. Germain Convention and aid in drafting a new Treaty. Such a Convention was finally signed by the United States in 1925. It provides for a general system of supervision and publicity for the international trade in arms and ammunition, prescribes a strict system of licenses for arms exports from every country, and excludes arms imports altogether from undeveloped areas, including nearly the whole of Africa and extensive coastal regions in South-West Asia. For the text of this Convention, see *Treaty Series*. For a summary, see 9 W. P. F., *Pamphlets* (1926), 234–37.

external aggression the territorial integrity and existing political independence of all Members of the League. In case of any such aggression or in case of any threat or danger of such aggression, the Council shall advise upon the means by which this obligation shall be fulfilled " (Art. 10).[35]

For comment, see 20 *A. J.* (1926), 151–54. For a protocol relating to Chemical and Bacteriological Warfare, see 9 W. P. F., *op. cit.*, 237.

At the same time the T. M. C. has been studying the question of the private manufacture of arms, and the preparation of a convention on this subject was ordered by the Fourth Assembly in 1924.

Considerable work has also been done in the way of securing knowledge regarding armaments. During 1922 and 1923 the T. M. C. published much statistical information, and in 1923 the Council authorized the Secretariat to begin the publication of a yearbook on armaments. The result is the annual known as the *Armaments Year-Book: General and Statistical Information.*

It should be noted that late in 1924 the Temporary Mixed Commission was reorganized under the name of the Coördination Commission.

But all this work is subsidiary to the main purpose of Arts. 8 and 9 which is to secure general reduction of armaments. In this main task little positive progress has as yet been made, though it is hoped that the foundations for important results may have been laid.

In 1922 the Assembly of the League applied itself anew to this task. A resolution was adopted which declared that "no scheme for the reduction of armaments can be fully successful unless it is general," and that "in the present state of the world many Governments would be unable to accept the responsibility for a successful reduction of armaments unless they received in exchange a satisfactory guarantee of the safety of their country."

Due to the labors of Lord Cecil and others, these principles found embodiment in the Draft Treaty of Mutual Assistance which was rejected by the Labor Government of Great Britain (cf. *supra*, p. 150). This project was replaced by the Geneva Protocol based upon the idea of combining disarmament with security through arbitration which was rejected by the British Tory Government (cf. *supra*, p. 151).

On the work of the League of Nations *re Disarmament*, see: Alexander, *The Revival of Europe* (1924), ch. 5; * Baker, *The Geneva Protocol* (1925), chs. 2 and 10; Buell, *Int. Relations* (1925), ch. 23; * Fanshawe, *Reconstruction* (1925), 86–117; Fry, *op. cit.*, ch. 10; Harris, *What the League of Nations Is* (1925), ch. 7; Lange, in 2 *Les origines et l'oeuvre de la societé des nations* (1924), 416–52; * Toynbee, *Survey of Int. Affairs, 1924* (1926), 1 ff.; * W. P. F., 8 *Pamphlets,* (1925) 463–84; and * Wheeler-Bennett, *Reduction of Armaments* (1925).

On the *Reduction of Armaments* generally, see especially: *Bliss in 4 *For. Aff.* (1926), 353–68, and in House and Seymour, *What Really Happened at Paris* (1921), ch. 16; Enock, *The Problem of Armaments* (1923); Picard, *La Limitation des armaments* (1911); Reely, *Disarmament* (selected articles, 1921); "The Staggering Burden of Armaments," in 4 W. P. F., *League of Nations* (1921), 213–72, 301–64; Wehberg, *Die Beschränkung der Rüstungen,* and *Limitations of Armaments* (1921); and * Wheeler-Bennett, *The Reduction of Armaments* (1925).

[35] This article, which was held erroneously by Ex-President Wilson to be the "heart of the Covenant," has been much criticised both on the grounds of

c. Action in Case of War or Threat of War.—" Any war or threat of war, whether immediately affecting any of the Members of the League or not, is hereby declared a matter

its being too weak and too strong. It was partly the fear of a Super-State engendered by this and other articles (particularly Arts. 16–17) that led to the rejection of the Treaty of Versailles by the United States Senate. On the other hand, the secondary States have been generally disposed to look upon Art. 10 as the "Keystone of the League."

On Dec. 3, 1920 Canada proposed the elimination of the article. The question as to what obligations are imposed by it was referred to a committee of five jurists who held its fundamental idea to be that no territorial changes (annexations) or loss of independence should result from war or aggression. For their report, see I *Bibliotheca Visseriana*, 129 ff.

At the Fourth Assembly in 1923, 29 States voted in favor of the following interpretative resolution:

"It is in conformity with the spirit of Article 10 that, in the event of the Council considering it to be its duty to recommend the application of military measures in consequence of an aggression or danger or threat of aggression, the Council shall be bound to take account, more particularly of the geographical situation and of the special conditions of each State.

"It is for the constitutional authorities of each Member to decide in reference to the obligation of preserving the independence and the integrity of the territory of Members, in what degree the Member is bound to assure the execution of this obligation by employment of its military forces.

"The recommendation made by the Council shall be regarded as being of the highest importance, and shall be taken into consideration by all Members of the League with the desire to execute their engagements in good faith." *L. of N. Official Journal*, Spec. Supp., No. 13, *Records of Fourth Assembly* (1923), 86.

It is interesting to note that Persia was the only State that voted against this interpretative resolution, but there were 22 absences or abstentions. The President announced that since unanimity was not obtained, he was unable to declare the resolution adopted. On the other hand, in accordance with a precedent in a similar case, he would not declare the motion rejected. He accordingly declared it not adopted.

By Art. 10 the Members of the League assume a double obligation: (1) to respect, and (2) to preserve the territorial integrity and *existing* political independence of one another *against external aggression*. The word *existing* has reference to the political status existing at the time of the aggression rather than at the time the agreement was made. The phrase *external aggression* appears to mean an attempt at conquest, annexation, or retention of occupied territory rather than a mere invasion in consequence of a war which may possibly not be illegal from the standpoint of the League, a reprisal or an act of self-help which might or might not constitute an external aggression. The use of the word *external* makes it clear that the League is no Holy Alliance aiming to crush revolutions or to interfere in the internal affairs of States.

Contrary to President Wilson's view (see *Hearings*, 66 Cong., 1st sess. Doc. No. 106, pp. 515, 535 ff.), the obligations assumed under Art. 10 are legal as well as moral in their nature. The guaranties are joint or collective, but are nevertheless severally and individually or separately binding. On the treaties of guarantee, see *supra*, No. 301.

Art. 10 does not guarantee the *status quo*. It only guarantees against

of concern to the whole League, and the League shall take any action that may be deemed wise and effectual to safeguard the peace of nations.   In case any such emergency should arise, the Secretary-General shall, on the request of any Member of the League, forthwith summon a meeting of the Council.

" It is also declared to be the friendly right of each Member of the League to bring to the attention of the Assembly or of the Council any circumstance whatever affecting international relations which threatens to disturb international peace or the good understanding between nations upon which peace depends " (Art. 11).[36]

territorial and political changes brought about by external aggression.   And it should not be overlooked that Art. 19 prescribes that "the Assembly may from time to time advise the reconsideration by Members of the League of treaties which have become inapplicable, and the consideration of international conditions whose continuance might endanger the peace of the world."

It should be also particularly noted that in case of aggression or danger of aggression, the Council shall merely advise upon the means by which the obligation is to be carried out, *i.e.*, the means of execution are left wholly to the discretion of the Member-States.

On *Article 10*, see especially: Adachi and Visscher, in 30 *Annuaire de l'Institut de Droit Int.* (1923), 22–47; Buell, *op. cit.*, ch. 24, pp. 557 ff.; Hoijer, *op. cit.*, 167–87; Pollock, *op. cit.*, 133–36; Rolin, in 2 *Les origines et l'oeuvre de la societé des nations* (1924), 453–88; Schücking and Wehberg, *op. cit.*, 449–66; Scott, in 18 *A. J.* (1924), 108–13; Struycken, in 1 *Bibliotheka Visseriana*, 93–157; and *Swiss Commentary*, in 3 W. P. F., *L. of N.* (1920), 123–25.

[36] This important article confers upon the League, more particularly upon the Council, a general right of mediation (cf. *supra*, No. 307), if not of collective intervention (cf. *supra*, Nos. 135–45, particularly note 15 on p. 240 and No. 143, p. 243.

Its importance was hardly realized at the time the League was established, but it has in practice proved to be one of the most useful articles of the Covenant.   Schücking and Wehberg (*op. cit.*, 469–500) mention no less than 25 instances of the application of Arts. 11 and 15.   The best example for the student is perhaps that of Aaland Islands.

On the *Case of the Aaland Islands*, see especially: Brown, in 15 *A. J.* (1921), 268–72; *Gregory, in 17 *A. J.* (1923), 63–76; * Kellor, 1 *Security Against War* (1924), ch. 13;   League of Nations, *Political Activities* (1925), 7–23; Schücking and Wehberg, *op. cit.*, 470–72; Stael-Holstein, in 12 *Z. V.*, (1923), 19 ff.; Strupp, 1 *Wörterbuch*, (1924) 19 ff.; and * Visscher, in 48 (3d ser. 2) *R. D. I.* (1921), 35 ff., 243 ff., 568 ff.; W. P. F., 8 *Yearbook of L. of N.* (1925), 425–28.

For other examples, both of successful and unsuccessful mediations and interventions by the Council, such as the dispute between Poland and Lithuania over the seizure of Vilna by the Poles (unsuccessful), the successful intervention of the League against the Jugo-Slavic invasion of Albania, the Upper Silesian Settlement, the Memel Dispute, the Corfu Incident (for special references on this incident, see above, note 28), etc., see: Alexander, *The Revival of*

d. **Submission of Disputes for Settlement.**—" The Members of the League agree that, if there should arise between them any dispute likely to lead to a rupture, they will submit the matter either to arbitration *or judicial settlement* or to inquiry by the Council, and they agree in no case to resort to war until three months after the award by the arbitrators *or the judicial decision*, or the report by the Council.

"In any case under this Article the award of the arbitrators *or the judicial decision* shall be made within a reasonable time, and the report of the Council shall be made within six months after the submission of the dispute " (Art. 12).[37]

e. **Arbitration and Judicial Settlement.**—" The Members of the League agree that, whenever any dispute shall arise between them which they recognize to be suitable for

Europe (1924), ch. 4; * Fanshawe, *Reconstruction* (1925), ch. 9, pp. 251–84; Harris, *What the League of Nations Is* (1924), ch. 6; * 1 Kellor, *op. cit.*, chs. 7–13 (hypercritical); Kohn, *Organization and work of the League* (1924), chs. 3–6; League of Nations, *op. cit.*, 24 ff.; Schücking and Wehberg, *op. cit.*, 469–500; * Williams, *op. cit.*, chs. 5–6; W. P. F., 13 *League of Nations* (1920), 280–85, *op. cit.*, (1922), 261–73 and * 8 *Pamphlets* (1925), 424–60.

The most recent application of Art. 11 (Art. 10 was also invoked) was in the case of the invasion of Bulgaria by Greek Soldiers on Oct. 21, 1925. The Bulgarian appeal to the League was received in Geneva early on the morning of Oct. 23d. The Council met at 6:00 P.M. on Oct. 26th and telegraphed its orders to the Greek and Bulgarian Governments to withdraw their troops behind their respective frontiers. At midnight of Oct. 28th, the last invading soldier was back on his territory.

On the *Greco-Bulgarian Affair*, see Glasgow, in 129 *Contemp. Rev.* (1925), 39 ff. and 108 ff.; * 9 W. P. F., *Pamphlets* (1925), 201–17, and 10 W. P. F., 7th *Yearbook* (1927), 201–04.

[37] The phrases set in italics came into force as an amendment on Sept. 26, 1924.

By this article the Members of the League obligate themselves: (1) to submit every dispute between them likely to lead to a rupture to (*a*) arbitration, (*b*) judicial settlement, or (*c*) inquiry by the Council; and (2) in no case to resort to war until three months after the arbitral award, the judicial decision, or the Council's report. The arbitral award and the judicial decision shall be made within a reasonable time and the Council's report within six months after the submission of the dispute. This insures at least nine months of delay before the disputants may resort to war. The Members of the League have pledged themselves to follow this procedure in case of dangerous controversies.

The observance of this agreement would exclude the possibility of an ultimatum or conditional declaration of war and a breaking of diplomatic relations, at least until the period of delay stipulated for has passed. It should also prevent military reprisals and pacific blockades. Cf. *infra*, Nos. 322–23. See also Schücking and Wehberg, *op. cit.*, 507 ff. For other good commentaries see *Swiss Commentary, op. cit.*, 126–32; and Hoijer, *op. cit.*, 218 ff.

submission to arbitration *or judicial settlement*, and which can not be satisfactorily settled by diplomacy, they will submit the whole subject matter to arbitration *or judicial settlement.*

" Disputes as to the interpretation of a treaty, as to any question of international law, as to the existence of any fact which if established would constitute a breach of any international obligation, or as to the extent and nature of the reparation to be made for any such breach, are declared to be among those which are generally suitable for submission to arbitration *or judicial settlement.*

" *For the consideration of any such dispute, the court to which the case is referred shall be the Permanent Court of International Justice, established in accordance with Article* 14,[38] *or any tribunal agreed to by the parties to the dispute or stipulated in any convention existing between them.*

" The Members of the League agree that they will carry out in full good faith any award *or decision* that may be rendered and that they will not resort to war against a Member of the League which complies therewith. In the event of any failure to carry out such an award *or decision*, the Council shall propose what steps should be taken to give effect thereto " (Art. 13).[39]

[For Article 14 on " The Permanent Court of International Justice, see *supra*, p. 481.]

[38] For Art. 14, see *supra*, p. 481.

[39] The parts set in italics came into force as an amendment on Sept. 26, 1924.

In Art. 13 the Members of the League agree that if diplomacy fails and the dispute is one which the parties recognize as suitable for arbitration or judicial settlement, they will submit the whole subject matter to one of these modes of decision. Four classes of disputes are enumerated as "among those" suitable for such methods of settlement. The disputants are free to choose between the Court of International Justice and any other tribunal agreed upon or stipulated by them in a treaty.

They further agree to execute in good faith any arbitral award or judicial decision and that they "will not resort to war against a Member of the League which complies therewith." The meaning of this seems to be that "the loser of a case may not make armed resistance to a State that has gained the verdict and is taking steps to secure the benefit of it." Harris, *What the League of Nations Is* (1924), 49.

The last sentence in Art. 13 is rather vague. But, judging from past experience, States will make little or no difficulty in the matter of executing arbitral awards or judicial decisions against them. The difficulty is in inducing them to submit their serious controversies to such modes of settlement.

f. **Disputes not Submitted to Arbitration or Judicial Settlement.**—-" If there should arise between Members of the League any dispute likely to lead to a rupture, which is not submitted to arbitration *or judicial settlement* in accordance with Article 13, the Members of the League agree that they will submit the matter to the Council. Any party to the dispute may effect such submission by giving notice of the existence of the dispute to the Secretary-General, who will make all necessary arrangements for a full investigation and consideration thereof.

" For this purpose the parties to the dispute will communicate to the Secretary-General, as promptly as possible, statements of their case with all the relevant facts and papers, and the Council may forthwith direct the publication thereof.

" The Council shall endeavor to effect a settlement of the dispute and, if such efforts are successful, a statement shall be made public giving such facts and explanations regarding the dispute and the terms of settlement thereof as the Council may deem appropriate.

" If the dispute is not thus settled, the Council, either unanimously or by a majority vote, shall make and publish a report containing a statement of the facts of the dispute and the recommendations which are deemed just and proper in regard thereto.

" Any Member of the League represented on the Council may make public a statement of the facts of the dispute and of its conclusions regarding the same.

" If a report by the Council is unanimously agreed to by the Members thereof other than the Representatives of one or more of the parties to the dispute, the Members of the League agree that they will not go to war with any party to the dispute which complies with the recommendations of the report.

" If the Council fails to reach a report which is unanimously agreed to by the members thereof, other than the Representatives of one or more of the parties to the dispute, the Members of the League reserve to themselves the right to take such action as they shall consider necessary for the maintenance of right and justice.

" If the dispute between the parties is claimed by one of them, and is found by the Council, to arise out of a matter which by international law is solely within the domestic jurisdiction [40] of that party, the Council shall so report, and shall make no recommendation as to its settlement.

" The Council may in any case under this Article refer the dispute to the Assembly. The dispute shall be so referred at the request of either party to the dispute, provided that such request be made within 14 days after the submission of the dispute to the Council.

" In any case referred to the Assembly, all the provisions of this Article and of Article 12 relating to the action and powers of the Council shall apply to the action and powers of the Assembly, provided that a report made by the Assembly, if concurred in by the Representatives of those Members of the League represented on the Council and of a majority of the other Members of the League, exclusive in

[40] The word *solely* in this paragraph should be particularly noted. It is generally believed that paragraph 8 of Art. 15 would exclude questions relating to immigration and tariff from the jurisdiction of the Council; but international agreements regarding these matters would certainly not be excluded, and such questions might have international aspects which would bring them within its jurisdiction. Certainly domestic questions threatening war or endangering good understanding between nations are not excluded from consideration by the League (see Art. 11).

In the advisory opinion respecting the Tunis-Morocco Nationality Questions (cf. *supra*, note 25 on p. 185), the Court of International Justice said: "The question whether a certain matter is or is not solely within the jurisdiction of a State is an essentially relative question; it depends upon the development of international relations. Thus, in the present state of International Law, questions of nationality are, in the opinion of the Court, in principle within the reserved domain." See *Advisory Opinions*, Series V, No. 4.

"The Court examined the French protectorates over Tunis and Morocco, and concluded that, while a State possesses exclusive jurisdiction in regard to nationality questions in its own territory, the question whether this extends to protected territory is a question of International Law." Hudson, *Court of Int. Justice* (1925), 51.

Fenwick (see editorial in 19 *A. J.* 1925, p. 144) defines domestic questions as "all questions upon which the members of the international community have not agreed to accept the regulation of a principle or rule of law. They are, in respect to their objects, the sum total of national interests minus the interests governed by International Law."

On "Matters of Domestic Jurisdiction," see also: Brierly, in *Brit. Yr. Book* (1925), 8–19; Castberg, in 49 (3 third ser.), *R. D. I.* (1922), 195–202; and Schücking and Wehberg, *op. cit.*, 588–92. The subject is one that deserves more consideration than it has received. See also above, note 36, p. 511 for references on the case of the Aaland Islands.

each case of the Representatives of the parties to the dispute, shall have the same force as a report by the Council concurred in by all the members thereof other than the Representatives of one or more of the parties to the dispute " (Art. 15).[41]

g. **Sanctions of Pacific Settlement.**—" Should any Member of the League resort to war in disregard of its covenants under Articles 12, 13 or 15, it shall *ipso facto* be deemed to have committed an act of war against all other Members of the League, which hereby undertake immediately to subject it to the severance of all trade or financial relations, the prohibition of all intercourse between their nationals and the nationals of the covenant-breaking State,

[41] By Art. 15 the Members of the League are free to submit *all* dangerous disputes that are not submitted to arbitration or judicial settlement to the Council (excepting those of domestic jurisdiction—see above) which shall try to effect a settlement of the dispute. If such efforts are successful, the Council shall publish such a statement regarding the facts and terms of settlement as it deems appropriate.

If the dispute is not thus settled, resort is had to publicity. The Council, either unanimously or by a majority vote, shall publish the facts, together with its recommendations; but provision is also made for a minority report. If the report of the Council is unanimous (other than the representatives of one or more of the parties to the dispute), the Members of the League agree that "they will not go to war with any party to the dispute which complies with the recommendations of the report." If the Council fails to agree on a report that is unanimous (other than, etc.), the Members of the League apparently reserve to themselves the right to go to war. It is not clear in what sense the phrase "Members of the League" is here used.

In the last two paragraphs of Art. 15, provision is made for reference of the dispute to the Assembly.

"Under Article 15 a dispute referred to the Council can be dealt with by it in several ways:

"(1) The Council can keep the matter in its own hands. . . .

"(2) It can submit any dispute of a legal nature for the opinion of the Permanent Court, though in this case the finding of the Court will have no force until endorsed by the Council.

"(3) While keeping the matter in its own hands, the Council can refer single points for judicial opinion.

"(4) There is nothing to prevent the Council from referring any matter to a committee, or to prevent such a committee from being a standing body. An opening is left, therefore, for the reference of suitable issues to such non-political bodies as the 'Commissions of Conciliation' which are desired in many quarters. . . .

"(5) The Council may at any time refer a dispute to the Assembly. . . ." *British Official Commentary on the Covenant*, in Pollock, *League of Nations*, 152–53 or 232–33. For commentaries on Art. 15, see also Hoijer, *op. cit.*, 263; and Schücking and Wehberg, *op. cit.*, 571–600; and Swiss Commentary, *op. cit.*, 136–40.

and the prevention of all financial, commercial or personal intercourse between the nationals of the covenant-breaking State and the nationals of any other State, whether a Member of the League or not.[42]

" It shall be the duty of the Council in such case to recommend to the several Governments concerned what effective military, naval or air force the Members of the League shall severally contribute to the armed forces to be used to protect the covenants of the League.

" The Members of the League agree, further, that they will mutually support one another in the financial and economic measures which are taken under this Article, in order to minimize the loss and inconvenience resulting from the above measures, and that they will mutually support one another in resisting any special measures aimed at one of their number by the covenant-breaking State, and that they will take the necessary steps to afford passage through their territory to the forces of any of the Members of the League which are coöperating to protect the covenants of the League.

[42] The Fifth Assembly on Sept. 27, 1924 voted the following amendments to Art. 16, to replace paragraph 1:

"Should any Member of the League resort to war in disregard of its covenants under Articles 12, 13 or 15, it shall *ipso facto* be deemed to have committed an act of war against all other Members of the League, which hereby undertake immediately to subject it to the severance of all trade or financial relations and to prohibit all intercourse at least between persons resident within their territories and persons resident within the territory of the covenant-breaking State, and, if they deem it expedient, also between their nationals and the nationals of the covenant-breaking State, and to prevent all financial, commercial or personal intercourse at least between persons resident within the territory of that State and persons resident within the territory of any other State, whether a Member of the League or not, and, if they deem it expedient, also between the nationals of that State and the nationals of any other State whether a Member of the League or not.

"It is for the Council to give an opinion whether or not a breach of the Covenant has taken place. In deliberations on this question in the Council, the votes of Members of the League alleged to have resorted to war and of Members against whom such action was directed shall not be counted.

"The Council will notify all Members of the League the date which it recommends for the application of the economic pressure under this Article.

"Nevertheless, the Council may, in the case of particular Members, postpone the coming into force of any of these measures for a specified period where it is satisfied that such a postponement will facilitate the attainment of the object of the measures referred to in the preceding paragraph, or that it is necessary in order to minimize the loss and inconvenience which will be caused to such Members."

" Any Member of the League which has violated any covenant of the League may be declared to be no longer a Member of the League by a vote of the Council concurred in by the Representatives of all the other Members of the League represented thereon " (Art. 16).[43]

[43] "The sanctions of Art. 16, with the exception of the last paragraph, apply only to breaches of the Covenant involving a resort to war.   In the first instance, it is left to individual States to decide whether or not such a breach has occurred and an act of war against the League has been thereby committed. . . . Any State, therefore, is justified in such a case in breaking off relations with the offending State on its own initiative, but it is probable, in fact, that the smaller States, unless directly attacked, will wait to see what decision is taken by the Great Powers or by the Council, which is bound to meet as soon as possible, and is certain to do so within a few hours.   It is the duty of the Council, with the help of its military, naval and air advisers, to recommend what effective force each Member of the League shall supply; for this purpose, each Member from which a contribution is required has the right to attend the Council, with power of veto, during the consideration of its particular case. . . .

"It is true that, in default of a strong international striking force, ready for instant action in all parts of the world, the Members of the League must make their own arrangements for immediate self-defense against any force that could be suddenly concentrated against them, relying on such understandings as they have come to with their neighbors previously for this purpose.   There is nothing in the Covenant (see Art. 21) to forbid defensive conventions between States, so long as they are really and solely defensive, and their contents are made public.   They will, in fact, be welcomed, in so far as they tend to preserve the peace of the world.

"To meet the first shock of sudden aggression, therefore, States must rely in their own resistance and the aid of their neighbors. . . .

"The last paragraph of Art. 16 is intended to meet the case of a State which, after violating its covenants, attempts to retain its position in the Assembly and Council." *British Commentary*, in Pollock, *op. cit.*, 233–35. For other commentaries, see Hoijer, *op. cit.*, 303 ff.; Pollock, *op. cit.*, 156–64; Schücking and Wehberg, *op. cit.*, 600–37; and *Swiss Commentary*, in 3 W. P. F., *L. of N.*, (1920) 140–50.

The sanctions provided for in Art. 16 are of two kinds—economic and military.   The economic sanctions include: (1) the immediate and general rupture of all trade and financial relations; (2) the prohibition of all intercourse, "at least between persons resident within their territories and persons resident within the territory of the covenant-breaking State," etc.; and (3) the prevention of "all financial, commercial or personal intercourse, at least between persons resident within the territory of that State and persons resident within the territory of any other State, whether a Member of the League or not," etc. (see amendment to parag. 1, quoted above in note 42). The Members of the League agree, further (in parag. 3 of Art. 16) to give one another mutual support in the execution of these financial and economic sanctions.

In case it is decided to apply military sanctions, the Council has merely the duty to *recommend* to the several Governments concerned what armed forces they shall severally contribute (parag. 2 of Art. 16).

h. **Disputes with and between Non-Members.**—" In the event of a dispute between a Member of the League and a State which is not a Member of the League, or between States not Members of the League, the State or States not Members of the League shall be invited to accept the obligations of Membership in the League for the purposes of such dispute, upon such conditions as the Council may deem just. If such invitation is accepted, the provisions of Articles 12 to 16 inclusive, shall be applied with such modifications as may be deemed necessary by the Council.

" Upon such invitation being given, the Council shall immediately institute an inquiry into the circumstances of the dispute and recommend such action as may seem best and most effectual in the circumstances.

" If a State so invited shall refuse to accept the obligations of Membership in the League for the purposes of such dispute, and shall resort to war against a Member of the League, the provisions of Article 16 shall be applicable as against the State taking such action.

" If both parties to the dispute, when so invited, refuse to accept the obligations of Membership in the League for the purposes of such dispute, the Council may take such measures and make such recommendations as will prevent hostilities and will result in the settlement of the dispute " (Art. 17).[44]

At the Paris Conference the French delegation repeatedly urged an international army or police force with a permanent international staff for the execution of the Treaty and Covenant and for security against sudden attack. But wiser counsels prevailed. The French view in favor of military sanctions has had considerable support on the Continent of Europe. In general, it may be said that in Europe more reliance is based upon force as a means of security than in Anglo-Saxon countries where there seems to be more confidence in public opinion and the so-called moral forces. Economic sanctions have never been adequately treated by publicists.

On *Sanctions* generally, see especially: Dumas, in 5 *A. J.* (1911), 934–57, and *Les sanctions de l'arbitrage int.* (1905); Hadjiscos, *Les sanctions int. de la Societé des Nations* (1920); Lammasch, *Völkermord oder Völkerbund* (1920), ch. 10; * Mitrany, *The Problem of Int. Sancturés* (1925); * Nippold, *Develop. of Int. Law after the World War* (1923), 54–93; Piccioni, in 30 *R. D. I. P.* (1923), 242–50; Rappard, *Int. Relations viewed from Geneva* (1925), ch. 5; Root, in 2 *A. J.* (1908) 451–57; Roxburgh, in 14 *A. J.* (1920), 26–37; and Visscher, *The Stabilization of Europe* (1924), chs. 4–5.

There has been thus far no occasion for the application of Art. 16.

[44] " Art. 17 asserts the claim of the League that no State, whether a Member of the League or not has the right to disturb the peace of the world till peaceful

320h. Treaties and Understandings. *a.* **Registration and Publication of Treaties.**—"Every treaty or international engagement entered into hereafter by any Member of the League shall be forthwith registered with the Secretariat and shall as soon as possible be published by it. No such treaty or international engagement shall be binding until so registered " (Art. 18).[45]

b. **Reconsideration of Treaties.**—"The Assembly may from time to time advise the reconsideration by Members of the League of treaties which have become inapplicable, and the consideration of international conditions whose continuance might endanger the peace of the world " (Art. 19).[46]

methods of settlement have been tried. As in early English law any act of violence, wherever committed, came to be regarded as a breach of the King's peace, so any and every sudden act of war is henceforward a breach of the peace of the League, which will exact due reparation." *British Commentary*, in Pollock, *op. cit.*, 235. See also Pollock, 164–70; Schücking and Wehberg, *op. cit.*, 637–44; and *Swiss Commentary*, 147–50.

[45] "Art. 18 makes registration, and not publication, the condition for the validity of treaties . . . ; but it is the duty of the Secretariat to publish all treaties as soon as this can be done." *British Commentary*, in Pollock, *op. cit.*, 235–36. Cf. Pollock, *op. cit.*, 171–72; Schücking and Wehberg, *op. cit.*, 644 ff.; and *Swiss Commentary*, 150.

This article constitutes at least a partial attempt to fulfil the first of Wilson's Fourteen Points. From July 5, 1920, when the first treaty was registered, to March 1, 1925, there had been registered and published in the League of Nation's *Treaty Series* (of which 32 vols. had been published) 829 conventions.

There has been little complaint of a failure to comply with Art. 18 which calls for the registration and publication of "*every* treaty or international engagement entered into *hereafter* by any Member of the League." There was considerable criticism of the failure of France and Belgium to present for registration the terms of a military understanding signed on Sept. 7, 1920 by the chiefs of staff of the French and Belgian armies, though the letters relating to the matter exchanged between the Ministers of Foreign Affairs were registered. The British Government notified the Secretary-General of the League on Feb. 15, 1921 that it had not presented for registration a large number of financial arrangements, many of them of small general importance.

In a memorandum submitted by the Secretary-General and approved by the Council of the League, registration was said to be required of "not only every formal treaty of whatsoever character and every international convention, but also any other international engagement or act by which nations or their governments intend to establish legal obligations between themselves and another State, nation or government." See Hudson, "The Registration and Publication of Treaties," in 19 *A. J.* (1925), 276–77.

[46] It should be noted that the functions of the Assembly, so far as the revision of treaties is concerned, are merely advisory; and that to give advice or express a wish, a majority vote appears to be sufficient. The advice is presumably addressed to the Members of the League concerned in the revision. The right of revision is not granted to the Assembly.

c. **Abrogation of Inconsistent Obligations.**—" The Members of the League severally agree that this Covenant is accepted as abrogating all obligations or understandings *inter se* which are inconsistent with the terms thereof, and solemnly undertake that they will not hereafter enter into any engagements inconsistent with the terms thereof.

" In case any Member of the League shall, before

"Art. 19 should be read together with Art. 11 which authorizes every Member of the League to call the attention of the Council or the Assembly to conditions appearing likely to endanger the peace.

"The weaknesses of these Articles, taken together or separately, is that they do not provide for any systematic revision or consolidation of the Law of Nations. That is a work which ought be to taken in hand and for which the League is competent." Pollock, *op. cit.*, 172.

The Advisory Committee of Jurists, which met at The Hague in July, 1920, recommended the institution of successive Conferences for the Advancement of International Law for the purposes of restating its "established rules" and formulating "amendments and additions," etc. (see Finch, in 19 *A. J.*, 1925, p. 538). But these proposals were not accepted by the Assembly at Geneva.

However, in Dec., 1924, the Council of the League appointed a Committee of Experts for the Progressive Codification of International Law, in accordance with a resolution adopted by the Fifth Assembly on Sept. 22, 1924. The prescribed duties of this Committee are: (1) to prepare a provisional list of the subjects of International Law, the regulation of which by international agreement would seem to be most desirable at the present moment; (2) tc examine replies received by the Governments to whom the list is communicated; and (3) to report to the Council on the questions which are sufficiently ripe, etc. (Finch, *op. cit.*, 534).

Such a committee, representing the main forms of civilization and the principle legal systems of the world, held its first meeting at Geneva early in April, 1925. A provisional list of subjects was selected for consideration and assigned to sub-committees. For the personnel of the Committee and provisional list of subjects, see Finch, *op. cit.*, 534–36.

Thus the work of official codification may be said to have begun. It is not codification in the old narrow sense of merely stating existing law in the form of a code, but also includes legislation or the adoption of new rules. What is needed for the advancement of International Law is not so much codification as legislation. In the international world, either can only be accomplished adequately through the treaty-making power, but this power can be set in motion through the agency or under the auspices of the League of Nations.

On *Codification* (both in the older and newer sense), see especially: Alvarez, *La codification de droit int.* (1912); *Baker, in *Brit. Yr. Bk.* (1924), 38–65; Crocker, in 18 *A. J.* (1924), 38–55; Fenwick, 72–75; * Garner, *Recent Developments in Int. Law* (1925), Sect. 14; Garner and Finch, in 19 *A. J.* (1925), 327 –33, and 534–42; Nys, in 5 *A. J.* (1911), 871–900; * 1 Oppenheim, §§ 30–36; * Root, in 5 *A. J.* (1911) 577–89, and in 19 *A. J.* (1925), 675–84; Scott, in 18 *A. J.* (1924), 260–80, and in 19 *A. J.* (1925), 333–37. See also *Procs. Am. Soc. I. L.* (1910), 208–87, and (1925), *passim.*

For further references, see 1 Oppenheim, p. 37; and Index to *A. J.* (1920).

becoming a Member of the League, have undertaken any obligations inconsistent with the terms of this Covenant, it shall be the duty of such Member to take immediate steps to procure its release from such obligations " (Art. 20).[47]

d. **Engagements that Are Valid.**—" Nothing in this Covenant shall be deemed to affect the validity of international engagements, such as treaties of arbitration or regional understandings like the Monroe doctrine, for securing the maintenance of peace " (Art. 21).[48]

[47] This article solemnly pronounces the supremacy of the Covenant over all obligations or understandings inconsistent therewith. Cf. Art. 6, parag. 2 of the Constitution of the United States which declares: "This Constitution, and the laws of the United States which shall be made in pursuance thereof, and all treaties made, or which shall be made, under the authority of the United States, shall be the supreme law of the land; and the judges in every State shall be bound thereby, any thing in the constitution or laws of any State to the contrary notwithstanding."

The possibilities of the first paragraph of Art. 20, if interpreted by a Chief Justice Marshall, do not seem to have attracted the attention of any commentator. However, the League of Nations is no super-State and even if the Court of International Justice included several Marshalls, it is not likely that it will ever develop such powers as are exercised by our Supreme Court. Yet the possibility of its some day declaring treaties null and void is by no means excluded. But, considering Continental ideas and practices, it is more likely that this function will be exercised by the Council or the Assembly of the League than by the Court of International Justice.

[48] Art. 21 asserts the validity of international engagements which have as their objects the maintenance of peace. Among these are mentioned treaties of arbitration and regional understandings such as the Monroe Doctrine. It seems to be generally conceded that purely *defensive* alliances are valid. But how are we to distinguish between an offensive and a defensive alliance?

The meaning of the phrase *regional understandings* of which the Monroe Doctrine is cited as an example, remains a mystery. But whatever they are. only those are valid which have as their object the maintenance of peace.

"The expression 'regional understandings' may be variously understood. It may be conceived that neighbor States form within the League of Nations something like close communities for developing more completely the principles of the League of Nations." *Swiss Commentary*, in 3 W. P. F., *L. of N.* (1920), 152. The Locarno Pact (see *supra*, pp. 151 ff.) would be a good example.

"'Regional understandings' is a strange and clumsy term, and the form of this Article is certainly capable of improvement. The Assembly, adopting the report of the Committee, has concluded on the whole that the time has not yet arrived for a revision, agreed that the Article shall be retained in its present form, and accepted the Committee's statement that 'agreements between Members of the League tending to define or complete the engagements in the Covenant for the maintenance of peace or the promotion of international coöperation may be regarded as of a nature likely to contribute to the progress of the League in the path of practical realization. Such agreements may also be negotiated under the auspices of the League of Nations, for example, in special conferences with its assistance.'" Pollock, *The League of Nations* (2d ed., 1922), 176–77.

[For Article 22 on the " Mandatory System," see *supra*, pp. 187 ff.]

320*i*. **Social and Other Activities.**—" Subject to and in accordance with the provisions of international conventions existing or hereafter to be agreed upon, the Members of the League:

" (*a*) will endeavor to secure and maintain fair and humane conditions of labor for men, women, and children, both in their own countries and in all countries to which their commercial and industrial relations extend, and for that

It is impossible to say what are included under the phrase "regional understandings" for the maintenance of peace. It certainly includes such arrangements as the neutralization of Switzerland and the Pan-American Union. It probably includes the Four Power or Pacific Pact. There is some evidence that the Anglo-Japanese Alliance and the Lansing-Ishii Agreement by which the United States recognized special interests of Japan in China were regarded in some quarters as regional understandings which did make for peace. Dr. Wellington Koo showed some concern over the possible application of the phrase to agreements or understandings regarding spheres of influence in China. It is apparently for the Council, the Assembly or the Court to decide when the occasion arises.

Art. 21 was inserted in the final text of the Covenant in deference to the wishes of the United States, strongly supported by Great Britain. See 1 Baker, *Wilson and World Settlement* (1922–23), ch. 18, pp. 323 ff.

"The origin of the Monroe Doctrine is well-known. . . . At first a principle of American foreign policy, it has become an international understanding, and it is not illegitimate for the people of the United States to ask that the Covenant should recognize this fact. In its essence it is consistent with the spirit of the Covenant, and indeed the principles of the League, as expressed in Article 10, represent the extension to the whole world of the principles of the doctrine; while, should any dispute as to the meaning of the latter ever arise between American and European Powers, the League is there to settle it." *British Commentary*, in Pollock, *op. cit.*, 236.

The Monroe Doctrine is recognized as valid, so far as the Covenant is concerned, *i.e.* it is not considered incompatible with it. There is no attempt at a definition, as the French at Paris desired. In case a question should arise involving the Monroe Policy, it would seem to be the duty of the Council or the Assembly, possibly of the Court of International Justice acting in an advisory capacity, to make such a definition or application of it as might be necessary to decide the particular case presented. On the *Monroe Doctrine*, see *supra*, No. 72 and p. 241. See pp. 87–88 for references.

On the "Monroe Doctrine and the League of Nations," see Brown, in 14 *A. J.* (1920), 207–10; Elliot, in 30 *I. L. A.* (1921), 74–105; Hoijer, *op. cit.*, 352–54; Inman, *Problems in Pan-Americanism* (1921), ch. 5, pp. 174–94; Klein, in 4 *Hispanic Am. Histor. Rev.* (May, 1921), 248 ff.; Lannay, in 47 (3d ser. 1), *R. D. I* (1920), 364 ff.; and Schücking and Wehberg, *Die Satzung des Völkerbundes* (1924), 670–80. On " Pan-Americanism and the League of Nations," see Lima, in 4 *Am. Histor. Rev.* (1921), 239 ff.

purpose will establish and maintain the necessary international organizations; [49]

" (b) undertake to secure just treatment of the native inhabitants of territories under their control; [50]

" (c) will intrust the League with the general supervision over the execution of agreements with regard to the traffic in women and children and the traffic in opium and other dangerous drugs; [51]

[49] On "The International Labor Organization," see Additional Note at the end of this chapter.

[50] The reference in parag. "b" is to the inhabitants of territories, colonies or dependencies which are not provided for in Art. 22. On "The Mandatory System," see *supra*, pp. 187–91.

[51] With respect to the White Slave Traffic, an International Conference on the Traffic in Women and Children was held under the auspices of the League of Nations at Geneva in the summer of 1921, which was attended by 34 States. It drew up a convention supplementing the Conventions of 1904 and 1910. This Convention was signed by 33 States and in 1924 had been ratified by 17 States with 3 adherents. For the text of this Convention, see 9 *L of N. Treaty Series* (1922), No. 269, pp. 417 ff.

In 1921 the Council of the League created an Advisory Committee on Traffic in Women and Children which examines the annual reports of the governments as to the traffic and supervises the working of the Convention. On "Traffic in Women and Children," see particularly a pamphlet entitled *Social and Humanitarian Work* by Information Section of L. of N. (Geneva, 1924), Pt. II, pp. 21–30.

With respect to the Opium Traffic, the Hague Convention of 1912 having remained largely unratified, the League Assembly of 1920 authorized the creation of an Advisory Committee. As a result of the activities of the League, most of the remaining States ratified the Hague Convention, there being 48 States bound by it in 1924.

The Hague Convention of 1912 was, however, regarded as very inadequate, especially in the United States. Until Jan., 1923 our Government had refused to work with the Opium Committee of the League. But the Harding Administration finally decided to coöperate and appointed "unofficial" representatives to attend the sessions of the Advisory Committee where the American delegation presented two strong resolutions designed to restrict the use of opium to medicinal and scientific purposes. These resolutions encountered opposition, but as a compromise the Advisory Committee finally recommended to the League the adoption of the American proposals, subject to a reservation by all the Powers except China and the United States.

The Fourth Assembly of the League passed a resolution providing for two Conferences—one to consist of the Governments having colonies in the Far East to secure a reduction of the amount of opium available for smoking in these colonies, and the other to conclude an agreement limiting the production of raw opium and the coca leaf for export to the amount needed for medicinal and scientific purposes.

The two Opium Conferences, which were in session between Nov., 1924 and Feb., 1925, adopted two agreements, two protocols and eight resolutions. It appears to be conceded that the Geneva Conventions of 1925 constitute at least

" (d) will intrust the League with the general supervision of the trade in arms and ammunition with the countries in which the control of this traffic is necessary in the common interest; [52]

" (e) will make provision to secure and maintain freedom of communications and of transit and equitable treatment for the commerce of all Members of the League.[53]   In this connection, the special necessities of the regions devastated during the war of 1914–1918 shall be borne in mind;

" (f) will endeavor to take steps in matters of international concern for the prevention and control of disease " (Art. 23).[54]

some improvement over the Hague Convention of 1912, but they cannot be deemed adequate for their purpose.   They did not meet the approval of the United States and China whose delegates withdrew from the Second Conference before it had completed its work.   On the "American Withdrawal from the Opium Conference," see Wright, in 19 A. J. (1925), 348–55.   For the official reasons given for withdrawal, see Ibid., 380–81.

On the various Opium Conferences, see especially: * Buell, Int. Relations (1925), ch. 11, and in 8 W. P. F., Pamphlets (1925), Nos. 2–3, pp. 41–194; * For. Policy Assoc., Int. Control of Traffic in Opium (May, 1925), pamphlet No. 1, 33; * League of Nations, Social and Humanitarian Work, Pt. I, pp. 7–20; * Willoughby, Opium as an Int. Problem (1925), passim, and Foreign Rights and Interests in China (1920), ch. 18; Wright, Hamilton, in A. J. (see Index vol., 1920); Wright, Quincy, in 18 and 19 A. J. (1924 and 1925), 281–95, and 559–68.

For the texts and documents, see Buell, 8 W. P. F., op. cit., 120 ff.; and Willoughby, op. cit., 438 ff.

[52] On the Conventions relating to the Trade in Arms and Ammunitions, see supra, note 34, p. 508, and note 47 on p. 143.

[53] On Freedom of Communication and Transit, see particularly: Ando, La liberte du commerce etc. (1925), Pt. II, pp. 59 ff.; Claveille, in The League of Nation Starts (London, 1920), ch. 12; Fanshawe, Reconstruction (1925), 149–61; Hoijer, op. cit., 417 ff.; Hostie, in 48 (3d ser. 2) R. D. I (1921), 83 ff., and 530 ff., in 51 (3d ser. 5) R. D. I. (1924), 680 ff. and in 52 (3d ser. 6) R. D. I. (1925), 115 ff.; Hollander, in 17 A. J. (1923), 470–88; League of Nations, Communications and Transit (pamphlet, 1924); Toulmin, in Brit. Yr. Bk. (1922–23), 167–78; 1 * Visschor, The Stabilization of Europe (1924), Lect. 3, and Le droit int. des communications (1924); and 8 W. P. F., Pamphlets (1925), 523–35, 9 W. P. F. (1926), 285–94.   Cf. supra, note 4, pp. 126–27 and note on p. 313.

It is a very important principle based on Wilson's Third Point, and like that of the freedom of the seas or of river navigation, capable of great possibilities of future application.

[54] In Feb., 1920 the Council of the League decided to summon an International Health Conference consisting of experts to draw up the constitution of the Health Organization.   This Conference met in April, 1920 and drew up a draft constitution which was accepted by the First Assembly in Nov., 1920.

The present constitution of the Health Organization of the League consists

(g) **International Bureaus.**—" There shall be placed under the direction of the League all international bureaus already established by general treaties, if the parties to such treaties consent.   All such international bureaus and all commissions for the regulation of matters of international interest hereafter constituted shall be placed under the direction of the League.

" In all matters of international interest which are regulated by general conventions but which are not placed

of: (1) An Advisory Council of government representatives which meet twice a year and are empowered to propose and discuss international conventions and which deals with any matter submitted to it by the Health Committee to which it also refers any question deemed proper for such a procedure. (2) The Health Committee, consisting of 16 members, which acts as an advisory organ of the Council and Assembly on all health matters.   It "directs the health work of the League, just as the Transit Committee and Financial and Economic Committees direct their respective branches of the League's technical activities."   This Committee also carries out investigations and makes an annual report to the Chairman of the Advisory Council on the work of the entire Health Organization during the proceeding year.   (3) A Health Section, forming part of the Secretariat of the League of Nations, of which it is the executive organ.   There is also a temporary Epidemic Commission whose object was to strengthen the health administration of countries in Eastern Europe in combating epidemics from Russia.   This Commission has acted through existing national health organizations rather than through its own agents.   Finally, it should be stated that the International Labor Office, the Pan-American Sanitary Bureau, and the League of Red Cross Societies are represented on the Health Committee, and that the Health Organization of the League collaborates with such other parts of the League machinery as the Opium, Mandates and Transit Committees.

In general, it may be said that "the object of the Health Organization is to advise the Assembly of the League in all international questions of public health, to establish closer relations between the health services in different countries, to act as a clearing house for information on public health questions, and finally, to help bring about the agreements necessary for all international action in public health matters."   *Health Organization of the L. of N.* (Information Section, L. of N. secretariat, 1923), 10–11.

The Health Organization has accomplished a great deal of useful work in fighting the spread of epidemics from Russia into Central and Southern Europe, the collection, publication and distribution of epidemiological intelligence and vital health statistics, the interchanges of public health personnel and individual fellowships, the coördination of scientific researches, and the securing of joint action in the combating of epidemic diseases.   On the organization and work of the *Health Organization of the League*, see Fanshawe, *op. cit.*, 161–74; Harris, *What the League of Nations Is* (1925), ch. 10; * *Health Organization*, L. of N., pamphlet cited above, Hoijer, *op. cit.*, 449 ff.; Strong, in *The League of Nations Starts* (London, 1920), ch. 10; Williams, *The League of Nations* (1923), ch. 7, pp. 87–96; and * 8 W. P. F. *Pamphlets* (1925), 494 ff.   For still more recent activities, see 9 W. P. F., *op. cit.*, (1926), 258–65; and 10 W. P. F., 7th *Yearbook* (1927), 280 ff.

under the control of international bureaus or commissions, the Secretariat of the League shall, subject to the consent of the Council and if desired by the parties, collect and distribute all relevant information and shall render any other assistance which may be necessary or desirable.

" The Council may include as part of the expenses of the Secretariat the expenses of any bureau or commission which is placed under the direction of the League " (Art. 24).[55]

(*h*) **Promotion of Red Cross and Health.**—" The Members of the League agree to encourage and promote the establishment and coöperation of duly authorized voluntary national Red Cross organizations having as purposes the improvement of health, the prevention of disease and the mitigation of suffering throughout the world " (Art. 25).

320*j*. **Amendments.**—" Amendments to this Covenant will take effect when ratified by the Members of the League whose Representatives compose the Council and by a majority of the Members of the League whose Representatives compose the Assembly.

[55] It should be particularly noted that international bureaus *already* established by general treaties can only be placed under the direction of the League of Nations, if the parties to such treaties give their consent. On International Bureaus, see *supra*, ch. 4, No. 79. For references, see note 59 on p. 92. For information as to what the League has done to carry out Art. 24, see 8 W. P. F. *Pamphlets* (1925), 561–65.

Arts. 23–25 on the "Social and Other Activities" of the League indicate a program rather than a series of definite legal obligations. They are merely instances of League activities and are not all inclusive. For example, at its very inception the League undertook a number of activities which were not included in the program, such as the repatriation of nearly a half million war prisoners and the relief of over three-quarters of a million Russian refugees. It also supervised the financial rehabilitation of Austria and Hungary. Particularly interesting to scholars is the program of the League's Committee on Intellectual Coöperation. See Fanshawe, *op. cit.*, 175–82; Hodges, in 24 *Cur. Hist.* (1926), 411 ff.; *League of Nations and Intellectual Coöperation* (Information section of L. of N. Secretariat, 1924); and 8 W. P. F. *Pamphlets* (1925), 536–43. See also 9 W. P. F. *Pamphlets* (1926), 295 ff. and 10 W. P. F., 7th *Yearbook* (1927), 323 ff.

On the *Social and Humanitarian Activities of the League* generally, see: Alexander, *Revival of Europe* (1924), ch. 3; * Buell, *Int. Relations* (1925), chs. 11–12; * Fanshawe, *op. cit.*, ch. 7, pp. 183–228; * Harris, *What the League of Nations Is* (1925), chs. 9–11; Hoijer, *op. cit.*, 387 ff.; Kohn, *op. cit.*, chs. 8–9; Schücking and Wehberg, *op. cit.*, 711–64; * *Social and Humanitarian Work of the League of Nations* (Information Section of L. of N. Secretariat); Williams, *The League of Nations Today*, chs. 7–8; and * 8 W. P. F. *Pamphlets* (1925), *passim*.

" No such amendment shall bind any Member of the League which signifies its dissent therefrom, but in that case it shall cease to be a Member of the League " (Art. 26).[56]

320*k*. **The Character and Work of the League.**—The League of Nations is no mere alliance. Nor is it, on the other hand, a super-State. It has no supreme or sovereign power with the right of command and coercion. It does not operate by virtue of its own authority and its powers are mainly advisory. It is essentially a Confederacy [57] of States (a Staatenbund) based on treaty, having organs and functions of its own that have been delegated to it by its Member-States which remain sovereign or independent. Voting is by States, though unanimity is not always necessary for a decision. The League is also a corporate body with rights and obligations and is an international person.[58]

[56] In 1921 the Assembly voted in favor of the following amendments to replace Art. 26, and the Members are now deciding upon its ratification:

"Amendments to the present Covenant the text of which shall have been voted by the Assembly on a three-fourths majority, in which there shall be included the votes of all the Members of the Council represented at the meeting, will take effect when ratified by the Members of the League whose Representatives composed the Council when the vote was taken and by the majority of those whose Representatives form the Assembly.

"If the required number of ratifications shall not have been obtained within twenty-two months after the vote of the Assembly, the proposed amendment shall remain without effect.

"The Secretary-General shall inform the Members of the taking effect of an amendment.

"Any Member of the League which has not at that time ratified the amendment is free to notify the Secretary-General within a year of its refusal to accept it, but in that case it shall cease to be a Member of the League."

The above amendment makes a three-fourths majority of the Assembly necessary instead of a bare majority of the Members of the League whose Representatives compose the Assembly. In this three-fourths majority there shall be included the votes of all the Members of the Council represented at the meeting of the Assembly.

For the amendments or proposed amendments to Arts. 4, 6, 12–13, 15 and 16, see above, pp. 501, 513, and 517.

On *Amendments*, see: Finch, in 16 *A. J.* (1922), 263–73; Hoijer, *op. cit.*, 467 ff.; Hudson, in 38 *Harv. Law Rev.* (1924–25), 903 ff.; Paulus, in 30 *R. D. I. P.* (1923), 525 ff.; Rolin. in 48 and 49 (3d ser., 2 and 3) *R. D. I.* (1921 and 1922), 56 ff., 225 ff. 171 ff., and 336 ff.: and Schücking and Wehberg, *op. cit.*, 764–81.

[57] On *Confederacies*, see *supra*, No. 101.

[58] On the legal character of the League, see particularly: 1 Fauchille, p.

The League is not directly endowed with legislative power, though it has already developed a large degree of initiative in international legislation and this points to one of its main functions.   This must, however, be accomplished through the treaty-making powers of its Members.   It may be said to perform considerable executive and administrative work, mainly through the Council and Secretariat, but it is by means of mediation, conciliation, arbitration and recommendation rather than by way of authority or command that it operates.   Economic and even military sanctions have been provided, but these must be executed through the Members of the League and they have never been called into effect.

Nevertheless, the League has done a vast deal of useful, necessary and effective work, and it cannot be gainsaid that the Covenant, both in respect to territory and population, is the supreme and fundamental law of by far the greater portion of mankind.[59]

215; Larnaude, *La Societé des Nations* (1920), 4 ff.; 1 Oppenheim, §§ 63, 167 c. and in 26 *R. D. I. P.* (1919), 234–44; and * Schücking and Wehberg, *op. cit.*, 102 ff. (for the correct view).

[59] For lists of Members and non-Members of the League, see *supra*, pp. 167–73.   Though not a Member, the United States has coöperated with the League to a much greater extent than is generally realized.   For instances, see Hudson, "American Coöperation with the League of Nations," in 7 W. P. F., *Pamphlets* (1924), 7–26.

Additional Note on the International Labor Organization.—This unique and important organization was called into being at Paris in 1919.   On Jan. 25 of that year the Paris Conference appointed a Commission on International Labor Legislation, consisting of 15 members.   This Commission held 35 sessions and framed a report which was substantially adopted at the fourth plenary session on April 11, 1919, and incorporated as Pt. XIII into the Treaty of Versailles (Arts. 387–427).   These same Labor sections were also incorporated into the main Paris Treaties.   For the Report of the Commission which includes a commentary on the Labor Section of the Treaties, see 9 *Am. Labor Leg. Rev.* (1919), 365 ff. or 2 *Int. Concil.* (1919), No. 140, pp. 851 ff.

The Preamble to the Labor Sections of the Paris Treaties declares that universal peace—the main object of the League of Nations—"can be established only if it is based upon social justice;" that "conditions of labor exist involving such injustice, hardship and privation as to produce unrest so great that the peace and harmony of the world are imperilled;" that "an improvement of these conditions is urgently required;" and that the "failure of any nation to adopt humane conditions of labor is an obstacle in the way of other nations which desire to improve the conditions in their own countries."   As examples of improved conditions urgently required are mentioned: the regulation of the hours of work, including the establishment of a maximum working day and week; the regulation of the labor supply; the prevention of unemploy-

BIBLIOGRAPHY

League of Nations.—Alexander, *The Revival of Europe* (1924); Baker, *The Geneva Protocol* (1925), *passim;* * Baker, *Woodrow Wilson and the World Settlement* (1922–23), in 3 vols., *passim;* Brett,

ment; the provision of an adequate living wage; the protection of the worker against sickness, disease and injury; the protection of children, young persons and women; provisions for old age and injury; protection of alien workers; recognition of the principle of freedom of association; and the organization of vocational and technical education.

In Art. 427 of the Treaty of Versailles are laid down the following guiding methods and principles: "(1) labor should not be regarded merely as a commodity or article of commerce; (2) the right of association for all lawful purposes by the employed as well as by the employers; (3) the payment of the employed of a wage adequate to maintain a reasonable standard of life as this is understood in their time and country; (4) the adoption of an eight hours' day or a forty-eight hours' week as the standard to be aimed at where it has not already been attained; (5) the adoption of a weekly rest of at least twenty-four hours, which should include Sunday wherever practicable; (6) the abolition of child labor and the imposition of such limitations on the labor of young persons as shall permit the continuation of their education and assure their proper physical development; (7) the principle that men and women should receive equal remuneration for work of equal value; (8) the standard set by law in each country with respect to the conditions of labor should have due regard to the equitable economic treatment of all workers lawfully resident therein; and (9) each State should make provision for a system of inspection in which women should take part, in order to ensure the enforcement of the laws and regulations for the protection of the employed."

In the application of the above principles, which have been aptly called the Charter of Labor, it is recognized that "differences of climate, habits and customs, of economic opportunity and industrial tradition, make strict uniformity in the conditions of labor difficult of immediate attainment."

The permanent International Organization of Labor is to consist of (1) a General Conference of Representatives of the Members, and (2) an International Labor Office. This Office is to be under the control of (3) a Governing Body. The Treaties also provide for the creation of a panel for the appointment of Commissions of Enquiry to hear and pass upon complaints against Members.

The General Conference shall meet at least once a year. "It shall be composed of four Representatives of each of the Members, of whom two shall be Government Delegates and the two others shall be Delegates representing respectively the employers and the workpeople of each of the Members. Each Delegate may be accompanied by advisers. . . . The non-Government delegates and advisers shall be chosen by the Governments in agreement with the industrial organizations which are most representative of employers or workpeople in their respective countries." (Art. 389 of the Treaty of Versailles).

Art. 390 contains the novel provision that "every Delegate shall be entitled *to vote individually* on all matters which are taken into consideration by the Conference."

The International Labor Office, which "shall be established at the seat of the League of Nations as part of the organization of the League" (Art. 392), shall be under the control of a Governing Body consisting of 24 persons.

The First Assembly (1921); * *British Official Commentary on the Covenant*, in Pollock, *League of Nations* (2d ed., 1922), 224–38; * Buell, *International Relations* (1925), ch. 28 and *passim* (see

Twelve persons represent the Governments; six, who are elected by the Delegates to the Conference, represent the employers; and six, also elected by the Delegates, represent the workers.   The Governing Body serves for three years, elects its own Chairman, regulates its own procedure, and fixes its own times of meeting (Art. 393).   It also appoints a Director of the International Labor Office who, subject to the instructions of the Governing Body, is responsible for the efficient conduct of the Office and who appoints its staff.   With due regard to the efficiency of the work of the Office, this staff shall consist of persons of different nationalities, a certain number of whom shall be women (Arts. 394–95).   The Director also acts as Secretary of the General Conferences (Art. 401).

There are three divisions of the International Labor Office: (1) the Research Division; (2) the Intelligence and Liaison Division for the collection of information, etc.; and (3) the Diplomatic Division, which organizes and prepares the work of the General Conference, and deals with official correspondence.   It also deals with questions connected with the Conventions and Recommendations adopted by the General Conference.   Each division is divided into numerous sections.   On these, see Fry, *Key-Book of the League of Nations*, pp. 67 ff.   See *Ibid.*, 72 ff. for Auxiliary Organizations of the International Labor Organization.

The staff of the Labor Office consists of over 300 officials of nearly 30 different nationalities.   Together with the staff of the Secretariat of the League (see *supra*, p. 505), they constitute a permanent International Civil Service.   See particularly Behrens, *The Int. Labor Office* (1924), ch. 2.

"The functions of the International Labor Office shall include the collection and distribution of information on all subjects relating to the international adjustment of conditions of industrial life and labor, and particularly the examination of subjects which it is proposed to bring before the Conference with a view to the conclusion of international conventions, and the conduct of such special investigations as may be ordered by the Conference" (Art. 396). The Office is also charged with the task of preparing the agenda for the meetings of the Conference as settled by the Governing Body, and the editing and publishing of a periodical dealing with problems of industry and employment of international interest.

As regards procedure (see Arts. 400–20) it is provided that "the agenda for all meetings of the Conference shall be settled by the Governing Body" (Art. 400).   See Arts. 400–02 for further details regarding the agenda. "The Conference shall regulate its own procedure, shall elect its own President, and may appoint committees to consider and report on any matter.   Except as otherwise expressly provided in this part of the present Treaty, all matters shall be decided by a *simple majority* of the votes cast by the Delegates present" (Art. 403).

The adoption of proposals by a General Conference takes the form either: (1) of a recommendation to be submitted to the Members for consideration with a view to effect being given it by national legislation or otherwise; or (2) of a draft international convention for ratification by the Members.   In either case a majority of two-thirds of the votes cast by the Delegates present shall be necessary on the final vote for adoption (Art. 405).   This constitutes the most important exception to the simple majority rule.

index); Bourgeois, *L'oeuvre de la Société des Nations* (1923); Butler, *A Handbook of the League of Nations* (1925); Cecil, Lord, *The Moral Basis of the League* (1923); Dickinson, *The United States*

"In framing any recommendation or draft convention of general application, the Conference shall have due regard to those countries in which climatic conditions, the imperfect development of industrial organization, or other special circumstances make the industrial conditions substantially different, and shall suggest the modifications, if any, which it considers may be required to meet the case of such countries." (Art. 405.)

"Each of the Members undertakes that it will, within the period of óne year at most . . . and in no case later than 18 months from the closing of the session of the Conference, bring the recommendation or draft convention before the authority or authorities within whose competence the matter lies for the enactment of legislation or other action." (Art. 405.)

A special provision was inserted in this same article for such backward countries as the United States where federal child labor legislation is still regarded as unconstitutional. "In case of a federal State, the power of which to enter into conventions on labor matters is subject to limitations, it shall be in the discretion of that Government to treat a draft convention to which such limitations apply as a recommendation only. . . ." On the "Power of the U. S. under the Constitution to Enter into Treaties," see Chamberlain, in 8 *Procs. Acad. Pol. Sci.* (1919), 90–99 or in 9 *Am. Labor Legis. Rev.* (1919), 330–38; and Parkinson, in *Ibid.*, 21–32.

Approved conventions are binding only upon the Members which have ratified them. If ratified they shall be registered by the Secretary-General of the League of Nations (Art. 406). "Each of the Members agrees to make an annual report to the International Labor Office on the measures which it has taken to give effect to the provisions of conventions to which it is a party. . . . The Director shall lay a summary of these reports before the next meeting of the Conference." (Art. 408).

"Any of the Members shall have the right to file a complaint with the International Labor Office if it is not satisfied that any other Member is securing the effective observance of any convention which both have ratified." (Art. 411.) The Governing Body may, at its discretion, either communicate the complaint to the Government in question, or refer it to a Commission of Enquiry for consideration and recommentation. See Art. 412 for the way in which the Commission of Enquiry shall be constituted.

After full consideration of the complaint, the Commission of Enquiry shall prepare a report embodying its findings on all questions relevant to determining the issue, and make such recommendations as it may deem proper. "It shall also indicate in this report the measures, if any, of an economic character against a defaulting Government which it considers to be appropriate, and which it considers other Governments would be justified in adopting." (Art. 414.) The Secretary-General of the League shall then communicate the report of the Commission of Enquiry to each of the Governments concerned in the complaint and cause it to be published. Within one month each of these Governments shall inform him whether or not it accepts the recommendations contained in the report; and if not, whether it proposes to refer the complaint to the Permanent Court of International Justice (Art. 415). The decision of this Court in regard to a complaint on any matter referred to it shall be final (Art. 417). It may "affirm, vary or reverse any of the findings or recommendations of the Commission of Enquiry, if any, and shall in its decision indicate

and the League (1923); Fosdick, etc., in *The League of Nations Starts* (1920); * Fanshawe, *Reconstruction* (1925); * Fry, *Key-Book of the League of Nations;* Garner, *Recent Developments in Int. Law* (1925),

the measures, if any, of an economic character which it considers to be appropriate, and which other Governments would be justified in adopting against a defaulting Government." (Art. 418.)

"In the event of any Member failing to carry out within the time specified the recommendations, if any, contained in the report of the Commissions of Enquiry, or in the decision of the Permanent Court of International Justice, as the case may be, any other Member may take against that Member the measures of an economic character indicated in the report of the Commission or in the decision of the Court as appropriate to the case" (Art. 419).

The expenses of the International Labor Organization (other than the travelling and subsistence expenses of the Delegates and their advisers and of the representatives attending the meetings of the Conference or Governing Body which are paid by each of its Members) are paid by the Secretary-General of the League of Nations out of the general funds of the League (Art. 399). During the year 1921, out of a total budget of 21,000,000 gold francs, the League of Nations allotted 7,000,000 gold francs, or one-third of its total income, to the International Labor Organization.

"The Members engage to apply conventions which they have ratified . . . to their colonies, protectorates and possessions which are not fully self-governing: (1) except where owing to local conditions the convention is inapplicable, or (2) subject to such modifications as may be necessary to adapt the convention to local conditions" (Art. 421).

Amendments to the Labor Sections of the Treaties "which are adopted by the Conference by a majority of two-thirds of the votes cast by the Delegates present shall take effect when ratified by the States whose representatives compose the Council of the League of Nations and by three-fourths of the Members" (Art. 422).

The First Session of the General Conference of Representatives of the Members of the International Labor Organization was held in Washington in October, 1919. It was called together by President Wilson and presided over by the American Secretary of Labor Wilson, but the United States, not being a Member, could not participate in the work of this important Conference. Though Germany and Austria were not Members of the League, they were admitted to membership in the International Labor Organization. Altogether 123 delegates representing 39 nations were present.

The Washington Conference adopted six Draft Conventions and six Recommendations. The Draft Conventions related to the following subjects: (1) the Limitation of the Hours of Work in Industrial Undertakings to Eight in the Day and Forty-eight in the Week (special provisions were made for Japan, and British India, and China was excepted from the obligations of the Convention); (2) Unemployment (each Member *e.g.* was to establish a system of free public employment agencies under control of a central authority); (3) Employment of Women before and after Childbirth; (4) Employment of Women during the Night; (5) Fixing the Minimum Age for Admission of Children in Industrial Employment (14 years except in Japan and India); (6) Night Work of Young Persons Employed in Industry.

The six Recommendations were concerned with (1) Unemployment; (2) Reciprocity of Treatment of Foreign Workers; (3) Prevention of Anthrax; (4) Protection of Women and Children against Lead Poisoning; (5) the

Sect. 12; Harris, *What the League of Nations Is* (1925), and *Geneva, 1923;* Hoijer, *Le pacte de la Société des Nations* (1926), and *La solution pacific,* etc. (1925), ch. 6; Keen, *Towards Int. Justice* (1923);

Establishment of Government Health Sections; and (6) Prohibition of the Use of White Phosphorus in the Manufacturing of Matches.

The Second Session of the General Conference, held at Genoa in 1920, was essentially a maritime conference which considered problems relating particularly to seamen.   It adopted three Draft Conventions and four Recommendations.   But it should be noted that the Main Draft Convention proposing a 48 hour week with certain modifications failed to secure the necessary two-thirds majority.

The Third Session of the International Labor Conference (Geneva, 1921) dealt largely with agricultural questions which, after some debate, were held to be within the jurisdiction of the Conference, and this view was later upheld by the Court of International Justice; but, failing the necessary two-thirds vote, the item calling for the adaptation to agricultural labor of the Washington decisions concerning hours of work was withdrawn from the agenda of the Conference.   The work at this Conference resulted in an unusual crop of Conventions and Recommendations—no less than seven of the former and eight of the latter.   They related largely to the rights and interests of agricultural workers.

A Fourth Session of the Conference was again held at Geneva in 1922.   But it may be regarded as a breathing space, for there was only one Recommendation adopted calling for statistics and other information concerning emigration, immigration, repatriation and transit of emigrants.   However, there was adopted an amendment to Art. 393 providing for the increase of the Governing Body to 320 members which was forwarded to the States for ratification.   A proposal was also adopted looking forward to alternative sessions in successive years of preparation and decision.   A proposal that the Conference should only meet every two years was not accepted.

Subsequent sessions of the International Labor Conference have apparently been less ambitious in their programs and more limited in output.   The Fifth Session, held at Geneva in 1923, had but one item on its agenda—General Principles for the Organization of Factory Inspection.

The Sixth Session (Geneva, 1924) *provisionally* adopted several Conventions and Recommendations; for under the new rule of procedure referred to above, final action was deferred until the next session.   At this session forty States were represented with 291 members of the Conference, including 165 advisers.   On the work of the Sixth Session see 10 *Int. Labor Rev.,* 549–82.

The Seventh Session (1925) discussed such matters as night work in bakeries, workmen's compensation for accidents and social insurance. 12 *Q. L. R.* (1925), 145 ff.

In reviewing the product of the International Labor Office and the Conferences, one is most favorably impressed by the amount of excellent work done and the number and quality of the Draft Conventions and Recommendations which have been adopted.   At its first five Sessions, the International Labor Conference adopted sixteen conventions and twenty recommendations.   "Of these in March 1924, 104 had been formally registered, 22 further ratifications had been authorized but not yet registered, and 137 further ratifications had been recommended for adoption in the various countries.   In addition, some 175 legislative measures had also been adopted, introduced or prepared, with a view to applying these conventions and recommendations."   Behrens, *Int.*

1 Kellor, *Security against War* (1924); Levermore, *League of Nations* (1921–24), in 4 annual vols.; Kohn, *The Organization and the Work of the League of Nations*, publ. by the Am. Acad. Pol. and Soc. Sci.

Labor Office (1924), 45 and Appendices VII and VIII for table and details. Cf. Johnston, *Int. Social Progress* (1924), ch. 7.

But there has been considerable disappointment because ratifications have not been more speedy and numerous. For example, the Convention on Hours of Work of the Washington Conference had been ratified by only five States— Bulgaria, Czecho-Slovakia, Greece, India and Rumania. On the "Attempt to Establish the Eight-Hour Day by International Action," see Feis, in 39 *Pol. Sci. Quar.* (1924), 373 ff. and 624 ff. Yet there are few countries in which the eight-hour day has not been accepted as the general rule. Other Conventions, such as the one on unemployment providing for the establishment of free employment exchanges and those relating to night work of women and the conditions of work for children and young persons, have been more fortunate. Especially gratifying have been the provisions for a sixty-hour week in India.

Like the League of Nations with which it is closely related but of which it is practically independent except in the matter of the budget, the International Labor Organization, which consists of 58 Members, constitutes a sort of Confederacy. Its powers, however, are legislative rather than executive or administrative as in the case of the League. It has certainly more initiative in international legislation than the league and is instrumental in creating a new body of international labor law which has been well-defined (by Mahaim, in 1 *Int. Labor Rev.*, 283) as "that part of International Law which regulates the mutual relations of States as touching those of their nationals who are workers." The organization has some unique features as an international body. The voting is by individuals instead of by States and a simple or two-thirds majority suffices. But it has none of the characteristics of a super-State; for it has no powers of coercion, and its Members have the right of withdrawal from the Confedereracy. Though there is a feeble provision for "economic" sanctions, they are to be enforced by the Members rather than by the organization, and the main reliance for enforcement is upon public opinion.

On the "Legal Character of the Int. Labor Organization," see Vilallonga, in 9 *Int. Labor Rev.* (1924), 196–207. This excellent article seems an adequate reply to the apparently erroneous views of Guerreau, *Une nouvelle institution de droit des gens. L'Organization permanente du Travail*—a work which I have been unable to consult.

On the *International Labor Organization*, see: Ayusawa, in 91 Columbia Univ. *Studies* (1926), No. 2: Barnes, in *Labor as an Int. Problem* (ed. Solano, 1920), ch. 1; * Behrens, *The Int. Labour Office* (1924); Butler, in *The League of Nations Starts* (London, 1920), ch. 9 and in *Labor as an Int. Problem* (ed. Solano, 1920), ch. 8; Fontaine, in *Labor as an Int. Problem* (ed. Solano, 1920), ch. 7; * Fry, *Key-Book of the L. of N.*, ch. 5; Gregory, in 15 *A. J.* (1921), 42–50; Guerreau, *Une nouvelle institution de droit des gens*, and in 29 *R. D. I. P.* (1922), 223 ff.; Hetherington, *Int. Labor Legislation* (1920); * Johnston, *Int. Social Progress* (1924); Lowe, *The Int. Protection of Labor* (1921, see for documents and bibliography); Miller, *Int. Relations of Labor* (1921); * National Industrial Conference Board, *The Int. Labor Organization*, Research Rep. No. 48, April, 1922; Perigord, *Int. Labor Organization* (1926); Pic, in 29 *R. D. I. P.* (1922), 60 ff.; Sanger, in 29 *I. L. A.* (1920), 329–42; Schiff, *Der Arbeiterschutz der Welt* (1920); Schücking and Wehberg, *Die Satzung des Völkerbundes* (1924), 95–102; Shotwell, in *Labor as an Int. Problem* (ed. Solano, 1920), ch. 2; Solano

(1924); * Laski, *A Grammer of Politics* (1926), Pt. I, ch. 11; Lodge, *The Senate and the League of Nations* (1925); Miller, *The Geneva Protocol* (1925), *passim;* * Munch (ed.), *Les origines et l'oeuvre de la Société des Nations*, in 2 vols. (1923–24); Newfang, *The Road to World Peace* (1924), Pt. III, chs. 23–32; Oppenheim, *The League of Nations* (1919); * Pollock, *League of Nations* (1922); Rappard, *Int. Relations Viewed from Geneva* (1925); Scelle, *Le Pacte des Nations;* * Schücking and Wehberg, *Die Satzung des Völkerbundes* (1924); * Smuts, *The League of Nations* (1923); Sweetser, *The League of Nations at Work* (1920); * *Swiss Commentary on the Covenant*, in 3 W. P. F., *L. of N.* (1920), No. 3, pp. 97–162; * Temperley, *A History of the Peace Conference of Paris*, in 6 vols. (1920–24), *passim* (see index at end of 6th vol.), and *The Second Year of the League* (1922); Visscher, *The Stabilization of Europe* (1924); Wehberg, *Grundprobleme des Völkerbundes* (1926); * Williams, *The League of To-day* (1923), *and The League, the Protocol, and the Empire* (1925); and W. P. F., *League of Nations* and *Pamphlets* since 1920, particularly * *Yearbook of the League* (1925, 1926 and 1927). See also various pamphlets published by the Information Section of the Secretariat of the League of Nations.

The most helpful publications of the League are the *Monthly Summary* and *The Official Journal*. The most useful general publications in this country are those of the *World's Peace Foundation*.

(ed.), *Labor as an Int. Problem* (1920), *passim;* 2 and 6 Temperley, 32–39 and 462–80; Thomas, in *Labor as an Int. Problem* (ed. Solano 1920), and in 1 *Int. Labor Rev.* (1921), 5 ff.; Vabre, *Le droit int. du travail* (1923); and 8 W. P. F., *Pamphlets* (1925), 585–93.

Consult also the *American Legislative Review*, and the various publications of the International Labor Office, such as the *International Labor Review* (monthly since 1921), the *Official Bulletin* (weekly since Nov. 15, 1920), the *Legislative Series, Special Reports, Studies and Reports*, the *Int. Labor Directory* (annual) and the *Documents of the Int. Labor Conference*.

For brief accounts of the *Int. Labor Organization*, see Buell, *Int. Relations* (1925), ch. 7, pp. 154–62; * Fanshawe, *Reconstruction* (1925), 56–68; Harris, *What the League of Nations Is* (1925), ch. 4; Hicks, *The New World Order* (1920), ch. 19; and Newfang, *The Road to World Peace* (1924), ch. 28.

CHAPTER XXIV

NON-AMICABLE OR FORCIBLE MODES OF SETTLEMENT OF INTERNATIONAL DISPUTES

There are at least six non-amicable methods of settling international disputes. These may also be considered as modes of self-help.

321. (I) **Retorsion.**—*Retorsion* is a species of retaliation in kind. It consists in treating in the same or similar manner a foreign State or its subjects chargeable with acts which, though perhaps not illegal,[1] are discourteous, unfair, offensive or otherwise injurious. It is usually applied by way of retaliation for discriminatory legislation or administrative action, such as hostile tariffs, exclusion or unfair treatment of foreigners of a particular nationality, or denial of civil rights to aliens. Retorsion is essentially a remedy for political, racial, or economic grievances, and should be used as a means of securing fair and honorable treatment rather than from motives of punishment or vengeance.[2]

322. (II) **Reprisals.**—*Reprisals*,[3] are general retaliatory measures for violations of law or international delinquencies, more particularly denials of justice.[4] They consist in such

---

[1] Oppenheim (II, § 29) maintains that retorsion can only be applied as a remedy for *political* differences. It is difficult to see why it cannot be applied to legal differences as well, though it is true that these should always be settled by arbitration, or other pacific mode of settlement, if at all possible. For a view contrary to that of Oppenheim, see 2 Westlake, 6.

[2] Several examples of retorsion may be found in 7 Moore, *Digest*, § 1090 and in 2 Hyde, § 588.

[3] Reprisal in time of peace should not be confounded with reprisals in time of war. For the latter, see *infra*, No. 337.

[4] On the "Responsibility of a State for International Delinquencies," see *supra*, ch. 11.

Reprisals were formerly classified as general and special, but special reprisals are obsolete. Down to the end of the eighteenth century States frequently issued licenses or "Letters of Marque and Reprisal" to such of their subjects as had been injured abroad, authorizing them to indemnify themselves upon the property of the subjects of the offending State. These were called special reprisals.

All reprisals are now, in a certain sense, *general* in character and, since the abolition of privateering, are executed by the State or government itself.

acts as the seizure at sea or on land of vessels or other property of a foreign State or its subjects as a means of securing redress or indemnity for an alleged wrong. They may take the form of a temporary occupation of a port,[5] the seizure of customs duties, or the institution of a pacific blockade.

Reprisals are *prima facie* acts of war, but they are not necessarily so intended by the State executing them, nor need they be so regarded by the State against which they are carried into effect. They furnish a rough means of obtaining redress for injuries of lesser importance in cases where all attempts at an amicable settlement have failed, or of putting stress upon a weak but obstinate State. They can and should be limited to the seizure and sequestration of vessels or goods belonging to the offending State, and the rights and property of individuals should be respected as much as possible.

This mode of self-help should not be resorted to until all diplomatic means of securing redress have been exhausted, and reprisals should bear somè proportion to the magnitude of the injury suffered and the amount of force necessary to obtain reparation. They are becoming more and more infrequent, and we may confidently look forward to the day when arbitration shall have wholly supplanted this crude and barbarous method of settling international differences.[6]

They may or may not be anticipatory of war. Reprisals are still classified by most authorities as *positive* and *negative*, but the distinction has little, if any, practical value.

[5] For example in 1895, Great Britain seized the port of Corinto in Nicaragua, and in 1901 France seized a portion of the island of Mitylene. A more recent instance of what seems to have been an unjustified reprisal was the occupation of Vera Cruz by United States troops in 1914 resulting from the arrest by Mexican authorities of two American sailors at Tampico. On the "Tampico Incident," see particularly; 2 Hyde, § 591; and 8 *A. J.* (1914), 579-85.

[6] For cases illustrating the use and abuse of reprisal, see 3 Calvo, §§ 1812 ff.; 1 Cobbett, 347-51; Evans, *Cases*, 364; Hall, (8th ed.), § 120, pp. 435 ff.; * 7 Moore, *Digest*, § 1096; 2 Oppenheim, §§ 34-35, 37; 3 Phillimore, §§ 21-23; * Scott, *Cases*, 514-21; Snow, *Cases*, 243-51. The most famous cases are: *Great Britain* v. *The Two Sicilies* (1840) and the case of *Don Pacifico* (1850). The latter case was certainly a gross abuse of the right of reprisal by Great Britain. A very interesting judicial opinion is that of Judge Davis, in *Gray* v. *U. S.* (1886), 21 Court of Claims, 340. See Evans, *Cases*, 364 or Scott, 517.

Apropos of the occupation of Corfu by Italy as a reprisal for the assassination of three Italian commissioners on Greek soil, the Commission of Jurists, which was appointed by the League Council to reply to certain legal questions

323. (III) **Embargo.**—A special form of reprisal is that of *hostile embargo*,[7] which consists in the sequestration of property (usually vessels) of the offending State in the ports of the embargoing State.   If a hostile embargo is followed by war, its commencement has a retroactive effect, and the vessels seized may be confiscated as enemy property.[8]

324. (IV) **Pacific Blockade.**—*Pacific blockade* [9] is the blockade of the ports of a foreign State in a time of peace without the intention of waging war.   The instances of its application have been so frequent since its first employment in the early part of the nineteenth century,[10] that it may be

involved in the case, declared: "Coercive measures which are not intended to constitute acts of war, may or may not be consistent with the provisions Articles 12 to 15 of the Covenant, and it is for the Council, when the dispute has been submitted to it, to decide immediately, having due regard to all the circumstances of the case and to the nature of the measures adopted, whether it should recommend the maintenance or the withdrawal of such measure."

This opinion of the jurists, which was unanimously adopted by the Council on March 13, 1924, is not enlightening on the point as to what coercive measures short of war constitute violations of Arts. 12–15.   In any case they could be considered under Art. 11 if they threaten to disturb international peace or good understanding.

It would seem that military reprisals or reprisals involving the use of the army or navy should not be permitted without action by the League, and that disputes should not be allowed to reach the stage of an ultimatum without arbitration, judicial settlement, or inquiry by the Council.

On the legal phases of the *Corfu Incident*, see Lowell and Hudson, in 6 W. P. F. *Pamphlets* (1923), 169 ff.; and Wright, in 18 *A. J.* (1924), 536–44. For further references on the Corfu Incident, see *supra*, p. 504, note 28.

[7] The term "hostile embargo" is used to distinguish this form of embargo from civil or pacific embargo—the detention by a State of its own vessels in port.

[8] So held by Lord Stowell in the case of *The Boedus Lust* (1803), 5 C. Rob. 245.   See Evans, 207 or Scott, 517.   It would seem that this same principle applies to captures at sea by way of reprisal, if not to reprisals generally.   See 2 Westlake, 10 and notes.

It is customary—a custom sanctioned by one of the Hague Conventions—to allow a certain time for the departure of foreign merchant vessels found in an enemy port at the outbreak of war.   See *infra*, Nos. 347–48.

[9] Pacific blockade is generally regarded as a form of reprisal, but is has also been used as a form of intervention or an act of international police, *e.g.* in Crete.

[10] The instances are about twenty in number.   The first case cited in the treatises is that connected with the intervention of the Powers in favor of Greece against Turkey, in 1827 but recent researches have unearthed a still earlier example, viz. the Anglo-Swedish blockade of Norwegian ports in 1814. See Söderquist, 60 ff., 282 ff.; and Staudacher, 32–34.

Since 1827, the most important and interesting instances of pacific blockade have perhaps been the following: The blockade of Greek ports by Great Britain

regarded as an established institute of the Law of Nations.[11]

325. **The Law of Pacific Blockade.**—The law of pacific blockade is perhaps best expressed by the rules adopted by the Institute of International Law in 1887:

" The establishment of a blockade without war cannot be considered as permitted by International Law except under the following conditions: (1) Ships under a foreign flag can enter freely notwithstanding the blockade. (2) The pacific blockade must be officially declared and notified, and maintained by a sufficient force. (3) The ships of the blockaded Power which do not respect such a blockade may be sequestered. When the blockade has ceased they must be restored to their owners with their cargoes, but without indemnity on any ground." [12]

326. **May Neutral Commerce be Interfered with?**— Among those publicists who admit the validity of pacific blockade, the main controversy has centered around the question whether the commerce of third Powers may be interfered with or their vessels seized and sequestered. International practice has varied considerably in regard to this matter,[13] but the great majority of authorities agree [14]

in 1856; that of the island of Formosa by France in 1884; the intervention in Greece by the Powers in 1886; that directed against Crete in 1897; and the Venezuelan Case in 1902.

For historical instances, see especially: 3 Calvo, §§ 1833 ff.; Falcke, *Le blocus pacifique* (1919), 13–222; Hall, § 121; * Hogan, *Pacific Blockade* (1908), 73–183; Holland, *Studies in Int. Law* (1898), 134 ff.; 7 Moore, *Digest*, § 1097; Söderquist, *Le blocus maritime* (1908), 60–119; Staudacher, *Die Friedens Blokade* (1909), 22–114.

[11] Among leading authorities who condemn pacific blockade are Bonfils, Despagnet, Fauchille, Geffcken, Hautefeuille, Kleen, F. de Martens, and P.-Fodéré.

Among those who justify this institution, with or without proper limitations, are Bluntschli, Bulmerincq, Calvo, Cauchy, Fiore, Hall, Heffter, Lawrence, Oppenheim, Perels, Rivier, Rolin-Jacquemyns, Westlake, and the Institute of International Law.

[12] As translated by 2 Westlake, 16. Cf. Scott, *Resolutions of the Institute of Int. Law*, 69–70. For the French text, see 9 *Annuaire* (1887), 300, or *Tableau*, 133.

Emphasis should be placed upon the fact that the penalty for violation of pacific blockade is detention or sequestration. In no case should vessels be confiscated. If they resist capture, they may of course be injured or destroyed in the course of the struggle. This rule has been generally observed in practice, though there are several instances of its violation.

[13] Prior to 1850 the commerce of third States was frequently interfered with.

that there is no obligation resting upon third States to respect such a blockade. Inasmuch, however, as this mode of self-help is a much milder remedy than war, and does not impose the burdens of neutrality, it may well be that third States sometimes acquiesce as a matter of policy and do not insist upon their full rights in the premises.[15]

327. (V) **Intervention.**—*Intervention*—a mode of action which has already been discussed,[16] and which may be employed as a means of self-help or of political action in general.

328. (VI) **War.**—*War*—the final resort (*ultimo ratio*) after all other means of securing redress have failed.[17]

During the blockades of Greece in 1850 and 1886, only Greek ships were excluded. In the Cretan blockade of 1897, non-Greek vessels were interfered with under certain circumstances. In 1884 France tried to enforce her blockade of Formosa against third States, but was forced to recognize a state of war with China, owing to the opposition of Great Britain. In 1902 the allied Powers enforced their blockade of Venezuelan ports against third States. The United States stated, however, that it adhered to its position in the case of the Cretan blockade of 1897, and did "not acquiesce in any extension of the doctrine of pacific blockade which may adversely affect the rights of States not parties to the controversy, or discriminate against the commerce of neutral nations." 7 Moore, *Digest*, § 1097, p. 140.

It is extremely doubtful whether the Venezuelan blockade of 1902 can be regarded as a pacific blockade. Great Britain seems to have regarded it as a war blockade from the first, and Germany performed acts which can scarcely be reconciled with the idea of a pacific blockade. Hogan (p. 51 and n.) mentions six pacific blockades in which the vessels of third States were not seized or detained.

[14] Exceptions to this rule are Bulmerincq, Heffter, Perels, and Staudacher. See Hogan, *op. cit.*, 52–53, for citations from the authorities on this point.

[15] I agree with Westlake (II, 17) on this point: "As the matter stands, it would be difficult to characterize the pacific blockader who sequestered quasi-neutral ships as a wrongdoer in an opprobrious sense, but it would be equally difficult to deny to the quasi-neutral the right of refusing to submit to the measure."

[16] See *supra*, Nos. 135–145.

[17] There are several non-amicable or forcible modes of showing a strong sense of disapproval, obtaining redress, or preventing an anticipated injury or attack which have not been indicated in the text. Such are the following: (1) A breach of diplomatic relations—a form of protest which usually indicates very strained relations and may be followed by war. (2) The passage of non-intercourse acts, such as were directed by the United States against France and England respectively in 1798 and 1809. (3) A display or limited use of force, *i.e.* a naval or military demonstration as a threat or form of constraint to insure the observance of alleged international rights or performance of duties. Such use or display of force may readily develop into intervention or war. For examples, see 7 Moore, *Digest*, § 1091.

On these modes of protest see, in general: 7 Moore, §§ 1089, 1091–93, 1099;

BIBLIOGRAPHY

Retorsion.—Bluntschli, Art. 505; Bonfils or 1 (3 Pt.) Fauchille, Nos. 972–74; Bulmerincq, in 4 Holtzendorff, 59–71; 3 Calvo, § 1807. Despagnet (2d ed.), Nos. 490–91; Fenwick, 420–21; 2 Fiore, Nos; 1226–27, and *Int. Law Cod.* Nos. 1391–95; Hall (8th ed.,) p. 433; *Heffter, §§ 27, 112; *2 Hyde, § 588; *Kamarowsky, *Le tribunal int.* (1887), 18–22; Liszt, § 55; 3 F. de Martens, § 105; 2 G. de Martens, § 254; *7 Moore, *Digest*, § 1096; *2 Oppenheim, §§ 29–32; 3 Phillimore, §§ 7–8; 2 Piédelièvre, Nos. 760–63; 6 P.-Fodéré, Nos. 2634–36; Rapisardi-Mirabelli, in 46 (2d ser. 16) *R. D. I.* (1914), 223–44, and *La retorsione* (1919); *2 Rivier, 189–91; Taylor, § 435; 2 Twiss, § 10; Ullmann, § 159; Vattel, liv. II, § 341; *2 Westlake, p. 6; Wharton, *Com. on Am. Law* (1884), § 206.

Reprisals and Hostile Embargo.—Bluntschli, Arts. 500–04; Bonfils or 1 (3 Pt.) Fauchille, Nos. 975–85; Bulmerincq, in 4 Holtzendorff, 72–116; *3 Calvo, §§ 1808–31; 1 Cobbett (4th ed.), 347–53; Dana, notes 151 and 152 to Wheaton, 370–73; Despagnet (2d ed.), Nos. 492–500; Ducrocq, *Représailles* (1901); Fenwick, 421–24; 2 Fiore, Nos. 1228–30, and *Int. Law Cod.*, Nos. 1396–1404; Funck-Brentano et Sorel, 229–30; Grotius, liv. III, cap. 2; *Hall, § 120; *1 Halleck (3d ed.), 471–85; Heffter (Geffcken), §§ 110–11; *2 Hyde, §§ 589–91, 593–94; Kamarowski, *op. cit.*, 22–38; Lafargue, *Les représailles* (1898); Lawrence, §§ 136–37; Liszt, § 55; 2 J. de Louter, § 41; 3 F. de Martens, § 105; 2 G. de Martens, § 255; *7 Moore, *Digest*, §§ 1095–96, 1098; McNair, in 11 *Grot. Soc.* (1926), 29 ff.; *2 Oppenheim, §§ 33–43; 1 Ortolan, *Règles int. et dip. de la mer* (1894), 346 ff.; *3 Phillimore, §§ 8–24; 2 Piédelièvre, Nos. 764–74; 6 P.-Fodéré, Nos. 2637–47; *2 Rivier, 191–98; *Scott, *Cases*, 514–21; Snow, *Cases*, 243–51, and *Int. Law*, § 35; Taylor, §§ 436–40; *2 Twiss, §§ 11–21; Ullmann, §§ 160–61; Vattell, liv. II, §§ 342–54; Walker, *Manual*, 94–95; 2 Westlake, 7–11, and in 25 *Law Quar. Rev.* (1909), 127–37 or *Collected Papers*, 590–606; *Wheaton, §§ 291–93; Wilson, §§ 90–91; Woolsey, § 118.

Pacific Blockade.—Barclay, in 29 *R. D. I.* (1897), 474 ff.; Barès, *Le blocus pacific* (1898); Basdevant, in 11 *R. D. I. P.* (1904), 362 ff.; Baty, in 30 *R. D. I.* (1898), 606 ff.: Bluntschli, Arts. 506–07; Bonfils or 1 (3 Pt.) Fauchille (for references, see p. 703), Nos. 986–94; Bulmerincq, in 4 Holtzendorff, 116–27; *3 Calvo, §§ 1832–49; 2 Cauchy,

6 P.-Fodéré, No. 2633; Taylor, §§ 433–34, 441; 3 Wharton, *Digest*, § 321; Wilson, §§ 88, 92–93.

Within recent years the economic boycott has also been resorted to as a means of pressure or reprisal to secure redress of grievances. The first instance of its application seems to have been by China against the United States in 1905. But thus far the boycott has been instituted by private individuals and corporations, and does not appear to have had public, official or direct governmental sanction. It has, however, been adopted as one of the sanctions of the League of Nations. See Art. 16 of the Covenant. Cf. *supra*, pp. 516–18. On the boycott see, 1 (3 Pt.) Fauchille, No. 985 [1–5] and references on p. 698.

Le droit maritime (1862), 426–28; 1 Cobbett, 359–62; Despagnet, Nos. 501–03; Ducrocq, *Représailles* (1901); * Falcke, *Le blocus pacifique*, and in 19 *Z. V.* (1909), 63 ff.; Fauchille, *Le blocus maritime* (1882), 38–67; Fenwick, 424–26; 2 Fiore, No. 1231, and *Int. Law Cod.*, Nos. 1409–19; Geffcken, in 19 *R. D. I.* (1887), 145 ff.; Gessner, *Le droit des neutres sur mer* (1886), 234–40; Hall, § 121; 2 Hautefeuille, *Des droits des neutres* (1868), tit. IX, 259 ff.; Heffter, § 111; * Hogan, *Pacific Blockade* (1908); Holland, *Studies in Int. Law* (1898), 130–50, and in 19 *Law Quar. Rev.* (1903), 133 ff.; * 2 Hyde, § 592; Kamarowski, *op. cit.*, 38–45; 1 Kleen, § 140; Lafargue, *Les représailles* (1898); Lawrence, § 138; 2 J. de Louter, § 41, pp. 207 ff.; 3 F. de Martens, § 105, pp. 165 ff.; Martiz, in 11 *Z. V.* (1919–20), 610–21; * 7 Moore, *Digest*, § 1097; * 2 Oppenheim, §§ 44–49; Perels, *Manuel*, 180–82, and in 19 *R. D. I.* (1887), 245 ff.; 2 Piédelièvre, Nos. 775–83; 5 and 6 P.-Fodéré, Nos. 2483–89, 2648; 2 Rivier, 198–99; Scott, *Cases*, 510–13; Snow, *Int. Law*, § 37; Söderquist, *Le blocus maritime* (1908), 60 ff.; Staudacher, *Die Friedensblockade* (1909); Streit, in 4 *R. D. I. P.* (1897), 61 ff., 446 ff., and 7 *Ibid.* (1900), 5 ff., 301 ff.; Taylor, § 444; Ullmann, § 162; * Walker, *Manual*, § 34, pp. 96–101, and *Science*, 157–58; Washburn, in 21 *Col. Law Rev.* (1921), 55 ff., 227 ff., 442 ff.; * 2 Westlake, 11–18, and in 25 *Law Quar. Rev.*, 13 ff. or *Collected Papers*, 572–89; Wheaton (Atlay's ed.), § 293 b; Wilson, § 94; Woolsey, § 119.

For Bibliographies, see Bonfils, Falcke, Fauchille, Hogan, Staudacher and Söderquist.

PART V

THE SO–CALLED LAW OF WAR

CHAPTER XXV

THE CAUSES, CHARACTERISTICS, AND FUNDAMENTAL PRINCIPLES OF WAR

329. Definition of War.—War, in a material sense, is a struggle or contention between States and belligerent or insurgent communities by means of organized armed forces. In a legal sense, war is the status or condition under which such a contest is carried on, and consists of the rules by which it is supposed to be regulated.[1]

330. War a Political Fact rather than a Legal Right.— War is a political fact recognized and, to a certain extent, regulated by the Law of Nations; but, though the source of legal rights and duties, it is not a *right* in the ordinary legal sense of this term. Like intervention,[2] for example, war is an exercise of sovereign or high political power—a quality assumed to be inherent in sovereignty itself. The State which goes to war performs a political act, whether from pure political motives or as a means of self-help, presumably after all attempts to arrive at an amicable mode of settlement have failed.[3]

---

[1] For various definitions of war, see 4 Calvo, § 1864; and 6 P.-Fodéré, No. 2650.

Ever since the days of Gentilis (who defined war as a "contention") and Grotius (who described it as a "condition"), authorities have differed on this point. As in the case of some other controversies of a similar nature, the truth is that both sides are in the right.

[2] Cf. *supra*, No. 145.

[3] War is not a mere means of execution or self-help, as claimed by some publicists, though a particular war may possibly have these motives. Such a claim is likely, however, to be more of a pretense than a reality. Nor is it a mode of legal procedure. As a means of execution or self-help, the remedy is entirely too dangerous and drastic; as a proper mode of procedure, it is too crude and defective. With modern facilities for settling international differences, it is seldom, if ever, that nations need have recourse to war in order to settle their controversies.

331. **Causes of War.**—Wars have been due to various and manifold causes.[4] They are partly psychological and in part social, economic, or political in origin. " They have their root in human nature, in the passions, appetites, aversions, and ambitions of mankind; and in the economic, political, or social conditions under which men seek for the means of existence and enjoyment. On the one hand, we have to reckon with certain human factors, such as hunger, greed, national jealousy, racial aversion, love of glory or national vanity, and a desire to gratify these passions; and on the other hand, man is often confronted with conditions in his physical, political, or social environment which make it difficult to gratify these desires without a resort to violence. . . . " [5]

Stated somewhat in the order of their relative importance, modern wars seem to be due to at least ten fundamental causes which deserve extended discussion, but can be here only briefly summarized:

(1) *Nationalism* or patriotism which in their excessive

[4] In his history of the Hannibalic War, Polybius (III, 6) carefully distinguishes between the real or fundamental causes of the struggle and the overt acts or events leading up to that great conflict. He justly remarks that we should look for real causes in the "motives which suggested such action and the policy which dictated it." The overt acts or events immediately preceding a war are apt to be mere irritants or pretexts. We should perhaps distinguish between: (*a*) the real or fundamental causes of a war; (*b*) its immediate causes; (*c*) the occasion or pretext.

[5] From an article by the writer, in the N. Y. *Independent* for November 4, 1899 (Vol. 57; 1036). Cf. *The Reader*, Vol. X, No. 4 (Sept., 1907).

The "Causes of War" is not a topic with which International Law, strictly speaking, is concerned. But, owing to its great interest and importance, it has been deemed advisable to include some discussion of it in this text.

On the *Causes of War*, see especially: Amos, *Remedies for War* (1880), 57–130; Anitchkow, *War and Labor* (1900), Pt. II; * Bakeless, *The Economic Causes of Modern War* (1921); Crosby, *Int. War: Its Causes and Cure* (1919), *passim*, especially dix. 25 ff.; Dickinson, *Causes of Int. War* (1920), and *The Choice Before Us* (1917), *passim*; Faguet, *Le pacifisme* (1908); Kamarowski, in 20 *R. D. I.* (1888), 132 ff.; * Kerr, in *Prevention of War* (1923), Lects. 1–3; * Lagorgette, *Le rôle de la guerre* (1906); Latourneau, *La guerre dans les diversos races humaines* (1895); Laveleye, *Des causes actuelles de la guerre en Europe et de l'arbitrage* (1873); Page, *War: Its Causes*, etc., (1923), ch. 1; Novicow, *Les luttes entre sociétés humaines* (3d ed., 1904); Peyronnard, *Des causes de la guerre* (1901); Perry, *Growth of Civilization* (1924), ch. 10; Richet, *Le passé de la guerre et l'avenir de la paix* (1907); Robinson, in 15 *Pol. Sci. Quar.* (1900), 581–622; Russell, *Why Men Fight* (1924); Saliéres, *La guerre*, etc. (1879); Seligman, *Problems of Readjustment* (1915), 37–72; and * Young, "Economics and War," in *Amer. Econ. Rev.* (1926), 1–13.

manifestations are perhaps the primary causes of irritation and strife between modern Nation-States. Nationalism is a product of group morality consisting in such qualities as national pride, vanity and self-respect, and appears to be a dangerous but inevitable factor in the development of the groupal organizations which form the units or centres of our political life.[6]

(2) Economic and political *imperialism* resulting mainly from economic, colonial and commercial rivalries between States that aim not merely at an ever increasing share in the world's trade, but often at a monopolitic control of such indispensable raw materials as coal, iron, petroleum and rubber. It appears to be a product of our modern capitalistic system and applies particularly to backward peoples or undeveloped regions. When these economic struggles are intensified by questions of national or political prestige, or rivalry in armaments (as *e.g.*, in the case of Britain and Germany prior to the World War), the strain becomes well-nigh intolerable, and it is increasingly difficult to maintain peace.[7]

[6] On Nationality, see especially: Buell, *Int. Relations* (1926), chs. 1–3; * Hayes, *Essays on Nationalism* (1926—see particularly ch. 4 on "Nationality as a Religion"); Herbert, *Nationality and its Problems* (1920); Muir, *Nationalism and Internationalism* (1916); the Article entitled "Nation" by * Renan, in 2 Lalor, *Cyc. Pol. Sci.*, 923–30; Pillisbury, *Psychology of Nationality and Internationalism* (1919); and Zimmern, *Nationality and Government* (1919). For references, see Krehbiel, *Nationalism, War and Society* (1916), p. 23; and Moon, *Syllabus on Int. Relations* (1925), Pt. II. On *Patriotism*, see particularly: Eastman, *Understanding Germany* (1916), 75–111; Inge, *Outspoken Essays* (1920), 35–58; * Nicolai, *The Biology of War* (1918), chs. 7–10; Stocks, *Patriotism*, etc. (1920, see this book for citations from Tolstoy's *Patriotism and Government*); and Veblen, *The Nature of Peace* (1917), ch. 2.

[7] A special phase of this imperialistic struggle is the export of capital that seeks, not merely ordinary investments, but opportunities for loans and concessions which may result in war.

On the *Export of Capital*, see especially: Brailsford, *The War of Steel and Gold* (1914), 63 ff.; Culbertson, *Int. Econ. Policies* (1925), ch. 10, and *Commercial Policy in War Time* (1919), ch. 17; Grunzel, *Economic Protectionism* (1916), 77–100, 254–73; and Hobson, *Export of Capital* (1914).

On *Imperialism* generally, see: * Angell, *The Great Illusion* (1911), particularly Pt. I, ch. 3; Bérard, *British Imperialism*, etc., (1906), and *L'Angle-terre et l'imperialism* (1915); * Brailsford, *op. cit.*, *passim*; Bowman, *The New World* (1921), ch. 2; * Buell, *Int. Relations* (1925), Pt. II, chs. 13 ff.; Cramb, *Imperial Britain, and Germany and England* (1914); Cromer, *Ancient and Modern Imperialism* (1910); * Culbertson, *Int. Econ. Policies* (1925), particularly chs. 9–11, and "Raw Materials," etc., in 112 *Annals*, etc., (March, 1924, No. 201),

(3) *Militarism* which has both psychological and institutional aspects.   On its psychological side, it might be described as a state of mind that is prone to believe in force as a solution of controversies and is strongly disposed to cut the Gordian knot when difficult problems present themselves.   As an institution it tends to perpetuate and even to increase its power and constantly preaches preparedness for war, forgetting that preparedness often only incites war. When Nation-States enter into a competitive struggle or rivalry in armaments they almost inevitably precipitate an armed conflict sooner or later.[8]

(4) *Machiavellian diplomacy, i.e.*, the pursuit of policies aiming at the maintenance and increase of political power by questionable means, such as the use of fraud, misrepresentation and secret intrigue.   Together with rivalry in armaments, this has been perhaps the greatest curse of European international politics, and is one of the main obstacles to the maintenance of truly pacific relations.[9]

(5) One of the most fundamental causes of war has undoubtedly been the *autocratic and oligarchical spirit and*

1–145, and in 112 *Annals Acad.*, etc. (March, 1924, No. 201), 1–145; Dawson, *What is Wrong with Germany* (1915), chs. 7–8; Friedjung, *Das Zeitalter des Imperialismus, 1884–1914* (1919);   Hill, *Rebuilding of Europe* (1917), ch. 3; Hobson, *Imperialism* (1922), and *Democracy after the War* (1917), Pt. I, ch. 4; Lair, *L'impérialism allemand* (1914); * Lippmann, *Stakes of Diplomacy* (1915), 71–128; * Moon, *Imperialism in World Politics* (1926), and *Syllabus on Int. Relations* (1925), Pt. III;   Reich, *Imperialism* (1905); Reinsch, *World Politics* (1900); Veblen, *Imperial Germany and the Industrial Revolution* (1915), ch. 7; Viallate, *Economic Imperialism* (1923), Pt. I, ch. 3:   Weyl, *American World Policies* (1917); Woolf, *Economic Imperialism* (1920), and *Empire and Commerce in Africa* (1919).   For references, see Moon, *Syllabus on Int. Relations* (1925), Pt. III.

[8] On *Militarism*, see, *e.g.*: Angell, *Arms and Industry* (1914), particularly ch. 4; * Bernhardi, *Germany and the Next War* (1912), particularly chs. 1–2; * Clausewitz, *On War* (1898), in 3 vols., particularly Bk. I, chs. 1–2, and Bk. VIII, ch. 6; Dawson, *op. cit.*, ch. 6; Dickinson, *The Choice Before Us* (1917), 1–159; Hobson, *Democracy after the War* (1917), chs. 1–3; Jordan, *The Blood of the Nation* (1902); Kellogg, in *Problems in Eugenics* (1912), 220–31; Lea, *The Valor of Ignorance* (1909, highly militaristic); * Liebknecht, *Militarism* (1917); Macdonald, *National Defense* (1918);   Mahan, *Armaments and Arbitration* (1912), chs. 1, 3, 4–5; * Smith, Munroe, *Militarism and Statecraft* (1918). For references on Militarism and Armaments, see Moon, *Syllabus*, etc. (1925), Pt. IV; and *supra*, p. 509 n.

[9] On *Machiavellian Diplomacy*, cf. *supra*, No. 6 and particularly note 9 on p. 4.   For references, see this note and the Bibliography on pp. 16–17.   See also Index.

methods which, in spite of democratic appearances and changes in forms of government pointing toward democracy, still govern individuals and classes in power. True it is that democracy furnishes no guarantee of pacific conduct, and that it may even be said to breed dangers and menaces of its own; [10] but, though it may be an illusion, there is a widespread belief that in the long run democracy and modern commercial relations make for internationalism and peace.[11]

There developed in the latter part of the nineteenth century, particularly in Germany, a positive *worship of the power of the State* which, though deeply rooted in Hegelian philosophy,[12] finds its most extreme exponent in the historian, Heinrich von Treitschke.[13]

(6) Exaggerated and absolutistic ideas of the *legal sovereignty of States*. Though closely related to autocracy, this is a juristic conception and a by-product of the political absolutism of an earlier historical period (particularly the seventeenth century). It resulted from the application of perhaps a necessary conception of absolute sovereignty in internal or domestic affairs, but was unfortunately applied to the State in its external relations as well and made to include the right to go to war for any reason whatsoever.

[10] As *e.g.*, the liability to sudden emotional outbursts, the machinations and cowardice of time-serving politicians, and the service of an unscrupulous, commercialized and sensational press.

[11] However, it must be said that this is largely speculative, for foreign policy has seldom, if ever, been under a real democratic control.

On *Democracy and Diplomacy*, see Barthélemy, *Démocratie et politique étrangère* (1917); Poole, *The Conduct of Foreign Relations* (1924), *passim*; Ponsonby, *Democracy and Diplomacy* (1915); and various pamphlets published by the Union of Democratic Control.

[12] See Dewey, *German Philosophy and Politics* (1915); and Willoughby, *Prussian Political Philosophy* (1918), *passim*.

[13] The two greatest works by Treitschke are the *Deutsche Geschichte Deutschlands* and the *Politik*. An English translation of the latter work appeared in 1916. Of the *History of Germany*, only one volume has apparently been translated into English. For *Selections from Treitschke's Lectures on Politics*, see Gowan (1914); and Scott, *Survey of the Int. Relations between U. S. and Germany* (1917), lxxiii-xci of the "Introduction."

On *Treitschke*, see: Barker, in *Oxford Pamphlets*, IV (1914), No. 20; * Cramb, *Germany and England* (1914), Lect. 3; * Davis, *The Pol. Thought of Treitschke*, (1915); Dawson, *What is Wrong with Germany* (1915), ch. 2; Durkheim, "Germany above all," in *Studies and Doc. on The War* (1916); Guilland, *Modern Germany and her Historians* (1915), 254–325; and Morgan, *German War Book* (1915), ch. 4.

This exaggerated idea of sovereignty or independence in international relations is still a serious obstacle to the development of a proper international organization, particularly in the United States, where our Senate appears to be the main custodian of this antiquated idea of the absolute nature of sovereignty.[14]

(7) *Neo-Darwinism* or the extreme and one-sided application of the Darwinian principle of natural selection or survival of the fittest (*i.e.* those best fitted to survive under a given environment). This pseudo-scientific view, which was not shared by Darwin himself,[15] places undue emphasis upon the struggle phase of existence as a factor in evolution, and neglects another even more important fact, or, viz., that of mutual aid or coöperation.[16]

(8) The operation of the *Malthusian law* of the increasing pressure on the means of subsistence resulting from the tendency of population to increase more rapidly than the food supply. The *Law of Diminishing Returns*, though it may be temporarily or partially suspended by such events in human history as the Industrial Revolution of the past century, appears to be a fundamental law of economics and a potent cause of migration and war.[17] To prevent these

---

[14] The idea of sovereignty has been particularly attacked by writers of the pluralistic school. For references, see ch. 7, note 1 on p. 175. For a good review of "Pluralistic Theories and the Attack on State Sovereignty" (with numerous references), see Coker, in Merriam, Barnes, etc., *Political Theories* (1924), ch. 3. For an excellent treatment of "Limitations on National Sovereignty in International Relations," see * Garner, in 19 *Am. Pol. Sci. Rev.* (1925), 1–24. (See note on p. 2 for list of publicists who attack the prevailing conception of sovereignty in international relations.) On *Sovereignty in International Law*, cf. *supra*, Nos. 93–95. For an orthodox view of sovereignty, see Lansing, *Notes on Sovereignty* (1921). Among more or less recent criticisms of sovereignty as an obstacle to international organization, see: Hill, *Rebuilding of Europe* (1916), ch. 1; Laski, *Grammer of Politics* (1926), 65–; and Potter, *Int. Organization* (1922), ch. 23, pp. 380–90.

[15] See Kropotkin, *Mutual Aid* (1902), p. 2.

[16] *Ibid.* Cf. *supra*, No. 11 and note 1.

On *Neo-Darwinism* as a cause of war, see particularly: Jordan, *The Blood of the Nation* (1902), *The Human Harvest* (1908), *War and the Breed* (1915), and *War's Aftermath* (1914); * Kellogg, in 120 *Atl. Mo.* (1917), 145 ff., 433 ff., and 10 *Unpopular Rev.* (1918), 146–59; Kropotkin, *Mutual Aid* (1902), especially chs. 1–3; Mitchell, *Evolution and the War* (1915), *passim*; Nasmyth, *Social Progress and the Darwinian Theory* (1916), *passim*; * Nicolai, *The Biology of War* (1918); Novicow, *La critique du darwinism social* (1910); Pearl, *Studies in Human Biology* (1924), ch. 22.

[17] On the *Law of Malthus* and *Over-Population* as a cause of war, see especi-

disastrous results, the obvious remedy is birth control [18] unless the means and rate of productivity of the food supply can be greatly increased.

(9) The establishment of *economic barriers in the way of protective tariffs, but more particularly tariffs of a preferential or discriminatory nature, to free trade between nations.* Though free trade seems to be an impractical ideal at the present stage of the world's industrial development, yet freer trade or more unrestricted commercial intercourse, unhampered by customs dues, would prevent much international friction and greatly tend to the maintenance of peace. The present ideal to be aimed at is, however, equality of treatment as expressed by the policy of the open door or principle of equal commercial opportunity and the most-favored-nation clause in its unconditional form.[19]

(10) *Relative international anarchy or the lack of adequate international law and organization* for the solution of international problems and the prevention and solution of inter-

ally: Carr-Saunders, *The Population Problem* (1922), particularly ch. 11, No. 20; * Cox, *The Problem of Population* (1923), particularly chs. 2, pp. 45 and ch. 3; Dunlop, in Paul (ed.), *Population and Birth Control* (1917), 195–97; East, *Mankind at the Crossroads* (1923), *passim*; Inge, *Outspoken Essays* (1920), 59–81; Leroy-Beaulien, *La question de la population* (1913), *passim*; * Malthus, *Essay on the Principle of Population* (1817), particularly Bk. I, chs. 1–2; * Pearl, *Studies in Human Biology* (1924), Pt. IV; Thompson, *Population: A Study in Malthusanism* (1921); * Wright, *Population* (1923), particularly chs. 2 and 7.

For Bibliographies, see Carr-Saunders and Thompson. *op, cit.*

[18] On *Birth Control*, see various books and contributions written or edited by Cox, De Villibiss, Drysdale, Ellis, Johnsen, Marchant, Meyer, Robinson and * Mrs. Sanger, particularly *The Pivot of Civilization* (1922). For bibliographies, see Johnsen and Schroeder.

[19] On the Most-Favored Nation Clause, cf. *supra*, No. 300. For references, see p. 449.

As early as 1623 Emeric Crucé (cf. *supra*, 67) called attention to the desirability of freedom of commerce and communication as a basis for international organization and peace.

On the *Effects of Tariffs*, more especially of a preferential or discriminatory nature, on international relations, see especially: * Culbertson, *Commercial Policy*, etc. (1919), particularly chs. 10–11, 14–16, *Int. Econ. Policies* (1925), particularly chs. 4–8, 11, in 94 *Annals Acad.* (March, 1921), 160–75, and in 9 *Procs. Am. Acad. Pol. Sci.* (Feb. 1921), 29–63; Fisk and Peirce, *Int. Commerc. Policies* (1923) particularly chs. 6–9, 11–12; Grunzel, *Economic Protectionism* (1916), 339 ff.; and Hobson, *Democracy and the War* (1919), ch. 4.

The economists do not seem to have adequately studied the effects of protective tarriffs on international relations. They almost invariably consider protection (or free trade) merely as a national or domestic problem.

national disputes. This cause, which is of a negative rather than a positive nature, is none the less one of the most important; and the relatively anarchical condition of world affairs is one that calls for an international economic organization as well as a political New World Order with proper agencies or machinery for enforcement.[20]

332. **The So-called Justice or Injustice of War.**—Earlier publicists usually devoted considerable space to the discussion of the conditions under which wars may be considered just or unjust. " The justice of war in general or of a certain war in particular, are questions of the gravest importance and of the most vital interest, but they belong to the domain of International Ethics or Morality rather than to that of International Law."[21]

[20] From a political standpoint, these anarchic conditions are well described in such works as Dickinson's *European Anarchy* (1916), and * *Int. Anarchy* (1926). For valuable suggestions of economic organization, see Garvin, *Economic Foundations of Peace* (1919), *passim*; and * Laski, *A Grammer of Politics* (1926), 610–24. For a valuable account of agencies of international control developed during the World War, but subsequently abandoned, see * Salter, *Allied Shipping Control* (1921).

"It may be noted that several prolific causes of war have almost ceased to operate in modern times. Religious wars have almost disappeared from the pages of European history, and for nearly a century there have been no wars in Europe for the sake of dynastic interests. . . .

"On the other hand, we have several new causes of war or sources of international friction which can scarcely be said to have operated on a large scale before the nineteenth century. The remarkable development of the twin ideas of democracy and nationality have brought into existence new and mighty forces which may ultimately insure peace, but which nevertheless increase the possibility of armed conflicts between modern nations.

"Commerce, like democracy, is Janus-like, facing both ways. Although it is believed that in the main modern industrial conditions make for peace, many so-called political wars have really been commercial wars in disguise, and the present struggle for economic supremacy has given rise to a new doctrine of commercial imperialism which is a serious menace to the peace of the world." *The Reader*, cited above, note 5.

It may be added that "if religious and dynastic wars are a thing of the past, recent contact between Orientals and Occidentals seems to indicate that there is a serious danger of a recrudescence of racial antipathies which, if they continue to grow, may furnish us with a new *casus belli* to which it will be extremely difficult to apply the principle of arbitration or judicial settlement." (See article in *Independent, op. cit.*, on p. 546.) But the student should be warned against the extravagancies of such a work as Stoddard's *Rising Tide of Color* (1920).

[21] Hershey, *Russo-Japanese War*, 67. Cf. Lawrence (7th ed.), p. 311.

On *Causes of War*, with special reference to their justice or injustice, see: Bluntschli, Arts. 515–21; Bonfils or 2 Fauchille, Nos. 1002–05; * 4 Calvo,

333. Classification of Wars.—Wars have been variously classified as public or private, international or civil, perfect or imperfect, principal and auxiliary, general or limited, just or unjust, offensive and defensive, wars of conquest, of intervention, etc., etc. The only distinctions which appear to have any value from a legal standpoint are those between (a) war in a material and legal sense,[22] and (b) between war on land and maritime warfare.

334. The Purpose of War.—A war has usually both a military and a political purpose. The military purpose is to overpower the enemy, *i.e.* to force his submission with the least possible sacrifice of life and property on both sides.

§§ 1884–96; Despagnet (2d ed.), Nos. 509–11; 3 Fiore, Nos. 1269 ff.; * Grotius, lib. I, c. 2 and lib. II, cc. 1, 22–26; * 1 Halleck, ch. 15; Heffter, § 113; Lueder, in 4 Holtzendorff, 221–28; 2 G. F. de Martens, §§ 265–66; 2 Oppenheim, § 63; 2 Piédelièvre, Nos. 798–803; 3 Phillimore, §§ 33–48; * 6 P.-Fodéré, Nos. 2663–70; 2 Rivier, 202–05; Taylor, § 452; * Vattel, liv. III, §§ 24–50, 183–87

The prevailing tendency among the best publicists is to justify war solely on the grounds of defense or necessity. It is the opinion of the writer that there are only three kinds of war which may ever be justified: (1) wars for the sake of defense or self-preservation; (2) struggles for liberty or freedom from oppression; and (3) the use of coercion to force a recalcitrant State to agree to a pacific settlement of a dispute.

The author is decidedly of the opinion that little, if any, advantage can be derived from a classification of wars into those that are just or unjust or even into defensive and offensive. From the standpoint of those that wage them, all wars seem to be defensive and therefore just. In his opinion the best formula yet discovered is that contained in the Geneva Protocol (Art. 10) where the aggressor was defined as "every State which resorts to war in violation of the undertakings in the Covenant or in the present Protocol," *i.e.*, any State that refuses arbitration or a pacific settlement-of the dispute. Cf. *supra*, p. 150 n.

[22] For this distinction, see Chief Justice Fuller in the case of *The "Three Friends"* (1896), 166 U. S. 1, and Evans, 66 or Scott, 830; and Wilson, § 96 (see the cases cited on p. 243 n.).

On the effects of a recognition of insurgency, or war in a material sense, see *supra*, Nos. 113–14.

Some of the Continental publicists maintain that a civil war has no international character. This view is incorrect. The same rules apply to a civil as to any other war. On the conditions essential for the recognition of belligerency, see *supra*, Nos. 115–116.

Since the acceptance of the Covenant of the League of Nations by the great majority of States, it might be said that, according to League Law, war may now be said to be: (a) illegal, *i.e.*, if involving a breach of the Covenant (more particularly Arts. 12–15); and (b) not illegal, *i.e.*, if purely defensive against a sudden or surprise attack, if carried on by or through the League itself, or "if the Council of the League fails to reach a report which is unanimously agreed to by the members thereof, other than the representatives of one or more of the parties to the dispute" (Art. 15, parag. 7).

The political purpose is to obtain that result for which the war was undertaken. This political purpose usually changes during the course of hostilities.

335. The Area or Region of War.—The area or region of war is " that part of the surface of the earth in which the belligerents can prepare and execute hostilities against each other." [23]   In general, this embraces all land and water outside of neutral jurisdiction, [24] including the open sea and the corresponding aërial space.   The possible war area of a belligerent State includes its colonies, protectorates, and regions or districts under disguised forms of occupation or cession. [25]   But it does not ordinarily include neutralized States or those portions of a State's territory, rivers, straits, canals, etc., which may have been neutralized. [26]   Nor does it include demilitarized zones.

336. The Fundamental Principles of Warfare.—There are several fundamental or underlying principles which are supposed to govern modern warfare in a general way:

(1) The principle of military necessity, but the kind and degree of force to be applied must be limited to the specific military end in view, and no more violence may be used at a given time than is necessary under the circumstances. [27]

[23] 2 Oppenheim, § 70.   Oppenheim adds: The "region of war ought to be distinguished from the theater of war," *i.e.* the area or theater of actual hostilities.

[24] It may include neutral territory in exceptional instances where the neutral State or territory is the main object of contention, as in the case of Korea and Manchuria during the Russo-Japanese War.

[25] See *supra*, Nos. 105–06, 178, 185.

[26] See *supra*, No. 109.

[27] As, for example, in case of bombardment and devastation, *infra*, pp. 601 ff. and 598 n.

The principle of military necessity is thus modified by considerations of enlightened self-interest as well as of humanity.   It must not be confounded with the false doctrine of military necessity (*Kriegsraison*) maintained by some German authorities.   See Westlake's criticism of the views of Lueder, in *Chapters*, 238 ff. or *Collected Papers*, 243 ff., and in 2 *Int. Law* (1st ed.), 115–17. Military necessity does not justify a violation of the rules of civilized warfare.

For an English translation of the *Kriegsbrauch im Landkriege* which gives expression to the ideas of the German General Staff on the subject of military necessity, see Morgan, *The German War Book* (1915); and 1 Rolin (1921) *Le droit moderne de la guerre*, Nos. 11 ff.   On the German doctrine, see also Andler, "*Frightfullness" in Theory and Practice* (1916).

For criticisms of the plea of military necessity as entered by Germany in justification of the violation of Belgian neutrality, see 2 Garner, §§ 439–42; and Visscher, *Belgium's Case* (1916), ch. 2, and in 24 *R. D. I. P.* (1917), 74–108.

(2) The principle of humanity, viz. that certain practices, such as the use of poison and submarine mines, are either wholly prohibited or limited because repugnant to the modern sense of humanity, honor, or fair play.

(3) War is primarily a relation between States, or between a State and the subjects of the enemy State in so far as the latter are identified with the State for military purposes,—not a relation between individuals.[28]

337. **Reprisals in War.**—The main sanction for the observance of the rules of warfare on the part of belligerents is ordinarily furnished by public opinion, but reprisals may be said to provide a sort of special sanction in serious or extreme cases of their persistent violation.[29] Reprisals [30] in war consist in acts of retaliation, such as the seizure of persons or property of the enemy by way of indemnity or to prevent repetition of the offense in case of violations of the rules of warfare by the opposing belligerent.

[28] I have adopted the compromise views of Westlake (see *Chapters*, 258–64 or *Collected Papers*, 264–71, and in 2 *Int. Law*, 32–38) on this much controverted subject. The controversy goes back to Portalis, who (in 1801) adopted Rousseau's doctrine that war is not a relation between individuals, but between States—a doctrine usually denied by Continental and supported by Anglo-American publicists.

It must be admitted that our experience during the World War has gone far to discredit the Rousseau point of view and to support the German doctrine declared by Clausewitz and others that modern war is a conflict between nations and peoples rather than merely or mainly between States and governments. It remains to be seen whether the distinction between combatants and non-combatants can be maintained in future great life and death struggles.

On these *Fundamental Principles of Modern Warfare*, see: Boidin, *Les lois de la guerre*, ch. 2; Bonfils and 2 Fauchille, Nos. 1000–09; Bordwell, ch. I; Creasy, 364 ff.; "Declaration of St. Petersburg of 1868" (preamble to), in Higgins, *Hague Peace Conferences*, 5; Despagnet (2d ed.), No. 513; Fenwick, 434 ff.; * Hall, Pt. I, ch. 3; Heffter, § 119; * Holland, *War on Land*, Nos. 1–3; Grotius, lib. III, cap. 7; Lawrence (7th ed.), § 205; * Lueder, in 4 Holtzendorff, 253–57, 371 ff.; Maine, 131 ff., especially 145; * 2 Oppenheim, §§ 57, 67, 69; 2 Piédelièvre, Nos. 792, 829, 868–70; 2 Rivier, 238 ff.; Taylor, § 451; Vattel, liv. III, §§ 136–38, 226; * 2 Westlake (1st ed.), 32–38, 52–59, 115–17; and *Chapters*, 232–67, or *Collected Papers*, 264 ff.; Wheaton, Nos. 342–43, 347.

[29] This applies more particularly to the rules of land warfare. The law of maritime capture is largely administered by prize courts.

See Art. 3 of the Fourth Hague Convention (4 H. C., 3) for special rules providing for compensation and responsibility in case of violation of the "Hague Regulations respecting War on Land." Cf. *infra*, No. 400.

[30] Reprisals in time of war must be carefully distinguished from reprisals as a means of self-help in time of peace. See *supra*, No. 322.

It is generally admitted: (1) That reprisals or retaliatory acts of warfare should never be resorted to out of mere revenge, but only as a means of protective retribution.   (2) They should only be admitted in grave cases of imperative necessity, and after careful inquiry into the nature of the alleged violations of the rules of warfare.   (3) Their nature or scope should not exceed the measure of such violations. (4) They may only be resorted to with the authorization of the commander-in-chief.   (5) They must be consistent with the laws of humanity and morality.   (6) Redress for the wrong complained of, or punishment of the real offenders, must be otherwise unattainable.[31]

[31] Arts. 27–28 of the *American Instructions;* the *Oxford Code* (1880) of the Institute of Int. Law, Arts. 85–86 (see Scott, *Resolutions*, 42); and the Russian proposals at the Brussels Conference of 1874 (see 2 Oppenheim, § 250).

The abuse of the right of reprisal has perhaps never been greater than during the World War.   In so far as they were admitted, the German atrocities in Belgium were defended on grounds of reprisal.   In consequence of repeated and indiscriminate attacks by German aviators upon undefended towns, villages and even hospitals in France and England, several important cities in Baden were bombed by French and British aviators in the summer and autumn of 1916.   On April 14, 1917 Freiburg was raided as an act of reprisal for the attacks of German submarines on British hospital ships.   By December 1, 1917, a general policy of air-raid reprisals appears to have been adopted by Great Britain and France.   The Germans resorted to counter reprisals.   On aerial reprisals, see 1 Garner, § 311.   See 2 *Ibid.*, §§ 349, 355–56 for reprisals because of treatment of prisoners.

The so-called Anglo-French blockade of Germany declared in March, 1915 was defended as a justifiable act of retaliation against Germany, on account of the latter's war decree of Feb. 1915, which had itself been declared an act of reprisal for alleged British violations of International Law.

The United States protested against these Anglo-French reprisals on the ground that they constituted a violation of neutral rights and that the *right of retaliation against an enemy did not include the right to interfere with the lawful commerce of neutrals.*   See the Notes of Secretary Lansing of July 21, and Oct. 21, 1915, in Spec. Supp. to 9 and 10 *A. J.* (1915 and 1916), 156 and 88.   The point involved is controversial.   The British Prize Courts upheld the legality of the Reprisal Orders in Council of Mar. 11, 1915 and Feb. 16, 1917 from the standpoint of International Law in the cases of *The Stigstad* (1916) 2 B. and C. P. C. 179 which were affirmed by the Privy Council, L. R. (1919), A. C. 219; and *The Leonora* (1918) 3 B. and C. P. C. 181, 385 affirmed by the Privy Council L. R. (1919), A. C. 974.   For these decisions of the Privy Council see also 13 *A. J.* (1919), 127 and 814.   For criticisms of these decisions, see Borchard in 23 *Yale Law J.* (1918–19), 583–87, and Yntema, in 17 *Mich. Law Rev.* (1918–19), 564–88.

These decisions are supported by Oppenheim, II, §§ 319, 360.   Richards (in *Brit. Year Bk.*, 1920–21, pp. 29 ff.) presents the arguments on both sides. See also 2 Garner, ch. 33, particularly the note on pp. 322–23.

On *Reprisals in War*, see: Baker and McKernan, *Laws of Warfare* (1919),

BIBLIOGRAPHY

Kinds, Nature or Characteristics, and Laws of War.—Atherley-Jones, *Commerce in War* (1907), *passim;* Barclay, *Law and Usage of War* (1914); Baty and Morgan, *War: Its Conduct and Legal Results* (1915); * Bernhardi, *Germany and the Next War* (1914); Bloch, *Der Krieg* (1899), in 6 vols., and * *The Future of War* (1899); Bluntschli, Arts. 510–21, and in 8 *R. D. I.*, 663 ff.; Boidin, *Les lois de la guerre*, etc. (1908); Bordwell, *Law of War* (1908); Bonfils or * 2 Fauchille, Nos. 1000–26; 4 Calvo, §§ 1860–98; Carpentier, *Les lois de la guerre continental* (1904); * Clausewitz, *Vom Kriege* (Eng. trans. in 3 vols., 1898); Descamps, in 7 *R. D. I. P.* (1900), 629 ff. and 705 ff.; Despagnet (2d ed.), Nos. 504–16; Dupuis, in 5 *R. D. I. P.* (1898), 35 ff.; Fenwick, ch. 26; 3 Fiore, Nos. 1261–89, and *Int. Law Cod.*, Nos. 1420–26; Funck-Brentano et Sorel, *Précis*, liv. II, ch. i; * Garner, *Int. Law and the World War* (1920), in 2 vols., *passim;* Geffcken, in 26 *R. D. I.*, 586 ff.; * Grotius, *De jure belli ac pacis*, lib. I, cap. 1, 2, and 3; lib. II, cap. 1, 22–26; lib. III, cap. 3; Guelle, *Précis des lois de la guerre* (1884), in 2 vols.; Hall, Pt. I, ch. 3; * 1 Halleck, chs. 15–16; Heffter, §§ 113–119; Heilborn, *System* (1896), 321 ff., and in 1 Stier-Somlo, *Handbuch des Völkerrechts*, 22–25; Higgins, *War and the Private Citizen* (1912); * Holland, *The Law of War on Land* (1908); 2 Hyde, §§ 596–601; Klüber, 235–37; Kamarowsky, *Le tribunal int.* (1887), 45–72; * Lagorgette, *Le rôle de la guerre* (1906); Lasson, *Das Culturideal und der Krieg* (1868); Lentner, *Das Recht im Kriege* (1886); Letourneau, *La guerre dans les diverses races humaines* (1895); Liszt, §§ 56 ff.; 2 Lorimer, *Institutes of the Law of Nations* (1883–84), Bk. IV, chs. 4–10; 2 J. de Louter, § 42; Lueder, *Krieg und Kriegsrecht* (1888), and in 4 Holtzendorf, 171 ff.; Manning, *Commentaries on the Law of Nations* (ed. by Amos, 1875), Bk. IV, ch. 1; 3 F. de Martens, *Traité*, § 106, and *La paix et la guerre* (1901); 2 G. F. de Martens, §§ 263–66; * Mérignhac, *Les lois de la guerre sur terre* (1903), and in 14 *R. D. I. P.* (1907), 197 ff.; 7 Moore, *Digest*, §§ 1100–05; Moynier, *Essai sur les lois de la guerre* (1895); * Novicow, *Les luttes entre sociétes*

491–520; Bluntschli, Arts. 567, 580, 685 n.; Bonfils or * 2 Fauchille, Nos. 1018–26; Bordwell, 305–06; 4 Calvo, §§ 2041–43; Davis (3d ed.), 325–27; Despagnet (2d ed.), No. 544; Fenwick, 489–91; Funck Brentano et Sorel, 293-96; Hall (8th ed.), 497–98, 640–41, 646; Halleck, in 6 *A. J.* (1912), 107–18; * Holland, *War on Land*, Nos. 119–20; 2 Hyde, § 667; Le Fur, *Des représailles* (1919); 3 F. de Martens, § 131; 7 Moore, *Digest*, § 1114 (for examples); Mérignhac, *La guerre sur terre* (1903), 210–18, 1 *La guerre de 1914-1918*), 210–18, and in 24 *R. D. I. P.* (1917), 9–26; * 2 Oppenheim, §§ 247–50; 2 Piédelièvre, Nos. 910–17; Pillet, *Les lois actuelles de la guerre* (1901), Nos. 144–46; * 8 P.-Fodéré, Nos. 3215–21; Renault, in 42 *J. D. I.* (1915), 313–44; 2 Rivier, 298–99; Rolin, Nos. 322–28; Spaight, *War Rights on Land* (1911), 462–65; Taylor, §§ 487 and 507; Vattel, liv. III, § 142; * 2 Westlake (1st ed.), 112–15, and *Chapters*, 253–58 or *Collected Papers*, 259–64; Wheaton, § 318; and Wilkinson, in 40 *Law Mag. and Rev.* (1914–15), 289–98.

humaines (1893), and *War and Its Alleged Benefits* (1911); 3 Nys, *Le droit int.*, ch. I, and *Le droit de la guerre* (1882); * 2 Oppenheim, §§ 53–73; 2 Piédelièvre, Nos. 784–805; * Pillet, *Le droit de la guerre* (1892), and *Les lois actuelles de la guerre* (1901); 6 P.-Fodéré, Nos. 2650–70; Rettich, *Zur Theorie und Geschichte des Rechts zum Kriege* (1888); 2 Rivier, §§ 61, 63, and in 13 *R. D. I.*, 79 ff.; Rolin, *La droit moderne de la guerre* (1921), in 3 vols.; Rougier, *Les guerres civiles*, etc. (1903); Taylor, §§ 449–54; Triepel *Die neuesen Forschritte auf dem Gebiete des Kriegsrechts* (1894); 2 Twiss, §§ 22–29; Ullmann, §§ 165–70, 174; Vattel, liv. III, §§ 1–5, 24–50, 69–72; Visscher, in 24 *R. D. I. P.* (1917), 74 ff.; War Dept. of U. S., *Rules of Land Warfare* (1917); * 2 Westlake, 1–5, and *Chapters*, 232–75 or *Collected Papers*, 237–82; Wilson, Art. on "War," in 40 *Cyc. of L. and P.*; Zorn, *Das Kriegerecht zu Lande* (1906).

For Bibliographies, see Bonfils, Bordwell, * Fauchille, Olivart, * Oppenheim, etc.

CHAPTER XXVI

DECLARATION OF WAR AND ITS EFFECTS

338. War an Abnormal Relation between States.—" War is an abnormal relation between . States, and produces abnormal conditions affecting the activities and interests of individuals as well. Consequently, its outbreak brings into existence a new set of rules affecting individuals and governments, which largely supplant or supplement those rights and obligations already existing in times of peace. In view of this fact, it is extremely important to fix upon a definite date for the beginning of these new and abnormal relations between belligerents on the one hand and the two or more belligerents on the other." [1]

339. Is a Declaration of War Necessary?—The question whether a formal notice of intention or declaration of war is necessary has been a subject of much controversy. The older as well as the more recent authorities have apparently been nearly equally divided on this subject.[2] And international practice has varied greatly, though in modern times declaration prior to hostilities has been, comparatively speaking, somewhat exceptional.[3]

[1] Hershey, *Russo-Japanese War* (1906), 62.

[2] Anglo-American publicists have generally insisted that a declaration of war is not necessary. They have maintained that the date of the first actual outbreak of hostilities furnishes a better criterion for the commencement of a war than the date of the formal declaration. Their view is perhaps best expressed by Hall (8th ed. 444):

"An act of hostility, unless it be done in the urgency of self-preservation or by way of reprisal, is in itself a full declaration of intention; any sort of previous declaration therefore is an empty formality, unless an enemy must be given time and opportunity to put himself in a state of defense, and it is needless to say that no one asserts such quixotism to be obligatory."

On the other hand, the majority of Continental publicists have insisted upon the utility or necessity of declaration, though they appear to be almost equally divided on this point. For more or less extensive citations of the authorities, see: 2 Fauchille, p. 34; 4 Calvo, § 1906; Hall, *op. cit.*, 446–49 and notes on pp. 448–50; Mérignhac, *La guerre sur terre*, 29–31 n.; 2 Oppenheim (3d ed., pp. 136 and 137 notes); 6 P.-Fodéré, No. 2673; and Rey, in 14 *R. D. I. P.* (1907), 306–07 n.

[3] Declarations were customary in Antiquity and the Middle Ages. The Romans were particularly strict in their observance of certain formalities connected with the declaration of war. See *supra*, No. 37.

340. A Sudden or Treacherous Attack Illegal.—However, the authorities are generally agreed that nations are bound to refrain from sudden or treacherous attacks upon one

Declarations prior to hostilities were no longer considered necessary during the seventeenth century. In his investigations on this subject, General Maurice of the British army (see his *Hostilities without Declaration*, 1883, and an article published in the *Nineteenth Century* for April, 1904) found less than ten cases out of 118 examined of declarations prior to hostilities between 1700 and 1872. For a list of wars begun without formal declaration, see 2 *A. J.* (1908), 57–62.

But it should be noted that there has been a tendency in recent times to revert to the older practice of beginning war with a declaration, *e.g.* in the cases of the Franco-German War of 1870 and the Russo-Turkish War of 1877. The Chino-Japanese War of 1894–1895 began, however, with the capture of the Chinese transport *Koshung* by a Japanese cruiser; and, in the case of the Spanish-American War, the United States formally declared war on April 25, 1898, after the capture of several Spanish vessels and the blockade of Cuban ports on April 22. The existence of hostilities or actual outbreak of the war was dated back to April 21 by the Declaration itself. But it should be noted that these were preceded by an ultimatum or conditional declaration. See Benton, *The Int. Law and Diplomacy of the Spanish-American War* (1908), 99, 109 ff.

Considerable controversy was aroused by the Russian charges of treachery against the Japanese because of the latter's attack on the Russian fleets at Chemulpo and at Port Arthur on Feb. 8, 1904, two days prior to Japan's declaration of war against Russia on Feb. 10.

Authorities are in substantial agreement in rendering a verdict of acquittal in favor of Japan as far as these charges are concerned. The attack on the Russian fleet could not have been in the nature of a surprise, as Japan had severed diplomatic relations on Feb. 6 and informed the Russian Government that "the Imperial Government of Japan reserve to themselves the right to take such independent action as they may deem best to consolidate and defend their menaced position, as well as to protect their established rights and legitimate interests."

It appears, however, that Japan actually began hostilities with the capture of the *Ekaterinoslav*, on the morning of Feb. 6, at least fourteen hours (allowing for the difference in time between Tokio and St. Petersburg) before the delivery of the Japanese note at the Russian capital, breaking off diplomatic relations. It seems that the decisive factor which determined the action of the Japanese was the appearance of the Russian fleet off the Shantung promontory between Port Arthur and the Japanese coast on Feb. 4. Under these circumstances, the Japanese Government may have been justified in ordering out its fleet even before the severance of diplomatic relations had been fully accomplished.

The following appears to have been the order of these occurrences:

February 4, 1904—Russian fleet seen off the Shantung promontory.

February 5 at 2 P.M.—Dispatch of note from Tokio to St. Petersburg, breaking off diplomatic relations and orders to Vice-Admiral Togo to go in search of the Russian fleet soon afterwards.

February 6 at 7 A.M.—Sailing of Japanese fleet from Sasebo.

February 6 at 9 A.M.—Capture of the *Ekaterinoslav*.

February 6 at 2 P.M.—Severance of diplomatic relations at Tokio.

another without negotiation or warning. " The use of a declaration does not exclude surprise, but it at least provides that notice shall be served an infinitesimal space of time before a blow is struck. . . . The truth is that no forms give security against disloyal conduct, and that when no disloyalty occurs, States always sufficiently well know when they stand on the brink of war." [4]

War is usually preceded by a long period of negotiations which may result in an ultimatum or a conditional declaration of war. With modern facilities for telegraphic and telephonic communication, a complete surprise would be well-nigh impossible.[5]

341. The Rules of the Second Hague Conference.—The controversy on the necessity or desirability of a declaration of war prior to hostilities was at least partly settled by the Convention relative to the Commencement of Hostilities, signed by nearly all the States [6] represented at the Second Hague Peace Conference.

This Convention declared: " The Contracting Powers recognize that hostilities between them are not (*ne doivent pas*) to commence without a previous and unequivocal warning, which shall take the form either of a declaration of war, giving reasons, or of an ultimatum with a conditional declaration of war " (Art. 1).

February 6 at 4 P.M.—Severance of diplomatic relations at St. Petersburg.
February 8, at noon—Japanese attack on Russian vessels at Chemulpo, Korea.
February 8, at midnight—Japanese attack on Russian fleet at Port Arthur.
February 10—Declaration of War.
On this controversy, see: Ariga, *La guerre russo-japonaise*, ch. 1; Bordwell, ch. 14; 2 Cobbett, 1–5; Ehrens and F. de Martens, in 11 *R. D. I. P.* (1904), 133 ff.; Hershey, ch. 1 and in 2 *A. J.* (1908), 944–45; Lawrence, *War and Neutrality*, ch. 2, and *Principles* § 140; Nagaoka, in 36 *R. D. I.* (1904), 461 ff.; Rey, in 14 *R. D. I. P.* (1907), 302 ff.; Smith and Sibley, ch. 3; and Takahashi, ch. I.
Though there were some exceptions, it would seem that the Powers generally observed the rule of declaring war before beginning hostilities at the outbreak of the World War. See 2 Fauchille, No. 1030; and Phillipson, *Int. Law and the Great War*, ch. 3. For a list of the declarations of the World War, see 1 Garner, 37–38; and 25 *R. D. I. P.* (1918), 85–87.

[4] Hall (8th ed.), 452.
[5] The surprise of a nation must not be confounded with that of an army or fleet. Thus Ariga (*op. cit.*, 26) admits that the Russian fleet at Port Arthur was surprised, not so Russia.
[6] The sole exceptions were China and Nicaragua. Nicaragua adhered later. Nearly half of them had ratified in July, 1911.

" The state of war should be notified to the neutral Powers without delay, and shall not take effect in regard to them until after the receipt of a notification, which may even be made by telegraph. Nevertheless, neutral Powers cannot plead the absence of notification if it be clearly established that they were in fact aware of the state of war " (Art. 2).[7]

The Hague Conference of 1907 has thus created an obligation not to commence hostilities without a previous conditional or formal declaration of war, as also to notify neutrals without delay; but there are some points not covered by these rules.

342. **War may Exist without Declaration.**—A declaration is, of course, unnecessary in the case of civil or purely defensive wars, and there can be no doubt that, in the future as in the past, war may exist without a declaration; and that in the absence of such a declaration of intention, the legal effects of the war date from the commencement of hostilities if these are an expression of hostile intent.[8] The failure to make a declaration would, however, constitute a breach of International Law.

The immediate effects of the outbreak of war may be thus summarized:

[7] 3 H. C. (1907), Arts. 1 and 2. It should be noted that Art. 2 merely renders an existing custom obligatory.

"Article 1 of the present Convention shall take effect in case of war between two or more of the Contracting Powers. Article 2 is binding as between a belligerent Power which is a party to the Convention and neutral Powers which are also parties to the Convention." Art. 3.

This Convention was based upon the rules adopted by the Institute of Int. Law in 1906. See Scott, *Resolutions*, 164.

An amendment providing that hostilities should not commence until twenty-four hours after the delivery of the declaration or ultimatum had elapsed was proposed by Holland and supported by Russia; but it was rejected by a vote of 16 to 13, with five abstentions.

On these *Hague Rules*, see 1 *Proceedings of the Hague Peace Conferences*, 131 ff.; Bordwell, 198–200; Boiden, 116–21; * Higgins, 198–205; Busta-mante y Sirven, *La seconde conférence de la paix* (1909), ch. 8; * Holland, *War on Land* (1908), 16–17; Lawrence, § 140; Lémonon, *La seconde confér-ence de la paix* (1908), Nos. 395–506; * 1 Rolin, Nos. 186 ff.; * 1 Scott 516–22; Stowell, in 2 *A. J.* (1908), 50 ff.; 2 Westlake, 267.

[8] So far as the writer is aware, judges of prize courts (at least in the United States and England), who have been called upon to pass upon the validity of captures made prior to a declaration, are unanimously of the opinion that war exists without a declaration. For cases, see Evans, *Cases*, 378–89 and Scott, *Cases*, 522–36.

343. The Effects of the Outbreak of War on (I) Diplomatic Relations.—Diplomatic intercourse ceases upon the outbreak of war, and this usually occurs prior to the opening of hostilities through the recall or dismissal of public ministers or ambassadors [9] representing the belligerent governments. The exequaturs of the consuls of the enemy State are also usually withdrawn.

344. Effect of War on (II) Treaties.—It was formerly held that all treaties between the belligerents, excepting those concluded with a view to hostile relations, were annulled by the outbreak of war.[10] This doctrine has been abandoned by the great majority of publicists, but authorities are by no means agreed on the question whether the abrogation of treaties as a consequence of war is the rule or the exception. Nor does a study of international practice afford a certain solution of the problem.

There is, however, a certain agreement between international practice and the bulk of the authorities on the following points:

(*a*) Transitory or dispositive treaties,[11] or agreements which purport to set up a permanent state of things, such as treaties of cession, boundary, independence, neutrality, and the like, are unaffected by war.[12]

---

[9] It is customary for each belligerent to ask the minister or consul of a friendly State to take charge of the archives, etc., and look after the interests of its nationals during the war. Thus the interests of Great Britain in South Africa during the Boer War were intrusted to the American consulate at Pretoria, as the interests of the United States had been intrusted to the British legation at Madrid during the Spanish-American War.

The mere recall or dismissal of public ministers only indicates very strained relations, and should not in itself be regarded as equivalent to a declaration of war.

[10] This untenable doctrine was held by a few leading authorities, *e.g.* 1 Kent, *Com.*, 177; 3 Phillimore, § 530; and 1 Twiss, § 252. But a reading of subsequent sections will show that Phillimore does not hold the doctrine in as absolute a form as has been represented.

[11] Cf. *supra*, Nos. 129–30, particularly pp. 218 and 223.

[12] "Where treaties contemplate a permanent arrangement of territorial, and other national rights, or which, in their terms, are meant to provide for the event of an intervening war, it would be against every principle of just interpretation to hold them extinguished by the event of war. If such were the law, even the treaty of 1783, so far as it fixed our limits, and acknowledged our independence, would be gone, and we should have had again to struggle for both upon original revolutionary principles. . . .

"We think, therefore, that treaties stipulating for permanent rights and

(b) Law-making treaties or conventions to which third Powers are parties, as, for example, the Hague Conventions, the International Postal Union, etc., remain in force. Such treaties, may, however, be suspended during a war, owing to the difficulty or impossibility of execution.

(c) Conventions entered into with a view to hostilities or which are applicable to a state of war are to be put into operation.

(d) Purely political conventions, such as treaties of alliance and agreements, the interpretation of which has given rise to the war, are abrogated.

(e) There is a difference of opinion respecting treaties of commerce, navigation, etc., but the better view would seem to be that their execution is merely suspended during the war. This is certainly the case with treaties of extradition, copyright, etc., dealing with matters having no connection with the war or its purpose. All such conventions may, of course, be treated as annulled, suspended, or as continuing in force at will of the belligerents, who usually define their status in the treaty of peace.

The general rule or principle governing this subject would seem to be that only such agreements as are incompatible with the ends of warfare are necessarily annulled or suspended, as the case may be; but that the belligerents may and should clearly indicate their position, more particularly in respect to commercial treaties and the like, in the treaty of peace.[13]

general arrangements, and professing to aim at perpetuity, and to deal with the case of war as well as of peace, do not cease on the occurrence of war, but are, at most, suspended while it lasts; and unless they are waived by the parties or new and repugnant stipulations are made, they revive in their operation at the return of peace." Judge Washington, in *Society for Propagation of the Gospel* v. *New Haven* (1823), 8 Wheaton, 464, 494; Evans, *Cases*, 402 or Scott, *Cases* 98. Cf. *Sutton* v. *Sutton* (1830), 1 R. and M. 663 or Scott, *Cases*, 468.

[13] International practice has varied greatly in this respect, but there is still a disposition to assume that treaties of commerce are annulled. A number of recent treaties of peace (*e.g.* those of Frankfort in 1871 between France and Germany and of Portsmouth in 1905 between Japan and Russia) place the commercial relations of the former belligerents upon the footing of the most-favored-nation clause, pending the negotiation of new conventions.

During the negotiations of the Treaty of Paris (1898) between Spain and the United States, the "American Commissioners proposed an article by which all the treaties in existence between the two countries at the outbreak of the war were enumerated and declared to continue in force." But the Spanish Com-

345. **Effects on** (III) **Subjects of Enemy State Found in Belligerent Territory at Outbreak of Hostilities.**—Prior to the World War, a continuous practice of several centuries had established the customary rule that nationals of the enemy State found in belligerent territory at the outbreak of war were permitted to remain during good behavior, unless their expulsion was required by military considerations.[14] Permission to remain carried with it, of course,

missioners insisted that the war had "terminated all agreements, compacts and conventions between the two countries" in accordance with the Spanish decree of April 23, 1898. Art. 29 of the Treaty of Friendship and General Relations between the United States and Spain (1902), provided that "all treaties, agreements, conventions, and contracts between the United States and Spain prior to the Treaty of Paris shall be expressly abrogated and annulled, with the exception of the treaty signed the 17th of February, 1834 . . . for the settlement of claims . . . which is continued in force by the present Convention." 5 Moore, *Digest*, pp. 376–77. Cf. Benton, *Int. Law and Diplomacy of the Sp.-Amer. War* (1908), 118 ff.

On the *Effect of War on Treaties*, see especially: * Baker and McKernan, *Laws of Warfare* (1919), 220–69, (for citations from the authorities); Bonfils or 2 Fauchille, No. 1049; Crandall, *Treaties*, § 181; Hall, § 125; * Hurst, in *Brit. Yr. Book* (1921–22), 37–47; 2 Hyde, §§ 547–51; Jacomet, *La guerre et les traités* (1909); Lawrence, §§ 144–46; 5 Moore, *Digest*, § 779, and in 1 *Columbia Law. Rev.*, 209 ff.; 2 Oppenheim, § 99; * Phillipson, *Termination of War*, 250–68; 1 Rolin, Nos. 217–31 ; and 2 Westlake (1st ed.), 29–32.

For fuller bibliographies, see Fauchille, Hurst, and Jacomet. For a "Table showing the Effect of War on Treaties," see Lawrence (4th ed.), § 146. It is omitted in the 7th edition. A *Project* on this subject was adopted by the Institute of Int. Law in 1912. See Scott, *Resolutions*, 172.

The Treaty of Versailles (Art. 282) enumerated 26 multilateral agreements of an economic or technical character that were to be applied between Germany and such of the Allied and Associated Powers as were parties thereto. Certain specified postal and telegraphic conventions were to be applied on condition that Germany fulfill expressed stipulations (Art. 283). Many treaty rights and principles which Germany had acquired were declared terminated in the Treaty. Each of the Allied or Associated Powers was to notify Germany of the bilateral treaties which it wished to revive with Germany, but no treaties were to be revived that were not in accordance with the Treaty of Versailles. In case of any difference of opinion, the League of Nations shall be called upon to decide. "Only those bilateral treaties and conventions which have been the subject of such a notification shall be revived between the Allied and Associated Powers and Germany; all the others are and shall be abrogated" (Art. 289).

[14] The only nineteenth century instances of expulsion prior to the World War were those of the Germans from Paris in 1870—a precautionary measure which has been much criticised; the expulsion of various categories of British subjects during the Boer War; and the forcible ejectment and cruel treatment of Japanese refugees in Manchuria and Siberia by the Russians during the Russo-Japanese War. In its Imperial Order of Feb. 28, 1904, the Russian Government had authorized Japanese subjects to "continue, under the protection of Russian law, to reside, and to follow peaceful callings in the Russian

the right to protection of life and property and obligations of temporary allegiance. If ordered to leave, it was held that alien enemies should be given a reasonable time for the withdrawal or disposal of their property. Nor might they be forcibly detained or held as prisoners.[15]

345a. The World War marked a wide departure from the practice of several centuries and a rule laid down by Vattel.[16] At the outbreak of the war the British Government accorded to German subjects a period of seven days during which they might leave and the French Government gave notice that all foreigners might leave France before the end of the first day of mobilization. Neither Germany nor Austria-Hungary allowed any period of grace. At first only suspects were arrested and interned in the United Kingdom, but later (in May, 1915), in consequence of mob outbreaks and a widespread popular demand, practically the entire enemy population, as well as the majority of naturalized British subjects of enemy origin, were interned in concentration camps.[17] In France the greater part of the enemy alien population,[18] particularly that of Paris, was placed in concentration camps in the early period of the war. Though less drastic at the beginning, the German Government

Empire except in territories forming part of the Imperial Lieutenancy in the Far East." In its "Instructions" of Feb. 10, 1905, the Japanese Government made no exceptions whatever, though it was made clear that such permission to continue residence in Japan should be considered as an act of grace and conditional upon good behavior. See Ariga, *op. cit.*, § 15; Hershey, *op. cit.*, 269, 282–83, 297–99; Lawrence, *War and Neutrality*, etc., ch. 3; Takahashi, *Russo-Jap. War* (1908), ch. 2.

[15] The last instance of forcible detention had occurred in 1803, when Napoleon I had ordered the arrest of all Englishmen residing in France between eighteen and sixty years of age as an unjustifiable reprisal for the British capture of French vessels with a prior declaration of war. Many of them were not freed before 1814.

Enemy merchants were generally given at least forty days for withdrawal and disposal of their goods, even in the Middle Ages.

[16] In 1758 Vattel (Bk. III, § 63) said: "A sovereign who declares war can not detain the subjects of the enemy, who happen to be in his State at the time of the declaration, nor can he seize their property. They came there in reliance upon the public faith; for in permitting them to enter his territory and to reside there the sovereign impliedly promised them full liberty and security for their return home."

[17] It was stated in the House of Commons on Dec. 14, 1915 that the number of aliens interned amounted to 45,749. Of these 32,274 were civilians, and 13,475 were described as "naval and military men."

[18] To the number, it is said of about 45,000.

adopted retaliatory measures of a similar nature.[19]   The German measures may perhaps be justified on this ground, but there seems to be no sound justification for the British and French internment of civilians.   Much may, however, be urged in favor of such treatment of reservists or persons liable to military service.

346. **Property Rights of Such Persons.**—The practice of confiscation of the property of the subjects of the enemy State found under belligerent jurisdiction at the outbreak of war is regarded as obsolete.   " Neither the principal nor the interest of a State debt can be confiscated or sequestered because the individuals to whom it is due are enemy subjects." [20]   Private debts, *i.e.* debts due from private individuals to subjects of the enemy State are no longer held to be confiscable, even from a purely legal standpoint, though the payment of such debts may be suspended during the war.[21]   The wars of the French Revolution furnish us

[19] On this subject, see particularly 1 Garner, ch. 3.   See also 2 Hyde, §§ 616–17; Phillipson, *op. cit.*, ch. 5; and Satow, in 2 *Grot. Soc.* (1917), 1–10.

[20] 2 Westlake, (1st ed.), 38.   There has been no attempt of this sort involving "the honor of the prince" since 1752, when Frederick the Great withheld payment to British subjects of the interest on the "Silesian Loan," by way of reprisal for the British capture of Prussian vessels under rules of maritime warfare which he held to be illegal.

On the *Silesian Loan Controversy*, see 1 Cobbett, *Cases*, 347–51; 2 Martens, *Causes célébrès*, 1–88; Snow, *Cases*, 243–46; and Wheaton, *History*, 206–17.

[21] The right to confiscate private enemy property was upheld by the older authorities.   It was still admitted by the Supreme Court of the United States in *Brown* v. *U. S.* (8 Cranch, 110, and Scott, *Cases*, 555) as late as 1814 that private debts due the enemy, as also other private enemy property found in belligerent territory at the commencement of hostilities, may be confiscated according to the strict law of war; but that, under the Constitution of the United States, it might only be done by Congressional authority.   But it is not likely that *Brown* v. *U. S.* would be followed to-day in the United States. The decisions even of a Chief Justice Marshall should not be deemed immortal. However, in *U. S.* v. *Chemical Foundation, Inc.*, (1926), the U. S. Supreme Court reaffirmed the opinion on the case of *U. S.* v. *Brown* and confirmed the confiscation by the Alien Property Custodian of some 4500 patents belonging to enemy Germans, in accordance with the powers granted by the Trading with the Enemy Act as amended in 1918.   It was held that there is "no, *constitutional* prohibition against the confiscation of enemy properties."   For this decision, see 47 Sup. Ct. Rep., Nov. 1, 1926.   For comment see, N. Y. *Nation*, Oct. 27, 1926, pp. 419 f.

In 1817 Lord Ellenborough held a Danish ordinance, confiscating private debts due British creditors from Danish debtors by way of reprisal, to be invalid and contrary to the Law of Nations, and refused to recognize the payment of such a debt to the Danish Government as an extinction of the obligation.   *Wolff* v. *Oxholm*, K. B., 6 M. and S. 92.

with the last important examples of the confiscation of the private property of enemy subjects found in belligerent territory upon the outbreak of hostilities.[22]

This decision has been much criticised, but "our own conclusion is that the time is fully ripe when a British Court should not lag behind the position taken by Governments, but should boldly follow Lord Ellenborough." 2 Westlake, 44.

[22] E.g., in 1793 upon the outbreak of war between France and European States. Art. 19 of the Treaty of Paris (1814) stipulated for restitution of all private property thus confiscated by France.

"Since the end of the Napoleonic Wars, the only instance of confiscation which has occurred was supplied by the American Civil War, in which the Congress of the Confederate States, by an Act passed in August, 1861, enacted that 'property of whatever nature, except public stocks and securities, held by an alien enemy since the 21st May, 1861, shall be sequestered and appropriated.' " Hall (8th ed.), 523–24.

"On the other hand, this rule does not prevent a belligerent from suspending the payment of enemy debts till after the war for the purpose of prohibiting the increase of enemy resources; from seizing public enemy property on his territory, such as funds, ammunition, provisions, and other valuables; and from preventing the withdrawal of private enemy property which may be made use of by the enemy for military operations, such as arms and munitions." 2 Oppenheim (1st ed.), § 102.

During the World War Great Britain enacted a series of Trading-with-the-Enemy-Acts and Amendments to or Extensions of these Acts. The Act of Nov. 27, 1914 directed the appointment of a custodian of enemy property for England and Wales and one for Scotland and Ireland. The custodian was charged with the duty of "receiving, holding, preserving and dealing with such property as might be paid to or vested in him in pursuance of the act." In general, he was to hold enemy property in his custody until the end of the war for the benefit of its owners. By the Act of Jan. 27, 1916 the powers of the controller were extended to include those of a liquidator and the Board of Trade was empowered, under certain conditions, to prohibit or wind up a business.

In France sequestrators were appointed with functions similar to those of the English custodians; but, contrary to the British procedure, no enemy business could be closed and its affairs wound up except by an order from a French court.

Though German policy, which might be described as one of mere supervision, was more liberal at first, Germany ultimately resorted to compulsory administration and liquidation as a means of reprisal.

In its war legislation and executive orders the United States followed, though with some differences, the policies of England and France. The Trading-with-the-Enemy Act of Oct. 6, 1917 authorized the President to appoint an "alien property custodian" with power to receive all money and other property in the United States due or belonging to an enemy or ally of an enemy, which might be paid, conveyed, transferred, assigned, or delivered to him, and to hold, administer, and account for the same under the general direction of the President. As compared with the English custodian and French sequestrator, it may be said that his powers were somewhat larger than either. They rather resembled those of the German administrator.

By a clause in the urgent deficiency bill approved March 28, 1918, the

347. **Effects on** (IV) **Enemy Merchantmen found in a Belligerent Port at the Outbreak of Hostilities.**—It is no longer customary to embargo, sequester, capture, or confiscate such vessels. " The uninterrupted practice of belligerent Powers since the outbreak of the Crimean War has been to allow enemy vessels *in their ports at the outbreak of hostilities*, to depart on their return voyage. The same privilege has been accorded enemy merchant vessels which sailed before the outbreak of hostilities, to enter and depart from a belligerent port without molestation on the homeward voyage." [23]

United States custodian was also given a general power to sell any property in his custody. The avowed purpose of this measure was to destroy German financial and economic power or influence in the United States. Considerable enemy property was disposed of under the terms of this Act which is impossible to justify as a military measure—its only valid justification. Unless this property is fully restored to its original private owners, the United States stands accused of having confiscated private enemy property for economic reasons.

The only possible defense would be that it was a justifiable measure of reprisal for Germany's action in unlawfully destroying the lives and property of our citizens by submarine warfare—a very doubtful plea. It was apparently the idea of Congress that at the end of the war American citizens could, if necessary, be indemnified for injuries and losses by payment from funds derived from the sale of German-owned property. The idea was that Germany should then indemnify her own citizens. But it would be highly unjust to hold individual Germans in the United States responsible for acts of the German Government.

On this subject, see especially: * 1 Garner, chs. 4 and 8, and *Recent Developments of Int. Law* (1925), 311–14. See also 2 Hyde, §§ 607, 610, 617, 619, 621–22; and 2 Oppenheim, § 101.

For detailed discussion of *Trading with the Enemy Acts during the World War*, see: Armstrong, *War and Treaty Legislation, 1914–1922* (2d ed., 1922); Hays, *Enemy Property in America* (1923); and Huberich, *Trading with the Enemy* (1918).

For the texts of the British Acts, Amendments, etc., see Armstrong, *op. cit.*, 123 ff. For those of the United States (with commentary and decisions), see Hays and Huberich, *op. cit.* See also *Alien Property Custodian Report* (Wash., 1919).

For certain confiscatory provisions of the Treaty of Versailles, see *supra*, ch. 5, note 29 on p. 138. For analyses of the economic clauses of the Paris Treaties, see Armstrong, *op. cit.*, Pt. IV; and Simonson, *Private Property and Rights in Enemy Countries* (1921).

[23] Report of the American Delegation to the Hague Conference of 1907. See 2 Scott, 219.

At the beginning of the Crimean War, in 1854, six weeks were allowed by Russia, England, and France. Similar concessions were made by Prussia in 1866, France and Prussia in 1870, and by Russia and Turkey in 1870. According to President McKinley's Proclamation of April 26, 1898, Spanish

348. The Rules of the Hague Conference of 1907.—The Hague Conference of 1907 must, therefore, be deemed to have taken several steps backward when it adopted the following Convention relative to the Status of Enemy Merchant Ships at the Outbreak of Hostilities:

" When a merchant-ship belonging to one of the belligerent Powers is found, at the commencement of hostilities, in any enemy port, it is *desirable* [24] that it should be allowed to depart freely, either immediately or after a sufficient term of grace, and, after being furnished with a passport, to proceed direct to its port of destination or some other designated port.

" The same rule shall apply in the case of a ship which, having left its port of departure before the commencement

merchant vessels in American ports were to be allowed until May 21, 1898, inclusive, for loading their cargoes and departing from such ports. They were not to be captured on their return voyage unless their cargoes included contraband of war, Spanish military officers, or any dispatches to or from the Spanish Government. It was further provided that "any Spanish merchant vessel which, prior to April 21, 1898, shall have sailed from any foreign port bound for any port of place in the United States, shall be permitted to enter such port or place, and to discharge her cargo, and afterwards forthwith to depart without molestation." Such a vessel, it was declared, was not to be captured on her return voyage.

For the text of this proclamation, see *House Doc.* of 55th Congress, 3d session (Foreign Relations, Vol. 1898), 772. See the case of the *Buena Ventura* (175 U. S. 388), for the liberal interpretation of this proclamation by our Supreme Court, which held that the enemy's vessels were included within the intention of the President's proclamation, even though their departure from an American port had taken place before the war had begun. Cf. the cases of *The Panama* (175 U. S. 535), and *The Pedro* (175 U. S. 354). See also 7 Moore, *Digest*, § 1196; and Benton, 130 ff., 166 ff.

The Japanese Imperial Decree of Feb. 9, 1904, permitted Russian merchantmen, having no contraband on board, to load and discharge their cargoes and remain in Japanese ports until Feb. 16; and, according to the Czar's Order of Feb. 28, Japanese merchant vessels without contraband might remain in Russian ports for a maximum period of forty-eight hours after the publication of the "present declaration by the local authorities." See Hershey, *op. cit.*, 269, 281, 295–97; Lawrence, *War and Neutrality*, ch. 3; and Takahashi, *op. cit.*, Pt. I, ch. 3.

[24] Russia proposed making the delay obligatory, but this was opposed by Great Britain, France, Japan, and the Argentine Republic. Consequently, the term *desirable* was adopted. This was a decided step backward. The Convention is also reactionary in several other respects, *e.g.* in the provisions making ignorance of the fact of hostilities a condition of immunity.

"The most important change in the old practice as introduced by the Convention was the abolition of the right of confiscation of both ships and their cargoes, and the substitution of detention with an obligation to restore the vessels at the close of the war. . . ." 1 Garner, p. 152.

of the war, has entered an enemy port in ignorance of hostilities " (Art. 1).

" A merchant-ship which, owing to circumstances of *force majeure*, may have been unable to leave the enemy port within the period contemplated in the preceding Article, or which may not have been allowed to leave, can not be confiscated.

" The belligerent may only detain it under an obligation to restore it after the war without indemnity, or he may requisition it on payment of indemnity " (Art. 2).

" Enemy merchant-ships which left their last port of departure before the commencement of the war, and are encountered at sea while ignorant of the outbreak of hostilities, can not be confiscated. They are only liable to detention under an obligation to restore them after the war without indemnity, or to be requisitioned, or even restored, with indemnity and under the obligation of providing for the safety of the persons as well as the preservation of the papers on board.

" After having touched at a port in their own country or at a neutral port, these ships are subject to the laws and customs of maritime warfare " (Art. 3).

" Enemy cargo on board the vessels referred to in Articles 1 and 2 is likewise liable to be detained and restored after the war without indemnity, or to be requisitioned on payment of indemnity, either together with the ship or separately.

" The same rule applies in the case of cargo on board the vessels referred to in Article 3 " (Art. 4).

" The present Convention does not affect merchant-ships whose construction indicates that thay are intended to be converted into warships " (Art. 5).[25]

[25] 6 H. C. (1907), Arts. 1–5. "The provisions of the present Convention are only applicable between the Contracting Powers, and only if all the belligerents are parties to the Convention." Art. 6.

The Convention was signed by all the Powers with the exception of the United States, China, and Nicaragua. Germany and Russia made reservations with respect to Article 3. In July, 1911, it had been ratified by eighteen States. The United States' refusal to sign was based on the ground that the Convention is an unsatisfactory "compromise between those who believed in the existence of a right and those who refuse to recognize the legal validity of the custom which has grown up in recent years. The Convention cannot be called progressive, for it questions a custom which seems generally established,

349. **Effects of War on** (V) **Non-intercourse between Belligerent Subjects.**—There are two contrasted views on this subject. The older authorities and the Anglo-American courts [26] have uniformly held that, unless specially licensed, trading or commercial intercourse between enemy subjects becomes *ipso facto* illegal upon the outbreak of war. This view is also shared by many modern authorities even on the Continent, [27] and has the support of considerable present-day international practice; but it is condemned or regarded as obsolete by an increasing number of authorities, [28] and international practice shows a growing

and its adoption would seem to sanction less liberal and enlightened practice."
1 Scott, *The Hague Peace Conferences*, 568.

On the *Sixth Hague Convention*, see: 3 *Actes et doc. de la deux. conférence*, 825–30, 852–53, 884–86; Bustamante y Sirven, *op. cit.*, ch. 9; Dupuis, *Le droit de le guerre maritime* (1911), Nos. 75–81; 1 Garner, §§ 102–03; * Higgins, 295–307; Lémonon, *op. cit.*, 647–61; * 1 Scott, 556–68, 2 *Ibid.*, 219–21, 415–21, and, in 2 *A. J.* (1908), 259 ff.; 2 Westlake, (1st ed.), 307.

On the practice during the World War, including reviews of numerous cases, see especially: Fenwick, 452–53; * 1 Garner, ch. 6; Hall, *Law of Naval Warfare* (1921), 29 ff.; * Higgins, in *Brit. Yr. Bk.* (1922–23), 55–78; 2 Hyde, § 765; and 2 Oppenheim, § 102a.

[26] The leading British case is that of *The Hoop* (1799), 1 Rob. 196, and Evans, *Cases*, 459 or Scott, *Cases* 622. In this case, one of particular hardship upon British merchants, Sir William Scott stated it as his opinion, based mainly on the authority of Bynkershoek, that "there exists such a general rule of maritime jurisprudence of this country, by which all trading with the public enemy, unless with the permission of the sovereign, is interdicted." He gives evidence to show that it was also the law of France, Spain, and Holland. Cf. *Potts* v. *Bell* (1800), Scott, *Cases*, 626.

The leading American case is that of *The Rapid* (1814), 8 Cranch, 155 and Scott, 621. The rule against trading was enforced against an American citizen who, after the outbreak of hostilities, had merely tried to bring home property which he had bought in England before the War of 1812 and deposited on a small British island "situated near the line between Nova Scotia and the United States." See, generally, the cases in Evans, ch. 13 or Scott, ch. 7.

[27] *E.g.* Bonfils or 2 Fauchille, Nos. 1060–65; Geffcken, note 5 to Heffter, § 123; Mérignhac, *La guerre sur la terre* (1903), Nos. 32–33; and Pillet, No. 40. This is also the view of 4 Calvo, §§ 1926 ff. and 1953 ff.; and of most of the Anglo-American authorities, as, *e.g.*, Hall, § 126; Lawrence (3d ed.), § 165; 3 Phillimore, § 69; Taylor, § 465; 2 Twiss, § 44; Wheaton, §§ 309 ff.; Woolsey, § 123.

[28] Among the authorities who regard the older view as obsolete, or who may at least be said to favor a more liberal and enlightened practice, are: Bluntschli, Art. 674; Bordwell, 202–03, 208–11; * Bentwich, *War and Private Property* (1907), ch. 5; Lawrence (7th ed.), § 143; Lueder, in 4 Holtzendorff, 358 ff.; Manche, *La déclaration de guerre* (1909), ch. 11; 3 F. de Martens, § 109, p. 202; Maurel, *De la déclaration de guerre* (1907), 339–43; 3 Nys, 60 ff.; * Phillipson, *Effect of War on Contracts* (1909), 53 ff.; 2 Piédelièvre, Nos. 841–46; 6

tendency toward the adoption of the more liberal rule that such trading as is not incompatible with military aims is permissible, unless specially prohibited by either of the belligerent governments. The main obstacles to the growth of a more enlightened practice would seem to be the existence of a number of contrary precedents embalmed in case law and the hide-bound conservatism of Anglo-American courts, which manifests itself in this as in every

P.-Fodéré, Nos. 2397–99; 2 Rivier, 231–32; 1 Rolin, Nos. 245 ff.; Ullmann, § 173; and 2 Westlake, (1st ed.), 44–51.

It is especially gratifying that the newer doctrine is gaining adherents in England and America. Bentwich (*op. cit.*, 50) observes: "A large part of the authority about trading with the enemy is really obsolete, but unfortunately, being embodied in case law, it has not been swept away." Lawrence (7th ed., § 143) has changed his former views on this sujbect. Westlake (II, 45) does not hesitate to call attention to the "conservative tendency of courts." And Bordwell (*op. cit.*, 203) says: "It is desirable that the view that war itself does not put an end to commercial intercourse, but that its illegality depends on its interdiction by the political authorities, should find even wider recognition than it has. . . . Where commerce is allowed, the rule that an alien enemy has no standing in court does not apply, and contracts can be made and enforced as in time of peace. Since the beginning of the Crimean War, a very large indulgence in commerce between belligerents has been allowed. Thus, in the Spanish-American War, neutral vessels, laden with American-owned cargoes other than contraband of war, cleared for Spanish ports." Cf. 7 Moore, *Digest*, § 1135, pp. 241–43. A tendency toward a more lenient practice was shown even by our Supreme Court in *Mathews* v. *McStea* (1875), 91 U. S. 7, and Scott (ed. of 1902), 508.

"By German law, a license to trade is presumed, and explicit notice is required to forbid specific kinds of commerce. But contraband trading is, of course, always prohibited, and the participation of a German citizen in the Morgan (English) war loan to France in 1870 was held illegal and invalid. In France and England the older principle prevails that all commerce is interdicted by the mere declaration of war, and that special licenses are required to permit any limitation of the rule." Bentwich, *op. cit.*, 51.

On *License to Trade*, see especially: Baker and McKernan, *op. cit.*, 374–411; Bordwell, 210–11; Bonfils or 2 Fauchille, No. 1062; * 4 Calvo, §§ 1969 ff.; * Hall, § 126; * 2 Halleck, ch. 30; Lawrence, § 214; 7 Moore, *Digest*, § 1141; 2 Oppenheim, § 217; Phillipson, *Effects of War on Contracts* (1909), 65–66; 6 and 7 P.-Fodéré, No. 2700, 2937; Scott, *Cases*, 635–43; Taylor, § 512; * Wheaton, §§ 409–10, and Dana's note, No. 198; Woolsey, § 155.

This subject is one which is really regulated by municipal law. Licenses are *general* when they permit a State's own subjects or all enemy or neutral subjects to trade in particular articles or at particular places; they are *special* when they permit particular individuals to carry on a trade in the manner described by the document itself. General licenses are granted only by the Government itself, special licenses may sometimes be granted by commanders-in-chief. Licenses were granted on a large scale by Napoleon I, but special licenses are now practically obsolete. This makes the jurisprudence bearing on the subject obsolete also. The most general rule is that they are strictly construed. Contracts under a license are valid.

other branch of jurisprudence. In view of the diversity of opinion and practice in this matter, it should be reasonably clear that there is no rule of International Law governing the subject, and that commercial intercourse between so-called enemy subjects is really regulated by municipal law.[29]

350. Trading with the Enemy. Anglo-American Practice. —Though there is no rule of International Law governing this subject, its importance demands a brief summary of Anglo-American practice. In general, the English and American courts hold that, with the exception of that class known as *commercia belli* (ransom bills,[30] bills of exchange drawn by prisoners of war and the like), all contracts concluded during war with enemy subjects are illegal and hence null and void. No action upon such contracts will be entertained, either during or after the war. But contracts made before the war are usually merely suspended as to their execution, and the enemy subject's right of suit revives at the close of the war.[31] Commercial partnerships are dissolved, as are in general all executed and executory contracts existing between enemy subjects which require further acting upon during hostilities, executory contracts which do not require to be further acted upon being merely suspended.[32]

[29] This is the opinion of Oppenheim (II, § 101.) He says (note 2, p. 111 of 1st ed.) Manning is the only British publicist who seems to agree with him. Bentwich (p. 47) and Phillipson (p. 48) appear to share this view, which obviously coincides with the facts of international practice, if not with the decisions and authorities. This view appears to have at least some support on the Continent. See, *e.g.*, 1 Rolin, Nos. 241–46.

[30] "Ransom is the repurchase by the original owner of the property acquired by the seizure of a prize. . . . When a vessel is released upon ransom the commander gives a ransom bill, by which he contracts for himself and the owner of the vessel and cargo that a stipulated sum shall be paid to the captor." Hall, § 151. Cf. 2 Hyde, § 760.

[31] But these rules do not apply to aliens of belligerent nationality who are permitted to reside in the enemy country. "An alien enemy residing in this country may contract and sue like a citizen (2 Kent, *Com.*, 63). When the creditor, although a subject of the enemy, remains in the country of the debtor, or has a known agent there authorized to receive the amount of the debt, throughout the war, payment then to such creditor or his agent can in no respect be construed into a violation of the duties imposed by a state of war upon the debtor." Justice Gray, in *Kershaw* v. *Kelsey* (1868), 100 Mass., 561, and Evans, *Cases*, 463 or Scott, *Cases* 654.

[32] Bentwich, *op. cit.*, 48–49. Bentwich cites *Esposito* v. *Bowden* (24 L. J. Q. B. 10, and 4 E. & B. 763)—a case growing out of the Crimean War—as the

BIBLIOGRAPHY

Declaration of War and its Immediate Effects.—Anis, *Du droit de déclarer la guerre* (1909); * Baker and McKernan, *Laws of Warfare* (1919), 1 ff. (for citations from the authorities); Bellat, *La déclaration*

leading case on this subject. For a note on this important case, which was decided in 1857, see Scott, *Cases*, 602.

The leading case on the dissolution of commercial partnerships is *Griswold v. Waddington* (Court of Errors of N. Y., 1819), 16 Johnson, 438 and Evans, 477 or Scott, 604. The leading case on ordinary contracts is *Ex parte Boussmaker* (Chancery, 1806), 13 Vesey Jr. 17, and Scott, 549. In *Hoare* v. *Allen* (Sup. Ct. of Pa., 1789), 2 Dallas, 102, 602, it was held that interest on a mortgage due a British subject residing in London in 1773 did not run during the Revolutionary War. But this decision is in conflict with *Ex parte Boussmaker* (see above). In *Hanger* v. *Abbott* (1867), 6 Wallace, 532, and Evans, 497 or Scott, 613, our Supreme Court held the Statute of Limitations did not run whilst the right of action is suspended by war.

In *N. Y. Life Ins. Co.* v. *Stathem* (1876), 93 U. S. 24, and Scott, 617, our Supreme Court decided that non-payment of premiums, due to the outbreak of the war, annuls a life insurance policy "in which time is material and of the essence of the contract"; but that the insured is "fairly entitled to have the equitable value of his policy," *i.e.* the amount of the premiums actually paid, minus the value of the insurance enjoyed.

In *Kershaw* v. *Kelsey* (see above) Justice Bray thus summarized the law governing intercourse between enemy subjects as judicially declared in Great Britain and the United States:

It "prohibits all intercourse between citizens of the two belligerents which is inconsistent with the state of war between their countries; and this includes . . . any act or contract which tends to increase his resources; and every kind of trading or commercial dealing or intercourse, whether by transmission of money or goods, or by orders for the delivery of either, between the two countries, directly or indirectly, or through intervention of third persons or partnerships, or by contracts in any form looking to or involving such transmission or by insurances upon trade or with the enemy. Beyond the principles of these cases the prohibition has not been carried by judicial decision. . . .

"At this age of the world," he continued, "when all the tendencies of the law of nations are to exempt individuals and private contracts from injury or restraint in consequence of war between their governments, we are not disposed to declare such contracts unlawful as have not been heretofore adjudged to be inconsistent with a state of war."

Consequently, the Supreme Court of Massachusetts unanimously decided that the plaintiff, the owner of a sugar plantation in Mississippi, might recover unpaid rent, etc., on land which he had leased to the defendant, a citizen of Massachusetts, during the Civil War. "It is perhaps not too much to say that this is the leading American case on this subject. It has been repeatedly cited and followed." Scott, 538 n. (ed. of 1902).

On the *Effect of War on Contracts, Corporations*, etc., see especially: Baker and McKernan, *Laws of Warfare* (1919), 68–122, 270–373, 831 ff. (for citations); Baty, *Int. Law in So. Africa* (1900), ch. 6, in 31 *Law Quar. Rev.* (1915), 30–49, and in *J. C. L.* (Aug., 1908); Baty and Morgan, *War: Its Conduct and Legal Results* (1915), particularly Pt. IV, chs. 1–5; * Bentwich, *War and Private Property* (1907), ch. 5, and in 9 *A. J.* (1915), 352 ff. and 642 ff.; Borchard,

de guerre (1909); Bluntschli, Arts. 521–56; Bonfils or * 2 Fauchille, Nos. 1027–65; Bordwell, Pt. II, ch. 1; 4 Calvo, §§ 1899–2003; Despagnet, Nos. 517–23; Dupuis, in 13 *R. D. I. P.* (1906), 725 ff.; Evans, *Cases*, 378–89; Fenwick, ch. 27; Féraud-Giraud, in 17 *R. D. I.* (1885), 19 ff.; Funck-Brentano et Sorel, *Précis*, liv. II, ch. 2; Garner, *Recent Developments in Int. Law* (1925), 308–24; Hall, Pt. III, ch. 1; 1 Hallack, ch. 17; Heffter (Geffcken), §§ 120–23; * 2 Hyde, §§ 602 ff.; * Lawrence, §§ 140, 143–46, 171–74; Longuet, *Le droit actuel de la guerre terrestre* (1901), §§ 1–15; 2 J. de Louter, § 43; Luedei, in 4 Holtzendorff, 332–62; Manche, *La déclaration de la guerre*, etc. (1909); 3 F. de Martens, §§ 108–09; Maurel, *De la déclaration de la guerre* (1907); * Maurice, *Hostilities without Declaration* (1883), and in *Nineteenth Century*, April, 1904; McNair, *Legal Effects of War* (1920); * Mérignhac, *De la guerre sur terre* (1903), 29–65; 7 Moore, *Digest*, §§ 1106–08; 3 Nys, chs. 2–3, and in 37 *R. D. I.* (1905), 517 ff.; * 2 Oppenheim, §§ 93–102; Owen, *Declaration of War* (1889); 3 Phillimore, Pt. IX, chs. 5–8; * Pillet, *Les lois actuelles de la guerre* (1901), ch. 3; 2 Piédelièvre, Nos. 806–49; 6 P.-Fodéré, Nos. 2671–2720; * 2 Rivier, 220–37; * 1 Rolin, liv. II, ch. 3; * Scott, *Cases*, Pt. III, ch. 2; Snow, *Cases*, 250–314; Taylor, §§ 455–68; Ullmann, §§ 171–73; Vattel, liv. III, §§ 51–65; Walker, *Manual*, §§ 37–50; * 2 Westlake (1st ed.), 18–51; Wheaton, Pt. IV, ch. 1, and Dana's notes, Nos. 156–58; Wilson, chs. 10–11; Woolsey, §§ 120–24.

For additional Bibliographies and references, see Fauchille and Oppenheim.

§ 46; Campbell, *Law of War and Contract* (1918); Chadwick, in 20 *Law Quar. Rev.* (1904), 167 ff.; 2 Cobbett, 82–125; * Evans, *Cases*, 477–97; * 1 Garner, §§ 146–74; Hall, in 18 *Col. Law Rev.*, 325 ff.; 2 Hyde, §§ 608–63; Latifi, *Effects of War on Property* (1909), particularly pp. 50 ff.; McNair, *Legal Effects of War* (1920); Page, *War and Alien Enemies* (1915), chs. 6–7; * Phillipson, *Effect of War on Contracts* (1909); Picciotto, in 27 *Yale Law Jour.* (1917–18), 167–78; * Schuster, in 2 *Grot. Soc.* (1917), 57 ff., and in *Brit. Yr. Bk.* (1920–21), 167–89; Scott, Leslie, *The Effect of War on Contracts* (1914); Scott, *Cases*, 585–621; Trotter, *Law of Contract During War* (1914); Westlake, in *J. C. L.* (April, 1909).

CHAPTER XXVII

THE LAWS OF LAND WARFARE

351. The Chief Means and Aims of Land Warfare.—
Land warfare has two main aims—the reduction or defeat of the enemy's armed land forces, and the temporary occupation and administration of the whole or a portion of the enemy's territory. The chief means by which it is sought to accomplish these ends are the application of armed force and the enforcement of military or martial law. The law of military occupation will be dealt with in the following chapter.

I. LAWFUL BELLIGERENTS

352. Who are Lawful Belligerents?—The Hague Regulations respecting the Law and Customs of War on Land lay down these definite rules relating to lawful belligerents:

" The laws, rights and duties of war apply not only to the army, but also to militia and volunteer corps fulfilling the following conditions: (1) To be commanded by a person responsible for his subordinates; (2) To have a distinctive emblem fixed and recognizable at a distance. (3) To carry arms openly; and (4) To conduct their operations in accordance with the laws and customs of war. In countries where militia or volunteer corps constitute the army, or form part of it, they are included under the denomination ' army ' " (Art. 1).[1]

[1] H. R. (1899 and 1907), Art. 1. Cf. B. D. (Brussels Declaration of 1874), Art. 9, of which H. R., 1 is almost an exact verbal reproduction. For the text of B. D., see Higgins, *The Hague Peace Conferences* (1909), 273 ff.; or Scott, *Texts of the Peace Conferences at the Hague* (1908), 382 ff.

These conditions were not observed by the Prussians during the Franco-German War of 1870–1871. They required that "every prisoner, in order to be treated as a prisoner of war, shall prove that he is a French soldier by showing that he has been called out and borne in the lists of a military organized corps, by an order emanating from the legal authority and addressed to him personally"—an impossible requirement. They also required an emblem or distinctive mark, clearly distinguishable at rifle distance—an absurd condition in these days of long-distance firing. See especially: Bordwell, 90 ff.; Hall, § 179; Lawrence, § 196; * Spaight, 41–46; and 2 Westlake (1st ed.), 61.

353. **Levies *en masse*.**—" The population of a territory which has not been occupied who, on the approach of the enemy, spontaneously take up arms to resist the invading troops without having had time to organize themselves in accordance with Article 1, shall be regarded as belligerents *if they carry arms openly* and if they respect the laws and customs of war " (Art. 2).[2]

It should be noted that H. R., 1 leaves several important questions, such as the use of guerrilla troops and savages in land warfare, to be dealt with by "the principles of the Law of Nations, as they result from the usages established between civilized nations, from the laws of humanity, and the requirements of the public conscience."   4 H. C., Preamble.   See Higgins, 211.

The Hague Regulations appear in the form of an annex to 4 H. C. (the Fourth Hague Convention of 1899 and 1907), by which the Contracting Parties agreed to issue to their armed land forces instructions which shall be in conformity with these Regulations.   The provisions contained in them are declared to be "only binding between Contracting Powers, and only if all the belligerents are parties to the Convention: "*A belligerent party which violates the provisions of the said Regulations shall, if the case demands, be liable to make compensation.   It shall be responsible for all acts committed by persons forming part of its armed forces.*"   4 H. C. (1907), Arts. 1–3.

Whether guerrilla, irregular, or detached bodies of men are entitled to the privileges of legitimate combatants, would seem to depend upon whether they fulfill the four conditions laid down in 1 H. R., 1.   On *Guerrilla Warfare*, see especially the somewhat lengthy citation from Leiber's *Miscellaneous Writings* (II, 277 ff.), in 1 *A. J.* (1907), 15–18.

The use of so-called savage or semi-barbarous troops in modern warfare would appear to be subject to the same conditions.   During the Russo-Japanese War, Admiral Alexieff issued an order offering special inducements to convicts from the island of Sakhalin to enlist in the Russian army.   Though this cannot be regarded as a positive violation of the Law of Nations, "there is something peculiarly revolting to modern conceptions of humanity in the employment of criminals for purposes of warfare."   Hershey, *Russo-Japanese War* (1906), 309–11.   Cf. Ariga, § 25.

[2] H. R., 2.   The italicized phrase was added in 1907.   Cf. B. D., Art. 10.

This article recognizes the legality of levies *en masse* provided they fulfill the two conditions laid down.   It represents a compromise between the opposing view of the larger and smaller States both at Brussels and at The Hague. The delegates from the weaker Powers desired a general recognition of levies *en masse* in occupied as well as in unoccupied territory, without reference to the requirements of Article 1.   But those from the more powerful States, particularly the German delegation, urged that the conditions laid down in Article 1 be applied to such risings.   It was finally agreed that levies *en masse* in occupied territory should be left to the customary Law of Nations.   As the matter stands, the status of so-called "war rebels" is uncertain.   See especially Bordwell, 232 ff.; and Hall, § 179.

"War rebels are persons within an occupied territory who rise in arms against the occupying or conquering army, or against the authorities established by the same.   If captured, they may suffer death, whether they rise singly, in small or large bands, and whether called upon to do so by their own, but expelled, Government or not. . . ."   1 *A. I.* (Lieber's *Instructions* of 1864

354. Division into Combatants and Non-combatants.—

" The armed forces of the belligerents may consist of combatants and non-combatants. In case of capture by the enemy, both have a right to be treated as prisoners of war " (Art. 3).[3]

2. PRISONERS OF WAR

355–368. Treatment of Prisoners of War.—" According

to the Hague Regulations, prisoners of war are in the power of the hostile Government, but not in that of the individuals or corps who captured them. They must be humanely treated. " All their personal belongings, except arms, horses, and military papers, remain their property " (Art. 4).[4]

for the Armies of the United States), Art. 85. For the text of these important "Instructions," see Scott, *Text*, etc., 350 ff.

This article is too harsh for present-day practice. Unauthorized individuals may be doubtless thus dealt with, and rigorous measures may be taken to prevent uprisings. But organized war insurgents on occupied territory are certainly entitled to treatment as lawful combatants if they fulfill the conditions laid down in H. R., 1.

On *Lawful Belligerents and Non-Combatants*, see: * Baker and Crocker, *Laws of Land Warfare* (1919), 9–37; Bluntschli, Arts. 569–72; * Bordwell, Pt. II, ch. 3, pp. 228–34; 4 Calvo, §§ 2044–65; Carpentier, *Les lois de la guerre continentale* (1902), 9–19; Despagnet, Nos. 524–27; Edmonds and Oppenheim, *Land Warfare* (1912), ch. 3, Nos. 17–38; * 2 Fauchille, Nos. 1067–77; Fenwick, ch. 28, pp. 460–63; 3 Fiore, Nos. 1303–16, and *Int. Law Cod.*, Nos. 1459–80; 1 Guelle *Précis des lois de la guerre sur terre* (1884), 69–90; * Hall, §§ 177–79; 1 Halleck (3d ed.), 555–62; Heffter, § 124; * Holland *War on Land*, 20–21, and *Studies*, 73 ff.; Holls, *Peace Conference at the Hague* (1900), 141–45; * 2 Hyde, §§ 649–54; *Kriegsbrauch im Land Kriege* (1902), 4–8; Lawrence, §§ 195–98; Longuet, *Le droit actuel*, etc. (1901), §§ 26–40; 2 J. de Louter, § 44; Lueder, in 4 Holtzendorff, 371–88; 3 F. de Martens, § 112; Mérignhac, *Les lois de la guerre sur terre* (1903), 67–87; 7 Moore, *Digest*, § 1109; 3 Nys 85–109; 2 * Oppenheim, §§ 60, 78–82; Pillet, ch. 2 and pp. 457–59; 6 P.-Fodéré, Nos. 2721–32; 2 Rivier, 242–53; * 1 Rolin, Nos. 281–94; * Spaight, ch. 3; Taylor, §§ 471–76; Ullmann, § 175; U. S. Army, *Rules of Land Warfare* (1914), ch. 3, Nos. 30–42; Vattel, liv. III, §§ 223–31; 2 Westlake (1st ed.), 60–63; Wheaton, § 356; Wilson, § 110; Zorn, *Das Kriegsrecht zur Lande* (1906), 36–72.

[3] For the two different senses in which the word "non-combatant" is used in war law, see Spaight, 58. For the views of authorities, see Baker and Crocker, *Laws of Land Warfare* (1919), 34–37.

[4] H. R., 4. Cf. B. D., 23. "Prisoners may of course be deprived for a time of the use of their property, for sufficient reasons; and it may be a question whether large sums of money found upon prisoners, or in their baggage, are in fact their private property." Holland, *The Laws of War on Land* (1908), No. 24. The *American Instructions* permitted the appropriation of *large* sums of money by the commander for the use of the army. *A. I.*, Art. 72. In the light of H. R., 4, even large sums (provided it be really private property) could only be sequestered.

Prisoners of war may be interned in any specified place or locality, and are " bound not to go beyond certain fixed limits," but they can only be confined as an " indispensable measure of safety." [5]

" The State may utilize the labor of prisoners of war, other than officers according to their rank and aptitude. There tasks shall not be excessive, and shall have nothing to do with the operations of war." They may be authorized to work for the public service, for private persons, or on their own account.[6]

" The Government into whose hands prisoners of war have fallen is bound to maintain them." Failing a special agreement between the belligerents, they " shall be treated as regards food, quarters, and clothing, on the same footing as the troops of the Government which has captured them." [7]

Military writers have sometimes asserted that a commander may kill his prisoners under circumstances of extreme danger or necessity, and Napoleon's destruction of 4000 prisoners at Jaffa is cited as an example of such necessity. But even in this case humanity would have been the better policy, as the sequel showed. "The massacre inspired the garrison of Acre with such desperate courage that the French failed in all their assaults on the place, and were obliged to abandon their dream of eastern conquest and retreat across the desert to Egypt." Lawrence (3d ed.), p. 337. Under modern conditions of warfare, it is difficult to imagine a case where the destruction of prisoners would be necessary for the sake of self-preservation.

[5] "The distinction here is between restriction to a specified locality and close confinement." Holland, *War on Land*, No. 25.

[6] "Work done for the State shall be paid for according to the tariffs in force for soldiers of the national army employed in similar tasks; or, if there are no such tariffs in force, at rates proportional to the work executed." H. R., 6. Cf. B. D., Arts. 25–26.

Art. 25 of the Brussels Declaration of 1874 provided that "prisoners of war may be employed on certain public works which have no immediate connection with the operations in the theater of war, provided," etc. But this provision was dropped at The Hague. This would seem to indicate that prisoners are not to be employed on fortifications even at a distance from military operations. This is the opinion of Westlake (1st ed.), II, 64. For the contrary view, see Bordwell, 240; and Holland, No. 26. Spaight (p. 282) observes that the "best modern opinion is adverse to permitting any military work whatever being exacted from prisoners." This is the safer rule.

Art. 6 H. R. also says: "The earnings of prisoners shall go to improving their position, and the balance shall be paid them at the time of their release, after deducting the cost of their maintenance."

[7] H. R., 7. Cf. B. D., 27. "The second paragraph here must, of course, be read subject to military necessities." Holland, No. 27. Bordwell (p. 241) calls attention to the special importance of the principle of the duty of maintenance as applied to reconcentration camps.

Prisoners are " subject to the laws, regulations and orders in force in the army of the State into whose hands they have fallen," and may be punished for acts of insubordination. " Escaped prisoners, recaptured before they have succeeded in rejoining their army, or before quitting the territory occupied by the army that captured them, are liable to disciplinary punishment "; but if they have succeeded in escaping and are again taken prisoners, they " are not liable to any punishment for the previous flight." [8]

The evidence seems to be overwhelming that during the World War Germany violated this and many other of the Hague Regulations regarding prisoners of war. The conditions in some of the camps, as, *e.g.*, in the civilian camp at Ruhleben and the military camps at Minden and Wittenberg, were deplorable; and, in general, the German authorities shifted the burden of maintaining the prisoners properly from their own shoulders to those of their friends and relatives. "The evidence is fairly abundant that in not a few cases prisoners were employed at work forbidden by the Hague convention, if the convention be interpreted to exclude forced labor which indirectly serves the military operations of the enemy, such as hauling coal, transportation of munitions, construction of military railroads, and the like." 2 Garner, 44. After considering some of the evidence, one must also agree with Garner (p. 35) that it is "hard to avoid the conclusion that the German Government fell far short of performing the human obligation which the laws of war impose upon belligerents in respect to the feeding of prisoners [and he might have added, furnishing them with adequate clothing]. It showed an indifference to the welfare of the prisoners which was inexcusable and indefensible."

It should be said by way of extenuation that the decentralization of the German Government due to war conditions was to a large extent responsible for such evil conditions as existed and that many of the camps were well-administered. The main source of the trouble seems to have been the great authority exercised by the Army Corps Commanders in charge who sometimes felt themselves more powerful than the Central Government. The mixing-up of the prisoners of different nationalities in one camp was another potent cause of trouble. Another criticism is the excessive military spirit in which the camps were administered.

On the *Treatment of Prisoners by Germany*, see especially: Dennett, *Prisoners of the Great War* (1919); 2 Fauchille, Nos. 1120–40, *passim*; * 2 Garner, *Int. Law and the World War*, chs. 21–22; Gerard, *Four Years in Germany* (1917) ch. 10; McCarthy, *The Prisoners of War in Germany* (1917); 1 Mérignhac, *Le droit de gens et la guerre de 1914–1918*, 250; *Régime des prisonniers de guerre* (Paris, 1916).

[8] H. R., Art. 8. Cf. B. D., 28. "H. R. 8 omits from B. D. 28 the express permission to use arms against a prisoner attempting to escape, after summoning him, but to fire on him certainly would be allowable. The disciplinary punishment mentioned in not understood to include death, but plots, rebellion, or riot would bring a prisoner under the former part of the article, and the penalty of death might be incurred for them." 2 Westlake (1st ed.), 64. Cf. Holland, No. 28; Bordwell, 241–42; Holls, *op. cit.*, 146–47; and Spaight, 286–89. For views of other publicists, see Baker and Crocker, *op. cit.*, 60–68.

Prisoners may be paroled if " the laws of their country authorize it, and, in such a case, they are bound, on their personal honor, scrupulously to fulfill, both as regards their own Government and the Government by which they were made prisoners, the engagements they have contracted." If paroled, " their own Government is bound not to require of nor accept from them any service incompatible with the parole given." [9]

Army followers, such as newspaper correspondents and reporters, sutlers and contractors, who fall into the enemy's hands, and whom the latter thinks fit to detain, have a right to be treated as prisoners of war, provided they can produce a certificate from the military authorities of the army they were accompanying." [10]

"Every prisoner of war, if questioned, is bound to declare his true name and rank, and if he disregards this rule, he is liable to a curtailment of the advantages accorded to prisoners of war of his class" (H. R., 9).

[9] H. R., 10. Cf. B. D., 31.   The terms of the parole are a matter of contract between the parties.   "The usual terms are that the prisoner, unless exchanged will not serve during the existing war against the captor or his allies engaged in the same war; and this is understood to refer only to active service in the field, and not to debar the paroled prisoner from performing military or administrative duties of any kind at places not within the seat of actual hostilities."   Westlake, (1st ed.), 65.   Cf. *A. I. (American Instructions)*, Art. 130, cited by Bordwell, 243.

It should be noted that a Government is only bound by the parole of its soldiers.   If the law forbids it, there is certainly no obligation.   If the law is silent and the Government disapprove, the paroled prisoner should be given an opportunity to return to captivity.   "In either case, however, the parole is personal and subjects the person who has broken it to punishment by the other side on recapture."   Bordwell, cited above.

In the American and British armies it has been customary to allow paroles to be given only through a commissioned officer except in cases of extreme hardship.   No such distinction seems to be made in France.   For the views of leading authorities on parole, see Baker and Crocker, *op. cit.*, 71–82.   For interesting details, see Spaight, 290–300.   The practice of parole as of exchange does not appear to have been resorted to much during the World War.

"A prisoner of war cannot be forced to accept his liberty on parole; similarly the hostile Government is not obliged to assent to the prisoner's request to be set at liberty on parole.   Any prisoner of war who is liberated on parole and recaptured bearing arms against the Government to which he had pledged his honor, or against the allies of that Government, forfeits his right to be treated as a prisoner of war, and can be brought before the Courts, "*i.e.*, the military courts.   (H. R., Arts. 11–12).

[10] H. R., 13.   Cf. B. D., 34.   As a rule such persons are not detained, but detention is often practiced for military reasons.

On the *Status and Treatment of War Correspondents*, see Hershey, *Russo-Japanese War*, 119–21 and notes for references and citations; and Takahashi,

The Hague Regulations (Art. 14) provide for the institution on the commencement of hostilities in each of the belligerent countries [11] of a Bureau of Information relative to prisoners of war.[12] The Bureau was to enjoy freedom of postage.[13]

Pt. III, ch. 5. See also Benton (for Spanish-American War), 153–55; * Higgins, in *War and the Private Citizen* (1912), ch. 3; * *International Law Situations* (1904); and 1 Rey, 350 ff. For further references, see Higgins, 92.

High civil functionaries are also liable to capture and treatment as prisoners, whether they belong to the army or not. There appears to be a difference of opinion respecting persons temporarily employed, such as guides, teamsters, messengers, etc. Such temporary employees are usually considered liable to capture, but Pillet (p. 194) thinks it would be unjustifiable to hold them as prisoners.

[11] "And, should the case happen, in the neutral countries in whose territory neutrals have been received."

[12] "This Bureau, being charged with answering all inquiries about prisoners or war, is furnished by the various services concerned with all the information respecting internments and transfers, releases on parole, exchanges, escapes, admissions into hospital, deaths, as well as all other information necessary to enable it to make out and keep up-to-date an individual return for each prisoner of war. The Bureau must state in this return the regimental number, surname and name, age, place of origin, rank, the corps, wounds, date and place of capture, of internment, the wounds and the death, as well as any observations of special character. The individual return shall be sent to the Government of the other belligerent after the conclusion of peace.

"It is also the duty of the Bureau of Information to gather and keep together all objects of personal use, valuables, letters, etc., found on the battlefield or left by prisoners who have been released on parole, or exchanged, or who have escaped, or died in hospitals or ambulances, and to forward them to those interested." H. R., 14.

Soon after the outbreak of the World War, the leading belligerents set up War Information Bureaus, in accordance with H. R. 14. There was some complaint of the failure of the German Government to answer the inquiries addressed to it directly by private persons. The German Government took the position that its Bureau was not obliged to answer any but official inquiries. It added that the task of replying to private inquiries had been assumed by the Red Cross Society, as in Russia and Japan. See 2 Garner, § 332. For a description of the organization and work of the British Bureau, see Roxburgh, *The Prisoners of War Information Bureau in London* (1915).

"Relief societies for prisoners of war, regularly constituted in accordance with the law of their country for the purpose of serving as intermediaries for charity, shall receive from the belligerents, for themselves and their duly accredited agents, every facility, within the bounds set by military necessities and administrative regulations, for the effective accomplishment of their humane task. Delegates of these Societies may be admitted to distribute relief at places of internment, as also at the halting places of repatriated prisoners, if furnished with a personal permit by the military authorities, and on giving an engagement in writing to comply with all regulations for order and police which the latter may prescribe" H. R., 15.

[13] "Letters, money orders, and valuables, as well as postal parcels destined

The Regulations also provide that " officers taken prisoners shall receive the same pay as officers of corresponding rank in the country where they are detained," [14] and prisoners are to enjoy freedom of religious worship, " including attendance at their own church service." [15] After the conclusion of peace, " the repatriation of prisoners of war shall take place with the least possible delay." [16]

for the prisoners of war or dispatched by them, shall be free of all postal rates, alike in the countries of origin and destination and in those they pass through. Gifts and relief in kind for prisoners of war shall be admitted free of all duties, as well as of payments for carriage by the Government railways" H. R., 16.

On Art. 16, Holland (No. 36) makes the following comments: "To give full effect to this article, new postal conventions would be necessary, as also, probably, fresh legislation. Letters, written to or received for, prisoners are liable to such censorship as may be ordered. The provision in the second paragraph would apply only to articles for personal use."

The adoption of the plan of a Bureau of Information, etc., for prisoners of war appears to have been largely due to the untiring efforts of M. Romberg, head of the Brussels committee for the care of prisoners during the Franco-German War. It was rejected at the Brussels Conference of 1874, but accepted at the Hague in 1899 with comparatively little discussion. Bordwell, 245–46. See also Holls, *op. cit.*, 150.

The plan was first put to an actual trial during the Russo-Japanese War, though voluntary or unofficial Bureaus of Information for the sick and wounded had been established in some previous wars. It appears to have been operated very successfully, especially by the Japanese, who however, made some complaint of delay and neglect on the part of the Russian Bureau. Hershey, *op. cit.*, 278 n., 284, 289–91, 319–23. Cf. Ariga, 97–100; 1 Rey, 427 ff.; and Takahashi 114–23.

[14] H. R., 17. This amount is to be repaid by their government unless, of course, the liability is undertaken, in the Treaty of Peace, by the other belligerent." Holland, No. 37.

[15] H. R., 18. "This article cannot, of course, be fully put into execution unless a chaplain of the prisoner's own persuasion happens to be present." Holland, No. 38.

"The wills of prisoners are received or drawn up on the same conditions as for soldiers of the national army" and the same rules "shall be observed regarding death certificates, as well as for the burial of prisoners of war, due regard being paid to their grade and rank." H. R., 19.

[16] H. R., 20. Holland (No. 40) justifies delay for the following reasons: (1) insufficiency of transport; (2) obvious risk; (3) punishment of offenses committed during imprisonment. The first reason is unquestionably a good one; the second is vague and extremely doubtful; and the third requires some explanation.

Prisoners may undoubtedly be detained after the conclusion of peace to serve out a sentence or imprisonment imposed for common law crimes and until they have paid any debts incurred during captivity, but it is a moot point whether they may be detained as a punishment for mere disciplinary offenses. I agree with Westlake (II, 67) that this would be a violation of sound principle.

3. THE SICK AND WOUNDED

369-374. Treatment of the Sick and Wounded of the Enemy.—" The obligations of belligerents with regard to

It appears that Japan released Russian prisoners who were serving disciplinary imprisonment.   2 Oppenheim, § 275.

Exchange of prisoners (which is not dealt with by the Hague Regulations) is regulated by cartels or agreements between the belligerents.   The general rule is "man for man, rank for rank, wounded for wounded."

Among savages, prisoners are often tortured and killed, sometimes sacrificed or eaten.   During Antiquity and the Middle Ages, they were usually sold into slavery or ransomed.   See *supra*, Nos. 29, 47.

The present practice is detention or internment, occasional exchange, and release on parole, rather than confinement or imprisonment.   Exchange has been rather exceptional during recent wars.   See Spaight, 301–04.

A very high standard—apparently the highest yet achieved—was set by the Japanese in their treatment of Russian prisoners during the Russo-Japanese War.   The Japanese methods of treatment of prisoners of war deserve special study and imitation.   See Akiyama, in 38 and 39 *R. D. I.* (1906 and 1907), 567 ff. and 211 ff. respectively;   Ariga, ch. 4;   Hershey, 284–91, 319–24; Nagaoka, in 36 *R. D. I* (1904), 497 ff.;   * 1 Rey, ch. 5;   Takahashi, Pt. II, ch. 2. On the Treatment of Prisoners by Germany, see above, note 7.

On *Treatment of Prisoners* generally, see: Ariga, *La guerre sino-japonaise* (1896);   ch. 4;   * Baker and Crocker, *Laws of Land Warfare* (1919), 38–108; Beinhauer, *Die Kriegsgefangenschaft* (1908);   Boiden, *Law of War*, etc. (1908), 89–100;   Bonfils or * 2 Fauchille, Nos. 1119–40;   * Bordwell, Pt. II, ch. 4; Bower, in 1 *Grot. Soc.* (1916), 23 ff.;   4 Calvo, §§ 2133–57;   Carpentier, *Les lois de la guerre continentale* (1904), 25–43;   Cros, *Condition et traitement des prisonniers de guerre* (1900);   Davis, in 7 *A. J.* (1913), 521–41;   Despagnet, Nos. 545–50;   Edmonds and Oppenheim, *Land Warfare*, ch. 5, Nos. 54–116;   Fenwick 470–72;   3 Fiore, Nos. 1355–62, and *Int. Law. Cod.*, Nos. 1569–90;   * Fooks, *Prisoners of War* (1924), particularly chs. 9–13;   * 2 Garner, chs. 21–22; 1 Guelle, *Précis*, etc., (1884) 187–215;   * Hall, §§ 131–35;   2 Halleck (3d ed.), 19–30, 326–29;   Heffter (Geffcken), §§ 127–29;   Higgins, 220–33;   Holland, *War on Land*, 21–27;   Holls, *The Peace Conference at the Hague* (1900), 145–51; * 2 Hyde, §§ 668–76;   *Kriegsbrauch*, (1902), 11–18;   Lawrence, § 164;   Longuet, *Le droit actuel de la guerre terrestre* (1901), §§ 77–83;   Lueder, in 4 Holtzendorff, 423–47;   3 F. de Martens, § 113;   McCarthy, *The Prisoner of War in Germany* (1917), particularly ch. 14;   Mérignhac, *Les lois de la guerre sur terre* (1903), and in 1 *La guerre de 1914–1918*, 250 ff.;   7 Moore, *Digest*, §§ 1127–31;   3 Nys ch. 15;   * 2 Oppenheim, §§ 125–32;   * Payrat, *Le prisonnier de guerre* (1910); Phillimore, in 5 *Grot. Soc.* (1920), 42–64;   * Pillet, *Les lois actuelles*, etc. (1901), ch. 6 and pp. 459–66;   7 P.-Fodéré, Nos. 2796–2842;   * 1 Rey, *La guerre japonaise*, etc. (1907), ch. 5 and annexes;   2 Rivier, 273–79;   * Romberg, *Des belligerents et des prisonniers de guerre* (1894);   * Spaight, ch. 10;   Taylor, §§ 519–24;   2 Twiss, § 177;   Triepel, *Die neusten Fortschritte*, etc. (1894), 41–55; Ullmann, § 177;   Vassaux, *Prisonniers de guerre*, etc. (1892);   Vattel, liv. III, §§ 148–54;   U. S. Army, *Rules of Land Warfare* (1914), ch. 4;   * 2 Westlake (1st ed.), 63–68, 288;   Wheaton, § 344;   Wilson, §§ 148–50;   Zorn, *Das Kriegsrecht zu Lande* (1906), 73–122.

The following constitute the main documentary material bearing on this interesting subject: *Am. Instructions*, Arts. 49–50, 56, 72–82, 105–10, 113,

the sick and wounded are governed by the Geneva Convention " (H. R., 21).[17]

" The soldiery and other persons officially attached to armies, who are sick and wounded, shall be respected and cared for by the belligerent in whose power they are, without distinction of nationality " (G. C., Art. 1).

" Subject to the treatment provided for them in pursuance of the preceding article, the sick and wounded of an army who fall into the hands of the other belligerent are prisoners of war, and the general rules of International Law concerning prisoners are applicable to them " (Art. 2).[18]

" After each engagement the belligerent in possession of the field of battle shall take measures to search for the wounded, and to insure the protection both of the wounded and the dead against pillage and ill treatment. He shall see to it that a careful examination of the bodies is made before the dead are buried or cremated " (Art. 3).[19]

in Scott, *Texts*, etc., 350 ff.; *Brussels Declaration*, Arts. 23–34, in Scott, 382 ff. or Higgins, 273 ff.; The *Oxford Code* or *Manual of the Institute of Int. Law*, Arts. 20–21, 61–88, in Scott, 389 ff.; and the *Hague Regulations*, Arts. 4–20. See also the appendices to Wilson and Tucker, *Int. Law*.

[17] *I.e.*, the Geneva Convention of 1906. This Convention replaced the Geneva Convention of 1864 for the ratifying States. It may be said to constitute the present law on the subject.

"Nevertheless, a belligerent who is compelled to abandon sick or wounded to the enemy shall, as far as military exigencies permit, leave with them a portion of his sanitary personnel and material to aid in caring for them." G. C. (1906), Art. 1. Cf. G. C. (1864), Art. 6. For English texts of the Geneva Conventions of 1864 and 1906 (the latter having practically supplanted the former), see Higgins, 8 ff., 20 ff.; or Scott, *Texts of the Peace Conferences at the Hague* (1908), 376 ff. and 402 ff.

[18] G. C., 2. See *supra*, Nos. 355–68. A portion of Art. 2, not being obligatory, is here omitted.

The Geneva Convention of 1906 appears to have been signed and ratified by about half of the members of the international community, including all the Great Powers excepting France. The Conference was originally attended by delegates from thirty-five Powers. The Convention of 1864 remains binding for those Powers which have not ratified or adhered to that of 1906, provided they are signatories of the former.

[19] G. C., 3. Cf. H. C. (1907), Art. 16, *infra*, No. 422. For the Japanese "Regulations Relative to the Clearing of the Battle-field," see Hershey, *Russo-Japanese War* (1906), 291 ff.

" Each belligerent shall, as soon as possible, send to the authorities of their country or army the military marks or tokens of identity found on the dead, and a list of the names of the sick or wounded collected by him.

" The belligerents shall keep each other mutually informed of any internments and transfers, as also of admissions into hospitals and deaths among

" Movable sanitary formations (that is to say, those which are intended to accompany armies in the field) and the fixed establishments belonging to the sanitary service shall be respected and protected by the belligerents " (Art. 6).[20]

" The personnel engaged exclusively in the collection, transportation, and treatment of the sick and wounded, as also in the administration of the sanitary formations and establishments, and the chaplains attached to armies, shall be respected and protected under all circumstances. If

the sick and wounded in their hands. They shall collect all the articles of personal use, valuables, letters, etc., found on the field of battle or left by the sick or wounded who have died in the sanitary establishments or formations, in order that such articles may be transmitted to the persons interested by the authorities of their country " (Art. 4).

Art. 5 is omitted.

[20] G. C., 6. Cf. G. C. (1864), 1; and 10 H. C. (1907), 1. The Geneva Convention of 1864 made use of the terms "ambulances" and "military hospitals." For these terms, the present Geneva Convention of 1906 substitutes the expressions "sanitary formations" and "establishments."

"Throughout the treaty the term 'sanitary formation' is applied to all establishments, whether fixed or movable, which are provided by public appropriation or private charity for the treatment of the sick or wounded in time of war. To each of the movable sanitary formations a surgical and administrative personnel is attached; tents, bedding, ambulances and other means of transportation are provided, together with a sufficient equipment of surgical instruments and medical and hospital supplies." Davis, in 1. A. J. (1907), 411–12.

Holland (No. 47) prefers the term "mobile medical units" to "movable sanitary formations." They include "all organizations which follow the troops on the field of battle (described in the British army as 'bearer companies' or 'field hospitals'); while 'fixed establishments' . . . would cover 'stationary' or 'general' hospitals (whether actually movable or not), placed on a line of communications, or at a base. Units of both kinds are to be 'respected,' i.e. not to be fired upon; and 'protected' afterwards in the discharge of their duties." Cf. Spaight, 436–39.

"The protection due to sanitary formations and establishments ceases if they are used to commit acts injurious to the enemy " (Art. 7).

"The following facts are not considered to be of such a nature as to deprive a sanitary formation or establishment of the protection guaranteed by Article 7:

"(1) That the personnel of the formation or establishment is armed, and that it uses its arms for its own defense or for that of its sick and wounded.

"(2) That in default of armed hospital attendants, the formation or establishment is guarded by an armed detachment or by sentinels duly authorized.

"(3) That arms or cartridges taken from the wounded and not yet handed over to the proper authority are found in the formation or establishment" (Art. 8).

they fall into the hands of the enemy, they shall not be treated as prisoners of war " (Art. 9).[21]

The personnel of Voluntary Aid Societies, duly recognized and authorized by their Government, who are employed in the sanitary formations and establishments of armies, is assimilated to the personnel referred to in the preceding article [Art. 9], provided always that the said personnel shall be subject to military laws and regulations.

" Each State shall make known to the other, either in time of peace or at the commencement of or during the course of hostilities—but in any case before actually employing them—the names of the Societies which it has authorized, under its responsibility, to render assistance to the regular sanitary service of its armies " (Art. 10).[22]

[21] G. C., 9.   "These provisions apply to the personnel of the guard of the sanitary formations and establishments under the circumstances indicated in Article 8, No. 2" (Art. 9).

"The persons here mentioned are bound to carefully abstain not only from acts of hostility against the enemy, but also from all acts, such as transmission of letters or messages, calculated to impede the success of operations."   Holland, No. 50.

"It would seem that the domestics of the sanitary personnel should receive the same treatment as themselves, but this is subject to some doubt."   Bordwell, 256.

[22] G. C., 10.   Cf. 3 H. C. (1899), 2; and 10 H. C. (1907), 2.

"This article makes it quite clear that Red Cross, or Aid Societies, unless affiliated to the regular medical organization of one or the other belligerent, and subject to its military law, enjoy none of the benefits conferred by the Convention. . . .   It makes no difference whether or not they are recognized by the Government of the State to which they belong, as available when needed for service with its own armies."   Holland, No. 51.   Cf. Spaight, 442.

"A recognized Society of a neutral country can only afford the assistance of its sanitary personnel and formations to a belligerent with the previous consent of its own Government and the authorization of the belligerent concerned.

"The belligerent who has accepted such assistance is bound to notify the fact to his enemy before making any use thereof" (Art. 11).

"The persons designated in Articles 9, 10, and 11 shall continue, after they have fallen into the hands of the enemy, to carry on their duties under his direction.

"When their assistance is no longer indispensable, they shall be sent back to their army of their country within such time and by such route as may be compatible with military necessity.

"They shall then take with them such effects, instruments, arms, and horses as are their private property" (Art. 12).

"While in his hands, the enemy shall secure to the personnel referred to in Article 9, the same allowances and the same pay as are granted to the persons holding the same rank in his own army" (Art. 13).

"Under Article XII, the *personnel* who fall into the enemy's hands may be

" If movable sanitary formations fall into the hands of the enemy, they shall retain their material, including their teams, irrespective of the means of transport and the driver employed " (Art. 14).[23]

" The buildings and material of fixed establishments remain subject to the laws of war, but they may not be diverted from their purpose so long as they are necessary for the sick and wounded " (Art. 15).[24]

" Convoys of evacuation [25] shall be treated like movable sanitary formations " (Art. 17).[26]

forced by him to carry on their duties so long as their services are indispensable." Spaight, 443–44. Cf. Bordwell, 259. Art. 13 does not apply to Voluntary Aid Societies.

[23] "Nevertheless, the competent military authority shall have the right to use the material for the care of the sick and wounded. It shall be restored under the conditions laid down for the sanitary personnel, and, so far as possible, at the same time" (Art. 14).

"This article cannot be supposed to debar the capturing commander from using, in case of necessity, some of the material of a medical unit (sanitary formation) for the benefit of his own wounded." Holland, No. 55. Cf. Bordwell, 260.

[24] "Nevertheless, the commanders of troops in the field may dispose of them, in case of urgent military necessity, provided they make previous arrangements for the welfare of the sick and wounded who are found there" (Art. 15).

"The provisions of this article, it must be observed, relate only to military establishments and material. Civil hospitals, even when State property, would be exempt from confiscation." Holland No. 56. Cf. Bordwell, 261.

"The material of Voluntary Aid Societies which are admitted to the benefits of the Convention in conformity with the conditions herein prescribed, is considered private property, and, as such, is to be respected under all circumstances, saving only the right of requisition as recognized by belligerents according to the laws and usages of war (Art. 16)."

"Medical stores, drugs, etc., except those held by a mobile medical unit (movable sanitary formation) or a convoy of evacuation, are not protected by the Convention and, are subject to seizure just like any other army property." Spaight, 449. Cf. Bordwell, 261–62.

[25] "Convoys of Evacuation" are convoys of sick and wounded in course of conveyance. Such convoys are not longer protected by an absolute neutrality." For valuable comments on G. C., 17, see Holland, No. 58; Fauchille et Politis, *Manuel de la Croix-Rouge*, 66–69; and Spaight, 451–54.

So-called "mixed or composite trains," consisting of both sick, and of wounded and military men or material, are not protected. An interesting case occurred during the Russo-Japanese War. See Hershey, *op. cit.*, 302; and Lawrence, *War and Neutrality*, 43–44. Cf. Ariga, § 48; Spaight, *op. cit.*; and Takahashi, 154–58.

[26] This, however, is subject to the following special provisions:

"A belligerent intercepting a convoy may break it up if military necessity requires it, provided he takes charge of the sick and wounded who are in it.

" As a compliment to Switzerland, the heraldic emblem of the Red Cross on a white ground, formed by reversing the federal colors, is retained as the emblem and distinctive sign of the sanitary service of armies " (Art. 18).[27]

" With the permission of the competent military authority, this emblem shall be shown on the flags and armlets (*brassards*), as well as on all the material belonging to the sanitary service " (Art. 19).

" The personnel protected in pursuance of Articles 9 (paragraph 1), 10, and 11 shall wear, fixed to the left arm, an armlet (*brassard*) with a Red Cross on a white ground, delivered and stamped by the competent military authority, and accompanied by a certificate of identity in the case of persons who are attached to the sanitary service of armies, but who do not have a military uniform " (Art. 20).[28]

"In this case, the obligation to send back the personnel, provided for in Article 12, shall be extended to the entire military personnel detailed for the transport or the protection of the convoy and furnished for this purpose with an authority in due form.

"The obligation to restore the sanitary material, provided for in Article 14, shall apply to railway trains and boats used in internal navigation which are specially arranged for evacuations, as also to the material belonging to the sanitary service for fitting up ordinary vehicles, trains and boats.

"Military vehicles, other than those of the sanitary service, may be captured with their teams.

"The civilian personnel and the various means of transport obtained by requisition, including railway material and boats used for convoys, shall be subject to the general rules of the Law of Nations" (Art. 17).

[27] "The phraseology of this article is intended to make it clear that the device has no religious significance, such as has been attributed to it by Mohammedan troops; so much so that although Turkey had signed the original Convention in 1865, it was thought desirable by that Power to distinguish its own medical services, in the wars of 1876 and 1897, by a Red Crescent, while undertaking to continue to respect the Red Cross in the service of the enemy.

"Turkey, the only important Power not represented at the Conference of 1906, acceded to the Geneva Convention of that year, on August 24, 1907, with however, the reservation 'that its armies will use the emblem of the Red Crescent for the protection of the ambulances'; adding, 'it is nevertheless well understood that the Imperial Government will scrupulously respect the inviolability of the Red Cross Flag.'" Holland, No. 59.

The representatives of Japan, China, Persia, and Siam expressed a willingness to accept the Red Cross, but at the Second Hague Peace Conference, Persia reserved the right to use the Lion and Red Sun.

[28] "A Register should be kept of the names and descriptions of the persons to whom these badges have been issued. Such persons, if not wearing a military uniform, should be furnished with an official certificate, bearing a number and a date corresponding with entries in the Register." Holland, No. 61. The arm badge is not always a prerequisite to protection, since they need not

" The sanitary formations belonging to neutral countries which may be authorized, under the conditions laid down in Article 11, should fly the national flag of the belligerent to which they are attached, along with the flag of the Convention " (Art. 22).[29]

" The emblem of the Red Cross on a white ground and the words ' Red Cross ' or ' Geneva Cross ' shall not be used, either in time of peace or in time of war, except to protect or to indicate the sanitary formations and establishments, the personnel and material protected by the Convention " (Art. 23).[30]

be worn by those temporarily in the sanitary service, as in the case of pickets or guards, litter-bearers, etc.   Bordwell, 264.

"The distinctive flag of the Convention shall only be hoisted over those sanitary formations and establishments which are entitled to be respected under the Convention, and with the consent of the military authority.   It should be accompanied by the national flag of the belligerent to whom the formation or establishment belongs.

"Nevertheless, sanitary formations which have fallen into the hands of the enemy, so long as they are in that situation, shall not fly any other flag than that of the Red Cross" (Art. 21).

"Article 21 makes it clear that the Red Cross flag must not be hoisted over civil hospitals or any buildings or ambulances other than those referred in to the Convention. . . .   It has, however, been the practice for civil hospitals to fly the Geneva flag, especially in bombarded towns." Spaight, 456–57.

"No national flag, it will be observed, is to be flown by a medical unit [formation] while in captivity.   It may, however, be supposed that an invader will hoist his own flag, accompanied by that of the Red Cross, over hospitals which he may find in the territory of which he is in occupation."   Holland, No. 62.

[29] "The provisions of the second paragraph of the preceding article are applicable to them" (Art. 22).

Holland (No. 63) says *apropos* of the article: "The only flags which, under any circumstances, can be flown by neutral Aid Societies are, it will be observed, that of the Red Cross, and that of the belligerent to whose army they are attached.   In captivity they can fly only the Red Cross flag."

[30] In Article 27 the Signatory Powers agreed to "adopt, or to propose to their legislative bodies, such measures as may be necessary to prevent at all times the employment of the emblem or the name of 'Red Cross' or 'Geneva Cross' by private individuals, or by Societies other than those which are entitled to do so under the present Convention, and in particular for commercial purposes as a trade mark or trading mark."

In Article 28 they undertook to adopt or propose to their legislative bodies "measures necessary for the repression in time of war of individual acts of pillage and maltreatment of the sick and wounded of armies, as well as for the punishment, as an unlawful employment of military insignia, of the improper use of the Red Cross flag and armlet (*brassard*) by soldiers or private individuals not protected by the present Conventions."

Arts. 25, 27 and 28 were not accepted by Great Britain.   The United

4. MEANS OF INJURING THE ENEMY ON LAND

375. Means of Injuring the Enemy.—"The right of belligerents to adopt means of injuring the enemy is not unlimited." [31]

States appears to have at least complied with the requirements of Article 27. 33 Stat. at Large, 600, cited by Bordwell, 267.

The remaining articles of the Geneva Convention of 1906 relate to the application, execution, ratification, etc., of the Convention. Article 24 declares that it is "only binding upon the Contracting Powers in case of war between two or more of them." Article 25 provides that "the Commanders-in-Chief of belligerent armies shall arrange the details for carrying out the preceding Articles, as well as for cases not provided for, in accordance with the instructions of their respective Governments and in conformity with the general provisions of the present Convention." In Article 26 the Signatory Governments agree that they will "take the necessary measures to instruct their troops, especially the personnel protected, in the provisions of the present Convention, and to bring them to the notice of the civil population."

On the *Geneva Convention of 1906*, see: * Bordwell, Pt. II, ch. 5; Delpech, in 13 *R. D. I. P.* (1906), 629 ff.; Davis, in 1 *A. J.* (1907), 409–17; Fauchille et Politis, *Manuel de la Croix Rouge* (1908); * Holland, *War on Land*, 27–40, and in *Fortn. Review* for August, 1907; * Higgins, 18–38; Meurer, in 1 *Z. V.* (1906), 521 ff.; * Spaight, ch. 13.

Accusations of violations of the Geneva Conventions are more or less common to all wars, and yet it cannot be said that their provisions are on the whole ignored or of no effect. On the violations by Germany during the World War, see especially 1 Garner, ch. 20, particularly §§ 314–18.

On *Treatment of the Sick, Wounded, and Dead*, see: * Ariga, *La guerre russo-japonaise* (1907), ch. 5; Bluntschli, Arts. 586–92; Bonfils or 2 Fauchille, Nos. 1108–18; * Bordwell, Pt. II, ch. 5; 4 Calvo, §§ 2161–65; Davis, in 1 *A. J.* (1907), 409–17; Despagnet, Nos. 551–54; * Dumant, *Souvenir de Solferino*, in Müller's *Entstehungsgeschichte des Rotenkranzes* (1897); Edmonds and Oppenheim, *Land Warfare*, ch. 6; * Fauchille et Politis, *Manuel de la Croix-Rouge* (1908); 3 Fiore, Nos. 1365–72, and *Int. Law Cod.*, Nos. 1594–1609; 1 Garner, ch. 20, §§ 313–18; Gillot, *La revision de la convention de Genève* (1902); 1 Guelle, *Précis*, etc. (1884), 144–86; Hall, § 130; 2 Halleck (3d ed.), 36–39; * Holland, *War on Land*, 27–40, and *Studies*, 61–65; * 2 Hyde, §§ 680–87; Lawrence, § 165; Longuet, *Le droit actuel*, etc. (1901), §§ 85–90; Lueder, in 4 Holtzendorff, 289–319, 398–421, and *La convention de Genève* (1876); Macpherson, in 5 *Z. V.* (1911), 253–77; Mérignhac, *La guerre sur terre* (1913), 114–42; 7 Moore, *Digest*, § 1134; 3 F. de Martens, § 114, and *La paix et la guerre* (1901), ch. 8; Moynier, *Étude sur la convention de Genève* (1870), *La Croix-Rouge* (1882), *La revision*, etc. (1898), and *La fondation de la Croix Rouge* (1903); Müller, *Entstehungsgeschichte des Rotenkranzes* (1897); 3 Nys, ch. 14; * 2 Oppenheim, §§ 118–24; Pillet, *Les lois actuelles*, etc., ch. 7; 6 and 7 P.-Fodéré, Nos. 2794, 2849–81; 2 Rivier, 269–73; * Spaight, ch. 13; Taylor, §§ 527–28; Triepel, *Die neusten Fortschritte*, etc. (1894), 1–41; Ullmann, § 178; U. S. Army, *Rules of Land Warfare* (1914), ch. 5; * 2 Westlake (1st ed.), 68–72, 271–73; Wilson, § 151.

[31] H. R., 22. Cf. B. D., 12. This declaration may be regarded as a solemn and official denial or repudiation of the doctrine of the *Kriegsraison* or military necessity (see *supra*, No. 336), as enunciated by leading German publicists

376. Declaration of St. Petersburg on Explosive Bullets.

—The Conference of military delegates from the European Powers and Brazil, which met at St. Petersburg in 1868, adopted the following Declaration and Preamble:

" Considering that the progress of civilization should have the effect of alleviating as much as possible the calamities of war;

" That the only legitimate object which States should endeavor to accomplish during war is to weaken the military forces of the enemy;

" That for this purpose it is sufficient to disable the greatest possible number of men;

" That this object would be exceeded by the employment of arms which would needlessly aggravate the sufferings of disabled men, or render their death inevitable;

" That the employment of such arms would, therefore, be contrary to the laws of humanity;

" The Contracting Parties engage mutually to renounce, in case of war among themselves, the employment by their military or naval troops of any projectile of a weight below 400 grammes (nearly fourteen ounces avoirdupois), which is either explosive or charged with fulminating or inflammable substances." [32]

and set forth in the *Kriegsbrauch im Landkriege* (1902), a German manual on the "Usages of Land Warfare," published by the historical section of the German Chief of Staff. For an English translation of the *Kriegsbrauch*, see Morgan, *The German War Book* (1915). For further references on the German doctrine, see note 27 on p. 554.

[32] "It is now very generally thought that clauses 2 and 3 of these Recitals are capable of being so read as to limit too narrowly the legitimate methods of making war." Holland, No. 41. However, this may be, "the civilized world has signed and sealed its approval of two great principles—the first, that the sole end of war is the overcoming of the military forces of the enemy; the second, that, to the means which may be adopted to secure this end, certain restrictive laws apply." Spaight, 75. The United States was not a party to this Declaration.

It should be noted that the only application made of the principles laid down in the Preamble to the Declaration of St. Petersburg is the prohibition of the use of explosive projectiles of a weight below 400 grammes, *i.e.* in bullets, not in shells. The Russian military authorities had invented a bullet which exploded on contact with either a hard or soft substance. The Russian Government was willing to forego the use of this dangerous explosive bullet, provided the other European Powers entered into a reciprocal engagement. This explains the immediate object of the Conference.

On the *Conference and Declaration of St. Petersburg of 1868*, see especially:

377. **The Hague Declarations on** (I) **Projectiles and Explosives from Balloons.**—" The great majority of the Powers represented at the First Hague Conference of 1899 signed the following Declarations:

" The Contracting Powers agree to prohibit, *for a term of five years*, the discharge of projectiles and explosives from balloons or by other new methods of a similar nature." For the phrase " for a term of five years," the Conference of 1907 substituted the expression *" for a period extending to the close of the Third Peace Conference."* [33]

378. (II) **On Asphyxiating or Deleterious Gases.**—" The Contracting Powers agree to abstain from the use of projectiles the sole object of which is the diffusion of asphyxiating or deleterious gases." [34]

379. (III) **On Expanding Bullets.**—" The Contracting Parties agree to abstain from the use of bullets which expand or flatten easily in the human body, such as bullets with a

Bordwell, 87–88, 278–79; * Higgins, 5–7; * Holland, *War on Land*, 41, 77–78, and *Studies*, 66–67; F. de Martens, *La paix et la guerre* (1901), 87–91; Mérignhac, *Guerre sur terre* (1903), Nos. 82–83; Pillet, No. 51; Spaight, 74 ff.; 2 Westlake, (1st ed.), 53–55.

[33] H. D. (1899 and 1907), 1. "This Declaration, having been originally drafted in 1899 by the First Peace Conference to operate for five years only, expired by the efflux of time. It had been ratified by almost all the Powers represented, except Great Britain [and the United States.] As redrafted in 1907 by the Second, it is to remain in force to the end of the third Conference." Holland, No. 73.

The Declaration of 1907 was signed and ratified by both Great Britain and the United States, but among the seventeen non-signatory Powers upon whom it was not binding were Germany, France, Italy, Japan, and Russia. Consequently, it can scarcely be deemed to have ever been an integral part of the Law of Nations.

"It was generally conceded at the Conference that balloons must not be allowed to attack undefended places; but it was thought that this was sufficiently provided for by the words 'by any means whatever,' now inserted in Art. 25 of the Hague Regulations." Holland, No. 73. Cf. *infra*, No. 382.

[34] H. D. (1899), 2. Holland, (No. 74) adds by way of comment: "This, and the following Declaration are, unless denounced, of perpetual obligation. They were ratified or acceded to by almost all the Powers represented at the Conference of 1899, except Great Britain, the United States, and Portugal, which, however, in the course of the proceedings of the Conference of 1907, signified their adhesion to both Declarations." This statement is inaccurate. The United States did not sign either of these Declarations. "It has been signed by all the other Powers represented at the First Peace Conference, but not by those which were represented only at the second." Higgins, 493. For the objections of the United States as expressed by Captain Mahan, see Higgins, 493; and Holls, 119.

hard envelope which does not entirely cover the core, or is pierced with incisions." [35]

380. **The Hague Prohibitions.**—" Besides the prohibitions established by special Conventions,[36] it is particularly forbidden:

" (a) To employ poison or poisoned weapons; [37]

[35] H. D. (1899), 3. This declaration was really aimed at the famous dumdum bullet so named from the arsenal near Calcutta where it was first made. It appears to have been designed for use against savages or barbarians whose wild onslaughts, it was claimed, could not be checked by ordinary bullets.

At the Conference of 1899, Captain Crozier of the American Delegation submitted an amendment which forbade the use of all bullets "which inflicted wounds of useless cruelty, such as explosive bullets and, in general, every kind of bullet which exceeds the limit necessary for placing a man *hors de combat.*" Holls, 103. This amendment had the support of Great Britain, but it failed of adoption. Consequently, both the United States and Great Britain withheld their signatures from the Declaration—a position which, however, has since been abandoned by Great Britain.

At the Conference of 1907, General Davis attempted to secure the consideration for a proposition couched in terms identical with Captain Crozier's amendment, but he was ruled out of order. Davis, in 2 *A. J.* (1908), 77.

The United States appears to be the only Power represented at the First Hague Conference which has not signed this Declaration.

On the *Hague Declaration*, see especially: Boiden *Les lois de la guerre*, etc., (1908), 100–15; Bordwell, 130–35, 279–80; Bustamante y Sirven, ch. 11; Davis, in 2 *A. J.* (1908), 74–77, 528–29; * Higgins, 484–97; Holland, 41–42, 80–81; * Holls, 93–120, 506–14; 2 Hyde, §§ 660–63; Lawrence § 205; Lémonon, 382–94; 1 Scott, 60–61, 649–54; * Spaight, 79–81, 101–03; 2 Westlake (1st ed.), 110, 274.

For complaints of the use of explosives and dumdum bullets during the Anglo-Boer and Russo-Japanese Wars, see Ariga, §§ 65, 71; Bordwell, 138–40; Despagnet, *La guerre sud-africaine, passim;* Hershey, 316–318; Takahashi, 173–74.

For charges and counter-charges of the use of "Forbidden Weapons and Instrumentables" during the World War, see particularly, 1 Garner, chs. 10 and 11. Practically all the belligerents on each side accused those on the other side of resorting to such practices.

For the provisions of the Washington Conference relating to gases, see *infra*, note 44 on p. 649.

[36] *I.e.* the Declaration of St. Petersburg and the Hague Declarations referred to in the preceding sections, "and any others which may have been or may be concluded, whether generally or between particular Powers." 2 Westlake, 72–73.

[37] H. R., 23 a. Cf. B. D., 13 a. The prohibition of the use of poisoned weapons is at least as old as the Laws of Manu. See *supra*, No. 20.

It appears that "cutting off an enemy's water supply is an allowable act of war," Spaight, 84. It has been suggested, on analogy, that the prohibition of poison extends to the spread of contagious diseases, and this is probably the case.

"*(b)* To kill or wound treacherously individuals belonging to the hostile nation or army; [38]

"*(c)* To kill or wound an enemy who, having laid down his arms, no longer having means of defense, has surrendered at discretion;

"*(d)* To declare that no quarter will be given; [39]

[38] H. R., 23 b. "This includes not only assassination of individuals, but also by implication, any offer for an individual 'dead or alive.'" Holland, No. 76.

"Modern International Law distinguishes between dashes made at a ruler or commander by an individual or a little band of individuals who come as open enemies, and similar attempts made by those who disguise their enemy character. A man who steals secretly into the opposing camp in the dark, and makes alone, or with others, a sudden attack in uniform upon the tent of king or general, is a brave and devoted soldier. A man who obtains admission to the same tent disguised as a pedlar, and stabs its occupant when lured into a false security, is a vile assassin, and the attempt to procure such murder is as criminal as the murder itself." Lawrence § 208. See also Art. 148 of the *American Instructions.*

"It is the essence of treachery that the offender assumes a false character by which he deceives his enemy and thereby is able to effect a hostile act which, had he come under his true colors, he could not have done." Spaight, 87. See *Ibid.*, 88, for examples.

[39] H. R., 23 d. "The admitted case in which it (quarter) is not practicable is that which occurs during the continuance of fighting, when the achievement of victory would be hindered and even endangered by stopping to give quarter instead of cutting down the enemy and rushing on, not to mention that during fighting it is often impracticable so to secure prisoners as to prevent their return to the combat. Hence it is especially difficult to avoid ruthless slaughter in the storm of a place or position, but the rule formerly dictated by military pride that those are not entitled to quarter who insult a superior force by defending a place after a breach has been made and the counterscarp thrown in, or who defend an ill-fortified place at all against a superior force, is entirely obsolete and condemned." 2 Westlake, (1st ed.), 75. Cf. Hall (8th ed.), 473–74 and note, and Lawrence § 163; and 2 Oppenheim, § 109.

The right of a commander to refuse quarter or to destroy prisoners "in case of imperative necessity, when there is no other means of keeping them and their presence constitutes a danger to the very existence of the captors," is still asserted by some authorities, notably in Germany. *Kriegsbrauch im Landkriege*, 16. Westlake (II, 76) agrees with Hall (474) that "prisoners who cannot safely be kept can be liberated." The Boers acted in this manner during the Anglo-Boer War. For examples of the difficulty of giving quarter or accepting surrender under certain circumstances, see Spaight, 91 ff.

"Willingness to surrender is usually indicated by the hoisting of a white flag, or some improvised substitute for it, but there is no settled procedure in this matter. Some troops throw down their arms; others hold up their hands (such was the Boer practice). The Prussian appeal for mercy in 1870 was to raise the butt end of the needle gun; this the French considered insufficient and made them fall on their knees. In the war of 1904 the Russians sometimes went to the length of embracing the enemy to whom they wished to surrender. There are so many diverse ways of indicating surrender that it seems desirable for one universal procedure to be settled by international agreement." Spaight,

" (e) To employ arms, projectiles, or material of a nature to cause superfluous injury; [40]

" (f) To make improper use of a flag of truce, of the national flag, or of military insignia and uniform of the enemy, as also the distinctive signs of the Geneva Convention; [41]

" (g) To destroy or seize enemy's property, unless such destruction or seizure be imperatively demanded by the necessities of war." [42]

95. See Ariga, § 29, for several amusing incidents which occurred during the Russo-Japanese War.

[40] H. R., 23 e. This is virtually an enactment into law of the principles laid down in the Declaration of St. Petersburg. See *supra*, No. 376.

Such forbidden missiles are "understood to include glass, nails, and bits of iron of irregular shape. Many writers include red-hot shot in the prohibition, which may be admitted when they would be directed only against men. . . ." 2 Westlake, 76.

"Explosive hand grenades, which were freely used in the Russo-Japanese War, as they were in the Crimean and Secession Wars, are not held to come under the prohibition of explosive bullets. Nor is there anything illegitimate in the use of [mines or] torpedoes in land war." Spaight, 81.

[41] H. R., 23 f. Cf. H. R., 24, *infra*, No. 381. There is some controversy as to what constitutes an "improper" use of the enemy's flag or uniform. The older jurists maintained that it is perfectly legitimate to use the distinctive emblems of an enemy in order to escape from him or to draw his forces into action; but it was held that "soldiers clothed in the uniforms of their enemy must put on a conspicuous mark by which they can be recognized before attacking, and that a vessel using the enemy's flag must hoist its own flag before firing." Hall (8th ed.), 649. Cf. Bluntschli, Art. 565; Bordwell, 283–84; 4 Calvo, No. 2106; Longuet, No. 54; Pillet, No. 55; and Taylor, § 488.

There is now a growing tendency on the part of publicists to reject the view that the enemy's flag or uniform may be used for purposes of approach. See, *e.g.* Bonfils, No. 1074; 2 Fauchille, No. 1087; Lawrence, § 207; Lueder, in 4 Holtzendorff, 458; Mérignhac, No. 89; 6 P.-Fodéré, No. 2760; and Spaight, 104 ff. I agree with Oppenheim (II, § 164) that Art. 23 f. of the Hague Regulations has left this question open.

"Troops may sometimes be obliged by lack of clothing, and with no fraudulent intent, to make use of uniforms belonging to the enemy. Care must be taken in such cases to make alterations in the uniform which will clearly indicate the side to which those who wear it belong." Holland, No. 79.

For examples of wearing enemy's uniforms during recent wars, see Spaight, 106–10. For instances during the Russo-Japanese War, see Ariga, §§ 67–68; Hershey, 307–08; Takahashi, 174–78.

[42] H. R., 23 g, "refers to pillage as distinguished from requisitions, and to devastation not directly necessary for a military purpose." 2 Westlake, 76. Cf. H. R., 46–47, 51–52, *infra*, Nos. 389–92, 394–95.

"It may be taken for granted that the necessities of war include the destruction of whatever property interferes with the operations of a conflict, an advance or a retreat." But "it is clear that the necessity must be fairly direct and immediate." Lawrence § 206, p. 536. "Devastation pure and simple,

" (h) To declare extinguished, suspended, or inadmissible

as an end in itself, as a self-contained measure of war, is not sanctioned by war law.   Permissible devastation presents itself invariably as a means to a military end, as a factor in a legitimate operation of war.   There must be some reasonably close connection between the destruction of property and the overcoming of the enemy's army.   To destroy with the intention of damaging the hostile Government's pocket is illegitimate. . . .   Devastation as an operation of war *per se* may be said to be wholly obsolete."   Spaight, 112.

But destruction of enemy property, which is incidental to a military operation or necessary for purposes of offense and defense, is justified.   This includes "war *material* and army supplies generally; property situated on the anticipated field of battle or in the zone of actual fighting; railways, telegraphs, etc. which are used by the enemy for his operations; . . . barracks, military storehouses, factories, and *depôts*, iron foundries and railway workshops which may be used to supply the enemy's army."   *Ibid.*, 128.   Cf. 2 Oppenheim, § 150. For exceptions, see H. R., 56, *infra*, No. 399.

The general devastation of a particular district or the destruction of a whole town is only permissible in extreme cases, as, *e.g.* if self-preservation should compel a belligerent to resort to severe measures in face of a threatened levy *en masse*, or "when, after the defeat of his main forces and occupation of his territory, an enemy disperses his remaining forces into small bands which carry on guerrilla tactics and receive food and information, so that there is no hope of ending the war except by a general devastation which cuts off supplies of every kind from the guerrilla bands."   2 Oppenheim, § 154.

The right of general devastation has been denied under any and all circumstances.   But this position can scarcely be reconciled with modern practice. Generals Sherman and Sheridan did not hesitate to destroy the granaries of the Southern armies in Georgia and the Shenandoah Valley during the Civil War, and during the Anglo-Boer War the British destroyed Boer farms on a large scale.   Vattel (liv. III, § 167), writing in the eighteenth century, still permitted devastation "for making a barrier, for covering a frontier against an enemy who cannot be stopped any other way."   But, as Lawrence (p. 535) says, such action "would now be held up to the execration of the civilized world."

In case devastation on a large scale is found imperative, the best possible provision should be made for the dispossessed inhabitants.   In several recent wars they have been herded in concentration or internment camps—a mode of procedure which has been criticised on the ground that non-combatants should not be made prisoners.   As pointed out by Spaight (p. 307), "generally speaking, the objection taken to such camps is sound in principle," and "such an extreme measure is only to be justified by very extreme circumstances."   The internment of the Boers in concentration camps by the British in 1901 was accompanied by a "terribly" high death rate, and met with severe criticism. The fearful sufferings of the Cubans which resulted from the reconcentration order of General Weyler in 1896 (see Benton, p. 27) was one of the main causes of intervention by the United States.   See also 7 Moore, *Digest*, § 1126.   Yet it is better to provide concentration camps for non-combatants than to turn them adrift as did General Sherman when he burnt Atlanta in 1864.   At least some of the evils which have hitherto been incident to concentration camps might be avoided by proper sanitary precautions and a more efficient management.

On *Devastation*, see especially: Bordwell, 284; 4 Calvo, §§ 2215 ff.; * Hall, § 186; Holland, 13–14, 43–44; 2 Hyde, §§ 657–58; * Lawrence § 207; 7

in a court of law the rights and actions of the nationals of the hostile party.[43]

" *A belligerent is likewise forbidden to compel the nationals*

Moore, *Digest*, § 1123; * 2 Oppenheim, §§ 149–54; 6 P.-Fodéré, Nos. 2770–74; * Spaight, 111–40, 307–10; Taylor, §§ 481–82; Wheaton, §§ 347–51.

For defenses of the devastations of Generals Sherman and Sheridan, see Bordwell, 77–79; and Spaight, 133–36.

For German devastations, more particularly of the Somme region of France before its evacuation by the German armies in March, 1917, see 1 Garner, ch. 13. Even shade trees, orchards and vineyards were not spared. Agricultural implements were destroyed. Perhaps the worst examples of unwarranted destruction were those of Lens in 1918 and the flooding of the coal mines there. As compensation for the destruction of these mines, Germany was required by the Treaty of Versailles to cede to France the coal mines of the Saar basin. See *supra*, p. 137.

[43] H. R. (1907), 23 h. The meaning of this paragraph is doubtful. If interpreted literally, it involves a clear denial of the Anglo-American doctrine that an alien enemy has no standing in court as such. This appears to have been the only view expressed in the discussions at the Hague Conference itself (see Higgins, 265), and this view is supported by Bonfils or 2 Fauchille, No. 1065; Bordwell, 210, 284–85; Kohler, in 5 *Zeitschrift* (1911), 384 ff.; Lawrence § 143; Phillipson, *Effect of War on Contracts* (1909), 46; Politis, in 18 *R. D. I. P.* (1911), 249 ff.; Ullmann (2d ed.), 474; and Whittuck, *Int. Doc.*, p. xxvii.

General Davis on the other hand, is of the opinion that it is merely one of a number of "reasonable and wholesome restrictions upon the authority of commanding generals and their subordinates in the theater of belligerent activity." Davis, in 2 *A. J.* (1908), 70. For a similar opinion expressed by Sir E. Grey in behalf of the British Government, see 5 *Zeitschrift* (1911), 389–91. This view is shared by Spaight, 140–42.

Professor Holland (No. 76) furnishes the following valuable comment:

"This clause, suggested by Germany, if intended only for the guidance of an invading commander, needs careful redrafting; if, as would rather appear, it is of general application, besides being quite out of place where it stands, it is so revolutionary of the doctrine which denies to an enemy any *persona standi in judicio*, that although it is included in the ratification of the Convention by the United States on March 10, and the signature of the same on June, 29 1908, by Great Britain, it can hardly, till its policy has been seriously discussed, be treated as a rule of International Law." Cf. Holland, in 28 *L. Q. R.* (1912), 94 ff.

Considering the form and manner of its adoption, it is difficult to avoid the conclusion that the clause is one of general application and constitutes an international obligation. But legislation is probably needed to carry it into effect, at least in England and the United States. It is, of course, highly desirable that it be recognized as a rule of International Law. For a very convincing argument in favor of so treating it, see Politis, in 18 *R. D. I. P.* (1911), 249 ff. See also 5 *Zeitschrift* (1911), 384 ff. For a very adequate treatment of this question in the light of legislation and judicial decisions during the World War, see * 1 Garner, ch. 5. See also 2 Hyde, §§ 611–13; and 2 Oppenheim, § 100 a. The leading British decision was that of *Porter* v. *Freudenberg* (Court of Appeals, 1915, 1 K. B. 8057) which reaffirmed the old Anglo-American common law doctrine. For this case, see Evans, 512 or Scott, 570.

of the hostile party to take part in the operations of war directed against their own country, even when they have been in his service before the commencement of the war." [44]

[44] H. R. (1907), 23 h. Cf. H. R. (1899 and 1907), 44. "This article, drafted by Germany, was in 1907 rather awkwardly annexed to H. R., 23, in substitution for Art. 44 of H. R. of 1899, which ran as follows: 'any compulsion on the population of occupied territory to take part in *military operations* against its own country is prohibited.' The immunity now accorded to subjects of the invaded States is considerably greater than that guaranteed by the old articles. In the first place, it relates to taking part in any *operations of war*, a term supposed to cover many acts not amounting to what would be described as *military operations*. An Austrian amendment which would have limited the exemption to taking part 'as combatants,' was accordingly rejected. In the second place, the subjects of that State are protected against compulsion to take part against their own country, even if they have previously been enrolled in the service of the invader.

"The terminology employed is, however, still ambiguous. Would this article render unlawful any compulsion on inhabitants of occupied territory to execute urgently required works, such as, *e.g.*, repairs to roads or bridges, although of ultimate military utility? A still more delicate question is whether it would protect the inhabitants from being compelled to act as guides to the enemy. The practice of exacting services of this kind was reprobated by many Powers at the Conference, but is still treated as admissible in 1902, by the *Kriegsbrauch* of the Prussian General Staff, p. 48. It must be noted that Germany, with several other first-class Powers, declines to accept H. R., 44." (See *infra*, No. 389). Holland, No. 77. Cf. Higgins, 265–69; and Spaight, 142–52.

Holland (No. 112) also thinks that the phrase *operations of war* "would probably not comprise works at a distance from the scene of hostilities," fortifications. On this point he is surely mistaken, though this was the view of the older jurists. There can be little doubt that H. R., 23 h. and 44, in principle at least, also apply to the use of forced guides. Cf. *infra*, No. 389.

On the other hand, the invading army may utilize the services of the inhabitants of the invaded or occupied district for transporting supplies, repairing roads or bridges, caring for the wounded, burying the dead, etc. "It is only such acts as are directly and distinctly subservient to military operations —such as building fortifications, making munitions, repairing arms, or giving information as to the enemy's position and numbers—that an invader is forbidden to demand of the 'passive enemy.'" Spaight, 152.

"Before quitting the Means of Injuring the Enemy, we must notice that it is considered unlawful to incite the enemy's troops to treason or desertion, a rule which was probably introduced for the mutual convenience of commanders and by a kind of chivalry between them, and which should carry with it the unlawfulness of enrolling deserters as recruits; also the allied rule that communications intended for the enemy can only be made to the highest officer in rank who is within reach. But it is not considered unlawful to stir up insurrection in the enemy's country. The projects of France in 1859 and of Prussia in 1866 to enroll Hungarian legions seem to be on the very border between incitement to desertion and incitement to insurrection." 2 Westlake, (1st ed.), 76.

On *Means of Injuring the Enemy on Land*, including *Ruses of War and Stratagems*, see: Baker and Crocker, *op. cit.*, 111–97; Bonfils, Nos. 1066–87;

381. Ruses or Strategems.—" Ruses of war and the employment of methods necessary for obtaining information about the enemy and the country are considered lawful " (Art. 24).[45]

382. Sieges and Bombardments.—" The attack or bombardment, *by any means whatever*, of towns, villages, dwellings, or buildings which are undefended, is prohibited " (Art. 25).[46]

Bordwell, Pt. II, ch. 6; 4 Calvo, liv. IV, §§ 2044 ff.; Despagnet, Nos. 528–30; Edmonds and Oppenheim, *op. cit.*, ch. 4, Nos. 39–53; * 2 Fauchille, Nos. 1078–99; 3 Fiore, Nos. 1303 ff., and *Int. Law Cod.*, Arts. 1481 ff.; 1 Guelle, *op. cit.*, Pt. II, ch. 2; * Hall, Pt. III, ch. 7, *passim*; 1 Halleck, ch. 18; Heffter, (3d ed.), § 125; * Holland, 40–45; * 2 Hyde, §§ 655–67; *Kriegsbrauch*, 9–24; Lawrence, Pt. III, ch. 6, *passim*; Longuet, *op. cit.*, §§ 41–61; Lueder, in 4 Holtzendorff, 388 ff.; 3 F. de Martens, § 110; Mérignhac, *op. cit.*, Nos. 78–91; 3 Nys, ch. 5; * 2 Oppenheim, §§ 107–17, 163–65; Pillet, ch. 4 and pp. 466–71; 6P.-Fodéré, Nos. 2742 ff.; 2 Rivier, 260–68; * 1 Rolin, Nos. 338 ff.; * Spaight, ch. 4; Taylor, §§ 477–93; Ullmann, § 176; U. S. Army, *Rules of Land Warfare*, *op. cit.*, ch. 6, Nos. 172–98; Walker, *Manual*, § 50; * 2 Westlake (1st ed.), 72–76, 269; Zorn, *op. cit.*, 127–61.

[45] H. R., 24. Cf. B. D., 14 and H. R., 44. "Good faith must, however, always be observed with the enemy, and this article must not be taken to authorize any such acts of treachery as are expressly forbidden." Holland, No. 78. Cf. H. R., 23 b and f, *supra*, No. 380 f. Ruses of war or strategems are considered unobjectionable "provided they do not involve treachery or a breach of an express or tacit convention." Spaight, 152. For examples of permissible ruses, see *Ibid.*, 153–56; and 2 Oppenheim, § 164.

A distinction must be here drawn between treachery or perfidy and mere deceit. The former are prohibited, the latter permitted. "War is a conflict of wits quite as much as a conflict of arms." Lawrence, § 207, p. 538.

[46] H. R., 25. Cf. B. D., 15; 9 H. C. (1907), 1. The phrase *by any means whatever* was inserted in 1907 in order to cover the bombardment of undefended towns, etc., by projectiles from balloons or airships. Cf. 1 H. D., *supra*, No. 377.

"The first Declaration of 1899 against the discharge of projectiles and explosives from balloons, a Declaration which was not limited to undefended places, was renewed in 1907, but it has not been accepted by many of the great military Powers." Higgins, 270 and 491.

"A place, although not fortified, may be bombarded if it is defended. This article is not to be taken to prohibit the use of any means for the destruction of buildings for military reasons. A place must not be bombarded with a view merely to the exaction from it of ransom." Holland, No. 80. Cf. 9 H. C. (1907), 4, *infra*, No. 435.

It appears that a place may also be bombarded if simply *occupied*, though not actually defended by the enemy. Spaight, 161.

"As war law now stands one may say that an undefended city, unoccupied by troops and not situated within the perimeter of defense of a neighboring fort or forts, may be bombarded in land war only in three cases and in those three cases only *if it is absolutely impossible to obtain the end in view by milder means:* the three cases being: (1) the destruction of military stores, factories,

" The Commander of an attacking force, before commencing a bombardment, except in case of an assault, should do all in his power to warn the authorities " (Art. 26).[47]

" In sieges and bombardments all necessary steps should be taken to spare, as far as possible, buildings devoted to religion, art, science, and charity, historic monuments, hospitals, and places where the sick and wounded are collected, provided they are not used at the same time for military purposes.

" It is the duty of the besieged to indicate these buildings or places by some special visible signs, which shall previously be notified to the assailants " (Art. 27).[48]

" The giving up to pillage of a town or place, even when taken by assault, is forbidden " (Art. 28).[49]

etc.; (2) to secure compliance with legitimate requisitions; and (3)—a very doubtful case—to inflict punishment, by way of reprisals, for infractions of the laws of war on the part of the enemy." *Ibid.*, 170.   Cf. Holland, *Studies*, 110.

[47] H. R., 26.   Cf. B. D., 16.   "By 'assault,' a surprise attack is here intended.   The besieger is under no absolute obligation to allow any portion of the population of a place to leave it, even when a bombardment is about to commence."   Holland, No. 81.

"On the other hand, to refuse exit to the non-combatants of a town which it is proposed to reduce by bombardment or assault, and not by famine, is to inflict unnecessary suffering on persons who are protected by the laws of war." Spaight, 174.   There appears to be no doubt that a usage is growing up in favor of the free exit of "useless mouths." For examples, see *Ibid.*, 175 ff.

[48] H. R., 27.   Cf. B. D., 17; and 9 H. C. (1907), 3 and 5.

"Thus firing on the houses of a fortified town is not forbidden, but when it can be avoided it is cruel, it is generally useless, and it ought to be forbidden unless there is reason to suspect that the houses are occupied by troops of the garrison, or are used as magazines." 2 Westlake, 78–79.

[49] H. R., 28.   Cf. H. R., 47; B. D., 18; and 9 H. C. (1907), 7.   "Much less may a garrison, . . . be put to the sword over an obstinate defense." Holland No. 83.

For charges and counter-charges of the bombardment of open and undefended towns, cities, and villages during the World War, see 1 Garner, ch. 18, particularly §§ 269–72.   For destruction of historic monuments, etc., see *Ibid.*, ch. 18.

On *Sieges and Bombardments*, see: * Barclay, in 20 *Eng. Rev.* (1915), 225–30; Baker and Crocker, *op. cit.*, 198–217; Bonfils, Nos. 1079–87; Bordwell, 286–88; * 4 Calvo, §§ 2067–97; Carpentier, *op. cit.*, 43–53; Despagnet, Nos. 531–37; Edmonds and Oppenheim, *op. cit.*, Nos. 117–38; * 2 Fauchille, Nos. 1093–99; 3 Fiore, Nos. 1322–30, and *Int. Law Cod.*, Arts. 1516–29; * 1 Garner, §§ 271–72; 1 Guelle, *op. cit.*, 109–22; Hall (8th ed.), 646–47; * Holland, *War on Land*, 46, and *Studies*, 96–111; Holls, *op. cit.*, 151–53; 2 Hyde, § 656; *Kriegsbrauch*, 18–22; Lawrence, § 204, and in 24 *R. D. I. P.* (1917), 56 ff.; Lueder, in 4 Holtzendorff, 448–57; Mérignhac, *op. cit.*, Nos. 92–97; 3 Nys, 148–60; * 2 Oppenheim, §§ 155–58; Phillimore, in 1 *Grot. Soc.* (1916), 61–66; Pillet, *op. cit.*, Nos.

5. SPIES AND ESPIONAGE

383. Spies.—" A person can only be considered a spy if, acting clandestinely or on false pretenses, he obtains or seeks to obtain information in the zone of operations of a belligerent, with the intention of communicating it to the hostile party.

" Thus, soldiers not in disguise who have penetrated into the zone of operations of the hostile army to obtain information are not considered spies. Similarly, the following are not considered spies: soldiers or civilians, carrying out their mission openly, charged with the delivery of dispatches destined either for their own army or for that of the enemy. To this class belong likewise individuals sent in balloons to deliver dispatches, and generally to maintain communication between the various parts of an army or a territory " (Art. 29).[50]

60–67 and p. 469; 6 P.-Fodéré, Nos. 2779–85; 2 Rivier, 284–88; * 1 Rolin, Nos. 365–78; * Spaight, ch. 5; Taylor, §§ 483–85; Ullmann, § 181; U. S. Army, Rules, etc., *op. cit.*, ch. 6, sect. 4, Nos. 212–29; Vattel, liv. III, §§ 168–70; * 2 Westlake (1st ed.), 76–79; Zorn, *op. cit.*, 171–74.

For examples of famous sieges and bombardments, see Calvo, P.-Fodéré, and Spaight. On the siege of Port Arthur, see Ariga, ch. 10; and Takahashi, Pt. II, ch. 6.

[50] H. R., 29. Cf. B. D., 19, 22. "To claim the benefit of the second clause of this article soldiers must be in uniform. Persons in balloons are not spies, even if engaged in observing the movements of the enemy. The examples given in this article are not intended to be exhaustive." Holland, No. 84.

Westlake (II, 80) observes that "the article leaves open the case of persons sent in balloons in order to gain information;" but he admits that the German treatment of spies (they were threatened with execution and actually imprisoned in fortresses) in 1870 was unjustifiable. For the strange declaration of Admiral Alexieff, soon after the outbreak of the Russo-Japanese War, that war correspondents, who may communicate news to the enemy by means of wireless telegraphy, shall be regarded as spies, see Hershey, *Russo-Japanese War*, 115 ff.; Higgins, *War and the Private Citizen*, 93; Lawrence, *War and Neutrality* (2d ed.), 83 ff.; 1 Rey, 368 ff.; and Smith and Sibley, 82–85.

"The essence of spying is false pretenses. . . . To establish the quality of a spy in the case of a soldier, there must be disguise; in the case of the civilian spy, disguise is not essential—the clandestine nature of the act is sufficient condemnation." Spaight, 203.

"Guides are not spies. If they are captured and are soldiers, they become prisoners of war. If they are civilians, an invading army might find it necessary to detain them; but subjects of the country who are caught guiding an invading army without being compelled to do so are liable to punishment for treason." 2 Westlake, 80.

" A spy taken in the act cannot be punished without previous trial " (Art. 30).[51]

" A spy who, after rejoining the army to which he belongs, is subsequently captured by the enemy, is treated as a prisoner of war, and incurs no responsibility for his previous acts of espionage " (Art. 31).[52]

6. NON-HOSTILE INTERCOURSE BETWEEN BELLIGERENTS

384. Flags of Truce.—" A person is considered as the bearer of a flag of truce who is authorized by one of the belligerents to enter into communications with the other, and who comes with a white flag. He has the right to inviolability, as have also the trumpeter, bugler or drummer,

---

[51] H. R., 30. Cf. B. D., 20. The trial is by court martial, and the punishment generally death.   Formerly spies were hanged; they are now usually shot. The severity of the punishment can hardly be justified, for it does not operate as an effective deterrent—the only ground upon which it is advocated.   The motives of the spy are immaterial and the practice is not necessarily dishonorable.

[52] H. R., 31.   Cf. B. D., 21.   Otherwise, he is not entitled to treatment as prisoner of war. "He may, of course, have incurred responsibility for acts of a different kind." Holland, No. 87.

On *Spies and Espionage*, see: * Adler, *Die Espionage* (1906); *American Instructions*, Arts. 88, 103–04; Ariga, *La guerre Russo-Japanaise* (1907), § 98; * Baker and Crocker, *op. cit.*, 218–31; Bluntschli, Arts. 628–31, 633, 639, 683; Bonfils or * 2 Fauchille, Nos. 1100–04; Bordwell, 291–92; 4 Calvo, §§ 2111–16; Despagnet, No. 539; Edmonds and Oppenheim, *op. cit.*, ch. 5; 3 Fiore, Nos. 1341, 1374–75, and *Int. Law Cod.*, Arts. 1492–97; 1 Guelle, *op. cit.*, 122–29; Hall, § 188; 1 Halleck (3d ed.), 571–74, and in 5 *A. J.* (1911), 590 ff.; * Holland, *War on Land*, 47–48; 2 Hyde, § 677; *Kriegsbrauch*, 30–31; Lawrence, § 199; Longuet, *op. cit.*, §§ 63–65; Lueder, in 4 Holtzendorff, 461 ff.; 3 F. de Martens, § 116; McKinney, in 12 *Ill. Law Rev.* (1918), 591–628; 7 Moore, *Digest*, § 1132; 3 Nys, 209 ff.; * 2 Oppenheim, §§ 159–61; Pillet, No. 57 and p. 472; 6 P.-Fodéré, Nos. 2765–68; 2 Rivier, 282–84; * 1 Rolin, Nos. 381–87; * Spaight, ch. 6; Takahashi, *Russo-Japanese War* (1908), Pt. II, ch. 5; Taylor, § 492; U. S. Army, *Rules of Land Warfare* (1914), ch. 6, Nos. 199–211; * 2 Westlake (1st ed.), 79–80; Wilson, §§ 110–41; Zorn, *op. cit.*, 174–95.

Distinct from spies are so-called "war traitors." See *infra*, note 4 on p. 615.   According to Oppenheim (II, § 160), Arnold was guilty of war treason rather than of espionage.   On the contrary, Capt. Hale was a spy. *Ibid.*, § 161. For the case of Miss Cavell, a British nurse who was condemned to death in Brussels in 1915 for aiding Belgian, British and French soldiers to escape, see 2 Garner, §§ 382–84; 2 Stowell and Munroe, 196–204; and 2 Whitlock, *Belgium*, chs. 7–11.   On "War Crimes" and "War Treason," see especially: 2 Garner, §§ 379–81; Hall (8th ed.), 498–99; 2 Hyde, § 178; 2 Oppenheim, §§ 162, 255 (which contains a list of such offenses), 257; Pillet, No. 142; Spaight, 333–35; and 2 Westlake (1st ed.), 90.   Cf. *infra*, note 4 on p. 615.

the flag bearer, and the interpreter who may accompany him " (Art. 32).[53]

" The Commander to whom a bearer of truce is sent is not obliged to receive him under all circumstances. He may take all steps necessary to prevent the bearer taking advantage of his mission to obtain information. In case of abuse, he has the right to detain the bearer temporarily " (Art. 33).[54]

" The bearer of a flag of truce loses his rights of inviolability if it is proved in a clear and incontestable manner that he has taken advantage of his privileged position to provoke or commit an act of treachery " (Art. 34).[55]

[53] H. R., 32. Cf. B. D., 43. All these persons enjoy the rights of inviolability, *i.e.*, "they may not be subjected to personal injury or detained as prisoners. It goes without saying that the bearer of a flag of truce is entitled to this immunity if he comes without attendants." Lawrence § 211. The immunity would probably also extend to his guide and any other necessary attendants not indicated in the text.

[54] H. R., 33. Cf. B. D., 44. The Hague Conference of 1899 suppressed the following paragraph of the Brussels Declaration: "He (the Commander) may equally declare beforehand that he will not receive bearers of flags of truce during a certain period. Envoys presenting themselves after such a notification from the side to which it has been given, forfeit their right to inviolability." It would seem, therefore, that such a declaration on the part of a Commander is no longer permissible. This is not, however, the view laid down in the British and German manuals, which still permit the practice. See Holland, No. 90; and *Kriegsbrauch*, 27, or Carpentier, *op. cit.*, 65. Cf. Spaight, 223.

The circumstances which excuse a Commander from receiving a bearer of a flag of truce are dictated by considerations of military necessity, as, *e.g.* in the midst of an assault or a pursuit, or during the execution of a secret movement.

In order to prevent the envoy from obtaining information, he is usually blindfolded while passing through the army or camp of the enemy. This is not regarded as in anywise humiliating. It is the duty of the Commander to take this or any other precautions which may be deemed necessary or advisable.

[55] H. R., 34. Cf. B. D., 45.

"If he purchases plans, or incites soldiers to desertion, or attempts to sketch defenses, he may be deprived of liberty, or perhaps, in extreme cases, executed as a spy." Lawrence, § 211. But it is only in the extremest cases that he may be so treated. If he gains important knowledge inadvertently or through the mere passive use of his senses, he is only subject to honorable and temporary detention. He is in honor bound not to seek information by illegitimate means, but he is under no obligation to refrain from reporting what he has seen and heard to his Commander. Spaight, 218–20.

For examples of the abuse of the white flag, see *Ibid.*, 224–25. See especially the translation of the Japanese Instructions from Ariga, pp. 226–27 For references on *Flags of Truce*, see 2 Oppenheim, p. 308 of 3d ed. or p. 377 of 4th ed.

The *Hague Regulations* are silent as to *Cartels*, *Passports*, *Safe-conducts* and *Safeguards*, which are usually discussed in this connection.

385. Capitulations.—"Capitulations agreed upon between the Contracting Parties must be in accordance with the rules of military honor. Once settled, they must be scrupulously observed by both parties " (Art. 35).[56]

Cartels are agreements between belligerents concluded for the purpose of regulating certain kinds of non-hostile intercourse, more especially the exchange of prisoners, the reception of flags of truce, and intercommunication by means of postal, telegraph, telephone, or railway facilities.

Passports, or *Safe-conducts*, are written permissions granted by a belligerent Commander to one or more enemy subjects to travel within the territory under his control. The terms seem to be convertible, though safe-conducts are sometimes held to apply only to a particular district or locality and to be issued for a particular purpose. The term "safe-conduct" is also applicable to the carriage of goods to a particular place. They are non-transferable and are revocable on grounds of military expediency. "They are only a matter of International Law when their granting of them has been arranged between the belligerents or their respective commanders, or between belligerents and neutral Powers. If they are granted without such an arrangement unilaterally on the part of one of the belligerents, they fall outside the scope of International Law." 2 Oppenheim, § 218. This is also the case with *Safeguards*.

A *Safeguard* is a "notification by a belligerent Commander that buildings or other property upon which the notification is usually posted up, are exempt from interference on the part of his troops. The term is also used to describe a guard, placed by a Commander to insure such exemption. 'Forcing a safeguard' is a serious offence." Holland, No. 101. "The object of a safeguard is generally to protect museums, historic monuments or the like; occasionally to show respect for a distinguished enemy, as in the case of the safeguard which McClellan placed over Mrs. R. E. Lee's residence, White House, Virginia, in 1862." Speight, 231.

"Soldiers employed as a safeguard are guaranteed against the application of the laws of war, and if the enemy occupies the locality it is usual to send them back to the army to which they belong; and in such a case their arms and baggage accompany them." *Ibid.*, cited from Pillet, 560; and Bonfils, No. 1247. For references on *Passports, Safe-conducts*, and *Safeguards*, see 2 Oppenheim, p. 306, of 3d ed. or p. 375 of 4th ed.

[56] H. R., 35. Cf. B. D., 46. "A capitulation is an agreement for the surrender of troops or places. A capitulation clearly in excess of the implied authority of the officer by whom it is made, when it is technically described as a mere 'sponsion,' as, for instance, that his troops shall never serve again against the same enemy, may be repudiated by his Government.

"It is an implied condition, in the capitulation of a place, that the capitulating force shall not destroy its fortifications or stores, *after* the conclusion of the agreement." Holland, No. 92.

The terms set forth in an agreement to capitulate may vary from absolute unconditional surrender to the grant of "all the honors of war," *i.e.* the right to depart armed with drums beating and colors flying. Usually troops which have surrendered become prisoners of war, and, unless otherwise agreed upon, a capitulating garrison must also be considered prisoners. "Usually, however, as an act of grace, the officers and functionaries of similar standing are allowed to return to their homes on giving their *parole d'honneur* and there are a few instances of the same privilege being extended to the rank and file." Speight, 255.

386. Armistices.—" An armistice suspends military operations by mutual agreement between the belligerent parties. If its duration is not fixed, the belligerent parties may resume operations at any time, provided always that the enemy is warned within the time agreed upon, in accordance with the terms of the armistice " (Art. 36).[57]

"The war *material* and public properties and moneys of a fortress or force which has capitulated pass to the conqueror. Private property, except arms, horses and military papers, are free from appropriation under Article IV of the *Reglement* (H. R., 4). Usually, officers are allowed to retain their swords, and when the capitulation is 'with the honors of war,' the men keep their arms as well." *Ibid.*

Stipulations or agreements in excess of powers are null and void. They are called *sponsions.* Such were the political provisions contained in the Capitulation agreed to by Generals Sherman and Johnston in 1865 to the effect that several State Governments were to be recognized, and that the people of the Confederacy were to be guaranteed their political rights and franchises as citizens of the Union. 5 Rhodes, *History of the U. S.*, 166.

"Stipulations affecting the political constitution or administration of a country or place, or making engagements with respect to its future independence, cannot be consented to even by an officer commanding in chief without the possession of special powers; and a subordinate commander cannot grant terms without reference to superior authority, under which the enemy gains any advantage more solid than permission to surrender with forms of honor." Hall § 194. Cited in part with approval, by 2 Westlake (1st ed.), 81. For references on *Capitulations,* see 1 Oppenheim, p. 314 of 3d ed., or pp. 382–83 of 4th ed.

[57] H. R., 36. Cf. B. D., 47. "There is no difference of meaning, according to British usage at least, between a 'truce,' and 'armistice,' and a 'suspension of arms.'" Holland, No. 93.

This statement is correct, at least from a legal standpoint, for the same rules apply in each case. It is customary, however, to distinguish between "armistices" or "truces" in the wider sense of these terms and a mere "suspension of arms," though even these terms are often used interchangeably in practice.

"Agreements for the temporary cessation of hostilities are called suspensions of arms when they are made for a passing and merely military end and take effect for a short time or within a limited space; and they are called truces or armistices when they are concluded for a longer term especially if they extend to the whole or a considerable portion of the forces of the belligerents, or have an entirely or partially political object." Hall, § 192. Hall adds in a note: "It is hardly possible to draw a clear line of distinction between suspensions of arms, truces, and armistices, though in their more marked forms they are readily to be distinguished." Cf. Lawrence, § 216. Oppenheim (II, §§ 231 ff.) distinguishes between (1) suspensions of arms, (2) general armistices, and (3) partial armistices.

An armistice is usually, though not necessarily, a precursor of peace. It need not apply to all the forces in the field of military operations, but whether general or partial, armistices or truces have nearly always an important political as well as military purpose. Mere suspensions of arms are generally concluded for such military purposes as collection of the wounded and burial of the dead;

" An armistice may be general or local.   The first suspends the military operations of the belligerent States
everywhere; the second, only those between certain frac-
tions of the belligerent armies and within a fixed radius "
(Art. 37).[58]

negotiations for surrender or capitulation; and the need for instructions from
superior authority.

In order to avoid misunderstanding and recrimination, it is very important
to fix upon a definite date (including the precise hour) for the beginning and
ending of an armistice.

[58] H. R., 37.   Cf. B. D., 48.   By "local" armistices are probably meant suspensions of arms and partial armistices.   "Every Commander has the power
to conclude a special, partial, or local armistice with repsect to the forces and
places under his immediate control, but a general armistice covering the whole
field of hostilities can be made only by the Commander in chief or diplomatic
representatives, . . .   Lawrence, § 216.

"An armistice should specify, as far as possible, the acts which are forbidden,
and those which are permitted, to the belligerents during its continuance."
Holland, No. 94.

The question of what is permissible during an armistice is much controverted.   There is general agreement that all actual hostilities should cease, but
that the belligerents may continue their preparations for offense and defense
"outside the line where the forces face each other. . . .   The majority of
writers, led by Vattel (III, § 245), maintain that in absence of special stipulations it is essentially implied in an armistice that within such line no alteration
of the *status quo* shall take place which the other party, were it not for the
armistice, could by application of force . . . prevent. . . .   On the other hand
a small [?] minority of writers, but led by Grotius (III, c. 21, § 7) and Pufendorf (VIII, § 7), assert that cessation of hostilities and of further advance only
are essentially implied in an armistice, all other acts such as strengthening of
positions by concentration of more troops on the spot, erection and strengthening of defenses, repairing of breaches of besieged fortresses, withdrawing of
troops, making of fresh batteries on the part of besiegers without advancing,
and the like being allowed."   2 Oppenheim, § 237.   Cf. Bonfils or 2 Fauchille,
Nos. 1254–56; Despagnet, No. 564; Hall, § 192; Lawrence, § 216; and Spaight,
235–39.

The latter or minority view is supported by such authorities as Bonfils,
Despagnet, Lawrence, Oppenheim, Pillet, and Spaight, and is more in accord
with modern practice.   To permit what is not expressly prohibited is, as
Spaight (p. 238) observes, "the only safe and satisfactory rule."   In his fourth
edition, Lawrence (§ 216) abandons the view expressed in former editions
(§ 237) that "during an armistice a belligerent may do in the actual theater of
war only such things as the enemy could not have prevented him from doing
at the moment when active hostilities ceased."   He now declares the "weight
of authority" to be in favor of this view, but the "weight of reasoning" and
"recent practice" to be on the side of the principle that the belligerent "may
do whatever is not forbidden expressly, except, of course, attack the enemy or
advance further into his territory."   It is strange that Westlake (I, 82) still
adheres to the older doctrine as laid down by Hall, § 192.

There is also a controversy respecting revictualling of a besieged place
during an armistice.   During the Franco-German War of 1870, Thiers claimed

" An armistice must be notified officially and in good time to the competent authorities and to the troops. Hostilities are suspended immediately after the notification, or on the date fixed " (Art. 38).[59]

" It rests with the Contracting Parties to settle, in the clauses of the armistice, what relation may be held, within the theater of war, *with and between the populations (avec les populations et entre elles)* " (Art. 39).[60]

that military usage permitted the revictualling of Paris on the ground that, "at the end of the armistice, each belligerent ought to find himself in the same situation as at the beginning." But the claim was denied by Bismarck "unless for some military equivalent." Spaight, 242. The question is one of those which should be specifically dealt with in the armistice. On the revictualling of a besieged place, see especially Hall, *op. cit.*,; and 7 P.-Fodéré, No. 2908.

[59] H. R., 38. Cf. B. D., 49. Each belligerent must notify his own troops. He is not bound to accept the notification from the enemy, "which may be a Greek gift." Spaight, 240. "Sometimes varying times are fixed for the commencement of the armistice, to allow of distant or isolated forces being notified without delaying the effect of the suspension in nearer places, and to prevent complications arising through such forces continuing hostilities should the armistice take effect from the date of signature. Hostilities cease from the moment of signing unless a later date is specified in the agreement. They need not cease during negotiations for an armistice; the negotiations must not be made the cover for a treacherous attack, but a belligerent is not bound to discontinue his operations because an armistice is being discussed. . . . Once the armistice is signed, if it is not to commence at a later date, any acts of war done in ignorance of it are null and void, and should be rectified as far as possible." *Ibid.*, 243–44.

In order to prevent hostilities during an armistice, it is customary to agree upon so-called lines of demarcation or a place of neutral ground between the opposing armies which must not be entered by the soldiers of either army. For examples, see Spaight, 244–45.

[60] H. R., 39. Cf. B. D. 50. Of the various translations consulted. Spaight's (p. 232) rendering of the phrase set in *italics* appears to be the only correct one. Nearly all the other versions translate the phrase *avec les populations et entre elles*, "with the populations and with each other." This is certainly both incorrect and misleading. "Of course, what is intended to be regulated is the intercourse of the population of the *occupied* territory with the population of the country still held by the enemy (in both cases nationals of the enemy State); and also between each belligerent force and the inhabitants of the localities held by the other." Spaight, 233 n.

"Article 39 lays down that the parties must settle what relations are to exist with and between the populations during an armistice. This provision is rendered necessary by the principle that an armistice suspends fighting but does not affect the state of war. . . . In the absence of a special provision, the invading belligerent's war rights as against the population continue unchanged. He can raise requisitions, billet his soldiers, demand services in kind and levy contributions, and his general martial law regulations remain in full force. And war conditions still hold good as regards the mutual relations

" Any serious violation of the armistice by one of the parties gives the other party the right to denounce it, and even, in case of urgency, to recommence hostilities immediately " (Art. 40).[61]

" A violation of the terms of the armistice by individuals acting on their own initiative, only gives the right of demanding the punishment of the offenders, and, if necessary, an indemnity for the losses sustained " (Art. 41).[62]

BIBLIOGRAPHY

The Laws of Land Warfare (for further references to the main treatises on Int. Law, see *supra*, notes).—Ariga, *La guerre Russo-Japonaise* (1908), *passim;* * Baker and Crocker, *The Laws of Land Warfare* (1916), and also * Baker and McKernan, *Laws of Warfare* (1919), *passim* (for citations from the authorities); Baty and Morgan, *War: Its Conduct and Legal Results* (1914); Boidin, *Les lois de la guerre et les deux conférences de la Haye* (1910); * Bordwell, *The Law of War between Belligerents* (1908), Pt. II; Carpentier, *Les lois de la guerre continentale* (1904); 2 Cobbett, *Leading Cases* (4th ed., 1924), Excursus I, 126–83; Edmonds and Oppenheim, *Land Warfare* (British Official Exposition); * 1 and 2 Garner, *Int. Law and the World War, passim;* 1 Guelle, *Précis des lois de la guerre* (1884), *passim;* Hershey, *Russo-Japanese War, passim,* particularly chs. 10–11; Higgins, *The Hague Peace Conferences* (1909), *passim,* particularly 207–80, and *War and the Private Citizen* (1912), chs. 1 and 3; * Holland, *The Laws of War on Land* (1908); Holls, *The Peace Conference at The*

of the inhabitants of the districts held by the two belligerents. In the absence of special conditions in the Protocol, the conclusion of the armistice does not free the inhabitants of the occupied territory from the obligation of holding no intercourse with the people in the other belligerent's zone of authority. They may be treated as spies or war traitors if they offend just as if hostilities continued." *Ibid.,* 245–46.

[61] H. R., 40. Cf. B. D., 51. As Oppenheim (II, § 239) points out: "Three rules may be formulated from this—(1) violations which are not serious do not even give the right to denounce an armistice; (2) serious violations do regularly empower the other party to denounce the armistice, but not, as a rule, to recommence hostilities at once without notice; (3) only in case of urgency is a party justified in recommencing hostilities without notice."

[62] H. R., 41. Cf. B. D., 52. It should be added that "a treaty of peace, after signature, but before ratification, operates as a general armistice." Holland, No. 99.

For Bibliographies on *Armistices,* see pp. 404–05 of the first edition of this work; and 2 Oppenheim, p. 320 of 3d ed., or pp. 387–88 of 4th ed. On the Armistice with Germany of Nov. 11, 1918, see 2 Hyde, § 647. For the views of leading authorities on Armistices, see Baker and Crocker, *Laws of Land Warfare,* 256 ff.

Hague (1900), ch. 4, pp. 134 ff.; * 2 Hyde, §§ 648–702; Jacomet, *Les lois de la guerre continentale* (publ. under the direction of the historical section of the Chief of Staff of the French army, 1913); *Kriegsbrauch im Landkriege* (publication of the German General Staff, 1902); Longuet, *Le droit actuel de la guerre terrestre* (1901); Morgan, *The German War Book* (1915), 51 ff.; Mérignhac, *Les lois et coutumes de la guerre sur terre* (1903), 8 *R. D. I. P.* (1901), 93 ff., and 14 *R. D. I. P.* (1907), 197 ff.; 2 Meurer, *Die Haager Friedens-konferenz, Das Kriegsrecht* (1907); * 2 Oppenheim, Pt. II, ch. 3; Pillet, *Les lois actuelles de la guerre* (1901); Pohl, *Deutsches Land Kriegsrecht* (1914); Renault, in 21 *R. D. I. P.* (1914), 468 ff.; Risley, *The Law of War* (1897), Pt. II; * 1 Rolin, *Le droit moderne de la guerre* (1920), *passim;* 1 Scott, *The Hague Peace Conferences* (1909), ch. 11; * Spaight, *War Rights on Land* (1911); 2 Stowell and Munro, *Int. Cases, passim;* Strupp, *Das. int. Landkriegsrecht* (1914); Takahashi, *Int. Law Applied to the Russo-Japanese War* (1908), *passim;* U. S. Army, *Rules of Land Warfare* (1914); * 2 Westlake, *War* (1907), ch. 4; and Zorn, *Das Kriegsrecht zu Lande* (1906).

For somewhat fuller Bibliographies, see 2 Fauchille, pp. 89–92; and 2 Oppenheim, Pt. II, ch. 3, *passim.*

CHAPTER XXVIII

WAR ON LAND (*Continued*)

THE LAW OF MILITARY OCCUPATION

387. Occupation Defined.—" Territory is considered occupied when it is actually placed under the authority of the hostile army. The occupation applies only to the territory where such authority is established and can be exercised " (Art. 42).[1]

[1] H. R., 42. Cf. B. D., 1. Like blockade at sea, occupation "in order to be binding must be effective," *i.e.* real and actually capable of enforcement. A mere proclamation or "paper" occupation will not suffice, though a formal notification may be taken as evidence of occupation.

"War law distinguishes between the invasion and the occupation of a hostile territory. . . . Invasion ripens into occupation when the national troops have been completely ousted from the invaded territory and the enemy has acquired control over it. . . . War law recognizes in the occupying belligerent a right of government which comes very near to the right of sovereignty." Spaight, 321.

Belligerent or military occupation should also be distinguished from conquest. Cf. *supra*, No. 171. The rights of a military occupant, however absolute, are in no wise those of a sovereign. They are merely provisional and are based upon military necessity. The occupant may not exact an oath of allegiance and his status is not even that of a temporary or substituted sovereign. The theory of the "temporary allegiance of the inhabitants" as laid down by some authorities (*e.g.* by Birkhimer, in *Military Government and Martial Law*, 2d ed., 1904) and our courts, is, therefore, erroneous.

Prior to the middle of the eighteenth century there was no distinction, either in theory or practice, between a mere occupation and a completed conquest. It was first made by Vattel (liv. III, § 197), but the full consequences of this distinction were not drawn before the appearance of Heffter's (§ 131) remarkable work in 1844.

On the older theory and practice, see especially: Hall, § 154; Lawrence, § 176; 2 Oppenheim, § 166; and 2 Westlake, (1st ed.), 85. The special student of this subject will find much illustrative material in the works of Lameire (see Bibliography at the close of this chapter).

There has been much controversy over the question as to what constitutes real or effective military occupation. It is now agreed that mere invasion is not occupation, and that constructive or presumptive occupation is insufficient. At the Brussels Conference of 1874, the smaller Powers stood up for the rights of the native inhabitants of an occupied district; the larger Powers (particularly Germany) championed the rights of the military occupant. The result was a compromise which is mainly in favor of the view of the smaller Powers and which certainly condemns some of the methods employed by the Germans

388. The Authority of the Occupant.—" The authority of the legitimate power having actually passed into the hands of the occupant, the latter shall take all steps in his power to reëstablish and insure, as far as possible, public order and safety (*l'ordre et la vie publics*) while respecting, unless absolutely prevented, the laws in force in the country " (Art. 43).[2]

during the Franco-German War of 1870. For a summary of the German theory and practice, see Spaight, 326–27.

Westlake (II, 84) agrees with Hall (§ 161, 8th ed., p. 576) that "a territory is occupied as soon as local resistance to the actual presence of an enemy has ceased, and continues to be occupied so long as the enemy's army is on the spot; or so long as it covers it, unless the operations of the national or an allied army, or local insurrection have reëstablished the public exercise of the legitimate sovereign authority." This is probably as good a statement of the law as can be found.

"But it would be unwise to interpret occupation too stringently as against the rights of the occupant. There is occupation so long as the occupant does actually exercise authority, to the exclusion of the legal government, in the area in question; and this he may do by means of flying columns quite as well as by maintaining garrisons. He must *police* the country and have it firmly under control. To establish an effective blockade there need not be a line of cruisers drawn across the mouth of a harbor, but there must be some force within striking distance, so as to make it difficult for any vessel to 'run the blockade' and gain entrance; and the same principle governs occupation. The whole population need not necessarily have been disarmed, nor is it essential that the occupation shall have been made known by proclamations. . . ." Spaight, 328.

[2] H. R., 43. Cf. B. D., 2–3. "The word 'safety' does not adequately render the *vie public* of the original, which describes the social and commercial life of the country." 2 Westlake, 84.

H. R., 43 "indicates that the law to be enforced by the occupant consists, first, of the territorial law in general, . . . and, secondly, of such variations of the territorial law as may be required by real necessity and are not expressly prohibited by any of the further rules which will come before us. Such variations will naturally be greatest in what concerns the relations of the communities and individuals within the district to the invading army and its followers. . . . Indeed, the entire relation between the invaders and the invaded, so far as it may fall within the criminal department whether by the intrinsic nature of the acts done or in consequence of the regulations made by the invaders, may be considered as taken out of the territorial law and referred to what is called martial law." 2 Westlake, 86.

"Martial law consists of such rules as are adopted, at his own discretion, by a commander-in-chief in the field, supplementing, or wholly or partially superseding the laws ordinarily in force in a given district. . . .

"'Martial law,' as thus defined, must be carefully distinghished from 'military law,' *i.e.* for the British Army, that fixed body of rules, now contained in the Army Act of 1881, as continued in force by the Army (Annual) Act, which is applicable in peace or in war, at home or abroad, to 'all persons subject to military law,' and to such persons only. [See *Manual of Military Law*, British War Office, 1914.]

389. Illegitimate Information.—"A belligerent is forbidden to force the population of occupied territory to

"In exercising his discretion in the administration of martial law, a commander should always be guided by the laws and customs of war, as generally accepted.

"Punishment under martial law should, as far as possible, be inflicted only after inquiry by a military court, convened for the purpose.

"Martial law applies to all persons, and to all property, within the district in which it is in force, irrespectively of the nationality of such persons, except in the case of diplomatic agents accredited by neutral States to the territorial sovereign." Holland, Nos. 4–7, 9. See also Nos. 8, 10–15. Cf. the articles cited from the *American Instructions*, in 7 Moore, *Digest*, § 1147.

It should also be noted that martial law is sometimes proclaimed and administered by the lawful sovereign in the face of invasion by a foreign foe or in times of riot or insurrection. But the distinction between "martial" and "military" law made by Birkhimer (Introduction and ch. 17) as applied to enemy and domestic territory respectively is not in accordance with usage. The terms are often used interchangeably, though military law is, properly speaking, the law for the government of the military forces themselves, whereas martial law is the law in accordance with which military authority is exercised in an occupied district. Both may exist in time of peace as well as war. On Military and Martial Law in the United States, see especially 2 Willoughby, *Const. Law of the U. S.*, chs. 61 and 62. For citations from the authorities on Martial Law, see Baker and McKernan, *Rules of Warfare* (1919), 412–76.

For examples of proclamations of martial law, see Spaight, 336–46. See especially the order of President McKinley, cited in 7 Moore, *Digest*, 1143, pp. 261–63.

"The practice of modern wars has been to leave existing laws in force, unless they are quite irreconcilable with a state of occupation, as recruiting laws are." Spaight, 356. This is held to apply particularly to civil and penal laws. "It may be necessary to vary the criminal, administrative, and other branches of Public Law, but hardly to interfere with the rules of Private Law, *e.g.* as to property, contracts, or family relations." Holland, No. 103. For violations of these principles by the German authorities in Belgium, see 2 Garner, ch. 24, §§ 373 ff.

In so far as the occupant does not exceed his powers, his acts are legally valid, and cannot be nullified by the succeeding Government. This is particularly true of judicial decisions (excepting sentences for "war treason") and of administrative acts which are not of a political nature or which do not operate beyond the period of occupation. "When the occupation comes to an end, . . . no redress can be had for what has been actually carried out, but nothing further can follow from the occupant's legislation." 2 Westlake, 87. See *Ibid.*, p. 88 for an exception.

"The occupant will often be glad to avail himself of the services of the native local authorities, so far as he can trust them, in case, and so long as, they are willing to continue in office." Holland, No. 103. Such has been the practice during recent wars and it is a usage which is obviously to the interest of both parties, but it is not obligatory. It applies especially to ordinary or local civil, financial, judicial, and police functionaries, not to important *political* officials. See especially: Bonfils or 2 Fauchille, Nos. 1164–1175; Bordwell, 307–10; and Spaight, 357–66. For fuller details, see Bray, *De l'occupation militaire* (1894), 178 ff.

*give information about the army of the other belligerent, or
about his means of defense* " (Art. 44).[3]

390. **Oath of Allegiance.**—" It is forbidden to compel
the population of occupied territory to take an oath [of
allegiance] to the hostile Power " (Art. 45).[4]

391. **Family Honor, etc. Respect for Private Property.**
—" Family honor and rights, the lives of individuals and
private property, as also religious convictions and freedom
of worship, must be respected.

" Private property cannot be confiscated " (Art. 46).[5]

[3] H. R., 44. Cf. B. D., 36. This virtually new article was added in 1907.
The old Article 44 (1899) was transferred to H. R., 23 h. Cf. *supra*, pp. 598 ff.
Holland (No. 104) still considers it doubtful whether even this additional article
forbids the use of "forced guides," but in this he is surely mistaken. Cf.
Higgins, 269; and Spaight, 368 ff. On the requisition of guides by Germany
during the World War, see 2 Garner, § 401.

It should, however, be pointed out that in signing the Convention, Germany,
Austria-Hungary, Japan, and Russia made reservations on the subject of this
article. But these Powers are bound by H. R., 23 h, which prohibits a belligerent to "compel the nationals of the hostile party to take part in operations
of war directed against the enemy."

[4] H. R., 45. Cf. B. D., 37. An *oath of neutrality* has, however, sometimes
been required. For an example during the Anglo-Boer War, see Spaight, 372.
Some publicists (*e.g.* Bordwell, 309) are of the opinion that an oath of fidelity
may be required of officials. No oath of obedience was required from the
Belgian judges by the German authorities in 1914. 2 Garner, 81 n.

"War crimes," whether committed by soldiers or by private individuals,
may be severely punished. For lists of such offenses, see 2 Oppenheim,
§§ 253, 255. The term "war treason" in this connection is objectionable. See
2 Westlake (1st ed.), 90. For a severe attack on the term "War Treason,"
see Morgan, in 2 *Grot. Soc.* (1917), 161 ff. For a defense of the term, see
Spaight, 333 ff. The term "war insurgent" would be preferable. Cf.
supra, note 52 on p. 604.

[5] H. R., 46. Cf. B. D., 38. This has been called the "Magna Charta of
War Law." Spaight, 374. But the article must unfortunately be read
"subject to military necessities."

"The freedom of worship secured by this article is obviously liable to restriction if it be used for the purpose of seditious propaganda or the encouragement of opposition to the occupant's Government." *Ibid.*, 375.

"By the prohibition of confiscation it is only meant that private property
cannot by any regulation of the invader be taken from its owner for no other
reason than that he is an enemy, not that it cannot be taken for military
necessity or by way of punishment for disobedience to a regulation or requisition." 2 Westlake, 92–93.

Though the practice of taking hostages from an occupied district (so as,
e.g. to insure the prompt payment of contributions and requisitions or as a
guarantee against insurrection) does not appear to be wholly obsolete, persons
detained as hostages cannot be put to death. The conduct of the Germans
during the Franco-German War in placing notable civilians upon the engines

392. **Pillage Forbidden.**—" Pillage is formally forbidden." [6]

393. **Taxes.**—" If, in the territory occupied, the occupant collects the taxes, dues, and tolls imposed for the benefit of the State, he shall do so, as far as possible, in accordance with the rules of assessment and incidence in force, and he shall in consequence be bound to defray the expenses of the administration of the occupied territory on the same scale as that to which the legitimate Government was bound (Art. 48)." [7]

of railway trains carrying German troops has been almost universally condemned.

On the "Taking of Hostages," see particularly: Bluntschli, No. 600; 2 Fauchille, No. 1146[1]; 2 Hyde, § 700; * 2 Oppenheim, § 258–59; * Spaight, 406–07, 465–70; and 2 Westlake (1st ed.), 102. For further references, see 2 Oppenheim, p. 350 of 3d ed.

During the World War the German military authorities in Belgium and Northern France resorted to a policy which was unprecedented in modern history—that of deporting large numbers of the civilian population from certain occupied districts either to Germany or to other occupied districts. This was apparently done for the purpose of supplying laborers to replace Germans for service in the army or in war industries. While "international conventions are silent on the question of the right of an invader to subject the conquered population to such treatment for the reason, no doubt, that it was not considered necessary in this age to prohibit formally a belligerent from resorting to a measure which the human conscience of the civilized world had so long condemned"; yet Art. 46 of the Hague Regulations expressly imposes upon belligerents the obligation to "respect family honor and rights," and Art. 43 requires the military occupant to "respect, unless absolutely prevented, the laws in force in the country." Art. 52 "likewise forbids the requisition of services except for the needs of the army of occupation." 2 Garner, § 429. Cf. Fenwick, 483–84; 2 Hyde, § 699; and 2 Oppenheim, § 170, p. 240.

On "Deportation of the Civilian Population from Occupied Territory," see particularly * 2 Garner, ch. 27 and the references therein cited. See especially: Basdavant, *Les déportations*, etc. (1917); Heuvel, in 24 *R. D. I. P.* (1917), 261 ff.; *The Deportation of Women and Girls from Lille* (1917); Passelecq, *Les déportations Belges* (1917); Toynbee, *The Belgian Deportations* (1917); and 2 Whitlock, *Belgium* (1919), chs. 38–45.

[6] H. R., 47.   Cf. B. D., 39, and H. R., 28.

"Pillage, or loot, was defined by General de Leer, at the Brussels Conference of 1874, as 'booty which is not permitted'; and Baron Jomini explained that 'there is a booty which is permissible on the field of battle—horses, etc. It is booty acquired at the expense of private property that the Commission means to prohibit.'" Holland, No. 107.

"As a term of modern law, it [pillage] may be defined as the unauthorized taking away of property, public or private, so that in order to appreciate the prohibition contained in this article we must know what taking away is authorized." 2 Westlake, 93. For this information, see *infra*, Nos. 394 ff.

[7] H. R., 48.   Cf. B. D., 5.   "The wording of this article was slightly altered

394. **Contributions.**—" If, besides the taxes referred to in the preceding Article, the occupant levies other money contributions in the occupied territory, this can only be for the needs of the army or of the administration of such territory (Art. 49)." [8]

" No general penalty, pecuniary or otherwise, can be inflicted on the population on account of individual acts for which it cannot be considered as collectively responsible (Art. 50)." [9]

from that of B. D., 5 in order not to seem to give the occupant a right to collect the taxes." 2 Westlake, (1st ed.), 94.

"The words 'imposed for the benefit of the State' are intended to exclude provincial and parochial taxes, or 'rates,' as they are called in England. The latter the occupant must not intercept; he can only supervise the expenditure of such revenue, to see that it is not devoted to a hostile purpose. The first charge upon the State revenue collected by the occupant is the cost of the local administration. When this has been provided for, any surplus that remains . . . may be devoted to the purposes of the occupant. . . .

No new taxes should be imposed by the occupant, for the imposition of taxation is, in modern times, an attribute of sovereignty. . . . But if the occupant cannot create taxes, he may levy contributions and requisitions, which serve the same end." Spaight, 378–79.

"As there would seldom be a law binding the legitimate Government to any scale of expense, the scale existing at the date of invasion would probably be understood as meant." 2 Westlake, 94.

[8] H. R., 49. Cf. B. D., 40 and 41. Contributions are not to be levied by way of securing riches or indemnity or for the purpose of inducing a stubborn enemy to submit. Even the official publication of the German General Chief of Staff (*Kriegsbrauch im Landkriege*, 63) only permits money contributions in the following cases:

(1) In places of taxes; (2) instead of requisitions in kind; (3) by way of penalty.

The exaction of money contributions has been defended on the ground that they sometimes make possible a more equitable distribution of military burdens than requisitions or contributions in kind. "It may sometimes be justifiable to levy a money contribution on one place, in order to spend it on the purchase of requisitions in another place. The burden of the war may thus be more equitably distributed, falling on the inhabitants generally, rather than upon individual owners of property which may be required." Holland, No. 109. Cf. Spaight, 387.

[9] H. R., 50. The usual mode of collective punishment is that of fines. "Of all the punishments used by war law, fines are the commonest and in many ways the most satisfactory and humane. They are, says the German *Kriegsbrauch im Landkriege* (p. 63), the most effective way of bringing a civil population to book. But they are a form of punishment which needs to be used with the greatest discretion and care. Bluntschli admits that the Germans stretched their war right of collective punishment altogether beyond its proper limit in 1870–71. A system of collective responsibility was established, which made not only the *commune* in which an offence was committed, but also that from which the delinquent came, liable for the offence. It is this practice which

" No contribution shall be collected except under a written order, and on the responsibility of a Commander in Chief.

" This collection shall only take place, as far as possible, in accordance with the rules in force for the assessment and incidence of taxes.

" For every contribution a receipt shall be given to the contributors (Art. 51)." [10]

395. **Requisitions.**—" Neither requisitions in kind nor services can be demanded from communities (*communes*) or inhabitants except for the needs of the army of occupation. They shall be in proportion to the resources of the country, and of such a nature as not to imply for the population any obligation to take part in military operations against their country.

" These requisitions and services shall only be demanded on the authority of the commander in the locality occupied.

" Supplies in kind shall, as far as possible, be paid for in cash; if not, their receipt shall be acknowledged, *and the*

the Hague Article aims at prohibiting; its intention is to confine collective punishment to such offences as the community has either committed or has allowed to be committed. Two important reservations to this general statement must, however, be made. First, the act punished need not necessarily be a violation of the laws and customs of war. . . . Any breach of the occupant's proclamations or martial law regulations may be punished in this way. Secondly, the provision of Article L does not prejudge the question of reprisals. Consequently, collective punishment may be inflicted in such circumstances as warrant the infliction of reprisals. There is nothing unfair in holding a town or village collectively responsible for damages done to railways, telegraphs, roads and bridges in the vicinity; it is the practice in all wars." Spaight, 408. See *Ibid.*, pp. 409–10 for examples. Cf. Bonfils, and 2 Fauchille, No. 1218; Bordwell, 316–17; Lawrence (7th ed.), 427–49; and 2 Westlake, (1st ed.), 95–96.

On the abuse of the system of "Collective Fines" and the theory of "Community Responsibility " by Germany during the World War, see * 2 Garner, ch. 26.

[10] H. R., 51. Cf. B. D., 41. "The receipt mentioned in this article is intended as evidence that money, goods, or services have been exacted, but implies, in itself, no promise to pay on the part of the occupant. He does not even thereby bind his Government, if victorious, to stipulate in the Treaty of Peace that the receipts shall be honored by the Government of the territory which has been under occupation. A Swiss proposal, making it obligatory to honor the receipts mentioned in this and the following article, was indeed deliberately rejected at the first Hague Conference.

"An occupant may, of course, incur a greater liability by the form which he chooses to give to his receipts, or under the terms of a general proclamation which he has issued." Holland, No. 111. Cf. Bordwell, 107 and 318.

payment of the sums due shall be made as soon as possible
(Art. 52)." [11]

[11] H. R., 52. Cf. B. D., 42. The ambiguous phrase set in italics was added in 1907. "The implication intended by those who would free the individual as far as possible from the burden of the war probably is that the amount is due from the belligerent giving the receipt, but the fact that the provision is not worded more definitely than it is, shows that the Governments were unwilling to agree to any absolute obligation in this regard and it is likely that whether the amounts indicated in these receipts are paid or not will be left to the Treaty of Peace or the action of the country in which the receiver was domiciled, as in the case of receipts given for war contributions." Bordwell, 319.

The original wording of this additional provision of H. R., 52 (1907) urged the payment of the receipts "as soon as possible, *even before the close of hostilities* so far as the military authority of the belligerent shall have the necessary pecuniary means in its power." 2 Westlake, 270. Cf. Higgins, 270; and Lémonon, 371. Westlake adds: "This addition leaves the matter much as it stood before. No obligation of the invading government to furnish its military authority with the means of satisfying the receipts is expressed. . . ."

But Spaight (p. 384) expresses a somewhat different view: "The last Hague Conference, in making the requisitioning belligerent responsible for payment, has struck a blow at the right of requisitioning—the extreme right recognized by jurists—which may change its whole nature, and complete a process which has already begun, of replacing requisitioning by the system of amicable purchase or at least by a right of preëmption. . . . The process is still far from complete. As war law stands to-day, contributions and requisitions remain as approved methods by which an invader can procure from the enemy's citizens such funds, goods, or services as his army needs—subject, in the case of requisitions, to his paying therefor either at the time or subsequently." Cf. *Ibid.*, 389 ff.

Supplies of any kind actually *needed by the army of occupation* are liable to requisition. They are usually collected through the medium of the local civil authorities. It should be strongly emphasized that they must not exceed the needs of the army or the resources of the country. In any case the native population should not be deprived of all means of subsistence and recovery.

"'Requisitions in kind' may, of course, relate not only to provisions, but also to horses, vehicles, clothing etc. The 'services' here intended are such as would be rendered by drivers, blacksmiths, and artisans and laborers of all kinds; as also by the occupiers of houses upon which troops are quartered." Holland, No. 112.

The "services" demanded must not be of such a nature as require participation in military operations. Holland (*op. cit.*) is of the opinion that "the 'operations of war' here intended would probably not comprise works at a distance from the scene of hostilities," but this is "probably" a mistaken view.

For the numerous and gross violations of the Hague Law pertaining to "Contributions, Requisitions, and Forced Labor" by Germany during the World War, see * 2 Garner, ch. 25. Particularly outrageous was the spoliation of Belgian and French factories and work-shops and the transportation of their tools and machinery to Germany. *Ibid.*, § 396.

On *Contributions and Requisitions*, see: Albrecht, *Requisitionen von neutralen Privateigentum*, etc. (1912); * Baker and Crocker, *op. cit.*, 357–92; Bonfils or * 2 Fauchille, Nos. 1207–26; Bordwell, 314–23; 4 Calvo, §§ 2231–84; Des-

396. **Appropriation of Movable State Property.**—" An army of occupation can only take possession of cash, funds, and realizable securities (*valeurs exigibles*) which are strictly the property of the State, depôts of arms, means of transport, stores and supplies, and, generally, all movable property of the State which is of a nature to be used for military operations.

" All appliances, whether on land, at sea, or in the air, adapted for the transmission of news or for the transport of persons or things (aside from cases governed by maritime law) depôts of arms, and, generally, all kinds of war material may be seized, even though they belong to private persons, but they must be restored and compensation arranged for at the peace (Art. 53)." [12]

pagnet, Nos. 586–88; Ferrand, *Des réquisition en matierè de droit int.* (1917); * 2 Garner, ch. 25; Gregory, *Contributions and Requisitions in War* (1915); 2 Guelle, *op. cit.*, 175–231; * Hall, § 140; Holland, *War on Land*, 55–57; 2 Hyde, §§ 692–93; Keller, *Requisition und Kontribution* (1898); *Kriegsbrauch*, 61–63; * Lawrence, § 180; Longuet, *op. cit.*, §§ 110–14; Lueder, in 4 Holtzendorff, 500–10; Mérignhac, *op. cit.*, Nos. 131–42; * 7 Moore, § 1149; 3 Nys, ch. 9; 2 Oppenheim, §§ 146–48; 2 Piédelièvre, Nos. 1024–41; Pillet, ch. 9; Pont, *Des requisitions militaires* (1905); 2 Rivier, 324–27; 1 Rolin, Nos. 497–520; * Spaight, ch. 12; Taylor, §§ 538–39; * 2 Westlake (1st ed.), 95–102. For further references, see 2 Fauchille, p. 281; and 2 Oppenheim, p. 207 of 3d ed.

[12] H. R., 53. Cf. B. D., 6. "It may be noted that considerable differences of opinion exist to the meaning of the purposely ambiguous term 'valeurs exigibles,' here translated 'realizable securities.' It has been officially translated into German by 'eintreibarre Forderungen.'" Holland, No. 113.

"All writers admit the occupants' right to appropriate and realize documents 'payable to bearer'; the difficulty is as to 'monies due' upon bills or checks requiring indorsement, or upon contract debts in any other form." Spaight, 411. The preponderant opinion at present seems to be that, while the occupant may appropriate *matured* debts, as also the interest on debts due the enemy State, he has no legal right to enforce the payment of debts which are not matured, or to indorse a check payable to order. See especially: Bonfils and 2 Fauchille, Nos. 1191–93; Despagnet, No. 602; Mérignhac, No. 149; Pillet, Nos. 170–71; Spaight, 411–12; and 2 Westlake, 103–04.

Among the *appliances*, etc., referred to in the second paragraph of H. R., 53 (1907), as liable to sequestration even though belonging to private persons, B. D., 6 (1874) had specifically named "railway plant, land telegraphs, steamers, and other ships." H. R., 53 (1899), added "telephones." In 1907 it was deemed best to proceed by way of general formula rather than specific enumeration.

It should be particularly noted that movable State property is liable to seizure and permanent appropriation, whereas private property (of the sort referred to in the second paragraph of the text), if seized, must be restored and compensation made to the owners at the conclusion of peace. This would seem to imply that receipts must be given

397. Submarine Cables.—" Submarine cables connecting an occupied territory with a neutral territory shall not be seized or destroyed except in case of absolute necessity. They must likewise be restored and compensation arranged for at the peace (Art. 54)." [13]

It should be added that "some forms of property, nominally belonging to the State, *e.g.* the funds of saving banks, may be in reality private property, under State management." Holland, No. 113. Any fund of which the State is mere custodian or trustee, such as State insurance or pension funds, would also be exempt.

On the "Seizure of Funds of Private Banks and Post-offices" by the Germans during the World War, see 2 Garner, § 399.

[13] H. R., 54 (1907). This wholly new article takes the place of H. R., 54 (1899), which dealt with railway material coming from neutral States and which now forms part of 5 H. C., 19. See *infra*, No. 456.

"There appears to be a general agreement that cables connecting neutral territory are inviolable, that cables connecting enemy territory may be cut anywhere except in neutral waters, and that under this Article, in case of necessity, cables connecting an occupied territory may be cut within such territory." Higgins, 271–72. Cf. Art. 5 of Stockton's *Naval War Code* (1902); The *Rules of the Institute of Int. Law on Submarine Cables* (1902); Hershey, *The Russo-Japanese War*, 122; and 2 Westlake, 280.

It has been a controverted question whether it is permissible for a belligerent to cut a cable connecting neutral with belligerent territory in the open sea. In 1902 the Institute of Int. Law (Scott, *Resolutions*, 162) laid it down that on the high sea such a cable "can only be cut if there is an effective blockade, and [then only] within the limits of the line of blockade, subject to the repair of the cable with the briefest possible delay."

This rule is criticized by Westlake (II, 1st ed., 281–283) as resting on compromise rather than principle, but the same criticism might be applied to many existing rules or usages of International Law.

The United States refused compensation to Great Britain as a matter of legal obligation for damages caused by the cutting of a British cable at Manila in 1898, but Chile recognized the duty of payment for a similar act in 1883. 2 Westlake, 283 n. The precedent set by Chile is the better one.

Reasoning from the analogy of H. R., 54, it would seem permissible to cut such a cable, subject to the duty of compensation, provided it is absolutely necessary from a military standpoint.

Soon after the outbreak of the World War the two German cables connecting Europe and America were cut near the Azores by the British. One British cable was cut by the Germans, but the other British cables connecting with America were not molested. At the Paris Peace Conference the question of the disposition of the German cables cut by the British was a subject of controversy. 2 Garner, § 560 and note on p. 410. By the Treaty of Versailles (Art. 244 and Annex VII), Germany renounced "on her own behalf and on behalf of her nationals in favor of the Principal Allied and Associated Powers all rights, titles or privileges of whatever nature" to a considerable number of submarine cables; but in so far as privately owned, their value was to be credited to the reparation account. There were similar provisions in some of the other Paris Treaties.

Mainly, I agree with Oppenheim (II, § 214 of 3d ed.) that "the question is

398. Immovable State Property.—" The occupying State shall regard itself only as administrator and usufructuary of the public buildings, immovable property, forests, and agricultural undertakings belonging to the hostile State and situated in the occupied country. It must protect the capital of these properties, and administer them according to the rules of usufruct (Art. 55)." [14]

399. Churches, Schools, Works of Art, etc.—" The property of communities (*communes*), that of institutions devoted to religious worship, charity and education, the

not settled how far belligerents are entitled to interfere with submarine telegraph cables."

On *Submarine Cables in Time of War*, see: 19 *Annuaire* (1902), 301–32: Bonfils, No. 1278; Cybichowski, in 17 *Z. I.* (1907), 160 ff.; Dupuis, in 10 *R. D. I. P.* (1903), 532–47; * 2 Fauchille, Nos. 1187, 1321; 2 Garner, § 560; Goffin, in 15 *Law Quar. Rev.* (1899), 145 ff.; * Higgins, 271–72; Holland, *War on Land*, 58, in 25 *J. I. P.* (1898), 648 ff.; * 2 Hyde, §§ 615 and 723; * Johannaud, *Les cables sousmarines* (1904); Kraemer, *Die unterseeischen Telegraphenkabel in Kriegszeiten* (1903); Latifi, *Effects of War on Property* (1909), 112–16; * Lawrence, § 230; 7 Moore, *Digest*, § 1176; Morse, in 25 *J. I. P.* (1898), 699 ff.; Perdrix, *Les cables sousmarines* (1902); 2 Oppenheim, § 214; * Phillipson, *Studies* (1908), 55–117; Rey, in 8 *R. D. I. P.* (1901), 681 ff.; * Rolland, *De la correspondance postale et télégraphique dans les relations int.* (1901); Roper, *Die Unterseekabel* (1910; * Scholtz, *Krieg und Seekabel* (1904); Spaight, 416–18; Stockton, *Outlines*, 351–53; * 2 Westlake (1st ed.) 280–83; Wilson, *Submarine Telegraphic Cables* (1901).

For fuller Bibliographies, see 2 Fauchille, pp. 414–15; and 2 Oppenheim, p. 297 of 3d ed.   For reference on *Submarine Cables in Time of Peace*, see *supra*, pp. 325–26 n.

[14] H. R., 55.   Cf. B. D., 7.   "A person is said, in continental systems of law, to be a 'usufructuary,' or to enjoy a 'usufruct,' in property in which he has an interest of a special kind, for life or some lesser period.   The 'rules of usufruct' may be shortly stated to be that the property subject to the right must be so used that its substance sustains no injury."   Holland, No. 115.

"There is no doubt that the occupant is entitled to get in the rents and dues of public immovables maturing during the occupation, and that his receipt for them will be a good discharge as against the enemy State. . . .

"In the case of forests, the right of a usufructuary is to cut the trees which regularly come to cutting during his tenancy; and this right the occupant has, subject to the condition that those who buy the timber from him must remove it during the continuance of the occupation, for the restored Government would not be bound to allow its removal.   And if the occupant sells timber which has not regularly come to cutting, the courts of the ligitimate Government will give no effect to any claims founded on such an illegal transaction." 2 Westlake, 106.

For the important case of the 15,000 oaks in the French State forests, sold by the Germans in 1870, see Latifi, *Effects of War on Property*, 19; Snow, *Cases*, 377; and Spaight, 367.   The original citation is 2 Dalloz (1872), 229.   On the "Cutting of Forests" by the Germans during the World War, see 2 Garner, § 398.

arts and sciences, even when belonging to the State, shall be treated as private property.

" All seizure, destruction, or intentional injury of such institutions, of historical monuments, or of works of art and science is forbidden and should be prosecuted (Art. 56)." [15]

400. Sanction of the Hague Regulations.—" A belligerent party which violates the provisions of the said Regulations shall, if the case demands, be held liable to make compensation. It shall be responsible for all acts committed by persons forming part of its armed forces." [16]

[15] H. R., 56. Cf. B. D., 8. "Roughly, one may give the gist of the Article as this: first, a Commander may, if necessary, turn a church into a hospital, but he may not auction the vestments or other church property to raise money. Secondly, he must not carry off or damage that class of property which may be generically described as 'starred by Baedecker.'" Spaight, 416. For "Destruction of Historic Monuments," etc., by Germany during the World War, see 1 Garner, ch. 18.

[16] 4 H. C., 1907, Art. 3. According to Art. 1 of the Hague Convention concerning the Laws and Customs of War on Land (4 H. C., 1899 and 1907), the Contracting Parties agreed "to issue to their armed land forces" instructions in conformity with the Hague Regulations. The provisions contained in these Regulations as also those in the Hague Convention are declared binding only between the Contracting Parties, and then only "if all the belligerents are parties to the Convention." Arts. 1 and 2.

The Convention was signed by all the States present at the Second Hague Conference, excepting China, Spain, and Nicaragua. The latter has since adhered. By July, 1911, it had been ratified by about half the States represented. But, in spite of their defects and frequent violation during the World War, the Hague Regulations still constitute the best code of the Laws of Land Warfare in existence.

This attempt made in 1907 to create a civil *sanction* for the Hague Regulations cannot be pronounced highly successful. It certainly did not prevent numerous violations, particularly by Germany during the World War; and, though the treaty of peace required compensation for "all damages done to the civilian population of the Allies and their property by the aggression of Germany by land, by sea, and from the air" (see *supra*, note 8 on p. 128), it can hardly be maintained that reparations were really assessed or collected on this basis. See *Report* of the Commission on the "Responsibility of the Authors of the War and on Enforcement of Penalties," in 14 *A. J.* (1920), 95 ff. Reprinted with the title "Violation of the Laws and Customs of War" by the Carnegie Endowment as Pamphlet No. 32 (1919). See pp. 144 f. or 17 f. for a list of violations.

In Arts. 228–30 of the Treaty of Versailles, Germany recognized the "right of the Allied and Associated Powers to bring before military tribunals persons accused of having committed acts in violation of the laws and customs of war"; and the German Government agreed to "hand over" all specified persons so accused, as also to furnish all necessary documents and information. The Paris Peace Conference thus set a new precedent looking forward to the

BIBLIOGRAPHY

Law of Military Occupation.—* Ariga, *La guerre sino-japonaise* (1896), chs. 12–13, and *La guerre russo-japonaise* (1908), chs. 12–18; * Baker and Crocker, *The Laws of Land Warfare* (for views of authorities), 292 ff.; Bentwich, in *Brit. Yr. Bk.* (1920–21), 139–48; Birkhimer, *Military Government and Martial Law* (1904), chs. 1–16; Bluntschli, Arts. 539–51, 644–63, 719–21; Bonfils or * 2 Fauchille, Nos. 1155–1236; Bordwell, Pt. II, chs. 8 and 9; Bray, *De l'occupation militaire* (1894); 4 Calvo, §§ 2166–93; Carpentier, *op. cit.*, 103–150; 2 Cobbett, *Leading Cases*, 165–75; Conner, *The Development of Belligerent Occupation* (Bulletin of State Univ. of Iowa, Apr. 6, 1912); Cybichowski, in 26 *Z. I.* (1916), 427 ff.; Depambour, *Des effets de l'occupation en temps de guerre* (1900); Despagnet, Nos. 566–602; Edmonds and Oppenheim, *Land Warfare*, Nos. 340–404; Fenwick, ch. 28, pp. 477–84; Féraud-Giraud, *Occupation militaire* (1881); 3 Fiore, Nos. 1454–81, and *Int. Law Cod.*, Arts. 1540–68; * 2 Garner, chs. 23–24; Grotius, III, cc. 5 and 6; 2 Guelle, *op. cit.*, 3–230; * Hall, Pt. III, chs. 3–4; 2 Halleck, chs. 21 and 33; Heffter (Geffcken), §§ 130–36;

establishment of the principle of individual responsibility and liability to punishment for criminal acts in violation of the laws and customs of war committed by members of the armed forces of one belligerent against the persons or property of the other belligerent. See especially: * 2 Garner, ch. 38 and the extensive literature on this subject cited in note on p. 472. *Ibid.*, in 14 *A. J.* (1920), 70 ff.

In accordance with Art. 228, lists of accused Germans were prepared by the principal Allied Governments, and a final extensive list, including many of the leading German military and naval officers, was compiled and presented to the German Government on Feb. 3, 1920. But the Allies accepted a German proposal that the accused be tried before the Supreme Court of the Empire in Leipzig.

In pursuance of this decision certain cases were selected for submission to the Court at Leipzig, and on May 7, 1920 an abridged list containing 45 names was handed to the German Government. To this list the British Government contributed seven names. Finally, there were twelve trials. These trials are said to have been fairly conducted, but the sentences imposed were very lenient from the British point of view, ranging from six months to four years imprisonment. However, barren the results may appear, the Leipzig Trials may be said to have set a precedent for the recognition of the principle that individual atrocities committed during a war may be punished after its cessation.

On the *Leipzig Trials*, see 16 *A. J.* (1922), 628–40; and Mullins, *The Leipzig Trials* (1921).

The German trials are not absolutely without precedent. On Nov. 10, 1865, Capt. Wirz was hanged after his trial and condemnation to death by a U. S. military commission because of his alleged responsibility for the "horrors" of Andersonville prison during the American Civil War. 5 Rhodes, *History of the United States*, 493, 495–96, 503, 506.

On the "Trial of Henry Wirz," see Exec. Doc. of H. of R., 2d sess., 40th Cong. (1867–68).

* Higgins, 245–55, 258 ff.; * Holland, *War on Land*, 52–59; * 2 Hyde, §§ 688–702; Jacomet, *Les lois de la guerre continental* (1913); *Kriegsbrauch im Landkriege*, 45–67; Latifi, *Effects of War on Property*, ch. 1; Lameire, *Théorie et pratique de la conquête dans l'ancien droit* (1902), *Les militaire occupations en Italie pendant les guerres de Louis XIV* (1903), *Les occupations militaires en Espagne pendant les guerres de l'ancien droit* (1905), and *Les occupations militaires de l'île de Minorque* (1908); * Lawrence, §§ 176–80; Longuet, *op. cit.*, §§ 110–33; Lönig, in 4 and 5 *R. D. I.* (1872 and 1873), 622 ff. and 69 ff.; Lorriat, *De la nature de l'occupation de guerre* (1903); 2 J. de Louter, § 46; Lueder, in 4 Holtzendorff, 468–524; Magoon, *Law of Civil Government under Military Occupation* (2d ed., 1900), *passim*; 3 F. de Martens, §§ 117–20; Mérignhac, *op. cit.*, Nos. 118–53; 1 Meurer, *Die Haagerfriedenskonferenz, Das Kriesrecht* (1907), 206 ff., and *Die völkerr. Stellung der vom Feind besetzen Gebiete* (1915); * 7 Moore, *Digest*, §§ 1143–55; * 3 Nys, chs. 6–9, 12, and *L'occupation de guerre* (1919); * 2 Oppenheim, §§ 133–48, 166–72, and in 33 *Law Quar. Rev.* (1917), 363 ff.; 2 Piédelièvre, Nos. 971–1046; Pillet, chs. 9–10, and pp. 477–84; 7 P.-Fodéré, Nos. 2939–3064; 2 Rivier, 299–327; Rolin, *Des occupations militaires* (1913); * 1 Rolin, Nos. 487–520; Rolin-Jacquemyns, in 2 and 3 *R. D. I.* (1870 and 1871), 666 ff. and 311 ff.; Ruzé, in 16 *R. D. I. P.* (1909), 134 ff.; * Scott, *Cases*, 694–732; Snow, *Cases*, 364–85; * Spaight, chs. 11–12; Stier-Somlo, in 8 *Z. V.* (1914), 581 ff.; 2 Stowell and Munro, *Int. Cases*, 146 ff.; Strupp, *Das int. Landkriegsrecht*, 93–126; * Takahashi, *Int. Law as Applied to the Russo-Japanese War*, Pt. II, chs. 9–10; Taylor, §§ 529–44, 568–79; 2 Twiss, §§ 62–71; Ullmann, §§ 183–84; Vattel, liv. III, §§ 73, 160–65, 197–200; Visscher, in 34 *Law Quar. Rev.* (1918), 72–81; Wehberg, *Capture in War on Land and Sea* (1911), chs. 1–4; * 2 Westlake (1st ed.), 83–107; Wheaton, §§ 346, 352–55; * Wilson, chs. 14 and 18; Zorn, *Das Kriegerecht zu Lande* (1906), 207–315.

For other bibliographies, see 2 Fauchille, pp. 213 f.; 2 Hyde, p. 361; and 2 Oppenheim, p. 230 of 3d ed.

CHAPTER XXIX

THE LAWS OF MARITIME WARFARE

401. The Aims and Means of Maritime Warfare.—The general purpose of warfare at sea is the same as that on land, viz. the overpowering or reduction of the enemy's forces with the least possible expenditure of life and property, but the specific aims are somewhat different.[1] The most important of these are: the defeat or destruction of the enemy's warships; the destruction of fortifications, arsenals, and military establishments on the enemy coast; the blockade [2] of particular ports or portions of such coast; the prevention of the carriage of contraband to the enemy, and various forms of unneutral service; the support or defeat of certain land operations, such as the landing of troops; and the defense and protection of the home coasts and of commerce.[3]

The chief means through which it is sought to realize these aims are: the seizure or destruction of enemy vessels; the seizure and appropriation of enemy goods on such vessels; the bombardment of fortified places on the enemy coast; the cutting of submarine cables connecting enemy territory;[4] blockade; ruses; espionage; and the capture of neutral vessels engaged in unneutral service or the carriage of contraband goods.

[1] On the *Aims and Means of Maritime Warfare*, see especially: Bonfils and Fauchille, No. 1268; * 2 Oppenheim, §§ 173–75; and 8 P.-Fodéré, Nos. 3066–68.

[2] Because of their bearing on the rights and duties of neutrals, the subjects of blockade and contraband will be dealt with in Part VI under the head of "Neutrality."

[3] "The special objects of maritime warfare are: the capture or destruction of the military and naval forces of the enemy; of his fortifications, arsenals, dry docks, and dockyards; of his various military and naval establishments, and of his maritime commerce; to prevent his procuring war material from neutral sources; to aid and assist military operations on land; and to protect and defend the national territory, property, and sea-borne commerce." Art. 1 of Stockton's Naval War Code.(officially promulgated in 1900, but withdrawn in 1904).

[4] On the rules governing the cutting of submarine cables, see *supra*, No. 397.

Though there is a great similarity between the rules of land and maritime warfare, there are also important differences. Consequently, a separate treatment of the subject is advisable. Unfortunately, we have no Hague Code to guide us in this enterprise as in the case of warfare on land; but we have fragments of such a Code in several of the Hague Conventions which have never been supplanted.[5]

402. The Theater of Naval Warfare.—"The area of maritime warfare comprises the high seas or other waters that are under no jurisdiction, and the territorial waters of belligerents. Neither hostilities nor any belligerent rights, such as that of visitation and search, shall be exercised in the territorial waters of neutral States."[6]

1. Lawful Belligerents in Maritime Warfare

403. Privateering and Conversion of Merchantmen into Warships.—"Privateering is and remains abolished."[7]

[5] Among the wishes expressed by the Hague Conference of 1907, was one that "the preparation of regulations relative to the laws and customs of naval warfare should figure in the program of the next Conference, and that in any case, the Powers may apply, as far as possible, to war by sea the principles of the Convention relative to the Laws and Customs of War on Land." Higgins, 69, or Scott, *Texts*, etc., 139. In may therefore be taken for granted that the laws of land warfare apply to the omissions in this chapter.

[6] Art. 5, § 1, of S. C. (Stockton's Code). On the "Theater of Maritime War," see especially 2 Fauchille, Nos. 1269–72. It may be recalled in this connection that the Suez Canal and certain rivers (the Congo, Niger, and a portion of the Danube) are neutralized. In this respect the Panama Canal may be said to be partially neutralized. See *supra*, No. 201.

[7] D. P. (Declaration of Paris of 1856), Art. 1. Higgins, 2. Cf. *supra*, No. 73.

Privateers have been defined as "vessels owned and manned by private persons, but empowered by a commission from the State, called a Letter of Marque, to carry on hostilities." Lawrence, § 200. They correspond somewhat to irregular troops in land warfare.

In 1870 Prussia attempted to create the first "Volunteer Navy," which was, however, to be placed under naval discipline and command during the Franco-German War. France protested against this plan as a disguised form of privateering, but the British Law Officers to whom the matter was referred gave it as their opinion that there was a "substantial difference" between such a scheme and privateering. In 1877–1878 Russia accepted the offer of a patriotic association to create a Volunteer Fleet, to be placed under the Command of naval officers and the crews subjected to military discipline. Great Britain and the United States have adopted a somewhat different system. They have entered into arrangements with great steamship lines, whereby, in return for sub-

The laws, rights, and duties of maritime warfare apply
not only to public warships, but to all properly commissioned merchantmen, fulfilling the following conditions:

(1) That of being " placed under the direct authority,
immediate control, and responsibility of the Power whose
flag " they fly.[8]

sidies, these companies agree to let or sell certain vessels to the Government at
a fixed price on short notice, and to build new vessels according to certain
specifications.   France, Japan, and other Powers have made similar arrangements.

On *Privateering* (now a subject of mere historical interest) and *Volunteer
Fleets*, see especially: Atherley-Jones, 315–21, 541–42, 544–45; Bluntschli,
Art. 670; Boeck, *De la propriété privée ennemie sous pavillon ennemie* (1882),
passim; Bonfils, Nos. 1362–95; 4 Calvo, §§ 2297 ff.; Despagnet, Nos. 638–39;
Dupuis, *Le droit de la guerre maritime* (1899 and 1911), ch. 3;   * 2 Fauchille,
Nos. 1273–1312; 3 Fiore, Nos. 1445–53, and *Droit Int. Cod.*, Nos. 1634–43; Geffcken in 17 *R. D. I.*, 369 ff.; * Hall, §§ 180–81; 2 Halleck (3d ed.), 108–23; * Higgins, 312–14; 2 Hyde, § 704; * Lawrence, §§ 200–01; Martin and Baker, *Laws of
Maritime Warfare* (1918), 471–85; * 7 Moore, *Digest*, §§ 1215 ff., 2 Oppenheim,
§§ 83–84;   Perels, *Manuel*, § 34;   8 P.-Fodéré.   Nos. 3092–3103;   2 Rivier, 253–59;   Stark, in 8 Columbia Univ. *Studies*, 11–163, No. 3;   Taylor,
§§ 438–39, 497; Wheaton, § 358, and Dana's note 173;   Wilson, §§ 133–34;
Woolsey, §§ 127–29.   For a fuller bibliography, see 2 Fauchille, pp. 357–58.

    [8] 7 H. C. (Hague Convention of 1907 on the Conversion of Merchant Ships
into Warships), Art. 1.   Higgins, 309, or Scott, *Texts*, etc., 247.   "The first
article presents a principle which is, so to speak, the corollary of the Declaration
of Paris, and has for its object to give every guarantee against a return more or
less disguised to privateering."   M. Fromageot, in 1 *Actes et doc. de la deuxième
conf.*, 244.   Cited by 1 Scott, 573.   This may, indeed, be said to be the purpose
of the Convention as a whole.

    The immediate cause of the insertion of this subject in the program of the
Second Hague Conference was a sensational incident of the Russo-Japanese
War.   In July, 1904, the world was electrified by the news that the *Peterburg*
and *Smolensk*, two cruisers belonging to the Russian Volunteer Fleet in the
Black Sea, had passed through the Straits and the Suez Canal disguised as
merchantmen, and were searching and seizing neutral vessels in the Red Sea.
There was great excitement in England when it was learned that the *Peterburg*
had captured the British Mail Steamer *Malacca* on a charge of carrying contraband, and was bringing her to Port Said through the Suez Canal as a prize.

    The British Government demanded the immediate release of the *Malacca*
and protested on the grounds that its alleged contraband consisted of government stores consigned to Hong Kong, and that merchantmen (such as the
Peterburg and *Smolensk* were assumed to be) could not lawfully exercise the
rights of visit and search.   Otherwise it would have been necessary to have
assumed a violation of the series of international treaties by which the Straits
were closed to warships.   For Russia had "either broken a long line of solemn
international compacts by sending commissioned warships through the Bosphorus and the Dardanelles in the guise of merchantmen, or she violated one
of the most cardinal principles of International Law by permitting or authorizing merchant vessels to exercise the strictly belligerent right of search on the
high seas."   Hershey, *Russo-Japanese War*, 151.

" (2) Merchant ships converted into warships must bear the external marks which distinguish the warships of their nationality.

" (3) The Commander must be in the service of the State and duly commissioned by the proper authorities. His name must figure on the list of the officers of the military fleet.

" (4) The crew must be subject to the rules of military discipline.

" (5) Every merchant ship converted into a warship is bound to observe, in its operations, the laws and customs of war.

" (6) A belligerent who converts a merchant ship must, as soon as possible, announce such conversion in the list of the ships of its military fleet." [9]

After a perfunctory or *pro forma* examination of the *Malacca's* cargo, she was released on July 27th, and the Russian Government agreed to instruct the officers of her Volunteer Navy to refrain from interference with neutral shipping in the future on the ground that "the present status of the Volunteer Fleet was not sufficiently well-defined, according to International Law, to render further searches and seizures advisable." But the *Smolensk* visited a British vessel as late as August 21, and the British Government was eventually forced to convey to the commanders of these cruisers the orders of the Russian Government.

On the case of the *Malacca*, see Hershey, *op. cit.*, 138–42, 148–52; Lawrence, *War and Neutrality*, etc. (2d ed.), 202–16; and Smith and Sibley, *Russo-Japanese War*, Pt. I, ch. 2.

[9] 7 H. C. (1907), 1–6. These rules lay down the conditions regulating the use of Auxiliary or Volunteer Vessels or Fleets. Cf. *supra*, note 7.

The Convention was signed by all the Powers mentioned in the Final Act except the United States, China, Dominica, Nicaragua, and Uruguay. Turkey signed under a general reservation. The United States withheld her signature of the same reason that she has never adhered in formal terms to the Declaration of Paris, viz. that our statesmen desire to see the abolition of the capture of unoffending private enemy property coupled with that of privateering. But there can be no doubt of our observance of these rules in practice. By July, 1911, the Convention had been ratified by 18 States.

Neither at The Hague nor at the London Conference of 1909 was it found possible to agree upon the important question of the place where the conversion of merchantmen may be effected. Great Britain, Japan, and the United States urged that such conversion should only be permitted in the ports of the country to which such vessels belonged, or in ports under military occupation. But the delegates of Germany, Russia, and France contended that it was permissible on the high seas, though M. Renault of France admitted it must not take place in neutral ports or neutral territorial waters. The Italian delegation proposed as a compromise that "ships which leave the territorial waters of their country after the opening of hostilities cannot change their character either on the high seas or in the territorial waters of another State."

2. Restrictions on Capture in Maritime Warfare

The Hague Conference of 1907 placed the following restrictions on the exercise of the right of capture in maritime war:

404. Inviolability of Postal Correspondence.—" The postal correspondence of neutrals or belligerents, whether official or private in character, found on board a neutral or enemy ship is inviolable. If the ship is detained, the correspondence is forwarded by the captor with the least possible delay.

" The provisions of the preceding paragraph do not apply, in case of violation of blockade, to correspondence destined for or proceeding from a blockaded port (Art. 1).

" The inviolability of postal correspondence does not exempt a neutral mail ship from the laws and customs of maritime war respecting neutral merchant ships in general.

This proposition failed to secure the support of the leading Continental Powers.

An attempt to decide the period of duration of the conversion met with a similar fate, as also Lord Reay's attempt on behalf of Great Britain to divide warships into two classes: (*a*) fighting ships (*vaisseaux de combat*); and (*b*) auxiliary vessels (*vaisseux auxiliares*), such as colliers, repairing vessels, supply ships, dispatch boats, transports, etc. He proposed the assimilation of auxiliary vessels to the status of fighting ships. But he met with the sound objection that the principles of "unneutral service" were involved in his proposition.

It would certainly seem that the conversion of merchantmen in neutral ports or waters is a gross violation of neutrality and that, if conversion on the high seas be permitted, it should be limited to vessels which have left their national ports before the outbreak of hostilities or to vessels captured from the enemy. Vessels once converted into warships should continue to bear that character during the whole period of the war.

The public character of a vessel is proved by her flag, her commission, and the presence of the proper naval officer in command. The word of the commander is usually regarded as conclusive evidence of her public character, though this can hardly be regarded as an absolute rule.

On the *Conversion of Merchantmen into Warships*, see especially: 1 and 3 *Actes et doc. de la deuxième conf., passim*; particularly I, 232–45 (from Fromageot's *Report*); Atherley-Jones, 538–42; Bonfils, No. 1395; Bustamente y Sirven, *La séconde conférence de la paix*, ch. 14; Despagnet, 641–43; * Dupuis, *Le droit de la guerre maritime* (1911), ch. 3; * 2 Fauchille, Nos. 1304–12; Hall, *Law of Naval Warfare* (1921), 49–53; * Higgins, 308–21, and *War and the Private Citizen* (1912), ch. 4; 2 Hyde, §§ 706–08; * Lawrence, § 202; Lémonon, *La seconde conférence de la paix* (1908), 611–22; Martin and Baker, *Laws of Maritime Warfare* (1918) 541–62; Naval War College, *Int. Law Situations* (1912), 158 ff.; * 1 Scott, 568–76; 2 Westlake (1st ed.), 304–06; Wilson, in 2 *A. J.* (1908), 271–75, and *Int. Law*, § 134.

The ship, however, may not be searched except when absolutely necessary, and then only with as much consideration and expedition as possible (Art. 2)." [10]

[10] 11 H. C. (1907), Arts. 1–2. Cf. Art. 20 of S. C. (Stockton's *Code*).

Herr Kriege (of Germany) deserves the credit for these proposals, which mark a distinct step in advance of the preëxisting law, since the rules on this subject were not clearly defined.

Within recent times there has developed a usage of exempting neutral mail steamers, not only from condemnation, but from visit, search, and capture as well. But such immunity was regarded as a matter of pure "grace and favor." In the future such vessels must not even be searched unless in case of absolute necessity.

It should be particularly noted that such limited exemption from search extends only to *neutral* mail steamers. On the other hand, all correspondence, whether found on board a neutral or *enemy* ship, is to be held inviolable unless it is "destined for or proceeding from an enemy port."

Belligerents are today less averse to the exemption of ordinary postal correspondence from search than formerly because they prefer to communicate by means of the telephone or wireless telegraphy. "The advantage to be drawn by belligerents from the control of the postal service therefore bears no proportion to the prejudicial effect of that control on legitimate commerce." Herr Kriege, in 3 *Actes et doc. de la deuxième conf.*, 861. The exemption, of course, does not include boats bearing special or noxious dispatches.

Russia was the only important State which did not sign this Convention. The explanation is probably to be found in the case of the *Prinz Heinrich* during the Russo-Japanese War. On this case, see Hershey, *Russo-Japanese War*, 139–40, 155–56; and Lawrence, *War and Neutrality*, etc. (2d ed.), 109 ff. The pioneer in this matter of giving exemption to postal correspondence was the United States. See especially: Atherley-Jones, 302; Dana, note 228 to Wheaton (Dana's ed.), 659–61; Hall, § 252; Hall, J. A., *Law of Naval Warfare* (1921), 90–94; Hershey, *op. cit.*, 154 n.; and Lawrence, *op. cit.*, 189, or *Principles*, p. 442 of 7th ed.

During the first year of the World War the British and French Governments did not interfere with the transportation of mails on neutral vessels. It was only after the Germans began to exploit the postal service, more particularly the parcels post, for military purposes and the importation of supplies that these Governments changed their policy and insisted upon their rights of search and seizure. There followed protests from the United States and other neutral governments. The United States, *e.g.*, did not deny the right to seize and detain postal parcels containing contraband destined for enemy use, but objected to the manner in which the belligerent right of search and detention was exercised, *i.e.*, to the bringing of neutral vessels into British ports for purposes of search and censorship. But the Allied Governments justified their action on ground of absolute necessity. In view of the danger from submarines and the German practice of submarining merchant vessels (including mail steamers) without warning or preliminary search, this was not an unreasonable contention.

On the "Interference with Mails . . . on Neutral Vessels" during the World War, see especially * 2 Garner, ch. 24, §§ 532–37. See also Allin, in 1 *Minn. Law Rev.* (1917), 293 ff.; Hall, *Law of Naval Warfare* (1921), 90–94; Hershey, in 10 *A. J.* (1916) 580–84; 2 Hyde, § 730; 2 Oppenheim, § 191.

On the general subject of the so-called *Inviolability of Postal Correspondence*,

405. **Exemption of Fishing Boats, etc.**—" Boats used exclusively in coast fisheries or in petty local navigation are exempt from capture, as also are their appliances, rigging, tackle, and cargo.

" This exemption ceases as soon as they participate in any manner of hostilities.

" The Contracting Parties bind themselves not to take advantage of the harmless character of said boats in order to use them for military purposes while preserving their peaceful appearance (Art. 3).

" Ships charged with religious, scientific, or philanthropic missions are equally exempt from capture " (Art. 4).[11]

see: Allin, in 1 *Minn. Law Rev.* (1917), 293 ff.; Atherley-Jones, 302 ff.; Baldwin, in 2 *A. J.* (1908), 307 ff.; Benton, *Spanish-American War*, 131, 168 ff.; Bonfils, No. 1354; Boeck, Nos. 207–208; Dupuis (1911), No. 112; 2 Fauchille, No. 1395[6]; * 2 Garner, ch. 34; * Hall, § 252; * Hershey, *Russo-Japanese War*, 153–56, and 10 *A. J.* (1916), 580–84; * Higgins, 401–02; * 2 Hyde, §§ 729–30; * Lawrence, *War and Neutrality*, ch. 9, pp. 185–200, and *Principles*, § 182, p. 442 of 7th ed.; Lémonon, *op. cit.*, 698–701; Martin and Baker, *Laws of Maritime War* (1918), 492–509; 2 Oppenheim, §§ 191, 411; Scott's *Cases* (for the case of the *Panama*), 756, and in 2 *Hague Conferences*, 614 ff.; Taylor, § 668; 2 Westlake (1st ed.), 264–65, 308; * Wheaton (Dana's ed.), note 228, pp. 659–61.

[11] 11 H. C. (1907), 3–4. Art. 3 safeguards and extends an immunity which has been generally observed, either as a matter of law or comity, and was not unknown even in the Middle Ages. It does not apply to deep-sea fishing. "Nor has the exemption been extended to ships or vessels employed on the high seas in taking whales or seals, or cod or other fish which are not brought fresh to market, but are salted or otherwise cured and made a regular article of commerce." Justice Gray, in the *Paquete Habana* and the *Lola*, 195 U. S. 677. For abridged reports of this decision, see Evans, 602 or Scott, *Cases*, 12.

The phrase "coast fisheries" has been left undefined. There can be no doubt that the term "coast" is not limited to that of the fishermen's own country, but includes any coast where they have a right to fish. On the other hand, the phrase "petty local navigation" does not include coasting steamers. Higgins, 404.

The exemption of vessels engaged in religious, scientific, or philanthropic missions (Art. 4) dates back to the eighteenth century. It must be held subject to the same conditions as those laid down for fishing boats. They should be furnished with safe-conducts. On the subject matter of these articles, see especially: Baldwin, in 2 *A. J.* (1908), 309–11; Benton, *Spanish American War*, 174–75; Bordwell, 222; Dupuis, (1911), Nos. 106–11; * Gray, Justice, in *Paquete Habana*, *op. cit.*; * Hall § 148; * Lawrence, § 182; Lémonon, *op. cit.*, 702–09; 2 Oppenheim, §§ 186–87; Taylor, § 546; * 2 Westlake (1st ed.), 133–38, 310.

For a very complete review of the authorities and precedents, see the opinion of Justice Gray in the case of the *Paquete Habana*, 175 U. S. Rep. 677, in which our Supreme Court held that "it is an established rule of International Law that coast fishing vessels, with their implements and supplies, cargoes and

3. REGULATIONS REGARDING THE CREWS OF ENEMY MERCHANT SHIPS CAPTURED BY A BELLIGERENT

406. Officers and Crew who are Nationals of a Neutral State.—" When an enemy merchant ship is captured by a belligerent, such of its crew as are nationals of a neutral State are not made prisoners of war.

" The same rule applies in the case of the captain and officers, likewise nationals of a neutral State, if they promise formally in writing not to serve on an enemy ship while the war lasts (Art. 5)."

407. When they are Nationals of the Enemy State.— " The captain, officers, and members of the crew, when nationals of the enemy State, are not made prisoners of war, on condition that they bind themselves, on the faith of a formal written promise, not to undertake, while hostilities last, any service connected with the operations of the war (Art. 6)."

" The names of the individuals retaining their liberty under the conditions laid down in Article 5, paragraph 2, and in Article 6, are notified by the belligerent captor to the other belligerent. The latter is forbidden knowingly to employ the said individuals (Art. 7)."

" The provisions of the three preceding Articles do not apply to ships taking part in hostilities (Art. 8)." [12]

crews, unarmed and honestly pursuing their lawful calling of catching and bringing in fresh fish, are exempt from capture as prize of war."

Other exemptions from capture are: (1) cartel ships, *i.e.* vessels used in the exchange of prisoners or other special services for the belligerents in accordance with agreements between them; (2) enemy ships protected by licenses so long as the terms of such permits are strictly observed; and (3) hospital ships, on which, see *infra*, 434 ff.

It has sometimes been claimed that vessels shipwrecked on an enemy's coast or driven into an enemy's port by stress of weather are exempt from capture, but there is no international obligation to this effect.

[12] 11 H. C., Arts. 5–8.   These Articles " mark an important alteration in the law of maritime warfare.   It is, apart from this Convention, a well-recognized rule of International Law that the officers and crews of captured enemy merchantmen are prisoners of war.   The practice was justified on the ground that it deprived the enemy of men who might render service on board ships which might be used as transports or for purposes of supply, or in the fighting navy. The rule was generally applied without regard to the nationality of the persons captured. . . .

" The Convention makes a definite and important change in a long-established rule of International Law, and confirms other usages which had been

4. Treatment of the Sick, Wounded, and Shipwrecked in Naval Warfare [13]

The Hague Convention of 1907 for the Adaptation of the Principles of the Geneva Convention [14] to Maritime War contains the following provisions relating to the treatment of the sick, wounded and shipwrecked in naval warfare.

408. Military Hospital Ships.—" Military hospital ships, that is to say, ships constructed or adapted by States specially and solely with the view of aiding the sick, wounded, and shipwrecked, the names of which have been communicated to the belligerent Powers at the commencement or during the course of hostilities, and in any case before they are employed, shall be respected, and cannot be captured while hostilities last " (Art. 1). [15]

almost universally observed in regard to a class of persons who take no part in hostilities, who are for the most part poor men, and whose imprisonment, while inflicting extreme hardship on their families, did not afford a corresponding gain to their captors. The distinction between combatants and non-combatants which has for many years been recognized in the case of land warfare has now become recognized also in naval warfare." Higgins, 405–06.

Articles 5–8 would of course not apply in case of resistance or an unprovoked attack on the part of the merchantman. The Convention of which they form a part was signed by all the Powers represented at the Second Hague Conference excepting China, Montenegro, Nicaragua, and Russia.

On the subject matter of these Articles, see Baldwin, in 2 *A. J.* (1908), 311; Bordwell, 222–23; Bustamante y Sirven, ch. 19; * Hall, note on pp. 485–86 of 8th ed.; Hall, J. A., *Laws of Naval Warfare* 122–23; * Higgins, 405–06; * Lawrence, § 149; Lémonon, 710–14; * 2 Oppenheim, §§ 85, 201; 1 Scott, 618–20; 2 Westlake (1st ed.), 130, 309.

During the World War, these Articles do not seem to have been observed. Of course they were not technically binding and did not form a part of customary law. According to Oppenheim (II, § 85), "all the belligerents interned the enemy crews of captured enemy vessels." The Germans of course violated them in their practice of submarine warfare.

[13] The treatment of prisoners taken in naval warfare is omitted as being substantially (though not formally) covered by H. R., 4–20, on Land Warfare. Cf. *supra*, Nos. 355 ff. See especially Arts. 10 and 11 of Stockton's Naval War Code. Cf. Holland, *Prize Law*, No. 240.

[14] *I.e.* the Geneva Convention of 1906. See *supra*, Nos. 369 ff. The Convention of 1907 is in form a new Convention, but it is really an amendment and enlargement of that of 1899 which had adapted the principles of the Geneva Convention of 1864 to maritime warfare. In consists, however, of twenty-eight articles instead of fourteen. The Additional Geneva Articles of 1868 served as a *modus vivendi* between 1868 and 1899, but they were never ratified. For the text of the "Additional Articles," see: Higgins, 14–17; Scott, *Text*, etc., 378–81; or Whittuck, 6–9.

[15] " These ships, moreover, are not on the same footing as warships as regards their stay in neutral port."

409. **Hospital Ships equipped by Private Individuals or Relief Societies.**—" Hospital ships equipped wholly or in part at the expense of private individuals or officially recognized relief societies shall be likewise respected and exempt from capture, if the belligerent Power to whom they belong has given them an official commission and has notified their names to the hostile Power at the commencement of or during hostilities, and in any case before they are employed " (Art. 2).[16]

410. **Hospital Ships equipped in Neutral Countries.**—" Hospital ships equipped wholly or in part at the cost of private individuals or officially recognized societies of neutral countries, shall be respected and exempt from capture, *on condition that they are placed under the control of one of the belligerents, with the previous consent of their own Government and with the authorization of the belligerent himself, and that the latter* has notified their name *to his adversary* at the commencement of or during hostilities, and in any case, before they are employed " (Art. 3).[17]

411. **Duties of Hospital Ships.**—" The ships mentioned in Articles 1, 2, and 3 shall afford relief and assistance to the wounded, sick, and shipwrecked of the belligerents without distinction of nationality. The Governments undertake not to use these ships for any military purpose. These vessels must in no wise hamper the movements of the combatants. During and after an engagement they will act at their own risk and peril."

3 H. C. (1899) and 10 H. C. (1907), 1. This article merely provides for the communication of the names of such vessels to belligerent powers; but, as Bordwell (pp. 267–68) points out: "The names of the hospital ships may also well be sent to neutral as well as to belligerent powers, in view of the exemption secured to them by this article from the rule applicable to warships in neutral ports."

16 *Ibid.*, 2. "These ships must be provided with a document from the proper authorities declaring that the vessels have been under their control while fitting out and on final departure."

"The privileges of this article were extended to ships equipped by individuals as well as those equipped by officially recognized societies, in order to encourage the placing of craft such as private yachts, in the medical service." Bordwell, 268.

17 *Ibid.*, 3. The italicized portion of this article was added in 1907. The Convention of 1899 had failed to regulate the relations between neutral hospital ships and belligerents. This defect is now remedied. Cf. G. C. (1906), 11.

412. **Rights of Belligerents over Hospital Ships.**—" The belligerents shall have the right to control and search them; they may decline their assistance, order them off, impose upon them a certain course, and put a commissioner on board; they may even detain them if serious circumstances require it.

" As far as possible the belligerents shall enter in the log book of the hospital ships the orders which they give them " (Art. 4).[18]

413. **Distinguishing Signs of Hospital Ships.**—" Military hospital ships shall be distinguished by being painted white outside with a horizontal band of green about a meter and a half in breadth.

" The ships mentioned in Articles 2 and 3 shall be distinguished by being painted white outside with a horizontal band of red about a meter and a half in breadth.

" The boats of the ships above mentioned, as also small craft which may be used for hospital work, shall be distinguished by similar painting.

" All hospital ships shall make themselves known by hoisting, with their national flag, the white flag with a red cross provided by the Geneva Convention, *and further, if they belong to a neutral State, by flying at the mainmast the national flag of the belligerent under whose control they are placed* " (Art. 5).[19]

414. **Sick Wards and Material on Hospital Ships.**—" In the case of a fight on board a warship, the sick wards shall be respected and spared as far as possible.

" These sick wards and the material belonging to them

---

[18] 3 H. C. (1899) and 10 H. C. (1907), 4.   Cf. Add. Articles, 10 and 13.

[19] *Ibid.*, 5.   Cf. G. C. (1906), 21 and 22.   Persia reserved the right to use the Lion and Sun instead of the Red Cross.

The Conference of 1907 added the following paragraphs to Article 5 (which are relegated to this note as being of minor importance):

"Hospital ships which under the terms of Article 4 are detained by the enemy must haul down the national flag of the belligerent to whom they belong.

"The ships and boats above mentioned which wish to insure by night the freedom from interference to which they are entitled, must, subject to the assent of the belligerent they are accompanying, take the necessary measures to render their special painting sufficiently plain."

"The distinguishing signs referred to in Article 5 can only be used, whether in time of peace or war, for protecting or indicating the ships therein mentioned" (Art. 6).

remain subject to the laws of war; they cannot, however, be used for any purpose other than that for which they were originally intended, so long as they are required for the wounded and sick.

" The Commander into whose power they have fallen may, however, in case of serious military necessity, apply them to other purposes, after first seeing that the wounded and sick on board are properly provided for " (Art. 7).

415. **Rights of the Staff of Such Vessels.**—" The protection to which hospital ships and sick wards are entitled ceases if they are used to commit acts harmful to the enemy.

" The fact of the staff of the said ships and sick wards being armed for maintaining order and defending the wounded and sick, and the presence of wireless telegraphy apparatus on board, are not sufficient reasons for withdrawing protection " (Art. 8).

416. **Private Vessels with Sick and Wounded on Board.** —" Belligerents may appeal to the charity of the commanders of neutral merchantmen, yachts, or boats to take on board and tend the sick and wounded.

" Vessels responding to this appeal, as also the vessels which have of their own accord rescued wounded, sick, or shipwrecked men, shall enjoy special protection and certain immunities. In no case can they be captured for having such persons on board; but, subject to any undertaking that may have been given to them, they remain liable to capture for any violations of neutrality they may have committed " (Art. 9).

417. **Rights and Duties of the Staff, etc., of Captured Vessels.**—" The religious, medical, and hospital staff of any captured ship is inviolable, and its members cannot be made prisoners of war. On leaving the ship they take with them the objects and surgical instruments which are their private property.

" This staff shall continue to discharge its duties while necessary, and can afterwards leave when the Commander-in-chief considers it possible.

" The belligerents must guarantee to the said staff that has fallen into their hands the same allowances and the same pay as are granted to the persons holding the same rank in their own navy " (Art. 10).

" Sailors and soldiers and other persons officially attached to fleets or armies who are taken on board when sick or wounded, whatever their nationality, shall be respected and tended by the captors " (Art. 11).

418. **Sick, Wounded, or Shipwrecked on Board Military Hospital Ships.**—" Any warship belonging to a belligerent may demand the surrender of the wounded, sick, or shipwrecked who are on board military hospital ships, hospital ships belonging to relief societies or to private individuals, merchant ships, yachts and boats, whatever the nationality of such vessels " (Art. 12).[20]

419. **On Board Neutral Warships.**—" If wounded, sick or shipwrecked persons are taken on board a neutral warship every possible precaution must be taken that they do not again take part in the operations of war " (Art. 13).[21]

420. **Treatment of Shipwrecked, Wounded, or Sick.**— " The shipwrecked, wounded, or sick of one of the belligerents who fall into the power of the other belligerent are prisoners of war. The captor must decide, according to circumstances, whether to keep them, send them to a port of his own country, to a neutral port, or even to an

---

[20] 10 H. C. (1907), 12.   This article was wholly new in 1907.   The Hague Conference of 1899 failed to agree upon a plan for the proper disposition of sick, wounded, or shipwrecked belligerents rescued by neutral vessels.   See Holls, 127–30, 500–06.

The British took a different view of their international obligations in the famous case of the *Deerhound* which arose during our Civil War.   "The owner of this yacht, acting at the request of Captain Winslow of the *Kearsarge*, helped to rescue the officers and crew of the *Alabama* upon the occasion of the latter's sinking at the hands of the *Kearsarge*.   To the surprise of Captain Winslow, the *Deerhound*, after picking up a certain number of men, largely officers (including Captain Semmes) of the *Alabama*, hastily and surreptitiously steamed off with its precious cargo to Southhampton. . . ."   Hershey, *Russo-Japanese War*, 77 n.   For the facts of the case, see *Claims against Great Britain*, III, 261–308 (1st sess., 41st Cong., 1869).   For a somewhat different view of the law and the facts, see Bernard, *Neutrality*, etc., 429–30.

[21] *Ibid.*, 13.   Inferentially, we may conclude that wounded, sick, or shipwrecked persons taken on board a neutral warship are not to be given up, but that they should be detained, interned, or paroled as in the analogous case of an army which has been forced to retreat into neutral territory.   This was the course followed in a case which arose during the Russo-Japanese War.   See Hershey, 75–77; and Lawrence, *War and Neutrality*, ch. 4.

enemy port.   In this last case, prisoners thus repatriated, cannot serve again while the war lasts " (Art. 14).[22]

421. **Those landed at a Neutral Port.**—" The ship-wrecked, wounded, or sick, who are landed at a neutral port with the consent of the local authorities, must, in default of an arrangement to the contrary between the neutral State and the belligerent States, be guarded by the neutral State so as to prevent them from again taking part in the operations of the war " (Art. 15).[23]

422. **Duties of Belligerents after each Engagement.**— " After each engagement, the two belligerents shall, so far as military interests permit, take measures to search for the shipwrecked, wounded, and sick, and protect them, as also the dead, against pillage and ill treatment.

" They shall see that the burial, whether by land or sea, or cremation of the dead shall be preceded by a careful examination of the corpses " (Art. 16).

" Each belligerent shall send, as early as possible, to the authorities of their country, navy or army, the military marks or documents of identity found on the dead and a list of the names of the sick and wounded picked up by him.

" The belligerents shall keep each other informed as to internments and transfers, as also admissions into hospitals and deaths which have occurred among the sick and wounded in their hands.   They shall collect all the objects of personal use, valuables, letters, etc., which are found in the captured ships, or which have been left by the wounded or sick who died in hospital, in order to have them for-warded to the persons concerned by the authorities of their own country " (Art. 17).[24]

[22] 10 H. C. (1907), 14, and 3 H. C. (1899), 9.   Bordwell (p. 275) considers the last paragraph of this article objectionable as amounting to compulsory parole.

[23] "The expenses of tending them in hospital and interning them shall be borne by the State to which the shipwrecked, wounded, or sick persons belong.

[24] 10 H. C. (1907), 17.   Cf. G. C. (1906), 4.   This article and the preceding one were wholly new in 1907.

The remaining articles of the Tenth Convention are of minor importance so far as the substance of International Law is concerned.

Art. 18 makes the usual reservation that "the provisions of the present Convention do not apply except between Contracting Parties, and only if all the belligerents are parties to the Convention."

Art. 19 provides that the "Commanders-in-chief of the belligerent fleets

5. Submarine Mines

One of the most fearful weapons of modern naval warfare is that of submarine mines. The Hague Conference of 1907 adopted the highly inadequate rules given below

shall arrange the details for carrying out the preceding articles as well as for cases not provided for, in accordance with the instructions of their respective Governments and in conformity with the general principles of the present Convention.

In Art. 20 the Signatory Powers agree "to take the necessary measures to instruct their naval forces, especially the personnel protected, in the provisions of the present Convention, and to bring them to the notice of the public."

In Art. 21 the Signatory Powers "undertake to enact or to propose to their Legislatures, if their criminal laws are inadequate, the measures necessary for checking in time of war individual acts of pillage and ill treatment in respect to the wounded and sick in the fleet, as well as for punishing, as an unjustifiable adoption of naval or military marks mentioned in Article 5 by vessels not protected by the present Convention." They also agree to "communicate to each other, through the Netherland Government, the enactments for preventing such acts at the latest within five years of the ratification of the present Convention."

"In the case of operations of war between the land and sea forces of belligerents, the provisions of the present Convention are only applicable to the forces on board ship (Art. 22)."

The Tenth Convention of 1907 was signed by all the Powers represented at the Conference except Nicaragua. China made a reservation of Art. 21, and Great Britain of Arts. 6 and 21. Only about half the Powers had, however, ratified the Convention by July, 1911.

In her submarine warfare during the World War, Germany seems to have utterly disregarded the Hague and Geneva Conventions relating to naval warfare, if, indeed, she did not deliberately and systematically violate them. On these "Violations," see especially * 1 Garner, ch. 20, §§ 319–27. See also Hall, *Law of Naval Warfare* (1921), ch. 4, pp. 99–115; 2 Hyde, § 782; and 2 Oppenheim, § 205.

The main British Prize Case was that of the *Ophelia* (1916), a German so-called hospital ship which was condemned on the grounds that the equipment of the vessel was wholly inadequate for hospital purposes, that she carried apparatus and appliances for signalling, and that, at the time of her capture, she was engaged in scouting. On the case of the *Ophelia*, see 1 Garner, § 327; and Scott, *Cases*, 772 n. Cf. the case of the *Orel* (Sasebo Prize Ct., 1905), a Russian hospital ship which was captured and condemned by the Japanese Prize Court during the Russo-Japanese War for having performed, while serving as a hospital ship, certain services to the Russian fleet that amounted to use for military purposes. This case is reported in Scott, *Cases*, 776. On the case of the *Orel*, see Higgins, *War and the Private Citizen* (1912), 74–76; and Takahashi, *Russo-Japanese War* (1908), 620–25.

On the *Hague Convention and Maritime Warfare*, see: Bonfils, No. 1280 [1-9]; * Bordwell, 267–77; Dupuis, *Le droit de la guerre mar.* (1911), Nos. 82–105; 2 Fauchille, No. 1395[28-43]; Fauchille et Politis, *Manuel de la Croix-Rouge* (1908), 122 ff.; Hall, § 130, pp. 478 ff. of 8th ed.; * Hall, J. A., *Law of Naval Warfare* (1921), ch. 4, pp. 99–115; * Higgins, 358–94, and *War and the Private Citizen* (1912), ch. 2; Holls, *The Peace Conference at the Hague* (1900), ch. 4

designed for the restriction and regulation of the laying of automatic submarine contact mines,[25] but it is hard to say whether or to what extent they are still in force.[26]

423. The Hague Prohibitions.—" It is forbidden:

" 1. To lay unanchored automatic contact mines, unless they be so constructed as to become harmless one hour at most after the person who laid them shall have lost control over them.

" 2. To lay anchored automatic contact mines which do not become harmless as soon as they have broken loose from their moorings.

" 3. To use torpedoes which do not become harmless when they have missed their mark " (Art. 1).[27]

" 4. It is forbidden to lay automatic contact mines off the coasts and ports of the enemy, with the *sole* object of intercepting commercial navigation (Art. 2).[28]

and App. C, pp. 497 ff.; 2 Hyde, §§ 769, 777–82; Lawrence, § 165, pp. 388 ff. of 7th ed.; Lémonon, *op. cit.*, 526–54; Martin and Baker, *op. cit.*, 563–96; 2 Oppenheim, §§ 204–09; * Renault, in 2 *A. J.* (1908), 295–306; 1 Scott, ch. 13, pp. 599–614; Takahashi, *op. cit.*, Pt. III, ch. 4; 2 Westlake (1st ed.), 275–79. For further references, see 2 Fauchille, p. 502 and 2 Oppenheim, p. 283 of 3d ed.

[25] The desirability of legislation on this subject was made evident by the menace to neutral life and property which existed during the Russo-Japanese War. For the main facts, see Hershey, *Russo-Japanese War*, 124 ff.; and Lawrence, *War and Neutrality* (2d ed.), 93 ff.

At the Hague Conference of 1907, the Chinese delegate stated that "the Chinese Government is even to-day obliged to furnish vessels engaged in coastal navigation with special apparatus to raise and destroy floating mines which are found, not only in the open sea, but even in its territorial waters. In spite of the precautions which have been taken, a very considerable number of coasting vessels, fishing boats, junks and sampans have been lost with all hands without the details of the disasters being known to the western world. It is calculated that from five to six hundred of our countrymen engaged in their peaceful occupations have there met a cruel death in consequence of these dangerous engines of war." Higgins, 329.

[26] See below, note 31.

[27] 8 H. C. (1907), 1. It would have been better to have accepted the British proposal to forbid the use of unanchored automatic submarine contact mines altogether. There seems to be no means of effective control over them.

"There is no certainty that floating mines, even if anchored at first, will not get loose, nor even much probability that a large percentage will not get loose." 2 Westlake (1st ed.), 322.

[28] *Ibid.*, 2. It will be readily seen that the insertion of the word *sole* renders this article largely illusory. All attempts to limit the area within which mines might be laid failed. Great Britain had proposed that they might only be laid in territorial or belligerent waters, excepting that "before fortified

424. Necessary Precautions.—" When anchored automatic contact mines are employed, every possible precaution must be taken for the security of peaceful navigation.

" The belligerents undertake to provide, as far as possible, that these mines become harmless after a limited time has elapsed, and, should they cease to be under surveillance, to notify the danger zones as soon as military exigencies permit, by a notice to mariners, which must also be communicated to the Governments through the diplomatic channel " (Art. 3).[29]

425. Duties of Neutral Powers.—" Neutral Powers which lay automatic mines off their coasts must observe the same rules and take the same precautions as are imposed on belligerents.

" The neutral Powers must give notice to mariners in advance of the places where automatic contact mines have been laid. This notice must be communicated at once to the Governments through the diplomatic channel " (Art. 4).[30]

426. Duties of Belligerents at the Close of the War.— " At the close of the war, the Contracting Powers undertake to do their utmost to remove the mines which they have laid, each Power removing its own mines.

" As regards anchored automatic contact mines laid by one of the belligerents off the coast of the other, their position must be notified to the other party by the Power which laid them, and each Power must proceed with the

military ports, however, this zone may be extended to a distance of ten miles from shore batteries, provided, etc." Higgins, 329–30.

[29] *Ibid.*, 3. This article is also largely illusory. There is no definite time limit within which anchored mines are to become harmless, and the phrase "military exigencies" may cover a multitude of sins of omission.

Arts. 1 and 3 were further weakened by the following provisions: "The Contracting Powers which do not at present own perfected mines of the description contemplated in the present Convention, and which, consequently, could not at present carry out the rules laid down in Articles 1 and 3, undertake to convert the *material* of their mines as soon as possible so as to bring it into conformity with the foregoing requirements" (Art. 6).

[30] *Ibid.*, 4. The limitation of the marine league imposed upon neutrals in the first draft Convention was suppressed. A Dutch proposal prohibiting mine laying in straits connecting the high seas was also suppressed, though the right of innocent passage is generally conceded.

least possible delay to remove the mines in its own waters "
(Art. 5).[31]

[31] *Ibid.*, 5. The Convention was concluded for seven years (Art. 11) and
to continue in force after the expiration of this period unless denounced.

The main defect of this Convention is its failure to prohibit the laying of
mines, floating or anchored, on the high seas with such exceptions as might be
deemed absolutely necessary. Belligerents should be forbidden to place mines
off the coasts of the enemy for all purposes of commercial blockade, though
they might well be permitted to use them for the protection of their own coasts
even beyond the three-mile limit in certain cases.

The Convention was clearly inadequate as a means of protecting neutral
shipping, and neutrals have a right to such protection, at least on the high
seas—the common international highway—and in narrow straits through which
they have the right of innocent passage.

The Convention was signed or ratified by all the Powers represented at the
Conference excepting China, Spain, Montenegro, Portugal, Russia, and
Sweden. France and Germany made reservations as to Article 2. In signing
the Convention, Great Britain made the following general reservation: "The
mere fact that the said Convention does not prohibit a particular act or proceeding must not be held to debar His Britannic Majesty's Government from
contesting its legitimacy." Turkey also made certain reservations respecting
Arts. 1, 3, and 6.

The Institute of International Law at Ghent, in 1906, and again in Paris, in
1910, condemned the laying of mines, whether fixed or floating, on the high
seas. But in other respects the rules of the Institute were not much in advance
of those of the Hague Conference. Art. 4 was, however, an improvement.
It interdicted the blockade of the ports or coasts of the enemy by means of
automatic contact mines, though it authorized them for naval or military, *i.e.*
strategic, ends. For a good criticism of the rules of the Institute, see Dupuis,
in 17 *R. D. I. P.* (1910), 597 ff.

For the rules of the Institute, see Scott, *Resolutions*, 167–68, 178–79.

On the *Eighth Hague Convention* and *Submarine Mines* generally, see:
* 21 *Annuaire* (1906), 88 ff. and 330 ff.; 22 *Annuaire* (1908), 222–27; 23
Annuaire (1910), 180 ff. and 440 ff.; 24 *Annuaire* (1911), 301 f.; 26 *Annuaire*
(1913), 227 ff.; Barclay, *Problems*, etc. (1907), 59 ff., 158; Boidin, *Les lois de la
guerre*, etc. (1908), 216–35; Bonfils, No. 1273; Bordwell, 280–82; Bustamante
y Sirven, *op. cit.*, ch. 13; Dupuis (1911), ch. 13, and in 14, 16, and 17 *R. D. I. P.*
(1907, 1909, and 1910), 381–86, 162–63, and 597–607 respectively; 2 Fauchille,
Nos. 1316[2-10]; Hall, *Law of Naval Warfare*, 60–69; * Hershey, *Russo-Japanese
War*, 124–35; * Higgins, 322–45; * 2 Hyde, §§ 713–19; * Lawrence, *War and
Neutrality* (2d ed.), 94 ff., and *Int. Problems* (1908), see index; Lémonon, *op.
cit.*, 472–502; * Martin and Baker, *op. cit.*, 421–48; Martitz, in 23 *Proceedings
of Int. Law Assoc.* (1906) 47–74; 2 Oppenheim, § 182 a; Rochall, *Die Frage
der Minen* (1910); Schüking, in 16 *Zeitschrift für int. Priv. u. Stafrecht* (1906),
121 ff.; 1 Scott, 576–87; Stockton, in 2 *A. J.* (1908), 276–84; * 2 Westlake
(1st ed.), 322–26; * *International Law Topics* (1905), 147–53 (1908), 98–113,
and (1914), 100–38.

The British Government accused the Germans of having planted mines in
the open waters of the North Sea on the first day of the World War. On
August 23, 1914 the British Admiralty warned neutrals that "the Germans are
continuing their practice of indiscriminatingly scattering mines upon the ordinary trade routes." On Oct. 2, 1914 the British Government announced that

6. BOMBARDMENT BY NAVAL FORCES

427. Hague Rules regulating Naval Bombardment.— Bombardment by naval forces presents much that is

in consequence of "the Germany policy of mine laying, combined with their submarine activity," it had authorized "a mine-laying policy in certain areas" of which due notice was given. On Nov. 3d the British Admiralty accused the Germans of having also "scattered mines indiscriminately in the open sea on the main trade route from America to Liverpool via the north of Ireland," and published an Order in Council declaring the whole of the North Sea "a military area." Ships of all countries wishing to trade with Norway, the Baltic, Denmark, and Holland were advised to come, if inward bound, by the English Channel and Straits of Dover and were to be given sailing directions to ensure safety. Later, at various times, the British mine fields were extended and otherwise altered.

On Feb. 4, 1915, the German Government, by way of retaliation, proclaimed "the waters surrounding Great Britain and Ireland, including the whole English Channel, to be comprised within the seat of war," and it declared that it would "prevent by all military means at its disposal all navigation by the enemy in those waters." Neutral powers were warned not to continue to intrust their crews, passengers, or merchandise to enemy merchant vessels. They were even urged to recommend to their own vessels to steer clear of these waters. For "in view of the hazard of war, and of the misuse of the neutral flag ordered by the British Government, it will not always be possible to prevent a neutral vessel from becoming the victim of an attack intended to be directed against a vessel of the enemy." In January, 1917 the German Government proclaimed a new war zone which "embraced the whole of the North Sea, including the waters around the British Isles, extending north to the Faroe Islands, westward from France and England for about 500 miles, and southward to within a few miles of the coast of Spain. A large portion of the Mediterranean Sea was also included within this 'barred' area. The aggregate area of the open sea embraced within the forbidden zones was estimated to exceed one million square miles. Within these zones, beginning on Feb. 1, 'all sea traffic was to be forthwith opposed by means of mines and submarines.' . . . All neutral merchant vessels entering the barred zones in violation of the above-mentioned conditions would be destroyed without warning and of course without provision being made for the safety of their crews or passengers." 1 Garner, 337–38. See *Ibid.* for the "above-mentioned conditions." The neutral governments, particularly the Dutch Government, protested vigorously against the planting of mines on the open sea.

On the *Use and Abuse of Submarine Mines during the World War*, see: 2 Fauchille, No. 1316[10]; Finch, in 9 *A. J.* (1915), 461 ff.; * 1 Garner, ch. 14, §§ 214–26; 2 Hyde, §§ 716–18; Naval War College, *Int. Law Situations* (see index vol., 1922); and Phillipson, *Int. Law and the Great War* (1915), ch. 20;

On *Maritime War Zones*, see: Baty, in 10 *A. J.* (1916), 47–48; Baty and Morgan, *War: Its Conduct and Legal Results* (1915), 223–26; Finch, in 9 *A. J.* (1915), 461 ff.; Hall, § 185, pp. 640–43 of 8th ed.; Hershey, in *Procs. Am. Soc. I. L.* (1916), 87–92; 2 Hyde, §§ 720–21; * 1 Garner, § 227; Lawrence and Carter, in 1 *Grot. Soc.* (1916), 48–49; and Naval War College, *Int. Law Situations* (see index vol., 1922).

For diplomatic correspondence between the U. S. and Germany relating to "Maritime Danger Zones and Mine Areas," see Spec. Supp. to 9 and 11 *A. J.* (1915 and 1917), 83 ff. and 4 ff. respectively.

analogous to bombardment by land troops.[32] On this subject the Hague Conference of 1907 formulated the following rules:

" The bombardment by naval forces of undefended ports, towns, villages, dwellings, or buildings, is forbidden.[33]

" A place cannot be bombarded solely because automatic submarine contact mines are anchored off the harbor " (Art. 1).[34]

" Military works, military or naval establishments, depôts of arms or war material, workshops, or plants which could be utilized for the needs of the hostile fleet or army, and ships of war in the harbor, are not, however, included in this prohibition. The commander of a naval force may destroy them by artillery, after a summons followed by a reasonable interval of time, if all other means are impossible, and when the local authorities have not themselves destroyed them within the time fixed.

" He incurs no responsibility for any unavoidable damage which may be caused by a bombardment under such circumstances.

" If for military reasons, immediate action is necessary, and no delay can be allowed to the enemy, it is nevertheless understood that the prohibition to bombard the undefended town holds good, as in the case given in paragraph 1, and that the commander shall take all due measures in order that the town may suffer as little harm as possible " (Art. 2).[35]

---

[32] Cf. *supra*, No. 382.

[33] Cf. H. R. (1907), 25. The all-inclusive phrase, *by any means whatever*, which was especially directed against certain much-feared practices of aërial warfare on land, inserted in the H. R., 25 (see *supra*, § 382), was omitted in 9 H. C., 1.

"The meaning of the term 'undefended' engaged the attention of the Committee, but owing to the difficulty of distinguishing between the defense of a coast and of a town near the coast, no definition was attempted." Higgins, 354.

[34] 9 H. C. (1907), 1. The second paragraph of this article was strongly opposed by Great Britain, Germany, France, and Japan, who entered reservations respecting this rule. Their attitude is approved by Westlake (II, 1st ed., 315). He says: "They were right. A place cannot be deemed undefended when means are taken to prevent an enemy from occupying it. The price of immunity from bombardment is that the place shall be left open to the enemy to enter." Cf. Bordwell, 289, Lawrence (4th ed.), p. 543, and Higgins, 354, to the same effect.

[35] 9 H. C., 2. Arts. 2 and 3 furnish exceptions to Art. 1. "This article

" After due notice has been given, the bombardment of undefended ports, towns, villages, dwellings, or buildings may be commenced, if the local authorities, on a formal summons being made to them, decline to comply with requisitions for provisions or supplies necessary for the immediate use of the naval force before the place in question.

" These requisitions shall be proportional to the resources of the place. They shall be demanded in the name of the commander of the said naval force, and they shall, as far as possible, be paid for in ready money; if not, their receipt shall be acknowledged " (Art. 3).[36]

" The bombardment of undefended ports, towns, villages, dwellings, or buildings, for the non-payment of money contributions, is forbidden " (Art. 4).[37]

" In bombardment by naval forces all necessary measures should be taken by the commander to spare as far as possible buildings devoted to public worship, art, science or charitable purposes, historic monuments, hospitals and places where the sick and wounded are collected, provided they are not used at the same time for military purposes.

" It is the duty of the inhabitants to indicate such monuments, buildings, or places by visible signs, which shall consist of large stiff rectangular panels, divided diagonally into two colored triangular portions, the upper portion black, the lower portion white " (Art. 5).[38]

" Unless military exigencies do not permit it, the commander of an attacking naval force must, before commencing the bombardment, do all in his power to warn the authorities " (Art. 6).[39]

might, and probably will, be held to confer a right on a commander to destroy by bombardment railway stations, bridges, entrepôts, coal, stocks, whether belonging to public authorities or private persons." Higgins, 355.

[36] *Ibid.*, 3. Cf. H. R., 42. As pointed out by Higgins (pp. 355–56), the punishment herein provided for a failure promptly to comply with a request for requisitions seems excessive. It would be more humane to follow the suggestion of Hall (8th ed., p. 518) to land a naval force and proceed as in the case of warfare on land.

[37] *Ibid.*, 4. This article finally disposes of the outrageous claim urged in some quarters that the exaction of ransom from coast towns or cities is permissible.

[38] *Ibid.*, 5. Cf. H. R., 27.

[39] *Ibid.*, 6. Cf. H. R., 26.

" It is forbidden to give over to pillage a town or place, even when taken by assault " (Art. 7).[40]

7. Capture of Enemy Goods and Vessels and Treatment of Prizes

428. Seizure of Enemy Vessels.—One of the most important means of maritime warfare is the attack upon and seizure of enemy vessels and the confiscation of enemy goods found on such vessels. All public vessels belonging to the enemy (especially warships) are subject to attack, seizure, or destruction by a belligerent man-of-war on the high seas or within the territorial waters of either belligerent. Enemy merchantmen can only be attacked if they refuse to submit to visit after having been duly signalled.[41]

429. How Seizure is Effected.—Seizure of an enemy merchantman is usually effected by sending an officer and a portion of the crew of the attacking ship on board the captured vessel.[42] She is then, as a rule, taken to a Prize Court of the captor and adjudicated upon.[43]

---

[40] 9 H. C., 7. Cf. H. R., 28. With several exceptions indicated above, this Convention must be pronounced satisfactory. It was signed or adhered to by all the Powers represented at the Conference except Spain.

On the *Ninth Convention and Naval Bombardments*, see especially; 1 *Actes et doc. de la dieuxième conf.*, 111–18; 15 *Annuaire* (1896), 145–51, 309–15; Barclay, *Problems*, etc., 51–52; Boidin, *op. cit.*, 201–15; Bonfils, No. 1277; Bordwell, 288–91; Bustamante y Sirven, *op. cit.*, ch. 16; * Dupuis, *Le droit de la guerre maritime* (1899), Nos. 67–72, and (1911), Nos. 42–47; 2 Fauchille, No. 1320; * 1 Garner, §§ 274–78; Hall, § 140; * Hall, J. A. *Law of Naval Warfare* (1921), 77–81; Hershey, *Russo-Japanese War*, 311–16 (see note on pp. 312–15 for citations from the authorities); * Higgins, 346–57; * Holland, *Studies*, 96 ff.; 2 Hyde, §§ 711–12; Lawrence, § 204, pp. 524–26 of the 7th ed., and *Int. Problems*, etc., 119 ff.; Lémonon, *op. cit.*, 503–25; Martin and Baker, *op. cit.*, 449–70; * 7 Moore, *Digest*, §§ 1166–74; 2 Oppenheim, §§ 212–13; 2 Rolin, Nos. 659–69; 1 Scott, 587–98, or 2 *A. J.* (1908), 285 ff.; * Stockton's *Naval War Code*, Art. 4; 2 Westlake (1st ed.), 315–17.

For the unjustified bombardment of the undefended British coast towns of Scarborough, Hartlepol, etc., without warning, during the World War, see 1 Garner, ch. 17, §§ 273–78.

[41] Most publicists contend that it is permissible for a man-of-war to use a false flag: (1) in approaching an enemy vessel for the purpose of drawing it into action; (2) when chasing an enemy ship; and (3) when attempting to escape. But it is agreed that she must fly her nation's flag before beginning the attack. 2 Oppenheim, § 211. For citation of authorities see *Ibid.*, note on p. 291 of 3d ed. On "Formalities of Visit, Search and Capture," see *infra*, p. 730 n.

[42] If this is impracticable, the captor orders the captured vessel to lower her flag and follow a prescribed course.

[43] On the *Origin of Prize Courts*, see especially: 2 Oppenheim, § 192; * 2 Twiss, §§ 74–75; and 2 Westlake (1st ed.), 122 ff.

430. **Destruction of Enemy Prizes.**—Enemy prizes may be directly appropriated, sold, or destroyed for exceptional reasons, such as unseaworthiness, the presence on board of infectious or contagious disease, stress of weather, serious danger of recapture, shortage of coal, lack of a prize crew, or serious danger to the success of military operations.[44]   If the destruction itself be lawful, it would

[44] See *Project* for the International Regulation of Maritime Prizes adopted by the *Institute of Int. Law* (1882–1887), Art. 50 in Scott, *Resolutions*, 55; *Russian Prize Regulations* (1895), Art. 21; *Japanese Regulations* (1904), Art. 91; Holland's *Manual of Prize Law* (1888), p. 86; Stockton's *Naval War Code* (1900), Art. 50 ; and *Instructions* issued by the Navy Department of the United States (1898), General Order 492.   The student will find these various articles collected by Wilson, note on pp. 305–07 (1st ed., 1910).

Great Britain only permits destruction in case the vessel is not in a condition to be sent into any port for adjudication or if the Commander is unable to spare a prize crew.   Holland, *op. cit.*, p. 86.

The Instructions issued by our Navy Department declare:

"The title to property seized as prize changes only by the decision rendered by the prize court.   But if the vessel itself or its cargo is needed for immediate public use, it may be converted to such use; a careful inventory and appraisal being made by impartial persons and certified to by the prize court.

"If there are controlling reasons why vessels may not be sent in for adjudication, as unseaworthiness, the existence of infectious disease, or the lack of a prize crew, they may be appraised and sold; and if this cannot be done, they may be destroyed.   The imminent danger of recapture would justify destruction, if there was no doubt that the vessel was good prize.   But in all such cases all the papers and other testimony shall be sent to the prize court in order that a decree may be duly entered."   7 Moore, *Digest*, p. 518; and Wilson, *op. cit.*, 304.

The case of the destruction of enemy prizes should be carefully distinguished from that of neutral prizes.   This distinction had not always been made.   Cf. *infra*, No. 522.

On the *Destruction of Enemy Prizes*, see especially: Atherley-Jones, 528–31; * Boeck, Nos. 268–85; Bonfils or 2 Fauchille, No. 1415; 5 Calvo, §§ 3028–34; * Dupuis (1899), Nos. 261–68, and (1911), No. 208; * 1 Garner, ch. 15, §§ 232 ff.; Hall, § 120, pp. 546–48 of 8th ed. (including notes); Hershey, *Russo-Japanese War*, 156–59; 2 Hyde, §§ 755–56; 2 Kleen, *De la neutralité*, 529–34; Lawrence, § 191; * 7 Moore, *Digest*, § 1212; 2 Oppenheim, § 194; * Smith, *The Destruction of Merchant Ships* (1917); 2 Westlake (1st ed.), 318–21; Wilson § 131; Wright, in 11 *A. J.* (1917), 358 ff.

Cf. references on *Destruction of Neutral Prizes*, *infra*, p. 739 n.

During the World War the Germans made drastic use of a new weapon of naval warfare of marvellous potency—the submarine torpedo-boat—with which they hoped to overpower their enemies.   Though tremendously effective, it was practically impossible for it to conform to the rules of modern maritime warfare, particularly the rules relating to visit and search and the one requiring that provision be made for the safety of the crew and passengers of vessels that they were obliged to sink.   The destruction without warning of the British liner *Lusitania* on May 7, 1915 with the loss of some 1200 non-combat-

seem that the neutral owners of goods thus destroyed
must not expect the payment of indemnity.[45]

ants (including 128 American citizens) made an indelible impression upon the
world.   In general German authorities argued that the rules of cruiser warfare
do not apply to submarines—an argument which amounts to a claim that the
law of the sea may be changed by a single belligerent.   Stated in this form,
its absurdity is evident.   In the further course of the World War, Germany destroyed a large number of neutral as well as enemy merchantmen by submarine
warfare.

On *Submarine Warfare*, see especially: Davidson, *The Freedom of the Seas*
(1918), ch. 4; François, in 30 *R. D. I. P.* (1923), 34 ff.; * 1 Garner, ch. 15;
Hall, in 5 *Grot. Soc.* (1920), 82–93; * Higgins, *Defensively-Armed Merchant
Ships and Submarine Warfare* (1917), 27 ff., and in *Brit. Yr. Bk.* (1920–21),
149–65; 2 Hyde, §§ 747–51; Naval War College, *Int. Law Situations* (see
index vol., 1922); Perrinjaquet, in 23 and 24 *R. D. I. P.* (1916 and 1917),
117 ff., 394 ff., 137 ff., and 365 ff.; Rogers, *America's Case against Germany*
(1917), chs. 2–7; * *Round Table* (June, 1916), No. 23, pp. 493–536.

For diplomatic correspondence relating to "Submarine Warfare" between
the U. S. and Germany, see Spec. Supp. to 9 and 11 *A. J.* (1915 and 1917),
129 ff. and 52 ff.

On the case of the *Lusitania*, see: Fleischmann, etc., in 9 *Z. V.* (1915–16),
135–237; 1 Garner, §§ 229 ff.; 2 Hyde, § 747, pp. 478–80; Meurer, *Der
Lusitania-Fall* (1915); Rogers, *op. cit.*, ch. 4.   For the decision of Judge
Meyer of the U. S. District Court that the liability of the Cunard S. S. Co. for
loss of life and property in consequence of the sinking of the Lusitania, see 12
A. J. (1918), 862 ff.   For abridged reports to this decision, see Evans, *Cases*,
561 and Scott, *Cases*, 784.

At the Washington Conference of 1921–22 (see *supra*, p. 146 n.) the United
States, the British Empire, France, Italy and Japan declared submarines under
no circumstances exempt from the established rules of visit and search and
that "a merchant vessel must not be·destroyed unless the crew and passengers
have been first placed in safety" (Art. 1).

"The Signatory Powers recognize the practical impossibliity of using submarines as commerce destroyers without violating . . . the requirements
universally accepted by civilized nations for the protection of the lives of
neutrals and non-combatants," and they accepted the prohibition of the use of
submarines as commerce destroyers as binding between themselves (Art. 4).

In this same treaty they also declared their assent to the prohibition of the
"use in war of asphyxiating, poisonous or other gases, and all analogous
liquids, materials or devices," and agreed to be bound by such prohibition as
between themselves (Art. 5).

All other civilized nations were invited to adhere to these agreements regarding poisons and submarines.   It remains to be seen whether or not they
will find adherents.   It must be admitted that there is much skepticism with
regard to these matters.

For the text of the Treaty, see Supp. to 15 *A. J.* (1921), or Buell, *The
Washington Conference* (1922), 395–98.   For discussions on submarines at the
Conference, see *Conference on the Limitation of Armaments* (Wash., 1922),
466–845, *passim*.   For an article on "Submarines at the Washington Conference," see Roxburgh, in *Brit. Yr. Bk.* (1922–23), 150–58.   For a valuable note
on the "Use of Gas, Vapor, Smoke and Bacteria," and references in Gas
Warfare, see McNair, in 2 Oppenheim (4th ed.), pp. 237–38.

[45] At least it was so held by the French *Conseil d'Etat in* 1870 in the cases

431. **Recapture.**—In case of recapture at sea, the vessels and other property recaptured from the enemy are usually restored to the original owners on the analogy of the Roman *jus postliminii* which restored to persons and things their original status upon rescue from the power of the enemy. The mode and conditions of restoration are determined by Municipal Law, since, according to International Law, the title to the recaptured vessel or property is really vested in the States whose forces have made the recapture.[45]

432. **Disposition of Prizes.**—After a prize is sold, it is usually condemned, and the whole or part of the net proceeds divided among the officers and crew of the vessel which made the capture.[46]

of the seizure of two German merchantmen. See 5 Calvo, § 3033; Dupuis (1899), No. 262; Hall, § 269, p. 877 of 8th ed.; and 2 Westlake (1st ed.), 318–19. On the "Destruction of Neutral Property in Neutral Vessels," see Wright, in 11 *A. J.* (1917), 358 ff.

The United States grants restoration to the original owners on payment of salvage awarded by the courts, provided the recapture is effected prior to condemnation by a properly constituted enemy prize court. France adopted the twenty-four rule as early as 1584, and restores on the payment of a thirtieth as salvage if the capture is effected within twenty-four hours of the original capture, though one tenth is demanded if a longer time has elapsed.

The most liberal rule is that of England. The Naval Prize Act of 1864 (§ 40) provides that, except in case of use as a warship, the recaptured vessel shall be restored to her former owner on payment of from one-eighth to one-fourth salvage if the recapture has been effected at any time during the war. Some of the smaller States follow the English usage; others, *e.g.* Prussia, follow the rule of the Consolato del Mare, which restored the vessel to the original owner on payment of a reasonable salvage in case of recapture before it had been taken into port or to a place of safety (*infra praesidia*) by her captors. The rule adopted by the United States would seem to be the most reasonable.

On *Recapture*, see especially: * Atherley-Jones, ch. 9; * De Boeck, Nos. 286–318; Bonfils, and 2 Fauchille, No. 1416; 5 Calvo, §§ 3186–2326; Davis (3d ed.), 366–68; Dupuis (1899), Nos. 278–81; * Hall, §§ 152, 166; * 2 Halleck (Baker's 3d ed.), 510–27 § 759; Lawrence, § 185; * 7 Moore, *Digest*, § 1213; 2 Oppenheim, §§ 196, 432; Perels, 226–28; * 3 Phillimore, Pt. X, ch. 6, §§ 403 ff.; 2 Rivier, 357–59; Scott, *Cases*, 772–78; Taylor, § 559; 2 Westlake (1st ed.), 156–58; Wheaton, §§ 367 ff.; Woolsey, §§ 151–52. See Scott, *Resolutions*, 77, 199, for rules adopted by the Institute of Int. Law.

[46] This practice is still followed by most States, but was abolished by the United States in 1899. See 7 Moore, *Digest*, § 1248. For information on this subject, see * Atherley-Jones, 560 ff.; Davis (3d ed.), 373; 2 Halleck (Baker's 3d ed.), 365 ff.; * Holland, *Manual*, 142 ff., for the British Royal Proclamation as to distribution of prize money; * 7 Moore, *Digest*, §§ 1245–48, for former distribution of prize money in the United States.

For a select Bibliography on *Prize Courts and Prize Procedure*, see *infra*, p. 742.

8. Enemy Character in Naval Warfare

433. Declaration of Paris.—The Declaration of Paris (1856) lays down the following important rules of exemption from the right of capture at sea:

" The neutral flag covers enemy's goods, with the exception of contraband of war.

" Neutral goods, with the exception of contraband of war, are not liable to capture under enemy's flag." [47]

According to the terms of this Declaration, with the exception of contraband goods, neutral goods on enemy vessels as well as enemy goods on neutral vessels are, generally speaking, exempt from capture;[48] but enemy goods found on board enemy vessels are still subject to capture.[49]

[47] Rules 2 and 3 of the *Declaration of Paris*. These rules adopt the principle of "free ships, free goods" without its supposed corollary "enemy ships, enemy goods."

On the *Declaration*, see especially * Higgins, 1–4. See *Ibid.*, p. 1 for select bibliography. Cf. *supra*, No. 73.

[48] Further exceptions to these rules are found in the case of blockade runners and vessels engaged in unneutral service or hostile aid. See *infra*, chs. 32 and 34.

[49] There has been for some time a powerful movement, championed by the United States, in favor of the adoption of the principle of the inviolability or total immunity from capture of private unoffending enemy property at sea. The first official sanction of the abolition of this remaining form of "pillage" is found in the treaty of 1785 negotiated by Franklin between Prussia and the United States. In 1823 John Quincy Adams, then Secretary of State, proposed exemption of private property at sea to Great Britain, France and Russia —a proposition which Russia expressed herself as willing to accept on condition that all the other naval Powers should join in it. When our Government was invited to give its adhesion to the Declaration of Paris of 1856, it declined to do so unless the Declaration should be extended to include this exemption.

The principle was adopted by Italy in her Marine Code of 1865 and in a treaty with the United States in 1871. It was acted upon by Prussia, Austria, and Italy in the War of 1866. In 1904 the Congress of the United States adopted a resolution in its favor, and a memorial in its behalf was presented by the American delegation to the First Hague Conference. At the Second Hague Conference the proposition of the United States in favor of immunity of private unoffending enemy property from capture at sea received twenty-one yeas and eleven nays, with twelve States abstaining or not voting. Since the opposition included such great maritime Powers as Great Britain, France, Russia and Japan, the proposal was considered lost.

The continued championship of this cause by the United States is all the more creditable from the fact that, in view of the strength of our navy and the small size of our merchant marine, it is somewhat doubtful whether our purely material interests lie in this direction. The interests of Great Britain with her powerful navy and enormous carrying trade are more difficult to determine.

434. **Tests of Enemy Character.**—In international practice there are applied two widely divergent criterions or tests of enemy character.   France and some of the other

They seem almost equally balanced, with the heavier weight inclining toward immunity.

Statesmen and international jurists appear to be equally divided in their opinions as to the desirability of this innovation.   On the Continent of Europe there seems to be a preponderance of opinion in favor of it; but in England the weight of authority and public opinion still appears to be strongly opposed, though there has long been a great and growing sentiment in its favor. Among statesmen and publicists favoring immunity might be cited: J. Q. Adams, Atherley-Jones, Azuni, Barbosa, Von Bar, Bluntschli, De Boeck, Bonfils, Bulmerincq, Butler, Calvo, Cauchy, Choate, Cobden, Desjardins, Despagnet, Fauchille, Field, Fiore, Fish, Foster, Geffcken, Gessner, Hall, Heffter, Holtzendorff, De Laveleye, T. J. Lawrence, Lord Loreburn, De Mably, Maine, Mancini, F. de Martens, Massé, Marcy, President McKinley, President Monroe, Napoleon I, Neumann, Nys, Piédelièvre, Perels, Pinheiro-Ferreira, de Beer Poortugael, Pradier-Fodéré, Rivier, Rolin-Jacquemyns, White, Wehberg, Woolsey, and the majority of the members of the Institute of International Law in 1875, 1877, and 1882.

Among those opposed to immunity might be cited: Admiral Aube, Bentwich, Bowles, Bynkerschoek, Dana, Funck-Brentano et Sorel, Sir Edw. Grey, Grotius, Hall, Halleck, Harcourt, Hautefeuille, Holland, Kent, Latifi, Lorimer, Mahan, Manning, Oppenheim, Ortolan, Lord Palmerston, Perels, Phillimore, Pillet, Pistoye et Duverdy, Renault, Röpcke, Lord Salisbury, Sir Wm. Scott, Admiral Stockton, Testa, Twiss, Vattel, Westlake, Wheaton, Wildman, Wilson.

Lack of space does not permit anything like an adequate discussion of this interesting and important subject.   The arguments of the advocates of immunity rest mainly upon considerations of humanity, progress, and the commercial interests of neutrals, if not of the belligerents themselves.   They also urge that war is essentially or exclusively a relation between States, point to the analogies or resemblances between land and maritime warfare, claim that immunity would constitute an important step toward the limitation of war, and deny that one of the main objects of maritime warfare is the destruction of the enemy's commerce.

The opponents of immunity, speaking generally, claim that war is a relation between individuals as well as States, minimize the resemblances and emphasize the differences between land and naval warfare, deny that the abolition of the capture of private unoffending enemy property would tend to lessen the number or duration of wars, and urge that the destruction of the enemy's commerce is an essential aim of modern warfare.

Some of the more recent authorities deem it necessary to preserve the right of capture in order to "deprive the enemy of important resources, both of ships which might be available as transports or for purposes of supply; and of men who might render service on board ships so employed or in the fighting navy. . . ." 2 Westlake, (1st ed.), 130.

But according to 11 H. C., 6 (see *supra*, Nos. 406 ff.), crews of captured enemy merchantmen are no longer to be made prisoners of war on certain conditions, and enemy vessels adapted or available for use as transports or for supply might be excepted from the rule of non-capture.   In any case it is difficult to see why it is necessary to confiscate either the vessel or the goods in the case of such merchantmen as may have been captured from a sense of military pre-

European States [50] apply the test of political nationality. The Anglo-American system, which is also applied in a somewhat modified form by Japan, makes enemy or neutral character in maritime warfare depend upon commercial or trade domicile.[51]

caution or necessity. Sequestration or preemption would surely be sufficient in such cases. A fuller agreement as to the conditions under which merchantmen may be converted into warships in time of war would also materially assist in the solution of this problem, which is not so difficult as it is made to appear.

It is probable that the conduct of belligerents during the World War has greatly weakened the likelihood of the abolition of the right of the capture of private unoffending property at sea. Cf. 2 Hyde, § 772.

For arguments pro and con on the *Abolition of the Capture of Private Unoffending Property at Sea*, see especially; Barclay, *Problems*, etc., 63–70, 172–79; Bentwich, *War and Property at Sea* (1907), 84–96; Bluntschli, in 9 and 10 *R. D. I.* 508 ff. and 60 ff.; * Boeck, Nos. 381 ff.; * Bonfils, Nos. 1281–1338; Bower, in 13 *A. J.* (1919), 60–78; Butler, in 168 *No. Am. Rev.* (1899), 54 ff.; 4 Calvo, §§ 2294–2410; * Choate, in *American Addresses*, 1–24; Corbett, in Mahan's *Neglected Aspects of War* 117 ff.; Despagnet, Nos. 643–45; Dupuis, *Le droit de la guerre maritime* (1899), Nos. 24 ff., and (1911), Nos. 25 ff.; * 2 Fauchille, Nos. 1324–82; 3 Fiore, Nos. 1399–1413; Fromagoet, in 2 Scott, 701–04; Hall, § 147, and in 26 *Contemp. Rev.* (1875), 737 ff.; Hays, in 12 *A. J.* (1918), 283–90; Holls, *Peace Conference*, 306–21; 2 Hyde, §§ 771–72; * Latifi, *Effects of War on Property* (1909), ch. 5; * Lawrence, § 194; Loreburn, *Capture at Sea*; * Mahan, in *Neglected Aspects of War* (1907), 157 ff.; 7 Moore, *Digest*, § 1198; 2 Oppenheim, § 178; 2 Piédelièvre, Nos. 1108–16; * 8 Pradier-Fodéré, Nos. 3066 ff.; Quigley, in 11 *A. J.* (1917), 22–45, 820 ff.; Röcke, *Das Seebeuterecht* (1904); Stockton, in 1 *A. J.* (1907), 930–43; Wehberg, *Capture*, etc.; * 2 Westlake (1st ed.), 129–32, in Latifi, 145 ff., and in 7 *R. D. I.*, 678 ff. For Bibliographies, see Boeck, Fauchille, (II, 421–22), Oppenheim (II, pp. 246 and 254 n of 3d ed.), Wehberg, etc.

[50] * *Le Hardy* v. *La Voltigeante*, 1 Pistoye et Duverdy, 321 and Scott, *Cases*, 686. In this leading case it was held that a neutral merchant domiciled in a belligerent country does not acquire a belligerent character, and that his property at sea is to be regarded as neutral.

[51] For the leading cases on *Commercial Domicile*, see Evans, ch. 12, pp. 411 ff. and Scott, ch. 8, pp. 659 ff. On "Domiciled Aliens," see *supra*, Nos. 237–43. For Bibliography, see p. 388.

"Residence in a neutral country will not protect [a merchant's] share in a house established in the enemy's country, though residence in the enemy's country will condemn his share in a house established in a neutral country." Wheaton, § 335. Indeed, Lord Stowell held that a merchant might have several trade domiciles, and the property of nationals has been ruthlessly confiscated by English and American courts because of its hostile origin.

The memorandum setting forth the views of the British Government for the benefit of the London Conference of 1909 gives the following summary of the Anglo-American doctrine:

"1. The principle adopted by the British Courts has been to treat the domicile of the owner as the dominant factor in deciding whether property captured in time of war is enemy property; but for this purpose the principle

435. Rules Respecting Enemy Character Adopted by the London Conference of 1909.

—The London Naval Conference which met in 1908–1909 discussed this subject at length, but was unable to come to any agreement beyond these general rules (which, however, were never ratified):

is not limited in all respects to the domicile of origin or residence, and is applied in the following way:

"(*a*) A person domiciled in a neutral country, but having a house of trade in an enemy country is deemed to acquire a commercial domicile in the enemy country in respect of transactions originating there; but the other property of such owner is not affected thereby.

"(*b*) A commercial domicile not being the domicile of nationality is terminated when actual steps are taken *bona fide* to abandon such domicile for a different one *sine animo revertendi*.

"2. This principle applies equally to the cases of an individual, a partnership, or a corporation, residence in the two latter cases being understood to mean the place whence the business is controlled.

"3. In the case of a partnership where one or more of the partners is domiciled in enemy territory, property not liable to be seized as enemy property on other grounds, is presumed to be divided proportionally between the partners and the share attributed to a partner domiciled in enemy territory is deemed to be enemy property." *Parl. Papers, Miscel.*, No. 4 (1909), p. 11.

Much of the law of domicile as applied to maritime capture is or should be regarded as obsolete. It is based upon the conception of war as a hostile relation between individuals as well as States, and an exaggerated idea of the importance of the capture of property *which might possibly* increase the enemy's resources. It is an illiberal and complicated system—a travesty upon justice supported by legal casuistry. Besides, it is a weak and ineffective weapon of warfare, and has, therefore, scant military justification.

At the London Conference of 1909, all the great maritime Powers (including Great Britain) finally ranged themselves on the side of the principle of nationality (with the exception practically of the United States) thus leaving us in the unenviable position of sole champion of this survival of Toryism in International Law.

During the World War Great Britain abandoned the old Anglo-American doctrine of commercial domicile as the real test of enemy character and substituted, to a certain extent at least, the continental test of nationality. Enemy persons were to include not only those residing in enemy territory, but also persons of "enemy nationality and association" residing in neutral countries. In order to prevent persons residing in the United Kingdom from trading with "any persons or bodies of persons not residing or carrying on business in enemy territory" . . . "black lists" of persons and firms in neutral countries with which trade was forbidden were published.

The total number of such persons and firms is said to have exceeded 1500 and the original "black list" contained the names of 85 persons and firms in the United States. Our Government addressed a formal protest to the British Government on the subject on July 26, 1916, but published similar lists after our entry into the war.

On this subject, see particularly * 1 Garner, §§ 156–61.

" Subject to the provisions [52] respecting transfer of flag, the neutral or enemy character of a vessel is determined by the flag which she has the right to fly.

" The case where a neutral vessel is engaged in a trade which is reserved in time of peace, remains outside the scope of, and is in no wise affected by this rule " (Art. 57).[53]

" The neutral or enemy character of goods found on board an enemy vessel is determined by the neutral or enemy character of the owner " (Art. 58).[54]

[52] See below, No. 436.

[53] D. L. (Declaration of London), Art. 57. The first paragraph embodies a recognized principle of International Law. See *supra*, No. 207. The second refers to the famous Rule of 1756, usually regarded as obsolete. See *supra*, No. 65 n.

For the text of these rules and the official *Report* to the Conference, see Higgins, 560–61, 567 ff.; or *Int. Law Topics* of the Naval War College (1909), 130 ff.

"Article 57 safeguards the provisions respecting transfer of flag, as to which it is sufficient to refer to Articles 55 and 56 (see below, No. 436); it might be that a vessel would really have the right to fly a neutral flag, from the point of view of the law of the country to which she claims to belong, but may be regarded as an enemy by a belligerent, because the transfer in virtue of which she has hoisted the neutral flag, is annulled by Article 55 or by Article 56." *Report* in Higgins, 603–04.

At the outbreak of the World War both the British and French Governments proclaimed those rules of the Declaration of London relating to transfers of flag to be in force. But it was soon discovered that the rule laid down in the first paragraph of Art. 57 afforded protection to German-owned ships flying a neutral flag. Consequently, the British Government abrogated the article and declared that in lieu thereof the British prize courts should "apply the rules and principles formerly observed in such courts." In order to meet the situation created by the action of German shipowners in the United States in using the American flag to protect cargoes shipped from America to neutral European ports (particularly Holland) for transshipment to Germany, the rule was adopted that the nationality of the owner should be taken as the test of enemy or friendly character. The French Government adopted the same policy. See 1 Garner, § 134.

[54] D. L., 58. But what is to determine the neutral or enemy character of the owner? Is it domicile or nationality? It was found impossible to agree on this point, the maritime Powers being about equally divided.

An unsuccessful attempt was made to agree upon the following rules as a compromise:

"The neutral or enemy character of goods found on board an enemy vessel is determined by the neutral or enemy nationality of their owner, or, in case of lack of nationality or of double nationality (neutral or enemy) of the owner, by his domicile in a neutral or enemy country.

"Provided that the goods belonging to a limited liability or joint stock company are, considered as neutral or enemy according as the company has its headquarters in a neutral or enemy country." Higgins, 604.

" If the neutral character of goods found on board an enemy vessel is not proven, they are presumed do be enemy goods (Art. 59).[55]

" The enemy character of goods on board an enemy vessel continues until they reach their destination, notwithstanding an intervening transfer after the opening of hostilities while the goods are being forwarded.

" If, however, prior to the capture, a former neutral owner exercises, on the bankruptcy of a present enemy owner, a legal right to recover the goods, they regain their neutral character" (Art. 60).[56]

436. **Transfer to Neutral Flag.**—" The transfer of an enemy vessel to a neutral flag, effected before the opening of hostilities, is valid, unless it is proved that such transfer was made in order to evade the consequences which the enemy character of the vessel would involve. There is, however, a presumption that the transfer is void if the bill of sale is not on board a vessel which has lost her belligerent nationality less than sixty days before the opening of hostilities. Proof to the contrary is admitted.

" There is absolute presumption of the validity of a transfer effected more than thirty days before the opening of hostilities if it is absolute, complete, and conforms to the laws of the countries concerned, and if its effect is such that the control of the vessel and the profits arising from her employment do not remain in the same hands as before the transfer. If, however, the vessel lost her belligerent nationality less than sixty days before the opening of hostilities, and if the bill of sale is not on board, the capture of the vessel would give no right to damages " (Art. 55).[57]

[55] D. L., 59. "Art. 59 enunciates the traditional rule according to which goods found on board an enemy vessel are, failing proof to the contrary, presumed to be enemy goods; this is merely a simple presumption, leaving to the claimant (not only) the right, but (also) the burden, of proving his rights." *Report* on the Declaration of London, in Higgins, 605; or in *Int. Law Topics* (1910), 135.

[56] D. L., 60. "This provision contemplates the case where goods which were enemy property at the time of departure have been the subject of a sale or transfer during the course of the voyage. . . ." *Report, op. cit.*

[57] D. L., 55. For commentaries on this article, see *Report, etc.,* in Higgins, 600 f.; *Int. Law Topics* (1909), 123 f.; and Bentwich, *The Dec. of London* (1911), 104–07.

"The transfer of an enemy vessel to a neutral flag, effected after the opening of hostilities, is void unless it is proved that such transfer was not made in order to evade the consequences which the enemy character of the vessel would involve.

"There is, however, absolute presumption that a transfer is void:

"(1) If the transfer has been made during a voyage or in a blockade port.

"(2) If there is a right of redemption or recovery.

"(3) If the requirements upon which the right to fly the flag depends according to the laws of the country under which the vessel is sailing, have not been observed" (Art. 56).[58]

BIBLIOGRAPHY

Laws of Naval Warfare generally (in addition to the general treatises on Int. Law).—Atherley-Jones, *Commerce in War* (1907); Azuni, *Le droit maritime de l'Europe* (1790); Bardas, *Das öffentliche Seerecht*

[58] D. L., 56. See commentaries *op. cit.* These rules apply to *vessels*.

It is a principle of Anglo-American Law that, in time of war or in contemplation thereof, *goods* shipped on account of the consignee are regarded as his goods from the time of shipment, and he cannot divest himself of this risk by special agreement. The *Packet De Bilboa* (1799), 2 C. Rob. 133, and Scott, 817. But it seems that the French rule permits the shipper to take such risk. *Les Trois Frères*, 1 Pistoye et Duverdy, 357, and Snow, *Cases*, 348.

For leading cases on the *Ownership and Transfer* of *Goods in Transit*, see Scott, *Cases*, ch. 14, pp. 811–22; or Snow, *Cases*, 339–55. For practice during the World War, see particularly 1 Garner, ch. 7. See especially the case of the *Dacia*, *Ibid.*, §§ 125–33. For the text of the decision of the French Prize Council (1915), see 9 *A. J.*, 1015.

On *Enemy Character*, see: Baty, in 9 (new ser., pt. 1), *J. C. L.* (1908), 157–66; * Bentwich, *The Declaration of London* (1911), chs. 5–6, and *The Law of Private Property in War* (1907), 79–82, 142–47; Bonfils, Nos. 1343–49; * Boeck, Nos. 159–90; Bordwell, 215–21; 4 Calvo, §§ 1932–52; * 2 Cobbett, 19–37, 62–70, 219–43; 2 Despagnet, Nos. 646–49; * Dupuis (1899), Nos. 92–129, and (1911), ch. 4; * Evans, *Cases*, ch. 12, pp. 411 ff.; 2 Fauchille, Nos. 1385–88; 3 Fiore, Nos. 1432–36; * 1 Garner, ch. 7 and 8, §§ 144, 155–61; Geffcken, in 4 Holtzendorff, 581–88; * Hall, Pt. III, ch. 6; Hall, J. A., *Law of Naval Warfare* (1921), ch. 9; * 2 Hyde, §§ 784–96; * Latifi, *Effects of War on Property* (1911), ch. 3; * Lawrence, Pt. III, ch. 2; 7 Moore, *Digest*, §§ 1189–94; 3 Nys, 70–84, and in 39 *R. D. I.* (1907), 149 ff.; * Naval War College, *Int. Law Situations* (see index vol., 1922); * 2 Oppenheim, §§ 87–92, and in 25 *Law Quar. Rev.* (1909), 372–84; 3 Phillimore, §§ 842–86; 2 Piédelièvre, Nos. 1117–25; 8 P.-Fodéré, Nos. 3166 ff.; * Scott, *Cases*, chs. 8 and 14; Taylor, §§ 468 and 517; 2 Twiss, §§ 152–62; Visscher, in 31 *Law Quar. Rev.* (1915), 289–98; Walker *Manual*, §§ 39–43; * 2 Westlake (1st ed.), 140–54; Wheaton, §§ 320–41.

Ostereichs (1909); Baty and Morgan, *War: Its Conduct and Legal Results* (1915), Pt. II, ch. 3; Bentwich, *The Law of Private Property in War* (1907), and in 9 *A. J.* (1915), 17–44; Bensten, *Das Seekriegsrecht* (1911); * Boeck, *De la propriété privée ennemie* (1882); Bowles, *The Declaration of Paris of 1856* (1900), and *Sea Law and Sea Power* (1910); Boidin, *Les lois de la guerre et les deux conférences de la Haye* (1908); Boyens-Lewis, *Das deutsche Seerecht* (1897 and 1901 in 2 vols.); * Cauchy, *Le droit mar. int.* (1862) in 2 vols.; 2 Cobbett, *Leading Cases*, particularly 184–96; * De Cussy, *Phases et causes célèbres de droit maritime* (1856); 1 Desjardins, *Le droit commercial maritime* (1898); * Dupuis, *Le droit de la guerre maritime d'après les doctrines anglaises* (1899), and *Le droit de la guerre maritime*, etc. (1911); Funck-Brentano, in 1 *R. D. I. P.* (1894), 324 ff.; Geffcken, *Das Seekriegsrecht*, in 4 Holtzendorff, 545 ff., and in 20 *R. D. I.*, 451 ff.; Gessner, in 10 *R. D. I.*, 489 ff.; Glass, *Maritime Int. Law* (1885); * Hall, J. A., *The Law of Naval Warfare* (1921); * Hautefeuille, *Histoire des origenes*, etc. (1869), and *Questions de droit maritime int.* (1861); Holland, *Manual of [British] Prize Law* (1888), and *Letters to the Times upon War and Neutrality* (1909); Hyde, *Maritime War* (1918); Latifi, *Effects of War on Property* (1909); Leroy, *La guerre maritime* (1900); Loreburn, *Capture at Sea* (1913); Lorimer, in 7 *R. D. I.*, 261–68; * Mahan, *The Influence of Sea Power on History* (1894), *passim*, *The Influence of Sea Power upon the French Revolution and Empire* (1892), *passim*, and *Sea Power and the War of 1812* (1905), *passim;* * Martin and Baker, *Laws of Maritime Warfare* (1918-views of authorities); Nys, *La guerre maritime* (1881), and in 7 *R. D. I.* (1875), *passim;* * Ortolan, *Règles int. et diplomatie de la mer* (1864), in 2 vols.; * Perels, *Manuel de droit mar. int.* (1884), and *Das int. öffent. Seerecht der Gegenwart* (2d ed., 1903); Pillet, in 5 *R. D. I. P.* (1898), 444 ff., *Les lois actuelles de la guerre* (2d ed., 1903), and in 23 *R. D. I. P.* (1916), 5 ff., 203 ff., and 423 ff.; Rosse, *Guide int. du commandant de bâtiment de guerre* (1888); Stockton's (U. S.), *Naval War Code* (1900); 2 Stowell and Munro, *Int. Cases* (1916), *passim;* Testa, *Le droit int. mar.* (1886); Twiss, in 16 *R. D. I.* (1884), 113 ff.; * Wehberg, *Capture in War on Land and Sea* (1911); *Das Seekriegsrecht* (1915); Wheaton, *History of the Law of Nations* (1845), *passim;* Zorn, *Die Fortschritte des Seekriegsrecht durch die zweiter Haager Friedenskonferenz* (1908).

For fuller Bibliographies, see Boeck, 2 Fauchille, pp. 339–42, Olivart, etc. For Bibliographies on particular topics, see footnotes to this chapter, *passim*.

For bibliography on prize law, see *infra*, pp. 741–42. For references on the *London Naval War Conference* of 1909, see *supra*, p. 101 n.

CHAPTER XXX

AËRIAL WARFARE [1]

Recent inventions in modes of aërial transportation and communication, notably by means of the aëroplane, dirigible balloons, and radio or wireless telegraphy, make it seem necessary (or at least desirable) to deal separately with aërial warfare.

437. Few Positive Rules of Aërial Warfare.—Very few positive rules or principles of International Law applicable to this field of future warfare have been thus far developed. The rules are largely inferential and speculative in their character, and are based upon generally recognized principles or analogous practices in land or naval warfare.

438. The Hague Declaration.—Many of the States represented at the Second Hague Peace Conference of 1907 agreed to " prohibit, *for a period extending to the close of the Third Peace Conference,* the discharge of projectiles and explosives from balloons or by other new methods of a similar nature." [2] But this " Declaration " was only signed by twenty-seven States, and the Signatories did not include four of the great maritime Powers. [3] It cannot, therefore, be regarded as an integral part of International Law and was not in force during the World War.

439. The Hague Regulations. (*a*) **As to Bombardment.**—The only positive rule of International Law bearing directly on the subject of aërial warfare which is based upon convention is found in the Hague Regulations respecting the Laws and Customs of War on Land:

" The attack or bombardment, *by any means whatever,*

---

[1] Cf. the *Law of Aërial Space in Time of Peace, supra,* ch. 16.

[2] 1 H. D. (1907). Higgins, 485–91. See, *Ibid.,* p. 488 for references.

[3] Viz., Germany, Italy, Russia, and Japan. The remaining non-Signatory Powers were Chile, Denmark, Spain, Guatemala, Mexico, Montenegro, Nicaragua (which has since adhered), Paraguay, Rumania, Servia, Sweden, and Venezuela. It should be noted that the United States was among the Signatories.

of towns, villages, habitations, or buildings which are not defended is forbidden " (Art. 25).[4]

440. (b) **On Wireless Telegraphy.**—But the following rules may be said to bear indirectly on the subject:

" Belligerents are also forbidden: (a) To erect on the territory of a neutral Power a wireless telegraphy station, or any apparatus intended to serve as a means of communication with belligerent forces on land or sea;

" (b) To use any installation of this kind established by them before the war on the territory of a neutral Power for purely military purposes, and which has not been opened for the service of public messages " (Art. 3).[5]

[4] H. R. (1907), 25.   Cf. *supra*, No. 382.

Though H. R. 25 may be said still to constitute the formal law pertaining to aërial as well as land bombardment, it is wholly unsatisfactory, at least as far as the former is concerned.   In fact, it may be said to be entirely impracticable, since the main purpose of aërial bombardment—that of the destruction of enemy property of possible military use—is altogether different from that of bombardment on land, the object of which is usually capture or military occupation.

Authority and practice alike tend to substitute the idea of the "military objective" for that of a "defended" place in aërial bombardment.   Thus, Art. 24 of the draft code on aërial warfare (see below, note 13) prepared by the Committee of Jurists which met at The Hague during Dec. to Feb., 1922–23, provides that "aërial bombardment is legitimate only when directed at a military objective that is to say, an object of which the destruction or injury would constitute a distinct military advantage to the belligerent.

"Such bombardment is legitimate only when directed exclusively at the following objectives: military forces; military works; military establishments or depots; factories constituting important and well-known centres engaged in the manufacture of arms, ammunition or distinctively military supplies; lines of communication or transportation used for military purposes."

This admirable code altogether prohibits aërial bombardment for the "purpose of terrorizing the civilian population, of destroying private property not of military character, or of injuring non-combatants," as also for the "purpose of enforcing compliance with requisitions in kind or payment of contributions in money" (Arts. 22 and 23).

On *Aërial Bombardment*, see especially: Fauchille, in 24 *R. D. I. P.* (1917), 56–74; * 1 Garner, ch. 19, particularly § 299, and in 18 *A. J.* (1924), 56 ff., especially pp. 64 ff.; Manisty, in 7 *Grot. Soc.* (1922), 33–40; * Moore, *Int. Law and Current Illusions* (1924), ch. 5, pp. 194–202, 240–48; and * Spaight, *Air Power and War Rights* (1924), 28–30, and chs. 8–11, and in *Brit. Yr. Bk.* (1923–24), 21–33.

[5] H. C. (1907), 3.   This article was suggested by the experiences of the Russo-Japanese War, when the Russians erected a receiving station at Chefoo in China for the purpose of communicating with Port Arthur by wireless telegraphy.   See Hershey, 122, 124, 266–67; Higgins, 282–83, 291; Lawrence, *War and Neutrality* (2d ed.), 213–20; and Scholtz, *Drahtlose Telegraphie u. Neutralität*, 13 ff.

" A neutral Power is not bound to forbid or restrict, on behalf of belligerents, the use of telegraphic or telephonic cables or wireless telegraphy apparatus, whether belonging to it or to companies or private individuals " (Art. 8).[6]

441. The Theater of Aërial Warfare.—Though there are no positive or conventional rules bearing on the subject, it is clear from general principles or analogous customs of warfare at sea or on land that belligerents have the right of waging aërial warfare in the aërial space surrounding the ocean as well as in that above their own territory or above territory under their military occupation (including the marginal seas bordering on such territory). But they do not have the right of using the aërial space surrounding the territory of neutral States (including their marginal waters) for military purposes.[7]

442. Restrictions on Neutrals.—It is also reasonably clear that belligerents have the right of forbidding or restricting the access to, or use of, the aërial space above belligerent territory by neutrals, if such restriction or prohibition is deemed necessary or desirable from a military standpoint.[8] They have probably also the right to impose

Art. 5 of 5 H. C. also makes it obligatory upon neutrals not to permit such acts on its territory.

According to 13 H. C. (1907), 5, belligerents are particularly forbidden to "erect wireless telegraphy stations, etc." in neutral ports or waters. Cf. *infra*, No. 461.

[6] 5 H. C., 8. Art. 9 adds: "Every restrictive or prohibitive measure taken by a neutral Power in regard to the matters referred to in Articles 7 and 8 must be applied impartially by it to the belligerents.

"The neutral Power shall see to it that the same obligation is observed by companies or private owners of telegraph or telephone cables or of wireless telegraphy apparatus."

[7] This principle was confirmed by general practice during the World War, so that it may now be considered a customary rule of the Law of Nations. Though violated in some instances, all the neutral States who had occasion to decide the question answered with a firm and unqualified negative any effort on the part of belligerent airships to enter or make use of their aërial territory even as a passageway. Even Germany showed by the nature of her excuses and assurances that she accepted the principle. In case of airmen in distress taking refuge in neutral territory, they, together with their equipment and material, should be interned. On "Violations of Neutrality by Belligerent Aircraft," see especially: 1 Garner, §§ 301 ff.; and Spaight, *op. cit.*, ch. 20, and *Aircraft in Peace* (1919), 1-4, 303-15.

[8] According to the Declaration of London, Art. 24, "wireless telegraphy as also balloons and flying machines and their distinctive component parts, together with accessories and articles recognizable as intended for use in con-

certain restrictions or prohibitions upon neutrals above the high seas within the zone or theater of military operations.[9] They may impose appropriate penalties for the violation of these rules.

443. Some Doubtful Points.—Whether the so-called innocent passage of public belligerent airships through neutral aërial space or the utilization by such airships of neutral territory for such relatively innocent purposes as repairs, the procuring of necessary supplies, etc., is permissible, may be considered more than doubtful.[10] It is also doubtful whether the custom of maritime warfare permitting the capture and confiscation of unoffending private enemy property on enemy vessels applies to aërial warfare, or whether such property is exempt from seizure except for a purely military purpose, as in the case of warfare on land.[11]

444. Rights of Balloonists and Aëronauts.—Balloonists and others engaged in aërial warfare, at least if properly enrolled and uniformed, are entitled to all the rights and privileges of lawful combatants. If captured, they should be treated as prisoners of war; [12] if killed, sick, or wounded,

nection with balloons and flying machines" may be declared conditional contraband.

Neutral airships would appear to be subject to the rights of visit and search, and liable to capture for carriage of contraband, for attempts to enter a blockaded port, or for unneutral services. They are liable to the appropriate penalties prescribed in such cases.

[9] "Belligerents may prevent the emission of waves, even by a neutral subject, upon the high sea within the zone which corresponds to the sphere of action of their military operations." Art. 6 of the Regulations on Wireless Telegraphy adopted by the Institute of International Law in 1906. Scott, *Resolutions*, 165. Cf. Art. 50 of the Oxford Manual of Naval War, *Ibid.*, 186.

[10] Total prohibition or abstention from such acts would be the preferable solution, as being more in accordance with the principles underlying the modern conception of neutral obligations. Cf. *infra*, No. 445. The prohibition would not necessarily apply to private belligerent airships.

[11] Here again, the rules governing land warfare should be preferred. The practice of pillage or the taking of booty in maritime warfare is a mere historic survival with no real justification on military grounds. There seems to be no good reason for applying it to aërial warfare.

[12] These statements appear necessary in view of a disposition shown in some quarters to treat them as spies upon several occasions.

During the Franco-German War of 1870, Prince Bismarck threatened to treat balloonists crossing the German lines as spies. See 1 Guelle, 136.

Early in 1904 Admiral Alexieff also threatened to treat as spies correspondents on board neutral vessels "who may communicate news to the enemy by

they should be dealt with in accordance with the provisions
of The Hague and Geneva Conventions.[13]

BIBLIOGRAPHY

Aërial Warfare or **The Law of Aërial Space in Time of War** (with
special reference to Balloons, Aëroplanes, and Wireless Telegraphy).
—* Baker and McKernan, *Laws of Warfare* (1919), 580–609; Bel-
lenger, *La guerre aérienne* (1912); Boiden, in 16 *R. D. I. P.* (1909),
261 ff.; Bonfils, liv. IV, No. 1440$^{4-21}$; Catellani, *Le droit aérien* (1912),
chs. 20–23; Colby, in 19 *A. J.* (1925), 702–15, and in 10 *Minn. Law
Rev.* (1926), 123 ff. and 207 ff.; Ellis, in 8 *A. J.* (1914), 256–73; * 2
Fauchille, liv. IV, Nos. 1440$^{5-50}$, 1476$^{12-23}$, in 24 *R. D. I. P.* (1917),
56–74, in 19 *Annuaire*, 19 ff., in 21 *Annuaire*, 76 ff., and 24 *Annuaire*,
23 ff.; Fenwick, ch. 34; * 1 Garner, ch. 19, in 18 *A. J.* (1924), 56–81,
in 30 *R. D. I. P.* (1923), 372 ff., and *Recent Developments in Int. Law*
(1925), Lect. 4, pp. 164 ff.; Hall, § 183 a; Hearn, *Airships in Peace
and War* (2d ed., 1910); 2 Hyde, § 663; Kausen, *Die Radiotelegraphie*,
etc. (1910), 75 ff.; Kebedgy, in 36 *R. D. I.* (1904), 445 ff.; Kuhn,
in *Procs. Am. Soc. I. L.* (1921, 77–80; Lanchester, *Aircraft in Warfare*
(1916), §§ 100 ff.; 3 Mérignhac, *Traité*, 299–349, and *Les lois de la
guerre sur terre* (1903), 197 ff.; * Meyer, *Die Luftschiffahrt in kriegs-
rechtlicher Bedeutung* (1909); Manisty, in 7 *Grot. Soc.* (1922), 33 ff.;

means of improved apparatus not yet provided for by existing conventions,"
in case any such "should be arrested off Kwan-tung or within the zone of operations of the Russian fleet." This declaration, which was communicated to the
Powers by the Russian Government, was provoked by the presence in the Gulf
of Pe-chi-li and adjacent waters near Port Arthur of Mr. Fraser, a London
Times war correspondent on board the Chinese dispatch boat *Haimun* equipped
with wireless telegraphy apparatus. His dispatches were sent to a neutral
station at the British port of Wei-hai-wei, whence they were transmitted to
London.

On the case of the *Haimun*, see especially: Fraser, *A Modern Campaign*
(1905); Hershey, *Russo-Japanese War*, 115 ff.; Lawrence, *War and Neutrality*
(2d ed.), 83 ff.; 1 Rey, *Russo-Japanese War*, 368 ff.; *Int. Law Situations* (1907),
159 ff.

The Hague Regulations (Arts. 13 and 29) include "newspaper correspondents and reporters" among the army followers entitled to treatment of
prisoners of war; and expressly exclude "individuals in balloons to deliver
dispatches, etc." from the category of spies. See *supra*, pp. 582 and 603.

[13] See *supra*, chs. 28 and 29, *passim*.

The student interested in this subject should study the admirable Report
of the Committee of Jurists which met at The Hague during Dec. to Feb.,
1922–23. It is divided into two Parts: Part I consists of a code of 12 Articles
or Rules for the Control of Radio in Time of War; and Pt. II, of 62 Articles or
Rules of Aërial Warfare. For the text of this *Report*, see Supp. to 17 *A. J.*
(1923), 242–60. For text and excellent commentary, see * Moore, *op. cit.*,
ch. 5. For discussion of these prepared rules, see also * Garner, in 18 *A. J.*
(1924), 56–81; Hamburg, in 50 (3d ser. 4) *R. D. I.* (1923), 421–35; Rodgers,
in 17 *A. J.* (1923), 629–40; and Spaight, *op. cit.*, *passim*.

Montmorency, in 7 *Grot. Soc.* (1922), 73 ff.; * Moore, *Int. Law and Current Illusions* (1924), ch. 5; Naval War College, *Int. Law Situations* (1907), 138 ff., and *Ibid.* (1912), 56 ff. (see also Index Vol., 1922); 2 Oppenheim, §§ 214^{a-c}; Phillipson, *Two Studies in Int. Law* (1908), 104 ff.; Philit, *La guerre aérienne* (1910); Picciati, in 15 *J. C. L.* (n. s., pt. II, 1915), 150–55; Rodgers, in 17 *A. J.* (1923), 629–40; Rolland, in 13 *R. D. I. P.* (1906), 58 ff., and 23 *R. D. I. P.* (1916), 497–604; Schneeli, *Radiotelegraphie und Völkerrecht* (1908), §§ 14–37; * Scholz, *Drahtlose Telegraphie u Neutralität* (1905); 1 Scott, *The Hague Conferences*, 649–54; * Spaight, *Air Power and War Rights* (1924), and *Aircraft in War* (1914); Stael-Holstein, *La reglementation de la guerre des airs* (1911); Winfield, in 40 *Law Mag. and Rev.* (1914–15); 257–71; Yvon, *La guerre aérienne* (1924).

For fuller Bibliographies, see Bonfils, Kausen, Meyer, etc.

Cf. Bibliography on *Law of Aërial Space in Time of Peace, supra,* pp. 345–46.   See also Bibliography, in 2 Fauchille, pp. 601–02.

PART VI

THE SO-CALLED LAW OF NEUTRALITY

CHAPTER XXXI

THE NATURE, HISTORICAL DEVELOPMENT, AND THE CHARACTERISTICS OR FUNDAMENTAL PRINCIPLES OF NEUTRALITY

445. Definition and Nature of Neutrality.—Neutrality has been well defined as " the condition of those States which in time of war take no part in the contest, but continue pacific intercourse with the belligerents." [1] It consists in the total abstention [2] from or absolute prohibition of certain acts (such as the sale of warships or the fitting and sending out of military expeditions [3] to aid either belligerent), as well as the observance of a strict impartiality in all cases where indirect assistance or support is still permissible (such as coaling or repair of belligerent warships in neutral ports). It also involves the acquiescence in or tolerance of certain acts (such as the exercise of the rights of visit and search) by the belligerents.

446. Historical Development of Neutrality.—The Law of Neutrality can scarcely be said to have existed in anything like its modern form prior to the close of the eighteenth century. [4] The theory of neutral rights and obligations was

---

[1] Lawrence (7th ed.), 582. For various definitions of neutrality, see 4 Calvo, § 2491; and 8 P.-Fodéré, No. 3224.

[2] "Neutrality does not consist in the mere impartial treatment of opposing belligerents, but in the entire abstinence from any direct assistance of either party in his warfare." Walker, *Science*, etc., 374.

[3] In such cases a State is bound to use "due diligence" or the "means at its disposal" for the prevention of these acts.

[4] The very idea of neutrality as a principle of public law or conduct appears to have been almost unknown to the nations of Antiquity and the peoples of the Middle Ages, at least prior to the publication of the *Consolato del Mare* in 1494; though, as Westlake (II, 1st ed., 161) observes, "the fact of neutrality" must be as old as war itself.

Even Grotius devotes only one short chapter (lib. III, cap. 17) to those whom he calls *medii*. The gist of his impracticable doctrine is contained in a single sentence: "It is the duty of those who stand apart from a war to do

formulated by Bynkershoek, Galiani, Hübner, De Martens, and Vattel in the eighteenth century, but it was first put into actual practice by the United States during the Washington administration.[5]

Owing to the outrageous conduct of " Citizen " Genêt,[6] a newly appointed French minister who arrived in the United States in April, 1793, in fitting out privateers and otherwise violating American neutrality, Jefferson, then Secretary of State, asserted that it is " the *right* of every nation to prohibit acts of sovereignty from being exercised by any other within its limits, and the *duty* of a neutral nation to prohibit such as would injure one of the warring Powers." [7]

nothing which may strengthen the side which has the worse cause or which may impede the motions of him who is carrying on a just war; and in a doubtful case, to act alike to both sides, in permitting transit, in supplying provisions, in not helping persons besieged."

Bynkershoek (in 1737) called neutrals *non hostes*, though Nys (2 *Études*, 59) has traced the use of the term *neutralité* back to French edicts and treaties belonging to the close of the fifteenth century. It appears that the first publicist to use the word "neutrality" was Neumayr de Ramsla in 1620. *Ibid.*, 60.

In the seventeenth century some progress was made in the regulation of the exercise of the rights of visit and search, as also in the law governing captures for carriage of contraband and breach of blockade. But the territorial sovereignty of neutral waters was frequently violated, and it was still customary to permit the levy of troops on neutral soil.

The principle of territorial sovereignty was better respected in the eighteenth century; but it was still regarded as permissible for a State remaining neutral to furnish troops to a belligerent in accordance with a treaty obligation, and levies of troops on neutral soil apart from treaty stipulations were not severely condemned.

[5] The First Armed Neutrality formed by Russia in 1780 to resist the maritime pretensions of England was an important step in this direction, but its principles were soon violated even by Russia. Cf. *supra*, No. 65.

[6] M. Genêt granted commissions to American citizens who fitted out privateers manned with Americans in American ports for the purpose of preying on British commerce. He also set up Prize Courts (in connection with French Consulates in the United States) which proceeded to try and condemn British vessels captured by French cruisers. When remonstrated with, Genêt's conduct was marked by extreme insolence.

For the story of Genêt's controversy with the Washington administration, see any good history of the United States. See especially 4 Moore, *Digest*, § 639; and Dana, note 215 to Wheaton, 536 ff.

[7] Jefferson to Genêt, June 5, 1793, 2 and 7 Moore's *Digest*, §§ 224 and 1295. In a communication to Mr. Morris, United States Minister to France, dated August 16, 1793, Jefferson thus stated the "principles of the Law of Nations" relating to the duties of neutral nations:

"A neutral nation must, in all things relating to the war, observe an exact impartiality toward the parties; that favors to one to the prejudice of the other

Because of this experience and the acquittal of Gideon Henfield,[8] who had been indicted for cruising in one of the privateers commissioned by Genêt, Congress passed the first Neutrality Act of 1794—a law which was strengthened in 1818 in consequence of violations of American neutrality during the Spanish-American wars of independence.[9]

would impart a fraudulent neutrality, of which no nation would be the dupe; that no succor should be given to either, unless stipulated by treaty, in men, arms, or anything else directly serving for war; that the right of raising troops being one of the rights of sovereignty, and consequently appertaining exclusively to the nation itself, no foreign power or person can levy men within its territory without its consent; and he who does may be rightfully and severely punished; that if the United States have a right to refuse the permission to arm vessels and raise men within their posts and territories, they are bound by the laws of neutrality to exercise that right, and to prohibit such armaments and enlistments." 7 Moore, § 1293, pp. 880–81.

[8] Wharton's *State Trials*, 49.

[9] Rev. St., §§ 5281–91 (U. S. Comp. St., 1901, pp. 3599–3602).

The neutrality Act of 1818 was thus summarized in President Roosevelt's Neutrality Proclamation of Feb. 11, 1904:

"1. Accepting and exercising a commission to serve either of the said belligerents by land or by sea against the other belligerent. [The phrase used throughout the Act is "any foreign prince, State, colony, district or people."]

"2. Enlisting or entering into the service of either of the said belligerents as a soldier, or as a marine, or seaman, on board of any vessel or war, letter of marque, or privateer.

"3. Hiring or retaining another person to enlist or enter himself in the service of either of the said belligerents as a soldier, or as a marine, or seaman on board of any vessel of war, letter of marque, or privateer.

"4. Hiring another person to go beyond the limits of or jurisdiction of the United States with intent to be enlisted as aforesaid.

"5. Hiring another person to go beyond the limits of the United States with intent to be entered into service as aforesaid.

"6. Retaining another person to go beyond the limits of the United States with intent to be enlisted as aforesaid.

"7. Retaining another person to go beyond the limits of the United States with intent to be entered into service as aforesaid.

"8. Fitting out and arming, or attempting to fit out and arm, or procuring to be fitted out and armed, or knowingly being concerned in the furnishing, fitting out, or arming of any ship or vessel with intent that such ship or vessel shall be employed in the service of either of the said belligerents.

"9. Issuing or delivering a commission within the territory or jurisdiction of the United States for any ship or vessel to the intent that she may be employed as aforesaid.

"10. Increasing or augmenting, or procuring to be increased or augmented, or knowingly being concerned in increasing or augmenting, the force of any ship of war, cruiser, or armed vessel in the service of either of the said belligerents, or belonging to the subjects of either, by adding to the number of guns of such vessels, or by changing those on board of her for guns of a larger caliber, or by the addition thereto of any equipment solely applicable to war.

"11. Beginning or setting on foot, or providing or preparing the means for,

Similar so-called " Enlistment " Acts were passed by the British Parliament in 1819 and 1870.[10]

447. General Characteristics or Fundamental Principles of Neutrality.—The following may be regarded as general characteristics or fundamental principles underlying or governing the positive rules of neutrality:

(1) War being " an abnormal or exceptional relation between States, the presumption, even in time of warfare, should be always in favor of the laws of peace, and therefore of the rights and privileges of neutrals in their peaceful relations with each other and with belligerents." [11]   " Unless proof to the contrary is shown, neutral States and their subjects are free to do in time of war between other States what they are free to do in time of universal peace." [12]

(2) An independent State has an inalienable right to remain neutral in a war, and a belligerent is bound to respect this neutrality, more particularly its territorial sovereignty.   The belligerent has a corresponding right to insist that the neutral State observe and enforce its neutral obligations.[13]

any military expedition or enterprise to be carried on from the territory or jurisdiction of the United States against the territories or dominions of either of the said belligerents."

Cited from *U. S. Foreign Relations* (1904), p. 32, by Wilson, § 173, pp. 389–90.   Cf. summary of the Act by Dana, note 215 to Wheaton, 542 f.

[10] For the text of the British Foreign Enlistment Act of 1870, see 2 Oppenheim, App. I, pp. 483 ff., or 33 and 34 Vict. 90.   For a convenient abridgment of those portions of the United States and British Acts which relate to the equipment of warships in neutral territory, see Scott, *Cases* (1st ed., 1902), 692–95.

The British Act of 1870 goes at least one step farther than the American Neutrality Acts.   It prohibits not only the commissioning, equipping, and dispatching, but also the building or construction of "any ship with intent or knowledge or having reasonable cause to believe that the same shall or will be employed in the military or naval service of any foreign State, at war with any friendly State."

[11] Hershey, *Russo-Japanese War*, 118.

[12] Lawrence, p. 583 of 7th ed.   For a remarkable exposition of this fundamental principle, see Descamps, *Le droit de la paix et de la guerre* (1898), and *Ibid.*, in 7 *R. D. I. P.* (1900), 629 ff. and 705.   It requires some modifications for Members of the League of Nations in view of their obligations under the Covenant.

[13] These principles are a corollary of sovereignty.   It is customary, though not strictly obligatory, for neutral States to issue Declarations of Neutrality soon after the outbreak of important wars.   These vary greatly in detail and content.   Some are very brief and general in their character.   For examples of such declarations, see *U. S. Foreign Relations* (1898), 14–36.   For the text of

(3) The characteristic attitude of neutrality is impartiality.   This attitude finds expression in absolute prohibition or total abstinence from all warlike operations, or it takes the form of equality of treatment of both belligerents in the case of acts which do not amount to a direct participation in the war.[14]

(4) A considerable portion of the Law of Neutrality, more particularly that relating to the so-called rights of visit and search, and to captures for carriage of contraband and unneutral service, is the result of a compromise between the opposing interests of neutrals and belligerents.

(5) In the study of this subject, it is necessary to keep in mind the distinction between the Law of Neutrality as existing between States and this Law as applied between States and individuals.   Some acts are permitted to the latter which are prohibited to the former.   It is also necessary to distinguish between the duties of a belligerent State toward neutral States and those of a neutral State towards belligerent States.

(6) In view of the example set by the Hague Conference of 1907, we have found it most convenient to abandon the above distinctions as the basis of our classification, and to deal with the Neutral Rights and Duties in Land and Maritime War respectively in separate chapters.[15]

President Wilson's Proclamation of Neutrality on Aug. 4, 1914, see Supp. to 9 *A. J.* (1915), 110–14.   For Neutrality Proclamations and Regulations relating to the World War, see Naval War College, *Int. Law Topics* (1916).

[14] Cf. *supra*, No. 445.

[15] The older distinctions between perfect and imperfect neutrality, voluntary and conventional neutrality, etc., have for the most part been abandoned by the more recent authorities.   They may have some basis in facts or conditions, but none in law,   The same may be said of such terms as "armed" and "benevolent" neutrality.   On permanent neutrality, or *Neutralization*, see *supra*, No. 109.

In an address at Cincinnati on Oct. 26, 1916, President Wilson is reported to have said: "This is the last war of the kind or of any kind that involves the world that the United States can keep out of.   I say this because I believe the *business of neutrality is over;* not because I want it to be over, but I mean this, that war now has such a scale that the position of neutrals sooner or later becomes intolerable."   Cited by the writer in an editorial in 11 *A. J.*(1917), 394.

While this is probably the case in a broad political sense, it is not true in a strict or legal sense.   There is still the possibility of wars in self-defense (the case of a sudden or surprise attack), the League of Nations may have to engage in wars in order to maintain and secure peace, and there is the possibility of wars that are not illegal under the Covenant or which are waged in defiance of the

BIBLIOGRAPHY

Historical Development of Neutrality.—Bergbohm, *Die bewaffnete Neutralität* (1884); * Bernard, *Neutrality of Great Britain during the American Civil War* (1870); * De Boeck, *De la privée proprieté ennemie*, etc. (1882); * Bonfils or 2 Fauchille, Nos. 1497–1521; Bynkershoek, *Questiones juris publici* (1737), lib. I, cc. 8–15; 4 Calvo, §§ 2495–2591: Cauchy, *Le droit mar. int.* (1862), *passim;* Fauchille, *La diplomatie française et la ligue des neutres de 1780* (1893); Fenwick, ch. 30, and *Neutrality Laws of the U. S.*, 1–14; 3 Fiore, Nos. 1503–35; Geffcken, in 4 Holtzendorff, 614–34; Gessner, *Le droit des neutres sur mer* (1876), 1–69; * Hall, Pt. IV, ch. 2; Hautefeuille, *Histoire des origines*, etc. (1858–1869), *passim,* and *Des droits et des devoirs des neutres* (1868), 160–66; * 1 Kleen, 1–70; * Lawrence, Pt. IV, ch. 1; 2 J. de Louter, § 53; 3 F. de Martens, § 130; * Moore, *American Diplomacy*, ch. 2; * 3 Nys, 535–46, and 2 *Études*, 47–163; * 2 Oppenheim, §§ 285–92; 3 Phillimore, §§ 161–226; Pyke, *Law of Contraband* (1915), chs. 4–5; 2 Rivier, 370–75; Scott, *Armed Neutralities of 1780 and 1800* (1918); Schuyler, *American Diplomacy*, 367–403; Taylor, §§ 596–613; 2 Twiss, §§ 208–12; 2 Verraes, 9–16; Walker, *History*, 195–202, and *Science*, 374–87; 2 Westlake (1st ed.), 169–81.

Characteristics or Fundamental Principles of Neutrality.—Bluntschli, Arts. 742–48; Bonfils and 2 Fauchille, Nos. 1441 and 1443; Bynkershoek, *Quest. jur. publ.*, lib. I, c. 9; 4 Calvo, §§ 2491–93; * Descamp, in 7 *R. D. I. P.* (1900), 629 ff. and 705 ff.; 3 Fiore, Nos. 1536–41, and *Int. Law. Cod.*, Nos. 1791–1827; Geffcken, in 4 Holtzendorff, 605–13; Grotius, lib. III, c. 17, § 3; * Hall, Pt. I, ch. 4; Hammarskjöld, in 3 *Bibliotheca Visseriania*, 53 ff.; 1 Hautefeuille, *Droit des neutres*, etc., 174–89; Heffter (Geffcken), §§ 144 and 146; Heilborn, *System*, 336–51; Hershey, in 26 *Int. J. of Ethics* (1915–16), 168–76; * Holland, in 2 *Proceedings of the British Academy* (1905) or 37 *R. D. I.* (1905), 359 ff.; * 2 Hyde, §§ 844–49; * 1 Kleen, §§ 1–4, 45–46; Lawrence, § 222; Lifschütz, in 27 *Z. I.* (1918), 40–124; 2 Lorimer, 121 ff.; 2 J. de Louter, § 54; 3 F. de Martens, § 131; 3 Mérignhac, 495–516; Liszt, § 66, 3 Nys; * 2 Oppenheim, §§ 293–319; Perels, § 38; Pillet, Nos. 184 ff.; 8 P.-Fodéré, Nos. 3222–33; * 2 Rivier, 381 ff.; Schopfer, *Le principe juridique de la neutralité* (1894); Ullmann, § 190; * Vattel, liv. III, §§ 103–04; Walker, *Manual*, § 54; 2 Westlake (1st ed.), 161–69.

obligations of Members of the League under the Covenant. No doubt the rôle and scope of neutrality in future wars will be much reduced, and the character of neutral rights and duties will be greatly modified. But it is impossible to foresee what course this development will take. It may, however, not be too hazardous to predict that in a war waged under the auspices of a powerful League, the freedom of the seas will hardly be respected even to the extent that has been the case in the past, and that the forces "coöperating to protect the covenants of the League," will not hesitate to cross the land frontiers of Members of the League, more particularly in view of their obligations under Art. 16 of the Covenant. For a study of "Neutralité et Société des Nations" by Cohn, see 1 *Les origines et l'œuvre de la Société des Nations* (1924), 153–204.

CHAPTER XXXII

NEUTRAL RIGHTS AND DUTIES IN LAND WARFARE

1. The Rights and Duties of Neutral Powers

The Hague Conference of 1907 adopted the following Convention respecting the " Rights and Duties of Neutral Powers and Persons in War on Land ":

448. Inviolability of Neutral Territory.—" The territory of neutral Powers is inviolable " (Art. 1).[1]

" Belligerents are forbidden to move troops or convoys, either of munitions of war or of supplies, across the territory of a neutral Power " (Art. 2).[2]

449. Enlistment and Levying of Troops.—" Corps of combatants cannot be formed, nor recruiting offices opened, on the territory of a neutral Power, in the interest of the belligerents " (Art. 4).[3]

[1] 5 H. C. (1907), Art. 1. Cf. 13 H. C. (1907), 1. See *infra*, No. 458. This article, which was adopted without discussion, embodies a fundamental principle of the Law of Neutrality always recognized in theory and, in modern times, nearly always observed in practice.

Japan was forced to violate this principle at the outbreak of the Russo-Japanese War by her attack on the Russian vessels at Chemulpo and her subsequent invasion of Korea and Manchuria. But the conditions were altogether anomalous. Korea was under the virtual protection of Japan, and Manchuria is a case of "double or ambiguous sovereignty." The maintenance of Korean independence and the securing of the Russian evacuation of Manchuria were among the ostensible objects of the war, and it was unavoidable that these regions should become theaters of military operations. The neutrality of China (outside of Manchuria) was secured through the acceptance by the Powers of the principles embodied in the Hay note of February 10, 1904. See Hershey, *Russo-Japanese War*, 70–73 and 246 ff.; and Lawrence, *War and Neutrality*, ch. 11.

Under very exceptional circumstances, a State might be forced to violate the territorial sovereignty of another as a means of self-preservation. In order to excuse such an act, one must "show a necessity of self-defense, instant, overwhelming, leaving no choice of means and no moment for deliberation." Webster, in the case of the *Caroline* (1841). Cf. *supra*, note on p. 233 n.

[2] 5 H. C., 2. It should be noted that this is a positive prohibition upon belligerents. For the corresponding obligation resting upon neutrals, see 5 H. C., 5, below, No. 449.

[3] 5 H. C., 4. (For Article 3, by which belligerents are forbidden to erect or use for military purposes wireless telegraphy stations or apparatus on neutral territory, see *supra*, No. 440.)

671

" A neutral Power ought not to allow on its territory any of the acts referred to in Articles 2 to 4.[4]

" It is not bound to punish acts in violation of neutrality unless such acts have been committed on its own territory " (Art. 5).[5]

" A neutral Power incurs no responsibility from the fact that individuals cross the frontier singly for the purpose of placing themselves at the service of one of the belligerents " (Art. 6).[6]

450. The Export of Arms, etc.—" A neutral Power is not bound to prevent the export or transit, on behalf of one or the other of the belligerents, of arms, munitions of war, or, generally, of anything which can be of use to an army or fleet " (Art. 7).[7]

Article 4 prohibits the enlistment or levying of troops on neutral territory. It does not forbid expressions of opinion or of sympathy, even through public meetings. Loans by neutral individuals to belligerents are not illegal, though loans by a neutral Government are inadmissible. See especially Benton, *Spanish American War*, 41–42, 59–60; Hershey, *Russo-Japanese War*, 79–82, 84–87; and 7 Moore, *Digest*, §§ 1311–13.

[4] Cf. 5 H. C., 2–4, *supra*, for the corresponding obligations upon belligerents referred to in the text.

[5] 5 H. C., 5. "A neutral State will, of course, not be expected to discharge the duties cast upon it by this article, and by Arts. 11–14 [*infra*, Nos. 451–53] should it be unprovided with forces sufficient to enable it to do so." Holland, No. 125.

[6] 5 H. C., 6. But it does incur responsibility if it knowingly permits, or does not by the exercise of due diligence prevent, foreign enlistment within its own jurisdiction. "Belligerent subjects who go home to perform their military duties, do not fall within the scope of this doctrine." 2 Westlake (1st ed.), 181.

The British Foreign Enlistment Act of 1870 prohibits enlistment or the acceptance of any commission or engagement on the part of a British subject (without a license from His Majesty), whether such engagement takes place within or without His Majesty's dominions. But our own Neutrality Laws (see *supra*, p. 667 for summary) merely prohibit enlistment or the acceptance of a foreign commission within the territory or jurisdiction of the United States. They also prohibit any one from hiring any person to enlist or from hiring another to go beyond the jurisdiction of the United States with intent to be enlisted; but they do not prohibit one from merely leaving the country with intent to enlist (*U. S.* v. *Kazinski*, 2 Sprague, 7).

It would seem that both the American and British laws are somewhat in advance of the actual requirements of International Law. On *Illegal Enlistment*, see especially Hall, § 218; Hershey, *op. cit.*, 82–83; * 1 Kleen, 255–85; Lawrence, § 236, pp. 639–40 of 7th ed.; * 7 Moore, *Digest*, § 1293; * 2 Westlake (1st ed.), 181–84.

[7] Cf. 13 H. C., 7, *infra*, No. 462. Official protests by belligerent Governments against the right of neutral individuals to trade in contraband are heard

" Every restrictive or prohibitive measure taken by a neutral Power in regard to the matters referred to in Articles 7 and 8 must be applied impartially by it to the belligerents " (Art. 9).[8]

" The fact that a neutral Power repels, even by force, attacks on its neutrality, cannot be considered as a hostile act " (Art. 10).[9]

2. INTERNMENT OF BELLIGERENTS AND CARE OF WOUNDED IN NEUTRAL TERRITORY

451. Duty of Internment.—" A Neutral Power which receives on its territory belligerent armies shall intern them, as far as possible, at a distance from the theater of war.

" It may keep them in camps, and even confine them in fortresses or in places assigned for this purpose.[10]

" It shall decide whether officers may be left at liberty on giving their parole that they will not leave the neutral territory without permission " (Art. 11).[11]

452. Treatment of Interned Troops.—" In the absence of a special Convention, the neutral Power shall supply the

during nearly every war. This view is also championed by a small band of publicists, notably by Hautefeuille, Phillimore, and Kleen. It is without sanction, either in theory or practice.

For a discussion of this question, with citations from Lawrence and Jefferson, see Hershey, *The Russo-Japanese War*, 183–87. For expressions of opinion on the part of American statesmen, see 7 Moore, *Digest*, §§ 1263 and 1308. For judicial opinions of the U. S. Supreme Court, see the cases of *The Commercen*, 1 Wheaton, 382; *The Peterhoff*, 5 Wallace, 28; and *The Santissima Trinidad*, 7 Wheaton, 283. For these cases, see also Evans, 656 and 788; and Scott, 973, 980, and 823. On the "Exportation of Arms and Munitions to Belligerents" during the World War, see * 2 Garner, ch. 35.

[8] 5 H. C., 9. Article 8 and part of Article 9 are here omitted as dealing with the subject of wireless telegraphy. See *supra*, No. 440.

[9] 5 H. C., 10. The neutral is, of course, bound to prevent the commission of such acts, if possible.

[10] With one exception (Art. 13), the articles under this head formed part of the Hague Regulations on Land Warfare adopted in 1899. In 1907 they were transferred to the Convention respecting the Rights and Duties of Neutral Powers and Persons in War on Land. Cf. also B. D., 53–56.

[11] 5 H. C. (1907), 11, and H. R. (1899), 57. "It will be noted that no duty is imposed upon the neutral to extend hospitality to belligerent fugitives." 1 Scott, 547.

"If a belligerent force even accompanied by prisoners, enters neutral territory in (proved) error, its immediate departure should be permitted." Holland, No. 131.

interned with the food, clothing, and relief prescribed by humanity.

" At the conclusion of peace, the expenses caused by the internment shall be made good " (Art. 12).[12]

" A neutral Power which receives prisoners of war who have escaped shall leave them at liberty. If it allows them to remain on its territory, it may assign them a place of residence.

" The same rule applies to prisoners of war brought by troops taking refuge in the territory of a neutral Power " (Art. 13).[13]

453. **Care of Sick and Wounded Belligerents.**—" A neutral Power may authorize the passage over its territory of wounded or sick belonging to the belligerent armies, on condition that the trains bringing them shall carry neither personnel nor war material. In such a case the neutral Power is bound to adopt such measures of safety and control as may be necessary for the purpose.

" Wounded or sick brought under these conditions into neutral territory by one of the belligerents, and belonging to the opposite party, must be guarded by the neutral Power, so as to insure their not taking part again in the operations of war. The same duty shall devolve on the neutral Power with respect to wounded or sick of the other army who may be committed to its care " (Art. 14).[14]

" The Geneva Convention applies to the sick and wounded interned in neutral territory." (Art. 15).[15]

[12] 5 H. C., 12 and H. R. 58. "Each belligerent will be responsible for the expenses caused by the internment of its own troops, in the absence of any treaty provision to the contrary." Holland, No. 132.

[13] 5 H. C., 13. This article was wholly new.

[14] 5 H. C., 14 or H. R., 59. "The neutral Power, though it may do so, is not bound to allow such passage as is here mentioned. The privilege should be accorded impartially, if at all, nor should one belligerent be permitted to send his sick and wounded through the neutral territory without consent of the other belligerent, previously obtained.

"Under the second pargaraph, wounded prisoners, brought into neutral territory by a belligerent, may not be carried through as prisoners to the territory of their captor, but must remain under neutral control as long as the war lasts, when they will be allowed to return to their own country." Holland, No. 134.

[15] 5 H. C., 15. Cf. H. R., 60 and B. D., 56. To these articles on *Internment*, it should perhaps be added that war material belonging to one of the belligerents brought into neutral territory, should, if admitted, be seized and

3. NEUTRAL PERSONS

454. Conditions under which a Neutral Individual cannot take Advantage of his Neutrality.—" The nationals of a State which takes no part in the war are considered to be neutrals." (Art. 16).[16]

" A neutral cannot take advantage of his neutrality:

" (*a*) If he commits hostile acts against a belligerent;

" (*b*) If he commits acts in favor of a belligerent, particularly if he voluntarily takes service in the ranks of the armed force of one of the parties.

" In such cases, the neutral shall not be more severely treated by the belligerent against whom he has abandoned his neutrality than a national of the other belligerent State could be [treated] for the same act " (Art. 17).[17]

455. Acts which are not to be considered Unneutral.—" The following acts shall not be considered as committed in favor of one of the belligerents, within the meaning of Article 17, letter (*b*):

" (*a*) The furnishing of supplies or the making of loans to one of the belligerents, provided that the person thus furnishing or lending lives neither in the territory of the other party nor in territory occupied by him, and that the supplies do not come from these territories;

" (*b*) The rendering of services in matters of police, or of civil administration " (Art. 18).[18]

detained until after the conclusion of peace, when it should be restored to its rightful owner. See especially 2 Oppenheim, § 341.

[16] 5 H. C., 16. "Neutral subjects, taking part in hostilities on behalf of one belligerent, are liable to be treated by the other belligerent in every respect as if they were enemy subjects, and their own Government has no right to object to their being so treated.

"Neutral subjects resident in the territory of a belligerent are, equally with the other inhabitants of the country, liable to suffer in person and property through the events of the war; and their Governments acquire thereby no right to claim compensation on their behalf. Such compensation, if not awarded by the special provisions of a treaty, is given only as a matter of grace and favor. They are, for instance, liable to be removed from their homes or even to be banished from the country, on suspicion of misconduct towards an occupying army, or for reasons of strategic convenience." Holland, No. 136.

[17] 5 H. C., 17. "It was agreed at the Conference of 1907 that expressions of sympathy are not 'acts' within the meaning of clause (*b*)." Holland, No. 137.

[18] 5 H. C., 18. Articles 16–18 are the surviving remnants of a German draft of twelve articles originally intended to form Chapter V of the Regulations for the Laws of War on Land. These articles, which constituted the first chapter of the German draft, were not accepted by Great Britain.

4. NEUTRAL PROPERTY

456. Railway Material.—" Railway material coming from the territory of neutral Powers, whether belonging to those Powers or to companies or private persons, and recognizable as such, cannot be requisitioned or utilized by a belligerent, unless in the case of and to the extent required by absolute necessity. It shall be sent back, as soon as possible, to the country of its origin.

" The neutral Power may likewise, in case of necessity, retain and make use, to a corresponding extent, of railway material coming from the territory of the belligerent Power.

" Compensation shall be paid, on either side, in proportion to the material used, and the duration of its use " (Art. 19).[19]

The main feature of the German proposals was the adoption of the principle of nationality instead of that of domicile as a test of status in belligerent territory. They provided, *e.g.* that military services should not be solicited from or required of neutral individuals during a war; that neutral Powers should engage to prevent their nationals from enlisting in the army of either belligerent; that no war taxes, *i.e.* specific requisitions or contributions for military purposes, should be demanded from neutral persons; that neutral property should not be injured or destroyed unless required by the exigencies of war, etc. For an English translation of the rejected German proposals, see De Bustamante, in 2 *A. J.* (1908), 109–10; or 1 Scott, 826–28.

The adoption of these proposals would have established "a *régime* highly favorable both to persons and property of neutrals in belligerent States. Great Britain, having large colonies with populations drawn from many States, would have been considerably handicapped if she had never been able to avail herself of the service of immigrants freely offered, who, not having resided long enough to acquire British nationality, still remained technically subjects of a neutral Power. The British delegate strongly objected to the German proposals, and he was supported by the delegates of France, Russia, and Japan, who also declined to accept the favored position created for subjects of neutral Powers in belligerent States." Higgins, 293–94.

These proposals were supported by Germany, Austria, Spain, Switzerland, and the United States.

The following wishes bearing on this subject were unanimously expressed by the Hague Conference of 1907:

"2. That, in case of war, the competent authorities, civil and military, should make it their special duty to insure and safeguard the maintenance of pacific relations, more particularly of a commercial and industrial nature, between the inhabitants of the belligerent States and neutral countries.

"3. That the Powers should regulate by special Conventions, the position as regards military charges, of foreigners residing without their territory." See Higgins, 69 and 85; and 2 Westlake (1st ed.), 285.

[19] 5 H. C., 19. Cf. H. R. (1899), 54, which it replaces. This article was the result of a compromise between the opposing views of France and Germany with reference to railway material coming from neutral countries like Belgium

457. Neutral Property of other Kinds.—" Property of neutrals of other kinds, found in territory which is the scene of hostilities, even though not placed by them at the disposal of the enemy, is liable to be taken possession of, or even destroyed, for strategic reasons, by either belligerent; but compensation must in this case be made, by the belligerent so acting, to the neutral owners for the loss they have sustained." [20]

and Luxemburg. The Conference adopted a middle course. But "the terms used in this Article leave the neutral very much at the mercy of the belligerent as regards the requisition and use of railway material. Who is to be the judge of the necessity, and what is to be the meaning of 'as soon as possible'?" Higgins, 294. For a contrary view, see 2 Westlake (1st ed.), 118 and 285–86.

On the *Convention on Neutral Powers and Persons in Land Warfare* as a whole, see: 1 and 3 *Actes et doc. de la deux confér.*, 125–29; 131–64, and 33–88, 179–230, respectively; * De Bustamante, in 2 *A. J.* (1908), 95–120; * Higgins, 182–294; * Holland, 62–68; Lémonon, 409–67; *Parl. Papers*, Misc. Nos. 4 and 5 (1908), *passim*; * 1 Scott, 541–55; 2 Westlake (1st ed.), 117–19, 284–87.

"This Convention affords, within modest limits, a starting point for future development and a basis on which may be built further rules safeguarding neutral interests. It contains on the whole well-accepted principles which were ready for codification.

"All the Powers except China and Nicaragua [which have since adhered] have signed this Convention, but Great Britain made reservations in regard to Articles 16, 17, and 18, and the Argentine Republic in regard to Article 18." Higgins, 294.

[20] Holland, No. 140. This paragraph, which is not a part of 5 H. C., may be regarded as a sort of corollary. In any event, it states a rule of International Law.

Analogous to this right of belligerents, in case of extreme urgency or necessity, to requisition, utilize, and even to destroy property belonging to neutrals in belligerent territory was the old so-called *right of angary* which arose in the Middle Ages (though the idea itself was derived from Roman Law) and was much practiced by Louis XIV. It consisted in the embargo on and seizure of neutral merchantmen in belligerent harbors and the use of such vessels, together with their crews, for the transportation of troops, munitions and provisions in payment of freight in advance. In the seventeenth and eighteenth centuries, many treaties forbade this practice and the so-called right fell into disuse during the latter half of the eighteenth century, though it was again revived by Napoleon in 1798 for the invasion of Egypt. There were few, if any, recorded instances in the nineteenth century, but many of the leading authorities continued to assert this belligerent right, at least in case of extreme urgency or necessity. The Institute of International Law, however, declared it abolished in 1898. See Art. 39, in Scott, *Resolutions*, 154.

During the World War the practice was revived, though there was no attempt made to compel the services of the crews of the vessels requisitioned. On March 31, 1918, President Wilson issued a proclamation (for text, see Supp. to 12 *A. J.*, 1918, p. 259) asserting that "the imperative military needs of the United States require the immediate utilization of vessels of Netherlands registry, now lying within the territorial waters of the United S†ates," and he authorized the Secretary of the Navy to take over such vessels as "may be necessary for essential purposes connected with the prosecution of the war against the German Government." The proclamation further stated that the United States Shipping Board shall make to the owners of the vessels full compensation, "in accordance with the principles of International Law."

In consequence of this proclamation, 77 Dutch vessels lying in American harbors were requisitioned, and Great Britain soon took similar action. The Dutch Government protested, but to no avail. Matters were subsequently adjusted with the Dutch Government. For the requisition of certain vessels under construction belonging to Norwegians, the United States Government paid under protest on Feb. 26, 1923, the sum of $12,239,852.47—the amount awarded by The Hague Court of Arbitration on June 30, 1921. For this award, see 17 A. J. (1923), 362. For the protest of Sec'y Hughes, see *Ibid.*, 287–89.

On *Requisitions of Neutral Vessels during the World War*, see: Basdavant, in 23 R. D. I. P. (1923), 268–79; * 1 Garner, §§ 119–20; 2 Hyde, § 635; Scott, in 12 A. J. (1918), 340–56.

On the so-called *Right of Angary*, see especially: * Albrecht, *Requisitionen von neutralem Privateigentum, insbesondere von Schiffen*, publ. as Supp. to 6 Z. V. (1912) and trans. by Henckels and Crocker (see below), 7–57; Allin, in 2 *Minn. Law Rev.* (1917–18), 415–28; Den Beer Poortugael in *Het Internationaal Maritiem Recht* (1888), 413, trans. by Henckels and Crocker, 68–71; * Bullock, in *Brit. Yr. Bk.* (1922–23), 99–129; 2 Cobbett, 376–78, 384–87; 2 Fauchille, Nos. 1490[5-6], 1493[4]; Fenwick, 529–31; Grotius, III, c. 17, § 1 (see also II, c. 2, §§ 6–9); 1 Garner, § 118; Hall, § 278, pp. 902 ff. of 8th ed.; Hall, *Law of Naval Warfare* (1921), 44–46; * Harley, in 13 A. J. (1919), 267–301; 3 Hautefeuville, 396 ff.; * Henckels and Crocker, *Memorandum of Authorities on Law of Angary* (1919); 2 Hyde, §§ 633–35; 2 Kleen, §§ 165, 230; Lawrence, § 233, pp. 623–27 of 7th ed.; 3 Mérignhac, 586–91; * 2 Oppenheim, §§ 364–67; 3 Phillimore, § 29; Rolin, in 47 (3 ser. 1) R. D. I. (1920), 19 ff.; Scott, *Cases*, 733 (case of the *Zamora*); Spaight, *War Rights on Land*, 510–13; Taylor, § 641; Vattel, II, § 121.

For selected references on the Law of Neutrality, whether at sea or on land, see Bibliography at the end of the next chapter.

CHAPTER XXXIII

NEUTRAL RIGHTS AND DUTIES IN MARITIME WARFARE

The Hague Conference of 1907 adopted the following Convention respecting the " Rights and Duties of Neutral Powers in Maritime War ":

1. PROHIBITIONS UPON BELLIGERENTS

458. General Principles.—" Belligerents are bound to respect the sovereign rights of neutral Powers and to abstain, in neutral territory or neutral waters, from all acts which would constitute a breach of neutrality on the part of the Powers which [knowingly] tolerated them " (Art. 1).[1]

" All acts of hostility, including capture and the exercise of the right of search, committed by belligerent warships in the territorial waters of a neutral Power, constitute a violation of neutrality and are strictly forbidden " (Art. 2).[2]

459. Prizes captured in Neutral Waters.—" When a ship has been captured in the territorial waters of a neutral

---

[1] 13 H. C. (1907), 1. Cf. 5 H. C., 1, *supra*, No. 448. "If a violation of neutrality occurs, it is a neutral's duty to take steps to obtain redress, especially where the other belligerent is injuriously affected, but this is not definitely stated in the Convention." Higgins, 461.

[2] This principle has been generally recognized both in theory and practice for over a century, though it was occasionally violated in the nineteenth century. The United States was guilty of at least two such violations during the Civil War—the seizure of the *Florida* in Brazilian, and the *Chesapeake* in British waters; but in both these cases the acts were disavowed and ample apology and reparation made. If possible, prizes thus captured must be restored. It is unnecessary to multiply references on this point. The leading case is that of the *Anna* (5 C. Rob. 373), decided by Sir William Scott (later Lord Stowell). For several instances of such violations during the World War, see 2 Garner, § 562.

The Japanese were guilty of a serious violation of this principle during the Russo-Japanese War. On the night of Aug. 11, 1904, the partially disarmed Russian torpedo boat destroyer *Ryeshitelni* was seized in and towed out of the Chinese harbor of Chefoo (where she had taken refuge) by two Japanese destroyers.

On the *Ryeshitelni Incident*, see * Hershey, *Russo-Japanese War*, 260–63; Higgins, 463; * Lawrence, § 229; Smith and Sibley, 116 ff.; * Takahashi, 437–44.

679

Power, this Power must, if the prize is still within its jurisdiction, employ the means at its disposal to release the prize with its officers and crew, and to intern the prize crew.

" If the prize is not within the jurisdiction of the neutral Power, the captor Government must, on the demand of that Power, release the prize with its officers and crew " (Art. 3).[3]

460. **Prize Courts in Neutral Territory.**—" A Prize Court cannot be set up by a belligerent on neutral territory or on a vessel in neutral waters " (Art. 4).[4]

461. **Neutral Territory as Base of Operations.**—" Belligerents are forbidden to use neutral ports and waters as a base of naval operations against their adversaries, particularly to erect wireless telegraph stations or any apparatus intended to serve as a means of communication with the belligerent forces on land or sea " (Art. 5).[5]

2. PROHIBITIONS UPON NEUTRAL POWERS

462. **Supply of War Materials, etc.**—" The supply, in any manner, directly or indirectly, by a neutral Power to a belligerent Power, of warships, ammunition, or war material of any kind whatever, is forbidden " (Art. 6).[6]

[3] 13 H. C., 3.   Cf. 12 H. C., 3.
[4] 13 H. C., 4.   This rule requires no comment.
[5] 13 H. C., 5.   Cf. 5. H. C., 3 (a) *supra*, No. 440 of which this article is in part a repetition.   A neutral Government is under the corresponding obligation to use due diligence, *i.e.* the means at its disposal, "not to permit or suffer either belligerent to make use of its ports or waters as the base of naval operations against the other, or for the purpose of a renewal or augmentation of military supplies or arms, or the recruitment of men."   Second rule of the Treaty of Washington.   See 7 Moore, § 1330.
[6] 13 H. C., 6.   The continued sale and delivery by the United States Government to agents of the French Government of arms and munitions of war after the outbreak of the Franco-German War of 1870 have been defended on the ground that the sales had begun prior to the opening of hostilities, but they cannot be justified.   See 7 Moore, *Digest*, § 1309.

Germany appears to have evaded this rule during the Russo-Japanese War by permitting the sale and delivery to Japan of a number of vessels practically forming part of her Auxiliary Navy, though belonging to the North German Lloyd and German Hamburg American Steamship Companies.   True it is that the sale of merchant vessels by neutral individuals to belligerents has been generally upheld in spite of the adaptability of many of these vessels to warlike purposes; but the fact that these vessels appear to have been auxiliary cruisers of the German navy puts a different face on the matter.   "In view of the close and intimate relations which subsist between these companies and the German Government, the sale and delivery of such vessels would seem to be impossible without the consent or connivance of that Government, and it can

" A neutral Power is not bound to prevent the export or transit, for the use of either belligerent, of arms, munitions of war, or, in general, of anything which could be of use to an army or fleet." (Art. 7).[7]

463. Fitting out or Arming of Ships on Neutral Territory.

—" A neutral Government is bound to employ the means at its disposal to prevent the fitting out or arming of any vessel within its jurisdiction which it has reason to believe is intended to cruise, or engage in hostile operations against a Power with which that Government is at peace.   It is also bound to display the same vigilance to prevent the departure from its jurisdiction of any vessel intended to cruise, or engage in hostile operations, which has been adapted in whole or in part within the said jurisdiction to warlike use " (Art. 8).[8]

hardly be contended that such consent or connivance could be given without a serious breach of neutral obligation." Hershey, *The Russo-Japanese War*, 110. For the facts and further discussion, see *Ibid.*, 91 ff.; Holland, in 37 *R. D. I.* (1905), 362 f.; Hyde, in 2 *A. J.* (1908), 511; 2 Oppenheim, § 321; and Takahashi, 485–89.

[7] 13 H. C., 7. Cf. 5 H. C., 7 which is couched in identical terms. See *supra*, No. 450 and note 7 for comment and references.

It should be noted that warships are not specifically mentioned in this article. Is this by way of exclusion or inclusion? This question appears to be unanswered. For discussion, see note 8, *below*.

[8] 13 H. C., 8. This is substantially a repetition of the First Rule of the Treaty of Washington (1871), relating to the arbitration of the Alabama Claims. For the text of these rules, see 7 Moore, *Digest*, § 1330. As to their origin, see 1 Moore, *Int. Arbitrations*, 495 ff. It will be noted that the phrase *due diligence* used in the Treaty of Washington is replaced by *means at its disposal* in 13 H. C., 8. Whether this furnishes a more definite test with a clearer meaning remains to be seen.

It should also be noted that 13 H. C., 8 adopts the Anglo-American doctrine of intent, but it is the intent which determined the probable destination or use of the vessel rather than that of the owner or shipbuilder. The British Act of 1870 goes further, and prohibits not only the actual commissioning, equipping, and dispatching, but also the building or equipping under contract of any "ship with intent or knowledge, or having reasonable cause to believe that the same shall or will be employed in the naval or military service of any foreign State at war with any friendly State."

Is the export, sale, or delivery of a warship to a belligerent purchaser or destination ever permissible? American statesmen and jurists have always held that "there is nothing in our laws, or in the Law of Nations, that forbids our citizens from sending armed vessels, as well as munitions of war, to foreign ports for sale. It is a commercial adventure which no nation is bound to prohibit, and which only exposes the persons engaged in it to the penalty of confiscation." Judge Story, in the *Santissima Trinidad* (1827), 7 Wheat. 283, and Evans, *Cases*, 788 or Scott, 823. Cf. *U. S.* v. *Quincy* (1832), 6 Peters, 445;

3. Application of the Rule of Impartiality

464. General Principles.—" A neutral Power must apply impartially to the two belligerents the conditions, the restrictions, or prohibitions, issued by it in regard to the

and *U. S.* v. *The Meteor* (1866), Scott, 828. For a brief review of these cases, see 2 Westlake (1st ed.), 188–89. For a digest of leading American cases, see Dana, note 215 to Wheaton, pp. 543–47. For opinions of American statesmen and judges, see 7 Moore, *Digest*, §§ 1295 ff. and 1307 ff.; and 3 Wharton, *Digest*, §§ 393 and 396.

But this view can scarcely be longer maintained in the face of the First Rule of the Treaty of Washington, now incorporated in 13 H. C., 8. As one of our leading American authorities, Dr. Freeman Snow, has well said: "In considering this question, it should be remembered that, by the introduction of steam as the motive power of ships, and of iron and steel as the material of their construction, the conditions of maritime warfare have been very radically changed. What might have been a reasonable rule as applied in the time of sailing ships might now in the age of swift ironclads, be intolerably oppressive. In the cases of *Santissima Trinidad*, *U. S.* v. *Quincy*, and the *Meteor*, the courts were dealing with small sailing vessels, which had been converted into privateers, the possession of which by one or the other belligerent Power made very little difference in the general result of the struggle; whereas, the possession of an iron-clad ship might well turn the scale one war or the other, as indeed it did in the war between Chile and Peru in 1880–1881. This great power of inflicting injury upon one of the belligerents, it is fair to say, ought not to be permitted to neutral citizens, and the neutral nation is alone in a position to restrain them.

"In view of these facts, it is believed that the doctrine set up by the United States Neutrality Act and the Federal Courts, that the 'intent' of the owner or shipbuilder is the criterion by which his guilt or innocence is to be judged, is wholly inadequate; it would not for a moment stand the test of due diligence as applied by the Geneva Tribunal." Snow, *Cases*, note on pp. 437–38. Cf. Scott, *Cases* (ed. of 1902), 720.

For a complete history of the "Alabama" cases and the Geneva Award of 1872, see U. S. *Diplomatic Correspondence* for the years 1863–1871; *Papers relating to the Treaty of Washington; Case of Great Britain* with Appendix; *Case of U. S.; Claims of the U. S.;* etc. For good abridgments of the proceedings of the Geneva Board, see 1 Moore, *Int. Arbitrations*, ch. 14, or 7 *Digest*, § 1330. For a good brief sketch, see Walker, *Science*, 458–502. For an excellent summary of the controversy from the British point of view, see Bernard, *The Neutrality of Great Britain during the American Civil War* (1870), *passim.* For a summary from the American point of view, see Cushing, *Treaty of Washington* (1873). See also Balch, *The Alabama Arbitration* (1900).

"In view of the unsatisfactory and inadequate character of the older body of doctrine, would it not be well to take a step or two even beyond the First Rule of the Treaty of Washington and broadly assert that a neutral State is bound to use the means at its disposal, not only to prevent the fitting out, arming, or equipping within its jurisdiction and departure from its territory of any vessel intended for the use of either belligerent, but also the construction, sale, and exportation of any warship whatsoever for or to any other than a *bona fide* neutral purchaser? Nay, would it not be well to go still farther and insist that a neutral State is bound to use the means at its disposal to prevent the construction for, or sale to, a belligerent purchaser, or the exportation to a

admission into its ports, roadsteads, or territorial waters, of belligerent warships or of their prizes.

" Nevertheless, a neutral Power may forbid a belligerent vessel which has failed to conform to the orders and regulations made by it, or which has violated neutrality, to enter its ports and roadsteads " (Art. 9).[9]

465. **Passage of Belligerent Warships through Territorial Waters.**—" The neutrality of a Power is not affected by the mere passage through its territorial waters of warships or prizes belonging to belligerents " (Art. 10).[10]

belligerent destination, of any vessel which is adapted or readily convertible to belligerent use?" Hershey, *The Russo-Japanese War*, 106. See *Ibid.*, pp. 106–09, for some arguments in favor of this position. See pp. 91 ff. for alleged violations of the rules governing this subject during the Russo-Japanese Conflict.

These rules are for the most part inadequately dealt with in works on International Law. Interesting discussions may be found in * Hall, §§ 224–25; 2 Hyde, §§ 853–54; Lawrence (3d ed.), §§ 261–63; 1 Kleen, 285–348; and * 2 Westlake (1st ed.), 184–98.

In the case of military expeditions, it should especially be noted that it is immaterial whether the various parts or elements of the expedition, such as ships, crews, or arms, are dispatched separately from the neutral territory or combined outside its limits. They are alike illegal. See especially the *Terceira* expedition of 1829 as reported in Hall, § 223; Lawrence, § 231; or * 2 Westlake, 194–95; and the *Horsa*, in 7 Moore, *Digest*, pp. 911–12.

Upon complaint of the German ambassador that submarines were being built in the United States for the use of the Entente Powers during the World War, the U. S. Government took steps to prevent further deliveries, but held hydro-aeroplanes to be essentially air craft which could be used for military purposes in the air only. See 2 Garner, p. 384 and n.

[9] 13 H. C., 9. "The right of a State to forbid in a general way access to its ports to the belligerents is not in question in Article 9, and follows from its right of issuing general regulations and prohibitions." Reply of M. Renault to Sir Ernest Satow, cited by Higgins, 467.

During the Russo-Japanese War, the Scandinavian States closed certain of their ports to all belligerent warships (except in case of distress and for hospital ships). Lawrence, *War and Neutrality*, 133.

[10] 13 H. C., 10. "Admiral Sperry declared that the United States could not accept this Article by reason of political considerations implied in the question of passage through territorial waters." Hyde, in 2 *A. J.* (1908), 515.

The question of passage through straits which form international passage-ways was left open. Several Scandinavian delegates proposed the addition of the rule adopted by the Institute of Int. Law in 1894: "Straits which form a channel from one open sea to another can never be closed." "The question was discussed by the Examining Committee but no resolutions were passed on these points. From the opinions expressed there it appeared to be the general feeling that a neutral State could forbid even the innocent passage through parts of its territorial waters so far as it was necessary to maintain its neutrality, but that this prohibition could not extend to straits uniting two open seas. Article 10 leaves these questions unsettled, they remain '*sous l'empire du droit*

466. **Neutral Pilots.**—" A neutral Power may allow belligerent warships to employ its licensed pilots " (Art. 11).[11]

467. **Duration of Sojourn of Belligerent Warships in Neutral Ports and Waters.**—" In default of special provision to the contrary in the legislation of a neutral Power, belligerent warships are forbidden to remain in the ports, roadsteads, or territorial waters of the said Power for more than twenty-four hours, except in the cases covered by the present Convention " (Art. 12).[12]

" If a Power which has been informed of the outbreak of hostilities learns that a warship of a belligerent is in one of its ports or roadsteads, or in its territorial waters, it must

des gens général.' All that it provides is that a State's neutrality is not compromised by the passage through its territorial waters of belligerent ships of war." Higgins, 468. For references and citations from Oppenheim, see *Ibid.*, note. Cf. *supra*, No. 193.

[11] 13 H. C., 11. It is not bound to provide them. It is extremely doubtful whether this permission extends to the employment of official pilots on the Open Sea.

[12] 13 H. C., 12. Cf. Art. 27. This Article represents a distinct step backward. Though the rule limiting the stay of belligerent warships in neutral ports (except for special reasons) to twenty-four hours was never officially accepted, *e.g.* by France, Germany, and Russia, it has been adopted by Great Britain, the United States, Japan, the Scandinavian countries, Brazil, Italy, Spain, China, etc., and it has been generally enforced during recent wars. The principle underlying the rule is that a belligerent armed vessel should not be permitted to remain in a neutral port longer than is absolutely necessary in order to procure innocent supplies or to effect repairs requisite for insuring seaworthiness.

An interesting German proposal supported by Russia was that the twenty-four hour rule should be obligatory in neutral ports and waters "situated in immediate proximity to the theater of war," but this was obviously impracticable.

"Article 12 makes no distinction between the belligerent war vessel which enters neutral waters simply *en route* to the theater of hostilities, and that which seeks refuge therein to escape capture. In the latter case, if special legislative provisions of the neutral so provided, a belligerent war vessel might, according to Article 12, be permitted to remain longer than twenty-four hours." Hyde, in 2 *A. J.* (1908), 517. This would violate a whole series of precedents set during the Russo-Japanese War.

On 13 H. C., 12, and the *24 Hours' Sojourn*, see especially: 17 *Annuaire* (for rule adopted by Institute of Int. Law), 285; * Benton (for the Spanish-American War), 185–87; Hall, § 231; * Hershey (for the Russo-Japanese War), ch. 7, *passim*; Higgins, 469–71; 2 Hyde, § 858, and in 2 *A. J.* (1908), 516–18; Lawrence, § 236, pp. 640–42; * Lémonon, 574–78; 7 Moore, § 1315; * Naval War College, *Int. Law Sit.* see general index, 1922; 2 Oppenheim, § 333, pp. 450–51; 1 Scott, 633–36; * 2 Westlake (1st ed.), 208–10, 329.

The 24 Hours Sojourn Rule appears to have been fairly well observed during

notify the said ship to depart within twenty-four hours or within the time prescribed by the local law " (Art. 13).[13]

" A belligerent warship may not prolong its stay in a neutral port beyond the time permitted except on account of damage or stress of weather. It must depart as soon as the cause of the delay is at an end." (Art. 14).[14]

468. Maximum Number of Belligerent Warships in Neutral Ports.—" In default of special provisions to the contrary in the laws of a neutral Power, the maximum number of warships belonging to a belligerent which may be in one of the ports or roadsteads of that Power simultaneously shall be three " (Art. 15).[15]

469. The Rule of Twenty-four Hours' Interval.—" When warships belonging to both belligerents are present simultaneously in a neutral port or roadstead, a period of not less than twenty-four hours must elapse between the departure of the ship belonging to one belligerent and the departure of the ship belonging to the other.

" The order of departure is determined by the order of arrival, unless the ship which arrived first is so circumstanced that an extension of its stay is permissible.

" A belligerent warship may not leave a neutral port or roadstead until twenty-four hours after the departure of a merchant ship flying the flag of its adversary " (Art. 16).[16]

470. Repairs in Neutral Ports.—" In neutral ports and roadsteads belligerent warships may only carry out such

the World War. See 2 Garner, § 563. See Supp. to 10 *A. J.* (1916), 121 ff., for Regulations Governing Visits of Men-of-War to Foreign Ports.

[13] 13 H. C., 13. Cf. Art. 24, *infra*, No. 474. On the case of the *Mandjur* (soon after the outbreak of Russo-Japanese War), see Hershey, 188–89; Higgins, 471; Lawrence, 137–39; and Takahashi, 418–29.

[14] " The regulations as to the length of time during which these vessels may remain in neutral ports, roadsteads, or waters do not apply to warships devoted exclusively to religious, scientific, or philanthropic purposes" (Art. 14).

[15] 13 H. C., 15. This rule was wholly new. The number three was selected as corresponding to the number usually allowed in time of peace.

[16] 13 H. C., 16. It should be noted that this article omits the saving clause "in default of special provisions to the contrary" contained in the previous articles.

The rule of the twenty-four hours' interval dates from the middle of the eighteenth century, whereas that of the twenty-four hours' sojourn was first introduced into international practice by Great Britain in 1862.

On the *24 Hours' Interval*, see especially: * Hall, § 231, pp. 750–53; Higgins, 472–73; Lawrence, § 236, p. 642; 2 Oppenheim, § 333, p. 447 and § 347, p. 469; and * 2 Westlake (1st ed.), 206–08.

repairs as are absolutely necessary to render them sea-
worthy, and may not add in any manner whatever to their
fighting force. The local authorities of the neutral Power
shall decide what repairs are necessary, and these must be
carried out with the least possible delay" (Art. 17).[17]

471. **Augmentation of Armaments in Neutral Waters.**—
" Belligerent warships may not make use of neutral ports,
roadsteads, and territorial waters for replenishing or increasing their supplies of war material or their armament,
or for completing their crews " (Art. 18).[18]

472. **Supply of Provisions and Fuel to Belligerent Warships in Neutral Ports.**—" Belligerent warships may only
revictual in neutral ports or roadsteads to bring up their
supplies to the peace standard.

" Similarly these vessels may only take sufficient fuel to
enable them to reach the nearest port in their own country.
They may, however, fill up their bunkers built to carry fuel,
when in neutral countries which have adopted this method
of determining the amount of fuel to be supplied.

" If, in accordance with the law of the neutral Power, the
ships are only supplied with coal twenty-four hours after
their arrival, the permissible duration of their stay is
extended by twenty-four hours " (Art. 19).[19]

[17] 13 H. C., 17. Cf. Arts. 13–15, *supra.* This is an admirable statement of
the rule governing repairs of belligerent armed vessels in neutral ports, except
that no repairs of injuries received in battle should be knowingly permitted by
the neutral. At least this was the precedent set by President Roosevelt in the
case of the three Russian cruisers interned at Manilla during the Russo-
Japanese War. See Hershey, 209 f.

On *Repairs and Internment of Belligerent Warships in Neutral Ports,* see
especially: 17 *Annuaire,* 285; Benton, 188–89; Donkier-Curtius, *Des navires
de guerre dans les eaux neutres* (1907); Gaborit, ch. 2; Hall, § 231; * Hershey,
204–10, 215; Higgins, 473–74; * 2 Hyde, § 860; * Lawrence, 644–45, and
War and Neutrality, 121; 7 Moore, §§ 1316–17; * Naval War College, *Int.
Law Sit.* (see general index, 1922); 2 Oppenheim, §§ 333 (5), 346–47 (3); * Takahashi, Pt. IV, ch. 1, pp. 417–58; 2 Westlake (1st ed.), 210–11. For the practice during the World War, see 2 Garner, § 563.

[18] 13 H. C., 18. Cf. 13 H. C., 5. Article 18 is in substance an enactment of
the second part of the Second Rule of the Treaty of Washington (1871) into
law. Cf. *supra,* No. 463.

[19] 13 H. C., 19. The discussion of the question of fuel supply to belligerent
warships in neutral ports was marked by divergent views. In accordance
with her practice since 1862—a practice followed by the United States, Japan,
and some other countries—Great Britain urged that the quantity of coal should
in no case exceed the amount necessary to enable the vessel to reach the nearest

" Belligerent warships which have taken fuel in a port belonging to a neutral Power may not replenish their supply in a port of the same Power within the succeeding three months " (Art. 20).[20]

473. **Prizes in Neutral Ports.**—" A prize may only be brought into a neutral port on account of unseaworthiness, stress of weather, or want of fuel or provisions.

" It must leave as soon as the circumstances which justified its entry are at an end.   If it does not, the neutral Power must order it to leave at once; should it fail to obey, the neutral Power must employ the means at its disposal to release it with its officers and crew and to intern the prize crew " (Art. 21).[21]

port of its own country or "some nearer named neutral destination."   Japan and Spain supported this view.   On the other hand, Germany, France and Russia claimed that belligerent vessels should be permitted to take in a normal peace supply.

The result was a compromise which cannot be regarded as satisfactory. The supply of coal or oil in any quantity in neutral waters to a modern battle fleet or warship engaged on an errand of destruction would seem to be a violation of the fundamental principles of neutrality.   But the discussion of this question is usually colored by a sense of national interest.   Thus, the main source of the Continental opposition to the limitation or prohibition of the supply of coal to belligerent warships in neutral ports lies in the fact that most of these States are poorly supplied with coaling stations as compared with Great Britain.   But, whatever the motive, there can be no doubt that British practice in this matter approaches most nearly the ideal or theoretical requirements.   The highest standard yet attained was set during the Russo-Japanese War by a proclamation issued by the Governor of Malta refusing hospitality to belligerent warships "proceeding to the seat of war" or proceeding to search for contraband.   For the text of this interesting proclamation, see Hershey, *Russo-Japanese War*, 200.

On *Coaling in Neutral Ports*, see especially: 17 *Annuaire*, 273; Benton, 190–94; 2 Fauchille, No. 1463[13–16]; Hall, § 221, pp. 726–27; * Hershey, ch. 7, *passim*, particularly pp. 198–203; * Higgins, 475–78; 2 Hyde, § 859, and in 2 *A. J.* (1908), 521–23; De Lapradelle, in 11 *R. D. I. P.* (1914), 531 ff.; * Lawrence, 645–49, and *War and Neutrality* (2d ed.), 120–37; * 7 Moore, *Digest*, § 1305; * Naval War College, *Int. Law Sit.* (see gen. index, 1922); 2 Oppenheim, §§ 333 (4), 346; Pilidi, *La combustible en temps de guerre* (1909); * 2 Westlake, (1st ed.), 210–13, 330.   For the practice during the World War, see Alvarez, *La Grande Guerre Européenne et la neutralité du Chile*, Pt. II, ch. 5; and 2 Garner, § 561.   For Chilean Neutrality Regulations regarding coal, etc., see *Int. Law Topics* (1916), 15 ff.

[20] 13 H. C., 20.   This has been the British practice since 1862.

[21] 13H. C., 21. Cf. Art. 3, *supra*.   Many States, *e. g.* Great Britain, Italy and Japan, prohibit belligerent warships from bringing their prizes into their ports when neutral except in case of distress.   France, Spain, and Brazil adhere to the older twenty-four hour rule for the sojourn in their ports of such vessels with their prizes.

" A neutral Power must, similarly, release a prize brought into one of its ports under circumstances other than those referred to in Article 21 " (Art. 22).[22]

" A neutral Power may allow prizes to enter its ports and roadsteads, whether under convoy or not, when they are brought there to be sequestered pending the decision of a Prize Court. It may have the prize taken to another of its ports.

On *Prizes in Neutral Ports* see especially: Hall (6th ed.), 614–15; * Higgins, 478–79; 3 Phillimore, § 379; * 2 Westlake, 214–15.

In Feb. 1916 the British S. S. *Appam*, captured by a German cruiser, was brought into the port of Newport News, Virginia by a small German prize crew assisted by the passengers and crew of the prize. The German ambassador at Washington informed our State Department of the intention of the prize master to remain with his prize in American waters until further notice and requested the internment in the United States of certain of her crew and passengers on the ground that the vessel had offered armed resistance when captured. This request was refused by the American authorities, and the ship's crew and passengers were set at liberty. But the German prize crew were kept on board the vessel as virtual prisoners.

Meanwhile, the British ambassador had made a formal demand for the release of the *Appam* to the British owners, and this demand was shortly followed by the filing of a libel against the vessel in the District Court by the owners. The American Secretary of State refused to sustain the German protest against the assumption of jurisdiction by the United States Court. The Federal District Court (234 Fed. Cases, 389) in which the case was tried held Arts. 21 and 22 of the 13th Hague Conventions (see above) were decisive. These articles, the court said, were declaratory of the existing Law of Nations and as such binding. And this in spite of the fact that Great Britain had not ratified the convention. The court concluded that "the manner of bringing the *Appam* into the waters of the United States, as well as her presence in these waters, constitutes a violation of the neutrality of the United States." Upon appeal to the United States Supreme Court the decision of the District Court was affirmed. For the Supreme Court decision in the case of the *Appam*, see 243 U. S. 124, or 11 *A. J.* (1917), 443. For abridged reports, see Evans, *Cases*, 779 or Scott, 858. For the diplomatic correspondence relating to the *Appam*, see Spec. Supp. to 10 *A. J.* (1916), 387 ff.

On the case of the *Appam*, see: Allin, in 1 *Minn. Law Rev.* (1917), 1–9; Bellot, in 2 *Grot. Soc.* (1917), 11–19; Borchard and Coudert, in 11 *A. J.* (1917), 270 ff. and 302 ff.; * 1 and 2 Garner, note on pp. 21–22 and § 567; 2 Hyde, § 862; and * Scott, in 10 *A. J.* (1917), 809–31.

In August, 1916 the Allies proposed that asylum be not granted by neutral Powers to submarines of any description. The United States declined to accede to this request, and allowed the German U-53 to enter the harbor of Newport. The Norwegian and Swedish Governments, however, pursued a different policy. On *Treatment of Submarines in Neutral Ports and Waters*, see: * 2 Garner, § 564; Hall, § 231 a; Hall, *Law of Naval Warfare* (1921), 158; 2 Oppenheim, § 344a; and Reeves, in 11 *A. J.* (1917), 147–53.

As to the *Deutschland*, a commercial submarine which was admitted to all the privileges of a merchantman in an American port, see 2 Garner, § 565.

[22] 13 H. C., 22.

" If the prize is convoyed by a warship, the prize crew may go on board the convoying ship.

" If the prize is not under convoy, the crew are left at liberty " (Art. 23).[23]

474. Internment of Belligerent Vessels in Neutral Ports and Detention of the Crew.—" If, notwithstanding the notification of the neutral Power, a belligerent warship does not leave a port where it is not entitled to remain, the neutral Power is entitled to take such measures as it considers necessary to render the ship incapable of putting to sea during the war, and the commanding officer of the ship must facilitate the execution of such measures.

" When a belligerent ship is detained by a neutral Power, the officers and crew are likewise detained.

" The officers and crew so detained may be left in the ship or kept either on another vessel or on land, and may be subjected to such measures of restriction as it may appear necessary to impose upon them. A sufficient number of men for looking after the vessel must, however, be always left on board.

" The officers may be left at liberty on giving their word not to quit the neutral territory without permission " (Art. 24).[24]

475. Measure of Due Diligence.—" A neutral Power is bound to exercise such surveillance as the means at its disposal allow to prevent any violation of the provisions of the above Articles occurring in its ports or roadsteads or in its waters " (Art. 25).[25]

476. Further Provisions.—" The exercise by a neutral Power of the rights laid down in the present Convention can

---

[23] 13 H. C., 23.   The purpose of this article is, according to M. Renault, "to render rarer, or to prevent, the destruction of prizes."   Whether this object will be attained remains to be seen.   It is certainly highly objectionable on principle.   The United States refused to accept this article.

[24] 13 H. C., 24.   Cf. 5 H. C., 11, par. 3.   For references on *Internment of Belligerent Armed Vessels*, see *supra*, p. 686 n.   The vessels are to be interned, the officers and crew detained.   This treatment is analogous to that accorded to belligerent troops seeking refuge on neutral territory.   Cf. *supra*, Nos. 451–52.

[25] 13 H. C., 25.   This article embodies the principle of the Third Rule of the Treaty of Washington (1871): "A neutral Government is bound to exercise due diligence in its own ports and waters and as to all persons within its jurisdiction, to prevent any violation of the foregoing obligations and duties."

never be considered as an unfriendly act by either belligerent who has accepted the Articles relating thereto " (Art. 26).[26]

" The Contracting Powers shall communicate to each other in due course all laws, ordinances, and other provisions regulating in their respective countries the status of belligerent warships in their ports and waters, by means of a communication addressed to the Government of the Netherlands and forwarded immediately by that Government to the other Contracting Powers." (Art. 27).[27]

[26] *Ibid.*, 26.

[27] *Ibid.*, 27. Art. 28 contains the usual stipulation that the "provisions of the present Convention are only applicable to the Contracting Powers and only if all the belligerents are parties to the Convention."

The force of this Convention is perhaps somewhat weakened by paragraph 7 of the *Preamble* which states that "these rules should not, in principle, be altered, in the course of the war, by a neutral Power, except where experience has shown the necessity for such change for the protection of the rights of that Power." This might conceivably be used as a pretext or loophole for the evasion of neutral obligations.

Other paragraphs in the *Preamble* emphasize the "desirability" of "specific enactments regulating the consequences of the status of neutrality" by neutral Powers; the obligation of impartiality in the application of the rules adopted; and that "in cases not covered by the present Convention, account must be taken of the general principles of the Law of Nations."

The following States did not sign this Convention: The United States, China, Cuba, Spain, and Nicaragua: but the United States and Nicaragua subsequently gave their adhesion. It seems Great Britain never ratified the Convention.

The following States made certain reservations: Germany in respect to Arts. 11–13 and 20; Great Britain, Arts. 19 and 23; Japan, Arts. 19 and 23; Turkey, as regards the Bosphorus and Dardanelles; the United States refused to accept Art. 23.

The Convention, as a whole, deserves praise for securing so much, but it has some glaring defects. Its greatest achievement is perhaps the successful incorporation of the substance of the Three Rules of the Treaty of Washington; its most striking defects are the failure to insist upon stricter rules limiting the sojourn of belligerent armed vessels in neutral ports and the supply of fuel to warships proceeding to the seat of hostilities, and the permission granted to neutral powers to admit prizes into their ports. "The rules laid down are nearly all accompanied by provisos enabling them to be excluded by a neutral strong enough and sufficiently interested to do so. The rights of neutrals are asserted, but their duties are not sufficiently emphasized." Higgins, 483.

On the 13th Hague Convention and Rights and Duties in Maritime War, see especially: 1 and 3 *Actes et doc. de la deux confér.*, 282, 295, and 460–518, 569–652, 695–735 respectively; 17 *Annuaire* (1898), 231–87; Barclay, *Problems*, etc., 83–90, 160–67, 348 ff.; * Benton, *Spanish-American War*, ch. 7; Bonfils or * 2 Fauchille, Nos. 1447–93; Bustamante y Sirven, *op. cit.*, ch. 22; Dupuis, *La droit de la guerre maritime* (1911), ch. 12; Einicke, *Rechte und Pflichten der neutralen Mächte im seekrieg* (1912); * Higgins, 445–83; * Holland, "Neutral Duties in a Maritime War," in *Proc. of the British Academy* (1905);

BIBLIOGRAPHY

Law of Neutrality generally (besides the general treatises on Int. Law).—21 *Annuaire* (1906), 100–88, 345-409; Ariga, *La guerre russojaponaise* (1908), *passim;* Asuni, *Droit maritime de l'Europe* (1805); Barclay, *Problems*, etc. (1907—see index); Barbosa, *Le devoir des neutres* (1917); Baty, *Britain and Sea Law* (1911); Benton, *Int. Law and Diplomacy of the Spanish-American War* (1908); Bernard, *Neutrality of Great Britain during the American Civil War* (1870); Bon, *La guerre russo-japonaise et la neutralité* (1909); Brewer, *Rights and Duties of Neutrals* (1916); Bynkershoek, *Questiones juris publici* (1737), lib. i, cc. 8–15; Campbell, *Neutral Rights and Obligations in the Anglo-Boer War* (1908); Descamp, *Le droit de la paix* (1898), and in 7 *R. D. I. P.* (1900), 629 ff. and 705 ff.; Donkier-Curtius, *Des navies de guerre dans les eaux neutres* (1907); Dupuis, *Le droit de la guerre maritime* (1911 and 1899); Einicke, *Rechte und Pflichten der neutralen Mächte im Seekrieg* (1912); Fenwick, *The Neutrality Laws of the U. S.* (1913); Féraud-Giraud, in 2 *R. D. I. P.* (1899), 291 ff.; Gaborit, *Questions de neutralité maritime soulévees par la guerre russo-japonais* (1906); Geffcken, "Die Neutralität," in 4 Holtzendorff; Gessner, *Le droit des neutres sur mer* (1876), and *Kriegführende u. neutrale Mächte* (1877); Hall, W. E., *The Rights and Duties of Neutrals* (1876); Hall, J. A., *The Law of Naval Warfare* (1921); 1 and 3 Hautefeuille, *Droits et devoirs des neutres* (1868); Heilborn, *Rechte und Pflichten der neutralen Staaten* (1887); Hershey, *Int. Law and Diplomacy of the Russo-Japanese War* (1906), *passim;* Holland, "Neutral Duties in a Maritime War," in 2 *Proceedings of the British Academy* (1905), or in 37 *R. D. I.* (1905), 359 ff., and *Letters to the "Times" upon War and Neutrality* (1909); Hübner, *De la saisie des bâtiments neutres* (1759); 1 and 2 Kleen, *Lois et usages de la neutralité* (1898–1900); Lawrence, *War and Neutrality in the Far East* (2d ed., 1904); Laws of Neutrality existing on August 1, 1914 (Wash., 1918); Ch. de Martens, *Causes célèbres* (1861); Mérignhac, in 32 *J. I. P.*, 592 ff., and *Les lois de la guerre sur terre* (1903), liv. V; 7 Moore, *Digest*, ch. 28, and *Am. Diplomacy* (1905), ch. 2; Nagaoka, in 31 *J. I. P.*, 285 ff.; Nys, *La guerre maritime* (1881), and 2 *Etudes*, 47–163 (see also 3 *Le droit int.*, 1912); Ortolan, *Règles int. et dip. de la mer* (1864); Perels, *Manuel de droit mar. int.* (1884), §§ 38 ff.; Pillet, *Les lois actuelles de la guerre* (1907), chs. 11–12; Rey, *La guerre russo-japonaise* (1911); 3 Rolin, *Le droit moderne de la guerre* (1921); Rosse, *Guide int. du commandant du bâtiment de guerre* (1891); Takahashi, *Int. Law applied to the Russo-Japanese War* (1908), Pt. IV; Testa, *Le droit public int. war* (1886), Pt. III, chs. 4–10; Vattel, liv. III, §§ 103–35; 2 Varreas, *Le lois de la guerre et la neutralité* (1906).

For a fuller Bibliography, see 2 Fauchille, pp. 635–38.

* 2 Hyde, §§ 848 ff., and in 2 *A. J.* (1908), 507–27; * Lawrence, Pt. IV, chs. 2–3, and *War and Neutrality*, ch. 6; Lémonon, *op. cit.*, 555–603; * 7 Moore, *Digest*, ch. 28; * 2 Oppenheim, Pt. III, ch. 2; 1 Scott, 620–48; Takahashi, *Russo-Japanese War*, Pt. IV, chs. 1–3; * 2 Westlake (1st ed.), ch. 8 and pp. 327–31.

CHAPTER XXXIV

THE SO-CALLED LAW OF BLOCKADE

477. Definition.—Blockade has been well defined as " the blocking of the approach to the enemy coast, or a part of it, for the purpose of preventing ingress and egress of vessels of all nations." [1]

478. Blockade as an Operation of War.—Blockade is an operation of war and " must be limited to the ports and coasts belonging to or occupied by the enemy." It can be directed only against an adversary. [2]

---

[1] 2 Oppenheim, § 368. Blockade should not be confounded with siege, though it has points of similarity as well as of dissimilarity. War blockade should also be distinguished from pacific blockades. Cf. *supra*, Nos. 324 ff. With reference to their purpose, war blockades are often spoken of as strategic or commercial, but these terms have no legal significance.

As an institute of maritime International Law, blockade dates from the sixteenth century and owes its origin to the Dutch who appear to have made the first applications of it as distinct from "siege" in 1584 and 1630. The Law of blockade may be said to have been elaborated by courts and jurists during the eighteenth century. On the *History of Blockade*, see especially: 2 Fauchille Nos. 1596–1609, and *De blocus maritime* (1882), 2–12; 1 Kleen, 542 ff.; * Söderquist, *Le blocus maritime* (1908), 7–119; 2 Westlake (1st ed.), 221–26, and *Collected Papers*, 325–37.

[2] Art. 1 of the unratified *Declaration of London* and *Report* on the Declaration, in Higgins, 542 and 572; or in Naval War College, *Int. Law Topics* (1909), 25 ff. Cf. D. L., 18 which declares that "the blockading forces must not bar access to neutral ports or coasts."

These rules, which were regarded as forming an undoubted part of the law of blockade prior to the World War, were violated in substance if not in form by the Allies during this great struggle, and it is not at all certain that they would not again be disregarded under similar circumstances.

On Feb. 4, 1915 the German Government issued its first war zone decree against Great Britain which has been frequently referred to as a submarine blockade. (This term is a misnomer, inasmuch as it possessed few, if any, of the elements of a lawful blockade.) On March 1, 1915, the British Government announced that it was the intention of the Allied Governments as a retaliatory measure "to seize all ships carrying goods of presumed enemy destination, ownership or origin." It declared, however, that these retaliatory measures would be enforced "without risk to neutral ships or to neutral or non-combatant life and in strict observance of the dictates of humanity. The British and French Governments will therefore hold themselves free to detain and take into ports ships carrying goods of presumed enemy destination, ownership, or origin. It is not intended to confiscate such vessels or cargoes unless they would other-

479. **A Blockade must be Effective.**—" In accordance with the Declaration of Paris of 1856, a blockade, in order to be binding, must be effective—that is to say—it must be maintained by a force sufficient really to prevent access to the enemy coast." (Art. 2).[3]

wise be liable to condemnation." Though not described as such, this was in effect a blockade, but it did not conform to the requirements regarded as essential to a legally valid blockade. By an Order in Council of March 11 and a French decree of March 13, 1915 the proposed measures against trade with Germany were definitely proclaimed.

The Governments of the United States, Denmark, the Netherlands, Norway and Sweden protested vigorously against these measures. The State Department at Washington declared that they "constituted an encroachment upon the rights of neutrals; that the effect was to establish a virtual blockade of the ports of neutral countries adjacent to Germany; that the right of retaliation against an enemy did not include the right to interfere with the lawful commerce of neutrals," etc. 2 Garner, § 325. For the British defense, see *Ibid.*, § 516.

The so-called blockade of Germany during the World War went much further than the application of the doctrine of continuous voyage to blockade forbidden by the unratified Declaration of London; it amounted to an attempt (for the most part successful) to control sea trade which had a presumptive enemy destination, ownership or origin, with neutral countries adjacent to Germany. It involved a practical violation of the second and third rules of the Declaration of Paris (see *supra*, No. 73). In order to make this "blockade" really effective, the Allies were forced (mainly, it is true, through diplomatic channels and through arrangements with such associations as the Netherlands Overseas Trust) to forbid the re-exportation of imported foods to Germany, or Austria-Hungary. They even went to the extent of "rationing" neutral countries like Holland by which importations into these countries were "limited to the estimated amount of their domestic requirements. Goods in excess thereof were seized under the application of the principle of destination." 2 Garner, § 528.

It should, however, be pointed out that the blockade of Germany by the Allies was in some respects more favorable to neutral trade than a technically legal blockade would have been, since vessels and cargoes were for the most part subject to preëmption instead of confiscation.

On the *Blockade of Germany during the World War*, see especially: Clapp, *Economic Aspects of the War* (1915), chs. 5–6; * 2 Garner, ch. 33, and *Prize Law during the World War* (1921, sects. 460–63); Hall, § 266 a; 2 Hyde, §§ 829–32; 2 Oppenheim, § 390 a; Parmelee, *Blockade and Sea-Power* (1924), chs. 3 ff.; and Perrinjaquet, in 24 *R. D. I. P.* (1915), 210–38.

For the diplomatic correspondence on the subject between the United States and Germany, see Supp. to 9–11 *A. J.* (1915–17, see indices).

[3] D. L., 2. On the *Declaration of Paris*, see especially: Higgins, 1–4; and *supra*, No. 73.

The phrase "really to prevent access" should not be taken too literally. It must mean "to make the attempt at access highly dangerous." This, at least, has been the universal practice. The abuse aimed at was that of so-called "paper" blockades of which the wars of the Napoleonic period furnish good illustrations.

" The question whether a blockade is effective is a question of fact." (Art. 3).[4]

480. **Effect of Bad Weather.**—" A blockade is not regarded as raised if the blockading forces are temporarily driven off by bad weather." (Art. 4).[5]

481. **Rule of Impartiality.**—" A blockade must be applied impartially to the ships of all nations." (Art. 5).[6]

" The commander of a blockading force may grant to a warship permission to enter, and subsequently to leave, a blockaded port." (Art. 6).[7]

482. **Circumstances of Distress.**—" In circumstances of

[4] D. L., 3. This is essentially a question for judicial decision. The number of the vessels or their position is in itself immaterial. They need not be anchored or stationary, as has been claimed by some Continental authorities (*e.g.* Fauchille, Hautefeuille, Heffter, Kleen, Ortolan, etc.), but an effective blockade may be maintained by cruisers at a considerable distance from the blockaded port or coast. Under certain circumstances one cruiser may be sufficient. The leading judicial decisions on this point are those of Lord Stowell and Dr. Lushington in the *Betsy* (1798), 1 C. Rob. 93, and Evans, *Cases*, 644, or Scott, 932; The *Franciska* (1854), 2 Spinks, 287. See also the decision of C. J. Fuller in the *Olinde Rodrigues* (1898), 174 U. S. 510, and Evans, 665. Cf. the *Nancy* (1809), 1 Acton, 57, and Scott, 941. Most German writers appear to agree with this view, *e.g.* Bluntschli, Art. 829; Liszt, § 64, II; and Perels, § 49.

In the controversy respecting the Allied blockade of Germany during the World War between the United States and Great Britain, the United States Government admitted that it was no longer practicable to render a blockade effective by means of a cordon of ships in the immediate offing of a blockaded port. See 2 Garner, § 516; and 2 Hyde, §§ 824 and 829. See particularly the middle paragraph in 2 Hyde, p. 648.

[5] D. L., 4. "It is not sufficient that the blockade be established; it must be maintained. If it is raised it may be reëstablished, but then it will require the same formalities as though it were established for the first time. . . . Article 4 must be considered restrictive in the sense that bad weather is the only form of compulsion which can be alleged. If the blockading forces are withdrawn for any other reason, the blockade would be regarded as raised, and, in case it should be reëstablished, Articles 12 (last rule) and 13 would apply." *Report*, *op. cit.*, in Higgins, 573–74.

[6] D. L., 5. In other words it must be universal. Unless it is thus universally and impartially applied, it need not be respected by neutrals. Cf. *The Rolla* (1807), 6 C. Rob. 372; and the *Franciska* (1855), 10 Moore, P. C. 37, and Evans, *Cases*, 648 or Scott, 944.

The failure of the allies to blockade the Baltic ports of Germany during the World War and thus prevent trade between Sweden and Germany was not a cause for just criticism on the part of the United States, inasmuch as it resulted from a geographical situation rather than deliberate intention or desire to favor Scandinavian trade as against American exporters. 2 Garner, § 518.

[7] D. L., 6. This is a matter left to his judgment or discretion. If he permits entrance to neutral warships, it is a matter of courtesy.

distress, acknowledged by an authority of the blockading forces, a neutral vessel may enter a place under blockade and subsequently leave it, provided that she has neither discharged nor shipped any cargo there." (Art. 7).[8]

483. **A Blockade must be Declared and Notified.**—A blockade, in order to be binding, should be declared and notified." (Art. 8).[9]

484. **Declaration of Blockade.**—" A declaration of blockade is made either by the blockading Power or by the naval authorities acting in its name. It specifies:

" (1) The date when the blockade begins;

" (2) The geographical limits of the coast blockaded;

" (3) The delay to be allowed to neutral vessels for coming out." (Art. 9).[10]

485. **Notification of Blockade.**—" A declaration of blockade is notified:

[8] D. L., 7. Among circumstances of distress the *Report* mentions want of food or water and need of immediate repairs. If the fact or state of distress is acknowledged, entrance is a matter of right. She has also a right to leave subsequently, provided, etc. Cf. the *Hiawatha*, Blatchford's P. C. 15.

[9] D. L., 8. Cf. D. L., 9, 11, and 16. "Independently of the condition prescribed by the Declaration of Paris that it must be effective, a blockade, to be binding, must be *declared* and *notified*.

" . . . The *declaration* of blockade is the act of the competent authority (a Government or commander of a squadron) stating that a blockade is, or is about to be, established under conditions to be specified (Article 9). The *notification* is the fact of bringing the declaration of the blockade to the knowledge of the neutral Powers or of certain authorities (Article 11).

"These two things—declaration and notification—will in most cases be done previously to the enforcement of the rules of blockade, that is to say, to the real prohibition of passage. Nevertheless, as we shall see later, it is sometimes possible for passage to be forbidden by the very fact of the blockade which is brought to the knowledge of a vessel approaching a blockaded port by means of a *notification* which is *special*, whereas notification which has just been defined, and which is spoken of in Article 11, is of a general character." *Report*, in Higgins, 575.

[10] D. L., 9. Cf. Art. 8, *supra*, and 16 (2), *infra*, No. 290.

" The declaration of blockade in most cases emanates from the belligerent Government itself. That Government may have left the commander of its naval forces the power to himself declare a blockade according to circumstances. There will not, perhaps, be as much reason as formerly to exercise this discretion, because of the ease and rapidity of communication. . . ." *Report*, *op. cit.* Cf. 2 Oppenheim, § 375.

It is assumed that a neutral vessel will be allowed a *reasonable* time for departure, though no definite time is fixed. Fifteen days have usually been granted. Art. 43 of the United States Naval Code (1900–1904) allowed thirty days.

" (1) To the neutral Powers, by the blockading Power by means of a communication addressed to the Governments directly, or to their representatives accredited to it;

" (2) To the local authorities by the officer in command of the blockading force. As soon as possible these authorities will, on their part, inform the foreign consuls who exercise their functions in the port or on the coast blockaded." (Art. 11).[11]

486. Extension or Reëstablishment of the Blockade.—

" The rules relative to the declaration and notification of blockade apply to cases where the limits of the blockade are extended, or where the blockade is reëstablished after having been raised." (Art. 12).[12]

[11] "A declaration of blockade is not valid unless notified. . . . Two notifications must be made [according to the Declaration of London]:

"(1) The first is addressed to neutral Powers by the belligerent Power, which communicates it to the Governments themselves or to their representative accredited to it. The communications to the Governments will in most cases be made through the diplomatic agents. . . . It is the duty of the neutral Governments advised of a declaration of blockade to take the necessary measures to dispatch the news to the different parts of their territory, especially their ports.

"(2) The second notification is made by the commander of the blockading force to the local authorities. These must inform, as soon as possible, the foreign consuls residing at the blockaded places or on the blockaded coastline. These authorities would be responsible for the neglect of this obligation. Neutrals might suffer loss from the fact of not having been informed of the blockade in sufficient time." *Report*, in Higgins, 576–77.

Article 11 seems to be a happy compromise between the extreme French view and practice, which prescribed special notification to every neutral vessel approaching the line of blockade, and the more reasonable Anglo-American view, which was that notification was not always necessary, and that knowledge might be presumed in case the existence of the blockade was one of general notoriety.

The legality of unnotified *de facto* blockades was upheld by our Supreme Court as late as 1899 in the case of the *Adula*, 176 U. S. 361, or Evans, 661. The so-called blockade of Germany by the Allied Powers during the World War was neither declared nor notified. In the interest of neutrals there is little, if any, question as to what the law of blockade should be. Blockades should be both officially declared and notified. The only questions are whether these rules will be observed in future wars and whether International Law imposes such an obligation in all cases.

[12] D. L., 12. "Suppose a blockade is extended beyond its original limits: as regards the new part, it is a new blockade, and, in consequence, the rules as to declaration and notification must be applied to it. The same is true in cases where a blockade is reëstablished after having been raised; the fact that a blockade has already existed in the same locality must not be taken into account." *Report*, in Higgins, 577.

487. Voluntary Raising or Restriction of the Blockade.— " The voluntary raising of a blockade, as also any restriction which may be introduced, should be notified in the manner prescribed by Article 11." (Art. 13).[13]

488. Knowledge a Condition of Liability for Breach of Blockade.—" The liability of a neutral vessel to capture for breach of blockade is contingent on her knowledge, actual or presumptive, of the blockade." (Art. 14).[14]

489. Presumptive Knowledge.—" Failing proof to the contrary, knowledge of the blockade is presumed if the vessel left a neutral port subsequently to the notification of the blockade made in sufficient time to the Power to which such port belongs." (Art. 15).[15]

[13] D. L., 13. Cf. Art. 11, *supra.* "Only it must be observed that the sanction could not be the same in the two cases. To insure the notification of the declaration of blockade there is a direct and adequate sanction: an unnotified blockade is not binding. In the case of the raising there can be no parallel to this. The public will really gain by the raising, even without being told of it officially. The blockading Power which did not notify the raising would expose itself to diplomatic remonstrance on the ground of the non-fulfillment of an international duty. This non-fulfillment will have more or less serious consequences, according to circumstances. Sometimes the raising of the blockade will really have become known at once, and official notification would add nothing to this effective publicity.

"It goes without saying that this relates only to the *voluntary* raising of a blockade; if the blockading force has been driven off by the arrival of enemy forces, it cannot be held bound to make known its defeat, which its adversary will undertake to announce without delay. Instead of raising a blockade, a belligerent may confine himself to restricting it; he only blockades one port instead of two. As to the port which ceases to be included in the blockade, it is as if there had been a voluntary raising; consequently, the same rule applies." *Report,* cited above.

[14] D. L., 14. "For a vessel to be liable to capture for breach of a blockade, the first condition is that she must have had knowledge of the blockade. . . . Nevertheless, there are circumstances in which even in the absence of proof of actual knowledge, knowledge may be presumed, the right of rebutting this presumption being reserved to the party concerned." *Report,* in Higgins, 578. Cf. Art. 15 and note 15, below.

[15] D. L., 15. "A vessel has left a neutral port subsequently to the notification of the blockade made to the Powers to which the port belongs. Was this notification made in sufficient time, that is to say, so as to reach the port in question, where it had to be published by the port authorities? That is a question of fact to be examined. If it is settled affirmatively, it is natural to suppose that the vessel was aware of the blockade at the time of her departure. This presumption is not absolute, however, and the right to adduce proof to the contrary is reserved. It is for the incriminated vessel to furnish it, by showing that circumstances existed which explain her ignorance." *Report, op. cit.*

490. **Special Notification Necessary in case of Total Lack of Knowledge.**—" If a vessel approaching a blockaded port has no knowledge, actual or presumptive, of the blockade, the notification should be made to the vessel itself by an officer of one of the ships of the blockading force. This notification should be entered in the vessel's log book, with entry of the day and hour, as also of the geographical position of the vessel at the time.

" A neutral vessel which leaves a blockaded port must be allowed to pass free if, through the negligence of the officer commanding the blockading force, no declaration of blockade has been notified to the local authorities, or if, in the declaration as notified, no period of delay has been indicated." (Art. 16).[16]

491. **Liability to Capture for Breach of Blockade.**—The Declaration of London attempted to restrict the " seizure of neutral vessels for breach of blockade " to within the " area of operations (*rayon d'action*) of the warships assigned to render the blockade effective " (Art. 17); but since this was a new rule not based on customary usage and the Declaration remained unratified, it can not be regarded as a rule of the Law of Nations. The rule of International Law is that, subject possibly to the restrictions upon capture laid down in No. 494 (see below), the vessel guilty of a violation of blockade may be taken either on her outward or return voyage.[17]

492. **Neutral Ports or Coasts cannot be Blockaded.**— " The blockading forces must not bar access to neutral ports or coasts." (Art. 18).[18]

The Anglo-American doctrine of presumptive or constructive knowledge was thus maintained by the Declaration of London, but its range limited to cases where there has been actual notification. The Declaration does not support the doctrine of notoriety. The leading case is that of the *Neptunus* (1799), 2 Rob. 110, and Evans, 646 or Scott, 935.

[16] D. L., 16. Cf. Art. 8, *supra*. This special notification "may be made to the vessels of a convoyed fleet by a neutral warship through the commander of the convoy."

[17] On *Liability to Capture* or *Acts which Constitute a Breach of Blockade*, and the *Penalty*, at least from the Anglo-American viewpoint, see especially: Hall, §§ 263–64; Hall, J. A., *Law of Naval Warfare* (1921), 204–09; 2 Hyde, § 837; Lawrence, §§ 251–52; 7 Moore, *Digest*, §§ 1272–79; 2 Oppenheim, §§ 383–90; 2 Westlake (1st ed.), 234–35, 237–38.

[18] D. L., 18. Cf. Art. 1 which Art. 18 completes. See *supra*, No. 478.

493. Doctrine of Continuous Voyage and Blockade.—
According to the Declaration of London, the doctrine of
continuous voyage is not applicable to blockade. It states:
" whatever may be the ulterior destination of a vessel or of
her cargo, the evidence of violation of blockade is not
sufficiently conclusive to authorize the seizure of the vessel
if, at the time, she is on her way to a non-blockaded port "
(Art. 19).[19] However, this doctrine was applied to blockade
by our Supreme Court during the Civil War, and the rule of
the Declaration of London was not observed during the
World War. In fact, it was definitely rejected by the
allies. Nor can the application of the doctrine to blockade
be said to be illogical or unsound in principle.[20]

**494. Restriction upon Capture to Pursuit during the
Return Voyage.—**" A vessel which, in violation of blockade,
has left a blockaded port or has attempted to enter the port
is liable to capture so long as she is pursued by a ship of the
blockading force. If the pursuit is abandoned, or if the
blockade is raised, her capture can no longer be effected."
(Art. 20).[21]

During our Civil War the *Peterhoff* (5 Wallace, 28), destined for Matamoras
on the Mexican side of the Rio Grande, was released on the ground that trade
with Mexico could not be prohibited. "It is a moot question whether the
mouth of a so-called international river may be the object of a blockade, in case
not all the riparian States are belligerents. Thus, when in 1854, during the
Crimean War, the allied fleets of Great Britain and France blockaded the mouth
of the Danube, Bavaria and Würtemburg, which remained neutral, protested.
When, in 1870, the French blockaded the whole of the German coast of the
North Sea, they exempted the mouth of the river Ems, because it runs partly
through Holland." 2 Oppenheim, § 373. Cf. 2 Westlake (1st ed.) 238–39.
For the *Peterhoff*, see Evans, *Cases*, 656 or Scott, 980.

It is generally held that straits forming international highways are not
subject to blockade, even though both states are within enemy jurisdiction.
Blockade of the Suez and Panama Canals is prohibited by treaty. See *supra*,
314.

[19] D. L., 19. Cf. Arts. 30 and 35 for the application of the doctrine of
"continuous voyage" to absolute contraband. On this doctrine as applied by
our courts to blockade during the Civil War, see the *Bermuda*, 3 Wallace, 514;
the *Stephen Hart*, Blatch. P. C., 387, 3 Wallace, 559, and Scott, *Cases*, 988;
and the *Springbok*, Blatch. P. C., 349, 5 Wallace 1, and Evans, 729.

[20] See 2 Garner, §§ 520–21.

[21] D. L., 20. "A vessel has left the blockaded port or has tried to enter it.
Shall she be indefinitely liable to capture? An absolutely affirmative reply
would be too extreme. This vessel must remain liable to capture so long as she
is pursued by a ship of the blockading force; and it would not suffice that she
be encountered by a cruiser of the blockading squadron. The question whether

495. Penalty for Breach of Blockade.—"A vessel found guilty of violation of blockade is liable to condemnation. The cargo is also condemned, unless it is proven that at the time the goods were shipped the shipper neither knew nor could have known of the intention to violate the blockade." (Art. 21).[22]

or not the pursuit is abandoned is one of fact; it does not suffice that the vessel should take refuge in a neutral port. The ship which is pursuing her can wait her departure, so that the pursuit is necessarily suspended, but not abandoned. Capture is no longer possible when the blockade has been raised." *Report*, in Higgins, 581–82.

The American Delegation accepted this article, under the reservation that "a pursuit it considered as continued and not abandoned within the meaning of the article, even if it is abandoned by one line of the blockading force to be resumed after an interval by a ship of the second line, until the limit of the area of the operations is reached. In certain conditions there might be several lines, each having its respective zone of pursuit."

Art. 20 somewhat modifies the Anglo-American doctrine that a ship which has successfully run a blockade is liable to capture at any time during her return voyage. See Art. 44 of the United States (Stockton's) Naval War Code.

[22] D. L., 21. "The vessel is condemned in all cases. The cargo is also condemned in principle, but the interested party may oppose a plea of good faith, that is to say, he may prove that when the goods were shipped, the shipper did not know and could not have known of the intention to break the blockade." *Report*, in Higgins, 582.

This makes the condemnation of the cargo turn upon the question of actual or presumptive knowledge on the part of the shipper. This presumption of knowledge would be absolute in case he were also the owner of the vessel, at least according to Anglo-American practice. See the leading case of *The Panaghia Rhomba* (1858), 120 Moore P. C., 168, and Scott, 951.

As late as the eighteenth century the crew of a blockade runner might be imprisoned or even put to death, but to-day they cannot even be made prisoners of war, though they may be detained as witnesses.

Though the rules on blockade laid down by the unratified London Naval Conference were on the whole very adequate and satisfactory, there were of course some points that were overlooked or omitted.

The most important omission was the failure to condemn blockade by submarine mines. Earlier, it had always been assumed that the use of warships was necessary in order to constitute an effective blockade, though they might be supported by shore batteries. During our Civil War the harbor of Charleston was obstructed by means of old sunken vessels laden with stones (7 Moore, *Digest*, § 1286), and this has been deemed a permissible mode of warfare as auxiliary to blockade.

In recent discussions it has sometimes been assumed that in future wars attempts will be made to institute blockades by means of submarine mines. 8 H. C., 2 (see *supra*, No. 431), forbids the "laying of automatic contact mines off the coasts and ports of the enemy, with the *sole* object of intercepting commercial navigation." Whether as a new and inhuman mode of warfare or as an unwarranted extension of the means of blockade, this method of interfering with neutral commerce should be absolutely prohibited. See especially:

495*a*. **Termination of Blockade.**—" A blockade ceases: (*a*) on the conclusion of peace, (*b*) when the blockading vessels voluntarily withdraw, (*c*) when these vessels are driven away by the enemy, however short the time of absence, (*d*) when it ceases to be effective, except because of stress of weather, (*e*) when the blockading place comes into the possession of the forces of the blockading belligerent." [23]

[23] Wilson, § 197. Cf. 2 Hyde, § 842; and 2 Oppenheim, § 378.

BIBLIOGRAPHY

Blockade.—Allessandri, *Contribution à l'étude des blocus nouveaux* (1919); * Atherley-Jones, *Commerce in War* (1907), ch. 2; Benton, *Spanish-American War* (1908), 124–25, 137–41, 200–05, 232; Bentwich, *Declaration of London* (1911), ch. 1; Bernard, *Neutrality*, etc. (1870, see index); Bluntschli, Nos. 827–40; * Boeck, Nos. 670–726; Bonfils, Nos. 1606–73; Bynkershoek, *Questiones juris publici*, lib. I, cc. 2–15; 5 Calvo, §§ 2827–2937; Carnazza-Amari, *Del blocco maritimo* (1897); 2 Cobbett, 530–54; * Dana, notes 232–35 to Wheaton, 671 ff.; Davis, ch. 14; Despagnet, Nos. 617–37; Deane, *The Law of Blockade* (1870); * Dupuis, *Le droit de la guerre maritime* (1899 and 1911), ch. 6; * Evans, *Cases*, ch. 17; * 2 Fauchille, Nos. 1589–1656, and *Du blocus maritime* (1882); 3 Fiore, Nos. 1606–29, and *Int. Law Cod.*, Nos. 1828–49; * 2 Garner, ch. 33, and *Prize Law during the World War* (1927), ch. 15; Geffcken, in 4 Holtzendorff, 738–71; Gregory, in 12 *Yale Law J.*, 339 ff.; Grotius, lib. III, c. 1, § 5; Güldenagel, *Verfolgung und Rechtsfolgen des Blockadenbruchs* (1911); Guynot-Boisière, *Du blocus maritime* (1899); * Hall, Pt. IV, ch. 8; Hall, J. A., *Law of Naval Warfare* (1921), ch. 6; 2 Hautefeuille, *Droits et devoirs des neutres* (1868), 177–274; 2 Halleck, ch. 25; Heffter (Geffcken), §§ 154–57; Historicus, *Letters of*, 89–118; Holland, *Prize Law*, Nos. 106–40; Holtzoff, in 10 *A. J.* (1916), 53–64; * 2 Hyde, §§ 824–43; Kennedy, in 25 *I. L. A.* (1908–09), 33 ff.; 1 Kleen, 542–644; Laurens, *Le blocus et la guerre sous-marine* (1924); * Lawrence, Pt. IV, ch. 5;

Bentwich, *War and Private Property*, 124; Lawrence § 203, pp. 512–13, and *International Problems*, etc., 189–92; and 2 Westlake (1st ed.), 326.

In case of insurrection, a Government cannot close ports in possession of the insurgents to neutrals by a mere declaration that they are no longer open to trade, though a State may of course exclude foreign as well as domestic trade from any of its harbors in which it actually exercises authority. For examples, see 7 Moore, *Digest*, § 1271.

There has been considerable opposition to purely commercial blockades, but the success of the great commercial blockade instituted by the United States against the Southern Confederacy during the Civil War went far to defeat this opposition. This view had official support even in the United States before the Civil War. For the argument of Secretary Cass (1859) against commercial blockades, see 7 Moore, *Digest*, § 1266, or 2 Westlake, 227.

Liszt, § 64; 2 J. de Louter, § 57; Malkin, in *Brit. Yr. Bk.* (1922–23), 87–98; Macdonell, in 1 *Grot. Soc.* (1916), 93 ff.; 3 F. de Martens, § 124; Martin, *Étude sur le blocus maritime* (1909); 7 Moore, *Digest*, ch. 27; Myers, in 4 *A. J.* (1910), 571 ff.; Naval War College, *Int. Law Topics* (see index, 1922); * 2 Oppenheim, Pt. III, ch. 3; 2 Ortolan, liv. III, ch. 9; * Parmalee, *Blockade and Sea Power* (1924), *passim;* Perels, §§ 48–51; Perrinjaquet, in 22 *R. D. I. P.* (1915), 127 ff.; 3 Phillimore, Pt. X, ch. 2; 6 and 8 P.-Fodéré, Nos. 2776–78, 3109–52; 2 Rivier, 288–98, 431–34; 3 Rolin, Nos. 1177–1200; * Scott, *Cases*, 938–54; Scott, *Resolutions*, see index (for rules adopted by Institute of Int. Law); Smith and Sibley, *Russo-Japanese War* (1905), ch. 15; Södersqist, *Le blocus maritime* (1908); Stockton, *Outlines*, ch. 25; Stockton's (U. S.) *Naval War Code*, Arts. 32–45; Takahashi, *Russo-Japanese War* (1908), Pt. III, ch. 3 and Pt. V, ch. 5 (for cases during the Russo-Japanese War); Taylor, Pt. V, ch. 7; Testa, *Le droit public int. maritime* (1886), 221–29; Triepel, *Konterbande, Blockade und Seesperre* (1918); 2 Twiss, ch. 6; Ullmann, § 182; Vattel, liv. III, § 117; 2 Verraes, *Droit int. les lois de la guerre et la neutralité* (1906), ch. 11; Walker, *Manual*, §§ 76–82; * 2 Westlake, ch. 9, and *Collected Papers*, 312–61; 3 Wharton, *Digest*, ch. 18; Wheaton, §§ 509–23; Wilson, ch. 25; Woolsey, §§ 202–06.

For Bibliographies, see Bonfils, Boeck, Fauchille, Oppenheim and Söderqvist.

CHAPTER XXXV

THE SO-CALLED LAW OF CONTRABAND

496. **Definition.**—Contraband of war consist of " those articles which belligerents prohibit neutrals from carrying to their enemies, not in connection with a blockade but because they are regarded as being objectionable in themselves, either generally or in the particular circumstances of a war." [1]

497. **List of Articles Absolute Contraband.**—The unratified Declaration of London (1909) declared that certain articles susceptible only of military use might, without notice,[2] be treated as contraband of war, under the name of absolute contraband.[3]

[1] 2 Westlake (1st ed.), 240. The term is derived from the Latin *contra bannum* or *bandum*, meaning contrary to the ban or edict.

The history of the modern theory and practice of the prohibition of the carriage of contraband appears to date from the sixteenth and seventeenth centuries. For historical treatment of the subject, see especially: * Atherley-Jones, ch. 1; 2 Fauchille, Nos. 1538–64; Hall, Pt. IV, ch. 5; 1 Kleen, 348 ff.; 7 Moore, *Digest*, ch. 26; Pyke, *Law of Contraband* (1915), chs. 4–5, 10; 2 Twiss, §§ 121 ff.; 2 Westlake, 241 ff.

"The notion of contraband connotes two elements: it concerns objects of a certain kind and with a certain destination. Cannons, for instance, are carried in a neutral vessel. Are they contraband? That depends: if they are destined for a neutral government, no; if destined for an enemy government,— yes. The trade in certain articles is by no means generally forbidden during war; it is the trade with the enemy in these articles which is illicit, and against which the belligerent to whose detriment it is carried on may protect himself by the measures allowed by International Law." *Report* on the Declaration of London, in Higgins, 582, or in Naval War College, *International Law Topics* (1909), 58–59.

[2] "The words *de plein droit* (without notice) imply that the provision becomes operative by the mere fact of the war, and that no declaration of the belligerents is necessary. Trade is already warned in time of peace." *Report*, cited above.

[3] D. L., 22. The list, now discarded, was as follows:

1. Arms of all kinds, including arms for sporting purposes, and their distinctive component parts. 2. Projectiles, charges, and cartridges of all kinds, and their distinctive component parts. 3. Powder and explosives specially adapted for use in war. 4. Gun mountings, limber boxes, limbers, military wagons, field forges, and their distinctive component parts. 5. Clothing and equipment of a distinctively military character. 6. All kinds of harness of a

498. Notification in Case Articles are added to the List of Absolute Contraband.

—" Articles and materials exclusively used for war may be added to the list of absolute contraband by means of a notified declaration.

" The notification is addressed to the Governments of other Powers, or to their representatives accredited to the Power making the declaration. A notification made after the opening of hostilities is addressed only to neutral Powers " (Art. 23).[4]

distinctively military character. 7. Saddle, draught, and pack animals suitable for use in war. 8. Articles of camp equipment, and the distinctive component parts. 9. Armor plates. 10. Warships including boats, and their distinctive component parts specially distinctive as being suitable only for use in vessels of war. 11. Implements and apparatus made exclusively for the manufacture of munitions of war, for the manufacture or repair of arms or of military material for use on land or sea.

This list was drawn up at the Second Peace Conference by the committee charged with the special study of the question of contraband. Cf. lists of contraband in Holland's *Manual*, Nos. 62 and 64; Stockton's *Naval War Code*, Art. 36; and the Japanese and Russian lists, in Hershey, *Russo-Japanese War*, 160–65.

Admiral Stockton, the leading American delegate, tells us that at least one half of the members of the London Conference were opposed to the inclusion of horses and mules in the list of absolute contraband. See 3 *A. J.* (1909), 605.

The above list of articles declared absolutely contraband proved absurdly inadequate during the World War. The first list announced by the British Government was identical with that of the Declaration of London, except that air craft, which is listed as conditional contraband in the Declaration, was put on the list of absolute contraband by the Order in Council. This list was greatly enlarged by subsequent Proclamations until by April 19, 1916 the distinction between absolute and conditional contraband was abandoned altogether and a single list of several hundred articles arranged alphabetically was published as mere contraband. Later (July 2, 1917) the distinction was again restored, there being two hundred items labelled absolute, and less than forty labelled conditional contraband. See especially: 2 Garner, § 496; Hall, § 247 a; Lawrence, § 255, pp. 718–20; and Pyke, *op. cit.*, 179–82. For lists, see Spec. Supp. to 9 and 10 *A. J.* (1915) and 1916, 9–54 and 49–57. For the final British list proclaimed July 2, 1917, see Hall, *Law of Naval Warfare* (1921), App. C., pp. 361 ff.

⁴ D. L., 23. "Certain discoveries or inventions might make the list in Article 22 insufficient. An addition may be made to it on condition that it concerns article *exclusively used for war*. This addition must be notified to the other Powers, which will take the measures necessary to make it known to their nationals. In theory, the notification may be made in time of peace or war. The former case will doubtless rarely occur, because a State which made such a notification might be suspected of meditating a war; it would, nevertheless, have the advantage of informing trade beforehand. There was no reason for excluding the possibility." *Report*, in Higgins, 583.

The condition indicated in *italics* in the above paragraph was not observed during the World War.

499. List of Articles Conditional Contraband.—According to the unratified Declaration of London, certain articles and materials susceptible of use in war as well as for purposes of peace might, without notice, be treated as contraband of war, under the name of conditional contraband.[5]

[5] D. L., 24.   The list of articles conditional contraband was as follows:

1. Foodstuffs. 2. Forage and grain, suitable for feeding animals. 3. Clothing and fabrics for clothing, boots, and shoes, suitable for military use. 4. Gold and silver in coin or bullion, paper money. 5. Vehicles of all kinds available for use in war, as also their component parts. 6. Vessels, craft, and boats of all kinds, floating docks, as also their component parts. 7. Fixed railway material or rolling stock, and materials for telegraphs, wireless telegraphs, and telephones. 8. Balloons and flying machines and their distinctive component parts, as also their accessories, articles and materials distinctive as intended for use in connection with balloons or flying machines. 9. Fuel; lubricants. 10. Powder and explosives not specially adapted for use in war. 11. Barbed wire, as also the implements for fixing and cutting the same. 12. Horseshoes and horseshoeing materials. 13. Harness and saddlery. 14. Field glasses, telescopes, chronometers, and all kinds of nautical instruments.

The *Report*, cited above, comments upon this article as follows (see Higgins, 584):

"The articles enumerated are only conditional contraband if they have the destination specified in Article 33.

"*Foodstuffs* include products necessary or useful for the sustenance of man, whether solid or liquid.

"*Paper money* includes only inconvertible paper money, *i.e.* banknotes which may or may not be legal tender. Bills of exchange and checks are not included.

"Engines and boilers are included in the category of (6).

"Railway materials include fixed material (such as rails, sleepers, turntables, parts designed for the construction of bridges) and rolling stock (such as locomotives and cars)."

In the early stages of the World War, foodstuffs were labelled as conditional contraband in the lists announced by Great Britain, France and Russia. On April 18, 1915, Germany also declared foodstuffs contraband. On April 13, 1916, the British Government declared that the distinction between absolute and conditional contraband had ceased to have any value for practical purposes. Consequently, they were simply labelled contraband.

In the Naval Instructions of the United States Governing Maritime Warfare, issued June 30, 1917, "all kinds of fuel, food, foodstuffs, feed, forage, and clothing and articles and materials used in their manufacture" were declared contraband when "actually destined for the use of the enemy government or its armed forces, unless exempted by treaty."

On *Foodstuffs as Contraband*, see especially: Hall, § 245; 2 Garner, § 499; 2 Hyde, §§ 800–02; and 2 Oppenheim, § 394 (1).

The so-called Anglo-American doctrine of conditional or occasional contraband has been strongly opposed by some continental publicists, *e.g.* Hautefeuille, Ortolan, Kleen, etc.; but the majority of them concede the application of the principle in exceptional cases. It may be noted that the Institute of International Law attempted (in 1896) to abolish what it termed relative or

500. Notification in Case Articles are added to the List of Conditional Contraband.—" Articles and material susceptible of use in war as well as for purposes of peace, other than those enumerated in Articles 22 and 24, may be added to the list of conditional contraband by means of a declaration which must be notified in the manner provided for in the second paragraph of Article 23 " (Art. 25).[6]

501. Notification in Case a Power waives its Right to treat Articles as Contraband.—" If a Power waives, so far as it is concerned, the right to treat as contraband of war articles and materials comprised in any of the classes enumerated in Articles 22 and 24, it shall make known its intention by a declaration notified in the manner provided for in the second paragraph of Article 23 " (Art. 26).[7]

accidental contraband, as applied to articles *ancipitis usus* (of dual or double use), and to limit contraband to a few categories. See Scott, *Resolutions*, 129.

For references to and citations from leading continental authorities opposed to the doctrine of conditional contraband, see especially: 5 Calvo, § 2709; Hall, § 240 and note on pp. 778–79; Hershey, *Russo-Japanese War*, note on pp. 161–63; Lawrence, § 255.

The following are leading cases on conditional contraband: *The Jonge Margaretha* (1799), 1. C. Rob. 189, and Evans, *Cases*, 672; *The Commercen* (1816), 1 Wheaton, 382, and Scott, *Cases*, 973; and *The Peterhoff* (1866), 5 Wallace, 28, 58, and Evans, 677 or Scott, 980.

The Anglo-American doctrine of conditional contraband is based upon the Grotian division of commodities into three classes: (1) articles of direct and immediate use in war, such as arms and ammunition, which are always contraband when they have a belligerent destination; (2) things absolutely useless in warfare, such as household furniture, which are never contraband under any circumstances; and (3) *res ancipitis usus*—things of double or dual use, *i.e.* useful in peace as well as war, such as coal, horses, provisions, cloth, etc. These are contraband of circumstance, *i.e.*, they are only to be treated as contraband under special circumstances, such as when destined to a place besieged, or when clearly intended for the direct use of the belligerent army or navy.

[6] D. L., 25. Cf. Art. 23, *supra*, No. 498.

[7] D. L., 26. Cf. Art. 23, *supra*, No. 498. "A belligerent may not wish to use the right to treat as contraband or war the articles included in the above lists. It may suit him either to add to conditional contraband an article included in absolute contraband or to declare free, so far as he is concerned, the trade in some article included in one class or the other. It is desirable that he should make known his intention on this subject, and he will probably do so in order to have credit for the measure. If he does not do so, but confines himself to giving instructions to his cruisers, the vessels visited will be agreeably surprised if the visiting officer does not reproach them with carrying what they themselves consider contraband. Nothing can prevent a Power from making such a declaration in time of peace. See what is said as regards Article 23." *Report, op. cit.*

502. The Free List.—The unratified Declaration of London also laid it down that " articles and materials which are not susceptible of use in war are not to be declared contraband of war " (Art. 27).[8]

" Neither may the following be treated as contraband of war:

" 1. Articles and materials serving exclusively for the care of the sick and wounded. They may, nevertheless, in case of urgent military necessity and subject to the payment of compensation, be requisitioned, if their destination is that specified in Article 30.

" 2. Articles and materials intended for the use of the

[8] It declared that the following articles may not be declared contraband of war:

1. Raw cotton, wool, silk, jute, flax, hemp, and other raw materials for the textile industries, as also yarns of the same. 2. Nuts and oil seeds; copra. 3. Rubber, resins, gums, and lacs; hops. 4. Raw hides, horns, bones, and ivory. 5. Natural and artificial manures, including nitrates and phosphates for agricultural purposes. 6. Metallic ores. 7. Earths, clays, lime, chalk, stone, marble, bricks, slates, and tiles. 8. Chinaware and glass. 9. Paper and materials prepared for its manufacture. 10. Soap, paint and colors, including articles exclusively used in their manufacture, and varnishes. 11. Bleaching powder, soda, ash caustic soda, salt cake, ammonia, sulphate of ammonia, and sulphate of copper. 12. Agricultural, mining, textile, and printing machinery. 13. Precious and semi-precious stones, pearls, mother-of-pearl, and coral. 14. Clocks and watches, other than chronometers. 15. Fashion and fancy goods. 16. Feathers of all kinds, hairs, and bristles. 17. Articles of household furniture and decoration; office furniture and accessories" (Art. 28).

The free list of the Declaration of London did not stand the test of the World War. The British Government for some time declined to treat cotton as contraband, but finally yielded to public opinion; and, on Aug. 20, 1915, placed raw cotton, cotton linters, cotton waste, and cotton yarns on the list of absolute contraband. See 2 Garner, § 498.

The *Report* (see Higgins, 585) furnishes the following comment upon the free list contained in D. L., 28: " To lessen the inconveniences of war as regards neutral trade it has been thought useful to prepare this so-called *free list* but this does not mean, as has been explained above, that all articles omitted might be declared contraband of war.

"The *ores* (6) are the products of mines from which metals are obtained.

"There was a demand that *dyestuffs* should be included in (10), but this seemed too general; for there are materials from which colors are produced, such as coal, but which also serve other uses. Products used only for making colors enjoy the exemption.

"'Articles de Paris,' the meaning of which is universally understood, come under (15).

"(16) refers to the hair of certain animals, such as pigs and wild boars.

"Carpets and mats are included in household furniture and ornaments (17)."

vessel in which they are found, as also those for the use of her crew and passengers during the voyage " (Art. 29).[9]

503. Destination in Case of Absolute Contraband. Application of the Doctrine of " Continuous Voyage."—

" Absolute contraband is liable to capture if it is shown to be destined to the territory belonging to or occupied by the enemy, or to the armed forces of the enemy. It is immaterial whether the carriage of the goods is direct or entails either transshipment or transport over land." (Art. 30).[10]

[9] D. L., 29. Cf. Art. 30, below.

"Motives of humanity have exempted articles and materials used exclusively to aid the sick and wounded, which naturally include drugs and different medicines. This does not refer to hospital ships, for which special immunity is provided by the Hague Convention of the 18th October, 1907, but to ordinary merchant vessels, whose cargo includes articles of the kind mentioned. . . .

"Articles and materials intended for use of the vessel, which might in themselves and by their nature be contraband of war, may not be so treated,—as, for instance, arms intended for the defense of the vessel against pirates or for making signals. The same is true of articles intended for the use of the crew and passengers during the voyage; the crew here includes all persons in the service of the vessel in general." Report, cited above.

The rules laid down in Art. 29 seem to have been observed during the World War.

[10] D. L., 30. Cf. Art. 22. "As has been said, the second element in the notion of contraband is *destination*. Great difficulties have arisen on this subject, which find expression in the *theory of continuous voyage*, often attacked or invoked without a clear comprehension of its exact meaning. One must simply consider cases by themselves to see how they can be settled without unnecessary annoyance to neutrals and without sacrificing the legitimate rights of belligerents." Report, in Higgins, 586.

A "continuous voyage" was thus defined by the British Government in a memorandum drawn up for the use of the London Naval Conference:

"When an adventure includes the carriage of goods to a neutral port, and thence to an ulterior destination, the doctrine of 'continuous voyage' consists in treating for certain purposes the whole journey as one transportation, with the consequences which would have attached had there been no interposition of the neutral port. The doctrine is only applicable when the whole transportation is made in pursuance of a single mercantile transaction preconceived from the outset. Thus it will not be applied where the evidence goes no further than to show that the goods were sent to the neutral port in the hopes of finding a market there for delivery elsewhere." Parl. Papers, Misc., No. 4 (1909), 7–8.

"The articles included in the list in Article 22 are absolute contraband when they are destined for territory belonging to or occupied by the enemy, or for his armed military or naval forces. These articles are liable to capture as soon as a similar final destination can be shown by the captor. It is not, therefore, the destination of the vessel which is decisive, but that of the goods. It makes no difference if these goods are on board a vessel which is to discharge them in a neutral port; as soon as the captor is able to show that they are to be forwarded from there by land or sea to an enemy country, that suffices to justify the cap-

504. Proof of Destination in Case of Absolute Contraband.—The unratified Declaration of London provided

ture and subsequent condemnation of the cargo. The very principle of continuous voyage, as regards absolute contraband, is thus established by Article 30. The journey made by the goods is regarded as a whole." *Report, op. cit.*

The doctrine of "continuous voyage" was first applied by England to neutral vessels engaged in the colonial trade—a trade prohibited to them in times of peace—of countries at war with Great Britain in violation of the so-called Rule of 1756. See the leading cases of the *William* (1806), 5 C. Rob. 385, and Evans, *Cases*, 725 or Scott, 982; and the *Immanuel* (1799), 2. C Rob. 186, and Evans, 632 or Scott, 928.

France appears to have made the first application of this doctrine to contraband during the Crimean War in 1855. See 4 and 5 Calvo, §§ 1961, 2767; and Pyke, *Law of Contraband* (1915), 151. But it was first applied on a large and greatly extended scale by the United States during the Civil War. Our courts applied the doctrine to blockade as well as to contraband and condemned cargoes consigned to Nassau and other West Indian ports or to Matamoras, Mexico, on the ground that they were to be transshipped to blockade runners or sent overland for the use of the Confederacy. The leading cases are those of the *Bermuda* (1865), 3 Wallace, 514; the *Peterhoff* (1866), 5 Wallace, 28 and Evans *Cases*, 677 or Scott, *Cases*, 980; the *Springbok* (1866), 5 Wallace 1, and Evans, 729; and the *Stephen Hart* (1863), Blatch. P. C., 387, and Scott, 988. The decision of Justice Betts in the latter case was affirmed by the United States Supreme Court (1865), 3 Wallace, 559. See also 7 Moore, *Digest*, §§ 1256 ff.

These decisions were severely criticised by leading British and Continental jurists, *e.g.* by Bernard, Hall, Twiss, Bluntschli, Bonfils, Fiore, Fauchille, Kleen, and many others. It may be admitted that some of the *dicta* of the judges and perhaps some of the decisions were open to criticism, but they were never officially questioned by the British Government, which assumed a similar position during the Anglo-Boer War in 1900 in the cases of the *Bundesrath, Herzog,* and the *General,* German vessels seized by British cruisers on suspicion of carrying contraband from German ports to the Portuguese port of Lorenzo Marques in Delogoa Bay. For the correspondence between England and Germany, see *Parl. Papers*, Africa No. 1 (1900), 1. Cf. 7 Moore, *Digest*, § 1262.

A similar position was taken by Italy in the case of the *Doelwijk* (1896). For discussion and references on this case, see Elliot, in 1 *A. J.* (1907), 97–99 and note on p. 99.

The London Naval Conference of 1909 effected what at the time seemed a happy compromise of this much-controverted question by sanctioning the application of the doctrine of "continuous voyage" to absolute contraband, but denying its applicability to conditional contraband and blockade. But this "happy" compromise has not stood the test of the World War.

During the World War, Great Britain and France strained the doctrine of contraband to the utmost not only by including practically everything in their lists of contraband that could possibly be of warlike use, but also by stretching the doctrines of continuous voyage and ultimate enemy destination to their extreme limits.

More than this—all ships carrying goods of *presumed* enemy origin or ownership as well as destination were liable to search and seizure. It might be said that the law of contraband was merged into that of blockade, and there

that proof of the destination specified in Article 30 is complete in the following cases:

" (1) When the goods are documented for discharge in an enemy port, or for delivery to the armed forces of the enemy.

" (2) When the vessel is to call at enemy ports only, or when she is to touch at an enemy port or to join his armed forces, before arriving at the neutral port for which the goods are documented." (Art. 31).[11]

virtually disappeared all distinction between contraband and blockade as well as between absolute and conditional contraband.

More even than this—neutral countries like Holland and the Scandinavian States were "rationed" and forced to place embargoes upon the exportation to enemy territory of many contraband articles. For embargo lists, see Naval War College, *Int. Law Sit.* (1915), 33 ff. Neutral trade with these countries could only be carried under the license of the British and French Governments. The amount of imports permitted to them was largely determined by pre-war statistics.

Moreover, the rules of procedure in British Prize Courts were changed during the World War to admit "extrinsic" evidence which could not otherwise have been introduced. See Garner, *Prize Law during the World War* (1927), pp. 114–15, 527–29; Hall, § 247; pp. 814–15 of Higgins, 8th ed.; and Richards, in *Brit. Yr. Bk.* (1920–21), 22 ff.

On the *Treatment of Contraband during the World War*, see: Clapp, *Econ. Aspects of the War* (1915), *passim*; 2 Fauchille, Nos. 1588[21]–[43]; * 2 Garner, ch. 32; Hall, § 247 a; 2 Hyde, §§ 803–05; 2 Oppenheim, Pt. III, ch. 4, *passim*; Perrinjaquet, in 22 *R. G. D. I.* (1915), 127–209; and Pyke, *Law of Contraband* (1915), ch. 14.

On the leading case of the *Kim* (1915), an application of the doctrine of continuous voyage to conditional contraband by Sir Samuel Evans, President of the Admiralty Division (in Prize) of the High Court of Justice in England, see: Anderson, in 11 *A. J.* (1917), 251 ff.; 2 Cobbett, 624 ff.; 2 Garner, § 506, and *Prize Law*, etc., 526–29; 2 Hyde, § 812. For the text of the decision, see 9 *A. J.* (1915), 979. For an abridged report, see Evans, *Cases*, 735.

On the doctrine of *Continuous Voyage*, see especially: 15 *Annuaire* (1896); Arias and Baldwin in 9 *A. J.* (1915), 583–93, 793–801; Atherley-Jones, ch. 3. * Baty, *Int. Law in South Africa*, ch. 1, and in 9 *Grot. Soc.* (1924), 101–17; * Elliot, in 1 *A. J.* (1907), 61–104; 2 Fauchille, No. 1567, and in 4 *R. D. I. P.* (1897), 297 ff.; * 2 Garner, §§ 501–05, and *Prize Law*, etc., 515 ff., 562 ff., and 590 ff.; Gregory, in 24 *Harvard Law Review* (1911), 167–81, and in 26 *I. L. A.* (1910), 120 ff.; Hart, in 17 *Law Quar. Rev.* (1901), 193 ff.; * 2 Hyde, §§ 808–13; Judson, in *Procs. Am. Soc. I. L.* (1915), 104–11; Naval War College, *Int. Law Topics* (1905), 77–106; * 2 Oppenheim, §§ 400–03 a; Pyke, *Law of Contraband* (1915), ch. 12; Remy, *Théorie de la continuité du voyage* (1902); Westlake, in 15 *L. Q. R.* (1899), 23–30; White, in 17 *L. Q. R.* (1901); Wilson, in *Procs. Am. Soc. I. L.* (1921), 45–55; Woolsey, in 4 *A. J.* (1910), 823–47.

[11] D. L., 31. Cf. Art. 30, *supra*. The *Report* (Higgins, 586) comments upon this Article as follows:

"As has been said, it is upon the captor that the obligation falls of proving that the contraband goods really have the destination specified in Article 30.

" The ship's papers are conclusive proof of the voyage of a vessel carrying absolute contraband, unless the vessel is encountered having manifestly deviated from the route which she ought to follow according to her papers and is unable to justify such deviation by adequate reasons " (Art. 32). [12]

505. Liability and Destination in Case of Conditional Contraband.—According to the Declaration of London, " conditional contraband is liable to capture if it is shown that it is destined for the use of the armed forces or of a government department of the enemy State, unless in this latter case the circumstances show that the articles cannot in fact be used for the purposes of the war in progress. This latter exception does not apply to a consignment coming under Article 24, (4) " (Art. 33). [13]

In certain cases specified in Article 31 proof of the destination is *conclusive*, that is to say, proof to the contrary is not admitted.

[12] D. L., 32. Cf. Art. 35, *infra*, No. 507. "The papers, therefore, are conclusive proof of the voyage of the vessel unless she is encountered under circumstances which show that their statements are not to be trusted." *Report*, cited above.

It is impossible to say what the law now is respecting the proof of destination required in case of absolute or conditional contraband.

The "Maritime Rights Order in Council" of July 7, 1916 (which superseded all previous orders on the subject) provided:

"(a) The hostile destination required for the condemnation of contraband articles shall be presumed to exist, until the contrary is shown, if the goods are consigned to or for an enemy authority, or an agent of the enemy State, or to or for a person in territory belonging to or occupied by the enemy, or to or for a person who, during the present hostilities, has forwarded contraband goods to an enemy authority, or an agent of the enemy State, or to or for a person in territory belonging to or occupied by the enemy, or if the goods are consigned 'to order,' or if the ship's papers do not show who is the real consignee of the goods.

"(b) The principle of continuous voyage or ultimate destination shall be applicable both in cases of contraband and of blockade.

"(c) A neutral vessel carrying contraband with papers indicating a neutral destination, which, notwithstanding the destination shown on the papers, proceeds to an enemy port, shall be liable to capture and condemnation if she is encountered before the end of her next voyage.

"(d) A vessel carrying contraband shall be liable to capture and condemnation if the contraband reckoned either by value, weight, volume, or freight, forms more than half the cargo."   Hall, pp. 807–08 of Higgins' 8th ed.

[13] D. L., 33.   Cf. Arts. 30–32 for absolute contraband.

"The rules concerning conditional contraband differ from those laid down for absolute contraband in two respects: (1) there is no question of destination for the enemy in general, but of destination for the use of his armed forces or government departments; (2) the doctrine of continuous voyage is excluded. Articles 33 and 34 refer to the first, and Article 35 to the second principle.

506. Presumption of Destination in Case of Conditional Contraband.

—" The destination referred to in Article 33 is presumed to exist if the consignment is addressed to enemy authorities, or to a trader (*commerçant*) established in the enemy country when it is well known that this trader supplies articles and material of this kind to the enemy. The presumption is the same if the consignment is destined to a fortified place of the enemy, or to another place serving as a base for the armed forces of the enemy. This presumption, however, does not apply to the merchant vessel herself bound for one of these places if it sought to prove the contraband character of the vessel.

" Failing the above presumption, the destination is presumed innocent.

" The presumptions set up in this Article admit proof to the contrary " (Art. 34).[14]

"The articles included in the list of conditional contraband may serve for peaceful uses as well as for hostile purposes. If, from the circumstances, the peaceful purpose is certain, their capture is not justified; it is otherwise if a hostile purpose is to be assumed, which happens, for instance, in the case of foodstuffs destined for an enemy army or fleet, or of coal destined for an enemy fleet. In such a case there is clearly no doubt. But what is the decision when the articles are destined for the civil authorities of the enemy State? It may be money sent to a civil authority for the use in the payment of official salaries, or rails sent to a department of public works. In these cases there is *enemy destination* rendering the goods liable in the first place to capture, and subsequently to condemnation. . . .

"War may be waged under circumstances such that the destination for the use of a civil authority cannot be questioned, and consequently cannot make the goods contraband. For instance, there is a war in Europe, and the colonies of the belligerent countries are not, in fact, affected by it. Foodstuffs or other articles in the list of conditional contraband destined for the use of a civil colonial administration would not be regarded as contraband of war, because the considerations adduced above do not apply in this case; the resources of the civil government could not be drawn on for the needs of the war. Gold, silver, or paper money are exceptions, because a sum of money can easily be sent from one end of the world to the other." *Report, op. cit.*, Higgins, 587–88.

[14] D. L., 34. Cf. Art. 33, *supra*.

"Ordinarily, contraband articles will not be directly addressed to the military or to the administrative authorities of the enemy State. Their true destination will be more or less concealed, and the captor must prove it in order to justify the capture. But it has been thought reasonable to set up presumptions based on the nature of the person to whom, or place for which, the articles are destined. It may be an enemy authority or a trader established in an enemy country who, as a matter of common knowledge, supplies the enemy Government with articles of the kind in question. It may be a fortified place of the enemy or a place serving as a base, whether of operations or supply, for the armed forces of the enemy.

507. The Doctrine of " Continuous Voyage " not Applicable to Conditional Contraband According to the Declaration of London.—" Conditional contraband is not liable to capture, except when found on board a vessel bound for territory belonging to or occupied by the enemy, or for the armed forces of the enemy, and when it is not to be discharged at an intervening neutral port.

" The ship's papers are conclusive proof of the voyage of the vessel as also of the port of discharge of the goods, unless the vessel is encountered having manifestly deviated from the route which she ought to follow according to her papers and is unable to justify such deviation by adequate reasons " (Art. 35).[15]

508. Exception in the Case the Enemy Territory has no Seaboard.—" Notwithstanding the provisions of Article 35, if the territory of the enemy has no seaboard, conditional contraband is liable to capture if it is shown that it has the destination referred to in Article 33 " (Art. 36).[16]

509. Place of Liability to Capture.—" A vessel carrying articles liable to capture as absolute or conditional contra-

"This general presumption may not be applied to the merchant vessel herself which is bound for a fortified place, except on condition that her destination for the use of the armed forces or authorities of the enemy State is directly proved, though she may in herself be conditional contraband.

"In the absence of the above presumption, the destination is presumed to be innocent.   This is the ordinary law according to which the captor must prove the illicit character of the goods which he claims to capture.

"Finally, all the presumptions thus set up in the interest of the captor or against him admit proof to the contrary.   The national tribunals, in the first place, and, in the second, the International Court, will exercise their judgment." *Report, op. cit.*   Cf. Bentwich, *The Dec. of London*, 70–74.

Arts. already pointed out (see above, notes 11 and 13), these rules did not stand the test of the World War.

[15] D. L., 35.   This Article must now be regarded as obsolete.   Cf. *supra*, note 11.   It represented a compromise that failed.

[16] D. L., 36.   Cf. Art. 33, *supra*.   "The case contemplated is certainly rare, but has nevertheless arisen in recent wars.   In the case of absolute contraband, there is no difficulty,·since destination for the enemy may always be proved, whatever the route which the goods are to follow (Article 30).   For conditional contraband the case is different, and an exception must be made to the general rule laid down in Article 35, paragraph 1, so as to allow the captor to prove that the suspected goods really have the special destination referred to in Article 33 without the possibility of being confronted by the objection that they were to be discharged in a neutral port." *Report, op. cit.*

This Article was designed to meet such cases as arose during the Anglo-Boer War.   It is probably good law.

band may be captured on the high seas or in the territorial waters of the belligerents throughout the whole course of her voyage, even if she has the intention of touching at a port of call before reaching the hostile destination " (Art. 37).[17]

" A capture may not be made on the ground of a previous carriage of contraband which is now at an end " (Art. 38).[18]

510. **Penalty for Carriage of Contraband.**—The Declaration of London laid down the following penalties for the carriage of contraband:

" Contraband goods are liable to condemnation " (Art. 39).[19]

" The confiscation of the vessel carrying contraband is allowed, if the contraband forms, reckoned either by value, by weight, by volume, or by freight, more than half the cargo " (Art. 40).[20]

---

[17] D. L., 37. "The vessel may be captured because of contraband during the whole of her voyage, provided that she is in waters where an act of war is lawful. The fact that she intends to touch at a port of call before reaching the enemy destination does not prevent capture, since in that case the enemy destination is proved in conformity with the rules laid down in Articles 30 to 32 for absolute contraband, and in Articles 33 to 35 for conditional contraband, and subject to the exception of Article 36." *Report*, in Higgins, 590.

[18] D. L., 38. "A vessel is liable to capture when it is carrying contraband, but not for having carried contraband," *i.e.* she is not liable on the return voyage or for a previous offense. As Lord Stowell said in the leading case of the *Imina* (3 C. Rob. 167 and Evans, 675): "The articles must be taken *in delicto*, in the actual prosecution of the voyage to an enemy's port." (The latter part of this dictum is not literally true or is subject to exceptions.) For a violation of this rule by Russia in the case of the *Allanton*, see Hershey, *Russo-Japanese War*, 171–72; and Lawrence, *War and Neutrality* (2d ed.), 221–47.

[19] D. L., 39. This Article "presents no difficulty."

[20] D. L., 40. "It was universally admitted, that in certain cases the condemnation of the contraband does not suffice, and that the vessel herself should be condemned, but opinions differ as to the determination of these cases. It was decided to fix upon a certain proportion between the contraband and the total cargo.

"But the question divides itself: (1) What shall be the proportion? The solution adopted holds the mean between those proposed, which varied from a quarter to three quarters. (2) How should this proportion be reckoned? Must the contraband form more than half the cargo in volume, weight, value, or freight? The adoption of a single fixed standard gives rise to theoretical objections, and also encourages practices intended to avoid condemnation of the vessel in spite of the importance of the cargo. If the standard of weight or volume is adopted, the master will ship innocent goods sufficiently bulky or weighty in order that the volume or weight of the contraband may be less. A

" If a vessel carrying contraband is released, the expenses incurred by the captor in the trial before the national prize court, as also for the custody of the ship and cargo during the proceedings, are to be borne by the ship " (Art. 41).[21]

" Goods which belong to the owner of the contraband and

similar remark may be made as regards the value or the freight. The consequence is that, in order to justify condemnation, it suffices that the contraband should form more than half the cargo according to any one of the points of view indicated. This may seem severe; but, on the one hand, any other system would make fraudulent calculations easy, and on the other, it may be said that the condemnation of the vessel is justified when the carriage of contraband formed an important part of her venture—a statement which applies to all the cases specified." *Report, op. cit.* in Higgins, 590–91.

In the Middle Ages, the vessel as well as the entire cargo were liable to be confiscated. Later (during the seventeenth and eighteenth centuries) it became customary only to exempt the vessel and the innocent part of the cargo. The Anglo-American practice has been to confiscate the vessel when the owner of the contraband was also the owner of the vessel, in case of guilty knowledge on the part of the latter, or if the ship offered resistance or sailed with false or simulated papers; and also to confiscate such part of the innocent cargo as belonged to the owner of the vessel. See Holland, *Manual* (1888), Nos. 80–87. The leading cases are the *Jonge Tobias* (1799), 1 C. Rob. 329; the *Neutralitaet* (1801), 3 C. Rob. 295, and Evans, *Cases,* 386; and *Carrington* v. *Ins. Co.* (1834), 8 Peters, 495, and Scott, *Cases,* 975.

In the case of the *Hakan* (see Evans, *Cases,* 693 or Scott, *Cases,* 968) the Judicial Committee of the Privy Council (1917) rejected the compromise proposed in Art. 40 of the Declaration of London as not embodying a rule of International Law binding on the Court. The underlying principle was found to be knowledge on the part of the owner. Consequently, the Court held that even the carriage of a complete cargo of contraband would not be sufficient of itself to justify the condemnation of the vessel.

[21] D. L., 41. "It is not just that, on one hand, the carriage of more than a certain proportion of contraband should involve the condemnation of the vessel, while if the contraband forms less than this proportion, it alone is confiscated. This often involves no loss for the master, the freight of this contraband having been paid in advance. Does this not encourage trade in contraband, and is it not proper to impose a certain penalty for the carriage of a proportion of contraband less than that required for condemnation? A kind of fine was proposed which should bear a relation to the value of the contraband articles. Objections of various kinds were expressed against this proposal, although the principle of the infliction of some pecuniary loss for the carriage of contraband seemed justified. The same object was attained in another way by providing that the expenses incurred by the captor in respect to the proceedings in the national prize court, as also for the custody of the vessel and her cargo during the proceedings, are to be borne by the vessel; the expense of the custody of the vessel including in this case the cost of the keep of the personnel of the captured vessel. It should be added that the loss caused to the vessel by being taken to and detained in a prize port is of such a nature as to constitute a most serious deterrent as regards the carriage of contraband." *Report,* cited above.

which are on board the same vessel are liable to condem·
nation." (Art. 42).[22]

511. **Effect of Ignorance.**—" If a vessel is encountered at
sea making a voyage in ignorance of hostilities or of the
declaration of contraband affecting her cargo, the contraband cannot be condemned except on payment of indemnity; the vessel herself and the remainder of the cargo
are exempt from condemnation and from the expenses
referred to in Article 41. The same rule applies if the
master, becoming aware of the opening of hostilities or of
the declaration of contraband, has not yet been able to
discharge the contraband.

" A vessel is deemed to be aware of the state of war or of
the declaration of contraband if she left a neutral port after
the notification of the opening of hostilities or the declaration of contraband made in sufficient time to the Power to
which such port belongs. A vessel is also deemed to be
aware of a state of war if she left an enemy port after the
opening of hostilities " (Art. 43).[23]

512. **Provision for Delivery of Contraband Goods to the
Belligerent Vessel.**—" A vessel stopped because carrying
contraband, and not liable to condemnation on account of
the proportion of contraband on board, may, when circumstances permit, be allowed to continue her voyage if the
master is willing to deliver the contraband to the belligerent
ship.

[22] D. L., 42. "The owner of the contraband is punished in the first place by
the condemnation of his unlawful property; and in the second by that of his
goods, even if innocent, which he may possess on board the same vessel."
This is in accordance with the Anglo-American practice.

[23] D. L., 43. Cf. Arts. 23 and 25, *supra*, Nos. 498 and 500. "This provision
is intended to spare neutrals who might in fact be carrying contraband, but
against whom no charge could be made. This may happen in two cases. The
first is that in which they do not know of the opening of hostilities; the second
is that in which, though aware of this, they do not know of the declaration of
contraband made by a belligerent, in accordance with Articles 23 and 25,
and which is properly applicable to the whole or a part of the cargo. It would
be unjust to capture the ship and condemn the contraband; on the other hand,
the cruiser cannot be obliged to allow to go on to the enemy goods suitable for
use in the war and of which he may be in urgent need. These opposing interests are reconciled by making condemnation conditional on the payment of a
compensation. (See for a similar idea the Convention of the 18th October,
1907, on the rules for enemy merchant vessels on the outbreak of hostilities)."
Report, op. cit. Cf. *supra*, No. 348.

" The delivery of the contraband is to be entered by the captor on the logbook of the vessel stopped, and the master of the vessel must give to the captor duly certified copies of all relevant papers.

" The captor is free to destroy the contraband which is thus delivered to him " (Art. 44).[24]

[24] D. L., 44. "A neutral vessel is stopped because of contraband. She is not liable to condemnation, because the contraband does not reach the proportion specified in Article 40. She can nevertheless be taken to a prize court in order that she may there receive judgment relative to the contraband. This right of the captor appears excessive in certain cases; if one compares the slight importance of the contraband (for instance, a case of guns or revolvers) with the heavy loss incurred by the vessel in being thus turned out of her course and detained during the time taken up by the proceedings. The question has, therefore, been asked whether the right of the neutral vessel to continue her voyage might not be admitted if the contraband articles were handed over to the captor, who, on his part, might only refuse them for sufficient reasons; for instance, the bad state of the sea, which would make transshipment impossible or difficult, well-founded suspicions as to the actual amount of contraband which the merchant vessel is carrying, the difficulty of stowing the articles on board the warship, etc. This proposal did not have sufficient support. It was alleged to be impossible to impose such an obligation on the cruiser, for which this handing over of goods would almost always have drawbacks. If, by chance, it has none, the cruiser will not refuse it, because she herself will have the advantage of not being turned out of her course by the necessity of taking the vessel to a port. The idea of an obligation having thus been excluded, it was decided to provide for the voluntary handing over of the contraband, which, it is hoped, will be carried out whenever possible, to the great advantage of both parties. The formalities provided for are very simple, and need no explanation.

"A judgment of a prize court must be rendered as regards the goods thus handed over. For this reason the captor must be furnished with the necessary papers. It may be supposed that there might be doubt as to the character of certain articles which the cruiser claims to be contraband; the master of the merchant vessel denies this, but prefers to deliver them so as to be free to continue the voyage. This is merely a capture which must be confined by the prize court.

"The contraband delivered by the merchant vessel may hamper the cruiser, which must be left free, to destroy it at the moment it is handed over." *Report*, in Higgins, 592.

In the main, the rules relating to contraband adopted by the London Naval Conference must be pronounced a happy compromise of Anglo-American and Continental views on the whole favorable to neutral trade. Since the Declaration was not ratified, it of course does not have the force of law. Consequently, each belligerent is free to revert to earlier practice which, however, is far from uniform.

There is one omission which should be particularly noted. The Declaration does not provide for *preëmption* except in the cases specified in Arts. 29 and 43. Some countries at times resort to the practice of preëmption, *i.e.* instead of absolutely confiscating the goods they prefer forcible purchase at the original cost of the goods plus expenses or freight and a reasonable profit. Thus, the

BIBLIOGRAPHY

Law of Contraband.—9 *A. J.* (1915), 210–20, 456–61, 680–87; 13–15 *Annuaire* (1894–96), *passim;* * Atherley-Jones, *Commerce in War* (1907), chs. 1 and 3; Bar, in 26 *R. D. I.* (1894), 401 ff.; * Barclay, *Problems,* etc., 91–98, 168–69; Baty, *Britain and Sea Law* (1911), ch. 2, and *Int. Law in S. Africa* (1900), ch. 1; Bentwich, *The Law of Private Property in War* (1907), chs. 8–9, and, *The Declaration of London* (1911), ch. 2; Bluntschli, Arts. 801–14; * Boeck, Nos. 606–59; Bonfils or * 2 Fauchille, Nos. 1535–88; Brocher de la Fléchère, in 31 *R. D. I.* (1899), 337 ff.; Brochet, *De la contrebande de guerre* (1900); Butte, in *Procs. Am. Soc. I. L.* (1916), 112 ff.; Bynkershoek, *Questiones juris publici,* lib. I, cc. 9–12; 5 Calvo, §§ 2708–95; 2 Cobbett, 555–88; Cros, *De la notion de la contrebande,* etc. (1905); * Dana, note 226 to Wheaton, 629 ff.; Davis, ch. 13; Despagnet, Nos. 687–90; * Dupuis, *La guerre maritime* (1899 and 1911), ch. 7; Elliot, in 42 *Am. Law Rev.* (1908), 578–97; * Evans, *Cases,* ch. 18; Fauchille, in 4 *R. G. D. I.* (1897), 297 ff.; 3 Fiore, Nos. 1591–1601, and *Int. Law Cod.,* Nos. 1850–75; Flourens, *De la notion de contrebande de guerre* (1907); Fromageot, in 27 *J. I. P.,* 29 ff.; * 2 Garner, ch. 32, and *Prize Law during the World War* (1927), chs. 13–14; Geffcken, in 4 Holtzendorff, 713–31; Grotius, lib. III, c. 1, § 5; * Hall, Pt. IV, ch. 5; Hall, J. A., *Law of Naval Warfare* (1921), ch. 7; 2 Halleck, ch. 26; Hart, in 17 *L. Q. R.* (1901), 193 ff.; 2 Hautefeuille, *Droits et devoirs des neutres* (1868), 65–176; Heineccius, *De navibus,* etc. (1740); Hershey, *Russo-Japanese War,* ch. 6; Heffter (Geffcken), §§ 158–61; Historicus,

British Admiralty Manual of 1888 (No. 84) states: "The carriage of goods conditionally contraband, and of such absolutely contraband goods as are in an unmanufactured state, and are the produce of the country exporting them, is usually followed only by the preëmption of such goods by the British Government, which then pays freight to the vessel carrying the goods." In such cases the British Courts of Admiralty have been accustomed to award the original price actually paid by the exporter plus his expenses and a reasonable profit, usually reckoned at ten per cent. See the *Haabet,* 2 C. Rob. 174, and Evans, *Cases,* 687 or Scott, *Cases,* 958. In March, 1915 Great Britain adopted the policy of preëmption for both vessels and goods accused of violating the so-called blockade of Germany.

In 1896 The Institute of International Law recognized the right of preëmption in the case of articles *ancipitis usus.* See Scott, *Resolutions,* 130.

Since preëmption is a mitigation of the rule prescribing confiscation as the penalty for the carriage of contraband, it is, of course, always open to belligerents to resort to it in all cases where the goods are undoubtedly contraband.

On *Preëmption,* see: Boeck, Nos. 730–31; Bonfils, Nos. 1314, 1411, 1583; 5 Calvo, §§ 2790–95; * 2 Fauchille, Nos. 1358, 1411, 1583; * Hall, 793–94 n. (8th ed.); 2 Halleck (3d ed.), 235–36; * 2 Kleen, § 230; Perels, § 46; 3 Phillimore, §§ 267–70; Pyke, *Law of Contraband* (1915), 225 ff.; 2 Twiss, § 146; Woolsey, § 197.

On *Penalty for Carriage of Contraband,* see especially; Hall, § 247; Hall, J. A., *Law of Naval Warfare* (1921), 223–26; 2 Hyde, §§ 815–16; Lawrence, § 259; 2 Oppenheim, §§ 405 ff.; * Pyke, *op. cit.,* ch. 14.

Letters of, 121–37; Hold de Ferneck, *Die Kriegskonterbande* (1907); Holland, in 31 *J. I. P.* 335 ff., and *Prize Law* (1888), Nos. 57–87; Hübner, *De la saisie des bâtiments neutres* (1759); * 2 Hyde, §§ 797–816; Kennedy and Rankin, in 24 *Law Quar. Rev.* (1908), 59 ff., 316 ff., and 449 ff.; * 1 Kleen, *De la Contrebande,* etc. (1893), 348–452, and in 25–27 *R. D. I.* (1893–1895), *passim;* Knight, *Des états neutres,* etc. (1903); * Lawrence, Pt. IV, ch. 6, and *War and Neutrality,* ch. 7; Liszt, § 68; 2 J. de Louter, § 58; Maine, *Int. Law* (2d ed., 1894), 96–112; Manning, *Commentaries,* etc. (1875), Bk. V, ch. 9; Manceaux, *De la contrebande de guerre* (1899); 3 F. de Martens, § 136; * 7 Moore, *Digest,* ch. 26, and *Int. Law and Current Illusions* (1924), ch. 2; Moseley, *What is Contraband and what is not* (1861); Naval War College, *Int. Law Topics* (see index, 1922); 3 Nys, 626–70; * 2 Oppenheim, Pt. III, ch. 4; 2 Ortolan, liv. III, ch. 6; Perels, §§ 45–46; Pilidi, *Le combustible en temps de guerre,* etc. (1909); 3 Phillimore, Pt. 10, ch. 1; * Pyke, *The Law of Contraband of War* (1915), and in 32 *Law Quar. Rev.* (1916), 50–69 (the *Kim* Case); Remy, *Théorie de la continuité du voyage* (1902); Richards, in *Brit. Yr. Bk.* (1922–23), 1–16; 2 Rivier, 416–23; 3 Rolin, 1201–46; * Scott, *Cases,* 955–81, and *Resolutions,* see index (for rules adopted by Institute of Int. Law); Smith and Sibley, *Russo-Japanese War,* ch. 13; Stockton, *Outlines,* etc., ch. 26; Stockton's (U. S.) *Naval War Code,* Arts. 34–36; * Takahashi, *Russo-Japanese War,* Pt. IV, ch. 4, and Pt. V, ch. 4 (cases); Taylor, Pt. V, ch. 5; Testa, *Le droit int. maritime* (1886), 201–20; Thonier, *De la notion de contrebande de guerre* (1904); Triepel, *Konterbande,* etc. (1918); 2 Twiss, ch. 7; Ullmann, §§ 193–94; Upton, *The Law of Nations affecting Commerce during War* (1863); Vattel, liv. III, §§ 111–13; 2 Verraes, *Droit int. Les lois de la guerre et la neutralité* (1906), ch. 10; Vossen, *Die Konterbande des Kriegs* (1896); Walker, *Manual,* §§ 73–75; * 2 Westlake, ch. 10, and *Collected Papers,* 362–92, 461–74, 519–22; Wheaton, §§ 476–501, 505–09; 3 Wharton, *Digest,* ch. 19; Wiegner, *Die Kriegskonterbande,* etc. (1904); * Wilson, ch. 24; Woolsey, §§ 193–97.

For Bibliographies, see Boeck, Bonfils, Fauchille, Kleen, Oppenheim, Pilidi, Thonier, and Wiegner.

CHAPTER XXXVI

THE SO-CALLED LAW OF UNNEUTRAL SERVICE OR HOSTILE AID

513. Difference between Contraband and Unneutral Service or Hostile Aid.—" In a general way, it may be said that the merchant vessel which violates neutrality, whether by carrying contraband of war or by breaking a blockade, affords aid to the enemy, and it is on this ground that the belligerent whom she injures by her acts is justified in inflicting on her certain losses. But there are cases where such unneutral service bears a particularly distinctive character, and for such cases it has been thought necessary to make special provision. These have been divided into two classes according to the gravity of the act charged against the neutral vessel." [1]

The offenses of carrying contraband and engaging in

---

[1] *Report on the Declaration of London* as translated in Naval War College, *Int. Law Topics* (1909), 99; or Higgins, 593. The *Report* continues:

"In the cases included in the first class (Article 45), the vessel is condemned, and receives the treatment of a vessel subject to condemnation for carrying contraband. This means that the vessel does not lose her neutral character and is entitled to the rights conceded to neutral vessels; for instance, she may not be destroyed by the captor except under the conditions laid down for neutral vessels (Articles 48 *et. seq.*) [Cf. *infra*, No. 522]: the rule that the *flag covers the goods* applies to the goods on board.

"In the more serious cases belonging to the second class (Article 46), the vessel is likewise condemned; but further, she is treated not only as a vessel liable to confiscation for carrying contraband, but as an enemy merchant vessel, which treatment entails certain consequences. The rule governing destruction of neutral prizes does not apply to the vessel, and, as she has become an enemy vessel, it is no longer the second but the third rule of the Declaration of Paris which is applicable. The goods on board will be presumed to be enemy goods; neutrals will have the right to reclaim their property on establishing their neutrality (Article 59). [Cf. *supra*, No. 443]. It would not, however, be necessary to go so far as to consider that the original neutral character of the vessel is completely lost, so that she should be treated as though she had always been an enemy vessel. The vessel may plead that the allegation made against her is not well-founded, that the act of which she is accused has not the character of unneutral service. She has therefore the right of appeal to the International Court in virtue of the provisions which protect neutral property." The Court referred to is the International Prize Court (see *infra*, add. note on pp. 740–41) which never came into existence.

unneutral service [2] are analogous in some respects, but there are also some marked contrasts. A former leading authority on this subject has thus expressed these differences: " They are unlike in nature, unlike in proof and unlike in penalty. To carry contraband is to engage in an ordinary trading transaction, which is directed toward a belligerent community simply because a better market is likely to be found there than elsewhere. To perform unneutral service is to interfere in the struggle by doing in aid of a belligerent, acts which are in themselves not mercantile, but warlike. In order that a cargo of contraband may be condemned as good prize, the captors must show that it was on the way to a belligerent destination. If without subterfuge it is bound to a neutral port, the voyage is innocent, whatever may be the nature of the goods. In the case of unneutral service the destination of the captured vessel is immaterial. The nature of her mission is the all-important point. She may be seized and confiscated when sailing between two neutral ports. The penalty for carrying contraband is the forfeiture of the forbidden goods, the ship being retained as prize of war only under special circumstances. The penalty for unneutral service is first and foremost the confiscation of the vessel, the goods on board being condemned when the owner is involved, or when fraud and concealment have been resorted to." [3]

514. **The Lesser Offenses of Unneutral Service.**— According to the unratified Declaration of London, " a neutral vessel will be condemned and will, in a general way, receive the same treatment as a neutral vessel liable to condemnation for carriage of contraband of war:

" 1. If she is on a voyage especially undertaken with a view to the transport of individual passengers who are embodied in the armed force of the enemy, or with a view to the transmission of intelligence in the interest of the enemy.

[2] The term "unneutral service" is decidedly preferable to "analogues of contraband" still preferred by some authorities. "Hostile aid" would perhaps be preferable to either.

[3] Lawrence, *Principles* (3d ed.), § 284, p. 633. Cf. *Ibid.* (7th ed.), § 260. The last sentence of the above citation needs some slight modification.

" 2. If, with the knowledge of the owner, the one who charters the vessel entire, or the master, she is transporting a military detachment of the enemy, or one or more persons who, during the voyage, directly assist the operations of the enemy.

" In the cases specified in the preceding paragraphs, goods belonging to the owner of the vessel are likewise liable to condemnation.

" The provisions of the present Article do not apply if when the vessel is encountered at sea she is unaware of the opening of hostilities, or if the master, after becoming aware of the opening of hostilities, has not yet been able to disembark the passengers. The vessel is deemed to be aware of the state of war if she left an enemy port after the opening of hostilities, or a neutral port after there had been made in sufficient time a notification of the opening of hostilities to the Power to which such port belongs " (Art. 45).[4]

[4] D. L., 45. Cf. Art. 42, *supra*, No. 510. "The first case supposes passengers traveling as *individuals;* the case of a *military detachment* is dealt with hereafter. It relates to individuals *embodied* in the armed military or naval forces of the enemy. There was some doubt as to the meaning of this word *embodied.* Does it include those individuals only who, summoned to serve in virtue of the law of their country, have really joined the corps to which they are to belong? Or does it also include such individuals from the time they are summoned, and before they have joined their corps? The question is of great practical importance. Suppose there are individuals who are natives of a country of continental Europe and settled in America; these individuals have military obligations towards their native country; they have, for instance, to belong to the reserve of the active army of that country. Their country being at war, they sail to perform their service. Shall they be considered as *embodied* in the sense of the provision which we are discussing? If we judged by the municipal law of certain countries, we might argue in the affirmative. But, apart from purely judicial reasons, the contrary opinion has seemed more in accordance with practical necessity and has been accepted by all in a spirit of conciliation. It would be difficult, or perhaps even impossible, without vexatious measures which neutral governments would not accept, to distinguish among the passengers in a vessel those who are bound to perform military service and are on their way to render it.

"The transmission of intelligence in the interest of the enemy is assimilated to the carriage of passengers embodied in his armed force. The reference to a vessel *especially* undertaking a voyage is intended to show that her usual service is not meant. She has been turned from her course; she has touched at a port where she does not ordinarily call, in order to embark the passengers in question. She need not be *exclusively* devoted to the service of the enemy; this last case would fall into the second class (Article 46, (4).).

"In the two cases just mentioned the vessel has performed but a single act;

515. The More Serious Offenses of Unneutral Service.
—"A neutral vessel will be condemned and will, in a

she has been employed to carry certain people, or to transmit certain intelligence; she is continuously in the service of the enemy. It results from this that she may be captured during the voyage on which she is performing the work which has been assigned to her; once that voyage is finished, all is over, in the sense that she may not be captured for having done the work in question; this (principle) is analogous to that recognized in the case of contraband (Article 38). Cf. *supra*, No. 509.

"The second case also falls under two heads:

"There is, first, the carriage of a military detachment of the enemy, or that of one or more persons who during the voyage directly assist his operations, for instance, by signalling. If they are soldiers or sailors in uniform there is no difficulty; the vessel is clearly liable to condemnation. If they are soldiers or sailors in citizen's dress who might be mistaken for ordinary passengers, knowledge on the part of the master or owner is required, the charterer being assimilated to the owner. The rule is the same in the case of persons directly assisting the enemy during the voyage.

"In these cases, if the vessel is condemned for unneutral service, the goods belonging to her owner are also liable to condemnation.

"These provisions assume that the state of war was known to the vessel engaged in the operations specified; such knowledge is the reason for and justification of her condemnation. The position is altogether different when the vessel is unaware of the opening of hostilities, so that she undertakes the service as in ordinary times. She may have learned of the opening of hostilities while at sea, but have had no chance of landing the persons whom she was carrying. Condemnation would then be unjust, and the equitable rule adopted is in accordance with the provisions already accepted in other matters. If a vessel has left an enemy port after such opening has been notified to the Powers to whom such port belongs, knowledge of a state of war will be presumed.

"The question here is merely one of preventing the condemnation of the vessel. The persons found on board who belong to the armed forces of the enemy may be made prisoners of war by the cruiser." *Report*, cited above.

Article 45 "is in a small measure a relaxation of the present English practice, by which a vessel might be condemned for carrying one or two officers of the enemy's forces, though in the course of an ordinary voyage, and though the masters and owners of the vessel were ignorant of the military character of the passengers." Bentwich, *The Dec. of London*, 87. Cf. the *Orozembo*, 6 C. Rob. 430, and Evans, *Cases*, 637 or Scott, *Cases*, 865.

For a digest of the leading cases, now perhaps no longer authoritative but still useful, see Dana, note 228 to Wheaton 637 ff.; and 7 Moore, *Digest*, § 1264.

"It would be intolerable to-day that a neutral ocean liner should be liable to condemnation, because a belligerent cruiser found among her passengers one or two persons who were proceeding to the enemy country to join the enemy forces, and who had come aboard without the knowledge of any responsible person, as could very easily be managed." Bentwich, *op. cit.*

On the immunity of ordinary mail, cf. *supra*, No. 412. Diplomatic dispatches are especially privileged. See the case of the *Caroline* (1808), 6 Rob. 464.

"According to the Naval Instructions Governing Maritime Warfare, of June 30, 1917, a neutral vessel is guilty of indirect unneutral service and may be sent in for adjudication as a neutral ship liable to condemnation:

general way, receive the same treatment as if she were a merchant vessel of the enemy:

" 1. If she takes a direct part in the hostilities.

" 2. If she is under the orders or under the control of an agent placed on board of the enemy Government.

" 3. If she is chartered entire by the enemy Government.

" 4. If she is at the time exclusively devoted either to the transport of enemy troops or to the transmission of intelligence in the interest of the enemy.

" In the cases dealt with by the present Article, the goods belonging to the owner of the vessel are likewise liable to condemnation " (Art. 46).[5]

"'(a) If she specially undertakes to transport individual passengers who are embodied in the armed forces of the enemy, and who are en route for military service of the enemy or to a hostile destination, or transmits intelligence in the interest of the enemy whether by radio or otherwise.

"'(b) If, to the knowledge of the owner, or the charterer, or of the agents thereof, or of the master, she is transporting a military detachment of the enemy, or one or more persons who are embodied in the military or naval service of the enemy and who are en route for military service of the enemy or to a hostile destination, or one or more persons who, during the voyage, lend direct assistance to the enemy, or is transmitting information in the interest of the enemy by radio or otherwise.'"   2 Hyde, § 822, p. 644.

[5] D. L., 46. "The cases here contemplated are more serious than those in Article 45, which justifies the severer treatment inflicted on the vessel, as has been explained above.

"*First Case.*—The vessel takes a direct part in the hostilities. This may take different forms. It goes without saying that if there is an armed conflict, the vessel is liable to all the risks of such a struggle. . . .

"*Second Case.*—The vessel is under the orders or control of an agent placed on board by the enemy Government. His presence marks the relation which exists between the enemy and the vessel. In other circumstances the vessel may also have relations with the enemy; but to be subject to condemnation, she must be in the third class.

"*Third Case.*—The vessel is chartered entire by the enemy Government, and is therefore entirely at its disposal; it can use her for different purposes more or less directly connected with the war, notably for purposes of transportation; such is the position of colliers which accompany a belligerent fleet. There will often be a charter-party between the belligerent Government and the owner or master of the vessel; but it is only a question of proof. The fact that the whole vessel has been chartered suffices, in whatever way it may be established.

"*Fourth Case*—The vessel is at the time exclusively devoted either to the carriage of enemy troops or to the transmission of intelligence in the enemy's interest. In distinction from cases dealt with by Article 45, the question here is one of a service to which the ship is permanently devoted. The decision accordingly is that, so long as such service lasts, the vessel is liable to capture, even if, at the moment, when an enemy cruiser searches her, she is engaged neither in the transport of troops nor in the transmission of intelligence.

" Any individual embodied in the armed force of the enemy, who is found on board a neutral merchant vessel, may be made a prisoner of war, even though there be no ground for the capture of the vessel " (Art. 47).[6]

"As in the cases in Article 45 and for the same reasons, goods belonging to the owner of the vessel found on board are also liable to condemnation.

"It was proposed to treat as an enemy merchant vessel a neutral vessel making at the same time, and with the authorization of the enemy Government, a voyage which she has only been permitted to make after the opening of hostilities or during the two preceding months. This rule would be applicable notably to merchant vessels admitted by a belligerent reserved in time of peace to the national marine of that belligerent—for instance, to the coasting trade. Several Delegations formally rejected this proposal, so that the question thus raised remains an open one." *Report, op. cit.*

If this latter proposal had been adopted, it would have revived the Rule of 1756.

Bentwich (*op. cit.*, 90–91) makes the following comment upon Article 46:

"The consequence of assimilating the treatment of neutral vessels, committing the more serious breaches of neutral duty specified in this Article (46), with the treatment of enemy vessels is that—

"(1) Not only goods belonging to the owner of the vessel, but all enemy goods found on board, though not contraband, may be confiscated, although when shipping the vessel was neutral. . . .

"(2) The vessel may be sunk by the captor without being brought in for adjudication by a Prize Court. . . .

"As to the four circumstances which are required to attach enemy characters to the vessel, the first, taking direct part in hostilities, would include acting as scout, or giving notice to a blockading squadron of the approach of an enemy fleet or neutral merchantman, or laying or removing mines at sea. . . . The distinctive characteristic of the second and third conditions is that the vessel should be in the exclusive service of the enemy Government at the time of the capture, which virtually makes her an addition to the enemy's forces. Thus if a neutral vessel were solely engaged in providing the enemy's forces with coal or provisions, it would be treated as an enemy vessel. . . . Lastly, if a neutral vessel, though hired in times of peace, continues after the outbreak of war to transport troops or carry war material exclusivel ,or the enemy, she is considered to identify herself with the enemy. . . . During the war between China and Japan in 1897 the Japanese sank an English vessel which was at the opening of hostilities captured in the act of transporting Chinese troops (*the Kowshing*); and no protest was made."

For the case of the *Kowshing*, see Takahashi, *Cases during the Chino-Japanese War* (1899). For the case of the *Cheltenham* during the *Russo-Japanese War*, see Hershey, 173 n. For the cases of the *Industrie* and the *Quangnam*, see Takahashi, *Russo-Japanese War*, 732–38.

[6] D. L., 47. This is a new rule. "Individuals embodied in the armed military or naval forces of a belligerent may be on board a neutral merchant vessel which is visited and searched. If the vessel is subject to condemnation, the cruiser will capture her and take her to one of her own ports with the persons on board. Clearly the soldiers or sailors of the enemy State will not be set free, but will be treated as prisoners or war. It may happen that the case will not be one for the capture of the ship—for instance, because the master was unaware of the status of an individual who had come on board as an ordinary

BIBLIOGRAPHY

Unneutral Service or Hostile Aid.—15 *Annuaire* (1896), 231–33; Atherley-Jones, 304–15; Bernard, *Neutrality*, etc. (1870), 187–225; Bluntschli, Arts. 815–18; Boeck, Nos. 660–69; 5 Calvo, §§ 2796–2825; 2 Cobbett, 589–607; * Dana, note 228 to Wheaton, 637 ff.; Despagnet, No. 691; * Dupuis, *La guerre maritime* (1899 and 1911), ch. 8; * Evans, *Cases*, ch. 16; 2 Fauchille, No. 1588¹⁵⁻¹⁷; 2 Garner, §§ 538–45, * *Prize Law during the World War*, ch. 14, sects. 446–50; Geffcken, in 4 Holtzendorff, 731–38; * Hall, Pt. IV, ch. 6; Hall, J. A., *Law of Naval Warfare*, ch. 8; 2 Halleck (Baker's 3d ed.), 289–301; 2 Hautefeuille, *Droits et devoirs des neutres* (1868), 170–76; Hirsh, *Kriegskonterbande und verbotene Transporte in Kriegszeiten* (1897); * Holland, *Prize Law*, Nos. 88–105; 2 Hyde, §§ 817–23; * 1 Kleen, 452–70; Lawrence, Pt. IV, ch. 7; 3 F. de Martens, § 136; * 7 Moore, *Digest*, §§ 1264–65; Naval War College, *Int. Law Topics* (see index, 1922); 3 Nys, 671–78; * 2 Oppenheim, Pt. III, ch. 5;

passenger. Must the soldier or soldiers on board the vessel be set free? This does not appear admissible. The belligerent cruiser cannot be compelled to set free active enemies who are physically in her power and are more dangerous than this or that contraband article; naturally she must act with great discretion, and it is at her own responsibility that she requires the surrender of these individuals, but she has the right to do so; it has therefore been thought necessary to explain the point." *Report*, in Higgins, 596–97; or *Int. Law Topics* (1909), 111.

"Article 47 gives the belligerent the right of removing from the neutral vessel any individual belonging to the enemy's forces; but to inculpate the vessel for such carriage there must be proof of unneutral intention shown by the fact that the vessel was not made in the ordinary course, but was specially undertaken in the enemy's interest." Bentwich, *op. cit.*, 87.

According to Article 47, Messrs. Slidell and Mason, agents of the Confederate Government, could not have been forcibly removed from the British mail steamer *Trent* (as they were by Captain Wilkes, the commander of the American cruiser *San Jacinto* in Novermber, 1861), since they were not "embodied in the armed force of the enemy."

On the *Trent Affair*, see especially, Atherley-Jones, *Commerce in War*, 311–15; * Bernard, *Neutrality*, etc., ch. 9; * Dana, note 228 to Wheaton, 644 ff.; Hall, § 253; 2 Halleck (3d ed.), 293–301; * Harris, *The Trent Affair* (1896); Historicus, II, 187–98; 2 Hyde, § 818; Lawrence (3d ed.), § 284; Marquardson, *Der Trent Fall* (1862); * 7 Moore, *Digest*, § 1265; 3 Wharton, § 374.

Upon the outbreak of the World War, the Allies adopted the rules relating to unneutral service contained in the Declaration of London, and applied them until the Declaration was abandoned in July, 1916. Thenceforth the earlier customary rules again became applicable.

During the War there were many instances of the removal from neutral vessels on the high seas of persons of enemy nationality by British and French cruisers. The most interesting and important cases were perhaps those of *Piepenbrink*, and the seizures on the *China* and the *Federico*. See 2 Garner, §§ 538–44. Cf. 2 Hyde, § 819. On "The *Trent* and the *China*," see Malkin, in *Brit. Yr. Bk.* (1924), 66–77.

For diplomatic correspondence between Great Britain and the United States relating to the *China*, see Spec. Supp. to 10 *A. J.* (1916), 427 ff.

Pastereau, *Des transports interdits aux neutres* (1912); Perels, § 47; 3 Phillimore, §§ 271–74; 2 Rivier, 388–91; 3 Rolin, Nos. 1247–71; * Scott, *Cases*, 865–91; Stockton, *Outlines*, ch. 27; Stockton's (U. S.) *Naval War Code*, Arts. 16 and 20; Takahashi (for cases during *Russo-Japanese War*), Pt. V, ch. 6, and *Cases during Chino-Japanese War* (1899), 52–72; Taylor, Pt. V, ch. 6; Vetzel, *De la contrebande par analogie* (1901); Walker, *Manual*, § 72; 2 Westlake (1st ed.), 261–65; Wheaton, §§ 502–04; * Wilson, ch. 27, and in *Procs. Am. Pol. Sci. Assoc.* (1904), 68–78.

CHAPTER XXXVII

RIGHTS OF VISIT AND SEARCH, OF CAPTURE, AND CONDEMNATION BY PRIZE COURTS

516. The Right of Visit and Search.—In order to discover whether neutral vessels are engaged in such acts as carriage of contraband, unneutral service, breach of blockade, etc., as well as to determine the enemy or neutral character of ships and their cargoes, it is necessary to concede to properly commissioned warships of belligerent Powers the right of visit and search as ancillary to the rights of capture and subsequent condemnation by properly constituted prize courts.[1]

As Lord Stowell (then Sir William Scott) said (in 1799) in the famous case of the *Maria* (1 C. Robinson 340, 359, and Evans, *Cases*, 535 or Scott, 1003):

" The right of visiting and searching merchant ships upon the high seas, whatever be the ships, whatever be the cargoes, whatever be the destinations, is an incontestible right of the lawfully commissioned cruisers of a belligerent nation. . . . This right is so clear in principle, that no man can deny it who admits the legality of maritime capture, because if you are not at liberty to ascertain by sufficient inquiry whether there is property that can legally be captured, it is impossible to capture. . . . The right is equally clear in practice; for the practice is uniform and universal upon the subject." [2]

[1] "It (the right of search) has been truly denominated a right growing out of, and ancillary to, the greater right of capture. Where this greater right may be legally exercised without search, the right of search can never rise or come into question." C. J. Marshall, in *The Nereide* (1815), 9 Cranch, 388, 427.

Strictly speaking, it is a belligerent right and there is no right of visit apart from that of search.

The only exceptions to the non-exercise of the right of visitation and search in time of peace are in the case of a well-grounded suspicion of piracy (see *supra*, No. 215), and when given by treaty to prevent slave trading (see *supra*, No. 216).

[2] But Lord Stowell added that "the right must unquestionably be exercised with as little of personal harshness and of vexation as possible."

517. The Mode of Exercising of this Right.—" Subject to any especial treaty stipulations," the United States prescribed (in 1900) the following mode of procedure, " to be followed by the boarding vessel, whose colors must be displayed at the time ":

" The vessel is brought to by firing a gun with blank charge. If this is not sufficient to cause her to lie to, a shot is fired across the bows, and in case of flight or resistance force can be used to compel the vessel to surrender.

" The boarding vessel should then send one of its smaller boats alongside, with an officer in charge wearing side arms, to conduct the search. Arms may be carried in the boat, but not upon the persons of the men. When the officer goes on board of the vessel he may be accompanied by not more than two men, unarmed, and he should at first examine the vessel's papers to ascertain her nationality, the nature of her cargo, and the ports of departure and destination. If the papers show contraband, an offense in respect of blockade, or enemy service, the vessel should be seized; otherwise she should be released, unless suspicious circumstances justify a further search. If the vessel be released, an entry in the log book to that effect should be made by the boarding officer." [3]

Other restrictions upon the right of visit and search are: (1) it is limited to properly commissioned belligerent cruisers; (2) it is restricted in its application to merchantmen; (3) it must not be exercised in neutral waters. Captures made in neutral territorial waters are invalid. Cf. *supra*, No. 458.

[3] Art. 32 of Stockton's *Naval War Code* (withdrawn in 1904). Cf. Art. 130 of the U. S. Instructions to Blockading Vessels and Cruisers issued in 1898, and the Draft Convention suggested in 1804 by Secretary Madison, in 7 Moore, *Digest*, § 1200; Holland's *Manual* of *Prize Law* (1888), Nos. 195–230; Arts. 51–73 of the Japanese Regulations in Takahashi, App. V, 784–86; and U. S. Naval Instructions Governing Maritime War (1917); Arts. 10–22 of the Project adopted by the Institute of Int. Law (1883 and 1887), Scott, *Resolutions*, 47–50.

The authorities seem agreed that the belligerent warship may chase under false colors, but must not fire until she has hoisted her national flag.

Many treaties still stipulate that the visiting ship shall approach the vessel about to be visited no nearer than a cannon shot, but this rule is based upon earlier treaties and practices, and is to-day regarded as impracticable.

The ceremony of the *semonce* or affirming gun is customary, but not obligatory. Hailing by signals is also practiced.

There is some authority and practice in favor of the view that the captain of the vessel visited may be summoned to send or present his ship's papers on board the visiting vessel for purposes of examination, but this is expressly

In case "suspicious circumstances justify a further search," [4] "care must be taken not to damage the vessel or the cargo, and no force whatever must be applied. No lock must be forcibly broken open by the search party, but the master is to be required to unlock it. . . .[5] Search being completed, everything has to be replaced with care." [6]

forbidden by Holland's *Manual*, No. 198, and § 12 of the Project of the Institutes, cited above.

On the *Formalities of Visit and Search*, see especially: * Atherley-Jones, ch. 6; Bonfils or 2 Fauchille, Nos. 1402–07; 5 Calvo, §§ 2955–56; Duboc, *Le droit de visites* (1902), *passim;* Hall, § 273; Holland, *Manual*, Nos. 196–230; 2 Kleen, § 193; 2 Oppenheim, §§ 418 ff.; Perels, § 54; and Taylor, §§ 687–88.

During the World War, the United States Government complained of the practice of British cruisers of taking American vessels into port for purposes of visit instead of searching them on the high seas. The practice, it was said, was not merely contrary to the established rules of visit and search, but it involved long delays and serious losses. The British Government justified its practice on the ground that modern conditions necessitated an adaptation of an old belligerent right to these changed conditions. The increased size of modern ships, the ease with which contraband, particularly copper, may be concealed in bales of hay, etc., the danger from enemy submarines—all rendered a thorough search on the high seas impracticable.

Under these new conditions, the British practice of taking neutral vessels into port for purposes of search seems to have been justified. In an editorial in 10 *A. J.* (1916), pp. 583 and 584, the writer expressed the opinion that our attitude was "needlessly obstructive, legalistic, and technical," and was based upon the letter rather than the spirit of our rights; and he asked the question whether our Government was not "straining at a gnat and swallowing a camel" (meaning the submarine camel)? This criticism was made with particular reference to British interference with our mails, but it appears to be equally revelant in this connection.

On this subject, see: 2 Garner, § 500; Hall, pp. 890–91 of 8th ed.; Hall, J. A., *Law of Naval Warfare* (1921), 264–69; 2 Hyde, §§ 727–28; and 2 Oppenheim, § 421 a.

[4] According to Art. 20 of the Project of the Institute of Int. Law (*op. cit.*), "there is ground for suspicion in the following cases:

"(1) When the vessel stopped does not heave to upon the invitation of the warship.

"(2) When it has resisted visit by means of hiding-places supposed to conceal papers on board or contraband of war.

"(3) When it has double, false, fraudulent or secret papers, in case its papers are insufficient, or if it has no papers at all.

"(4) When the papers have been thrown into the sea or destroyed in some manner, especially if these acts were done after the vessel was able to perceive the approach of the warship.

"(5) When the vessel stopped sails under a false flag."

[5] A failure to comply with this demand would be construed as resistance and as justifying seizure.

[6] 2 Oppenheim, § 421. See especially Holland's *Manual*, Nos. 217–30.

518. Right of Capture.—" Irrespective of the character of her cargo, or her purported destination, a neutral vessel should be seized if she—

" (1) Attempts to avoid search by escape;[7] but this must be clearly evident.

" (2) Resists search by violence.

" (3) Presents fraudulent papers.

" (4) Is not supplied with the necessary papers to establish the objects of search.

" (5) Destroys, defaces, or conceals papers."[8]

519. Resistance to Visit and Search.—" Forcible resistance to the legitimate exercise of the right of stoppage, visit and search, and capture involves in all cases the condemnation of the vessel. The cargo is liable to the same treatment which the cargo of an enemy vessel would

[7] "A mere attempt on the part of a neutral merchantman to escape visitation does not in itself constitute resistance." 2 Oppenheim, § 423.

"A belligerent cruiser encounters a merchant and summons her to stop in order that it may proceed to visit and search. The vessel summoned does not stop, but tries to avoid visit and search by flight. The cruiser may employ force to stop her, and if the merchant vessel is damaged or sunk, she has no right to complain, since she has acted contrary to all obligation imposed upon her by the Law of Nations. If the vessel is stopped, and if it is shown that it was only in order to escape the inconvenience of visit and search that she had recourse to flight, and that otherwise she had done nothing contrary to neutrality, she will not be punished for her attempt. If, on the other hand, it is established that the vessel has contraband on board, or that she has in any way whatever violated her neutral obligations, she will suffer the consequences of her infraction of neutrality, but she will not undergo any further punishment for her attempt at flight. Some thought, on the contrary, that the ship should be punished for an obvious attempt at flight as much as for forcible resistance. It was said that the possibility of condemnation of the escaping vessel would lead the cruiser to spare her so far as possible. But this view did not prevail." *Report* to the London Naval Conference, in Naval War College, *Int. Law Topics* (1909), 145; or Higgins, 608.

[8] Stockton's *Code, op. cit.*, Art. 33; and *Instructions* to U. S. Blockading Vessels and Cruisers (1898), Art. 14, in 7 Moore, *Digest*, p. 485.

"The papers generally expected to be on board a vessel are:

"1. The register. 2. The crew and passenger list. 3. The log book. 4. A bill of health. 5. The manifest of cargo. 6. A charter party if the vessel is chartered. 7. Invoices and bills of lading." *Ibid.*

For definitions of these and other terms and the requirements on this head of the leading maritime nations, see Atherley-Jones, *Commerce in War*, 345–52.

Mere deficiency of papers does not arouse the same degree of suspicion as spoliation, destruction, defacement, or concealment of papers. The highest suspicion is aroused by false or double papers. Grave suspicion of such offenses justifies capture. See especially Hall, § 276; 2 Halleck (3d ed.), 270–72; *2 Oppenheim, §§ 426–28; Taylor, § 690.

undergo.   Goods belonging to the master or owner of the vessel are regarded as enemy goods." [9]

[9] D. L. (Declaration of London), Art. 63.   Forcible resistance is construed as an act of hostility and renders the vessel liable to condemnation, even in cases where no acts contrary to neutrality were committed.

The cargo is assimilated to cargo on board an enemy vessel.   "This assimilation involves the following consequences: the neutral vessel which has resisted becomes an enemy vessel, the goods on board are presumed to be enemy goods.   Neutrals who are interested may claim their property, in accordance with Article 3 of the Declaration of Paris; but enemy goods will be condemned because the rule the *flag covers the goods* cannot be adduced, as the captured vessel on which they are found is considered an enemy.   It will be noticed that the right to claim the goods is recognized for all neutrals, even for those who are of the nationality of the captured vessel; it would seem to be excessive to make such persons suffer for the action of the master.   There is, however, an exception as regards the goods belonging to the owner of the vessel.   It seems natural that he should bear the consequences of the acts of his agent.   His property on board the vessel is therefore treated as enemy goods.   *A fortiore* the same rule applies to the master."   *Report*, cited above.

"The assimilation of the prize which resists capture has the consequence (1) that it may be sunk by the captor, subject only to his obligation to pay compensation to any innocent neutral who proves that he had an innocent cargo on board, (2) that all the cargo is presumed to be enemy property, and (3) that any enemy goods on board are confiscated.   Goods belonging to the master or owner of the vessel are also confiscated; but any other neutral who owns part of the cargo may prove the innocent character of his property and obtain restitution of his property, or, if it has been destroyed, compensation, because neutral goods on enemy vessels are free from capture."   Bentwich, *The Dec. of London*, 121.

In the case of *The Fanny* (1814, 1 Dodson, 443 and Scott, 1012), Lord Stowell condemned neutral goods found on board an armed enemy merchantman on the ground that the shipper might have intended to resist visitation and search.   But the Supreme Court of the United States maintained the opposite view in the case of *The Nereide* (9 Cranch, 388, and Evans, 544 or Scott, 1014), decided the year following (1815).   Story dissented from the opinion of the majority of the Court as expressed by C. J. Marshall.   The more reasonable view expressed by Lord Stowell and J. Story has generally been preferred by commentators.

During the World War the question arose as to whether belligerent merchantmen had a right to arm for defensive purposes and to defend themselves in case of attack.   Great Britain maintained and Germany denied this right.   Great Britain and her allies seem to have had the better of the argument and their views probably represent existing law.

On "The Status of Defensively-Armed Merchant Ships," see particularly: Anderson and Stowell, in *Procs. Am. Soc. I. L.* (1917), 11–23; * Higgins, *Defensively-Armed Merchant Ships and Submarine Warfare* (1917), and in 8 *A. J.* (1914), 705–22; Oppenheim, in 8 *Z. V.* (1914), 154 ff.; Scott, in 10 *A. J.* (1916), 113–18; and Smith, *The Destruction of Merchant Ships* (1917).   For the German viewpoint, see Schram, *Das Prisenrecht*, 266–67; and Triepel, in 8 *Z. V.* (1914), 378 ff.   For diplomatic correspondence relating to the subject, see 9–11 Spec. Supp. to *A. J.* (1915–17), 222 ff., 310 ff., and 225 ff. respectively. For the Circular of the U. S. Department of State issued Sept. 19, 1914, see Supp. to 9 *A. J.* (1915), 121–22.

520. **Convoy.**—" Neutral vessels under convoy of their national flag are exempt from search. The commander of a convoy gives, in writing, at the request of the commander of a belligerent warship, all information as to the character of the vessels and their cargoes, which could be obtained by visit and search " (Art. 61).[10]

" If the commander of the belligerent warship has reason to suspect that the confidence of the commander of the convoy has been abused, he communicates his suspicions to him. In such a case it is for the commander of the convoy alone to conduct an investigation. He must record the result of such investigation in a report, of which a copy is furnished to the officer of the warship. If, in the opinion of the commander of the convoy, the facts thus stated justify the capture of one or more vessels,

---

[10] D. L., 61. The *Report*, cited above, furnishes the following comments upon this article:

"The principle laid down is simple; a neutral vessel convoyed by a warship of her own nationality is exempt from visit and search. The reason for this is that the commander of the belligerent cruiser ought to find in the assurances of the commander of the convoy the guarantee that the exercise of the right of visit and search itself would afford; in fact, he cannot question the assurances given by the official representative of a neutral Government, without failing in international courtesy. If neutral Governments allow belligerents to visit and search vessels sailing under their flag, it is because they do not wish to assume the responsibility for the supervision of such vessels, and therefore allow belligerents to protect themselves. The situation changes when a neutral Government consents to assume that responsibility; the right of visit and search has no longer the same ground.

"But it follows from the explanation of the rule given respecting convoy that the neutral Government undertakes to give the belligerents every guarantee that the vessels convoyed shall not take advantage of the protection which is accorded to them in order to do anything contrary to neutrality, for example, to carry contraband of war, to render unneutral service to the belligerent, to attempt to violate blockade. There is need, therefore, of a genuine supervision to be exercised from the outset over the vessels about to be convoyed, and that supervision should be continued throughout the voyage. The Government must act with vigilance so as to prevent all abuse of convoy, and will give to this end precise instructions to the officer placed in command of a convoy.

"A belligerent cruiser encounters a convoy; she communicates with the commander of the convoy, who should, at her request, give in writing all relevant information respecting the vessels under his protection. A written declaration is required, because it prevents all ambiguities and misunderstandings, and because it binds more fully the responsibility of the commander. This declaration has for its aims to make visit and search unnecessary by the mere fact that this would afford to the cruiser the information which the visit and search would have supplied."

the protection of the convoy must be withdrawn from
such vessels " (Art. 62).[11]

[11] D. L., 62. "Usually the commander of the cruiser will accept the declaration which the commander of the convoy will have given to him, but he may
have serious grounds for believing that the confidence of the commander has
been betrayed, that a convoyed ship of which the papers are apparently regular
and exhibit nothing suspicious is, in fact, carrying contraband cleverly concealed.   The commander of the cruiser may communicate her suspicions to the
commander of the convoy.   An investigation may be considered necessary.
It is made by the commander of the convoy; it is he alone who exercises authority over the vessels placed under his protection.   It appeared, nevertheless,
that much difficulty might be avoided if the belligerent were allowed to be
present at this investigation; otherwise he might still suspect, if not the good
faith, at least the vigilance and perspicacity of the one who makes the search.
But it was not thought that an obligation to allow the officer of the cruiser to
be present should be imposed upon the commander of the convoy.   He will
act as he judges best; if he agrees to the presence of an officer of the cruiser, it
will be as an act of courtesy or good policy.   He must in every case make a
report of the investigation and give a copy to the officer of the cruiser.

"Differences may arise between the two officers, particularly in regard to
conditional contraband.   The character of a port to which grain is destined
may be disputed.   Is it an ordinary commercial port?   Is it a port which serves
as a base of supplies for the armed forces?   The situation which arises out of
the fact of the convoy must in such a case prevail.   The officer of the cruiser
can do no more than make his protest, and the difficulty will be settled through
the diplomatic channel.

"The situation is altogether different if a convoyed vessel is found beyond
the possibility of dispute to be carrying contraband.   The vessel has no longer
a right to protection, since the condition upon which such protection depends
has not been fulfilled.   She has deceived her own Government, and has tried
to deceive the belligerent.   She must therefore be treated as a neutral merchant
vessel which, in the ordinary way, encounters a belligerent cruiser and is
visited and searched by her.   She cannot complain at being treated thus
rigorously, since there is in her case an aggravation of the offense, committed
by a carrier of contraband." Report, op. cit., in Int. Law Topics (1909), 138–
42; or Higgins, 606–08.

"Neutral vessels seeking to break blockade enjoy no immunity by reason of
convoy, if after notice to the convoying ship, they come within the sphere of
operations of the blockading force." Bentwich, The Dec. of London (1911),
118.

It is to be hoped that articles 61–62 of the Declaration of London furnish a
happy ending and final solution of a long-standing controversy.   Continental
jurists and international practice generally have favored exemption from search
of neutral merchantmen under warships of their own nationality.   And the
United States has usually followed the Continental practice, though her jurists
and publicists have almost uniformly opposed it.   In more recent times Great
Britain remained practically the sole champion of the opposition to the right of
convoy, though in practice, as pointed out by Viscount Grey, the British
doctrine was waived in 1854 and has not been enforced in any recent war.
Parl. Papers, Misc., No. 4 (1909), p. 25.   The leading case was that of The
Maria (1799), 1 C. Rob. 340.   See Evans, Cases, 535 or Scott, 1003.   However,
during the World War, Great Britain continued to refuse to recognize the right

521. **Prizes sent in for Adjudication.**—In case there is evidence or serious ground for suspicion of carriage of contraband, breach of blockade, unneutral service, or of the commission of any of the acts enumerated in No. 518, the captured neutral prize should be conducted to a port where a Prize Court is in session for the purposes of adjudication.[12]

" Prizes should be sent in for adjudication, unless otherwise directed, to the nearest suitable port, within the territory of the United States, in which a Prize Court may take action.

" The prize should be delivered to the court as nearly as possible in the condition in which she was at the time of seizure; and to this end her papers should be carefully sealed at the time of seizure, and kept in the custody of the prize master.

" All witnesses whose testimony is necessary to the adjudication of the prize should be detained and sent in with her, and if circumstances permit, it is preferable that the officer making the search should act as prize master." [13]

of convoy and in a controversy with The Netherlands only agreed to refrain from exercising the right of visit and search upon the fulfillment of specific conditions that were accepted by the Dutch Government. *Parl. Papers,* Misc. No. 13 (1918).

Belligerent or enemy convoy constitutes constructive resistance and entails condemnation and confiscation. See *The Schooner Nancy* (1892), 27 Ct. Cl. 99, and Scott, *Cases,* (ed., 1902), 861; *The Brig Sea Nymph* (1901), 36 Ct. Cl. 369, and Scott (ed., 1902), 869; and the dissenting opinion of J. Story, in *The Nereide,* 9. Cranch, 388, 445, 453–54.

On *Convoy,* see especially: Atherley-Jones, 322–28, 331–37; * Bentwich, *The Dec. of London,* ch. 7; Bonfils, Nos. 1597–1605; 5 Calvo, §§ 2969 ff.; Cobbett, 655–61; Dana, note 242 to Wheaton, pp. 692–96; * Dupuis (1899 and 1911), ch. 9; * 2 Fauchille, Nos. 1664–71; * Hall, § 272; Hall, J. A., *Law of Naval Warfare* (1921), 271–73; 2 Halleck (3d ed.), 260–68; Heffter, § 170; Hershey, *Russo-Japanese War,* note on pp. 150–51; 3 Hautefeuille, Tit. XI, ch. 3; 2 Hyde, §§ 734–35; * 2 Kleen, 356–90; Lawrence, § 245; * 7 Moore, *Digest,* §§ 1204–05; 2 Oppenheim, § 417; 2 Ortolan, liv. III, ch. 7; Perels, § 56; 3 Phillimore, § 338; * Pyke, *Law of Contraband* (1915), 195–205; Taylor, § 693; 2 Westlake (1st ed.), 259–61; Wheaton, §§ 525 ff.; Wilson, § 181; Woolsey, §§ 209–11.

[12] Cf. *supra,* No. 436, on the capture of enemy vessels. On the treatment of officers and crew, see *supra,* No. 414.

[13] Stockton's (U. S.) *Naval War Code,* Arts. 46–48. Cf. the U. S. Instructions to Blockading Vessels and Cruisers issued in 1898, and §§ 4615–17 of the Revised Statutes of 1878, in 7 Moore, *Digest,* § 1212, pp. 514–15; Hol-

522. **Destruction of Neutral Prizes.**—" A captured neutral vessel is not to be destroyed by the captor, but must be taken into such port as is proper in order to determine there the rights respecting the validity of the capture " (Art. 48).[14]

" As an exception, a neutral vessel captured by a belligerent ship, and which would be liable to condemnation, may be destroyed if the observance of Article 48 would involve danger to the warship, or to the success of the operations in which she is engaged at the time " (Art. 49).[15]

" Before the destruction, the persons on board must be placed in safety, and all the ship's papers and other documents which the parties interested consider relevant for the decision as to the validity of the capture must be taken on board the warship " (Art. 50).[16]

" A captor who has destroyed a neutral vessel must, as a condition precedent to any decision upon the validity of the capture, establish in fact that he only acted in the

land's *Manual of (British) Prize Law* (1888), Nos. 231–314; §§ 45–62 of the Project adopted by the Institute of Int. Law. in Scott, *Resolutions*, 197 ff.; and ch. 8, Arts. 74–97, of the Japanese Regulations (1904), in Takahashi, 786–88.

[14] D. L., 48. "The general principle is very simple. A captured neutral vessel which has been seized may not be destroyed by the captor; that may be admitted by every one, whatever view is taken as to the effect produced by the capture. The vessel must be taken into a port for the determination there as to the validity of the prize. A prize crew will or will not be put on board, according to circumstances." *Report* on the Dec. of London, in *Int. Law Topics* (1909), 113; or Higgins, 598.

For the conditions justifying the admission of prizes into neutral ports, see 13 H. C., Arts. 21–23, *supra*, No. 473.

[15] D. L., 49. "The first condition necessary in order to justify the destruction of the captured vessel is that she should be liable to condemnation upon the facts of the case. If the captor cannot even hope to obtain the condemnation of the vessel, how can he lay claim to destroy her?

"The second condition is that the observance of the general principle would naturally involve danger to the safety of the warship or to the success of the operations in which she is engaged at the time. This is the regulation on which agreement was reached after various tentative propositions. It was understood that the phrase *compromettre la sécurité* was synonymous with *mettre en danger le navire*, and might be translated into English by *involve danger*. It is, of course, the situation that the moment when the destruction takes place which must be considered in order to decide whether the conditions are or are not fulfilled. A danger which did not exist at the actual moment of the capture may have appeared some time afterwards." *Report*, cited above.

[16] D. L., 50. "This provision lays down the precautions to be taken in the interest of the persons (on board) and of the administration of justice."

face of an exceptional necessity such as is contemplated in Article 49. If he fails to do this, he must compensate the parties interested without examination as to whether the capture was valid or not " (Art. 51).[17]

" If the capture of a neutral vessel, of which the destruction has been justified, is subsequently held to be invalid, the captor must compensate those interested, in place of the restitution to which they would have been entitled " (Art. 52).

" If neutral goods which were not liable to condemnation have been destroyed with the vessel, the owner of such goods is entitled to compensation " (Art. 53).[18]

" The captor has the right to require the handing over, or to proceed himself to the destruction, of any goods liable to condemnation found on board a vessel which is

[17] D. L., 51. "This provision gives a guarantee against the arbitrary destruction of prizes by establishing a real responsibility of the captor who has carried out the destruction. Before any decision respecting the validity of the prize is given, the captor must actually prove that he was really in such an exceptional situation as was specified. This must be proved in proceedings to which the neutral is a party who, if not satisfied with the decision of the National Prize Court, may take his case before the International Court. [The reference here is to the International Prize Court provided for by the Second Hague Conference which never came into existence. See below, add. note, pp. 740–41.] This proof is, therefore, a condition precedent which the captor must fulfil. If he does not do this, he must compensate those interested in the vessel and the cargo, without any investigation as to whether the capture was valid or not. In this way a positive sanction is provided in respect to the obligation not to destroy a prize except in the cases specified; this sanction is a fine inflicted on the captor. If, on the other hand, this proof is given, the prize procedure follows the usual course; if the prize is declared valid, no compensation is due; if it is declared void, those interested have a right to be compensated. Resort to the International Court can be had only after the decision of the prize court has been rendered on the whole matter, and not immediately after the preliminary question has been decided." *Report, op. cit.*

[18] D. L., 52–53. "Suppose a vessel which has been destroyed carried neutral goods not liable to condemnation: the owner of such goods has, in every case, a right to compensation, that is to say, without having to distinguish as to whether the destruction was or was not justified. This is equitable and is a further guarantee against arbitrary destruction." *Report*, cited above.

"As regards innocent neutral goods sunk with *enemy* prizes, the Declaration does not strictly apply. . . . The full recognition, however, in the Declaration of the right of the owner to recover compensation, when his innocent goods are sunk with a neutral prize, must strengthen the argument of those who hold that he should be entitled to compensation whenever a belligerent interferes with his innocent trade. It is likely that the International Prize Court would find in the neutral's favor if the point were brought before them." Bentwich, *op. cit.*, 100.

not herself liable to condemnation, provided that the circumstances are such as would, according to Article 49, justify the destruction of a vessel liable to condemnation. The captor must enter the goods delivered or destroyed in the log book of the vessel stopped, and must obtain from the master duly certified copies of all relevant papers. When the goods have been handed over or destroyed, and the formalities carried out, the master must be allowed to continue his voyage.

" The provisions of Articles 51 and 52 respecting the obligations of a captor who has destroyed a neutral vessel are applicable " (Art. 54).[19]

[19] D. L., 54.   Cf. D. L., 44, *supra*, § 512.   The *Report*, cited above, furnishes the following comment upon this Article, which seeks to introduce an innovation into international practice:

"A cruiser encounters a neutral merchant vessel carrying contraband in a proportion less than that specified in Article 40.   [Cf. *supra*, No. 510.]   The captain of the cruiser may put a prize crew on board the vessel and take her into port for adjudication.   He may, in conformity with the provisions of Article 44, accept the delivery of the contraband which is offered to him by the vessel stopped.   But what is to happen if neither of these solutions is reached?   The vessel stopped does not offer to deliver the contraband, and the cruiser is not in a position to take the vessel into one of her ports.   Is the cruiser obliged to let the neutral vessel go with the contraband on board?   This has seemed excessive, at least in certain exceptional circumstances.   These are in fact the same which would have justified the destruction of the vessel, if she had been liable to condemnation.   In such a case the cruiser may require the delivery or proceed to the destruction of the goods liable to condemnation.   The reasons which warrant the destruction of the vessel would justify the destruction of the contraband goods, the more so as the considerations of humanity which may be invoked in case of the destruction of a vessel do not apply here. Against an arbitrary demand by the cruiser there are the same guarantees as those which made it possible to recognize the right to destroy the vessel.   The captor must, as a condition precedent, prove that he found himself in the exceptional circumstances specified; failing this, he is penalized to the value of the goods delivered or destroyed, without investigation as to whether they were or were not contraband.

"The Article prescribes certain formalities which are necessary to establish the facts of the case and to enable the prize court to adjudicate.

"Of course when once the goods have been delivered or destroyed, and the formalities carried out, the vessel which has been stopped must be left free to continue her voyage."

Prior to the adoption of the above rules on the "Destruction of Neutral Prizes" by the London Naval Conference of 1909, there had been much disagreement among the authorities and differences in recent international practice on this subject.   The Second Hague Peace Conference of 1907 had vainly attempted a solution of the problem.   The solution effected by the London Conference appears to be as satisfactory as could be expected under the circumstances.   It remains to be seen whether and to what extent it will be

523. National Prize Courts.—National Prize Courts are municipal tribunals set by belligerent States for the purposes of adjudicating upon captured or destroyed prizes.[20] They are supposed to administer International Law, and usually make an honest effort to do so; but in case the rules laid down by superior legislative or administrative authority conflict with the Law of Nations, they are bound by municipal rather than by International Law.[21]

524. Their Jurisdiction.—" The jurisdiction of prize courts extends over all captures made in war by their country's cruisers, over all captures made on land by a naval force acting alone or in conjunction with military forces, and over seizures made afloat by the joint operation of land and sea forces. It also includes all recaptures, ransoms, and ransom bills, and all incidental questions growing out of the circumstances of capture such as freights and damages. And when it was customary for States to make seizures afloat in anticipation of war, the cases that arose

observed in future wars. Certainly the rules laid down in the unratified Declaration were grossly violated by Germany during the World War. See especially 2 Garner, ch. 31.

On the *Destruction of Neutral Prizes*, see: * Atherley-Jones, 531–38; Barclay, *Problems*, etc., 99–102; Bonfils or 2 Fauchille, No. 1415; Bentwich, *Dec. of London* (1911), ch. 4; 5 Calvo, §§ 3019, 3028–34; Dana, note 186 to Wheaton, p. 485; * Dupuis (1899 and 1911), Nos. 261–68 and 206–17 respectively; * 2 Garner, ch. 31; Hall, § 277; Hall, J. A., *Law of Naval Warfare* (1921), 294 ff.; Hershey, *Russo-Japanese War* (especially for case of *The Knight Commander*), 156–59; * Holland, *Prize Law* (for British rule), No. 303, *Neutral Duties*, etc., in 2 *Procs. British Academy* (1905), 12–13, and in *War and Neutrality*, 140–50; * 2 Hyde, §§ 757–58; 2 Kleen, 529–34; Lawrence, § 191, and *War and Neutrality* (2d ed.), 250 ff.; * 7 Moore, *Digest*, § 1212; Naval War College, *Int. Law Sit.* (1905 and 1907), 62–76 and 74–108; 2 Oppenheim, § 431; Pyke, *Law of Contraband* (1915), 205–10, 214; 1 Scott (for Hague Conference), 725–30; Smith, *The Destruction of Merchant Ships* (1917), 70 ff.; Smith and Sibley *Russo-Japansese War*, ch. 12; Takahashi, *Cases on Int. Law during the Chino-Japansese War* (for the case of the *Kowshing*), 26–31, 46–47, and *Int. Law during the Russo-Japanese War*, 310–36; * 2 Westlake (1st ed., 1907), 318–21; * Wilson, §§ 131 and 185.

Cf. *Destruction of Enemy Prizes*, *supra*, No. 438.

[20] They may not be set up in neutral territory. Cf. *supra*, No. 460.

[21] There is some good authority to the contrary (*e.g.* 2 Halleck, 3d ed., 411–12), but such a view would be anarchical in its effects if put into practice. The establishment of an International Prize Court would doubtless result in a more internationalized body of prize court jurisprudence. Whether the Permanent Court of International Justice will function in this capacity remains to be seen.

therefrom were taken before the prize courts. Speaking generally, we may lay down the proposition that the courts of neutrals have no jurisdiction over the captures of belligerents." [22]

[22] Lawrence, *Principles*, § 189. Lawrence adds: "But to this rule there are exceptions. Jurisdiction exists and can be exercised when the capture is made within the territorial limits of the neutral State, or when a vessel, originally equipped for war within neutral jurisdiction, or afterwards made efficient by an augmentation of warlike force therein, takes a prize at sea and brings it within the waters of the injured neutral during the voyage in which the illegal equipment or augmentation took place. In both cases neutral sovereignty is violated by one belligerent, and in consequence the neutral is exposed to claims and remonstrances from the other. Jurisdiction is therefore conferred upon it for its own protection, and in order that it may insist upon the restoration of the property unlawfully taken." See case of the *Santissima Trinidad* (1822), 7 Wheat. 283 in Evans, 788 or Scott, 823.

Adjudication in a national prize court is usually rather in the nature of an inquest upon property than of an issue between parties as in ordinary trials. The inquest begins with an inquiry by the Government of the captors into the facts. This involves an examination by the court of the vessel and its cargo, the ship's papers, and the persons on board. The parties litigant do not themselves appear at this stage of the inquest. Then follow arguments by counsel. The burden of proof lies on the claimants, *i.e.* there is a presumption in favor of the captors. If the evidence *in preparatory, i.e.* the evidence thus far discovered, is sufficient for condemnation, the court gives its decision accordingly. If this evidence is insufficient, the court may call for further proof, *i.e.* proof beyond the vessel, cargo, papers, and persons on board. The proceedings now assume more closely the form of a trial between litigants, though there are, strictly speaking, no pleadings.

On *Prize Court Procedure*, see especially: Boeck, Nos. 363–80, 769–90; * Dana, note 186 to Wheaton, 480 ff.; * Garner, *Prize Law during the World War* (1927), ch. 3; Hall, J. A., *Law of Naval Warfare* (1921), ch. 11; Holland, *Manual of Prize Law* (1888), ch. 22; * 2 Hyde, §§ 897–901; Lawrence, §§ 189–90, Pyke, in 32 *Law Quar. Rev.*, 144–67; and Roscoe, in *Brit. Yr. Bk.* (1921–22), 90–98.

Additional Note on the International Prize Court.—As a remedy for the imperfections of the system of National Courts, the Second Hague Conference of 1907 had agreed upon a Convention (for the text, see Higgins, 407 ff. or 2 Scott, 472 ff.) for the establishment of an International Prize Court. It was to be a Court of Appeal from the judgments of National Prize Courts. Appeals might, in certain cases, be made by neutral or even enemy individuals as well as by neutral Powers (Arts. 3 and 4). If the legal question to be decided was governed by a treaty in force, the Court was to be governed by the provisions of said treaty. "In the absence of such provisions, the Court shall apply the principles of International Law. If no generally recognized rule exists, the Court shall give judgment in accordance with the general principles of justice and equity" (Art. 7).

The Court was to be composed of fifteen judges appointed for a term (renewable) of six years. The eight leading Powers were to have permanent seats, the remaining seven judges being appointed by the other Contracting Powers sitting in rotation as shown by a Table annexed to the Convention (see Higgins, 430 or 2 Scott, 504–05).

BIBLIOGRAPHY

Rights of Visit and Search.—* Atherley-Jones (1907), chs. 5–6; Barclay, *Problems*, etc., 71–72; Bluntschli, Arts. 819–26; Bonfils, Nos. 1589 ff.; 5 Calvo, §§ 2939–91; 2 Cobbett, 655 ff.; Dana, notes, 242–243 to Wheaton, 692–96, 698–700; Despagnet, Nos. 693–95; Duboc, in 4 *R. D. I. P.* (1897), 382 ff., and *Le droit de visites*, etc. (1902); * Dupuis, *Le droit de la guerre maritime* (1899 and 1911), ch. 9; Evans, *Cases*, 535 ff.; 2 Fauchille, Nos. 1657 ff.; 3 Fiore, Nos. 1630–41, and *Int. Law Cod.*, Nos. 1876 ff.; Geffcken, in 4 Holtzendorff, 773–81; * Hall, Pt. IV, ch. 10; Hall, J. A., *Law of Naval Warfare* (1921), ch. 10; * 2 Halleck, ch. 27; 3 Hautefeuille, *Des droits des neutres*, 1–202; Heffter, §§ 169–71; Hirschmann, *Das int. Prisenrecht* (1912), §§ 33–34; * Holland, *Manual of [British] Prize Law* (1888), Nos. 1–17, 151–230; * 2 Hyde, §§ 724–35; * 2 Kleen, 246–389; Lawrence, § 186; Lawrence, W. B., *Visitation and Search* (1858); Loewenthal, *Das Untersuchungsrecht*, etc. (1905); Manning, *Law of Nations*, ch. 11; Mirbach, *Die völkerr. Grundsätze des Durchsuchungsrecht* (1903); * 7 Moore, *Digest*, §§ 1199 ff.; Naval War College, *Int. Law*

The radical character of several of these provisions should be particularly noted. The jurisdiction of the Court was in effect obligatory and it was given power to give decisions on the basis of justice and equity, *i.e.*, it was expressly empowered to make law.

The Convention was signed by most of the States represented at the Conference, but was ratified by only a few of the more important ones. The United States Senate consented to ratification after a Protocol had been signed in 1910 which revised certain provisions of the Convention. This Protocol provided in effect that appeals to the Court might take the form of actions against the nation for damages, instead of appeals in the original cases as tried in the national courts.

But our President never ratified the Convention inasmuch as Great Britain delayed ratification both of the Convention for the Establishment of an International Prize Court and of the Declaration of London which had laid down rules for its guidance. The defeat in the House of Lords of the bill that would have enabled the British Government at once to adopt the Declaration and establish the Court settled its fate and the Court never came into existence.

On the *International Prize Court*, see: 1 and 2 *Actes et doc. de la deuxième confér.*, 165, 188–229, and 11–33, 783–856, 1071–1106 respectively; Barclay, *Problems*, etc., 105–08; Bonfils or 2 Fauchille, Nos. 1440 and 1691; Brown, in 2 *A. J.* (1908), 476 ff.; Bustamante y Sirven, *La seconde conférence de la paix* (1909), ch. 27; Curtius, in 41 *R. D. I.* (1909), 5 ff.; * Dupuis *Le droit de la guerre maritime* (1899 and 1911), ch. 11; Fried, *Die zweite Haager Konferenz*, 121–30; Gregory, in 2 *A. J.* (1908), 458 ff.; Hershey, in 19 *Green Bag* (1907), 652 ff.; * Higgins, 407–44; * Holland, *War and Neutrality*, 150–62; * Lawrence, § 192, and in *International Problems*, etc., 141–59, 182–97; * Lémonon, *La seconde conférence de la paix* (1908), 280–335; * 2 Oppenheim, §§ 438–47; Ozanan, *La juridsiction int. des prises maritimes* (1910), Pt. II, 121 ff.; 1 Pohl, *Deutsche Prisengerichtsbarkeit* (1911), 47 ff.; * Potter, *Int. Organization* (1922), 241, 243–52; * Renault, in 1 Scott, 492–93, 501; * 1 Scott, ch. 10, and in 5 *A. J.* (1911), 302 ff.; Scott, *Resolutions* (for Project of the Institute of Int. Law), 22–23; * 2 Westlake (ed., 1907), 288–97; White, in 2 *A. J.* (1908), 490 ff.

Topics (1905), 48–61; * 2 Oppenheim, §§ 414–28; 2 Ortolan, 249–82; Perels, §§ 52–55; 3 Phillimore, §§ 322–44; Pyke, *Law of Contraband* (1915), 191–205; 2 Rivier, 423–28; * Scott, *Cases*, 1003 ff.; * Stockton's *Naval (U. S.) War Code*, Arts. 30–33, 46–50; Taylor, §§ 685 ff.; 2 Twiss, §§ 91–97; Vattel, liv. III, § 114; 3 Wharton, ch. 16; Wheaton, §§ 524–37; Wilson, ch. 23; Woolsey, §§ 208 ff.

Capture, Prize Courts, and Procedure.—6–9 *Annuaire* (1881–1887), *passim;* * Atherley-Jones, chs. 7–9; Bardas, *Das öffent. Seerecht Ostreichs* (1909); Bluntschli, Arts. 841–62; * Boeck, Nos. 329–80, 740–90; * Boyens, *Das deutsche Seerecht* (1897 and 1901, in 2 vols.); Bulmerincq, in 10–14 *R. D. I.* (1878–1882), *passim*, especially 11 *R. D. I.* (1879), 152 ff. and 321 ff.; 5 Calvo, §§ 3004–3114; 2 Cobbett, 211 ff., 259 ff., 279 ff.; De Cussy, *Causes célèbres* (1865), *passim;* Dana, note 186 to Wheaton, 450 ff.; Despagnet, Nos. 664–70; * Dupuis, *op. cit.* (1899 and 1911), ch. 10; Evans, *Cases*, ch. 15; * 2 Fauchille, Nos. 1396 ff.; 3 Fiore, Nos. 1681–91, and *Int. Law Cod.*, Nos. 1892 ff.; * Garner, *Prize Law during the World War* (1927); Geffcken, in 4 Holtzendorff, 781–88; Gessner, *Le droit des neutres sur mer* (1876), 369 ff., and in 13 *R. D. I.*, 260 ff.; Grotius, *De jure praedae* (1604–1605), ed. Hamaker (1868); Hall, J. A., *Law of Naval Warfare* (1921), ch. 11; 2 Halleck, chs. 31–32; 3 Hautefeuille, *op. cit.*, 203–395; Heffter, §§ 172–73; Hirschmann, *Das int. Prisenrecht* (1912); * Holland, *Manual [British] Prize Law* (1888), Nos. 231–314; Huberich, *German Prize Code* (1915); Hübner, *De la saisi des bâtiments neutres* (1759); * 2 Hyde, §§ 736 ff., 752 ff., 890 ff.; * 2 Kleen, 390 ff.; * Lawrence, §§ 188–90; 2 J. de Louter, §§ 50, 59; Manning, *op. cit.*, ch. 13; Marstrand-Mecklenburg, *Das Japanische Prisenrecht*, etc. (1908); Ch. de Martens, *Causes célèbres, passim;* * 7 Moore, *Digest*, §§ 1206–14, 1222 ff.; *Naval Instructions [of U. S.] Governing Maritime Warfare* (1917); * 2 Oppenheim, §§ 429–37; Ozanan, *La jurisdiction int. des prises maritime* (1910); 2 Ortolan, liv. III, ch. 5; * Perels, *Das allg. öffent. Seerecht im Deutschen Reiche* (1901); Perels, *Manuel*, §§ 55–60; * 3 Phillimore, Pt. IX, chs. 4–6 and Pt. XI, §§ 345 ff.; Pistoye et Duverdy, *Traité des prises maritimes* (1859), in 2 vols.; Pohl, *Deutsche Gerichtsbarkeit* (1911); Pyke, *op. cit.*, 205–19; 2 Rivier, 339–59; * Richards, "British Prize Courts and the War," in *Brit. Yr. Bk.* (1920–21), 11–34; 2 Rolin, 296 ff., 359 ff.; Roscoe, *Lord Stowell* (1916), *passim;* Schramm, *Das Prisenrecht* (1913); Story, *Notes on the Principles and Practice of Prize Courts* (1854); * Scott, *Cases*, 744 ff., 1036 ff., and *Resolutions* (for Project adopted by Institute of Int. Law), 45 ff.; Taylor, §§ 563–67, 691; Takahashi (cases during the Russo-Japanese War), Pt. V, and *Cases during Chino-Japanese War* (1899); 2 Twiss, ch. 9; Valin, *Traité des prises* (1758–1760); Verzijl, *Le droit des prises et la grande guerre* (1924); Vigiére, *La jurisdiction des prises maritime* (1901); * Wehberg, *Capture in War on Land and Sea* (1911), *passim;* 3 Wharton, *Digest*, §§ 328 ff.; Wheaton, §§ 385–97; Wilson, ch. 28.

For fuller Bibliographies, see Bonfils, Fauchille, Ozanan, and Wehberg.

INDEX

(References are to pages)